	What Happens in the **BRAIN?**	 How we *Develop*	HOW we Differ	When Things Go **Wrong**
CHAPTER 8 **Memory**	When We Give Eyewitness Testimony: What Happens in the Brain? Memory: What Happens in the Brain?	The Effect of Aging on Memory: How We Develop	Gender and Dementia: How We Differ	Disorders of Memory: When Things Go Wrong
CHAPTER 9 **Language and Thought**	Language: What Happens in the Brain? Theory of Mind: What Happens in the Brain? When We Learn a Second Language: What Happens in the Brain?	Language: How We Develop Metacognition: How We Develop	Language: How We Differ	Thought: When Things Go Wrong
CHAPTER 10 **Intelligence**	Intelligence: What Happens in the Brain?	Cortical Thickness and Intelligence: How We Develop	Extremes in Intelligence: How We Differ	Moderate, Severe, and Profound Retardation: When Things Go Wrong
CHAPTER 11 **Motivation**	Hunger: What Happens in the Brain? Sex: What Happens in the Brain? When We're Motivated to Run a Marathon: What Happens in the Brain?	Achievement: How We Develop	Hunger: How We Differ Sex: How We Differ Achievement: How We Differ	Hunger: When Things Go Wrong Sex: When Things Go Wrong Affiliation: When Things Go Wrong
CHAPTER 12 **Emotion**	Emotion: What Happens in the Brain?	Emotion: How We Develop	Emotion: How We Differ	Disorders of Emotion: When Things Go Wrong
CHAPTER 13 **Personality**	Personality: What Happens in the Brain?	Freud's Psychosexual Stages: How We Develop How Much Do Genetic Factors Contribute to Personality? How We Develop	Personality: How We Differ	Personality Disorders: When Things Go Wrong
CHAPTER 14 **Social Psychology**	Social Functioning: What Happens in the Brain?	Attitudes: How We Develop	Roles, Gender, and Social Skills: How We Differ	Disorders of Social Functioning: When Things Go Wrong
CHAPTER 15 **Stress, Coping, and Health**	Physiological Responses to Stress: What Happens in the Brain? When Public Speaking Stresses Us Out: What Happens in the Brain?	Life Changes: How We Develop	Individual Responses to Stress: How We Differ	Posttraumatic Stress Disorder: When Things Go Wrong
CHAPTER 16 **Psychological Disorders and Treatment**	The Neuroscience Model: What Happens in the Brain? When a Depressed Person Takes an Antidepressant: What Happens in the Brain?	Freud, Psychosexual Stages, and Abnormality: How We Develop	Socioeconomic Class: How We Differ Cultural Factors: How We Differ	Throughout

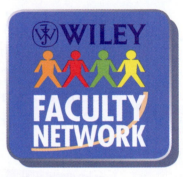

Psychology
Around Us

Psychology
Around Us

Ronald Comer
Princeton University

Elizabeth Gould
Princeton University

WILEY

John Wiley & Sons, Inc.

VICE PRESIDENT AND EXECUTIVE PUBLISHER	Jay O'Callaghan
EXECUTIVE EDITOR	Christopher Johnson
ASSISTANT EDITOR	Eileen McKeever
SENIOR DEVELOPMENT EDITOR	Marian Dolan Provenzano
MARKETING MANAGER	Danielle Torio
SENIOR PRODUCTION EDITOR	Trish McFadden
MEDIA MANAGER	Lynn Pearlman/Bridget O'Lavin
CREATIVE DIRECTOR	Harry Nolan
INTERIOR DESIGN	Amy Rosen
COVER DESIGN	Howard Grossman
COVER PHOTO	© Ed Kinsman/Photo Researchers, Inc.
SENIOR ILLUSTRATION EDITOR	Anna Melhorn
PHOTO DEPARTMENT MANAGER	Hilary Newman
EDITORIAL ASSISTANT	Sean Boda/Brittany Cheetham/Mariah Maguire-Fong
PRODUCTION SERVICES	Furino Production

This book was set in Minion by Prepare Inc. and printed and bound by RR Donnelley/Jefferson City. The cover was printed by RR Donnelly/Jefferson City.

This book is printed on acid free paper. ∞

To order books or for customer service please, call 1-800-CALL WILEY (225-5945).

Library of Congress Cataloging in Publication Data:
ISBN-13   978- 0-471-38519-6

Printed in the United States of America

10 9 8 7 6 5 4 3 2

About the Authors

Ronald Comer has taught in Princeton University's Department of Psychology for the past 35 years and has served as Director of Clinical Psychology Studies for most of that time. He has received the President's Award for Distinguished Teaching at the university. Comer also is the author of the textbooks *Abnormal Psychology*, now in its seventh edition, and *Fundamentals of Abnormal Psychology*, now in its sixth edition, and the coauthor of *Case Studies in Abnormal Psychology*. He is the producer of various educational videos, including *The Introduction to Psychology Video Library Series*. In addition, he has published journal articles in clinical psychology, personality, social psychology, and family medicine.

Elizabeth Gould has taught in Princeton University's Department of Psychology for the past 12 years. A leading researcher in the study of adult neurogenesis, she has published numerous journal articles on the production of new neurons in the adult mammalian brain. Gould has been honored for her breakthrough work with a number of awards, including the 2006 NARSAD Distinguished Investigator Award and the 2009 Royal Society of the Arts Benjamin Franklin Medal. She serves on the editorial boards of *The Journal of Neuroscience*, *Neurobiology of Learning and Memory*, *Biological Psychology*, and *Cell Stem Cell*.

To our children

Lindsey, Sean, and William

E.G.

Jon and Jami

Greg and Emily

R.C.

Brief Contents

Contents

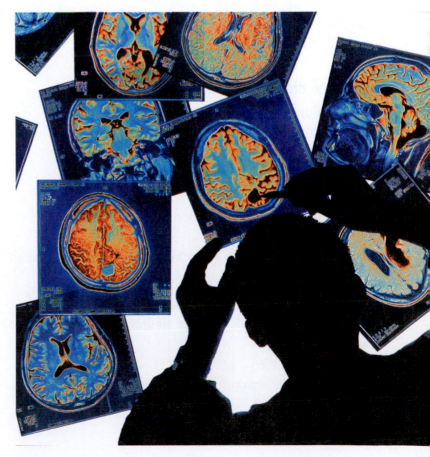

CHAPTER 5 | Sensation and Perception 128

CHAPTER 15 | Stress, Coping, and Health 500

To the Instructor

Psychology is all around us. If ever there was a subject that permeates our everyday lives, it is psychology. Behavior occurs everywhere, and the study of behavior can help shed light on the widest range of events and issues.

This textbook **Psychology Around Us** helps to open students' minds to the notion that psychology is indeed around them every day and that its principles are immediately applicable to a whole host of life's questions. It also features classroom-proven pedagogy to keep students engaged and help them master the material.

Between the two of us, we have taught Introductory Psychology, Abnormal Psychology, and Neuroscience for about 50 years. Throughout those years, we have always been struck by how differently students react to various subjects of psychology. For example, most students find Abnormal Psychology fascinating, relevant, and "alive," while many consider other areas of psychology to be flat and removed from their lives. Thus, while excited by their abnormal psychology text, they are often disappointed by their introductory psychology text.

There is something very wrong with this. After all, like abnormal psychology, general psychology deals with people and with behavior; and what can be more interesting than that? Granted, abnormal behaviors are often exotic and puzzling, and people who display them generate empathy, sympathy, and curiosity; but, certainly, normal behavior is every bit as remarkable.

This gap between the appeal of abnormal behavior and that of normal behavior occurs throughout psychology. Students are fascinated by instances of "memory gone bad" yet take for granted that people can remember in the first place. They love to follow the activity of serotonin and dopamine when studying mood disorders and schizophrenia, but not when learning about these neurotransmitters in an introductory psychology course. Students are captivated by failures in attention (ADHD), thought (schizophrenia), communication (autism), or coping (posttraumatic stress disorder), yet almost nonchalant about the fact that people usually attend, think, communicate, and cope quite well. They keenly appreciate the importance and effects of psychotherapy, yet almost overlook everyday instances of attitude, behavior, and mood change.

Our textbook is dedicated to helping students appreciate that both normal and abnormal behavior are fascinating, and to energizing, exciting, and demonstrating for them the enormous relevance of psychology. It encourages students to examine what they know about human behavior and how they know it, and opens them up to an appreciation of psychology outside of the classroom.

About the Text

As instructors and researchers, we (the authors) are both passionate about the study of psychology and genuinely fascinated by behavior, thought, and emotion. When we teach a course, we consider ourselves successful if we have engaged our students in the rigorous study of psychology while simultaneously transferring our passion for the subject. These same criteria of success should be applied to a textbook in psychology: It should broaden the reader's knowledge about the field and, at the same time, move, excite, and motivate the student. To achieve this goal, our textbook includes a range of features—some traditional, others innovative.

While implementing the traditional introductory psychology concepts and theories, this textbook also introduces two special pedagogical tools, the *Cut Across Connection* and *What Happens in the Brain When...* These features help to demonstrate how psychology's various topics are relevant to each other and also to everyday life.

Special Pedagogical Tools

Cut Across Connection

One of the most important ways that this text will help students "see the big picture" are recurring sections that highlight how the different fields of psychology are connected to each other and how they connect to everyday life. We highlight *human development, brain function, abnormal psychology, and individual differences* as ideas that literally cut across our discipline.

Following a long-standing tradition, for example, most of today's textbooks offer detailed chapters on *developmental psychology* early in the book and detailed chapters on psychological disorders late in the textbook. In between are chapters on other subfields of psychology — from sensation, perception, language, and thought, to emotion, personality, and social behavior. These middle chapters focus on the nature, explanations, and applications of each subfield, but they typically do not explore how such areas of psychological functioning *develop* or what *dysfunctions* may occur in each area.

It is left to the reader to remember developmental material from earlier chapters and see its implications for the material at hand, or to place the current material on hold and tie it weeks later to subsequent chapters on related psychological disorders and treatments. No wonder some students are impatient to "get to the psychology!" They are not set up to appreciate the full range of the field.

To achieve our goal of showing students how psychology is indeed all around us, and to bring our textbook in line with the course curricula of most professors, we have structured each of the chapters in our textbook in a very particular way — a cross-sectional presentation.

Every chapter on a substantive area of psychology not only offers a thorough presentation of the nature, explanations, and applications of that area, but also includes "*Cut-Across*" sections on the *development, brain function, individual differences, and dysfunctions* that occur in that realm of mental life. The Sensation and Perception chapter (Chapter 5), for example, includes the sections "How Does Hearing Develop?", "What Happens in the Brain When We Hear?", "Hearing: How We Differ", and "When Hearing Goes Wrong," along with comparable sections on smell, taste, touch, and sight. Similarly, the Emotion chapter (Chapter 12) includes the sections "How Do Emotions Develop?", "What Happens in the Brain When We are Feeling Emotions?", "Emotions: How We Differ", and "When Emotions Go Wrong."

What Happens in the Brain When ...

Many introductory psychology students consider the study of neuroscience to be difficult and at times irrelevant to the study of human behavior. In recent years, however, neuroscience has been tied to virtually every subfield of psychology. Remarkable brain imaging studies, in conjunction with animal studies, have helped us to identify the neural mechanisms of everyday experience. Accordingly, *Psychology Around Us* incorporates neuroscience information into chapters where it has been traditionally absent, such as Social Psychology and Consciousness. In addition, the text offers a key teaching feature that helps bring neuroscience directly into the lives of readers: Exciting and accessible two-page layouts appear throughout the book illustrating what happens in the brain when people are performing such common behaviors as eating pizza, learning a video game, acquiring a second language, giving a speech in public, and running a marathon. These layouts, which include neuroimages and findings from both human studies and relevant animal experiments, draw students into the brain and provide them with up-to-date information about the neural mechanisms at work during their everyday experiences. Regardless of their background in neuroscience, students come away intrigued by material that has traditionally been considered difficult.

Additional Features

Chapter-Opening Vignettes

Every chapter begins with a vignette that shows the power of psychology in understanding a range of human behaviors. This theme is reinforced throughout the chapter, celebrating the extraordinary processes that make the everyday possible.

Guided Learning

A **Learning Objective** for each chapter section identifies the most important material for students to understand while reading that section. These learning objectives also serve as the driving principle in *WileyPLUS*.

Following each section is a **Before You Go On** feature that helps students check their mastery of the important items covered. • **What Do You Know?** questions prompt students to stop and review the key concepts just presented. • **What Do You Think?** questions encourage students to think critically on key questions in the chapter.

Special topics on psychology around us

Each chapter highlights interesting news stories, current controversies in psychology, and relevant research findings that demonstrate psychology around us. The *Practically Speaking* box emphasizes the practical application of everyday psychology.

Helpful study tools...

Key Terms are listed at the end of each chapter with page references.
Marginal Definitions are defined in the margin next to their discussion in the text.
Marginal Notes present interesting facts and quotes throughout the chapter.

Chapter Summary

The end-of-chapter Summary reviews the main concepts presented in the chapter with reference to the specific Learning Objectives. It provides students with another opportunity to review what they have learned as well as to see how the key topics within the chapter fit together.

Resources

Psychology Around Us is accompanied by a host of resources and ancillary materials designed to facilitate a mastery of psychology.

Powerful Media Resources

WileyPLUS is an online teaching and learning environment that integrates the entire digital textbook with the most effective instructor and student resources to fit every learning style. With *WileyPLUS*,

- Students achieve concept mastery in a rich, structured environment that's available 24/7 and

- Instructors can personalize and manage their course more effectively with assessment, assignments, grade tracking, and more. For more information, visit **www.wileyplus.com**

Instructor Resources

Instructor Resources can be found within the **Psychology Around Us** WileyPlus course and on the text's companion website, www.wiley.com/college/comer.

"Lecture-Launcher" Videos

The **Psychology Around Us** series of "lecture-launcher" videos helps bring lectures to life and, most importantly, captivate students. They help demonstrate the most important theme of an introductory psychology course — that psychology is all around us and that behavior, from everyday normal behavior to abnormal behavior, is truly fascinating. Averaging about five minutes in length, this collection covers a range of relevant topics.

Each video is a cream-of-the-crop excerpt from the CBS, BBC, NBC, ABC, Public Broadcasting, or Independent video libraries chosen from a televised news report, documentary, lab study, or the like, and illustrating a particular lecture point, bringing the topic to life in exciting ways.

In addition, the package has been produced by Professor Comer and other leading university educators whose extensive teaching, video, and psychology backgrounds enable them to develop video materials that perfectly address the lecture needs and goals of teachers and students.

The clips in this 75-piece package focus on topics ranging from the split-brain phenomenon to conformity and obedience, emotions of fear or disgust, sensations of taste and smell, infant facial recognition, gender orientation, and brain development.

The videos are accompanied by an extensive *Instructor's Guide*. This guide offers a description of each module in the package, its length and source, features of special interest, and relevant textbook/lecture topics.

The video program is readily accessible and easily integrated into the Introductory Psychology course through the *Psychology Around Us* WileyPlus course. Instructors have the option of assigning videos to students for viewing outside of class along with quizzes that test understanding of the video's content and relevance.

Psychology Around Us Video Lab Activities

Psychology Around Us offers a series of 14 active learning projects that students can conduct on their own. Traditionally, such exercises have been presented in book form, with *written* exercises guiding students through paper-and-pencil tasks. Today students can *interact* with computerized exercises, become more engaged by video and animated material, and receive immediate feedback about the effects and accuracy of their choices.

These lab activities use extensive video material to drive student learning. The combination of video footage and digital interactive technology bring the lab exercises to life for students in ways that were previously impossible, actively engaging the students and helping them to better process the lesson at hand. The kinds of video material included in the *Video Lab Activities* range from laboratory brain footage to videos of everyday events to psychology documentary excerpts.

For example, one video-digital lab exercise on *Memory Manufacturing and Eyewitness Testimony* unfolds as a cluster of video-digital lab exercises on memory. They guide the student to also explore (1) *pre-event and post-event memory interference*, (2) *childhood memory limits*, (3) *snapshot memories*, and (4) *the creation of false memories*.

Like the "Lecture-Launcher" videos, the Video Labs are accessible through the *Psychology Around Us* WileyPlus course. Instructors have the option of assigning the Videos Labs to students for completion outside of class; the student's work is then viewable by the instructor in WileyPlus's Gradebook section.

Instructor's Manual

Prepared by Elaine Cassel, *Lord Fairfax Community College*
This Instructor's Manual is designed to help instructors maximize student learning and encourage critical thinking. It presents teaching suggestions for every chapter using the book's objectives as well as including ideas for lecture classroom discussions, demonstrations, and videos. This manual will also share activity-based applications to everyday life.

Lecture PowerPoint Presentation

Prepared by Lisa Hagan, *Metropolitan State College of Denver*
Every chapter contains a *Lecture PowerPoint Presentation* with a combination of key concepts, figures and tables, and problems and examples from the textbook.

TestBank

Prepared by Christopher Mayhorn, *North Carolina State University,* **Matthew Isaak,** *University of Louisiana at Lafayette,* **and Susan Weldon of** *Henry Ford Community College*
The *Test Bank* is available in a Word® document format or through Respondus®. The questions are available to instructors to create and print multiple versions of the same test by scrambling the order of all questions found in the Word version of the test bank. This allows users to customize exams by altering or adding new problems.

Prelecture Quizzes

Prepared by Brenda Walker-Moore, *Kirkwood Community College*
This resource offers 10-15 questions per chapter that are assignable to students prior to the lecture or for general review purposes.

In-Class Concept Checks

Prepared by Brenda Walker-Moore, *Kirkwood Community College*
This resource offers 10-15 questions per chapter that can be used with a variety of person response (or "clicker") systems.

Student Resources

Student Resources can be found within the *Psychology Around Us* WileyPlus course and on the text's companion website, www.wiley.com/college/comer.

Online Study Tools

Prepared by Brenda Walker-Moore, *Kirkwood Community College* **and Arthur Olguin of** *Santa Barbara City College*

Psychology Around Us provides students with a website containing a wealth of support materials to develop their understanding of class material and increase their ability to solve problems in the classroom. On this website students will find Practice Chapter Exams for every chapter that will allow them to assess their understanding of chapter concepts. Students will be able to study using tools available on the webstite that include: Interactive Flash Cards, Chapter Summaries, Learning Objectives, Web Resources, and more!

Acknowledgments

The writing of this text has been a group effort involving the input and support of many individuals. On a personal note, we thank our families, friends, and colleagues for their support and availability, particularly Marlene Comer and Jon Cohen. We greatly appreciate the significant help provided by Linda Chamberlin, Sean Allan, and Emily Graham. We are enormously grateful to those individuals who made important research and writing contributions to early drafts of various elements of the book, including Dina Altshuler, Leslie Carr, Greg Comer, Jon Comer, Lindsay Downs, Jami Furr, Jamie Hambrick, Rob Holaway, and Art Pomponio. And we offer our sincere gratitude and admiration to the terrific team of professionals assembled by John Wiley & Sons who guided the development and production of this book so effectively, particularly those individuals with whom we worked most closely— Chris Johnson, Jay O' Callaghan, Marian Provenzano, Barbara Heaney, Sheralee Connors, Suzanne Thibodeau, Beverly Peavler, Hilary Newman, Jeanine Furino, Elizabeth Morales, and Danielle Torio.

Finally, a very special thank you goes out to the hundreds of faculty who have contributed to the development of this first edition text, its art program, its digital resources and its powerful supplemental program.

To the reviewers, focus group and workshop participants who gave their time and constructive criticism, we offer our deep appreciation. We are deeply indebted to the following individuals and trust they will recognize their contributions throughout the text.

Reviewers

David Alfano, *Community College of Rhode Island*
Evelyn Blanch-Payne, *Albany State University*
Amanda Bozack, *University of New Haven*
Jennifer Breneiser, *Valdosta State University*
Tina Burns, *Florida International University*
Jarrod Calloway, *Northwest Mississippi Community College*
Jill Carlivati, *George Washington University*
Daneen Deptula, *Fitchburg State College*
Dale V. Doty, *Monroe Community College*
Kimberley J. Duff, *Cerritos College*
Jane Dwyer, *Rivier College*
Darlene Earley-Hereford, *Southern Union State Community College*
Julie Evey-Johnson, *University of Southern Indiana*
Linda Fayard, *Mississippi Gulf Coast Community College*
Angela Fellner, *University of Cincinnati*
Christopher M. France, *Cleveland State University*
Adia J. Garrett Butler, *University of Maryland-Baltimore County*
Linda Bolser Gilmore, *DeKalb Technical College*
Marvin Gordon, *University of Illinois-Chicago*
Gladys S. Green, *Manatee Community College-Bradenton*
Laura Gruntmeir, *Redlands Community College*
Alexandria Guzman, *University of New Haven*
Sheryl Hartman, *Miami Dade College*
Myra M. Harville, *Holmes Community College*
Bert Hayslip, Jr., *University of North Texas-Denton*
Tonya Honeycutt, *Johnson County Community College*
Charles Jacob Huffman, *James Madison University*

Jessica Jablonski, *The Richard Stockton College of New Jersey*
Cheri L. Kittrell, *Manatee Community College-Bradenton*
Juliana K. Leding, *University of North Florida*
Angela Lipsitz, *Northern Kentucky University*
Missy Madden-Schlegel, *Marist College*
Gregory Manley, *University of Texas at San Antonio*
Christopher B. Mayhorn, *North Carolina State University*
Tamara J. Musumeci-Szabo, *Rutgers, The State University of New Jersey*
Ronnie Naramore, *Angelina College*
Dominic J. Parrott, *Georgia State University*
Terry F. Pettijohn, *The Ohio State University-Marion*
Sean P. Reilley, *Morehead State University*
Karen Rhines, *Northampton Community College*
Margherita Rossi, *Broome Community College*
Maria Shpurik, *Florida International University*
Morgan Slusher, *Community College of Baltimore County-Essex*
Mark Stewart, *American River College*
Inger Thompson, *Glendale Community College*
Suzanne Tomasso, *Manatee Community College-Bradenton*
Katherine Urquhart, *Lake-Sumter Community College*
Andrew S. Walters, *Northern Arizona University*
C. Edward Watkins, *University of North Texas-Denton*
Mark Watman, *South Suburban College*
Sheree Watson, *University of Southern Mississippi*
Shannon Michelle Welch, *University of Idaho*
Diane Keyser Wentworth, *Fairleigh Dickinson University*
Judith Wightman, *Kirkwood Community College*

Ann Brandt-Williams, *Glendale Community College*
Manda J. Williamson, *University of Nebraska-Lincoln*
Melissa Wright, *Victoria College*

Workshop Participants

Marion F. Cahill, *Our Lady of the Lake College*
Jarrod Calloway, *Northwest Mississippi Community College*
Mark Covey, *Concordia College*
Dale V. Doty, *Monroe Community College*
Adia J. Garrett Butler, *University of Maryland, Baltimore County*
Esther Hanson, *Prince George's Community College*
Sheila Kennison, *Oklahoma State University*
Cheri Kittrell, *State College of Florida, Manatee-Sarasota*
Ronnie Naramore, *Angelina College*
Marylou Robins, *San Jacinto College*
Maria Shpurik, *Florida International University*
Inger Thompson, *Glendale Community College*

Focus Group Participants

Jake Benfield, *Colorado State University*
Ann Brandt-Williams, *Glendale Community College*
Baine Craft, *Seattle Pacific University*
Linda Bolser Gilmore, *DeKalb Technical College*
Elaine Cassel, *Lord Fairfax Community College*
Shawn Robert Charlton, *University of Central Arkansas*
Laurie Corey, *Westchester Community College*
Angela Fellner, *University of Cincinnati*
Andrew M. Guest, *University of Portland*

James E. Hall, *Montgomery College*
Alishia Huntoon, *Oregon Institute of Technology*
Heide D. Island, *Seattle Pacific University*
Dale V. Klopfer, *Bowling Green State University*
Heather LaCost, *Waubonsee Community College*
Fred Leavitt, *California State University-Hayward*
Irv Lichtman, *Houston Community College*
Wade Lueck, *Mesa Community College*
Gregory Manley, *University of Texas at San Antonio*
Timothy D. Matthews, *The Citadel*
Dawn McBride, *Illinois State University*
Eleanor E. Midkiff, *Santa Barbara Community College*
Richard Miller, *Western Kentucky University*
Robin Musselman, *Lehigh Carbon Community College*
Kathryn C. Oleson, *Reed College*
Sean P. Reilley, *Morehead State University*
N. Clayton Silver, *University of Nevada-Las Vegas*
Nancy Wiggins, *Lurleen B. Wallace Community College*
Judith Wightman, *Kirkwood Community College*
Jason Young, *Hunter College*

Content Consultants

Eileen Achorn, *University of Texas-San Antonio*
Bill Altman, *Broome Community College*
Kim Anderson, *Brigham Young Universtiy-Idaho*
Harold E. Arnold, *Judson College*
Eileen Astor-Stetson, *Bloomsburg University*
Kerri Augusto, *Becker College*
Anisah Bagasra, *Claflin University*
Ted Barker, *Northwest Florida State College*
Jacob Benfield, *Colorado State University*
John Billimek, *California State University-Long Beach*
Ann Brandt-Williams, *Glendale Community College*
Laurel Brooke Poerstel, *University of North Carolina-Wilmington*
Kimberly Carmitchel, *Colorado Mountain College*
Patrick Carmody, *University of Tennessee-Knoxville*
Juan Casas, *University of Nebraska at Omaha*
Kinho Chan, *Hartwick College*
Shawn Robert Charlton, *University of Central Arkansas*
Kimberly Christopherson, *Morningside College*
Wanda Clark, *South Plains College*
Job Clement, *Daytona State College*
Frank Conner, *Grand Rapids Community College*
Verne Cox, *University of Texas at Arlington*

Gregory Cutler, *Bay de Noc Community College*
Matthew Dohn, *Kutztown University*
Joan Doolittle, *Anne Arundel Community College*
Darryl L. Douglas, *University of Michigan-Flint*
Vera Dunwoody, *Chaffey College*
Christopher Dyszelski, *Madison Area Technical College*
Melanie Evans, *Eastern Connecticut State University*
Kimberly Fairchild, *Manhattan College*
Sue Frantz, *Highline Community College*
Michael K. Garza, *Brookhaven College*
David Gersh, *Houston Community College*
William Goggin, *University of Southern Mississippi*
Mark Grabe, *University of North Dakota*
Jonathan Grimes, *Community College of Baltimore County*
Gretchen Groth, *Metropolitan State College of Denver*
Nancy Hartshorne, *Central Michigan University*
Jeffrey B. Henriques, *University of Wisconsin-Madison*
Raquel Henry, *Lone Star College-Kingwood*
Rick Herbert, *South Plains College*
James Hess, *Black Hills State University*
James Higley, *Brigham Young University*
Jameson K. Hirsch, *East Tennessee State University*
Farrah Jacquez, *University of Cincinnati*
Richard Kandus, *Mt. San Jacinto College-Menifee Campus*
Dan Klaus, *Community College of Beaver County*
Heather LaCost, *Waubonsee Community College*
Gerard LaMorte, *Rutgers, The State University of New Jersey*
Mark Laumakis, *San Diego State College*
Laura Lauzen-Collins, *Moraine Valley Community College*
Nicolette Lopez, *University of Texas at Arlington*
Tim Maxwell, *Hendrix College*
Barbara McMillan, *Alabama Southern University*
Lisa R. Milford, *State University of New York-Buffalo*
Hal Miller, *Brigham Young University*
Robin Musselman, *Lehigh Carbon Community College*
Ronnie Naramore, *Angelina College*
Jane A. Noll, *University of South Florida*
Christine Offutt, *Lock Haven University*
Andrew Peck, *Pennsylvania State University*
Thomas Peterson, *Grand View University*
Daniel Philip, *University of North Florida*
Ralph Pifer, *Sauk Valley Community College*
William Pithers, *Edinboro University*
Brian Pope, *Tusculum College*

Diane M. Reddy, *University of Wisconsin-Milwaukee*
Heather Rice, *Washington University in St. Louis*
Marylou Robins, *San Jacinto College*
Richard Rogers, *Daytona State College*
Steve Rouse, *Pepperdine University*
Lisa Routh, *Pikes Peak Community College*
Catherine Sanderson, *Amherst College*
Alan Schlossman, *Daytona State College*
Gloria Shadid, *University of Central Oklahoma*
David Simpson, *Carroll University*
Wayne S. Stein, *Brevard Community College*
Mark Strauss, *University of Pittsburgh*
Marla Sturm, *Montgomery County Community College*
Dr Éva Szeli, *Arizona State University*
Pamela M. Terry, *Gordon College*
Elayne Thompson, *Harper College*
Natasha Trame, *Lincoln Land Community College*
Shaun Vecera, *University of Iowa*
Larry Ventis, *College of William and Mary*
Kurt Wallen, *Neumann College*
Susan Weldon, *Henry Ford Community College*
Jane Whitaker, *University of the Cumberlands*
Nancy Wiggins, *Lurleen B. Wallace Community College*
Robert W. Wildblood, *Indiana University-Kokomo*
Kip Williams, *Purdue University*
Patrick Wise, *Monroe Community College*
Lynn Yankowski, *Maui Community College*
Jennifer Yates, *Ohio Wesleyan University*
Michael Young, *Valdosta Technical College*
Edmond S. Zuromski, *Community College of Rhode Island*

Cover Consultants

Laurie Corey, *Westchester Community College*
Katherine Dowdell, *Des Moines Area Community College*
Kimberley J. Duff, *Cerritos College*
Christopher M. France, *Cleveland State University*
Linda Bolser Gilmore, *DeKalb Technical College*
Andrew M. Guest, *University of Portland*
Charles Jacob Huffman, *James Madison University*
Alishia Huntoon, *Oregon Institute of Technology*
Christopher B. Mayhorn, *North Carolina State University*
Deana Julka, *University of Portland*
Kathryn C. Oleson, *Reed College*
Maria Shpurik, *Florida International University*
Jason Young, *Hunter College*

To the Student

How to Use This Book

The features in this book promote your reading comprehension, reflection, problem-solving skills, and critical-thinking skills. These skills are key to success in the course and in your life beyond. Let's walk through the pedagogical features that will help you learn the material in this book.

CHAPTER 10

Intelligence

Chapter Outline

- What Do We Mean by Intelligence?
- Additional Types of Intelligence
- How Do We Measure Intelligence?
- Is Intelligence Governed by Genetic or Environmental Factors?
- Intelligence
- Extremes in Intelligence

As Smart as They Look?

Each week on the reality show America's Most Smartest Model, producers ask male and female models to compete in a series of tasks designed to test both their intelligence and their modeling skills. An intelligence-testing task, for example, may require rapid-fire responding to trivia questions that will determine how fast a partner has to run on a treadmill or dissecting and correctly identifying the organs from a fetal pig. Winning the intelligence challenge gives a model a decided edge in the modeling challenge. In one episode, for example, the winning team members were assigned a runway show with their dressing room next to the stage, while the losing team had to complete an obstacle course to make it to the runway. Models who fail to compete strongly in both tasks are eliminated from the show.

Obviously, much of the show's humor comes from stereotypes that models are generally not very smart, and certainly the show takes great delight in having models who cannot name the vice president of the United States (or, for that matter, do not know a judge's last name). However, the show is equally derisive of contestants who cannot name an Italian designer under time pressure or do not demonstrate appropriate interpersonal skills during a surprise networking challenge. Further confounding the stereotype of the not-so-smart model, contestants include

Andre, a son of Romanian diplomats who speaks five languages and delights in scheming people off the show, and Daniel, a Ph.D. candidate in psychology at a major California university who correctly spells both phosphorescence and Bacchanalian during a spelling bee.

Clearly, America's Most Smartest Model is built on common conceptions of what intelligence is. Like many other aspects of human behavior, however, intelligence is a concept that appears simple at first glance, only to become more and more complicated the closer we look at it. Start with the basic question: How do you define intelligence? Most people use smart or stupid to characterize the other people in their lives all the time, and they generally have a great deal of confidence in their assessments. But answer this: When you describe a friend as a generally smart person, how are you assessing smartness? Are you thinking about how your friend performs in all situations, or are you just impressed by how sophisticated her answers are in English class and ignoring the fact that she's just scraping by in Chemistry? If you were watching the TV show just described, would you be sympathetic to a contestant's protest that "street smarts" make him an intelligent person, even if he can't successfully identify a city in Iraq? And what about that friend of yours who seems to be "book smart" but lacks common sense? Is that person, book smarts and all, the one you want leading you if your plane crashes on a remote island?

Okay, then, so what do we mean by intelligence? Does it mean the same thing in every instance? How do we understand it, and how do we measure it? To these basic questions we must add several others: Can we distinguish between intelligence and talent? Are intelligence and wisdom the same thing? Are intelligence and creativity related? And, finally,

310 Chapter 10 Intelligence

Intelligence 311

Chapter-Opening Vignettes

Every chapter begins with a vignette that shows the power of psychology in understanding a range of human behaviors. This theme is reinforced throughout the chapter, celebrating the extraordinary processes that make the everyday possible.

Guided Learning

Chapter Learning Objectives summarize what you should be able to do once you have studied the chapter. You can use the learning goals in two ways. First, study them before reading the chapter to get an overall picture of how the concepts in the chapter are related to each other and what you will be learning. Then, after reading the chapter, use the learning goals to review what you have learned, either individually or in peer study groups. Advance organizers can improve learning and retention without significantly increasing study time.

Helpful study tools...

Following each section is a Before You Go On feature that helps you check your mastery of the important items covered. **• What Do You Know?** questions ask you to stop and review the key concepts just presented. **• What Do You Think?** questions encourage you to think critically on key questions in the chapter.

What is Science

LEARNING OBJECTIVE 1 Describe the steps in the scientific method.

Before we consider psychology as a science, take a moment to try to an
tion, what is a science? You might have answered that question by listin
ences, such as chemistry, biology, or physics. You might have envisione
coated guy or gal in a lab somewhere, mixing strangely bubbling chemica

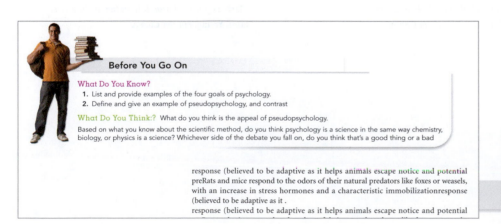

Before You Go On

What Do You Know?
1. List and provide examples of the four goals of psychology.
2. Define and give an example of pseudopsychology, and contrast

What Do You Think?: What do you think is the appeal of pseudopsychology.

Based on what you know about the scientific method, do you think psychology is a science in the same way chemistry, biology, or physics is a science? Whichever side of the debate you fall on, do you think that's a good thing or a bad

response (believed to be adaptive as it helps animals escape notice and potential
preRats and mice respond to the odors of their natural predators like foxes or weasels,
with an increase in stress hormones and a characteristic immobilizationresponse
(believed to be adaptive as it .
response (believed to be adaptive as it helps animals escape notice and potential

This text is designed to allow text discussions to intersect at precise points with side notes that are placed in the page margins—interesting and relevant psychology facts, contemporary news stories, historical points, material from movies, and the like. Also intersecting with the text material at just the right points on each page are elements such as relevant exciting boxes, current controversies in psychology, research surprises, and perfectly selected photos.

---

to relieve pressure on your skin. The parts of your skin under continuous pressure would develop sores or bruises. Since many everyday experiences would be damaging to our bodies if we were not able to detect discomfort, a lack of ability to detect pain can be very dangerous.

PRACTICALLYSPEAKING | **Quick Ways to Reduce Acute Pain**

As we discuss in this chapter, medical practitioners are constantly seeking ways to provide relief to patients in chronic, or continuing, pain. But what about acute pain, the short-term pain you feel when you bump your leg on a table, for example?

Gate control theory suggests that touch sensations, which frequently travel along fast fibers, can help prevent some pain sensations traveling on the slow pathways from reaching areas of your brain where they are perceived. According to this theory, the brain only processes so much input, so touch can help to set up a "gate" that stops pain. This explains why we have a tendency to rub the skin of areas of our body that have been injured. For example, if you walk into a piece of furniture, you might rub your leg to dampen the pain.

Focusing on your breathing may also help. We often tend to gasp and then hold our breath when we injure ourselves, such as bumping a leg. Formal methods of pain control, such as the Lamaze method for childbirth, work in part by altering this natural tendency, by teaching people to breathe in short, panting gasps (Leventhal et al., 1989).

Distraction can also help, whereas anxiously focusing on pain can make it worse (al Absi & Rokke, 1991). Some studies have suggested that simply looking at a pleasant view, can affect pain tolerance (Ulrich, 1984). Other evidence suggests that in order for a distraction to be effective, the experience must be active. Studies have shown that playing an interesting videogame can dampen pain detection, whereas passive watching of a TV show has little effect. Stress and sexual experience also decrease the perception of pain. So, if you bump your leg on the way into a big job interview or on a hot date, perhaps you would not notice the pain as much as you would under other circumstances!

144 Chapter 5 Sensation and Perception

---

s of many communal side
l from each. People in India
meal, often including por-
d with social interactions.
hen they are in a social set-
compared to when eating
that involve business meet-
at more than those whose
ample. This may be due to
s well as the fact that peo-
n they are engaged in con-

e an individual **body weight**
eral level. We may fluctuate in a small range around that weight, but
n to the original set point, even after major deviations from it (Pasquet
)4). This is particularly evident when people diet. A reduction in body
llowed by a rebound back toward the original weight. The *Practically*
iscusses why so many dieters fail to achieve lasting weight loss. This
se, however. Some people do undergo dramatic weight changes in one
her and maintain their new weights for a considerable period of time.
tain a lower body weight typically make permanent changes in their
persistently monitor their weight (Dansinger et al., 2005; Warziski et
er et al., 2005).
ch suggests, however, that body weight set point is not the only
determining how much we eat. The availability of food we like
Many individuals in societies such as much of the United States,
lentiful, find their weights steadily creeping up over the years
). This can be seen with laboratory rodents, too. Presenting them
of highly palatable foods will cause more eating and weight gain
agan et al., 2002). This suggests that a firm body weight set point
experimental animals or humans. When presented with highly
d a diminishing level of activity, most people have a tendency to
they age.

body weight set point a weight that individuals typically return to even after dieting or overeating.

> "A man seldom thinks with more earnestness of anything than he does of his dinner."
>
> —*Samuel Johnson, writer*

Key Terms are listed at the end of each chapter with page references.

Margin Definitions define the key terms discussion in the text.

Margin Notes present interesting facts and quotes throughout the chapter.

Seeing the "Big Picture" in Psychology

Cut Across Connections

Every chapter on a substantive area of psychology not only offers a thorough presentation of the nature, explanations, and applications of that area, but also includes *"Cut-Across"* sections on the *development, brain function, individual differences*, and *dysfunctions* that occur in that realm of mental life. Your success in this course will depend on how well you can integrate this information meaningfully. The more often you review your prior knowledge and connect it with new knowledge, the more automatic and refined learned knowledge and skills become.

Hearing When Things Go Wrong

There are many conditions that lead to abnormalities in the auditory system. Some cause either partial or total **deafness**, the loss of hearing. Abnormalities in the auditory system can also add unwanted auditory perceptions.

Deafness Deafness has a variety of causes. It can be genetic or caused by infection, physical trauma or exposure to toxins, including overdose of common medications such as aspirin.

Since speech is an important mode of communication for humans, deafness can have dramatic consequences for socialization. This is particularly a concern for children, because young children need auditory stimulation in order to develop normal spoken language skills. For this reason, physicians try to identify auditory deficits at an early life stage. Parents can then make choices among different options to help their children with deafness. Some deaf individuals learn to use sign language and other methods of communication that rely on the senses other than hearing. Research over the past years has made progress in the construction of cochlear implants that help individuals with deafness to hear sounds (Sharma et al., 2009). Although this work is developing at a rapid pace, there remain many deaf people who are not helped by cochlear implants, however. (Battmer et al., 2009). This is one reason that many individuals and families choose to avoid them. Some in the deaf community also believe that hearing is not necessary in order to lead a productive and fulfilling life. For them, the potential benefits of implants may not outweigh the potential risks of surgery required to place them in the cochlea (Hyde & Power, 2006).

A world of new possibilities After undergoing successful cochlear implant surgery, this four-year-old child practices the violin under the instruction of his music teacher at the Memphis Oral School for the Deaf.

Hearing HOW we Differ

We differ greatly in our ability to detect specific sounds. People show particular differences in their ability to identify certain notes in a scale. **Absolute pitch** refers to the ability to recognize an individual note in isolation. This is very difficult for most people. Only about 1 in 10,000 people in Western countries has absolute pitch. This ability seems to originate in childhood, between the ages of three and six years, through musical training, and it is associated with differences in brain anatomy (Zatorre, 2003). Research has shown that portions of the cortex are actually thinner in individuals with absolute pitch (Bermudez et al., 2009). Although it's not clear whether people with absolute pitch start out with a thinner cortex or whether they develop it through training, it's possible that synaptic pruning contributes to this structural difference.

Studies have shown, however, that people who speak tonal languages, or languages in which differences in tone convey meaning, such as Vietnamese and Mandarin Chinese, are more likely to develop absolute pitch than those speaking Western languages. This again suggests the possibility that early learning of auditory information related to tones can have a permanent effect on the functioning of this sensory system.

Just as some people exhibit absolute pitch, others are tone deaf, or unable to discern differences in pitch. Although tone deafness or *amusia* is sometimes the result of damage to the auditory system, it can be present at birth, and researchers believe it may be related to genetics (Peretz et al., 2007). Tone deafness affects up to 4 percent of the population and mostly results in a diminished appreciation for music. Although music appreciation is an important enriching ability, people with tone deafness are able to enjoy all other aspects of life. This condition only presents serious social problems when it occurs in cultures where the language is tonal.

Breaking the bad news One of the guilty pleasures for many *American Idol* fans is that special moment when judge Simon Cowell calls a contestant "tone deaf." The show includes performers whose musical abilities vary from absolute pitch to tone deafness.

Hearing How we Develop

Our ears are formed and capable of transducing sound waves before we are even born. In fact, human fetuses have been shown to respond to noises long before birth. Research has shown that fetuses respond to loud noises with a startle reflex and that after birth, they are capable of recognizing some sounds they heard while in utero. However, the ability to recognize and respond appropriately to a wide variety of sound stimuli is acquired over many years of postnatal life. Sounds associated with language, for example, become recognizable over postnatal development, as do those associated with music. We describe language development in more detail in Chapter 9.

Sensitive periods exist for the development of both language and music learning (Knudson, 2004). As we described in Chapter 3, we acquire certain abilities during sensitive periods of development much more easily that we do after the sensitive period has ended. The tonotopic map in the primary auditory cortex of the brain is organized during such a sensitive period of development (deVillers-Sidani et al., 2007). Studies in experimental animals have shown that exposing animals to pure tones during a certain time in development, leads to a larger representations of those sounds in the auditory cortex. The same exposure after the sensitive period in development is over has no such effect. If a sound is made important to the animal, however, by pairing it either with a reward, such as water, or a punishment, such as an electric shock, the primary auditory cortex can be reorganized so that more of it responds to the relevant tone (Bakin et al., 1996). Such top-down processing of tones indicates that this region of the brain still shows plasticity after the sensitive period is over. It is not as easy, however, to remap the brain after a sensitive period as it is during one. The stimuli needed to produce changes in older animals must be very strong and important, compared to those needed for younger animals (Kuboshima & Sawaguchi,

A bit too early A pregnant woman tries to introduce music to her fetus by positioning headphones on her stomach. Although fetuses do indeed respond to loud noises and can detect certain sounds, the acquisition of musical skills cannot take place until sensitive periods unfold during the pre-school years.

Hearing What Happens in the BRAIN?

After auditory information is transduced from sound waves by the hair cells in the basilar membrane of the cochlea, it travels as signals from nerves in the cochlea to the brainstem, the thalamus, and then the auditory cortex, which is located in the temporal lobe. Part of the primary auditory cortex is organized in a **tonotopic map**. That is, information transmitted from different parts of the cochlea (sound waves of different frequency and, hence, sounds of different pitch) is projected to specific parts of the auditory cortex, so that our cortex maps the different pitches of sounds we hear. Auditory information from one ear is sent to the auditory cortex areas on both sides of the brain. This enables us to integrate auditory information from both sides of the head and helps us to locate the sources of sounds.

From the primary auditory cortex, auditory information moves on to the auditory *association areas* in the cortex. As we described in Chapter 4, association areas of the brain's cortex are involved in higher-order mental processes. Association areas help to link the sounds we hear with parts of the brain involved in language comprehension.

Association areas also integrate, or coordinate auditory information with signals from other sensory modalities. Have you ever noticed how distracting it is to watch a movie that has an audio slightly out of synchrony with the video image? This is because the brain is set up to integrate information from multiple sensory systems. Over time, we learn to have expectations about the coincidence of certain visual stimuli with specific sounds. When the sounds in a movie do not match the visual images the way they would in real life, our expectations are violated and our attention

They can't fool the brain (yet) M.I.T. professor Neil

Cut Across Connections shown above are taken from Chapter 5 Sensation and Perception.

What Happens in the Brain When . . .

It's our hope that you will come to see the fascination of psychology and develop a passion for this field of study. One example of how we demonstrate this to you is a regular feature throughout the textbook—a two-page spread called *What Happens in the Brain When . . . .* Centering on a common everyday activity, these lively spreads clarify the remarkable brain events that help give life to the activity and serve as an awe-inspiring reminder that psychology is everywhere.

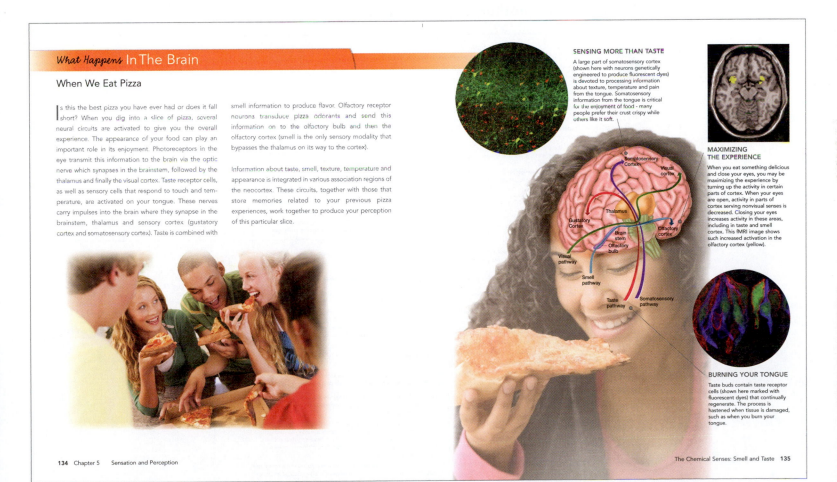

What Happens in the Brain feature shown above taken from Chapter 5 Sensation and Perception.

Review Main Concepts

Chapter Summary

Each chapter ends with a summary and list of key terms aimed at representing the scope and emphasis of a relatively large amount of material in an efficient and concise form. The end-of-chapter Summary reviews the main concepts presented in the chapter with reference to the specific Learning Objectives. It provides you with another opportunity to review what you have learned as well as to see how the key topics within the chapter fit together. You can write your own summary first, as a review strategy, and then check your work against the text summary to self-evaluate your understanding of the big picture in each chapter.

Summary

Understanding How We Develop

LEARNING OBJECTIVE 1 Understand the key debates underlying research and theory in child development.

- Developmental psychology is the study of changes in our behavior and mental processes over time and the various factors that influence the course of those changes.
- Key philosophical issues in the study of developmental psychology are what drives change (biological or environmental factors); what's the nature of the change (qualitative or quantitative); and the role of early experiences in shaping later development.

How Is Developmental Psychology Investigated?

LEARNING OBJECTIVE 2 Describe and discuss the advantages and disadvantages of cross-sectional and longitudinal designs for researching development.

- Two major research approaches in developmental psychology are cross-sectional (comparing different age groups to assess change) and longitudinal (studying the same group to see how responses change over time).
- The cohort-sequential research design combines elements of the cross-sectional and longitudinal approaches.

Before We Are Born

LEARNING OBJECTIVE 3 Discuss patterns of genetic inheritance and describe stages and potential problems during prenatal development.

- Our genetic inheritance comes from both parents, who each contribute half our chromosomes. Genes can combine in various ways to make up our phenotype, or observable traits.
- Genetics can influence the manifestation of both physical traits and psychological traits, including temperament, although environment also plays a role.
- Prenatal development begins with conception and is divided into three stages: germinal, embryonic, and fetal, each characterized by specific patterns of development.
- Individuals are susceptible to multiple influences by biological and environmental forces before they are even born, during the prenatal period.

Infancy

LEARNING OBJECTIVE 4 Summarize the major physical, cognitive, and emotional developments that take place during infancy.

- Infants make dramatic gains in both physical and psychological capabilities. Our brains grow during this period, preparing us to learn and encode the information that will organize those changes.
- One of the most important developmental theorists, Jean Piaget, proposed a theory of cognitive development that suggested that through learning and self-experimentation, we help our thinking to grow progressively more complex.
- Piaget believed we passed through multiple stages on the way to formal adult reasoning and that each transition was accompanied by the acquisition of a new cognitive capability. During the sensorimotor stage, in infancy, we become able to hold memories of objects in our minds.
- Information-processing researchers have suggested that babies may develop mental capacities at earlier ages than Piaget believed they did.
- Attachment [...] posed to b[...] ensuring th[...] attachment [...] secure the [...] capabilities [...]
- Baumrind f[...] also affect [...] quent resea[...] on other en[...]

Childhood

LEARNING OBJECTIVE 5 Summarize the major physical, cognitive, and emotional developments that take place during childhood.

- Physical growth continues at a generally slower pace in childhood than in infancy. Myelination and synaptic pruning continue to shape the brain.
- Piaget believed that children pass through the stages of preoperational and concrete operations thinking, learning to manipulate their mental schema. Other researchers have suggested children's thinking may not be as limited during these stages as Piaget thought it was.
- Theories of moral development have often focused on moral reasoning (the reasons why a child would do one thing or another) rather than values. Generally, research supports the movement from morality rooted in submitting to authority to morality rooted in more autonomous decisions about right and wrong.
- Some researchers suggest that moral reasoning may vary across gender and culture. Other researchers have questioned whether morality theories would be better served by measuring behavior instead of expressed reasoning or attitudes.

Key Terms

developmental psychology 57	recessive trait 63	assimilation 69	puberty 82
maturation 57	codominance 63	accommodation 69	primary sex characteristics 82
stage 57	discrete trait 63	equilibrium 69	secondary sex characteristics 82
critical periods 59	polygenic trait 63	object permanence 70	formal operations 84
cross-sectional design 59	temperament 63	information-processing theory 70	menopause 87
longitudinal design 60	zygote 64	habituation 70	cellular clock theory 88
cohort-sequential design 60	placenta 64	attachment 72	wear-and-tear theory 88
prenatal period 60	miscarriage 64	reciprocal socialization 74	

92 Chapter 3 Human Development

Summary and Key Terms shown above taken from Chapter 3 Human Development.

Psychology Around Us

Memory Manufacturing and Eyewitness Testimony

"This is a stick-up!"

Memory plays a big role in our lives and in psychology. Generally, most people believe that they can remember things pretty well. Indeed, retrieving past memories, including "buried" memories, is a major part of daily functioning. Similarly, in the criminal justice system, the memories of eyewitnesses are relied upon heavily and lead to many convictions. BUT are our memories as accurate as we like to believe? Should we have great confidence in our recollections of recent everyday events, let alone our adult memories of childhood events, the recollections of eyewitnesses, and the like?

As you are working on this online exercise, consider the following questions...

- What do you think this lab exercise says about the accuracy of our memories?
- What implications might this lab exercise hold for the field of psychology's assumptions, techniques, and interpretations?
- How might this contrived situation differ from a real-life event? Does this contrivance help account for the accuracy or inaccuracy of your memories? Pro or con?

Psychology Around Us **275**

This Video Lab Exercise shown above is taken from Chapter 8 Memory.

Video Lab Activities

These activities use extensive video material to drive student learning. The combination of video footage and digital interactive technology brings the lab exercises to life in ways that were previously impossible. In actively engaging with the material you will better process the concepts. The kinds of video material included in the *Video Lab Exercises* range from laboratory brain footage to videos of everyday events to psychology documentary excerpts. These activities are accessible via WileyPlus, the optional on-line companion to this textbook

CUT/ACROSS CONNECTION

What Happens in the BRAIN?

- The main language areas are on the left side of the brain for most people—but not all.
- Thinking about images (or smells or tests) activates the same brain areas as if we were actually seeing (or smelling or tasting). Thoughts that involve language activate language areas of the brain.
- When we watch other people do things, mirror neurons in our brain can activate just as though we were doing the same things.

When Things Go Wrong

- Damage near Broca's area of the brain can cause us to lose our ability to use grammar.
- Obsessive-compulsive disorder involves unavoidable thoughts called obsessions and irresistible urges, or compulsions, to perform certain behaviors.
  - About 1 percent of all people in the United States display schizophrenia, a disorder marked by disorganized thoughts and loss of contact with reality.

HOW we Differ

- Girls tend to learn to talk earlier than boys. However, the difference soon disappears.
- Babies who learn two languages at home begin talking slightly later than those who learn just one.
- The number of words we have in our language for a certain object or concept (such as a color) may influence how we can think about that object or concept.

How we Develop

- Very young infants are able to perceive all the sounds of every language. As time passes, however, we lose the ability to distinguish phonemes of other languages.
- Our ability to learn languages is at its best before school age. After we pass age 13, it is much more difficult for us to learn new languages than it was earlier.
- We naturally tend to use child-directed speech with babies. It may be an evolutionary adaptation that helps humans learn language.
- One of the reasons toddlers don't play hide-and-seek very well is because their theory of mind abilities are still undeveloped.

This Cut Across Connection feature shown above is taken from Chapter 9 Language and Thought.

Cut/Across Connections Summary

This section pulls together **fascinating and relevant facts and concepts** from the chapter's Cut Across sections. Used in combination with the Chapter Summary, Cut/Across Connections will help keep you focused on psychology's "big picture."

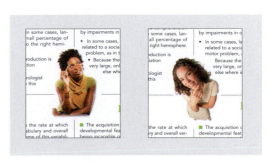

Hopefully, by understanding the rationale for the pedagogical elements in this text, you will become more motivated to use them while you study. We hope you enjoy using this book as much as we enjoyed writing it for you!

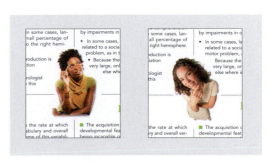

To the Student **xliii**

Psychology
Around Us

CHAPTER 1

Psychology: Yesterday and Today

chapter outline

- What is Psychology?
- Psychology's Roots in Philosophy
- The Early Days of Psychology
- Twentieth Century Approaches
- Psychology Today

"Trolling" the Internet

Trolls are no longer villains confined to fairy tales and fantasy stories. In Internet terminology, troll is a name for someone who seeks to intentionally disrupt online communities. Trolls ask distracting questions in comment chains, post wildly inappropriate and disruptive notes on message boards, and, like their fictional namesakes, basically seek to sow confusion and havoc anywhere where there's a community of users that appears ripe for pranking.

Troll pranks can involve relatively mild provocations, such as stealing another person's alias on a site and posting under that name, or taking on wild personas and posting bizarre statements that almost force people to respond. Trolls are credited, for example, with originating "Rick-rolling," the Internet term for posting a misleading link. Rick-rolling is named after a prank that took unsuspecting users who clicked a link to a videogame site, not to the game they wanted but instead, to a video for the Rick Astley song "Never Gonna Give You Up." Rick-rolling actually gave the song a huge boost in popularity and entertained mainstream Web programmers so much that YouTube pulled the same prank on its own users one April Fool's Day, sending everybody who clicked the day's featured videos to Rick's video.

Sometimes, however, trolls dip into much darker territory, such as stealing people's social security numbers or harassment. In one infamous case, a troll happened upon a MySpace memorial to a teen who had committed suicide. That troll proceeded to mock, on a well-known troll message board, a typo in one of the tributes. The mockery expanded to contempt for the victim himself and eventually to a series of cruel events outside the online world. The teen's bereaved parents were barraged for a year and a half with anonymous "prank" phone calls from people pretending to be the teen or asking for him.

Some observers see trolling as evidence of the increasing detachment and moral deterioration of society. Others see it as merely a technology-aided extension of tendencies people have always expressed. How can we understand this bizarre behavior and its implications for society? Is it within the normal range of human experience, or does it exemplify some deviance within our culture or within a select set of individuals? These are the types of questions that the science of psychology is set up to answer. But they're not the only questions.

Trolling along. Psychologists study all kinds of mental processes and behaviors, including new ones such as trolling.

While psychology can help us try to understand unusual behavior, like that of trolls, it also helps us understand far more common things that we all do. Why do people even use Facebook or MySpace in the first place, for example? Psychology can provide some insights. As you read this book, you'll see that all the topics we examine contribute not only to understanding of unusual or problematic behaviors but also to things that happen all around us, every day.

We'll discuss human development, examining how we mature and what shapes us as we age. Maybe trolls experienced some events in childhood that shaped their view of other Internet users. We'll look at motivation and emotion, getting some ideas about why people do things and how we experience our feelings. What drives people to spend hours every day on the Internet, for example? We'll look at theories of intelligence, including one that suggests that the kind of intelligence needed to hack into websites and steal social security numbers is different from the kind of intelligence needed to empathize with people such as parents who have lost a child. Along the way, our goal is to help you get insights not only into the attention-grabbing and sometimes bizarre things that can go wrong but also into the often-overlooked but miraculous things that usually go right. We've also included several "Practically Speaking" boxes that we hope can help you to use what you learn to make even more things go right in your own life.

 Every journey begins with a first step, and in this chapter, the first step is to learn what psychology is. After that, we'll discuss where psychology originated and how it developed. Finally, we'll learn more about psychology today, including what psychologists do, where they do it, and what's new and changing in what they do.

Psychology: Myth vs. Reality

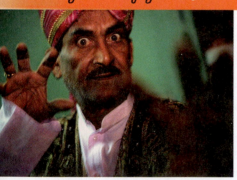

Go to a party and tell strangers that you're a psychologist, and they will most likely tell you about their anxieties or phobias. Alternatively, they might smile nervously and comment that you're probably analyzing their behavior right there. Most people assume that all psychologists are therapists, when, in fact, clinical psychology is but one specialty in a field that includes cognitive, social, developmental, and sports psychology, among many others. Psychology, like most scientific fields, has many myths that lead to inaccurate stereotypes about psychologists and the phenomena that they study. Here are a few others:

MYTH #1: The nature versus nurture debate was put to rest years ago. *In fact, it is still very much alive in psychology.*

MYTH #2: Most mental disorders have clear and dominant biological causes. *It just seems that way because so many drug treatments are available for people with psychological problems. In fact, we still have much to learn in this realm.*

MYTH #3: The brain does not produce new neurons after childhood. *Actually, current research indicates that new neurons continue to be formed throughout life, even in old age.*

MYTH #4: As most people age, their neurons die. *In fact, in normal non-pathological aging, there is little or no loss of neurons.*

What is Psychology?

Define psychology, and describe the goals and levels of analysis psychologists use.

Curiosity about the inner workings of the mind has probably existed since humans first began to communicate their ideas to others and to recognize that other people have thoughts and emotions that are distinct from their own. **Psychology** is the study of *mental processes* and *behavior*. The term also refers to the application of that knowledge to various realms of human life, including mental dysfunction, education, and business.

Mental processes describe the activity of our brains when we are engaged in thinking, observing the environment, and using language. Mental processes include complex experiences, such as joy, love, and even the act of lying. During psychology's early history, the primary method for exploring internal mental processes was to observe outward **behavior**, our observable actions, and make inferences, or guesses, about what was happening in the mind. Since psychology became an experimental science in the nineteenth century, however, psychological researchers have sought more direct ways to examine mental processes. In fact, in the past decade, the advent of brain imaging and other forms of technology has enabled scientists to uncover fascinating connections between behavior and mental processes and to move toward a more comprehensive view of how mental processes occur in various individuals and situations.

When psychologists study mental processes and behavior, they generally have one of four goals in mind:

- *Description.* Psychologists seek to *describe* very specifically the things that they observe. As you read this book, you'll see that psychologists have described phenomena ranging from how babies learn to talk to how we fall in love, how we make decisions, and more.

- *Explanation.* Telling what, where, when, and how are sometimes not enough. A key goal for many psychologists is to answer the question of, "Why?" As we'll see in Chapter 2, psychologists have developed hypotheses and theories to *explain* a huge variety of events, from why we get hungry to why we either like or don't like parties.

- *Prediction.* Psychologists also seek to *predict* the circumstances under which a variety of behaviors and mental process are likely. You'll learn later in this book, for example, about research that predicts the conditions under which we are most likely to offer help to a stranger in need.

- *Control.* We often encounter situations in which we want to either limit or increase certain behaviors or mental processes—whether our own or those of others. Psychology can give students advice on controlling their own behaviors that ranges from how to limit unhealthy stress or how to increase what we remember from a class.

In order to describe, explain, predict, or control mental processes and behaviors, we need to recognize the many various influences on them. All our thoughts and actions, down to the simplest tasks, involve complex activation and coordination of a number of levels—the levels of the *brain*, the *individual*, and the *group*. As you will see throughout this textbook, no psychological process occurs solely at one of these levels. Analyzing how the brain, the individual, and the group influence each other reveals much about how we function—insights that might be overlooked if we were to focus on one of these levels alone (see **Table 1-1**).

> " Man is the only animal for whom his own existence is a problem which he has to solve "
>
> —*Erich Fromm, psychologist and philosopher*

psychology the study of mental processes and behaviors.

mental processes activities of our brain when engaged in thinking, observing the environment, and using language.

behavior observable activities of an organism, often in response to environmental cues.

TABLE 1-1 The Levels of Analysis in Psychology

Level	What Is Analyzed	"Trolling"
The brain	How brain structure and brain cell activity differ from person to person and situation to situation	What are the patterns of brain activation in trolls as they seek to upset others?
The person	How the content of the individual's mental processes form and influence behavior	What values do the trolls hold? Do they have limited capacity for empathy? Are they selfish, narcissistic, or angry persons?
The group	How behavior is shaped by the social and cultural environments	How is troll participation affected by anonymity, sense of affiliation with other troll groups, or decreased connection to the larger society?

At the *level of the brain*, psychologists consider the brain cell activity that occurs during the transmission and storage of information. They also focus on the design of the brain, including the chemicals and tissues that it is composed of and the genes that guide its formation. As we'll see later in this chapter, technological advances in the fields of molecular biology and brain imaging have made it possible to study how brain structure and activity differ from person to person and situation to situation. A psychologist studying the brain can now look, for example, at what parts of the brain are activated by the administration of a pharmaceutical or street drug or the brain changes that accompany anxiety and depression (Damsa et al., 2009).

At the *level of the person*, psychologists analyze how the *content* of mental processes—including emotions, thoughts, and ideas—form and influence behavior. To use a computer analogy, this level relates to the *software* rather than the mechanical functioning, or *hardware*, of the brain. The level of the person includes many of the things that people think of first when they discuss psychology—ideas such as consciousness, intelligence, personality, and motivation. Although internal biological structures of the brain allow such person-level processes to occur, we cannot understand the processes unique to each individual, such as personality or motivation, without also studying this content.

Psychologists may strive to understand the brain activities and mental processes of an individual, but their understanding remains incomplete without analysis at the *level of the group*. This perspective acknowledges that humans are shaped by their social environment and that this environment varies over time. *Groups* can refer to friends, to family members, or to a large population. Often a large group shares a **culture**, a set of common beliefs, practices, values, and history that are transmitted across generations. The groups to which people belong or perceive themselves to belong, can influence their thoughts and behaviors in fundamental ways (Prinstein & Dodge, 2008).

When they conduct research, psychologists may focus on different levels of analysis, but it is important to recognize that activity is happening simultaneously at all three different levels during even our most everyday decisions and tasks. The levels also interact. Brain activity is detectable only with special instruments, like microscopes or neuroimaging machines, but is nevertheless affected by other levels, even by our broad cultural contexts. Similarly, barely noticeable changes in the biology of our brains can cause major changes in our general state of being or how we respond to others.

> "Everything that irritates us about others can lead us to an understanding of ourselves."
>
> *–Carl Jung, psychiatrist and philosopher*

culture a set of shared beliefs and practices that are transmitted across generations.

Let's go back for a moment to our earlier discussion on Internet trolling. If psychologists set out to understand trolling behavior, they could examine it at various levels. Operating at the level of the brain, they could explore patterns of brain activation in trolls in order to see what brain changes occur when trolls go online or seek to upset or empathize with others. At the level of the person, psychologists could explore questions of intelligence and personality to see whether there are certain characteristics common to most trolls. Finally, at the level of the group, psychologists might examine how anonymity buffers trolls as they disregard general standards of polite behavior or how trolls' participation on their own message boards strengthens bonds to other trolls and decreases their broader sense of connection to the population at large. As you'll see throughout this book, the notion of multiple levels of analysis has played an important role in the development of psychological theories (Fodor, 2007, 2006, 1968).

Having examined what psychologists study and how they do it, let us next consider how psychology got its start, how historical and societal factors have affected the way psychologists study the mind and behavior, and how psychologists have shifted their energies among the different goals and levels of analysis throughout psychology's history. We will then consider where the field of psychology is today and where it may be going tomorrow.

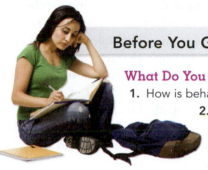

Before You Go On

What Do You Know?
1. How is behavior different from mental processes? How are they the same?
2. What are the three levels of analysis in psychology?

What Do You Think?
What would be the focus of each of the four goals of psychology when studying Internet trolling? How would the questions and actions of a psychologist who seeks to describe trolling differ from those of someone who wants to control trolls, for example?

Psychology's Roots in Philosophy

LEARNING OBJECTIVE 2 Describe the influences of early myths and ancient Greek philosophies on psychology.

Before the development of science as we know it today, humans attempted to explain the natural environment through *myths*, tales that often gave human qualities to natural events. A volcano might be the result of an angry mountain goddess, for example. In order to control both natural and human behavior, people of past times also developed a number of magical ceremonies and rituals. Some theorists today believe that these methods for influencing and understanding events were the first forms of religious practice and that such practices reflect an innate human need to understand and make sense of people and the natural world. In fact, according to such theorists, the science of today is somewhat similar to primitive myths in that it represents our attempts to describe, explain, predict, and control our reality (Waterfield, 2000).

Although they focused on supernatural, life-giving forces, the early rudimentary belief systems contributed to the explosion of intellectual curiosity and information

Mythical explanations. Before the development of science, myths were used to explain natural events. Some have survived. Here a Hawaiian woman places offerings to the Fire Goddess during a ceremony at the crater of Halemaumau Volcano.

"Sure, we need more research in alchemy, necromancy, and sorcery, but where is the money going to come from?"

that occurred in the fourth and fifth centuries B.C.E. It was around that time that the great thinkers of ancient Greece began moving beyond supernatural explanations. Instead, they tried to find ways to determine the nature of reality and the limitations of human awareness of reality. To accomplish these difficult goals, they engaged in open, critical discussions of each other's ideas. Such intellectual dialogue created a flow of ideas, and new ideas of any nature were both respected and challenged. In such open forums, students and nonintellectuals could challenge prevailing doctrines and even their instructors.

The history of psychology (and most other sciences) starts with the history of philosophy, as the Greeks' efforts came to be called. *Philosophy* is defined as the study of knowledge and reality. The ancient philosophers' method of introducing problems and then questioning proposed solutions is at the core of today's modern scientific method, which we will discuss in greater detail in Chapter 2. The freedom of thought found in Greek society emphasized that theories, ideas about the way things work, are never final but rather always capable of improvement. Today's psychologists still take that view.

Hippocrates (ca. 460–377 B.C.E.) actually produced one of the first psychological theories, suggesting that an individual's physical and psychological health is influenced by *humours*—four bodily fluids (blood, phlegm, yellow bile, and black bile)

FIGURE 1-1 Hippocrates' psychological theory
This medieval manuscript illustrates the psychological effects of the humours proposed by the Greek physician. The illustration on the left demonstrates the melancholia produced by black bile, while the one on the right depicts the joyous, musical, and passionate personality produced by blood.

that collectively determine a person's character and well-being and predict the individual's responses to various situations. He also correctly identified the brain as the organ of mental life. Hippocrates tested his theories with direct observation and at least some dissections. Because of such efforts, academic study became rooted firmly in detailed scientific methods of study (see **Figure 1-1**).

Other Greek philosophers, such as *Socrates* (ca. 470–399 B.C.E.) and *Plato* (ca. 427–347 B.C.E.), believed that "truth" lies in the mind and is highly dependent upon our perceived, or subjective, states. Socrates looked for concepts that are the "essence" of human nature and searched for elements that various concepts have in common. He tried, for example, to identify *why* something – anything – is beautiful and what essential factors an object must possess in order to be beautiful. His student, Plato, believed that certain ideas and concepts are pure and signify an ultimate reality. Plato believed that we could use reasoning to uncover these *core ideas* deeply imbedded in every human soul. The ideas of these two philosophers represented early studies of mental states and processes.

Similarly, *Aristotle* (ca. 384–322 B.C.E.), the most famous thinker of the Greek period, made key contributions to the foundations of psychology. His writings represent some of the first important theories about many of the topics you will be coming across throughout this book, such as sensations, dreams, sleep, and learning (Hergenhahn, 2005) although, at the same time, he mistakenly believed that the brain was an organ of minor importance. Aristotle was one of the first to promote empirical, or testable, investigations of the natural world. He looked inward at sensory experiences and also scrutinized his environment carefully, searching for the basic purpose of all objects and creatures. In his studies, he formed ideas about how living things are hierarchically categorized, concluding—centuries before Charles Darwin—that humans are closely related to animals.

What Do You Know?

3. What do the earliest myths have in common with today's scientific studies?

4. Greek philosophers who believed reasoning would uncover ideals or core ideas were focused on which aspect of psychology?

5. How did the Greek philosopher Hippocrates explain mental processes and behavior? How did his research methods influence today's study of psychology?

What Do You Think? What advantages do you think a scientific approach has for explaining behavior and mental processes compared to a supernatural approach?

The Early Days of Psychology

LEARNING OBJECTIVE 3 Name important early psychologists and describe their major theories and research methods.

Approximately 2,000 years after they lived, the philosophies of the ancient Greeks re-emerged to influence European thinkers during the Renaissance period of the 1400s through the 1600s. In the centuries both during and after the Renaissance, European society underwent a scientific revolution. A spiritual worldview, which had dominated for several centuries, was replaced increasingly by a view of the world based on mathematics and mechanics. By 1800, both the universe and human beings were believed to be machines that were subject to fixed natural laws. The roles of magic and mysticism in science essentially disappeared (Leahey, 2000).

Although mysticism declined as a form of explanation for human nature, there remained great confusion and disagreement regarding human motives and origins. In the latter part of the nineteenth century, *Charles Darwin* proposed the theory of evolution, making the radical suggestion that all life on Earth was related and that human beings were just one outcome of many variations from a common ancestral point. Darwin also suggested natural selection as the mechanism through which some variations survive over the years while others fall out of existence. Natural selection proposes that although all kinds of variations can be passed down from parent to offspring, some variations are *adaptive*—better suited to an organism's environment. These adaptive variations help the organism to thrive. On the other hand, less-adaptive variations reduce the ability of an organism to survive. Darwin's theories about man's evolution from the ape shifted scientific interest toward an understanding of the origins of humans and our behavior.

Social and technological developments during the 1800s also helped set the stage further for the science of psychology. Improvements in transportation, communication, and education allowed information to flow more freely to more levels of society than ever before, leading to a rise of popular interest in science.

The Founding of Psychology

In this atmosphere, psychology emerged finally as a distinct scientific field of investigation. As we have observed, prior to the late nineteenth century, psychology was virtually indistinguishable from the study of philosophy. In 1879, however, the physiologist *Wilhelm Wundt* (1832–1920) opened a laboratory in Leipzig, Germany, dedicated exclusively to the study of psychology. As a natural scientist, Wundt believed that the exper-

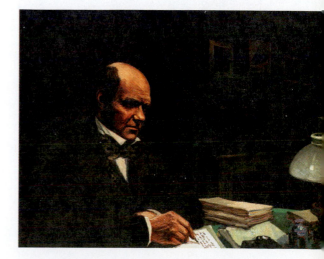

Charles Darwin (1809-1882). The theories by the English naturalist about human evolution shifted scientific attention toward human origins and behavior.

"To be, or not to be," from Shakespeare's play *Hamlet*, is the famous line uttered by the play's main character to indicate his psychological struggle with suicide as a way to end his mental suffering. Hamlet's father is murdered by his uncle (his father's brother), who then marries Hamlet's mother. After Hamlet learns of his uncle's brutality from a ghostly vision, he struggles with the ethical and moral contradictions of how to avenge his father's murder. *Hamlet* is arguably Shakespeare's greatest tragedy and through its brilliant prose, both the characters of *Hamlet* and the audience explore the themes of suicide, revenge, incest, moral corruption, and mental dysfunctioning.

One aspect of Shakespeare's genius was his ability to portray the mental lives of his characters in disturbing and realistic detail. Through his keen observations of the human condition, he examined the intricacies of mental disturbances and individuals' struggles with self-knowledge, themes that did not fully emerge in psychological science until the late nineteenth and early twentieth centuries.

Indeed, Shakespeare's unique understanding of mental dysfunction predated Western psychology by almost 300 years. Through the characters in his plays, he presented many of the classic symptoms associated with contemporary psychological maladies, including sociopathy (*Richard III*), alcoholism (*Henry V*), anxiety (*Macbeth*), depression (*King Lear* and *Hamlet*), dementia (*Hamlet*), epilepsy (*Julius Caeser*), obsessive compulsive patterns (*Macbeth*), palsy (*Troilus and Cressida*), eating disturbances (*Henry IV Parts I & II* and *The Merry Wives of Windsor*) and paranoia (*Coriolanus, Othello, Hamlet, Macbeth,* and *Richard, III*), to name a few (Cummings, 2003). Altogether, the Bard speculated on the nature and causes of behavior in at least 20 of his 38 plays and many of his sonnets.

---

imental methods of other sciences were the best way to study the mind and behavior, so he established a program that trained students to perform such experiments in psychology. Psychology's emphasis on rigorous, scientific experimentation continues to this day, as we'll see in Chapter 2.

Wundt exposed research participants to simple, standardized, repeatable situations and then asked them to make observations, an approach similar to ones used in the study of physiology. One of Wundt's most famous experiments, for example, involved a clock and pendulum. Wundt found that when determining the exact location of the pendulum at a specific time, his observations were always off by 1/10 of a second. He believed that he had found evidence that humans have a limited attention capacity and that it requires 1/10 of a second to shift focus from one object to another.

The father of experimental psychology. Wilhelm Wundt works with colleagues in his laboratory at the University of Leipzig, one of the first laboratories devoted exclusively to psychological research.

Wundt studied the content and processes of **consciousness**, the behaviors and mental processes that we're aware are happening. In his laboratory, he was particularly interested in studying the idea of *will* and how it influences what individuals choose to attend to in their environments. He believed that much of behavior is motivated and that attention is focused for an explicit purpose. Wundt called this branch of investigation **voluntarism**.

Later, Wundt also went on to form theories about emotion and the importance of historical and social forces in human behavior. His ideas about cultural psychology are in fact appreciated today for their early recognition that an individual's social context must also be taken into account in order to fully explain his or her mental processes and behavior (Benjamin, 2007, 1997).

Structuralism: Looking for the Components of Consciousness

One of Wundt's students, *Edward Titchener* (1867–1927), expanded upon his ideas and formed the school of **structuralism** in the United States. Titchener's goal was to uncover the structure, or basic elements, of the conscious mind, much like looking at the parts that make up a car engine or bicycle, or the individual bricks in a complicated Lego® sculpture.

To study the conscious mind, the structuralists relied heavily on a method originated by Wundt, called **introspection**, which literally means "looking inward." This method involved the careful observation of the details of mental processes and how they expand simple thoughts into complex ideas. If shown a house made of Legos, for example, an introspecting structuralist would describe the smooth, shiny texture of each brick, the color of the brick, the tiny gap between it and the adjoining bricks, and so forth.

Toward the end of the 1800s, arguments began to emerge against the use of introspection as an experimental technique. Skeptics pointed out that scientists using introspection often arrived at diverse findings, depending on who was using the technique and on what they were trying to find. The school of structuralism also came under attack for its failure to incorporate the study of animals and to examine issues of abnormal behavior.

The major concern many psychologists had with structuralism, however, was its emphasis on gathering knowledge for its own sake without any further agendas such as a desire to apply our knowledge of the mind in practical ways. Recall the four goals of psychology discussed earlier. The goal of the structuralists was to use introspection to *describe* observable mental processes rather than to *explain* the mechanisms underlying consciousness or to try to *control* such mechanisms. They believed that speculation about unobservable events had no place in the scientific study of psychology. Ultimately, even Titchener himself acknowledged the need to understand the purpose of human thought and behavior rather than to merely describe it.

Although many of structuralism's principles did not survive, its propositions that psychologists should focus largely on observable events and that scientific study should focus on simple elements as building blocks of complex experience have lived on in certain modern schools of thought.

Functionalism: Toward the Practical Application of Psychology

William James (1842–1910), one of America's most important psychologists (and philosophers) was instrumental in shifting attention away from the structure of mental content to the purposes and functions of our mental processes. James set up the first psychology laboratory in the United States at Harvard University and wrote one of the first important psychology texts, *Principles of Psychology*. His view of psychology was that mental events and overt behaviors have functions (Richardson, 2006; Keller, 1973). Thus, James's approach was called **functionalism**. To use our earlier analogy, functionalists would be less interested in describing the parts of a car engine or bicycle, and more interested in what the engine or bicycle can do under a variety of conditions.

Functionalists viewed the mind as an ever-changing stream of mental events rather than the more or less static set of components that the structuralists were seeking. For this reason, James and his colleagues were also interested in understanding how the mind adapts and functions in a changing environment.

Functionalism did not rely primarily on a single research method, such as introspection. It used a variety of methods, and it also highlighted differences among individuals rather than similarities. And unlike structuralism, functionalism emphasized the need for research to include animals, children, and persons with mental disorders

consciousness personal awareness of ongoing mental processes, behaviors, and environmental events.

voluntarism belief that much of behavior is motivated and that attention is focused for an explicit purpose.

structuralism belief that mind is a collection of sensory experiences and that study should be focused on mental processes rather than explanation of mechanisms underlying those processes.

introspection method of psychological study endorsed by Wundt and his followers, involving careful evaluation of mental processes and how they expand simple thoughts into complex ideas.

functionalism belief that mental processes have purpose and focus of study should be on how mind adapts those purposes to changing environments.

William James. The influential psychologist and philosopher investigated the purposes and functions of our mental processes. His book *Principles of Psychology* took 12 years to write and was 1200 pages in length.

Gestalt psychology field of psychology arguing that we have inborn tendencies to structure what we see in particular ways and to structure our perceptions into broad perceptual units.

in order to understand both normal and abnormal psychological functioning (Richardson, 2006; Keller, 1973).

The shift from structuralism to functionalism was apparent in an early experiment on how humans locate sound. Participants in the experiment were asked to point to the location of a sound (Angell, 1903). A structuralist would have asked each participant to provide an introspective report of his or her conscious experience of the sound. Functionalists, however, were more concerned with issues, such as how accurately participants could point in the direction in which the sound was physically located.

Although it never really became a formal school of psychology, functionalism helped to focus psychologists' attention on what the mind can and does accomplish. Spurred by the emphasis of functionalists on providing applicable and concrete information, psychology began to tackle socially relevant topics. The researchers William Lowe Bryan and Noble Harter (1897), for example, performed a famous investigation regarding how quickly telegraph operators could learn necessary typing skills. Their findings were used to improve training for railroad telegraphers, and the study is now widely regarded as one of the first to have a significant social and commercial impact. Functionalism also marked the beginning of exploration into socially important issues, such as learning and education, and indeed, *educational psychology* remains a significant area of research in the field today.

Gestalt Psychology: More than Putting Together the Building Blocks

While opponents of structuralism in the United States were raising concerns that structuralism did not examine the uses of consciousness, other psychologists in Germany were questioning in a more basic way the structuralist idea that consciousness can be reduced to basic mental elements. **Gestalt psychology** is based on the idea that we have inborn tendencies to impose structure on what we see, and these tendencies cause us to perceive things as broad "perceptual units" rather than as individual sensations. Indeed, the word *Gestalt* is of German origin, meaning "whole" or "form." The school subscribed to the idea that "the whole is greater than the sum of its parts."

For example, when you watch TV, you see complete pictures. In fact, each picture is made up of thousands of small dots, called *pixels*. If you get close enough to the screen, you can see the picture break down, but our brains still favor integrating those dots into a cohesive whole. Similar findings have been gathered regarding our tendency to group eyes, noses, and mouths into recognizable human faces. Children three months of age or younger show a preference for human faces but only when the component parts of faces are arranged correctly in a facial orientation (Gava et al., 2008; Morton & Johnson, 1991).

Gestaltists developed over 100 perceptual principles to describe how the brain and sensory systems perceive environmental stimuli. Some of the Gestalt laws are shown in **Figure 1-2**. Gestaltists also viewed learning as tied to perception. They believed that problem solving occurs when a person develops a sudden and complete insight into a solution—indeed, they believed that problems remain in an unsolved state until such points of insight occur.

Facial recognition. Even babies younger than 3-months-old can piece together the component parts of a face and recognize it as a whole object. In particular, they can recognize the familiar face of their mother.

The Gestalt school helped guide psychology away from the study of component parts and toward a more comprehensive view of the human mind and functioning. Many of its concepts and the importance of the study of perception are still present in modern psychology, although Gestalt psychology is no longer a prominent, distinct school.

Figure Ground:
The tendency to perceive one aspect as the figure and the other as the background. You see a vase or two faces, but not both at the same time.

FIGURE 1-2 Gestalt laws Gestalt psychologists studied how we perceive stimuli as whole forms or figures rather than individual lines and curves.

Proximity:
Objects that are physically close together are grouped together. (In this figure, we see 3 groups of 6 hearts, not 18 separate hearts.)

Continuity:
Objects that continue a pattern are grouped together.

When we see this,

we normally see this

plus this.

Not this.

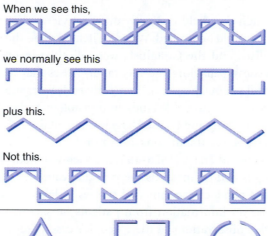

Closure:
The tendency to see a finished unit (triangle, square, or circle) from an incomplete stimulus.

Similarity:
Similar objects are grouped together (the green colored dots are grouped together and perceived as the number 5).

Before You Go On

What Do You Know?

6. What is introspection, and which early school of psychologists relied most heavily upon it?
7. What was the main difference in approach between functionalism and structuralism?
8. What did the Gestalt psychologists study?

What Do You Think? Which early school of psychology most closely resembles the way you view the human mind? Why?

Twentieth-Century Approaches

Eye to eye. Sigmund Freud, founder of psychoanalytic theory, examines a sculptured bust of himself at his village home in 1931.

From the late 1800s into the twentieth century, psychology continued to grow as a science. In the years leading up to World War I and through World War II, there was tremendous growth in the field of psychology. The number of psychologists rapidly expanded, and popular interest in psychology grew to unprecedented levels.

As more people became interested in the field, more viewpoints on behavior and mental processes continued to emerge. Several twentieth-century schools of thought had major influence on the field, including the psychodynamic approach, the behaviorist approach, the humanistic approach, the cognitive approach, and the sociobiological approach. We'll explore next the defining features of all of these approaches.

Psychoanalysis: Psychology of the Unconscious

Although they held distinctly different views about how the mind is structured and how it should be studied, Wundt, Titchener and the structuralists, James and the functionalists, and the Gestaltists were all alike in one way: They all focused on consciousness, behaviors and mental processes that we are aware are happening. And, as you will see in Chapter 6, their early endeavors into the conscious experience remain an area of considerable study in psychology today. Other theorists, however, eventually came along and focused largely on mental processes of which we are unaware, those that happen in the **unconscious** mind.

Sigmund Freud (1856–1939), a Viennese neurologist, suggested that many of our thoughts and feelings exist beyond the realm of awareness, in the unconscious. Freud did not conduct experimental studies of laboratory participants. He built his theory instead on information from patients he saw in his medical practice. Based on his detailed observations of these people's cases, Freud came to believe that the mind is a complex interaction of those thoughts and memories that exist at different levels of awareness, some conscious and some unconscious. He saw mental life as a competition among forces that strive to reach the upper levels of awareness. Freud's theory was developed over decades and is called the **psychoanalytic theory**.

Freud further believed that childhood experiences help set the stage for later psychological functioning by contributing to effective or ineffective interactions among conscious and unconscious forces. According to Freud, certain developmental milestones must be achieved successfully in order for a person to achieve emotional adjustment. He also was interested in how children unconsciously adopt social and moral norms from their parents and, in turn, develop a conscious awareness of what constitutes acceptable and unacceptable expressions of their internal desires. Freud suggested that these conscious standards lead to unavoidable tensions between our unconscious, primal needs and our conscious, social or moral restraints. According to Freud, the back-and-forth tension within and between the conscious and unconscious mind is what shapes personality, helps produce abnormal behaviors in some cases, and governs virtually all behavior.

In fact, Freud and his followers saw the conscious mind as a thin mask over a deep unconscious mental world, a world that contains impulses and urges that cannot be expressed freely given the constraints of a person's social environment. Let's return again to our friends, the Internet trolls. Freud would likely perceive the trolls' explanations that their behavior is intended to educate the ignorant as tissue-thin justifications for deeper feelings of mistrust or hostility toward the world. He would also be interested

" Freud: If it's not one thing, it's your mother.**"**

—*Robin Williams, comedian*

in why many people become so upset by the deeds of trolls. After all, most of the actions of trolls amount to goofy behavior and anonymous slurs from strangers (trolls) with zero credibility, yet they send many people into a state of near apoplexy. As trolls often state triumphantly, "If you need to write a page-long comment to say that a troll isn't bothering you, you've already lost."

As we shall see later in the textbook, psychoanalytic notions typically have not held up well when subjected to rigorous scientific study. For evidence, Freud relied on anecdotes and case histories of remarkable changes in his patients. Researchers have not been able to find much support for his claims when they test them with larger groups of people (Wallerstein, 2006). The lack of research support, as well as philosophical differences, prevented many of his contemporaries from accepting Freud's theories. William James, the functionalist, for example, rejected the psychoanalytic notion of the unconscious. To him, conscious ideas were not a product of underlying machinery: what was observed in the conscious mind was the complete experience.

Nevertheless, to this day, psychoanalysis remains an influential theory of mental functioning and personality in the field of psychology. Clearly, his theory increased the applications of psychology to many new aspects of everyday life. It stirred interest in motivation, sexuality, child development, dreams, and abnormal behavior—all topics we will discuss later in this book. Freud's use of discussion as a therapeutic technique helped lead to the creation of psychiatry and clinical psychology as influential therapeutic methods, and these methods continue to thrive.

Although many of Freud's ideas have been challenged, they certainly marked a turning point in the understanding of human nature. Psychoanalytic theory was among the first psychological theories to provide a comprehensive view of human nature, and it helped make psychology relevant to more people than ever before.

unconscious hypothesized repository of thoughts, feelings and sensations outside human awareness, thought in some theories to have a strong bearing on human behavior.

psychoanalytic theory psychological theory that human mental processes are influenced by the competition between unconscious forces to come into awareness.

behaviorism branch of psychological thought arguing that psychology should study only directly observable behaviors rather than abstract mental processes.

stimuli elements of the environment that trigger changes in our internal or external states.

response ways we react to stimuli.

Behaviorism: Psychology of Adaptation

In addition to theories about the conscious mind and the unconscious mind, a third area of psychology, called **behaviorism**, emerged in the early part of the twentieth century. This school of thought was founded on the belief that psychology should study only behaviors that are directly observable rather than abstract mental processes.

Early behaviorists tended to focus on the relationships between **stimuli**—things that trigger changes in our internal or external states—and **responses**—the ways we react to stimuli. As you'll read in Chapter 7 on Learning, these behaviorists developed a number of influential ideas about how responses produce consequences and how those consequences in turn affect an organism's future responses to stimuli.

Behaviorism originated in America and Russia. In the United States, animal research was growing in popularity, while in Russia, *Ivan Pavlov's* (1849–1936) discovery of a phenomenon that came to be called *conditioning* linked various animal behaviors to events in the animals' environments (Bitterman, 2006; Bauer, 1952). Such successful studies of nonhuman behavior called into question the methods being used to investigate human behavior. Even though animals could not introspect, scientists seemed to be learning a great deal by observing their behavior.

Edward Thorndike (1874–1949), who was technically a functionalist, helped transition the field of psychology toward behaviorism by proposing that animal findings could help explain human behavior. As behaviorism proved increasingly fruitful and popular, tensions grew between investigators who used introspection and those who relied on observation.

John Watson (1878–1958) is generally credited with pioneering the school of behaviorism. He agreed with Thorndike that animals could be useful in guiding our understanding of human psychology, and he sharply disagreed with psychoanalysis and with

The box! B.F. Skinner developed the so-called "Skinner box" to help him investigate how consequences reinforce behavior. Here he uses the box to train a rat to press a lever for a food reward.

reinforcement learning process in which the consequence resulting from a behavior will increase or decrease the likelihood that the behavior will occur again.

humanistic psychology theory of psychology that sought to give greater prominence to special and unique features of human functioning.

client-centered therapy approach to therapy founded by Carl Rogers, based on the notion that the client is an equal and positive gains are made by mirroring clients' thoughts and feelings in an atmosphere of unconditional positive regard.

The real teachers. Behaviorists use principles of conditioning, reinforcement, and modeling to teach animals various behaviors in laboratory settings. However, like this young Bonobo chimpanzee, animals (and humans) usually learn behaviors in their natural environments where their parents and other important figures inadvertently apply learning principles.

the notion of unobservable mental processes. As we'll discuss in Chapter 7, he was able to extend Pavlov's animal work to young children, and he essentially launched modern psychological theory by demonstrating that children could be conditioned by researchers to fear various objects and situations.

B.F. Skinner (1904–1990), who emerged as the leading behaviorist after World War II, helped expand behaviorism's perspective by acknowledging that internal, mental processes may indeed be at work in some situations, such as when an animal runs to get food. But even here, Skinner argued, empirical—observable—information should be gathered first, and then theories about causation could be formulated from that. That is, even when behaviorists acknowledged that internal mental processes were probably at work, they held that their primary job was to describe empirical phenomena not to explain them. For example, when observing the behavior of a monkey who is attempting to obtain food, a behaviorist might describe how the animal distinguishes a particular food from other stimuli, how it approaches the food, and what steps it takes to obtain it – observations meant to reveal how particular responses come to be associated with the food stimulus.

An idea central to behaviorism is that the consequence resulting from a particular behavior serves to either increase or decrease the likelihood that an individual will perform that same behavior again in the future. If the consequence of a given behavior is rewarding, it is regarded as **reinforcing**, and the individual will be more likely to repeat the behavior down the road. A behavior is *positively* reinforcing when it brings about a desired outcome (such as food or a prize), and *negatively* reinforcing when it helps an organism avoid undesirable outcomes. For example, procrastination may be negatively reinforcing to the extent that it helps people avoid the pain of actually sitting down to do their homework. Remember, if a behavior is either positively or negatively reinforcing, we are more likely to do it again later.

The term *negative reinforcement* is sometimes confused with *punishment*, but the latter is really a very different factor in behavior. Unlike negative reinforcements, *punishments* render behaviors less likely to be repeated. Back to our Internet trolling behavior, some comment board moderators have tried to control trolling by "disemvoweling," removing all the vowels from the offending comments of trolls. This punishing practice makes troll comments easier to detect and harder to read, and therefore, less likely to generate the kind of outraged response a troll finds rewarding. Disemvoweling punishes the troll and effectively has decreased the numbers of offensive comments and hijacked comment threads on many message boards.

The principles of behaviorism became widely used in advertising and in helping businesses address personnel problems. As behaviorism grew in popularity, its principles were applied to numerous industries as well as to courts, schools, and even the military. During this period, researchers also placed great emphasis on the development of controlled scientific methods that might establish psychology once and for all as a true science. Given the appeal of its objective and controlled methods of investigation, behaviorism reached considerable prominence in the academic field, and it continues to have a strong influence on psychology today. Indeed, most of today's experimental studies continue to adhere to rigorous research standards similar to those laid down by behaviorists.

Behaviorism was not embraced by all, however. Some psychologists criticized John Watson and other prominent behaviorists for popularizing and, in their view, cheapening psychology. In 1929, for example, psychologist Joseph Jastrow wrote that behaviorism's portrayal in popular magazines and newspapers undermined psychology's role as a valid science (Jastrow, 1929). Similarly, other psychologists raised questions about the merits of this area of psychology.

In addition, over time, the behaviorists themselves began to disagree with each other and to divide into competing schools of thought. In the 1960s, for example, the psychologist *Albert Bandura* (1925–) demonstrated that children often seem to learn not by conditioning or clear rewards and punishments but by *social observation*, or *modeling*. Bandura and other psychologists also showed that people could learn without any apparent change in their overt behavior, a phenomenon that suggested individual changes might reflect some kind of internal representations and mental processes. With these and related developments, pure behaviorism (that is, behaviorism with no attention to mental processes, such as beliefs or thoughts) began to lose some of its influence.

Humanistic Psychology: A New Direction

By the 1950s and 1960s, psychoanalytic and behaviorist theories were at opposite ends of the psychology spectrum, one focusing exclusively on mental processes and the other exclusively on behavior. The 1960s were a particularly troubled time socially and economically in the United States and also a time when heated debates took place regarding the relationship between people and authority figures and when questions were raised about essential human rights. In this atmosphere, **humanistic psychology** emerged as an alternative theory that sought to give greater prominence to the special and unique features of human functioning than to the mechanistic principles that characterized psychoanalysis and behaviorism.

Founding humanistic theorists *Carl Rogers* (1902–1987) and *Abraham Maslow* (1908–1970) rejected the approach of behaviorists. They felt that behaviorists looked at humans just as they looked at animals, largely regarding people as machines that could be predicted and controlled but giving little or no weight to consciousness and other distinctly human characteristics. Humanism, in contrast, focused on the potential of individuals and highlighted each person's subjectivity, consciousness, free will, and other special human qualities. According to humanistic psychologists, all people have the potential for creativity, positive outlook, and the pursuit of higher values. They claimed that if we can fulfill our full potential, we will inevitably lead a positive life of psychological growth.

Maslow, in fact, proposed that each of us has a basic, broad motive to fulfill our special potential as human beings, which he called the drive for *self-actualization*. He suggested that anyone who achieved this broad motive would indeed lead a positive and fulfilling life. Maslow's hierarchy of human needs summarized his theory and is shown in **Figure 1-3**.

Carl Rogers developed a humanistic alternative to the psychoanalytic approach to psychotherapy, which he called **client-centered therapy**. According to Rogers, therapists should respect their clients as equals. The therapist establishes a trusting and warm relationship with the client by "mirroring" feelings and conveying unconditional support and positive regard for the client. This very human approach to therapy played an important role in the establishment of the fields of clinical and counseling psychology after World War II.

In certain respects, the humanists were not actually seeking to prove behaviorists and psychoanalysts wrong but rather to complete their ideas. They believed that behaviorism was too limited to the objective realm and that psychoanalysis failed to acknowledge the free will and autonomy of individuals. The goal of humanists, in contrast, was to jolt people from a psychological rut and to help them realize their innate and grand potential. Although humanism did

Humanistic pioneer. Carl Rogers was the founder of client-centered therapy, which promotes an equal relationship between therapists and clients and helps clients to achieve their full potential.

FIGURE 1-3 **Maslow's hierarchy of needs** Maslow prioritized our numerous needs and believed that we must satisfy basic physiological and safety needs first. Only then can we progress up the hierarchy and achieve self-actualization.

Self-actualization needs: to find self-fulfillment and realize one's potential

Esteem needs: to achieve, be competent, gain approval, and excel

Belonging and love needs: to affiliate with others, be accepted, and give and receive attention

Safety needs: to feel secure and safe, to seek pleasure and avoid pain

Physiological needs: hunger, thirst, and maintenance of internal state of the body

cognitive psychology field of psychology studying mental processes as forms of information processing, or the ways in which information is stored and operated in our minds.

information processing means by which information is stored and operated internally.

cultural psychology the study of how cognitive processing varies across different populations.

neuroscience study of psychological functions by looking at biological foundations of those functions. Previously known as *psychobiology*.

behavioral genetics subfield of psychology looking at the influence of genes on human behavior.

sociobiologists theorists who believe humans have a genetically innate concept of how social behavior should be organized.

evolutionary psychology field of study believing that the body and brain are products of evolution and that genetic inheritance plays an important role in shaping the complete range of thoughts and behaviors.

not ultimately have as great an impact on psychology as the schools of behaviorism and psychoanalysis, it sparked a greater appreciation of human consciousness and helped to establish a balance between the prevailing views of psychology. Perhaps most importantly, the movement triggered an increased interest in mental processes.

Cognitive Psychology: Revitalization of Study of the Mind

In the years after World War II, a new school of psychology emerged whose goal was to measure mental processes effectively. The famous psychologist *George A. Miller* has recalled that period as a time when "cognition [mental process] was a dirty word because cognitive psychologists were seen as fuzzy, hand-waving, imprecise people who really never did anything that was testable" (Baars, 1986, p. 254). While serving as president of the American Psychological Association in 1960, the Canadian psychologist *Donald Hebb* (1904–1985) urged the psychological community to apply the rigorous experimental standards seen in behavioral studies—that is controlled and objective methods—to the study of human thought.

In 1967, *Ulric Neisser*, a student of Miller's, published the influential text *Cognitive Psychology* in which he described *cognition* as "all the processes by which....sensory input is transformed, reduced, elaborated, stored, recovered, and used" (Neisser, 1967, pg. 4). Neisser went on to define **cognitive psychology** as the study of **information processing**, the means by which information is stored and operates internally.

Cognitive psychologists compared the human mind to a computer, likening mental processes to the mind's *software* and the human nervous system to the system's *hardware*. Early cognitive psychologists reasoned that if modifying software can control the "behavior" of computers, identifying and modifying mental processes can control human behavior. Cognitive psychology soon became the dominant model of the mind.

Under this engineering model, cognitive psychologists focused their attention on the *functioning* of cognitive mechanisms rather than on their content. Cognitive researchers were able to observe the "inputs" and "outputs" of the mental system through carefully controlled experimentation and then to theorize about the internal mechanisms that must underlie such mental functioning.

Cognitive psychology continues to influence contemporary theory and research into memory, perception, and consciousness, among other areas that we will discuss in this text. The rigorous experimental standards established by cognitive scientists continue to define current methods for studying how information is stored and manipulated by the brain across different situations. Moreover, at the core of a relatively new field called **cultural psychology** is an interest in how cognitive processing may vary across different populations. *Cross-cultural* research uses cognitive experimental methods to help distinguish mental processes that are universal to all humans from those that are shaped by particular variables in the social and physical environment (Byrne et al, 2009; Cole, 1996).

Psychobiology/Neuroscience: Exploring the Origins of the Mind

Interest in the biological basis of psychological phenomena can be traced through the work of Hippocrates, Aristotle, Pavlov, and even Freud. Thus it is not surprising that eventually a distinct area of psychology, called *psychobiology*, emerged. Psychobiology attempted to explain psychological functions by looking primarily at their biological foundations (Gariepy & Blair, 2008; Hergenhahn, 2005). In particular, psychobiology explored brain structure and brain activity and the ways they might be related to individual behaviors and group dynamics. The term psychobiology has fallen into disuse, although this subfield of psychology has continued to grow. It is now referred to as **neuroscience.**

Early psychobiology gained momentum with the advancement of scientific and medical techniques. *Karl Lashley* (1890–1958), one of the most influential psychobiologists, based his work on the study of animal neurological functioning. He used surgical techniques to destroy certain areas in the brains of animals and then observed the effects of such destruction on memory, learning, and other cognitive processes. Lashley found that the tissues within certain areas of the brain were often linked to particular cognitive functions. His ultimate goal was to pinpoint all areas of the brain responsible for memory, learning, and other higher functions. He was never able to accomplish this goal fully, and it continues to be a major interest in contemporary research.

Roger Sperry (1913–1994), a researcher who was influenced greatly by Lashley, pioneered *split-brain* research on animals. Sperry and his colleagues severed the connections responsible for relaying information between the left and right hemispheres, or halves, of the brain. They found that even after the brain is split surgically, the two hemispheres of animals can often function and learn independently. Later investigators found similar results when they studied human beings who had undergone a similar split-brain surgery to treat severe seizures (Colvin & Gazzaniga, 2007). Split-brain research on both animals and humans made it possible to study the separate functioning of the brain's hemispheres, which, as we'll see in Chapter 4, remains a popular topic in contemporary psychology.

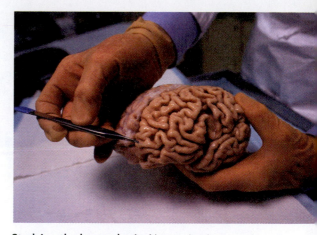

Studying the human brain Neuroscientists examine brain structure and brain activity to determine how they are related to behavior. Here a researcher dissects the brain of a former patient with dementia as part of a study to learn more about memory and memory disorders.

A number of psychological subfields have been influenced by the field of neuroscience, as well as by Darwin's early work on evolution. **Behavioral genetics**, for example, studies the influence of genes on cognition and behavior. This is not a completely new field. Early in the twentieth century, and even during the rise of behaviorism, a number of animal researchers used evolutionary principles to help explain human behavior.

Similarly, **sociobiologists**, as they were initially called, theorized that humans have an innate concept of how social behavior should be organized. In 1975 Harvard biologist Edward O. Wilson, a specialist on ants, brought great attention to this view with his book *Sociobiology: The New Synthesis*. He and other sociobiologists suggested that humans are genetically more predisposed than other organisms to learn language, create culture, protect territory, and acquire specific societal rules and regulations. Sociobiologists did not claim that genetic influences are necessarily more important than environmental factors, such as parenting or the mass media. Rather, they proposed that our social behavior is the result of biological *and* cultural influences. One sociobiologist, David Barash (1979, p. 45), commented, "For too long social science and biological science have pursued 'nothing but' approaches. Sociobiology may just help redress that imbalance."

The subfield of sociobiology is now part of a still broader subfield called **evolutionary psychology**. Evolutionary psychologists continue to hold that the body and brain are largely products of evolution and that inheritance plays an important role in shaping thought and behavior (see **Table 1-2**). The laws of evolutionary psychology are thought to apply to all organisms and to all kinds of mental functions and behaviors (not only social ones), just as the laws of physics apply to all bodies in space.

Evolutionary psychology has become one of the most popular topics in contemporary psychology (Buss, 2009, 2005, 1999). Evolutionary psychologists suggest that some behaviors and mental processes are more effective than others at solving problems of living – namely, those that help people to survive and reproduce. These successful strategies are passed on to people's children, as well as taught to others, and they eventually become important parts of each individual's inborn makeup.

"I'm a social scientist, Michael. That means I can't explain electricity or anything like that, but if you ever want to know about people I'm your man."

That certain look. Facial expressions of sadness (left two photos) and happiness (right two photos) are universal across all cultures. Are these commonalities related to our evolutionary history?

One goal of evolutionary psychologists is to identify **cultural universality**, human behaviors and practices that occur across all cultures. Just as behaviorists study animal behavior to identify simple actions that form the basis of more complex human behaviors, evolutionary psychologists believe that uncovering universal human behaviors will help identify inborn functions common to all humans. Theoretically, such knowledge will answer important questions about the relative impact of biological factors and life experiences on our development.

Throughout this book, we'll be observing a number of common practices displayed by people across cultures, such as using specific facial expressions to express emotions, displaying a fear of snakes, telling stories, and giving gifts (Chomsky, 2005; Brown, 1991). But are such commonalities the direct result of evolutionary forces? Have these behaviors and reactions been passed on from generation to generation largely because they remain highly adaptive? In fact, two evolutionary biologists, Stephen Jay Gould and Richard Lewontin (1979), did not think so. They argued that some of the traits and behaviors seen across cultures are no longer evolutionarily advantageous and instead may be *byproducts* of behaviors that served adaptive functions a long time ago. Initially, for example, the human smile may have represented a submissive baring of teeth often seen in animals, designed to ward off attacks by enemies. Over many, many years, however, it has come to be used in human social environments to signal the presence of a friend, or to signal humor.

Although it can be difficult and at times misleading to identify evolutionary roots for today's behaviors, the study of genetics and inheritance continues to play an important role in psychology. Indeed, many investigations conducted over the past two decades have established the importance of genetic influences on human development. We'll see later in this book, for example, that studies of twins who were separated at birth and reared in different families often find that the twins continue to share many characteristics (Bouchard, 1984). The verdict on evolutionary psychology may still be out, but few of today's psychologists question the contribution of genetic factors to mental functioning and behavior.

TABLE 1-2 The Major Perspectives in Psychology Today

Perspectives	Major emphases
Psychoanalytic	Interactions between the conscious and unconscious mind govern virtually all behavior; childhood experiences set the stage for later psychological functioning
Behaviorist	Only observable behavior can be studied scientifically. Perspective focuses on stimulus-response relationships and the consequences for behavior
Humanist	People can be helped to realize their full and grand potential, which will inevitably lead to their positive psychological growth
Cognitive	Mental processes are studied using an information processing model (inputs/outputs)
Neuroscience/ Psychobiological	Psychological functions are explained primarily in terms of their biological foundations
Evolutionary	Behavior and mental processes are explained in terms of evolution, inheritance, and adaptation.

Before You Go On

What Do You Know?

9. Which theorist is most closely associated with psychoanalytic theory—the theory that unconscious conflicts, rooted in childhood, affect much of our behavior?
10. According to behaviorist theorists, what are the various reinforcement principles, and what impact does each have on behavior?
11. What did humanist theorist Abraham Maslow suggest is the ultimate goal of human beings?
12. What are cognitions?
13. What is the main contention of evolutionary psychology?

What Do You Think?
Which of the theories presented here depend largely on biological principles? Which of the theories seem to be based more on environmental explanations? And which appear to rely on an interaction of factors?

Psychology Today

LEARNING OBJECTIVE 5 Describe the three major branches of psychology and summarize key trends in psychology.

In the contemporary field of psychology, we can recognize the influence of various schools of thought that date back to the days of Greek philosophers. The psychological orientations we have discussed in this chapter, such as functionalism, behaviorism, and cognitive science, have not disappeared but rather continue to develop and interact with one another. Indeed, today there is broad recognition that psychology must be as diverse as the humans whose behavior it attempts to explain (Sternberg & Grigorenko, 2001).

More detailed information is available now than ever before about how the brain functions, and this information has in fact served to emphasize the importance of analyzing human thought and behavior at a variety of levels. Brain imaging studies have, for example, been used to test behavioral principles, identifying which areas of the brain are activated when a behavior is performed or when an outcome is better (or worse) than expected (Cumming, 2009). Similarly, cognitive psychologists and biologists have examined psychoanalytic notions, such as the proposal that our unconscious minds hold memories that might be too anxiety-provoking for our conscious minds. Recent investigations have, for example, linked real memories to one pattern of brain activity and false memories to another (Garoff-Eaton, Slotnick, & Schacter, 2006).

As the diversity of the field has increased, so too has the need for there to be communication among its various voices. Indeed, today's psychologists are represented in various professional organizations including the American Psychological Association (150,000 members), the Association for Psychological Science (20,000 members), and the Society for Neuroscience (38,000 members), which collectivity address the interests and needs of more than 50 different specialities in psychology. **Figure 1-4** shows the variety of fields of study in psychology today.

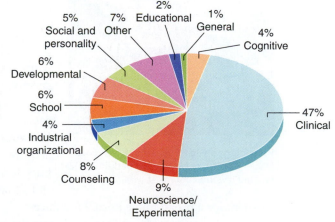

FIGURE 1-4 Percentage of recent doctorates awarded in each subfield of psychology Psychologists today have a wide variety of areas to pursue (APA, 2008).

cultural universality behaviors and practices that occur across all cultures.

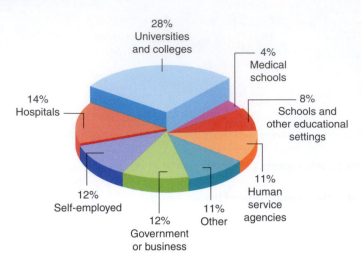

28%
Universities
and colleges

4%
Medical
schools

14%
Hospitals

8%
Schools and
other educational
settings

12%
Self-employed

12%
Government
or business

11%
Other

11%
Human
service
agencies

FIGURE 1-5 Where do new psychologists work? The primary work settings for recent PhDs in psychology are colleges, hospitals, the government, businesses, and human service agencies (APA, 2009).

Branches of Psychology

There are currently three key branches of psychology –*academic psychology*, *applied psychology*, and *clinical and counseling psychology*. Psychologists from all three branches share an interest in mental processes and behavior. They differ in the amount of emphasis they each place on the psychology of individuals, the discovery of general principles of psychology, and the application of psychological knowledge to groups of people. **Figure 1-5** summarizes the range of settings in which academic, applied, and clinical and counseling psychologists work.

Academic Psychology When Wilhelm Wundt founded psychology as a discipline distinct from philosophy in 1879, his goal was to examine human nature. He did not focus on questions of how psychology could be applied or used outside the laboratory. Today, the branch of psychology known as **academic psychology** carries on Wundt's mission. Academic psychology involves research and instruction on a wide variety of psychological topics.

Academic psychologists typically work at colleges and universities, where they often divide their time between teaching and conducting research in their particular fields of interest. A *developmental psychologist*, for example, may teach courses on child devel-

Psychology's wide influence. Psychologist Daniel Kahneman (left) is awarded the 2002 Nobel Prize in Economics.

Psychology is the study of behavior and mental life. Students who major in psychology gain a broad understanding of what makes people "tick" from a wide range of perspectives, including developmental, social, clinical, and biological. They also acquire a body of knowledge and set of skills that help qualify them for a broad range of career choices.

If people want to become psychologists, they will find that an undergraduate degree in psychology prepares them to pursue graduate degrees in any number of psychology subfields, including clinical, health, cognitive, social, neuroscience, organizational, educational, and sports psychology. Alternatively, being an undergraduate major in psychology can help open the door to graduate study in many other fields, such as law, business management, economics, and medicine.

Even if graduate study is not for you, an undergraduate degree in psychology can lead to interesting jobs and careers. Psychology majors are typically viewed by prospective employers as well qualified to work in fields that require people skills, as well as, analytical, research, and writing abilities. "But," you might say, "just about every job deals with people." Yes, that's the point.

An undergraduate degree in psychology particularly qualifies individuals for entry-level jobs in people-oriented careers such as communications, marketing, human resources, sales, and business. Beyond people skills, the analytic, research and writing skills of psychology majors enhance their eligibility for human-service, legal, and law-enforcement jobs, including positions as paralegals and corrections officers. Furthermore, the same skills may make individuals good candidates for careers in general business, marketing research, management consulting, computer game design, and investment banking.

In short, psychology is related to so much in our world that a degree in this discipline can lead to work and careers in more areas and fields than you might imagine. Keep in mind, for example, that the psychologists Daniel Kahneman (2002) and Herbert Simon (1978) are Nobel Laureates in *economics*, while the neuroscientists Eric Kandel (2000), Rita Levi-Montalcini (1986), and Roger Sperry (1981) won their Nobel Prizes in *medicine* and *physiology*.

opment while also researching how children think and behave. The efforts of academic researchers have resulted in a large body of psychological knowledge, and, for the most part, the chapters throughout this textbook reflect their considerable work and findings.

Applied Psychology   Although Wilhelm Wundt intended for psychology to pursue "pure" scientific knowledge, many of his students went on to apply their knowledge to a variety of disciplines (Hergenhahn, 2005). Functionalism, founded by William James, marked the first formal branch of applied psychology. As you'll recall, this orientation was influenced by evolutionary theory and focused on applying psychological principles to social issues. Today, the branch of psychology called **applied psychology** involves the application of psychological principles to help solve practical problems in education, marketing, and other fields (Steg et al., 2008). Lawyers may consult with psychologists to help determine whom to select for a jury. Advertisers may consult with psychologists to conduct research to determine how best to market products to teenagers. Throughout this book, we shall examine a wide range of research developments, both those that have immediate practical applications and those that simply further our insights about the human mind and behavior.

Applied psychologists have earned either a master's degree, which requires two years of graduate study, or a Ph.D. (doctorate of philosophy). Many applied psychologists specialize in a broad traditional academic field, such as developmental or social psychology, and use their expertise further to help guide decisions and work outside of academic settings. There are also a number of specialized programs of study within applied psychology. *Sports psychologists*, for example, may provide guidance to athletes or teams, helping them overcome feelings of anxiety or frustration or teaching them to focus their energy more effectively.

Clinical and Counseling Psychology   **Clinical and counseling psychology** help individuals to cope more effectively or to overcome abnormal functioning. Actually, there are several different types of mental-health practitioners.

- *Clinical psychologists* generally provide *psychotherapy*, which involves helping people to modify thoughts, feelings, and behaviors that are causing them distress or inhibiting their functioning. They also may administer and interpret psychological tests to provide further information relevant to treatment. Many clinical psychologists earn a Ph.D. degree awarded by a university graduate program, which typically requires training in therapeutic practices and in the conduct and interpretation of research. Some clinical psychologists earn a Psy.D. (doctorate of psychology) degree. This degree is awarded by graduate programs that place less emphasis on research and greater emphasis on psychotherapy and psychological testing.

- *Counseling psychologists* and *psychiatric social workers* also provide psychotherapy for people with psychological problems. These professionals may also help individuals and families deal with issues tied to relationships, careers, child-rearing, and other important areas of functioning. In addition, some social workers provide aid to families through social service systems that are available in a community. Counseling psychologists earn a Ph.D. or Psy.D. in their field, while social workers earn either an M.S.W. (masters of social work) or D.S.W. (doctorate of social work) degree from a school of social work.

- *Psychiatrists*, who may also provide guidance and therapy to individuals, are professionals who attend medical school and earn an M.D. (doctorate of medicine). Psychiatrists generally have less training in psychological research and

academic psychology branch of psychology focusing on research and instruction in the various areas or fields of study in psychology.

applied psychology branch of psychology applying psychological principles to practical problems in other fields, such as education, marketing, or industry.

clinical and counseling psychology the study of abnormal psychological behavior and interventions designed to change that behavior.

The couch! Sigmund Freud's signature therapy procedure was to have patients lie on a couch and say whatever came to mind, while he took notes behind them. This wax recreation of the neurologist and his office is on display at a museum in Berlin, Germany.

New Mexico and Louisiana currently are the only states that grant prescription privileges to psychologists who receive special pharmacological training. The U.S. territory of Guam also grants such privileges to psychologists.

testing than clinical psychologists, but they have medical knowledge and the ability to prescribe medications for abnormal emotional states or behavior problems, a professional privilege that most states do not grant to clinical or counseling psychologists or social workers.

Shared Values

Although the three branches of psychology—academic, applied, and clinical and counseling—have different goals and ways of meeting those goals, they do share important values that guide their work. Many of those values will shape our discussions throughout this textbook, so let's take a look at them here.

- *Psychology is theory-driven.* If you're going to explain human behavior, you have to have a theory. We will describe the elements of a good theory in Chapter 2. Psychologists have developed theories, or potential answers, for many key questions: Do mental processes exist? What are the relative roles of biological inheritance and environmental influence in shaping human psychology? How do we explain deviant behavior, such as Internet trolling? Each school of psychology provides ideas to help answer such questions. And every branch of psychology uses its potential answers to guide research or improve psychological interventions.
- *Psychology is empirical.* From its very start, what separated psychology from other human disciplines, such as philosophy was its emphasis on controlled observations and experimentation. Psychology finds more use and value in ideas that receive strong empirical, or research, support, than in ideas, even seemingly compelling ones, that cannot be supported with evidence from systematic testing.
- *Psychology is multilevel.* As we discussed at the beginning of this chapter, to understand the complete picture of human mental processes and behavior, psychologists must account for what is happening at the levels of the brain, the person, and the group. Although certain theories place more emphasis on one level than another, all of the levels are indeed operating to influence whatever mental process or behavior we may be observing. Thus, in chapters throughout this textbook, we will be presenting evidence about what happens at each of these three levels.
- *Psychology is contextual.* As recently as 20 years ago, the thought of Internet trolls—actually, even the thought of the Internet—was unimaginable to most people. As the history of psychology shows, however, technological advances have had a strong influence on the development, rise, and fall of particular theories. Without the computer, for example, the field of cognitive psychology would have been described very differently. In fact, technological and other societal changes force us to look at human behavior from new perspectives that broaden our awareness. All of this means that some of the theories you're studying today may eventually go the way of structuralism—influential but dramatically changed in nature. This is the way that science progresses.

Current Trends in Psychology

The values of psychology, as theory-driven, empirical, multilevel, and contextual, work together to drive constant progress and change in the field. Today, those values, as well as larger social developments, are shaping several trends in psychology. In particular, the field is growing more diverse, continuing to profit from technological advances, and continuing to give birth to new schools of thought.

collectivist culture whose members focus more on the needs of the group and less on individual desires.

individualistic culture that places the wants or desires of the person over the needs of the group.

cognitive neuroscience study of mental processes and how they relate to the biological functions of the brain.

social neuroscience study of social functioning and how it is tied to brain activity.

Growing Diversity Early in the history of psychology, few women or members of racial minority groups were able to obtain the advanced education and professional status necessary to contribute to the field. As psychology itself has grown more diverse, however, so have psychologists (see **Figure 1-6**). Psychology now has more women earning graduate degrees than does any other science. Indeed, 71 percent of newly earned Ph.D.s in psychology are awarded to women (APA, 2009). In addition, 16 percent of newly earned Ph.D.s are awarded to minority group members, compared to 7 percent thirty years ago (APA, 2009).

Growing diversity among psychologists has overlapped with an increased interest in the diversity of the people they study, treat, and influence. *Cultural psychology* has, for example, become an important area of investigation. As we observed earlier, this field of study seeks to uncover mental processes that exist across all cultures, as well as important cultural differences.

Cultural psychologists often focus on differences between *collectivist* cultures and *individualistic* cultures. Members of **collectivist** cultures emphasize the needs of the group and subsume individual desires to those of the family or peer group. In contrast, **individualistic** cultures stress the needs of persons over those of the group. One study of differences between these two types of cultures examined positive emotions, such as happiness. Individuals from Eastern cultures, which tend to be more collectivist, and Western cultures, which tend to be more individualistic, appear to hold different beliefs about the sources of happiness. When asked to talk about events that make them feel happy, Chinese research participants focused on interpersonal interactions and evaluations from others, while Western participants pointed to personal achievement and self-evaluation (Lu & Shih, 1997).

Research has also indicated that even within a broad culture, subcultures may differ with regard to happiness. Studies have shown, for example, that positive emotions, such as strong self-acceptance are, on average, a bit lower among individuals from southern parts of the United States than among those from the West or Midwest. Some researchers have hypothesized that these lower levels of well-being and self-acceptance may reflect a subculture that is relatively more concerned with showing hospitality and respecting tradition than with fostering positive self-concepts and promoting personal growth (Markus et al., 2004). Given psychology's growing interest in these and related differences among people and between groups, we have included throughout the textbook sections called "How We Differ." These sections examine how memory, emotions, social values, and the like differ from situation to situation, person to person, and group to group.

Advances in Technology As we observed earlier, technological shifts also contribute to shifts in psychological theory. The development of computers in the 1950s and 1960s contributed to the cognitive psychology revolution. Technology has continued to change the face of science and psychology in more recent years. Innovations such as brain imaging and effective pharmacological, or drug, treatments for mental disorders have revealed a great deal about human mental processes and behavior. As you'll see in Chapter 4, for example, the development of brain-imaging technology has made it possible for researchers to observe activity in the brain directly.

In fact, in recent years a new area of psychological study and theory has emerged: **Cognitive neuroscience** focuses not only on mental processes but also on how mental processes interact with the biological functions of the brain. That is, what happens in the brain when we are remembering something, making a decision, or paying attention to something? One goal of cognitive neuroscientists is to link specific mental processes to particular brain activities. Similarly, a field called **social neuroscience** has

Mary Whilton Calkins, who worked with William James and was the first female president of the American Psychological Association, completed all her coursework at Harvard but was denied a Ph.D. because she was a woman.

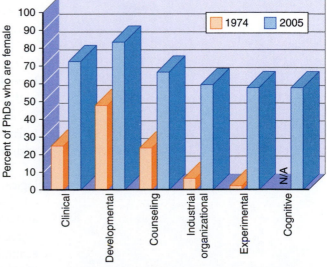

FIGURE 1-6 Growth of women Ph.D.s in psychology Over a 30-year period, the increase in the percentage of women earning Ph.D.s has been dramatic, especially in the clinical, developmental, and counseling fields (Cynkar, 2007).

Since the beginnings of psychology as a science, women have made important discoveries and contributions to psychology. Here are but a few of the field's female pioneers.

The work of *Mary Whiton Calkins* (1863–1930) was noteworthy for her emphasis on the self, consciousness, emotions, and dreams, which stood in stark contrast to John Watson's behaviorist movement at the time. Calkins was the first woman president of the American Psychological Association (APA).

Margaret Floy Washburn (1871–1939), was the first woman to receive a Ph.D. in psychology (1894) and the first woman elected to the National Academy of Sciences (1932). She was one of the earliest experimental psychologists to insist that mental phenomena were as important for scientific study as observable behaviors.

Karen Horney (1885-1952), was one of the most influential early psychoanalytic theorists, a pioneer in the discipline of "feminine psychiatry," and a leader in the Neo-Freudian movement that challenged traditional Freudian views. She was especially critical of Freud's theory of sexuality, challenging many of his notions in this area of functioning.

Leta Hollingsworth (1886-1939), was best known for her studies of "mentally deficient" and "mentally gifted" individuals and for her views on gender differences in mental functioning. She was one of the first theorists of her time to challenge the notion that relatively fewer female achievements reflected biologically inferiority, arguing instead that women were victims of a male-dominated social order.

Nancy Bayley (1899–1994) was best known for her work in the measurement of infant intelligence and human development, which remain the standard today. Bayley was the first woman to receive the Distinguished Scientific Contribution Award from the APA.

Mamie Phipps Clark (1917–1983) and her psychologist husband Kenneth Clark were two of the first well-known African-American psychologists. She and her husband were best known for their work on the effects of segregation on the self-images of minority children.

Brenda Milner (1918-) has been a pioneer in the study of memory and other cognitive functions in humans. She was the first to investigate how damage to the brain's hippocampus affects memory through her study of a famous amnesia patient known as H.M. in the research literature.

Carol Gilligan (1936–) is best known for her pioneering work on gender differences, which has forever changed society's understanding of the human experience. Gilligan was named one of the 25 most influential Americans in 1996 by *Time* Magazine and received the fourth annual Heinz Award in the Human Condition in 1998.

Anne Treisman (1935-) has been a leading researcher of visual attention, object perception, and memory. She was the first psychologist to propose that different kinds of attention enable people to combine the observed separate features of an object into a consciously experienced whole.

---

emerged, which seeks to link social functioning to particular brain activities. Recent studies have, for example, found that there is a network of nerve cells in the brain that is activated when we show empathy, our ability to understand the intentions of others.

Cognitive and social neuroscience are currently among psychology's more active areas of theory and research. Given the enormous growth and impact of such areas, we have also included throughout the book a section called "What Happens in the Brain?" In these sections, you'll learn about the neuroscience of memory, emotions, social behavior, and the like. You'll discover, for example, what happens in the brain when you are learning new material before an important test and then again when you get together with friends to celebrate the completion of that test.

The development of imaging tools, computer technology, and a number of biological techniques has also helped enhance our understanding and treatment of mental dysfunctioning in recent years. These tools have enabled researchers to look directly at the brains of disturbed persons while they are feeling sad or anxious, hearing voices, or recalling repressed memories. Such studies have helped reveal that depression, for example, is related not only to traumatic childhood experiences, significant losses in life, and feelings of helplessness but also to abnormal activity of key chemicals in the brain. Given such wide-ranging insights, we also have included in most chapters a section called "When Things Go Wrong." We discuss in these sections what happens when normal psychological processes, such as memory, emotional coping, social engagement, and the like, go astray.

At first glance, psychology's intensified focus on the brain may make it appear that technology and biology are dominating contemporary psychology. However, it is unlikely that psychology will ever be overtaken by biology. Indeed, recent findings in cognitive neuroscience and other areas suggest that our insights about mental functions (and dysfunctions) and about behavior are most complete when the different branches of the field intersect and cooperate. In clinical psychology, for example, it is now clear that many mental disorders are best understood and treated when explanations and techniques from different schools of thought are combined.

One important area of psychology that has intersected with other areas of the field for many years is developmental psychology, the study of how we change over the course of our lives. Developmental psychology has both incorporated and contributed to research in areas, such as our use of language, our emotions, our personalities, and the structure of our brains. We emphasize the cross-fertilization of development and other areas by including in most chapters a section called "How We Develop."

New Schools of Thought   As we saw earlier, historical schools of thought in psychology sow the seeds for related but new ideas. We can see, for example, influences of the functionalists, who were interested in applying psychological research, and the humanists, who were interested in helping people achieve their highest potential, when we look at a relatively new movement in the field called *positive psychology*. Positive psychology gives special focus to more upbeat features of human functioning, including happiness, meaning in life, and character strengths, as well as increased attention to how those features of positive living might be developed more readily (Baumgardner & Crothers, 2009; Seligman & Csikszentmihalyi, 2000).

Accentuating the positive. Residents of a small Spanish village cry out in joy as they are drenched with 30 tons of water during a water festival. Positive psychologists study the impact that happiness and positive emotions have on human functioning.

Happiness seems to have become a buzz word of the twenty-first century. It has been embraced particularly by the popular media, fueling a self-help industry that claims to give people tools for achieving emotional well-being. This heightened interest in positive functioning has been used to help market nutritional advice, as seen, for example, in the book *The Good Mood Diet: Feel Great While You Lose Weight* (Kleiner & Condor, 2007), and has appeared even in fields not associated primarily with psychology, as in the book *The Architecture of Happiness* (Botton, 2006). The field of positive psychology has tried to devote scholarly discussion and scientific study to happiness and its positive counterparts. In fact, an estimated 150 psychology departments in the United States now offer courses in positive psychology (Senior, 2006).

A growing body of research does indeed suggest that positive emotions can have a profound impact on development and behavior. As you'll see in Chapter 15, for example, when we discuss stress, coping, and health, a number of studies have found that having a positive outlook promotes *resilience*, the ability to bounce back in the face of adversity (Bonanno, 2008, 2005, 2004). Similarly, studies indicate that positive emotions may boost the functioning of our immune systems. Research even suggests that our emotions help influence how well we resist common colds (Cohen et al., 2008, 2003)!

In Chapter 12 on emotions, we'll also come upon a line of research that suggests that each of us has a particular "set-point" on our happiness thermometer, a relatively stable level of well-being that we may carry with us to each situation in our lives. We may depart from that set-point for short periods of time, but many of us return to our particular level of happiness within weeks or months of a destabilizing event (Headey, 2008).

In Chapter 16, we'll see that some psychologists have even developed a new form of therapy, called *positive psychotherapy*, that does not target specific symptoms of mental dysfunction but rather focuses on increasing the positive emotions and sense of engagement and meaning experienced by clients (Seligman et al., 2006). According to

Socrates' approach to teaching involved leading students through their assumptions and logic by asking them specific, precise questions. This approach, called the Socratic method, remains an important part of a clinical psychologist's therapeutic practice to this day.

proponents of positive psychology, certain techniques and behaviors can be of particular help to people in their efforts to achieve happiness or return to happiness after unpleasant events.

What Changes and What Remains Constant?   Since the early years of Greek philosophy, theorists have attempted to determine how the human mind operates and whether there are universal laws that govern mental processes and behaviors. Those questions remain at the forefront of contemporary psychology as today's neuroscientists, cultural theorists, and other psychologists try to determine how the mind and body are related, whether there are knowable universal truths about mental processes and human behaviors, and whether such truths are best understood through the perspective of the brain, the individual, or the group, or a particular combination of the three. It is not likely that psychology can ever provide complete answers to these complex questions, but striving to uncover even partial answers has already uncovered a wealth of information about how human beings function and has produced a range of compelling theories and research findings.

As you read about these theories and findings throughout this textbook, you will do well to keep asking yourself a question raised by *Carl Jung (1875–1961)*, one of the field's most famous clinical theorists, "How much truth [is] captured by this [particular] viewpoint?" Ideas move in and out of vogue, and what is accepted today as a useful or accurate outlook might not be seen the same way tomorrow.

Both historical and social forces determine the focus of scientific energy. Psychology, perhaps more than any other field, struggles constantly to achieve a proper balance between popular trends and interests, societal influences, and scientific objectivity (Leahey, 2000, p. 544). Although fads and fashions will likely continue to exert some influence on the development of psychology in the coming years, it is important to recognize that such fads hardly comprise the substance of the field. Moreover, we must always keep in mind the limitations of psychology (or of any discipline) in answering the basic questions of human existence. As we noted at the beginning of this chapter, scientific knowledge serves as a *means* for exploring such questions rather than an end.

Before You Go On

What Do You Know?

14. What are the three major branches of psychology?

15. What is cultural universality, and which psychologists are interested in it?

16. What is the focus of positive psychology?

What Do You Think?   Which branch of psychology most appeals to you as a potential profession? Why? What kinds of things do you think would be important for positive psychologists to study?

Summary

What is Psychology?

LEARNING OBJECTIVE 1   Define psychology, and describe the goals and levels of analysis psychologists use.

- Psychology is the study of mental processes and behavior.

- The goals of psychology are to *describe*, *explain*, *predict*, and *control* behavior and mental processes. Psychologists vary in the degree to which they focus on some of these goals more than others.

- The study of psychology must occur at multiple levels, including the level of the *brain* (the biological activity associated with mental processes and behavior), the level of the *person* (the content of mental processes), and the level of the *group* (social influences on behavior).

Psychology's Roots in Philosophy

LEARNING OBJECTIVE 2 Describe the influences of early myths and ancient Greek philosophies on psychology.

- Early explanations of human behavior were rooted in superstition and magic.
- Later, philosophers, beginning with the ancient Greeks, tried to develop more objective theories of human consciousness and reality.
- The work of such early philosophers as Hippocrates, Socrates, Plato, and Aristotle contributed to the later formation of psychology as a natural science.

The Early Days of Psychology

LEARNING OBJECTIVE 3 Name important early psychologists and describe their major theories and research methods.

- The development of psychology has been strongly influenced by shifts in the social environment and development of new technology.
- The first psychology laboratory was founded in Leipzig, Germany by physiologist Wilhelm Wundt. Wundt was interested in human consciousness and will, which he studied through small, structured activities that could be easily watched and replicated.
- Structuralism, a school of thought developed by one of Wundt's students, relied upon the use of introspection, the careful observation of human perception. The goal of the structuralists was to find the smallest building blocks of consciousness.
- William James established the first psychology laboratory in the United States at Harvard and helped shift the field's focus to the functions of the mental events and behaviors, forming a school of thought known as functionalism.
- Gestalt psychologists, rather than divide consciousness into its smallest parts, studied human tendencies to perceive pattern, putting together the "parts," or individual sensations, to create a "whole" or perception that went beyond the sum of the parts.

Twentieth-Century Approaches

LEARNING OBJECTIVE 4 Summarize the major principles of the psychoanalytical, behaviorist, humanistic, cognitive, and neuroscience approaches to psychology.

- Over the years, different fields of psychology emerged, with different ideas about what was the appropriate area of study for human psychology. Some of the most influential fields were the psychoanalytic, behaviorist, humanistic, cognitive, and neuroscience schools of thought.
- Sigmund Freud's psychoanalytical theory focused on the importance of unconscious mental processes.
- Behaviorists believed strongly that psychology should restrict its focus to the careful study of observable behaviors.
- Humanistic psychologists reacted against the mechanical portrayals of people by the behaviorists, and emphasized individuals' potential for growth and self-actualization.
- Cognitive psychologists reignited interest in the study of mental processes, comparing the workings of the mind to the workings of computers.
- Biological science, including interest in the workings of the brain and in our genetic inheritance, is the major influence on neuroscience approaches.

Psychology Today

LEARNING OBJECTIVE 5 Describe the three major branches of psychology and summarize key trends in psychology.

- The theoretical and cultural diversity of the field of psychology has increased dramatically over recent years.
- There are three key branches of psychology: academic, applied, and clinical/counseling.
- Across the three branches and many specialty areas in psychology, psychologists are united by their shared values. Psychologists generally agree that psychology is *theory-driven*, *empirical*, *multilevel*, and *contextual*.
- Currently, psychology appears to be developing as a science in response to a growing *diversity* throughout the field, advances in *technology* (such as brain scanning), and the development of *new schools* such as positive psychology.

Key Terms

CHAPTER 2

Psychology as a Science

chapter outline

- What is a Science?
- Is Psychology a Science?
- How Do Psychologists Conduct Research?
- How Do Psychologists Make Sense of Research Results?
- What Ethical Research Guidelines Do Psychologists Follow?

Ugly Reality?

Reality television has become an increasingly present and controversial part of the world media over the past decade. Shows, such as *American Idol*, *Survivor*, *Dancing with the Stars*, and *The Amazing Race* currently dominate network television. And their cousins—*Flavor of Love*, *Jackass*, and *Real Housewives of Atlanta*—receive huge ratings on cable television. Actually, there are various kinds of reality shows— for example, the *competition* realities, in which people vie for a job, recognition, or a dream mate; the *real-life* realities, which have people conduct their lives as usual, for all the world to see; and the *advice* realities, in which professionals tell individuals how to improve their behaviors.

Among the most popular reality shows are the *give-away/makeover* programs: shows in which people who are poor, down on their luck, or appearance-challenged are chosen to receive special gifts, makeovers, or opportunities that will improve their lives markedly. Today's giveaway/makeover shows have roots dating back to 1956 when *Queen for a Day* hit the TV airways. In this popular show, several women would each tell their hard-luck life story to a studio audience who would then decide, by way of applause, which woman should receive a refrigerator and other life-changing prizes.

Similarly, one of today's most popular giveaway/makeover shows, *Extreme Makeover: Home Edition*, invites people from across the world to nominate a "deserving family that des-perately needs" improvements in their house. Then the *Extreme Makeover* team—designers, workers, even neighbors—spend a week renovating the chosen family's entire house and property. The moments in which a family first learns that it has been selected for a makeover and those in which the family later sees their renovated home are the emotional highlights of each show.

Many criticisms have been leveled at reality TV (Hirschorn, 2007). It's crass, say its detractors. It's exploitative. It lowers the level of cultural discussion and encourages audiences to take pleasure in the humiliation of other human beings.

Defenders of reality TV counter that such criticisms are "snobbery." They point out that participants on reality TV include individuals from a variety of racial and socioeconomic backgrounds who rarely receive much exposure on scripted television shows. At their best, defenders argue, reality shows, particularly the giveaway/makeover ones, bring out admirable qualities in viewers, tapping into positive feelings such as altruism, empathy, and concern for others, and, in turn, offering a window into social instincts, behaviors, and interactions.

Is reality TV a barbaric force? Is it a force for good, giving a voice to the voiceless and providing natural demonstrations of human behavior? Or is it, after all, just television?

Viewers may base their answers to these questions on their personal experiences. Journalists and media critics may use comparisons to other televisions shows or look at trends over time. Sociologists and anthropologists might look for large-scale cultural shifts in moral or other standards. Psychologists try to

Reality mania Supporters of reality television contestant Susan Boyle gather to watch her compete on the final episode of "Britain's Got Talent" in 2009. Viewers often seem to be enormously affected by the people and events on display in today's reality TV shows.

answer questions like these by using scientific research methods to look for relationships between reality TV and systematic changes in individual people's mental processes and behavior.

In this chapter, you'll find out exactly what the scientific research methods of psychologists are and how psychologists use them. We'll begin the chapter by defining what science is. Then we'll consider just how well psychology fits with the definition of a science, particularly in comparison to other fields. Next we'll examine in some detail the methods that psychologists use to conduct research, including, by way of example, research into the nature and impact of television viewing habits. Finally, we'll look at the statistics that help researchers interpret their results and the ethical rules that guide them when working with humans or animals.

What is a Science?

LEARNING OBJECTIVE 1 List two core beliefs of science, and describe the steps in the scientific method.

Before we look at psychology in particular, take a moment to try to answer the general question, what is a science? You might answer by listing types of sciences, such as chemistry, biology, or physics. You might envision a white-coated person in a lab somewhere, mixing strangely bubbling chemicals or lecturing students about where to start an incision on the frog in the tray in front of them. Such things are only *sometimes* associated with science. Two characteristics that all sciences share, however, are similar principles, or beliefs, about how best to understand the world and reliance on the *scientific method* as a way to discovering knowledge.

Scientific Principles

Science is built on a foundation of core beliefs about the world. Two essential beliefs are that:

- *The universe operates according to certain natural laws.* Scientists believe that things happen in and around us in some kind of orderly fashion that can be described using rules or laws. The natural law of cause and effect, for example, suggests that when something is set in motion, it has an effect on other things. Psychologists look for the laws that describe mental processes and behavior.

- *Such laws are discoverable and testable.* By carefully observing what happens in the natural world, we can figure out the laws governing those events. In turn, we can use these laws to make predictions about what might happen, and we can then experiment to see whether those predictions come true.

As a natural science, psychology operates according to these two core beliefs. Psychology also shares with other sciences a similar logical approach to discovering and testing laws about how things happen: the scientific method.

The Scientific Method

The scientific method relies upon a process of logical reasoning derived from philosophy. Early perspectives on human knowledge were governed by **deductive reasoning**, a process that starts with broad basic principles and applies them in specific situations to prove hundreds and thousands of other, smaller truths. If you ever applied the Pythagorean theorem to calculate the length of a side of a right triangle, you were using deductive reasoning; you were applying a broad principle to a specific case.

Sir Francis Bacon, a British philosopher and statesman in the early 1600s, was one of the first to question the deductive reasoning approach. Bacon felt deductive reasoning was too susceptible to the thinker's **biases**—personal beliefs or conventional wisdom that a particular thinker mistakenly accepts as broad, basic truths. We'll see throughout this book that psychological research has shown many times that widely accepted conventional wisdom can be biased. For example, people typically consider themselves to be free and independent thinkers who will always stand up for what they believe to be right. As we'll discuss in Chapter 14, however, scientists have been able to demonstrate that, when confronted by an authority figure or even just a small group of people with opposite views, many people go along with the higher authority or the crowd rather than follow their own beliefs.

Bacon argued that, to avoid bias, science and philosophy should proceed in an opposite direction of deductive reasoning, using a process called **inductive reasoning** instead. Here, thinkers use controlled direct observations to generate broad conclusions, and over time such conclusions are combined to achieve nonbiased truths about the laws of the universe.

Psychologists using inductive reasoning would begin the search for natural laws by making **empirical**, or objectively testable, observations of mental processes and behaviors. Their observations would in turn lead them to develop **theories**, ideas about the laws that govern those processes and behavior.

Inductive reasoning is still a key idea in much scientific research. There are so many factors governing human behavior, however, that if psychologists were to rely entirely on induction, or observation, they could never discover and specify all of the potential factors affecting human behavior—the factors needed to generate accurate broad theories. Thus, to build on the best of both deductive and inductive reasoning approaches, psychologists today typically employ a blended model known as the **hypothetico-deductive approach** (Locke, 2007). They begin with a deductive process: they identify a hypothesis. According to the famous philosopher *Karl Popper* (1902–1942), a sound scientific theory must establish, in advance, the observations that would refute it (Popper, 1963, 1959). In other words, a sound theory runs the risk of being proven false. To test the soundness of their theories, researchers create **hypotheses**, specific statements that are objectively falsifiable (that is, they can be disproved). A physicist, for example, might generate a hypothesis based on the theory of cause and effect, which states that hitting

Law seeking This meteorologist relies on physical laws to describe and predict the force and path of hurricanes. Similarly, psychologists seek out laws to describe and predict mental processes and behavior.

deductive reasoning reasoning proceeding from broad basic principles applied to specific situations.

biases distorted beliefs based on a person's subjective sense of reality.

inductive reasoning reasoning process proceeding from small specific situations to more general truths.

empirical able to be tested in objective ways.

theories ideas about laws that govern phenomena.

hypothetico-deductive reasoning process of modern science where scientists begin with an educated guess about how the world works, and then set about designing small controlled observations to support or invalidate that hypothesis.

hypothesis a general statement about the way variables relate that is objectively falsifiable.

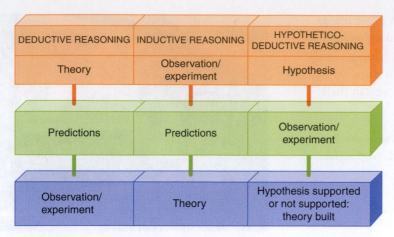

DEDUCTIVE REASONING	INDUCTIVE REASONING	HYPOTHETICO-DEDUCTIVE REASONING
Theory	Observation/experiment	Hypothesis
Predictions	Predictions	Observation/experiment
Observation/experiment	Theory	Hypothesis supported or not supported: theory built

FIGURE 2-1 Reasoning and the scientific method
Several different kinds of reasoning may be used as scientists carry out their work. Most psychological researchers use the hypothetico-deductive approach.

a baseball with a bat causes the ball to move in a new direction. If researchers were then to discover that baseballs keep going straight into the catcher's mitt, even after being hit, the hypothesis would be disproved and scientists would have to reconsider their theory of the law of cause and effect.

Similarly, in the hypothetico-deductive approach, psychologists set out to create controlled observations that will prove or disprove their hypotheses. In many cases, research results do indeed disprove their hypotheses. Psychologists may then reject or modify their theories and generate new hypotheses for further testing. Through repetition of this process, theories evolve over time to become more and more accurate explanations of human thought and behavior. This approach is outlined in **Figure 2-1**.

As we discussed at the beginning of the chapter, many people have ideas about whether reality TV has good or bad effects or indeed any effects at all on viewers. To produce a scientific theory about the effects of reality TV, a person would need to step outside his or her personal beliefs in order to avoid bias. A scientific approach would involve the steps described below:

- *Make observation.* We might first examine what viewers do after watching a reality TV show. Do, for example, they exhibit moral behavior after watching an episode of *Extreme Makeover: Home Edition.* That is, do they engage in behaviors that suggest increased empathy and awareness of others' beliefs and needs?

- *Develop hypotheses.* After making such observations, we would generate hypotheses about what led to the behavior we observed. If viewers acted more morally, for example, did positive behavior on the show cause viewers to think of their fellow human beings in a more positive light? Or were the viewers simply modeling themselves after the television cast? Whatever our explanation, we would generate a falsifiable hypothesis to test. One hypothesis, for example, might be that viewers change their behavior to be more like the people they see on reality TV shows.

- *Test hypotheses.* As we'll see in this chapter, there are several kinds of research studies we could conduct to see if this hypothesis can be disproved.

- *Build a theory.* If the hypothesis is, indeed, disproved, we might modify or even throw it out and develop and test a new hypothesis. If our hypothesis that people who watch reality TV change their behavior to be more like the cast of the show is not disproved, we might test it further. We might, for example, decide to study the viewers of a variety of reality shows. If the results continue to support our hypothesis, the hypothesis can become a theory. A theory, in turn, can become a framework to generate additional hypotheses.

Before You Go On

What Do You Know?
1. What are the two core beliefs of a science?
2. What is the difference between inductive and deductive reasoning?
3. What is the difference between a hypothesis and a theory?
4. What is the hypothetico-deductive method?

What Do You Think? Based on what you know about the scientific method, do you think psychology is a science in the same way chemistry, biology, and physics are sciences?

Is Psychology a Science?

LEARNING OBJECTIVE 2 Compare and contrast psychology with other natural sciences, such as biology, chemistry, and physics, and with pseudosciences, such as astrology.

As we saw in Chapter 1, prior to the nineteenth century, psychology was a field based largely on philosophy, religion, and even mysticism. With a rise in the popularity of animal research in the nineteenth century, however, scientists began to develop an increased interest in physiology and how human actions are tied to innate biological functions. Charles Darwin's theories on evolution, along with advances in the field of biology, raised questions about the interactions between humans and our environments. Given such roots, many credit the influence of biological science for shifting psychology from a philosophy toward becoming a science (Hergenhahn, 2005).

Although psychology is now defined as a natural science that uses experimental methods to study mental processes and behavior, it does differ from the physical sciences, such as biology, in key ways, including how it pursues scientific goals and its role in influencing personal and social values.

Francis Bacon was so committed to the scientific method that it may have killed him. In 1626, he hypothesized that snow might be a good way to preserve meat. He went out, bought a goose, and stuffed it with snow, but in the process he contracted pneumonia and died.

Goals of Psychology

As we saw in Chapter 1, all sciences share the goals of describing, explaining, predicting, and controlling the phenomena they study. However, the emphasis each field places on these goals may vary. One key difference between psychology and the physical sciences, for example, is in the area of description. A core goal of many physical sciences is to isolate and describe the smallest elements that contribute to a larger whole. Biologists look at how a cell contributes to the overall functioning of an organism, for example. Chemists and physicists examine how atoms and subatomic particles make up the structure of, well, everything. Although psychology also attempts to isolate fundamental elements of behavior and mental processes, psychologists face an additional task because behavior is determined by many such factors simultaneously. These factors can be temporary or permanent fixtures in a person's life. The atomic structure of gold, for example, is the same in all gold all over the world, but a complex behavior, such as reading this textbook cannot be broken down into a standard set of elements that work the same for every person. The reading behavior of a student might be influenced by a temporary factor, such as anticipation of an upcoming exam, that does not affect the reading behavior of nonstudents. The idea behind psychological research is both to *isolate* the relative contribution of such factors and to think about how these factors *come together* to influence human behavior.

Multiple influences Behavior is complex and is determined by many factors operating simultaneously. What factors—temporary, permanent, or both—might be influencing this man to take a dip in the ocean on a cold day?

Psychologists face an additional challenge because much of what they study does not have a clear and observable physical reality like the basic units of study in other scientific fields. With the help of special tools, scientists in those fields can observe even the tiniest bits of matter, including atoms and DNA. Of course, this is also true of psychology *to some degree*. Behaviors, sensations, or physiological responses, for example, can be directly observed, measured, and explained. In his review of science, the great German philosopher Immanuel Kant suggested that when studying phenomena such as these, psychology is indeed empirical and very close to a "real" science (Kant, 2003). Other psychologists, such as the behaviorist B. F. Skinner, also advocated this view of psychology, and in fact, as we saw in Chapter 1, many behaviorists have stated that, as scientists, psychologists should study *only* what is directly observable.

Thoughts versus behaviors Thoughts cannot be observed directly, but behaviors can. Thus psychologists can be more certain about the romantic feelings of the woman on the right than those of the woman on the left.

On the other hand, as Kant himself observed, many of the processes that form the basis of psychology cannot be observed or described directly. We have no microscopes or tests that will allow us to see a thought or an emotion, for example, with the same clarity as a cell. Granted, good scientific work and sound experimental study have enabled us to look at many of the ways thoughts and feelings can influence behaviors, and psychologists are always seeking out new ways of objectively defining these and other elusive features of mental functioning. But direct observation continues to be a difficult task in the field of psychology.

Values and the Application of Psychology

Psychology is also distinct from other scientific fields inasmuch as it deals in major ways with issues associated with values, morality, and personal preference—issues that historically were addressed exclusively by spiritual and political leaders. Like all scientists, psychologists try to provide society with useful information that has practical applications. But people are particularly inclined to use psychological information to decide issues that overlap with philosophy, religion, the law, and other such realms of life. For example, the American Psychological Association recently gave testimony to the Supreme Court about adolescent brain function and risk-taking behavior. The Association reported findings that many adolescents' brains are not yet developed enough to allow them to understand fully the consequences of their behaviors. Based on this testimony, the Court ruled on an important moral, ethical, and legal question—deciding that adolescents who commit murder should not be faced with the possibility of the death penalty.

Happy Birthday! Yangyang, a female goat cloned by Chinese scientists in 2000, wears a wreath at her 6th birthday party. Advances in genetic research and genetic engineering hold much promise but the ethical implications are important to consider.

Of course, other sciences also influence the values and ethics of human beings to various degrees. The field of genetic research, for example, was pioneered by biological scientists who were looking for better farming practices, but some early geneticists soon came to believe that selective breeding could be applied to humans to increase the likelihood of desired offspring. Their research contributed to a field eventually known as *eugenics*, which influenced not only many people's personal childbearing decisions, but also contributed to policies of governments and social agencies in some locations that required forced sterilization surgery for people deemed unfit to reproduce (Whitaker, 2002). Indeed, eugenics often was associated with racism and homophobia. Today the field of genetic research sparks concerns and debate about food practices, stem cell research, human cloning, and other such issues. Every scientific field must wrestle with questions of how to ethically apply the knowledge it discovers about the world, but few more so than the field of psychology. In addition, few sciences are as plagued as psychology is with popular imitations and misrepresentations of their work.

Misrepresentation of Psychology

It is natural for people to seek guidance periodically on how to live their lives. And psychologists certainly do not shy away from helping people with their problems, as evidenced by the thriving areas of clinical and counseling psychology and other applied disciplines described in Chapter 1. Ultimately, however, science—even psychology—cannot answer fundamental and subjective questions about human nature. People who claim to do so are misrepresenting the science of psychology with *pseudopsychology*. Pseudopsychology, or *pop psychology*, has no basis in the scientific method, yet it takes on the trappings of science, often with the goal of promoting certain moral or religious values (Hergenhan, 2005). A fundamental difference between pseudopsychology and psychology is that psychology does not claim to address all human issues, whereas pseudoscientists argue that psychological principles can provide the answers to all of life's major questions (Leahey, 2005).

Astrology is a good example of pseudopsychology. It uses Zodiac "signs" to predict one's future and give advice about one's relationships and decisions. Astrology's guiding principle is that all human beings have particular personality traits that are based upon the alignment of planets on the dates of their births and those traits determine

> "Do you believe in UFOs, astral projections, mental telepathy, ESP, [and] clairvoyance…? Uh, if there's a steady paycheck in it, I'll believe anything you say."
>
> *–Dialogue from the 1984 movie* Ghostbusters

Making Psychology More Popular

Within many scientific disciplines, there are charismatic researchers and practitioners who are able to describe their complex topics so that almost anyone can understand the concepts. These individuals present facts about science in ways that engage the public's imagination. As a result, some of them become well known figures in the popular media, such as in mass-market books, magazines, television, and radio. Psychology too has its share of such individuals.

Antonio Damasio, MD, Ph.D., for example, is an award-winning, internationally recognized neuroscientist. He is director of the University of Southern California's Brain and Creativity Institute. Damasio is also the author of best-selling books that explain the underlying neurobiological systems for emotion, memory, language, consciousness, and ethics (Damasio, 2003, 1999, 1994). His books have made neuroscience accessible to a wide audience.

Another popular researcher is psychologist Steven Pinker, Ph.D. who teaches at Harvard University. His specialties include visual cognition and language development. He is the author of award-winning and best-selling books that explore the idea that language is instinctual for human beings (Pinker, 2007, 2002, 1999, 1997, 1994). Pinker was named one of *Time Magazine's* 100 most influential people in the world in 2004 and received the Humanist of the Year award in 2006.

And then, of course, there are the celebrity practitioners—professionals who are very well known to the public as talk show hosts on radio and television. Some such practitioners are well trained and have appropriate professional credentials. Celebrity talk-show host, Drew Pinsky, M.D., for example, is a board certified internist, addiction medicine specialist with psychological training, and licensed private practitioner. Since 1995, Pinsky has hosted a national radio advice show called *Loveline,* and he also hosts television programs on VH1 and MTV. He is known to listeners as "Dr. Drew" and provides them with medical, sexual, relationship, and drug-addiction advice.

But a word to the wise. For each Pinsky, who is well qualified, there are many more celebrity practitioners who do not have proper training or appropriate credentials in their supposed areas of expertise, including some of the media's most popular TV and radio advisors. Before listening too closely, it is always best to check the qualifications of a psychologist or other professional who is dispensing advice on radio, television, or the Web.

how people will react to events and interact with others. Although they have no scientific foundation, the methods and tests used in astrology resemble psychological personality tests. Astrologers often adopt the terminology and topics of psychology, and so confuse many individuals—including many astrologers themselves—into believing that their field is scientifically based.

Clearly, psychologists must maintain a difficult balance. On the one hand, it is important to encourage the human drive to seek guidance and derive meaning about how to live effectively. On the other hand, psychology must distance itself from pseudoscience to maintain its status as a natural, empirically-based science. As one researcher wrote, "Mainstream psychologists have a problem differentiating themselves from what they regard as a pseudoscience without seeming dogmatically intolerant" (Hergenhahn, 2005, p. 532).

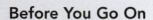

Before You Go On

What Do You Know?
5. What are the four goals of psychology?
6. What is the main difference between psychology and pseudopsychology?

What Do You Think?   Why do you think that pseudopsychology appeals to so many people even though it is not based on science and does not reflect the truth?

How Do Psychologists Conduct Research?

LEARNING OBJECTIVE 3 List steps in the research process and key characteristics of descriptive and experimental psychological research methods.

Let's go back to the controversy over reality TV. Suppose that you frequently watch *Extreme Makeover: Home Edition,* the giveaway/makeover show in which workers and friends renovate the homes of deserving and needy families. Let's say that after viewing the show, you notice that you're more charitable toward your friends. You wonder whether all people who watch this particular show become morally superior to those people who do not. How would you, as a psychological researcher, study this question?

As we described earlier, the scientific method begins with observation. So, after noting your own reaction, you may decide to observe other viewers. Maybe you get together with some friends or sit in a common area when the reality show is on, and you watch how everyone interacts with each other during and after the show.

"Well, you don't look like an experimental psychologist to me."

State a Hypothesis

After you've made such observations, you need to generate a prediction; this is your research hypothesis (see **Figure 2-2**). As we have noted, a hypothesis defines what you think will happen and states your prediction in a way that can be tested and found to be either true or false. Your hypothesis might be: Watching *Extreme Makeover: Home Edition* typically increases viewers' charitable behavior.

Notice in your hypothesis that you are saying that one thing results in another thing. The two things are called *variables*. A **variable** is a condition or event or situation—it can really be many things. A condition or event that is thought to be a factor in changing another condition or event is known as an **independent variable**. In this study, watching or not watching the giveaway/makeover show is an independent variable. A researcher could change this variable to see how it affects charitable behavior. Charitable behavior would be a **dependent variable**, the condition or event you expect to change as a result of varying the independent variable.

In addition to defining these variables, you also have to **operationalize** the variables—develop very precise definitions of the independent and dependent variables that allow you to measure and test them. In this case, you might define the independent variable as the length of time viewers watch the show. As a researcher, you may require the participants in your study to watch part of an episode, a whole episode, or even a series of episodes.

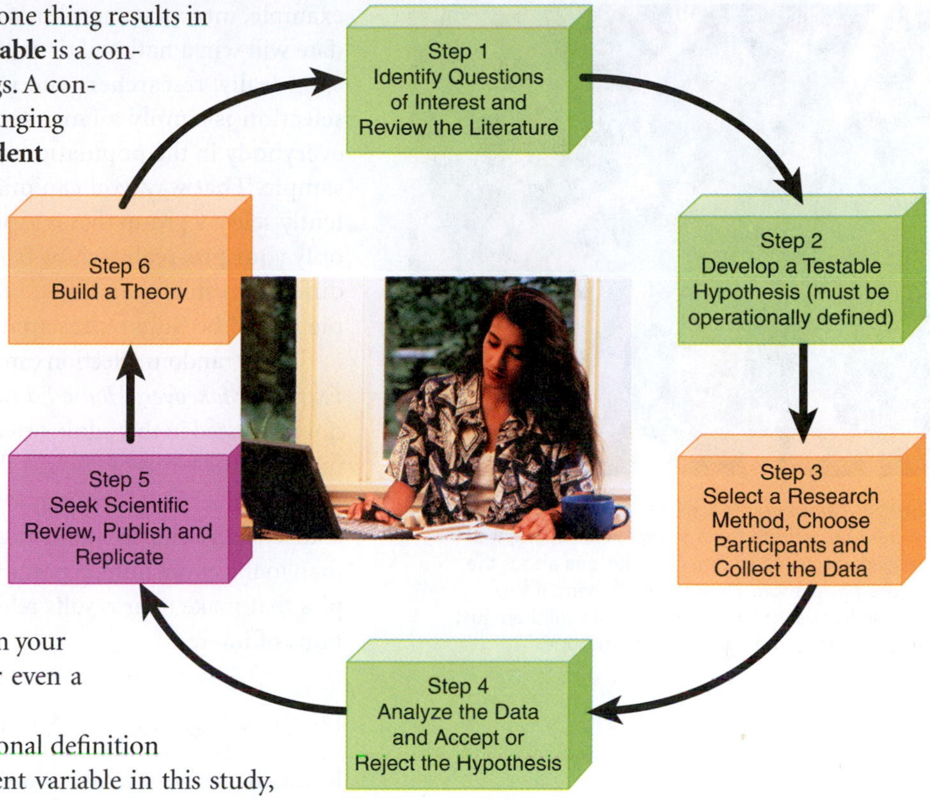

While it may be relatively easy to create an operational definition of watching, it is harder to operationalize the dependent variable in this study, charitable behavior. You might have participants fill out a questionnaire asking about their charitable feelings and their intentions to volunteer their time, give money to good causes, or help out friends. If you did this, however, you would not know for sure that the attitudes and intentions stated on the questionnaire reflect actual charitable behavior. Many people think a lot about volunteering or helping others without actually doing so. Thus, you might prefer to have participants in your study demonstrate some kind of actual charitable behavior. You could, for example, set up a situation in which each participant has to make a donation to other participants in the study or to a charity, and then see who gives larger contributions. Even here, however, you would not be sure that your operational definition of charitable behavior is on target. You might not be measuring "true-life" moral behavior; the participants might be altering their research behavior because they know they are being watched. There are yet other ways researchers could operationally define charitable behavior. Each definition would have advantages and disadvantages and each would have implications for the conclusions the researchers can draw.

FIGURE 2-2 How do psychologists conduct research? Psychologists follow certain steps and confront a number of choice points as they study questions about mental processes and behaviors.

Choose Participants

Once you've identified your variables, you need to select the people who will participate in your study. It generally isn't feasible for researchers to go out into the world and study the entire population of people whose behavior interests them. Indeed, a population of interest could sometimes include everybody in the whole world. Even when psychologists are not interested in the entire human population, their populations of interest may be very large groups, such as all Americans, adults, teenagers, men, or women. In your reality show study, the population of interest includes everyone who watches *Extreme Makeover: Home Edition* and everyone who doesn't.

Because they cannot usually study an entire population, researchers must obtain a subset, or **sample**, from their population of interest, to stand in for the population as a whole. Population sampling of this kind is used very frequently. Political pollsters, for

variable condition, event, or situation that is studied in an experiment.

independent variable condition or event that is thought to be a factor in changing another condition or event.

dependent variable condition or event that you expect to change as a result of variations in the independent variable.

operationalize to develop a working definition of a variable that allows you to test it.

sample the group of people studied in an experiment, used to stand in for an entire group of people.

Proper sampling Which of the people in this photo should be included in a study? All of them, if a researcher wants to draw conclusions about the entire population. Only some of them, if the researcher seeks to understand just children, just adults, just women, or other subgroups.

example, interview samples of the voting population in order to predict which candidate will win a national or statewide election.

Ideally, researchers choose their samples through **random selection**. Random selection is simply a fancy term for choosing your participants in such a way that everybody in the population of interest has an equal chance of becoming part of the sample. That way, you can minimize *sampling biases*—that is, you will not inadvertently select a group that is especially likely to confirm your hypothesis. If you include only your pro-reality show friends in your sample, the study probably will yield very different results than if you include only elite television critics. Indeed, neither sample would be fully representative of the population at large.

Truly random selection can be elusive. The part of your population who do not watch *Extreme Makeover: Home Edition* includes, for example, 4-year-olds, who probably are not interested in this adult-oriented program and who probably are not capable of making the same kinds of choices about charitable behavior that 25- or 45-year-old persons might make. Thus, you may decide to narrow your sample to include adults only. Of course, such a choice would mean that your findings will be relevant to adults only, rather than to the entire human population. Researchers in psychology often try to choose samples that make their results relevant to the broadest possible segments of their populations of interest.

Pick a Research Method

Researchers have several options when designing studies to test their hypotheses. Research methods differ in their goals, samples, and the ability of researchers to generalize their results to a population. Most of the methods we describe next, including case studies, naturalistic observation, and surveys, are known as **descriptive research methods**. They allow researchers to pursue the goal of description: to determine the existence (and sometimes the strength) of a relationship between the variables of interest. In addition to such descriptive methods, we will also describe *experiments*, which allow researchers to explain the *causes* of behavior (see **Figure 2-3**).

Case Studies   A **case study** focuses on a single person. Medical and psychological practitioners who treat people with problems often conduct case studies to help deter-

FIGURE 2-3 Descriptive versus experimental research Because descriptive methods and experimental methods each serve particular purposes and have different advantages and disadvantages, psychological research includes both kinds of approaches.

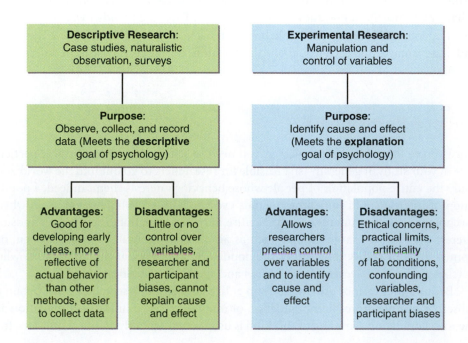

mine whether therapeutic interventions affect their client's symptoms (Martin & Hull, 2007). A case study can be a good resource for developing early ideas about phenomena. One disadvantage of a case study, however, is that it can be affected greatly by *researcher bias*, which occurs when researchers see only what they expect to see in their studies. Some clinician/researchers may, for example, note only the healthy behaviors of persons after they have provided treatment to those individuals. Another disadvantage of case studies is that researchers cannot confidently generalize to other situations from the study of a single person. Suppose, for example, that in order to test your hypothesis that watching a give-away/makeover reality show increases charitable behavior, you conduct a case study: you closely observe one man who watches such a show, and you find that he later reports himself to be generous and charitable, giving hours of service to a homeless shelter every weekend. Your case study observation might indicate that your hypothesis is worthy of further research, but without comparison participants, it is impossible to say much about other viewers of the show. You would not know whether this person's behavior after watching the show is the norm or an exception.

A first-hand look Unlike case studies or surveys, naturalistic observations enable researchers to directly observe people in their natural settings. Here, for example, a psychologist observes a preschool classroom through a one-way mirror.

Naturalistic Observation   In **naturalistic observations**, researchers watch as unobtrusively as possible while people behave as they normally do. Researchers often make naturalistic observations of children in schools or day-care centers. Perhaps as a researcher you could go into participants' homes over multiple weeks and see whether they watch a particular giveaway/makeover show. You could then observe whether those people who watch the show engage in more moral behavior and whether those who don't watch behave less morally. Naturalistic observations have the advantage of being more reflective of actual human behavior than most other research designs. A disadvantage of this type of research, however, is that naturalistic observations can be subject once again to researcher bias—observers may notice only what they expect to see (Connor-Greene, 2007). Another potential problem is that the mere presence of a researcher or even a video camera in an otherwise natural environment can change the behavior of the participants. Many people become nicer or more considerate when they are aware that they are being watched, for example.

Surveys   A third descriptive approach, frequently used in psychological research, is the **survey**. In a survey, researchers ask people a series of questions. Researchers can conduct surveys using in-person, telephone, or e-mail interviews, or they may ask the questions via a written questionnaire. To test your reality show hypothesis, for example, you might design a questionnaire that asks people about their *Extreme Makeover: Home Edition* watching habits and about their charitable attitudes, and use their answers to determine whether or not a relationship exists between the two variables.

The advantage of a survey approach is that surveys allow researchers to obtain information that they might not be able to gather using case studies or naturalistic observations. It might be hard, for example, to tell whether a person in a case study is engaging in moral behavior because he or she wishes to do the right thing, or whether the individual is behaving morally in order to get some kind of reward. A survey can help pin down such issues. Another reason surveys are sometimes favored by psychologists is that they can also provide data that enables researchers to measure how strong the relationship is between two variables of interest.

Surveys do suffer some disadvantages, however. Their data can be unreliable because people frequently answer in ways that are socially acceptable rather than in ways that are

random selection identifying a sample in such a way that everyone in the population of interest has an equal chance of being involved in the study.

descriptive research methods studies that allow researchers to demonstrate a relationship between the variables of interest, without specifying a causal relationship.

case study study focusing on a single person.

naturalistic observation study in which researchers directly observe people in a study behaving as they normally do.

survey study in which researchers give participants a questionnaire or interview them.

experiment controlled observation, in which researchers manipulate the presence or amount of the independent variable to see what effect it has on the dependent variable.

experimental group group that is exposed to the independent variable.

control group group that has not been or will not be exposed to the independent variable.

double-blind procedure study in which neither the participant nor the researcher knows what treatment or procedure the participant is receiving.

reflective of their true attitudes, a problem known as *subject bias*. Thus, people in your giveaway/makeover show study may describe themselves on a survey as more charitable than they actually are because they know that being charitable is considered a more socially appropriate trait than being selfish or stingy. Similarly, participants in a survey study may have inflated views of just how charitable they are. Although subject bias obviously is a common concern for survey researchers, it can also occur in experiments and other types of research as well, as we shall soon see.

Another problem is that survey data cannot tell us the *direction* of the relationship between variables. Do people who watch a particular reality show a lot become more charitable, or are highly charitable people drawn to watch that show a lot? A survey cannot help you answer this question.

Experiments   If you want to know what *causes* what, you have to design an experiment. An **experiment** is a controlled observation in which researchers manipulate levels of one variable—the independent variable—and then observe any changes in another variable—the dependent variable—that result from their manipulation.

One way of experimentally testing your reality show hypothesis in this kind of study would be to divide your sample into two groups: an **experimental group** and a **control group**. An experimental group is the one exposed to the independent variable. In our example, the experimental group would consist of people who are instructed to watch *Extreme Makeover: Home Edition.* A control group, in contrast, consists of people who are similar to those in the experimental group but who are not exposed to the independent variable—for example, people not instructed to view that show. By comparing the charitable behavior of the two groups after one group watches the show and the other does not, you might conclude with some degree of confidence that differences in charitable behavior are caused by exposure to *Extreme Makeover: Home Edition.* You could also create a more complex experiment, in which multiple experimental groups watch varying amounts of this reality show, and compare them with the nonwatching control group participants in order to determine how much viewing of the show it takes to produce changes in charitable behavior.

The composition of experimental and control groups needs careful attention. In our example, no one in the control group has ever seen *Extreme Makeover: Home Edition* (see **Figure 2-4**) and none will be instructed to do so for the study. But what about the experimental group? Should you include people who've watched the show previously, or should you begin with a group of participants who—like the control group—have never, ever watched the show, and then expose the experimental group to a marathon of this reality show's episodes. Either approach is acceptable, but the two approaches may lead to different conclusions.

Other kinds of differences—past or present—between the experimental and control groups may also influence the results of an experiment. Even when they use *random assignment* to make sure that everyone in their sample has an equal chance of being in either the control or experimental group, researchers still run the risk that the groups will differ in some important ways. Suppose that you randomly assign your reality TV participants to each of your groups, but nevertheless wind up with wealthy individuals in one group and poor individuals in the other group. Such an unintended group difference may affect the participants' subsequent charitable behaviors and so may lead you to draw incorrect conclusions. Some researchers pre-interview or give questionnaires to participants in both the experimental and control groups to make sure that the groups are comparable to one another. Their goal is to help guarantee that whatever effects emerge in the study are caused by the experimental manipulation of the independent variable and are not attributable to other, pre-existing variables, such as income level.

FIGURE 2-4 **The experimental design** Key features of experimental designs are independent and dependent variables and random assignment of experimental and control groups.

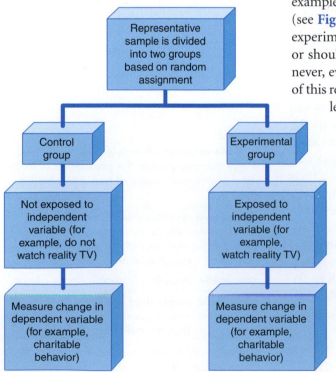

In addition, experimenters must be careful when deciding what tasks will be performed by participants in the control group. Researchers often have the participants in a control group engage in an activity of some kind, just to make sure that the changes seen in the experimental participants are indeed due to the impact of the independent variable and not the result of the experimental participants being particularly active during the study. You might, for example, have your control group participants view another—nonreality—TV show that is just as engaging as *Extreme Makeover: Home Edition*. You could, for example, show the animated cartoon series *Pokemon* to the control group. If the experimental participants still demonstrate more charitable behavior than the control participants afterwards, you can be more certain that the reality show is in fact responsible.

Finally, experimenters must be careful to avoid bias in their studies. Once again, they must avoid subject bias and researcher bias—sources of bias that we discussed earlier. In addition, they must set up their studies so that they do not unintentionally convey to participants the outcome that they (the experimenters) expect to see, an undesired effect known as a *demand characteristic*. If a researcher were to tell participants in the experimental group of the reality TV study that their answers to a charitability questionnaire will indicate how much reality TV contributes to positive real-life behavior, the researcher might be creating a demand characteristic that is encouraging those participants to overstate their charitable inclinations. For this reason, many studies, particularly pharmaceutical ones, are designed so that the persons who administer the study or who evaluate the behavior of participants are unaware of the hypotheses of the study. Indeed, a number of studies use a specialized method known as a **double-blind procedure**, in which neither the participant nor the researcher knows which group—experimental or control—the participant is in. Double-blind studies help keep researchers from observing or creating what they want to observe and participants from intentionally acting in ways that confirm a researcher's hypothesis.

Experimental answer Do complex visual images stimulate babies? To answer this causal question, experimenters have shown swirling designs to one group of babies (experimental group) and bland designs to another group (control group). Babies in the experimental group typically attend to their designs longer than do those in the control group, suggesting that complex images do indeed attract the attention of babies.

Before You Go On

What Do You Know?

7. Which variable is controlled or manipulated by an experimenter?
8. What are three descriptive research methods used in psychology?
9. Which research method allows research to say that one variable causes another?

What Do You Think?   What would you conclude if people's charitable behavior increased after a single exposure to *Extreme Makeover: Home Edition*? How would that conclusion be different if charitable behavior only increased after a marathon viewing of the show?

How Do Psychologists Make Sense of Research Results?

LEARNING OBJECTIVE 4 Tell what information is conveyed by statistics, including correlation coefficients, means, and standard deviations, and explain how psychologists draw conclusions about cause and effect.

Once researchers obtain results from an experiment or descriptive study, what do they do with them? Can they simply eyeball their findings and say that there's a relationship between this and that variable, or that the two groups under study are different? No. Scientists cannot depend just on impressions or logic. If they tried, they would have no way of knowing whether a relationship found between variables or a difference between groups actually matters.

correlation predictable relationship between two or more variables.

correlation coefficient statistic expressing the strength and nature of a relationship between two variables.

positive correlation relationship in which scores on two variables increase together.

negative correlation relationship in which scores on one variable increase as scores on another variable decrease.

perfect correlation one in which two variables are exactly related, such that low, medium, and high scores on both variables are always exactly related.

Psychologists use *statistics* to describe and measure relationships between variables. There are many statistical analyses that scientists use to look at the differences and similarities between groups. We won't go into a lot of depth about statistics here. We will, however, give you a few tips to help you understand the research findings you'll be reading about in this book and elsewhere. We'll discuss correlations, which describe the relationships between variables, and then go on to discuss the statistical tests researchers use to determine how likely it is that their results might be occurring simply by chance. Then, we will examine how researchers use the statistical results to decide whether or not their hypothesis has been supported and to guide the next steps in the research process.

Correlations: Measures of Relationships

A predictable relationship between two or more variables is called a **correlation**. To describe correlations, especially in descriptive studies, psychologists use a statistic called a **correlation coefficient**.

A correlation coefficient can range from -1.00 to $+1.00$. The number itself and the positive or negative sign in the correlation coefficient each convey different information. The positive or negative signs tell you the direction of the relationship. When scores on both variables get bigger together, the relationship is known as a **positive correlation**. In our example of a reality show study, we predicted a positive correlation between *Extreme Makeover: Home Edition* watching and charitable behavior: As watching increases, so will charitable behavior. If we had suggested that charitable behavior does not increase, but actually drops, as people watch more and more reality TV, then we would be predicting a **negative correlation**. When the variables are negatively correlated, higher scores on one variable are related to lower scores on another variable. **Figure 2-5** shows various such relationships.

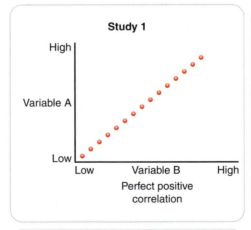

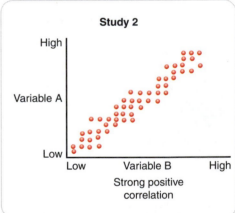

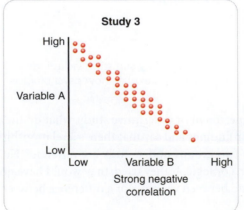

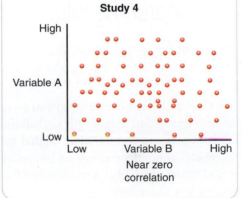

FIGURE 2-5 **Graphing correlations** If we were to plot each participant's score on Variable A and Variable B on a graph, we would see that the variables display a perfect positive correlation in Study 1, strong positive correlation in Study 2, strong negative correlation in Study 3, and near zero correlation in Study 4.

In addition to looking at the positive or negative sign, we must consider the value of the number in the correlation coefficient. The number tells the size, or strength, of the relationship between variables—that is, how well can we predict one variable if we know the other. The larger the number, the stronger the relationship. Thus, a correlation coefficient of 0.00 means that there is no relationship between the two variables. Knowing a person's score on one variable tells you nothing about the person's score on the other. The farther a correlation coefficient gets from 0 in either the positive or negative direction, the stronger the relationship between the two variables. A high positive correlation coefficient means that scores on the two variables under examination typically rise and fall together, and a high negative correlation coefficient means that a rise in one of the variables usually is accompanied by a fall in the other. A correlation of −1.00 or +1.00 is known as a **perfect correlation**, one in which the variables' scores are always perfectly related.

Again, it is important to keep in mind that in correlation coefficients, the positive and negative sign and the number itself provide two different pieces of information. A correlation with a negative coefficient is not weaker than one with a positive coefficient. In fact, the relationship may be stronger if, for example, the negative correlation is −0.7 and the positive correlation is +0.2. A negative correlation of −0.7 would mean that the two variables are quite strongly related in such a way that low scores on one variable very often are associated with high scores on the other (see **Figure 2-6**).

In psychology, really exciting relationships are often reflected by a correlation coefficient of 0.3 and above. This is far from a perfect correlation, largely because relationships between behaviors, thoughts, and emotions can be so complex and because so many other variables may also be at work in such relationships. Nevertheless, 0.3 or above typically means that the two variables in question do indeed have some kind of predictable relationship.

Correlations offer lots of useful information, particularly when we are interested in the scientific goal of prediction. The correlation coefficient tells us just how well we can use one piece of information about someone, such as how much the person watches a giveaway/makeover reality show, to predict his or her behavior in another realm, in this case charitable behavior. One key piece of information correlations do *not* tell us, however, is *causality*, whether or not a change in one variable actually causes the change in the other (see **Figure 2-7**). As we mentioned earlier, only experimental studies and experimental analyses can tell us whether causality is at work.

+1.00	Perfect positive relationship
+.88	Very strong positive relationship
+.62	Strong positive relationship
+.38	Moderate positive relationship
+.12	Weak positive relationship
0.00	No relationship
−.12	Weak negative relationship
−.38	Moderate negative relationship
−.62	Strong negative relationship
−.88	Very strong negative relationship
−1.00	Perfect negative relationship

FIGURE 2-6 How to read a correlation coefficient The sign of the coefficient tells us the direction and the number tells us the magnitude, or strength, of the relationship between two variables.

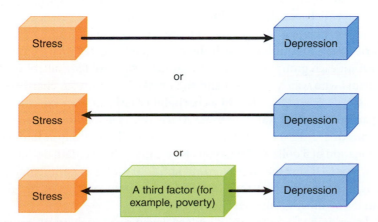

FIGURE 2-7 Correlation versus causation Research has found a strong correlation between stress and clinical depression. However, this correlation does not tell us whether stress causes depression, depression causes stressful events, or other factors, such as poverty, produce both stress and depression.

Correlation versus causality The repeated co-occurrence of two events (correlation) does not necessarily mean that one is causing the other. Children who eat ice cream, for example, tend to have bike accidents. It may be that eating ice cream while riding causes young bikers to have more accidents. Or, it may be that parents typically treat their children to ice cream whenever they have accidents. Or, perhaps hot summer days lead to increases in both ice cream eating and bike riding.

Experimental Analyses: Establishing Cause and Effect

If you want to examine differences between groups and establish causality, you have to do a different set of statistical analyses. Collectively, these are called *experimental analyses* because they are associated with experiments. Researchers sometimes divide experimental analyses into two categories: *descriptive statistics*, which describe or summarize the data gathered from a study, and *inferential statistics*, which tell researchers what they can conclude, or infer, more broadly from their results.

In order to describe differences between the scores of experimental group and control groups, researchers calculate the *mean* and *standard deviation* of each group. The **mean** is the arithmetic average of the scores of all participants in a group. This is the same average you've been calculating since fourth grade math class. Big differences between the mean—the average score—of an experimental group and the mean of a control group may indeed suggest big differences between the participants in the groups.

To be certain of this, however, researchers also look at the **standard deviation**, an index of how much the participants' scores *vary* from one another within each group. Suppose, for example, you have ten control-group participants who watch *Pokemon* and then make donations to charity of 4, 5, 4, 6, 5, 4, 4, 7, 5, and 6 dollars in a charitability task, and ten experimental-group participants who watch *Extreme Makeover: Home Edition*, then make donations of 1, 2, 12, 11, 5, 9, 4, 1, 3, and 2 dollars. Each group would have a mean donation of 5 dollars. Unless you also examine the standard deviations for both groups (1.05 for the control group and 4.20 for the experimental group), you might not realize that there are more extreme reactions in the reality show group than in the other group (see **Figure 2-8**).

After determining the mean and standard deviation of each group, researchers can compare the two groups. Psychologists typically compare means using statistical procedures known as *t-tests* (for two groups) or *analyses of variance* (for two or more groups). These procedures look both at the mean differences and at the variance within

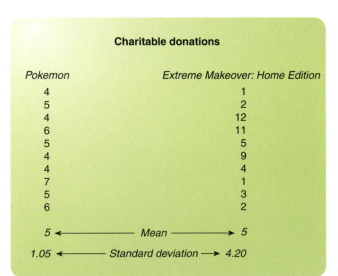

Charitable donations	
Pokemon	Extreme Makeover: Home Edition
4	1
5	2
4	12
6	11
5	5
4	9
4	4
7	1
5	3
6	2
5 ← Mean → 5	
1.05 ← Standard deviation → 4.20	

FIGURE 2-8 Variability and the standard deviation Although these two sets of data have the same mean, or average, score of charitability in our fictitious study, viewers of *Extreme Makeover: Home Edition* are much more varied in their charitable behaviors (high standard deviation) than are viewers of *Pokemon* (low standard deviation).

the groups, as well as at the size of the groups. The statistical procedures are known as significance tests because they measure whether the differences found between groups are *statistically significant*. In statistics, the word *significant* has a slightly different meaning from most people's everyday use of the same word. A test of statistical significance tells us how likely it is that the differences found between groups are due to experimental manipulations rather than due to chance. Such tests indicate this likelihood by calculating a *probability statistic*.

If a test of statistical significance yields a probability statistic of $p < .05$, it means that if researchers were to conduct the same study 100 times, they would, by chance alone, get the same result found in the current study less than 5 percent of the time. In other words, there's an extremely low probability that the result found in the current study occurred simply as a random act of chance. Most likely, it occurred because of a real difference between the two groups of subjects in the study. By convention, when a test of statistical analysis yields a probability of less than .05 ($p < .05$), psychological researchers conclude that the difference they have found between groups in their study is statistically significant—i.e., likely to be a real difference that is due to the manipulations carried out in the study.

Keep in mind that the numerical difference between group means and the probability statistic says nothing about how big an effect you're seeing in your study. Let's say that participants who watch *Extreme Makeover: Home Edition* later display a higher mean charity score than do those who watch *Pokemon*, and that the probability statistic is less than 0.01 ($p < .01$). This does not necessarily mean that the reality show viewers have become *much* more charitable than the nonviewers. It just means that there's less than 1 chance in 100 that you obtained that result by chance. If you want to know how big the effect of watching reality TV is, you need to calculate yet another statistic, known as *effect size*, which describes the strength of the relationship between two variables. If you were to find a large effect size in your study, it would suggest that watching the reality show strongly increases charitable behavior.

"I just feel fortunate to live in a world with so much disinformation at my fingertips."

Using Statistics to Evaluate and Plan Research

If you get a result like this—a difference between groups that is very unlikely to have occurred by chance—does it mean you have fully supported your hypothesis and should sit back and toast your success? Well, not yet. Scientists need to be sure. They need to go back and test their hypotheses some more. It is only through **replication**, taking the data from one observation and expanding on it to see if it holds up under multiple conditions and in multiple samples, that we can determine whether what we hypothesize is correct. Over time, replication enables hypotheses to become theories and theories to become laws.

Another important feature of science is to use different research methods to explore the same research question. If researchers use several approaches, including surveys, experimentation, and independent observations, and obtain the same results, they can be more certain that their hypotheses are accurate and have confidence about incorporating those hypotheses into theories.

As we described earlier, in our discussion of the scientific method, a theory is also a framework to generate additional hypotheses. If your hypothesis about *Extreme Makeover: Home Edition* proves correct, and people on average report themselves to be more charitable and exhibit more charitable behaviors on experimental tasks, you have reason to continue your line of research. You can conduct the same experiment with

mean arithmetic average of a set of scores.

standard deviation statistical index of how much scores vary within a group.

replication repeated testing of a hypothesis to insure that the results you achieve in one experiment are not due to chance.

other reality shows, such as *Survivor* or *American Idol* and see whether the hypothesis continues to hold up for all kinds of reality shows. You may also decide to look at other forms of moral behavior besides charity, such as empathy or sense of fair play. If you continue to replicate these results with other shows and other moral behaviors, you are effectively supporting the theory that watching reality TV in fact contributes to increased moral behavior within a culture. A Nobel Prize is inevitable.

PRACTICALLYSPEAKING Tips on Reading a Scientific Journal Article

As a psychology student, particularly if you major in psychology, you will most likely read journal articles for some of your required classes. Initially, this task may seem overwhelming. The authors of journal articles tend to use unfamiliar language, condense complex concepts into a small space, and make assumptions about the reader's knowledge of their topic. However, you can turn this task into something interesting and worthwhile by following a few simple steps.

When you read a research paper, try to understand the scientific contributions the authors are making. You should read the paper critically and not assume that the authors are always correct.

You do not need to read the paper sequentially to get the gist of it. First, you might read the abstract, the introduction, and the conclusions. Next look through the references to determine whose work is at the root of the current research. After this first read through, try to summarize the article in one or two sentences.

Then, go back and read the entire paper from beginning to end. Study the figures, re-read parts that are difficult to understand, and look up unfamiliar words. Make notes in the margins or on separate sheets of paper. And answer the following questions as you work:

- **Title:** What does this tell you about the problem?
- **Abstract:** What does this general overview tell you about the current paper?
- **Introduction:** What are the authors' assumptions, important ideas, and hypotheses?
- **Methods:** Do the methods seem to effectively test the authors' hypotheses?
- **Related work:** How does the current work relate to past work? What is new or different about the current study?
- **Conclusions:** What were the study's results, and do they make sense? What were the study's limitations? What do the authors propose for future research? How does the study contribute to a better understanding of the problem?

You also may choose to outline, summarize, or keep more detailed notes, especially if you are using the article for a term paper.

Before You Go On

What Do You Know?

10. What two pieces of information does a correlation coefficient give about the relationship between variables?
11. What do the mean and standard deviation tell you about scores of a group?
12. What do *t*-tests tell experimenters?

What Do You Think? What are some examples of positive and negative correlations you've observed in everyday life?

What Ethical Research Guidelines Do Psychologists Follow?

LEARNING OBJECTIVE 5 Tell what ethical steps psychologists take to protect the rights of human research participants.

For 40 years between 1932 and 1972, the American government committed a grave breach of ethics in the now-infamous Tuskegee Syphilis Study, an extensive clinical investigation concerning the course and treatment of syphilis in African-American men. Many of the men in the study who tested positive for syphilis were not treated, or were treated only minimally for the disease, to ensure that they would not benefit from treatment because researchers wanted to study the course of the disease when left untreated. In a later interview, John Heller, one of the medical directors of the project stated, "The men's status did not warrant ethical debate. They were subjects, not patients; clinical material, not sick people" (Jones, 1981, p. 179). Horrors, such as the Tuskegee experiment alarmed the public and heightened awareness and concern about the ethical practices of scientists, including psychologists, who conduct research with human and animal participants (Katz et al., 2008; McGaha & Korn, 1995).

A nation apologizes In a 1997 White House ceremony, President Bill Clinton offers an official apology to 94-year-old Herman Shaw and other African American men whose syphilis went untreated by government doctors and researchers in the infamous Tuskegee Syphilis Study.

Today, psychological research must be designed with the goal of protecting the participants involved with the study. Psychology researchers are bound by the same broad ethical principles that govern doctors and other clinicians. The Code of Ethics of the American Psychological Association states it clearly: "Psychologists . . . take care to do no harm" (APA Code of Ethics, 2002).

To ensure that researchers follow proper ethical practices, **institutional review boards (IRBs)** provide oversight in academic and other research settings across the world. Any institution (university, private corporation, government agency, or medical school) conducting research involving human participants is expected to appoint an IRB, which often consists of a mixture of researchers from inside and outside the field and of individuals from the community. IRBs examine research proposals and rule on the potential risks and benefits of each study's procedures. If the risk or discomfort associated with a proposed study is deemed to outweigh the potential scientific benefit from the study, then the undertaking is rejected. IRBs generally require that psychologists studying human participants take the following steps to protect human participants:

- *Obtain informed consent.* **Informed consent** from participants requires that researchers give as much information as possible about the purpose, procedures, risks, and benefits of a study, so participants can make informed decisions about whether they want to be involved in the study. If participants include children, researchers must obtain informed consent from both the parents or caregivers and the child.
- *Protect participants from harm and discomfort.* In addition to medical or physical risks, such as those faced by the men in the Tuskegee studies, researchers must avoid putting participants in situations that could cause them undue emotional stress, for example.
- *Protect confidentiality.* Researchers must have in place, and explain to participants, careful plans to protect information about the identities of participants and the confidentiality of their research responses.

institutional review board (IRB) research oversight group that evaluates research to protect the rights of participants in the study.

informed consent requirement that researchers give as much information as possible about the purpose, procedures, risks, and benefits of the study so that a participant can make an informed decision about whether or not to participate.

Consent has its limits To protect children who participate in studies, researchers must also obtain informed consent from their parents or caregivers.

- *Provide complete debriefing.* In some cases, if participants were to have full knowledge about the purposes and goals of a study before it began, their responses during the study might be influenced by that knowledge. Researchers often try to balance giving participants enough information before a study to protect their rights, yet withholding information that may affect participants' responses. Thus, at the end of a study, researchers are required to offer a **debriefing** to participants—an information session during which they reveal any information that was withheld earlier.

In addition to ruling on the costs and benefits of the study, review boards also assess other issues. They look, for example, at the compensation individuals receive for their participation (to make sure that participants are not tempted to participate in potentially dangerous studies by high levels of compensation), and they determine whether particular groups (such as men, women, or members of minority ethnic groups) are singled out unnecessarily.

In a related development, the ethics of psychological research involving animals has come under scrutiny. Animal rights advocates point out that animals are especially vulnerable research participants, since they cannot give their consent to be part of a study. They also argue that animals may be exposed to more extreme risks than humans, for sometimes unclear benefits.

Although animal rights activists are certainly correct in pointing to such problems as consent and enhanced risk for animals, they are not correct when some of them suggest that the study of human psychology has derived little benefit from the study of animals. Much of our knowledge about learning and motivation began with studies of animals, such as Pavlov's famous dogs (which we will talk more about in Chapter 7). We also have gained substantial knowledge about the nervous system from work on animals, using research procedures that could never be conducted on human beings. And animal research has played a major role in the development of medications, including medications for psychological and neurological disorders. The American Psychological Association, the Society for Neuroscience, and the National Institutes for Health have issued specific ethical guidelines regarding research with animals. These guidelines mandate that the research must advance both human and animal welfare, should only be used when it advances our knowledge of behavior or neuropsycho-

debriefing supplying full information to participants at the end of their participation in a research study.

As you have seen in this chapter, research involving animals has been the focus of scrutiny and debate in recent years. Thus let's clarify some important facts and figures about animal research (APA, 2009; ILAR, 2009; MORI, 2005, 1999).

1. The welfare of animal subjects is of great interest and concern not only to animals activists but also to animal researchers, government agencies, scientific organizations, and the public.

2. Around 8 percent of psychological research involves the use of animals; 90 percent of the animals used are rodents and birds (mostly rats and mice); only 5 percent are monkeys and other primates.

3. Every regulated institution that conducts animal research is required by law to have an *Institutional Animal Care and Use Committee (IACUC),* which carefully reviews and oversees all such studies at their institution. The IACUC ensures that each study follows all ethical, legal, and humane guidelines, and the commitee pays close attention to such issues as the prevention or alleviation of animal pain, alternatives to the use of animals, and the clinical and scientific importance of the study.

4. In surveys, 75 percent of the public say that they can accept animal research as long as it is for scientific purposes. And most respondents even approve of experiments that bring some pain to animals when those investigations are seeking a cure for childhood leukemia, AIDS, or other significant problems.

logical functioning, and must first consider alternatives to the use of animals (such as computer modeling or the use of different procedures with human participants) (ILAR, 2009; APA Code of Ethics, 2002).

All such guidelines—for both animal and human research undertakings—help ensure not only more ethical procedures but better science as well.

Before You Go On

What Do You Know?

13. What does an institutional review board do?

14. What is informed consent and how does it relate to debriefing?

What Do You Think? Are ethical standards different for psychology than those for other sciences? Should they be?

Summary

What is a Science?

LEARNING OBJECTIVE 1 List two core beliefs of science, and describe the steps in the scientific method.

- *Science* is an approach to knowing the world built on the core principles that (1) the universe operates according to certain natural laws and (2) these laws are discoverable and testable.

- Science is founded upon the scientific method, a process that moves from making controlled, direct observations to generating progressively broader conclusions and tests and attempting to disprove hypotheses.

Is Psychology Really a Science?

LEARNING OBJECTIVE 2 Compare and contrast psychology with other natural sciences, such as biology, chemistry, and physics, and with pseudopsychologies, such as astrology.

- Psychology shares with every science the primary goals of describing, explaining, predicting, and controlling the objects of study. The goals of psychology differ from those of other sciences because the search for elements of mental processes and behavior is complicated by constantly shifting human factors.

- Psychology also shares more similarity with the fields of religion and philosophy than many sciences do because psychological findings are more often associated with values, morality, and personal preference.

- Psychology is different from pseudopsychology. Although the latter also attempts to answer fundamental questions about human nature and behavior, it has no basis in the scientific method.

How Do Psychologists Conduct Research?

LEARNING OBJECTIVE 3 List steps in the research process and key characteristics of descriptive and experimental psychological research methods.

- Psychological research is rooted in first generating a hypothesis, or prediction, about the relationship between two or more variables based on observations.

- Psychologists conduct research with a sample, a small group meant to represent the larger population of interest. The best means of selecting a sample is random selection, a procedure in which everyone in the population has an equal chance of being selected to be in the sample.

- Descriptive research methods include case studies, naturalistic observations, and surveys.

- Case studies are in-depth observations of a single individual.

- Naturalistic observation involves observing people in settings outside of laboratories where their behavior occurs naturally.

- Surveys may be conducted in interviews or with questionnaires.

- Only experiments allow researchers to draw conclusions about cause-and-effect relationships.

- All research methods have advantages for particular uses and all are subject to various drawbacks. Researchers must plan carefully to avoid subject bias, researcher bias, and demand characteristics.

How Do Psychologists Make Sense of Research Results?

LEARNING OBJECTIVE 4 Tell what information is conveyed by statistics, including correlation coefficients, means, and standard deviations, and explain how psychologists draw conclusions about cause and effect.

- Correlations allow us to describe and measure relationships between two or more variables. A *correlation coefficient* tells the direction and size of a correlation.

- Researchers use the mean and standard deviation to describe and summarize their results.

- Researchers use *p values* to determine the statistical significance of results. *Effect size* tells how strong the relationship is between variables.

- Replication of experiments and repeated study of the same predictions using different methods help hypotheses become theories.

What Ethical Research Guidelines Do Psychologists Follow?

LEARNING OBJECTIVE 5 Tell what ethical steps psychologists take to protect the rights of human research participants.

- As egregious ethical practices came to light in the United States in the 1960s and 1970s, people took action to protect the rights of research participants.

- Today, oversight boards called institutional review boards (IRBs) help to protect human rights.

- Psychological researchers must obtain informed consent from human participants, protect them from harm and discomfort, protect their confidentiality, and completely debrief them at the end of their participation.

- The use of animal participants in research has also raised ethical concerns. Oversight boards called Institutional Animal Care and Use Committees (IACUC) help to protect animals needs and comfort in experiments.

Key Terms

deductive reasoning 33

biases 33

inductive reasoning 33

empirical 33

theories 33

hypothetico-deductive
   reasoning 33

hypothesis 33

variable 39

independent variable 39

dependent variable 39

operationalize 39

sample 39

random selection 41

descriptive research methods 41

case study 41

naturalistic observation 41

survey 41

experiment 42

experimental group 42

control group 42

double-blind procedure 42

correlation 44

correlation coefficient 44

positive correlation 44

negative correlation 44

perfect correlation 44

mean 47

standard deviation 47

replication 47

institutional review board
   (IRB) 49

informed consent 49

debriefing 50

CHAPTER 3

Human Development

chapter outline

- Understanding How We Develop • How Is Developmental Psychology Investigated?
- Before We Are Born • Infancy • Childhood • Adolescence • Adulthood
- Developmental Psychopathology

Growing Up Super

Did you ever think about what it takes to become a super-hero? Many seem to be shaped by early tragedy. Superman is the last survivor of a doomed alien race, adopted and raised by a human couple in Kansas. Batman's will to fight evil was forged after a thug killed his parents in front of him when he was 12 years old.

Perhaps the most complicated and tragic is Peter Parker, your friendly neighborhood Spider-Man. Like Bruce Wayne and Clark Kent, Peter is an orphan. Raised by his elderly aunt and uncle, Peter is a good student, but shy and constantly worried. When he is bitten by a radioactive spider, and acquires super strength and agility, Peter's first thought is not heroism, but freedom. His newfound superpowers lead to a short but exciting career in wrestling, earning him money and stardom and the chance to be that outgoing, wisecracking, popular person he always wanted to be. All that comes to an end when, in a moment of selfishness, he allows a thief to run past him, and the same thief later kills his Uncle Ben. Peter's crime fighting career as Spider-Man is sparked by this tragedy as he reflects on his uncle's greatest lesson: "With great power comes great responsibility."

If you were charting the development of a superhero, what would you focus on? Unlike other fields in psychology, which often focus on what a person is like at a particular moment in his or her life, **developmental psychology** is interested in changes in our behavior and mental processes over time and how various factors influence the course of those changes. Developmental psychologists might wonder whether the fact that Batman, Superman, and Spider-Man are all orphans helps explain their heroism. They might notice that, even though Bruce Wayne, Clark Kent, and Peter Parker were orphaned, they each had caregivers who helped to buffer the loss of their parents. Bruce Wayne's family butler, Alfred, stepped in as his father figure, Clark had the kindly Kents, and Peter had his aunt and uncle.

In addition to noticing similarities between groups of people, developmental psychologists are interested in differences between individuals. Clark Kent's trauma happened before he was born, and he was raised by parents with strong values about right and wrong; perhaps as a result, he appears to be the least conflicted about his role in the world. Bruce Wayne saw his parents murdered right in front of him. His outlook on life appears to be much darker and more cynical than Superman's, although he is equally single-minded in his pursuit of justice. Peter Parker feels burdened consistently by the role of Spider-Man and often tries to give it up, only to remember his guilt over his uncle's murder and resume his crime fighting.

Pondering the development of superheroes is interesting, but most of us are even more interested in our own origins. What happened to make us into the women and men we are? Was it genes, or parents, or friends, or other, more individualized factors that led to you being where you are right at this moment? Do changes occur because of biological factors or because of our experiences? Are we all doomed to turn into our mothers or fathers?

Unfortunately, development is too complex and depends on too many influences that steer the course of our lives in one direction or another for developmental psychologists to state with precision what causes us to be the way we are. Instead, they try to identify several general factors that work together to influence how we grow and change across our lifespan.

It's worth noting that the terms *developmental psychology* and *child psychology* have often been treated interchangeably. If you take a developmental psychology course, you'll probably wind up spending most of your time on child psychology; you'll be lucky if you make it to adolescence (we mean in the course, not in life). And this chapter will in some ways be more of the same. We're going to spend a lot of time talking about childhood, simply because that's what most of the pioneering theorists in developmental psychology spent their time thinking about and studying.

However, a revolution has started over the last few years. Developmental psychologists now acknowledge that developmental changes do not stop when we leave childhood (see Table 3-1). As we'll see later in the chapter, a trend toward longer human lifespans has also given rise to fields of study, such as *gerontology* and the *psychology of aging*.

We'll also need to talk about how things go wrong, an area in which another revolution has been brewing. A new field of study called *developmental psychopathology* has provided a new way to help us think closely about the factors over the course of a lifetime that contribute to one person becoming a superhero and another becoming a supervillain.

We worry about what a child will become tomorrow, yet we forget that he is someone today.

—Stacia Tauscher, author

TABLE 3-1 Developmental Stages Over the Lifespan

Stage	Approximate Age
Prenatal	Conception to birth
Infancy	Birth to 2 years
Early childhood	2–6 years
Middle childhood	6–12 years
Adolescence	12–20 years
Young adulthood	20–45 years
Middle adulthood	45–60 years
Later adulthood	60 years to death

Understanding How We Develop

LEARNING OBJECTIVE 1 Understand the key debates underlying research and theory in child development.

Before we discuss what happens in development, it's useful to consider some of the key issues that concern developmental psychologists. These issues are often foundations for theory, research, and clinical work, but they are not always directly tested. As you read through the rest of the chapter, you may want to think about how the theories we will discuss later fit with these big ideas about human development.

What Drives Change? Nature versus Nurture

The key debate in human development is: how much of our growth, personality, and behavior is influenced by *nature*, our genetic inheritance, and how much is influenced by *nurture*, a term that encompasses the environment around us as well as our experiences as we grow.

Scientists who take a strong view of the influence of genetics or biology on development are said to view development *endogenously*. They look at development as biologically programmed to happen sequentially, a process known as **maturation**. Other scientists believe that our experiences have a greater influence on how we develop, a perspective known as an *exogenous* view of development.

Going back to our superhero examples, Superman's superpowers are the product of endogenous developmental factors. His alien nature makes him stronger than a locomotive and able to leap tall buildings in a single bound. Batman's development is more exogenous. The early experience of losing his parents led him to commit himself to a study and workout regimen designed to bring him to the point of human perfection.

It is not as easy, however, to attribute the characteristics of people outside the superhero world exclusively to either nature or nurture. In the real world, our traits and behaviors are almost always influenced by an interaction between such factors. Still, researchers continue to have robust debates about whether endogenous or exogenous factors are more important. You will see that the so-called nature-nurture issue applies not only to questions about development but also to ideas about intelligence (discussed in Chapter 10), social behavior (Chapter 14), and pretty much all of the psychological disorders that we discuss at the end of each chapter.

Qualitative versus Quantitative Shifts in Development

Throughout this chapter, whether we are referring to physical development, social development, or cognitive development, you will notice that we talk a lot about stages. A **stage** is a developmental point at which we achieve certain levels of functioning, such as saying a first word, taking a first step, or getting a driver's license.

Developmental researchers have significant arguments about whether or not these stages represent *qualitative* shifts in the growth of persons, meaning that individuals make developmental jumps that result in them becoming different than they were before (see **Figure 3-1**). Qualitative theorists would argue that once we acquire language, for example, we think of the world in a different way because we are able to give things

developmental psychology the study of changes in behavior and mental processes over time and the factors that influence the course of those changes.

maturation the unfolding of development in a particular sequence and time frame.

stage developmental point at which organisms achieve certain levels of functioning.

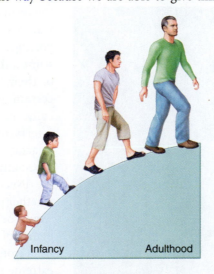

Infancy   Adulthood   Infancy   Adulthood

(a) Qualitative development   (b) Quantitative development

FIGURE 3-1 Do stages represent qualitative or quantitative shifts in development? (a) Some theorists believe that individuals make qualitative jumps in development as they move from stage to stage. (b) Others think that development is a steady continuous process.

"We've been thinking a lot about what we want to do with your life."

names and even to think about things that don't have a concrete reality. Without the word "love," they argue, it would be hard to conceive of the various things that love means, because one cannot point to love or sense it in a direct way (at least not the same way you do a ball or a favorite toy). Stage theories are largely endogenous; they hold that major qualitative shifts are biologically programmed to happen in a certain sequence and at a certain time, leading people to progress through development in the same general way and hit milestones at around the same time. For example, the majority of humans begin to walk sometime close to the age of 1 year.

Even though human development is sequential in many ways, the *timing* of developmental milestones does often vary. Some children take their first steps weeks or even months earlier than others. Many theorists believe the individual variations in timing indicate that development often represents more of a *quantitative* shift. According to these theorists, development is the result of an ongoing acquisition of new information and new experiences, and what seem like big, sudden developmental changes actually are the result of a gradual accumulation of many small changes, often so small that they are hard to notice. Theorists and researchers in the quantitative camp believe that walking comes as a result of a series of small developmental changes, including the steady growth of our muscles until they can hold our body weight and the development of our brains until they can control physical coordination. Quantitative theorists have an easier time accounting for individual differences in the timing of milestones but a harder time explaining why most people go through similar sequences of development during similar times of life, despite considerable variations in their experiences.

Do Early Experiences Matter? Critical Periods and Sensitive Periods

Related to the question of stage theories versus continuous theories of development is the question of whether there are *critical* periods in development. A **critical period** is a point in development when the organism is extremely sensitive to a particular kind of environmental input, making it easier for the organism to acquire certain brain functions. If the environmental input does not occur at that point, development will be thrown off track (hence, the term *critical*). For example, the pioneering critical period theorist, Konrad Lorenz, found that goslings will forever connect with whatever moving stimuli they see most often during the first 36 hours of their lives. In Lorenz's work, he was able to get certain goslings to think of him (or more specifically, his boots) as their mother. He used the term *imprinting* to describe the development of this attachment. Take a look at the accompanying photo, especially if you are having trouble believing this.

Psychologists have long been curious about whether people also have critical periods. Of course, it would be unethical for researchers to deprive human beings of their usual early experiences in order to see what would happen, but cases of human deprivation—extreme poverty or death of one's parents, for exam-

The followers By exposing these baby geese to him alone during their first day of life, ethology pioneer Konrad Lorenz manipulated them into viewing him as their mother. For geese, the first 36 hours after birth is a critical learning period during which they become imprinted to their mother—or a mother substitute.

ple—do sometimes occur naturally. By studying the histories of children in these unfortunate situations, researchers have learned that serious psychological disabilities may result from early deprivations (Michel & Tyler, 2005). At the same time, however, other studies have found that subsequent changes in environmental input (for example, removing deprived children from their early negative environments and placing them in more positive ones) can help the children recover partially or, in some cases, completely.

Because individuals can recover at least partially even after deprivation during key time periods in their lives, most of today's psychologists and biologists believe that critical periods are better defined as *sensitive periods*, times when we are especially receptive to environmental input, but not rigidly so (Michel & Tyler, 2005). Theorists today are less inclined to believe that input is essential during a critical period, like a countdown that is running out on your opportunity to develop particular traits or functions. Instead, they view sensitive periods as largely *experience-driven*, flexible enough to extend past typical time frames for development (Armstrong et al., 2006).

All is not lost Early deprivation, such as that experienced by these young children at a Vietnamese orphanage, can result in severe psychological disabilities. Moving the children to more positive and stimulating settings, however, can help many of them to recover at least partially.

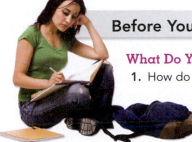

Before You Go On

What Do You Know?

1. How do quantitative theories of development differ from qualitative theories of development?
2. What is the difference between a critical period and a sensitive period?

What Do You Think? Do you see biological or environmental factors as playing a more major role in your development?

How is Developmental Psychology Investigated?

LEARNING OBJECTIVE 2 Describe and discuss the advantages and disadvantages of cross-sectional and longitudinal designs for researching development.

As we've noted, developmental psychologists are interested in learning about changes that happen as we age. How do they go about measuring those changes?

One approach is the **cross-sectional design**. In this approach, researchers compare groups of different-aged people to one another. For example, they might compare a group of 60-year-olds to a group of 30-year-olds on a memory task to see how memory changes over time. The benefit of the cross-sectional approach is that it's easy and straightforward, as well as convenient, for both researchers and participants.

The big problem with the cross-sectional approach is that it assumes that any changes found in a study are the result of age. Researchers must remember to also consider other factors that might influence their results. Let's say that the task used to measure memory differences between the two age groups mentioned above is computer-based. If the 30-year-olds perform better on the memory task, the researchers might conclude that the results are due to age-related changes in memory. But the findings could be related more to the fact that 30-year-olds are more familiar with and less intimidated by computer technology than 60-year-olds are.

critical periods points in development when an organism is extremely sensitive to environmental input, making it easier for the organism to acquire certain brain functions and behaviors.

cross-sectional design research comparisons of groups of different-aged people to one another.

FIGURE 3-2 **Cross-sectional versus longitudinal research design** Cross-sectional research uses participants of various ages to examine age-related differences. Longitudinal research studies the same participants over time to determine age-related changes.

CROSS-SECTIONAL DESIGN

Different participants of various ages are compared at one point in time to determine age-related *differences*

Group One
30-year-old participants

Group Two
60-year-old participants

Group Three
90-year-old participants

Research done in 2011

LONGITUDINAL DESIGN

The **same** participants are studied at various ages to determine age-related changes

Study One
Participants are 30 years old

Study Two
Same participants are now 60 years old

Study Three
Same participants are now 90 years old

Research done in 2011

Research done in 2041

Research done in 2071

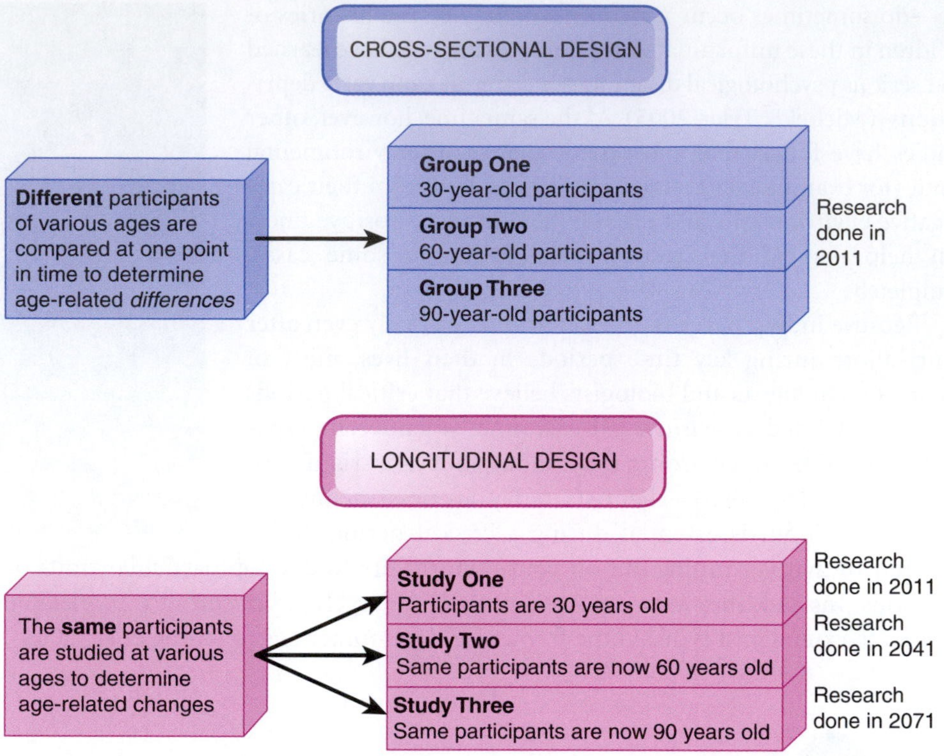

Another drawback of cross-sectional research is that it does not provide much explanation of how or when age-related changes may have occurred. If older participants actually have memory declines, for example, did those declines occur suddenly, in their early 50s, or accumulate gradually over the past 30 years?

For these reasons, many developmental researchers prefer a **longitudinal design** (see **Figure 3-2**). This research follows the same group of people over a period of time, administering the same tasks or questionnaires to them at different points in their lives to see how their responses change. We'll discuss one of the most famous of these longitudinal studies in Chapter 10 when we talk about a long-term longitudinal study of extremely intelligent people (Feldhusen, 2003).

The main benefit of longitudinal research is that researchers can be reasonably confident that the observed changes are a function of time and developmental experiences. Unfortunately, longitudinal studies require considerable time and money. The study you'll read about in Chapter 10 went on for 85 years! Moreover, many participants in longitudinal studies drop out of the studies over the course of their lives because they move away, lose interest, become ill, or even die (see **Table 3-2**).

longitudinal design research following the same people over a period of time by administering the same tasks or questionnaires and seeing how their responses change.

cohort-sequential design blended cross-sectional and longitudinal research, designed to look at both how individuals from different age groups compare to one another and also follow them over time.

prenatal period period of development stretching from conception to birth.

genes basic building blocks of our biological inheritance.

deoxyribonucleic acid (DNA) molecules in which genetic information is enclosed.

chromosomes strands of DNA; each human being has 46 chromosomes, distributed in pairs.

genotype a person's genetic inheritance.

phenotype the observable manifestation of a person's genetic inheritance.

allele variation of a gene.

homozygous both parents contribute the same genetic material for a particular trait.

TABLE 3-2 Cross-sectional and Longitudinal Research Designs Compared

	Cross-sectional design	Longitudinal design
Advantages	• Easy and straightforward • Convenient for both researchers and participants	• Gives reasonably reliable information about age changes
Disadvantages	• Cohort effects are difficult to separate • Does not explain how or when changes may have occurred	• Requires considerable time and money • Many participants drop out over the course of study

Seeking to obtain the advantages and avoid the drawbacks of cross-sectional and longitudinal designs, some developmental researchers design studies that combine the two. A **cohort-sequential design** looks at both how age groups compare to one another at various points in the research but also takes a longitudinal approach to see how those differences vary over time.

Before You Go On

What Do You Know?

3. What is the main advantage of using a longitudinal design instead of a cross-sectional design?

What Do You Think? If a researcher today finds differences between a group of 20-year-olds and a group of 60-year-olds, what historical, social, and cultural factors might have contributed to those differences?

Before We are Born How we *Develop*

LEARNING OBJECTIVE 3 Discuss patterns of genetic inheritance and describe stages and potential problems during prenatal development.

An enormous amount goes into shaping human development during the **prenatal period**, the nine months or so stretching from conception to birth. Growth during this period happens incredibly quickly. Our biological parents are the starting point for our development by contributing parts of their own genetic inheritance. We'll see that the contributions from a mother and a father can form a variety of combinations—some matching exactly, some differing completely.

In the Beginning: Genetics

Genes are the most basic building blocks of our biological inheritance. Each gene is composed of a specific sequence of **deoxyribonucleic acid**, or **DNA**, molecules. DNA and genes are arranged in strands called **chromosomes**, found in each cell of our bodies. Each of us has 23 pairs, or 46 total, chromosomes. Twenty-three chromosomes are contributed by each of our biological parents, and the resulting combination is called our **genotype**, which broadly refers to a person's genetic inheritance. A person's **phenotype** is the observable manifestation of that genotype, the physical and psychological characteristics that are on display in each individual.

It is difficult to determine a person's genotype solely on the basis of his or her phenotype—appearance or behavior. Consider the ability to roll your tongue. Tongue rolling is genetically determined; either you are born with the ability or you will never have it (Fry, 1988). If you can roll your tongue, you display a tongue-rolling phenotype. Without further information, however, we cannot say exactly what your genotype is. As we have noted, each parent contributes half of a child's chromosomal makeup; half of the offspring's genes come from the biological mother and half from the father. Variations of the same gene, such as the gene for tongue rolling, are called **alleles**. If both parents contribute the same allele, then the person is **homozygous** for the trait—

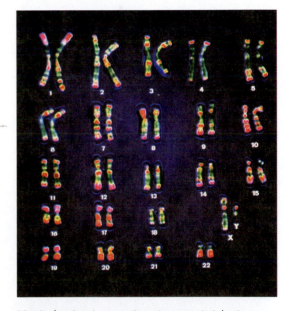

Magical pairs A person's entire genetic inheritance is contained in 23 pairs of chromosomes, with each parent contributing one chromosome to each pair. Here we see an individual's chromosomes stained with dyes and photographed under a microscope.

To roll or not to roll In this family, the father can roll his tongue (a dominant trait), while the mother cannot (a recessive trait). As a result, their daughter displays a tongue-rolling phenotype, which is rooted in a heterozygous tongue-rolling genotype.

that is, he or she has two matching alleles of the same gene. If you can roll your tongue, you *may* be homozygous for the tongue-rolling gene.

It turns out, however, that people can still roll their tongues if they inherit a tongue-rolling allele from one of their parents and a nonrolling allele from the other. In such instances, the individuals have the observable phenotype of tongue rolling, but their genotype is **heterozygous**, a combination of two different alleles. Thus, if you can roll your tongue, you are displaying a tongue-rolling phenotype, and this phenotype may reflect either a homozygous or a heterozygous genotype (see **Figure 3-3**).

Depending on the trait in question, any of three different phenotypes can result when a person has a heterozygous combination of different alleles (Adapted from Truett et al., 1994):

- One possibility is that the trait either will be expressed in its entirety or will not be expressed at all. This is the case with heterozygous tongue rolling. If you have one "rolling" allele and one "nonrolling" allele, you will be able to roll your tongue. Tongue rolling is a **dominant trait**, a trait that is expressed in your phenotype regardless of whether your genotype is homozygous or heterozygous for the trait. A **recessive trait**, on the other hand, is one that is expressed in your phenotype only when you are homozygous for that trait. The inability to roll your tongue is recessive. You must have two matching "nonrolling" alleles in order to be prevented from rolling your tongue.

- For some traits, a person with a heterozygous pair of alleles may show a *mixture* of genetic coding. For example, children of couples who have different racial backgrounds can have features associated with the backgrounds of both parents, such as blended skin color or eye shape.

- For yet other traits, persons with a heterozygous pair of alleles may express *both* of the parents' genes in their phenotype. This outcome is called **codominance**. An example of codominance is found in blood type. If one parent has blood Type A and the other parent has Type B, the child can express both in the form blood Type AB.

The thing that makes the study of genetics particularly challenging is that only a few of our traits are **discrete traits**, the product of a single gene pair. Instead, most human traits are **polygenic traits**, ones that involve the combined impact of multiple genes. It is especially likely that traits affecting our behavior are polygenetic.

As we noted in Chapter 1, many psychological researchers are interested in trying to determine how much of the way we think and act is influenced by our genetic inheritance, a field of study called behavioral genetics. Developmental psychologists are often in a position to examine the influence of genetics. One of the key areas of focus of both

FIGURE 3-3 Genotype versus phenotype
Individuals who are able to roll their tongues may have either a homozygous or a heterozygous genotype for tongue rolling. In contrast, people who cannot roll their tongues must have a homozygous genotype for non-tongue rolling.

Genotype:	Homozygous		Heterozygous		Homozygous	
Parent Contributions:	Mother: tongue rolling allele	Father: tongue rolling allele	Mother: tongue rolling allele	Father: non-tongue rolling allele	Mother: non-tongue rolling allele	Father: non-tongue rolling allele
Phenotype:	Tongue rolling trait will be expressed		Tongue rolling trait will be expressed		Tongue rolling trait will not be expressed	

behavioral genetics and developmental psychology, for example, has been **temperament**, often defined as a biologically-based tendency to respond to certain situations in similar ways throughout our lifetimes (Henderson & Wachs, 2007; Bates, 1989). In a longitudinal study that began in the 1950s, researchers Stella Chess and Alexander Thomas (1996) suggested that, as infants, people tend to fall into one of three temperament categories:

- *Easy.* Babies with easy temperaments were described as playful, regular in bodily functions, such as eating and sleeping, and open to novelty.

- *Difficult.*—Babies with difficult temperaments tend to be irritable and likely to have intensely negative reactions to changes or new situations.

- *Slow-to-warm-up.* Babies in this category are less active and less responsive than babies in the other two categories. In general, they tend to withdraw in the face of change, but their withdrawal is not as sharply negative as those with difficult temperaments.

Following Chess and Thomas's studies, many researchers have examined how our temperament relates to our later personality characteristics. In a famous line of work, biologist and psychologist Jerome Kagan (2008, 2001) conducted a longitudinal study examining the relationship between babies' levels of *behavioral inhibition*, the tendency to withdraw from new or different situations, and levels of shyness later in life. He found that children who were highly inhibited at 21 months of age were more likely than uninhibited toddlers to be shy when they were 12 to 14 years old.

Kagan's research seems to illustrate two key aspects of temperament:

1. *Temperament is inborn.* For an attribute to be temperamentally based, it must appear early (for example, shortly after birth). Considering that Kagan tested babies at such a young age, it is doubtful that they had much of an opportunity to learn to be fearful of new situations. Thus, many researchers believe that inhibited temperaments are biologically inherited.

2. *Temperament is stable across situations and time.* The participants in Kagan's study who were most shy temperamentally were the ones who were most inhibited at different times and in different situations. Researchers have also established that other aspects of a person's temperament are stable over time and place (Henderson & Wachs, 2007). This is not to say, however, that there is no variability at all from time to time and situation to situation. Indeed, investigators have found greater stability of temperament when measuring behavior across similar situations, such as in various family situations, than when comparing temperamental influences on children's behavior across different situations, such as school versus home.

Despite the biological factors implied above, it is important to recognize that our environments also play important roles in how we behave. Kagan's studies revealed, for example, that not all of the babies who were inhibited at birth later developed into shy teenagers. Similarly, being highly extroverted around new toys as a newborn did not always lead his infant participants to become life-of-the-party teenagers. In fact, if genetics were destiny, we'd all have a much easier time predicting how people will turn out, and this would be a much shorter chapter. As we'll see, however, our environment plays a very strong role in determining our development, beginning before we are even born.

> "The first half of our lives is ruined by our parents, and the second half by our children."
>
> —*Clarence Darrow, attorney*

heterozygous parents contribute two different alleles to offspring.

dominant trait trait that is expressed in a phenotype, no matter whether the genotype is homozygous or heterozygous for the trait.

recessive trait trait that is only expressed if a person carries the same two genetic alleles (e.g., is homozygous for the trait).

codominance in a heterozygous combination of alleles, both traits are expressed in the offspring.

discrete trait trait that results as the product of a single gene pairing.

polygenic trait trait that manifests as the result of the contributions of multiple genes.

temperament biologically-based tendencies to respond to certain situations in similar ways throughout our lifetimes.

Have you ever explained yourself by referring to your birth order? "Oh, I'm the middle child, so I just don't feel like I belong." Or perhaps, "I'm spoiled and act out because I'm an only child." In reality, the effect of birth order on personality is hotly debated by psychologists, and most of the "effects" of birth order may be more anecdotal than they are actual.

In 1996, scientist and scholar Frank Sulloway published the book *Born to Rebel* in which he argued that first-borns tend to be more responsible while later-borns tend to be more rebellious. He further hypothesized that later-borns tend to be more open to experience and more agreeable than first-borns, and, at the same time, less neurotic, less extraverted, and less conscientious (Jefferson, Herbst, & McCrae, 1998).

Although Sulloway's book was widely praised at first, many psychologists eventually questioned his methodology and noted inconsistencies in his data. Most notably, in 2000, the journal *Politics and the Life Sciences* attempted to publish a roundtable issue devoted to a discussion of Sulloway's book. The issue was to include articles and commentaries from a number of scholars who rejected or questioned Sulloway's work (Townsend, 2000, p. 135). The debate became so heated that, according to the journal's editor, Sulloway threatened legal action and the publication of the issue was delayed for four years, eventually appearing in 2004.

Scientists typically subject research to peer review, in which an article is read by fellow scientists and intensely scrutinized and revised before it is published. Books, however, do not have to go through this process, which was one of the criticisms leveled against Sulloway's research (Townsend, 2000). In contrast to Sulloway's findings, a peer-reviewed article that examined over 1000 birth order studies has concluded that birth order does not influence personality in a clear and consistent way (Jefferson et al., 1998).

Perhaps that is why birth order research seems to be shifting away from the area of personality and toward other areas, such as intelligence and physical features. It has been found, for example, that first-borns tend to score about three points higher on IQ tests compared to second-borns. Similarly, children born earlier in a family are, on average, taller and weigh more than those born later (Kluger, 2007).

Despite the fact that birth order studies have not yet yielded clear or compelling findings, the topic remains very popular in the public domain. Indeed, in recent years, *Time* and other newsmagazines have presented several cover stories on the relationship between birth order and psychological and social functioning, an indicator that even as many psychologists believe birth order to be a subject unworthy of research, the public's fascination with the topic continues to grow (Kluger, 2007).

Prenatal Development

Prenatal development begins with *conception*, when a sperm fertilizes an egg, resulting in the creation of a single cell, called a **zygote**. The first 2 weeks after conception is known as the *germinal stage*. During the first 36 hours of this stage, the single cell zygote divides and becomes two cells. Then these two cells divide to become four, those four divide and become eight, and so on. As its cells keep multiplying, the zygote moves up through the mother's fallopian tube (where it was first fertilized) to her uterus. About a week after fertilization, the zygote attaches itself inside the uterus. The other major transition that occurs during the germinal stage is the formation of a nutrient-rich structure called the **placenta** that will allow the swiftly developing individual to begin performing the basic functions of life, such as breathing, feeding, and waste excretion.

The second stage of the prenatal period is the *embryonic stage* (2 to 8 weeks). Most of the major systems of the body, such as the nervous and circulatory systems, as well as the basic structure of the body, begin to take shape during this stage. It is during this stage that the new organism is most vulnerable to **miscarriage**, discharge from the uterus before it is able to function on its own, or to the development of defects. Given

zygote single cell resulting from successful fertilization of the egg by sperm.

placenta nutrient-rich structure that serves to feed the developing fetus.

miscarriage discharge of the fetus from the uterus before it is able to function on its own.

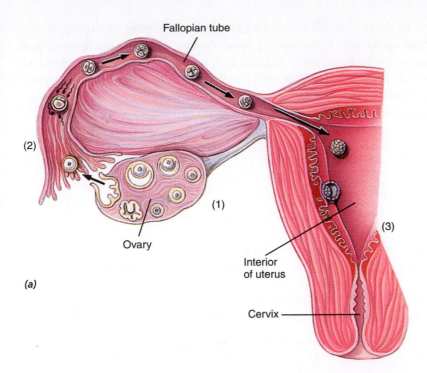

Fallopian tube

Ovary

(2)

(1)

(3)

Interior
of uterus

Cervix

(a)

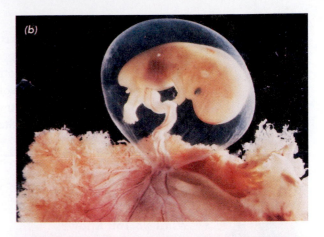

(b)

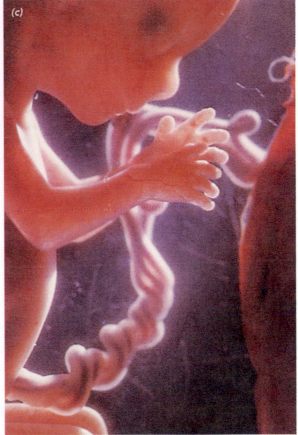

(c)

FIGURE 3-4 Prenatal development *(a) Germinal period: From ovulation to implantation:* After the egg leaves the ovary (1), it travels to the opening of the fallopian tube (2) where it is fertilized and becomes a zygote. About a week later, the zygote reaches the uterus, implants itself in the wall of the uterus (3), and triggers the formation of the nutrient-rich placenta. *(b) Embryonic stage:* Once the zygote is implanted it grows rapidly. By 8 weeks, many external body structures and internal organs have been formed. Notice that the head grows faster than the rest of the body. At this stage, the embryo is vulnerable to miscarriage. *(c) Fetal stage:* From 8 weeks to birth, the fetus continues to enlarge rapidly and the basic structures undergo substantial change.

such possibilities, new parents often wait until the pregnancy has lasted well into the last stage, or *fetal stage*, before announcing it (see **Figure 3-4**).

The fetal stage lasts from the end of the embryonic stage until the birth of the baby. The fetus has several characteristics, including a developing muscular and skeletal system, that lead to a sudden ability to move. Especially during the last three months, the fetus' brain begins to grow at a remarkable pace. Organs that began to emerge in the embryonic stage now start to function independently, and the fetus begins to hiccup, see, hear, and sleep. All of these functions contribute to the fetus' eventual ability to function independently of the mother.

Prior to Birth When Things Go Wrong

The fetus is vulnerable to any number of problems soon after it moves beyond being a twinkle in someone's eye. As you will see throughout the book, many disorders are inherited from the parents. Some of these disorders, such as sickle-cell anemia, cystic fibrosis, or phenylketonuria (PKU) are linked to recessive genes. Still other disorders are linked to chromosomal problems. In Chapter 10, for example, when we talk about intelligence, we'll also talk about *Down Syndrome*, a pattern caused by the presence of an extra chromosome in the twenty-first chromosome pair.

In addition to genetic and chromosomal problems, a number of environmental risks, called **teratogens**, can influence the fetus' development during the prenatal period. Pregnant women should avoid risks, such as smoking or ingesting alcohol and other substances, legal and illegal, all of which have been linked to birth defects. Even soft cheeses and deli meats can pose certain risks because of the possibility of contracting *listeria*, a bacterium that can put the fetus at significant risk (Guevara, 2008; Stehlin, 1996).

Before You Go On

What Do You Know?

4. What are the possible phenotypic outcomes from a heterozygous genotype?
5. How did Chess and Thomas categorize the temperaments of babies in their studies, and what were the major attributes of each temperament category?
6. What are the key things that identify a behavior as temperamentally-based?
7. What are the three stages of prenatal development, and what happens at each stage?

What Do You Think? How do you think environment might influence a genetically-influenced trait, such as behavioral inhibition? For example, what might parents or teachers of an inhibited toddler do that would either contribute to or tend to decrease later shyness?

Infancy  How we *Develop*

LEARNING OBJECTIVE 4 Summarize the major physical, cognitive, and emotional developments that take place during infancy.

Families of newborns often think of their infants as factories for eating, drooling, and excreting. It's true, a baby's capabilities are limited at this point in some ways, but in other important ways they are ready to go.

Physical Development

Compared to some other species, human infants are still relatively "unfinished" at birth. Our key senses develop fully during our first months and we learn to walk after about a year or so, but our brains—although they also show amazing development during infancy—are not fully developed until we are teenagers or young adults.

What Happens in the Body During Infancy? The senses of taste, smell, and touch are all highly developed at birth. A baby can distinguish the scent of his or her mother's milk from another woman's milk and can make fine distinctions between various tastes after only a few days out of the womb.

Other senses are less developed. Hearing is still immature and affected by fluid from the mother's womb that continues to take up space in the newborn's ears. If you've ever spent a day swimming, you've probably had a sense of what it's like to hear like a baby. Things sound a little muddled, with greater sensitivity to high and low pitched sounds. These limitations change quickly, however. Within a few days the baby can distinguish familiar speech from new sounds and words that they have not heard before.

teratogens environmental risks to a fetus's development during gestation.

TABLE 3-3 **Common Newborn Reflexes**

Reflex	Stimulation	Response	Function
Rooting	Touch the corner of the infant's mouth	Infant turns toward the stimulation and begins to suck	Helps infant begin feeding
Grasping	Press finger against infant's palm	Infant grasps finger and holds on	Allows infant to hold on to caregiver for safety
Moro	Let infant's head lose support	Infant flings arms outward and then inward in a hugging motion	May have helped infant to hold on to caregiver when support is lost
Babinski	Stroke sole of infant's foot	Toes spread apart	Unknown

Vision is a baby's least developed sense (Kellman & Arterberry, 1998; Maurer & Salapatek, 1976). Newborns cannot clearly see objects much more than 7 or 10 inches away. Similarly, their ability to scan objects is limited. If they look at a triangle, they will focus only on one of its corners. If they look at a face, they will focus largely on the chin or hairline. And they do not develop good color vision until they are 3 months of age. At first, these visual limitations are not a big deal; after all, babies do not travel very far, and they can see far enough to make eye contact with their mothers while nursing. Interestingly, their vision improves steadily, and by the time babies start moving around, about 7 to 8 months of age, their vision has approached adult levels.

In addition to our senses, we are also born with certain **reflexes**, programmed reactions to certain cues that do not require any conscious thought to perform. For example, babies pucker their lips and begin to suck whenever something brushes their cheeks or is put in their mouths, a response called the *rooting reflex*. Other common reflexes are listed in **Table 3-3**.

What Happens in the

Infancy B R A I N ? Perhaps you have heard popular claims that most of our brain development happens before age 3. Are they right? As with many questions in psychology, the answer here is yes and no. Infancy is, indeed, a time of remarkable changes in our brains. Although a newborn's head is only about one-fourth the size of an adult's, there is a lot going on in there! As you'll see throughout this book, however, the brain continues to change and develop throughout our whole lives.

Two key processes are responsible for the amazing growth of the brain in the earliest years of life. The first is a sheer increase in connections among *neurons*, the brain's nerve cells. As we will describe in detail in Chapter 4, information is passed from neuron to neuron at transmission points called **synapses**. Born with 100 billion neurons, the child acquires synaptic connections at a staggering rate during its first few years, expanding from 2500 such connections per neuron at birth to around 15,000 per neuron by age 2 or 3 years (Bock, 2005; Di Pietro, 2000). Many of these connections develop as a function of normal maturation, regardless of the baby's experiences and, in fact, serve as a way of helping the baby process new experiences. As babies, we actually develop far greater numbers of synapses than we will eventually need. As we grow older, two-thirds of our early synaptic connections fall away (Bock, 2005; Di Pietro, 2000). Our experiences help to stimulate and strengthen some of the connections, while

Brain growth in the first two years This illustration shows the increases in the complexity of neurons that occur over the course of infancy.

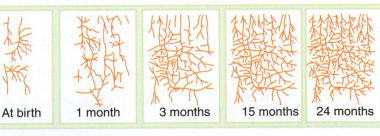

At birth | 1 month | 3 months | 15 months | 24 months

reflexes programmed physical reactions to certain cues that do not require any conscious thought to perform.

synapses transmission points between neurons.

synaptic pruning developmental reduction of neuronal connections, allowing stronger connections to flourish.

myelination development of fatty deposits on neurons that allow electric impulses to pass through neurons more efficiently.

proximodistal growth from more central areas of the body to parts at the outer edges.

motor skills ability to control our bodily movements.

synapses that are not used weaken and dissipate. This process is called **synaptic pruning** because of its similarity to pruning, or cutting away, the dead branches of a tree or bush in order to help the healthy, live branches flourish (Edin et al., 2007).

The other process that accounts for increased brain growth is **myelination**. Myelin is a fatty white deposit that forms around and insulates portions of many neurons, helping electric impulses pass through a neuron more efficiently. During infancy, much of myelination occurs in the spinal cord and in areas of the brain primarily associated with movement, reflexes, sensory responses, and certain low-level learning processes. For the most part, brain and body development follow a **proximodistal** pattern, in which parts closer to the center (that is, the spine) develop sooner than parts at the outer edges (the extremities). In this way, our most vital organs and body parts form first.

How Do We Learn to Control Our Movements?   By the end of their first year, most babies are up and moving. **Motor skills**, the ability to control one's bodily movements, include achievements such as grasping objects, crawling, and eventually walking. **Table 3-4** shows the typical ages at which children in the United States reach particular motor-development milestones. As we noted earlier in the chapter, most babies acquire motor skills in roughly the same order, which suggests that there may be a maturational explanation for the way in which they unfold.

At the same time, and as Table 3-4 also shows, there is considerable variability regarding when a child hits a particular milestone. The timing of motor development can be influenced by a number of environmental factors.

Negative influences, such as abuse, neglect, or poor nutrition, can slow a child's motor development. Cultural practices that either encourage or discourage early motor development can also influence the timetable. For example, the Kipsigis people in Kenya begin working with babies shortly after birth to help them sit up, stand, and walk (Super, 1976). In turn, Kipsigis children achieve these milestones about a month before children raised in the United States. On the other hand, the Ache parents in Paraguay worry about their children moving more than a few feet away, and they actively discourage independent motor development in their children. As a result, Ache children do not walk until an average of one year later than children in the United States (Kaplan & Dove, 1987).

TABLE 3-4   Milestones in Motor Development

Motor Milestone	Average Age Achieved	Age Range
When prone, lifts chin up	2 months	3 weeks–4 months
Rolls over	2 months	3 weeks–5 months
Sits alone	7 months	5–9 months
Crawls	7 months	5–11 months
Stands holding furniture	8 months	5–12 months
Stands alone	11 months	9–16 months
Walks alone	11 months, 3 weeks	9–17 months
Walks up steps	17 months	12–23 months

Based on Laura E. Berk, *Infants, Children, and Adolescents, 6e* (Boston: Allyn & Bacon, 2008) Table 5.2, p. 188.

As we noted at the beginning of this chapter, the timetable for learning to walk provides an excellent example of the interaction of nature and nurture in our development. Although achieving a developmental milestone three months early or one year late is significant (particularly to a worried or proud parent), it is equally significant that the process keeps moving forward—that most everyone eventually hits this particular milestone.

Cognitive Development

Amazingly, in just two short years, people proceed from wordless, vague (but cute) babies who are completely dependent on others to little yappers who can get into just about everything and figure out how to get a glass of juice that catches their eye. What happens during this period of time that triggers such a dramatic shift? We will talk about how we learn our languages in Chapter 9. Here, we discuss the important changes in thinking ability that happen during those first two years.

"I still don't have all the answers, but I'm beginning to ask the right questions."

Piaget's Theory   One of the world's most influential developmental psychologists, Jean Piaget, focused on **cognitive development**, how thinking changes (Piaget, 2003, 2000, 1985). Piaget's theory began with naturalistic observations of children, including his own, in real life situations (Mayer, 2005). On the basis of his observations, Piaget hypothesized that young children's thinking processes might differ from that of adults. He then proceeded to test his hypotheses by making small changes in the children's situations and watching to see how they responded to those changes (Phillips, 1975). Based on the results of these tests, Piaget developed a theory of how we acquire knowledge and the abilities to use it.

According to Piaget, all of us have mental frameworks or structures for understanding and thinking about the world. He called these frameworks **schemata**, and he believed that people acquire and continuously build their schemata through their experiences in the world. For example, you may have acquired a schema about Chinese restaurants, based on your experiences. When you go to a Chinese restaurant in your community, you can predict some of the dishes that are going to be on the menu, and you know not to look for pizza or a hamburger.

Piaget believed that when children gain new knowledge, their schemata change. This can happen in two ways. The first, **assimilation**, was defined by Piaget as the inclusion of new information or experiences into pre-existing schemata. During your first few visits to Chinese restaurants, for example, you may have ordered only General Tso's chicken. In later visits, however, you may have expanded, but not drastically altered, your schema with new information by trying other chicken dishes.

Sometimes, we come across new information so different from what we already know that we cannot simply add it to our old schemata. We must alter a pre-existing schema significantly to fit in new information or experiences, an adjustment Piaget called **accommodation**. Let's say that you traveled for the first time to New York's Chinatown neighborhood. There you learned not only that there are several different styles of Chinese cooking but also that your favorite dish, General Tso's chicken, is not even really Chinese. It is a dish created in New York to interest Americans in Chinese cuisine. Based on this experience, you would have to radically revise your mental framework for Chinese restaurants.

According to Piaget, engaging in assimilation and accommodation helps us to reach a mental balance, or **equilibrium**. As a result of your experiences in Chinese restaurants at home and in New York, you may now feel comfortable in a variety of Chinese restaurants.

Piaget's theory is a stage theory. He suggested that we travel through several stages of cognitive development in life, progressing from being, as babies, unable to even form schemata to being able, as teenagers and adults, to perform complicated mental feats

cognitive development changes in thinking that occur over the course of time.

schemata Piaget's proposed mental structures or frameworks for understanding or thinking about the world.

assimilation one of two ways of acquiring knowledge, defined by Piaget as the inclusion of new information or experiences into pre-existing schemata.

accommodation one of two ways of acquiring knowledge, defined by Piaget as the alteration of pre-existing mental frameworks to take in new information.

equilibrium balance in a mental framework.

TABLE 3-5 Piaget's Four Stages of Cognitive Development

Stage	Age	Description
Sensorimotor	Birth to age 2	"Thinks" by using senses and motor skills; no thought beyond immediate experience
Preoperational	Age 2–7	Able to hold ideas of objects in imagination; unable to consider another's point of view or distinguish between cause and effect
Concrete operational	Age 7–11	Can think about complex relationships (cause and effect, categorization); understands conservation; unable to think abstractly or hypothetically
Formal operational	Age 11 on	Able to think abstractly and hypothetically

of logic using schemata. Piaget believed strongly that, as we move from stage to stage, *qualitative* shifts occur in our thinking. Children in one stage not only know more but actually become different sorts of thinkers than they were at earlier stages. **Table 3-5** shows the four developmental stages proposed by Piaget. He proposed that, during infancy, we are in the earliest, or sensorimotor, stage.

Piaget named this first stage sensorimotor because he thought that, early on, babies can think only about the world in terms of what they can sense directly or encounter through simple motor actions—that is, a ball, a favorite toy, or a parent is present only insofar as the baby can sense it directly or lay hold on it in some way. Once that pacifier is under the couch, it's gone. Out of sight, out of mind.

Piaget believed that much of our early learning happens as a result of our reflexes. He observed that even though they are "hardwired" into us, reflexes are susceptible to change. As the baby engages in reflex behaviors, he or she gets feedback about how those responses affect him or her and the surrounding world. The rooting reflex often brings food to a hungry infant, for example. In this way, babies are acquiring knowledge that contributes to the formation of schemata. The baby may come to develop a schema relating rooting behavior to feeding.

A major cognitive milestone of the sensorimotor stage is the development of **object permanence** at around 8 months of age, the realization that objects continue to exist even when they are out of a baby's immediate sensory awareness. A child may cry when a toy rolls under the couch, for example. When children eventually begin to demonstrate awareness of things out of their sensory awareness, it suggests that they are beginning to hold concepts in mind. They have developed mental schemata of those objects.

Eventually, babies become able not only to hold objects in their minds, but also to manipulate and make predictions about those objects and how they interact with other objects. A baby may try to lift a cloth to look under it for a hidden toy, for example. By the end of the sensorimotor stage, Piaget believed that the young child's schemata have changed from needing a direct experience of the world to one in which ideas and concepts stand in for those objects.

Information Processing Views of Cognitive Development   Piaget often looked at what children could not do and then used their mistakes to determine their cognitive abilities. Today, however, psychologists who adhere to the **information-processing theory**— who study how children take in information—look to see what children *can* do, as opposed to what they cannot. Such theorists have found that Piaget probably underestimated children's competencies at various developmental stages (Lourenç & Machado, 1996).

object permanence an infant's realization that objects continue to exist even when they are outside one's immediate sensory awareness.

information-processing theory developmental theory focusing on how children take in and use information from their environment.

habituation process in which individuals pay less attention to a stimulus after it is presented to them over and over again.

Out of sight, out of mind Prior to 8 months of age, babies have no recognition of *object permanence*. For example, here a young infant plays happily with a stuffed dog (left), but displays no awareness that the animal continues to exist after an experimenter removes it from sight (middle). In contrast, the 10-month-old on the right immediately seeks out and finds a favorite toy that has been hidden from him under a cloth.

To see when a baby developed object permanence, for example, Piaget would hide the object and see whether the baby looked for it. Searching suggests that the baby still had the object in his or her mind. As we have noted, however, it takes some time for babies to master control over their bodies enough to move purposefully and conduct a search. If you cannot grab a cloth that is hiding a toy, you cannot lift it and look under it. Thus, other researchers have suggested that a better indicator of object permanence is whether or not babies react with surprise when hidden objects are revealed again (Baillargeon, 1987). After all, to be surprised, you have to have an expectation that is challenged in some way. Such surprise implies that you have a mental representation of the situation. Studies focusing on the surprise reaction suggest that babies as young as 3 months may display some form of object permanence.

Researchers also have found evidence that babies can *learn* and *remember* right after birth. Throughout life, individuals often learn to perform and repeat certain behaviors by experiencing positive consequences after they first manifest the behaviors, a process called *operant conditioning* that we'll talk about much more in Chapter 7 (Lipsitt et al., 1966). It turns out that even very young babies learn to perform certain behaviors when they are systematically rewarded by researchers. If babies can shift their strategies to bring about positive outcomes or avoid negative ones, they must have some concepts (and, by extension, memories) of the relationships between behaviors and outcomes. Babies also display **habituation**—that is, they stop responding over time to the same stimulus if it is presented again and again. If babies had no memory or no idea of external objects, they would not be able to become bored by repeated presentations. Habituation has also become a crucial research tool for measuring infant perceptions of colors, sounds, faces, and other such things.

Believe it or not, researchers also have been able to demonstrate that babies may be able to do math! As you can see in **Figure 3-5**, psychologist Karen Wynn conducted a series of studies in which she showed 5-month-old babies a sequence of events where one doll is put in a case behind a screen followed by another doll (McCrink & Wynn, 2004, 2002; Wynn 2002, 1992). She found that when the screen was dropped, the babies expressed surprise and looked longer if only one doll was in the case than if both dolls were present. The babies seemed to know that the case should hold two dolls. This result has been replicated with even larger numbers (five to ten dolls) in 9-month-old children!

By adjusting their approaches to focus more on the child's capacities, information-processing researchers have found that cognitive development may involve fewer qualitative shifts and more quantitative growth than Piaget believed. Nevertheless, Piaget remains very influential. His stages still provide a general guideline for the cognitive development of children, and for that reason, we will continue to look at his later stages in this chapter. In addition, his theory remains influential in generating research that

1. Object placed in case   2. Screen comes up

3. Second object added   4. Hand leaves empty

5. Screen drops   ...revealing 1 object

FIGURE 3-5 Baby math To see whether 5-month-old infants have an appreciation of addition and subtraction, Wynn showed them the sequence of events illustrated above. If the infants express surprise when the screen drops and they see only one object, it suggests that they understand that 1 + 1 = 2. (Adapted from Wynn, 1992)

seeks both to support the theory and to rebut it. If nothing else, the controversy ignited by Piaget's ideas has helped us think about how to best study children's thought processes. Perhaps most importantly, Piaget encouraged psychologists to stop thinking of children as organisms programmed by biology or by early experiences but rather as active interpreters of their world. Piaget considered children to be little scientists constantly drawing conclusions about the world on the basis of their own personal research, conducted through their experiences in the world.

Social and Emotional Development

Parents are at the center of an infant's social world, and many psychologists have focused on the importance of the early experiences children have with their parents. *Attachment theory* has made the best empirical case for how crucial this relationship is (Nelson & Bennett, 2008). In this section, we'll talk about the principles of this theory and how parent-child relationships may influence a child's social and emotional development.

Attachment Theory   Theorist John Bowlby believed that human beings are born with a drive to form an **attachment**, to become emotionally close to one particular caregiver, usually their mother. He suggested that early positive experiences with that caregiver are critical to health and well-being and that they shape how well the individual will function emotionally, socially, and even cognitively later in life.

Bowlby also argued that all the behaviors of infants are targeted at bringing them closer to their mothers. He believed, for example, that reflexes such as rooting or reaching out help babies build relationships with their mothers (Bowlby 1958). To Bowlby, the presence of these reflexes provided evidence that attachment processes are inborn and crucial to the survival and well-being of babies. Bowlby also thought that children with strong attachments to their parents will actually feel safer than children who are more independent and less attached to their parents. Indeed, he suggested that steady, consistent responsiveness to a baby's needs is actually the best way for a mother to eventually bring about a truly independent and well-functioning child. Initially, the scientific community reacted to this assertion negatively. The psychological wisdom of Bowlby's day had held that parents who respond to children's needs by drawing the children in will succeed only in fostering neediness and dependence.

Mary Ainsworth, a student of Bowlby's who had conducted naturalistic observations in Uganda, supported Bowlby's ideas that mother-child attachment occurs around the world (Ainsworth, 1993, 1985, 1967). Ainsworth further noticed that some mothers, whom she labeled "highly sensitive," seemed to form attachments that were more successful in fostering their children's independence. Ainsworth developed a way to test the attachment between babies and their mothers in a laboratory setting. Using her procedure, called the *Strange Situation* (see **Figure 3-6**), Ainsworth observed systematically how various babies and mothers work together to cope with new and moderately stressful situations. Based on her experimental findings, Ainsworth, like Bowlby, argued that babies attach to their mothers because that is how their needs get met (Bretherton, 1992).

Ainsworth identified three basic attachment styles: *secure, anxious/avoidant*, and *anxious/ambivalent* (see **Figure 3-7**). Later, psychologist Mary Main noted that some children fail to show any reliable way of coping with separations and reunions, exhibiting features of all three of the other styles, without any pattern or consistency. She added a fourth category to describe this pattern: *disorganized/disoriented* (Main & Solomon, 1990).

Based on Ainsworth's work, Bowlby (1969) later suggested that early attachment experiences help people create an *internal working model* of the world and themselves. If children come to think of other people as supportive and helpful, as a result of having sensitive mothers, Bowlby suggested that this positive model will influence their later

attachment   a close emotional bond to another person, such as a baby to a caregiver.

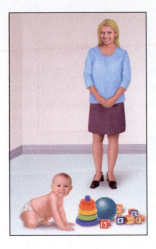
(a)

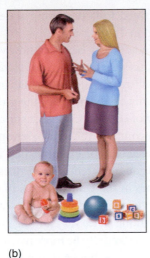
(b)

(c)

(d)

(e)

FIGURE 3-6 **The Strange Situation procedure**
(a) The baby plays while the mother is nearby. (b) A stranger enters the room, speaks to the mother, and approaches the child. (c) The mother leaves and the stranger stays in the room with an unhappy baby. (d) The mother returns and the stranger leaves. (e) The baby is reunited with the mother.

relationships in a healthy way. In contrast, children who develop a working model that the world is insensitive or does not care may be at risk for poor adjustment or difficult relationships with other people later in their lives.

The vast majority of attachment research has focused on mothers, and indeed, cultural practice bears out the importance of the mother-child relationship; in almost every society, mothers do the majority of child care (Parke, 1995). Evidence also indicates, however, that fathers are indeed capable of responding in highly sensitive ways (as defined by Ainsworth) and that if a father is highly sensitive, a baby generally turns out to be securely attached (Howes, 1999).

Parenting Styles HOW we Differ

Once attachment theory gave psychologists a way of *operationalizing* (or defining in a measurable way) the relationship between parents and children, other researchers began applying those insights to understanding how parent behaviors might contribute to development. For example, Diana Baumrind, a psychologist at University of California-Berkley, conducted interviews and observations of primarily white, middle-class preschool children and their parents and found that two characteristics of parental behavior seem particularly important: how many demands the parent puts on the child and how responsive the parent is to the child (Baumrind, 1991). Combining those two

60%
Secure attachment

15%
Disorganized/
disoriented
attachment

10%
Anxious/
ambivalent
attachment

15%
Anxious/
avoidant
attachment

FIGURE 3-7 **Styles of attachment** Ainsworth and Main identified four styles of attachment. *Secure attachment (60 percent):* The infant uses the mother as a secure base from which to explore and as a support in time of trouble. When the mother leaves the room, the infant is moderately distressed and happy when she returns. *Anxious/avoidant attachment (15 percent):* The infant is unresponsive with the mother and is usually indifferent when she leaves the room and when she returns. *Anxious/ambivalent attachment (10 percent):* The infant reacts strongly when the mother leaves the room. When she returns, the infant shows mixed emotions, seeking close contact and then squirming away angrily. *Disorganized/disoriented attachment (15 percent):* The infant displays confused and contradictory behavior when the mother returns; for example, ignoring the mother while being held, appearing flat and depressed, looking dazed, crying out, and/or showing a rigid posture.

reciprocal socialization the transactional relationship between parent and child.

dimensions, Baumrind has identified four parenting styles and the child outcomes associated with them, as depicted in Table 3-6.

A key question about Baumrind's theory has been how well it applies outside white, individualistic cultures. As we discussed in Chapter 1, *individualistic cultures* are those in which people are expected to be self-reliant and self-achieving, while *collectivist cultures* expect people to be focused primarily on the needs of the group. Cross-cultural research has found that parents in a variety of cultures can be classified into the same four styles. It is not clear, however, that the outcomes of the four parenting styles are the same across different cultures. Research has suggested, for example, that in Asian cultures, the high-demand, low-responsiveness authoritarian parenting style does not necessarily lead to negative child outcomes as it often does in the United States. In fact, the authoritarian style can benefit children's academic performances during adolescence (Chao, 2001). Research also suggests that outcomes of parenting styles vary among cultural groups in the United States. An authoritarian parenting style seems to be more harmful to middle-class boys than to middle-class girls, to white American preschool girls than to African-American preschool girls, and to white American boys than to Hispanic-American boys (Baumrind, 1991).

Another important question researchers have examined is how children's behaviors affect parenting styles, a transaction known as **reciprocal socialization**. Highly rambunctious children are, for example, more likely to evoke authoritarian control behaviors in their parents (Caspi, 1998). Most of today's research on reciprocal socialization emphasizes the transaction between the parent and the child and holds that the *fit* between a parent and child's behavioral styles is more important than some objectively right or wrong style.

What Do Fathers Have to Do With Development? A Lot!

It takes both a sperm and an egg to create a child. Yet if you looked at child development research conducted prior to the mid-70s, you would have thought that researchers were unaware of this fact! Case in point: upon reviewing the existing literature in 1975, psychologist Michael Lamb declared that fathers were "forgotten contributors to child development" (Lewis & Lamb, 2003). Why were fathers so long ignored, and what do we now know about their impact on children?

Fathers were left out of developmental research for decades for both pragmatic and stereotype-based reasons. Mothers were more likely to be the primary caregivers of children, leading researchers to believe that their impact was more important to study. In addition, fathers were more difficult to recruit for research because they tended to work outside of the home during regular business hours. Early childhood educators also tended to have more frequent contact with mothers than fathers, leading mothers to be most salient when those educators conducted studies of "parenting" effects (Gadsden & Ray, 2003). There were also implicit biases driving the oversight, such as the widely-held belief that fathers lacked the sensitivity toward children that could only come from "maternal instinct" (Solantaus & Salo, 2005).

In recent years, however, it has been found that parenting styles are largely equivalent between the sexes. Research on families with same-sex parents has helped clarify this point. Moreover, while mothers in more conventional family structures do tend to be slightly more sensitive caregivers than fathers, particularly after the child reaches 1 year of age, the amount of parenting experience seems to underlie much of this effect. That is, if a father spends more time taking care of the child, his sensitivity tends to be higher. For a variety of cultural reasons, American fathers tend to be more involved in play with their children than in caretaking. In fact, given the choice, infants prefer to play with their fathers than with their mothers. Such differences in interaction styles, however, are not large (Lewis & Lamb, 2003).

Research suggests that, on average, children from families in which two parents are present and active have many advantages over those raised in mother-only families (NFI, 2009; Cuff et al., 2005; Harpet et al., 2004; Hoffman, 2002). They have, for example, fewer accidents as toddlers, are less likely to be depressed as children and adults, and display lower rates of juvenile delinquency, teenage pregnancy, drug use, and incarceration.

Although developmental research still focuses more heavily on mothers than on fathers, the field has come a long way over the past 30 years. Moreover, the number of articles and books devoted to fathers seems to be on the increase (e.g., Lamb & Day, 2004; Tamis-LeMonda & Cabrera, 2002).

TABLE 3-6 Parenting Styles

Parental style	Parental behavior	Associated outcome in children
Authoritative	Warm, sensitive to child's needs, nurturing; makes reasonable demands and encourages appropriate autonomy	High self esteem, cooperativeness, self control, social maturity
Authoritarian	Cold, rejecting; makes coercive demands; frequently critical of child	Low self esteem, anxious, unhappy, often angry and aggressive
Permissive	Warm, accepting but overindulgent and inattentive	Impulsive, disobedient, overly dependent on adults, low initiative
Uninvolved	Emotionally detached and depressed; little time or energy for child rearing	Anxious, poor communication skills, antisocial behavior

Before You Go On

What Do You Know?

8. What is the role of myelination in the development of the brain?
9. What is the Strange Situation?
10. What are the major parenting styles, and what are the major child outcomes associated with each style?

What Do You Think?
How do you think the various attachment styles correlate with Baumrind's parenting styles? Do you think there is one optimal form of parenting?

Childhood How we Develop

LEARNING OBJECTIVE 5 Summarize the major physical, cognitive, and emotional developments that take place during childhood.

Although physical growth slows somewhat during childhood, our inner and outer lives become increasingly complex. We develop the cognitive capacity to think and talk about the world in new ways that do not involve the concrete reality right in front of us. Our social and emotional lives also become more complex and expand to include peers and teachers. In this section, we'll focus on how the world gets a lot bigger during childhood and how children manage to keep up.

Physical Development

Growth during early childhood, which lasts from about the ages of 2 to 6 years, and middle childhood, which lasts from about age 6 until 12, is not as dramatic as it was during infancy. Although progress is more gradual, children's brains and bodies still experience major changes. Both become much more efficient, as we'll see.

How Does the Body Grow During Childhood? The dramatic physical growth that occurs from conception through our second year slows down during early childhood, such that we grow only about $2\frac{1}{2}$ to 3 inches a year. We master a good deal of motor and physical control during this period. Children develop basic control over their urination and bowel movements, and they solidify a preference for their right or left hand for most tasks. Of course, during early childhood many aspects of development remain works-in-progress. Although our coordination improves and we can work the buttons, zippers, and shoelaces necessary to dress ourselves, that doesn't necessarily mean that we can coordinate clothes effectively. Remember those embarrassing family pictures?

As children move from early into middle childhood, around age 6, things begin to rev-up again. Children's motor abilities improve dramatically as they gain coordination, agility, and strength. At the same time, the first major distinctions between boys and girls begin to appear. Girls experience a growth spurt in height and weight during their tenth or eleventh year, while boys have to wait a couple of years more for their spurt. On the other hand, boys develop somewhat more muscle mass, meaning they can throw and jump a little farther and run a little faster. Girls tend to be a bit more agile on average. As we'll see later in the chapter, these average differences become much more pronounced as children move into adolescence.

What Happens in the
Childhood B R A I N ?

Throughout early and middle childhood, the brain becomes more efficient through a continued combination of the myelination and synaptic pruning that began in infancy. During childhood, myelination is concentrated in the brain areas known as the *association regions*. These are the areas of the brain that coordinate the activity and operation of other regions of the brain (Paus et al., 1999). The increased efficiency of the association regions as they become myelinated leads to more sophisticated planning and problem-solving abilities. Most 4-year-olds cannot play chess very effectively, for example, but many elementary school children have the strategic skills to be good chess players.

As we discussed earlier, synaptic pruning helps solidify the neural connections that are most beneficial to the child. As childhood draws to a close, pruning slows some. The numbers of synaptic connections between particular neurons and the overall electric activity in the brain both begin to stabilize.

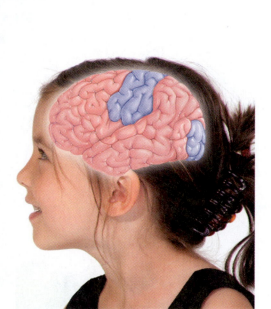

Association regions of the brain The association regions (all areas of the cortex not colored blue in this illustration) undergo extensive development during childhood, leading to further growth of the cognitive processes.

Cognitive Development

One of the major activities of childhood is going to school, and in most countries, formal education begins around the age of 6 or 7. We'll see in this section that school entry coincides with the development of the cognitive skills that Piaget called **operations**, the ability to hold an idea in mind and manipulate it mentally. Piaget suggested that between the ages of about 2 and 12 children go through two stages of cognitive development: the *preoperational stage*, which lasts from age 2 through 7, followed by the *concrete operational stage*, lasting from age 7 through 12. Schools also provide rich social environments, a factor that another cognitive development theorist, Lev Vygotsky, believed is crucial to learning.

Piaget's Preoperational Stage According to Piaget, as children move into the **preoperational stage**, they become able to hold memories, or representations, of objects in their imaginations and to work with them as ideas. This represents a dramatic shift from the earlier sensorimotor stage in which they were able to manipulate actual objects only. The thinking of children at this stage still shows some limitations, compared to adult thinking, however.

One major limitation is what Piaget called *irreversibility*. Although they can work with symbols and concepts that stand in for real-world objects, children at the preoperational stage still think in rather simplistic ways about the relationships between those concepts and objects. For them, changes in relationships happen in one direction only. One researcher offers the following example of a 4-year-old who was asked about his family:

> "Do you have a brother?"
> "Yes."
> "What's his name?"
> "Jim."
> "Does Jim have a brother?"
> "No."
>
> (Phillips, 1975)

The boy is able to hold the idea of his brother Jim in his head, even though Jim is not there, indicating he has developed object permanence. At the same time, he has adopted this concept in one direction only: Jim is *my* brother. The boy is unable to think about the reverse relationship—that he is Jim's brother also.

The reason this child cannot think of himself as Jim's brother, according to Piaget, is because he cannot take Jim's point of view, an inability Piaget referred to as **egocentrism**. Piaget did not use the term *egocentrism* to mean the boy is arrogant. His use of the term refers strictly to children's flaws in logical reasoning. This boy cannot yet realize that other people also have brothers. Piaget believed that *perspective-taking*, the ability to take another person's point of view, is not mastered until a later stage.

Irreversibility is also related to a lack of **conservation**, the ability to understand that something can stay the same even though its appearance changes. Piaget used a now-famous task to demonstrate young children's problems with conservation. He gave a child two identical beakers with equal amounts of water in each and asked which of the beakers held more water. Children over 2 years old were usually able to say that both beakers held the same amount. Piaget would then ask the child to pour the water into two new beakers that were shaped differently, one shallow and wide and the other tall and narrow. After the children poured the water, Piaget again asked which held more water. Children between the ages of 2 and 7—even after they themselves had poured the water into the new beakers—were more likely to say the tall, narrow beaker held more water. Piaget believed this indicated that the children could not mentally reverse

operations Piagetian description of a child's ability to hold an idea in his or her mind and mentally manipulate it.

preoperational stage according to Piaget, a developmental stage during which the child begins to develop ideas of objects in the external world and the ability to work with them in his or her mind.

egocentrism flaws in a child's reasoning based on his or her inability to take other perspectives.

conservation the understanding that certain properties of an object (such as volume and number) remain the same despite changes in the object's outward appearance.

Shapes can be misleading In the classic test for conservation, a child is shown two identical short thick glasses, each filled with liquid. The child then watches as the liquid from one glass is poured into a tall thin glass and is asked to indicate which glass now has more liquid. Most children between 2 and 7 years incorrectly pick the tall thin glass.

the pouring of the water to imagine that the two amounts of water would once again match if both were returned to their original containers.

Children's lack of conservation also may be related to difficulty in making distinctions between *appearance* and *reality*. In one classic example of this confusion, researcher Rheta DeVries (1969) allowed children to play with her cat, Maynard. After a while, DeVries and her assistants would hide Maynard's front half from view while they strapped a dog mask onto the cat's face. (We have no idea how she got a cat to agree to wear a dog mask.) DeVries then asked the toddlers what kind of animal Maynard was. Even though Maynard was never completely out of view, the majority of the 3-year-old participants, and a good number of 4- and 5-year-olds thought the cat had magically become a dog. By the age of 6, when they were nearing the concrete operational stage, none of the children made this mistake.

Piaget's Concrete Operational Stage   During the stage of **concrete operations**, children demonstrate the ability to think about ideas. They start to talk authoritatively about complex relationships, such as cause and effect and categorization. They can take others' perspectives and reverse operations. By now, they consider the notion that a cat can mysteriously become a dog ridiculous. They know dogs and cats fit into certain hard and fast categories, and they can now extend those categories to other organisms that share the same features.

Children at this stage show a mastery of real-world relationships. This mastery is limited, however, to ideas that have real-world counterparts, such as brothers and sisters and other family members, categories of plants or animals, or causes of weather conditions. That's why Piaget refers to the stage as *concrete* operations. Children in this stage have difficulty with abstract relationships between objects that do not exist in the real world, such as abstract mathematical relationships. They also find it difficult to think about hypothetical, alternate possibilities and have trouble speculating on questions, such as "What ways can this situation play out?" A mastery of those kinds of relationships is left for the next stage of development.

Criticisms of the Preoperational and Concrete Operations Stages   Many critics have challenged Piaget's belief that children in the preoperational and concrete operations stages have problems taking others' point of view. In fact, some researchers have become very interested in young children's beliefs about how their own minds and the minds of others work, a field of research called **theory of mind**.

Theory of mind was first studied in an experiment with children between the ages of 3 and 9. Each child participant was told a story about a boy named Maxi who tries to sneak some chocolate from his mom (Wimmer & Perner, 1983). According to the story, Maxi's mother brings home some chocolate to make a cake, and while Maxi is watching, she puts the chocolate in a blue cupboard (see **Figure 3-8**). Maxi then goes out to play. While he is outside, his mother makes the cake and puts the remaining chocolate in a green cupboard. Next, Maxi comes back in, wanting some chocolate. The researchers then asked the children in the study where Maxi would look for the chocolate.

This deceptively simple task actually requires a high level of thought. Children have to not only remember where the chocolate has traveled, but also take the viewpoint of Maxi and realize that Maxi has no way of knowing that his mom moved the chocolate. Three- and four-year-olds regularly fail such tests, suggesting this task is too complicated for them, while six-year-olds regularly succeed. Experiments such as these support Piaget's notion that young children are highly egocentric, but also suggest that many such children are able to take other people's thoughts and feelings into account much sooner than Piaget had predicted.

concrete operations Piagetian stage during which children are able to talk about complex relationships, such as categorization and cause and effect, but are still limited to understanding ideas in terms of real-world relationships.

theory of mind a recognition that other people base their behaviors on their own perspectives, not on information that is unavailable to them.

scaffolding developmental adjustments that adults make to give children the help that they need, but not so much that they fail to move forward.

zone of proximal development the gap between what a child could accomplish alone and what the child can accomplish with help from others.

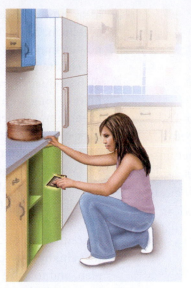

FIGURE 3-8 **Theory of mind** Young research participants are told a story in which a child first sees his mother place chocolate in a upper cupboard, then he leaves while she makes a chocolate cake. In his absence, the mother places the leftover chocolate in a lower cupboard, and the child then returns looking for leftover chocolate. Participants with a theory of mind recognize that the child in the story will look for the leftover chocolate in the original upper cupboard, because the child is not aware of the mother's switch of locations.

In part, Piaget's approach may have been limited by a failure to listen to his own theory. Piaget believed that thought preceded language, that our thinking develops faster than our ability to use words. Yet, his tests of his theories rested on observations of children's performances on language-based tasks, such as the question about Jim's brother. Other researchers, by focusing on nonverbal responses or by making their questions more age-appropriate or child-friendly, have found evidence that children develop certain cognitive competencies sooner: for example, pictures accompanied the story of Maxi.

Still other critics have charged that Piaget's theory fails to account fully for *social* factors, the influences that other people may have on a child's cognitive development. Piaget's theory, instead, focuses on how children guide their own development through experimentation and reflection. Later in his life, Piaget himself also wondered whether his theory said enough about the role of social experiences in development (Inhelder & Piaget, 1979; Piaget, 1972). As we'll see next, a contemporary of Piaget's had more to say about social influences on cognitive development.

Vygotsky and the Role of Cultural Factors While Piaget was focusing on how children's private experiments and reflections shape their thinking, a Russian psychologist named Lev Vygotsky was becoming increasingly interested in how social interactions with parents might drive the development of children. Unlike Piaget, who viewed a child's development as a process of individual achievement, Vygotsky (2004, 1991, 1978) believed that constructive interactions with parents, older children, teachers, and siblings help the child develop ways of thinking about and functioning in the world. In Vygotsky's view, an older "mentor," such as a parent, helps the child by initially taking responsibility for the basic skills and capabilities the child is developing. Over time, the "mentor" takes less and less responsibility. Vygotsky referred to the mentor's step-by-step assistance as **scaffolding**. Vygotsky labeled the gap between what children can accomplish by themselves and what they can accomplish with the help of others as the **zone of proximal development**.

Because of his death at the young age of 37 and the chilly political climate between the former Soviet Union and the West, Vygotsky's ideas have come to light only in recent years. Developmental psychologists have found numerous ways to apply Vygotsky's

" Parents can only give good advice or put them on the right path, but the final forming of a person's character lies in their own hands. "

—*Anne Frank, diarist and Holocaust victim*

ideas, however. He has become one of today's most influential developmental theorists (Feldman, 2003). Indeed, ideas of scaffolding and zones of proximal development are now an important part of educational systems throughout the United States. When helping children learn to read, for example, many teachers begin by reading books to them, then gradually turn over responsibility for various reading skills. The children may first follow along with the pictures as the teacher reads the words, then point to letters. Eventually, they learn to read single words, then sentences, and finally entire books on their own, as the teacher provides less and less scaffolding and the children's zone of proximal development becomes smaller.

"Every function in the child's cultural development appears twice: first, between people (interpsychological) and then inside the child (intrapsychological). This applies equally to voluntary attention, to logical memory, and to the formation of ideas. All the higher functions originate as actual relationships between individuals."

–Lev Vygotsky, Russian psychologist

Whereas Piaget believed that thinking preceded language, Vygotsky believed that language is crucial to cognitive development because a great deal of mentoring relies on talking and listening. Both theorists noticed that preschool-aged children seem to talk to themselves a lot. Piaget regarded this incessant chatter as largely unimportant, egocentric babble. Vygotsky, however, called that chatter **private speech**. He believed that children use private speech to regulate their behavior and internal experiences, to plan, and to solve problems, often repeating or imitating the words of their mentors. Vygotsky believed that, eventually, these private chats turn into silent, internal dialogues, perhaps similar to the conversations adults have in their heads each morning about whether to hit the snooze button on their alarm clocks one more time and risk being late for that first appointment.

Because Vygotsky believed that other individuals are critical to helping children develop, he also believed that there is a great deal more variability in how children develop. He believed that each culture has its own specific challenges, and that those challenges change over the course of life, meaning that development has to meet those challenges.

Social and Emotional Development

We will focus on many features of a child's social and emotional development in Chapters 12 and 14. Here, our main focus will be on *moral* development, how children acquire an understanding of right and wrong and how to function in a complex society.

Kohlberg's Theory of Moral Development

Lawrence Kohlberg was a student of Jean Piaget who was interested in Piaget's ideas on moral development. Piaget believed that, as with general logical reasoning, children learn how to reason morally by translating their behaviors and experiences into general moral principles that they can apply across different situations. He proposed that children's morality is based initially on obeying adults. As they get older, the basis of their moral reasoning shifts toward cooperation with peers (Piaget, 1965). Kohlberg expanded upon Piaget's ideas and developed a method to evaluate the moral reasoning processes of children. He presented them with stories about moral dilemmas, such as the story of Heinz in **Figure 3-9**, and asked them to say what the main characters in the stories should do and why.

Heinz and the Drug

In Europe, a woman was near death from a special kind of cancer. There was one drug that the doctors thought might save her. It was a form of radium that a druggist in the same town had recently discovered. The drug was expensive to make, but the druggist was charging ten times what the drug cost him to make. He paid $400 for the radium and charged $4,000 for a small dose of the drug. The sick woman's husband, Heinz, went to everyone he knew to borrow the money and tried every legal means, but he could only get together about $2,000, which is half of what it cost. He told the druggist that his wife was dying, and asked him to sell it cheaper or let him pay later. But the druggist said, "No, I discovered the drug and I'm going to make money from it." So, having tried every legal means, Heinz gets desperate and considers breaking into the man's store to steal the drug.

Question: Should Heinz steal the drug? Why or why not?

FIGURE 3-9 **Kohlberg's moral dilemma story** (Paragraph excerpted from Scot Lilienfeld, Steven Lynn, Laura Namy, and Nancy Wolf, *Psychology: From Inquiry to Understanding* (Boston: Pearson: Allyn & Bacon.)

On the basis of his studies, Kohlberg developed a stage theory of moral development, depicted in **Table 3-7** (Kohlberg, 2008, 1994, 1963). The focus of this theory is *moral reasoning*, how children come to their decisions about what is right and wrong rather than on the particular decisions that they make. Like Piaget, Kohlberg believed that young children make moral choices that seem likely to ensure the least amount of

TABLE 3-7 Kohlberg's Stage Theory of Moral Development

Stage	Reason to steal drug	Reason not to steal drug
Preconventional: Morality centers on what you can get away with	He can get away with it.	He will be caught and go to jail
Conventional: Morality centers on avoiding others' disapproval and obeying society's rules	If he doesn't steal the drug people will think he is a terrible person.	If he steals people will think he is a criminal; it's against the law.
Postconventional: Morality is determined by abstract ethical principles	Sometimes the law is unjust and it is right to break it.	He will not have lived up to his own standards of honesty and will lose his self-respect.

trouble with authority figures. However, Kohlberg also looked beyond childhood to adolescence and described how older children and adults become more independent in their moral reasoning.

Although Kohlberg believed that moral reasoning often is correlated with other areas of development, such as cognition or intelligence, he held that it develops along its own track. As the ability of children to take another person's point of view grows, their moral reasoning also becomes more complex. To reach the highest stages of moral reasoning, Kohlberg believed, individuals must be exposed to complex social situations, such as working at jobs that involve lots of people or going to college.

Like Piaget's theory of general cognitive development, Kohlberg's theory suggests that each stage of moral development is not just a shift in complexity but instead represents a new framework for making moral decisions. Each such stage forms a foundation for the next stage, and children must travel through the stages of moral development in sequence. A child may be delayed, or perhaps even fail to reach some of the higher stages, but he or she must go through each earlier stage to reach the next one.

Finally, Kohlberg believed that the process of moral development is universal and happens the same way in every culture. Kohlberg's original research included boys only, but he later studied girls and conducted moral dilemma interviews in villages in Mexico, Taiwan, and Turkey.

Gilligan's Theory of Moral Development   One of Kohlberg's collaborators, Carol Gilligan, eventually questioned some of his findings and ideas, partly because his studies initially focused on boys alone and also because his later studies that did include girls seemed to suggest that girls are morally less developed than boys. Kohlberg believed that girls do not have as many complex social opportunities as boys and, as a result, are excessively concerned with the standards of others and often fail to achieve higher stages of moral reasoning.

Gilligan interpreted the boy-girl findings differently. She argued that the moral reasoning used by girls is indeed different from that of boys but not inferior. She noticed that boys tend to base their decisions about moral dilemmas on abstract moral values, such as justice and fairness. Many girls look at the situations differently. Instead of the abstract values involved, they focus more on the value relationships between the principal players. A boy's answer to the Heinz dilemma might center on the importance of property value for the druggist, for example, while a girl's answer might stress that Heinz will not be able to help his wife if he is jailed for stealing the drug (Gilligan, 1993). Gilligan argued that the reasoning of boys and girls is equally sophisticated, but their goals and the aspects of the dilemma that they notice differ. Gilligan went on to conduct her own interviews with men and women and found further support for her theory that women are inclined to make moral judgments based more on caring and managing relationships than on Kohlberg's notions of justice and fairness.

private speech a child's self-talk, which Vygotsky believed the child uses to regulate behavior and internal experiences.

puberty development of full sexual maturity during adolescence.

primary sex characteristics changes in body structure that occur during puberty that have to do specifically with the reproductive system, including the growth of the testes and the ovaries.

secondary sex characteristics changes that occur during puberty and that differ according to gender, but aren't directly related to sex.

Other studies have not always supported Gilligan's theory that women and men differ in their moral orientation. Nor, however, have they always supported Kohlberg's notions of moral superiority among males (Walker, 2006). Some recent studies, for example, suggest that differences in the education levels of their research participants may have accounted for the apparent moral differences between males and females observed by these two investigators; when education level is controlled for, females and males often earn similar moral stage scores (Dawson, 2002).

Gilligan's ideas have had a broad influence on psychology, anthropology, and other social sciences. In a classic book, *In A Different Voice*, Gilligan (1993) noted that over the years many psychological theorists have embraced male development patterns as the norm and viewed differences from that norm as inferior. Similarly, she argued that women have been underrepresented in many of psychology's most influential studies and theories. As a result of her arguments, many researchers now include more females in their studies. In addition, most of today's researchers think of differences among participants as individual variations rather than positive or negative characteristics.

Current Directions in Moral Development Much research in moral development over the last 50 years has been influenced by Kohlberg's and Gilligan's theories. Many researchers have focused on Kohlberg's notion that the stages of moral development are the same for everyone, and indeed a review of 45 studies conducted across a wide range of cultures has found that Kohlberg's claims of universality hold up pretty well for the early stages of moral development (Snarey, 1985). Such research also has suggested that people from different cultures rarely skip stages or revert to previous ones.

Cross-cultural researchers have also noted cultural differences that support Gilligan's ideas. Some researchers have found, for example, that respondents from *collectivist* cultures tend to score lower on the Kohlberg scales than do those from *individualistic* cultures (Gibbs et al., 2007). Close examinations indicate, however, that these score differences reflect differences in the kinds of moral problems faced by people in each of these cultures, not moral superiority or inferiority. As described in Chapter 1, collectivistic cultures put greater emphasis on society and relationships than individualistic cultures, which tend to emphasize individual justice and fairness.

Finally, a number of moral development researchers have wondered how much the expressed moral attitudes of people reflect their actual decision-making (Krebs & Denton, 2006). As we will see in our discussion of attitudes in Chapter 14, people do not always actually do what they say they will do (an experience you've probably had once or twice in your own life). Because the vast majority of research into moral reasoning has relied on Kohlberg's moral dilemma interviews, many researchers argue that we may be able to say a fair amount about people's moral *philosophies* but little about their *behavior*.

Before You Go On

What Do You Know?

11. In what areas of the brain is myelination concentrated during childhood, and how does myelination of these areas affect the child's cognitive functioning?

12. What are the crucial differences between Piaget's view of cognitive development and Vygotsky's view of cognitive development?

13. How are the ideas of scaffolding and zone of proximal development reflected in contemporary American educational practices?

14. How do contemporary theories of moral reasoning differ from Piaget, Kohlberg, and Gilligan?

What Do You Think?
Do you think that men and women reason differently about morality? If the outcome is the same in our moral choices, does the reasoning we used to achieve that outcome matter?

Adolescence | How we *Develop*

LEARNING OBJECTIVE 6 Summarize the major physical, cognitive, and emotional changes that take place during adolescence.

With the possible exception of the first couple years of life, the amount of change that occurs during adolescence rivals that of any other developmental passage. Most crucially, puberty begins. In the cognitive sphere, adolescents display features of both children and adults, and they begin to learn how to function independently. In this section, we will describe the key biological, cognitive, and social transitions that characterize this dramatic period.

Physical Development

Puberty refers to the physical development of primary and secondary sex characteristics. **Primary sex characteristics** are the body structures that have to do specifically with the reproductive system, including growth of the testes and the ovaries. **Secondary sex characteristics** refer to nonreproductive body events that differ according to gender, such as the deepening of the male voice or the increase in female breast size (see **Figure 3-10**).

The onset and course of puberty is influenced largely by the *pituitary gland,* which coordinates the activities of the rest of the endocrine system. As you'll see in Chapter 4, the endocrine system includes the *adrenal glands, testes,* and *ovaries.* During adolescence, events throughout this system stimulate the growth of body hair and muscle tissue and trigger the onset of the female menstrual cycle, among other changes. One of the most important changes is a *growth spurt* triggered by the thyroid gland that, as we observed earlier, actually begins for girls in middle childhood and for boys during early adolescence (see **Figure 3-11**). The growth spurt happens about two years before the primary sex characteristics kick in and is not only a harbinger of those later changes, but also helps prepare the body for them (Rekers, 1992).

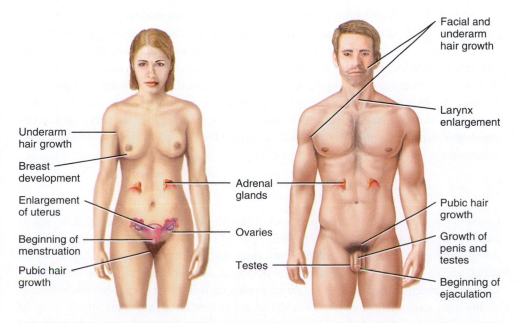

FIGURE 3-10 Primary and secondary sex characteristics The complex changes in puberty primarily result when hormones are released from the pituitary gland, adrenal gland, and ovaries and testes.

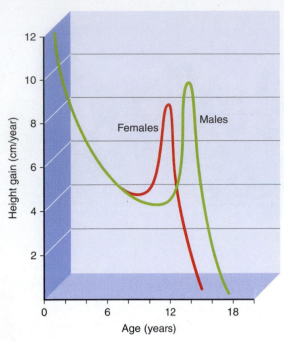

FIGURE 3-11 Adolescent growth spurt The growth spurt of girls occurs, on average, two years before that of boys. Thus, between the ages of 10 and 14 years, the average girl is taller than most boys.

The changes of puberty stabilize after a couple years. In the meantime, however, many of those changes can be very disruptive to adolescents. Of course, we're all familiar with the big ones: hair (or the lack of hair) in embarrassing places, acne, cracking voices. For both boys and girls, variations from age norms for puberty can be upsetting; girls who mature early and boys who mature late report more problems making the transitions through adolescence than those who hit puberty "on time" (Hayatbakhsh et al., 2009).

The brain also goes through significant changes during adolescence. Myelination continues to increase and synaptic connections continue to decrease as a result of synaptic pruning. As with middle childhood, many of these changes appear to be localized; they now focus on the *prefrontal cortex*, the brain area that helps coordinate brain functions and is instrumental in making sound judgments. Many psychologists point to the pruning that occurs in the prefrontal cortex as the reason teenagers often display poor judgment in their daily functioning for a while (Compas, 2004).

Cognitive Development

As we mentioned above, adolescent thinking has features of both child cognition and adult cognition. Teenagers show increased capacity for reasoning about abstract things but also have deficits in their abilities to see outside of the moment or to take others' points of view. These strengths and limitations both come into play in their social and emotional growth as adolescents attempt to define themselves as persons.

Piaget's Formal Operations Stage   Piaget suggested that at around the age of 12, we cross over into mature adult thinking processes, a final stage known as **formal operations**. Piaget believed that the hallmark achievement of this stage is the ability to think about ideas conceptually without needing concrete referents from the real world. The successful transition to formal operations means that teens are no longer bound by the concrete realities of their world. For example, in math class they have moved beyond using real-life representations of numbers, such as counters, and now can use rules to solve problems, even algebra problems involving variables. They can conceive of other worlds and other possible realities, even ones that do not exist outside their own imaginations.

Although formal operations represent the apex of cognitive development, teenagers continue to experience some egocentric thought. They may, for example, display the so-called *personal fable*: over the course of searching for a sense of identity and spending time in deep focus on their own thoughts and feelings, teens may become convinced that they are special—the first persons in history to have those particular thoughts and feelings. Another form of egocentric thought that marks adolescence is the *imaginary audience*. The imaginary audience describes the teenager's feeling that everyone is scrutinizing him or her, a notion that leads to strong feelings of inhibition and self-consciousness.

Social and Emotional Development

German psychologist Erik Erikson is one of the few major developmental theorists to look at development across the *entire* lifespan (Erikson, 1985, 1984, 1959). Erikson divided the span from birth to old age into eight stages. Each of Erikson's stages is associated with a "main task," a challenge the person must meet and reconcile. An individual's achievement at each stage has a direct impact on how he or she meets the challenges of the next stage. Erikson believed that culture and relationships play strong roles in personality formation, and so he referred to his work as a stage theory of *psychosocial* development.

formal operations Piaget's final stage of cognitive development; the child achieves formal adult reasoning and the ability to think about things that don't have a concrete reality.

TABLE 3-8 Erikson's Stages of Psychosocial Development

Stage 1 Trust versus mistrust (birth –age 1) Infants develop a basic trust in others. If their needs are not met by their caregivers, mistrust develops.

Stage 2 Autonomy versus shame and doubt (ages 1–3) Children exercise their new motor and mental skills. If caregivers are encouraging, children develop a sense of autonomy versus shame and doubt.

Stage 3 Initiative versus guilt (ages 3–6) Children enjoy initiating activities and mastering new tasks. Supportive caregivers promote feelings of power and self-confidence versus guilt.

Stage 4 Industry versus inferiority (ages 6–12) Children learn productive skills and develop the capacity to work with others; if not, they feel inferior.

Stage 5 Identity versus role confusion (ages 12–20) Adolescents seek to develop a satisfying identity and a sense of their role in society. Failure may lead to a lack of stable identity and confusion about their adult roles.

Stage 6 Intimacy versus isolation (ages 20–30) Young adults work to establish intimate relationships with others; if they cannot, they face isolation.

Stage 7 Generativity versus self-absorption (ages 30–65) Middle aged-adults seek ways to influence the welfare of the next generation. If they fail, they may become self-absorbed.

Stage 8 Integrity versus despair (ages 65+) Older people reflect on the lives they have lived. If they do not feel a sense of accomplishment and satisfaction with their lives, they live in fear of death.

As Table 3-8 shows, Erikson believed that each stage of development is associated with a potentially positive outcome versus a potentially negative outcome. For example, the conflicts and challenges associated with infancy determine whether a baby will develop a basic trust of the world (positive outcome) or mistrust (negative outcome). Babies whose parents respond attentively when they cry with hunger, learn that the world is a good place and that other people can be trusted.

The key developmental task faced by adolescents is to resolve the conflict between *identity* and *role confusion*. During adolescence, teenagers start making decisions that affect their future roles, such as where they want to go to college or what they want to do with their lives, as well as decisions about abstract aspects of their identities, such as political or religious beliefs.

According to Erikson, if we do not reach a successful resolution of the conflict confronted at a particular stage, we may find it harder to meet the challenges of subsequent stages. Teenagers who did not effectively resolve the conflicts of their earlier psychosocial stages may enter adolescence with heightened feelings of mistrust and shame. These lingering feelings may render the teens particularly confused about which roles and beliefs truly reflect their own values and which ones reflect excessive peer and family influences. Peer relationships are extremely important to all teenagers, and Erikson believed that vulnerable teens are particularly likely to be confused about where their own beliefs start and the wishes of others end.

A number of other theorists and researchers have also highlighted the critical role that identity formation plays while teens are seeking to negotiate their way through adolescence successfully. James Marcia (2007, 1994), for example, expanded Erikson's theory, suggesting that a combination of identity "crises" (and identity explorations) and personal decisions to make commitments in life help to define a teen's identity.

" The best way to keep children home is to make the home atmosphere pleasant— and let the air out of the tires. "

—*Dorothy Parker, author*

You are in college now and your parents inform you that you are a responsible grown-up. Such a pronouncement can create an internal conflict for you because you do not feel all that grown up, yet. But don't despair. If you are feeling confused and uncertain about yourself, your abilities, your relationships, and your future, you actually are in the majority.

College-aged, young adults are still maturing both physically and psychologically. From the ages of 18–23, significant changes occur in your brain (Bennett & Baird 2006). Along with profound changes in mental and cognitive capacities, emerging adults experience psychological transformations as they become more self-aware, develop a sense of purpose, find their moral compass and value system, and make decisions about long-term goals—career, intimate partnerships, and family (Perry, 1970). In the face of such changes, you will most likely experiment with different roles and experiences to help you find what is "right" for you. In fact, this period of your life has been called a "psychosocial moratorium" (Erikson, 1968). Welcome to one of your most significant periods of developmental change!

Fortunately, there are some things that might help you cope with the developmental roller-coaster ride that takes you into adulthood. First of all, accept that you are changing. Your physical and psychological development occur over a very long period of time, and some of these changes creep up on you when you least expect them. This developmental period is very different from the stages and changes that characterized your childhood; in particular, you have a much greater mental capacity to examine what is happening to you and to determine how best to cope.

One useful coping strategy during this period is to share your concerns with a trusted friend or close family member. If you do not want to share with someone you know, try talking to a school counselor. One of the least productive things you can do is isolate yourself by either withdrawing or pushing people away—whether by inappropriate behavior, constant partying, or offensive remarks.

Sometimes, just letting off steam is enough to let go of what is bothering you. If you find yourself talking about the same problems repeatedly, however, it may be time to work on a proactive solution and implement it. Bounce around ideas, search for solutions, and then try them out. And, while you are evolving, you might try to keep a version of the golden rule in mind; treat others as you would like to be treated. Try to show kindness and respect both for yourself and those around you.

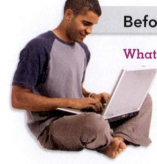

Before You Go On

What Do You Know?

15. If a child arrives at puberty significantly earlier or later than his/her peer group, how might that affect his/her adjustment?

16. Define formal operations.

17. Describe what Erikson believed was the major dilemma and risk for adolescence.

What Do You Think?   How might Erikson explain Bruce Wayne's or Peter Parker's difficulties with adjustment during these developmental stages?

LEARNING OBJECTIVE 7 Describe key physical, social, and emotional changes that take place throughout adulthood.

Traditionally, developmental psychology viewed adulthood as an outcome rather than a period of time worthy of study. As we'll see, however, adulthood is in fact a time of continuing change—and by change, we do not necessarily mean decline. Let's look at some of the developmental changes that happen during adulthood.

Physical and Cognitive Development

With the end of adolescence comes full maturity. Nevertheless, the body continues to go through changes during adulthood. And, as we'll see, so does the brain.

What Happens in the Body During Adulthood? Generally, physical attributes, such as strength, reaction time, and overall body function are at their peak during our 20s. As we move into our 30s, the body begins to decline slowly. Our metabolism slows, for example, so it takes a bit more work to keep some roundness from appearing around the waist.

During our 30s and 40s, we begin to show the first significant signs of aging. Skin begins to lose some of its tautness and grey hairs begin to sprout. Although we're significantly past our sensory peak, only in their 40s do most people begin to notice decline in that area of functioning (Fozard et al., 1977). We become more farsighted, finding it hard to read or see small objects close to us, and we have difficulty seeing in the dark or recovering from sudden glares of light. We also become less sensitive to high-frequency noises.

Women in their 50s typically go through a major change called *menopause* (Nelson, 2008). **Menopause** involves a series of changes in hormonal function that eventually lead to the end of the menstrual cycle and reproductive capabilities. The early phase of menopause is often associated with a variety of physical experiences, such as hot flashes, headaches, and sudden shifts in mood.

As we move into late adulthood, during our 60s and 70s, we may become a bit shorter and thinner due to changes in our skeletal structure and metabolism (Bord-Hoffman & Donius, 2005). Our immune systems also begin to decline in function, leaving us at higher risk for illness. Our vision and hearing continue to decline, joined by our sense of taste. Our pupils shrink, so that less light reaches the retina, making it harder for us to see in low light.

The story is not as simple as a long, slow, inevitable decline, however. Exogenous factors, such as exercise, stress, diet, and life experience, can have a dramatic influence on the course and impact of these changes (Larson et al., 2006; Brach et al., 2003). Although declines are common, many of the changes can be subtle and have minimal impact on how well we function in the world.

What Happens in the Adulthood B R A I N ? Until recently, neuroscientists believed that our brains begin to shrink during adulthood, both in terms of volume and weight, and that much of this loss is attributable to the shrinkage and loss of active brain cells (Miller & O'Callaghan, 2005). Research over the past decade, however, has revealed that no significant loss of neurons occurs in adulthood, except in cases of brain pathology (Miller & O'Callaghan, 2005); that new neurons keep being formed in certain parts of the brain

menopause series of changes in hormonal function occurring in women during their 50s, which lead to the end of the menstrual cycle and reproductive capabilities.

Downward slide In this computer illustration, the green-glowing proteins at the end of the chromosomes are telomeres, tiny structures that help cells to reproduce. The structures appear to grow shorter and shorter with repeated use, leading eventually to reduced cell reproduction and poor self-repair by the body.

cellular clock theory theory suggesting that we age because our cells have built-in limits on their ability to reproduce.

wear-and-tear theory theory suggesting we age because use of our body wears it out.

free-radical theory theory suggesting we age because special negatively charged oxygen molecules become more prevalent in our body as we get older, destabilizing cellular structures and causing the effects of aging.

developmental psychopathology the study of how problematic behaviors evolve as a function of a person's genetics and early experiences and how those early problematic issues affect the person at later life stages.

risk factors biological and environmental factors that contribute to problematic outcomes.

conduct disorder clinical disorder in children and adolescence associated with emotional and behavioral problems, such as rule-breaking, trouble with limit-setting from authority figures, bullying and fighting with other people, and cruelty.

throughout life, including during adulthood (Gould, 2007); and that such neurons may be the result of new learning, play a role in further learning, or both (Leuner, Gould, & Shors, 2006). Given the stability and even addition of neurons during adulthood, it is not surprising that most of our broad intellectual capabilities remain intact throughout our lives. We're able to solve problems and process information in our adult years about as quickly as we could in our 20s (Park & Gutchess, 2006; Park et al., 2002).

As we move into our 40s and 50s, however, we do begin to see *some* intellectual shifts. Recovering information from long-term memory starts to take a little longer, and it takes a bit longer to learn new material. During our 60s and 70s, our memories decline, as does our confidence in our ability to remember and to solve problems (Freedman et al., 2001). Overall, as we'll discuss in Chapter 8, such declines tend to have a more significant impact on our ability to recall information than on our skill at solving problems or dealing with new situations.

Why Do We Age?   Scientists have offered many theories about why we age; no single explanation is widely accepted (Pierpaoli, 2005). One important theory of aging, the **cellular clock theory**, suggests that aging is built into our cells. Tiny structures on the ends of DNA strands, called *telomeres*, aid in cell reproduction but grow shorter each time they are used. Eventually they become too short, and cells can no longer reproduce themselves. As a result, the body is less able to repair itself. The various changes of aging—saggy skin and decreases in vision and memory, for example—are the direct result of those events.

Two other theories of aging are more rooted in our experiences and the impact that life events can have on us. The *wear-and-tear* and *free-radical* theories suggest that years of use help wear out our bodies. The **wear-and-tear theory** boils down to: the more mileage we put on our bodies through living (augmented by factors, such as stress, poor diet, and exposure to environmental teratogens), the sooner we wear out (Hawkley et al., 2005). The **free-radical theory** provides a chemistry-oriented explanation (Boldyrev & Johnson, 2007). Free radicals are oxygen molecules that are negatively charged. A negative charge on a molecule can attract small particles of matter called *electrons* from other molecules. According to the free-radical theory of aging, free radicals become more prevalent in our system as we get older, increasingly destabilizing cell structures and doing progressively more damage to our bodies—resulting in the aging effects described above.

Social and Emotional Development

Although the social and emotional changes that occur in adulthood are more gradual than those that characterize childhood, adults experience multiple transitions in these areas (Roberts et al., 2002, 2006; Palkovitz et al., 2001). As you saw in Table 3-8, Erikson proposed that adults travel through three major life stages—stages marked by the need to resolve conflicts between *intimacy* and *isolation* (our ability to form sustaining relationships with others), *generativity* and *self-absorption* (our ability to give back to the world and provide for the future), and *integrity* and *despair* (our ability to face our mortality with a sense of a life well lived).

The journeys through each of these stages correspond to many of the rites of passage associated with adulthood, including marriage, parenting, retirement, and death—events that we'll be discussing further throughout the book. It is worth noting that, in many societies, the timing and form of such milestones of adulthood are now more variable than they were in earlier days. In the past, for example, the length of time a couple would spend married before having their first child was relatively short. That time has extended greatly in recent decades; moreover, the number of couples who choose to remain childless has doubled since 1960 (Demo et al., 2000). It has also become more acceptable in some societies for people who are not married to raise children (Weinraub et al., 2002).

Similarly, the average human lifespan continues to increase, lengthening the time that older adults remain part of the workforce, as well as part of the retired population, before dying (Volz, 2000). Such cultural shifts have opened new areas of study for psychologists, who are seeking to understand how these shifts may affect adult development.

Before You Go On

What Do You Know?

18. What is the difference between the wear-and-tear theory of aging and the free-radical theory of aging?
19. Describe and define Erikson's major crises of adult development.

What Do You Think?
Do you think that life experiences may actually increase adults' cognitive, or mental, abilities? Why might this be so?

Developmental Psychopathology *When Things Go Wrong*

LEARNING OBJECTIVE 8 Understand how the developmental psychopathology approach uses a developmental perspective to look at problematic behaviors.

Throughout the textbook, we will consider the ways that different psychological attributes and faculties develop and how those attributes and faculties may go wrong. We'll examine in depth, for example, memory disorders in Chapter 8 and autism in Chapter 16. For now, however, we'll offer just a broad understanding of how things can go wrong during development.

Psychologists in the field of **developmental psychopathology** are interested in how problematic behavior patterns evolve, based on both genetics and early childhood experiences, and in how those early problematic patterns affect functioning as individuals move through later life stages (Hinshaw, 2008; Hudziak, 2008). Developmental psychopathologists also compare and contrast problematic behavior patterns with more normal behavior patterns, seeking to identify **risk factors**—biological and environmental factors that contribute to problematic outcomes. In addition, they seek to identify other factors that can help children avoid or recover from such negative outcomes.

One disorder of special interest is called *conduct disorder*, a diagnosis applied strictly to children and adolescents. **Conduct disorder** (and its less severe cousin, *oppositional defiant disorder*) is characterized by a number of emotional and behavioral problems, including frequent rule-breaking, trouble following the limits imposed by authority figures, bullying and fighting, and cruelty. Looking at how developmental psychopathologists approach this disorder can help us understand how they approach all psychological disorders.

Developmental psychopathologists focus first on the various behaviors shown by children with conduct disorders (Hinshaw, 2002) to distinguish the conduct disorder from other disorders and see whether it has any relationships to milder problems, such as impulsiveness and distractibility. The negative behaviors of conduct disorder, such as defying authority, breaking rules, and fighting, are categorized as *externalizing behaviors* (as opposed to *internalizing behaviors*, such as fearful responses, crying, or withdrawal).

Violating, hurting, and disregarding others Many children with conduct disorder wind up in trouble with the law. Here a teenager and two ten-year-olds are led from a courtroom after being accused of attacking a homeless day laborer.

A report examining the many school shootings that have occurred across the United States over the past decade found that bullying was a factor in most of them (Crisp, 2001). Sometimes, the shooters had been bullies; more often, they had been the *victims* of bullying. One survey asked children aged 8 to 15 what issues in school troubled them most, and the children pointed to teasing and bullying as "big problems" that ranked even higher than racial discrimination, AIDS, and sex or alcohol peer pressures (Cukan, 2001). Overall, over one-quarter of students report being bullied frequently and more than 70 percent report having been victimized at least once, leading in many cases to feelings of humiliation or anxiety (Jacobs, 2008; Nishina et al., 2005). In addition, our online world has broadened the ways in which children and adolescents can be bullied, and today cyberbullying—bullying by e-mail, text-messaging, or the like—is increasing (Jacobs, 2008).

In response to these alarming trends, many schools—elementary through high school—have started programs that teach students how to deal more effectively with bullies, work to change the thinking of bullies, train teachers, conduct parent discussion groups, and applied classroom prevention measures (Jacobs, 2008; Frey et al., 2005; Twemlow, 2003). Furthermore, public health campaigns have tried to educate the public about antibullying programs, including the U.S. Government's "Stop Bullying Now" campaign.

Although recognizing the negative—and potentially tragic—impact of bullying, some experts worry that the sheer prevalence of bullying may make it a very difficult problem to overcome. It is hard, for example, for educators and clinicians to identify which bullies or bullied children will turn violent given that a full 70 percent of children have experienced bullying. Can we really rid our schools and communities of a problem as common as this? One observer has even argued, "Short of raising kids in isolation chambers...bullying behaviors can never be eliminated entirely from the sustained hazing ritual known as growing up" (Angier, 2001).

Like other developmental psychologists, developmental psychopathologists look for patterns and changes over time. Some studies have suggested, for example, that when externalizing behaviors begin in early childhood, they are more likely to be due to biological factors, such as genetic inheritance (Taylor, Iacono, & McGue, 2000), placing children with early-onset conduct disorders at greater risk for problems later in life than those whose conduct problems begin in adolescence. Still other studies indicate that, although externalizing behaviors tend to be moderately stable over time, the specific forms of the behaviors do shift with age. For example, explicitly aggressive acts, such as picking fights, typically decrease over time, while less overt acts of aggression tend to increase during early adolescence (Hinshaw, 2002). It seems that many children with conduct disorder learn as a result of the negative consequences for their bad behavior, but they do not really change internally. They learn primarily to hide their aggressive behavior so that they do not get into as much trouble.

Again, like other kinds of developmental psychologists, those interested in developmental psychopathology hold that behavior can be analyzed in a variety of ways. According to this view, a full accounting of how children get off-track (or stay on-track) requires looking at how genetics, environmental influences, and the children's own psychological processes all collaborate to bring about their current pattern of behavior and functioning.

Two concepts that developmental psychopathologists have provided to the field of psychology are *equifinality* and *multifinality* (Mitchell et al., 2004; Cicchetti & Rogosch, 1996). The concept of **equifinality** holds that individuals can start out from all sorts of different places and yet, through their life experiences, wind up functioning (or dysfunctioning) in similar ways. **Multifinality** follows the opposite principle. It suggests

equifinality the idea that different individuals can start out from different places and wind up at the same outcome.

multifinality the idea that children can start from the same spot and wind up in any numbers of other outcomes.

resilience the ability to recover from or avoid the serious effects of negative circumstances.

that children can start from the same point and wind up in any number of different psychological places. Applying these two concepts to conduct disorders, it appears that various roads may lead to the development of a conduct disorder during adolescence. A child with conduct disorder may have been born with a difficult temperament, experienced poor parenting, or developed poor social skills. **Table 3-9** lists risk factors that link conduct disorders to the likelihood of committing serious and violent crimes during adolescence or adulthood. As suggested by the notion of equifinality, regardless of which set of risk factors is at play, the outcome is often similar.

At the same time, multifinality assures us that not every difficult baby and not every baby with ineffective parents will wind up with a conduct disorder. Indeed, the vast majority will wind up with no pathology at all. Developmental psychopathologists are very interested in the biological, psychological, or environmental factors that help buffer against or negate the impact of risk factors—factors that help produce **resilience**, an ability to recover from or avoid the serious effects of negative circumstances (Greene, 2008; Hudziak & Bartels, 2008). In short, according to this viewpoint, it is just as critical to understand what goes right as it is to understand what goes wrong.

Let's return one more time to one of the superheroes at the start of this chapter. A developmental psychopathologist might hypothesize that Bruce Wayne faced several major risk factors for conduct disorder, including the loss of his parents when he was 8 years old, witnessing the trauma unfold, and living in social isolation afterward. The psychologist would be equally interested in identifying those factors that may have helped contribute to Bruce Wayne's resilience, including his high socioeconomic status (he's impossibly wealthy), his surrogate father-son relationship with his butler Alfred, his later positive parent-like relationship with his ward Dick Grayson (a.k.a. Robin), and his peer relationship with Commissioner Gordon.

TABLE 3-9 Risk Factors that Link Conduct Disorders to the Commission of Violent Crimes During Adolescence or Adulthood

Family violence	Multiple clinical disorders
Family dysfunction/conflict	Risky behavior
Family distress	Gun availability/risk
Childhood exposure to violence	Antisocial parent
Childhood maltreatment	Gang membership
Childhood neglect	Peer violence
Childhood adversity	Personality disorder
Substance abuse	Academic failure
Hyperactivity	Social incompetence

Source: FAS, 2008; Weaver et al, 2008; Gonzales et al., 2007; Lahey & Waldman, 2007; Mueser et al., 2006; Panko, 2005.

Before You Go On

What Do You Know?

20. How do externalizing behaviors differ from internalizing behaviors?
21. Why is resilience important to developmental psychopathology?
22. What is the difference between equifinality and multifinality?

What Do You Think?
Consider problems such as anxiety and depression. Do you see any advantages to looking at emotional or mental problems from a developmental perspective, as the product of a lifetime of biological and environmental experiences, rather than just examining the symptoms displayed by people with these problems? Do you see any disadvantages to this approach?

Summary

Understanding How We Develop

LEARNING OBJECTIVE 1 Understand the key debates underlying research and theory in child development.

- Developmental psychology is the study of changes in our behavior and mental processes over time and the various factors that influence the course of those changes.
- Key philosophical issues in the study of developmental psychology are what drives change (biological or environmental factors); what's the nature of the change (qualitative or quantitative); and the role of early experiences in shaping later development.

How Is Developmental Psychology Investigated?

LEARNING OBJECTIVE 2 Describe and discuss the advantages and disadvantages of cross-sectional and longitudinal designs for researching development.

- Two major research approaches in developmental psychology are cross-sectional (comparing different age groups to assess change) and longitudinal (studying the same group to see how responses change over time).
- The cohort-sequential research design combines elements of the cross-sectional and longitudinal approaches.

Before We Are Born

LEARNING OBJECTIVE 3 Discuss patterns of genetic inheritance and describe stages and potential problems during prenatal development.

- Our genetic inheritance comes from both parents, who each contribute half our chromosomes. Genes can combine in various ways to make up our phenotype, or observable traits.
- Genetics can influence the manifestation of both physical traits and psychological traits, including temperament, although environment also plays a role.
- Prenatal development begins with conception and is divided into three stages: germinal, embryonic, and fetal, each characterized by specific patterns of development.
- Individuals are susceptible to multiple influences by biological and environmental forces before they are even born, during the prenatal period.

Infancy

LEARNING OBJECTIVE 4 Summarize the major physical, cognitive, and emotional developments that take place during infancy.

- Infants make dramatic gains in both physical and psychological capabilities. Our brains grow during this period, preparing us to learn and encode the information that will organize those changes.
- One of the most important developmental theorists, Jean Piaget, proposed a theory of cognitive development that suggested that through learning and self-experimentation, we help our thinking to grow progressively more complex.
- Piaget believed we passed through multiple stages on the way to formal adult reasoning and that each transition was accompanied by the acquisition of a new cognitive capability. During the sensorimotor stage, in infancy, we become able to hold memories of objects in our minds.
- Information-processing researchers have suggested that babies may develop mental capacities at earlier ages than Piaget believed they did.
- Attachment theory suggests that the baby is biologically predisposed to bond and form a relationship with a key caregiver, thus ensuring that his or her needs are met. The security of the attachment relationship will have later implications for how secure the person feels in his or her emotional and social capabilities.
- Baumrind found evidence that different parenting styles could also affect the overall well-being of the child, although subsequent research suggested that outcomes might vary depending on other environmental and cultural influences.

Childhood

LEARNING OBJECTIVE 5 Summarize the major physical, cognitive, and emotional developments that take place during childhood.

- Physical growth continues at a generally slower pace in childhood than in infancy. Myelination and synaptic pruning continue to shape the brain.
- Piaget believed that children pass through the stages of preoperational and concrete operations thinking, learning to manipulate their mental schema. Other researchers have suggested children's thinking may not be as limited during these stages as Piaget thought it was.
- Theories of moral development have often focused on moral reasoning (the reasons why a child would do one thing or another) rather than values. Generally, research supports the movement from morality rooted in submitting to authority to morality rooted in more autonomous decisions about right and wrong.
- Some researchers suggest that moral reasoning may vary across gender and culture. Other researchers have questioned whether morality theories would be better served by measuring behavior instead of expressed reasoning or attitudes.

Adolescence

LEARNING OBJECTIVE 6 Summarize the major physical, cognitive, and emotional changes that take place during adolescence.

- Adolescence is generally associated with many substantial changes, including the onset of full sexual and physical maturity, as well as reasoning capabilities that approach adult levels. However, the teenager has certain limitations that influence his or her ability to make sound judgments and avoid risky situations.
- Erikson proposed a theory of development that stretched across the lifespan and incorporated various dilemmas that needed to be successfully reconciled in order for development to stay on track.

Adulthood *How We Develop*

LEARNING OBJECTIVE 7 Describe key physical, social, and emotional changes that take place throughout adulthood.

- Adult physical and psychological development is often characterized by some degree of decline. However, most basic faculties remain intact across the lifespan.
- The ages at which adults are expected to reach major social and emotional milestones, such as marriage and parenting, are more flexible now in many societies than they were in the past.

Developmental Psychopathology

LEARNING OBJECTIVE 8 Understand how the developmental psychopathology approach uses a developmental perspective to look at problematic behaviors.

- The developmental psychopathology approach studies how early problematic behaviors evolve as a function of a person's genetics and early experiences and how those behaviors affect the person in later life.
- Developmental psychopathologists are particularly interested in identifying the risk factors that contribute to problematic outcomes.
- The concept of equifinality holds that although children may start out at different places, through their life experiences they wind up functioning (or dysfunctioning) in similar ways. The concept of multifinality holds that children can start out at the same place but may wind up in a number of different psychological places.
- Developmental psychopathologists are also interested in the factors that contribute to resilience, the ability to recover from or avoid the serious effects of negative circumstances.

Key Terms

developmental psychology 57
maturation 57
stage 57
critical periods 59
cross-sectional design 59
longitudinal design 60
cohort-sequential design 60
prenatal period 60
genes 60
deoxyribonucleic acid (DNA) 60
chromosomes 60
genotype 60
phenotype 60
allele 62
homozygous 62
heterozygous 63
dominant trait 63

recessive trait 63
codominance 63
discrete trait 63
polygenic trait 63
temperament 63
zygote 64
placenta 64
miscarriage 64
teratogens 66
reflexes 67
synapses 67
synaptic pruning 68
myelination 68
proximodistal 68
motor skills 68
cognitive development 69
schemata 69

assimilation 69
accommodation 69
equilibrium 69
object permanence 70
information-processing theory 70
habituation 70
attachment 72
reciprocal socialization 74
operations 77
preoperational stage 77
egocentrism 77
conservation 77
concrete operations 78
theory of mind 78
scaffolding 78
zone of proximal development 78
private speech 81

puberty 82
primary sex characteristics 82
secondary sex characteristics 82
formal operations 84
menopause 87
cellular clock theory 88
wear-and-tear theory 88
free-radical theory 88
developmental psychopathology 88
risk factors 88
conduct disorder 88
equifinality 90
multifinality 90
resilience 90

CUT/ACROSS CONNECTION

What Happens in the BRAIN?

- At birth we have aproximately 100 billion neurons. A newborn has around 2500 synaptic connections per neuron while a 3-year-old has six times that many connections! But a 20-year-old has only around one-third the synaptic connections per neuron of a 3-year-old, a huge reduction due to synaptic pruning.
- *Myelination*, the formation of fatty white coverings around neurons, helps neurons transmit information more efficiently. During infancy, much of myelination occurs in brain areas tied to movement, reflexes, and sensory responses. During childhood, myelination is concentrated in brain areas that help coordinate activity, planning, and problem solving.
- Despite past beliefs, no significant loss of neurons occurs in adulthood, except in cases of brain pathology.
- New neurons keep being formed in certain parts of the brain throughout life, including during adulthood.

When Things Go Wrong

- Environmental risks, called *teratogens*, can influence prenatal development adversely. Thus, pregnant women should avoid risks, such as smoking or ingesting alcohol, each of which has been linked to birth defects.
- Developmental psychopathologists seek to identify biological, psychological, and environmental *risk factors* that contribute to the development of behavioral problems and psychological disorders.
- Risk factors for the development of *conduct disorders* in children and adults include family violence or dysfunction, childhood maltreatment, substance abuse, peer violence, and personality disorders.
- Despite the appearance of such risk factors, many children do not develop conduct disorders—a phenomenon attributed to their *resilience*. Like risk factors, the biological, psychological, and environmental factors that help produce resilience are of enormous interest to developmental psychopathologists.

HOW we Differ

- Only a few human traits are the product of a single gene pair. Most traits, particularly behavioral ones, are *polygenic*, helping to produce many variations in how traits are expressed from person to person.
- Babies tend to display either an *easy, difficult,* or *slow-to-warm-up* temperament, and their particular infant temperament often helps predict their reactions to situations throughout the lifespan.
- On average, Kipsigis in Kenya walk a month before babies in the United States, and Ache babies in Paraguay begin walking a year later than U.S. children—variations due to cultural differences in parenting.
- Babies may display either a *secure, anxious/avoidant, anxious/resistant,* or *disorganized attachment style*—a style that helps predict later relationship needs.
- On average, girls experience a growth spurt during their tenth or eleventh year, a couple of years prior to boys.
- Primary sex characteristics during puberty include growth of the testes for boys and growth of the ovaries for girls. Secondary sex characteristics include a deepening of the voice for boys and increase in breast size for girls.
- According to some research, the higher stages of moral development of males tend to focus on justice, fairness, and other abstract moral values, whereas those of females factor in relationship needs and responsibilities.

How we Develop

- At birth, the senses of taste, smell, and touch are highly developed, hearing is somewhat immature, and vision is extremely limited.
- Babies may have some sense of mathematics as early as 5 months of age.
- Most children do not develop a *theory of mind*, the ability to recognize that other persons have a perspective different from their own, prior to 3 years of age.
- Young children tend to make moral decisions that help ensure they will not get into trouble with parents or adults. In contrast, the moral decisions of adolescents and young adults tend to be more complex and guided by broader principles of right and wrong.
- Although less egocentric than younger children, many teenagers often display *personal fables* in which they are convinced that they are special—the first persons to have various thoughts and feelings—and perceive an *imaginary audience* in which they believe everyone is scrutinizing them.
- It is not entirely clear why we age and grow old.
- The human lifespan has continued to increase with each generation.

Video Lab Exercise

Psychology Around Us

School Days, "Cool" Days

Young children spending recess in their elementary schoolyard—breaking into different groups, playing various games, having all kinds of interactions. Each doing their own thing? Not really. The schoolyard conversations, physical activities, and mental processes generally follow the principles, milestones, and even rules cited in developmental stage theories. While the children recess away, your job is to identify and explain the stages of physical, cognitive, and social-emotional development reflected by their recess activities.

Fast forward to adolescence and to a teenage party. Individuals finally doing their own thing? Once again, the answer is no. And once again, your job is to detect the developmental stages and principles that their "cool" behaviors, talk, and posturing reflect.

As you are working on this online exercise, consider the following questions:

- What does this lab exercise say about the nature-versus-nurture debate in developmental psychology?
- Do the behaviors and interactions on display in the lab exercise indicate that stage differences are *qualitative* or *quantitative*?
- What events and steps have helped transform the enthusiastic (but awkward) elementary school kids of one video into the "cool" (though still awkward) high school kids of the second video?
- Stages or no stages, the children and teenagers in the lab exercise also show many individual differences. How did that happen?

CHAPTER 4

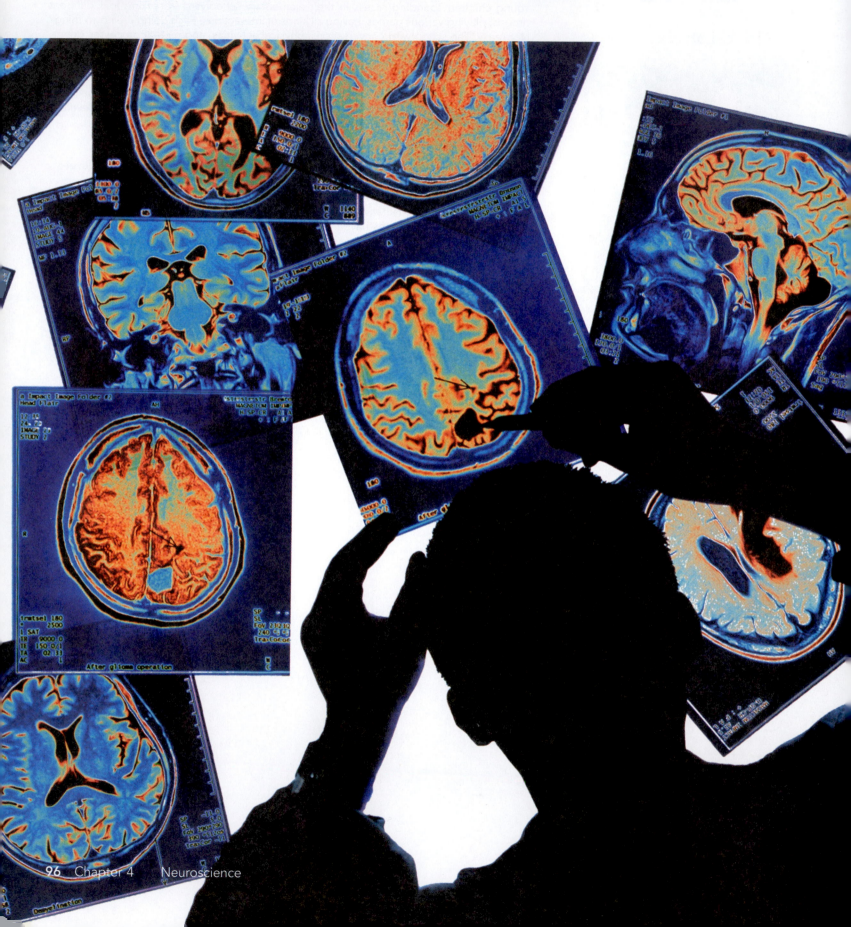

Neuroscience

chapter outline

Your Brain in *Jeopardy!*

For decades, one of the most popular game shows on television has been *Jeopardy!* Maybe you've watched it yourself, or even tried to play along at home. If so, you know that *Jeopardy!* is all about demonstrating brain power. It is a quiz show where contestants compete to be the first to correctly supply "questions" in response to answer clues in a number of categories. Winning contestants must be strategic and fast, as well as having a lot of facts memorized. Even as they listen to the host preview the categories, contestants must quickly plan their strategies, deciding for example whether they know more about "British Playwrights" or "American Poets." Then, they need speed and physical coordination; the only way to be allowed to answer a question is to be the first to press a buzzer. And of course, throughout the show, contestants must control their emotions. *Jeopardy!* contestants are never shown bursting into anxious tears or having angry confrontations with one another or the host.

Like the *Jeopardy!* contestants, we all rely on our brains and our nervous systems all day long. We remember things we have learned, and we learn new things. Without a nervous system, we wouldn't be able to register changes in the environment, nor would we be able to react to those changes.

Whenever we see, hear, and speak, whether about *Jeopardy!* clues or what's for dinner, we're using our nervous system. We use it as we experience a variety of emotions over the course of the day. Like the *Jeopardy!* contestants, we rely on it to form plans and strategies. Sometimes, we even need it to enable us to take quick physical actions, such as pressing a buzzer. **Neuroscience** is the study of the nervous system. In this chapter—and in *What Happens in the Brain* sections of other chapters of the book—we'll examine many of the discoveries of this fascinating field.

The complexity of the adult human brain is so staggering that its study has been referred to as the "final frontier." We'll see in this chapter that, although considerable progress has been made in understanding the organization and function of the brain, there remain large gaps in our knowledge about how the actions of the billions of microscopic cells in the brain produce complex behaviors, such as thought.

No less perplexing and impressive is the consideration of how the brain developed in the first place. Before we are even born, many millions of brain cells are arranged in an orderly fashion. Each one of them must hook up with other appropriate brain cells in order to transmit the messages that will let us breathe, eat, see, hear and think. Just as with the adult brain, we are still far from understanding exactly how the cellular events that occur during brain development are appropriately orchestrated, but progress has been made on many fronts.

Amazingly, this highly complicated process works right almost all the time. Sometimes things go wrong in the nervous system, as we'll see later in this chapter, but the overwhelming majority of people have normally functioning brains.

neuroscience the study of the nervous system.

neuroimaging techniques that allow for studying brain activity by obtaining visual images in awake humans.

neuron a nerve cell.

dendrites the parts of neurons that collect input from other neurons.

axon the part of the neuron that carries information away from the cell body toward other neurons.

axon terminal the end of a neuron's axon, from which neurotransmitters are released.

How Do Scientists Study the Nervous System?

LEARNING OBJECTIVE 1 Understand the key methods that scientists use to learn about brain anatomy and functioning.

In the past, researchers on psychological issues in humans often avoided analyzing the brain, mainly for technical reasons. Until recently, it was difficult, if not impossible, to study what goes on in the human brain without causing damage to brain tissue. As a result, human neuroscience relied on one of the following methods:

- *Examining autopsy tissue.* This method allows neuroscientists to see what our brains look like, but has the obvious drawback of telling them little about how these systems worked while the person was alive and using them.

- *Testing the behavior of patients with damage to certain parts of the brain.* Scientists called *neuropsychologists* have learned a lot about the brain from studying patients with brain damage. Patients with localized brain damage often have loss of some function. The loss of function then suggests what the brain region does when it is undamaged. The obvious drawback of this approach is that it involves inferring information about the normally functioning brain from the damaged brain. Even patients with localized brain damage may have smaller undetectable abnormalities in other areas of the brain. Also, the damaged brain may undergo reorganization over time so abnormalities in behavior may not reflect what goes on in the intact brain.

- *Recording brain activity, or brain waves, from the surface of the scalp.* Scientists have used *electroencephalograms*, or EEGs, to learn about the activity of our brains during certain states (awake and asleep) as well as during certain behavioral tasks. The drawback of this type of analysis is that surface recordings only provide a summary of activity over a large expanse of tissue—pinpointing the location of activity using this method can only be done in a general sense.

These findings have been combined with those from animal studies where specific brain regions are examined microscopically, recorded from electrically or targeted for destruction, a process called *lesioning*. Taken together, these approaches have provided us with a great deal of information about the brain and the nervous system in general, but they all share drawbacks. They can tell us little about activity in specific regions of healthy, living, human brains.

Over the past few decades, however, several new techniques, collectively referred to as **neuroimaging**, have been developed to study brain activity in awake, healthy humans. These techniques enable researchers to identify brain regions that become active under certain conditions. Among the most useful neuroimaging methods are positron emission tomography (PET) and functional magnetic resonance imaging (fMRI). PET scans enable the detection of uptake of certain molecules so that brain areas of increased activity can be identified. fMRI allows for the detection of changes in blood flow, a presumed indicator of changes in the activity of neurons. The availability of these neuroimaging technologies has produced an explosion of research that has infused neuroscience into virtually every area of psychological investigation. The results have confirmed many previously held claims about brain function and raised additional new questions. As the technology is rapidly developing, and neuroimaging methods become more and more sensitive, there is no doubt we will gain a better understanding of the organ that serves most human behavior: the brain.

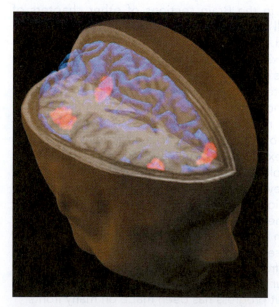

The brain at work This 3D computer generated image of a human brain shows areas of brain activation (colored areas) in individuals undergoing a moral decision-making task. This study employed fMRI technology which uses changes in blood flow as a measure of changes in neural activity.

Before You Go On

What Do You Know?

1. Describe how studies of people with brain damage and EEGs have contributed to our knowledge of the brain and nervous system.

2. What are the main advantages of neuroimaging methods over earlier neuroscience research methods?

What Do You Think? Do you think it will be possible to use neuroimaging techniques to determine what a person is thinking? What are the ethical implications of using this technology?

What Cells Make Up the Nervous System?

LEARNING OBJECTIVE 2 Name the two major types of cells in the nervous system and describe the primary functions of each.

We know that the **neuron**, or nerve cell, is the fundamental unit of the nervous system (Jones, 2007) and that communication among neurons is necessary for normal functioning of the brain and spinal cord. The peripheral nervous system that runs throughout the rest of our bodies, outside the brain and spinal cord, is also made up of neurons.

The structure and function of individual neurons, as well as how these cells work individually and in groups, called *networks*, has been the subject of considerable scientific inquiry for over a century (Jones, 2007). Neuroscientists have discovered that neurons have specialized structures that enable them to communicate with other neurons using both electrical and chemical signals.

But neurons are not the only cells in the nervous system. As we'll see, neuroscientists have increased their attention to *glia*, the other type of cell found in our nervous systems.

Neurons

The human brain contains about 100 billion neurons. The basic structure of a neuron is shown in Figure 4-1. Like most of our other cells, neurons have a cell body filled with cytoplasm that contains a nucleus (the residence of chromosomes that contain the genetic material). In addition, neurons contain organelles that enable the cell to make proteins and other molecules, produce energy, as well as permit the breakdown and elimination of toxic substances.

However, as **Figure 4-1** shows, neurons are different from other cells, in that they have specialized structures called *dendrites* and *axons* that are important for communication with other neurons.

Dendrites extend like branches from the cell body to collect inputs from other neurons. Neurons can have many dendrites and, indeed, some have very extensive dendritic "trees" that allow a single neuron to receive more than 200,000 inputs from other neurons.

Axons also extend from the cell body. Unlike dendrites, however, axons typically function to carry information away from the cell body, toward other neurons. Axons have a specialized region at the end, called the **axon terminal**. Unlike the case with dendrites, neurons usually have only one axon. The axon can be very long. One of your axons, for example, runs from your spinal cord all the way to the end of your big toe. In addition, axons can be highly branched. These branches, or collaterals, greatly increase the number of neurons that the axon contacts.

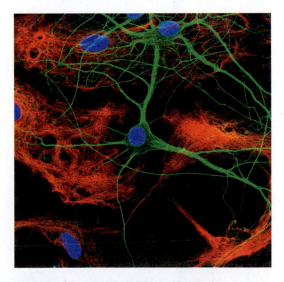

Neurons have a cell body (shown here in this fluorescent image in blue), as well as axons and dendrites (shown in green) for communicating with other neurons.

FIGURE 4-1 The neuron The major structures of the neuron include the cell body, the axon, and the dendrites. Dendrites typically receive information from other neurons, while axons send information away from the cell body to communicate with other neurons. Arrows indicate the direction of information flow.

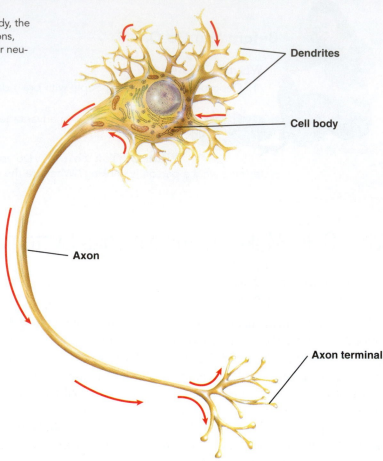

Dendrites

Cell body

Axon

Axon terminal

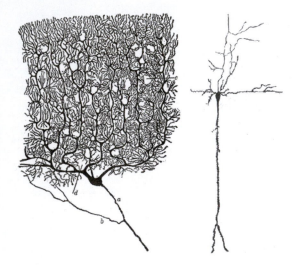

Various shapes These drawings by the early neuroanatomist Santiago Ramon y Cajal are just two examples of the vast diversity in the shape of neurons in the brain.

There are many different kinds of neurons. Some are large, while others are relatively small. Some have very elaborate dendritic trees, while others possess a single unbranched dendrite. Although these cells all look quite different from one another, they have two features in common. All neurons are covered by a membrane that surrounds the entire neuron, including its axon and dendrites, and all have the capability of communicating with other cells by producing and sending electrical signals.

Glia

In addition to neurons, the nervous system contains a large number of nonneuronal cells called **glia**. In fact, in some parts of the human brain, glia outnumber neurons by a factor of about 10. Their vast numbers make it surprising that glia have received relatively little attention by neuroscientists. In the past, glia were considered to be support cells, which implies a passive structural function. Discoveries over the past two decades, however, have confirmed that these cells are diverse and actively serve many purposes, that are critical for normal functioning of neurons. Although most of the rest of this chapter focuses on neurons and systems made up of neurons, glia are actively involved in nervous system function. We will return to glial cells periodically throughout the rest of this chapter.

Before You Go On

What Do You Know?

3. What are the two types of cells in the nervous system?

4. What are the three major types of glia and the functions of each type?

What Do You Think?   Why do you think the function of glia was overlooked by researchers for so long?

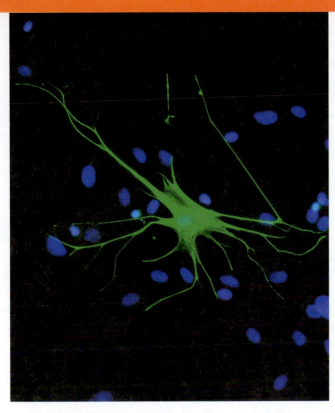

ical for normal function. There are three major categories of glia, *astroglia, oligodendroglia,* and *microglia.* Astroglia are so-named because most are shaped like stars (see photo on left) – this glial type is important for creating the blood-brain barrier, a system that monitors the passage of molecules from the blood to the brain, and for regulating the flow of blood into regions with changes in neuronal activity (Iadecola and Nedergaard, 2007). Astroglia also function to take in chemicals released by neighboring neurons and to provide important growth-promoting molecules to neurons. Astrocytes will migrate to the site of brain injury, enlarge, and multiply to form a glial scar (Fitch and Silver, 2008). Astroglia also serve to communicate with neurons, influencing their electrical activity (Haydon et al., 2009). Another type of astroglia serves as a stem cell in the adult brain (Doetsch, 2003). These cells are capable of dividing and producing new cells, including new neurons.

The *oligodendroglia* are important for providing a protective fatty sheath, or coating, called *myelin* that wraps around the axons of neurons. Myelin serves to insulate axons from nearby neurons. This is particularly important in the brain and spinal cord, where neurons are very closely packed and axons are often organized into bundles. Myelin also enables more efficient transfer of electrical signals down the axon.

Finally, *microglia,* so-named because they are very small, are important for cleaning up the debris of dead cells so that brain regions can continue with their normal functioning. Microglia are an important brain defense against infection and illness.

When glial cells were first discovered, they were given a Greek name that means "glue" because scientists believed their chief function was to hold the brain together. Now more than 100 years later, we know that glia play many roles in the brain that are crit-

How Do Neurons Work?

LEARNING OBJECTIVE 3 Describe what happens when a neuron "fires" and how neurons send messages to one another.

Neurons send messages to one another via electrochemical events. A sudden change in the electrical charge of a neuron's axon causes it to release a chemical that can be received by other neurons.

Your brain uses 20% of your body's energy, but it makes up only 2% of your body's weight.

The Action Potential

As we have discussed, neurons are covered by a membrane. On both sides of this membrane, inside and outside the neuron, are fluids. Like other bodily fluids, the *extracellular fluid* that surrounds the outside of nerve cells contains charged particles called *ions.* Ions can be either positive or negative in charge.

Ions are also found in the cytoplasm that fills the neuron. This gives neurons an electrical charge, even when they are resting. (When a neuron is not sending a message,

glia the cells that, in addition to neurons, make up the nervous system.

resting potential the electrical charge of a neuron when it is at rest.

ion channels pores in the cell membrane that open and close to allow certain ions into and out of the cell.

action potential a sudden positive change in the electrical charge of a neuron's axon. Also known as a spike, or firing, action potentials rapidly transmit an excitatory charge down the axon.

it is said to be resting) This charge, called the **resting potential**, is negative; the fluid inside the neuron is more negatively charged than the fluid outside the cell. If you put a very small recording electrode into an axon, it will read a negative charge, typically around −70 millivolts, relative to outside of the cell.

The neuron's membrane exhibits *selective permeability* to ions. Embedded in the membrane are specialized **ion channels**, or pores, that only allow the passage of certain ions into and out of the cell. These ion channels can open or close depending on information the cell receives from other neurons. Some of the key ions that are involved in determining the resting potential are the positively charged ions sodium $(Na+)$ and potassium $(K+)$ and the negatively charged chloride $(Cl-)$ ion. When the neuron is at rest, positive sodium ions are higher in concentration outside of the cell. This concentration gradient changes dramatically when the cell is activated by other neurons.

When information received from other neurons is positively charged, or *excitatory*, and reaches a certain *threshold*, an event begins at the axon, known as an **action potential**. The action potential is shown in **Figure 4-2.** During an action potential (also known as a *spike*), ion channels that allow the passage of sodium $(Na+)$ through the membrane open rapidly. This enables $Na+$, which is present in higher concentrations outside of the axon, to rush through the $Na+$ channels into the axon. The sudden influx of positive ions shifts the electrical charge of the axon, from negative to positive. At the peak of the action potential, the membrane charge is about $+50$ mV.

As Figure 4-2 shows, the action potential travels down the axon, away from the cell body toward the terminal. As each portion of the axon spikes, or *fires*, the $Na+$ channels on the next patch of membrane open, letting the spike continue its progress toward the axon terminal. After the action potential has passed a particular segment of the axon, the membrane works to restore the resting potential by using specialized proteins to pump $K+$ ions out of the cell.

Action potentials are not graded—there cannot be weaker or stronger action potentials. They follow an *all-or-none* principle. If the stimulation reaching the neuron exceeds a certain threshold, it fires; otherwise, it does not. To facilitate the transfer of the action potential down the axon, the axons of many neurons are insulated by **myelin**, produced by specialized glial cells. Wrapped areas of the axon are broken up at regular intervals by regions that expose the neuronal membrane to the extracellular fluid. These regions are called *nodes of Ranvier*. As shown in **Figure 4-3**, action potentials travel very quickly down myelinated axons by jumping from node to node.

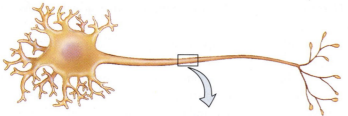

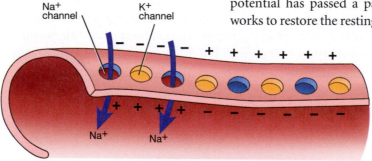

(a) This figure shows an action potential occurring along a segment of the axon membrane. During an action potential, Na+ channels in the axon membrane open and Na+ enters the cell, giving the membrane a more positive charge.

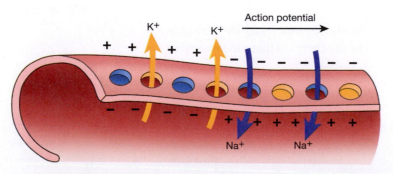

(b) As the action potential moves past a certain patch of membrane, the membrane works to restore the resting potential by closing the Na+ channels so no more Na+ enters the cell. K+ channels are opened and K+, which is more concentrated inside the cell, exits through the channels. Thus, the resting potential is restored.

FIGURE 4-2
The action potential

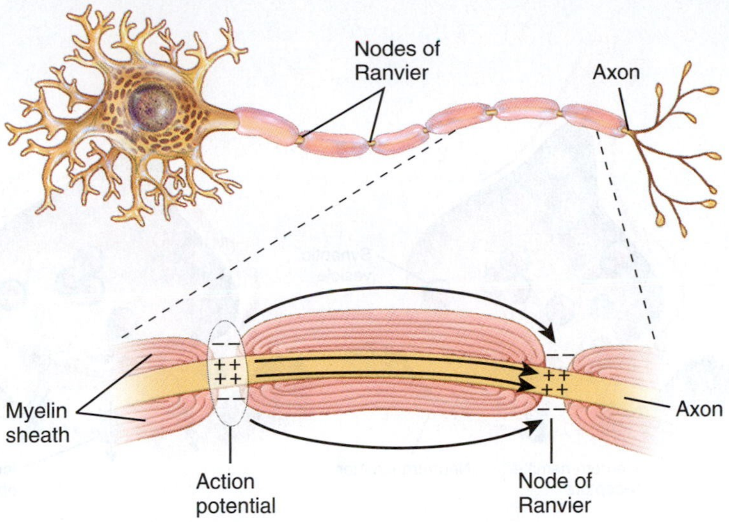

FIGURE 4-3 **Nodes of Ranvier** The nodes of Ranvier are the regions of bare axon that are between areas wrapped in myelin. Action potentials travel down the axon by jumping from node to node.

After it fires, the neuron cannot fire again for a short time, known as a *refractory period*. Immediately following an action potential, the axon is completely unable to fire no matter how strong the stimulus to the neuron. This time is called the **absolute refractory period**. During the **relative refractory period**, which begins a little later, the cell can fire if it is given a strong enough stimulus, but the threshold for spiking is higher than usual.

Since action potentials are all-or-none, they don't convey a lot of specific information. However, the pattern of action potentials, whether they occur in rapid succession or at a slow pace, whether they are regular or more sporadic, can provide a neural code that is specific.

Communication Across the Synapse

Once the positive charge of an action potential reaches the axon terminal, it stimulates special events that enable the passage of information to other neurons. Neurons are not physically connected to one another; they are separated by small gaps. These gaps, called **synapses**, are tiny spaces (about 20 nm or 0.00002 mm wide) usually between the axon terminal of one cell and the dendrite of another cell by which neurons communicate. Communication across these spaces involves specialized chemicals called **neurotransmitters**. Neurotransmitter molecules are usually contained within small **synaptic vesicles** in the axon terminal, also known as the *presynaptic* terminal, of the neuron sending information.

When the spike reaches the presynaptic axon terminal, it causes the release of neurotransmitter molecules into the synapse. As **Figure 4-4** shows, the neurotransmitter then diffuses across the synapse and binds to neurotransmitter receptors on the dendrite of the receiving, or *postsynaptic*, neuron. **Neurotransmitter receptors** are proteins in the cell membrane that recognize specific molecules. They operate in a lock and key fashion, so that receptors can only receive the specific neurotransmitter that "fits" them.

When a neurotransmitter binds to a receptor, the combination stimulates an electrical event in the postsynaptic membrane. These electrical events, called **postsynaptic potentials**, can be *excitatory* or *inhibitory*. The electrical response of the postsynaptic cell is determined by the receptor. If the receptor has an excitatory action, then the postsynaptic cell will be depolarized; the membrane potential will become less negative. Depolarizations that arise from inputs of a single neuron may not be

myelin a fatty, white substance, formed from glial cells, that insulates the axons of many neurons.

absolute refractory period a short time after an action potential, during which a neuron is completely unable to fire again.

relative refractory period just after the absolute refractory period during which a neuron can only fire if it receives a stimulus stronger than its usual threshold level.

synapses tiny spaces between the axon terminal of one neuron and the next neuron through which communication occurs.

neurotransmitters specialized chemicals that travel across synapses to allow communication between neurons.

synaptic vesicles membrane-bound spheres in the axon terminals of neurons where neurotransmitters are stored before their release.

neurotransmitter receptors proteins in the membranes of neurons that bind to neurotransmitters.

postsynaptic potentials electrical events in postsynaptic neurons, that occur when a neurotransmitter binds to one of its receptors.

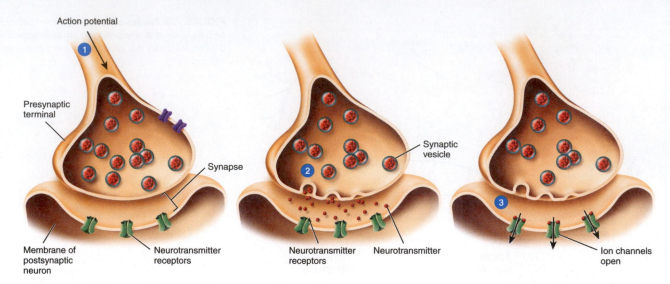

Action potential

Presynaptic terminal

Synapse

Synaptic vesicle

Membrane of postsynaptic neuron

Neurotransmitter receptors

Neurotransmitter receptors

Neurotransmitter

Ion channels open

FIGURE 4-4 Communication across the synapse (1) A positive charge reaches the end of the axon; (2) the positive charge stimulates release of neurotransmitters contained in membrane-bound vesicles into the synapse; (3) neurotransmitters bind to receptors on the postsynaptic neuron; ion channels open and electrical charge in postsynaptic neuron changes.

great enough to trigger an action potential in the postsynaptic neuron, but when summed with other excitatory inputs to the same neuron, the threshold will be reached and the neuron will fire. This will then send the information on to the next neuron in the chain. Alternatively, if the neurotransmitter has an inhibitory action, then the postsynaptic cell will be hyperpolarized: its membrane potential will become more negative. Hyperpolarization makes it less likely that the postsynaptic neuron will fire an action potential.

Compared to the action potential, which is an all-or-none depolarization, postsynaptic electrical events are much more varied. As described above, they can be depolarizing or hyperpolarizing and graded in strength. In addition, postsynaptic events at individual synapses can change with experience.

Repeated release of neurotransmitter into the synapse can result in long-lasting changes in neurotransmitter receptors located on the postsynaptic membrane (Costa-Mattioli et al., 2009). Glial cells also release chemicals, called *gliotransmitters*, that can cause long-term changes in postsynaptic membranes (Angulo et al., 2008). These receptor changes may make the postsynaptic response stronger or weaker, depending on the characteristics of the input. Change in the nervous system is generally referred to as **plasticity**. Plasticity at the synapse, such as the changes that occur from repeated release of neurotransmitters, is called *synaptic plasticity*. Neuroscientists have studied synaptic plasticity extensively because evidence suggests that it may explain some types of learning as we will describe further in Chapter 7.

Neural Networks

In the brain, the number of neurons involved in a neural circuit is typically much greater than two. Collections of neurons that communicate with one another are referred to as *neural circuits* or *neural networks*. Given that the human brain contains about 100 billion neurons, each of which receives numerous synaptic inputs from a multitude of other neurons, the computational power of this organ is vast. Some clusters of neurons in specific brain regions communicate more heavily with those of other specific regions—these combinations participate in certain functions. Neuroscientists have focused attention on individual neural systems in order to better grasp the functioning of neural circuits related to specific behaviors.

Neural network Neurons form circuits or networks that expand the communications among different brain regions. This image shows axons and dendrites (red) extending from the neuronal cell bodies (shown in blue).

What Do You Know?

5. How do neurons work?
6. What happens in the axon of a neuron during an action potential?
7. When an action potential reaches the axon terminal, what happens?
8. How does a postsynaptic neuron receive and respond to messages from other neurons?

What Do You Think?   Long axons are vulnerable to damage – what do you think some advantages might be of having a neuron with a very long axon (for example, one with a cell body in the spinal cord and axon terminal in the toe or finger)?

How is the Nervous System Organized?

LEARNING OBJECTIVE 4   Name and describe the functions and subdivisions of the two major parts of the nervous system.

As shown in **Figure 4-5**, the human nervous system can be divided into two main components: the central nervous system and the peripheral nervous system. The *central nervous system* consists of the brain and spinal cord. The *peripheral nervous system* consists of the nerves that extend throughout our bodies to provide a means for sending information back and forth between the periphery (for example, your arm) and the central nervous system.

The Peripheral Nervous System

The peripheral nervous system consists of the somatic nervous system and the autonomic nervous system. The **somatic nervous system** consists of all of the nerves that gather sensory information (typically about touch and pain) from all over the body, neck, and head, and deliver it to the spinal cord and brain, as well as the nerves that send information about movement from the central nervous system to the muscles of

plasticity change in the nervous system.

somatic nervous system all the peripheral nerves that transmit information about the senses and movement to and from the central nervous system.

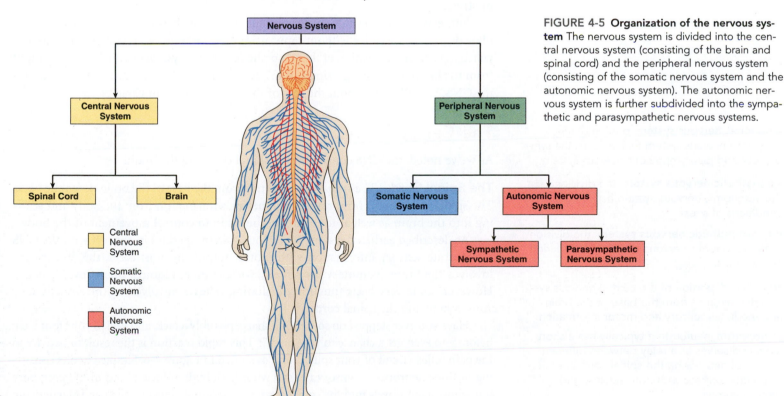

FIGURE 4-5 Organization of the nervous system The nervous system is divided into the central nervous system (consisting of the brain and spinal cord) and the peripheral nervous system (consisting of the somatic nervous system and the autonomic nervous system). The autonomic nervous system is further subdivided into the sympathetic and parasympathetic nervous systems.

The social kind of threat The sympathetic nervous system doesn't distinguish between threats of physical harm or situations of social stress. It arouses the body to respond to both, with physiological reactions such as dry mouth, lack of appetite, or pounding heart.

the body, neck, and head. As we will see shortly, the somatic nervous system doesn't serve any function without the integrating capacity of the central nervous system. Even very simple reflexes require the central nervous system.

By contrast, parts of the **autonomic nervous system** operate, in large part, without help from the central nervous system. The autonomic nervous system can be subdivided into two parts: the *sympathetic nervous system* and *parasympathetic nervous system*. Both components of the autonomic nervous system consist of collections of nerve cells and their axons distributed throughout the body. However, they serve opposing functions. The sympathetic nervous system is activated under conditions of stress, whereas the parasympathetic nervous system is inhibited during those times, but active during more restful times.

The **sympathetic nervous system** is responsible for the "fight-or-flight" reaction, the physiological response that enables us to respond to potentially life-threatening situations. The **parasympathetic nervous system**, on the other hand, is important for controlling basic functions that occur when the individual is not at immediate risk. For instance, digestion is a function under the control of the parasympathetic nervous system. Not surprisingly, when stressful situations occur and the sympathetic nervous system is activated, digestion stops. This makes good adaptive sense. Energy spent digesting food could be diverted to serve other functions (such as increasing blood flow to the leg muscles) so that the individual can escape the threatening situation.

Sometimes the sympathetic nervous system is activated when humans are not necessarily at risk of bodily harm, but under social situations where the major fear is one of embarrassment and humiliation, such as competing on *Jeopardy!* You don't have to be on television to experience a sympathetic nervous system response, however. Have you ever given a speech in front of a group of people? Many people experience a strong stress response to such situations. They develop a rapid heart rate and a dry mouth, signs that the sympathetic nervous system has kicked in. Although this reaction can be particularly disturbing, given that it often lessens the quality of your speech, it is a clear example of stress activating a physiological system. Mentally reframing such experiences as exciting opportunities can lessen the negative effects of stress.

Some aspects of the autonomic nervous system, such as the components that regulate digestion, are active without input from the central nervous system, often abbreviated as CNS, but activation of the sympathetic nervous system definitely requires input from the brain, since recognizing and responding to an experience as stressful requires the CNS. We talk more about the role of the brain in stress in Chapter 15.

The Central Nervous System

As we've noted, the CNS consists of the spinal cord and the brain.

The Spinal Cord   The **spinal cord** extends from the base of the brain down the back. The spinal cord is very important for gathering information from the body and sending it to the brain as well as for enabling the brain to control movement of the body.

As described earlier, the somatic nervous system operates in concert with the CNS to integrate sensory information with motor output. In most cases, this integration involves the brain (voluntary movement, for example, requires brain involvement). However, some very basic functions, including reflexes, involve just the somatic nervous system and the spinal cord.

Have you ever stepped on something sharp, possibly a tack, and pulled your foot back before you even get a chance to yell "ouch"? This rapid reaction is the result of activity in the pain reflex circuit of your spinal cord, as shown in **Figure 4-6**. Simple circuits consisting of three neurons—a sensory neuron whose cell body is located out in the periphery but whose axon travels into the spinal cord; a connecting neuron, called an **interneuron**;

autonomic nervous system portion of the peripheral nervous system that includes the sympathetic and parasympathetic nervous systems.

sympathetic nervous system the division of the autonomic nervous system activated under conditions of stress.

parasympathetic nervous system the division of the autonomic nervous system active during restful times.

spinal cord portion of the central nervous system that extends from the base of the brain and mediates sensory and motor information.

interneuron neuron that typically has a short axon and serves as a relay between different classes of neurons. In the spinal cord, interneurons communicate with both sensory and motor neurons.

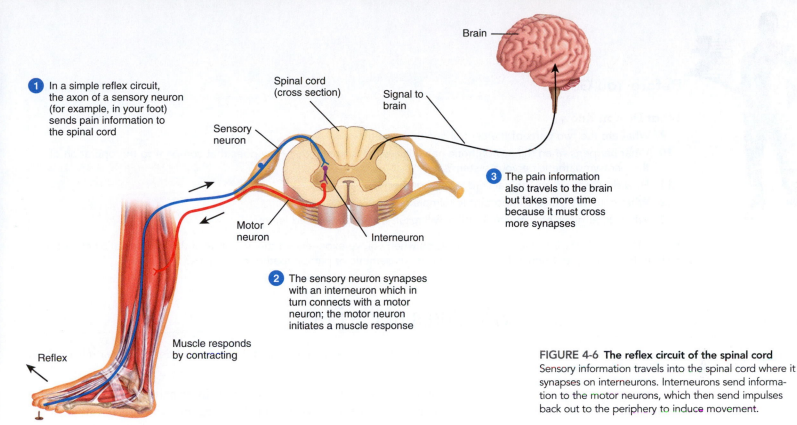

1 In a simple reflex circuit, the axon of a sensory neuron (for example, in your foot) sends pain information to the spinal cord

Spinal cord (cross section)

Signal to brain

Brain

Sensory neuron

3 The pain information also travels to the brain but takes more time because it must cross more synapses

Motor neuron

Interneuron

2 The sensory neuron synapses with an interneuron which in turn connects with a motor neuron; the motor neuron initiates a muscle response

Muscle responds by contracting

Reflex

FIGURE 4-6 The reflex circuit of the spinal cord
Sensory information travels into the spinal cord where it synapses on interneurons. Interneurons send information to the motor neurons, which then send impulses back out to the periphery to induce movement.

and a motor neuron whose cell body is located in the spinal cord and whose axon travels out to the body—can control pain reflexes without any communication with the brain.

Pain information also travels up to the brain and enables you to vocalize about the pain and carry out other movements, such as hobbling to a chair, sitting down, and pulling the tack out, but these reactions are slower than the reflex because the information must travel greater distances and more importantly, it must travel across many more synapses (information flows more slowly across synapses because synaptic communication involves the flow of chemicals as well as receptor events, both of which take more time than it takes for action potentials to travel down the axon).

Spinal Cord Injuries   When Things Go **Wrong**

In addition to controlling simple reflexes, the spinal cord is very important for carrying sensory information up to the brain and motor information back out to the body. When the spinal cord is damaged such that the flow of information to and from the brain is disrupted, individuals become paralyzed, as well as incapable of noticing touch or pain sensations on the body. The higher up the spinal cord the damage occurs (the closer it occurs to the brain), the larger the proportion of the body that is afflicted. Thus, when individuals break their necks and permanently damage the spinal cord close to the brain, they lose touch and pain sensation everywhere but their heads and faces, and they become *quadriplegic,* paralyzed everywhere but the head and neck. If the damage occurs farther down the back, then they may retain sensation and usage of the upper limbs and torso but not of the lower limbs.

Since spinal cord damage is so devastating and afflicts such a large number of young people (about 11,000 new cases in the U.S. each year, the majority of which are between the ages of 18 and 30), scientists have directed attention to finding ways to enhance regeneration of severed axons in the spinal cord, as well as the potential replenishment of motor neurons destroyed by injury (Barnabé-Heider et al., 2008). Although some progress has been made in the treatment of spinal cord injury, there is much work to be done. In most cases, spinal cord injury results in permanent loss of function.

Before You Go On

What Do You Know?

9. What are the two parts of the central nervous system?
10. What happens when the sympathetic nervous system is operating? How does that compare to the operation of the parasympathetic nervous system?
11. How do the brain and spinal cord work together?
12. What neuron types are important for simple reflexes?
13. What determines how much disability will result from a spinal cord injury?

What Do You Think?   Describe an occasion when you've experienced the workings of the sympathetic nervous system. Have you ever been able to control your sympathetic or parasympathetic reactions? If so, how?

Structures of the Brain

brainstem or **medulla** the part of the brain closest to the spinal cord that serves basic functions.

reticular formation a brain structure important for sleep and wakefulness.

serotonin neurotransmitter involved in activity levels and mood regulation.

LEARNING OBJECTIVE 5 List key structures of the brain and describe their relationships to our behavior.

Like the spinal cord, different parts of which integrate information from and about different parts of the body, the brain is also divided into regions, which serve varying functions. **Figure 4-7** shows the major structures of the brain.

The Brainstem

The part of the brain closest to the spinal cord is called the **brainstem** or **medulla**. The brainstem is important for basic bodily functions, including respiration and heart rate regulation. Although most of the actions of the brainstem occur without our conscious knowledge or involvement, this part of the brain is critical for survival and normal functioning. Damage to the brainstem, as a result of stroke or trauma, is often fatal.

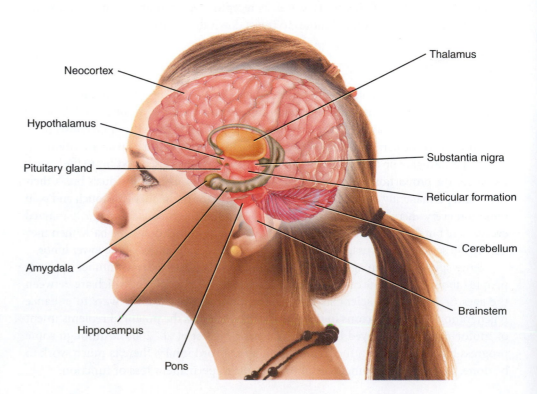

FIGURE 4-7 Major structures of the brain The brain is subdivided into several major structures, each with specific functions.

The brainstem is also important for integrating information about pain and touch from the head and neck with motor output. Neurons from the face, mouth, and tongue related to touch, pain, pressure, and vibration send inputs into the CNS that connect first in the brainstem. Parts of the brainstem are important for controlling eye movement, tongue movement, and facial expressions.

Several neuron groups, or *nuclei*, in the brainstem work together to form an area known as the **reticular formation**, which is important for sleep and wakefulness. Groups of neurons in the reticular formation are the major brain source of the neurotransmitter **serotonin**. These serotonin neurons send axons throughout the brain. Brain serotonin has been implicated in a number of important functions, such as activity levels and mood regulation (Lowry et al., 2008). Several popular drugs for depression and anxiety are those that increase the action of serotonin.

The Pons

Above the brainstem is a region called the **pons**. This part of the brain also contains cell groups, such as the *locus coeruleus*, that belong to the reticular formation. Neurons of the locus coeruleus have long axons projecting throughout the brain and spinal cord. These neurons use the neurotransmitter **norepinephrine** and are important for arousal and attention (Viggiano et al., 2004).

The Cerebellum

Sitting at the back of the brain, connected to the brainstem by the pons, is the highly convoluted **cerebellum**. This part of the brain is important for motor coordination. People with cerebellar damage often have an awkward gait and have difficulty reaching for objects without trembling. In addition to its role in motor coordination, the cerebellum is important for certain types of learning involving movement. For example, when you learn to tie your shoelaces or to play the piano, your cerebellum is at work. Other parts of the brain participate as well, particularly in cases where the task involves paying attention to a complicated series of instructions. The cerebellum then stores the learned motor information to be recalled automatically once it's completely learned.

The Midbrain

Above the pons sits a collection of brain regions collectively called the *midbrain*. The midbrain contains a number of different nuclei, including an area called the **substantia nigra**. Like the cerebellum, the substantia nigra is important for movement, but this area serves different functions from those of the cerebellum. Neurons in the substantia nigra that produce a neurotransmitter called **dopamine** communicate with other brain regions located in the forebrain. These pathways are critical for fluidity of movement as well as inhibition of movement. This brain region is the major structure damaged in a neurological disorder called *Parkinson's disease* (Cenci, 2007) that we discuss in more detail later in this chapter.

The Thalamus

The **thalamus** is a large collection of nuclei located anterior to, or in front of, the substantia nigra. Many of the thalamic nuclei serve as relay stations for incoming sensory information. In fact, all of our sensory systems, with the exception of the sense of smell, have a major pathway that synapses in the thalamus. Two major components of the thalamus are the *lateral geniculate nucleus* (LGN) and the *medial geniculate nucleus* (MGN). The LGN is important for relaying information about visual stimuli and the MGN is important for relaying information about auditory stimuli.

pons part of the brain anterior to the brainstem that includes the locus coeruleus.

norepinephrine neurotransmitter important for arousal and attention.

cerebellum part of the brain, near the back of the head, important for motor coordination.

substantia nigra brain region important in fluidity of movement and inhibiting movements.

dopamine neurotransmitter plentiful in brain areas involving movement and rewards.

thalamus an area of the brain that serves as a relay station for incoming sensory information.

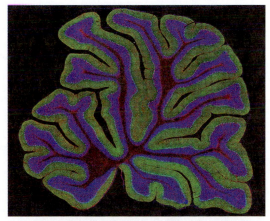

A convoluted brain region The cerebellum has many folds on its surface, shown here in this fluorescent image of a slice through this part of the brain.

The Hypothalamus

The **hypothalamus** is aptly named because this collection of nuclei sits beneath the thalamus (the prefix *hypo-* comes from ancient Greek for below or under). Regions of the hypothalamus are important for a number of motivational processes, including eating, drinking, sex, and maternal behavior. Damage to discrete parts of the hypothalamus can alter these basic behaviors dramatically. The hypothalamus is also critical for the control of the **endocrine**, or hormonal, **system**.

The Pituitary Gland and the Endocrine System

The hypothalamus is connected to a structure called the **pituitary gland**. The pituitary works with the hypothalamus to control a particular class of chemical messengers in the body—*hormones*—that are important for growth, reproduction, metabolism, and stress.

There are two parts of the pituitary gland, the *anterior pituitary* and the *posterior pituitary*. The anterior pituitary is connected to the hypothalamus via blood vessels that allow it to receive signaling molecules from specific neuron groups of the hypothalamus. These parts of the hypothalamus communicate with the anterior pituitary to release various *peptides*, chemicals that can act as hormones themselves (such as growth hormone) or that can work to stimulate the release of hormones from endocrine glands in the periphery.

There are a number of key endocrine glands. The anterior pituitary produces releasing factors that control endocrine glands, such as the ovaries, the testes, the thyroid, and the adrenal glands. The ovaries and testes are sex glands, or gonads. They produce our reproductive hormones: estrogen and progesterone for the ovaries, testosterone for the testes. The thyroid gland produces thyroid hormones that are important for metabolism.

The *adrenal glands* produce hormones that are critical for responding to stressful situations. As shown in **Figure 4-8**, the hypothalamus, pituitary, and adrenals work together in a system called the *hypothalamic-pituitary-adrenal (HPA) axis*, which is an important component of the stress response. The HPA axis works in concert with activation of the sympathetic nervous system to maximize our chances of survival under adverse conditions.

Our hormones not only affect organs and muscles throughout the body, they also provide feedback and interact with the brain. Hormones of the ovaries, testes, thyroid, and adrenals are small molecules that readily cross the blood-brain barrier. In the brain, one of their major actions is to provide a negative feedback signal. For example, when high enough levels of adrenal stress hormones (called *glucocorticoids* or *cortisol* in humans) reach the hypothalamus, they provide a feedback signal to stop further stimulation to the HPA axis. In addition to their actions in negative feedback, hormones of the ovaries, testes, thyroid, and adrenals have been shown to influence the functioning of our neurons as well as biochemistry and growth, both during development and in adulthood. Thus, the appropriate control of the pituitary releasing factors by the anterior pituitary is critical for numerous functions.

Like the anterior pituitary, the posterior pituitary is also connected to the hypothalamus, this time by a bundle of axons. The parts of the hypothalamus that communicate with the posterior pituitary do so by sending nerve impulses to the posterior pituitary. The posterior pituitary also plays a role in the endocrine system. Activation of the posterior pituitary leads to the release of hormones called *neuropeptides* into

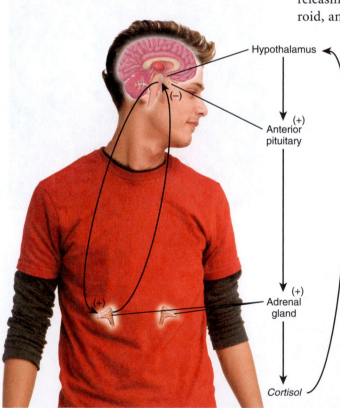

Hypothalamus
(−)
(+)
Anterior pituitary
Negative feedback (−)
(+)
Adrenal gland
(+)
Cortisol

FIGURE 4-8 **The hypothalamic-pituitary-adrenal (HPA) axis** In response to stress, the HPA axis is activated. The hypothalamus produces a hormone that stimulates the anterior pituitary to release another hormone into the blood stream. The adrenal gland then releases the stress hormone cortisol. Cortisol travels to the brain and shuts off the HPA axis via negative feedback.

the blood stream. These hormones are *oxytocin,* important for nursing, and *vasopression,* important in regulating blood pressure. Oxytocin and vasopressin are also produced by neurons within the rest of the brain, where they act as *neuromodulators,* chemicals that work at the synapse to modify the actions of neurotransmitters. Brain oxytocin and vasopressin have been implicated in social behavior, including pair bonding and parental care, as well as in stress responses (Donaldson & Young, 2008).

The Amygdala

The **amygdala** is located deep within the brain, in a region referred to as the temporal lobe. Like the thalamus and hypothalamus, the amygdala is not a homogeneous structure. Instead, it is a collection of nuclei that serve different functions. The amygdala is involved in recognizing, learning about, and responding to stimuli that induce fear (LeDoux, 2007). This brain region has been the focus of considerable attention by neuroscientists because it may be involved in the development of phobias, or abnormal fears. In addition, the amygdala has been implicated in processing information about more positive emotions.

The Hippocampus

The amygdala communicates with the **hippocampus**, a brain region important for certain types of learning and memory. Neuroscientists have extensively studied individuals with damage to the hippocampus and found that they are incapable of forming new *episodic* memories, or memories about events (described in more detail in Chapter 8). Destruction of the hippocampus in adulthood doesn't wipe out all memories of early life or one's identity, merely those that occurred relatively close to the time of brain damage. This suggests that the hippocampus only temporarily stores information about events (Squire et al., 2004). In addition to its role in the formation and transient storage of episodic memories, the hippocampus is important for learning about one's spatial environment. Learning how to navigate around a new campus, for instance, requires the hippocampus. Animal research shows that the hippocampus has neurons called "*place cells*" that show changes in activity only when the animal is located in a specific location in space (Moser et al., 2008). Unlike the situation for the temporary role of the hippocampus in episodic memory, the hippocampus seems to retain its critical role in the storage of spatial navigation information for a long time, perhaps an entire lifetime.

The hippocampus doesn't consist of well-delineated collections of neurons or nuclei. Instead, it is organized in regions and layers. Because of the layered structure of the hippocampus, neuroscientists have been able to both record from and stimulate individual parts of the hippocampus, so that much of the function and connectivity of this brain region has been studied. The hippocampus is a major site of plasticity, or the ability of neurons to change, as we described earlier. Neurons in the hippocampus show both synaptic and structural plasticity. In fact, it is a region known to produce entirely new neurons in adulthood (Gould, 2007, Cameron & McKay, 2001). The function of these new neurons remains unknown, but their presence suggests that the adult brain is capable of regenerative processes, and furthermore, that the process of neuron birth, or neurogenesis (which we discuss in more detail later in this chapter), may be harnessed for purposes of brain repair. We will return to the hippocampus at length when we discuss learning and memory in Chapters 7 and 8.

The Striatum

Located more toward the midline of the brain are the **striatum** and its related structures. This brain region works with the substantia nigra to produce fluid movements, such as those needed to hit the buzzer as a *Jeopardy!* contestant. Damage to either of these brain

The amygdala in action The amygdala processes the stimuli that elicit fear, such as when one is out alone on a dark night.

hypothalamus brain structure important for motivation and control of the endocrine system.

endocrine system the system that controls levels of hormones throughout the body.

pituitary gland brain structure that plays a central role in controlling the endocrine system.

amygdala brain area involved in processing information about emotions, particularly fear.

hippocampus brain region important for certain types of learning and memory.

striatum a brain area that works with the substantia nigra to enable fluid movements.

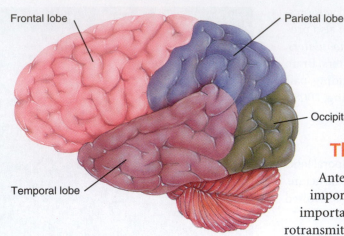

Frontal lobe

Parietal lobe

Occipital lobe

Temporal lobe

FIGURE 4-9 **The lobes of the neocortex** The neocortex can be subdivided into four lobes—frontal, parietal, occipital, and temporal.

regions produces a collection of debilitating motor symptoms, such as uncontrollable shaking. In addition to its role in movement, the striatum is important for certain types of learning and memory (Grahn et al., 2008), namely those that do not require conscious awareness. As we will see in the later chapters on learning and memory, we learn some information unintentionally and often are unaware that learning has occurred. Under some circumstances, this ability involves the striatum.

The Nucleus Accumbens

Anterior to the striatum is a brain region called the **nucleus accumbens**, an area important for motivation and reward learning (Goto & Grace, 2008). It receives important projections from neurons in the midbrain that use dopamine as a neurotransmitter. Dopamine release in the nucleus accumbens has been associated with reward learning and has been implicated in drug abuse (Nestler, 2004).

All of the above-mentioned brain regions are collectively referred to as *subcortical* because they are located beneath the largest and most complex part of the human brain: the neocortex.

The Neocortex

The human neocortex is huge, much too large to fit in the skull if it were stretched out. This is the reason why the human brain is all folded on the surface. The neocortex has many convolutions or folds that enable it to cram a large number of neurons into a head small enough to be supported by the human neck.

The **neocortex** is highly developed in humans and is responsible for many of our most complex behaviors, including language and thought. Although some of the functions of neocortical regions are not well understood, there is consensus among neuroscientists that within the neocortex, there is localization of function. This means that certain parts of the neocortex are important for specific behaviors or abilities.

At the most macroscopic level, the neocortex can be subdivided into four different parts or *lobes*, as shown in **Figure 4-9**: occipital, temporal, parietal and frontal. Within each of these regions, there are two major classifications:

Parallel processing Air traffic controllers must react to an array of sensory stimuli and make quick decisions. Communication among the association cortex within and between the lobes of the brain allows us to perform such complex functions simultaneously.

1. *Primary sensory and/or motor areas.* These areas are responsible for processing basic information about the senses as well as for producing signals that lead to voluntary movement. As we will see, many of the primary sensory and motor parts of the neocortex process information related to the opposite, or *contralateral*, side of the body.

2. *Association cortex.* **Association cortex** in each region is responsible for many complex functions, including higher-order sensory processing, integrating information from different senses (how you know that an object that looks like a violin is producing the music), thinking, planning, and other complex functions.

The Occipital Cortex The **occipital cortex**, the cortical area at the back of the skull, contains primary sensory regions important for processing very basic information about visual stimuli, such as orientation and lines. As shown in **Figure 4-10**, visual information arrives in the occipital cortex via partially crossed connections. The visual information from each eye that is closest to the midline between the two eyes is actually projected to the opposite side of the brain. As a result, the representation of your left visual field is on your right primary visual cortex, and vice versa.

Association areas in the occipital cortex integrate information about color, complex patterns, and motion. Since vision is such an important sense for primates, the occipital

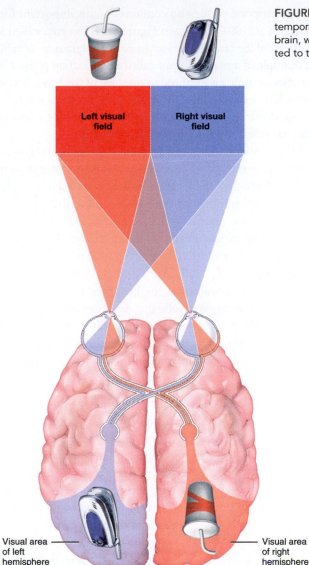

FIGURE 4-10 **The visual system is a partially crossed pathway** Visual cues from the temporal (toward the side) part of the visual field are sent to the opposite side of the brain, while those of the medial (toward the nose) part of the visual field are transmitted to the same side of the brain.

Left visual field

Right visual field

Visual area of left hemisphere

Visual area of right hemisphere

cortex is very well developed in humans. Although the occipital cortex is often referred to as the visual cortex, it's important to realize that visual information is also processed in other parts of the neocortex. In fact, some estimates suggest that 50 percent of the human neocortex is devoted to some sort of visual task! Connections to other parts of the neocortex enable us to hook up visual information with information from other sensory modalities as well as with our memory stores (for example, connecting the sight of a potato chip with its smell, taste, sound when crunched, feel, and memories of having that type of food in your past). This serves as an important reminder that no brain region operates entirely on its own. Each receives input from other areas and communicates with many other regions to produce integrated responses.

The Temporal Cortex The **temporal cortex** is located on the sides of the head within the temporal lobe. It wraps around the hippocampus and amygdala. The temporal cortex includes areas important for processing information about auditory stimuli, or sounds. Abnormal electrical activity in the temporal cortex, such as what occurs with seizures or epilepsy, has been shown to result in auditory hallucinations. People who have epileptic seizures centered in this region sometimes "hear" in their minds very loud music during seizures. Neurosurgery to remove a region causing seizures is particularly dangerous in this part of the brain since there are so many critical functions that may be disrupted.

nucleus accumbens a brain area important for motivation and reward.

neocortex the largest portion of the brain, responsible for complex behaviors including language and thought.

association cortex areas of the neocortex responsible for complex functions, including higher-order sensory processing, thinking, and planning.

occipital cortex lobe of the neocortex at the back of the skull, important for processing very visual information.

temporal cortex part of the neocortex important in processing sounds, in speech comprehension, and in recognizing complex visual stimuli, such as faces.

For instance, the temporal cortex also contains regions important for language comprehension (Damasio et al., 2004). Shown in **Figure 4-11**, this area, called **Wernicke's area**, is located on the left side of the brain in the vast majority of humans (over 90 percent). (This is a good example of a phenomenon called *lateralization of function,* which means that the particular ability is localized to one side of the brain. We will return to this general issue later in the chapter.) Wernicke's area communicates with other areas, including a region located in another cortical area important for the recognition of appropriate syntax (language rules) and the production of speech.

In addition to the temporal cortex involvement in hearing and language comprehension, this lobe plays important roles in learning and memory as well as in recognition of objects via visual cues. Regions of the temporal cortex respond to complex visual stimuli, such as faces (Gross, 2005). Neuroimaging studies have shown that parts of this brain region are activated when people view photos of faces, particularly those of familiar faces. These findings are strengthened by the fact that recording electrodes placed into these same brain regions show changes in neuronal activity, or firing rate, when the same complex visual stimuli are presented (Seeck et al., 1993). At first consideration, the presence of neurons that respond to faces in the temporal cortex might suggest that direct projections from the eye activate a set of cells in the temporal lobe that are programmed to respond to complex visual stimuli. This is not the case though. The "face cells" in the temporal cortex respond to faces because they receive inputs from visual areas in the occipital cortex as well as memory centers in the brain, allowing for the recognition of faces previously seen.

The Parietal Cortex The **parietal cortex** is localized on the top middle of the brain. The primary sensory parts of this cortical region are critical for processing information about touch or somatosensory stimuli: our senses of touch, pressure, vibration, and pain. The parietal cortex contains a region known as the **somatosensory strip**, a band of cortex that processes tactile information about different body parts. As **Figure 4-12** shows, this area of the brain forms a systematic body map, but one in which some parts of the body are represented more than others. For instance, somatosensory information about the lips (which are particularly sensitive) occupies a greater amount of cortex than does somatosensory information about the elbow.

In addition, the parietal cortex plays an important role in the higher-order processing of visual stimuli. As we will see in Chapter 5 on sensation and perception, processing visual stimuli involves localizing visual cues in space. The parietal cortex contains a system known as the "where pathway" that enables us to see and respond to visual information in a spatially appropriate way. People with damage to the "where pathway" can find it impossible to pour water from a pitcher into a glass. This deficiency is not due to a motor disturbance, but rather to an inability to properly determine where the glass is located relative to the pitcher.

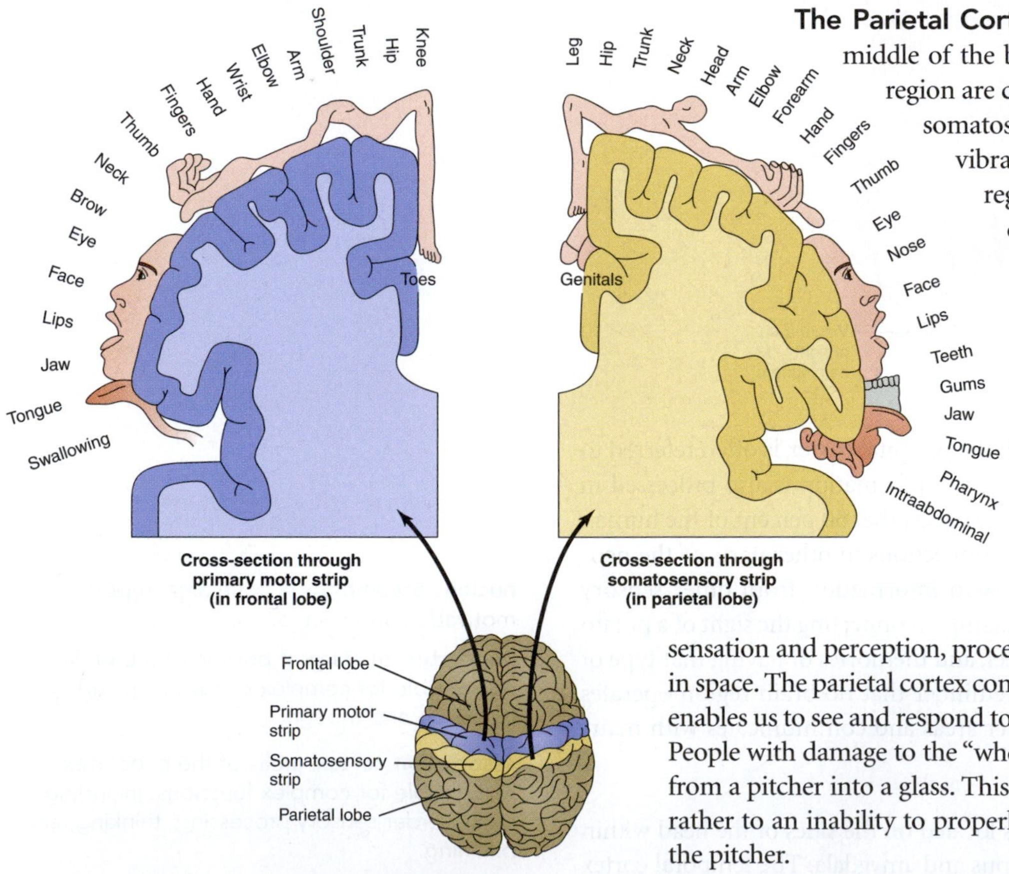

The Frontal Cortex Located at the front of the brain (behind the forehead) is the **frontal cortex**. The frontal cortex is a relatively large cortical region and is proportionately larger in humans compared to less complex animals. Like the other cortical regions, however, the frontal cortex is not just one area, but a large collection of regions that serve numerous functions. The frontal cortex is important for planning and movement. Voluntary movements begin in the frontal cortex, in a part referred to as the *primary motor strip,* also

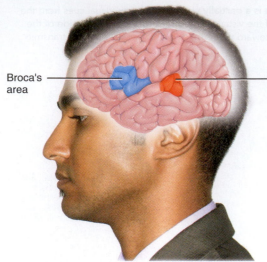

Broca's area

Wernicke's area

FIGURE 4-11 Major brain regions important for speech production and language comprehension Broca's area, located in the frontal lobe, is critical for speaking and Wernicke's area, located in the temporal lobe, is critical for understanding language.

Shoulder, Trunk, Hip, Knee, Arm, Elbow, Wrist, Hand, Fingers, Thumb, Neck, Brow, Eye, Face, Lips, Jaw, Tongue, Swallowing, Toes

Cross-section through primary motor strip (in frontal lobe)

Leg, Hip, Trunk, Neck, Head, Arm, Elbow, Forearm, Hand, Fingers, Thumb, Eye, Nose, Face, Lips, Teeth, Gums, Jaw, Tongue, Pharynx, Intraabdominal, Genitals

Cross-section through somatosensory strip (in parietal lobe)

Frontal lobe
Primary motor strip
Somatosensory strip
Parietal lobe

FIGURE 4-12 Motor and sensory cortices are organized according to body parts Areas of motor cortex that control the movement of specific body parts and those of somatosensory cortex that receive tactile information are grouped according to body parts. Some regions are overrepresented, including the mouth and hands.

shown in Figure 4-12. For a long time it has been known that stimulation of different parts of the primary motor strip invokes movement in specific groups of muscles. However, recent research suggests that parts of motor cortex are not just involved in contracting specific muscles but in coordinating the use of these muscles in complex movements (Graziano, 2006). In addition to its role in controlling movement, the frontal cortex contains a region called **Broca's area**, which is critical for speech production. Individuals with damage to this region, or to the connections between Wernicke's and Broca's area, find it impossible to generate speech, despite normal language comprehension.

The part of the frontal cortex closest to the front of the head is referred to as the **prefrontal cortex** and it is important for a large number of functions. Among them is short-term memory or working memory (Soto et al., 2008). When you call information for a phone number and hold that number in your mind while you dial, you are using your prefrontal cortex. In addition, when you execute complex plans, such as planning and hosting a party or creating a *Jeopardy!* strategy, you are using your prefrontal cortex.

FIGURE 4-13 After the accident Phineas Gage holds the railroad spike that impaled his brain (left). A reconstruction shows how the spike likely entered Gage's head, damaging the frontal cortex (right). After the accident, Gage's personality drastically changed.

Moral reasoning (discussed in Chapter 3) has also been localized, at least in part, to a component of the prefrontal cortex. Children with damage to the prefrontal cortex can have difficulty understanding ethical principles despite normal IQ (Anderson et al., 1999). The prefrontal cortex has also been implicated in some aspects of mood regulation. Studies have shown that individuals with a positive outlook on life tend to have more activity on one side of their prefrontal cortex (Urry et al., 2004).

One of the earliest examples of localization of function involved an individual with damage to the prefrontal cortex. In the mid-1800s, a railroad worker named Phineas Gage experienced severe brain damage when a metal railroad spike penetrated his frontal lobes during an explosion (**Figure 4-13**). Gage miraculously recovered physically, but those who knew him previously reported that his personality was never the same again. Once a mild-mannered individual, Gage became hot-tempered and prone to outbursts of anger. Stories such as this, as well as some experimental data, led to the suggestion that the prefrontal cortex is important for personality. Such claims, which do have some basis but were perhaps overstated, led to the development of a once popular procedure called a *prefrontal lobotomy* that was used to treat individuals with problems ranging from severe mental illness to nonconformity and rebellion (Heller et al., 2006). Due to the lack of scientific basis and the side effects of its application, this surgery has (appropriately) fallen out of fashion. However, more limited destruction of the prefrontal cortex is still used for a small number of patients suffering from severe depression or other forms of mental illness who do not respond to drug therapy (Abosch & Cosgrove, 2008).

The four general regions of the neocortex can be further subdivided into many areas, which serve different functions and have different neural connections. However, all parts of the neocortex share some neuroanatomical features. The neocortex consists of six layers, whether occipital, temporal, parietal, or frontal. Although some variations exist in the composition of the layers across regions, in general, the output neurons (those that project to subcortical structures) are located in the deepest layers.

The Corpus Callosum

Communication from one side of the neocortex to the other occurs via a bundle of axons that make up a large structure called the **corpus callosum**, shown in **Figure 4-14**.

The corpus callosum appears to connect two relatively equal halves of the brain, called **hemispheres**, but the brain is actually not completely symmetrical, nor do the hemispheres work quite the way you might expect. For instance, you might expect the right hemisphere to control things that happen on the right half of the body, and

Wernicke's area an area of the temporal cortex important in helping us understand language.

parietal cortex lobe of the neocortex involved in processing information related to touch and complex visual information, particularly about locations.

somatosensory strip an area of the parietal cortex that processes tactile information coming from our body parts.

frontal cortex lobe of the neocortex involved in many functions including movement and speech production.

Broca's area brain region located in the frontal lobe that's important for speech production.

prefrontal cortex portion of the frontal cortex involved in higher-order thinking, such as memory, moral reasoning, and planning.

corpus callosum bundle of axons that allows communication from one side of neocortex to the other.

hemispheres halves of the brain.

A popular claim about brain function is that we only use a small fraction of our brains while the rest lies dormant. Many claim that we could transcend what we commonly consider human limitations if we could only tap into the potential of this large, "unused" percentage of the brain. The idea that we only use 10 percent of our brain is false and has no support at all in the scientific literature of today. In fact, scientists have shown that large parts of our brains are activated at all times, both during wakefulness and sleep.

The myth that we use very little of our brains was probably based, in part, on neuroscience studies done by the psychologist Karl Lashley in the early part of the 20th century (Lashley, 1929). Lashley showed that rats could learn some mazes even after very large parts of their brains had been removed. Those who supported this myth also pointed out that in some instances, large parts of the brain can be damaged in humans with little functional deficit; people with major brain damage often seem "as good as new."

It's important to consider that although a brain region may not be critical for solving a maze or carrying out another task, it may be active nonetheless. Neuroimaging studies have shown that even when humans engage in relatively simple tasks, such as pressing an elevator button, visual, motor, memory, and attention areas are activated. Thus, people without brain damage actually are using large areas of the brain in these tasks (Bédard & Sanes, 2009), even though we could get along without some of those regions if we had to.

Some of us may seem at times to be using only 10 percent of the abilities but how *well* we are putting our brains to use is a whole other question. The research is clear about the brain's activity: Most of the brain is active, much of the time.

---

the left to control the left. Things are not that simple, however. There are many crossed connections to and from the primary cortex, leading to asymmetries, or differences in function between the hemispheres. Input from our visual, auditory, and somatosensory systems is at least partially crossed, for example. The left part of somatosensory cortex receives tactile input from the right part of the body and vice versa. Crossed connections also contribute to asymmetries in the primary motor cortex. The left part of the primary motor cortex controls movement on the right part of the brain and vice versa. Furthermore, as we describe later in this chapter, not everybody's hemispheres are the same. There are some fascinating individual differences in the two halves of our brain.

A treatment sometimes used when people have severe epilepsy is to sever the corpus callosum, to stop the spread of seizures from one side of the brain to the other. People who have undergone this surgery are called *split-brain patients*. These patients are normal in many respects, but they lack the ability to integrate information from the two hemispheres (Gazzaniga, 2005). Studies on these patients have highlighted the fact that the two hemispheres need the corpus callosum to communicate. Preventing this can sometimes result in one part of the brain acting in opposition to the other.

The Integrated Brain

It's important to remember that many of the above mentioned brain areas, including the cortical regions, can be subdivided into multiple areas or nuclei, each of which is involved in different functions. However, no brain region works alone. To process information, integrate it with previous information, and then to formulate and execute a reaction requires neural circuitry undoubtedly not contained within a single brain region. For example, a person whose brain contained only a hippocampus would not be able to store information about anything because it would lack the sensory pathways necessary to provide stimuli about events or the spatial environment. Understanding how a brain region works requires sophisticated knowledge about information that flows into the area, that which flows out of the areas, and of course, the important computations that occur within the neurons of that given brain region.

Corpus Callosum

FIGURE 4-14 The corpus callosum This cross section of the human brain shows the large bundle of axons that allows communication between the two hemispheres.

What Do You Know?

14. Which part of the brain is essential to basic functioning, such as breathing?

15. Describe the role of the brain in regulating hormones throughout the body.

16. Which part of the brain has been linked with our fear responses?

17. What behavior is most closely linked to the hippocampus?

18. Which of our senses is linked primarily with the occipital cortex? Which with the temporal cortex? Which with the parietal cortex?

19. What are the primary functions of Broca's and Wernicke's areas, and where are they located?

20. What mental functions are associated with the frontal cortex?

21. How do the two hemispheres of the brain communicate, and how are functions distributed between the two?

What Do You Think? What are the potential pitfalls in making inferences about brain function from studying a single brain area?

Building the Brain | How we *Develop*

LEARNING OBJECTIVE 6 Describe the processes of neurogenesis, synaptogenesis, and programmed cell death, and their role during development and throughout the lifespan.

Development of the nervous system begins during the embryonic phase of prenatal life, before we are born, and continues throughout the lifespan.

Brain Development Before We Are Born

Embryos have three layers of rather undefined tissue that later specialize to become all of our recognizable body parts. Nervous tissue originates from one of the layers, called the *ectoderm*. A portion of the ectoderm thickens and eventually folds to form a tube called the **neural tube**. As cells lining the wall of the neural tube divide and produce more cells, eventually the process of *differentiation* begins. Differentiation refers to the achievement of characteristics specific to a certain type of cell—in this case a neuron. The production of new neurons is called **neurogenesis**.

Young neurons are born near the center of the neural tube and migrate away from their birthplaces to create new brain regions, as shown in **Figure 4-15**. The migrating young neurons can travel in several different ways, including moving along the specialized glia called *radial glia* (Marín & Rubenstein, 2003). They can also move along axons of other neurons that have already been formed or travel through the extracellular space itself.

As these new neurons take up residence in areas where certain brain regions are forming, they grow axons and dendrites and quickly make synaptic contact with other neurons. The process of forming new synapses is called **synaptogenesis**. Gradually, through neurogenesis and synaptogenesis, a young brain is formed with many functions, including hearing and touch, working before we are even born.

It seems most intuitive that brain development would require mostly constructive processes—a new brain needs to synthesize new neurons and those new neurons need to make dendrites, axons, and synapses. However, neuroscientists were surprised to find that destructive cellular events are just as important for brain development as are constructive events. As we described in Chapter 3, during development, our brains overproduced neurons in large numbers. The extra, unused neurons are culled, through a process called *programmed cell death* (Levi-Montalcini, 1988). In some brain regions, cell death claims the lives of over three-fourths of the neurons originally produced by the brain.

Why would the brain waste so much energy making neurons only to kill them off? The answer seems to be that producing a large number of neurons will insure that a

neural tube area of an embryo from which the CNS arises.

neurogenesis the production of new neurons.

synaptogenesis the process of forming new synapses.

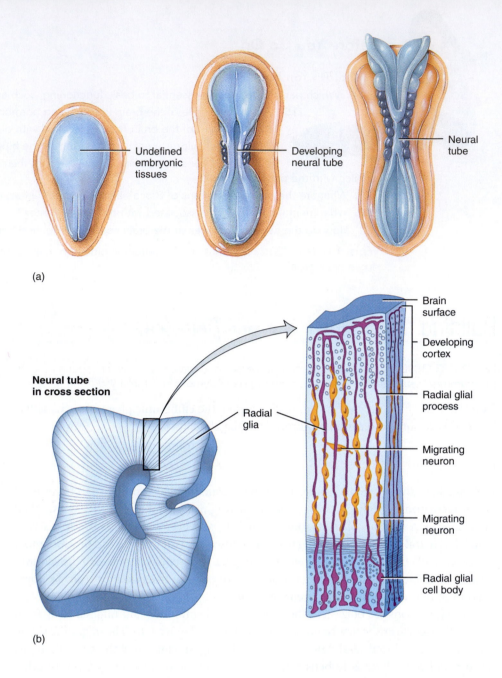

FIGURE 4-15 How the nervous system develops
(a) The brain and spinal cord originate from the embryonic neural tube. (b) Neurons are born in tissue that surrounds the central canal (the ventricle) and migrate away from the center to build the CNS.

(a)

Undefined embryonic tissues

Developing neural tube

Neural tube

Neural tube in cross section

Radial glia

Brain surface

Developing cortex

Radial glial process

Migrating neuron

Migrating neuron

Radial glial cell body

(b)

reasonable number make appropriate connections. Those that fail to make the needed connections ultimately die. Developmental cell death is special because it involves the activation of a program of suicide genes within the neuron itself (Steller, 1995). Importantly, it does not trigger any inflammation or reactive events as occurs with other types of cell death as a result of trauma. For example, developmental cell death does not attract microglia or *astroglia*, nor does it lead to the formation of a glial scar. This insures that the young neurons that did not make the cut were eliminated without wreaking havoc on the brain region.

Of those neurons that survive, most undergo some form of regressive structural remodeling before development is complete. That is, many neurons initially develop more dendrites and synapses, or more elaborate axons, than they will eventually need. Only those that are necessary and make appropriate connections survive (Luo & O'Leary, 2005). The rest are retracted and reabsorbed, so that in the long-term, the brain spends energy only on those circuits that work most efficiently.

Brain Development Across the Lifespan

For humans, many of the cellular events, such as neurogenesis, neuronal migration, dendrite formation, axon extension, synaptogenesis, and their regressive counterparts that take place before birth, reflect the unfolding of a preprogrammed, maturational plan that can only be altered by toxic influences, such as the ingestion of drugs or alcohol by a pregnant woman. Although there are some interesting exceptions, presented in Chapters 5 and 7, that describe evidence for fetal sensation and learning, our brains are generally much more open to being physically shaped by our experiences after we are born than before. Both progressive and regressive developmental events occur after birth, too—these are affected by experience. For example, our experiences may determine which synapses are maintained and which are pruned during infancy and childhood.

Other events, such as myelination, occur at different time points in our development, depending on the brain region. As described in Chapter 3, myelination in humans occurs mostly after we are born. It begins relatively rapidly in some of the primary sensory areas and continues through late adolescence or early adulthood. Myelination of the prefrontal cortex, for example, is not finished until after puberty, which may explain why adolescents are generally less efficient at planning and executing complex behaviors than are adults.

You may think that developmental events in the nervous system stop once you became an adult. In fact, a very common myth about the brain is that you have all of the neurons you will ever have once you are born and any that die cannot be replaced. Neuroscientists have recently overturned this fallacy by showing that some populations of neurons continue to be produced well into adulthood (Gould, 2007).

As discussed earlier in this chapter, a brain region that exhibits substantial neurogenesis in adulthood is the hippocampus (Cameron & McKay, 2001). Adult neurogenesis may be important for the functions of the hippocampus, which as we saw earlier, is involved in learning and memory (Leuner et al., 2006). Although still a controversial issue, it is possible that the plastic nature of new neurons may provide the substrate needed for us to change as a result of our experiences, in other words, to learn.

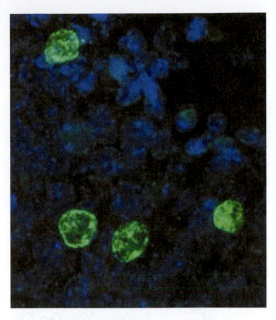

New neurons (green), shown here in this fluorescent photomicrograph, are produced in the hippocampus of adult mammals, including humans.

Dying Cells in a New Brain?

Early neuroanatomists studied growth and development of the nervous systems in a variety of species. One important developmental phenomenon they overlooked, however, was the role of cell death in sculpting the brain. It wasn't until the 1940s that an Italian medical doctor, Rita Levi-Montalcini, began investigating this possibility.

Ousted from her post at the Turin medical school during World War II because she was Jewish, Levi-Montalcini made a discovery that changed how we view brain development and eventually led to a Nobel Prize. Though she was under constant threat of deportation and death, Levi-Montalcini continued to study neural development in her apartment, using fertilized eggs from a nearby farm as her experimental animal. Through careful microscopic work, she was the first to discover that neurons are overproduced during development and that neural circuits are sculpted by cell death, as we described in this chapter.

She was also able to determine which neurons were most likely to survive. The survival of a new neuron, she found, was critically dependent on whether or not that neuron made contact with an appropriate target site. Levi-Montalcini found that amputating a limb bud from a developing chick embryo resulted in the survival of fewer motor neurons, whereas grafting an extra limb to a developing chick embryo led to the survival of more neurons.

Levi-Montalcini eventually made it to the United States where she was the first to identify trophic factors, the chemicals that promote neuron growth. In 1986 she was awarded the Nobel Prize in Medicine (Levi-Montalcini, 1988). She later returned to Italy, where she continues her active life, serving in the Italian Senate past the age of 100.

In addition to the incorporation of entirely new neurons into pre-existing neural circuits, the adult brain also shows evidence of ongoing dendritic remodeling (McEwen, 2001) and synaptogenesis, or forming of new synapses (Cooke & Woolley, 2005). Although evidence for these changes was first observed decades ago, using traditional methods of examining brain sections under the microscope, recent studies using genetically-engineered mice with fluorescent neurons have allowed researchers to examine and determine the size and shape of individual neurons in live animals through transparent windows implanted into their skulls. These studies have confirmed the earlier reports by showing that dendrites and synapses change in shape, size, and number throughout adult life (Knott et al., 2006).

The extent to which this structural plasticity contributes to normal brain function remains unknown, but its occurrence indicates that the adult brain is not a rigid, static place. Researchers studying structural plasticity in the adult brain hope that identifying the mechanisms controlling these events may someday help us to actually change the shape and connections of neurons in order to repair circuits that are abnormal as a result of brain damage or birth defects.

Before You Go On

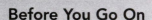

What Do You Know?

22. How are neurons formed before we are born?
23. What is synaptogenesis? Does it ever stop?

What Do You Think? What advantages does cell death have for the developing brain?

Brain Side and Brain Size HOW weDiffer

LEARNING OBJECTIVE 7 Explain the neuroscience evidence about brain lateralization and the significance of brain size.

You may have heard popular theories about "left-brained" or "right-brained" types of people, or jokes about the female brain versus the male brain. Neuroscience tells us that, although the importance of them may be exaggerated in the public mind, there are, indeed, some differences among the brains of different groups of individuals.

Differences in Brain Lateralization

In most people, there are some parts of cortex that exist only on one side of the brain. Wernicke's and Broca's areas related to speech and language, for example, are on the left side of most people's brains; but not everybody's. The exceptions occur most often in left-handed individuals. Left-handers are more likely to have these language areas located on the right side of their brains or on both sides, than are right-handers, suggesting that lateralization of more than one function (handedness and language) may be linked in some way.

In addition to these rather clear-cut functional and anatomical asymmetries, many people believe that more general thought processes are lateralized, such that people who think a certain way are using proportionately more of one side of their brain than they are the other side. Although this remains controversial, the "word on the street" is that individuals who rely heavily on their right brain are more likely to be creative and use abstract reasoning and imagery to solve problems. This side of the brain is thought to

"Can the brain understand the brain?"
—*David Hubel, neuroscientist and Nobel laureate in medicine*

be dominant in artists and engineers. By contrast, the left side of the brain is thought to be dominant in individuals with strong analytical and verbal skills. This distinction has been so popularized that it's difficult to separate fact from fiction.

What then is the scientific evidence for "right-brain" and "left-brain" dominant thinking? Neuroscientists have been able to temporarily inactivate one hemisphere, by infusing drugs into the circulatory system that feeds that side of the brain, in order to determine which functions are affected most and fastest. Another way neuroscientists study the hemispheres is by taking advantage of the fact that part of the visual field of each eye crosses over to the opposite side of the brain. Researchers can present visual stimuli to only one hemisphere by requiring the participant to fixate on a point and/or use a special contact lens. They then ask participants to complete a task using just one side of the brain.

Studies such as these have shown that the right-brain–left-brain dichotomy is only a general theme, and there are notable exceptions. For instance, the right brain, which is typically believed to excel at spatial perceptual tasks, is actually less accurate at making some spatial perceptual distinctions, such as determining the location of objects in relation to one another. Overall, the research shows that, aside from the language areas noted above, the two hemispheres are more similar than they are different. Indeed, even when right-left differences are detected in function, these differences are usually relative. For example, the left brain can accomplish what the right brain can accomplish, it's just less efficient at some tasks and more efficient at others.

Gender Differences

On average, the brains of women are smaller than those of men. Does this mean men are smarter than women? It does not. The overall size of the brain appears to be more closely related to the size of the body than to function. In fact, a relationship between

> "What it comes down to is that modern society discriminates against the right hemisphere."
>
> —*Roger Sperry, neuroscientist and Nobel laureate in medicine*

PRACTICALLYSPEAKING — How Can You Prevent Age-Related Decline in Brain Function?

A common adage used today with regard to the aging brain is "Use it or lose it!" Stories in the media encourage aging individuals to keep their brains active by spending time on crossword puzzles, Sudoku, or other brainteasers. Some companies have even developed and marketed brain puzzles they claim are specifically designed to keep the brain agile and prevent declines in a wide range of general cognitive abilities, such as day-to-day problem solving and memory.

Unfortunately, the scientific evidence available does not support these claims. While it's true that people with a higher level of education and also those with multiple interests and socially active lives seem somewhat protected from age-related cognitive dysfunction (Perneczky et al., 2008), there is no evidence that engaging in brain puzzles is beneficial for any purpose other than making you better at solving similar brain puzzles! In other words, mastery of these tasks does not generalize to overall cognitive performance.

One type of experience, however, that does seem to make a difference in cognitive performance is physical exercise. In humans, aerobic exercise increases blood flow to the brain, improves performance on cognitive tasks, and elevates mood (Pereira et al., 2007). Studies in experimental animals have shown that physical exercise increases the birth of new neurons in the hippocampus and also stimulates the growth of neurons in general throughout brain structures that support cognitive function (Stranahan et al., 2006; 2007).

So add protection of your brain to the list of other reasons of why it's a good idea to hit the gym regularly. There's good scientific evidence to support this claim!

brain size and intelligence doesn't exist, except at the two ends of the spectrum; people with abnormally small or abnormally large brains are both more likely to exhibit mental deficiencies than those with brains whose size falls in the normal range.

In addition to the overall size difference, researchers have reported some differences in the size of certain brain regions in humans. For example, part of the corpus callosum, connecting the two hemispheres of the brain, has been shown to be larger in women (Johnson et al., 1994). This finding has contributed to the much-overstated suggestion that women are more likely to use both sides of their brains than men are. Even in cases where differences have been reported in the size of brain regions, the overall differences between men and women are very small, so much so that they really don't tell us much about the individual person of either gender. An exception to this exists in the hypothalamus where certain nuclei that control the release of reproductive hormones differ in men and women.

Before You Go On

What Do You Know?

24. What does research show about "right-brained" creative thinking versus "left-brained" analytical thinking?
25. On which side of the brain do most people have their language-related areas? What about left-handed people?
26. Does overall brain size matter in how well brains function?

What Do You Think?
What are some of the ethical problems associated with searching for structural differences in the brains of different groups of people?

Neurological Diseases When Things Go Wrong

> "All the most acute, most powerful, and most deadly diseases, and those which are most difficult to be understood by the inexperienced, fall upon the brain."
>
> —Hippocrates, 4th century B.C.E.
> Greek philospher

LEARNING OBJECTIVE 8 Describe four neurological disorders and the current directions in research for treating them.

In general, diseases of the nervous system can be divided into two broad classes characterized by the type of physician designated to care for the patient. These classes are psychiatric illnesses and neurological illnesses. In the case of psychiatric illnesses, such as depression and schizophrenia, the underlying problem is often thought of as primarily a biochemical or neurotransmitter imbalance. In the case of neurological illnesses, such as Parkinson's disease and Alzheimer's disease (discussed in Chapter 8), the main problem is thought to be structural, generally involving the degeneration of neurons. Although there is certainly overlap between these two classes of brain diseases (for instance, people with depression are known to have a smaller hippocampus (Sheline et al., 2003) and people with Parkinson's disease have a deficiency in the neurotransmitter dopamine (Jankovic & Aguilar, 2008), this general distinction holds true. Because psychiatric diseases are taken up in other chapters of this book, we will focus here on some key neurological diseases:

- **Multiple sclerosis** involves demyelination, or loss of myelin, on the axons of neurons. This leads to the inefficient transmission of electrical information among neurons and a range of symptoms, including vision loss, pain, and muscle weakness, depending on where the demyelination occurs. Research on multiple sclerosis has focused on finding ways to stimulate myelination (Franklin & Ffrench-Constant, 2008).

- **Amyotrophic lateral sclerosis** (ALS or Lou Gehrig's disease, so-named after a famous athlete who had the illness) is another condition that affects movement.

People with ALS experience degeneration of motor neurons in the spinal cord. The symptoms of this disease begin with localized muscle weakness and ultimately, the entire body is afflicted. People with ALS typically die when the motor neurons that control basic functions, including breathing, die.

Interestingly, some populations of motor neurons appear to be more resistant to ALS than others. Examples of the resistant populations include the cells that control eye movements (Laslo et al., 2001) and those that are involved in motor control of the anus and genitals (Mannen et al., 1982). Investigators are studying these neuron groups to determine whether molecular differences between vulnerable and resistant populations of cells can be used to stimulate protective mechanisms in motor neurons that degenerate in this devastating disease.

- **Parkinson's disease** is a neurological condition that involves the death of dopaminergic neurons—those that rely on the neurotransmitter dopamine—in the substantia nigra. Patients with this condition often have a tremor in their hands and muscle rigidity. Parkinson's disease can have many different causes and affects a relatively large percentage of the population. In most cases, however the cause is not known.

  People with Parkinson's disease can be treated with drugs that replace the dopamine that is lost when the neurons in the substantia nigra die. However, this replacement is only temporary. As time passes, patients become resistant to the dopamine drugs and/or develop intolerable side effects to the drugs. Because drug therapy is only temporary and so many people suffer from the condition, scientists have spent considerable effort searching for novel therapies. Among them include the transplantation of stem cells, which can be induced to produce new neurons that make dopamine. Although these treatments are promising, there is much work to be done before they can be used routinely (Isacson & Kordower, 2008).

- **Huntington's disease** is an inherited condition that results in the death of neurons in the striatum. People suffering from this disease exhibit awkward movements and often, symptoms of psychosis (Paulsen, 2009). Like ALS and Parkinson's disease, Huntington's disease is progressive and as yet, there is no cure.

Transplanting Stem Cells to Treat Neurological Disorders

Medical and neuroscience researchers have not yet developed truly effective medicines for these devastating neurological diseases, so some neuroscientists have turned their attention to the possibility of repairing damaged brain regions by transplanting new tissue into the brain.

Early work ruled out the possibility of transplanting fully differentiated brain tissue into a damaged region. In most cases, these transplants did not survive or integrate properly into the existing circuitry. Subsequent attempts to transplant fetal brain tissue into brains of adults suffering from Alzheimer's or Parkinson's disease also met with limited, if any, success. Fetal tissue may integrate into the damaged brain, but it remains foreign and often does not function normally for extended periods of time.

Thus, transplantation research has focused primarily on the possibility of restoring damaged circuits by transplanting stem cells. **Stem cells**, as described earlier, are undifferentiated cells that have the potential to grow into any cell type if given the appropriate environmental cues. The most versatile stem cells come from embryonic tissue (Srivastava et al., 2008). Researchers have obtained stem cells from embryos created as part in vitro fertilization, a procedure sometimes used to help infertile couples have babies. Eggs are fertilized with sperm in the laboratory, and some of the resulting embryos are implanted into a woman's uterus. Remaining, or extra, embryos, at very early stages of development, can provide a source for stem cells. This source, however, is very controversial among those who question whether the embryos could be considered humans yet.

multiple sclerosis neurological disease that causes a loss of myelin on the axons of neurons.

amyotrophic lateral sclerosis (**ALS** or Lou Gehrig's disease) neurological disease that causes degeneration of motor neurons in the spinal cord, leading to loss of movement and eventual death.

Parkinson's disease neurological disease that involves the death of dopaminergic neurons in the substantia nigra, leading to tremors, muscle rigidity, and other motor problems.

Huntington's disease inherited neurological condition that results in the death of neurons in the striatum.

stem cell undifferentiated cell that can divide to replace itself and create new cells that have the potential to become all other cells of the body, including neurons.

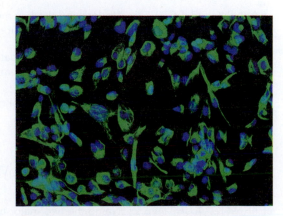

Neural stem cells shown in this microscopic image have been used to repopulate damaged brain regions. These cells can divide and produce different types of neurons depending on their environment.

Because, as we will see, stem-cell research has shown great promise, researchers are now working to find other sources of stem cells, including reproducing them from adult tissue.

Thus far, stem cell transplantation studies in animals have been successful in some cases, particularly in animal models of Parkinson's disease (Takahashi et al., 2009; Hovakimyan et al., 2008). The effectiveness of stem-cell treatment may depend on what kind of brain cell is damaged and where the damaged cells are located. For instance, Parkinson's disease arises predominantly from the death of dopaminergic neurons in the substantia nigra. Thus, restoring this population of neurons, providing they make appropriate connections and synthesize the correct neurotransmitter, is likely to repair the deficit. Other neurological diseases that cause more widespread damage might not respond as well. For example, patients with Alzheimer's disease (which we discuss in some detail in Chapter 8) lose neurons throughout their brains. The disease also causes the formation of abnormal clusters of nondegradable protein that interfere with neuronal function (Rafii & Aisen, 2009). Replacing only certain types of dead neurons may not be sufficient to overcome the widespread devastation characteristic of this disease.

Before You Go On

What Do You Know?

27. What goes wrong in the nervous system to cause multiple sclerosis, ALS, Parkinson's disease, and Huntington's disease?

28. What have neuroscientists learned to date about transplants of brain tissue as a way to treat neurological diseases?

What Do You Think?
What are the technical and ethical pitfalls stem cell researchers must contend with?

Summary

How Do Scientists Study the Nervous System?

LEARNING OBJECTIVE 1 Understand the key methods that scientists use to learn about brain anatomy and functioning.

- Neuroscientists examine autopsy tissue and patients with localized brain damage to learn about brain anatomy and brain function.
- EEGs and neuroimaging, such as PET scans and fMRI, allow us to study brain function in the living brain.

What Cells Make Up the Nervous System?

LEARNING OBJECTIVE 2 Name the two major types of cells in the nervous system, and describe the primary functions of each.

- The two major types of brain cells are neurons and glia.

- Neurons communicate with other cells by producing and sending electrochemical signals.
- Glia are involved in various functions, such as forming the blood-brain barrier, producing myelin, and clearing the brain of debris.

How Do Neurons Work?

LEARNING OBJECTIVE 3 Describe what happens when a neuron "fires," and how neurons send messages to one another.

- Communication within a neuron occurs electrically by means of the action potential, whereas communication between neurons occurs at the synapse via chemical signals called *neurotransmitters*.
- Neurotransmitters are released by the presynaptic neuron, diffuse across the synapse, and bind to receptors on the postsynaptic site.
- The response of a receiving neuron to a neurotransmitter is determined by the receptor on the postsynaptic, or receiving, neuron's membrane. Depending on the type of receptor, the postsynaptic neurons will fire or not.

How is the Nervous System Organized?

LEARNING OBJECTIVE 4   Name and describe the functions and subdivisions of the two major parts of the nervous system.

- The two major divisions of the nervous system are the central nervous system, which consists of the brain and spinal cord, and the peripheral nervous system, which consists of nerves that extend throughout the body outside the central nervous system.
- The peripheral nervous system has two divisions: the somatic nervous system, which sends information about the senses and movement, and the autonomic nervous system, which controls involuntary functions and responses to stress.
- The autonomic nervous system is divided into the sympathetic nervous system, which responds to stress, and the parasympathetic nervous systems, which is responsible for digestion and other processes that occur when the body is at rest.

Structures of the Brain

LEARNING OBJECTIVE 5   List key structures of the brain, and describe their relationships to our behavior.

- The brain can be subdivided into many regions, each of which serves one or more specialized functions.
- The brainstem participates in movement and sensation of the head and neck as well as in basic bodily functions, such as respiration and heart rate.
- The midbrain includes the substantia nigra, an area important for movement.
- The hypothalamus controls basic drives (food, drink, sex) and hormones while the thalamus serves as a relay station for sensory information on its way to the cerebral cortex.
- Many brain regions participate in different types of learning—the hippocampus is important for spatial navigation learning and learning about life's events; the amygdala is important for fear learning; the cerebellum and striatum are important for motor learning; and the nucleus accumbens is important for reward learning.
- A large part of the brain consists of the neocortex. The neocortex can be subdivided into frontal, parietal, temporal, and occipital regions. The cortex controls movement, integrates sensory information, and serves numerous cognitive functions.

Building the Brain

LEARNING OBJECTIVE 6   Describe the processes of neurogenesis, synaptogenesis, and programmed cell death, and their roles during development and throughout the lifespan.

- Cellular processes that build the brain are neurogenesis, which produces new neurons, and synaptogenesis, which forms new synaptic connections with other neurons.
- Cellular processes that sculpt or fine-tune the brain are cell death, axon retraction, and synapse elimination.
- Changes in brain structure, including neurogenesis and synaptogenesis, occur throughout life, into old age.

Brain Side and Brain Size

LEARNING OBJECTIVE 7   Explain the neuroscience evidence about brain lateralization and the significance of brain size.

- Research shows that the two hemispheres are more similar than different and that any differences are usually relative.
- Brain size appears to be related to overall body size and not to brain function.

Neurological Diseases

LEARNING OBJECTIVE 8   Describe four neurological disorders and the current directions in research for treating them.

- Multiple sclerosis involves the loss of myelin on the axons of neurons.
- In amyotrophic lateral sclerosis, the motor neurons in the spinal cord degenerate.
- Parkinson's and Huntington's diseases are primarily the result of neuronal destruction in the substantia nigra and striatum, respectively.
- Some regeneration occurs in the brain after it is injured, but repair is typically not complete and functional impairment often remains. Researchers believe transplantation of brain tissue, particularly embryonic stem cells, may provide relief for some neurological diseases.

Key Terms

CUT/ACROSS CONNECTION

What Happens in the BRAIN?

- The human brain contains about 100 billion neurons. In addition, some parts of the brain contain 10 times that many non-neuronal cells, called glia.
- If you put a recording electron into a "resting" neuron, it will read a negative charge of approximately –70 millivolts. At the peak of a neuron's action potential, the membrane charge is around +50 millivolts.
- Action potentials of neurons follow an all-or-none principle. When sufficiently stimulated, a neuron fires; otherwise, it does not.
- Synaptic spaces are about 20 nanometers wide. A nanometer is 1 billionth of a meter.
- The sympathetic nervous system is responsible for the "fight-or-flight" reaction; the parasympathetic nervous system helps control the basic functions of life, such as digestion.
- The hypothalamus helps regulate eating, drinking, sex, maternal behavior, and the endocrine system.
- Although the two halves of the brain are called *hemispheres*, the brain is not completely symmetrical.

When Things Go Wrong

- When the spinal cord is damaged and information to and from the brain interrupted, individuals become paralyzed. The higher up the damage—the closer it occurs to the brain—the larger the proportion of body affliction.
- People with damage to the frontal cortex region called *Broca's area*, cannot generate speech but can understand language.
- With some notable exceptions, psychiatric disorders (for example, clinical depression) seem tied most often to biochemical imbalances in the brain, while neurological disorders (for example, Parkinson's disease and Alzheimer's disease) seem tied to brain-structure abnormalities, including the degeneration of neurons.
- Many neuroscientists currently are trying to develop treatments for certain neurological diseases in which they restore damaged neural circuits by transplanting new tissue into those areas of the brain, particularly by transplanting stem cells—undifferentiated cells that can grow into particular cell types.

HOW we Differ

- Although the speech and language areas—Wernicke's and Broca's areas—are on the left side of most people's brains, these areas may be located on the right side or both sides for some people—particularly left-handed people.
- On average, the brains of women are smaller than those of men, although such size differences have no relationship to intelligence or other faculties.
- Some theorists believe that women are more likely than men to use both sides of their brain.

How we Develop

- Over the course of development, a process of programmed cell death, or cellular pruning, results in the death of over 75 percent of the neurons initially produced by the brain.
- Our environmental experiences also help determine which synapses are maintained and which are pruned during infancy and childhood.
- Myelination of the frontal cortex is not completed until after puberty.
- Contrary to past beliefs, some populations of neurons continue to be produced well into adulthood—for example, neurons in the hippocampus.
- Adult brains also continue to undergo dendrite remodeling and synaptogenesis.

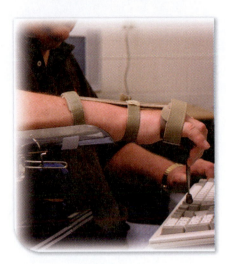

Psychology Around Us

The Amazing Brain

A teenager who's had his left-brain hemisphere removed to alleviate very severe epilepsy. A young woman recovering from a car accident. A middle-aged man undergoing rehabilitation after a stroke. The cognitive and physical functioning of each of these individuals reflects various kinds of brain damage. For years, prior to the development of neuroimaging technologies, neuroscientists learned about the brain largely by observing the behaviors of brain-impaired individuals, and then working backward, figuring out what those altered behaviors seemed to say about the operation of the affected brain areas.

You have a similar task in this video lab exercise. Observe the behaviors and functioning of each of the individuals in the video and suggest which of their brain areas have been damaged, how those brain areas probably operate when they are not damaged, and how rehabilitation might help change the brain and restore the behaviors and functioning of the individuals.

As you are working on this online exercise, consider the following questions:

1. What examples of *brain lateralization* are on display for each of the individuals in the lab video?
2. What do the treatment gains of each individual reveal about *brain integration* and *brain plasticity*?
3. How might *stem cell transplantations*, if such techniques are successfully developed and socially approved, improve on the rehabilitation techniques applied in this lab video?

CHAPTER 5

Sensation and Perception

chapter outline

On and Off Sensation

Have you ever noticed how enticing the aroma of your favorite restaurant is when you first walk through the front door? The smell of foods you enjoy coming from the kitchen make your mouth water. Depending on how long it's been since you last ate a meal, you might develop an urgent craving to order as soon as possible!

After you order, while you wait for your meal to arrive, you may not even notice it, but your awareness of the food odors in the room is probably gradually diminishing. By the time your meal is delivered to your table, you are probably not even noticing the smells that seemed so strong when you first entered the restaurant. When the server places your plate on the table, right under your nose, however, you might suddenly begin to notice the smell of food again—this time your own.

Our sense of smell contributes greatly to our enjoyment of a good meal. In fact, all of our senses become involved when we enjoy a meal. We use vision, our sense of sight, to admire the food on the plate. Hearing lets us listen to the sizzle of a particularly hot dish, or enjoy conversation with our dining companions. Obviously, our sense of taste is involved once we actually take a bite of food, but so are our senses of touch, as we discern the temperature and texture of the food. Without our touch senses, we could not tell a rough, cool salad from a smooth, warm soup.

Psychologists have generally agreed that there are five senses: smell, taste, touch, sound, and sight. Touch is actually a complex of senses collectively referred to as the *cutaneous senses* or the *somatosenses*. These include pressure, vibration, pain, temperature, and position. Although we will discuss each of these five major senses separately in this chapter, in most of our day-to-day experiences, we actually use these sensory systems or *modalities* to experience the world.

We use our senses in two almost inseparable processes. One process is **sensation**, the act of using our sensory systems to detect stimuli present in the environment around us. Once acquired, sensory information must be interpreted in the context of past and present sensory stimuli. This process, which also involves recognition and identification (for example, the realization that you recognize the smell in a restaurant as pizza cooking), is broadly defined as **perception**.

Sensation and perception are both critical for our interpretation of, and interaction with, the environment. Accurate functioning of our sensory systems is critical for survival. Imagine how greatly diminished your chances of survival would be if you could not see a fire, feel its heat, hear others crying "fire," smell the smoke, or interpret any of these sensations appropriately. Aside from the clear adaptive significance of our ability to sense and perceive the world, our life experiences are greatly enriched by these processes. Let's explore them in more detail.

sensation the act of using our sensory systems to detect environmental stimuli.

perception recognition and identification of a sensory stimulus.

sensory receptor cells specialized cells that convert a specific form of environmental stimuli into neural impulses.

sensory transduction the process of converting a specific form of environmental stimuli into neural impulses.

absolute threshold the minimal stimulus necessary for detection by an individual.

Common Features of Sensation and Perception

LEARNING OBJECTIVE 1 Describe characteristics shared by all the senses, including receptor cells, transduction, and thresholds, and differentiate between top-down and bottom-up processes of perception.

Each of our sensory systems is set up to convert the physical stimuli we receive from the world outside our bodies into neural information. Sensation and perception occur differently in each of our sensory modalities, but our senses also share some common processes. Each of the senses has a set of specialized cells called **sensory receptor cells** that convert a specific form of environmental stimuli into neural impulses, the form of communication used in our brains and nervous systems (see **Figure 5-1**). This conversion is called **sensory transduction**. For each sensory system, the different physical stimuli that are converted to brain activity through sensory transduction are listed in **Table 5-1**.

Our sensory receptors can be activated by very weak stimuli. A stimulus must, however, reach a certain level of intensity before we can detect it, because the conversion of physical stimuli into neural impulses only occurs when the stimuli reach this level or threshold. The minimal stimulus necessary for detection by an individual is called the **absolute threshold** (**Table 5-2**). Although the absolute threshold varies from person to person, in most cases, it is surprisingly small. For instance, many normal humans are capable of detecting a candle flame a mile away on a clear night (Galanter, 1962). Researchers have also worked to determine the smallest difference that we can detect between two stimuli, called the **difference threshold** or **just noticeable difference**. When sensory systems are working optimally, the difference threshold is also remarkably small.

Our senses are generally organized to detect change. This makes adaptive sense since most stimuli we are exposed to are not important enough to warrant our attention. Imagine how difficult it would be to concentrate on reading this chapter if sensory information about the odors of your breath, the taste of your mouth, the sound of the clock ticking, and the touch of your clothing were all competing with your ability to read! To combat the possibility of being unable to focus on the salient or important cues, our sensory systems respond to the continual presence of the same stimulus with a decreased response to that stimulus, a process called **sensory adaptation**.

Although it's possible that the diminished sense of smell people experience as they sit in a restaurant may be due to blocked sinuses, it's

Smell   Taste   Touch   Hearing   Sight

FIGURE 5-1 Sensory receptor cells Each sensory system contains specialized cells that are activated by particular physical stimuli.

TABLE 5-1 **Sensory Transduction Converts Environmental Stimuli into Neural Activity**

Sensory System	Physical Stimuli
Olfactory (smell)	Odorants (airborne chemicals)
Gustatory (taste)	Chemicals (typically in food)
Somatosensory (touch, heat, pain)	Pressure or damage to the skin
Auditory (hearing)	Sound waves
Visual (sight)	Light (photons)

TABLE 5-2 Absolute Thresholds for Various Senses

Sense	Absolute threshold
Smell	A drop of perfume diffused throughout a six-room apartment
Taste	One teaspoon of sugar in two gallons of water
Touch	An insect's wing falling on your cheek from a height of about half an inch
Hearing	The tick of a watch at 20 feet in a quiet room
Sight	A candle flame 30 miles away on a clear, dark night

difference threshold or **just noticeable difference** the minimal difference between two stimuli necessary for detection of a difference between the two.

sensory adaptation the process whereby repeated stimulation of a sensory cell leads to a reduced response.

bottom-up processing perception that proceeds by transducing environmental stimuli into neural impulses that move onto successively more complex brain regions.

top-down processing perception processes led by cognitive processes, such as memory or expectations.

much more likely that this experience occurs as a result of sensory adaptation. Our ability to detect odors gradually fades when we are in their presence for a prolonged period. Sensory adaptation can be overcome by providing a much stronger stimulus, which is what happens when your restaurant meal is delivered to your table. Now that the source of the smell is more concentrated in your vicinity, your ability to smell is renewed. Although the sense of smell is perhaps most prone to this response, all of our sensory systems exhibit some form of adaptation.

Sensation and perception almost always happen together. Researchers, however, have worked to study each process separately and to determine how the two work together. Perception can occur through **bottom-up processing**, which begins with the physical stimuli from the environment, and proceeds through transduction of those stimuli into neural impulses. The signals are passed along to successively more complex brain regions, and ultimately result in the recognition of a visual stimulus. For example, when you look at the face of your grandmother, your eyes convert light energy into neural impulses, which travel into the brain to visual regions. This information forms the basis for sensing the visual stimulus and ultimately its perception. Equally important to perception, however, is **top-down processing**, which involves previously acquired knowledge. When you look at grandma's face, for example, brain regions that store information about what faces look like, particularly those that are familiar to us, can help you to perceive and recognize the specific visual stimulus.

Typically, perception involves both bottom-up and top-down processing occurring at the same time. The combination lets us rapidly recognize familiar faces and other stimuli. Bottom-up and top-down processing are involved in sensation and perception of all sensory modalities. For example, recognizing familiar songs involves not only information carried from the ear to the brain but also the matching of that information with previously stored information about the music. We also combine bottom-up and top-down processes to help us recognize the smell or taste of a familiar food.

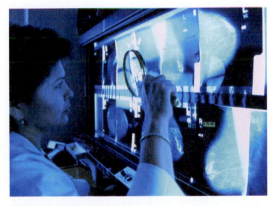

A critical difference A radiologist carefully examines a mammogram, looking for the slightest indication of a tumor. An individual's ability to detect a difference between two visual stimuli (such as normal versus abnormal tissue) can be increased by special training, practice, and instruments, but it is still limited to some degree by sensory difference thresholds.

Before You Go On

What Do You Know?
1. What is sensory transduction?
2. What are absolute and difference thresholds?
3. Compare and contrast bottom-up and top-down processing.

What Do You Think? Describe examples of sensory adaptation that you have experienced in two or more of your sensory modalities.

The Chemical Senses: Smell and Taste

LEARNING OBJECTIVE 2 Summarize the biological changes that underlie smell and taste.

Smell and taste are usually called the *chemical senses* because they involve responses to particular chemicals. Smell, our **olfactory sense**, and taste, our **gustatory sense**, emerged early in our evolutionary history (Doty, 1986). The sense of smell, in particular, is more sensitive and of greater significance to less complex animals, who use it for social communication as well as finding food and avoiding predators (Yahr, 1997; Mech & Boitani, 2003). This is less so for humans who rely more heavily on vision. However, the contributions of both smell and taste to the safety, social communication, and overall quality of life in humans are often underestimated. The ability to detect dangerous odors, such as smoke or a gas leak, or dangerous flavors, such as tainted food or poison, can be critical to our survival. In addition, some of our greatest pleasures in life come from the ability to smell and taste—to smell a rose or, as we all know, to enjoy a good meal.

In this section, we'll explore the environmental stimuli that create aromas and flavors, the organs we use to sense those stimuli, and how we transform environmental stimuli into brain signals that eventually help us perceive different smells and tastes. We'll also discuss the development of these abilities, some very interesting differences among people in their ability to taste and smell things, and some problems that can go wrong in the olfactory and gustatory systems.

Taste and Smell: How They Work

Sensation in the smell or olfactory system begins when chemicals called **odorants** enter the nose, as shown in "What Happens in the Brain When We Eat Pizza" on the following pages. Odorants are converted to neural signals at sensory receptors located in our nasal mucosa. These sensory receptors are located on the *cilia*, or hairlike structures, of **olfactory receptor neurons** (McEwen, 2008).

When odorants enter the nose, these chemicals bind to specific receptors located on the olfactory receptor neurons in a lock-and-key fashion. Only certain airborne chemicals bind to specific receptors (Buck, 1996). When enough odorant molecules have bound to receptors, the combination sets off an action potential in the olfactory receptor neuron. As we described in Chapter 4, the action potential or *firing* of a neuron sends a message to other neurons. The firing of olfactory receptor neurons is transmitted to the brain, as we'll see next.

Continuous binding of certain odorants, such as those contained in the main ingredients of a restaurant dinner, will result in fatigue of the olfactory receptor neurons to which they bind. In other words, the cell will stop responding to the odorant unless it's given a chance to recover so it can fire again (Dalton, 2000). If you were to step outside the restaurant to make a phone call, for example, you would probably notice the food smells again when you stepped back into the restaurant, because your olfactory receptor neurons would have gotten a break from constant exposure to the food odorants. When a stimulus is continuously present, however, as when you remain sitting in the restaurant, the only way the olfactory receptor neurons will respond to the odorant would be if the stimulus is increased in magnitude. As we saw, this is the case when the food is brought directly to your table. Many more odorant molecules are now available to your nose and its olfactory receptor neurons.

In humans, the sense of smell is very closely tied to the sense of taste. Have you ever noticed how dull your sense of taste is when you have a bad cold? This is due, in large part, to mucous blocking the access of odorants to the olfactory receptors located on the cilia. What we normally refer to as *taste* is really *flavor*, a combination of smell and taste.

olfactory sense our sense of smell.

gustatory sense our sense of taste.

odorants airborne chemicals that are detected as odors.

olfactory receptor neurons sensory receptor cells that convert chemical signals from odorants into neural impulses that travel to the brain.

papillae bumps on the tongue that contain clumps of taste buds.

taste buds clusters of sensory receptor cells that convert chemical signals from food into neural impulses that travel to the brain.

olfactory bulb the first region where olfactory information reaches the brain on its way from the nose.

Taste, the gustatory sense, is itself independent of smell and its major organ is the tongue. Your tongue is covered with bumps, called **papillae**. As shown in **Figure 5-2**, papillae contain clumps of **taste buds**, each of which contains sixty to one hundred sensory receptor cells for taste. Taste receptor cells have cilia that contain the actual receptors. These cilia extend through the pores of the taste receptor and are exposed to the contents of your mouth.

There are four major kinds of taste receptors. Each responds to a specific taste in our food: 1) sweet, 2) sour, 3) bitter, and 4) salt (Sugita, 2006). A fifth type of taste receptor has also been discovered—*umami*. Umami is the taste of monosodium glutamate (MSG). It is a chemical additive used in cooking some Asian food and American fast food. Each of these five types of taste receptors uses a slightly different mechanism for transduction of the chemicals in food to neural impulses in the gustatory system. For example, salt activates its taste receptors by sending sodium ions into the channels on the taste receptor cell. Since sodium ions are positively charged, the electrical charge of the taste receptor then becomes more positive. Taste buds are not evenly distributed across the tongue but most tastes can be recognized to a greater or lesser degree on most parts of the tongue.

The overall sensations we experience when we eat food are not just the result of combined interactions between olfactory and gustatory senses. Much of the information we get about food is delivered to us through one of the touch or *tactile* senses. The consistency of a particular food is not relayed to the brain via the taste receptors, but rather by inputs from touch receptors located on the tongue. The role of food consistency in determining preference is much greater than you might imagine. Many adult humans reject certain foods, such as raw oysters or cooked okra, specifically because those foods have a "slimy" texture.

In addition, the sensation we experience when we eat a "hot," as in spicy, meal is related to a component of the tactile system that communicates information about pain. A chemical called *capsaicin*, from chili peppers, activates pain receptors located in the tongue (Numazaki & Tominaga, 2004). These pain impulses, in conjunction with tactile information about the food texture, as well as the flavors (smell and taste) associated with the food, can combine to produce a sensation that is pleasurable to many people.

Suppose a food is not spicy, but is hot in the other meaning of the word in that it just came out of the oven. We've all had the experience of burning our mouths, which can damage the taste receptors on the tongue. As the box accompanying this section points out, the sensory receptors of taste are unusual because they regenerate when this happens.

What Happens in the Smell and Taste B R A I N ?

Signals from our olfactory receptor neurons travel to the brain via the olfactory nerve. As the figure on the right shows, information carried along the olfactory nerves travels first to a structure called the **olfactory bulb**, located at the base of the front of the brain, beneath the frontal lobes. Olfactory information is then sent to regions of the cerebral cortex that are important for recognizing and discriminating among odors, including the piriform cortex (Wilson, 2001).

The ability of our cortex to recognize patterns of inputs from a variety of olfactory receptors is most likely responsible for our detection of certain odors. Studies have shown that the piriform cortex is *plastic* or changeable in adulthood (Li et al., 2008). That is, the parts of piriform cortex that normally recognize specific odorants can change with experience, actually remapping this brain region. The chemical structures of some pairs of molecules are so similar that untrained humans can't discriminate between them (the two odors are usually below the just noticeable difference).

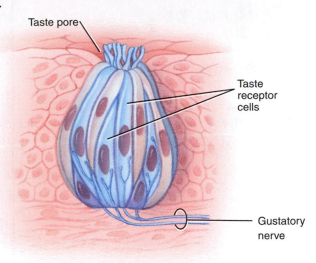

FIGURE 5-2 **A taste bud** The receptor cells for taste are clustered within the taste buds found in the bumps, or papillae, covering your tongue.

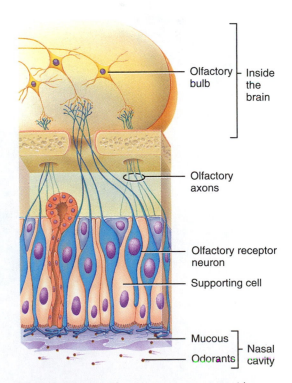

The smell route Olfactory receptor neurons (shown here in blue) transduce information from odorant molecules that enter the nose. This information is carried by the olfactory nerve into the brain where it synapses in the olfactory bulb.

The Chemical Senses: Smell and Taste **133**

When We Eat Pizza

Is this the best pizza you have ever had or does it fall short? When you dig into a slice of pizza, several neural circuits are activated to give you the overall experience. The appearance of your food can play an important role in its enjoyment. Photoreceptors in the eye transmit this information to the brain via the optic nerve which synapses in the brainstem, followed by the thalamus and finally the visual cortex. Taste receptor cells, as well as sensory cells that respond to touch and temperature, are activated on your tongue. These nerves carry impulses into the brain where they synapse in the brainstem, thalamus and sensory cortex (gustatory cortex and somatosensory cortex). Taste is combined with smell information to produce flavor. Olfactory receptor neurons transduce pizza odorants and send this information on to the olfactory bulb and then the olfactory cortex (smell is the only sensory modality that bypasses the thalamus on its way to the cortex).

Information about taste, smell, texture, temperature and appearance is integrated in various association regions of the neocortex. These circuits, together with those that store memories related to your previous pizza experiences, work together to produce your perception of this particular slice.

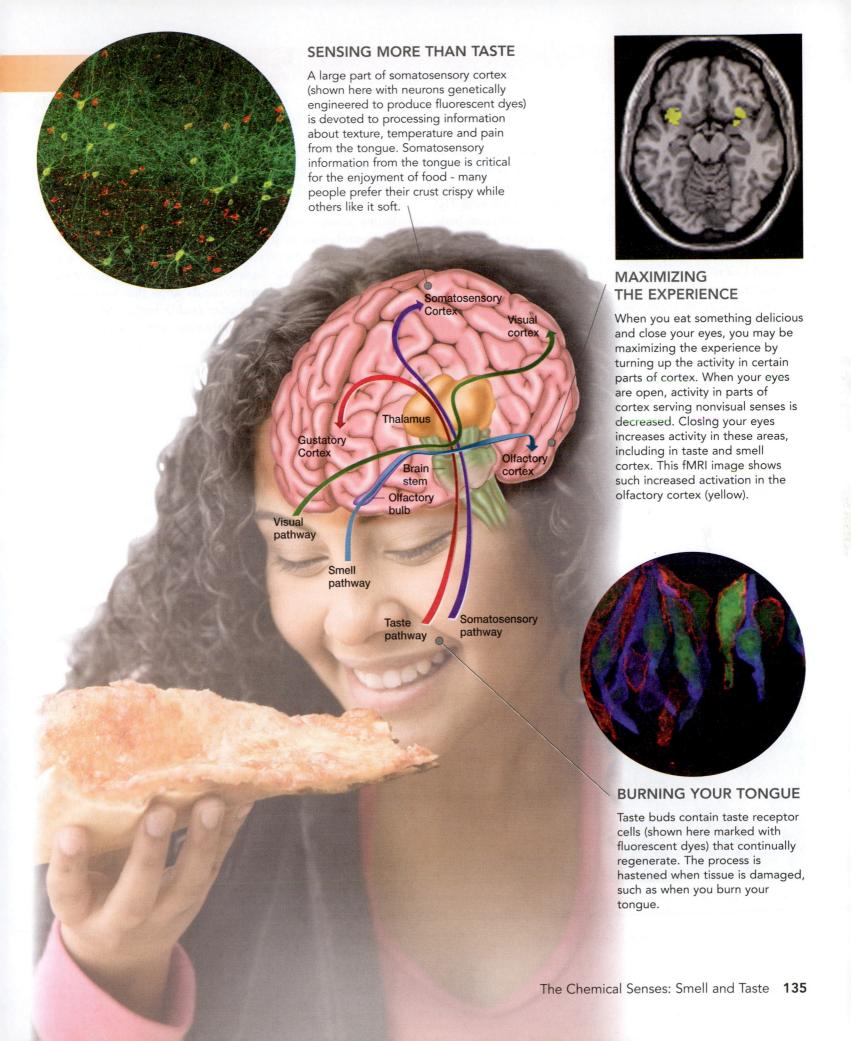

SENSING MORE THAN TASTE

A large part of somatosensory cortex (shown here with neurons genetically engineered to produce fluorescent dyes) is devoted to processing information about texture, temperature and pain from the tongue. Somatosensory information from the tongue is critical for the enjoyment of food - many people prefer their crust crispy while others like it soft.

MAXIMIZING THE EXPERIENCE

When you eat something delicious and close your eyes, you may be maximizing the experience by turning up the activity in certain parts of cortex. When your eyes are open, activity in parts of cortex serving nonvisual senses is decreased. Closing your eyes increases activity in these areas, including in taste and smell cortex. This fMRI image shows such increased activation in the olfactory cortex (yellow).

Somatosensory Cortex

Visual cortex

Thalamus

Gustatory Cortex

Brain stem

Olfactory cortex

Olfactory bulb

Visual pathway

Smell pathway

Taste pathway

Somatosensory pathway

BURNING YOUR TONGUE

Taste buds contain taste receptor cells (shown here marked with fluorescent dyes) that continually regenerate. The process is hastened when tissue is damaged, such as when you burn your tongue.

The Chemical Senses: Smell and Taste   **135**

If you, like most people, have had the experience of burning your tongue on too-hot food, you've probably noticed that by the next day or so, your ability to taste has returned and your tongue is no longer painful. This is due to the remarkable regenerative characteristics of the taste buds. Taste receptor cells normally turn over—they die and are replaced—in a matter of days. The process happens even faster when they are damaged. Our olfactory receptor neurons are also constantly turning over under normal circumstances (Farbman, 1997).

The capacity to regenerate on such a large scale and so rapidly is probably necessary because the receptor neurons for both taste and smell are exposed to the external environment.

Unlike the sensory receptors of the eye, which are protected by the eyeball, or those of the ear, which are protected by the eardrum, the surface of the tongue and the mucosa of the nose are directly exposed to any number of noxious chemical molecules that may enter our mouths or noses. Because destruction of receptors is likely under such circumstances, we need to constantly regenerate receptor cells just to continue normal functioning of our smell and taste systems.

Neurobiologists study the regenerative capabilities of the taste buds and olfactory receptor neurons in hopes of understanding exactly *how* these cells are constantly rejuvenating. Scientists and medical professionals hope that understanding these mechanisms may someday enable replacement of other types of cells, ones that currently don't seem capable of repair when they are damaged.

However, if exposure to one of the chemicals is paired with a painful shock to the leg, humans can be taught to discriminate between the odors (Li et al., 2008). This is a remarkable example of top-down processing. Learning about associations between odors and other experiences (such as a shock) can influence our ability to perceive sensory information in the future. In parallel with the new ability to discriminate the odors of closely related molecules, the areas of the piriform cortex that are activated by each of the previously indistinguishable molecules become more distinct from each other.

The olfactory bulb also sends information to the amygdala, an area important for emotions and fear, as well as indirectly to the hippocampus, an area important for learning and memory. Many people report that certain smells are evocative of past events (Lehrer, 2007). The smell of baking might remind you of visiting your grandmother as a young child, the smell of peanut butter might remind you of your elementary-school cafeteria, and so on. The ability of smells to call up memories is probably related in part to olfactory connections to the hippocampus and amygdala.

Unspeakable pleasure The ecstasy demonstrated on this woman's face as she bites into a chocolate covered strawberry serves as a vivid reminder that taste information is integrated with the reward circuits in the brain.

Taste receptor cells do not have axons but instead synapse with sensory neurons in the tongue to send information to our brains. Taste information is sent to the *thalamus* and eventually, the cerebral cortex. We'll see throughout this chapter that the thalamus is a relay station for incoming sensory information of many kinds; all of our sensory systems except olfaction have a main pathway through the thalamus.

Taste information is integrated with reward circuits in the brain (Norgren et al., 2006) and rewarding tastes seem to be processed separately from aversive tastes. Tastes that are considered to be rewarding, such as salty and sweet, activate overlapping areas in the taste cortex. By contrast, tastes generally considered to be less pleasurable, such as bitter and sour, activate regions that overlap less with rewarding tastes and more with one another in the taste cortex (Accolla et al., 2007). Taste and smell information are processed through separate pathways but there is convergence in the association parts of neocortex, namely in the prefrontal cortex.

In addition to integrating information about taste in general, part of the cortex that receives taste information, called the *insula*, is associated with the emotion of disgust.

Neuroimaging studies have shown that this brain region becomes activated not only when we smell or taste something revolting but also when we view repulsive visual images (Calder et al., 2007; Schienle et al., 2008).

Smell and Taste | How we *Develop*

The sense of smell is relatively well developed at birth. Research suggests that, within hours of birth, a newborn baby is capable of telling his or her own mother from another woman using only the sense of smell. In fact, olfactory functioning seems to be in place even before birth. Newborn infants show a learned preference to the odors of their mother's amniotic fluid. After birth, infants quickly learn to recognize the smell of their own mother's milk. Exposure to odors of their mother's milk has a calming effect on infants when they are experiencing a brief, minor painful stimulus, such as a needle stick in the heel (Nishitani et al., 2009). This effect doesn't appear to be as specific to the milk as it is to the mother—exposure to other odors that the baby has associated with the mother, such as vanillin, has the same calming effect as mother's milk odor (Goubet et al., 2007).

The ability to taste is also well formed at birth in humans. Newborn humans show an innate preference for sugar and aversion to bitter or sour tastes. Babies move their faces toward a sweet substance and make sucking movements with their mouths, but turn away and grimace when presented with a sour or bitter substance (Rosenstein & Oster, 1988).

Researchers have shown that by about seven years of age, children develop a preference for sour tastes (Liem & Mennella, 2003). This may explain the popularity of candies such as Sour Patch Kids. However, the aversion to bitter tastes typically lasts until adulthood. At this time, bitter foods, such as blue cheese and dark chocolate can emerge as favorites.

Many of these developmental changes are the result of learning. As children grow, they become accustomed to different tastes. However, there is some evidence to suggest that the gustatory system itself changes from infancy to adulthood. We form taste buds before we are even born, and as newborns, have higher concentrations of them on our tongues than we will as adults. Children also have taste buds on their palates, inside the cheeks, and the back of their mouths (Nilsson, 1979). Although these regions continue to contain taste buds in adults, their numbers decline with time.

The high number of taste buds in children may explain why they are often picky eaters. The tastes of certain foods may seem too strong to children, because their larger number of taste buds produces more neural impulses than adults would generate from the same food. Some researchers suggest that this developmental phenomenon might actually be adaptive in helping us survive. If young children enjoyed ingesting substances with strong or bitter tastes, they might be at higher risk of poisoning.

Children often refuse or eat very little of unfamiliar foods (Koivisto Hursti, 1999). Although neuroimaging studies on developing humans have yet to be done with regard to taste, it's tempting to speculate that as individuals grow and their tastes broaden, areas in the taste cortex represented by certain tastes are modified. It's likely that increased exposure to certain foods, especially when paired with positive social interactions and encouragement from parents, result in a remapping of previously aversive taste information on the gustatory cortex.

Smell and Taste HOW we Differ

Among humans, there is a wide range in the ability to detect certain odors. Some people seem relatively insensitive to even pungent odors, while others are particularly sensitive. Some of these individual differences are related to learning. Childhood exposure to particular odors decreases the reaction to those odors in adulthood.

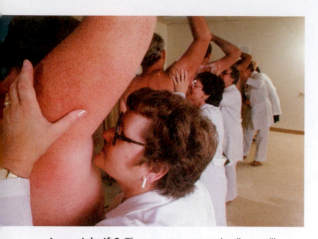

A special gift? These scent testers (or "noses") determine whether a new deodorant produces a pleasant result. People who are highly sensitive to odors often find employment that puts their special ability to use.

In addition to these learned differences, research suggests that females are generally more sensitive to smell than males are, and that this sensitivity varies with the stage of the menstrual cycle (Pause et al., 1996). Around the time of ovulation, women are more sensitive to odors than during other stages of the cycle. Women's ability to detect different odors also diminishes after menopause (Hughes et al., 2002). The exact biological mechanisms that underlie these differences are not known, but it is possible that reproductive hormones, such as estrogen, alter the excitability, or the likelihood of firing of olfactory neurons.

There is also considerable individual variability in the ability to taste. Researchers group people into three different categories with respect to taste sensitivity: nontasters (25 percent of people), medium tasters (50 percent), and supertasters (25 percent). These groups are distinguished based on their ability to detect and respond negatively to a specific bitter substance (Bartoshuk et al., 1996). Supertasters are repulsed by the bitter chemical. Nontasters do not even notice the bitter taste although they are capable of detecting other tastes. Medium tasters notice it, but do not find the taste particularly offensive. These functional differences are the result of variations in the concentration of taste buds on the tongue.

Women make up a higher proportion of supertasters than do men (Bartoshuk et al.,1994). This heightened sensitivity of both chemical sensory systems, smell and taste, is likely to have had adaptive significance for women. Since the chemicals in women's diets are passed along to their children when women are pregnant or nursing, the ability to detect and avoid potentially harmful odors and tastes may have contributed to survival of the species by protecting infants from toxic substances.

Smell and Taste When Things Go Wrong

True taste disorders are rare. In fact, most people who seek medical assistance complaining that they cannot taste are actually suffering from problems with their olfactory, as opposed to gustatory, systems. People with a condition called **anosmia** have lost the ability to smell. They can often still taste sweet, salt, sour, bitter, and umami, but they can no longer detect other flavors, since those require the additional information provided by food odorants.

In some rare cases—typically as a result of head trauma or oral surgery—humans lose the ability to taste itself, a condition called **ageusia**. Head trauma is also a leading cause of anosmia (Haxel et al., 2008). Sometimes the nerves that carry olfactory information from the olfactory receptor neurons to the olfactory bulb can be sheared, cutting off the pathway by which information about smell reaches the brain. People with Alzheimer's disease also suffer from a diminished sense of smell that is probably due to a combined degeneration of olfactory receptor neurons and neurons located in olfactory brain regions (Djordjevic et al., 2008).

Although humans can certainly survive without the ability to smell, their quality of life is considerably diminished. Many people with anosmia report feelings of depression. In addition, there are safety and social issues to consider. Since we use our sense of smell to detect dangers, such as smoke or spoiled food, anosmia increases the risk of injury. Moreover, socially acceptable cultural practices of hygiene may become difficult to follow with anosmia, since humans often use olfactory cues to make decisions about bathing, washing clothes, and brushing teeth. People with anosmia can learn to cope effectively with their condition by using other sensory systems to detect danger. They might, for example, use sound cues, such as a blaring smoke detector to notice smoke, or visual cues, such as appearance and freshness dates, to detect spoiled food.

anosmia inability to smell.

ageusia inability to taste.

free nerve endings sensory receptors that convert physical stimuli into touch, pressure, or pain impulses.

Meissner's corpuscles sensory receptors that convert physical stimuli about sensory touch on the fingertips, lips, and palms.

Merkel's discs sensory receptors that convert information about light to moderate pressure on the skin.

The chemical senses are also involved in the symptoms of some people with migraine headaches or epilepsy. For instance, a specific odor can initiate the onset of a migraine (Kelman, 2007). Likewise, patients with a certain form of epilepsy, called *reflex epilepsy*, will experience a seizure only after exposure to a specific odor. Although the reasons for this remain unknown, these individuals find it necessary to avoid specific intense odorants. In other patients suffering from migraines or epilepsy, stimuli from the other sensory systems, such as touch, sound, and sight, can initiate the headaches or seizures.

Some people experience hallucinations called *auras* either before or during migraine headaches or epileptic seizures. Auras can involve any of the sensory systems. People with these conditions might have touch, sound, or sight hallucinations, and some experience strong, often unpleasant, smells or tastes. The involvement of different senses indicates which brain circuits are compromised in these conditions. For example, if a person's seizure is preceded by strong olfactory hallucinations, it's likely that his or her olfactory pathways are initiating the seizure, or at least participating in its generation.

Migraines and the senses Migraine sufferers often experience sensory distortions—for example, a strange light or unpleasant smell—just before or during their headaches. In some cases, specific odors actually trigger migraines.

Before You Go On

What Do You Know?

4. What five tastes have specific receptors?
5. Which parts of the brain are involved in sensing and perceiving odors?
6. What are supertasters?
7. How are smell and taste involved with migraines and epileptic seizures?

What Do You Think?
This section of the chapter listed some ways, such as using smoke detectors, for people with anosmia to compensate for their lack of smell. What other ways can you suggest that people with anosmia might use to replace the safety and pleasures that a sense of smell provides?

The Tactile or Cutaneous Senses: Touch, Pressure, Pain, Vibration

LEARNING OBJECTIVE 3 Describe how the different senses of touch work and what can happen when things go wrong.

As with the chemical senses, there are rewarding and aversive types of tactile stimuli. The pleasure associated with a relaxing back massage or stroking a baby's cheek stands in stark contrast to the discomfort of getting a scrape or burn. The tactile or somatosensory system is actually a complex sense. As shown in **Figure 5-3**, our skin contains a variety of sensory receptors to register different types of physical stimuli (Munger & Ide, 1988).

- **Free nerve endings** are located mostly near the surface of the skin and function to detect touch, pressure, pain, and temperature.
- **Meissner's corpuscles** transduce information about sensitive touch and are found in the hairless regions of the body, such as the fingertips, lips, and palms.
- **Merkel's discs** transduce information about light to moderate pressure against the skin.

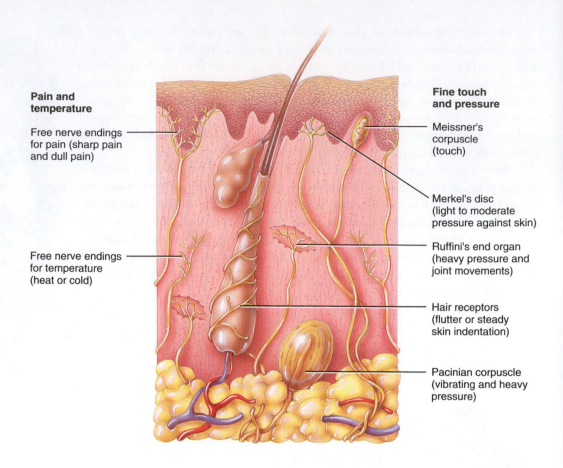

Pain and temperature

Free nerve endings for pain (sharp pain and dull pain)

Free nerve endings for temperature (heat or cold)

Fine touch and pressure

Meissner's corpuscle (touch)

Merkel's disc (light to moderate pressure against skin)

Ruffini's end organ (heavy pressure and joint movements)

Hair receptors (flutter or steady skin indentation)

Pacinian corpuscle (vibrating and heavy pressure)

- **Ruffini's end-organs** are located deep in the skin. They register heavy pressure and movement of the joints.
- **Pacinian corpuscles** are also buried deep in the skin and respond to vibrations and heavy pressure.

Depression of the skin activates free nerve endings that give us the sense of being touched. As you may have noticed, your skin is not equally sensitive to tactile stimuli over your whole body. Certain parts of your body, for example, the skin on your elbow, are much less sensitive to touch than other areas, such as your face and hands. These differences likely arise as a result of different densities of free nerve endings. Areas that are more sensitive have more free nerve endings.

We can also experience sensory adaptation, resulting in reduced tactile sensation from depression of the skin that continues for a period of time. This happens to you every day when you put on your clothing; shortly after getting dressed, you are no longer aware of the tactile stimulus your clothing provides (unless of course it is too tight).

What Happens in the Tactile Senses B R A I N ?

Our brains use a variety of related processes to help us perceive general information about a range of nonpainful touch sensations, including pressure, temperature, and general touch. Pain perception is also an important, but not yet fully understood, function.

The Touching Brain   When we touch something, or something touches us, our free nerve endings send tactile information into the spinal cord. The signals travel up the spinal cord to the brain, as shown in **Figure 5-4**. In the brain, touch information is

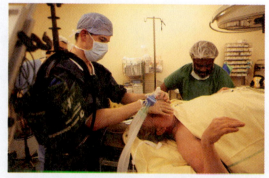

Using the brain to counteract pain Anesthesia is a procedure that helps block pain sensations, enabling patients to undergo surgery. Drug-induced anesthetic approaches that act through the brain are *general anesthesia* (seen here) and sedation.

first received in the thalamus, and then routed from there to the somatosensory cortex (located in the parietal lobe). Information about pressure and vibration is generally transmitted to the brain in a similar way, after being converted to neural impulses by the specialized receptors described above.

Our brain processes tactile information *contralaterally*, or on the opposite side of the brain from the side of the body where the touch occurred. So, if you touch something with your left hand, the information is eventually processed by the somatosensory cortex on the right side of your brain.

As we discussed in Chapter 4, the somatosensory cortex does not have an equal representation of all parts of the body (Kakigi et al., 2000). For example, tactile inputs from the hands take up proportionately more space in the somatosensory cortex than those from the back. This seems reasonable, given the fact that our hands are specialized for object manipulation, and we need to process information from them in great detail. As described in the box accompanying this section, other animals have somatosensory systems that are adapted to provide high-resolution tactile information from the parts of their bodies that are especially important to their daily lives. Information about pressure and vibration is generally transmitted to the brain in a similar way after being converted to neural impulses by the specialized receptors described above.

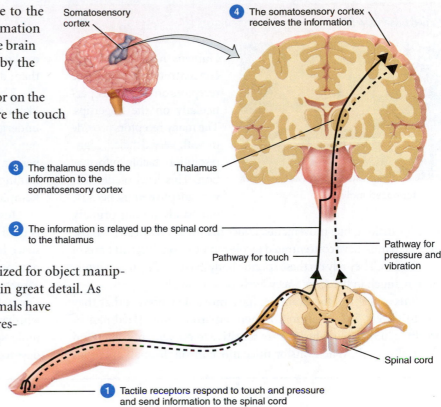

FIGURE 5-4 Somatosensory pathways in the central nervous system

Pain and the Brain   Like general touch information, painful sensations are also transmitted to the brain via free nerve endings. Pain information travels to the brain via two different types of pain fibers. One system, called the *fast pathway*, uses myelinated axons that, as we discussed in Chapter 4, carry signals faster than unmyelinated axons. Messages about sharp, localized pain travel along the fast pathway directly up the spinal cord to the thalamus and to areas of the somatosensory cortex. Pain information received via the fast pathway helps us to respond quickly with a withdrawal reflex, such as pulling a hand away after touching a hot stove. The slower pain pathway uses more unmyelinated axons—these inputs communicate with brain regions involved in processing emotions. Pain we perceive via the slow pathway is more often burning pain than sharp pain.

Like all other sensory systems we've discussed so far, the pain system shows evidence of sensory adaptation. A common example of this can be experienced when eating a spicy meal. Recall that the sensation of eating chili peppers is mostly due to the activation of pain fibers located on the tongue. Oftentimes, when a very "hot" food is first ingested, the pain response seems great. However, as the meal progresses, the response diminishes and we are less likely to experience discomfort. This is due to adaptation of the pain fibers and a subsequent decrease in their activity. However, when pain is associated with actual tissue damage or an abnormality in the pain system, as discussed below, pain can be persistent and debilitating.

The Tactile Senses | How we Develop

The tactile senses are generally in place at birth. In fact, studies have shown that fetuses can respond to the touch of a hair at a relatively early stage in prenatal development (Lagercrantz & Changeux, 2009). However, the ability to recognize and respond to different somatosensory stimuli occurs only after birth and involves further brain development as well as learning.

Ruffini's end-organs sensory receptors that respond to heavy pressure and joint movement.

Pacinian corpuscles sensory receptors that respond to vibrations and heavy pressure.

The star-nosed mole

Humans have a very high concentration of tactile receptors on our hands, particularly on the fingertips. The many receptors provide us with very detailed, high-resolution tactile information. This level of detail is very adaptive to us, because our hands are our primary tools for making fine movements. Other mammals, particularly those without hands, have concentrated tactile receptors on different parts of their bodies. They rely on these specific body parts for fine touch information, much in the same way we rely on our hands.

Rats and mice, for example, have movable whiskers that they use to detect information in their environments (Feldman & Brecht, 2005). Their whiskers are sensitive to movements of air and physical stimuli. When rats or mice move through small openings or dig tunnels, they use the movement of their whiskers to help them determine the location of the walls of these confined spaces.

The star-nosed mole is named for its specialized nose, shaped like a star, which has 21 appendages. This creature lives mostly underground and is almost completely blind. It navigates throughout its dark environment by using its star-shaped nose as a blind person would use his or her hands, to accomplish such tasks as finding food and exploring its spatial environment (Catania & Remple, 2004).

Just as a good deal of the somatosensory cortex in our brains is used to process information from the hands, a large amount of space in the brains of other animals is devoted to processing information from their specialized somatosensory features, The somatosensory cortex in the brain of a rodent devotes a proportionately large amount of space to processing information from the whiskers, for example, and the nose representation in the star-nosed mole somatosensory cortex is proportionately larger than that devoted to other body parts.

For children, one of the most enjoyable types of somatosensory input is being tickled. Although rough or prolonged tickling can become abusive, when tickled under the right circumstances, children often explode with laughter. The reaction we have to tickling is a result of activation of somatosensory pathways in an uneven, uncontrollable and unexpected manner. Not only are our sensory systems organized to detect change, but they are most tuned to stimuli that are unexpected and surprising. When you move your body and produce tactile sensations, these stimuli are less noticeable to you than are sensations produced by another individual. The sensations of your own legs touching one another when you cross your legs, for example, is generally less noticeable than a similar touch on your leg would be if someone sitting next to you brushed their leg against yours. Likewise, your reaction to your cat jumping onto your lap is likely to be much greater if you have your eyes closed when it happens. This differential response to surprising tactile stimuli appears to be a defense mechanism that has adaptive significance. It is probably also the reason why being tickled by someone else is more effective at producing an emotional reaction than trying to tickle yourself. Our enjoyment of being tickled generally diminishes as we age. This is likely due to the fact that adults are better at anticipating stimuli, and hence are more difficult to surprise, than are children.

Tactile Senses HOW we Differ

Humans differ greatly in their ability to detect physical stimuli on the skin. In addition, they differ in the degree to which they find certain tactile stimulation pleasurable or aversive. For example, some people enjoy an intense back massage while others do not. Of all the somatosensory experiences, the one that has received the most research attention is that of pain. Pain management for surgical procedures and other medical conditions is a critical part of patient care. There are dramatic differences in both the threshold to detect pain and the degree to which pain causes emotional suffering. Some of these differences can be attributed to ethnicity. For example, studies have shown that Japanese people have a lower pain threshold than Caucasians. These differences extend to reports of the detection of nonpainful stimuli as well (Komiyama et al., 2009).

Although learning plays some role, groups of people also differ in the actual sensation and perception of pain as a result of physical differences in their sensory systems. Studies have shown, for example, that women have a lower threshold for detecting pain than do men. They report greater pain intensity than men in response to the same stimulus (Garcia et al., 2007). One interpretation of this sex difference is that women are just less able to cope psychologically with painful stimuli since they haven't been "toughened up." In fact, research suggests that women may have about twice as many pain receptors in their facial skin than men. This suggests a physical cause for at least some of the differences in pain sensitivity. It is not yet known whether this difference exists throughout the body or whether it is specific to the face.

Neuroimaging studies show that people's brains react differently depending on their sensitivity to pain (Dubé et al., 2009). People exposed to a high temperature stimulus in one study exhibited varied responses, for example. Those who reported feeling pain showed changes in activity in their thalamus, somatosensory cortex, and cingulate cortex areas. Those who did not report feeling pain, showed similar activity in the thalamus, but no changes in the cortical regions. Although there may be differences in the two groups' sensory receptors in their skin, these findings suggest that differences in activation of brain circuitry may also underlie varied responses to painful stimuli.

One theory, the **gate control theory of pain** attempts to explain the relationship of brain activity to pain by suggesting that some patterns of neural activity can actually create a "gate" that prevents messages from reaching parts of the brain where they are perceived as pain (Melzack, 1999).

Early versions of this theory hypothesized that pain signals were blocked in the spinal cord, but later research has focused on neurochemicals or patterns of activity in the brain itself. Individual differences in gating mechanisms may result in the wide range of pain sensitivity across people.

High pain threshold This performer lifts concrete blocks and other heavy objects with a chain attached to his pierced tongue—an act that is unbearable for most people to even watch. Although hours of practice and conditioning and certain tricks of the trade each play a role in this behavior, a high pain threshold is certainly a prerequisite.

Tactile Senses When Things Go Wrong

As we've seen, sensing and perceiving pain are normal, and important, functions of our tactile senses. Some people, however, experience either too much pain or too little. Sometimes, people even feel pain and other sensations in limbs or other body parts that have actually been removed.

Chronic Pain The most common abnormality associated with the somatosensory system is that of chronic pain, pain that lasts longer than three months. In the United States, a relatively large percentage of the population, about one in six people, suffers from chronic pain. There are multiple causes of chronic pain, although in some cases the cause cannot be identified. In all cases, however, pain management is a critical issue, since prolonged pain sensations can interfere with daily functioning, and may lead to depression or even suicide.

Researchers have identified two groups of chemicals naturally produced by our nervous systems that have pain relieving properties, **endorphins** and **enkephalins**. Endorphins and enkephalins belong to a class of molecules called *opiates*. As we will see in Chapter 6, this class of chemicals also includes pain-killing drugs, such as morphine and heroin. When opiates are present in the nervous system naturally, they are referred to as *endogenous opiates*. These molecules are released by neurons after intense physical exercise, stress, and sexual experience. They are thought to be responsible for the so-called *runner's high* as well as for the ability of some people to perform heroic physical actions under extreme duress.

gate control theory of pain suggests that certain patterns of neural activity can close a "gate" to keep pain information from traveling to parts of the brain where it is perceived.

endorphins naturally-occurring pain-killing chemicals in the brain.

enkephalins naturally-occurring pain-killing chemicals in the brain.

Medical practitioners use opiate drugs that mimic or stimulate the endogenous opiate system for pain relief. However, this approach has been problematic because people easily become addicted to opiate drugs. Opiate drugs are not only addictive when they are abused illegally, such as heroin, but when they are prescribed medically, as happens with morphine. Repeated use of these drugs to treat chronic pain can produce a physiological dependence that is very difficult to overcome. In addition, these drugs become less effective with continual use, so higher and higher doses are needed to achieve pain relief. Opiates suppress breathing, however, so they can be very dangerous at high doses. Eventually, people with chronic pain can reach a point where the dose of medicine needed to reduce their pain would be enough to stop their breathing and kill them, but lower doses do not provide them with pain relief. Scientists continue to explore new avenues for pain relief that do not produce addictions or unwanted side effects.

In extreme debilitating cases of chronic pain, physicians have turned to neurosurgery. Destroying the pathways that carry information about pain stimuli to the brain can be effective for some people. An extreme form of neurosurgery to relieve intractable chronic pain is a *cingulotomy*, destruction of the cingulate cortex (Cetas et al., 2008).

No Pain   Some people are incapable of detecting painful stimuli. While the idea of feeling no pain may sound appealing at first, the fact is that our ability to recognize and respond to discomfort is critical for preventing physical damage to the body. Consider how often you shift position in your chair when you are studying or sitting in a lecture. If you were unable to receive signals of discomfort from your body, you would not move to relieve pressure on your skin. The parts of your skin under continuous pressure would develop sores or bruises. Since many everyday experiences would be damaging to our bodies if we were not able to detect discomfort, a lack of ability to detect pain can be very dangerous.

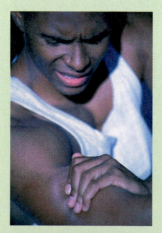

As we discuss in this chapter, medical practitioners are constantly seeking ways to provide relief to patients in chronic, or continuing, pain. But what about acute pain, the short-term pain you feel when you bump your leg on a table, for example?

Gate control theory suggests that touch sensations, which frequently travel along fast fibers, can help prevent some pain sensations traveling on the slow pathways from reaching areas of your brain where they are perceived. According to this theory, the brain only processes so much input, so touch can help to set up a "gate" that stops pain. This explains why we have a tendency to rub the skin of areas of our body that have been injured. For example, if you walk into a piece of furniture, you might rub your leg to dampen the pain.

Focusing on your breathing may also help. We often tend to gasp and then hold our breath when we injure ourselves, such as bumping a leg. Formal methods of pain control, such as the Lamaze method for childbirth, work in part by altering this natural tendency, by teaching people to breathe in short, panting gasps (Leventhal et al., 1989).

Distraction can also help, whereas anxiously focusing on pain can make it worse (al Absi & Rokke, 1991). Some studies have suggested that simply looking at a pleasant view, can affect pain tolerance (Ulrich, 1984). Other evidence suggests that in order for a distraction to be effective, the experience must be active. Studies have shown that playing an interesting videogame can dampen pain detection, whereas passive watching of a TV show has little effect. Stress and sexual experience also decrease the perception of pain. So, if you bump your leg on the way into a big job interview or on a hot date, perhaps you would not notice the pain as much as you would under other circumstances!

Some people are born unable to feel pain. A rare genetic condition called *familial dysautonomia* is associated with an inability to detect pain or temperature (Axelrod, 2004). Children with this disorder are at grave risk of life-threatening injuries and must be monitored very carefully. Loss of pain sensation can also be acquired later in life. Some medical conditions, including diabetes, can cause *neuropathies*, or nerve dysfunction, that block pain sensations arising from the person's extremities. People with such neuropathies may not notice if they sustain an injury in an affected area, such as a toe. Sometimes tissue can get so damaged that it must be amputated.

Phantom Limb Sensations   Many individuals with amputated limbs report tactile hallucinations or *phantom* sensations of touch, pressure, vibration, pins and needles, hot, cold, and pain in the body part that no longer exists. Some people even feel the sensation of a ring on the finger or a watch on the wrist of an amputated arm. Similar phantom experiences have been reported in woman who have undergone mastectomy for the treatment of breast cancer (Björkman et al., 2008).

Researchers believe that such phantom sensations are the result of abnormal activity in the somatosensory cortex of the brain. When a body part is removed, the part of somatosensory cortex that previously received its input does not become inactive. Instead, somatosensory inputs from intact body parts expand to occupy those regions of the cortex (Ramachandran, 2005). Since information from the face is represented in an area of the somatosensory cortex located near that of the arm and hand, a person whose arm was amputated is likely to experience an expansion of the somatosensory inputs from his or her face into the arm and hand regions of cortex.

Although researchers do not fully understand how reorganization of somatosensory cortex produces phantom sensations, there is clearly a memory component to the phenomenon. People are more likely to experience phantom sensations that they actually felt previously, as opposed to random sensations. For example, someone who previously wore a ring or a watch is more likely have the sense of wearing one after an amputation than is a person who didn't wear a watch or ring. Similarly, people who previously experienced considerable pain in their now-missing body part are much more likely to feel phantom pain.

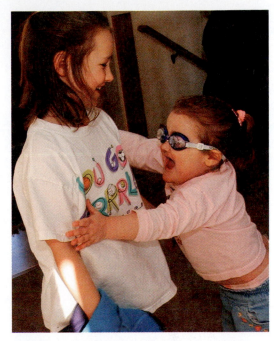

She feels no pain The child on the right looks like any other 3-year-old welcoming her big sister home from school, except for the goggles she is wearing. The child, who suffers from a severe case of familial dysautonomia, cannot detect any pain to her body and must wear goggles to protect her eyes from excessive rubbing and scratching and the effects of various injuries. She has lost one eye, damaged the other, and inadvertently chewed apart portions of her tongue and mouth.

Before You Go On

What Do You Know?

8. List the different types of tactile receptors in the skin and the primary functions of each.
9. Compare and contrast slow and fast pain pathways.
10. Why do children so often enjoy getting tickled?
11. What are some possible explanations for individual differences in pain sensitivity?

What Do You Think?   Have you experienced an occasion when your senses have worked together to either enhance or diminish pain or another touch sense? For example, did certain sights or sounds make pain better or worse?

The Auditory Sense: Hearing

LEARNING OBJECTIVE 4 Summarize what happens when we hear.

Hearing, the auditory sense, plays a very important role in social communication as well as in our ability to detect danger. In addition to these clearly adaptive roles, the ability to hear enriches our lives through music and other pleasurable sounds.

sound waves vibrations of the air in the frequency of hearing.

tympanic membrane the ear drum.

ossicles tiny bones in the ear called the *hammer, anvil,* and *stirrup*.

oval window a membrane separating the ossicles and the inner ear, deflection of which causes a wave to form in the cochlea.

cochlea fluid-filled structure in the inner ear, contains the hair cells.

basilar membrane structure in the cochlea where the hair cells are located.

hair cells sensory receptors that convert sound waves into neural impulses.

The auditory system is designed to convert **sound waves**, vibrations of the air, into neural impulses. Sound waves have two major qualities that produce our perceptions of different sounds:

- *Frequency.* The *frequency* of a sound wave refers to the number of cycles the wave completes in a certain amount of time. Frequency of a sound wave is measured in units called *Hertz* (Hz) which represent cycles per second. The frequency of a sound wave is responsible for producing the *pitch* of a sound. The voice of Mickey Mouse is a high-frequency sound wave that produces a high-pitched sound. Although the range of human hearing is quite large, we hear sounds best within the range of 2,000–5,000 Hz, which encompasses the frequencies of most sounds that humans actually make, such as babies crying and people talking.

- *Amplitude.* The *amplitude* of a sound wave refers to the strength of a given cycle. Waves with higher peaks and lower bottoms are higher amplitude than those that do not reach such extremes. The amplitude of a sound wave is responsible for our detection of *loudness*. Waves with high amplitudes produce loud sounds, while those with low amplitudes sound soft. Loudness is measured in units called *decibels* (dB).

Our detection of sound begins, of course, in the ear. Sound waves are converted to neural impulses in the ear through several steps, as shown in **Figure 5-5**.

1. First, sound waves enter the outer ear and at its deepest part, deflect the ear drum or **tympanic membrane**.

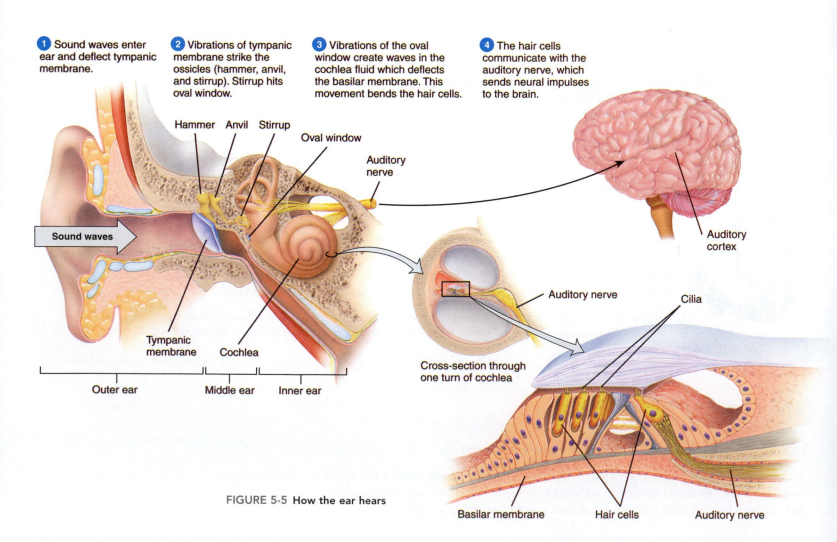

① Sound waves enter ear and deflect tympanic membrane.

② Vibrations of tympanic membrane strike the ossicles (hammer, anvil, and stirrup). Stirrup hits oval window.

③ Vibrations of the oval window create waves in the cochlea fluid which deflects the basilar membrane. This movement bends the hair cells.

④ The hair cells communicate with the auditory nerve, which sends neural impulses to the brain.

Hammer Anvil Stirrup

Oval window

Auditory nerve

Sound waves

Auditory cortex

Tympanic membrane Cochlea

Outer ear Middle ear Inner ear

Auditory nerve

Cilia

Cross-section through one turn of cochlea

Basilar membrane Hair cells Auditory nerve

FIGURE 5-5 **How the ear hears**

2. Vibrations of the tympanic membrane set in motion a series of three tiny bones or **ossicles**, called the *hammer, anvil,* and *stirrup*. The stirrup, which is the last bone in the chain, hits the **oval window**, a membrane separating the ossicles and the inner ear.

3. Deflection of the oval window causes a wave to form in the fluid-filled **cochlea** of the inner ear. When fluid moves in the cochlea, it deflects the **basilar membrane** that runs down the middle of the cochlea. The basilar membrane is covered with rows of **hair cells**, the auditory sensory receptors. Movement of the basilar membrane bends the hair cells that transduce the "fluid sound wave" into electrical activity.

4. The hair cells communicate with nerves in the cochlea that, in turn, send the neural impulses to the brain.

There are two major theories about how the auditory system converts sound waves into all the various sounds we can perceive. The first, called *frequency theory*, suggests that different sound frequencies are converted into different rates of action potentials or firing in our auditory nerves. According to this theory, high-frequency sounds produce a more rapid firing than do low-frequency sounds. Although there may be some truth to frequency theory—different firing rates contribute to sound perception of low tones—researchers agree that this theory cannot fully explain sound perception.

The second theory, called *place theory*, seems to account for a greater degree of auditory perception. Place theory holds that differences in sound frequency activate different regions on the basilar membrane. Regions along the basilar membrane send inputs to the brain that are encoded according to the place along the membrane where the inputs originated.

As with the other sensory systems we've discussed, adaptation also occurs in the auditory system when we are continuously exposed to sounds. We can adapt to sounds in several ways. First, our ears respond to very loud sounds by contracting muscles around the ear's opening so that less of the sound wave can enter the ear. This also happens when you talk, so that the sound of your own voice, which is so close to your ear, is not deafening. Second, the hair cells of the ear also become less sensitive to continuous noises. Unfortunately, if the noise is loud enough, it can actually damage the hair cells (Petrescu, 2008). Unlike receptors for the chemical senses, our sensory receptors in the ear are not readily replaced, so such damage to the hair cells makes the ear permanently less sensitive. To protect your own hair cells from such permanent damage, which is associated with hearing loss, avoid prolonged exposure to loud noises—including the music coming through your iPod!

Finally, the brain can filter out many sounds that are not important, even if they are relatively loud. This ability enables you to carry on a conversation with your friends at a noisy party. This phenomenon, often referred to as the *cocktail party effect*, is another example of top-down processing. The brain is able to attend to, and pick up on, relevant sounds even in a very noisy environment. These relevant sounds, such as your name or the names of people who interest you, grab your attention and focus your auditory perception because you have previously learned their importance. So background noise, even if it's also the sounds of people talking, interferes minimally with hearing a conversation, as long as the conversation is of interest to us.

To determine the importance of a particular sound, it's necessary to localize it in space, to figure out where it is coming from. For example, if you're driving in a car and you hear the sound of an ambulance siren, you need to determine whether the ambulance is far away or close up in order to decide whether or not to pull over to the side of the road to let the ambulance pass. You also need to determine from which direction the sound is approaching you. The auditory system uses several cues to help localize sound:

- *General loudness* We learn from many early experiences that loud sounds are usually closer to us than are quiet sounds, so that eventually we automatically use the loudness of a sound to assess the distance between ourselves and the source of the sound.

Unlike in humans, damaged hair cells in the bird cochlea are regenerated. Scientists are studying the regeneration of bird hair cells to find ways to repair hearing loss in humans.

What television? This father, who has set up shop in his family room, seems oblivious to the loud sounds coming from the television that his son is watching. He is concentrating on his phone conversation and professional work while filtering out the irrelevant TV noise.

tonotopic map representation in the auditory cortex of different sound frequencies.

- *Loudness in each ear* Because of the distance between our ears and the presence of the head between our ears, there are slight differences between each ear in the loudness of the same sound wave. The ear closer to the sound hears a louder noise than the ear farther from the sound. This difference is particularly useful in detecting the location of high-frequency sounds.
- *Timing* Another cue used to localize sound is differences in the time at which sound waves hit each ear. Sound waves will reach the ear closer to the source of the sound before they reach the ear farther away. Since the ears are separated in space, a sound wave will also hit each ear at a slightly different part of its wave cycle, creating a phase difference. This cue is particularly useful to us in localizing sounds with low frequencies.

We also adjust our heads and bodies to assess the location of sounds. These movements allow us to hear how the sound changes while we're in different positions and to use those changes to help make a reasonable approximation of its location. Finally, the use of other sensory systems, such as vision, may come into play. For instance, you might confirm the location of the ambulance when you look into your rearview mirror and see it approaching.

What Happens in the
Hearing B R A I N ?

After auditory information is transduced from sound waves by the hair cells in the basilar membrane of the cochlea, it travels as signals from nerves in the cochlea to the brainstem, the thalamus, and then the auditory cortex, which is located in the temporal lobe. Part of the primary auditory cortex is organized in a **tonotopic map**. That is, information transmitted from different parts of the cochlea (sound waves of different frequency and, hence, sounds of different pitch) is projected to specific parts of the auditory cortex, so that our cortex maps the different pitches of sounds we hear. Auditory information from one ear is sent to the auditory cortex areas on both sides of the brain. This enables us to integrate auditory information from both sides of the head and helps us to locate the sources of sounds.

From the primary auditory cortex, auditory information moves on to the auditory *association areas* in the cortex. As we described in Chapter 4, association areas of the brain's cortex are involved in higher-order mental processes. Association areas help to link the sounds we hear with parts of the brain involved in language comprehension.

Association areas also integrate, or coordinate auditory information with signals from other sensory modalities. Have you ever noticed how distracting it is to watch a movie that has an audio slightly out of synchrony with the video image? This is because the brain is set up to integrate information from multiple sensory systems. Over time, we learn to have expectations about the coincidence of certain visual stimuli with specific sounds. When the sounds in a movie do not match the visual images the way they would in real life, our expectations are violated and our attention is drawn to this discrepancy from the norm.

In some people, the integration of sensory systems in the brain can sometimes lead to abnormal crossover of different modalities. As described in the box accompanying this section, people who experience a condition known as *synesthesia,* perceive sensations in a different modality from that of the original stimulus. Synesthesia is not a debilitating abnormality; in fact it has sometimes been described as enriching, particularly when it occurs in artistic or musical individuals.

They can't fool the brain (yet) M.I.T. professor Neil Gershenfield and a graduate student work on project *Digital Stradivarius,* an attempt to build a digital model that can match the sound of the great violins of Stradivarius. When digital-produced and instrument-produced sound waves are each converted into neural impulses in the brains of musical experts, the experts can detect a difference. The instrument remains the champ.

"The best kaleidoscope ever"
Performer and songwriter Tori Amos has said that she often experiences the notes and chords in her music as colors and light filaments. She says, "Try to imagine the best kaleidoscope ever."

Can you see noise or taste words? Some people can. This condition is called *synesthesia*. The name comes from two Greek words: *syn*, meaning together, and *aesthesis*, meaning perception, and therefore refers to "joined perception." People who have synesthesia experience a stimulus that normally would be perceived by one sense in a different sensory modality. They may actually see colors or images when they hear music.

The most common form of synesthesia is called *colored letters or numbers*. A person who has this form always sees a color in response to a specific letter or number. There are also synesthetes who smell particular odors in response to touch, who hear noises in response to smell, or who feel a tactile stimulus in response to sight. There are even some individuals who possess synesthesia involving three or more senses, but this is especially unusual.

People who experience synesthesia are not simply imagining their unusual sensations. Neuroimaging studies have shown that sensory areas normally not affected by particular stimuli are activated if that sense is involved in the synesthetic experience (Nunn el al., 2002). For example, the auditory cortex of sight–sound synesthetes, as well as the visual cortex, becomes active in response to particular visual stimuli that cause synesthesia. The brain of a person who can hear a picture or color really does respond as though the stimulus were producing sound waves, as well as reflecting light waves.

Hearing How we *Develop*

Our ears are formed and capable of transducing sound waves before we are even born. In fact, human fetuses have been shown to respond to noises long before birth. Research has shown that fetuses respond to loud noises with a startle reflex and that after birth, they are capable of recognizing some sounds they heard while in utero. However, the ability to recognize and respond appropriately to a wide variety of sound stimuli is acquired over many years of postnatal life. Sounds associated with language, for example, become recognizable over postnatal development, as do those associated with music. We describe language development in more detail in Chapter 9.

Sensitive periods exist for the development of both language and music learning (Knudson, 2004). As we described in Chapter 3, we acquire certain abilities during sensitive periods of development much more easily that we do after the sensitive period has ended. The tonotopic map in the primary auditory cortex of the brain is organized during such a sensitive period of development (deVillers-Sidani et al., 2007). Studies in experimental animals have shown that exposing animals to pure tones during a certain time in development, leads to a larger representations of those sounds in the auditory cortex. The same exposure after the sensitive period in development is over has no such effect. If a sound is made important to the animal, however, by pairing it either with a reward, such as water, or a punishment, such as an electric shock, the primary auditory cortex can be reorganized so that more of it responds to the relevant tone (Bakin et al., 1996). Such top-down processing of tones indicates that this region of the brain still shows plasticity after the sensitive period is over. It is not as easy, however, to remap the brain after a sensitive period as it is during one. The stimuli needed to produce changes in older animals must be very strong and important, compared to those needed for younger animals (Kuboshima & Sawaguchi, 2007). In humans, the auditory brain is set up to acquire information about speaking and music most readily relatively early in life, during the preschool years. It is more difficult, but by no means impossible, for us to learn additional languages or certain music skills after we mature.

A bit too early A pregnant woman tries to introduce music to her fetus by positioning headphones on her stomach. Although fetuses do indeed respond to loud noises and can detect certain sounds, the acquisition of musical skills cannot take place until sensitive periods unfold during the pre-school years.

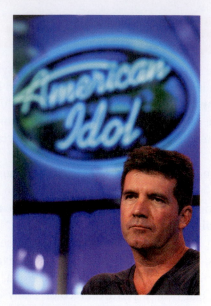

Breaking the bad news One of the guilty pleasures for many *American Idol* fans is that special moment when judge Simon Cowell calls a contestant "tone deaf." The show includes performers whose musical abilities vary from absolute pitch to tone deafness.

Hearing HOW we Differ

We differ greatly in our ability to detect specific sounds. People show particular differences in their ability to identify certain notes in a scale. **Absolute pitch** refers to the ability to recognize an individual note in isolation. This is very difficult for most people. Only about 1 in 10,000 people in Western countries has absolute pitch. This ability seems to originate in childhood, between the ages of three and six years, through musical training, and it is associated with differences in brain anatomy (Zatorre, 2003). Research has shown that portions of the cortex are actually thinner in individuals with absolute pitch (Bermudez et al., 2009). Although it's not clear whether people with absolute pitch start out with a thinner cortex or whether they develop it through training, it's possible that synaptic pruning contributes to this structural difference.

Studies have shown, however, that people who speak tonal languages, or languages in which differences in tone convey meaning, such as Vietnamese and Mandarin Chinese, are more likely to develop absolute pitch than those speaking Western languages. This again suggests the possibility that early learning of auditory information related to tones can have a permanent effect on the functioning of this sensory system.

Just as some people exhibit absolute pitch, others are tone deaf, or unable to discern differences in pitch. Although tone deafness or *amusia* is sometimes the result of damage to the auditory system, it can be present from birth, and researchers believe it may be related to genetics (Peretz et al., 2007). Tone deafness affects up to 4 percent of the population and mostly results in a diminished appreciation for music. Although music appreciation is an important enriching ability, people with tone deafness are able to enjoy all other aspects of life. This condition only presents serious social problems when it occurs in cultures where the language is tonal.

Hearing When Things Go Wrong

There are many conditions that lead to abnormalities in the auditory system. Some cause either partial or total **deafness**, the loss of hearing. Abnormalities in the auditory system can also add unwanted auditory perceptions.

Deafness   Deafness has a variety of causes. It can be genetic or caused by infection, physical trauma or exposure to toxins, including overdose of common medications such as aspirin.

Since speech is an important mode of communication for humans, deafness can have dramatic consequences for socialization. This is particularly a concern for children, because young children need auditory stimulation in order to develop normal spoken language skills. For this reason, physicians try to identify auditory deficits at an early life stage. Parents can then make choices among different options to help their children with deafness. Some deaf individuals learn to use sign language and other methods of communication that rely on the senses other than hearing. Research over the past years has made progress in the construction of cochlear implants that help individuals with deafness to hear sounds (Sharma et al., 2009). Although this work is developing at a rapid pace, there remain many deaf people who are not helped by cochlear implants, however. (Battmer et al., 2009). This is one reason that many individuals and families choose to avoid them. Some in the deaf community also believe that hearing is not necessary in order to lead a productive and fulfilling life. For them, the potential benefits of implants may not outweigh the potential risks of surgery required to place them in the cochlea (Hyde & Power, 2006).

A world of new possibilities After undergoing successful cochlear implant surgery, this four-year-old child practices the violin under the instruction of his music teacher at the Memphis Oral School for the Deaf.

Hearing Unwanted Sounds   About one of every 200 people is affected by *tinnitus*, or ringing in the ear. Tinnitus has multiple causes, some of which are related to abnormalities in the ear itself (Lanting et al., 2009). Most people are able to cope with the noise, but some find it too loud and distracting to ignore.

Patients with epilepsy in the temporal cortex have reported the perception of hearing complex auditory stimuli, such as a musical tune (Wieser, 2003). This symptom, which can be completely distracting and disturbing to the patient, is the result of abnormal electrical activity in brain circuits that store complex auditory memories. Treatment for epilepsy sometimes involves neurosurgery to remove the part of the brain that is responsible for starting the seizures. Brain surgery in the temporal lobes, where auditory information is processed is particularly dangerous, however, because the temporal lobe also houses Wernicke's area, which is critical for language comprehension.

> "I have unwittingly helped to invent and refine a type of music that makes its principal exponents deaf. Hearing loss is a terrible thing because it cannot be repaired."
>
> —*Pete Townshend, rock musician of the band The Who*

Before You Go On

What Do You Know?

12. What happens in the ear to transduce sound waves into neural signals?
13. What is a tonotopic map?
14. What are sensitive periods and how are they important for hearing?
15. What is tinnitus?

What Do You Think?   What would you suggest including in an ideal early school curriculum, to develop children's auditory systems to their maximum capabilities?

The Visual Sense: Sight

LEARNING OBJECTIVE 5 Describe key processes in visual sensation and perception.

The ability to see and make sense of the visual world around us plays a very important role in human life. We use our vision in virtually all of our activities. Most of our social experiences have a visual component, for example. Vision is important for communication: facial expressions and "body language" or nonverbal communication help to convey information that is often lost in spoken language. No doubt related to its importance to us, the visual sense is particularly well developed in humans. Some estimates suggest that about half of the cerebral cortex of our brains is devoted to processing some type of visual stimuli.

The stimulus for vision is light. Light is made up of particles called *photons*. The light that we can see is part of the electromagnetic spectrum of energy that also includes many forms we cannot see, such as X-rays and radio waves. Like sound, light travels in waves. The visible spectrum of light ranges from about 400 to 700 nanometers in wavelength (a nanometer is a billionth of a meter). As shown in **Figure 5-6**, different wavelengths within our visible spectrum appear to us as different colors. Objects in the world absorb and reflect light in varying levels and patterns—those that reflect more light are perceived as brighter.

absolute pitch the ability to recognize or produce any note on a musical scale.

deafness loss or lack of hearing.

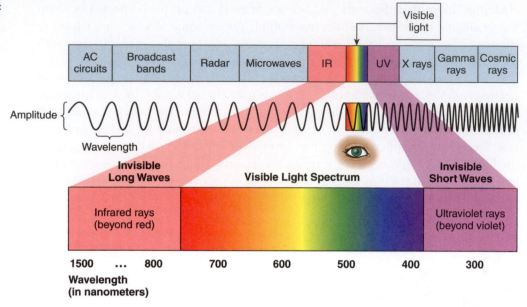

Visible light

| AC circuits | Broadcast bands | Radar | Microwaves | IR | | UV | X rays | Gamma rays | Cosmic rays |

Amplitude

Wavelength

Invisible Long Waves   **Visible Light Spectrum**   **Invisible Short Waves**

Infrared rays (beyond red)   Ultraviolet rays (beyond violet)

| 1500 | ... | 800 | 700 | 600 | 500 | 400 | 300 |

Wavelength (in nanometers)

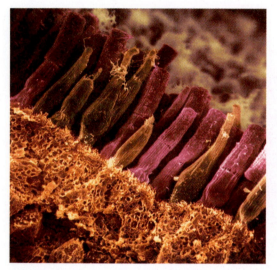

The photoreceptors This colorized scanning electron micrograph shows the retina's photoreceptors—the rods and cones—which help pass visual signals through the optic nerve to the brain. Rods (*pink*) are the photoreceptors that detect light. Cones (*olive*) are photoreceptors that detect color.

retina a specialized sheet of nerve cells in the back of the eye containing the sensory receptors for vision.

photoreceptors the sensory receptor cells for vision, located in the retina.

rods photoreceptors most responsive to levels of light and dark.

cones photoreceptors responsive to colors.

Seeing the Light

Vision begins when light enters the eye, as shown in **Figure 5-7**. Muscles in the iris—the colored part of the eye that you can see—adjust the size of our pupils to let in more or less of the light reflected from objects around us. These muscles also adjust the shape of the lens, focusing the light that enters the eye onto a specialized sheet of nerve cells in the back of the eye, called the **retina**. The retina is where we transduce light waves into neural impulses that the brain can process. Two major classes of visual receptors or **photoreceptors** exist in the retina, the **rods** and the **cones**. The rods predominate. There are over 100 million rods in the human retina. Rods are important for detecting light; they are highly sensitive to small amounts of light and are critical for night vision. The cones are much fewer in number, with only about 6 million per human retina. Cones respond to light of different wavelengths, which is how we detect color.

When light reaches the photoreceptors, a series of chemical reactions take place. The rods and cones stimulate the bipolar cells that, in turn, cause ganglion cells to then fire. The axons of the ganglion cells are bundled together to form the **optic nerve**. Signals from the ganglion cells travel along the optic nerve out of the eye and into the brain.

Rods and cones are not evenly distributed throughout the retina. Cones are concentrated more in the center than the periphery of the retina. The **fovea**, the region of the retina where our vision is at its sharpest, is entirely made up of cones. Rods are distributed throughout the rest of the retina and, unlike cones, are concentrated at the peripheral edges of the retina. Have you ever noticed that your peripheral vision is not particularly acute? It mostly enables you to detect movement, but not necessarily details. This is due to that fact that rods dominate the peripheral parts of the retina. The retina also contains a region that is completely lacking in rods and cones. This area produces a blind spot in your visual field. The *blind spot* is the location where your optic nerve leaves your retina. Because the visual parts of the brain are very good at filling in incomplete images, the blind spot is not noticeable under normal circumstances. With some manipulation of your visual inputs as instructed in Figure 5-7, however, you can experience your blind spot.

Like the other sensory systems we previously discussed, the visual system undergoes sensory adaptation. Dilation and constriction of the pupil, the opening in the center of the iris, is one way that the visual system adapts to the light. When you go from inside your home to outside on a bright, sunny day, you may immediately feel the need

FIGURE 5-7
How the eye sees

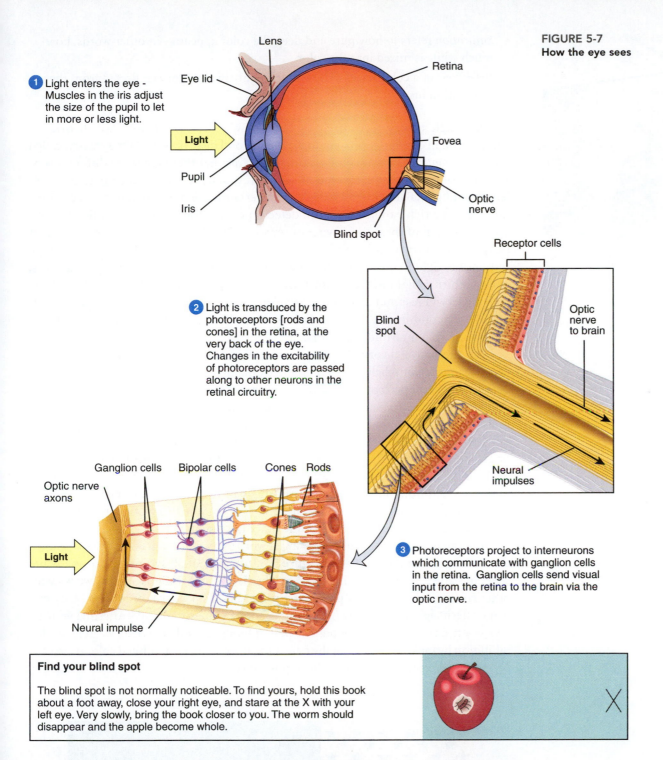

1. Light enters the eye - Muscles in the iris adjust the size of the pupil to let in more or less light.

Lens

Eye lid

Light

Pupil

Iris

Retina

Fovea

Optic nerve

Blind spot

Receptor cells

Blind spot

Optic nerve to brain

2. Light is transduced by the photoreceptors [rods and cones] in the retina, at the very back of the eye. Changes in the excitability of photoreceptors are passed along to other neurons in the retinal circuitry.

Neural impulses

Ganglion cells   Bipolar cells   Cones   Rods

Optic nerve axons

Light

Neural impulse

3. Photoreceptors project to interneurons which communicate with ganglion cells in the retina. Ganglion cells send visual input from the retina to the brain via the optic nerve.

Find your blind spot

The blind spot is not normally noticeable. To find yours, hold this book about a foot away, close your right eye, and stare at the X with your left eye. Very slowly, bring the book closer to you. The worm should disappear and the apple become whole.

X

to squint, and shade your eyes. Your eyes quickly adapt to light, however, in part by constriction of the pupil that decreases the amount of light entering the eye. Conversely, to allow vision to occur in dark places, the pupil will open further to let in more light.

Seeing in Color

As we noted earlier, cones enable us to see color. The color of a visual stimulus can be described along three dimensions: hue, saturation, and brightness. The variety of colors we can perceive is related to the different combinations of these three characteristics.

- *Hue* refers to the wavelength of light that the visual stimulus produces. This is the most basic aspect of color, whether the stimulus is red, blue, yellow, or some other color.

optic nerve the bundle of axons of ganglion cells that carries visual information from the eye to the brain.

fovea center of the retina, containing only cones, where vision is most clear.

Changing one's view These two people at the Sensorium museum exhibit at M.I.T. wear wireless head gear that causes each of them to view the world from the visual perspective of the other. This visual manipulation is eventually adjusted to, but, for a while, it interferes with many aspects of visual functioning, including shape, light, and color perceptions; activity in visual regions of the brain; depth perception; and perceptual constancies.

- *Saturation* refers to how pure and deep the color appears—in other words, how much white is mixed into the color.
- *Brightness* of a color refers to how much light emanates or is reflected from the visual stimulus.

No single theory yet entirely explains how we perceive color. Two theories of color vision in combination help to explain a good deal, however. One theory, called the *trichromatic theory* of color vision, maintains that there are three different sensors for color and that each type of sensor responds to a different range of wavelengths of light (Balaraman, 1962). We can certainly see more than just three colors, however. The rich variations we can detect in color arise from combinations in relative activation of these three types of sensors. This theory is largely correct, in that people with normal color vision have three different kinds of cones. One type responds to light in the yellowish-red wavelengths, another to the green wavelengths, and the third to light in the bluish-purple wavelengths. Typically, at least two of the cone types will respond to a certain wavelength of visible light, but in varying increments. The combination of the signals produced by cones is what enables the brain to respond to a multitude of colors.

An alternative theory about color vision is called the *opponent process theory* (Buchsbaum & Gottschalk, 1983). This theory maintains that color pairs work to inhibit one another in the perception of color. For example, red inhibits the perception of green, yellow inhibits the perception of blue, and black inhibits the perception of white. There is also some truth to this theory because we cannot mix certain combinations of colors. For example, we cannot see reddish green or bluish yellow; instead we see brown or green, respectively. Opponent processing may be the result of activity in a region of the thalamus that receives visual information, called the *lateral geniculate nucleus*. Inputs to this nucleus from one color of an opposing pair inhibit those from the other color in the pair. So inputs carrying red information prevent the firing of neurons that convey green information, and so on for the other opponent pairs.

You can observe opponent processing at work by staring at the white dot in the middle of the green and black flag in **Figure 5-8**. After about 30 seconds, stare at a white sheet of paper. You will see an *afterimage* that is red and white. This also works with other colors in the opponent pairs. A white-on-black image will produce a black-on-white afterimage, and a yellow image will produce a blue afterimage. Afterimages happen when one color in an opponent pair inhibits the other. When we release this inhibition by looking away from the first color, the previously inhibited color overcompensates and creates an image in the opponent color.

FIGURE 5-8 The afterimage effect Afterimages occur when one color in an opponent pair inhibits the other. When you look away from the first color, the previously inhibited color is turned on. To see opponent processing in action, stare at the white dot in the center of the flag for about 30 seconds, then look away at a white sheet of paper.

The two theories can be used together to explain color blindness. Very few people are actually unable to see any colors at all. Most people who have what is called *color blindness* are really just unable to distinguish certain colors. Most common is red-green color blindness, which is tested with images, such as the one shown in **Figure 5-9**. Studies suggest that people with this problem have a shortage of cones that respond to either the greenish or reddish wavelengths. Therefore, the lateral geniculate nucleus of their thalamus does not receive sufficient inputs that enable it to inhibit either red or green colors, making people unable to distinguish between the two colors (Weale, 1983; Wertenbaker, 1981).

Sight What Happens in the BRAIN?

Visual information leaving the retina travels via the optic nerve to the brainstem. After synapsing with neurons in the *superior colliculus*, visual information then communicates with the thalamus. From the thalamus, visual input travels to the primary visual cortex, located in the occipital lobe.

Basic visual information is transmitted throughout the brain via a partially crossed set of axons (**Figure 5-10**). Visual information from the middle part of your visual field, closest to your nose, is sent, via axons that cross to the other side of your brain, to the opposite side of your visual cortex. Visual information from the lateral part of your visual field, closest to your temples, travels to the same side of the visual cortex.

Once visual information reaches the primary visual cortex, it is processed to enable the detection of very simple features, such as lines and edges (Hubel & Wiesel, 1959). However, we don't see the world as a collection of lines and edges. Instead, we see a rich set of complex visual stimuli that change as we and the world around us move. Detection of complex visual stimuli occurs as a result of circuitry that involves association areas of visual cortex. Recall from our discussion of hearing that association areas are involved with higher-order processes of perception: thinking and memory.

The pathways that process information about complex visual stimuli can be roughly divided into the "*what*" and the "*where*" pathways, as shown in **Figure 5-11** (Ungerleider & Haxby, 1994). That is, the regions that process visual information to help us determine *what* is the identity of an object (is it an apple, a car, or a house) are different from those where

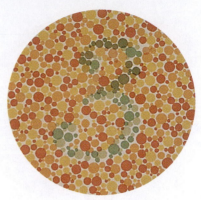

FIGURE 5-9 Color blindness Most people who are color blind cannot distinguish between red and green; they would see only a random pattern of dots in this figure.

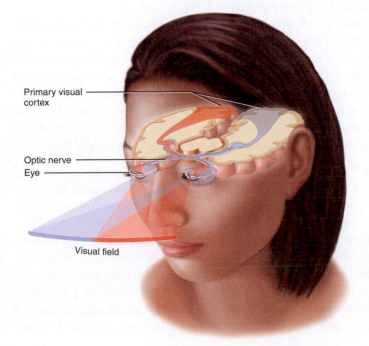

Primary visual cortex

Optic nerve
Eye

Visual field

FIGURE 5-10 The crossed visual pathway Before entering the brain the optic nerves partially cross. Visual information from the middle part of your visual field travels to opposite sides of your visual cortex, while information from the lateral part of the field (closest to your temples) travels to the same side of the visual cortex.

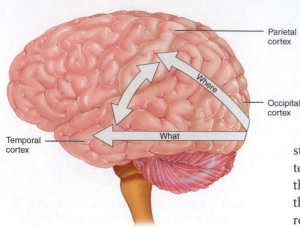

FIGURE 5-11 The "what" and "where" pathways The "what" pathway of the brain processes information that helps us identify an object, while the "where" pathway helps us identify its location in space. Communication between the two pathways allows us to integrate complex visual stimuli.

FIGURE 5-12 Seeing only half the picture When asked to copy a drawing of a house with a driveway, parked car, and garden to its left, a patient with hemi-neglect copies only the right side of the drawing—the house and a tree. She completely ignores the left side of her visual field.

we process the visual information to figure out *where* in space the object is located (is the apple on the table, under the table, or behind the table). The "what" pathway involves axons that travel from the occipital cortex to the temporal cortex. The "where" pathway involves axons that travel from the occipital cortex to the parietal cortex.

How do researchers know about the brain regions that serve these complex functions? Recall from Chapter 4 that one way scientists have determined the function of certain brain regions is by examining the deficits displayed by people who have sustained damage in particular areas of their brains, usually as a result of stroke, disease, or head trauma. Patients with damage to the parts of the temporal cortex, which houses the "what" pathway, exhibit a condition called *visual agnosia*. Although their vision remains intact, they cannot recognize objects visually. When shown a rose, they can describe it, but they cannot name it. If they are allowed to touch or smell the rose, however, they can immediately identify it as a rose. A more specified form of visual agnosia that happens to people with damage to a certain part of the "what" pathway is called *prosopagnosia*. Individuals with prosopagnosia cannot recognize faces (Farah et al., 1995). Sometimes these patients can recognize familiar individuals by concentrating on some visual characteristic that is not directly related to facial features, such as the person's hairstyle or eyeglasses, but their ability to recognize the face itself is lost (Sacks, 1985).

Patients with damage to the "where" pathway also have normal vision, but they have lost the ability to locate objects in space. For example, when given the task of pouring water from a pitcher into a glass, they will invariably miss and pour the water onto the table or floor. A very interesting form of damage to the "where" pathway results in a condition called *hemi-neglect* (Mesulam, 1981). Patients with hemi-neglect completely ignore one side of their visual field. Because nerves that carry visual information cross to the opposite sides of the brain, people with damage to the left side of their "where" pathways neglect the right side, and vice versa (**Figure 5-12**). When asked to copy a drawing, people with hemi-neglect will leave out one half of it. Women with this condition have been known to apply makeup and do their hair only on one side.

In addition to the information researchers have gained from studying patients with brain damage, neuroimaging studies of people without brain damage have confirmed the presence of the "what" and "where" pathways. Indeed, these types of studies have shown that brain activity changes in specific parts of the "what" pathways when the participants are viewing objects (Reddy & Kanwisher, 2006).

So far we have discussed vision from a bottom-up perspective. Light comes in through the eye and the neural impulses generated are passed to successively more complex brain regions that ultimately result in the perception of a visual stimulus. Equally important to visual perception, however, is top-down processing, which involves previously acquired knowledge. Like perception involving the other sensory systems, visual perception involves both bottom-up and top-down processing occurring at the same time. Brain regions that store information about what objects look like can help us to perceive visual stimuli that are partially hidden or of different size from when we originally encountered them.

Putting Together the Parts: Gestalt Principles We don't see images as a series of small patches of color or a series of simple features. Instead, our visual system assembles this information into coherent objects and scenes. Even when we see a small part of an object or scene partially obscured by another object, we are able to perceive it as a whole, given limited visual information. Our brains are organized to fill in the missing parts so that we perceive and recognize meaningful stimuli. As we described earlier, part of our ability to perceive images comes from our use of cognitive processes, such as memory and learning, to help us recall from prior experience images that match the stimuli we are sensing.

The area of study focused on understanding principles by which we perceive and recognize visual stimuli in their entirety despite limited information is called *Gestalt* psychology. As mentioned in Chapter 1, Gestalt psychologists believe that perception helps us to add meaning to visual information, so that "the whole is greater than the sum of the parts" of what we see. Gestalt psychologists have identified several laws by which visual information is organized into coherent images:

- *Proximity* The law of proximity indicates that visual stimuli near to one another tend to be grouped together. For example, AA AA AA is seen as three groups while AAA AAA is seen as two groups despite the fact that each set has six *A*s.
- *Similarity* The law of similarity indicates that stimuli resembling one another tend to be grouped together. So AAaa is viewed as two groups because of the dissimilar appearance of upper and lowercase letters.
- *Continuity* The law of continuity indicates that stimuli falling along the same plane tend to be grouped together. AAA ^{AAA} would be organized into two perceptual groups because they are not on the same line.
- *Good form* The law of good form indicates that stimuli forming a shape tend to be grouped together while those that do not remain ungrouped. Compare ☺ to O:). The former are perceived as a smiley face while the latter are perceived as three separate symbols.
- *Closure* The law of closure indicates that we tend to fill in small gaps in objects so that they are still perceived as whole objects.

These laws of visual organization work to create meaningful information out of the vast array of photons our eyes typically encounter when we look at something.

Sometimes, however, our brain's tendency to impose order can lead us to perceive sights that are, in fact, illusions, such as those shown in **Figure 5-13**. Only careful examination reveals that the drawings depict physically impossible situations.

FIGURE 5-13 Impossible figure The brain is organized to perceive meaningful images; with impossible figures such as this, the brain tries but cannot form a stable perception. (M.C. Escher's "Convex and Concave" ©2009 The M.C. Escher Company-Holland. All rights reserved. www.mcescher.com)

Getting in Deep When you look at the items on the table in a restaurant, how do you know which items are closer to you and which are farther away? We use a number of methods for depth perception, determining the distance of objects away from us and in relation to one another.

Because our eyes are set a slight distance apart, we do not see exactly the same thing with each eye. This **retinal disparity**, the slightly different stimuli recorded by the retina of each eye, provide us with a *binocular* cue of depth. Our brains use the discrepancies between the visual information received from our two eyes to help us judge the distance of objects from us. You can observe your own retinal disparity by holding up a finger at arm's length away from your face. Close first one eye, then the other, and note how the position of your finger seems to change relative to objects in the background beyond the finger.

Another binocular cue to depth is actually tactile. We feel the changes in the muscles around our eyes as we shift them to look at objects at various distances. Closer objects require more **convergence**, turning our eyes inward toward our noses. Use your finger again to demonstrate convergence. Start with the finger at arm's length from you and watch it as you bring it closer and closer to your face. Note the sensations you feel as you do so.

We also use a number of other cues to determine depth. The following are sometimes called **monocular cues**, because, if needed, they can help us judge depth based on information from only one eye. You can see them all in the photo in **Figure 5-14**:

- *Interposition* When one object blocks part of another from our view, we see the blocked object as farther away.
- *Elevation* We see objects that are higher in our visual plane as farther away than those that are lower.

retinal disparity the slight difference in images processed by the retinas of each eye.

convergence inward movement of the eyes to view objects close to oneself.

monocular cues visual clues about depth and distance that can be perceived using information from only one eye.

FIGURE 5-14 **Monocular depth cues** How many monocular depth cues can you identify in this photograph of the Taj Mahal in India?

- *Texture gradient* We can see more details of textured surfaces, such as the wood grain on a restaurant table, that are closer to us.
- *Linear perspective* Parallel lines seem to converge in the distance.
- *Shading* We are accustomed to light, such as sunlight, coming from above us. We use differences in the shading of light from the top to the bottom of our field of view to judge size and distance of objects.
- *Familiar size* Once we have learned the sizes of objects, such as people or restaurant plates, we assume that they stay the same size, so objects that look smaller than usual must be farther away than usual.
- *Relative size* When we look at two objects we know are about the same size, if one seems smaller than the other, we see it as farther away than the other.

Although some studies show that we can perceive depth at very early ages, and may even be born with some depth perception abilities, top-down processing also plays a part in depth processing (Banks & Salapatek, 1983). We use our memories of the sizes of objects around us, for example, to help judge depth.

Artists use monocular depth cues to help us "see" depth in their two-dimensional representations. In essence, they create an illusion of depth. Because visual perception happens nearly automatically, we are quite susceptible to such visual illusions. For example, people from cultures that have a lot of architecture and structures featuring straight edges, such as the United States, are easily fooled by the Ponzo illusion and Müller-Lyer illusion, shown in **Figure 5-15**, which both take advantage of our tendency to use linear perspective to judge distance (Berry et al, 1992; Brislin & Keating, 1976).

Seeing What We Expect to See: Perceptual Constancies Top-down processing also contributes to **perceptual constancies**, our tendencies to view objects as unchanging in some ways, even though the actual visual sensations we receive are constantly shifting. We tend to see the food on our plate as the same colors, for example, even when a restaurant owner dims the lights for the evening and the actual light waves we are receiving change in intensity, a phenomenon known as color *constancy* (Schiffman, 1996). Once we have learned the shape of an object, we also experience shape constancy (Gazzaniga, 1995). We may get visual input of only the edge of a plate as server sets it on a restaurant table in front of us, but we perceive the plate as a round disk.

Another consistency, size consistency, helps us in depth perception, as noted above. Once we have learned the size of an object, we expect it to stay the same. Top-down processing, based on our memory of the object's size, leads us to assume that if it looks smaller than usual, it is probably far away, instead of thinking that the object has somehow shrunk. As with our other perceptual processes, perceptual constancies, while usually very useful in helping us understand the world, can sometimes lead us to "see" illusions. A common size illusion, for example, is the moon illusion. The moon stays the

perceptual constancies our top-down tendency to view objects as unchanging, despite shifts in the environmental stimuli we receive.

(a)

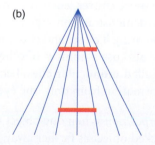

(b)

FIGURE 5-15 **Perceptual illusions** (a) The Müller-Lyer illusion: The line on the right appears longer, but both lines are the same length.

(b) The Ponzo illusion: The converging lines make the upper bar seem larger, but both bars are identical in length.

same size all the time, but when we view it close to a horizon it appears much bigger than when we see it farther from the horizon (see **Figure 5-16**) (Kaufman & Rock, 1989).

Sight | How we *Develop*

Newborn infants are capable of seeing, but their visual acuity is much less than it will be after a few months. For a short time after birth, human babies focus mostly on contrasts. For example, a baby will stare at the hairline of his or her caregiver, instead of the face.

By the time we are about two months old, visual acuity has improved and infants seem to focus intently on faces. Their focal range is limited, though. They see objects best that are within a foot away. Perhaps not coincidentally, this is about the distance people tend to place their faces when interacting with babies. Over the next several months, our visual acuity improves so that by the end of the eighth month, vision in babies is quite similar to that of normal adults. These early life changes in vision are due to the postnatal development of the visual nervous system. As we'll see next, proper development of the visual system requires visual experience during a specific part of early life.

Sight | When Things Go *Wrong*

Many common vision problems can be corrected today. Increasingly common laser surgeries or the lenses in glasses or contacts can help people cope with nearsightedness, or difficulty seeing things clearly far away, and farsightedness, problems seeing near objects clearly, for example. Eye-care practitioners help with a variety of other problems as well. Sometimes, however, there is no treatment available, or treatment is begun too late to prevent people from losing vision in one or both eyes.

Amblyopia To see the world as a whole, both eyes must work together to produce not two separate images, but one comprehensive image. To do this, motor control of both eyes is important. Newborn infants often do not move their eyes in tandem. It is not uncommon for parents to report concern that their young infants sometimes appear to have crossed eyes. This is a normal characteristic that typically resolves itself within a few months after birth as the eye muscles and the motor system that controls them mature.

Some people, however, do not naturally develop coordinated movement of both eyes. This condition is called *strabismus* and affects about 2 percent of the population. To avoid seeing double images, children with strabismus will rely on the visual information from one eye while ignoring information from other. Strabismus is commonly treated by having the child wear a patch over the stronger eye, thus forcing the child to use the weaker one, or by surgery. If children are treated during early life, their normal binocular vision can be preserved.

If strabismus remains uncorrected past the age of about six years, however, it will eventually lead to a loss of visual abilities in the weaker eye, or *amblyopia*. Amblyopia can be a permanent condition that results from abnormal development of the brain's visual cortex. As we discussed in Chapter 3, many development psychologists suggest that there are not only sensitive periods, when we can develop certain skills with greater ease than at other time in our lives, but also "critical periods," which are the *only* times during which certain developments can take place. Amblyopia develops if we do not receive visual stimulation from both eyes during the critical period of development for the normal maturation of the visual brain. After about the age of six, the brains of children with strabismus seem to lose the ability to use information from both eyes and instead process inputs only from one eye.

FIGURE 5-16 The moon illusion The moon is the same size all the time but it appears larger near the horizon than higher in the sky, partly because no depth cues exist in space.

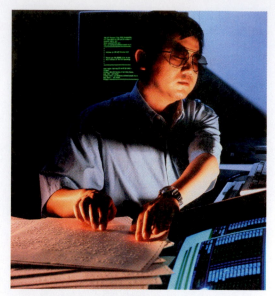

A life of accomplishment Braille, devised in 1821 by blind Frenchman Louis Braille, has greatly improved the level of accomplishment and quality of life of people who are sightless. Here a blind computer developer reads Braille at his workstation.

Blindness About 12 million people in the United States suffer from visual impairments that are either total or so severe and uncorrectable that these individuals are characterized as blind. There are many potential causes of blindness. Some are congenital, or present at birth, while others are acquired later in life. Diseases that can produce blindness include diabetes, glaucoma, and macular degeneration.

Since humans rely so heavily on visual information, living without adequate visual input is very challenging. A number of devices have been created to help blind people live independently. Braille, a system of reading that involves touch, has significantly improved quality of life for the blind. Braille uses various combinations of raised dots to replace traditional printed letters and numbers.

Visually impaired individuals can become so proficient at reading Braille that they can actually read faster than people with normal vision typically read printed material. Researchers have found that blind individuals who become experts at reading Braille are actually using parts of their "visual" brain to process the sophisticated tactile information. Neuroimaging studies have shown that parts of the occipital and temporal cortices that normally process visual information are activated in blind individuals while they read Braille. It is also noteworthy that the individuals with congenital blindness use more of their visual brains to read Braille than did those who became blind later in life. This may be another example of a critical period at work. The acquisition of Braille reading skills as a child may allow for the reorganization of the visual system to serve some new function. Learning Braille later in life may lead to less dramatic reorganization because those parts of the visual brain have already become "hard-wired," or less plastic and open to change.

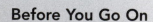

Before You Go On

What Do You Know?

16. What are rods and cones?

17. What are the two theories of color vision and how do they work together?

18. What do the "what" and "where" pathways in the brain do?

19. What are the two major types of depth perception cues and what is the difference between them?

20. What is strabismus, how is it treated, and what can happen if it is not treated promptly?

What Do You Think? Is the cliché, "Seeing is believing," really true? Why or why not?

Summary

Sensation is the process of converting physical stimuli from our environment into neural impulses that the brain can process. Perception is the process of interpreting the neural signals to understand the information we receive.

Common Features of Sensation and Perception

LEARNING OBJECTIVE 1   Describe characteristics shared by all the senses, including receptor cells, transduction, and thresholds, and differentiate between top-down and bottom-up processes of perception.

- Our sensory systems convert physical stimuli into neural information with specialized cells called *sensory receptor cells* that convert a specific form of environmental stimuli into neural impulses by a process called *sensory transduction*.
- The conversion of physical stimuli into neural impulses only occurs when the stimuli reach a certain level, or threshold. The absolute threshold is the minimum level of a stimulus we can detect. The difference threshold is the smallest difference we can detect between two similar stimuli.
- Our sensory systems are set up to detect change. With continuous exposure to a stimulus, adaptation occurs.

The Chemical Senses: Smell and Taste

LEARNING OBJECTIVE 2   Summarize what happens when we smell and taste.

- Smell, our olfactory sense, converts chemical odorants into neural signals that the brain can use. Taste, our gustatory sense, is closely intertwined with smell. Most flavors are a combination of scents with the five basic tastes we can discern: sweet, salty, sour, bitter, and umami.
- Our tactile sense combines with taste and smell, to help us appreciate, or dislike the textures of foods and to experience temperature and "hot" sensations from capsaicin in spicy foods.
- Taste buds in papillae on the tongue convert chemicals in our food to neural signals the brain can use. Taste receptors and smell receptors are routinely replaced, since they are more vulnerable to damage than other sensory receptors.
- Information about smell goes directly from the olfactory bulb to the olfactory cortex. Areas of the brain that process smells and tastes are plastic, or changeable. Processing of smells also sometimes overlaps with emotions and memories.
- Our preferred tastes change as we mature from childhood to adulthood, probably from a combination of learning and physical changes in the mouth.
- True disorders of taste are rare; people more frequently lose part or all of their sense of smell. Anosmia can present safety risks and diminish pleasure in life.

The Tactile or Cutaneous Senses: Touch, Pressure, Pain, Vibration

LEARNING OBJECTIVE 3   Describe how the different senses of touch work and what can happen when things go wrong.

- A variety of sensory receptors throughout our bodies convert touch, pressure, or temperature stimuli into neural impulses that our brains can perceive.
- The sensory cortex of the brain maps touch sensations. Especially sensitive or important body parts receive disproportionately large representation in the cortex.
- Pain travels to the brain via both a fast pathway and a slow pathway.
- People differ greatly in the perception of pain. Some of the differences are related to culture and gender. Others are individual.
- The gate control theory of pain suggests that certain patterns of neural activity can close a "gate" so that pain information does not reach parts of the brain where it is perceived.
- Medical professionals continue to search for ways to relieve people's chronic pain. Opiate drugs that simulate natural pain-killing endorphins or enkephalins are addictive. Sometimes practitioners resort to neurosurgery, which stops a patient from receiving all touch signals.
- The inability to feel pain can put people at high risk for injuries.
- People who have lost body parts surgically or through accidents often feel phantom sensations in the missing body part. These may be related to reorganization of the somatosensory cortex after an amputation.

The Auditory Sense: Hearing

LEARNING OBJECTIVE 4 Summarize what happens when we hear.

- The frequency and amplitude of sound waves produce our perceptions of pitch and loudness of sounds.

- When sounds enter the ear, they move the ear drum, which sets in motion the ossicles. The last of these, the stirrup, vibrates the oval window, setting into motion fluid in the cochlea. Hair cells on the basilar membrane in the cochlea transduce movements along the basilar membrane into neural signals the brain can interpret.

- Frequency theory suggests that patterns in the firing rates of the neurons are perceived as different sounds. Place theory suggests that information from different locations along the basilar membrane is related to different qualities of sound.

- Top-down processing lets us use the general loudness of sounds, as well as differences in the signals received from each ear, to determine location of a sound.

- Different pitches are represented in a tonotopic map in the auditory cortex of the brain. Association areas of the cortex help us recognize familiar sounds, including speech.

- The brain integrates information from multiple sensory systems to enable the appropriate recognition and response to stimuli. Some people experience an overlap of sensory systems known as synesthesia.

- As young children, we experience a sensitive period during which it is especially easy for us to learn auditory information, including language and music. Some people, particularly those exposed to pure tones during this sensitive period, develop absolute pitch.

- Common hearing problems include hearing loss and deafness, as well as hearing unwanted sounds, such as tinnitus.

The Visual Sense: Sight

LEARNING OBJECTIVE 5 Describe key processes in visual sensation and perception.

- Vision is very important to humans, and a great deal of our brain is involved in processing visual information.

- Rods and cones in the retina at the back of the eye change light into neural impulses. Cones provide detailed vision and help us perceive color, while rods provide information about intensity of light.

- Two different theories in combination—trichomatic theory and opponent process theory—explain a good deal of how we perceive color.

- The fovea at the center of the retina contains only cones and provides our sharpest vision. We have a blind spot where the optic nerve leaves the retina to carry information to the brain.

- In the brain, visual information is processed through the "what" and "where" pathways.

- Damage to the brain can produce deficits in sensation, as well as abnormal sensory experiences.

- Top-down processing is involved in much visual perception. Gestalt theorists have identified several principles by which we recognize stimuli even when visual inputs are limited. We use binocular and monocular cues for depth perception. Perceptual constancies, based on learning from previous experiences, help us to see things as stable despite constant shifts in our visual inputs. These top-down processes can be "fooled" by visual illusions.

- Without adequate visual stimulation through both eyes during a critical period of life, we may not develop binocular vision, a condition known as amblyopia.

- Blind individuals can use other sensory modalities to compensation for the loss of visual information. Learning Braille with touch involves the use of brain areas normally used for vision.

Key Terms

CUT/ACROSS CONNECTION

What Happens in the BRAIN?

- The brain normally integrates information from multiple sensory systems. In people who experience synesthesia, brain areas for one sense are activated by stimuli related to different senses, so that they might, for example, hear colors.
- Different parts of our brains are active in figuring out what we see from those that help us figure out where things are when we see them.
- Blind people who learn to read Braille at early ages actually use parts of their visual cortex to do so, in addition to areas normally associated with touch.

When Things Go Wrong

- People rarely lose their sense of taste. Most problems with taste are related to loss of sense of smell.
- When we damage taste buds or odor receptors in the nose, they are replaced, but damage to other sensory receptors, such as photoreceptors and hair cells, is permanent. They are not replaced.
- People who experience phantom sensations in missing body parts usually feel things they actually felt before losing the body part.

HOW we Differ

- About a fourth of all people are supertasters, able to discern bitter tastes that many others do not even notice.
- On average, women have more sensory receptors for pain in their faces than men do.
- Only about 1 person in 10,000 in Western countries develops absolute pitch, the ability to identify tones heard in isolation. More people who speak tonal languages have absolute pitch.
- About 4 people in 100 in the United States are tone deaf.

How we Develop

- All of our sensory systems begin to develop during fetal life. We can hear, feel, smell, and taste before we are born.
- Sight is our least developed sense at birth.
- Children have more taste buds in more locations in their mouths than adults, which may explain in part why they dislike many new foods.

Video Lab Exercise

www.wileyplus.com

Psychology Around Us

The Ups and Downs of Visual Perception

Seeing is Not Always Believing

Whether driving through the streets of a city, looking out a train window at the passing landscape, or viewing events on the ground from a plane above, you are relying on your visual senses. Come along for a video ride in which nothing can be taken for granted and during which you will be asked to not only enjoy the view, but to explain it, ignore it, adjust to it, or change it.

As you are working on this on-line exercise, consider the following questions:

- What does this lab exercise say about both the power and the limits of visual perception?
- What's going on in your brain as you correctly observe objects, adapt to visual events, or are fooled by visual illusions?
- What role does attention play in visual perception?
- How might your auditory sense affect what you see?

CHAPTER 6

Consciousness

chapter outline

- When We Are Awake: Conscious Awareness
- Preconscious and Unconscious States
- Hypnosis • Meditation
- When We Are Asleep • Psychoactive Drugs

Love and Awareness on an Errand

Imagine yourself driving a car, perhaps to drop off some clothes at the dry cleaners on a Saturday morning. You've slept in, so you're feeling pretty relaxed and alert. Traffic is light and driving easy. You're singing along with some music playing. One song reminds you of a former love, and you begin to recall a special intimate moment with that person. But since he or she dumped you, you try to shift your focus to your psychology homework assignment. You slow as you see a stoplight turn yellow, then stop for the red light. What will you write about, you wonder, as you wait for the light? Maybe the pain of ending relationships would be a good paper topic.

You begin to accelerate as the light turns green, but then jerk to a halt when you notice another car sailing through the intersection against the red light on the cross street. The driver is obviously distracted by yakking on his cell phone, and you wonder whether he might be drunk, too, judging by his excessive speed. You're suddenly back to thinking entirely about driving as you avoid this driver. Crisis averted, you notice the song that made you think of your ex is over and a new song is playing. This one reminds of your new sweetie, and you recall a nice dream you had last night, in which your current love featured quite heavily....

Quite a lot can occur to you when running a simple errand, such as going to the dry cleaners!

Consciousness is often defined as our immediate awareness of our internal and external states. But how aware is "aware"? Sometimes we are keenly aware of something and other times only dimly so. In addition, sometimes we do not seem to be paying much attention to complex stimuli, yet we wind up recalling information from them later. Consider people who are just learning how to drive. New drivers must concentrate carefully on checking the rearview mirror, gauging how hard to press on the gas and brake pedals, and the like. In time and with experience, drivers come to perform most of these activities almost automatically; they stop being particularly aware of them while driving. An experienced driver can stop the car while simultaneously pondering a topic for his or her psychology paper, for example.

Heightened awareness Navigating an automobile requires full concentration for new drivers such as this nervous individual. This is not the case, however, for people who have been at it for years, many of whom are barely conscious of the driving-related tasks they are performing.

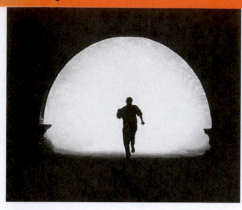

A man lies dying. He hears himself pronounced dead by his doctor. He feels himself rushing through a long, dark tunnel and suddenly finds himself outside his body, observing it from a distance as the doctor tries to revive him Soon, a loving, warm spirit—a being of light—comes to meet him and directs him through a panoramic review of the major events of his life. He feels himself approaching a barrier—a sort of border between earthly existence and some other state. He is overwhelmed by joy but must return to his body, for the time has not come for him to die. Later, he has trouble describing this experience, but it profoundly affects his life and his feelings about death.

Thus does Dr. Raymond Moody describe a typical near-death experience (NDE) in his best-selling 1975 book, *Life after Life*, which introduced NDEs into the popular culture. Typically these experiences include some or all of the features just described—the tunnel, the out-of-body experience, the bright light, and so forth. Over the past several decades, many people have reported having such experiences (Carey, 2009). The question is, what causes them?

Some observers offer a religious or supernatural explanation, that the soul leaves the body during an NDE and encounters a "spirit of light" (Sheikh et al., 2007). Moody himself has adopted this view.

But many researchers disagree and look instead to more scientific explanations (Nelson et al., 2006). Some point out, for example, that certain drugs produce the same effects as NDEs. Perhaps the brain, under great stress, releases chemicals that, like these drugs, induce hallucinations (Augustine, 2007). Others attribute NDEs to the brain's constant efforts to process our sensory experiences and maintain a stable sense of reality. As a person nears death, the senses shut down, sending faulty information that the brain tries to interpret as best it can. This effort may lead to misinterpretations about where the body is in space or produce the sensation of being in a dark tunnel with bright light at the end. These and other scientific explanations share the notion that NDEs often reflect an altered state of consciousness that is brought about by sensory arousal, a heightened state of awareness, and the brain's ongoing efforts to determine what we experience as real.

In addition to these constant, mostly effortless, shifts in our awareness, we can also experience shifts that occur as the result of special events or efforts, such as being asleep, dreaming, meditating, or ingesting alcohol or other substances. In this chapter, we shall examine conscious awareness, changes in consciousness, and some of the major ways in which these changes come about.

The study of consciousness has undergone many historical shifts. As you may recall from Chapter 1, early psychologists defined psychology entirely as the study of consciousness. The influential American psychologist William James, for example, noted that our conscious awareness continually shifts based on what we're paying attention to and how intensely we are attending (Singer, 2003). Nevertheless, we feel continuity from moment to moment. As the opening story describes, many thoughts and fantasies—all different in meaning and feeling—can occur within a short period of time, yet we maintain a sense of sameness. Whether thinking of former lovers or dry cleaning, we have a sense of ourselves as the same person. James coined the term "stream of consciousness" to signify how we experience our conscious life, because consciousness, like a running stream, keeps moving, yet seems to be the same.

You may also recall from Chapter 1 that one of psychology's most influential theories of consciousness has been Sigmund Freud's psychoanalytic theory. Freud introduced the idea that we can have *unconscious* thoughts and feelings of which we are not even aware. Right up to his death in 1939, Freud kept defining and revising his ideas about states of consciousness, and we will discuss these in some detail later in this chapter.

consciousness our immediate awareness of our internal and external states.

Partly in response to the difficulties of conducting research on elusive concepts, such as the unconscious mind, many researchers during the first half of the twentieth century, especially those in North America, shifted their interest from consciousness to observable behavior and, as you read in Chapter 1, equated psychology with *behaviorism* (Baars, 2003). Theorists and researchers in Europe, however, continued to pay significant attention to consciousness and even unconsciousness.

During the latter part of the twentieth century, with important developments in neuroscience and computer technology, consciousness reemerged as a topic of major interest in psychology (Frith, 2003). With the help of neuroimaging techniques, investigators have been able to explore meaningfully the relationship between brain activity and various states of consciousness (Keenan, Gallup, & Falk, 2003). Indeed, a considerable body of research now is directed at the study of conscious, less conscious, and nonconscious states (Baruss, 2003).

Test your own powers of attention. Before finishing this introduction, take a break and watch the video at http://viscog.beckman.illinois.edu/flashmovie/15.php. Count how many times the players in white shirts complete a pass of the basketball.

When We Are Awake: Conscious Awareness

LEARNING OBJECTIVE 1 Define different levels of conscious awareness and describe key brain structures and functions associated with those levels.

As the opening vignette illustrates, *attention* plays a key role in conscious awareness. Psychiatric researcher John Ratey (2001) has pointed out, "Before we can be conscious of something...we have to pay attention to it." At the same time, attention does not equal consciousness. We need something more. To be fully conscious of something, we must be *aware* that we are attending to it.

Conscious awareness of ourselves, our needs, and how to satisfy them has directly aided us in survival, contributing mightily to our evolutionary progress. To be conscious of our thirst, for example, is to understand that water is necessary to quench it, and to know that certain actions are necessary to obtain water, helps us compete successfully for water—more successfully than creatures that operate without consciousness. Clearly, conscious awareness involves elements beyond attention, and in fact, a number of such elements have been suggested by theorists. Three of the most prominent are *monitoring*, *remembering*, and *planning*:

- We *monitor* ourselves and our environment as we decide (implicitly) what items to be aware of (Glaser & Kihlstrom, 2005). A quickly moving car approaching us might catch our awareness, for example.

- In order to be aware of a current event, we often must bring forth *memories* of past experiences and previously acquired knowledge and skills (Baars, 2003; Osaka, 2003). Such memories establish a context for our current situation, provide us with the motivation and ability to focus on it, and may even become part of the present situation. A driver has to have a memory related to red lights in order to be aware that a yellow light is a signal to slow down.

- *Control* and *planning* are also often at work. In fact, to help us plan for the future—from which route to take to the dry cleaners to our choice of a mate or career—we often bring into conscious awareness images, events, and scenarios that have never occurred. In such cases, conscious awareness may help us to initiate more effective behaviors or make wiser decisions.

No room for error As we interact with our environment, we constantly monitor both ourselves and the situations at hand to help ensure that we attend to key features of the interactions. When performing a dangerous task, such as climbing a mountain, careful monitoring can take on life-and-death importance.

Multiple brain processes and structures must be operating simultaneously in order for us to be conscious of our world or ourselves (Kolb & Whishaw, 2009). In fact, research has shown that when we are awake, most if not all the neurons in our brains are constantly active. Of course, certain neurons become particularly active when an individual is stimulated by objects or events, but even in the absence of such stimulation, neurons are still active at a steady, low level and are communicating with other neurons (Llinas, 2001; Llinas & Ribary, 2001).

Recall from Chapter 4 that neurons tend to work together in groups, or *networks*, and those networks become more and more efficient with repeated use. For us to experience conscious awareness of something, such as a thought or an oncoming car, many of these networks must become particularly active at once. While one set of networks is enabling us to pay attention to the stimulus, other biological events must also be at work, enabling us to be aware and recognize that we are attending. Still others are allowing us to monitor, remember, and control.

Think back to the basketball video. Did you immediately notice the gorilla among the players, or did you miss it? What do you think that implies about your consciousness?

Researchers have not yet pinpointed all of the brain areas and events that are responsible for such *parallel processing*, but research has suggested that two areas of great importance to consciousness are the *cerebral cortex*, the brain's outer covering of cells, and the *thalamus*, the brain structure that often relays sensory information from various parts of the brain to the cerebral cortex.

The Cerebral Cortex   Evidence has accumulated that some areas of the brain are responsible for attention, while other areas—particularly ones in the cerebral cortex—are in charge of one's awareness of that attention. Investigations by Lawrence Weiskrantz (2002, 2000, 1997) on *blindsight* illustrate how this works in the visual realm.

Weiskrantz studied people whose visual areas in the cerebral cortex had been destroyed, leaving them blind, so far as they were aware. When Weiskrantz presented such people with a spot of light on a screen and asked them to point to it, the individuals were totally unaware of the light and could not fulfill the request. Yet, when he told the same individuals to "just point anywhere," they typically pointed in the direction of the light. Similarly, these individuals could generally avoid chairs, tables, and other objects as they walked through a room, denying all the while that they were seeing anything at all. In short, the patients in Weiskrantz's studies could and did readily attend to visual objects, yet because the visual areas in their cerebral cortex had been destroyed, they were unaware of those objects. Weiskrantz and others have concluded that the areas of the brain that help us *attend* to visual stimuli are different from the visual areas in the cerebral cortex that help us to be *aware* that we are attending to such stimuli.

Remarkable studies of "split-brain" patients, conducted by investigators Roger Sperry (1998, 1995, 1985, 1982) and Michael Gazzaniga (2000, 1995, 1988, 1983), also point to the cerebral cortex as a center of conscious awareness. As you'll recall from Chapter 4, people with severe seizure disorders can sometimes be helped by cutting the nerve fibers of their *corpus callosum,* the brain structure that connects the two hemispheres of the brain, to keep abnormal activity from traveling from one side of the brain to the other. By carefully studying such split-brain patients, Sperry and Gazzaniga learned that the left and right sides of the cerebral cortex may play different roles in conscious awareness.

As shown in **Figure 6-1**, in the split-brain patients, the objects in the left visual field project only to the visual area in the right hemisphere (Thompson, 2000). Similarly,

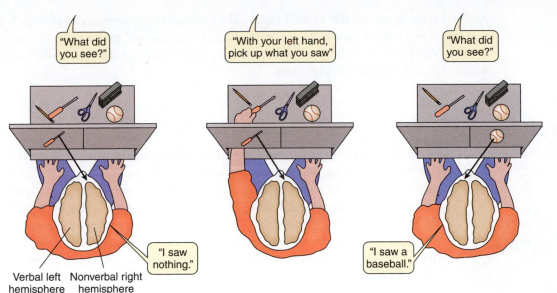

"What did you see?"

"With your left hand, pick up what you saw"

"What did you see?"

"I saw nothing."

"I saw a baseball."

Verbal left hemisphere   Nonverbal right hemisphere

FIGURE 6-1 **Split-brain research** (a) When a picture of a screwdriver is flashed to a split-brain patient's left visual field, the information goes to his nonverbal right hemisphere and he cannot name the object. (b) When instructed to feel behind a screen among a variety of objects and select the one that matches the picture just seen, the patient correctly selects the screwdriver. (c) When a picture of a baseball is flashed to the patient's right visual field, he easily names it.

visual information presented to the right visual field projects only to the visual area in the left cortex.

Using this information, the investigators found that when they showed a word to a patient's left hemisphere, the individual was readily able to say and write the word. When a word was flashed to the right hemisphere, however, the individual could *not* say or write it. Apparently, the left cerebral cortex is responsible for verbal awareness.

In contrast, the right cerebral cortex seems to be responsible for nonverbal forms of conscious awareness. In one study, for example, the experimenters flashed a picture of a screwdriver to each patient's right hemisphere. The individuals were then instructed to feel, from behind a screen, a variety of real objects, including a real screwdriver, and on the basis of touch, to select the object that matched the picture they had just seen: all correctly selected a screwdriver. Apparently, the right cerebral cortex can produce tactile awareness and perhaps other kinds of nonverbal awareness as well, but not verbal awareness. Of course, for most of us, our two hemispheres are connected and these various kinds of awareness occur simultaneously, helping to produce a broad and complete sense of conscious awareness.

The Thalamus We might think of the networks of neurons in the brain as similar to the different train lines in a complicated subway system, like that of New York City. In order for trains to get from place to place on schedule without collision, a train conductor (or even a whole group of them) must oversee the process. Researchers have nominated several brain areas as potential conductors, involved in routing messages along the proper neural network "subway lines" of our brains. Two of the most prominent candidates are the *intralaminar nuclei* and *midline nuclei* of the *thalamus* (Van der Werf et al., 2002; Ratey, 2001). Research indicates that the intralaminar and midline nuclei receive and project long axons to neurons throughout the cerebral cortex, including areas that, as we have seen, are involved in conscious awareness (Ratey, 2001).

Consistent with this theory, investigators have observed that people actually lose all consciousness and enter a deep coma if their intralaminar and midline nuclei are broadly damaged. If, however, the damage to the nuclei occurs in only one hemisphere, individuals lose awareness of only half of their bodies. They become unaware of all events that occur on one side of their visual field, for example, or unaware of all objects that touch one side of their body. In short, the intralaminar and midline nuclei seem to play an important role in conscious awareness, with different nuclei responsible for different dimensions of consciousness.

Alert Consciousness How we *Develop*

There have been a number of attempts to identity consciousness in infants. As we saw in Chapter 3, there is evidence that even before the age of 2, babies may be able to direct their attention, hold concepts in mind, and engage in planned or intentional behaviors—the component skills of consciousness. Because babies are not yet able to talk very well, however, it's difficult to determine how aware they are that their experiences are things happening to them, or even whether they are fully aware of themselves as separate beings from others, a concept known as *sense of self.*

Researchers have developed some ingenious ways to try to determine when babies first experience a sense of self. In one test, experimenters secretly dabbed red make-up on babies' foreheads while pretending to wipe them. Then they placed the babies in front of a mirror. The researchers reasoned that babies who had developed a sense of self would see the makeup and touch their own heads, while those who did not understand they were looking them-selves in the mirror would try to touch the makeup by touching the mirror. Based on such tests, it seems that most children develop a stable concept of the self by around 18 months of age (Gallup, 1970; Lewis & Brooks-Gunn, 1979).

Some researchers suggest that the early cognitive development we discussed in Chapter 3 and the development of consciousness contribute to one another. That is, if infants demonstrate the ability to develop concepts and to think through their behaviors—even if they cannot express such thinking—they should be viewed as having a rudimentary sense of self-consciousness. Without this rudimentary sense of consciousness, babies would not be able to develop any concept at all (Mandler, 2004).

Other theorists suggest that consciousness itself is rooted in language. Because babies do not have language, they cannot reflect on their thoughts and behaviors and do not have consciousness yet (Rakison, 2007; Zelazo, 2004). These theorists suggest that a shift happens at around 22 months of age, when babies show the abilities to reason inductively and to name and categorize concepts, which in turn enable them to represent concepts in a richer and deeper way.

Thus, describing how consciousness develops during awake states remains both a philosophical and empirical question, influenced in large part by how we define consciousness. The matter is further complicated by the question we asked at the beginning of this chapter: Just how aware is "aware"? We'll see next that there may be levels of alert consciousness at which we are not fully aware of all our thoughts.

Hello there When babies look into a mirror and realize that they are looking at themselves, it means that they are finally experiencing a sense of self. That is, they are aware of themselves as separate beings from others.

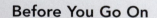

Before You Go On

What Do You Know?

1. List the core cognitive processes of consciousness.
2. What is blindsight?

What Do You Think?   What characteristics do you believe are essential to define alert consciousness?

Preconscious and Unconscious States

preconsciousness level of awareness in which information can become readily available to consciousness if necessary.

unconscious state state in which information is not easily accessible to conscious awareness.

LEARNING OBJECTIVE 2 Summarize the ideas of preconscious and unconscious states, including Freud's thinking on the unconscious.

Theorists often talk about different "levels of consciousness" or "degrees of consciousness," and some believe that consciousness should be distinguished from two alternative states, *preconsciousness* and *unconsciousness.*

Preconsciousness is a level of awareness in which information can become readily available to consciousness if necessary. Have you ever tried to remember something that you're certain you know but just cannot recall at the moment? When something is on the tip-of-your-tongue (a phenomenon we'll talk about again in Chapter 8), it is in your preconsciousness. When (or if) you finally do remember it, the memory has reached consciousness.

Many of our most familiar behaviors occur during preconsciousness. Take a second—can you remember exactly what your morning ritual was this morning? What song was playing when you woke up? Did you count every tooth as you brushed it? For many morning activities, you probably do things in the same order, but you do not necessarily need to plan all the steps or think about what you're doing as you move through your ritual. Preconscious behaviors of this kind are sometimes called *automatic behaviors.* As we saw at the beginning of the chapter, driving can involve automatic behaviors.

An **unconscious state** is one in which information is not easily accessible to conscious awareness. Perhaps at a particularly beautiful moment while watching a movie, you become teary-eyed, with no idea why. Psychoanalytic theorists, influenced by the ideas of Sigmund Freud, would suggest that the movie triggered a memory in your unconscious. It may be a memory of an especially happy or difficult time in your childhood, but chances are, you will never find out for sure. Information, feelings, and memories held in the unconscious are—by definition—not readily available to conscious awareness. So, at the movies, you may just have to enjoy the tearful moment without fully appreciating why you are so moved.

"If you ask me, all three of us are in different states of awareness."

Freud's Views of the Unconscious

Although there are many current views about the unconscious, most have some relationship to the explanation advanced by Sigmund Freud (Kihlstrom, 1999). As we discussed in Chapter 1, Freud believed that the vast majority of our personal knowledge is located in our unconsciousness, and thus is not readily accessible (see **Figure 6-2**). According to him, one of the key functions of the unconsciousness is to house thoughts and memories too painful or disturbing to us to remain in our consciousness (Gomes, 2003). Indeed, he maintained that at some level, we may *repress* such thoughts and memories, keeping them in our unconscious and preventing them from entering our conscious experience. Even though we cannot access unconscious material directly, Freud still believed the unconscious is an important driver of human behavior.

Freud also suggested that, although it is typically inaccessible, unconscious material does come into conscious awareness on occasion (Ross, 2003). Have you ever meant to say one thing, but something very different comes out, often to your embarrassment? Freud identified this slip of the tongue (called a *Freudian slip*) as a moment when the mind inadvertently allows a repressed idea into consciousness. Let's say that you do not

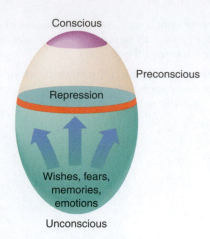

FIGURE 6-2 Freud's view of the unconscious
According to Freud, material that is relegated to the unconscious, such as repressed material, enters preconscious awareness or conscious awareness only accidentally or indirectly.

enjoy your job but you're not sure why. One day you arrive at work 15 minutes late and your boss is waiting for you. Whereas you intend to say, "I'm sorry I'm late, boss," you say instead, "I'm sorry I hate boss." Suddenly you—and your boss—are well aware of why you don't like your job!

Freud also believed that our unconscious can work against us and that people who store too many emotionally-charged memories and needs in their unconscious may eventually develop psychological disorders (as we will discuss in further detail in Chapters 13 and 16). His theory suggests that the knowledge and memories stored in the unconscious maintain their ability to influence how we think, feel, and relate to others. If we repress too much, we may experience distortions in how we feel or relate to others, and, at the same time, we may feel helpless to change. Based on this part of Freud's theory, psychoanalytic psychotherapy attempts to bring patients' unconscious material into their conscious awareness.

Cognitive Views of the Unconscious

Throughout much of the twentieth century, scientists paid little, if any, attention to the unconscious. Rejecting Freud's psychoanalytic ideas, they also rejected the notion that people's behaviors, thoughts, and feelings may be influenced by mental forces of which they are totally unaware. This dismissal of the unconscious has shifted dramatically in recent decades. Today, most psychologists believe that unconscious functioning does occur and a number of explanations—particularly cognitive explanations—have been proposed.

Perhaps the most prominent cognitive explanation for unconscious processing points to the concept of **implicit memory** (Kihlstrom et al., 2007, 2000). As we shall observe more closely in Chapter 8, cognitive theorists distinguish two basic kinds of memory—*explicit memory* and *implicit memory*. Explicit memories are pieces of knowledge that we are fully aware of. Knowing the date of your birth is an explicit memory. Implicit memories refer to knowledge that we are not typically aware of — information that we cannot recall at will—but that we use in the performance of various tasks in life.

Implicit memory is usually on display in the *skills* we acquire, such as reading, playing an instrument, driving a car, or speaking a second language. Our performance of such skills improves as we gain more and more of the knowledge, motor behaviors, and perceptual information required for the skills. These gains—that is, these implicit memories—are usually revealed to us indirectly by our improved performances, not by our consciously recalling the acquired information and experiences that led to the improvements. Shortly after learning to drive, you may realize one day that you are able to drive and talk to a passenger at the same time, for example, but not recall the exact moment you learned how to control the wheel and pedals well enough to add the additional activity of carrying on a conversation.

Implicit memory may also involve factual information. When we vote for a particular candidate on election day, a wealth of past experiences and information may be at the root of that behavior—childhood discussions with our parents about political parties, Web sites we've seen, articles we've read, political science classes we've taken, interviews or "news-bites" we have heard, and more. As we pull the election lever, however, we typically are not aware of all these past experiences or pieces of information.

Cognitive and cognitive neuroscience theorists see implicit memories as a part of everyday functioning rather than as a way to keep difficult information from reaching our awareness (Kihlstrom et al., 2007, 2000). They have discovered research methods to test our unconscious—implicit—memories and have gathered evidence that explicit and implicit memories are stored in different pathways in the brain.

implicit memory knowledge that we have stored in memory that we are not typically aware of or able to recall at will.

hypnosis a seemingly altered state of consciousness during which individuals can be directed to act or experience the world in unusual ways.

What Do You Know?

3. What is the difference between preconscious and unconscious states?

4. What is the importance of implicit memory to the notion of the unconscious?

What Do You Think?   Do you think there are unconscious forces driving people's behaviors? If not, is it all conscious choice, or do you believe there are other explanations?

Hypnosis

LEARNING OBJECTIVE 3 Discuss theories and evidence about what hypnosis is, how it works, and how it can be used.

In movie and cartoon portrayals of hypnosis, a creepy guy dressed in black tells an unsuspecting person to stare at a swinging pocket watch and says, "Relax, just relax." Soon, the person is completely under the power of the hypnotist, who often makes him or her do something completely out of character or, in more sinister films, illegal and dangerous. As you might expect, this image is exaggerated and distorted.

It is true, however, that in real life, **hypnosis** is considered by many psychologists to be an altered state of consciousness (Kihlstrom, 2007; Farvolden & Woody, 2004). During hypnosis, people can be directed to act in unusual ways, experience unusual sensations, remember forgotten events, or forget remembered events.

People typically are guided into this suggestible state by a trained hypnotist or hypnotherapist. The process involves their willing relinquishment of control over certain behaviors and their acceptance of distortions of reality. In order for hypnosis to work, individuals must be open and responsive to suggestions made by the hypnotist.

Some people are more open to a hypnotist's suggestions than others, a quality that often runs in families (Kihlstrom, 2007). Approximately 15 percent of adults are very susceptible to hypnosis, while 10 percent are not at all hypnotizable. Most adults fall somewhere in between (Hilgard, 1991, 1982). People who are especially suggestible, in touch with their fantasy worlds, and comfortable playing with their imaginations are particularly likely to approach the experience with a positive and receptive attitude (Roche & McConkey, 1990). Perhaps not surprisingly, therefore, children tend to be particularly open to hypnotic suggestion (Wallace & Persanyi, 1989).

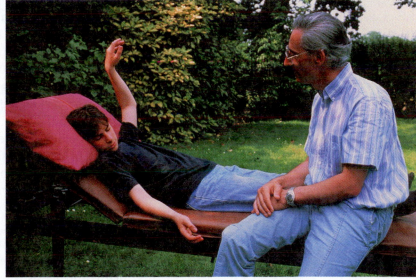

The power of suggestion People can be directed to experience unusual sensations and act in unusual ways when in a hypnotic state—a trance-like altered state of consciousness marked by extreme suggestibility. Here a hypnotized young man believes that a balloon is tied to his left hand and that his right hand is extremely heavy.

Hypnotic Procedures and Effects

Hypnotists use various methods to induce the hypnotic state. Sometimes—in a much tamer version than the movie portrayals—a person is asked to relax while concentrating on a single small target, such as a watch or an item in a painting on the wall. At other times, the hypnotist induces a *hyperalert* hypnotic trance that actually guides the individual to heightened tension and awareness. In either case, the hypnotist delivers "suggestions" to the subject, not the authoritarian commands on display in the movies.

dissociation a splitting of consciousness into two dimensions.

One area of functioning that can be readily influenced by hypnotists is motor control. If the hypnotist suggests that a person's hand is being drawn like a magnet to a nearby stapler, the individual's hand will soon move to the stapler, as if propelled by an external force.

In some cases, people can be directed to respond *after* being roused from the hypnotic trance. A predetermined signal prompts such *posthypnotic responses*. During hypnosis the hypnotist may suggest, for example, that the person will later stand up whenever the hypnotist touches a desktop. After being roused, and with no understanding of why, the person will in fact stand when the hypnotist touches the desk.

Related to posthypnotic responses is the phenomenon of *posthypnotic amnesia*. The hypnotist directs the person to later forget information learned during hypnosis. Once again, after being roused from the hypnotic trance, the person does not remember the learned material until the hypnotist provides a predetermined signal to remember. The degree to which the earlier information is forgotten varies. Some people will not remember any of the learned material, while others will remember quite a bit.

Hypnosis can also induce *hallucinations*, mental perceptions that do not match the physical stimulations coming from the world around us. Researchers have distinguished two kinds of *hypnotic hallucinations*: positive and negative. Positive hallucinations are those in which people under hypnosis are guided to see objects or hear sounds that are not present. Negative hallucinations are those in which hypnotized people fail to see or hear stimuli that are present. Negative hallucinations are often used to control pain. The hypnotized person is directed to ignore—basically, to simply not perceive—pain. The hallucination may result in a total or partial reduction of pain (Gruzelier, 2003). Some practitioners have even applied hypnosis to help control pain during dental and other forms of surgery (Auld, 2007). Although only some people are able to undergo surgery while anesthetized by hypnosis alone, combining hypnosis with chemical forms of anesthesia apparently helps many individuals (Hammond, 2008; Fredericks, 2001). Beyond its use in the control of pain, hypnosis has been used successfully to help treat problems, such as anxiety, skin diseases, asthma, insomnia, stuttering, high blood pressure, warts, and other forms of infection (Shenefelt, 2003).

Many people also turn to hypnosis to help break bad habits, such as smoking, nail biting, and overeating. Does hypnosis help? Research has shown that hypnosis has little effect in helping people to quit smoking over the long term (Spanos et al, 1995; Valbo & Eide, 1996). However, greater success has been noted in efforts at weight loss, particularly if hypnosis is paired with cognitive treatments, interventions that help people change their conscious ways of thinking (Ginandes, 2006; Lynn & Kirsch, 2006).

Why Does Hypnosis Work?

There are various theories about why hypnosis works (Kallio & Revonsuo, 2003). One, proposed by the pioneering researcher Ernest Hilgard, views hypnosis as a state of *divided consciousness*. Another theory sees it as an implementation of *common social and cognitive processes* (see **Figure 6-3**).

As a professor, Hilgard hypnotized a student to become deaf during a classroom demonstration. The student could not hear even loud noises. Another student asked Hilgard whether "some part" of the hypnotized student could still hear noise. In response, Hilgard instructed the hypnotized student to raise his finger if some part of him could still hear. Surprisingly, the student did raise a finger.

FIGURE 6-3 **Explaining hypnosis** Two theories explain how a hypnotized individual is able to ignore pain.

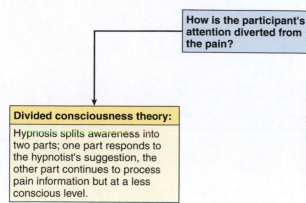

How is the participant's attention diverted from the pain?

Divided consciousness theory:
Hypnosis splits awareness into two parts; one part responds to the hypnotist's suggestion, the other part continues to process pain information but at a less conscious level.

Social/cognitive process theory:
The participant is highly motivated to believe in hypnosis, and, without awareness, works hard to ignore the pain.

From this experience, Hilgard concluded that consciousness splits into two parts and that both act at once during hypnosis, an experience called **dissociation** (Hilgard, 1992). One part of our consciousness becomes fully tuned into and responsive to the hypnotist's suggestions. The second part, which Hilgard called the *hidden observer*, operates at a subtler, less conscious level, continuing to process information that is seemingly unavailable to the hypnotized person. According to Hilgard, the hidden observer was the part of the student's mind that was still able to hear while hypnotized.

Another leading theory of hypnosis is that, instead of resulting from a divided consciousness, hypnotic phenomena consist simply of highly motivated people performing tasks or enacting roles that are asked of them. Because of their strong beliefs in hypnosis, the people fail to recognize their own active contributions to the process (Spanos et al., 1995).

What Happens in the Hypnosis B R A I N ?

Neuroimaging studies show that hypnosis affects neuron activity in brain areas previously implicated in conscious awareness, suggesting to some theorists that the procedure does indeed produce altered consciousness, as suggested by Hilgard's theory (Rainville et al., 2002, 1999, 1997).

When people are hypnotized, they are usually first guided into a state of *mental relaxation*. Studies have found that during this state, neural activity in key areas of the cerebral cortex and thalamus—brain regions that, as we noted earlier, are implicated in conscious awareness—slows down significantly (Rainville et al., 2002). Hypnotized individuals are next guided into a state of *mental absorption*, during which they focus carefully on the hypnotist's voice and instructions and actively block out other sources of stimulation, both internal and environmental. In fact, mental absorption has often been described as a state of *total focus*. During this state, cerebral blood flow and neural activity actually pick back up in key areas of the cerebral cortex, thalamus, and other parts of the brain's attention and conscious awareness systems (Rainville et al., 2002).

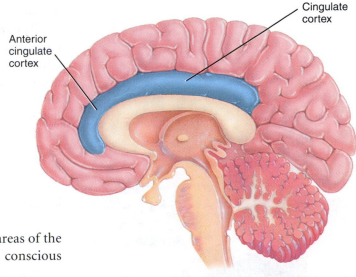

Neuroimaging research suggests that one part of the brain's cerebral cortex, the *anterior cingulate cortex*, may be particularly involved when hypnosis is used to anesthetize or reduce pain. This region has been implicated both in general awareness and in the unpleasantness we feel during pain. In one study, participants were hypnotically induced to ignore their pain while placing their hands in painfully hot water (Rainville et al., 1997). While the individuals were in a hypnotic pain-free state, neurons in their anterior cingulate cortex became markedly less active. Although the activity of other neurons that receive pain messages continued as usual in these people's brains—suggesting that they were indeed receiving sensations of pain—the decreased activity in the anterior cingulate cortex seemed to reduce their *awareness* of the pain. They did not perceive the pain sensations.

Before You Go On

What Do You Know?

5. What are hypnotic hallucinations and how might they be useful?
6. How does Hilgard use the idea of a divided consciousness to explain hypnosis?

What Do You Think? What are the ethical implications of using hypnosis to control behavior?

meditation technique designed to turn one's consciousness away from the outer world toward one's inner cues and awareness.

adaptive theory of sleep theory that organisms sleep for the purposes of self-preservation, to keep away from predators that are more active at night.

restorative theory of sleep theory that we sleep in order to allow the brain and body to restore certain depleted chemical resources and eliminate chemical wastes that have accumulated during the waking day.

circadian rhythm pattern of sleep-wake cycles that in human beings roughly corresponds to periods of daylight and night.

Meditation

LEARNING OBJECTIVE 4 Describe the techniques and effects of meditation.

Meditation is a technique designed to turn one's consciousness away from the outer world, toward inner cues and awareness, ignoring all stressors (Fontana, 2007). The technique typically involves going to a quiet place, assuming either a specific body position or simply a comfortable position, controlling one's breathing, limiting one's outward attention, and forming internal images. The result of such efforts is an altered state of consciousness, accompanied by deeply relaxing and pleasant feelings. Experienced meditators are often said to attain a "wider consciousness."

Meditation is an ancient practice that can be traced through the history of all the world's major religions. Perhaps the best known practices derive from the *yoga* traditions of the Hindu religion and from the Zen traditions of Buddhism. *Yoga* is a form of meditation that involves adjusting the body into different positions, or *poses*, in an attempt to also regulate blood flow, heart rate, and digestive processes.

Two major techniques to meditation seem to use opposite approaches. In *opening-up* approaches, the meditator seeks to clear his or her mind in order to receive new experiences. One opening-up technique is to imagine oneself as another person; a related opening-up technique involves the performance of a common task in a slightly different way, in order to call better attention to one's daily routine. In the other kind of meditation approach, *concentrative meditation,* the person actively concentrates on an object, word, or idea, called a *mantra.* In some versions of this approach, the person concentrates instead on a riddle, called a *koan.* A well-known koan involves answering the question, "What is the sound of one hand clapping?"

One of meditation's greatest appeals is that it can help people relax. In fact, studies have shown that people in meditative states experience increases in the same brain waves that are associated with the relaxation phase individuals experience just prior to falling sleep (Aftanas & Golasheiken, 2003). Research has found that meditation also can lower respiration, heart rate, blood pressure, and muscle tension. Because of its positive impact on physical functioning, it has been used to help treat pain, asthma, high blood pressure, heart problems, skin disorders, diabetes, and viral infections (Wootton, 2008; Goodman et al., 2003). One form of meditation that has been applied in particular to patients suffering from severe pain is *mindfulness meditation* (Carey, 2008; Kabat-Zinn, 2005). Here, meditators pay attention to the feelings, thoughts, and sensations that are flowing through their minds during meditation, but they do so with detachment and without judgment. By just being mindful but not judgmental of their feelings and thoughts, including feelings of pain, the individuals are less inclined to label or fixate on them and, in turn, less likely to react negatively to them.

Before You Go On

What Do You Know?

7. What are the physical effects of meditation?
8. What are the main benefits of altering consciousness through meditation?

What Do You Think? Which approach to meditation appeals more to you, opening-up meditation or concentrative meditation? Why?

When We Are Asleep

LEARNING OBJECTIVE 5 Describe what happens when people sleep, key theories of why we sleep and dream, and problems with sleep and how they affect functioning.

To Benjamin Franklin's famous acknowledgment that the only sure things in life are death and taxes could be added a third: that sooner or later we must—absolutely must—fall and stay asleep. Sleep is so central to our lives—indeed, most people spend 25 years of their lives asleep—that we first need to ask what important purpose does it serve?

Why Do We Sleep?

Interestingly, despite considerable research into the matter, no consensus exists about why people need to sleep (Moorcroft, 2003). After all, as we shall see, the brain does not rest when we are sleeping, nor, on the surface, does sleep offer the body much more rest than it would get by sitting down and relaxing for awhile. Yet all animals sleep, and they would, in fact, die if they were deprived of sleep for too long (see **Figure 6-4**).

One theory, the **adaptive theory of sleep**, suggests that sleep is the evolutionary outcome of self-preservation. Proponents of this view suggest that organisms sleep in order to keep themselves away from predators that are more active at night. Our ancestors, for example, tucked themselves away in safe places to keep from being eaten by nocturnal animals on the prowl. Animals that need to graze and so have less chance of hiding from predators tend to sleep less. An elephant, for example, sleeps only two or three hours a day, whereas a bat sleeps around twenty. This evolutionary argument, however, seems to account more for why we sleep at night than for why we sleep in the first place.

Several biological theories of sleep have also been proposed. One suggests that sleep plays a role in the growth process, a notion consistent with the finding that the *pituitary gland* releases growth hormones during sleep. In fact, as we age, we release fewer of these hormones, grow less, and sleep less (Gais et al., 2006).

Researchers have also observed changes in neuron activity in other areas of the brain during sleep, including the *reticular formation* and the *pons*, as well as the *forebrain region*. As we described in Chapter 4, these regions are important in alertness and arousal. Researchers have not established, however, that changes in the activity of these areas *cause* us to sleep.

Another biological theory, the **restorative theory of sleep**, suggests that sleep allows the brain and body to restore certain depleted chemical resources, while eliminating chemical wastes that have accumulated during the waking day (Smith & Baum, 2003; Irwin, 2001). Which chemicals might be depleted, and which ones might build to excess? We do not really know (Thompson, 2000). While we may not yet know exactly what causes sleep, we do know that sleep occurs in regular patterns, or *rhythms*, and that these rhythms reflect changes in the body's chemistry (Moorcroft, 2003).

Rhythms of Sleep

Human beings' basic pattern is called the **circadian rhythm** (see **Figure 6-5**). Within each 24-hour cycle, we experience a sustained period of wakefulness that gives way to a period of sleep. Although we tend to be awake during the day and to sleep at night, our circadian rhythms are not fully dependent on the cycles of daylight (Schultz & Kay, 2003; Thompson, 2000).

"Everyone needs to sleep" These two bees take time out from their busy agenda to sleep in a comfortable flower.

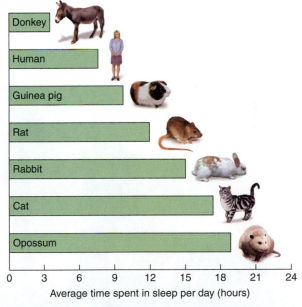

FIGURE 6-4 Sleep needs of various animals Animals vary greatly in how much sleep they need each day. Their sleep needs are related in part to how much awake time is needed to obtain food and protect themselves from predators.

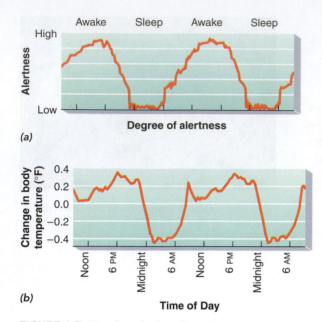

Awake Sleep Awake Sleep

High

Alertness

Low

Degree of alertness

(a)

0.4
0.2
0.0
−0.2
−0.4

Change in body temperature (°F)

Noon 6 PM Midnight 6 AM Noon 6 PM Midnight 6 AM

(b)

Time of Day

FIGURE 6-5 Circadian rhythms Two prime examples of circadian rhythms are our cycles of alertness and shifts in body temperature.

During the circadian cycle, we also experience other, more subtle patterns of biochemical activity. As morning nears, for example, our temperature rises and continues to rise until it peaks at midday. Then it dips and we feel fatigued. Many people around the world take naps during this early afternoon lull. Later in the afternoon, body temperature rises once more, only to drop again as we approach our full evening sleep (Johnson et al., 2004). Research has suggested that, on average, we are most alert during the late morning peak in the circadian rhythm. This "rule," however, varies with age (Yoon et al., 2003). Younger people tend to peak later in the day, while older people peak earlier.

Along with shifts in body temperature, we also experience changes throughout the 24-hour period in blood pressure, the secretion of hormones, and sensitivity to pain. As we have discussed, for example, the release of growth hormones tends to occur during periods of sleep.

The circadian rhythm has been called our *biological clock* because the pattern repeats itself from one 24-hour period to the next. This clock, however, can be made to go haywire by certain events (Waterhouse & DeCoursey, 2004). For example, the clock can be disrupted by long-distance airplane flights when we are awake at times that we should be sleeping—a problem compounded by crossing time zones. The result: jet lag. Similarly, people who work nightshifts, particularly those who keep irregular schedules of dayshifts and nightshifts, may experience sleep disorders and, in some instances, develop problems such as depression or health difficulties. People with a pattern called *circadian rhythm sleep disorder* experience excessive sleepiness or insomnia as a result of a mismatch between their own sleep-wake pattern and the sleep-wake schedule of most other people in their environment (Lack & Bootzin, 2003).

"Owls" and "Larks" HOW we Differ

Do you get up at the crack of dawn, head to the gym, and complete all of your class assignments before noon? Then you are probably a morning person (a "lark"). Or do you have trouble getting up before noon and can't really concentrate on your work until much later in the day? If so, you are likely an evening person (an "owl").

Most people have no preference for the time of day when they are most alert and active; they may shift their sleep-wake rhythms two hours earlier or later than normal with no adverse affects on their alertness or activity level (Sack et al., 2007). But for some, there is a strong preference for either earlier or later in the day.

Researchers now believe that genetics plays an important role in determining these variations in sleep-wake rhythms, and that age, ethnicity, gender, and socioeconomic factors have almost no influence (Paine, Gander & Travier, 2006). Every cell in your body has its own internal clock, and scientists are able to measure your unique body clock at the cellular level (Cuninkova & Brown, 2008). As we shall see, the master control center for your body's internal clock and your own sleep-wake rhythm is found in the brain area known as the *suprachiasmatic nucleus*.

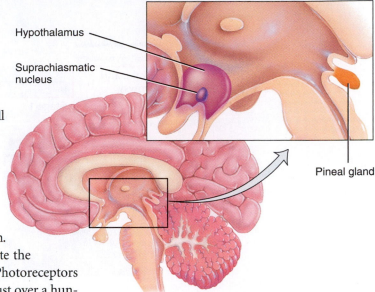

Hypothalamus

Suprachiasmatic
nucleus

Pineal gland

When We Sleep *What Happens in the* B R A I N ?

Research has uncovered what happens in our brains to control the circadian rhythms of when we wake and sleep, as well as what happens in the brain while we sleep.

Controlling the Clock   The **suprachiasmatic nucleus (SCN)**, a small group of neurons in the *hypothalamus*, is ultimately responsible for coordinating the many rhythms of the body (Waterhouse & DeCoursey, 2004; Honma et al., 2003). As daylight fades into night, the SCN "notices" the change and directs the *pineal gland* to secrete the hormone *melatonin*. Increased quantities of melatonin, traveling through the blood to various organs, cause sleepiness. Melatonin production peaks between 1:00 and 3:00 A.M. As dawn approaches, this production decreases and sleepers soon awaken.

During the day, photoreceptors in the retina of the eye communicate the presence of sunlight to the SCN and melatonin secretions remain low. Photoreceptors are also sensitive to artificial light. In fact, the invention of the lightbulb just over a hundred years ago has disturbed the human experience of the circadian rhythm by increasing the number of hours of light people are exposed to in a given day. This may be one reason why many people today sleep much less than our forbearers.

What happens if a person is entirely deprived of access to environmental shifts in sunlight and darkness? In a number of sleep studies, participants have been placed in special settings where they are totally deprived of natural light. In such settings, the SCN extends the body's "day," by as much as an hour, to about 25 hours (Lavie, 2001). When we are deprived of light, the various circadian rhythms also become out-of-synch with each other. The normal cycles of body temperature and melatonin production, for example, no longer coordinate with one another (Lavie, 2001).

If we speak of a biological clock, we should also be able to speak of *setting*, or *resetting*, the clock (Waterhouse & DeCoursey; 2004). In fact, when a person who has been kept in an environment without sunlight is returned to normal living conditions, the usual 24-hour circadian rhythm is quickly restored.

Patterns of Sleep   Every 90 to 100 minutes while we sleep, we pass through a sleep cycle that consists of five different stages (Lavie, 2001). Researchers have identified these stages by examining people's brain-wave patterns while they sleep, using a device called an *electroencephalograph* (*EEG*). EEG readings indicate that each stage of sleep is characterized by a different brain-wave pattern, as shown in **Figure 6-6**.

When we first go to bed and, still awake, begin to relax, EEG readings show that we experience what are called *alpha waves*. As we settle into this drowsy presleep period, called the **hypnagogic state**, we sometimes experience strange sensations. We may feel that we are falling or floating in space, or "hear" our name called out, or we may hear a loud crash. All of these sensations seem very real, but none actually has happened. Such sensory phenomena are called *hypnagogic hallucinations* (Sherwood, 2002). Also common during this presleep stage is a *myoclonic jerk*, a sharp muscular spasm that generally accompanies the hypnagogic hallucination of falling.

When we finally doze off, EEG readings show that our brain waves become smaller and irregular, signaling that we have entered *Stage 1 sleep*. Alpha-wave patterns are replaced by slower waves, called *theta waves*. This first stage of sleep actually represents a bridge between wakefulness and sleep; it lasts only a few minutes. Our conscious awareness of street noises or the hum of an air conditioner fades. If we are roused from this stage, we might recall having just had ideas that seem nonsensical.

Falling deeper into sleep, we next pass into *Stage 2 sleep*. A still further slowing of brain-wave activity occurs during this stage, although we may also exhibit **sleep spindles—**

suprachiasmatic nucleus (SCN) small group of neurons in the hypothalamus responsible for coordinating the many rhythms of the body.

hypnagogic state a presleep period often characterized by vivid sensory phenomena.

sleep spindles bursts of brain activity lasting a second or two; occur during Stage 2 sleep.

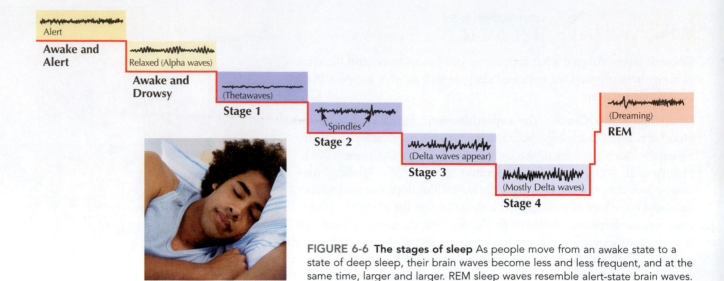

Alert

Awake and Alert

Relaxed (Alpha waves)

Awake and Drowsy

(Theta waves)

Stage 1

Spindles

Stage 2

(Delta waves appear)

Stage 3

(Mostly Delta waves)

Stage 4

(Dreaming)

REM

FIGURE 6-6 The stages of sleep As people move from an awake state to a state of deep sleep, their brain waves become less and less frequent, and at the same time, larger and larger. REM sleep waves resemble alert-state brain waves.

bursts of brain activity that last a second or two. During Stage 2, breathing becomes steadily rhythmic. Occasionally, the body twitches, although generally our muscle tension relaxes. During this stage, which lasts 15 to 20 minutes, we can still be awakened fairly easily. Towards the end of Stage 2 sleep, our brain waves slow even further and *delta waves* start to appear in addition to the theta waves. Delta waves indicate *delta sleep,* or deep sleep.

The next two stages of sleep, *Stage 3* and *Stage 4,* are characterized by very deep sleep. In Stage 3, between 20 and 50 percent of our EEG waves are delta waves. During Stage 4, the percentage of delta waves increases to more than 50 percent (Bertini et al., 2007; Cooper, 1994). During Stage 4, heart rate, blood pressure, and breathing rates all drop to their lowest levels and the sleeper seems "dead to the world." Interestingly, although our muscles are most relaxed during this deepest phase of sleep, this is also the time that people are prone to sleepwalking and might go for a stroll. Similarly, children who wet their beds tend to do so during this stage.

Passing through all of the first four stages takes a little more than an hour of each 90 to 100-minute sleep cycle. After that, we experience the most interesting stage of sleep, **rapid eye movement,** or **REM, sleep.** In fact, all the preceding stages (Stages 1–4) are collectively called **nonREM sleep,** or **NREM.** During REM sleep, we experience rapid and jagged brain-wave patterns, in contrast to the slow waves of NREM sleep. REM sleep has been called *paradoxical sleep* because, even though the body remains deeply relaxed on the surface—almost paralyzed—we experience considerable activity internally (Wickwire et al., 2008). The rapid brain-wave pattern of REM sleep is accompanied by increased heart rate and rapid and irregular breathing, for example. Moreover, every 30 seconds or so, our eyes dart around rapidly behind our closed eyelids. Perhaps most interesting, people's brains behave during REM sleep just as they do when we are awake and active (Ratey, 2001).

Along with this brain activity, the genitals become aroused during REM sleep. Indeed, except during nightmares, men are usually experiencing erections and women vaginal lubrication and clitoral engorgement during REM sleep, even if the content of the dream is not sexual (Mann et al., 2003; Solms, 2007). Men often retain their erections beyond the REM stage, explaining the occurrence of "morning erections."

As we will discuss shortly, dreams usually occur throughout REM sleep. If people are awakened during this stage, they almost always report that they have been dreaming. Unlike the hypnagogic hallucinations of presleep, which are often fleeting and isolated images, dreams tend to be emotional and are experienced in a story-like form. Dreams are less common during NREM sleep, and when they do happen, they are less vivid or fantastic than REM dreams.

rapid eye movement sleep (REM) stage of sleep associated with rapid and jagged brainwave patterns, increased heart rate, rapid and irregular breathing, rapid eye movements, and dreaming.

nonREM sleep (NREM) Stages 1 through 4 of normal sleep pattern.

Many researchers believe that REM sleep serves a particularly important function—the consolidation of memories of newly learned material, a process that we will be talking about more in the coming chapters on learning and memory (Fenn et al., 2003). In fact, REM sleep tends to extend longer than usual in both animals and humans if the organisms go to sleep after just having learned a new task (Smith, 2006, 1996). In one study, a group of volunteers were trained on a perceptual task just before going to sleep (Karni et al., 1994). Half of the sleepers were awakened during REM sleep, while the other half were awakened later, during the next cycle of NREM sleep. The next day, those who had been awakened during REM sleep performed more poorly on the perceptual task than those who had been awakened during the later NREM phases. Presumably, the REM-awakened volunteers had not yet had the opportunity to fully consolidate their memories of the newly learned task.

This memory consolidation theory has, however, been challenged by some studies showing that when animals are administered antidepressant drugs, which typically disrupt REM sleep, they nevertheless continue to learn and remember quite well (Vertes & Eastman, 2003). Research also finds that people with lesions to the *pons* portion of the brain, which is active during REM sleep, learn, remember, and function quite normally.

It is worth noting that every kind of mammal whose sleep patterns have been studied, including birds, experience both NREM and REM sleep. Thus, many theorists believe that animals also dream. Of course, this comes as no surprise to dog owners who have, no doubt, frequently observed their pets twitch their paws in a regular rhythm during REM sleep, as if running in a dream (Thompson, 2000).

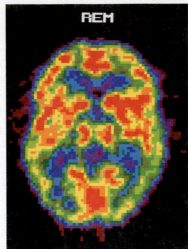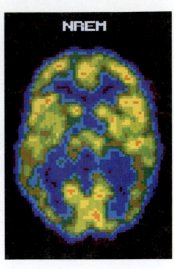

Almost like being awake When we are in REM sleep, our brains behave much like they do when we are awake and active, and indeed it is during this stage of sleep that we dream. The PET scan of a brain during REM sleep (left) reveals much more activity (indicated by the colors "red" and "orange") than does the scan of a brain during nonREM sleep (right).

Dreams

Dreams—emotional, story-like sensory experiences that usually occur during REM sleep—have proven to be endlessly fascinating to scientists, clinicians, philosophers, artists, and laypeople, probably because of how vivid and mysterious they are. A woman dreams of being punched in the stomach and doubling over in pain. In thinking about the dream the next day, she notices that she feels very vulnerable. She also recalls that earlier on the day of the dream she had learned that her investment portfolio lost a great deal of money, and she remembers having felt vulnerable because all of that money was gone. Could the dream and the loss of money be related? Some psychologists would say yes, while others would be skeptical. In this section we shall examine ways in which different theorists and researchers have come to understand dreams (Moorcroft, 2003).

Research suggests that actions in dreams run in real time—that is, it takes you as long to accomplish something in the dream as it would if you were performing the action while you were awake.

Freudian Dream Theory   Sigmund Freud argued that dreams represent the expression of unconscious wishes or desires. He believed that dreams allow us to discharge internal energy associated with unacceptable feelings (Freud, 1900). Freud suggested that *dream interpretation,* in which a psychoanalytic therapist facilitates insight into the possible meaning behind a dream, may help clients appreciate their underlying needs and conflicts with the goal of being less constrained by them during waking life. For example, if a lonely and morally upstanding young man is sexually attracted to his brother's wife, he might have a dream in which he goes swimming in a private pool that is marked "No Trespassing." His therapist might help the man arrive at the conclusion that the dream about swimming in an off-limits pool symbolizes his wish to be with his sister-in-law. Such an insight eventually might help the man to overcome inhibitions he feels about finding a suitable partner for himself.

Freud called the dream images that people are able to recall the *manifest content.* The unconscious elements of dreams are called the *latent content.* In our example, the young man's desire for his sister-in-law (latent content)—a scandalous idea that he would never allow himself to have—is symbolized in the dream by a swim in the pool

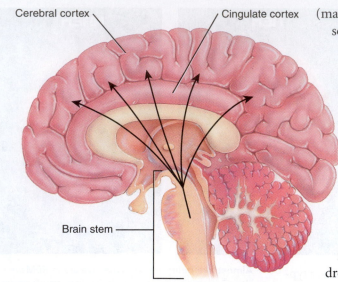

Cerebral cortex   Cingulate cortex

Brain stem

FIGURE 6-7 **Activation-synthesis** According to the activation-synthesis theory of dreaming, neurons in the brainstem activate neurons in other areas throughout the brain. The brain combines these various signals into a story, or dream.

Dream stories People often experience similar dream stories. For example, 80 percent of all people have had repeated dreams of running toward or away from something.

(manifest content). His dream of a happy swim in forbidden territory is his mind's solution to a problem that he could not work out consciously.

Many of today's theorists, including a number of psychoanalytic ones, criticize Freud's theory. For example, *object-relations theorists,* psychoanalytic theorists who place greater emphasis on the role of relationships in development, focus more on relationship issues when interpreting dream material. Regarding the earlier dream in which a woman gets punched, an object-relations therapist might be inclined to help the patient explore her feelings of vulnerability in various relationships rather than her financial fears.

Information-Processing Theory Information-processing theory offers an alternative, more cognitive, view of dreaming. According to this view, dreams are the mind's attempt to sort out and organize the day's experiences and to fix them in memory. Consistent with this perspective, studies have revealed that interrupting REM sleep—and so interrupting dreams—impedes a person's ability to remember material that he or she has learned just before going to sleep (Empson, 2002). Also, in support of this view, researchers have found that periods of REM sleep (during which we dream) tend to extend longer when people's days have been filled with multiple stressful events or marked by extensive learning experiences (Palumbo, 1978). Thus, according to an information-processing perspective, the woman who dreamed of being punched may simply have been attempting to process and give order to the stressful financial events that she had experienced earlier in the day.

Activation-Synthesis Hypothesis Researchers J. Allan Hobson and Robert W. McCarley have proposed a more biological hypothesis about dreaming, the **activation-synthesis model** (Hobson, 2005; Hobson & McCarley, 1977) (see **Figure 6-7**). They argue that as people sleep, their brains activate all kinds of signals. In particular, when dreams occur, neurons in the *brainstem* are activated. These, in turn, activate neurons in the *cerebral cortex* to produce visual and auditory signals. Also aroused are the emotion centers of the brain, including the *cingulate cortex, amygdala,* and *hippocampus.* Neuroimaging scans of people who are experiencing REM sleep confirm heightened activity and neuron communication in each of these brain regions.

Hobson and McCarley suggest that the activated brain combines—or *synthesizes*—these internally generated signals and tries to give them meaning. Each person organizes and synthesizes this random collection of images, feelings, memories, and thoughts in his or her own personal way—in the form of a particular dream story (Hobson et al., 1998). The woman who dreamed of being punched might be trying to synthesize activation in brain areas that normally receive signals from the muscles of the stomach with signals from areas of the brain that process emotions, for example.

What remains unclear in this model is why different people synthesize their onslaught of brain signals in different ways. Freud, of course, might suggest that each person's particular synthesis is influenced by his or her unfulfilled needs and unresolved conflicts.

Nightmares, Lucid Dreams, and Daydreams

Dreams evoke many different feelings. Dreams filled with intense anxiety are called *nightmares.* The feeling of terror can be so great that the dreamer awakens from the dream, often crying out. Nightmares generally evoke feelings of helplessness or powerlessness, usually in situations of great danger. They tend to be more common among people who are under stress. People who experience frequent nightmares and become very distressed by their nightmares are considered to have a *nightmare disorder.*

It appears that nightmares are more common among children than adults, although there is some dispute on this issue. When children have a nightmare, simple reassurances that they are safe and that the dream does not reflect real danger are usually helpful. It is important to help the child appreciate the difference between inner and outer reality (Halliday, 2004; Josephs, 1987).

In contrast to nightmares, during which dreamers feel they are caught in a real and terrifying situation, **lucid dreams** are dreams in which people fully recognize that they are dreaming (Baars et al., 2003). Some lucid dreamers can even willfully guide the outcome of their dreams (LaBerge, 2007). In a lucid dream, the woman who dreamed of being punched might tell herself—while still asleep—that she is only dreaming and is actually fine; she even might try to guide the outcome of the dream so that she prevails over her attacker. Although not necessarily subscribing to psychoanalytic theory, people who attempt to engage in lucid dreaming often believe that it is a way to open up another phase of human consciousness.

A third dream-related phenomenon is actually associated with waking states of consciousness—the daydream. Fantasies that occur while one is awake and mindful of external reality, but not fully conscious, are called *daydreams* (Schon, 2003; Singer, 2003). Recall, for example, that the driver in the opening story of this chapter had an elaborate daydream about an old romantic interest. Sometimes a daydream can become so strong that we lose track of external reality for a brief while. Although we may be embarrassed when caught daydreaming, such experiences may also afford us opportunities for creativity; we are, after all, less constrained during the fantasies than we would be if attending strictly to the outside world.

Sleep | How we *Develop*

Parents or older siblings know all too well that young babies do not sleep quite like older children or adults. Through the first four months of life, babies sleep between 14 and 17 hours each day. The amount of time that they spend sleeping declines steadily as they get older (Sadeh et al., 2009). Although babies spend a lot of time asleep overall, the lengths of their sleep periods can last anywhere from minutes to hours before they are stirred and crying out for attention. For parents, the good news is that sleep tends to become more structured at around six months of age.

Babies appear to spend a great deal more time than adults in REM sleep—around 8 hours per day for infants, compared with 2 hours for adults (Siegel, 2005). The size of this difference has led theorists to suspect that infant sleep patterns are crucial to development in various ways. Several have speculated, for example, that REM sleep aids in the development of the central nervous system by facilitating synaptic pruning and preventing the formation of unnecessary connections, although research has not yet confirmed this belief. Also, by slowing body activity, the extended REM sleep of babies may help to regulate the temperature of their developing brains. REM sleep tends to decrease to adult levels somewhere between the ages of two and six years (Curzi-Dascalova & Challamel, 2000).

By early childhood, an individual's total daily sleep requirement also decreases significantly (see **Figure 6-8**). Most children sleep around 9 hours each day, although pediatricians recommend between 12 and 15 hours of sleep for anyone between two and five years of age (Acebo et al., 2005). Teenagers average around 7 hours of daily sleep although pediatricians recommend at least 8 hours for them. As adults, our sleep patterns continue to change. As we age, we spend less and less time in deep sleep and

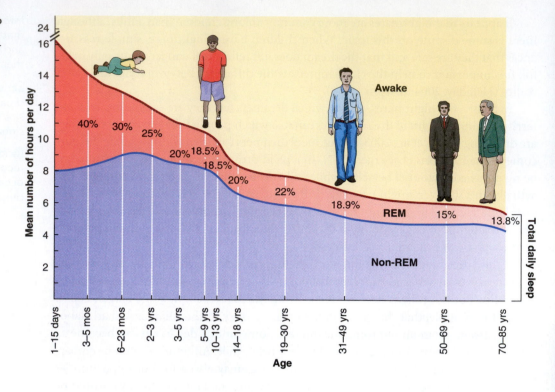

FIGURE 6-8 The effects of aging on the sleep cycle As we get older, our total daily sleep and our REM sleep decrease. The largest shifts occur during out first three years of life.

A graduate student in physiology, Eugene Aserinsky, discovered REM sleep when he attached electronic leads to his 8-year-old son's head and eyelids to monitor his sleep and waking brain waves and found unexpected brain-wave activity, suggesting his son "had woken up even though he hadn't. (Aserinsky, 1996)."

REM sleep, our sleep is more readily interrupted, and we take longer to get back to sleep when awakened (Garcia-Rill et al., 2008).

As discussed earlier, our sleep-awake cycle is tied to our bodies' circadian rhythms. These biological clocks are also affected by environmental demands and expectations. Studies have, for example, contrasted parenting practices in the United States with those in the Kipsigis tribe (you may remember them from Chapter 2). Many American parents structure their babies' sleep by putting them down at designated times and not responding to their cries. In contrast, Kipsigis mothers keep their babies with them constantly. As a result, Kipsigis babies sleep for much shorter periods of time later into infancy than do American babies; in many cases, they do not sleep for long stretches even as adults (Super & Harkness, 2002, 1972). The body clocks of teenagers also seem to be compromised by the increased social and academic pressures that they encounter (Crowley, Acebo, & Carskadon, 2007). Many adolescents in the United States, for example, stay up late largely because that's what it takes for them to finish their homework or to keep up with their friends.

Sleep Deprivation and Sleep Disorders When Things Go Wrong

How much sleep a person needs varies, depending on factors such as age, lifestyle, and genetic disposition. The amount of sleep a person actually gets may also be different from how much they need. Their lifestyles deprive many people of sleep, and sleep disorders and may also make it impossible to sleep properly.

Sleep Deprivation Left unhindered, most people would sleep for nine or ten hours a day in order to awaken alert and refreshed. However, we've all had the opposite experience—that of not getting enough sleep. We become generally sleepy and maybe a little cranky. After a while, we may yearn for sleep. Researchers have found that without enough sleep, people also experience a general malaise (Fredriksen et al., 2004). They display lower productivity and are more apt to make mistakes (Van Dongen, 2007,

2003). Not surprisingly, accidents and deaths sometimes occur when drivers and pilots do not get enough sleep. While it is possible to make up for the lost sleep of one night by sleeping a little longer the next night, it becomes increasingly difficult for persons to "pay off" their "sleep debt" if they chronically miss sleep (Moorcroft, 2003).

Adolescents are particularly likely to be sleep deprived (Carskadon, 2002). Interestingly, teenagers today get about two hours less sleep per night than teens did 80 years ago. In fact, the distinguished sleep researcher William Dement has asserted that 80 percent of students at his institution, Stanford University, are "dangerously sleep deprived" (Dement & Vaughan, 1999). Ironically, students who pull all-nighters in order to complete their work actually wind up working less efficiently and effectively than they would if they were to sleep the eight or nine hours that they need. Despite such problems among young persons, researchers have not conducted much research on how sleep deprivation specifically affects physical, cognitive, and emotional development (Loessl et al., 2008).

Sleep researchers used to spend most of their time examining the impact of lost sleep on simple or monotonous tasks. Today's researchers, however, often look at the impact of sleep deprivation on more complex activities (Moorcroft, 2003; Harrison & Horne, 2000). Studies suggest, on the one hand, that sleep deprivation does *not* necessarily lower one's performance on complex logical tasks. Sleep-deprived participants in such tasks often are able to avoid poor performances by being highly interested in the complex tasks at hand. Many sleep-deprived college students, for example, seem able to conduct research or write papers, particularly if those works interest them a lot. Problems arise, on the other hand, when a sleep-deprived person faces unexpected turns of events, distractions, or innovations while working on a complex task, or needs to revise the task. If, for example, someone turns on the television while you're studying in a sleep-deprived state, your learning is likely to suffer considerably.

In an important set of findings, researchers have also learned that sleep loss can lower the effectiveness of people's immune systems (Benedict et. al., 2007; Dement & Vaughan, 1999). Sleep deprived people apparently have a more difficult time fighting off viral infections and cancer, for example. Thus, it may not be surprising that people who average at least eight hours of sleep a night tend to outlive those who get less sleep (Dement & Vaughn, 1999).

Sleep Disorders   Sleep disorders occur when normal sleep patterns are disturbed, causing impaired daytime functioning and feelings of distress (Espie, 2002; APA, 2000). Almost everyone suffers from some kind of sleep disorder at one time or another in their lives. The sleep disorder may be part of a larger problem, such as life stress, a medical condition, or substance misuse, or it may be a *primary* sleep disorder, in which sleep difficulties are the central problem. Primary sleep disorders typically arise from abnormalities in the people's circadian rhythms and sleep-wake mechanisms.

People who suffer from **insomnia**, the most common sleep disorder, regularly cannot fall asleep or stay asleep (Taylor et al., 2008; Morin & Espie, 2003). More than 20 percent of the entire population experience significant extended episodes of insomnia each year (APA, 2000). The National Sleep Foundation claims that 43 percent of adults experience at least one symptom of insomnia a few nights or more each week.

As you might expect, many cases of insomnia are triggered by day-to-day stressors. In particular, job or school pressures, troubled relationships, and financial problems have been implicated. For many people, a subtle additional stress is worrying about not getting enough sleep while trying to fall asleep. This vicious cycle can further intensify anxiety and make sleep all the more elusive (Espie, 2002).

Insomnia is more common among older people than younger ones (Knight et al., 2006). Elderly individuals are particularly prone to this problem because so many

Sleep wins Whether it's a bassist collapsing in mid-play on a couch or a gardener dozing on a bench, the need to drift off eventually catches up with those who are sleep deprived.

insomnia sleep disorder characterized by a regular inability to fall asleep or stay asleep.

of them have medical ailments, experience pain, take medications, or grapple with depression and anxiety—each a known contributor to insomnia (Taylor et al., 2008). In addition, some of the normal age-related sleep changes we described earlier may heighten the chances of insomnia among elderly people. As individuals age, for example, they naturally spend less time in deep sleep and their sleep is interrupted more readily (Edelstein et al., 2008).

Twenty million people—typically older men who are heavy snorers—suffer from **sleep apnea**, the second most common sleep disorder. People with this condition repeatedly stop breathing during the night, depriving the brain of oxygen and leading to frequent awakenings. Sleep apnea can result when the brain fails to send a "breathe signal" to the diaphragm and other breathing muscles or when muscles at the top of the throat become too relaxed, allowing the windpipe to partially close. Sufferers stop breathing for up to 30 seconds or more as they sleep. Hundreds of episodes may occur each night. Often the individual will not remember any of them, but will feel sleepy the next day.

Narcolepsy, marked by an uncontrollable urge to fall asleep, afflicts more than 135,000 people in the United States (NINDS, 2006). People with this disorder may suddenly fall into REM sleep in the midst of an argument or during an exciting football game. When they wake, they feel refreshed. The narcoleptic episode is experienced as a loss of consciousness that can last up to 15 minutes. This disorder can obviously have serious consequences for people driving cars, operating tools, or performing highly precise work. Its cause is not fully known. Narcolepsy seems to run in families, and some studies have linked the disorder to a specific gene or combination of genes (Quinnell et al., 2007).

Sleepwalking most often takes place during the first three hours of sleep. Sleepwalkers will often sit up, get out of bed, and walk around. They usually manage to avoid obstacles, climb stairs, and perform complex activities. Accidents do happen, however: tripping, bumping into furniture, and even falling out of windows have all been reported. People who are awakened while sleepwalking are confused for several moments. If allowed to continue sleepwalking, they eventually return to bed. The disorder appears to be inherited (Hublin et al., 2001). Up to 5 percent of children experience this disorder for a period of time (Wickwire et al, 2008).

Related to sleepwalking is *night terror disorder*. Individuals who suffer from this pattern awaken suddenly, sit up in bed, scream in extreme fear and agitation, and experience heightened heart and breathing rates. They appear to be in a state of panic and are often incoherent. Usually people suffering from night terrors do not remember the episodes the next morning. Night terror disorder is not the same thing as a *nightmare disorder,* discussed earlier in the chapter, in which sufferers experience frequent nightmares. Sleepwalking and night terrors are more common among children than among adolescents or adults. They tend to occur during Stages 3 and 4, the deepest stages of NREM sleep (Hublin et al., 1999).

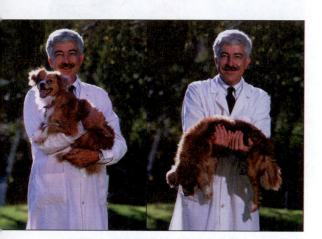

Studying narcolepsy Some people with narcolepsy, a sleep disorder marked by uncontrollable urges to fall asleep, further experience sudden losses of muscle tone during their narcoleptic episodes. To learn more about this abnormal pattern, famous sleep researcher William Dement studies dogs such as Tucker, seen here before and during a sudden narcoleptic episode.

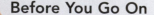

Before You Go On

What Do You Know?

9. What are the major theories of why people sleep?
10. What is the difference between the manifest content of a dream and its latent content?
11. What is the role of the suprachiasmatic nucleus in human consciousness?
12. What is the difference between a nightmare and a night terror?

What Do You Think?
Which of the theories of dreams described in this section seems to make most sense to you and why? Could another idea or a combination of theories better explain dreaming?

Psychoactive Drugs

LEARNING OBJECTIVE 6 List and describe common depressant, stimulant, and hallucinogenic psychoactive drugs and their effects.

What is one of the first things you do every day? For millions of people, the answer is to have a cup of coffee (maybe more than one). Why do so many people do this? For most, it is to give themselves a bit of a jolt and get the day going. Similarly, people often use other substances to help improve, or at least change, how they feel or function. Many people smoke cigarettes to feel more alert, less anxious, or both. Others may have a glass of wine or beer in the evening in order to wind down from a hectic day.

These substances—coffee, cigarettes, and alcohol—along with many others, alter our state of consciousness and influence our moods and behaviors. Collectively, they are examples of **psychoactive drugs**, chemicals that affect awareness, behavior, sensation, perception, or mood. Some such drugs are illegal chemicals (heroin, ecstasy, marijuana), while others are common and legal. **Table 6-1** shows the three broad categories of drugs and lists examples of specific drugs that fall within those categories.

"No thanks, I'm fine."

TABLE 6-1 Psychoactive Drugs and Their Effects

DRUG CLASS	EFFECTS
Depressants	**Depress activity of central nervous system**
Alcohol	Slows down brain areas that control judgment, inhibition, behavior (speech, motor functioning, emotional expression)
Sedative-hypnotics (benzodiazepines)	Produce relaxation and drowsiness, relieves anxiety
Opioids (opium heroin, morphine, codeine, methadone)	Reduce pain and emotional tension, produce pleasurable and calming feelings
Stimulants	**Increase activity of central nervous system**
Caffeine	Increases alertness
Nicotine	Increases alertness, reduces stress
Cocaine	Increases energy and alertness, produces euphoric feelings of well-being and confidence
Amphetamines	Increase energy and alertness, reduce appetite, produce euphoric feelings
Hallucinogens	**Enhance normal perceptions**
LSD	Dramatically strengthens visual perceptions (including illusions and hallucinations) along with profound psychological and physical changes
Cannabis (marijuana, THC)	Produces a mixture of hallucinogenic, depressant, and stimulant effects
MDMA (Ecstasy)	Enhances sensory perceptions, increases energy and alertness, produces feelings of empathy and emotional well-being

sleep apnea sleep disorder characterized by repeatedly ceasing to sleep during the night, depriving the brain of oxygen and leading to frequent awakenings.

narcolepsy sleep disorder marked by uncontrollable urge to fall asleep.

psychoactive drugs chemicals that affect awareness, behavior, sensation, perception, or mood.

Fighting addiction Thousands of people from alcohol and drug recovery programs march across the Brooklyn Bridge in 2008 as part of The Recovery Rally, a campaign to spread the message that addiction is treatable.

Most of us know someone who has an addiction problem. According to some clinical theorists, addictions are not only about alcohol and substance abuse; they may also cover dependencies such as food, the Internet, gambling, caffeine, shopping, sex, and exercise, to name a few (Page & Brewster, 2009; Stein, 2008). Addictive patterns do not suddenly appear; they are usually long-standing and may be rooted in various psychological problems. Whereas it takes time for an individual to lose control of his or her life to a dependency, it also takes time, motivation, commitment, discipline, and often the help of a professional treatment program to regain control and recover from an addiction. There are no quick fixes for recovery.

How do you know whether you or someone close to you is experiencing an addiction? This is a complex issue that typically requires careful clinical assessment for a definitive answer. Nevertheless, there are some straightforward questions that you can use to determine whether professional attention is in order. For example, is the person unable to meet responsibilities at home, school, or the office? Has the person tried to stop the repeated behavior but cannot, and continues to engage in it despite the apparent dangers?

Although most clinicians agree that there is no substitute for careful clinical assessment and treatment of addictions, some have developed basic detection devices that can help get the ball rolling. For example, a brief tool to detect alcohol addiction is known as the CAGE questionnaire. It asks these questions: 1) Has the person ever felt that he or she should **CUT DOWN** on the drinking? 2) Has the person ever been **ANNOYED** by people criticizing the drinking? 3) Has the person ever expressed remorse or **GUILT** about drinking? 4) Has the person ever started to drink in the morning as an **EYE-OPENER** to start the day or get rid of a hangover? A "yes"' answer to at least two of these questions may indicate a problem with alcohol addiction and a corresponding need for professional assessment and treatment. More than a quarter century after the CAGE questionnaire was first developed, it has been validated in many studies as an effective, quick indicator of the need for help (O'Brien, 2008).

Some of the changes brought about by psychoactive drugs are temporary, lasting only as long as the chemicals remain in the brain and body. But certain psychoactive drugs can also bring about long-term changes and problems. People who regularly ingest them may develop maladaptive patterns of behavior and changes in their body's physical responses, a pattern commonly called **addiction**. We will also be discussing addiction in Chapter 11 when we examine the motives and drives that direct behavior, including chronic drug-taking behavior.

Those addicted to a drug feel compelled psychologically and physically to keep taking it. They rely on the drug excessively and chronically and may damage their family and social relationships, function poorly at work, or put themselves and others in danger. Addicted individuals may also acquire a physical dependence on the drug. They may develop a **tolerance** for the drug, meaning they need larger and larger doses in order to keep feeling its desired effect. And, if they try to stop taking or cut back on the drug, they may experience unpleasant and even dangerous **withdrawal symptoms**, such as nausea, cramps, sweating, or anxiety. People in withdrawal may also *crave* the drug that they had been taking regularly. Even if they want to quit taking it, the knowledge that they can quickly eliminate the unpleasant withdrawal symptoms by simply ingesting the drug makes it difficult for many users to persevere through the withdrawal period. In any given year, 9.2 percent of all teens and adults in the United States, around 23 million people, display addiction (NSDUH, 2008).

Depressants

Psychoactive drugs that slow down the central nervous system are called **depressants**. They reduce tension and inhibitions and may interfere with a person's judgment, motor activity, and concentration. The three most widely used groups of depressants are *alcohol*, *sedative-hypnotic drugs*, and *opioids*.

Alcohol *Alcohol*, a depressant that is taken in liquid form, is one of the most commonly used psychoactive drugs. More than half of the people in the United States drink beverages that contain alcohol, at least from time to time (NSDUH, 2008). Purchases of beer, wine, and liquor amount to many billions of dollars each year in the United States alone. Nearly 7 percent of people over 11 years of age are heavy drinkers, having at least five drinks in a row on at least five occasions each month (NSDUH, 2008). Among heavy drinkers, males outnumber females by more than two to one, around 8 percent to 4 percent.

All alcoholic beverages contain *ethyl alcohol*, a chemical that is quickly absorbed into the blood through the lining of the stomach and the intestine. The ethyl alcohol immediately begins to take effect as it is carried in the bloodstream to the central nervous system (the brain and spinal cord), where it acts to slow functioning by binding to various neurons, particularly those that normally receive a neurotransmitter called *gamma aminobutyric acid*, or *GABA*.

addiction psychological or physical compulsion to take a drug, resulting from regular ingestion and leading to maladaptive patterns of behavior and changes in physical response.

tolerance mark of physical dependence on drug, in which person is required to take incrementally larger doses of the drug to achieve the same effect.

withdrawal symptoms unpleasant and sometimes dangerous side effects of reducing intake of a drug after a person has become addicted.

depressants class of drugs that slow the activity of the central nervous system.

Binge Drinking and College Students

Binge drinking—the consumption of five or more drinks in a row—is a major problem in many settings, not the least of which are college campuses (NSDUH, 2008, Read et al., 2008). According to research, 40 percent of college students binge drink at least once each year, many of them multiple times per month (NCASA, 2007; Wechsler et al., 2004). These are higher rates than those among similar aged individuals who do not attend college (Ksir et al., 2008). On many campuses, alcohol use often is an accepted part of college life. But consider these statistics:

- Binge drinking by college students has been associated with 1,700 deaths each year, 500,000 injuries, and tens of thousands of cases of sexual assault, including date rape (NCASA, 2007; Wechsler et al., 2000).
- Alcohol-related arrests account for 83 percent of all campus arrests (NCASA, 2007).

- Binge drinking by female college students has increased 31 percent over the past decade.
- Alcohol may be a factor in 40 percent of college problems (Anderson, 1994).

Given such trends, many researchers and clinicians have turned their attention to the problem of college binge drinking. Surveys of more than 50,000 students across the United States find that the students most likely to binge drink are those who live in a fraternity or sorority house, pursue a party-centered lifestyle, and engage in high-risk behaviors, such as substance misuse or having multiple sex partners (Wechsler & Nelson, 2008; Wechsler et al., 2004, 1995, 1994).

Efforts to reduce college binge drinking have begun to make a difference. Some universities, for example, now provide substance-free dorms. One study found that 36 percent of the residents in such dorms were binge drinkers, compared to 75 percent of students who lived in a fraternity or sorority house (Wechsler et al., 2002). The implications are clear: college drinking, including binge drinking, is more common and harmful than previously believed. And most experts agree that the time has come to attack this enormous problem head on.

TABLE 6-2 **Alcohol's Effects on the Body and Behavior**

Number of drinks[a] in two hours	Blood alcohol content (%)[b]	Effect
(2)	0.06	Relaxed state; increased sociability
(3)	0.09	Everyday stress lessened
(4)	0.10	Movements and speech become clumsy
(7)	0.20	Very drunk; loud and difficult to understand; emotions unstable
(12)	0.40	Difficult to wake up; incapable of voluntary action
(15)	0.55	Coma and/or death

[a] A drink refers to one 12-ounce beer, a 4-ounce glass of wine, or a 1.25-ounce shot of hard liquor.

[b] In America, the legal blood alcohol lever for "drunk driving" varies from 0.05 to 0.12.

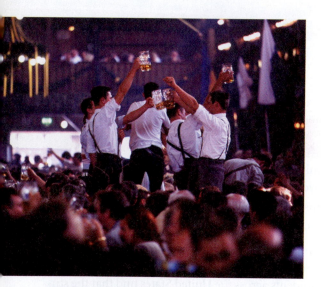

Cultural endorsement? Five men and hundreds of others around them celebrate at Oktoberfest, Germany's annual 16-day festival, marked by eating, special events, and perhaps most prominently, drinking. Almost 7 million liters of beer are served to thousands of revelers at each year's festival, an excessiveness that many believe contributes to binge drinking and alcoholism.

At first, ethyl alcohol slows down the brain areas that control judgment and inhibition; people become looser and more talkative, relaxed, and happy. When more alcohol is absorbed, it slows down additional areas in the central nervous system, causing the drinkers to make poorer judgments, become careless, and remember less well. Many people become highly emotional, and some become loud and aggressive.

As drinking continues, the motor responses of individuals decline and their reaction times slow. They may be unsteady when they stand or walk, for example, Their vision becomes blurred and they may misjudge distances. They can also have trouble hearing. As a result, people who have drunk too much alcohol may have enormous difficulty driving or solving simple problems.

As summarized in **Table 6-2**, the *concentration*, or proportion, of ethyl alcohol in the blood determines how much it will affect a person (Ksir et al, 2008). When the alcohol concentration reaches 0.06 percent of the blood volume, a person usually feels relaxed and comfortable. By the time it reaches 0.09 percent, the drinker crosses the line into *intoxication*. If the level goes as high as 0.55 percent, death will probably result. Most people, however, lose consciousness before they can drink enough to reach this level. The effects of alcohol subside only when the alcohol concentration in the blood falls.

Though legal, alcohol is actually one of society's most dangerous drugs, and its risks extend to all age groups. In fact, 10 percent of elementary school students admit to some alcohol use and nearly 45 percent of high school seniors drink alcohol each month (usually to the point of intoxication), with 3 percent of them drinking every day (Johnston et al., 2007). Surveys indicate that over a one-year period, 6.6 percent of all adults in the world fall into a long-term pattern of alcohol addiction, known as **alcoholism** (Somers et al., 2004). More than 13 percent of adults experience the pattern at some time in their lives, with men outnumbering women by at least two to one (Kessler et al., 2005).

The prevalence of alcoholism in a given year is similar (from 7 to 9 percent) for white Americans, African Americans, and Hispanic Americans (SAMHSA, 2008). Native Americans, particularly men, display a higher alcoholism rate (15 percent) than any of these groups. Generally, Asians in the United States and elsewhere have lower rates of alcoholism than do people from other cultures. As many as one-half of Asians have a deficiency of *alcohol dehydrogenase*, a chemical responsible for breaking down and eliminating alcohol from the body, so they react very negatively to even a small intake of alcohol. Such extreme reactions help prevent heavy use (Wall et al., 2001; APA, 2000).

People who abuse alcohol drink large amounts regularly and rely on it to help them to do things that would otherwise make them nervous. Eventually the drinking disrupts their social behavior and their ability to think clearly and work effectively. Many build up a tolerance for alcohol and they need to drink greater and greater amounts to feel its effects. They also experience withdrawal when they stop drinking. Within hours, for example, their hands and eyelids begin to shake, they feel weak, they sweat heavily, their heart beats rapidly, and their blood pressure rises (APA, 2000).

Alcoholism can wreak havoc on an individual's family, social, and occupational life (Murphy et al., 2005). Medical treatment, lost productivity, and losses due to deaths from alcoholism cost society many billions of dollars each year. The disorder also has been implicated in more than one-third of all suicides, homicides, assaults, rapes, and accidental deaths, including 30 percent of all fatal automobile accidents in the United States (Ksir et al., 2008). Intoxicated drivers are responsible for 12,000 deaths each year. One of every eight persons has driven while intoxicated at least once in the past year (NSDUH, 2008).

The 30 million children whose parents have alcoholism are also severely affected by this disorder. The home life of these children often features much conflict and, in some cases, sexual or other forms of abuse. The children themselves have elevated rates of psychological problems and substance-related disorders over the course of their lives (Hall & Webster, 2002). Many display low self-esteem, weak communication skills, poor sociability, and marital problems (Watt, 2002; Lewis-Harter, 2000).

Long-term excessive drinking can also cause severe damage to one's physical health (Myrick & Wright, 2008). It so overworks the liver—the body organ that breaks down alcohol—that people may develop an irreversible condition called *cirrhosis,* in which the liver becomes scarred and dysfunctional (CDC, 2008). Alcohol abuse may also damage the heart and lower the immune system's ability to fight off infections and cancer and to resist the onset of AIDS after infection.

Finally, women who drink during pregnancy place their fetuses at risk (Finnegan & Kandall, 2008). Heavy drinking early in pregnancy often leads to a miscarriage. Excessive alcohol use during pregnancy may also cause a baby to be born with *fetal alcohol syndrome*, a pattern that can include mental retardation, hyperactivity, head and face deformities, heart defects, and slow growth. It has been estimated that in the overall population approximately 1 of every 1,000 babies is born with this syndrome (Ksir et al., 2008). The rate increases to as many as 29 of every 1,000 babies of women who are heavy drinkers.

Sedative-Hypnotic Drugs

At low dosages, **sedative-hypnotic drugs** produce feelings of relaxation and drowsiness. At higher dosages, they are sleep inducers, or hypnotics. *Benzodiazepines,* antianxiety drugs developed in the 1950s, are today's most popular sedative-hypnotic drugs available. More than 100 million prescriptions are written each year for this group of chemical compounds (Bisaga, 2008). Xanax®, Ativan®, and Valium® are three of the benzodiazepines in wide clinical use.

This group of drugs reduces anxiety without making people as overly drowsy as alcohol or other depressant substances. Nevertheless, in high enough doses, benzodiazepines can cause intoxication and lead to addiction (Dupont & Dupont, 2005). As many as 1 percent of the adults in the United States become addicted to these drugs at some point in their lives (Sareen, Enns, & Cox, 2004).

Spreading the word Perhaps the most successful public effort to reduce drunk driving fatalities has been undertaken by Mothers Against Drunk Driving (MADD). Raising public awareness through ads, campaigns, and lobbying efforts, this organization has helped reduce the number of alcohol-related automobile deaths by 47 percent since it was formed in 1980.

alcoholism long-term pattern of alcohol addiction.

sedative-hypnotic drugs class of drugs, the members of which produce feelings of relaxation and drowsiness.

Opioids   The term **opioids** refers to *opium* and drugs derived from it, including *heroin*, *morphine*, and *codeine*. Opium, a substance taken from the sap of the opium poppy, has been used for thousands of years. In the past, it was used widely in the treatment of medical disorders because of its ability to reduce both physical pain and emotional distress. Physicians eventually discovered, however, that the drug was addictive. Morphine and heroin, each of which was later derived from opium for use as a safer painkiller, also proved to be highly addictive. In fact, heroin is even more addictive than the other opioids.

Additional drugs have been derived from opium, and several synthetic (laboratory-blended) opioids such as *methadone* have also been developed. Each of these various drugs has a different strength, speed of action, and tolerance level. Today, morphine and codeine are used as medical opioids, usually prescribed to relieve pain. Heroin is illegal in the United States under all circumstances.

Outside of medical settings, opioids are smoked, inhaled, snorted (inhaled through the nose), injected by needle just beneath the skin ("skin popped"), or injected directly into the blood stream ("mainlined"). An injection quickly produces a *rush*—a spasm of warmth and joy that is sometimes compared with an orgasm. The brief spasm is followed by several hours of a pleasant feeling and shift in consciousness called a *high* or *nod*. During a high, the opioid user feels very relaxed and happy and is unconcerned about food or other bodily needs.

Opioids depress the central nervous system, particularly the brain areas that control emotion. The drugs attach to brain receptors that ordinarily receive **endorphins**, neurotransmitters discussed in the previous chapter, that help reduce pain and emotional tension (Ksir et al., 2008). When neurons receive opioids at these receptors, the opioids produce the same kinds of pleasant and relaxing feelings that endorphins would produce.

The most direct danger of heroin use is an overdose, which shuts down the respiratory center in the brain, almost paralyzing breathing and in many cases causing death. Death is particularly likely during sleep, when individuals cannot fight the respiratory effects by consciously working at breathing. Each year 2 percent of those addicted to heroin and other opioids are killed by the drugs, usually from an overdose (Theodorou & Haber, 2005; APA, 2000).

Stimulants

Psychoactive drugs that speed up the central nervous system are called **stimulants**. They produce increases in blood pressure, heart rate, alertness, thinking, and behavior. Among the most problematic stimulants are *caffeine, nicotine, cocaine*, and *amphetamines*,

Caffeine   *Caffeine*, a mild (and legal) stimulant, is the world's most widely used stimulant. It is found in coffee, tea, chocolate, cola, and so-called *energy drinks*. Worldwide, 80 percent of all people consume caffeine in one form or another every day (Rogers, 2005). Like many other psychoactive drugs, caffeine is addictive, although this addiction does not cause the significant social problems that are associated with substances such as alcohol, heroin, and cocaine (Paton & Beer, 2001; Silverman et al., 1992). Still, quitting caffeine can cause unpleasant withdrawal symptoms for chronic users, including lethargy, sleepiness, anxiety, irritability, depression, constipation, and headaches. Withdrawal symptoms can start only a few hours after the individual's last consumption of caffeine.

Nicotine   Although legal, *nicotine* is one of the most highly addictive substances known (Ksir et al., 2008). Most commonly, it is taken into the body by smoking tobacco. Nicotine is then absorbed through the respiratory tract, the mucous membranes of the nasal area, and the gastrointestinal tract. The drug procedes to activate nicotine receptors located throughout the brain and body. Inhaling a puff of cigarette smoke delivers a dose of nicotine to the brain faster than it could be delivered by injection into the blood stream.

" Caffeine. The gateway drug. **"**

—*Eddie Vedder, singer/guitarist, Pearl Jam*

Regular smokers develop a tolerance for nicotine and must smoke more and more in order to achieve the same results (Hymowitz, 2005). When they try to stop smoking, they experience withdrawal symptoms such as irritability, increased appetite, sleep disturbances, and a powerful desire to smoke (Dodgen, 2005; APA, 2000).

Almost one third of all individuals over the age of 12 in the United States regularly smoke tobacco (NSDUH, 2008). Surveys also find that nearly 22 percent of all high school seniors have smoked within the past month (Johnston et al., 2007). All of this smoking eventually takes a heavy toll: 440,000 people in the United States alone die each year as a result of smoking (George & Weinberger, 2008). Chronic smoking is directly tied to lung disease, high blood pressure, coronary heart disease, cancer, strokes, and other fatal medical problems. Moreover, pregnant women who smoke are much more likely than non-smokers to deliver premature and underweight babies (NSDUH, 2008).

Cocaine *Cocaine,* the key active ingredient of South America's coca plant, is the most powerful natural stimulant currently known. The drug was first separated from the plant in 1865. For many centuries however, native people, have chewed the leaves of the plant to raise their energy and increase their alertness.

Processed cocaine—a white, fluffy powder—is snorted and absorbed through the mucous membrane of the nose. Some users, however, prefer the more powerful effects of injecting cocaine intravenously or smoking it in a pipe or cigarette. Around 28 million people have tried cocaine, and 2.4 million—the majority of them teenagers or young adults—are using it currently (NSDUH, 2008). In fact, 6 percent of all high school seniors have used cocaine within the past year (Johnston et al., 2007).

Cocaine brings on a rush of euphoria and well-being—an orgasmic-like reaction if the dose is high enough. Initially, cocaine stimulates the higher centers of the central nervous system, shifting users' levels of awareness and making them excited, energetic, and talkative. As more cocaine is taken, it stimulates additional areas of the central nervous system, resulting in increases in heart rate, blood pressure, breathing, arousal, and wakefulness. Cocaine apparently produces these effects largely by increasing activity of the neurotransmitter *dopamine* at key neurons throughout the brain (Haney, 2008). As the stimulating effects of cocaine subside, the user experiences a depression-like letdown, popularly called *crashing* (Doweiko, 2006).

Regular use of cocaine may lead to a pattern of addiction. Tolerance to the drug may develop, and suddenly withdrawing from it results in depression, fatigue, sleep problems, anxiety, and irritability (Ksir et al., 2008). Today, almost 1 out of every 100 persons over the age of 12 in the United States is addicted to cocaine (NSDUH, 2008).

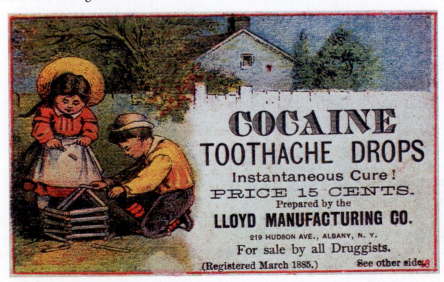

The early days In the early twentieth century, cocaine was an ingredient in such products as Cocaine Toothache Drops and Coca-Cola soft drinks.

Cocaine also poses serious physical dangers (Kosten et al., 2008). Use of the drug in powerful, smokable, forms known as *freebasing* and *crack,* has caused the annual number of cocaine-related emergency room incidents in the United States to increase 100-fold since 1982, from around 4,000 cases to 450,000 (SAMHSA, 2008). In addition, cocaine use has been linked to as many as 20 percent of all suicides among people under 61 years of age (Garlow, 2002). The greatest danger of cocaine use is an overdose, which may impair breathing, produce major—even fatal—heart irregularities, or cause brain seizures (Doweiko, 2006).

Amphetamines *Amphetamines* are manufactured in the laboratory. These stimulants are most often taken in pill or capsule form, although some individuals inject the drugs intravenously or smoke them for a quicker and more powerful effect. Like cocaine, amphetamines increase energy and alertness and lower appetite in small doses, produce intoxication and psychosis in higher doses, and cause an emotional letdown when they leave the body. Also like cocaine, these drugs produce such effects by increasing the activity of the neurotransmitter *dopamine* (Haney, 2008).

Tolerance to amphetamines builds very rapidly, thus increasing the chances of users becoming addicted (Acosta, Haller, & Schnoll, 2005). People who start using the drug to help reduce their appetite, for example, may soon find they are as hungry as ever and increase their dose in response. Athletes who use amphetamines to increase their energy may also soon find that they need increasing amounts of the drug. When people who are addicted to the drug stop taking it, they fall into a pattern of deep depression and extended sleep identical to the withdrawal from cocaine. Around 1.5 to 2 percent of the population in the United States become addicted to amphetamines at some point in their lives (APA, 2000; Anthony et al., 1995).

One powerful kind of amphetamine, *methamphetamine* (nicknamed *crank*), currently is experiencing a major surge in popularity. Almost 6 percent of all persons over the age of 12 in the United States have now used this stimulant at least once. It is available in the form of crystals (known as *ice* or *crystal meth*) which are smoked by users.

Most of the nonmedical methamphetamine in the United States is made in small, illegal "stovetop laboratories," which typically operate for a few days and then move on to a new location (Ksir et al., 2008). Although such laboratories have been around since the 1960s, they have increased eightfold over the past decade. A major health concern is that the secret laboratories produce dangerous fumes and residue (Burgess, 2001).

Since 1989, when reports first emerged about the dangers of smoking methamphetamine crystals, the rise in usage has been dramatic. In 1994, fewer than 4 million Americans had tried this stimulant at least once. That number rose to more than 9 million in 1999 and is 15 million today (NSDUH, 2008). Initially, the drug was available primarily in western parts of the United States (NSDUH, 2007), but its use has been spreading east steadily. Indeed, treatment admissions for methamphetamine abuse are on the increase in New York, Atlanta, Minneapolis/St. Paul, and St. Louis (Ksir et al., 2008; CEWG, 2004), and methamphetamine-linked emergency room visits are rising in hospitals throughout all parts of the country (DAWN, 2008).

Around 60 percent of current methamphetamine users are men (NSDUH, 2008). The drug is particularly popular among biker gangs, rural Americans, and urban gay communities, and has gained wide use as a "club drug," the term for drugs of choice at all-night dance parties, or "raves" (Ksir et al., 2008).

Like other kinds of amphetamines, methamphetamine increases activity of the neurotransmitter dopamine, producing increased arousal, attention, and related effects. This particular drug also may damage nerve endings—a *neurotoxicity* that is

"Drugs are a bet with your mind."
—*Jim Morrison, singer, The Doors. Died of suspected overdose in 1971*

hallucinogens substances that dramatically change one's state of awareness causing powerful changes in sensory perception.

flashbacks recurrence of the sensory and emotional changes after the LSD has left the body.

compounded by the drug's tendency to remain in the brain and body for a long time—more than six hours (Rawson & Ling, 2008). But, among users, such dangers are less important than methamphetamine's immediate positive impact, including perceptions by many that it makes them feel hypersexual and uninhibited (Jefferson, 2005). All of this has contributed to major public health problems. For example, one-third of all men who tested positive for HIV in Los Angeles in 2004 reported having used this drug (Jefferson, 2005). Similarly, according to surveys, a growing number of domestic-violence incidents, assaults, and robberies have been tied to the use of methamphetamine (Jefferson, 2005).

Hallucinogens

Hallucinogens, or *psychedelic drugs*, are substances that dramatically change one's state of awareness by causing powerful changes in sensory perception, such as enhancing a person's normal perceptions and producing illusions and hallucinations. The substance-induced sensory changes are sometimes called "trips," and these trips may be exciting or frightening, depending on how a person's mind reacts to the drugs. Many hallucinogens come from plants or animals; others are laboratory-produced.

Bad trip Ingesting LSD brings on hallucinosis, a state of sensory and perceptual distortions. Sometimes this state can be very frightening and disorienting, as captured in this photo illustration of a hallucination of hands and arms burning.

LSD *Lysergic acid diethylamide*, or *LSD*, is a very powerful hallucinogen that was derived by the Swiss chemist Albert Hoffman in 1938 from a group of naturally occurring substances. During the 1960s, a period of rebellion and experimentation, millions of users turned to the drug in an effort to raise their consciousness and expand their experiences. Within two hours of being swallowed, LSD brings on *hallucinosis*, a state marked by a strengthening of visual perceptions and profound psychological and physical changes. People may focus on small details—each hair on the skin, for example. Colors may seem brighter or take on a shade of purple. Users often experience illusions in which objects seem distorted and seem to move, breathe, or change shape. LSD can also produce strong emotions, from joy to anxiety or depression. Past thoughts and feelings may return. All these effects take place while the user is fully alert, and wear off in about six hours. Scientists believe that LSD produces these effects primarily by binding to many of the neurons that normally receive the neurotransmitter *serotonin*, changing the neurotransmitter's activity at those sites (Julien, 2008).

More than 14 percent of all people in the United States have used LSD or another hallucinogen during their lives (NSDUH, 2008). A key problem is that LSD is so powerful that any dose, no matter how small, is likely to produce very strong reactions. Sometimes the reactions are quite unpleasant, an experience called a "bad trip." In addition, some LSD users have **flashbacks**, recurrences of the sensory and emotional changes even after the LSD has left the body (Doweiko, 2006).

Cannabis The hemp plant *Cannabis sativa* grows in warm climates. Collectively, the drugs produced from varieties of hemp are called *cannabis*. The most powerful of them is *hashish*; the weaker ones include the best-known form of cannabis, *marijuana*, a mixture derived from the buds, crushed leaves, and flowering tops of hemp plants. Although there are several hundred active chemicals in cannabis, *tetrahydrocannabinol* (*THC*) is the one most responsible for its effects. The greater the THC content, the more powerful the cannabis.

When smoked, cannabis changes one's conscious experiences by producing a mixture of hallucinogenic, depressant, and stimulant effects. At low doses, the smoker typically has feelings of happiness and relaxation, although some smokers become anxious or irritated, especially if they have been in a bad mood. Many smokers have sharpened perceptions and become fascinated with the intensified sounds and sights that they are experiencing. Time seems to slow down, and distances and sizes become greater. This

reward learning pathway brain circuitry that is important for learning about rewarding stimuli.

reward-deficiency syndrome theory that people might abuse drugs because their reward center is not readily activated by usual life events.

overall reaction is often called getting "high." In strong doses, cannabis produces particularly unusual visual experiences, changes in body image, and even hallucinations (Mathew et al., 1993). Most of the drug's effects last two to six hours.

Because marijuana can interfere with complex sensorimotor tasks and cognitive functioning, it has been tied to many automobile accidents (Kauert & Iwersen-Bergmann, 2004). In addition, many people on a marijuana high fail to remember information, especially recently learned material; thus, heavy marijuana smokers may function poorly at school or work (Lundqvist, 2005). Some research also suggests that regular marijuana smoking may contribute to long-term medical problems, including lung disease (Ksir et al., 2008; NIDA, 2002), lower sperm counts in men, and abnormal ovulation in women (Schuel et al., 2002).

Due to changes in growing patterns, today's marijuana is at least four times higher in THC content than was the marijuana of the early 1970s (Doweiko, 2006; APA, 2000). As a result, many people, including 5 percent of high school seniors, are now caught in a pattern of heavy and regular use, getting high on marijuana daily, although it is not clear whether such use represents a true addiction or a strong habit (Johnston et al., 2007). Either way, a number of these users do indeed find their social, occupational, or academic lives affected greatly. Around 1.7 percent of people in the United States have displayed heavy and regular marijuana use in the past year; between 4 and 5 percent have fallen into a pattern of such use at some point in their lives (NSDUH, 2008; APA, 2000).

Marijuana as Medicine

An uncommon medicine A man suffering from chronic arthritis smokes marijuana at a protest rally, calling on the government to implement a medical marijuana program.

Movies, such as *Dazed and Confused, Half Baked,* and *The Big Lebowski*—so-called "stoner films"—have helped to popularize the image of a marijuana user as a mellow hippie trying to avoid the wrath of inept authority figures (Meltzer, 2007). In fact, however, the many millions of individuals who have tried marijuana come in all sizes, shapes, and personalities (Earleywine, 2007). Indeed, tens of thousands of them use marijuana for a very serious purpose—as medicine.

Common medicinal uses of marijuana, or cannabis, include treatment of chronic pain, nausea associated with chemotherapy, glaucoma, and disease-related anorexia (Okie, 2005). A key difficulty for many patients, however, lies in gaining access to the drug; in the United States, federal law holds that possession or distribution of marijuana for any purpose is illegal—a law upheld by the Supreme Court in 2005 (Sunil, Carter, & Steinborn, 2005). Despite this, 31 states formally recognize that marijuana can have medicinal value, and 14 of them allow their residents to grow, possess, or use marijuana when approved by a physician. Moreover, the U.S. Attorney General recently announced that federal prosecutors would not prosecute cases against medical marijuana users as long as they are complying with the laws of their states.

The federal anti-marijuana laws are based, in part, on assessment by the National Institute for Drug Abuse and the Food and Drug Administration that evidence to support medical marijuana usage is lacking. To address this concern, a randomized, double-blind, placebo-controlled study—the gold standard of research design—was recently conducted to investigate the effectiveness of marijuana in reducing pain associated with nerve damage. The researchers found that smoking marijuana, even at a low dose, did indeed reduce pain in comparison to a placebo. In this study, the patients considered the negative side effects to be minimal and tolerable, although the effects did include slight declines in learning and recall abilities, especially with higher doses (Wilsey et al., 2008).

Some countries are already convinced—the Netherlands and Canada now allow the sale of medical marijuana in select pharmacies. In the United States, however, it appears that more studies of the kind just described will be required before the medical use of marijuana is accepted by the federal government and its legislators. In the meantime, the mind of the public may already be set; surveys indicate that more than 70 percent support medical marijuana use (Earleywine, 2007).

Psychoactive Drugs *What Happens in the* B R A I N ?

As you have seen, an ingested drug increases the activity of certain neurotransmitters in the brain—chemicals whose normal purpose is to reduce pain, calm us, lift our mood, or increase our alertness—and these neurotransmitters, in turn, help produce the particular effects of the drug. Alcohol, for example, heightens activity of the neurotransmitter *GABA;* opioids raise *endorphin* activity; and cocaine and amphetamines increase *dopamine* activity. Similarly, researchers have identified a neurotransmitter called *anandamide* (from the Sanskrit word for "bliss") that operates much like THC (Hitti, 2004).

It used to be thought that each drug, along with its corresponding neurotransmitters, sets in motion a unique set of brain reactions. However, recent brain-imaging studies suggest that while each drug has its own starting point in the brain, most (perhaps all) of them eventually activate a single **reward learning pathway**, or "pleasure pathway," in the brain (Haney, 2008; Koob & LeMoal, 2008). This brain reward learning pathway apparently extends from the midbrain to the nucleus accumbens and on to the frontal cortex (see Chapter 4). The key neurotransmitter in this pathway appears to be *dopamine*. When dopamine is activated there, a person wants—at times, even craves—pleasurable rewards, such as music, a hug, or, for some people, a drug (Higgins & George, 2007; Higgins et al., 2004).

Certain drugs apparently stimulate the reward learning pathway directly. You'll recall that cocaine and amphetamines directly increase dopamine activity. Other drugs seem to stimulate it in roundabout ways. The biochemical reactions triggered by alcohol and opioids each set in motion a series of chemical events that eventually lead to increased dopamine activity in the reward learning pathway.

Research also suggests that people prone to abuse drugs may suffer from a **reward-deficiency syndrome**—their reward learning pathway is not activated readily by the events in their lives (Blum et al., 2000; Nash, 1997)—so they are more inclined than other people to turn to drugs to keep their pathway stimulated. Abnormal genes have been pointed to as a possible cause of this syndrome (Finckh, 2001; Lawford et al., 1997).

But how might persons become ensnared in a broad pattern of addiction, marked by tolerance and withdrawal effects? According to one explanation, when a person takes a particular drug chronically, the brain eventually makes an adjustment and reduces its own production of the neurotransmitter whose activity is being increased by the ingested drug (Kleber & Galanter, 2008; Kosten, George, & Kleber, 2005). That is, because the drug is increasing neurotransmitter activity, natural release of the neurotransmitter by the brain is less necessary. As drug intake increases, the body's production of the neurotransmitter continues to decrease, and the person needs to take more and more of the drug to feel its positive effects. In short, drug takers are building tolerance for a drug, becoming more and more dependent on it, rather than on their own biological processes to feel comfortable or alert. In addition, if they suddenly stop taking the drug, their supply of neurotransmitters will be low for a time, producing symptoms of withdrawal that will continue until the brain resumes its normal production of the necessary neurotransmitters.

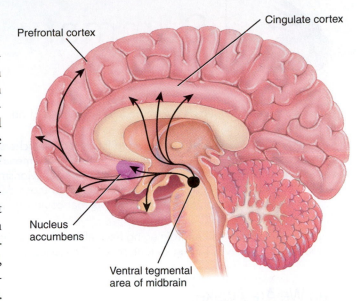

The brain's reward learning pathway, or "pleasure pathway," extends from an area in the midbrain called the ventral tegmental area to the nucleus accumbens, as well as to the prefrontal cortex.

Before You Go On

What Do You Know?

13. What are the major drug categories and the characteristics of each category?
14. What is addiction, and what are two key features of addiction to a drug?
15. Why is alcoholism realtively less common among Asians than in individuals of other ethnic groups?

What Do You Think?
Why do you think alcohol is more acceptable culturally than some of the other drugs we are discussing here?

Summary

- Consciousness is defined as our immediate awareness of our internal and external states.
- The study of consciousness has proven difficult for researchers, because of the difficulty measuring its associated phenomena, such as dreams and awareness. In part, the rise of behaviorism in the United States during the 1950s was a reaction to these difficulties, focusing more on objective behaviors that could be easily measured.
- Recent developments in neuroimaging have allowed researchers to look at brain activity during various states of consciousness.

When We Are Awake: Conscious Awareness

LEARNING OBJECTIVE 1   Define different levels of conscious awareness and describe key brain structures and functions associated with those levels.

- Attention is one of the key aspects of conscious awareness. Other key cognitive activities underlying cognitive awareness include monitoring (our implicit decisions about what to attend to), memory, and planning.
- Most biological investigators believe that consciousness results from a combination of brain activities in several brain regions. Two key brain structures appear to be the cerebral cortex, which helps regulate our awareness of attentional processes, and the thalamus, which relays sensory information from various parts of the brain to the cerebral cortex for processing.

Preconscious and Unconscious States

LEARNING OBJECTIVE 2   Summarize the ideas of preconscious and unconscious states, including Freud's thinking on the unconscious.

- In addition to our conscious level of awareness, many psychologists believe there are other levels or degrees of consciousness, and distinguish conscious awareness from two other states—unconsciousness and preconsciousness.
- Preconsciousness is a level of awareness in which information can become readily available to consciousness if necessary.
- Unconsciousness is a state in which information is not easily accessible to conscious awareness.
- Freud viewed the human unconscious as an important storehouse for knowledge and experience, which although not directly accessible to our conscious awareness, still influences our behavior.
- Although Freud's ideas fell into disfavor for several years, in recent years, scientists have begun to reexamine the unconscious

from different points of view. For example, implicit memory describes knowledge that we have and are able to apply to various tasks, without being able to recall it at will.

Hypnosis

LEARNING OBJECTIVE 3   Define hypnosis and discuss theories and evidence about what hypnosis is, how it works, and how it can be used.

- Hypnosis is a suggestible state during which people can be directed to act in unusual ways, experience unusual sensations, remember forgotten events, or forget remembered events.
- Ernest Hilgard's theory suggests that hypnosis divides consciousness into two parts: one focused on the suggestions of the hypnotist, and the other a hidden observer. Other theorists suggest that motivated role-playing is at work in hypnosis.
- Hypnosis has been used to successfully help control pain, as well as treat problems , such as anxiety, skin diseases, asthma, insomnia, stuttering, high blood pressure, warts, and other forms of infection.

Meditation

LEARNING OBJECTIVE 4   Define meditation and describe the techniques and effects of meditation.

- Meditation is designed to help turn one's consciousness away from the outer world toward inner cues and awareness, and to ignore all stressors.
- Like hypnosis, meditation has been suggested to have numerous positive benefits, including successfully treating many of the same illnesses, and helping people to relax.

When We Are Asleep

LEARNING OBJECTIVE 5   Describe what happens when people sleep, key theories of why we sleep and dream, and problems with sleep and how they affect functioning.

- Every 90 to 100 minutes when we sleep, we pass through a sleep cycle consisting of five different stages. The fifth stage of sleep, rapid eye movement, or REM sleep, is characterized by rapid and jagged brain-wave patterns and eye movements and irregularities in heart rate and breathing. Dreaming usually occurs during this phase of sleep.
- Scientists have identified brain activities that maintain the regular rhythms of life. Our move from a sustained period of wakefulness into a period of sleep during each 24-hour period is known as a *circadian rhythm.*

- Scientists have not reached a definitive conclusion about why people sleep, although some scientists have suggested sleep serves an evolutionarily adaptive function, keeping our ancestors away from predators that hunted at night. Others have suggested that sleep might play a role in growth, or allow us time to restore depleted chemical resources in the brain and body and eliminate chemical wastes that have accumulated throughout the day.

- We also do not understand why people dream. Freud believed that dreams represent expressions of the internal desires and wishes that have been repressed and stored in the unconscious. Recent theories about dreams emphasize more cognitive approaches. The information-processing theory of dreams suggests that dreams are the mind's attempt to sort out and organize the day's experiences and fix them in memory. The attention-synthesis hypothesis suggests that dreams are the mind's attempts to give meaning to internally generated signals firing throughout the brain during deep sleep.

- Sleep deprivation can lead to feelings of fatigue, irritability, and malaise, resulting in lower productivity and a tendency to make mistakes. Loss of sleep can also affect the functioning of the immune system. The regular inability to fall asleep or stay asleep is called insomnia. Other sleep disorders include sleep apnea, narcolepsy, sleepwalking, and night terrors.

Psychoactive Drugs

LEARNING OBJECTIVE 6   Define and describe common depressant, stimulant, and hallucinogenic psychoactive drugs and their effects.

- The three main classes of psychoactive drugs are depressants (substances that slow down brain activity), stimulants (substances that excite brain activity), and psychedelic or hallucinogenic drugs (substances that distort sensory perceptions).

- Regular ingestion of some drugs can lead to maladaptive changes in a person's behavior patterns and physical responses, a pattern known as *addiction*. Signs of addiction can include increased tolerance, the need for larger and larger doses of a substance to get the desired effect, and symptoms of withdrawal when one discontinues the drug.

Key Terms

consciousness 166

preconsciousness 171

unconscious state 171

implicit memory 172

hypnosis 172

dissociation 174

meditation 176

adaptive theory of sleep 176

restorative theory of sleep 176

circadian rhythm 176

suprachiasmatic nucleus (SCN) 177

hypnagogic state 177

sleep spindles 177

rapid eye movement sleep (REM) 180

nonREM sleep (NREM) 180

information-processing theory of dreams 183

activation-synthesis model 183

lucid dreams 183

insomnia 185

sleep apnea 187

narcolepsy 187

psychoactive drugs 187

addiction 189

tolerance 189

withdrawal symptoms 189

depressants 189

alcoholism 191

sedative-hypnotic drugs 191

opioids 192

endorphins 192

stimulants 192

hallucinogens 194

flashbacks 194

reward learning pathway 196

reward-deficiency syndrome 196

CUT/ACROSS CONNECTION

What Happens in the B R A I N ?

- People who are blind because of damage to visual areas in the cerebral cortex are still able to point in the direction of light projected onto a screen, even though they are not aware of attending to the light. That's because the areas in the cerebral cortex that are in charge of *awareness* of attention are not the same as the areas responsible for attention itself.

- Similarly, hypnosis used to anesthetize or reduce pain doesn't keep sensations of pain from reaching neurons. Instead, it reduces awareness of the pain by decreasing activity in a particular part of the cerebral cortex.

- Humans are probably not the only animals that dream. Dreaming takes place during rapid eye movement (REM) sleep, the final stage of the brain's five-stage sleep cycle, and every kind of mammal that has been tested experiences these sleep stages.

- There are various theories to explain dreaming. Some researchers, for instance, believe that we dream because the brain, while we sleep, produces a variety of visual and auditory signals and then tries to combine these self-produced signals in a way that makes sense.

- Most, or perhaps all, psychoactive drugs eventually work by activating a single reward learning pathway in the brain. The key neurotransmitter in this reward learning pathway is dopamine.

When Things Go **Wrong**

- Adolescents are especially likely to suffer from sleep deprivation. In fact, teenagers today get about two hours less sleep per night than teens 80 years ago.

- Going without sleep, over time, causes a variety of problems: general malaise, lower productivity, and an increased tendency to make mistakes, and even lower immune system functioning.

- The most common sleep disorder is insomnia. Insomnia sufferers, who are generally older people, regularly have trouble falling asleep or staying asleep. Less common is narcolepsy, which involves suddenly falling asleep for short periods of time—sometimes even in the midst of an argument or during an exciting football game.

- In any given year, more than 9 percent of all teens and adults in the United States display drug or alcohol addiction.

- Intoxicated drivers cause 12,000 deaths each year.

HOW we Differ

- Although most of us don't have a strong preference, some of us are "morning people" who like to get everything done early in the day, while others are "night people" who prefer to sleep late and do our work in the evening.

- Such preferences depend on our internal clocks, and the settings of those clocks are thought to be determined primarily by genetic factors.

- Alcoholism is displayed by at least twice as many men as women.

- Native Americans, particularly men, display a higher rate of alcoholism than other racial minority groups or white Americans.

How we *Develop*

- The question of when babies develop alert consciousness is a matter of debate. On the one hand, some researchers argue that early cognitive development, such as that discussed in Chapter 3, shows that babies do have a rudimentary sense of consciousness. Others argue that consciousness comes later, with the development of language.

- During the first four months of life, babies sleep between 14 and 17 hours a day, but the time spent sleeping declines steadily as they get older.

- Environmental demands and expectations affect babies' sleep-awake cycles. In the Kipsigis tribe, for example, babies sleep for much shorter stretches longer into infancy than American babies. That's because Kipsigis mothers keep their babies with them constantly, while American parents structure their babies' sleep by putting them to bed at regular times.

Video Lab Exercise

Psychology Around Us

Sleep's Impact on Daily Functioning

It's Not Nice to Fool Mother Nature

Try though we might, we cannot exercise a lot of control over sleep. Whether we like it or not, we are at the mercy of our circadian rhythms; once we are asleep, we are along for a ride through our sleep cycle; and if we deprive ourselves of too much sleep, we function poorly while we are awake.

In this video lab exercise, your job is to perform video tasks and react to various scenes at various times throughout the day and under various states of sleep deprivation. You may think you're on top of your game most of the time, but as you'll see, sleep-awake rhythms and sleep deprivation strongly affect how you think, how you learn, and how you feel about various people, objects, and situations.

As you are working on this on-line exercise, consider the following questions:

- What does this lab exercise say about our sleep needs and the impact of sleep on our daily lives?
- Do we become "morning people" or "night owls" based on our experiences or on our biological predispositions?
- How might dreams fit into the equation?
- Are there any ways to get around sleep rhythms and sleep needs?

CHAPTER 7

Learning

Chapter Outline

- What Is Learning? • Classical Conditioning • Operant Conditioning
- Observational Learning • Factors that Facilitate Learning
- When We Learn *What Happens in the Brain?* • Prenatal and Postnatal Learning
- Learning and Gender • Learning Disabilities

Name that Tune

If you have a favorite musical group, you probably eagerly await the release of their latest album and scan the Internet for signs that they will be touring in your area. When you first hear a new song performed by the group, it's likely to feel a little familiar, given your attachment to the group's style. The lyrics and tune will be new, however, and you won't know them right away. If you listen to the album several times on your iPod, even if you are not intently concentrating on the music and are instead engaged in other activities while listening, the music will seem increasingly familiar each time you hear it. You may find yourself humming or whistling the tune without realizing it. After you've heard the song a few times, you will probably know most, if not all, of the lyrics. All of this learning is likely to occur without much effort. For most people, it's much easier than learning a poem or an essay of comparable length. The reasons for the ease with which learning occurs in this situation are multifaceted and most likely involve emotional engagement with the material and the fact that having the lyrics set to music makes them "catchier."

This type of automatic learning experience may stand in stark contrast to your efforts to master the information presented in a course that is dense with facts and figures, such as organic chemistry. For a course like this, students often use specific study techniques to learn the material. At the very least, concentration and extensive studying are critical for learning in such a course.

Why are these two learning experiences so different? There are most likely several reasons. First, there is the difficulty factor. Material in your most challenging courses is likely to be conceptually difficult. Thus, learning the material requires first gaining an understanding of it and then finding a way to remember it. By contrast, information presented to you in most entertainment is relatively simple and usually does not require concentrated effort to understand.

Second, attention probably plays an important role. Attention is critical for certain types of learning and it's probably not difficult to attend to the lyrics of a new song from your favorite group. Even for organic chemistry aficionados, however, it may be difficult to sustain attention long enough to learn labor-intensive course material effectively in one sitting. This type of material often requires repeated presentation, perhaps first in class, then by reading in your text, and finally by studying your notes.

Third, emotional factors facilitate learning information. Numerous studies have shown that emotionally charged material is easier to learn (although this can sometimes present a problem, as we will see later in the chapter). Since new music from your favorite group is likely to elicit an emotional reaction, be it one of sadness or happiness, this material is learned more readily.

Finally, differences between these two types of learning experiences may be related to our biology. Humans evolved living in groups where social cooperation was essential for survival. Thus, we are biologically ready to learn about social interactions and relationships, the subject matter of many song lyrics. Facts about organic chemistry, on the other hand, were not critical information for the survival of early people, and as a result, our brains are not as prepared to learn this type of information.

All of these variables—task difficulty, attention, emotions, and biological readiness—are important for learning. The study of each will come up later in this chapter. The overall picture underscores how learning is complex and multidimensional.

What Is Learning?

learning a lasting change caused by experience.

learning curve a graph that shows change in performance on a learning task over time.

associative learning learning that involves forming associations between stimuli.

nonassociative learning learning that does not involve forming associations between stimuli.

habituation a form of nonassociative learning whereby repeated presentation of a stimulus leads to a reduction in response.

sensitization a form of nonassociative learning whereby a strong stimulus results in an exaggerated response to the subsequent presentation of weaker stimuli.

LEARNING OBJECTIVE 1 Define learning and distinguish between associative and nonassociative learning.

Put simply, **learning** is defined as a lasting change caused by experience. In the laboratory, scientists study learning by measuring changes in behavioral responses. This is particularly true for studies of animals, where it's impossible to verbally assess the degree to which the subject has learned. However, it's clear that considerable learning occurs in the absence of overt behavioral change. You might not show any new behavior for example, even though you've learned the lyrics of a new song from hearing it several times. This is likely to be the case if the song does not end up as one of your favorites.

It may seem strange to separate a discussion about learning with a closely related subject: memory, which is covered in the next chapter. Although learning and memory are indeed interrelated and many of the biological mechanisms (and brain regions) that underlie learning are also critical for memory, the study of these topics has diverged in the laboratory. Traditionally, animals (dogs, monkeys, rats, and mice) were the focus of studies on learning, whereas humans were the predominant focus of studies on memory. With the advent of neuroimaging technology and a greater public concern for understanding learning disabilities, more research on learning is focused on humans as well. Wherever possible throughout this chapter, we'll apply information that scientists have gained from animal experimentation to questions of human learning.

Scientists typically display data from learning studies in a **learning curve**, a graph that shows change in performance on the learning task over time, as shown in **Figure 7-1**. The learning curve can be used to determine whether or not mastery of the task occurs rapidly (in other words, is the task relatively easy?) or whether it occurs gradually, which is the case when the task is relatively difficult. The graph of a learning curve for an easy task will be very steep initially, perhaps leading to a plateau when peak performance is reached.

In general, learning can be divided into two major categories: *associative* and *nonassociative*. **Associative learning** is a change that occurs as the result of experiences that lead us to link two or more stimuli together. An example of associative learning would be learning the words to a song in conjunction with the tune. **Nonassociative learning** also involves change based on experience, but happens without a person connecting two or more different pieces of information.

Nonassociative Learning

Nonassociative learning is by far the simpler of the two types; the most basic forms of learning are nonassociative. This means that they do not involve linking together information about more than one stimulus. Rather, nonassociative learning refers to a change that occurs as a result of our experiences with a single sensory cue. There are two major types of nonassociative learning, *habituation* and *sensitization*.

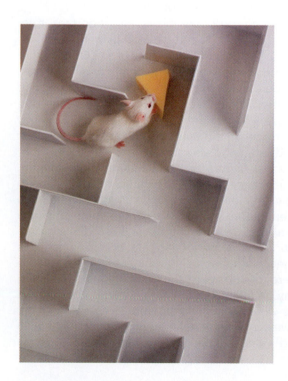

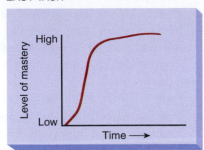
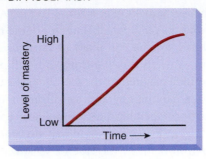

EASY TASK

DIFFICULT TASK

FIGURE 7-1 Learning curves Learning study data are typically displayed on learning curve graphs that show the mastering of a task over time. The learning curves reveal whether the task was an easy or difficult one.

Habituation We discussed habituation of our senses in Chapter 5: Sensation and Perception. Habituation happens when our senses begin to respond less strongly to repeated presentations of the same sensory cue. A smell, such as baking cookies, might hit you with the power of a freight train when you first walk into your home, but after a while, you may barely notice it. Even though the cookies continue to give off just as much aroma, you have become habituated. You respond less and less strongly, though the same stimulus repeatedly reaches the sensory receptors in your nose. In most cases, sensory habituation occurs without our awareness. You might notice it occurred afterwards, but it does not require attention to the stimulus for learning to occur.

When we use the term **habituation** to talk about learning, it also refers to a decrement in response after repeated stimulus presentation. Learned habituation, however, is not the exclusive result of sensory adaptation or fatigue of neurons in the sensory receptors. Instead, learning theorists study habituation that involves changes in neurons in our central nervous system. If a decrease in response occurs because of a change in neurons in the brain or spinal cord, then the effect qualifies as learning.

Sensitization **Sensitization** is another form of nonassociative learning that involves an altered response after the presentation of a single sensory cue. Unlike habituation, sensitization involves an increase, as opposed to a decrease, in response with learning. A good example of this can be drawn from a common experience we've all had: being

Habituation in action When this child is initially presented with letter blocks, she responds to them happily and learns various ways to enjoy them (*left*). However, after months of repeated presentations with the same stimuli, her response to the blocks is decidedly more muted and less enthusiastic (*right*).

startled. Imagine you are home alone at night reading quietly. Without any warning, your pet cat knocks over a lamp. You may jump or even shout out in fear before realizing what has happened. And, for some time after you regain your senses and scold poor kitty, you are still likely to startle again, even in response to a normal auditory stimulus, such as the ring from your cell phone. Your enhanced response to this typical stimulus may reflect the fact that sensitization has occurred.

Both habituation and sensitization make good adaptive sense. In the case of habituation, when harmless stimuli are repeatedly presented, continuing to respond to them is a waste of energy and may prevent you from noticing an important change in the environment. In the case of sensitization, an extreme unexpected stimulus may signal danger, so a greater than usual response to stimuli that follow may be helpful for survival.

Nonassociative Learning: B R A I N ?   Since habituation and sensitization are very basic forms of learning, they occur in animals with very simple nervous systems. Neuroscientists have taken advantage of this and used one of the simplest—the nervous system of a sea slug—to study the biological basis of nonassociative learning (Kandel, 2001).

Sea slugs do not have brains or spinal cords. They do, however, have some of the largest neurons in the animal kingdom; their neurons can actually be seen with the naked eye. This makes it easy to record from the neurons, using electrodes as described in Chapter 4. Researchers have been able to use electrode recordings from sea slugs to develop a thorough understanding of how simple nervous systems change in response to learning.

If you touch a sea slug once lightly, it will withdraw two vulnerable parts of its body, the gill and the siphon. If you touch it multiple times lightly, eventually this response will diminish as habituation sets in. Recordings from the sea slug's neurons have shown that in habituation, the amount of neural activity in the motor neurons (the neurons that control the gill and siphon muscles) goes down as the animal is repeatedly touched (Gingrich & Byrne, 1985). The decrease in activity is largely due to the fact that the neurotransmitter in the synapse between the sea slug's sensory neuron and the motor neuron gets depleted with repeated presentations of the tactile stimulus. Eventually, the same level of sensory stimulus becomes ineffective at causing the gill and siphon withdrawal response because the amount of neurotransmitter has diminished to the point that the synapse can no longer be activated (**Figure 7-2**).

To study sensitization, scientists apply an electric shock to the tail of the sea slug. The slug responds with a strong gill and siphon withdrawal reflex. Then they apply a very mild tactile stimulus to the slug's body. It still strongly withdraws its gill and siphon because it is sensitized.

Sensitization can occur even when a slug has undergone trials of habituation (Hawkins Cohen, & Kandel, 2006). If habituation occurs as a result of neurotransmitter depletion, how can sensitization result in an almost immediate restoration of activity in the same motor neuron? The answer lies in the fact that the tail shock recruits another population of neurons, called *interneurons*, into the circuitry. Interneurons work to enhance the weakened sensory neuron input to the synapse of the sensory and motor nerves. The combined action stimulates the motor neurons enough to produce the augmented withdrawal response.

You may be wondering what all of these experiments on sea slugs can tell us about learning in more complex animals, including humans. Although there are many important differences between sea slugs and humans, it's likely that these basic mechanisms, or something very close to them, also operate in more complex nervous systems, such

Learning from the slug   By studying sea slugs, scientists have gained insights about how the nervous system changes in response to learning.

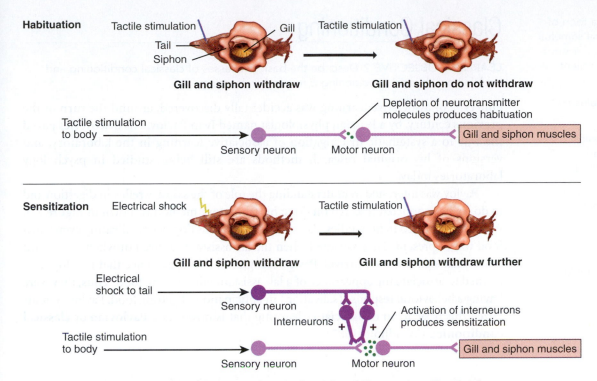

Habituation

Tactile stimulation · Tail · Siphon · Gill

Gill and siphon withdraw → Tactile stimulation **Gill and siphon do not withdraw**

Depletion of neurotransmitter molecules produces habituation

Tactile stimulation to body → Sensory neuron → Motor neuron → Gill and siphon muscles

Sensitization

Electrical shock

Gill and siphon withdraw → Tactile stimulation **Gill and siphon withdraw further**

Electrical shock to tail → Sensory neuron — Interneurons + + — Activation of interneurons produces sensitization

Tactile stimulation to body → Sensory neuron → Motor neuron → Gill and siphon muscles

FIGURE 7-2 **Habituation and sensitization in the sea slug** (Above) The sea slug gill and siphon withdrawal reflex becomes habituated to a repeated tactile stimulus when the neurotransmitter needed to activate its motor neurons has been depleted. (Below) The sea slug can experience sensitization to mild tactile stimulation if it is first exposed to a noxious stimulus like electric shock—a stimulus that activates a group of neurons called interneurons. These latter neurons stimulate the animal's motor neurons, which in turn produce responses to mild tactile stimuli.

as our own. We, too, may experience habituation because of depleted neurotransmitter and sensitization because of the added recruitment of interneurons.

Associative Learning

Nonassociative learning does not account for the majority of learning that engages more complex organisms, such as humans. The majority of learning is considered to be associative. It involves making connections between two or more stimuli. Most of the learning you engage in as a student is highly associative. Course material involves connecting numerous concepts and facts to produce an overall picture of a certain subject. Learning song melodies or lyrics also involves forming associations. Two major types of associative learning are *classical conditioning* and *operant, or instrumental, conditioning*. In classical conditioning, as we'll see next, we come to associate two stimuli, eventually responding the same way to both. We'll then examine operant conditioning, by which we come to associate stimuli with our behaviors.

"I can't explain it. I see that guy coming up the walkway and I go postal."

Before You Go On

What Do You Know?

1. What is learning?

2. What happens in synapses during habituation? What happens during sensitization?

What Do You Think? Give an example from your own life of nonassociative learning.

Pavlovian or **classical conditioning** a form of associative learning whereby a neutral stimulus is paired with a salient stimulus so that eventually the neutral stimulus predicts the salient stimulus.

unconditioned stimulus (US) a stimulus that on its own elicits a response.

unconditioned response (UR) a physical response elicited by an unconditioned stimulus; it does not need to be learned.

conditioned stimulus (CS) a neutral stimulus that eventually elicits the same response as an unconditioned stimulus with which it has been paired.

conditioned response (CR) a physical response elicited by a conditioned stimulus; it is usually the same as the unconditioned response.

extinction reduction of a conditioned response after repeated presentations of the conditioned stimulus alone.

Classical Conditioning

LEARNING OBJECTIVE 2 Describe the basic processes of classical conditioning and explain how classical conditioning is relevant to learning.

One type of associative learning was accidentally discovered, around the turn of the previous century, by a Russian physiologist named Ivan Pavlov. His discoveries paved the way to a systematic investigation of associative learning in the laboratory, and versions of his original research methods are still being studied in psychology laboratories today.

Pavlov was interested in understanding the role of the salivary reflex in digestion and to do so, he conducted research on dogs; his laboratory method is shown in **Figure 7-3**. As time progressed in his studies, Pavlov noticed that his dogs were salivating even when food wasn't present. They salivated when the lab assistants arrived or when they heard noises that signaled their arrival. Pavlov recognized this as evidence that the dogs had learned to associate the appearance of a lab assistant with getting food. Thus, they were having a behavioral response (salivation) in anticipation of getting food. Pavlov systematized this basic form of associative learning that is now called **Pavlovian** or **classical conditioning** (Windholz, 1987).

How Does Classical Conditioning Work?

In classical conditioning, a person or animal learns to associate a previously neutral stimulus with an **unconditioned stimulus (US)**, one that normally elicits a physiological response. Because the response doesn't have to be learned, it is called the **unconditioned response (UR)**. With repeated pairings, the neutral stimulus alone elicits the physiological response. After that happens the stimulus is no longer neutral. It is now called the **conditioned stimulus (CS)**, and the physiological response it elicits is called the **conditioned response (CR)**. This process is summarized in **Figure 7-4**.

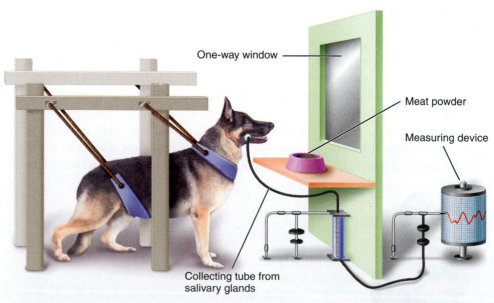

One-way window

Meat powder

Measuring device

Collecting tube from salivary glands

FIGURE 7-3 Pavlov's setup for collecting and measuring salivation in dogs The dog is placed in a harness and given a bowl of meat powder. A tube from the salivary gland collects the saliva, which is measured and recorded.

For Pavlov's dogs, the unconditioned stimulus was food. Their unconditioned response was to salivate. The arrival of a lab assistant was, originally, a neutral stimulus to the dogs. After repeated pairings of the assistant with food, however, the assistant's arrival became a conditioned stimulus. The dogs salivated when they heard or saw the assistant show up. Their salivation, once an unconditioned response to the food, was now a conditioned response to the assistant.

Classical conditioning is not just for the dogs, however. It happens to people, too. Suppose classroom exams (US) made you nervous (UR). If all your exams were given in the same room on campus, the room itself (CS) might begin to make you feel nervous (CR), even though it probably didn't affect you much one way or another the first time you entered.

Timing plays an important role in the formation of learned associations. An effective presentation schedule would be to pair the US and the CS together, with the CS slightly before the US, so that it has predictive value. You enter the room, and then you take the exam, for example. A neutral stimulus that follows an unconditioned one has little or no predictive value and makes it unlikely that an association between the stimuli will form. If you went to the room later in the day after you took exams, instead of taking the test there, the room would probably never grow to make you nervous. Not surprisingly, learning is more robust when the number of CS-US pairings is high.

Pavlov also showed that the learned response could be eliminated, by presenting the conditioned stimulus over and over again, without the unconditioned stimulus. The lab assistant might show up many times without offering any food to the dogs. This phenomenon, called **extinction**, does not represent "unlearning" or forgetting, but rather a process by which the previously learned CR is actively inhibited (Quirk, 2006).

Evidence that the information about the previous CS-US pairing still exists after extinction training can be observed by allowing time to pass with no training after

A classic moment In this famous photo, Ivan Pavlov (*center, with beard*) stands with his assistants and students prior to demonstrating his classical conditioning experiment on a dog.

“ While you are experimenting, do not remain content with the surface of things. Don't become a mere recorder of facts, but try to penetrate the mystery of their origin. ”

—Ivan Pavlov, Russian physiologist

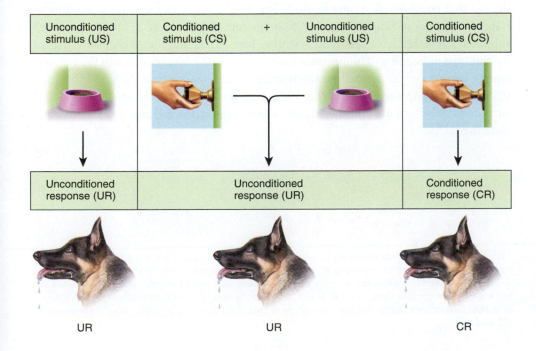

FIGURE 7-4 **Classical conditioning** The sequence of classical conditioning is shown here, from left to right. (1) The US (meat powder) produces the UR (salivation). (2) During conditioning, the US is paired with a CS, a neutral or conditioned stimulus (a sound such as a doorknob being turned). (3) After conditioning, the CS alone produces the conditioned (learned) response of salivation.

spontaneous recovery re-emergence of a conditioned response some time after extinction has occurred.

stimulus generalization when similar stimuli elicit the same response as a conditioned stimulus after classical conditioning has occured.

phobia an abnormal fear, often of a stimulus that is not inherently dangerous, that may arise as a result of fear conditioning.

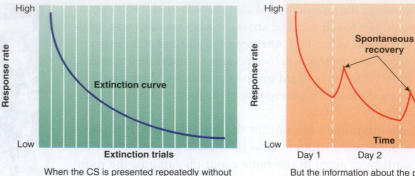

When the CS is presented repeatedly without the US, the individual's learned response gradually decreases until extinction occurs.

But the information about the previous CS-US pairing is not lost, and the extinguished response spontaneously reappears.

FIGURE 7-5 **Extinction and spontaneous recovery**

extinction has occurred. In this case, the CR will often re-emerge at a later date, a phenomenon called **spontaneous recovery** (**Figure 7-5**). Even though the assistant didn't bring food for several visits, the dogs might still salivate a week later when the assistant arrived. Even if you revisited the classroom you took exams in several times to hear a guest lecture, you might re-experience the nervous feeling at a later time when you happen to walk by.

Classical Conditioning *What Happens in the* BRAIN?

Extinction training and spontaneous recovery show that classical conditioning creates lasting changes in the nervous system in order for us to make a CS-US association. After extinction training, these changes persist; the nervous system does not go back to the way it was before conditioning. Instead, the newer extinction learning creates further changes that allow us to suppress the conditioned response.

Researchers have used another form of classical conditioning, conditioning of the eye-blink response, to learn more about the location of nervous system changes that occur in classical conditioning. In this procedure, humans or animals are conditioned to associate a tone (CS) with a US, such as a mild shock to the eyelid or a puff of air to the eye that normally elicits an eye blink. Eventually, eye blink becomes a conditioned response, elicited in response to the CS tone alone (**Figure 7-6**). By studying animals subjected to eye-blink conditioning, scientists have found that the cerebellum is critical for this type of learning (Thompson & Steinmetz, 2009). Changes occur in the synapses among neurons in the cerebellum when animals learn to associate the CS with the US (Christian & Thompson, 2003). This was a very surprising finding, since prior to this work, the cerebellum was considered to be a brain region devoted mainly to coordinated movement.

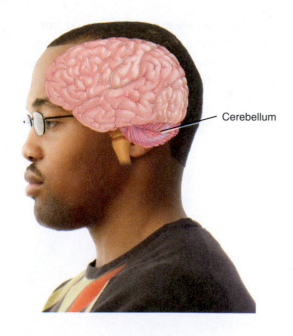

— Cerebellum

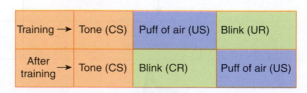

Training →	Tone (CS)	Puff of air (US)	Blink (UR)
After training →	Tone (CS)	Blink (CR)	Puff of air (US)

FIGURE 7-6 **Eye blink conditioning** Researchers have relied on eye blink conditioning in animals to learn more about the brain processes involved in classical conditioning. In this procedure, a CS or neutral stimulus (a tone) is followed by a stimulus (such as a puff of air) that causes the animal to blink (UR). After conditioning, the animal will blink after hearing the tone and before receiving the stimulus. Researchers found that the cerebellum is critical for learning the association between the CS and UR.

Classical Conditioning and Fears

Although the work on classical conditioning of the salivary reflex and the eye-blink response was groundbreaking, you may have trouble seeing what its relevance is to human learning outside of the laboratory. Although some of us experience a mild version of classical conditioning when our stomachs growl around a certain time of day, some other forms of classical conditioning are probably much more relevant to human life.

One such example is called *fear conditioning*. Fear conditioning was first studied by the American psychologist, John Watson, whose most well-known study was classical conditioning of a human baby named "little Albert." Watson exposed baby Albert to an initially neutral stimulus, a white rat. Immediately after the appearance of the white rat, little Albert was subjected to a loud crashing noise that startled him so much he burst into tears. Repeated pairings of the white rat with the loud noise made Albert cry at the mere presence of the rat. There are serious ethical problems associated with Watson's line of research. Little Albert's mother was never informed of the studies, which were carried out without regard for their cruelty or the possibility that they would have a lasting negative effect on his emotional state (Field & Nightingale, 2009). They are, however, the first example of classical conditioning in humans and of fear conditioning in any species.

Watson's studies also led to the discovery of **stimulus generalization**, which refers to the fact that similar, but not identical, stimuli can take the place of a CS. Albert, for example, came to fear not only the white rat, but also other white stimuli, including a human with a white beard.

Subsequent laboratory studies with animals show that fears are very easily learned. Fear conditioning of laboratory rodents involves training them to associate a neutral cue (usually a tone) with a painful stimulus, usually an electric shock to the feet (**Figure 7-7**). Naïve rodents will respond to foot shock by adopting a characteristic posture of immobilization, or "freezing." This response probably reflects adaptive behavior small mammals engage in when confronted with a predator and no way to escape; they minimize movement to escape detection. Typically just a few pairings of a tone with foot shock are needed to lead to a lasting CS-US association. The rat will freeze at the CS tone alone (LeDoux, 2003). This type of learning involves the amygdala (LeDoux, 2000).

Animal fear-conditioning studies, such as these also provide examples of how emotion can facilitate the learning process. Since shock is painful, and thus fear-inducing, its presence in a learning situation can speed up the formation of an association between the CS and US.

Phobias

When Things Go Wrong

Phobias   Some scientists believe fear conditioning is the basis of the development of a category of anxiety disorders called *phobias* (LeDoux, 1998; Morgan, Romanski, & LeDoux, 1993). **Phobias** are exaggerated fears of stimuli, many of which have little or no inherent danger. Little Albert was conditioned to have a phobia to white fur. People who suffer from phobias are believed to have learned an association (hopefully not in the laboratory) between neutral and dangerous stimuli, thus being conditioned to fear a relatively harmless cue.

Teaching a child to fear   In an ethically-questionable study by today's standards, John Watson and his colleague Rosalie Rayner used classical conditioning principles to teach 11-month-old "Little Albert" to fear white rats.

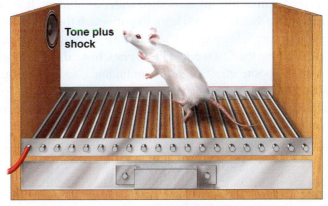

Rat is given electrical shock to the feet in combination with a tone.

Tone plus shock

Later
Rat freezes in fear to the tone alone.

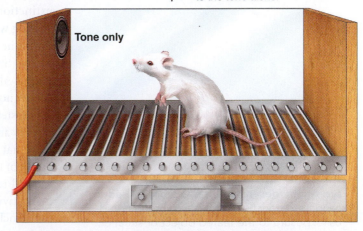

Tone only

FIGURE 7-7 Fear conditioning in rats   In fear conditioning, a laboratory rat is given an electrical shock (US) to the feet just after exposure to a neutral stimulus (CS), such as a tone. Only a few pairings of the US and CS are needed for the rat to freeze in fear at the tone alone.

Tough love This peaceful domestic scene belies the fact that female rats are often very rough with their young pups—perhaps explaining why many rat pups are attracted to, instead of repelled by, stimuli associated with pain.

Some researchers made an interesting discovery when attempting to use olfactory cues to fear condition very young rat pups. Adult rats will avoid stimuli that are associated with punishment. If an odor is paired with a shock, rats will learn to distinguish that odor and avoid it in the future. This response to olfactory learning, however, is not present during the first week of life for rats. Instead, rat pups will display the opposite effect of such conditioning. Odor pairings with shock produce an approach response in the pups (Moriceau & Sullivan, 2006). Why would rat pups learn to move toward, instead of away from, an odor that predicts pain?

The answer may lie in rats' normal lifestyles. Rat pups live in the nest, staying close to their mothers for the first two weeks of life, until they start weaning. During this early time in the nest, the mother is likely to do many things to the pups that elicit pain. Mothers retrieve pups by picking them up by their teeth, and they routinely step on their babies. Thus, a tendency to form avoidant reactions to odors associated with pain would be detrimental to the survival of a very young rat.

As time passes, however, and the pup becomes less dependent on the mother and more capable of avoiding her sharp teeth and heavy foot, pups develop a healthy aversion to painful stimuli. Around this time, avoidance becomes the natural response to odor pairings with noxious stimuli; rats at this age learn, for example, to avoid smells associated with electric shock.

Some investigators have speculated that a similar conditioning process may contribute to the development of *attachment disorder* in humans. This condition is characterized by an inability to form healthy emotional relationships with others. People with attachment disorder do not respond positively to nurturing behavior, and they often seek out situations that are likely to result in physical and emotional pain. Since a major cause of this condition is early childhood abuse and neglect, it's possible that excessive strengthening of associations between painful stimuli and one's caregiver during development lead to persistent maladaptive responses to social interactions.

systematic desensitization a process used to condition extinction of phobias through gradual exposure to the feared object or situation.

conditioned taste aversion a form of classical conditioning whereby a previously neutral stimulus (often an odor or taste) elicits an aversive reaction after it's paired with illness (nausea).

The theory that phobias arise from fear conditioning has led to the development of therapies that are also based on classical conditioning. In one common process, known as **systematic desensitization,** people who suffer phobias undergo a series extinction trials, repeated exposure to the feared object or situation in the absence of pairing with a US. There was no follow up on Little Albert, so we don't know whether or not he carried his phobia throughout his life. If he had been treated with systematic desensitization, however, Watson might have created a pleasant, quiet situation and placed Albert and the white rat together in this pleasant situation many times until Albert no longer cried at the sight of the rat.

Systematic desensitization sometimes helps people with phobias to overcome their anxiety and function normally in the presence of the fear-inducing cue. Remember, however, that extinction trials do not produce "unlearning," but instead involve active inhibition of the previously learned association (Quirk, 2006). This means that the previously learned fear may reappear. Neuroimaging studies suggest that phobias involve abnormal activity in the amygdala, a part of the brain that is active when we experience emotions, including fear. People with phobias show rapid activation of this brain region when exposed to the stimuli they fear most. Extinction training, by contrast, is known to activate part of the prefrontal cortex as phobias diminish (Quirk, Garcia, & González-Lima, 2006). Recall from Chapter 4 that our prefrontal cortex can help us to inhibit emotional impulses. Thus, phobias that have been desensitized still exist. As a result, they are prone to spontaneous recovery, similar to other classically-conditioned behaviors.

Arachnophobia An extreme fear of spiders is one of the most common of all phobias. Around half of all women and 10 percent of all men have at least a mild fear of spiders.

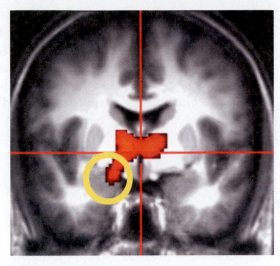

Phobias and the brain This colored brain scan of a cross section of the brain reveals increased activity in a phobic individual's amygdala (*region circled in yellow*) while the person is looking at a feared object.

Classical Conditioning and Taste Aversions

Another type of classical conditioning that has been studied in the laboratory has relevance to human learning. **Conditioned taste aversion** involves learning an association between a particular food and a subsequent stomach illness (Garcia et al., 1985). Many of us have had this type of experience. You eat a certain type of food and a short time later, you are stricken with nausea and vomiting. Whether or not the symptoms are related to the food, you will probably have an aversion to that particular dish for some time afterwards. In this case, the US is whatever agent actually made you nauseous, be it bacterial, viral, or chemical. The food is the CS. The unconditioned physiological response (UR), which becomes the CR, is nausea itself. Nausea will be elicited by exposure to the food in the future.

Some people are especially vulnerable to conditioned taste aversions. Pregnant women with severe morning sickness may develop intense aversions to foods that are followed by nausea. Similarly, people undergoing chemotherapy for cancer treatment can develop aversions to foods they ingest right before a chemotherapy session, due to the nausea that is a side effect of the drug.

Conditioned taste aversions happen very quickly. Laboratory research has shown that a single pairing of food and nausea may be all that's necessary. Maybe you still feel queasy at the thought of a food that was associated with stomach sickness in your past. This is particularly impressive, given the length of time that can intervene between exposure to the CS and the illness—sometimes on the order of several hours. Separation of a tone from a shock by several hours would make it very difficult, if not impossible, to produce fear conditioning, and yet conditioned taste aversion is highly successful with just one pairing.

Scientists suggest that we have a biological readiness to learn certain associations (Gaston, 1978). Clearly, the link between taste and stomach illness is physiological. This biological readiness may be rooted in our evolutionary history. The ability to associate potentially tainted food with a subsequent illness was most likely highly adaptive during human evolution. Those who could not do this were more likely to be poisoned and to risk poisoning members of their families. Those who readily formed such associations and avoided potentially risky food were more likely to survive and successfully reproduce.

Producing a taste aversion In pioneering work, researcher John Garcia and his colleagues used classical conditioning to teach coyotes to not eat sheep. The researchers laced freshly killed sheep with a vomit-inducing chemical. Whenever the coyotes ate such tainted meat, they became ill; eventually, they ran away from the mere sight and smell of sheep.

Biological preparedness also may help explain why taste aversions are easy to learn for animals that use odor and taste for food detection. In these same animals, it is difficult to form an association between a visual or auditory cue and nausea. However, in animals such as birds, that select their food using visual cues, conditioned aversions to flavors or odors are difficult to produce. Birds can be more readily conditioned to avoid visual cues (such as a certain colored bead) when those cues have been paired with stomach illness. Since birds often search out food using vision (consider the bird searching for a wiggly worm), it's more natural for them to associate a visual cue, than a gustatory or olfactory one, with a subsequent stomach illness.

Before You Go On

What Do You Know?

3. You take your dog in the car when going to the veterinarian. After several visits, Rover cowers and whimpers whenever he sees the car. Identify the US, UR, CS, and CR in this example of conditioned fear.

4. What is conditioned taste aversion? How does it happen?

What Do You Think? How might the principles of classical conditioning be used in advertising?

Operant Conditioning

LEARNING OBJECTIVE 3 Describe the basic processes of operant conditioning and explain how shaping can be used to teach new behaviors.

Classical conditioning, although relevant outside of the laboratory, does not account for the vast majority of learning by complex organisms. Classical conditioning is a passive form of learning that does not involve the active participation of the learner. In fact, most forms of classical conditioning occur without awareness that the association is being formed.

In everyday life, however, the majority of our learning is active. Most of us are not passive participants in the environment. Instead, we seek out pleasurable experiences, such as good food, good company, and good grades, and we do our best to avoid unpleasant experiences. We react to our environments and modify our behavior according to the responses we receive. As we continue to learn more about the environment, we change our behavior accordingly. Psychologists use the terms **operant** or **instrumental conditioning** to describe learning that occurs in an attempt to receive rewards and avoid punishment.

For some of the earliest laboratory studies of operant conditioning, psychologist Edward Thorndike created a contraption called a "puzzle box." This was a cage, into which Thorndike placed a hungry cat. As shown in **Figure 7-8**, the animal could escape from the box by pressing a pedal that pulled a string. Escape from the box led to a food reward. The first escape from the box probably occurred through the random actions of the experimental animal. In moving about, the cat would accidentally step on the pedal and thus receive temporary freedom and a fish reward. Once this occurred, however, Thorndike's cats began to more quickly engage in that same behavior when he put them back into the box. Eventually, the cat would immediately step on the pedal when placed into the puzzle box. This work led Thorndike to develop a theory known as the **law of effect** (Thorndike, 1933), which states that behaviors leading to rewards are more likely to occur again, and behaviors producing unpleasantness are less likely to occur again. He proposed that the law of effect applied not only to other animals, but also to humans.

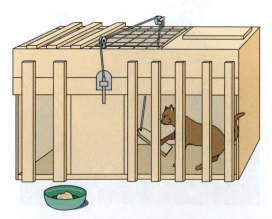

FIGURE 7-8 Thorndike's puzzle box Edward Thorndike used a puzzle box to study operant conditioning in cats. When the cat accidentally stepped on a pedal that pulled a string, the cat escaped from the box and received a fish reward. Once the cat had done this, it performed the action more quickly when it was put back into the box, until eventually it stepped on the pedal immediately each time.

How Does Operant Conditioning Work?

Thorndike's ideas about instrumental conditioning eventually became highly influential. For several decades of the twentieth century, the dominant school of thought in psychology was **behaviorism**, the systematic study of observable behavior (Gantt, 1980). A major goal of behaviorist psychologists was to understand the principles of instrumental, or operant, conditioning. Many researchers, such as leading behaviorist, B. F. Skinner, conducted learning research with laboratory animals such as rats and pigeons.

Reinforcement and Punishment   In typical experiments, stimuli are provided in response to the animal's behavior. These stimuli make it more or less likely that the animal will engage in the behavior again. For example, if a laboratory rat presses a lever and receives a food pellet reward, the food works as a **reinforcer**, a consequence that increases the likelihood that the rat will repeat the behavior or press the lever again. If, on the other hand, the rat receives an electric shock in response to a lever press, the shock works as **punishment**, a consequence that decreases the likelihood that the rat will press the lever again.

What happens in the brain during instrumental conditioning? It appears that somewhat different areas of our brains respond to reinforcement and punishment. Regions important for reward include the ventral tegmental area (Matsumoto & Hikosaka, 2009), the nucleus accumbens, and the prefrontal cortex (Kalivas & Nakamura, 1999), regions that all rely on the neurotransmitter dopamine (we will return to this subject in Chapter 11 on motivation). Learning from punishment, involves some of the same brain regions (Matsumoto & Hikosaka, 2009), as well as those important for fear and pain, including the amygdala and somatosensory cortex (**Figure 7-9**).

Reinforcement and punishment can be either negative or positive. Both forms of reinforcement—positive and negative—increase the likelihood that a response will occur, and both forms of punishment decrease the likelihood of a response recurring.

- **Positive reinforcement** is what we consider to be a reward—providing a motivating stimulus.
- **Negative reinforcement** involves removing an aversive stimulus.
- **Positive punishment** involves administering an unpleasant consequence for behavior.
- **Negative punishment** takes away something pleasant.

operant or **instrumental conditioning** a form of associative learning whereby behavior is modified depending on its consequences.

law of effect behaviors leading to rewards are more likely to occur again, while behaviors producing unpleasantness are less likely to occur again.

behaviorism the systematic study and manipulation of observable behavior.

reinforcer an experience that produces an increase in a certain behavior.

punishment an unpleasurable experience that produces a decrease in a certain behavior.

positive reinforcement presentation of a pleasant consequence following a behavior.

negative reinforcement removal of a negative consequence as a result of behavior.

positive punishment presentation of an unpleasant consequence following a behavior.

negative punishment removal of a pleasant stimulus as a consequence of a behavior.

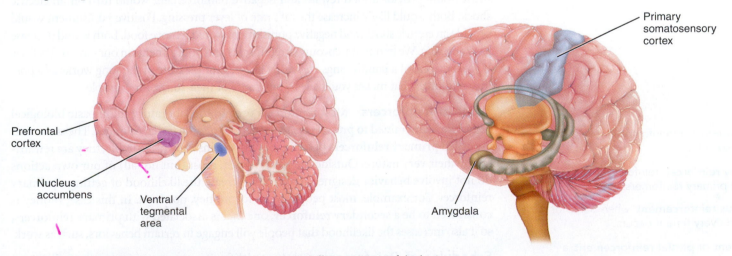

FIGURE 7-9 Brain areas involved in instrumental learning Different regions of the brain are involved in reward and in punishment. Learning from reward involves the ventral tegmental area, nucleus accumbens, and prefrontal cortex. Learning from punishment involves the amygdala and the somatosensory cortex.

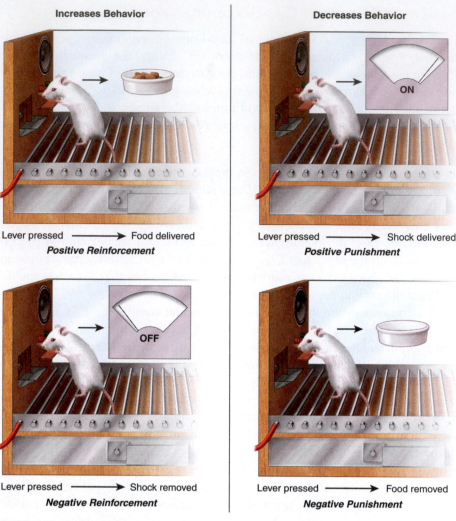

Increases Behavior	Decreases Behavior

Lever pressed ──→ Food delivered
Positive Reinforcement

Lever pressed ──→ Shock delivered
Positive Punishment

Lever pressed ──→ Shock removed
Negative Reinforcement

Lever pressed ──→ Food removed
Negative Punishment

FIGURE 7-10 Reinforcement and punishment The apparatus shown here is called a *Skinner box*. The rat can press a lever to receive a food pellet. The floor of the box is wired to give an electric shock. The box is used to test the effects of positive and negative reinforcement and punishment on behavior.

If we take the case of our lever-pressing rat, as shown in **Figure 7-10,** positive reinforcement would provide a food reward and negative reinforcement would turn off an electric shock. Both would likely increase the rat's rate of lever pressing. Positive punishment would provide an electric shock, and negative punishment would remove food. Both would decrease lever pressing. We frequently encounter reinforcers and punishments in our day-to-day lives. If you buy one of a band's songs and really like it, your pleasure in the song works as a positive reinforcer that makes you likely to buy more of their songs, for example.

Types of Reinforcers   Most reinforcers used in the laboratory fulfill basic biological needs. Rats are trained to press levers to get access to food, water, or mates. These rewards are called **primary reinforcers** because they are intrinsically pleasurable; they are rewarding by their very nature. Outside the lab, however, most (but not all) of our own actions do not involve behavior designed to directly increase the likelihood of getting a primary reinforcer. For example, most people work for money, not food. In this case, money is considered to be a **secondary reinforcer**, one that is associated with primary reinforcers, so it also increases the likelihood that people will engage in certain behaviors, such as work.

Schedules of Reinforcement   In real-life situations, we are not usually reinforced or punished every single time we perform a behavior. You may, for example, hold the door open for the person who walks in behind you many times a day, but

---

primary reinforcer reinforcer that is intrinsically pleasurable.

secondary reinforcer reinforcer that is associated with primary reinforcers.

continuous reinforcement when behavior is reinforced every time it occurs.

intermittent or **partial reinforcement** a schedule of reinforcement where the behavior is only followed by reinforcement some of the time.

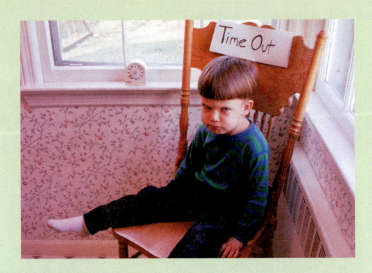

Although both reinforcement and punishment are effective ways of altering behavior in laboratory learning studies, evidence from real-life situations suggests these two approaches may not be equally effective. Positive reinforcement seems to be more effective than punishment for teaching young children, for example. One exception to this general rule is in cases where children put themselves in immediate danger. At such times, a harsh scolding might be much more effective at stopping the behavior.

One reason that positive reinforcement seems more effective may be because punishment is often misused. Research suggests the following guidelines for using punishment effectively to promote learning:

• Positive punishment is most effective when it occurs immediately after the incorrect behavior.

• Punishment is effective only when it is clear that the punishment is a consequence of a specific behavior, rather than, say, a result of the teacher or caregiver's bad mood or general dislike for the child.

• Punishment works only when its aversive component outweighs any reward obtained by the behavior. It is difficult and often unethical to devise a punishment that far outweighs the rewarding aspect of the behavior.

Negative punishment seems to be less problematic ethically than positive punishment, but still may fail in some circumstances. Many parents and preschool teachers use a negative punishment technique called "time out" as a consequence for unwanted behavior. This method involves removing the child from his or her surroundings, generally by putting them in a separate location in the classroom or home. The child has thus had a pleasurable stimulus (access to playthings and classmates) removed. Time out also removes the child from the environment that may have contributed to the bad behavior and allows quiet time to think about the situation. The effectiveness of time out depends on the circumstances and the individual. If the child was acting out to gain attention, then intervening, even in a negative manner, may not effectively eliminate the behavior. Also, removal from a certain environment, such as the classroom or the dinner table, may not be sufficiently negative to alter the offensive behavior. It might even be rewarding to some children. In general, educators and child psychologists conclude that wherever possible, positive reinforcement of desired behavior is the best motivator for behavioral change.

only receive a pleasant "thank you" once or twice. Researchers have studied the effects of different schedules of reinforcement on behavior (Skinner, 1958; Skinner & Morse, 1958). When a behavior is reinforced every single time it occurs, reinforcement is said to be **continuous**. In contrast, there are also several possible schedules of **intermittent** or **partial reinforcement**, by which the behavior is only sometimes reinforced. The most common types of intermittent reinforcement schedules are described in Table 7-1.

In a *ratio schedule*, reinforcement is based on the number of behavioral responses. In a **fixed ratio schedule**, a person or animal is rewarded every time they make a predetermined number of responses. The "frequent drinker" card at your local coffee shop may offer you a free cup of coffee after you pay for a dozen other cups, for example. In a **variable ratio schedule**, reinforcement occurs for a predetermined average number of responses. You may have a new message on average every three times you look at your phone, but sometimes you can look six times in a row and see no messages, and other times you might have a message twice in a row.

In an *interval schedule*, reinforcement is based on elapsed time, rather than on the number of behavioral responses. In a **fixed interval schedule**, such as occurs with a

fixed ratio schedule reinforcement occurs after a specific number of responses.

variable ratio schedule the number of responses required for reinforcement varies.

fixed interval schedule reinforcement occurs every time a specific time period has elapsed.

variable interval schedule reinforcement occurs after varying amounts of time.

behavior modification a planned effort to change behavior.

shaping introducing new behavior by reinforcing small approximations of the desired behavior.

learned helplessness a situation in which repeated exposure to inescapable punishment eventually produces a failure to make escape attempts.

TABLE 7-1   Intermittent Reinforcement Schedules

Schedules Based on Number of Responses			
	Definition	Response rate	Example
Fixed ratio	Reinforcement occurs after a predetermined number of responses	High	Field workers paid by the amount they harvest
Variable ratio	Reinforcement occurs after an average number of responses	High	A slot machine pays out after an average of 20 tries but the payout intervals are unpredictable
Schedules Based on Time Intervals			
Fixed interval	Reinforcement occurs after a fixed period of time	Increases with time	A worker receives a paycheck every week
Variable interval	Reinforcement occurs after varying lengths of time	Low	Work breaks occur at unpredictable intervals, such as 60 minutes, 72 minutes, and 54 minutes.

weekly salaried paycheck, you are reinforced every time a certain period of time passes. Like a variable ratio schedule, a **variable interval schedule** provides reinforcement after varying lengths of time have passed.

Intermittent or partial reinforcement schedules are more effective than continuous reinforcement at maintaining behavior. With continuous reinforcement, the behavior is always paired with the reward. If reinforcement stops, the elimination signals a major change in the relationship between stimulus and response. By contrast, with intermittent reinforcement, the behavior is only followed by reinforcement some of the time. When a response occurs but is not reinforced, it's not readily apparent whether or not the reward has stopped altogether. Continuing to engage in the behavior makes sense in case a reward might happen.

The principles of partial reinforcement can be applied to **behavior modification**, a planned effort to change behavior, in children. Parents, teachers, and caregivers should avoid providing intermittent reinforcement for behaviors they want to stop. When parents are trying to wean children off a bottle or pacifier, for example, experts agree it is best to do so in an absolute manner. If parents sometimes allow a child who cries or whines to have the bottle or pacifier, he or she will be more likely to cry or whine again in the future than if the crying and whining are never, ever reinforced.

Using Operant Conditioning to Teach New Behaviors

Until now, we have described how operant conditioning can lead people and animals to increase or decrease behaviors that they already display at least some of the time. Thorndike's cats, for example, learned to press the pedal in

"Oh, not bad. The light comes on, I press the bar, they write me a check. How about you?"

the puzzle box more often than they would have by chance, but they already pressed the pedal at least once in a trial and error fashion before learning the association. Operant conditioning can also be used to teach people and animals entirely new complex behaviors.

This method, called **shaping**, rewards actions that are increasingly closer to a desired final behavior, rather than waiting for the exact behavior to happen before providing reinforcement. Consider training a dog to roll over. First you might provide a treat if the animal lies down on its stomach. Eventually, you would require the dog to perform something closer to rolling over in order to get the same reward. You might offer a treat only when the dog lies down and turns a bit to the side. You carry on in this way, rewarding *successive approximations* of the desired behavior until the complete behavioral sequence emerges. Shaping is highly effective in modifying the behavior of animals and can be used to teach people, too. Humans regularly learn behavior through shaping. If you are learning to dance the Tango, for instance, your instructor may praise you lavishly at first for simply moving your feet in the correct order. Later, you may win praise only for moving them without stepping on your partner's toes, and so on, until only graceful, coordinated steps earn positive remarks.

A natural surfer? No. This boogie boarding terrier underwent many learning trials and received rewards for many successive approximations of this behavior before it became a skilled wave rider.

As with classical conditioning, we should note that biology plays a role in determining how easy or difficult a particular learning task will be for a certain species. Although some trainers appear to be quite capable of teaching animals to engage in a wide range of unnatural behaviors, it turns out there are, of course, limits to this.

Some researchers have tried to train raccoons to put coins in a piggy bank, for example. Through shaping techniques, raccoons can be trained to pick up a single coin and place it in a piggy bank. However, raccoons are known for their natural tendency to wash food before eating it. If they are given more than one coin at a time, their natural tendency to wash objects seems to interfere with the shaping techniques. Instead of putting the coins into the bank, they rub them together. One of the most prominent examples of biological constraints on learning concerns language learning. Other than humans, only certain species of birds, like parrots, can be taught to speak (although their speech is generally thought to be a form of mimicry). No matter how much reinforcement or punishment is provided, biological factors make speech impossible for most animals. (We will return to this topic in Chapter 9.)

Learned Helplessness *When Things Go Wrong*

Sometimes our prior learning experiences can cause problems with later learning situations. One problem that can arise as the result of operant conditioning is a phenomenon, known as **learned helplessness**, in which prior experiences with inescapable punishment condition people or animals to accept punishing consequences in later situations when they could actually avoid them (Seligman et al., 1980). For instance, research with rats has found that, after repeated inescapable shocks to the tail, if rats are given the option of escaping a foot shock by moving to a different area in the testing cage, many of them fail to do so (Weiss & Glazer, 1975). The rats that could not escape the tail shocks initially failed later to learn how to stop a shock to the foot. Instead, they stayed put and took the punishment. Learned helplessness is thought by some researchers to be an animal model of depression (Porsolt, 2000). Humans with depression are often unmotivated to act in order to change the stimuli they receive from their environments, and some theorists suggest that these people have learned this pattern of inaction from earlier, perhaps unrelated, experiences in which they were unable to make the changes they wanted. Learned helplessness also may partially explain some of the characteristics of battered spouse syndrome (Clements & Sawhney, 2000).

Why do they stay? Spousal abuse occurs in at least 4 million American homes each year. Psychologists believe that many victims develop feelings of helplessness and become convinced that they are incapable of changing the situation.

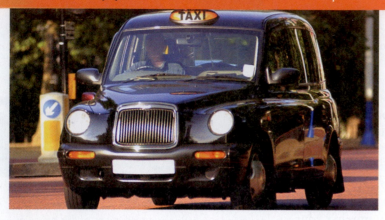

Taxicab drivers, particularly those in London, must learn and remember a large amount of spatial navigation information to perform their jobs efficiently. Perhaps it is not surprising then that this job has been linked to differences in brain regions that are important for spatial navigation learning. MRI studies of London taxi drivers, for example, showed that they have a slightly larger hippocampus than people of the same age who do not have taxicab training (Maguire et al., 2000).

Whether this finding reflects cause or effect remains unknown. It may be that individuals with larger hippocampi gravitate toward jobs that make use of their spatial navigation skills. Alternatively, exposure to a significant amount of spatial information may enlarge the hippocampus through training. Some studies in experimental animals suggest that the second explanation is likely: the hippocampus may grow in response to experience. Living in a complex environment, learning, and physical activity all increase the size and number of neurons in the hippocampus in lab animals (Shors, 2009; Leuner, Gould, & Shors, 2006; Mirescu & Gould, 2006). Something similar many occur in humans as well.

Repeated, inescapable abuse may cause learned helplessness. The victim can become withdrawn and unable to respond in an adaptive way, even if there is an option to escape an abusive situation.

Learning and Thinking

Strict behavioral psychologists have argued that all types of learning are forms of conditioning. During the twentieth century, some prominent behaviorist psychologists argued that everything we do comes about as a result of either classical or operant conditioning. Many also suggested that only observable changes in behavior should be taken as evidence of learning. This interpretation of learning as strictly based on behavioral conditioning, however, seems overly simplistic when you consider the wealth of knowledge you have amassed without any overt reinforcement. Indeed, research has shown that learning does seem to happen without any obvious reinforcement.

Spatial Navigation Learning   One good example of learning without reinforcement arose from laboratory studies designed to assess the ability of reinforcement to train rats to learn information about spatial navigation. Perhaps not surprisingly, laboratory rodents can be trained to navigate through a maze by providing them with reinforcement along the way. This approach, which is a form of shaping, involves the presentation of food rewards as rats move in the correct direction.

In the absence of reinforcers, rats typically explore a maze, but are not motivated to find the quickest route from start to finish. However, when rats are allowed to first explore the maze and are then provided with reinforcement, they learn the task much faster than naïve rats. Studies of this type show that the rats were learning information about the spatial environment while they were randomly exploring the maze—even though they were not receiving any reinforcement for learning. When reinforcement was introduced, the rats displayed their latent learning (**Figure 7-11**) (Tolman & Gleitman, 1949).

spatial navigation learning learning that involves forming associations among stimuli relevant to navigating in space.

insight learning a sudden realization of a solution to a problem or leap in understanding new concepts.

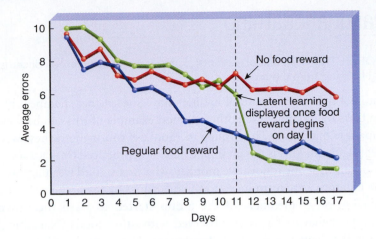

FIGURE 7-11 **Latent learning in rats** Rats are motivated to explore a maze, but when given a food reward, they make fewer errors in finding the quickest route to the end of the maze and the reward. When the reward is introduced after the rats explore the maze, the error rate drops sharply, indicating that learning occured all along.

(Graph labels: Average errors (y-axis, 0 to 10); Days (x-axis, 0 to 17); No food reward; Latent learning displayed once food reward begins on day II; Regular food reward)

It might be easy to imagine yourself in a similar situation. Exploring a particular environment, perhaps by riding your bicycle for fun or as a passenger in a car, would make finding a location in that same environment, such as a new job or a new restaurant, much easier than doing so in a completely unfamiliar locale.

This particular example of spatial navigation learning probably represents another form of biological readiness for certain types of learning. Rodents, and probably humans, seem predisposed to form spatial maps of their environments through learning (O'Keefe, 1990). Learning spatial information about their environments would have had adaptive value to our ancestors—and it still does for modern-day rats—in terms of finding food, shelter, and escape routes. Spatial navigation learning requires an intact hippocampus, a brain region that is also important for learning about other nonspatial events (Morris, 1990).

Insight Learning   In addition to spatial navigation learning, there are other types of learning that cannot be readily explained in behaviorist terms. One additional example of this is **insight learning**. Most of us have had this experience. We may puzzle and struggle over a difficult problem. Then, some time later—perhaps while we are not even working on the problem—we may have an "ah-ha!" or "eureka" moment, when the solution suddenly becomes evident. Some individuals even report solving problems in their dreams. The Nobel laureate Otto Loewi, the discoverer of the actions of neurotransmitter chemicals, claims to have come up with his definitive study while sleeping, after pondering the question over and over while awake (Loewi, 1957). Although finding the solutions to our problems in our dreams is fairly rare, insight learning is widespread and is another type of learning that doesn't involve any obvious reinforcement.

Language learning also does not neatly fit into a behavioral explanation. As we discuss in detail in Chapter 9, the principles of association and reinforcement cannot fully explain a number aspects of how we learn to understand and use our native languages.

"Ah-hah" During the 1920s, psychologist Wolfgang Kohler conducted pioneering studies on insight learning. Here one of Kohler's chimpanzees piles three crates on top of each other to reach a banana that had been placed out of its reach. When first confronted with this complex task, the chimp sat and contemplated the situation; then, in an apparent flash of insight, it stacked and climbed up the crates.

Before You Go On

What Do You Know?
5. What are positive reinforcement and negative reinforcement? What are the effects of each on behavior?
6. What is learned helplessness?
7. What is spatial navigation learning and why is it difficult to explain using operant conditioning?

What Do You Think?   How could you use operant conditioning principles to get a roommate or child to regularly hang up his or her coat instead of throwing it on the floor?

Imitating Imo A Japanese macaque washes its sweet potatoes in ocean water. This behavior is displayed only by members of the monkey's particular troupe. Apparently, they learned it by imitating the innovative behavior of a young monkey named Imo.

Observational Learning

LEARNING OBJECTIVE 4 Define observational learning and summarize concerns about observational learning from the media.

Studies of animal behavior in natural habitats have shown that members of certain species learn tasks by watching each other. A good example of this can be seen with a troupe of Japanese macaques. This troupe of monkeys routinely washes sweet potatoes before eating them. This is not an innate behavior, practiced by macaques all over the world. It began with one innovative monkey, who first started washing sweet potatoes after the potatoes were introduced to the macaques by researchers. After observing this behavior, other members of the group started to wash their own sweet potatoes—similar behavior has been observed with other foods (Nakamichi et al., 1998). Other studies have reported that **observational learning**, learning from watching the behavior of others, led to the use of novel tools by dolphins and certain primate and bird species (Krüetzen et al., 2005). Through observational learning, animals can culturally transmit behaviors across generations. That is, parents or older members of a group engage in behavior that the young observe. Observation leads to mimicry, or **modeling**, which is concrete proof that learning occurred.

In addition to contributing to learning through mimicry, observation can affect other types of behavior that indirectly signal learning has occurred. A good example of this can be seen with reward studies in capuchin monkeys (Brosnan & De Waal, 2003). This species can be rather easily trained to perform a task for a food reward, such as a cucumber slice. If, however, the trained monkey observes another monkey receiving a more desirable reward (for example, a grape) for performing the same task, the monkey will respond by refusing to carry out the task again. This suggests not only that capuchin monkeys have an internal concept of fairness, but also that they have used the experience of observing the consequences of another monkey's behavior to modify their own.

Similar examples abound in our own lives. We learn by observation, using others as positive and negative role models and, perhaps, modifying our own behavior in new ways to accommodate the new information. Suppose a classmate is warmly rewarded with praise for asking a question in lecture. You now have information that the instructor welcomes questions. As a consequence of observing your classmate's rewarding experience, you may be more likely to ask a question of your own in the future.

Observational Learning and Violence

Some of the most famous experiments of observational learning in children were carried out by a psychologist named Albert Bandura. Bandura was interested in whether children learned violent behavioral responses by observing aggression. He showed children a movie of a woman beating up an inflatable clown punching bag, called a Bobo doll (see **Figure 7-12**) (Bandura, Ross, & Ross, 1961). After the movie, the children were allowed to play in a room full of toys, including a Bobo doll. Those who had previously watched the Bobo video were twice as likely as those who did not watch it to display violent behavior toward the doll.

The researchers further investigated whether observational learning would be influenced by information about reward and punishment. Indeed, they found such a relationship. The children who saw a video in which beating up the Bobo doll led to rewards, such as candy and praise, were more likely to act aggressively toward the doll than those who observed the woman being punished for beating Bobo.

Bandura's studies, and a great deal of research that followed, raised concerns that violence on television, in movies, and in videogames promotes aggressive behavior among

observational learning learning that occurs without overt training in response to watching the behavior.

modeling mimicking others' behavior.

viewers, especially children (Bandura, 1978). Some studies have demonstrated a convincing link between excessive television watching and aggressive behavior in children (Johnson et al., 2002). The number of violent acts in a short stretch of children's programming can be disturbingly high. The number of such acts is typically highest in cartoons, where the consequences of violent actions are usually nonexistent. In fact, cartoon characters seem to have many lives, often returning unscathed after experiencing all manner of horrors.

Although there is strong correlational evidence that television watching is associated with aggressive behavior in children, remember from our discussion of correlations in Chapter 2 that a correlation can only tell us that two variables are related. Correlations do not tell whether one variable causes the other. Some studies suggest that kids who already behave aggressively may prefer to watch more violent TV. Recall, too, that correlations only describe the relationship between the two variables specified. Other factors may influence both of those variables. In the studies of TV watching, for example it's clear that media violence is not the only factor contributing to children's aggression. Some studies have shown that children who watch excessive television are also less likely than children whose viewing is limited to have other positive environmental influences in their lives. Heavy TV watching is associated with low socioeconomic status and low parental involvement, so these children may lack parental or neighborhood influences against aggression.

FIGURE 7-12 **Aggressive modeling** Bandura found that children learned to abuse an inflatable clown doll by observing an adult hit the doll.

Before You Go On

What Do You Know?
8. What is observational learning and what does it demonstrate when it happens?
9. What has research shown about media violence and aggressive behavior in child viewers?

What Do You Think?
How might the media be used to get children—or adults—to mimic positive social behaviors?

Factors that Facilitate Learning

LEARNING OBJECTIVE 5 Define massed and spaced practice and tell what conditions are best for learning semantic material, such as facts in your classes.

It's clear that we can learn in a variety of ways: through simple habituation and sensitization, by linking stimuli in classical conditioning, by associating our behavior to its consequences through operant conditioning, or by using our observations of the consequences of another's behaviors as a model for our own. We also know that several factors can affect how well each of these learning methods works. Timing, as we have seen, is crucial in classical conditioning. It can also affect other types of learning. The amount of attention we pay when trying to learn is another factor that can facilitate, or alternatively, impede our learning, depending on the type of learning.

Timing

You have probably noticed that you learn more information when you study for an exam over an extended period of time, as opposed to cramming for the test by pulling an "all-nighter." Why is this?

Oh, those all-nighters! Cramming for a test the night before an exam leads to the acquisition of less information than studying for the test over an extended period of time.

Much of the learning that you, as a student, undertake on a daily basis involves acquiring information about facts. Psychologists distinguish between this type of learning, called *semantic learning*, and *episodic learning*, which is learning about events in our own lives. We will return to the distinction between episodic and semantic learning in the next chapter dealing with memory, but we can offer some advice now about how to improve your learning of semantic material.

Most importantly, repetition helps. Semantic learning is facilitated by multiple exposures to the same material, such as reading the textbook, then listening carefully in class, and then reviewing your notes and textbook. Multiple exposures make it more likely that learning will occur, compared to a single exposure, such as just reading the book or just going to class.

Your learning will also be facilitated by having time intervals between these exposures. When learning trials occur close together, as they do when you try to cram reading the book and reviewing all into the night before a big test, they are referred to as *massed*. When they are separated in time, they are referred to as *spaced*. The difference in efficiency between massed and spaced trials for learning has been demonstrated not only in the laboratory, but also in real life. Massed studying, or cramming, is ineffective for two reasons. First, it does not allow enough time between learning trials to maximize learning, and, second, it leads to sleep deprivation.

Awareness and Attention

It's clear that much learning occurs without our awareness. Nonassociative learning and some forms of associative learning—including some forms of classical conditioning and procedural, or motor-skill, learning—often occur without the individual realizing that information has been acquired. Another good example of this is learning the lyrics and tune to a new song, described at the start of this chapter, which often occurs without the intention to memorize. Observational learning also often occurs without awareness, as in the case of children modeling aggressive behavior observed on television. In some instances, awareness and excessive attention can actually interfere with learning. Gymnasts, for example, sometimes find that explicit mental rehearsal breaks their concentration and interferes with their performance when they are trying to learn a new move.

In most instances, however, awareness and attention enhance learning. Many forms of associative learning, including semantic and episodic learning, require awareness and are greatly enhanced by attentional processes. You have probably experienced this first-hand on days when you are feeling out of sorts and have difficulty concentrating on your coursework. The information you read or hear in lectures at such times is much less likely to be learned than material presented at a time when you are more attentive.

Given the role of attention in learning, it is worth considering an important question: How does attention work? Scientists have found that the answer to this question depends on the circumstances. Some attentional processes are automatic and occur when a particular stimulus is very different from those that surround it. Psychologist Anne Treisman studied attention to visual stimuli and showed that in the case of a simple scene, if one stimulus differs considerably from others, it will immediately grab our attention, a phenomenon referred to as "*pop-out*". In order for pop-out to work, the stimulus must be singularly different from the surroundings (Treisman & Kanwisher, 1998). As scenes get more and more complicated, pop-out is less likely to help in guiding attentional processes. Instead, we must rely on an active searching method, where we examine material in search of the most relevant stimuli. Anyone who has enjoyed children's books like "Where's Waldo" or "I Spy", where a relevant stimulus is buried in a complex visual scene, has engaged an *active searching* attentional process. Recall from Chapter 5 the distinction between bottom-up and top-down processing. Pop-out, because of its simplicity and speed, employs bottom-up processing while active searching, because of the need to draw on cognitive processes and memory, uses top-down processing.

Sometimes attentional processes can get in the way—if information is inherently contradictory, for example, attending to one stimulus can block our ability to attend to the relevant one. A good example of this is the *Stroop Effect*, a psychological test that involves presenting a list of words printed in different colors. Each of the words is a color word (green, red, black, blue), but each is printed in color that differs from that of the word (green, red, black, blue). Participants are asked to list the colors of the ink, thus ignoring the word color—this is very difficult to do quickly because bottom-up attentional processing interferes with the ability to focus on just one contradictory stimulus (Herd et al., 2006).

What can we do then to maximize our attention to relevant information while trying to learn? First, it's a good idea to identify relevant information and focus on those throughout your reading. If your professor mentions topics repeatedly in class, you might use an active searching method to find additional similar material in your readings. Second, avoid dividing your attention. Our attentional processes are generally at their best when they are focused on one task. Performing other behaviors, such as answering text messages or watching TV, while trying to study usually interferes with our ability to attend to relevant material. In fact, a recent study showed that people who engage in a high degree of "multi-tasking" are less likely to perform well overall (Ophira et al., 2009).

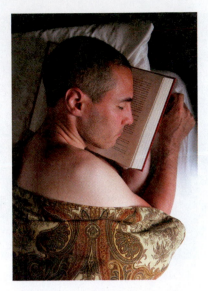

Sleep deprivation, attention, and learning Sleep deprivation makes it difficult to pay attention, thus impairing our ability to learn. In addition, sleep deprivation *after* learning reduces our ability to retain newly learned material.

Before You Go On

What Do You Know?
10. Which would be better for helping you learn psychology facts: massed or spaced practice? Why?

11. What kinds of learning benefit from focused attention?

What Do You Think?
How could you modify your own schedule or study habits to allow for spaced practice of your material or to take advantage of your most alert and attentive times of day?

When We Learn *What Happens in the* B R A I N ?

LEARNING OBJECTIVE 6 Discuss synaptic changes that occur in learning, such as long term potentiation.

Throughout this chapter, we have mentioned different brain regions and neural mechanisms that might underlie certain types of learning. One general conclusion we can draw about the neuroscience of learning is that a single learning center does not exist. As we have seen, different types of learning are served by different neural systems:

- Habituation and sensitization arise from changes in the sensory neurons themselves and their related corresponding interneurons and motor neurons.
- Classical conditioning of the eye blink response is associated with the cerebellum, while fear conditioning involves the amygdala.
- Reward learning relies on the midbrain dopamine system, and motor learning involves activation of the basal ganglia, a region near the thalamus.
- Spatial navigation learning and episodic learning in general involve the hippocampus.

Complex environments and learning Humans exposed to stimulating environments and animals raised in stimulating cages each seem to perform better on many learning tests, compared to those living in more deprived settings. This finding is consistent with what we now know about how the brain changes during learning (Pham et al., 2002; Rosenzweig & Bennett, 1996).

> **"** Cells that fire together, wire together. **"**
>
> —*Donald Hebb, psychologist*

The evidence that some kinds of learning can take place without our awareness, while others require close attention, also emphasizes the fact that there is no single learning system in the brain. See, for example, "What Happens in the Brain When We Learn to Play a Video Game" at the end of this section.

Although there are multiple neural systems that underlie different types of learning, neuroscientists suspect that all learning involves some kind of change in the strength of the synapse, the connection between neurons. One of the first ideas about learning involving changes in synaptic strength was put forth in the 1950s by the Canadian psychologist Donald Hebb. Hebb suggested that cells that were activated at or around the same time as one another would have stronger synapses than those that were out of step with one another (Cooper, 2005).

Scientists have gathered considerable evidence to support Hebb's view. Many forms of associative learning have been linked to a form of synaptic plasticity, or change, discussed in Chapter 4, called **long-term potentiation (LTP)**. Recall that a synapse is the tiny gap across which neurons communicate via neurotransmitters. Long-term potentiation refers to a change in activity at the synapse that results in a long-term enhancement in the activity of the postsynaptic neuron—the one that receives the neurotransmitter message (**Figure 7-13**) (Bliss & Lomo, 1973). LTP has been demonstrated in the synapses in brain areas involved in eye blink conditioning, fear conditioning, and spatial navigation learning (Scelfo, Sacchetti, & Strata, 2008; Whitlock et al., 2006; Maren, 2005). LTP can be associative in nature, occurring only when electrical activity in two related areas occurs around the same time. Moreover, researchers have demonstrated, by blocking the neurotransmitter receptors in the postsynaptic neuron, that preventing LTP inhibits some forms of learning.

Another possible mechanism for learning, one that could actually work in tandem with LTP, is the formation of new synapses in our brains. The possibility that learning is accompanied by growth of synapses was first suggested by the early neuroanatomist Ramon y Cajal in the late nineteenth century (DeFelipe, 2002). Since then, numerous studies have shown that Ramon y Cajal was correct. Changes in the number, size, and shape of synapses and dendritic spines, sites of excitatory synapses, have been observed with learning (Leuner, Falduto, & Shors, 2003; O'Malley,

long-term potentiation (LTP) a form of synaptic change that involves increased activity in the postsynaptic cells after strong, repetitive stimulation.

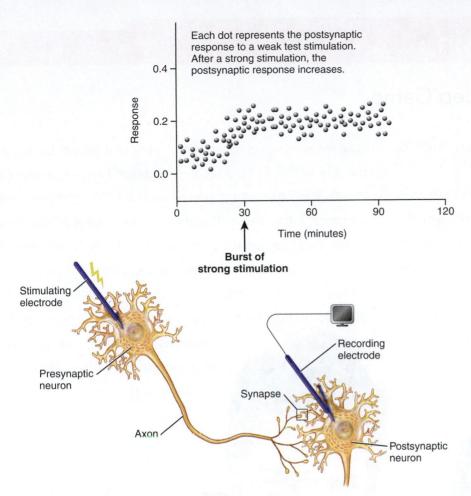

Each dot represents the postsynaptic response to a weak test stimulation. After a strong stimulation, the postsynaptic response increases.

Burst of strong stimulation

FIGURE 7-13 **Long-term potentiation** When a presynaptic neuron is given a strong burst of stimulation, it changes the activity at the synapse of the postsynaptic neuron. Subsequently, a weak stimulation reaching the postsynaptic neuron produces a greater effect than would have occurred before.

O'Connell, & Regan, 1998; Moser, Trommald, & Andersen, 1994). Even the number of entirely new neurons in our hippocampus can increase with certain types of learning (Shors, 2009). These studies present the possibility that structural change may not only occur with learning, but may actually underlie learning.

Some evidence suggests that preventing the production of new neurons can inhibit certain types of learning, but not others (Shors, 2009; Leuner et al., 2006). It's likely that if structural changes participate in learning, then they do so in concert with changes in the function and biochemistry in the relevant circuits.

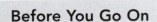

Before You Go On

What Do You Know?

12. Which brain regions are associated with reward and punishment?
13. Name and describe a process referred to in the quotation, "Cells that fire together, wire together."

What Do You Think? Why are so many different brains regions involved in learning?

When We Learn to Play a Video Game

You need to find that key, but watch out for those obstacles!

How do we learn to navigate through virtual reality, avoiding dangers that prevent us from moving through the game to mastery? What parts of the brain enable us to learn the rules of the game and respond to changes in the electronic world as we play?

When we learn a new video game that involves spatial navigation through a virtual three-dimensional space, trying to avoid punishments and obtain rewards all along the way, we are engaging a number of neural circuits throughout the brain. First, spatial navigation learning requires inputs from the visual cortex to the hippocampus and temporal lobe. Second, learning about rewards involves dopamine projections extending from the ventral tegmental area to the nucleus accumbens and prefrontal cortex. And third, integration and long-term storage of the information from these systems involves other cortical regions, including the parietal and temporal cortex. Will you make it to the next level?

PICKING A STRATEGY

People use different strategies to solve tasks that involve navigating in space. Some people use a 3D strategy, using their position relative to the environment to find their way. Others use landmarks and numbering strategies (for example, enter the second door on your right). The different strategies engage different neural systems, shown on these fMRI images. Spatial 3D strategies activate the hippocampus (top, yellow) while landmark strategies activate the basal ganglia (bottom, yellow).

STRENGTHENING YOUR SYNAPSES

When you learn a task that involves spatial navigation and reward, synapses in a number of brain regions, including the hippocampus and nucleus accumbens, likely undergo long-term potentiation (LTP), a form of synapse strengthening. Most postsynaptic sites that undergo synapse strengthening are located on small extensions off of dendrites, called dendritic spines (shown here labeled with a green fluorescent tracer).

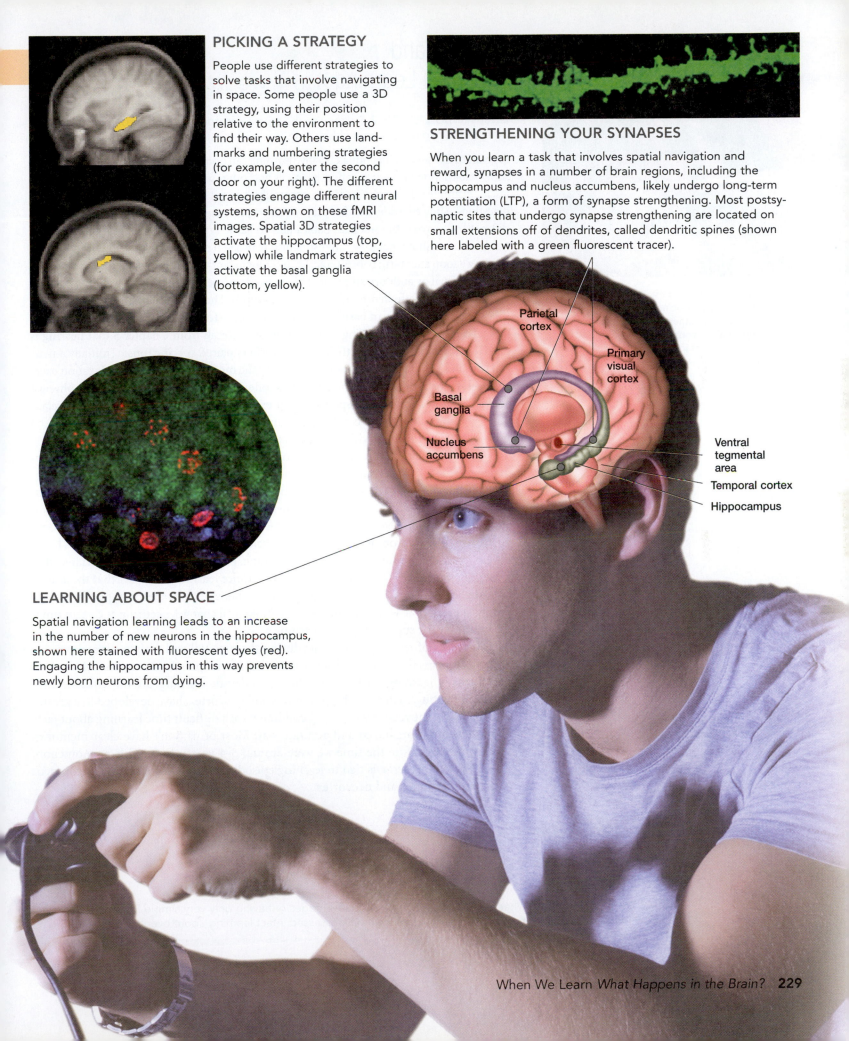

Parietal cortex

Primary visual cortex

Basal ganglia

Nucleus accumbens

Ventral tegmental area

Temporal cortex

Hippocampus

LEARNING ABOUT SPACE

Spatial navigation learning leads to an increase in the number of new neurons in the hippocampus, shown here stained with fluorescent dyes (red). Engaging the hippocampus in this way prevents newly born neurons from dying.

Prenatal and Postnatal Learning | How we *Develop*

Early olfactory learning In this study infants are exposed to bottles containing smells of their mothers, their fathers, and other people. In such research undertakings, babies consistently show highest preference for the smell of their mothers and second highest for that of their fathers.

LEARNING OBJECTIVE 7 Summarize the types of learning that occur before we are born and during early postnatal life.

Several studies suggest that nonassociative learning can occur before we are even born. Fetuses show habituation and sensitization to smells and other sensory stimuli. In one set of studies, for example infants who had been prenatally exposed to garlic—through their mothers' digestion—showed evidence, after they were born, that they recognized the garlic odor. They did not try to avoid the smell, as babies new to garlic typically do. Habituation studies of newborns also show that they can distinguish between new and familiar sights and sounds. Even very soon after birth babies typically stop moving for a brief time when they are exposed to a new visual or auditory stimulus. This response suggests that they have already become accustomed, or habituated, to "old" sights and sounds. They have learned to recognize them.

We are also capable of basic associative learning before birth. One team of researchers reported classical conditioning of human fetuses. Recall from Chapter 5 that hearing is partially developed before birth. These researchers paired specific music (initially a neutral stimulus) with relaxation exercises done by the mother. The maternal relaxation exercises served as an unconditioned stimulus, often leading to a slowing of fetal physical activity (an unconditioned response). After enough pairings of the music and the relaxation, the music became a conditioned stimulus, leading directly to a decrease in fetal movement (CR), with or without the relaxation exercises.

Newborn humans also demonstrate olfactory learning by showing an almost immediate preference for their own mothers' odor, by turning their heads in the direction of their mothers' odor much more often than toward odors of strangers. The preference for maternal odor has clear adaptive consequences in helping babies to identify the person who, throughout our evolutionary history, has been their primary source of food and care.

As we develop from infancy onward, it's clear that biological factors, such as brain development, guide the development of learning. Psychologists and pediatricians often refer to *developmental milestones*, many that require learning. The fact that these abilities, such as crawling, walking, language comprehension, and speech, typically emerge during specific time windows suggests that biological changes occuring at certain times are necessary for specific types of learning.

The types of learning that occur during the prenatal and early postnatal periods are simple forms that don't critically involve late-developing brain regions. More complex forms of learning, such as episodic and semantic learning, are not efficient until forebrain regions, such as the hippocampus and neocortex, have developed to a greater extent. This is one reason why young children have a difficult time learning about facts and events in an organized and accurate way. Most of us don't have clear memories about our lives before the time we were around 3-4 years of age. This phenomenon, called *infantile amnesia*, is tied to learning episodic information and the development of the hippocampus and neocortex.

Before You Go On

What Do You Know?

14. What kinds of learning can happen before we are born?

What Do You Think? What are the advantages and disadvantages of having only very simple forms of learning intact during fetal life? What consequences would arise if we possessed intact learning about events before birth?

Learning and Gender HOW weDiffer

LEARNING OBJECTIVE 8 Summarize gender differences in learning and discuss their potential sources.

Within the range of what is considered normal, learning abilities vary greatly. You have likely experienced this firsthand by comparing study techniques and learning requirements of some of your friends and family with your own. Some individuals are gifted at certain subjects and are capable of acquiring that information much more readily than others. Studies of twins have suggested a genetic factor in certain forms of learning, but that does not account for the majority of variability in learning. Other factors clearly play a role. Environmental factors, as well as nongenetic biological factors, are likely to modulate learning abilities.

Gender Differences

One highly controversial topic in the study of individual differences in learning is the issue of gender. Many individuals have preconceived notions about learning performance in boys and girls. For instance, it is a relatively common claim that boys are better at mathematics while girls excel at language arts. Since the social and educational implications of such claims are significant, it is important to carefully evaluate scientific evidence related to them. The first question we need ask is whether significant sex differences in learning actually exist. If so, then the cause of these differences becomes the critical issue. Are they biologically governed by chromosomes and/or hormones, or do they arise as a result of environmental influences?

Numerous studies have claimed that gender differences exist in a number of different learning tasks. Tasks that require mental rotation of images tend to favor males, while verbal-learning tasks sometimes favor females. Although these overall differences are sometimes statistically significant when a relatively large number of individuals are tested, there is still a substantial overlap between the two genders in performance on both tasks. In addition, the difference between the average for each sex is smaller than the range within a given sex, leading to the conclusion that reports of gender differences in learning ability do not mean much for the individual. In other words, there are plenty of spatially gifted girls and verbally talented boys.

Examination of performance on standardized tests, such as the SAT, reveals higher average math scores among boys than girls. Again, these differences are not enormous and say very little about the individual, since the range within a gender far exceeds the average differences. In fact, the range in scores among boys is greater than the range for girls. In other words, although the average for boys is higher, boys earn some of the lowest scores, as well as some of the highest scores. We should also note that standardized tests are typically not actual tests of learning ability, because differences in preparation for such examinations are huge; someone with a high score may have studied for months, while someone with a lower score may have gone into the test without any advance preparation.

Even though they are small, and there is a lot of overlap between genders, these consistent gender differences are enough to raise issues about whether biological or environmental factors, such as schooling, influence math learning. Cultural perceptions may influence teachers' attitudes about gender differences in math ability, for example, leading to unintentional discouragement of girls in math.

Studies done by social psychologist Claude Steele have identified a phenomenon called **stereotype threat**, in which awareness of negative stereotypes about oneself can interfere significantly with test performance. In these studies, Steele and his colleagues observed that mentioning, before a test, a gender difference disadvantaging one gender

Self-fulfilling prophecy? In this math class, a male teacher calls on a male student for the answer. Many psychologists suspect that findings of male superiority in the learning of mathematical tasks and female superiority in the acquisition of language skills have more to do with expectations, biased teaching, misinterpretation of findings, sociocultural factors, and stress reactions than with actual differences in learning potential.

stereotype threat awareness of a negative stereotype that affects oneself and often leads to impairment in performance.

led to poorer performance on the part of the group experiencing the bias. Members of stereotyped groups performed worse even if researchers called attention to the stereotype in an encouraging way, such as, "Come on girls, I know you can score well on this test and disprove the belief that boys are better at math!" In fact, trying hard to overcome such a stereotype seems to worsen performance even more. This phenomenon, which is incompletely understood, is not specific to gender differences or to math performance. Stereotype threat can also impair the performance of white males on an athletic test if they are informed of the stereotype that Caucasians are less athletically gifted than African Americans. In Chapter 11, we discuss additional effects of stereotype threat on IQ test performance.

A biological factor that could affect learning may be our responses to stress. Some studies have shown that gender differences in response to stress can affect not only learning, but also test performance. On average, girls are more emotionally perturbed than boys by the anxiety of test taking. These studies also show that helping girls to reduce test stress by teaching them relaxation exercises or pre-exposing them to the testing environment can eliminate many gender differences in performance. (We discuss stress and coping techniques in further detail in Chapter 15.) This work emphasizes the need to consider other factors, such as stress, when we evaluate claims of individual differences in learning ability.

Before You Go On

What Do You Know?

15. What is stereotype threat and what effect does it have on learning?

What Do You Think? What are the ethical problems associated with investigating gender differences in learning abilities? How might positive or negative findings of sex differences in learning affect society's attitude toward men and women in the workplace?

Learning Disabilities When Things Go Wrong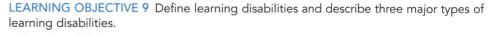

LEARNING OBJECTIVE 9 Define learning disabilities and describe three major types of learning disabilities.

A **learning disability** is a specific deficiency in one aspect of cognitive functioning, while other aspects function normally. Learning disabilities are different from mental retardation, which is a more global deficit in intellectual abilities. Individuals with learning disabilities can even have very high IQs with impairment only in one type of learning.

Dyslexia

The most common form of learning disability is **dyslexia**, a deficiency in learning to read. Some estimates suggest that between 5 and 10 percent of school age children have dyslexia. The condition is two to three times more prevalent in boys than girls.

Contrary to popular belief, dyslexia doesn't primarily manifest itself as a reversal of letters of words. Reversal of letters or words is common in young children in the process of learning to read. Most children outgrow this as they acquire reading skills. People with dyslexia display this characteristic for longer periods of time, until they are older than average, in part because they are not as far along on the reading learning curve, but it is a symptom of their larger problems in learning to read.

Studying dyslexia A range of factors have been proposed to explain dyslexia, a deficiency in the ability to read, including deficits in visual processing, speech skills, auditory processing, and object or letter identification. Here a young boy with the disorder undergoes a reading test with prism glasses.

There is some evidence that the same people with dyslexia have visual processing deficits that may produce perceptual problems, which in turn, contribute to their difficulty in recognizing written words. Neuroimaging studies comparing children with dyslexia to those without the disability have shown that some children with dyslexia have reduced blood flow in brain regions associated with acquisition of reading skills, such as the left parietal and temporal cortex (Hoeft et al., 2006). Most people with dyslexia can overcome their difficulties in learning to read with the help of extensive tutoring and specific educational programs.

Dyscalculia

A slightly less prevalent learning disability, which may exist with or without dyslexia, is a condition known as **dyscalculia**. This refers to an inability to readily acquire information about mathematics. Dyscalculia afflicts less than 5 percent of the population and is more prevalent in boys than girls.

Dyscalculia can occur in individuals with normal, or even higher than average, reading abilities, suggesting a deficit in specific brain circuitry associated with acquisition of mathematical skills. Less information is available about dyscalculia than about dyslexia, but some evidence suggests that parts of the left parietal and frontal cortex of the brain are less active in individuals with dyscalculia (Price et al., 2007). As with dyslexia, intensive tutoring and specific educational programs can help students with dyscalculia learn mathematical information.

Attention Deficit Disorders

As we have noted, attention greatly aids some types of learning, especially the semantic learning required in school. Although not specifically designated as learning disabilities, two attention disorders often contribute to difficulties in learning. **Attention deficit disorder (ADD)** is characterized primarily by an inability to concentrate. **Attention deficit hyperactivity disorder (ADHD)** is a similar disorder in which concentration problems are accompanied by problematically high activity levels. These attention disorders are sometimes associated with dyslexia and dyscalculia. Both disorders are more prevalent in boys than girls.

Neuroimaging studies have identified some brain regions that appear to be different in children with ADD or ADHD, compared to children without these disorders. Some evidence suggests that ADHD is associated with structural abnormalities in the cerebral cortex (Qiu et al., 2009; Wolosin et al., 2009; Shaw et al., 2007). Studies have also shown decreased blood flow in the basal ganglia (Bush, Valera, & Seidman, 2005) and also a portion of the prefrontal cortex called the *anterior cingulate* (Smith et al., 2008). Some studies have even shown an overall decrease in the size of these brain regions in people with ADHD (Hill et al., 2003).

ADD and ADHD can be successfully treated with stimulant drugs, including methylphenidate, widely known by the trade name Ritalin®, and dextroamphetamine, which has the trade name Adderall®. Both drugs enhance attention and, even though they are stimulants, paradoxically diminish hyperactivity. The extent to which these drugs correct abnormalities in the cerebral cortex of people with ADD and ADHD remains undetermined.

The identification and study of learning disabilities and attention deficit disorder raise important ethical considerations. First, it is paramount that diagnoses be made early, so that intervention can occur before significant developmental delays occur. Second, it is equally important that diagnoses are accurate, so that children with other behavioral problems are not incorrectly medicated.

A third issue concerns misuse of stimulant drugs. The increased diagnosis of attention disorder and subsequent stimulant prescriptions have led to stimulant abuse by some people who most likely do not have attention disorders. Some recent studies have

learning disability a specific deficiency in one aspect of cognitive function while other aspects function normally.

dyslexia a learning disability that involves deficits in learning to read and write.

dyscalculia an inability to readily acquire information about mathematics.

attention deficit disorder (ADD) a disorder characterized by an inability to pay attention.

attention deficit hyperactivity disorder (ADHD) a disorder characterized by an inability to pay attention, accompanied by excessive activity.

Learning to "play" attention Various techniques have been used to help explain and treat ADHD, including a computer program called *Play Attention*. Here a child wears a helmet that measures brain waves while he performs computer tasks requiring various degrees of attention.

estimated that a significant percentage of college students have used Ritalin and similar drugs without a prescription. Most students surveyed report that they use the drugs to help them study. Since attention-disorder drugs enhance attention and thus learning in normal individuals, this raises ethical questions (Greely et al., 2008). Do stimulants provide an unfair advantage to students who take them in settings—such as college—where success is determined by cognitive function? Is stimulant use among people without attention disorders comparable, for example, to athletes using performance enhancing drugs to improve their competitive standing?

Before You Go On

What Do You Know?

16. What are dyslexia and dyscalculia?

What Do You Think?   What, in your opinion, are the ethical pros and cons of taking attention-enhancing drugs when they are not needed to treat a disorder?

Summary

What Is Learning?

LEARNING OBJECTIVE 1   Define learning and distinguish between associative and nonassociative learning.

- Learning is a lasting change in the brain caused by experience.

- Nonassociative learning is a lasting change that happens as a result of experience with a single cue. Types of nonassociative learning include habituation, in which we display decreased responses to familiar stimuli, and sensitization, in which we display increased responses to stimuli of normal strength after being exposed to an unusually strong stimulus.

- Associative learning is a lasting change that happens as a result of associating two or more stimuli. Types of associative learning include classical and operant conditioning.

Classical Conditioning

LEARNING OBJECTIVE 2   Describe the basic processes of classical conditioning and tell how classical conditioning is relevant to human fears and taste aversions.

- As a result of classical conditioning, a previously neutral stimulus comes to elicit a response by being paired with an unconditioned stimulus (US) that already generates the response, known as an unconditioned response (UR). The neutral stimulus becomes a conditioned stimulus (CS) when it elicits the same response as the US. The response to the CS is known as a conditioned response (CR).

- Repeated presentation of the CS without the US can lead to extinction, or suppression of the CR. Extinction does not mean we forget the CS-US association, however. The CR can be spontaneously recovered.

- Eye blink conditioning shows that classical conditioning requires changes in the cerebellum.

- Phobias and conditioned taste aversions can result from classical conditioning. Systematic desensitization uses classical conditioning to extinguish phobia responses. Conditioned taste aversions suggest that we are biologically prepared to quickly learn responses important to our survival.

Operant Conditioning

LEARNING OBJECTIVE 3   Describe the basic processes of operant conditioning and explain how shaping can be used to teach new behaviors.

- Operant conditioning is a learned association between stimuli in the environment and our own behavior. The law of effect states that we learn to repeat behaviors that will increase our rewards and help us avoid punishment.

- Reinforcers are rewarding stimuli from the environment. Positive reinforcement provides a desired stimulus; negative reinforcement takes away an unpleasant stimulus. Both increase the chance a behavior will be repeated. Primary reinforcers are reinforcing in and of themselves. Secondary reinforcers become reinforcing because of their association with primary reinforcers.

- Positive punishment provides an unpleasant stimulus; negative punishment takes away a rewarding one. Both types lower the chances that a behavior will be repeated.
- Schedules of intermittent reinforcement provide reinforcements after either fixed of variable intervals of time or numbers of responses. Any intermittent reinforcement modifies behavior more effectively than continuous reinforcement.
- Shaping, or rewarding successive approximations of a behavior, uses operant conditioning principles to teach new behaviors. People and animals are limited in the behaviors they can learn, however, by their biological endowments.
- Learned helplessness occurs when previous learning that punishment is inescapable interferes with the later ability to learn how to avoid escapable punishment. It may be related to depression or the behavior of abuse victims.
- Insight learning and spatial navigation learning seem to take place in the absence of any obvious reinforcement.

Observational Learning

LEARNING OBJECTIVE 4   Define observational learning and summarize concerns about learning violent behavior from the media.

- Observational learning is learning by watching the behavior of others. We are likely to model, or imitate, others' behavior that we see rewarded.
- Many people are concerned that high levels of violence in the media encourage viewers to model such aggression. Studies about the causal nature of media encouraging violence have been inconclusive.

Factors that Aid Learning

LEARNING OBJECTIVE 5   Define massed and spaced practice and tell what conditions are best for learning semantic material, such as facts in your classes.

- Repeated, spaced practice aids learning of semantic material, such as classroom information.
- We can learn without paying attention and some tasks are easier to learn that way, but focused attention aids semantic learning.

When We Learn *What Happens in the Brain*

LEARNING OBJECTIVE 6   Define long-term potentiation and discuss synaptic changes that occur in learning.

- Long-term potentiation is a change in the ability of networks of neurons, in which the postsynaptic neuron becomes more active in response to certain presynaptic inputs.

- Learning may also be linked to the addition of more synapses in the brain, either through growing new neurons or by adding dendritic material to existing ones.
- Many regions of the brain, including the hippocampus, neocortex, and cerebellum, are involved in different types of learning and have been shown to exhibit LTP and neuron growth.

Prenatal and Postnatal Learning

LEARNING OBJECTIVE 7   Summarize the types of learning that occur before we are born and during postnatal life.

- We are capable of nonassociative learning, both habituation and sensitization, before birth, as well as basic associative learning, such as classical conditioning.
- We become capable of increasingly complex forms of learning as relevant areas of our brains mature after we are born.

Learning and Gender

LEARNING OBJECTIVE 8   Summarize gender differences in learning and discuss their potential sources.

- Studies show small, but consistent average differences between males and females in learning, with males performing better at spatial rotation tasks and females better at verbal learning. Males also tend to average higher mathematics scores on standardized tests. However, the range of abilities within a sex is much greater than the difference between males and females.
- Environmental factors, such as stereotype threat, may contribute these gender differences. Biological differences in stress reactions may also play a role in test-score differences.

Learning Disabilities

LEARNING OBJECTIVE 9   Define learning disabilities and describe major types of learning disabilities.

- A learning disability is a specific deficiency in one area of learning, while learning in other areas takes place normally. Dyslexia is a common disability in learning to read. Dyscalculia is a disability in learning mathematics.
- Attention Deficit Disorder (ADD) and Attention Deficit Hyperactivity Disorder (ADHD) affect concentration and can impair learning. Both are commonly treated with stimulant drugs. The use and misuse of these drugs raises many ethical concerns.

Key Terms

CUT/ACROSS CONNECTION

What Happens in the BRAIN?

- All types of learning actually involve changes in our brains, although different types of learning involve different brain regions.
- London taxicab drivers, who have intricate spatial knowledge of their cities, tend to have a larger hippocampus than people without similar geographical knowledge.
- Some research suggests that our brains might rehearse new information in our sleep, which could explain why sleep deprivation makes learning more difficult.

When Things Go Wrong

- Phobias might result from classical conditioning, in which we learn to respond with fear to something that isn't necessarily threatening. We can learn to extinguish phobic behavior, but can't "unlearn" the phobia.
  - We can learn a long-lasting aversion to a food if it makes us sick only once, even several hours after we eat it.
  - Learned helplessness might play a role in depression. If people have previously been unable to escape punishment, they may fail to act to escape unpleasant situations, even when it becomes possible.

HOW we Differ

- People who watch a lot of violent media or play violent videogames may be more likely to behave aggressively than those who watch less, but no definitive studies have shown this.
- There are very small average differences in learning between males and females, but average differences cannot help you predict how well any individual will learn.
- If we learn about a negative stereotype about a group to which we belong, our learning and performance often change to reflect that stereotype.

How we Develop

- We can learn simple associations before we are even born.
- Very early in life, we fail to display efficient complex learning, such as episodic or semantic learning. These forms of learning depend on further development of the hippocampus and neocortex.
- Reinforcement is generally more effective and ethical than punishment for teaching children.

Video Lab Exercise

Psychology Around Us

Bringing Learning and Conditioning Principles to Life

You Can So Teach an Old Dog New Tricks

We're constantly learning in life—learning new behaviors, new reactions, new lessons, new skills, and new ideas. Sometimes we are aware of it, sometimes not. We learn some things faster than others. And we learn better in some contexts than others. But we do indeed keep learning.

At the same time, we don't take advantage of every learning opportunity. Moreover, when we do learn something, it may not stay learned indefinitely. And, as we know all too well, we learn a lot of things (certain fears, for example) that we wish we hadn't learned.

This video lab exercise will bring learning principles to life by teaching you some new behaviors and skills—sometimes with your cooperation and sometimes in spite of yourself. And, by the way, while you're learning, you'll also be required to identify the conditioning principles and variables at play—just to show that you learned some new material while reading this chapter.

As you are working on this on-line exercise, consider the following questions:

- How readily does classical, operant, and observational learning occur?
- How easy is it to resist conditioning or, at the other end, to extinguish a newly-learned behavior or skill?
- How do attention, timing, and insight come into play?
- How can learning be enhanced?

CHAPTER 8

Memory

A Man with No Past

Now a cult classic, the 2000 film *Memento* fascinated viewers with a series of harrowing situations that confronted the main character, Leonard. In the movie, Leonard is looking for the person or people who attacked him and brutally murdered his wife. His search is hard and frightening, however, because the attack left Leonard unable to form new memories. To cope with this problem, Leonard takes Polaroid instant pictures and makes notes on them as he acquires information. He also tattoos on his body to help him put the puzzle together. Despite these efforts, however, scenes in the movie frequently open with Leonard being attacked by people he does not know or chased for reasons he cannot explain until he has time to piece the information together.

At the same time, Leonard finds himself confronted with other characters who may—or may not—have his best interests at heart as they try to "help" him along his way. On top of everything, Leonard has doubts. Given his own memory loss, how can he be sure that he didn't kill his wife and then somehow cause his own memory loss to protect himself from his guilt?

Consider everything that memory lets you do. Obviously there are the everyday tasks, such as passing tests, turning in a paper on time, or remembering a friend's birthday. But go deeper: Think of the things memory lets you do that you take for granted. Because of memory, you can have favorite foods, favorite musicians, favorite movies, and favorite TV shows. Not only can you remember friends' birthdays, you can also remember their typical behaviors and their preferences and then predict what they might want for their birthday.

You can go deeper still. If you did not somehow encode events and people in your mind, you would not know about anything that you were not directly sensing at that moment. You would only know what was in your line of sight and have no idea how the things that you were seeing connected to you or had any significance or meaning. Without memory, you would, like Leonard, be a stranger to yourself, unable to form the identity, or sense of self, that comes from linking one's present to one's past and using this information to make decisions about the future (Kihlstrom, Beer, & Klein, 2003). By keeping a record of our past, our memory takes us out of an infinite present.

memory the faculty for recalling past events and past learning.

encoding a basic activity of memory, involving the recording of information in our brain.

storage a basic activity of memory, involving retention of information for later use.

retrieval a basic activity of memory, involving recovery of information when we need it later.

information-processing model view of memory suggesting that information moves among three memory stores during encoding, storage, and retrieval.

parallel distributed-processing (PDP) (or connectionist) model theory of memory suggesting information is represented in the brain as a pattern of activation across entire neural networks.

What is Memory?

LEARNING OBJECTIVE 1 Define the basic activities of memory and describe two major models of memory.

Simply put, **memory** is the faculty for recalling past events and past learning. This definition is perhaps the only thing about memory that is simple. Although psychologists often differ in their ideas about memory, they generally agree that it involves three basic activities:

- *Encoding*—Getting information into memory in the first place
- *Storage*—Retaining memories for future use
- *Retrieval*—Recapturing memories when we need them

When, for example, you attend a musical concert, you may transform the sights and sounds produced by the performing band into a kind of memory code and record them in your brain (encoding). This information then remains stored in the brain until you retrieve it at later times—when, for example, you see photos of the band online, watch their music videos, or decide which of the band's songs to download. At such times of retrieval, the original concert event, including the feelings of exhilaration and discovery that you experienced at the concert, may come rushing back.

How do we manage to encode, store, and retrieve information? Psychologists have developed a number of models of explanation, including the *information-processing model* and the *parallel distributed-processing model*, or *connectionist model*.

The **information-processing model** of memory holds that information must pass through three stages, or systems, of mental functioning in order to become a firmly implanted memory—sensory memory, working memory, and long-term memory (see **Figure 8-1**) (Nee et al., 2008; Buchner & Brandt, 2003). When we first confront a stimulus, our brain retains a sensory image—or *sensory memory*—of it for less than a second. Sensory memories help us to keep alive a bit longer items that we have experienced briefly, so that we can, in a sense, decide whether to pay further attention to them. If, for example, we look up a person's e-mail address, our sensory memory records the address and quickly passes it on to our *working memory*. We can help

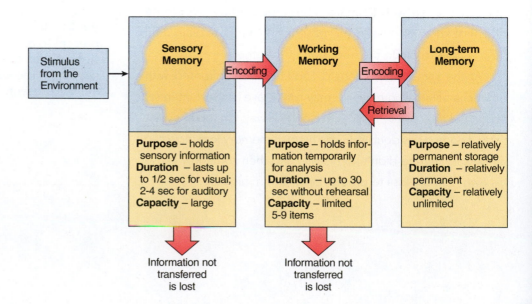

FIGURE 8-1 **The three-stage memory model** This model is a useful framework for thinking about the three basic memory stages. Each stage differs in purpose, duration, and capacity.

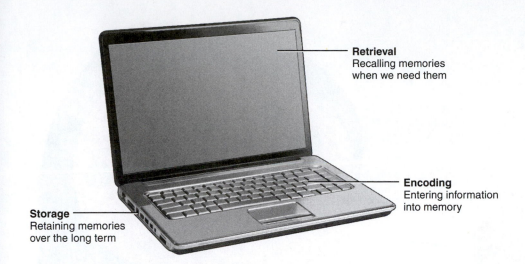

Retrieval
Recalling memories
when we need them

Encoding
Entering information
into memory

Storage
Retaining memories
over the long term

FIGURE 8-2 **Memory as a computer** In the information-processing model of memory, the basic memory stages are analogous to a computer: encoding allows us to enter information into our brain; storage to retain the information over the long term; and retrieval to call up the information as we need it.

retain the new address in working memory by concentrating hard and repeating it over and over as we address an e-mail or type it into our computer's address book. But working memory itself can hold only so much information at a time. It will eventually fail us and the information will disappear unless it is further passed on to our *long-term memory* system—the system that can retain a seemingly unlimited number of pieces of information for an indefinite period of time.

The three systems of memory proposed by the information-processing model are comparable to the operation of a computer (see **Figure 8-2**). Have you ever typed faster than your computer can process and then watched it spit out several characters at once? *Sensory memory* works in a similar way, giving us a quick copy of the information in our environment. In addition, information saved to *working memory* is equivalent to the information that a computer retains for as long as a document or website is open, but which disappears if you do not save it. And the final memory system, *long-term memory*, is the equivalent of the computer hard drive, storing information until something causes disruption or loss of the memory. These three systems are sometimes referred to as *memory stores*. The information-processing model has generated a great deal of research that we will explore further in the sections of this chapter that focus on encoding, storage, retrieval, and forgetting.

Although the information-processing model suggests that sensory memory, working memory, and long-term memory correspond roughly to computer memory structures, we need to be clear that this is just a metaphor. If you break open a computer, you can find the dedicated modules where the various forms of memory are in operation. When we look at the human brain, however, there are no equivalent dedicated structures where short-term memory and long-term memory exist.

Unlike the information-processing model, which suggests that information is stored and retrieved piece by piece, an alternative model of memory, the **parallel distributed-processing model (PDP),** or **connectionist model,** holds that newly encountered pieces of information immediately join with other, previously encountered pieces of relevant information to help form and grow networks of information (Rogers & McClelland, 2008). Such networks result in sophisticated memories, broad knowledge, and the ability to make better decisions and plans in life. Look, for example, at **Figure 8-3**. When the person in the figure sees an apple, connections to information involving things that are round, the color red, or possibly grandma (because of the apple tree in her backyard) are all activated, while other, less relevant connections are inhibited. These connections are all part of the network of information related to apples that this person has stored. When one part of the

> " Memory isn't like reading a book; it's more like writing a book from fragmentary notes. "
>
> —*John Kihlström, psychologist*

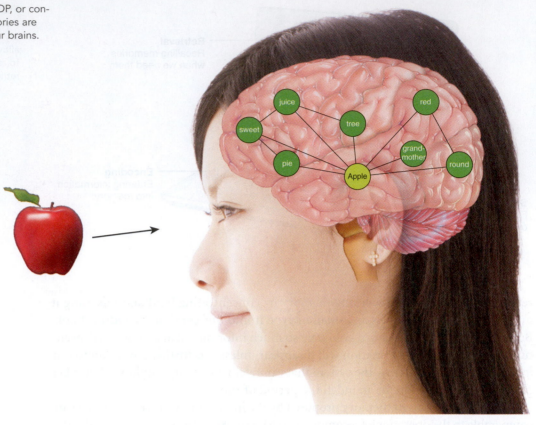

FIGURE 8-3 The PDP model of memory The PDP, or connectionist, model of memory suggests that memories are stored in a network of associations throughout our brains.

"apple" network is activated, related neurons throughout the brain also become active and richer memories spring forth. The PDP model of memory has gained many proponents, largely because its principles fit well with the field's growing recognition that neurons throughout our brains form networks of association as we respond to repeated learning experiences and events in life.

Before You Go On

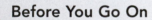

What Do You Know?

1. What are encoding, storage, and retrieval?

2. What are the three memory stores suggested by the information-processing model of memory?

What Do You Think?   Judging from your own experiences, do you think memory works more like a computer, with different memory stores, or more in a connectionist fashion? Could the two ideas both be useful in explaining some of your experiences?

How Do We Encode Information Into Memory?

LEARNING OBJECTIVE 2 Describe how information is encoded and transferred among different memory stores and what we can do to enhance encoding.

How many steps are there from the front door of your building to your room? Can't remember? How about an easier question: what was the first word you said yesterday morning? Most of us probably cannot recall an answer to either of these questions.

"As I get older, I find I rely more and more on these sticky notes to remind me."

Contestants in the annual USA National Memory Championship are asked to memorize thousands of numbers and words, pages of faces and names, lengthy poems, and decks of cards (Schacter, 2001). Would it surprise you to learn that a recent winner considers herself dangerously forgetful? That's right. "I'm incredibly absentminded," winner Tatiana Cooley told a reporter. Fearful that she will forget to carry out everyday tasks, Cooley depends on to-do lists and notes scribbled on sticky pads, "I live by Post-Its," she admitted ruefully.

The image of a National Memory Champion dependent on Post-Its in her everyday life has a paradoxical, even surreal quality: Why does someone with a capacity for prodigious recall need to write down anything at all? Can't she call on the same memory abilities and strategies that she uses to memorize hundreds of words or thousands of numbers to help remember that she needs to pick up a jug of milk at the store? Apparently not.

The kinds of everyday memory failures that Cooley seeks to remedy with Post-It notes—errands to run, appointments to keep, and the like—reflect *absentmindedness*: lapses of memory caused by inattentiveness, improper encoding, or carelessly overlooking available memories at the time of information retrieval.

Your lack of recall may be because the information was never *encoded,* or entered into your memory. Because we fail to encode many pieces of information that we come across in life, we do not actually remember most of the things that we experience. Encoding requires *attention*—that is, we need to focus on or notice the information in the first place. We can encode only what we attend to.

Using Automatic and Effortful Processing to Encode

We are not always aware that we are attending to things in our environment. Sometimes we attend to information—particularly, information about *time, space,* or *frequency*—without much conscious awareness and indeed with little or no effort. Even though you might not know how many steps there are from the front door of your building to the door of your room, you probably do not get lost very often along the way and you probably did not need to practice the route to figure out how to get to your room. The encoding process that allowed you to learn this basic route is called **automatic processing** (Hassin, 2005).

Although we use automatic processing to encode many kinds of information, the encoding of other information requires that we make conscious efforts and pay very close attention. This is the type of processing you are engaging in right now as you read this chapter, whether you are preparing for tomorrow's class or studying for a test. As you read through the present material, you are trying to find ways to bring this new information into your memory, because the facts won't settle there without your careful attention. This kind of encoding—which is typically needed when a person learns new information, such as new names, songs, or tasks—is called **effortful processing** (Hassin, 2005).

Keep in mind that whether we are encoding information through automatic or effortful processing, we must be paying attention. Our attention might be less apparent

> **"**The true art of memory is the art of attention.**"**
>
> *—Samuel Johnson, writer*

automatic processing encoding of information with little conscious awareness or effort.

effortful processing encoding of information through careful attention and conscious effort.

Memory buster This student's upcoming test performance is clearly at risk. *Effortful processing,* such as acquiring new information from a textbook, is easily disrupted when one also attends to other tasks during the encoding process.

in automatic processing, but if we do not attend sufficiently to information, in one way or another, we will simply not be able to encode it.

There are key differences between these two kinds of processing. First, the encoding of information by effortful processing tends to be disrupted when a person is forced to perform other tasks or to attend to other information while trying to encode the information at hand. You probably will not gather much from this book if you try to read it while carrying on a lively phone or text conversation, for example. In contrast, automatic processing, being so effortless, is disrupted only slightly by the performance of other tasks.

Second, as the name might suggest, putting extra effort into effortful processing makes it more effective. Automatic processing is not significantly enhanced by a person's extra efforts to attend and encode. You could go and rehearse the path from your front door to your room and count the steps, but it's unlikely that you'll know any more about the route than you knew this morning. In contrast, extra efforts can make an enormous difference in effortful processing. Reading over the material in this chapter again and again will affect considerably your ability to recall it on a test.

Encoding Information into Working Memory: Transferring from Sensory Memory into Working Memory

As we observed earlier, when we first confront a stimulus, our brains retain a very brief sensory image of it—an image called a **sensory memory**. If, for example, we are shown a photograph for just a moment, we retain a detailed image of all the shapes and items in the photograph for a few hundred milliseconds. Studies by researcher George Sperling in the late 1950s and early 1960s provided psychologists with important insights about how sensory memories operate (Sperling, 1960).

Sperling wanted to demonstrate the presence of a brief visual storehouse—equivalent to the buffer memory of a computer—that would hold a picture of our environment for a very brief period of time. He also wanted to measure how long this buffer would last. To do so, he exposed participants to a list of random letters, similar to what you might see on an eye chart (although always the same size) (**Figure 8-4**). He presented those letters extremely quickly and found that, generally speaking, participants did a pretty good job reporting the letters if asked to do so right away. The longer Sperling waited after showing the letters, however, the more performance declined. After about half a second, participants had trouble remembering any letters from the grid.

If we do not pay much attention to our sensory memories, as is usually the case, they will disappear forever. Those that are attended to, however, may enter the **working memory**, the second system of memory. Working memory serves several important functions in our day-to-day lives (Hambrick & Engle, 2003). One of the most important is that of enabling us to hold on to information—such as a phone number—that we need for short periods. We use working memory in this way much of the time. Whenever we read, for example, our working memory enables us to keep the beginning of a sentence in mind while we are reading the last part of the sentence, so that the whole phrase will make sense to us (Just & Carpenter, 2002). It also enables us to relate new sentences, such as this one, to previous sentences we have just read. Similarly, in a conversation, working memory helps us link new comments to previous ones so that we can follow what we are hearing.

```
K  Z  R  A

Q  B  T  P

S  G  N  Y
```

FIGURE 8-4 Test of sensory memory In his study of the duration of sensory memory, George Sperling flashed a chart of letters, similar to this one, for 1/20 of a second. He found that participants could recall almost all the letters in a particular row if asked to do so immediately, but half a second later, their performance declined.

One way of helping to make sure that information is encoded into working memory is **rehearsal**, consciously repeating the information. As far back as 400 B.C.E., the ancient Greek philosophers recognized the value of rehearsal in memory. They advised students to repeat whatever they heard, on the assumption that hearing and saying the same things would transfer new information into memory (Turkington & Harris, 2009, 2001). We are rehearsing when we keep repeating a phone number we've just heard until we can call it or add it to our phone's contact list. Such rehearsal increases the likelihood that the information will indeed enter our working memory and be available to us as we dial or punch in the phone number.

Encoding Information into Long-Term Memory: Transferring Working Memory into Long-Term Memory

Although concentrated efforts, such as rehearsal, can lengthen the availability of information in working memory, eventually that information is either passed on to the long-term memory system or lost (Jonides et al., 2008, 2003). It is in **long-term memory** that we hold all of the information we have gathered, available for use—often at a moment's notice—in a new situation or task. When we remember past events, previously-gathered information, people we once met, past feelings, or acquired skills, we are using our long-term memory system.

Just as rehearsal can help move information from the sensory memory system to the working memory system, it can help us move short-term, working memories into the long-term memory system (Neuschatz et al., 2005). Most of us rehearse information from a course's textbook and lectures, for example, when we are studying for an examination. Information passes into long-term memory best when our rehearsal sessions are spread out over a period of time rather than attempting to take in a great deal of information all at once. As we observed in Chapter 7, this phenomenon is known as the **spacing effect**. Thus, *distributed practice*, such as studying material weekly, followed by reviews closer to the time of an exam, is usually more profitable than *massed practice*, such as studying in one "cram" session just before the exam.

As we also saw in Chapter 7, sleep can help or hurt rehearsal. Information acquired in the hours before falling asleep tends to be encoded into long-term memory, as long as we have time to process it before sleep sets in (Backhaus et al, 2008; Stickgold & Walker, 2007). Information learned just as sleep is approaching is rarely retained, however, partly because we fall asleep before we can rehearse. Furthermore, information that comes to us during sleep—a language tape, for example—does not typically enter our memories at all.

In What Form is Information Encoded?

We must use some kind of code or representation to encode information. Different codes are available to us (Martin, 2009). When encoding information into working memory—for example, trying to keep a phone number in memory long enough to dial it—we can use a *phonological code*, repeating the sounds of the numbers again and again, or we can employ a *visual code*, holding an image of how the digits would look if written down. Research suggests that people tend to favor phonological codes when recording verbal information, such as digits, letters, and words. We rely more on visual codes for nonverbal information, such as a person's face or a speeding car (Just & Carpenter, 2002).

sensory memory memory involving detailed, brief sensory image or sound retained for a brief period of time.

working memory a short-term memory store that can hold about seven items at once.

rehearsal conscious repetition of information in an attempt to make sure the information is encoded.

long-term memory the memory system in which we hold all of the information we have previously gathered, available for retrieval and use in a new situation or task.

spacing effect facilitated encoding of material through rehearsal situations spread out over time.

Putting working memory to good use As people surf through TV channels with their valued remote control, they are making use of working memory. They must briefly remember each video snippet that they come across so that they can make a wise decision about what to watch for the next half-hour.

What subway? Because people tend to use semantic codes (codes based on meaning) to record important events into long-term memory, everyone at this nontraditional wedding in Beijing may later remember the day's events differently. A few may even leave out the fact that it took place on a subway platform!

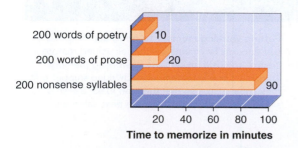

FIGURE 8-5 **Meaning matters in memory** Meaning helped people memorize poetry and prose much faster than nonsense syllables. (*Based on* Turkington & Harris, 2009, 2001)

Although adequate for most purposes, the phonological or visual codes that people use to record information in their working memory tend to be flawed. Some people, however, produce visual images with extraordinary detail and near-perfect accuracy. When recalling an object or scene that they have just witnessed, these people almost seem to be looking at a photograph. Thus their detailed images are called *eidetic memories*, or photographic memories. Eidetic memories usually occur among children: as many as 5 percent of children encode images with this level of detail. The eidetic images can last for several minutes (Hochman, 2001).

When we encode *nonverbal information* into long-term memory, we once again tend to use phonological or visual codes. Similarly, we may use olfactory, gustatory, or tactile codes to help record smells, tastes, or physical sensations. Long after a concert, for example, audience members may remember its intensity by visualizing images of the stage and the lighting effects, re-experiencing the smells of the arena and the crowd, and calling to mind the sounds of the musical instruments, the performers' voices, and the crowd's cheers.

In contrast, to encode *verbal information* into long-term memory, people tend to use **semantic codes**, representations based on the *meaning* of information. Because we often rely on the meaning of information when transferring items into long-term memory, our later recall of events may be flawed to some degree. Many a family gathering has been spent sharing different versions of an important event—for example, the day Sarah received the news that she was accepted into medical school. Everyone at the gathering may remember the key elements of that special day, but the specific memories of each person—from the size and thickness of the envelope that bore the announcement to the wording of the announcement or the exclamation of various family members—may differ dramatically. Why? In part, because each member used semantic coding to record the important family happening into their long-term memory.

It is worth noting that the various codes may operate simultaneously when information is being encoded (Kessels & Postma, 2002). One of these codes—semantic, phonological, or visual—may be used more actively than the others in particular instances, but when we use multiple codes, the combined impact of the these codes increases the likelihood and strength of the memory.

Meaning and Encoding Inasmuch as meaning often plays a key role in long-term memory, we should not be surprised that the more meaningful information is, the more readily it is encoded and later remembered. In one study, for example, people were asked to memorize 200 words of poetry, 200 nonsense syllables, and a 200-word prose passage (see **Figure 8-5**). The poetry took 10 minutes to learn and the prose less than 20 minutes, but the nonsense syllables took an hour and a half!

Similarly, the more meaningful a personal event, the more readily it is encoded and later remembered. Sarah's acceptance into medical school was recognized by everyone in the family as a significant turning point in her life. Thus, Sarah, her parents, and her siblings all remembered the day of her acceptance. A lesser event, such as a day at the circus or a trip to a department store, might not be encoded as readily.

People can help ensure that less meaningful information proceeds into long-term memory by artificially *adding* meaning to it (Ceci et al., 2003). Many a new music student, for example, has come to appreciate that the five lines of printed music of the treble clef are called *E-G-B-D-F*, by first tying those letters to the sentence "*Every Good Boy Does Fine*." The first letter of each word in the sentence is the same as one of the lines of printed music. By giving more meaning to the musical language, the sentence helps the students to encode the information into their long-term memory.

As we have seen, you can use the technique of *elaboration,* or *elaborative rehearsal,* to impose meanings on seemingly unrelated pieces of information, such as the names of musical notes. Many mnemonic systems, based on processes and principles discovered by memory researchers, rely on elaboration to help you better encode, store, and retrieve information that you need to remember (Cavallini et al., 2003; Ceci et al., 2003; Kail, 2003).

One of the best ways to elaborate is by making the target information personally meaningful. For example, if you want to remember the difference between the spelling of the words *dessert* (a treat that follows a meal) and *desert* (a dry, hot, arid place), you might say to yourself, "I like something super sweet after dinner," to remind you that the food item is spelled with a double *s.*

Two other mnemonic techniques involve *imagery,* taking a mental picture of something meaningful to you and using information from the picture to increase your memory potential.

- *Key Word Method* This visualization method was developed by researcher Richard Atkinson (1975) for the learning of foreign-language words. A student trying to learn Spanish, for example, will think about an image that ties the Spanish word to an English key word that sounds similar to a portion of the foreign word. The Spanish word *caballo,* which means "horse," sounds like *eye* in its middle syllable. So a student might imagine a horse kicking a giant eye. When confronted with the word *caballo,* the sound of the key word, *eye,* should cue the student to see the image in his or her mind and to retrieve the information that *caballo* means "horse." In one experiment, students who were instructed to use this method of study scored an average of 88 percent correct on a test, while those who studied by repetition alone for the same duration scored only 28 percent correct (Pressley, Levin, & Delaney, 1982; Raugh & Atkinson, 1975). The method has also proven helpful in studying unfamiliar vocabulary within a student's native language, such as medical terms (Troutt-Ervin, 1990).

- *Method of Loci* This method (*loci* is Latin for "places") can help you remember information that must be recalled in a specific order, such as a list of words. First, imagine a place that you know well, such as your home. Visualize the layout of that place as you walk through it. At home, for example, you might imagine yourself walking through the front door, past a couch, toward a round table, then past a television set, and finally into the kitchen. Next, form a picture in your mind that connects each word or object to a location in the house. If the first word on a list to be remembered is *cat,* you might imagine a cat scratching at the front door, for example. Once you have tied the items on the list to these images and practiced them, you can mentally walk through the "place" and list the items one-by-one in the correct order.

Such applications are known as **mnemonic devices.** Similarly, if people *elaborate* on the meaning of information, they increase the likelihood that it will be encoded into long-term memory. Throughout this book, we include relevant examples that we hope will make the information more applicable and more relevant and, in turn, make your memories more accessible.

semantic code cognitive representation of information or an event based on the meaning of the information.

mnemonic devices techniques used to enhance the meaningfulness of information, as a way of making them more memorable.

As you know by now, organizing information is necessary for the proper storage and retrieval of memories. *Chunking* is one way of organizing information to help enhance memory. Another organizational technique—organizing a list of unrelated words into a story—has also been shown to be very successful. In one study, participants who used this approach were able to recall, on average, over 90 percent of the words presented to them from twelve lists, compared to only 10 percent recalled by participants who did not use this approach.

A third way to organize new material is to create a *hierarchy* of the information, separating it into sections and subsections, much like the chapter of a textbook. For example, if you need to memorize the names of all the muscles of the body for an anatomy class, you might group them according to their locations or by their actions.

One very useful study technique for helping readers—such as yourself—to learn and remember textbook information is, once again, based on the principle of organization (West et al., 2008). The **PQRST** method is named for its five steps, which are to be undertaken in order.

- *Preview* Skim the entire section you are required to learn. Look for the basic themes, and try to get a rough idea of the information you will have to process when reading the section in more detail. If you were reading a section of a textbook about the assassination of U.S. President John F. Kennedy, your preview might focus on figuring out the principal events and people involved in the assassination.
- *Question* Examine the organization of the section and turn each subsection into a question that you want to answer over the course of your reading. If one of the subheads was, "The Assassination of an Assassin," ask yourself, "How did the assassin of President Kennedy come to be killed himself?"
- *Read* Read the section with the goal of finding the answers to your questions.
- *Self-Recitation* Ask yourself and answer aloud a set of questions that arose from the reading material, such as: "Who shot John Kennedy?" and "From what location was he shot?"
- *Test* Test yourself by trying to recall as much of the learned information as you can.

By organizing your reading in this way—by asking yourself questions about the information at hand before, during, and after reading—you stand a better chance of retaining the information than if you were to spend your time simply reading through the section several times.

Organization and Encoding   Another important variable that can enhance the encoding of information into long-term memory is *organization*. Actually, when people add to or elaborate on the meaning of certain pieces of information or events, they are organizing them. That is, they are giving the information a structure that is more familiar and available to them. As such, they are making it easier to encode into long-term memory. Typically, people do this intuitively. If we asked you to memorize a list of words that included FOX, BEAR, ITALY, ENGLAND, RABBIT, SPAIN, and MOUSE, you might naturally sort the words into rough categories of "Animals" and "European Countries."

Organization by categories can be particularly useful in helping us to encode complicated situations. Cognitive psychologists have identified structures called **schemas**, knowledge bases that we develop based on prior exposure to similar experiences or other knowledge bases. Schemas can be helpful in allowing us to attend to and encode a lot of information in a hurry. Think about the first time you walked into a new restaurant. Did it feel awkward or strange because you weren't sure of the rules or what to order? If you had visited other, similar restaurants before that one, the schemas you developed during your experiences at those restaurants probably helped you know what to do and what to order in the new restaurant with less effort than you would have needed if you had never been in a restaurant at all.

In need of a schema This young patron seems confused about how things work at Round House Restaurant in Brno, Czech Republic. His previous restaurant schemas simply have not prepared him for the Round House's unusual use of a model train to deliver food and drinks to its customers.

Before You Go On

What Do You Know?

3. How does increased attention affect automatic and effortful processing?
4. Why is it more effective to study all term long, rather than in one massive session right before a final exam?
5. Which type of coding would most people use to remember someone's face? Which type would most people use to remember a person's name?

What Do You Think? As we noted earlier in the chapter, the author Samuel Johnson wrote, "The true art of memory is the art of attention." Can you think of experiences from your own or others' lives that bring this statement to life?

How Do We Store Memories?

LEARNING OBJECTIVE 3 Describe how we organize and store information in working and long-term memory and how we can enhance our long-term memories.

As you have seen, after entering the working memory system, information remains there for only a short period of time, sometimes only a matter of seconds. In contrast, when information moves on to the long-term memory system, it can remain there for hours or a lifetime. The retention of information—whether brief or long—in either of these memory systems is called **storage**.

Storage in Working Memory

Information may enter working memory from two major sources. New information, as we have seen, can be encoded after a short trip through the sensory memory system. In addition, we can bring back into the working memory system information that previously has been encoded in the long-term memory system, for use in a current situation or task.

schemas knowledge bases that we develop based on prior exposure to similar experiences or other knowledge bases.

storage the retention of information—whether brief or long—in either working memory or long-term memory.

During the time that information from either of these sources is residing in the working memory system, it can, as we have seen, serve many important functions in our daily lives, from enabling us to read or carry on conversations to helping us solve current problems. The information stored in working memory also helps us do mental computations, such as mathematical problems (Maybery & Do, 2003). We could not, for example, add together the numbers 12 plus 13 if our working memory were not reminding us that we are computing those particular numbers, that addition is the task at hand, and that 3 plus 2 equals 5 and 10 plus 10 equals 20. In fact, because working memory helps us do mental computations, it is often characterized as a "temporary notepad" that briefly retains intermediate information while we think and solve larger problems.

Research suggests that memory and related cognitive functions peak at approximately age 25 (McGaugh, 2003, 1999).

The Storage Limits of Working Memory

Once information enters working memory, it can be stored for just a limited period of time (Just & Carpenter, 2002). Concentrated efforts, such as rehearsal can lengthen the availability of information in working memory, but eventually it is either passed on to the long-term memory system or lost (Jonides et al., 2008, 2003).

Just as striking as the limited *duration* of working memory is its limited *capacity*. On average, only five to nine items can be stored there at a given moment. This number was first uncovered back in 1885 by the German researcher Hermann Ebbinghaus (1850–1909) who pioneered memory research by studying his own memory, and it was confirmed over 70 years later by psychologist George Miller (1956).

In a typical study of this phenomenon, researchers present people with a sequence of unrelated digits, letters, words, or the like, and then ask them to restate the items in the correct order. Because the items are unrelated and presented rapidly, it is likely that this procedure is tapping into the storage capacity of working memory only, not into some related information that has been stored in long-term memory. In study after study, almost every adult can recall sequences that consist of five items, but very few can recall lists consisting of more than nine items. Each individual displays his or her own **memory span**—the maximum number of items that can be recalled in the correct order—but no memory span strays very far from seven. Because research shows that almost everyone has a working memory capacity in this range, Miller described it as the "magical number seven, plus or minus two."

Enhancing Working Memory

Actually, the storage capacity of working memory is not quite as limited as it may seem from the Ebbinghaus and Miller studies. Each of the seven or so items that working memory holds can consist of more than a single digit, letter, or word. An item can consist of a "chunk" of information. **Chunking** pieces of information together into larger units enables us to encode more information in our working memory system, and it also enables our working memory to store more information at a given moment.

Let us say that we are presented with a string of 23 letters, *o-u-t-l-a-s-t-d-r-i-v-i-n-g-n-i-g-h-t-w-a-s-i*. Because our capacity in working memory is only 7 ± 2 items, we would, on the face of it, be unable to store this entire sequence of items. If, however, we recognized that these letters can be chunked into words—"out," "last," "driving," "night," "was," and "I"—our task changes. We now need to store only 6 items (that is, 6 words) in working memory, rather than 23, and the task becomes manageable. In fact, these words can be further chunked into one item: the sentence "Last night I was out driving." If we store the information in this way, we still have room in our working memory for several other items. Similarly, without realizing it, we may be taking advantage of chunking when we first try to master a song's lyrics. Rather than learn the song letter by letter or word by word, we may hold on to seven new lines at a time, repeating the lines again and again until we "nail" them.

memory span maximum number of items that can be recalled in correct order.

chunking grouping bits of information together to enhance ability to hold that information in working memory.

explicit memory memory that a person can consciously bring to mind, such as one's date of birth.

implicit memory memory that a person is not consciously aware of, such as learned motor behaviors, skills, and habits.

Our ability to chunk actually comes from our long-term memory system (Cowan & Chen, 2009). Recall that information may enter working memory as either new information arriving from sensory memory or through retrieval from long-term memory. In chunking, we use our stored, long-term knowledge that certain letters spell certain words or that words can be organized to form sentences to guide us in chunking new information.

Storage in Long-Term Memory

Whereas the sensory memory and working memory systems deal only with a limited number of short-term memories, our long-term memory system retains a seemingly unlimited number of pieces of information for an indefinite period of time, extending from minutes to a lifetime (Nairne, 2003). Indeed, memory researcher Elizabeth Loftus has estimated that our long-term memory system may hold as many as one quadrillion separate pieces of information. This expansive capacity and duration is critical to our functioning, for it is in this vast memory store that we hold—ready for use—all of the information that we have ever gathered. When we remember previously-gathered knowledge, past events and people, or acquired skills, we are using our long-term memory system.

Several factors influence whether particular events are stored in long-term memory. As we have observed, new information must first be attended to in order to have any chance of eventually winding up in this memory system. Furthermore, items that are attended to must be encoded and briefly stored in working memory and then encoded into long-term memory before they can be stored in this memory system (Ceci et al., 2003). Any shortcomings in these attention and encoding activities may prevent the information from being stored in the long-term system (McGaugh, 2003). Moreover, even after information is successfully stored in long-term memory, some of it may become inaccessible (Loftus & Loftus, 1980). That is, some of the information that we have previously acquired cannot be retrieved from long-term memory. Most of the research on long-term memory storage, including the loss of stored information, has been conducted in the biological realm, as we shall soon see.

We have observed that the number of items that can be stored in working memory is rather similar from person to person (7 ± 2). The capacity for long-term memory storage, while enormous for most of us, does, however, vary greatly among people. The differences from person to person may be due to factors, such as attention and the ability to move information from working memory to long-term memory.

Surveys indicate that 16 percent of adults have forgotten their wedding anniversaries (22 percent of men and 11 percent of women). People married only a few years are as likely to forget as those married for many years (Kanner, 1995).

What Types of Memories Do We Store in Long-Term Memory?

Various kinds of information are stored in long-term memory, as shown in **Figure 8-6**. **Explicit memories** consist of the types of memories that you can consciously bring to mind, such as your mother's birthday, or the movie discussed at the beginning of this chapter. But there are other types of memories that we are not consciously aware of, such as learned motor behaviors and perceptual information that help us to develop various skills and habits. These **implicit memories** might include reacting with disgust when you are given a plate of food that made you sick sometime in the past—you might not recall the initial bad meal, but you remember to avoid the food.

Neuroimaging studies of patients with brain damage suggest that these two kinds of information are stored in different brain regions (Kandel, 2007; Squire & Schacter, 2002). Explicit memories are converted into long-term memories in the hippocampus and then are stored permanently in various areas of the neocortex.

FIGURE 8-6 **The long-term memories we store** Our long-term memories are of two main types, with various subdivisions within each.

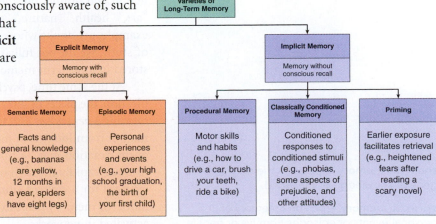

Explicit versus implicit memories (Left) The many details of Star Trek movies that this onlooker and other Trekkies love to recall are *explicit* memories. (Right) In contrast, the learned motor behaviors and perceptual information that enable this skateboarder to artfully do her thing are *implicit* memories.

(In a sense, the hippocampus serves as a temporary storage site within the long-term explicit memory system). In contrast, the striatum, the region located toward the midline in the brain, plays a key role in the storage of implicit memories. As we observed in Chapters 4 and 7, when people need to call upon implicit memories to help them carry out various skills and habits, their striatum and its related structures become particularly active. In fact, an individual whose striatum is damaged by injury or disease may have enormous difficulty performing longtime skills and habits, yet retain most of his or her explicit memories.

To make things even a bit more complicated, there are two types of explicit memories: **semantic memories**, your general knowledge, and **episodic memories**, knowledge of personal episodes from your own life. Some studies further hint that these two subgroups of explicit memories may, themselves, be stored in different ways from one another, but this possibility is far from certain (Rugg et al., 2003).

How Are Long-Term Memories Organized? How does the long-term memory system organize the many pieces of information that are stored there? Is it set up like a bookstore in which the various items are organized first by broad categories, such as fiction and nonfiction, then by subcategories (in the case of nonfiction, for example, "art," "health," "nature," "science," or "travel"), and finally by sub-subcategories (for example, art books whose authors' names begin with *A, B*, and so on)? Despite years of study, we do not fully understand how pieces of information are organized when stored in long-term memory.

At the same time, psychologists do now know that, regardless of their precise organization, the pieces of information stored in long-term memory are linked to each other, forming a *network of interwoven associations*. Thus, when we retrieve one piece of information from long-term memory, a related one will often spring forth, and that piece of information may, in turn, trigger another one. This web of associations enables us to travel rapidly through our long-term memory to retrieve much of the information we need for a current situation or task. As we saw earlier, the PDP, or connectionist, model of memory helps explain such networks by suggesting that our neurons also are activated in networks.

semantic memory a person's memory of general knowledge of the world.

episodic memory a person's memory of personal events or episodes from his or her life.

Before You Go On

What Do You Know?

6. What is chunking, and why would you want to use it?
7. What kind of information is stored in semantic memory and episodic memory? Are semantic and episodic memories implicit or explicit memories?

What Do You Think? What are some examples of elaboration and organizational strategies that have helped you in school or other areas of your life? What new ones are you going to try after reading this chapter?

How Do We Retrieve Memories?

LEARNING OBJECTIVE 4 Describe how we retrieve information from memory and how retrieval cues, priming, context, and emotion can affect retrieval.

As we have noted, when information is successfully encoded from working memory into long-term memory, it is not only stored there, but is available for retrieval later. When we retrieve information from our long-term memory, it moves to the front and center of our thinking and becomes available once again for use in our working memory system. Upon its return to working memory, the retrieved information may be used to help clarify current issues, solve new problems, or simply re-experience past events (Hambrick & Engle, 2003; Cook, 2001). Retrieved memories of past political readings and experiences may, for example, enable us to push the right lever in a voting booth. Similarly, retrieved memories of learned math tables help us calculate new mathematical problems, and retrieved memories of how to drive guide us to park our cars in tight spaces. The kind or amount of information stored in long-term memory would mean little if we were unable to retrieve it. Like a library or the Internet, the information in long-term memory must be navigated efficiently and accurately in order to yield needed information.

Just as researchers do not fully understand how information is organized when stored in long-term memory, they do not know for sure how retrieval is carried out. Some theorists propose that it is a kind of "search" process (Raaijmakers & Shiffrin, 2002, 1992). In other words, the person focuses on a specific question and scans his or her memory for the specific answer to that question. Other theorists believe that retrieval is more like an "activation" process in which the questions people pose to themselves activate relevant pieces of information that have been stored in long-term memory, after which this activation then spreads *simultaneously* to every other associated piece of information. The difference between these two operations is akin to the difference between the specific results you get on a Wikipedia search versus the hundreds of results you get from a Google search.

If we fail to locate a particular book in a library or bookstore, it can mean either that the book is not there or that we are looking for it in the wrong section. Similarly, our failure to locate a piece of information in our long-term memory may mean that it is not stored there (encoding failure or storage loss) or that we have committed a *retrieval failure* of some kind.

"And here I am at two years of age. Remember? Mom? Pop? No? Or how about this one. My first day of school. Anyone?"

retrieval cues words, sights, or other stimuli that remind us of the information we need to retrieve from our memory.

priming activation of one piece of information, which in turns leads to activation of another piece, and ultimately to the retrieval of a specific memory.

recognition tasks memory tasks in which people are asked to identify whether or not they have seen a particular item before.

recall tasks memory tasks in which people are asked to produce information using little or no retrieval cues.

We experience many retrieval failures in our daily travels. Often we find ourselves unable to recall a face, an event, or a scheduled appointment, yet it comes to mind later. Obviously the information was available in our memory all along, or we would not recall it later. Similarly, all of us have experienced the frustration of being unable to recall the answer to an exam question, only to remember it soon after the test. And in some instances we may become particularly frustrated when a piece of information feels right at the edge of our consciousness, an experience called the *tip-of-the-tongue* phenomenon.

The retrieval of information from memory is facilitated by **retrieval cues**—words, sights, or other stimuli that remind us of the information that we need. Essentially, when we come across a retrieval cue, we enter our long-term memory system and activate a relevant piece of information. Because the pieces of information in this memory system are linked to each other in a network of associations, the activation of the first piece of information will trigger the activation of related pieces until a complete memory emerges.

Priming and Retrieval

If the pieces of information stored in long-term memory are indeed linked together in a network of associations, then the key to retrieving a specific memory is to locate one piece of information and follow associated pieces until arriving at the memory. This activation of one piece of information, which then triggers the activation of other pieces and leads to the retrieval of a specific memory, is called **priming** (Ramponi et al., 2007). Sometimes we consciously try to prime a memory. If, for example, we are having trouble remembering the name of a woman whom we met last week, we may bring the letter *M* to mind, recalling vaguely that her name began with that letter and hoping that the *M* sound will lead to her name. Or we may try to recall our conversation with the nameless acquaintance, hoping that this recollection will eventually lead us back to her name.

Priming may also take place without our conscious awareness. Say you are in a store and you vaguely notice the classic jazz standard *Summertime* playing on the store's sound system. If you were to walk out of the store and a friend were to ask you what song had just been playing on the store's speaker, you might not be able to recall it. However, if a short while later, in an unlikely turn of events, a quiz show host were to pop up and ask you to name three classic jazz songs for $500, research suggests that you would be particularly likely to include *Summertime* in your answer. Although you had no choice in the matter and were not even aware that it was happening—and even if you dislike jazz and were trying to ignore the song while in the store—it would have served as a retrieval cue and primed you to recall *Summertime* when later quizzed about jazz hits.

Given the operation of priming, we should not be surprised that the more retrieval cues we encounter, or the more informative they are, the better our retrieval of memory. This is why people perform better on **recognition tasks**, ones in which they must report whether or not they have seen a particular item before, than on **recall tasks**, those in which they are forced to produce memories using no or few retrieval cues (**Figure 8-7**) (Turkington & Harris, 2009, 2001; Tulving, 1974). If you are asked to name everyone who was enrolled in your tenth-grade history class—a recall task—you will probably be able to remember some of the individuals, but far from all of them. If, on the other hand, you are shown pictures one-by-one from your high school yearbook and asked to point to, identify, and name those individuals who were in your history class—a recognition task—you probably will perform better. The reason? The latter task offers more retrieval cues. Not surprisingly, students usually perform better on multiple-choice exams, which are recognition tasks, than on essay or short-answer exams, which are recall tasks.

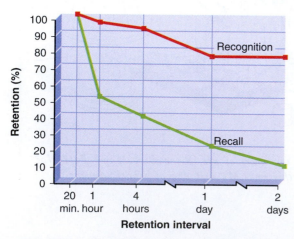

FIGURE 8-7 Recognition versus recall In one study of retrieval, participants were tested for either recognition or recall of nonsense syllables over the course of two days. Retrieval on the recognition test was far superior than on the recall test. (*Data from:* Schwanenflugel et al., 1992; Luh, 1922)

"Oh, yes, I remember them well" If asked to name several members of the Chicago Bulls 1998 championship team (a *recall task*), even ardent basketball fans will have difficulty. If, however, they were shown this team photo (a *recognition task*), many fans would readily come up with such names as Phil Jackson (top row) and Michael Jordan, Scotty Pippen, and Dennis Rodman (bottom row).

Context and Retrieval

It is often easier to retrieve particular information when we return to the setting or situation in which we first encoded it. Most of us have had personal experiences that attest to this. Upon returning to our old home or school, for example, we may find ourselves almost overrun by memories of events that we have not thought about for years. Similarly, a return to the scene of an argument or romantic encounter may evoke detailed memories of the original event. Not surprisingly, then, some educators believe that people perform best on exams when the exams are administered in the same rooms where the material was taught.

Clearly, returning to or duplicating the *context* in which information was learned may help us to retrieve it (Postle, 2003). Why? Once again, the answer appears to be retrieval cues. The original context, the location or situation in which we learn material, is loaded with retrieval cues, each of which activates a piece of information, setting off the activation of associated pieces and leading to memories of the original event. The likely impact of these many retrieval cues is an increase in the number, intensity, and accuracy of relevant memories.

Emotion: A Special Retrieval Cue

Just as a letter, word, song, or setting may serve as a retrieval cue and lead to specific memories, so may an emotional state, or mood. If people learn something while in a particular state of mind, they may recall it more readily when they are in that state again. Gordon Bower was one of the first psychologists to recognize this phenomenon, called

It is not always possible to return to the original site of our learning. In such cases, one can mentally revisit the context. If, in an exam, you are unable to remember something you learned in a class, perhaps you should imagine the classroom and try to hear in your mind the instructor's voice telling you the information.

state-dependent memory memory retrieval facilitated by being in the same state of mind in which you encoded the memory in the first place.

flashbulb memory detailed and near-permanent memories of an emotionally significant event, or of the circumstances surrounding the moment we learned about the event.

forgetting the inability to recall information that was previously encoded into memory.

state-dependent memory (Bower, 2008, 1981; Forgas, 2008). In one study, he had people learn a list of words while they were in a hypnotically induced happy state of mind. He found that they remembered the words better if they were in a happy mood when tested later than if they were in a sad mood. Conversely, those who learned the words when in a sad mood recalled them better if they were sad during later testing than if they were happy. Apparently, a feeling can serve as a cue for retrieving information that was encoded while experiencing that feeling.

Some theorists further believe that a person's emotions may be more than just another retrieval cue (McGaugh, 2003). As we shall see in the following sections, they suggest that strong emotions may enhance memories by leading to increased *rehearsal, elaboration,* and *organization* of a particular event, or that intense emotions may trigger a *special memory mechanism*, producing emotional memories.

Emotional Memory: Rehearsal, Elaboration, and Organization   If an event makes us particularly happy, or for that matter, distinctly upset, we will probably think about it again and again. We are likely to talk about highly emotional events with friends and relatives, perhaps write about them in a personal journal, or even try to revisit the scene or recreate the context of the event. Such behaviors are commonly displayed by people who have achieved a special personal accomplishment, observers of exciting sporting events, or victims of accidents, hurricanes, or other catastrophes, Together, responses of this kind amount to repeated rehearsals, elaborations, and organization of the emotionally-charged events. Think back to Sarah's medical school acceptance. Talking about the day with her relatives not only helped Sarah repeat the event, but probably also helped her link it to other important events in the family and to organize her recall of the event, perhaps chronologically from the moment the acceptance letter arrived until the moment she read it. We have seen already that rehearsal, elaboration, and organization all are ways to improve the encoding and storage of memories; thus, we should not be surprised that exciting or upsetting events tend to be retrieved more readily than bland ones (McGaugh, 2003).

Special Emotional Memory Mechanisms: Flashbulb Memories   If we were asked where we were at 9:00 A.M. a few Tuesdays back, what we were doing, and who we were talking to, few of us would be able to answer off the top of our heads. Yet, if we were asked the same questions about our whereabouts on Tuesday, September 11, 2001, at 9:00 A.M., the fateful hour when two planes crashed into and brought down the twin towers of the World Trade Center, many of us could state with apparent accuracy and remarkable confidence these and other details (Romeu, 2006; Pezdek, 2003). Such detailed and near-permanent memories of emotionally significant events, or of the circumstances surrounding our learning of the events, are called **flashbulb memories**. Beyond widely shared events, such as the 9/11 attacks, people also have flashbulb memories of emotional events that have more personal significance, such as the birth or death of a loved one.

The kinds of details retained in flashbulb memories seem unavailable to us in our memories of other events (Edery-Halpern & Nachson, 2004). What is it about these special events that enables us to retrieve such details? According to some theorists, it is the extraordinary level of emotionality that we experience during the event. Specifically, our intense emotions may help trigger a special memory mechanism—a mechanism above and beyond the usual memory processes—that produces a near-permanent record and more likely retrieval of nearly everything we encountered during the event (McGaugh, 2003).

This proposed memory mechanism has yet to be fully identified, but certain studies do support the notion that emotionally-charged memories involve mechanisms beyond those operating for more neutral memories (Kensinger & Corkin, 2003). In one

The ultimate flashbulb memory Most people have detailed memories of their whereabouts and actions on September 11, 2001. Flashbulb memories of this kind are helped along by the extraordinary level of emotionality that people experience during the event.

study, for example, some participants were given a tranquilizer drug while hearing an emotional story about a boy who received emergency surgery, whereas other participants were given a placebo drug during the same story (Cahill et al., 1994). One week later, the participants who had been tranquilized—and due to the tranquilizer, had experienced little emotionality during the intense story—remembered less about the story than did the placebo participants, whose emotions had been allowed to rise during the story. In contrast, when the study's participants were asked to recall a more neutral story, participants from both groups showed equal accuracy in their later recollections (**Figure 8-8**).

On the other hand, some recent research has called into question whether flash-bulb memories are, in fact, as highly accurate as they have been purported to be (Marsh, 2007). One study, for example, compared undergraduates' memories of the 9/11 attacks with their memories of everyday events (Talarico & Rubin, 2007, 2003). Although the participants in the study reported a high level of confidence in the accuracy of their 9/11 memories, the data indicated that, in fact, such memories were no more accurate than those of more neutral events.

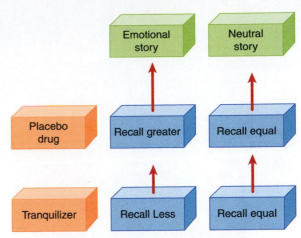

FIGURE 8-8 Emotional arousal and memory In Cahill's study of emotion's role in memory, participants heard either an emotional or neutral story. Those given a tranquilizer while hearing the emotional story recalled less than those given the placebo. However, both groups recalled the same for the neutral story.

Before You Go On

What Do You Know?

8. If researchers show people several pictures of small rodents, then find that a lot of people include hamsters and mice when asked to name animals that make good pets, what has happened? Why did it happen?
9. Why do many educators believe it is helpful to take an exam in the same room where you learned the material?
10. How do strong emotions affect our memory processes?

What Do You Think?   Have you experienced flashbulb memories or state-dependent memory? If so, when?

Why Do We Forget and Misremember?

LEARNING OBJECTIVE 5 Summarize key theories of why we forget information and sometimes distort or manufacture memories.

Throughout most of this chapter, we have considered which variables help us to accurately remember events and information. But as you well know, people do not always remember things as well as they would like. The elusive name, the missed meeting, and the overlooked birthday of a friend or relative are all instances of **forgetting**—the inability to recall information that was previously encoded. Sometimes we not only forget information, we distort or manufacture memories. We recall events differently from the way in which they occurred or we remember things that never occurred at all.

Theories of Forgetting

As we have observed, some apparent losses of memory are not really instances of forgetting at all, but rather failures of attention. If our mind is elsewhere when we are putting down a set of keys or a treasured remote control, we simply cannot encode such acts. Correspondingly, the location of such items will not be stored in memory and available for later retrieval. At the other end of the spectrum, some material is indeed stored and available, but has weak or few retrieval cues attached to it, making it difficult for people to activate—or prime—the relevant memories from storage.

Beyond these common causes of forgetting, theorists have uncovered a number of variables that may actively interfere with memory and, in turn, produce forgetting (Wixted, 2004). Each of today's leading explanations of forgetting has received some research support, but as you will see, each also has key limitations and raises significant questions.

Decay   As we observed earlier, German researcher Herman Ebbinghaus pioneered the study of forgetting over a century ago by systematically testing his own memory of lists of syllables (for example, *lin, wee, sul*). After rehearsing and mastering a particular list, Ebbinghaus would measure how well he had retained the syllables after various intervals of time: twenty minutes, two days, a month later, and so on. He found that there was a huge drop in his retention of a list soon after learning it. However, the amount that he forgot eventually leveled off; in fact, most of the information that had been retained ten hours after first memorizing a list remained in his memory three weeks later. Known as the *"forgetting curve"* (see **Figure 8-9**), this pattern of rapid memory loss followed by a stable retention of the remaining information has been supported again and again by research (Deffenbacher et al., 2008).

Many theorists explain patterns of forgetting, such as that observed by Ebbinghaus, by pointing to *decay*. According to the **decay theory,** memories often fade away on their own simply because they are neglected or not used for a long period of time (Wixted, 2004; McGaugh, 2003). This theory is built on the notion that memories leave a physical trace in the brain—a so-called *memory trace*—when they are acquired. Theoretically, these traces fade away over time if the person does not use them.

Decay theory is not as popular an explanation for forgetting as it once was. It cannot account for the repeated finding that people learn seemingly forgotten information or skills much more rapidly the second time around than the first time. In other words, *relearning* is faster than initial learning. If forgotten information has, in fact, eroded because of disuse—that is, if memory traces have been lost—relearning should be occurring from scratch, and it should take just as long as the initial learning did.

Interference   According to the **interference theory**, forgetting is affected primarily by what happens to people before or after they learn information. This theory holds that information will be retained in memory as long as competing, similar information does not interfere with it (Wixted, 2004). Suppose your friend moves to a new house and receives a new telephone number in which the first three digits are the same as the old number. Perhaps when dialing the new number, you find yourself mistakenly dialing her old number. According to the interference theory, the new phone number was forgotten because competing information—the old number—interfered with its retrieval.

When the competing information that prevents recall has been learned *before* the forgotten item, as in the case of the forgotten phone number, the process is called **proactive interference**. Alternatively, **retroactive interference** occurs when new information disrupts the retrieval of previously learned information (see **Figure 8-10**). Suppose, for example, you wish to call your friend's old number—perhaps to reach her mother who is still living at the old location—but you mistakenly dial the new number. In this scenario, you forgot the old number because competing information—the new number—interfered with its retrieval.

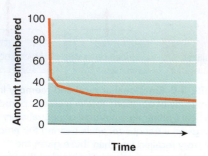

FIGURE 8-9 **The forgetting curve** We forget a great deal very rapidly but the forgetting levels off and the amount of information we retain stabilizes.

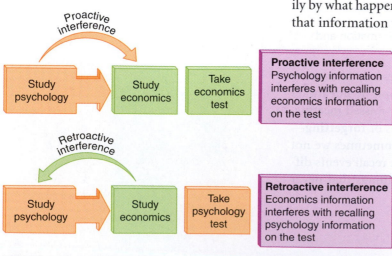

FIGURE 8-10 **Proactive and retroactive interference** Forgetting is affected by interference from other information. Proactive interference occurs when information already learned interferes with learning new information; retroactive interference occurs when new information disrupts recalling previously learned information.

Proactive interference Psychology information interferes with recalling economics information on the test

Retroactive interference Economics information interferes with recalling psychology information on the test

Can you spell "anxiety"? Two children each await their turn at the annual Scripps National Spelling Bee. Both are fully prepared, but their emotional states are another story. Who is likely to perform better?

We should keep in mind that old information does not always interfere with the learning or remembering of new information. Sometimes it can even help us learn and retain new information. People who know how to roller skate often pick up ice skating faster than other people. Speakers of Spanish may have an easier time learning to speak Portuguese. Interference occurs only when old and new information conflict with one another.

We have observed how emotions—both positive and negative—often enhance memory by either providing powerful retrieval cues, setting up additional rounds of rehearsal, or triggering special memory mechanisms. At the same time, all of us have had experiences in which negative emotions, such as anxiety, actually interfere with memory and cause us to forget (McGaugh, 2003).

Some students experience severe test anxiety, for example. They may prepare fully for an examination, retain all of the necessary information, and score high on practice tests. Yet, on the day of the examination, they experience feelings of anxiety that grow from butterflies in their stomach to a consuming fear that they will "not do well on the exam ... not pass the course ... perhaps not even complete college." Their anxiety grows so out of control as the test sits in front of them that they are unable to retrieve many of the answers that had been so available to them during practice tests the evening before. Many counselors who work with such individuals suggest that the negative thoughts accompanying their anxiety (for example, "I will not pass this course") interfere with the retrieval of memories and cause the students to forget.

Motivated Forgetting   Sometimes we seem to almost purposely forget information that is unpleasant, embarrassing, or painful (Kennedy, Mather, & Carstensen, 2004). Suppose, for example, that during your freshman year, you completely bungle a conversation with a classmate on whom you have a crush. Humiliated, you give up all hopes of pursuing the relationship, and by the end of the semester, the two of you are hardly acknowledging each other. Fast-forward three years. By now, you have become much more suave, and, as it turns out, you and your former crush meet again at a graduation party. As the two of you laugh together, talk comfortably, and discover shared values, you wonder aloud how it is that you never got together during your four years at college. Taken aback by your comment, your new friend recalls for you the freshman year bungling incident. You are shocked by this revelation. On reflection, you recall vaguely that a discussion took place three years ago, but, for the life of you, you have no recollection of the stammering, falling, and other embarrassing moves you made. In fact, you do not even recall having been all that interested in this person in the first place.

decay theory   theory of forgetting, suggesting memories fade over time due to neglect or failure to access over long period of time.

interference theory   theory that forgetting is influenced by what happens to people before or after they take information in.

proactive interference   competing information that is learned before the forgotten material, preventing its subsequent recall.

retroactive interference   learning of new information that disrupts access to previously recalled information.

"The wedding was perfect" Left to her own devices and the power of motivated forgetting, this bride might eventually forget that she tripped on her wedding dress on that most important of days. If only she could get rid of this photo.

Clearly, you have forgotten an incident and related information that was unpleasant. But why? One possibility is that because the event was so painful, you actively worked to forget it. You avoided opportunities for rehearsal, such as sharing the terrible experience with friends or relatives or writing about it in your personal journal. You may have even avoided retrieval cues, such as the walkway where the catastrophic interaction occurred. In short, you avoided rehearsing, elaborating, or organizing the information, making it less available for later retrieval from memory.

Of course, anyone who has *actively* tried to forget an upsetting event knows that this is not so easy to do. Even if we do not share the event with others, we often find ourselves thinking about it (that is, privately rehearsing it) again and again. Moreover, like a flashbulb memory, the special emotional component of such an event often increases, rather than decreases, the likelihood of our remembering it.

Why then do we seem to forget certain unpleasant events or information? The leading explanation of such motivated forgetting is Sigmund Freud's theory of **repression**. Freud held that all people employ repression on occasion, a process in which we unconsciously prevent some traumatic events from entering our awareness, so that we do not have to experience the anxiety or blows to our self-concept that the memories would bring. According to Freud, the repressed material is not lost, but rather *hidden* from consciousness. He believed that our experiences, especially childhood experiences, are too rich and powerful to slip away altogether. In fact, the hidden material may influence later decisions or interpretations of events, although we are not aware of its impact in such cases. In short, the repressed information takes on the form of an implicit memory.

According to Freud, repressed memories may be jogged and brought forth under certain circumstances. Indeed, as we saw in Chapter 1, a key feature of psychoanalytic therapy, the treatment approach first developed by Freud, is to help clients rediscover their repressed memories of past traumas and, in turn, open the door to more effective functioning. Despite the wide influence of this theory and of psychoanalytic therapy, it is important to recognize that research has failed to demonstrate consistently that people repress unpleasant events (Kihlström, 2006; Baddeley, 1990).

Distorted or Manufactured Memories

Our memories can be subject to distortions. In large part, this is because, as we observed earlier, we tend to rely on semantic codes when we encode information into long-term memory. That is, we encode the *meaning* of an event, rather than its specific words or images. In turn, when we later retrieve the memory, we have to *reconstruct* it. We must fill in details from our earlier recollection. Thus, when five persons later try to remember the same event—for example, when Sarah and her family members recall her acceptance into medical school—they may each recall the details of the event quite differently.

A number of factors may contribute to faulty reconstructions of memory—that is, to the distortion or manufacture of memories. Three of the most common are *source misattributions,* exposure to *misinformation,* and the effects of *imagination* (**Table 8-1**).

Source Misattributions When we encode and store information in long-term memory, we often fail to record where it came from. Years ago, millions of viewers watched a popular television game show named *To Tell the Truth* each evening. On this show, three persons would claim to be an individual who was famous for a particular skill or accomplishment, for example, a famous dog trainer. Only one of the three was, in fact, the real expert; the other two were imposters. A celebrity panel would fire questions at the three individuals. They might ask questions about dogs, dog instincts, effective training techniques, and the like. Then, on the basis of the answers, they would try to decide who the real expert was. Finally, the expert would stand up and identify himself or herself.

repression process in which we unconsciously prevent some traumatic events from entering our awareness, so that we do not have to experience the anxiety or blows to our self-concept that the memories would bring.

source misattribution remembering information, but not the source it came from; can lead to remembering as true information from unreliable sources.

TABLE 8-1	Common Reasons Why We Distort or Manufacture Memories
Source misattribution	We often fail to record where the information came from when we encode and store the information in long-term memory
Exposure to misinformation	New information that is inaccurate or misleading can distort our recall or lead us to manufacture new memories
Effects of imagination	Our own imagination can lead us to recall events that never took place

During the questioning period, television viewers were exposed to a good deal of information. In the case of a famous dog trainer, for example, viewers would hear answers about which breeds are easier to train, which training techniques are most effective, how long training typically takes, and so on. The problem was that only one-third of this information was necessarily accurate. Only the actual trainer was "sworn to tell the truth." The two impostors were making up answers. Later, it was often impossible for viewers to remember whether a particular piece of information came from the expert (and was therefore accurate) or from one of the impostors (and was inaccurate). Unable to remember that the information came from a dubious source, many viewers carried away from each program false information, which they continued to believe for months or years.

In a similar manner, we often forget or are confused about where we have gathered information that is now stored in our long-term memory system. Such **source misattributions** can render our memories of certain events distorted, or in some cases, manufactured (Lindsay et al., 2004). Is our detailed recollection of getting lost at the mall when we were six years old a direct memory of that event? Or, are we actually remembering our parents' many stories about the event? Or are we confusing our own life with that of one of the children on a rerun episode of the perpetually syndicated 1970s TV series *The Brady Bunch*? We may have supreme confidence in our memory of the event and even "remember" vivid details about it, yet the memory may be inaccurate or even entirely false. We are remembering something, but it may not be the event itself.

Exposure to Misinformation Earlier we noted that retroactive interference often causes us to forget something when we are later exposed to new competing information. For example, an old phone number may be lost from memory when a fairly similar, new phone number is mastered. Similarly, exposure to new information, particularly misinformation, can lead to the distortion or the manufacture of memories (Wixted, 2004).

Consider a situation in which a man witnesses a robbery. If a week later the eyewitness is asked, "Could you please describe the robber," he is being called upon to rely exclusively on his memory for a description. If, however, the eyewitness is told in passing, as part of the questioning process, "We've had a number of similar robberies lately, involving a heavy, blond-haired guy with a beard," this new information may greatly influence the witness's recall of the robber and the robbery. Such exposures to new information—often misinformation—are of great concern

Confident eyewitnesses are just as likely to be wrong as less-confident eyewitnesses (Gruneberg & Sykes, 1993).

A terrible error A woman talks to the man whom she had previously identified as her rapist. Her memory was eventually proved wrong by DNA evidence—after he had served 11 years of a life sentence in prison! Mistaken eyewitness memories and testimony are responsible for most wrongful convictions in the U.S. justice system.

Mistaken eyewitness testimony is the primary cause of the conviction of innocent people (Wells et al, 1998).

in police cases. Many a defendant has been accused or even convicted of a crime based on testimony from witnesses whose memories were unintentionally distorted or manufactured (Wells & Loftus, 2003). (See "What Happens in the Brain When We Give Eyewitness Testimony" at the end of this section for more information.)

The impact of misinformation on memory has received considerable study in psychology laboratories. How do researchers "plant" misinformation in memory studies? A clever investigation by psychologist Elizabeth Loftus and her colleagues (1978) illustrates how this is done. Participants in her study observed a film of a traffic accident and were then asked to remember certain details of the accident. One group of subjects was asked, "How fast were the cars going when they *smashed* into each other?" A second group was asked, "How fast were the cars going when they *hit* each other?" The experimenter's use of the word *smash* implies as very severe accident, whereas the word *hit* implies a milder accident. Not surprisingly, people who heard *smash* remembered the cars going at a faster speed than did those who heard *hit*. The researchers also asked, "Did you see any broken glass?" Those who heard *smash* were much more likely to say yes than those who heard *hit*. In fact, there had been no broken glass in the film.

Study after study has demonstrated the distorting effects of misinformation on memory. In each, participants first observe an event and later receive from experimenters new, misleading information about the event (Sacchi, Agnoli, & Loftus, 2007; Loftus, 2005). A short while after observing an uneventful interaction between two spouses, for example, participants in a study may be told, in passing, that one of the spouses is a rather hostile person, or amorous, or devious. Sure enough, in their later recollections of the observed interaction, many participants "remember" hostile, amorous, or devious acts by the spouse in question. Similarly, people have been induced, by subsequent exposures to misinformation, to "remember" objects—glasses, paintings, revolvers—that were not actually present in an observed event.

A particularly powerful way of being exposed to misinformation is through *hypnosis*. As we first saw in Chapter 6, people who are hypnotized enter a sleeplike state in which they become very suggestible. While in this state, they can be led to behave, perceive, and think in ways that would ordinarily seem impossible. They may, for example, become temporarily blind, deaf, or insensitive to pain. Hypnosis can also help people remember events that occurred and were forgotten years ago, a capability used by many psychotherapists. On the other hand, in recent years, it has come to the attention of researchers that hypnosis can also make people forget, distort, or manufacture memories by supplying misinformation (Barnier et al., 2004). Witnesses who are hypnotized to help them remember an observed crime are, in fact, likely to remember details offered or implied by the hypnotist. These details, such as the time of the crime, the clothes worn by the perpetrator, or the presence of a weapon, may be inconsistent with their actual observations. For this reason, police hypnotists must be extraordinarily careful when questioning witnesses. Even so, state courts across the United States no longer admit as evidence eyewitness recollections that have been gathered initially under hypnosis.

Hypnosis and memory A police hypnotist uses the procedure to help a woman remember details of a crime that she witnessed. In fact, however, hypnosis often causes people to distort or manufacture memories, rather than rediscover them.

The Effect of Imagination It turns out that our memories can be distorted not only by misinformation supplied by others, but also by false information that comes from within, from our imaginations. Researchers have found repeatedly that when people are instructed to imagine the occurrence of certain events, many come to believe that they have in fact experienced the events (Thomas et al., 2007; Thomas & Loftus, 2002).

In one study, a team of researchers asked the parents of college students to list events that had, in fact, occurred during the students' childhoods (Hyman & Kleinknecht, 1999). In later interviews, the students themselves were instructed to recall those real events, along with another event, one that had not actually occurred according to the parents' reports. The students were not told that this event was false. A student might, for example, be instructed to recall the false event of accidentally knocking over a table at a wedding, as well as a number of events that actually had occurred. When interviewed some days later, about one-fourth of the students fully believed that the false events had occurred during their childhood, and, in fact, they could "remember" many details of the unfortunate experiences. Clearly, misinformation from others or from our own imaginations, or from a combination of the two, can greatly influence our recollections, leading at times to forgetting, distortions, or even the manufacture of memories.

The Effect of Aging on Memory How we *Develop* In Chapters 3 and 7, we observed that babies can remember and learn right after birth and that memory skills continue to develop and strengthen as we move through childhood and adolescence. It is also the case that as we travel through middle adulthood and old age, we become more susceptible to forgetting, distortions, and misremembering. Researchers suggest that older adults rely more on gist memory—the "gist" of things rather than hard facts—and the elderly also tend to remember positive information while ignoring the negative (Park & Reuter-Lorenz, 2009; Jacoby et al., 2005). For these reasons, some older individuals fall prey to scams.

Brain fitness A growing number of cognitive fitness centers are now being developed, where elderly people work on computer tasks designed to help improve their memories and cognitive functioning. However, research has not yet clarified that brain exercises prevent cognitive decline.

Although the age-related changes in the way our memory functions are gradual, they actually begin in our twenties (Park & Reuter-Lorenz, 2009). Certain parts of the brain, such as the hippocampus, begin to shrink. A study of the brains of elderly individuals found that the hippocampus was about 20 percent larger in those with excellent memories than those suffering from Alzheimer's disease (Erten-Lyons et al., 2009), a finding that may also have implications for non-pathological aging processes.

As the elderly population continues to grow, an increasing amount of research is focusing on how to improve memory and prevent, or at the very least, lessen the impairments mentioned above. Brain fitness approaches —using computer exercises and various mental games to keep the mind "in shape"—have become very popular and are often recommended to elderly patients by health-care professionals. Although this approach has received support in a few studies (Basak et al., 2008), many of today's researchers remain skeptical about whether brain puzzles and the like can in fact prevent cognitive decline. On the other hand, as we observed in Chapter 4, research has demonstrated repeatedly that physical exercise does indeed help to prevent or slow down cognitive deficiencies and impairments.

Before You Go On

What Do You Know?

11. How does the decay theory explain forgetting?

12. What is repression?

13. A late night TV comedy show host suggests that members of one political party have better sex lives than members of the others. Although this person is obviously unqualified to know, your friends have started to tell you it's proven that members of this party have more fun, so they're thinking of switching parties. What might be happening to your friends' memories?

14. The saying, "Elementary, my dear Watson," did not appear in any of the writings of Sir Arthur Conan Doyle, the author of the Sherlock Holmes series, yet millions of fans vividly remember reading these words. What processes can explain this manufactured memory?

What Do You Think? What examples of proactive and retroactive interference or memory distortions have you experienced in your own life?

When We Give Eyewitness Testimony

Imagine you have witnessed a car accident where someone was injured. You dialed 911 and stayed at the scene to tell the police officer what happened. A few months later, you were called to testify as an eyewitness at the trial. How accurate do you think your memory would be?

When people give eyewitness testimony, many regions of their brains are involved, including the hippocampus, amygdala, prefrontal cortex, visual cortex, thalamus, and mammillary bodies, among others. Let's see how several of these regions are involved in such eyewitness testimony.

DISTORTING THE MEMORY

Memories are often susceptible to distortions when they are recalled. Wrong information can be incorporated into an eyewitness's memory if leading questions are asked or if circumstances surrounding the inquiry are particularly frightening.

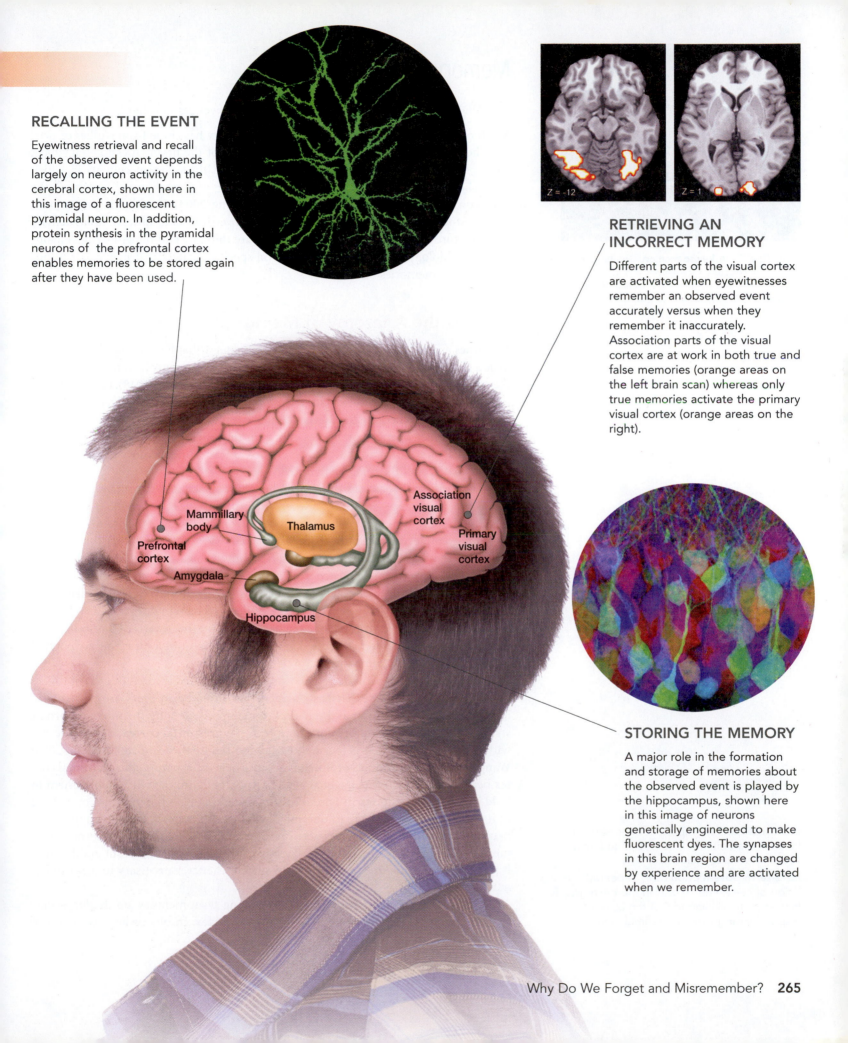

RECALLING THE EVENT

Eyewitness retrieval and recall of the observed event depends largely on neuron activity in the cerebral cortex, shown here in this image of a fluorescent pyramidal neuron. In addition, protein synthesis in the pyramidal neurons of the prefrontal cortex enables memories to be stored again after they have been used.

RETRIEVING AN INCORRECT MEMORY

Different parts of the visual cortex are activated when eyewitnesses remember an observed event accurately versus when they remember it inaccurately. Association parts of the visual cortex are at work in both true and false memories (orange areas on the left brain scan) whereas only true memories activate the primary visual cortex (orange areas on the right).

Z = -12

Z = 1

Prefrontal cortex

Mammillary body

Thalamus

Amygdala

Hippocampus

Association visual cortex

Primary visual cortex

STORING THE MEMORY

A major role in the formation and storage of memories about the observed event is played by the hippocampus, shown here in this image of neurons genetically engineered to make fluorescent dyes. The synapses in this brain region are changed by experience and are activated when we remember.

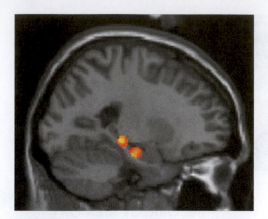

FIGURE 8-11 A key to memory The hippocampus is a crucial structure for memory. It is activated when people recall information about facts and events (shown on this fMRI scan in yellow).

LEARNING OBJECTIVE 6 Describe how the brain is involved in memory.

Much of what we know about the biology of memory has come from studies of people who have suffered injuries to specific locations of the brain (Alessio et al., 2006, 2004). Important information has also been gained through experiments in which researchers surgically or chemically change the brains of animals and then observe the effects on old memories and new learning (Schwarting, 2003). In addition, over the past decade, studies using brain scans have enabled investigators to observe brain activity and structure at the very moment that people are thinking and remembering. Finally, molecular biology studies have shed light on specific changes that may occur in our brain cells as memories form.

What Is the Anatomy of Memory?

Memories are difficult to locate. Recall from Chapter 4 that back in the 1920s, neurological researcher Karl Lashley undertook a series of experiments with rats, in search of the specific places in the brain where memories are stored (Lashley, 1948). He would train a rat to run through a maze, then cut out a snippet of its brain tissue and set the rat loose in the maze again, checking to see whether it still remembered how to navigate through the maze. Lashley operated on hordes of rats, cutting out different sections of brain tissue for each one. He found that all rats retained at least some memory of the maze, no matter what part of the brain he removed.

Based on studies such as this, researchers have concluded that there is no single place—no storehouse—in the brain where memories reside (Gaffan, 2003), that information in the brain is encoded across various neurons throughout the brain. As we have seen, for example, connectionist theorists see memory as a *process* rather than a place, an activity that involves changes in networks of multiple neurons throughout the brain. When such networking is activated, a memory is triggered and comes forth. This conclusion that there is no single place in the brain where memories reside is similar to the Chapter 7 conclusion that a single learning center in the brain does not exist. Indeed, because memory and learning go hand in hand, you'll see that several of the brain structures and activities that were discussed in Chapter 7 to account for learning are pointed to again here as we examine the neuroscience of memory.

Although today's theorists believe that neurons located throughout the brain are involved in memory, research has clarified that some brain areas are particularly important in the formation and retrieval of memories. Among the most important structures in working memory, for example, is the **prefrontal cortex**, a key structure within the neocortex that is located just behind the forehead (Öztekin et al., 2009; Wang, 2005). When animals or humans acquire new information, the prefrontal cortex becomes more active (Lian et al., 2002). Apparently this activity enables them to hold information temporarily and to continue working with the information as long as it is needed. To refer back to our analogy between the brain and a computer, the neurons in the prefrontal cortex seem to operate like a computer's random access memory (RAM), drawing information from various parts of the brain and holding it temporarily for use in a task, yet able to switch whenever necessary to other information and tasks.

Among the most important structures in long-term memory are the *hippocampus* (see **Figure 8-11**) and other parts of the neocortex. In our earlier discussion of

prefrontal cortex important brain structure located just behind the forehead and implicated in working memory.

long-term potentiation (LTP) repeated stimulation of certain nerve cells in the brain greatly increases the likelihood that the cells will respond strongly to future stimulation.

explicit memories, we noted that the hippocampus converts such memories into long-term status, stores the memories temporarily, and then sends them on to various areas of the neocortex for genuine long-term storage. As we saw in Chapter 4, destruction of the hippocampus in adulthood does not wipe out all long-term memories, only those that occurred just prior to the brain damage (Squire et al., 2004). In contrast, destruction of certain parts of the neocortex results in the loss of older memories. These findings suggest that the hippocampus is indeed an important temporary storage site for long-term memories and a key player in the transfer of such memories into genuine long-term status in the neocortex.

What is the Biochemistry of Memory?

As we have discussed, the PDP, or connectionist, model of memory describes the storage of information in long-term memory as a *network* of associations. When we activate one piece of information, related ones spring into action, enabling us to travel through our long-term memory system rapidly and retrieve particular memories. But how, in fact, does the brain manage to link such pieces of information to each other? Research increasingly points to biochemical and electrical changes in certain neurons, particularly those neurons located in the key brain regions that we have just noted.

Neural Circuits   As we observed in Chapter 4, communication throughout the brain proceeds from neuron to neuron in a particular way. A given message arrives at a neuron as an impulse, travels down the axon of the neuron, and is then carried by a chemical—a *neurotransmitter*—across the synaptic space to another neuron. The next neuron is then triggered and, like the preceding neuron, passes along a message to yet another neuron, and so on. When we talk about certain pieces of information being closely linked to other pieces of information in the long-term memory system, we are really saying that certain neurons in the brain become predisposed to trigger other neurons.

"The matters about which I'm being questioned, Your Honor, are all things I should have included in my long-term memory but which I mistakenly inserted in my short-term memory."

The question for memory researchers is how such neural circuits form. How is it that some neurons become predisposed to trigger other neurons, enabling us to retrieve a given memory? It appears that the repeated stimulation of certain neurons greatly increases the likelihood that these neurons will respond—and respond strongly—to future stimulation of the same kind, a phenomenon called **long-term potentiation (LTP)** (Wixted, 2004). LTP affects not just single neurons, but the networks of neurons that make up neural circuits. The effects of LTP can last quite a long time (hence the name *long-term* potentiation), long enough to be a key factor in the formation and retrieval of memories. Think of many sleds ridden one after another down a snowy slope, creating a groove that later sledders can easily find. LTP seems to create a kind of groove that helps memories form, so a person can more easily retrieve a memory later by following the well-worn path.

You already know from Chapter 7 that LTP plays a role in learning. Researchers have gathered considerable evidence that it also plays a role in long-term memory. If experimental animals are given substances known to block the development of LTP, they have difficulty transferring information from their working memory into their long-term memory (Sanberg et al., 2006; Lynch et al., 1991). Conversely, drugs that enhance the development of LTP seem to improve the acquisition of long-term memories. In one study, for example, rats that were given an LTP-enhancing drug learned and remembered a maze better than rats that were not administered the drug.

amnestic disorders organic disorders in which memory loss is the primary symptom.

retrograde amnesia inability to remember things that occurred before an organic event.

anterograde amnesia ongoing inability to form new memories after an amnesia-inducing event.

dementia severe memory problems combine with losses in at least one other cognitive function, such as abstract thinking or language.

Many of the neurons and neural circuits that use *glutamate* as their neurotransmitter are particularly likely to exhibit LTP. This is not surprising because glutamate is a very common neurotransmitter, being present in about 90 percent of all excitatory synapses. Glutamate is also a key neurotransmitter in the formation of memories, as you shall soon see. Moreover, neurons that exhibit LTP are commonly located in the hippocampus and neocortex, brain regions that play such important roles in the formation of long-term memories, as we have just observed (Thompson, 2000).

Proteins   Still other memory researchers have tried to identify biochemical changes that occur within neurons as memories are forming (Rosenzweig, 1996: Turkington & Harris, 2009, 2001). When neurons receive neurotransmitters at their receptor sites, chemical changes immediately begin to occur within the neurons. For example, *ribonucleic acid* (*RNA*) and *calcium* are increased in the cells, and these chemicals help manufacture proteins (Greenspan, 2003).

Proteins are believed to help memories form. Although researchers have yet to identify all of the proteins involved in memory formation, they have found that disruptions in the production of proteins often interfere with the proper encoding, storage, or retrieval of memories (Martinez & Derrick, 1996). For example, by blocking calcium or the production of RNA, researchers have been able to interrupt the formation of long-term memories.

All of these findings suggest that memory occurs as a result of changes both within and among neurons. Clearly, although no one has yet discovered all of the biological changes that account for memory, researchers are shedding more and more light on how the brain manages to provide this critical faculty.

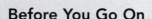

Before You Go On

What Do You Know?

15. Which parts of the brain are most active in memory? How are these parts related to neurotransmitters involved in memory?

16. What is a neural network and how might long-term potentiation contribute to its formation?

What Do You Think?   What side effects might occur if drugs were taken that could manipulate memory-related neurotransmitters and proteins? Should such drugs be legally available to anyone who wants them?

Disorders of Memory
When Things Go Wrong

LEARNING OBJECTIVE 7 Describe physical and psychological disorders that disrupt memory.

At times, each of us has been inconvenienced by flawed memories or by outright forgetting. When our memories fail to operate as we would like, we may experience dismay, frustration, or embarrassment. Imagine how upsetting and confusing life would be if memory failure were the rule rather than the exception, as it became for Leonard, the character in the movie *Memento*. This is the experience of people who have memory disorders (McGaugh, 2003).

There are two basic groups of memory disorders: *organic memory disorders*, in which physical causes of memory impairment can be identified, and *dissociative disorders*, in which the disruptions in memory lack a clear physical cause. The latter disorders are much less common than the former.

Organic Memory Disorders

Some changes in memory have clear organic causes, such as brain injury, medical conditions, and substance misuse. The most common kinds of organic memory disorders are *amnestic disorders*, which primarily affect memory, and *dementias*, which affect both memory and other cognitive functions.

Amnestic Disorders People with **amnestic disorders**, organic disorders in which memory loss is the primary symptom, experience retrograde amnesia, anterograde amnesia, or both (**Figure 8-12**). **Retrograde amnesia** is an inability to remember things that occurred before the organic disorder or event that triggered amnesia. **Anterograde amnesia** is an ongoing inability to form new memories after the onset of the disorder or event. Not surprisingly, the anterograde amnesia observed in amnestic disorders is often the result of damage to the brain's *temporal lobes* or *mammillary bodies*, areas that play a role in transferring information from working memory into long-term memory.

In severe forms of anterograde amnesia, such as that suffered by Leonard, the main character in the film *Memento*, new acquaintances are forgotten almost immediately and problems solved one day must be tackled again the next. The person may not remember anything that has happened since the physical problem first occurred. A middle-aged patient who suffered a physical trauma more than 25 years ago, for example, may still believe that Ronald Reagan is president of the United States.

Head injuries are a common cause of amnestic disorders. Although *mild* head injuries—for example, a mild concussion—rarely cause much memory loss, almost half of all *severe* head injuries do cause some permanent learning and memory problems (Sadock & Sadock, 2007). Brain surgery can also cause amnestic disorders. The most famous case of memory loss as a result of brain surgery is that of H.M., a man whose identity was protected for decades until his death in 2008 (Kensinger et al., 2001; Corkin, 1984). H.M. suffered from severe epilepsy, a disorder that produced seizures in his temporal lobes. To reduce his symptoms, doctors performed surgery in 1953 that removed parts of both his temporal lobes, the amygdala, and the hippocampus. At that time, the role of these brain areas in the formation of memories was not known. (Today temporal lobe surgery is usually done on only the right or left side of the brain.) H.M. experienced severe anterograde amnesia from the time of his surgery until his death. He kept failing to recognize anyone he met after the operation.

Dementias In **dementia**, severe memory problems combine with losses in at least one other cognitive function, such as abstract thinking or language (APA, 2000). As you have seen in this chapter, forgetfulness is quite normal. In fact, as people move through middle age, memory difficulties, lapses of attention, and related cognitive difficulties increase and may occur with regularity by the age of 60 or 70. Sometimes, however, people experience memory and other cognitive changes that are far more extensive. They may be victims of dementia.

Between 3 and 9 percent of the world's adult population suffer from some form of dementia (Berr et al., 2005). Its occurrence is closely related to age. Among people 65 years of age, the prevalence of dementia is around 1 to 2 percent, increasing to as much as 50 percent of those over the age of 85 (Apostolova & Cummings, 2008). Altogether, 5 million persons in the United States experience some form of dementia (Soukup, 2006). More than 70 forms have been identified. Some result from metabolic, nutritional, or other problems that can be corrected. Most forms of dementia, however, are caused by neurological problems, which are currently difficult or impossible to correct.

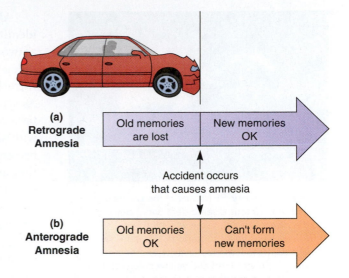

(a) **Retrograde Amnesia** — Old memories are lost / New memories OK

Accident occurs that causes amnesia

(b) **Anterograde Amnesia** — Old memories OK / Can't form new memories

FIGURE 8-12 Two types of amnesia An organic event can lead to two types of inability to remember. In retrograde amnesia, the individual loses memories of things that occurred before the event. In anterograde amnesia, the individual can recall the past but cannot form new memories.

Part of the sport? Hard hits to the head are common in boxing, football, and hockey, leading, in many cases, to brain injuries that produce permanent memory and learning problems. As many as 350,000 athletes endure consciousness-losing injuries each year (Gioia, 2007).

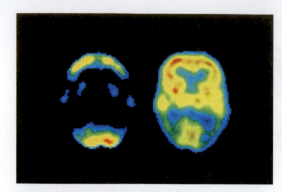

Scans tell the story PET scans of the brains of a person with Alzheimer's disease (*left*) and a person without the disease (*right*), taken while the two individuals were trying to perform the same task, reveal how much less brain activity occurs in the Alzheimer's patient. Red and yellow colors on PET scans indicate areas of high brain activity.

Alzheimer's disease most common form of dementia, usually beginning with mild memory problems, lapses of attention, and problems in language and progressing to difficulty with even simple tasks and recall of long-held memories.

neurofibrillary tangles twisted protein fibers found *within* the cells of the hippocampus and certain other brain areas.

senile plaques sphere-shaped deposits of a protein known as *beta-amyloid* that form in the spaces *between* cells in the hippocampus, cerebral cortex, and certain other brain regions, as well as in some nearby blood vessels.

Alzheimer's disease, named after Alois Alzheimer, the German physician who first identified it in 1907, is the most common form of dementia, accounting for as many as two-thirds of all cases. This gradually progressive disease sometimes appears in middle age, but most often it occurs after the age of 65. The disease usually begins with mild memory problems, lapses of attention, and difficulties in language and communication. As symptoms worsen over the years, the person has trouble completing complicated tasks or remembering important appointments. Eventually patients also have difficulty with simple tasks, distant memories are forgotten, and changes in personality often become very noticeable. They may withdraw from others, become more confused about time and place, wander, and show very poor judgment. They may lose almost all knowledge of the past and fail to recognize the faces of even close relatives.

Usually, Alzheimer's disease can be diagnosed with certainty only after death, when structural changes in the person's brain can be fully identified in autopsy (Julien, 2008; APA, 2000). People with Alzheimer's disease, for example, form far more than ordinary numbers of *neurofibrillary tangles* and *senile plaques*, brain changes that are normal features of aging up to a point (Selkoe, 2002, 2000, 1991). **Neurofibrillary tangles** are twisted protein fibers found within the cells of the hippocampus and several other brain areas. **Senile plaques** are sphere-shaped deposits of a protein known as *beta-amyloid protein* that form in the spaces between cells in the hippocampus, cerebral cortex, and several other brain regions, as well as in some nearby blood vessels. The presence of so many tangles and plaques indicates that enormously destructive processes take place in the brains of Alzheimer victims (Meyer-Luehmann et al., 2008; O'Connor et al., 2008). Researchers do not yet fully understand what those processes are, but they have begun to zero in on several possibilities.

One line of research suggests that two proteins involved in memory formation—*beta-amyloid protein* and *tau protein*—take an abnormal form and essentially run amok in people with Alzheimer's disease (Apostolova & Cummings, 2008). Abnormal changes in the structure of the beta-amyloid protein seem to be involved in the formation of plaques in the hippocampus and other brain areas. Similarly, abnormal changes in the structure of the tau protein lead to the formation of tangles in those brain areas. Related studies suggest that Alzheimer patients may display an imbalance in the metabolism of calcium, which, as we have seen, is used in making proteins related to memory. Still other research has linked particular genes to abnormal protein production, leading some researchers to identify certain families that carry an increased likelihood of plaque formation and of Alzheimer's disease (Turkington & Harris, 2009, 2001; Drachman, 2006).

Yet another line of research points to reduced activity of neurotransmitters that are typically related to memory. Many studies have found, for example, that acetylcholine and glutamate are in low supply in the brains of people with Alzheimer's disease (Chin et al., 2007; Bissette et al., 1996). This decrease is probably related to the death of neurons by plaque and tangle formations.

Gender and Dementia HOW we Differ Depending on whether you are a male or a female, you may be susceptible to different risk factors for dementia and Alzheimer's disease. Older women are more likely to develop dementia than men. Although this may be because women tend to live longer, natural age-related declines in estrogen, which is known to have a protective effect in the brain, could also be a factor (Sun, 2007). In men, there is evidence to suggest that decreases in testosterone cause increases in beta-amyloid proteins that, as we mentioned previously, are involved in Alzheimer's disease (Rosario & Pike, 2008).

As we age, certain conditions in men and women may increase the likelihood of developing dementia. A study of adults with mild cognitive impairment showed that stroke in men and depression in women increase the risk for dementia (Artero et al., 2008). In addition to risk factors, Alzheimer's disease also may "look" different in men and women. The brains of women with the disease, for example, typically have many more neurofibrillary tangles than do those of men (Barnes et al., 2005). Also, men with Alzheimer's disease tend to be more aggressive, while women are more likely to become depressed (Lovheim et al., 2009).

Dissociative Disorders

People with **dissociative disorders** experience major losses of memory without any clear physical causes. Many memorable books and movies have portrayed such disorders. Some clinicians, however, believe that they are quite rare. There are several different kinds of dissociative disorders, including *dissociative amnesia, dissociative fugue,* and *dissociative identity disorder (multiple personality disorder):*

Progressive deterioration A staff member at a special residential facility helps a woman with Alzheimer's disease eat dinner. As memory deficits and other features of the disease worsen over the years, victims have trouble performing even simple tasks.

- *Dissociative amnesia* People with **dissociative amnesia** are unable to recall important information, usually of an upsetting nature, about their lives (APA, 2000). The loss of memory is much more extensive than instances of normal forgetting and is often triggered directly by a traumatic event—typically a serious threat to health and safety—as in wartime and natural disasters (Cardena & Gleaves, 2007). Dissociative amnesia interferes mostly with memories of personal material; that is, memories of general knowledge (such as who is the president of the United States) usually remain. Similarly, people with this disorder typically retain their *implicit* memories, recollections of how to write, read, drive, and other skills.

- *Dissociative fugue* In addition to forgetting their personal identities and details of their past lives, people with **dissociative fugue** flee to an entirely different location. Although some individuals travel but a short distance and make few social contacts in the new setting, others travel far from home, take new names and establish new identities, develop new relationships, and even seek new lines of work (APA, 2000; Kihlström, 2001).

- *Dissociative identity disorder* People with **dissociative identity disorder**, formerly known as *multiple personality disorder,* develop two or more distinct personalities—called **subpersonalities**—each having a unique set of memories, behaviors, thoughts, and emotions. Often one of the subpersonalities has little or no recall of the experiences, thoughts, feelings, or behaviors of the others. During activities and interactions, one of the subpersonalities takes center stage and dominates the person's functioning.

  Most cases of dissociative identity disorder are first diagnosed in late adolescence or early adulthood, but the symptoms usually begin in early childhood, often after episodes of abuse, perhaps even before the age of 5 (Maldonado & Spiegel, 2007). Women receive this diagnosis at least three times as often as men (APA, 2000).

  In the famous case of "Eve White," depicted in the book and movie *The Three Faces of Eve*, a woman had three subpersonalities—Eve White, Eve Black, and Jane (Thigpen & Cleckley, 1957). Eve White, the primary personality, was quiet and serious; Eve Black was carefree and mischievous; and Jane was mature and intelligent. According to the book, these three subpersonalities eventually merged into a single, integrated personality named Evelyn. However, in an autobiography decades later, this woman revealed that altogether twenty-two subpersonalities had come forth during her life, including nine subpersonalities after Evelyn (Sizemore, 1991).

dissociative disorders psychological disorder characterized by major loss of memory without a clear physical cause.

dissociative amnesia psychological disorder characterized by inability to recall important information, usually of an upsetting nature, about one's life.

dissociative fugue psychological disorder characterized by loss of memory of personal identities and details of one's past life and flight to an entirely different location.

dissociative identity disorder psychological disorder characterized by the development of two or more distinct personalities.

subpersonalities alternate personalities developed in dissociative identity disorder, each with a unique set of memories, behaviors, thoughts, and emotions.

Identity restored Cheryl Ann Barnes is comforted by her grandmother aboard an airplane on her way back home to Florida in 1996. The 17-year-old high school student had disappeared from her home and was found five weeks later in a New York hospital, apparently suffering from fugue.

A variety of theories have been proposed to explain dissociative disorders, although none of them has received much research support. Three of the leading explanations point to phenomena that we have come across earlier in this chapter—*state-dependent memory*, *hypnosis*, and *exposure to misinformation*.

State-Dependent Memory   As we have noted, if people learn something when they are in a particular mood or state of mind, they may remember it best when they are again in that same condition. People who are prone to develop dissociative disorders may have mood-to-memory links that are extremely rigid and narrow (Dorahy & Huntjens, 2007). Each of their memories may be tied exclusively to a particular state of arousal, so that they recall a given event from the past only when they experience an arousal state almost identical to the state in which the memory was acquired. When such people are relaxed, for example, they may forget what occurred during stressful times, thus setting the stage for a dissociative disorder.

Self-Hypnosis   As you have seen, by introducing misinformation and drawing on the powers of imagination and suggestion, hypnosis can make people forget or distort facts, events, and even their personal identities. When a hypnotist induces a person to forget important information, the effect is called *hypnotic amnesia* (Barnier et al., 2004).

Many parallels exist between hypnotic amnesia and dissociative disorders. For example, both are conditions in which people forget certain material without any insight that something is being forgotten. Such parallels have led some theorists to conclude that dissociative disorders may be a form of *self-hypnosis* in which people hypnotize themselves—consciously or unconsciously—to forget unpleasant events that have occurred in their lives (Maldonado & Spiegel, 2007). In short, dissociative disorders may represent extreme cases of motivated forgetting.

Exposure to Misinformation   Some psychologists suggest that the symptoms of dissociative disorders may originate not from within the individual, but in a therapist's office. We have seen how easy it is for people to distort or manufacture memories based on even casual suggestions. According to this explanation, therapists may unintentionally create dissociative disorders, particularly dissociative identity disorders, by subtly suggesting to their clients over the course of treatment that they may have other personalities or by asking the clients to produce different personalities while in a hypnotic state (Loewenstein, 2007; Piper & Merskey, 2004).

Before You Go On

What Do You Know?

17. Compare and contrast retrograde and anterograde amnesia. What are the likely causes of both?
18. What changes happen in the brains of people with Alzheimer's disease?
19. How might state-dependent memory and self-hypnosis be linked to dissociative disorders?

What Do You Think?   Do you think that media portrayals of amnesia and dissociative disorders have actually influenced psychotherapists and members of the public to increase the number of diagnoses of these conditions? What other reasons might explain increased diagnoses?

Summary

What is Memory?

LEARNING OBJECTIVE 1   Define the basic activities of memory and describe two major models of memory.

- Memory is our faculty for holding onto past events and past learning. It involves three basic activities: encoding, storage, and retrieval.
- Researchers typically take an information-processing approach to memory, talking about different memory stores that work together in a similar way to part of a computer, each serving particular functions and holding information for varying lengths of time.
- PDP or connectionist models of memory suggest that information is stored not in a particular neuron or location in the brain, but instead across a network of connections.

How Do We Encode Information Into Memory?

LEARNING OBJECTIVE 2   Describe how information is encoded and transferred among different memory stores and what we can do to enhance encoding.

- Encoding refers to taking information in and putting it into memory.
- Encoding can happen either automatically or through effortful processing. Either way, however, a person must attend to something to put it into memory.
- One of the most common means of effortful processing is rehearsal of material.
- Encoding takes place in the form of phonological, sound, or visual codes.

How Do We Store Memories?

LEARNING OBJECTIVE 3   Describe how we organize and store information in working and long-term memory and how we can enhance our long-term memories.

- The retention of information in memory is known as *storage*. Information can be stored in memory for anywhere from fractions of a second to a lifetime.
- Sensory memory is the equivalent of the small buffer on your computer, holding a very brief visual or auditory copy of information so you can decide whether or not to encode it into working or long-term memory. Sensory memory may also help maintain the continuity of your sensory input.
- Working memory is a short-term store of slightly more information that allows us to conduct simple calculations, such as memorizing a phone number so we can dial it immediately, or remembering the beginning of a sentence as we come to the end of the sentence.

- It appears that, without rehearsal, we can hold 7 ± 2 pieces of information in working memory, although we can expand that capacity through techniques, such as chunking.
- Long-term memory appears to be both infinite in capacity and storage time.
- Information taken from working memory into long-term memory appears to be organized according to its meaningfulness and relation to other concepts in long-term storage.
- Information in long-term memory may be stored in the form of explicit memories of facts or in implicit memories, knowledge about how to do something. A person cannot always articulate implicit knowledge.

How Do We Retrieve Memories?

LEARNING OBJECTIVE 4   Describe how we retrieve information from memory and how retrieval cues, priming, context, and emotion can affect retrieval.

- The access of information from memory is known as retrieval. Retrieval can be facilitated by retrieval cues that make memories easier to access.
- Retrieval cues can include priming, context, and enhancing meaningfulness of the memory by making them more personally or emotionally relevant.

Why Do We Forget and Misremember?

LEARNING OBJECTIVE 5   Summarize key theories of why we forget information and sometimes distort or manufacture memories.

- Forgetting is the inability to recall information that has previously been encoded.
- Initially, researchers believed that failure to access information regularly led to its loss from awareness, a theory known as *decay theory*. This theory is less popular now, and researchers instead emphasize other problems with remembering.
- Interference theory suggests that information gets in the way of proper encoding of information, preventing it from being remembered later. Retroactive interference comes from new information that interferes with previous memories. Proactive interference comes from earlier memories that interfere with new ones.
- Motivated forgetting hypothesizes that we try to purposely forget information that is unpleasant, embarrassing, or painful.
- In addition to being forgotten, memories can also be distorted or manufactured. We can make source misattributions, where we forget where information came from. We can also be exposed to new information that distorts previous information (as described in interference theory). Also, our own imaginations can play a role in distorting how our memories play out.

Memory *What Happens in The Brain*

LEARNING OBJECTIVE 6 Describe how the brain is involved in memory.

- Because scientists have not been able to pinpoint the place where memories are stored in the brain, they have concluded that there is no single storehouse. Instead, memory appears to be a process, resulting from activation patterns throughout the brain.

- However, structures like the prefrontal cortex are extremely important in helping people hold information in working memory and to work with it as long as it is needed. Also, the hippocampus and other parts of the neocortex appear to be important in the transfer of memories into long-term memory.

- Memory itself appears to be a neural circuit, a network of neurons predisposed to trigger one another whenever one is activated. Through a phenomenon called *long-term potentiation*, repeated stimulation of certain nerve cells increases the likelihood that the neurons will respond strongly whenever stimulated.

Disorders of Memory

LEARNING OBJECTIVE 7 Describe physical and psychological disorders that disrupt memory.

- Disorders of memory can come about through aging, brain trauma, or the experience of traumatic events. Organic memory disorders, involving physical causes, include disorders such as amnesia and dementia. Major losses of memory without a clear physical cause are known as *dissociative disorders*.

- Amnesia refers to the inability to remember things before (retrograde) or after (anterograde) an organic event, such as a head injury or brain surgery.

- The other major class of organic memory disorders is dementia, characterized by severe memory problems combined with losses in at least one other cognitive function, such as abstract thinking or language.

- The most common form of dementia is Alzheimer's disease, a severe progressive form of dementia that accounts for at least half of all dementia cases.

- The brains of people with Alzheimer's disease have an extraordinarily high number of neurofibrillary tangles and senile plaques. The disease may stem from malfunctions of certain proteins or neurotransmitters involved in the normal formation of memories. A tendency toward developing these biochemical problems may be genetically inherited.

- Most of the time, dissociative disorders are triggered by a serious trauma or upsetting event and the memory loss is specifically related to that trauma.

- Dissociative amnesia refers to the inability to remember important, upsetting information about one's life.

- Dissociative fugue involves the complete loss of one's identity, combined with a flight to another location.

- Dissociative identity disorder describes a disorder in which a person develops two or more distinct personalities, each with a unique set of memories, behaviors, thoughts, and emotions.

- Dissociative disorders may be a form of extreme state-dependent memory or an example of self-hypnosis, although some theorists suspect that dissociative identity disorder can also be inadvertently triggered by therapy discussions or events.

Key Terms

CUT/ACROSS CONNECTION

What Happens in the BRAIN?

- In his pioneering neurosurgical studies, Karl Lashley found that rats retained at least some memory of their mazes, even when he removed large parts of their brains.
- Memory is not confined to any single area of the brain, although the prefrontal cortex is especially active in working memory and the hippocampus and other parts of the neocortex are heavily involved in long-term memory.
- If experimental animals are given substances that block the development of long-term potentiation (LTP) in their neurons, they have difficulty transferring information from working memory into long-term memory.
- The brains of people with Alzheimer's disease form an unusually large number of plaques, although these deposits may not be the actual cause of the disease.

HOW we Differ

- The storage capacity of everyone's working memory seems to be about the same, but storage capacity in long-term memory varies greatly from person to person.
- Everyone uses phonological, visual, and semantic codes to encode information into meaning, but individuals may differ in how much they use each of these codes.
- The hippocampus size of elderly adults with excellent memories is, on average, 20 percent larger than that of people with Alzheimer's disease.
- Women are somewhat more likely than men to develop dementia.

When Things Go Wrong

- Head injuries are a common cause of amnestic disorders, organic disorders in which memory loss is the key symptom.
- From the moment that he had both of his temporal lobes surgically removed, the famous patient H.M. was never again able to form and hold new long-term memories.
- Only 1 to 2 percent of 65-year-olds experience Alzheimer's disease and other forms of dementia, compared to as many as 50 percent of those over the age of 85.
  - The symptoms of dissociative identity disorder, formerly known as multiple personality disorder, usually begin in early chilhood, often after episodes of abuse.

How we Develop

- Children are more likely than adults to have eidetic, or photographic, memories.
- An adult's recall of a childhood event can be influenced by emotions tied to the event, other events that have occurred since the initial one, motivated forgetting, exposure to misinformation, and the effects of imagination.
- As we age, we become more susceptible to forgetting, distortions, and misremembering.
- Although changes in the functioning of our memories unfold gradually throughout adulthood, specific declines in memory may actually begin in our twenties.
- Although forgetfulness becomes increasingly common as we age, dementia is not a normal part of aging.

View this in Action

www.wileyplus.com

Video Lab Exercise

Psychology Around Us

Memory Manufacturing and Eyewitness Testimony

"This is a stick-up!"

Memory plays a big role in our lives and in psychology. Generally, most people believe that they can remember things pretty well. Indeed, retrieving past memories, including "buried" memories, is a major part of daily functioning. Similarly, in the criminal justice system, the memories of eyewitnesses are relied upon heavily and lead to many convictions. BUT are our memories as accurate as we like to believe? Should we have great confidence in our recollections of recent everyday events, let alone our adult memories of childhood events, the recollections of eyewitnesses, and the like?

As you are working on this online exercise, consider the following questions…

- What do you think this lab exercise says about the accuracy of our memories?
- What implications might this lab exercise hold for the field of psychology's assumptions, techniques, and interpretations?
- How might this contrived situation differ from a real-life event? Does this contrivance help account for the accuracy or inaccuracy of your memories? Pro or con?

CHAPTER 9

Language and Thought

chapter outline

- Language • Language and Thought • Thought

"I'd Like to Phone a Friend, Please."

If you're like the vast majority of the college students who responded to one recent survey (Elliot, 2007), you own and use a cell phone. In fact, you probably use it a lot. In the United States, people in the traditional college age group, 18 to 24 years old, send an average of nearly 1,000 text messages every month; they average more text messages than they do phone calls (Keane, 2008). Today's cell phones can help you not only make and receive calls and texts, but also take and share pictures, get your e-mail, and search the Internet, or use an ever-expanding variety of other applications. Nearly every day, news reports feature stories of lost hikers or others who were rescued after calling for help from their cell phones, or when rescuers tracked them using the automatic global-positioning information generated by their phones. All you need to do to get benefits from your handy device is to figure out how to use it. That is, after you've decided which carrier to use, what phone to buy, and which service plan to get.

Using your cell phone requires language skills. You need to speak and understand the speech of your callers. When you text or scroll through the menus, you need to read, and perhaps write. You're also using language if you happen to read the instructions that come with your phone. Not only are you using language skills, you are also using a variety of different thinking skills. You may be mentally envisioning the person you're calling or texting. You may use what you know about their habits to try to determine when would be the best time to reach them, or to leave a voice mail, if you don't really want to reach them. Of course, as we've noted, the process of acquiring the device and learning to operate it in the first place also involved some key thinking skills. You had to make several key decisions and likely solve some problems, such as how to make sure that you could transfer all of your contacts from your old phone to your new one.

Language and thought are characteristics that distinguish humans from other creatures. Language enables us to communicate in a precise and often creative way. We use language, for example, to specify to a phone salesperson exactly which model of phone, in which color, and with which accessories, we would like to buy. We also use language to tell stories or jokes in exciting ways that make our friends gasp or laugh with us. Language has allowed us, as a species, to learn from past generations, originally by oral story telling and then by written language. Language is a critical component of human behavior because it greatly facilitates progressive social interactions. Consider the difficulty involved in organizing a large group of people to build an ancient city. Such a feat would be nearly impossible without the use of language.

Although language is communicative, sometimes we use language only in our own heads. We often think using words, but many of our thoughts are not shared. Some people write extensively but only for themselves, never intending or wanting others to read their written words. Although the processes of language and thought overlap, a clear difference exists between them. In general, psychologists study these processes separately.

Human thought is highly complex, varies from individual to individual, and takes on many different forms. While much thought involves the use of words, some does not, instead relying on visual imagery or sounds. Consider, for example, what happens when a particular tune is stuck in your head. Even if you can't remember the lyrics, you can often imagine the music.

The study of thought is a major component of cognitive psychology. As we saw in Chapter 1, the word **cognition** refers to a variety of mental processes that contribute to thinking and knowing. Cognition is involved in learning and memory, as well as thinking. In this chapter, we'll discuss a number of different types of thinking, which can involve accumulating knowledge, solving problems, making decisions, and even thinking about thinking!

Language

LEARNING OBJECTIVE 1 Define language, describe how we learn languages, describe parts of the brain that are involved in language, and discuss differences and problems that can affect people's language skills.

Language, whether spoken, signed, or written, is a set of symbols used to communicate. We use symbols, mainly words, to convey our thoughts and desires to others who share an understanding of the symbols. Language can be divided into two main components: language production and language comprehension. **Language production** occurs when we generate communicative vocalizations or gestures. Human language production is *generative* or creative; we make new sentences whenever we speak, rather than just restating old ones. In fact, humans have a remarkable capacity for producing new sentences, and we rarely repeat previously-heard sentences exactly. The ability to produce new sentences almost automatically is an important feature of human communication. We know that many other species communicate with sounds, but the vocalizations uttered by most species are inborn and do not change. A lion does not need to learn how to roar, for example, and it does not phrase its roar differently every time.

Very few species other than humans can learn new vocalizations, sounds produced in an effort to communicate (Pinker & Jackendoff, 2005). Vocal learning occurs in some species of songbirds (canaries, zebra finches), bats, aquatic mammals (whales and dolphins), and humans. It may come as a surprise to you that no primates other than humans learn language naturally, although monkeys and apes have an extensive repertoire of species-specific vocalizations. Those that have learned some vocalizations are not capable of the complexities that characterize human language. Despite years of training in the laboratory, for example, no ape has ever learned to speak.

Humans are also endowed with an impressive capacity for **language comprehension**, the ability to understand communicative vocalizations or gestures. We can generally comprehend fragments of sentences or words that are mispronounced. We can understand people who speak with accents, people with speech impediments, such as lisps or stutters, and even the speech of toddlers. Our ability to understand speech that is incomplete or unclear is related to the fact that much of language comprehension is automatic. Typically we understand spoken language without concentrating, which is the reason we are able to carry on a conversation with limited pauses before responding.

Vocal learners These canaries are among the very few species other than humans that actually learn their vocalizations. Canary song is re-learned every year just before the breeding season.

The study of speech can be divided into four general areas: *phonology, semantics, syntax,* and *pragmatics.* The building blocks of language are shown in **Figure 9-1**. The smallest units of sound in any language are called **phonemes**, and the study of how sounds are put together to form words is called **phonology**. The word *tip* has three phonemes—*t, i,* and *p*. The number of phonemes differs from language to language (Halle, 1990). The English language has about 40 phonemes (give or take a few depending on the dialect). At the two ends of the spectrum are the language Pirahã (an indigenous language of Brazilian people living in the Amazon), which has only ten phonemes, and the Taa language (also known as !Xóõ), a language of indigenous people of Botswana and Namibia, which has 141 phonemes.

Speakers of one language often cannot distinguish sounds of other languages if their own language does not include the phoneme (Dietrich, Swingley, & Werker, 2007). For example, Spanish does not include the sound used in English to pronounce the letter *J*. Spanish speakers pronounce *J* like English speakers pronounce *H*, as in the case of the boy's name *Juan*. In the process of learning Spanish in the absence of other languages, the ability to make the English /j/ sound decreases. Spanish speakers who are exposed to both languages early in their lives, however, acquire the correct pronunciation for the English phoneme of the letter *J* much more readily. We discuss later in this chapter how it is much easier for us to learn languages during an early stage of life.

While phonemes are sounds, **morphemes** are the smallest units of language that convey *meaning* (Miller, 1978). For example, the word *tips* has two morphemes. One is *tip* and the other is *s*, which is used to communicate that the word is plural. The study of the meaning of words is referred to as **semantics**. The dictionary meaning of a word is referred to as its **lexical meaning**. Lexical meaning changes over time. Consider the word *gay*, which, prior to the twentieth century, meant "happy." *Gay* now not only has an additional meaning of homosexual, but its original meaning has also fallen largely into disuse.

Knowing the meaning of individual words is important, but a word's meaning is often communicated through the position of the word in a sentence. For example, the word *blue* can mean a color or a depressed emotional state. When heard alone, it's impossible to tell the intended meaning, but when we hear *blue* in the context of a particular sentence, such as, "She wore a beautiful blue dress," or, "He's feeling blue today," the distinction becomes instantly clear. The way in which words are constructed into sentences is referred to as **syntax**.

Phonology, semantics, and syntax bring us to the point where we have sounds, words, and sentences. Communication also requires adhering to social norms, such as speed of speech, responding at appropriate intervals, making eye contact, and using acceptable body language. These aspects of communication are called **pragmatics**, because they refer to the practical use of language.

cognition mental processes of thinking and knowing.

language a set of symbols used to communicate.

language production the process of using movement to produce speech. Language production can also encompass signing by using hand signals.

language comprehension the process of understanding spoken, written, or signed language.

phoneme the smallest unit of language, an individual sound.

phonology the study of how individual sounds or phonemes are used to produce language.

morpheme the smallest unit of meaning in language.

semantics the study of how meaning in language is constructed of individual words and sentences.

lexical meaning dictionary meaning of a word.

syntax the grammatical positioning of words in a sentence.

pragmatics the practical aspects of language usage, including speech pace, gesturing, and body language.

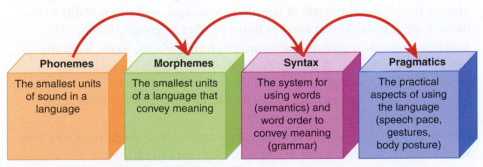

FIGURE 9-1 **The building blocks of language**

Getting his message across The facial expression, hands on hip, body posture, and other nonverbal cues of President Barack Obama, as he talks to his chief of staff, help communicate his feelings of concern and unhappiness.

One aspect of pragmatics is our use of body language, or **nonverbal communication**. The way we move our hands, bodies, and faces can change the connotations of our speech. Suppose your instructor said, "I would like to meet with you after class." If this statement was delivered with one raised eyebrow, a sneer, and arms folded across the chest, you would likely interpret it differently than you would if the instructor said the sentence with a warm smile, while leaning forward with hands on the desk. Some people are not aware of the body language they are using and unwittingly send the wrong messages when they attempt to communicate. An employee may believe, for example, that a boss is making inappropriate advances, because the boss is unaware of the message he or she sends by standing close and touching the worker's arm while talking.

Nonverbal communication seems to be acquired automatically, often by observing the actions of others. Nonverbal communication is related to, but not identical to, gesturing, which refers to communicative movements of the arms and hands. Gesturing facilitates speech production. While the ancient Greeks provided orators with explicit lessons in gesturing to enhance their speeches, studies have shown that gesturing appears to be innate (Acredolo & Goodwyn, 1988). For example, people blind from birth, who have not had the chance to learn gestures by watching others, nevertheless use gestures. Gesturing is often difficult to inhibit; blind people will gesture even when they realize they are talking to another blind person (Goldin-Meadow, 1999).

Language | How we *Develop*

You were probably too young at the time you started to speak your native language to remember learning it. Your parents may have proudly kept a record of your first words. If they did, they probably abandoned the list pretty quickly, as it became too long very fast. Within just a few years, almost every human baby goes from being incapable of speaking or understanding language to having an extensive vocabulary in one of over 4,000 languages. The general sequence of language learning is the same for most people:

- *Prevocal learning* Between two and four months of age, babies are capable of perceiving all possible phonemes, including those that are not needed for the language(s) they will ultimately learn (Aslin, Jusczyk, & Pisoni, 2000). During this time, babies have a remarkable ability to distinguish among these sounds. Researchers investigated babies' abilities to distinguish among different phonemes by training the babies to turn their heads toward an interesting visual reward when they hear a change in speech sounds. Results of studies using this type of training (which is a form of operant or instrumental conditioning, as described in Chapter 7) suggests that young babies can discern a much wider range of phonemes than older children or adults can (Werker, 1989). This ability declines, however, as babies begin to learn their native languages (Eimas et al., 1971). With practice in only the phonemes of our native languages, we lose the ability to distinguish among sounds that are only heard in other languages (Eimas, 1975).

- *Babbling* By about six months, babies start to babble (Sachs, 2009). **Babbling** refers to the production of meaningless sounds that enable the infant to experiment with vocalizations in a way that gradually approaches their soon-to-be-acquired native language. All babies babble, including those who are deaf (Wallace, Menn, & Yoshinaga-Itano, 1999).

- *First words* By about one year, speaking begins, typically in the form of very simple words, such as *mama, dada,* or *hi* (Ingram, 1986). At this early stage, our ability to comprehend is much greater than the ability to speak (see **Figure 9-2**). At about one year of age, the average baby can understand approximately fifty words, but

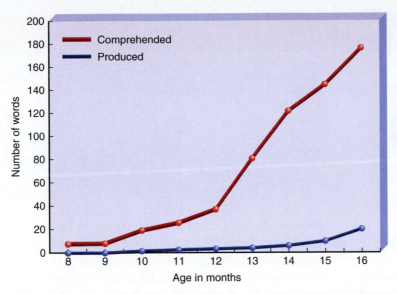

FIGURE 9-2 Babies' comprehension of words Babies can comprehend more words than they can speak. One-year-old babies understand about 50 words but will not be able to speak them until about six months later. (Adapted from Fenson at al., 1994.)

he or she will not be able to speak that many until about six months later (Fenson et al., 1994). One-year-olds can often follow commands, such as, "Get the ball and bring it to mommy," even though their spoken vocabulary may only include *ball* and *mama*.

- *Telegraphic speech* By age two, most toddlers speak in very short (typically two-word) sentences (Bloom, 1970). This is called **telegraphic speech** because, as in old-fashioned telegraph messages (for which senders were charged by the word), all but the essential words are omitted. Instead of saying, "I want a cookie," a two-year-old is more likely to say simply, "Want cookie."

- *Pragmatics* By three years of age, the average toddler has naturally acquired some practical information about language use, including the need to pause between sentences and the knowledge that certain sentences are statements, whereas others are requests (Garvey, 1974). If you were similar to the average bright English-speaking three year old, your vocabulary probably included about 1,000 words.

- *Grammar* By age four, children have automatically absorbed many of the rules of grammar, even though they have received no formal education about the grammar of their native languages (Tager-Flusberg, 2001). As discussed below, some of the early stages of reading often emerge around this time when children are exposed to written words at home or preschool. By age six, the average child uses almost 3,000 words and likely understands a great many more, about 14,000 words (depending on the amount of language they were previously exposed to—see Poverty and Language Development on page 282). By age nine, practical aspects of language, such as inferring meaning of obscure language, interpreting metaphors, and understanding sophisticated humor, emerge (Wellman & Hickling, 1994).

Even though the majority of language learning occurs relatively early in life, vocabulary and its usage can continue to increase in size and sophistication for decades to come. In studying for the SAT or other college-admission exams, many teenagers find themselves learning words they haven't used before. Vocabulary can increase throughout adulthood and seems to be one type of memory that is not adversely affected by the normal aging process. Elderly people with slowed reaction times and impaired memory for events in their own lives often score as high, if not higher, than young adults on vocabulary tests.

nonverbal communication body language.

babbling babies' production of meaningless sounds.

telegraphic speech speech that consists of minimalistic sentences. This form of speech characterizes early toddlerhood and is the first evidence of sentence formation.

Socioeconomic status	Words per hour	Affirmations	Prohibitions
Low SES	176	5	11
Mid SES	251	12	7
High SES	487	32	5

Children from socioeconomically disadvantaged backgrounds often struggle in academic settings. In fact, several studies suggest that poor children have deficient vocabularies when they first enter elementary school and that these differences often get exaggerated as the years pass because vocabulary builds on itself (Hart & Risley, 1995).

Research has shown that the initial language deficits of poor children are due to environmental differences. On average, as infants, toddlers, and young children, students from lower socioeconomic status (SES) households are exposed to fewer words than are students from households with higher socioeconomic status. As shown in the table, one study found that, in any given hour, children in poor homes heard less than half the number of words than children in high SES homes did (Hart & Risley, 1995). In addition, much more of the speech to which poor children were exposed was prohibitive, for example when a parent says, "Stop it!" or "Don't touch that."

The exact reasons why poor parents communicate less and less positively with their children remain unknown. The stress of poverty and the potential lack of suitable role models for parents (parenting skills are largely acquired through one's own upbringing) are two likely causes. The good news is that the problem of reduced vocabularies in lower SES children can be prevented by preschool intervention that includes educating parents about the benefits of talking and reading to children in the home.

> " *Language is a process of free creation.* "
> —*Noam Chomsky, American linguist*

Theories of Language Development Recall recent experiences you've had building your vocabulary, perhaps to take exams in your school classes or as you studied for a college standardized test. You may also have had experience learning a second or third language later in your education, perhaps starting in late elementary school or even in high school. In either situation, whether expanding your vocabulary in your first language, or adding an entirely new language, you probably experienced a much slower learning rate than you did when you learned your first language as a very young child. Language-related learning later in life probably also required concentrated attention to your studies; it most likely did not occur automatically.

The ease with which language is acquired by human infants has led many researchers to speculate that language has a biological basis. The linguist Noam Chomsky was among the first to suggest that language learning is built into our brains (Chomsky, 1964). The brain does appear to be set up to understand and communicate using language. As we have noted, the ability to detect all phonemes used in any human language exists in all human babies (as long as their hearing is intact). Other studies have also shown that the very young brain is wired to acquire language rapidly and automatically, because it is in a highly plastic, or changeable, state, ready to absorb new information about language. As humans grow and reach adulthood, the brain maintains the ability to change, but that ability has diminished (Johnson & Newport, 1989)—language learning becomes much slower and requires more effort.

Chomsky described our early capacity for language learning as a sort of *language acquisition device* built in to our brains. As we have seen, this "device" seems to become less efficient as we age. Psychologists often refer to the childhood years before age 13 as an especially important period for language acquisition. Some debate exists as to whether language systems have a critical or a sensitive period (Kyle, 1980). Recall from Chapter 3 that a *critical period* refers to a window of time during which certain influences are *necessary* for appropriate formation of the brain. After the **critical period**, these influences are no longer capable of having as profound an impact on the brain. A *sensitive period* refers to a developmental time during which the brain is more *susceptible* to influences. After the **sensitive period**, change can still occur but it doesn't happen as readily. As we have seen, we can still expand our vocabularies or learn new languages later in life, suggesting that, in normal cases, we go through more of a sensitive period than a critical period for language learning. Some evidence, however, such as from the sad case described in the accompanying box on the case of Genie, suggests that there is a critical period during which we must have *some* language input or we do not acquire normal fluency with speech.

It's clear that our brains have a biological propensity to help us acquire at least one language, but the process of language learning is not exclusively hardwired into us. Much evidence suggests that the environment plays a critical role, too. Early behaviorists, including B. F. Skinner (1957), suggested that language is acquired as a result of instrumental conditioning. Toddlers are rewarded with praise for producing appropriate speech, and ignored or scolded for failure to do so. As you may have noticed, however, parents, caregivers, and other older people do not usually systematically reward toddlers for correct speech. The two year old who says, "Want cookie," is just as likely to get one as another child who can ask, "Please, may I have a cookie?" Conditioning alone, therefore, cannot explain language learning.

Interactive theories suggest that experience works along with biological developmental periods to enhance and guide language learning (Goldberg, 2008). As we have described, for instance, if a baby isn't exposed to certain phonemes, his or her capacity to distinguish among these sounds diminishes.

The environments of most babies and young children also typically offer a high degree of very interactive speech. Most adults talk to babies with a special intonation in their voices: a high-pitched and sometimes exaggerated speech that is called **child-directed speech** (Fernald et al., 1989). Child-directed speech may help babies learn words by keeping them interested in the stimulus generating them. The patterns of child-directed speech are often rich in emotions, which may have the added benefit of fostering a close emotional relationship between caregiver and child, thus enhancing the quality and quantity of communication. Child-directed speech is also observed when parents use sign language to communicate with babies. Whether the adult, child, or both are deaf, the use of sign language during the learning phase naturally takes the form of a child-directed speech—slower in the formation of the hand signs, with longer pauses in between signs and exaggeration of facial expressions of emotions (Masataka, 1998). Child-directed speech arises naturally; people adopt it without any formal instruction, suggesting that humans seem to have a biological predisposition to teach effective communication to the very young (Cooper & Aslin, 1994; Bornstein et al., 1992).

The development of syntax, or grammatical rules, also suggests an interaction of biology and environment. Even in children with hearing loss who are not formally trained in sign language but develop their own form of signing, there is evidence of a grammatical structure. These findings suggest that the brain is predisposed to create a set of rules by which language will be used. Grammar rules differ from language to language, but within a given language, they remain the same and are followed fairly consistently by speakers of the language.

Even with such a strong biological basis, however, grammar is still affected by environment. We can see the effects of environment when children begin formal education. Children typically acquire a large vocabulary and the ability to form grammatically correct sentences by about age four, generally before they receive formal

Baby sign This mother is using child-directed speech to communicate with her toddler, including special intonations in her voice and a modified form of sign language. In turn, the child's responses include a form of sign language sometimes called "baby sign."

critical period a time during development after which we cannot develop certain capabilities.

sensitive period a time during development after which it becomes more difficult to develop certain capabilities.

child-directed speech speech characterized by exaggerated emotional responses and a slower pace that is common among caregivers communicating with babies and young children.

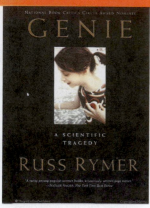

In 1970, an adolescent girl and her blind mother were delivered to a welfare office in California (Rymer, 1994). At the hands of her sadistic father, the girl, named Genie, had spent her entire life in isolation chained to a potty chair. She was rarely spoken to except in a punitive way ("stop it"). Her father communicated with her mostly by grunting and barking. At age 13, when her mother finally left the father, Genie had been exposed to almost no speech and appeared to be nearly mute. Her vocabulary consisted of about 20 words.

Age 13 is the time at which most researchers had assumed that the critical period for language acquisition is over. This assumption is based on the fact that after this age, people learn new languages with greater difficulty and typically don't lose their accents Because Genie was 13 years old at the time when she was rescued, she was an interesting, although tragic, test case of whether a critical period for language exists.

Genie's experiences tended to provide support for the theory that a sensitive period for language learning does exist. During the years that followed her rescue, Genie received extensive, interactive language training. Although she did initially show progress in expanding her vocabulary, it was always limited and didn't include the acquisition of grammatical rules. Unfortunately, Genie's vocabulary regressed even further when she was under stress.

Although the case of Genie seems to support the language critical period theory, it's important to keep in mind that Genie was not only deprived of language, but also subjected to extreme physical and emotional abuse that may have contributed significantly to her inability to learn (Kyle, 1980).

---

training in grammar (Tager-Flusberg, 2001). Once formal grammar education begins in elementary school and grammatical rules are consciously learned, however, children become more prone to errors. For example, once children learn that the suffix *-ed* refers to the past tense, they apply *-ed* to verbs that are irregular. A child who previously used the past tense of "*think*" correctly as "*thought*," may begin to say "*thinked*." Such mistakes are referred to as **overregularization** (Maratsos, 2000). They provide evidence that, while the tendency to readily pick up syntax exists in the very young, some aspects of grammar are learned. At the very least, there are two systems for language acquisition: one that is automatic and the other that requires conscious attention and can be learned explicitly. Overregularization is an example of how the conscious learning system can interfere with—and actually do a worse job than—the unconscious system of language acquisition.

Learning to Read   As we noted, many children begin formal education and start learning to read at around the ages of five or six years old. Reading is a complicated behavior that emerges considerably after the foundations of language production and comprehension have been laid down.

Children typically begin the process of learning to read by telling stories from looking at pictures in a book and attempting to recognize a few simple words (Sénéchal & LeFevre, 2001). In schools in the United States, reading and writing are usually a main focus of the first- and second-grade years. By the end of second grade (around age eight), reading becomes much less laborious for most children, as it transitions to an automatic process, one that requires little or no conscious thought (Ely, 1997). A trip in a car with a bright eight year old often results in exclamations of surprise that the printed words on billboards and store signs suddenly make sense.

Once reading becomes automatic, most people become very proficient at it. Just as we are capable of understanding spoken fragments of sentences or words spoken in for-

Identical genes, different reading skills These 5-year-old identical twins are reading as part of a study in Australia investigating how much of one's reading and spelling abilities are related to genes and how much are related to upbringing and schooling.

eign accents, we can understand written abbreviations with ease. Consider the abbreviated writing of the text message: U R L8. It's very easy to determine that this means, "You are late," because the phonemes are identical to those that are used to correctly spell out these words. More complicated and nonphonetic written messages require explicit learning. Consider the abbreviated writing of the text message: I ctn I g2g il ttyl. Without prior knowledge of the acronyms *ctn*, *g2g* and *ttyl*, the message, "I can't talk now, I've got to go, I'll talk to you later," would remain a mystery.

What Happens in the Language BRAIN?

In most people, language production and comprehension centers are located in the left hemisphere of the brain. In a small percentage of people (about 5 percent), the language centers are lateralized to the right hemisphere of the brain. In some cases, language involves both hemispheres. One area of the left hemisphere of the brain, known as Broca's area, is important for our ability to speak, while another area, called Wernicke's area, is important in language comprehension. In a typical conversation, both areas would be active at once, along with other parts of the brain.

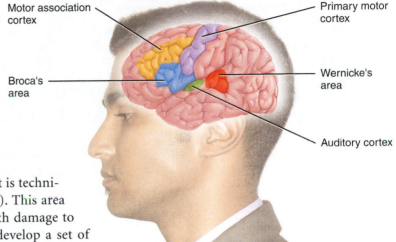

Broca's Area Broca's area is located in the frontal lobe in what is technically the motor association cortex (Damasio & Geschwind, 1984). This area was named after the neurologist who first described patients with damage to this region. People who suffer damage in or near Broca's area develop a set of symptoms called **Broca's aphasia**. The term *aphasia* can refer to an inability either in language production or in language comprehension. In Broca's aphasia, the problem is with production; people have great difficulty speaking. They speak unusually slowly and have trouble with pronunciations.

Because Broca's area is located in the motor association cortex, many researchers believe that the difficulty in speaking that characterizes Broca's aphasia is caused by difficulties in making the necessary movements. Speaking requires a complex set of movements of the lips, tongue, and larynx and movements are largely controlled by the primary motor cortex in the brain. The content of patients' speech supports the theory that difficulties in movement, rather than in thinking, are the major problems when Broca's area is damaged. Although difficult to follow, the speech of most people with Broca's aphasia makes sense. They have clear thoughts to communicate, but they have great difficulty getting them out.

Damage to Broca's area can, however, also produce an inability to speak with proper grammar, a condition referred to as **agrammatism**. This deficit suggests that our ability to use grammar is stored close to or within the same neural tissue that is responsible for speech production. This close neuroanatomical relationship probably explains how once learned, grammar is automatic. When we speak, we don't need to carefully construct grammatically correct sentences.

The agrammatism suffered by people with Broca's aphasia also tends to be linked to mild impairments in language comprehension. For instance, people with Broca's aphasia who were asked to point, from a group of pictures, to the correct one that illustrated a phrase such as "the cat ate the food" could do so. If researchers asked these people to point to a nonsense picture illustrating the phrase, "the cow was on the car," however, they were almost as likely to choose a picture of a car on a cow as to choose the correct one. The researchers concluded that people with Broca's aphasia were not

overregularization the process by which elementary school children apply learned grammatical rules to improperly "correct" an irregular verb.

Broca's area a region in the frontal lobes near the motor cortex that is important for speech production.

Broca's aphasia a neurological condition arising from damage to Broca's area where the patient is unable to produce coherent speech.

agrammatism a neurological condition arising from damage to a brain region just anterior to Broca's area where the patient is incapable of using words in grammatical sequence.

Frontal cortex

Parietal cortex

Temporal cortex

Scanning for language comprehension This PET scan displays the brain activity of a person who is repeating the words of another individual. Such vocal repetitions activate (*red and orange*) his Broca's area for speech production (*left*), Wernicke's area for language comprehension (*right*), and a motor region tied to vocalizations.

Making the grade This student at the Mississippi School for the Deaf uses sign language to answer questions on a vocabulary test. Similar to students who hear and talk, her brain's Wernicke's area and Broca's area become active as she comprehends and answers the test questions.

Wernicke's area a brain region located in the temporal lobe that is important for language comprehension.

Wernicke's aphasia a neurological condition associated with damage to Wernicke's area where a person cannot understand language.

able to use clues such as grammar and word order to determine the meaning of a sentence that was not obvious from its individual words.

Neuroimaging studies of people without brain damage have confirmed much of what neurologists and neuropsychologists have discovered from studying the behavior of people with Broca's aphasia (Gernsbacher & Kaschak, 2003). Broca's area itself is active during speaking, and a closely located area just in front of Broca's area becomes active when we try to comprehend sentences with complicated grammar.

Sign language uses brain areas similar to those important in spoken language. Neuroimaging studies show that, in people with intact brains, Broca's area and Wernicke's area are activated during signing. Since producing sign language does not require actual speech production, it does not involve as much activation of Broca's area. However, because sign language does involve use of grammar to construct meaningful sentences, using sign language activates the same neural tissue near Broca's area, involved in the use of grammar when speaking. Deaf people with brain damage around Broca's area can experience deficits in grammar use with signing.

Wernicke's Area Although the tissue near Broca's area seems to contribute to the comprehension of grammar in language, other parts of the brain are even more important for language comprehension. Because speech comprehension begins when we hear, it is not surprising that the brain regions most important for understanding speech are located near the auditory cortex in the upper part of the left temporal lobe. **Wernicke's area** was first identified by a neurologist named Wernicke, who studied patients with brain damage. People who suffer destruction to this part of the brain have **Wernicke's aphasia**. They cannot understand speech. Patients with Wernicke's aphasia are fully capable of talking, but their speech makes no sense.

Other Brain Regions In addition to Broca's and Wernicke's areas, other brain regions have important functions in specific aspects of language. For instance, the box on cursing accompanying this section describes how the amygdala, a brain region important for fear and aggression, appears to be involved in the use of profanity.

Most people also typically use regions in the right hemisphere to understand figurative language, such as metaphors. In figurative language, the meaning of a phrase is different from the literal meaning of the words used in the phrase. Damage to the right hemisphere can lead to taking figurative language literally. For instance, a person might think the phrase "hold your horses" means to grab hold of an actual horse. Metaphors are figures of speech that compare unlike things. Damage to the right hemisphere might lead a person to think that you live with an actual farm animal when you say, "My roommate is a total pig." Perhaps because understanding humor requires a grasp of abstract language—humor often involves the use of puns and metaphors—right hemisphere damage can also disrupt the ability to understand a joke.

A role for the right hemisphere in processing information about metaphors has been demonstrated using a relatively new technique in brain science called *transcranial magnetic stimulation* or *TMS*. Researchers can aim TMS, which delivers a strong magnetic signal, into a participant's head to temporarily inactivate a specific brain region. One such study found that TMS of the right hemisphere temporarily impaired the ability of humans to understand metaphors and that this impairment was greatest when the metaphors were unfamiliar to the participants (Pobric et al., 2008).

If a person learns two or more languages simultaneously as a child, Broca's and Wernicke's areas are involved in the use of all languages. Interestingly, however, if we do not learn a second language (or third or fourth) until adulthood, the brain does not rely as heavily on Broca's and Wernicke's areas. Instead, it recruits other circuits to aid in the

All languages have taboo words, those that are controversial and not considered to be part of neutral conversation. Across cultures, taboo or curse words seem to fall into one of three general categories: religious references, sexual references, and excrement references. The relative weight of each of these categories of curse words differs according to cultural beliefs. Religious profanity (such as *G— damn it*) is considered to be much milder in the United States than in cultures where belief in God is universal.

People swear for a variety of reasons, including for intimidation, to show off, to emphasize a point, and to express negative emotions in response to a mishap. Expletives are often used to get attention and intimidate. They are commonly associated with anger. It is not surprising that the brain regions activated by swearing or hearing swear words are those that are involved in aggression and fear. Use of profanity involves activation of the amygdala, a primitive brain region that is important for emotions, including fear and rage.

It appears that the same neural circuitry humans use for swearing is also important to other animals for responding to basic emotions, even though the manner of expressing these emotions is different. The amygdala is involved in expressions of fear and aggression in nonhumans, including monkeys, cats, and rats. While these animals are known to vocalize loudly under threatening circumstances, they don't use language and they can't speak. We can only imagine what they might say.

---

learning process. Among these are parts of the prefrontal cortex, important for working memory, and the temporal lobe, active in the acquisition of semantic information. The recruitment of additional brain regions not involved in language learning early in life may contribute to the greater difficulty of learning a language later in life.

Reading also involves a wide range of brain regions. The physical actions required to read activate areas of the brain that aid in visual processing and motor functions. Since reading involves eye movements, for example, it recruits a brain region in the frontal lobe called the *frontal eye fields*. The content of what we read also affects which brain areas become more active during reading. Words of particular emotional importance, such as obscenities or disgust words, activate the amygdala. When we read words that evoke odors, such as *garlic* or *cinnamon*, the primary olfactory, or smell-related, regions of the brain become activated (González et al., 2006).

Language HOW we Differ

There is considerable variability among the normal population in the rate at which language is acquired and the size of vocabulary and overall verbal skills. Some evidence suggests that males and females may differ in language skills. There are even differences in the number of languages that we acquire. Although all normal people become proficient in at least one language, some people are multilingual and can become fluent in many different languages.

Differences Among Individuals Some of the variability in the rate of language acquisition is due to our environments. Our vocabulary size, for example, is affected by our environment, particularly early in life. As described in the box earlier in the chapter, children in low-income households often hear fewer words and have smaller vocabularies when they start school than those from more affluent families.

There is also a great degree of variability in the normal population with regard to reading and writing skills. For instance, people differ substantially in the speed with which they can read. This skill seems to be tied to eye movements. In English, words are written on the page from left to right, and reading speed is greatest for individuals whose

Language diversity Although most people in the United States can speak one language only, many acquire two or more. This six-year-old reads a Spanish book in her "dual language" first grade classroom in Kansas.

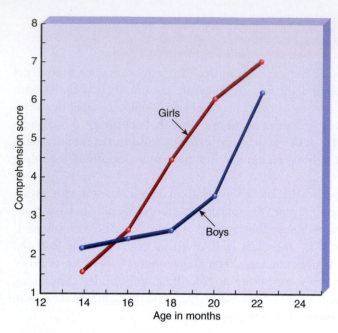

FIGURE 9-3 Gender differences in speech comprehension Early on, there is a notable difference in language comprehension between girls and boys. Girls comprehend language at a faster rate, but this gender gap disappears by about age two (Reznick & Goldfield, 1992).

"Your vocabulary is enlarged."

eyes move in the same left-to-right direction as the printed words, with no backtracking. Slower readers tend to not only pause for longer periods of time over individual words, but also to backtrack, moving their eyes back to words already passed (Lahey et al., 1982). It's not clear whether the less fluid eye movements occur because reading is more difficult or whether the backtracking eye movements are a distraction that interferes with rapid reading.

Gender Differences in Language   One difference in verbal learning and overall skills that may be related, at least in part, to genetics is a notable gender difference in early language learning. Girls tend to learn to talk earlier: On average, girls acquire speech and language comprehension at a faster rate than boys (**Figure 9-3**) (Reznick & Goldfield, 1992). These early differences often diminish by about age two, however, when those slower to acquire language catch up.

Although boys may catch up in speaking skills, girls still seem to outpace boys in the language skills used in elementary school, where, as a group, they seem to score higher on tests of English ability. It's not clear, however, whether this difference is related to a real gender difference in language ability or to a gender difference in some of the skills necessary to be a good student, such as paying attention, taking legible notes, and studying. By young adulthood, these differences seem to be gone. There are no substantial male-female differences in overall critical reading or writing scores on the SAT.

As discussed in Chapter 7, when considering gender differences, remember to keep in mind that, even though statistical differences may exist between average scores of boys and girls or men and women, this doesn't mean much for the individual. Many boys acquire language skills very rapidly and become talented writers and speakers as adults.

Another important point to consider is that the gender difference in language acquisition may have an experiential component. Because boys tend to be more active than girls, and girls tend to be more social than boys, it's possible that girls are exposed to a higher degree of interactive language than boys. If young boys are constantly on the move, exploring the environment may occupy more time than language learning.

Despite the fact that there do not appear to be significant differences in overall verbal ability between adult men and women, some evidence suggests a difference in the way that women and men process language information. Neuroimaging studies have shown that, on average, women are more likely to use both hemispheres of the brain to process language information, whereas language processing in men tends to be more lateralized (Clements et al., 2006). The extent to which these differences in recruitment of neural circuitry during language processing between men and women have any functional consequence remains to be determined.

Learning More Than One Language   Many children grow up in multilingual homes, where two or more languages are spoken. Such children tend to learn to speak and understand language at slightly later ages than children who only need to learn a single language. The greater amount of information and decoding necessary to learn two or more languages simultaneously may explain the very slight lag.

Like first languages, multiple languages are also most readily acquired by the very young. In adulthood, the language learning process is labor intensive and often remains incomplete. By the age of 13, our language learning ability has declined substantially (**Figure 9-4**) (Johnson & Newport, 1989). The difference can be seen with accents. People who immigrate to the United States as children learn to speak English without an accent, whereas those who immigrate as teens or adults speak English less fluidly and typically with the accent of their native tongue. A similar phenomenon exists for deaf children learn-

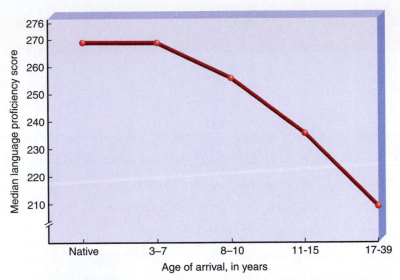

FIGURE 9-4 **The earlier we learn a new language, the more proficient we become** Immigrants' mastery of English depends on when they begin the learning process. The proficiency of those adults who started learning their new language before age 7 is comparable to that of native speakers. However, the proficiency of those who started acquiring the language in young adulthood is much poorer (Johnson & Newport, 1989).

ing sign language. After about age 13, it becomes more difficult to learn this skill. Knowing this, many of us wish we had been exposed to multiple languages as youngsters. Those fortunate enough to have this experience can become fluent in several languages without any formal study. See "What Happens in the Brain When We Learn a Second Language" on the following pages.

Before You Go On

What Do You Know?

1. What is language and how does language production differ from language comprehension?
2. What are phonology, morphology, syntax, and pragmatics?
3. What is the typical sequence of language acquisition for most babies?
4. Where are Broca's and Wernicke's areas located in the brain and what is the primary function of each?

What Do You Think? Should preschools and early grades of elementary schools in the United States be required to teach children multiple languages? What might be the advantages and drawbacks for children of such schooling?

Language and Thought

LEARNING OBJECTIVE 2 Describe thinking that happens without words and summarize the linguistic relativity hypothesis.

Many of us consider our thoughts to be primarily related to language. Since we often have no trouble responding automatically with words in a conversation, it can seem that language is the natural driving force of thought, and one influential psychological theory suggests that our language controls and limits our thoughts. In many cases, however, complex thoughts occur in the absence of language.

When We Learn a Second Language

Do you speak more than one language, or are you learning a second language now? Then you probably know that it takes a lot of time to become fluent in a second language, particularly if you didn't start to learn as a young child. Learning a second language not only engages brain regions that are involved in language production and comprehension, it also activates areas important for learning semantic information, such as the hippocampus, and those important for working memory, such as the prefrontal cortex. As we acquire grammatical rules and become more fluent, the regions in our brain that are associated with learning a first language—such as Broca's area and Wernicke's area—become primarily involved. As we activate these language production and comprehension areas more and more, we rely less and less on semantic and working memory regions.

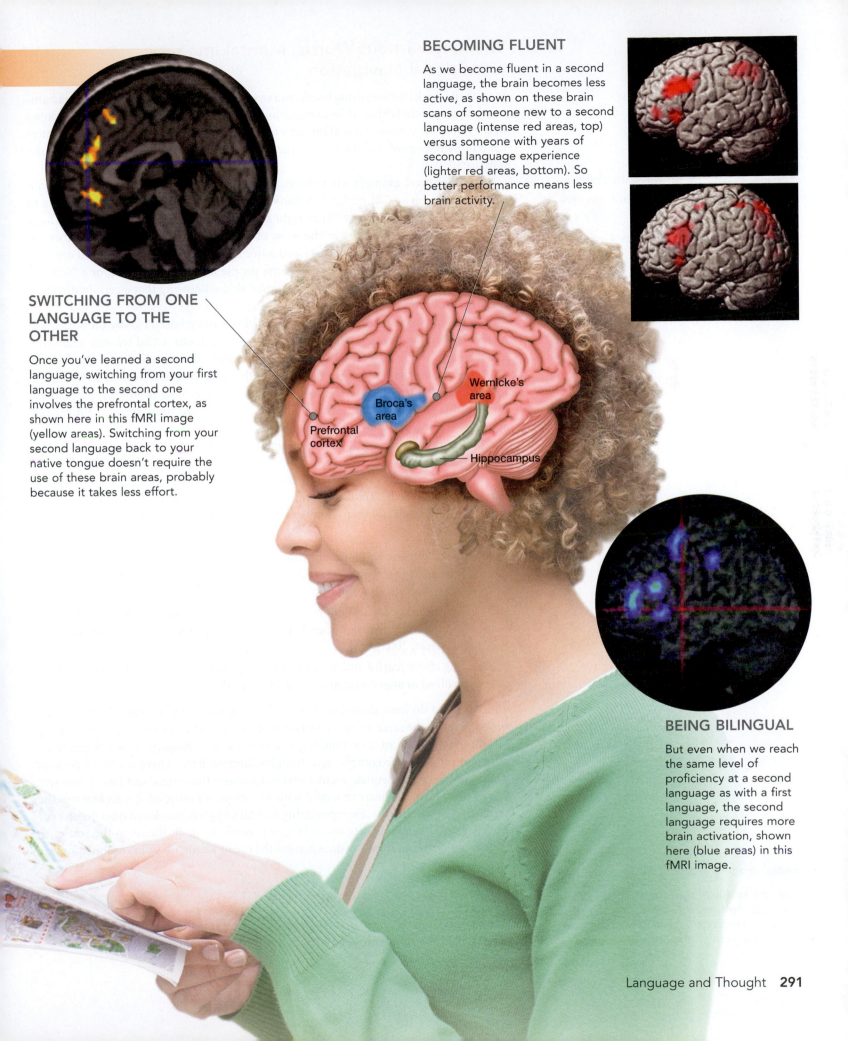

BECOMING FLUENT

As we become fluent in a second language, the brain becomes less active, as shown on these brain scans of someone new to a second language (intense red areas, top) versus someone with years of second language experience (lighter red areas, bottom). So better performance means less brain activity.

SWITCHING FROM ONE LANGUAGE TO THE OTHER

Once you've learned a second language, switching from your first language to the second one involves the prefrontal cortex, as shown here in this fMRI image (yellow areas). Switching from your second language back to your native tongue doesn't require the use of these brain areas, probably because it takes less effort.

Wernicke's area

Broca's area

Prefrontal cortex

Hippocampus

BEING BILINGUAL

But even when we reach the same level of proficiency at a second language as with a first language, the second language requires more brain activation, shown here (blue areas) in this fMRI image.

Language and Thought   **291**

Thinking without Words: Mental Imagery and Spatial Navigation

During the weeks before spring break, you may enjoy picturing yourself lying in a hammock sipping a cool drink while overlooking the Florida coast or skiing down the slopes of the Rocky Mountains. **Mental imagery** refers to thoughts that involve conjuring internal representations of stored sensory input. Most of our mental imagery does not involve language.

Another good example where language doesn't play a major role in thinking can be observed with spatial navigation thinking. Although some people use narrative to remember directions, such as, "Turn right at the second light on Main Street," in many cases, spatial thinking occurs in the form of visual imagery. You may remember the appearance of certain street corners and automatically turn right when you are triggered to do so by your visual system. Some people use dead reckoning or a "sense of direction" to navigate. This kind of directional skill—knowing that a certain direction is north, for example—is not language driven.

Our ability to use imagery to solve problems is often based closely on our spatial memories. Studies have shown that we appear to search our actual relevant memories to solve tasks requiring mental imagery. For example, if researchers give participants photos of rooms that are long and narrow, with regularly spaced objects in them, and later ask the participants to describe the objects located in those rooms, the participants do so with a greater lag time between objects than if asked to carry out a similar task after looking at a photo of a smaller room.

Interestingly, using mental imagery activates many of the same brain regions as are used for the sensory experience itself. Neuroimaging technology has allowed us to observe which regions of the brain become most active when people think. This type of research suggests that thinking about something can actually activate the same brain regions as sensing or doing it (Goldberg, Perfetti, & Schneider, 2006). There are many examples:

- When you visualize or picture in your mind an event or scene, your brain activates the visual areas that would be active if you were actually gazing at the event or scene (O'Craven & Kanwisher, 2000).
- Thinking about tastes and odors activates many of the same gustatory and olfactory brain regions involved when you really do taste or smell something (Bensafi, Sobel, & Khan, 2009).
- Thinking about fearful and anxiety-provoking subjects activates the amygdala, an area involved in anger, fear, and stress (Shin et al., 2004).

And when we do have thoughts that involve language, they activate the frontal and temporal lobes, the same areas used when we comprehend or produce spoken language.

Although some of our thinking involves mental imagery, it is obviously not sufficient for all of the complicated thoughts humans have. There are many concepts that do not have an adequate mental image. Consider thinking about love. Some symbols of love, such as a heart or Cupid with his arrow, are associated with love but they hardly tell the whole story. Even conjuring mental images of our loved ones doesn't adequately express our thoughts about love in general. As we'll discuss in the rest of the chapter, much of our thinking does involve the use of words, often in combination with imagery.

The Influence of Language on Thought

Many psychologists believe that language influences our thinking a great deal, an idea that is called the **linguistic relativity hypothesis**, which suggests that the number of

"Most events are inexpressible, taking place in a realm which no word has ever entered."

—*Rainer Maria Rilke, German poet*

mental imagery picturing things in your mind.

linguistic relativity hypothesis suggests that the vocabulary available for objects or concepts in a language influences how speakers of that language think about them.

words we have available to us related to a single concept, the more complex and detailed our thoughts are about that object or idea.

Evidence in support of the linguistic relativity hypothesis comes from cross-cultural studies that reveal large discrepancies in the number of words various languages dedicate to certain characteristics or objects. Studies have shown that extensive vocabularies for certain characteristics can lead to an ability to make finer distinctions along that dimension (Davies & Corbett, 1997). The English language, for example, has many words used to distinguish different colors. We can describe nuances of difference in shades of the color blue, for example, by using words such as *azure, cobalt, cyan, indigo, turquoise, aquamarine,* and more. By contrast, members of the Dani tribe of Papua New Guinea have in their entire language only two words to distinguish color, one word for light and the other for dark. These people are not colorblind. They can perceive differences in color, but they do not have words to describe them. The linguistic relativity hypothesis suggests that because English-speaking people have words for subtle concepts or distinctions regarding color, we are encouraged to think more about them than we would if, like the Dani, our vocabulary did not include those words.

Far from colorblind The colorful and carefully-blended war decorations of Dani tribesmen show that these individuals from Papua New Guinea are not colorblind, despite their limited vocabulary for colors.

Before You Go On

What Do You Know?

5. What is mental imagery and what parts of the brain does it involve?
6. What research evidence suggests that we use mental imagery to solve problems involving our spatial memories?
7. What does the linguistic relativity hypothesis suggest about the influence of our language on our thinking and what research has been done?

What Do You Think? In what ways do you believe your language influences your thoughts?

Thought

LEARNING OBJECTIVE 3 Describe and summarize research on thinking processes, including problem solving, decision making, and metacognition.

We can think in many different ways. The study of cognition includes, for example, mental imagery and spatial navigation, as we have seen. Cognitive scientists also study the development of our thinking abilities, how we solve problems, how we make decisions, and even how we think about our own thoughts. We will take a look at some of their major findings in the remainder of this chapter. Our thinking abilities are truly impressive, but the variety and complexity of thought also means we are sometimes vulnerable to problems in our thinking. We'll also discuss two psychological disorders that are characterized primarily by disruptions in thought processes.

Different forms of thinking develop at different rates. Thoughts that involve language emerge around the time that language capabilities are forming, whereas those that involve reasoning emerge later. Formulating long-term plans and carrying them out is a type of thought that develops relatively late (Chandler & Carpendale, 1998). Changes in our thinking continue to occur throughout life. Teenagers and young adults become increasingly capable of making and carrying out long-term plans for their futures.

Thinking and Effort: Controlled and Automatic Processing

The distinction between controlled and automatic thinking is an important concept in cognitive psychology. As we discussed in Chapter 8 on memory, *controlled processing* is effortful and relies on a limited-capacity system, while *automatic processing* seems effortless. Automatic processing is not usually disrupted very much if we are distracted by other tasks. Experienced drivers can carry on a conversation while driving a car, for example. However, automatic processing, such as driving, can be severely disrupted by simultaneously engaging in a task that requires more attention than speaking, such as reading or sending a text message. Controlled processing requires more attention. Most of us cannot carry on a conversation while conducting multidigit mental arithmetic. We must direct our thoughts toward the math problem.

Cognitive control refers to the ability to direct thought and action in accord with one's intentions (Carter, Botvinick, & Cohen, 1999). Some examples of this include:

- the ability to direct attention to a specific stimulus within other competing, and perhaps stronger stimuli, such as finding the face you are looking for within a crowd
- maintaining a new piece of information in mind against distraction, such as remembering a telephone number until you dial while on your cell phone in a crowded mall
- overcoming a compelling behavior, such as not scratching a very itchy mosquito bite
- pursuing a complex but unfamiliar behavior, such as learning the moves of a new sport or how to work the controls of a new videogame
- responding flexibly and productively in new situations, such as playing a complex videogame that requires anticipating future consequences

The brain's ability of exert control over mental processing is referred to as *executive function*. People with damage to the frontal lobes often display a condition called *dysexecutive syndrome*, characterized by impairments in cognitive functions that depend on control, such as planning or the ability to flexibly respond in new situations. This deficit was dramatically documented in the classic case of Phineas Gage. As we discussed in Chapter 4, Gage was a railroad foreman who suffered damage to his prefrontal cortex when a metal spike was driven through his head in a construction accident. Before the accident, acquaintances described him as thoughtful, responsible, and of sound judgment, but following his injury, he was considered to be

Automatic processing has its limits
Even automatic processing, such as that used when driving a car, can be severely interrupted by tasks that require significant attention, such as texting. Thus, to prevent car accidents, state laws typically allow people to converse (a relatively non-distracting activity) on a hands-free phone while driving, but forbid them to use a hand-held cell phone.

"capricious . . . and unable to settle on any of the plans he devised for future action." Changes such as these have been observed repeatedly in patients with damage to the frontal cortex.

As we age, we also develop more capacity for cognitive control. Very young children, for example, often make decisions based on impulse; if they want the cookie and it's in view, they will grab it. Problems arise with social interactions for this reason. Preschool-aged children will often fight over toys because they don't understand the concepts of waiting and fairness. As children grow, however, their decision-making process becomes more sophisticated. Usually by the time they are six to eight years old, children are able to modulate their impulses for the good of their peers. During snack-time, William may save a cookie for Lydia, who is out of the room, rather than eat it himself. At an even later stage, between the ages of nine and twelve, children become able to make decisions with the long-term future in mind. They are more willing to make sacrifices in the immediate future in order to get a larger pay off later on. If given the option of getting one square of chocolate after completing a single math problem or an entire chocolate bar after a 24-hour waiting period, older children will often decide to hold out for the whole bar.

Enough for everyone By the age of 6 to 8 years old, children have learned to better control their thoughts and actions in accord with their various intentions. Sharing everything from ice cream to toys becomes a more common occurrence.

Thinking to Solve Problems

One aspect of thinking that has received considerable attention from psychologists is that of *problem solving*. **Problem solving** is triggered by our desire to reach a goal. We must figure out how to get from our current state of affairs, which is in some way unsatisfactory, to our desired end state (Bourne, Dominowski, & Loftus, 1979). We use problem-solving skills in many avenues of life, from the formal mathematics problems we've all solved in school to the informal day-to-day problems, such as how to get along with a roommate.

Defining Our Problems The first step in solving a problem is to figure out exactly what your problem is—to develop a representation of the problem.

On one end of the spectrum, we use formal problem-solving skills to solve math problems. Our goal in arithmetic is usually straightforward, to move from not knowing the correct answer to knowing it. Researchers refer to problems, such as arithmetic with easy-to-discern beginning and end states, as *well-defined problems*. We often find it fairly easy to find a strategy for solving well-defined problems.

On the other end of the problem-solving spectrum are *ill-defined problems*, such as how to deal with a less than helpful roommate. Our goal in this case might be difficult to define in precise terms. We may want to stop doing what we feel is an unfair share of housecleaning, but how will we know when we've reached that goal? As you might imagine, it's often more difficult to find solution strategies for ill-defined problems than it is for well-defined ones.

To define a problem, you must figure out your current state and your goal, and identify the differences between them. Consider the following problem. When driving home on a particular road, you need to make a left onto Main Street at a traffic light that is always very backed up at the time of day you travel. Your current state is frustration with the long wait at the light.

Your goal might be to find a faster way to make the turn. With this goal in mind, you could consider several ways to speed up the turn, such as altering the time of day you travel, driving faster to arrive at the intersection earlier, or merging into the line of waiting cars closer to the intersection. None of these solutions is ideal. If the problem is represented in a different way, however, a new solution may come to mind. You might, for example, change your question from, "How do I make a left onto Main Street?" to, "How can I get onto Main Street faster?"

> **"** We only think when we are confronted with problems. **"**
>
> –John Dewey, American psychologist

algorithm problem-solving strategy that always leads to a solution.

heuristic shortcut thinking strategy.

mental set tendency to use problem-solving strategies that have worked in the past.

functional fixedness tendency to view objects as having only one function.

confirmation bias tendency to look for information that meets our expectations.

Adopting a new goal such as this may cause you to notice that you could turn right into the parking lot of a shopping center at the corner, then exit the lot quickly and legally onto Main Street in the direction you want to go—avoiding the left-hand turn entirely. Changing the representation of a problem doesn't guarantee a solution, but it increases your chances of finding one if your new representation triggers you to consider new alternatives.

Strategies for Problem Solving   After you have represented the problem, you must choose a strategy for finding a solution. Two major types of strategies—algorithms and heuristics—are used. An **algorithm** is a strategy that, if followed methodically, will always lead to a solution. For example, an algorithm strategy could be used to solve an arithmetic problem that includes adding up a series of ten single-digit numbers by adding each number to the overall sum. Following this algorithm will produce a correct answer but it can be time consuming. If you had to add up the total of fifty or a hundred different numbers, you might begin to look for faster ways to solve the problem.

To save time and effort when solving problems, we often use a set of **heuristics**, or shortcut strategies. Instead of taking the time to add together a long list of numbers, you might just estimate the total. Heuristics often help us reach a satisfactory solution, but they do not guarantee a correct answer to a problem.

Algorithm and heuristic strategies can be used to solve problems in everyday life. Consider the steps you would take to find out whether or not a particular professor will be a good teacher for you before enrolling in his or her course. Using an algorithm method, you might question every student enrolled in the class the previous term. This method would give you the maximum amount of information and the greatest chance of reaching the correct answer. Using a heuristic strategy, you might ask a few students you know who took the course or examine the drop rate in the class for evidence of how many students decide against the course once enrolled. The heuristic methods save time and effort, but they are also riskier. Your few acquaintances might not learn as well from a teaching style that you like, for example.

Some helpful heuristic strategies in problem solving include working backward, forming subgoals, and searching for analogies:

Two heads are better than one For many problems, better solutions are reached when multiple persons think the problem through together. Such collaborations may increase the likelihood of gathering sufficient information and reduce the chance of falling into common problem-solving traps.

- *Working backward* is helpful for problems with well-defined goals. Starting from your goal, you think backward, imaging a series of steps it would take you to move backward from your goal to your current state. Once you've determined the steps between your current state and the goal, you can actually follow them in a forward order. Working backward to figure out if a professor is a good teacher for you, you may define your goal as enjoying the teacher's lectures. A good step to find out if you enjoy the lectures is to sit through one, so you may decide to visit and sample one of the professor's class sessions in the current term.

- *Forming subgoals* involves dividing a larger problem into smaller ones (Catrambone, 1998). If your ultimate goal is to find out if a professor will be a good teacher for you, you may form subgoals, such as asking three former students about the professor and arranging to sit in on one lecture.

- *Searching for analogies* involves recalling similar problems that you've encountered (Holyoak, & Morrison, 2005). If you've successfully sought information about an unknown professor's teaching style before, you might just reuse the methods that worked best for you in that instance to learn more about the current professor.

We're not always aware of using a method in order to solve a problem. Sometimes we seem to solve a problem quickly, without intensive effort or concentration, through a phenomenon known as *insight*. In fact, several groundbreaking scientific discoveries have been described as "eureka" moments of insight. Sometimes sudden solutions occur after an *incubation period,* during which we have mentally "set aside" a problem that we've been working on. When we return to the problem after a period of time, the solution comes to mind without further conscious strategizing. Some studies suggest that type of problem solving is automatic (Novick & Bassock, 2005).

Problems in Problem Solving   Sometimes we fall into patterns of thinking that make it difficult to solve problems to which those patterns don't apply. One common difficulty can happen early in representing the problem. We must define the problem using relevant information and ignore any irrelevant information. When considering the problem of finding out whether or not a professor has a good teaching style for you, you might not be terribly interested in that professor's interesting line of research, for example, if the professor's research has little impact on his or her teaching.

Other difficulties can occur when we get to the point of actually solving problems. Some of these are the result of heuristics. When we use the heuristic of looking for analogies, for example, we risk falling into a **mental set**, a tendency to use problem-solving strategies that have always worked in the past. If you have a certain solution in mind, you may see the problem as fitting that solution, when it does not. If you view getting onto Main Street with a mental set that sees the problem as how to make a left turn, you miss possible solutions that do not involve left turns. The nine-dot problem shown in **Figure 9-5** is a good way to practice overcoming mental sets.

One particular version of a mental set is referred to as **functional fixedness**, the tendency to view objects as having only one use or function. If you have ever used a coin to turn the head of a screw when you didn't have a screwdriver handy, you have overcome functional fixedness. The string problem, shown in **Figure 9-6** is one test that psychologists have used to reveal when people are experiencing functional fixedness.

We can also hamper our ability to solve problems by adopting a **confirmation bias**, a tendency in solving problems to look for information that meets our expectations. If you have heard that all of the professors in the department in which you are thinking of taking a class are good teachers, you may only seek out opinions from students who completed the class taught by the professor whose class you are thinking of taking, rather than undertaking the more difficult task of finding people who have dropped the course. The problem with this approach is that students who stayed through the whole course would be more likely to confirm what you expect to hear, that the teacher is good, than to give you a negative, but potentially helpful, evaluation.

In one classic study, researchers revealed confirmation bias by giving participants a series of numbers: 2, 4, and 6 (Wason, 1960). They asked the participants to figure out the rule for that set by generating their own sets of numbers. Each time the participants offered a series, the experimenters told them only whether their set did or did not follow the same rule as the original set. Many participants became convinced that the rule was to increase each number by 2. They offered repeated sets of numbers, such as 8, 10, 12 or −4, −2, 0. The researchers told them that their sets conformed to the original rule, but when asked to state the original rule, these participants got it wrong. The original rule was simply that each number had to have a numerical value larger than the one before it.

The way to overcome confirmation bias is to purposely look for information that disconfirms your ideas. Participants who generated random series of numbers, such as 54, 3, 12, would have been more likely to correctly figure out the rule.

" If the only tool you have is a hammer, it is tempting to treat everything as if it were a nail.**"**

—Abraham Maslow, American psychologist

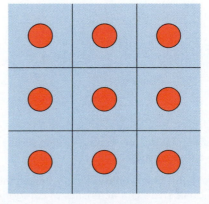

FIGURE 9-5 **The nine-dot problem** Without lifting your pencil, draw no more than four lines to connect all the dots. (The solution is on page 298.)

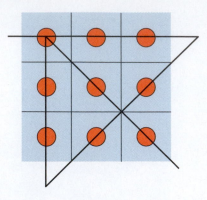

Solution to the nine-dot problem Most people have difficulty with this problem because they see the arrangement of dots as a square and try to keep within the boundaries of the dots. This mental set limits their ability to solve the problem.

FIGURE 9-6 **The string problem** Two strings are suspended from above, and you cannot reach both of them at the same time. How can you tie them together? (The solution is on page 300.)

Thinking to Make Decisions

Decision making involves evaluating and choosing from among the alternatives available to us. Many of your everyday thoughts involve weighing options and making choices. First you must decide what time to wake up. A series of decisions follow, including choices about what to wear, what to eat for breakfast, with whom to spend your time, and what to do. Even when we're on a regular schedule, we don't behave like robots. We often have options to deviate from our regular course of action, and we must decide whether or not to take them.

Information for Decision Making   To make decisions, we need to gather or recall information relevant to each alternative. Suppose you're trying to decide which of two movies to go see. You would probably like a little information about each film to help you make your choice. You can gather information from sources outside yourself, such as movie reviews and the comments of your friends. You can also recall relevant information that you already have. You may, for example, recognize the names of some of the actors or one of the directors.

When we draw from our memories to get information, we often use heuristic short-cuts. The use of heuristics is sometimes successful, but often leads to reaching the incorrect decision (Stanovich, 2008; Tversky & Kahneman, 1993, 1974). One such heuristic is that of representativeness. The **representativeness heuristic** makes the assumption that individual objects or people are members of a category if they share similar characteristics. This leads to drawing conclusions about that object, or person, with a small

decision making evaluating and choosing from among options.

representativeness heuristic assumes that individuals share characteristics of category of which they are a member.

availability heuristic judging easily-recalled events as more common.

set of specific data while ignoring other relevant information. If, for example, one of the movies you noted is a romantic comedy, you have a set of expectations about what the plot of the movie might be like.

Two researchers, Amos Tversky and Danny Kahneman (1974), nicely demonstrated people's use of the representativeness heuristic by asking research participants to read a description of an individual that included personal attributes such as, "shows no interest in political and social issues," and, "spends most of his free time on . . . mathematical puzzles." After they read this paragraph, participants were also told that the individual was randomly selected from a pool that contained 70 percent lawyers and 30 percent engineers. Ignoring the strong statistical probability that the individual was more likely to be a lawyer than an engineer, most of the participants used the personal characteristics of the individual to identify him as an engineer.

Another approximation used to make decisions is known as the **availability heuristic**. This refers to the likelihood that we will judge an event as more common if it is easier to think about it (Keller, Siegrist, & Gutcher, 2006; Oppenheimer, 2004; McKelvie & Drumheller, 2001). You may easily remember the one really great film made by an actor in one of the movies you're thinking about attending, but not be able to recall much about the actor's so-so work in several other films. The availability heuristic also explains why we tend to think that infrequent but highly salient and memorable events, such as plane crashes, are more common than they are. Because such events are easy to call to mind, we assume they commonly occur when, in fact, they are very rare (Foster, 2009).

Another aspect of the availability heuristic that affects decision making is the fact that we tend to rely on more recently stored memories to make judgments about events. For example, patients who underwent painful medical colonoscopy procedures are more likely to remember the event as excruciatingly painful if it is over quickly and ends at a time of maximal pain, then if the procedure is extended for a longer period of time with some time at the end of diminished pain (Redelmeier, Katz, & Kahneman, 2003). Because it's easier to call more recent information to mind, we assume that it is more indicative of the overall experience.

Rational Decision Making   After we've gathered or brought to mind information about the alternatives, how do we evaluate each one and go about picking one of them? For thousands of years, since the time of the ancient Greek philosopher Plato, philosophers have argued that it is better to rely on logical reasoning than on emotions or instinct when making decisions. And, until relatively recently, many of the theorists and researchers who studied decision making assumed that people's decisions—particularly financial decisions about what products to buy, whether to save or spend, and how to invest—were based on purely logical reasoning. Many models of such rational decision-making processes exist. Many assume that we choose a set of criteria and rank each alternative on its *utility*, or its ability to satisfy each criterion (Edwards & Newman, 1986; Edwards, 1977). If you are looking for a new phone, for instance, you might evaluate its size, cost, and the number of apps you like to use that the phone makes available. Some models of rational decision making suggest that we may go even farther and give more importance or "weight" to certain criteria. If, for example, it is very important to have certain apps available on the new phone, you' may weigh that criterion more highly than the phone's size and cost. According to these models, after gathering and evaluating information on each phone, we could mathematically calculate which phone is the best for us. A model of such a calculation is shown in **Table 9-1**. According to this model, you would choose Phone C.

For some decisions, rational models of decision making suggest that we might also take into account the *probability* that we can attain our choices. If, for example, you are choosing classes for next term, the course that ranks as your top choice may be so

Unforgettable Because horrific scenes of airplane crashes stay in our memories, we tend to think that such crashes are more common than they actually are.

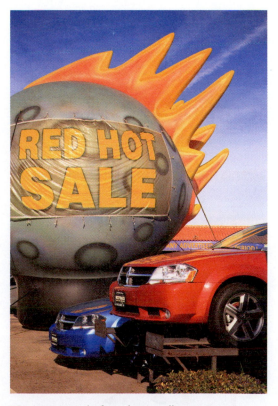

"Buy one now, before they're all gone." Recognizing that emotions can interfere with careful decision-making, automobile dealers typically try to create a sense of urgency and excitement when selling their products.

Criterion	Weight of criteria	Phone A		Phone B		Phone C	
		Rank	Rank × weight	Rank	Rank × weight	Rank	Rank × weight
Size	+3	8	24	5	15	5	15
Cost	+6	8	48	6	36	4	24
Apps	+10	0	0	5	50	8	80
Total of rank × weight		**Phone A: 72**		**Phone B: 101**		**Phone C: 119**	

popular on campus that you rate your chance of getting into the class as low. In this case, you may decide to sign up for another course, instead of your top choice.

Reason-based decision-making methods such as these can help us when we have fairly few choices and evaluate them using fairly few attributes (Payne & Bettman, 2004). Sometimes we cannot use such a model until we narrow down the choices (Slovic, 1990; Tversky, 1972). You may, for example, have eliminated 15 other phones that were entirely beyond your budget before choosing only 3 to consider further. Sometimes the method of eliminating alternatives is the only one we need. If every phone but one is beyond your budget, you don't need to perform a complicated analysis before deciding which phone you can get.

Rational decision-making models tend to be based on assumptions that we have information available to us about all our alternatives and that we have time to ponder this information. As you may have experienced, a lot of decisions in real life don't fit these criteria (Gigerenzer & Goldstein, 1996). After you buy your phone, for example, you may want to stop in the food court at the mall for a snack. With only a few minutes to decide, you may focus on only a few of the available options—maybe the first couple restaurants you walk by—or a few attributes of the choices—such as whether they offer a vegetarian dish. You may still think rationally about your choice, but you are using a model known as *bounded rationality*, that limits the cognitive effort you need to invest (Simon, 1957). Research suggests that we successfully use bounded rationality to make many of our decisions, doing the best we can with the cognitive resources and information that we have available at a given moment (Gigerenzer, 2004; Simon, 1990).

Emotions and Decision Making   Suppose you're perusing the food court for your snack and you get a craving for some French fries. You might just buy some and eat them, without putting much, if any, rational thought into your decision. For a long time, decisions such as this troubled rational decision-making theorists, because such choices are not based on logical reasons. Because of the work of Danny Kahneman, however, we now know that decision making often involves irrational processes that can be driven by our emotions. In fact, people *often* rely heavily on their emotions, or "gut instinct," rather than pure reason to make decisions.

The involvement of emotions in decision making makes predicting human behavior very difficult. There are individual differences in emotional reactions, and many of these are driven by developmental experience and temperament. Even our moods can affect our decision making. Research suggests, for example, that when we are in a positive mood, we tend to make more efficient decisions with less rational consideration of the alternatives. We also tend to be content with those choices (Schwartz et al., 2002).

Solution to the string problem Tie the pliers to one string and use it as a weight to swing the string closer to you. Functional fixedness can limit your ability to recognize this use for the pliers.

Researchers have discovered a few situations in which our emotions are likely to influence decisions somewhat predictably. One of these is when we try to estimate risks in anticipating the consequences of our decisions. For example, if you buy the wrong new phone, you risk being unhappy with it or needing to take it in for lots of repairs. Research suggests that we base our decisions, at least in part, on our anticipation of how we'll feel (Mellers, Schwartz, & Cooke, 1998; Mellers et al., 1997; Kahneman & Tversky, 1979) if we make a bad choice, and that, in general, we try hard to avoid making decisions we will regret later (Connolly & Zeelenberg, 2002). For many of us, "bad" outweighs "good" in our anticipation, so we might make less than optimal choices just to avoid the risk of feeling bad later. Given the option to receive ten cents of a shared dollar, for example, most people will opt out altogether, taking nothing instead of the ten cents, because they would feel they had been treated unfairly by having to share the dollar. This is irrational behavior since clearly, ten cents is better than nothing at all.

Understanding how emotions can shift the likelihood of a purchase is of particular interest to advertisers. If the context that produces positive emotion can be identified in all situations, it can be used effectively to persuade consumers to buy. In many cases, language can play a role in producing this context by framing choices in positive or negative ways. We are more likely to buy a food that is labeled "75 percent fat-free" than one that is described as "25 percent fat," for example (Sanford et al., 2002). Framing is especially effective in arousing emotions when we are estimating risks. Most college students would feel safer using condoms that prevent the transmission of HIV 95 percent of the time than the same condoms when they are described as failing to prevent HIV transmission 5 percent of the time (Linville, Fischer, & Fischhoff, 1993).

The interference of emotions in making decisions is not all negative. Although it's true that being upset, anxious, feeling cheated, or irrationally hopeful may impair our judgment and increase the chance that we will make an impulsive and unnecessary purchase, it is sometimes the case that emotions help us make better decisions. Research has shown that individuals often make better decisions in games with a chance element when they claim to be operating on a "hunch". Intuition is not well understood, but it is an irrational characteristic that sometimes improves decision-making capabilities. The Practically Speaking feature gives you some tips about when it can be helpful to "go with your gut."

metacognition thinking about one's own thoughts.

Metacognition

One of the most complicated forms of thought is **metacognition**, thinking about thinking. When we consider our own memories, for example, we engage in a form of metacognition. We may mull over specific facts we remember, thinking about their sources and when we learned them. We may also think about how information we have learned in the past is influencing our current interpretations of events. Metacognition involving thinking about the source of memories involves activation of the frontal cortex of the brain, as well as the hippocampus, a region important for storage of information. Damage to the hippocampus can result in source amnesia, a condition that prevents accurate thinking about one's own memories (Lakhan, 2007).

Self-reflection is another form of metacognition. It involves thinking about our own identities, how we influence other people, and our relative self-worth. Self-reflection is an important human behavior because it enables us to evaluate and modify our responses based on our past experience. We may reflect on our behavior at a recent party, for example, and decide that we would feel better about ourselves if we were more, or perhaps less, outgoing. Then we might take steps either to overcome shyness or tone down our party persona. Self-reflection can sometimes have negative consequences if it leads to repetitive thoughts of worthlessness and anxiety. For people with specific

Assessing metacognition in animals Because chimps and gorillas cannot vocalize as humans do, researchers can assess their capacity for metacognition only with special strategies, such as by having them point to symbols on a keyboard or by observing their behavior in certain learning tasks.

Intuition, hunches, inner voice, gut instinct. Emotional decision making goes by many names and its importance is often downplayed compared to rational thought. However, using emotion to make decisions is particularly important for interacting in social situations. In some cases, your survival may even depend on it.

For example, being able to judge a person by how you feel allows you to make quick decisions about interacting with them. You may conclude that you don't trust the individual but be unable to offer a rational explanation. After all, you don't even know them. Subtle characteristics about the individual from their body language to their facial expression may have led you to that conclusion. Researchers have also discovered that the same areas of the brain that are activated when you make a negative judgment about a person are also activated in response to painful or aversive stimuli (Critchley et al., 2000).

Emotional decision making also comes into play when groups cooperate. When you and your friends are deciding on which movie to see, you don't make a pie chart. You gauge the interest of the others for the particular movie choices and the choice with the most enthusiastic response is the movie everyone usually decides to see (Thagard & Kroon, 2006). Of course, emotion alone rarely makes an appropriate decision—a combination of rational thinking and emotional processes probably leads to the best possible outcome.

biological tendencies, excessive self-reflection can lead to psychological disorders, such as depression and anxiety disorders (Takano & Tanno, 2009).

Another type of metacognition occurs when we infer what someone else is thinking by watching or hearing about that person's actions. This phenomenon, called *theory of mind*, is an important aspect of human thought, although as the box, "Can Animals Think?" discusses, it may also exist in a few other species. Theory of mind is an adaptive trait because it facilitates communication and peaceful living with other people. If we did not have theory of mind and instead needed explicit verbal information about the feelings and intentions of another person, social communication would be stilted.

Once we acquire this ability during development, it becomes automatic. You probably exercise your theory of mind many times a day, while assessing your roommate's mood on the basis of his or her actions, gauging a professor's expectations based on his or her demeanor, or trying to figure out what type of a person your date is from the cues you receive on the first date.

"Try verbalizing it."

Metacognition How we *Develop*   Children develop theory of mind gradually, starting during the toddler years. Young children, ages two to three years, demonstrate that they lack the ability to infer the thinking of the person who is searching for them when trying to play hide-and-seek. Children this age will often "hide" by covering their eyes while remaining in a location that is not out of view. Rather than take the point of view of the searcher, they rely on their own experience, "If I can't see because my eyes are covered, no one else can see me." This lack of theory of mind disappears by about age four (Sabbagh et al., 2009; Aschersleben, Hofer, & Jovanovic, 2008).

Pet owners have long noted that their dogs seem to watch their faces and respond as if they are inferring the owner's thoughts. A dog that sees the owner smiling might eagerly approach with tail wagging, looking for a food treat, while one who sees the owner scowling might retreat, whimpering. It's impossible to determine, however, whether the dog is just responding to stimulus cues as a result of operant conditioning or learning based on past experiences. Do animals have a theory of mind?

Increasing evidence suggests that many animals are, indeed, capable of complicated thought and seem to possess a theory of mind (Hirata, 2009; Reid, 2009). Researchers have devised methods to study theory of mind in experimental animals, including nonhuman primates and birds. Chimpanzees and capuchin monkeys can be trained to trade certain less palatable food items for rewards the monkeys prefer. These animals seem to infer a negative reaction on the part of an experimenter to a partially eaten piece of food and attempt to hide the evidence by passing off an apple with the bite mark hidden from view.

Outside the lab, some species of birds seem to infer the intentions of other birds. Western scrub jays, for example, will rehide stored food if they notice they were being watched when the food was hidden. This evidence strongly suggests that the scrub jay has a theory of mind. The scrub jay seems to infer that the intentions of a watching bird is to steal hidden food. In response to this inference, the scrub jay moves the food to a new secret location after the watcher stops looking.

Young children's developing theory of mind may contribute to jealousy and an inability to share when it enables a child to think of another child as a rival, with intentions to take away the child's toys. Another behavior that is tied to thinking about what's going on in another person's head is lying. In general, people lie for two main reasons: to prevent themselves from being punished or to make someone else feel good. Children learn very early to lie in order to avoid punishment. This behavior seems to emerge around age three for most children, and by age five it is a fairly universal phenomenon (Talwar & Lee, 2008). If "backed into a corner" so that a child believes it's likely he or she will be punished, almost all five year olds will lie. Theory of mind allows people to lie in hopes of preventing punishment, even if they have not explicitly been warned about the punishment (Talwar, Gordon, & Lee, 2007). Because the child is able to imagine that an adult believes the child's behavior is wrong, he or she can then infer that the adult intends to punish the child for the wrong behavior.

Lying in order to make another person feel better, such as giving false compliments or reassurances, is another behavior that arises during the preschool years. Unlike lying to avoid punishment, however, this type of lying seems to increase in frequency as we get older. Have you ever complimented a friend on a new haircut or new outfit that you actually feel is less than flattering? The chances are, you did not feel particularly guilty afterward because your thoughts about how your friend feels are stronger than your desire to always tell the truth.

Although theory of mind seems to be present in very young children, other forms of metacognition are not evident until much later in development. For example, thinking about one's memories and evaluating current information in the context of the past is not a common thought process of young children. Young children often suffer from source amnesia (not remembering where they heard about certain information), which not only makes them prone to develop false memories, but also interferes with their ability to think about their memories in a meaningful way (Zola, 1998).

What Happens in the

Theory of Mind B R A I N ? Neuroscientists believe that the ability to think about another person's intentions is directly linked to a set of cells in the brain called **mirror neurons** (Rizzolatti & Fabbri-Destro, 2008). Mirror neurons are located in the frontal and parietal cortex. These cells are activated not only when an individual engages in a particular task, but also when he or she watches another person engage in this task. Activation of the same set of neurons, whether it is you or another person who acts, produces overlap in the neural circuitry that probably leads to predictions about behavior.

Consider, for instance, what might happen in your brain when you reach into a cookie jar. Usually when you reach into a cookie jar, you are hungry and looking for something good to eat. This might activate several neurons in your frontal cortex, including those involved in movement, as well as those important for anticipation and for reward. For the sake of this discussion, let's refer to these neurons as A, B, and C. Reaching into the jar activates neuron A, which in turn activates B and C. If neuron A is a mirror neuron, your neuron A can also be activated in your brain when you watch somebody else reach into a cookie jar. Activating your neuron A will, in turn, activate your neurons B and C, which carry information about intention. They tell you that the anticipated reward of reaching in the cookie jar is finding the cookie. Based on this activation in your brain, you may infer that the other person is reaching into the jar because they hope to find a cookie in there.

Thought When Things Go **Wrong**

Many disorders include problems with thinking. In many cases, however these conditions are primarily associated with deficits in other psychological processes; impairments in the person's thinking are not the main difficulty. Individuals with Alzheimer's disease are often in a confused state, for example, but the reason they are not thinking clearly is because their memories are disrupted. In other cases, problems with thinking are tied to aberrant emotional states. Depression is often accompanied by repetitive thoughts about worthlessness and hopelessness, and cognitive therapy that targets these thoughts can often be a successful form of treatment (Rupke, Blecke, & Renfrow, 2006). Although the thought components of dementia and mood disorders are real and significant symptoms, we discuss them in other chapters because these conditions are primarily associated with other psychological processes. Instead, we focus in this chapter on two disorders, obsessive-compulsive disorder and schizophrenia, that are characterized primarily by difficulties in controlling one's thoughts.

Obsessive-Compulsive Disorder

Obsessive-compulsive disorder (OCD) is defined by having uncontrollable, anxiety-provoking thoughts called *obsessions*. Many people with this disorder feel *compulsions*, or irresistible urges, to perform mental or physical ritual actions to help reduce their anxiety. People with OCD know that their thoughts are out of contact with reality, but they often find the thoughts impossible to inhibit and ignore. The impulse to engage in compulsive behavior, such as washing one's hands over and over or repeatedly checking whether a stove has been turned off, is so strong that anxiety builds with each passing moment that the behavior is inhibited (Magee & Teachman, 2007). OCD can range from relatively mild to extremes that render people unable to participate in normal life activities. Estimates of the prevalence of OCD

"I have schizophrenia" A young woman diagnosed with schizophrenia looks over some notes before shooting an episode of the MTV documentary series "True Life." The episode, titled "I Have Schizophrenia," followed her struggles to pursue academic goals and achievements after having battled the mental disorder.

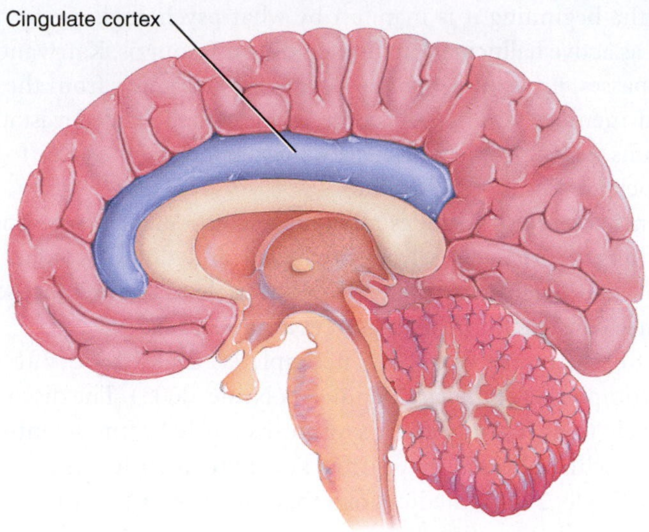

Cingulate cortex

FIGURE 9-7 **Brain treatment for OCD** Surgery that selectively damages part of the cingulate cortex can bring relief to people with otherwise untreatable OCD.

are uncertain because many people with mild OCD do not receive a formal diagnosis. Conservative estimates suggest that OCD affects about 1 percent of the population (Kessler et al., 2005).

The biological basis of OCD remains incompletely understood, but most researchers believe that an imbalance in the neurotransmitter serotonin may play some role. People with OCD often respond positively to treatment with antidepressant medications that target serotonin neurons, such as Prozac® and Paxil® (Soomro et al., 2008). Behavioral therapy is also often effective in treating people with OCD. A typical behavioral therapy approach involves exposing the patient to conditions that provoke anxiety, such as touching food, while preventing the ritualistic behavior that typically diminishes the anxiety, such as hand washing. With repeated exposures, the patient sometimes learns that withholding the ritual behavior does not have negative consequences (Fenske, & Schwenk, 2009). In some cases, however, neither antidepressant treatment nor behavioral therapy helps relieve people's OCD. In extreme cases, where anxiety and ritualistic behavior are preventing normal functioning, patients may undergo brain surgery. This treatment involves selectively damaging part of the prefrontal cortex, called the cingulate cortex (**Figure 9-7**). In about 30 percent of patients with otherwise untreatable OCD, cingulate damage is effective at reducing symptoms (Baer et al., 1995).

Schizophrenia

Schizophrenia is a relatively common psychotic disorder, characterized by extreme disorganization of thinking. About one in one hundred people in the United States have been diagnosed with some form of schizophrenia (Regier et al., 1993). Although schizophrenia can exist in multiple forms, a common theme in the disease is a break from reality in thoughts and actions. People with schizophrenia experience distortions of reality, distortions in the form of *hallucinations* (usually auditory) and *delusions*, beliefs that are not based in reality (APA, 2000). They also exhibit a devastating inability to plan and control their own thoughts (Berenbaum & Barch, 1995). Furthermore, many people with this disorder suffer impaired working memory and find it impossible to keep track of information necessary to execute a simple series of actions (Piskulic et al., 2007).

Schizophrenia is typically diagnosed in the transition period between late adolescence and early adulthood (Keith, Regier, & Rae, 1991). The disorder is

mirror neurons neurons located in the frontal and parietal cortex, which respond similarly when the individual engages in an activity and when the individual watches someone else engage in the activity.

obsessive-compulsive disorder (OCD) a mental disorder associated with abnormal anxiety-provoking thoughts that can lead to ritualistic behaviors.

schizophrenia a mental disorder characterized by disorganized thoughts, lack of contact with reality, and sometimes auditory hallucinations.

progressive: In the beginning it is manifest by what psychologists refer to as *positive symptoms*, such as active hallucinations and delusions (Gourzis, Katrivanou, & Beratis, 2002). As time passes, *negative symptoms*—behavior stemming from the person's loss of thinking and memory abilities—become more evident and devastating than the positive symptoms. Many people with schizophrenia find it impossible to hold a job or participate in social or family relationships.

Schizophrenia often also includes a language component. Sometimes a person's speech and writing become entirely disorganized and out of contact with reality (Covington et al., 2005). However, many people are able to retain intact semantics and syntax in sentence construction (Covington et al., 2005).

The causes of schizophrenia remain incompletely understood, but there appears to be a genetic component (Sullivan, Kendler, & Neale, 2003). The discovery of drugs that can effectively treat schizophrenic symptoms has led some scientists to suggest that people with schizophrenia may suffer key abnormalities in neurotransmitter activity (Goff & Coyle, 2001). Medications that block receptors for the neurotransmitter dopamine, called *antipsychotics* or *neuroleptics*, can reduce some of the symptoms of schizophrenia, including delusions and hallucinations (Tandon et al., 2008). This has led researchers to speculate that schizophrenia may be the result of overactivity in the brain's dopamine systems or of an abnormal distribution of specific dopamine receptors in the brain (Carlsson & Lindqvist, 1963). New classes of drugs that target the neurotransmitter glutamate receptors have been used successfully to treat cognitive symptoms in schizophrenia that are not relieved by neuroleptic medications, suggesting that glutamate may also be involved in the disorder (Patil et al., 2007).

One major problem with antipsychotic medications is the high rate of side effects, some of which are permanent. In addition to weight gain, which can lead to other health problems, certain neuroleptics can produce a condition called *tardive dyskinesia*, a permanent motor disturbance of the mouth and tongue. Tardive dyskinesia often does not subside even when medication is stopped, and may be the result of a permanent restructuring of dopamine systems serving motor function (Larach et al., 1997). Recall from the discussion of dopamine in Chapter 4, that this neurotransmitter is importantly involved in movement. Clearly, more research is needed to investigate the biological basis of schizophrenia with an aim toward its prevention and the development of new drugs that treat the symptoms without creating major side effects.

Before You Go On

What Do You Know?

8. Compare and contrast controlled and automatic cognitive processing.
9. What are the two main types of strategies for solving problems and how do they differ? Give at least one example of each type.
10. What are the representativeness and availability heuristics and how do they affect decision making?
11. How can emotions affect our decision making?
12. What are metacognition and theory of mind?
13. How is thinking disturbed in OCD and schizophrenia?

What Do You Think?
Which of the barriers to problem solving described in this chapter most often seem to affect you? Which problem-solving strategies seem to work best for you?

Summary

Language

LEARNING OBJECTIVE 1 Define language, describe how we learn languages and parts of the brain that are active in language, and discuss differences and problems that can affect people's language skills.

- Language is a set of symbols used to communicate. Language comprehension is understanding verbal messages, and language production is creating them.
- The study of language can be broken into phonology (sounds), semantics (meaning), syntax (grammar), and pragmatics (practical usage).
- Most people follow a typical sequence of language acquisition that includes the ability to distinguish, but not produce, all possible phonemes at about two to four months of age, babbling at about six months, and speaking first words at around one year of age.
- The standard way we learn language suggests that we have an inborn capacity for language learning, although environment contributes as well. There appears be a sensitive or critical period before about 13 years old when it is easiest to acquire language.
- In most people the language centers in the brain are in the left hemisphere. The main brain region important for speech production is Broca's area. The main region for language comprehension is called Wernicke's area. Several other areas of the brain are also active in language, including the frontal eye fields when we read.
- There are small average gender differences in early language learning, with girls learning faster initially. These differences disappear with time.

Language and Thought

LEARNING OBJECTIVE 2 Describe thinking that happens without words and summarize the linguistic relativity hypothesis.

- Some thoughts, including mental imagery and spatial navigation, require no words.
- The linguistic relativity hypothesis suggests that the amount of vocabulary we have available in our language for objects or concepts influences the way we think about those objects or concepts.

Thought

LEARNING OBJECTIVE 3 Describe and summarize research on thinking processes, including problem solving, decision making, and metacognition.

- We are capable of several different kinds of thought, and different types of thinking involve different brain regions, often including those related to the specific thoughts. We develop various thinking abilities gradually with age.
- Controlled processing relies on the executive function of the brain. We become increasingly able to exert cognitive control as we age.
- Problem solving is finding a way to reach a goal. Algorithms, problem-solving strategies that guarantee a solution if followed methodically, work best for well-defined problems. Shortcut strategies called heuristics may help with ill-defined problems.
- Common problem-solving heuristics include working backwards, finding analogies to other problems, and forming subgoals. Heuristics can lead to difficulties in problem solving, including mental sets, functional fixedness, and confirmation bias.
- Decision-making involves evaluating and choosing from among the options available to us. We often use heuristics to recall information in order to make decisions, but some, including the representativeness and availability heuristics, can bias our evaluations.
- Rational models of problem solving suggest that we make elimination options and/or make weighted evaluations of the utility and probability of options. We often lack time, information, or cognitive resources for rational decision making, however, so we use a strategy of limited or bounded rationality.
- Emotions often play a role in decision making, sometimes interfering with our ability to make rational decisions, but other times helping us to make efficient choices.
- Metacognition is thinking about our own thoughts. It includes reviewing and evaluating our own memories, self-reflection, and theory of mind—inferring the intentions of other people. Mirror neurons in the brain contribute to theory of mind.
- Obsessive-compulsive disorder (OCD) and schizophrenia are two mental disorders that include a major thought disruption.

Key Terms

CUT/ACROSS CONNECTION

What Happens in the BRAIN?

- The main language areas are on the left side of the brain for most people—but not all.
- Thinking about images (or smells or tests) activates the same brain areas as if we were actually seeing (or smelling or tasting). Thoughts that involve language activate language areas of the brain.
- When we watch other people do things, mirror neurons in our brain can activate just as though we were doing the same things.

When Things Go Wrong

- Damage near Broca's area of the brain can cause us to lose our ability to use grammar.
- Obsessive-compulsive disorder involves unavoidable thoughts called obsessions and irresistible urges, or compulsions, to perform certain behaviors.
  - About 1 percent of all people in the United States display schizophrenia, a disorder marked by disorganized thoughts and loss of contact with reality.

HOW we Differ

- Girls tend to learn to talk earlier than boys. However, the difference soon disappears.
- Babies who learn two languages at home begin talking slightly later than those who learn just one.
- The number of words we have in our language for a certain object or concept (such as a color) may influence how we can think about that object or concept.

How we Develop

- Very young infants are able to perceive all the sounds of every language. As time passes, however, we lose the ability to distinguish phonemes of other languages.
- Our ability to learn languages is at its best before school age. After we pass age 13, it is much more difficult for us to learn new languages than it was earlier.
- We naturally tend to use child-directed speech with babies. It may be an evolutionary adaptation that helps humans learn language.
- One of the reasons toddlers don't play hide-and-seek very well is because their theory of mind abilities are still undeveloped.

Psychology Around Us

Differences in Language and Communication

Speaking the Same Language

Everybody says it. Living in this age of cell phones and the Internet, we are witnessing a communication explosion. People are said to be more closely connected than ever, and, correspondingly, the world is supposedly getting smaller. But is this true? Are language and communication in today's world better, or even different, than in the past? Are we becoming one, or is communication across people and the world as complex and flawed as ever?

For this video lab exercise, you'll become a communications expert, observing a range of encounters and communications, judging their effectiveness, accounting for the weaknesses and strengths of each, and then working to improve the communications. You'll be observing two people texting messages, a parent talking to a child, animals vocalizing to each other, a trainer communicating with an animal, and a man and woman having a heart-to-heart.

As you are working on this on-line exercise, consider the following questions:

- What does this lab exercise suggest about how language and communication develop, within species and across species?
- Do men and women listen differently and/or speak different languages?
- How does language affect thinking, decision making, perception, and behavior?
- What's going on in the brain while all this communication is happening?

Intelligence

Chapter Outline

- What Do We Mean by Intelligence?
- Additional Types of Intelligence
- How Do We Measure Intelligence?
- Is Intelligence Governed by Genetic or Environmental Factors?
- Intelligence
- Extremes in Intelligence

As Smart as They Look?

Each week on the reality show *America's Most Smartest Model*, producers ask male and female models to compete in a series of tasks designed to test both their intelligence and their modeling skills. An intelligence-testing task, for example, may require rapid-fire responding to trivia questions that will determine how fast a partner has to run on a treadmill or dissecting and correctly identifying the organs from a fetal pig. Winning the intelligence challenge gives a model a decided edge in the modeling challenge. In one episode, for example, the winning team members were assigned a runway show with their dressing room next to the stage, while the losing team had to complete an obstacle course to make it to the runway. Models who fail to compete strongly in both tasks are eliminated from the show.

Obviously, much of the show's humor comes from stereotypes that models are generally not very smart, and certainly the show takes great delight in featuring models who cannot name the vice president of the United States (or, for that matter, do not know a judge's last name). However, the show is equally derisive of contestants who cannot name an Italian designer under time pressure or do not demonstrate appropriate interpersonal skills during a surprise networking challenge. Further confounding the stereotype of the not-so-smart model, contestants include Andre, a son of Romanian diplomats who speaks five languages and delights in scheming people off the show, and Daniel, a Ph.D. candidate in psychology at a major California university who correctly spells both phosphorescence and Bacchanalian during a spelling bee.

Clearly, *America's Most Smartest Model* is built on common conceptions of what intelligence is. Like many other aspects of human behavior, however, intelligence is a concept that appears simple at first glance, only to become more and more complicated the closer we look at it. Start with the basic question: How do you define intelligence? Most people use *smart* or *stupid* to characterize the other people in their lives all the time, and they generally have a great deal of confidence in their assessments. But answer this: When you describe a friend as a generally smart person, how are you assessing smartness? Are you thinking about how your friend performs in all situations, or are you just impressed by how sophisticated her answers are in English class and ignoring the fact that she's just scraping by in Chemistry? If you were watching the TV show just described, would you be sympathetic to a contestant's protest that "street smarts" make him an intelligent person, even if he can't successfully identify a city in Iraq? And what about that friend of yours who seems to be "book smart" but lacks common sense? Is that person, book smarts and all, the one you want leading you if your plane crashes on a remote island?

Okay, then, so what do we mean by intelligence? Does it mean the same thing in every instance? How do we understand it, and how do we measure it? To these basic questions we must add several others: Can we distinguish between intelligence and talent? Are intelligence and wisdom the same thing? Are intelligence and creativity related? And, finally, how do we value intelligence? Our answers to such questions will influence how we define intelligence and whether we decide that anyone is particularly high in intelligence.

What Do We Mean By Intelligence?

LEARNING OBJECTIVE 1 Describe various ways in which intelligence has been defined and summarize the current thinking on whether intelligence is general or specific.

Although Western thinkers as far back in history as Socrates, Plato, and Aristotle have commented on intelligence, it was not until the nineteenth and early twentieth centuries that psychologists and others began to form our present notions about it. In 1921, a group of scholars attended a symposium on the subject of intelligence. In their report, they emphasized that whatever else might be involved, **intelligence** involves the *ability to learn* and the *ability to meet the demands of the environment effectively*. People who hope to master algebra, for example, must have the capacity to grasp mathematical principles and profit from mathematical instruction, and they must be able to apply what they learn to various problem sets and life situations.

Years later, another survey of scholars pointed to the same abilities as keys to intelligence and added a third: the *ability to understand and control one's mental activities*. This additional mental capacity was termed **metacognition** (Hertzog & Robinson, 2005). Sometimes metacognition is understood as the ability to think about one's own thinking. The ancient philosopher Socrates gave us an early example of metacognitive thinking when he proclaimed, "Know thyself."

Defining intelligence in terms of our ability to learn, to adapt to the demands of our environment, and to reflect on and understand our own mental processes makes intuitive sense. However, this definition encompasses a wide variety of notions about what intelligence might be. To develop a more precise definition, let's begin by considering a very basic question: Is intelligence just one thing or a combination of many different skill sets? All current theories of intelligence in one way or another consider this question.

Is Intelligence General or Specific?

Suppose you were joining a challenging mountain-climbing expedition. Which of your team members do you think would be more likely to complete the climb successfully: a generally smart person, or a person who had mastered, one by one, a large number of important tasks associated with mountain climbing? That is, is intelligence largely the result of a single, general factor, or does it come from a cluster of different abilities?

Spearman and the g Factor   Charles Spearman (1863–1945) was a philosopher and soldier who also became an influential figure in the study of intelligence. Spearman helped to develop a tool for analyzing intelligence, called **factor analysis**. Factor analysis is a statistical method for determining whether certain items on a test correlate highly, thus forming a unified set, or cluster, of items. In the case of intelligence tests, for example, people who do well on vocabulary items also tend to do well on other verbal items, such as reading comprehension. Taken together, all of the test items relating to words and reading form a verbal-reasoning cluster that can be used to assess a person's overall verbal-reasoning skill. On Western intelligence tests, other clusters include those related to logical, spatial, and mechanical reasoning.

While Spearman granted that some people have a particular strength in one area or another, he also noticed that those who scored high on one cluster tend to score high on other clusters as well. As he put it: "A bright child tends to score higher on all aspects

intelligence the ability to learn, to meet the demands of the environment effectively, and to understand and control one's mental activities.

metacognition the ability to understand and control one's mental activities.

factor analysis a statistical method for determining whether certain items on a test correlate highly, thus forming a unified set, or cluster, of items.

g factor a theoretical general factor of intelligence underlying all distinct clusters of mental ability; part of Spearman's two-factor theory of intelligence.

s factor a theoretical specific factor uniquely tied to a distinct mental ability or area of functioning; part of Spearman's two-factor theory of intelligence.

primary mental abilities seven distinct mental abilities identified by Thurstone as the basic components of intelligence.

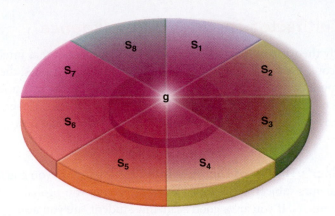

FIGURE 10-1 Spearman's two-factor theory of intelligence
In Spearman's model, the *g* factor of intelligence represents a broad and deep capability that underlies all other specific mental abilities, or the *s* factors.

of an intelligence test than a dull one." Thus, he hypothesized that a general factor, the **g factor**, of intelligence underlies all distinct clusters of mental ability. At the same time, he believed that each cluster of intelligence is further affected by a *specific factor*, an **s factor**, which is uniquely tied to that particular area of functioning (**Figure 10-1**) (Spearman, 1937, 1927, 1923, 1904).

To illustrate this *two-factor view* of intelligence, think again about the reality show we discussed at the beginning of the chapter, *America's Most Smartest Model*. The show tests intelligence in specific areas every week, ranging from science to spelling, and a contestant may be kicked off the show for not having a skill set in that area. Such an approach is more consistent with the notion that intelligence is made up of a number of different skill sets. At the same time, the idea is that in the end the smartest person will show the fewest deficits in knowledge—an assumption consistent with the existence of a general intelligence.

Over the years, many theorists have embraced Spearman's notion of a *g* factor, and researchers have repeatedly found indications that such a factor may indeed be at work (Johnson et al., 2004). These theorists typically agree that the *g* factor "is not merely book learning, a narrow academic skill, or test-taking smarts. Rather, it reflects a broader and deeper capability for comprehending our surroundings—'catching on,' 'making sense' of things, or 'figuring out' what to do" (Gottfredson, 1997, p. 13).

Thurstone and Primary Mental Abilities   Although many theorists continue to embrace Spearman's notion of a g factor of intelligence, the idea of such a general factor was controversial in Spearman's day and remains so to the present. An early critic of Spearman's ideas was Lewis L. Thurstone (1887–1955), a pioneer in psychological measurement and statistics. He argued that intelligence is made up of seven distinct mental abilities: verbal comprehension, word fluency, numerical skill, spatial ability, associative memory, perceptual speed, and reasoning (Thurstone, 1938). He termed these factors **primary mental abilities**.

Observing such differences from person to person, Thurstone argued that each of the primary mental abilities on his list is distinct, not a reflection of general underlying intelligence. And, in fact, his initial work seemed to suggest that these abilities are not related. However, recognizing this theory as a direct challenge to the notion of the *g* factor, other researchers used factor analyses to reevaluate Thurstone's ideas, and they detected at least a slight tendency of those who scored high in one mental ability to score high in another (Spearman, 1939). In short, Thurstone's work did not fully dispel the notion of the *g* factor.

Despite the limitations of Thurstone's theory, the idea of distinct areas of intelligence has continued to drive theorizing about intelligence, even among those who believe that a *g* factor is at least partly at play in intellectual functioning. Let's turn next to the work of three modern theorists who have carried on Thurstone's quest to identify separate components of intelligence.

Who was the smartest person ever? It depends on your criteria. Although Albert Einstein's name has become synonymous with the term "brilliance," his cognitive functioning was below average in certain ways. Viewed as the ultimate absent-minded professor, he once had to call the dean's office at the Princeton Institute for Advanced Study to ask for directions to his home—located a block from campus.

Who's more intelligent? According to Howard Gardner's theory of multiple intelligences, these three extraordinary individuals each have a different kind of intelligence. For Bruce Springsteen, it's musical intelligence. For Nobel-prize winning author Toni Morrison, it's linguistic intelligence. And for physicist Stephen Hawking, it's mathematical intelligence.

Current Multifactor Theories of Intelligence

Most of the early theorists on intelligence agreed with Spearman that intelligence has a *g* factor at its core. Today's psychologists have increasingly questioned the *g* factor or at least placed more emphasis on specific abilities, or *s* factors, that may affect intellectual performance. Three theorists in particular—Howard Gardner, Robert Sternberg, and Stephen Ceci—have broadened the definition of intelligence and deemphasized the *g* factor.

Howard Gardner's Theory of Multiple Intelligences Are you equally successful in every academic subject? If you are like most people, you probably do better in some areas than others. If you are a good academic student, are you also a good artist? Musician? Cook? Do you know someone who does not do well on academic tests but nevertheless seems intelligent? Perhaps this person has strong leadership skills, social intuition, street smarts, or a razor-sharp sense of humor.

Psychologist Howard Gardner, influenced in part by the work of Thurstone, has advanced the **theory of multiple intelligences**, which argues that there is no such thing as a single unified intelligence (Gardner, 2008, 2004; Kornhaber & Gardner, 2006). Instead, Gardner believes that there are several independent intelligences. Drawing on research from the fields of neuroscience and developmental, evolutionary, and cognitive psychology, he claims that the different intelligences come from different areas of the brain. In support of this view, he notes that damage to specific areas of the brain does not necessarily lead to a universal collapse of mental functioning. Rather, some types of functioning may be affected while others remain intact.

Gardner's research regarding people of exceptional ability has also contributed to the notion of multiple and independent intelligences. His work with *savant syndrome* individuals, for example, seems consistent with this view. Individuals with savant syndrome often score low, sometimes extremely low, on traditional intelligence tests, yet possess startling ability in a specific area. Some have little verbal ability but are able to compute numbers with the speed of a calculator, others can draw with great skill, and still others have a keen memory for music.

Table 10-1 depicts the eight basic intelligences identified by Gardner: linguistic, logical-mathematical, musical, spatial, bodily-kinesthetic, interpersonal, intrapersonal, and naturalistic. In addition, Gardner has raised the possibility that there may be two additional intelligences: spiritual intelligence, which enables persons to focus on cosmic and spiritual issues; and existential intelligence, which is needed to consider ultimate issues, such as the meaning of life.

Although Gardner's theory has roots in Thurstone's ideas, it is, in fact, different from Thurstone's theory in several ways. First, Thurstone held that the mental functions he identified *collectively* constitute intelligence. He did not believe, as Gardner does, that each factor is itself an "intelligence." Further, Gardner believes that the various intelligences are best measured in the contexts in which they occur. Thus, assessments conducted in real-world settings are more useful than paper-and-pencil examinations for assessing several of the intelligences (Tirri & Nokelainen, 2008). Finally, Gardner's definition of multiple intelligences includes an important cultural component: Each intelligence, he suggests, reflects "the ability to solve problems, or to create products, that are valuable within one or more cultural settings" (Gardner, 1993).

Because the various intelligences are thought to emanate from different areas, or modules, of the brain, Gardner's theory is often called a *modular model* of mental functioning. Nevertheless, according to Gardner, the various intelligences can influence one another. For example, in addition to a well-developed musical intelligence, a cellist might need a high bodily-kinesthetic intelligence to physically handle the instrument and a high interpersonal intelligence to work in perfect harmony with other players in an

TABLE 10-1 Gardner's Multiple Intelligences

Type of intelligence	Characteristics	Possible vocations
Linguistic	Sensitivity to the sounds and meaning of words	Author, journalist, teacher
Logical/mathematical	Capacity for scientific analysis and logical and mathematical problem solving	Scientist, engineer, mathematician
Musical	Sensitivity to sounds and rhythm; capacity for musical expression	Musician, composer, singer
Spatial	Ability to perceive spatial relationships accurately	Architect, navigator, sculptor, engineer
Bodily/kinesthetic	Ability to control body movements and manipulate objects	Athlete, dancer, surgeon
Interpersonal	Sensitivity to the emotions and motivations of others; skillful at managing others	Manager, therapist, teacher
Intrapersonal	Ability to understand one's self and one's strengths and weaknesses	Leader in many fields
Naturalistic	Ability to understand patterns and processes in nature	Biologist, naturalist, ecologist, farmer
(Possible) Spiritual/existential	Ability to focus on spiritual issues and the meaning of life	Philosopher, theologian

Source: Adapted from Gardner, 1993

theory of multiple intelligences Theory that there is no single, unified intelligence, but instead several independent intelligences arising from different portions of the brain.

triarchic theory of intelligence Sternberg's theory that intelligence is made up of three interacting components: internal, external, and experiential components.

orchestra. Critics of Gardner's ideas, however, maintain that still deeper relationships exist among the various intelligences and mental functions.

Robert Sternberg's Triarchic Theory of Intelligence Psychologist Robert Sternberg has proposed a **triarchic theory of intelligence** (Sternberg et al., 2008; Sternberg, 2003). Sternberg shares Gardner's view that intelligence is not a unitary mental function. According to Sternberg, however, intelligence is made up not of numerous independent intelligences but of three interacting components, as shown in **Figure 10-2**: the internal, external, and experiential components—sometimes referred to as the analytic, creative, and practical components.

- *Internal (analytic)* This component of intelligence relates to the internal processing of information: acquiring information; planning, monitoring, and evaluating problems; or carrying out directions. The internal aspect of intelligence is the one most often measured by today's intelligence tests—the sort of intelligence needed for straightforward tasks and problems that we confront at school or work or in life.
- *External (creative)* Sternberg notes that some tasks are novel and so require a special way of thinking. Traveling to Russia for the first time, for example, requires

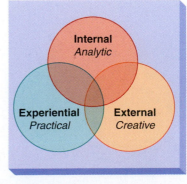

FIGURE 10-2 **Sternberg's triarchic theory of intelligence** Robert Sternberg proposes that there are three components to intelligence, not multiple independent ones. In his model, intelligence is related to the successful interaction among these three: the internal (analytic), the external (creative), and the experiential (practical) components.

bioecological model of intelligence Ceci's theory that intelligence is a function of the interactions among innate potential abilities, environmental context, and internal motivation.

emotional intelligence an individual's ability to perceive, express, assimilate, and regulate emotion.

more creative thinking than purchasing a can of soda. Among other things, a traveler would have to figure out how to get through Russian customs, find his or her way to a hotel, and order meals in restaurants—all, perhaps, without knowing the language. This component of intelligence clearly requires creativity, and it also must interact with the internal component of intelligence to bring about successful results.

- *Experiential (practical)* This type of thinking helps us adapt to or improve our environments or select new environments. Let's say you move into a new home and find that the neighbors make a lot of noise when you are trying to go to sleep. At first, you might try to solve the problem by moving to another bedroom in the house (adapting to the environment). If this doesn't work, you might try installing soundproof windows or complaining to the neighbors or to the landlord (changing the environment). And, finally, if that doesn't work, you might decide to move to another house (selecting a new environment).

Sternberg suggests that practical intelligence often relies on *tacit knowledge*, "action-oriented knowledge, acquired without direct help from others, that allows individuals to achieve goals they personally value" (Sternberg et al., 1995, p. 916). A successful businessperson who earned only average grades in school has probably acquired considerable tacit knowledge, or "know-how," by working in the business environment and figuring out what is needed to get the work done. Not surprisingly, research shows that tacit knowledge is related to job success (Sternberg, 2003; Sternberg et al., 1995).

Sternberg argues that effective interactions among the internal, external, and experiential components are key to achieving successful intelligence—an advantageous balance between adapting to, shaping, and selecting problems encountered within one's environment. Because each intellectual component in Sternberg's theory actively relates to the others, his model is considered more dynamic, or interactive, than Gardner's.

Stephen Ceci's Bioecological Theory of Intelligence Psychologist Stephen Ceci has proposed the **bioecological model of intelligence**, which holds that intelligence is "a function of the interactions between innate potential abilities, environmental context (ecology), and internal motivation" (**Figure 10-3**) (Barnett & Ceci, 2005; Ceci et al., 1997). According to Ceci, each person's innate abilities derive from a system of biological factors, or "resource pools." These resource pools are independent of each other, and each is responsible for different aspects of one's information-processing capabilities. Further, Ceci claims that a person's innate abilities will develop more or less based on how they interact with the individual's environmental resources, or context.

Consider, for example, a child whose biological resource pool endows her with the potential to succeed in math. Her abilities might lead to early successes in arithmetic, prompting her parents to provide environmental changes—her own computer, special tutoring in math, and so forth—that will help her to further develop her innate math potential. This encouraging environmental context will likely lead to further successes, which in turn may lead to additional environmental changes, such as enrollment in a special school.

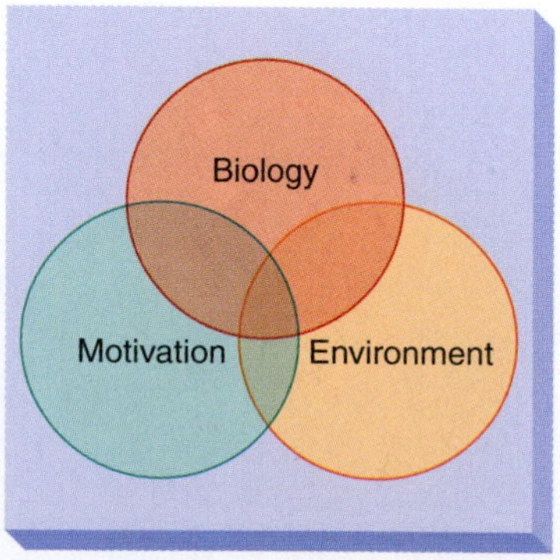

FIGURE 10-3 **Ceci's bioecological model of intelligence** Stephen Ceci proposes that intelligence is the product of interaction among biological, environmental, and motivational resources, and that each resource is responsible for a different aspect of intelligence.

Finally, according to the bioecological model, individuals must be internally *motivated* in order to fulfill their innate abilities and take advantage of their particular environments. When people feel motivated in certain areas, they tend to focus on their intellectual skills in those areas and to seek out environmental resources that are relevant. In an interesting study, Ceci found that men who were successful at race track betting and who produced complicated strategies for predicting winning horses did not demonstrate sophisticated thinking in other areas of functioning (Ceci & Liker, 1986).

Clearly, such men were motivated to "hit it big" and so developed complex intellectual processing and personal environmental opportunities that might lead to that particular result.

Where are We Today?

Obviously, many theories on the nature of intelligence have been proposed and investigated. Is there a basic view upon which today's theorists agree? On the one hand, it would be fair to say that the majority do believe that intelligence *includes* a *g* factor—an overriding intellectual ability (Larsen et al., 2008). On the other hand, few current theorists believe that the *g* factor is the be-all and end-all of intelligence. Most consider specific abilities (verbal, numerical, spatial skills, for example) and special factors (motivation, context, experience, and the like) to also be important in the expression of intelligence. The *g* factor is at work in every task that we confront in life, while the specific abilities and special factors come into play for some tasks but not others. This prevailing view is called a *hierarchical model* of intelligence (Lubinski, 2004).

Because the *g* factor seems to play a role across all kinds of tasks, it is, of course, desirable to have a high degree of general intelligence. But the *g* factor alone will not consistently lead to outstanding performances or successes in school, work, or other areas of life. Conversely, verbal ability, high motivation, or proper environment alone rarely guarantees high intellectual achievement. Intelligence truly appears to be a complex, multifaceted phenomenon.

> "Knowing others is intelligence; knowing yourself is true wisdom. Mastering others is strength; mastering yourself is true power."
>
> –*Tao Te Ching, Chinese philosopher*

Before You Go On

What Do You Know?

1. Identify and define the two factors in Spearman's model of intelligence.
2. How does Thurstone's theory of primary mental abilities differ from Gardner's theory of multiple intelligences?
3. What are the three components of the triarchic theory of intelligence, and how do they contribute to mental functioning?

What Do You Think? How would you define intelligence?

Additional Types of Intelligence

LEARNING OBJECTIVE 2 Discuss several proposed types of intelligence that go beyond intellectual functioning.

The ideas and work that we have encountered so far consider a wide range of intellectual skills. But have they captured all aspects of intelligence? A growing number of theorists are focusing on the role of intelligence in emotions, social functioning, wisdom, creativity, and personality.

Emotional Intelligence

The concept of emotional intelligence is rather new: researchers began to actively study it in the 1990s. **Emotional intelligence** refers to an individual's ability to perceive, express, and assimilate emotion, and to regulate emotion in the self and others (Mayer et al., 2008; Goleman, 1995). Emotionally intelligent people are thought to be self-aware,

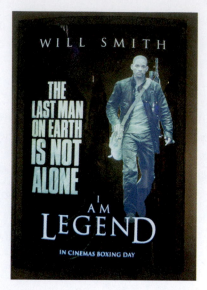

Emotional intelligence and acting Their abilities to perceive and regulate emotions in themselves and in others enable successful actors to portray a wide range of characters. Will Smith, for example, has always had the highest grossing film on the weekend of his movie openings, regardless of the kind of role he is playing.

sensitive to how they feel and how their feelings change, and able to manage their emotions so that they are not overwhelmed by them. People with well-developed emotional intelligence also tend to be empathic, knowing how to comfort and encourage others. Not surprisingly, they often succeed in their careers and marriages, as parents and as leaders (Martin, 2008).

If we grant the existence of emotional intelligence, then the question arises: Can it be measured? In fact, researchers have devised a number of ways to measure it (Austin et al., 2008). One test is the *Multifactor Emotional Intelligence Scale* (Mayer et al., 2003, 2003; Salovey et al., 2003). This test measures twelve emotional abilities that are, in turn, grouped into four "branches of abilities"—perceiving, facilitating, understanding, and managing emotion. Although some theorists believe that certain individuals are inherently more skilled than others in the emotional sphere, other theorists argue that emotional intelligence can be learned and they call for schools and businesses to offer systematic instruction in the understanding and management of emotions (Thomas et al., 2008; Wall, 2008).

Social Intelligence

Most people know someone who displays remarkable social savvy, a person who can walk right into a party or a meeting and just take over the room. Such people seem to know intuitively what is important to others, how to charm their way out of difficult situations, and how to gain the affection of everyone with whom they interact. Would you say these individuals are highly intelligent? Some theorists would say yes (Furnham, 2008; Goleman, 2006). Specifically, they would say that the individuals are high in *social intelligence*.

The notion of social intelligence is older than that of emotional intelligence. In fact, early in the twentieth century, the learning pioneer Edward Thorndike (whom you may remember from Chapter 7) suggested that intelligence consists of three facets: the ability to understand and manage ideas (abstract intelligence), concrete objects (mechanical intelligence), and people (social intelligence) (Thorndike, 1920). By social intelligence, Thorndike meant "the ability to understand and manage men and women, boys and girls—to act wisely in human relationships." Other theorists have described social intelligence more simply as the ability to get along with others. Either way, it is clearly an important asset, not only in interpersonal relationships but also at school and work and in leadership roles (Furnham, 2008; Bass, 2002).

Wisdom

In myth, art, and popular culture, we often encounter characters who do not possess much formal education but who seem to have an insightful appreciation of life and the world. They are generally portrayed as experienced in the ways of the world; little about life appears to surprise them. These people are considered to possess *wisdom*, the ability to make sound judgments about important, difficult, or uncertain situations and to choose the best course of action (Fowers, 2005, 2003). Are intelligence and wisdom the same thing?

Robert Sternberg (2008, 2003) believes that wisdom is a special version of intelligence and has developed the *balance theory of wisdom* to account for this special capacity. Recall that in Sternberg's triarchic theory, intelligence consists of three aspects—analytic, creative, and practical—with practical intelligence involving the ability to effectively apply one's experiences and learning to everyday decisions. According to Sternberg, wisdom is primarily (though not entirely) the product of practical intelligence. He says that wisdom is the application of tacit knowledge—"know-how"—to solve problems in such a way that a common good is achieved and a balance main-

Social intelligence for profit People with high social intelligence seem to have a natural grasp of what is important to others and an ability to help other people "open up." Here, television's most acclaimed interviewers—Larry King and Oprah Winfrey—discuss how they have used their social intelligence to achieve professional success.

tained among the interests of the individual, the community, and society. Sternberg distinguishes wisdom from other expressions of practical intelligence by noting that wisdom involves a particular concern for the community at large and a careful balancing of interests.

More than any other dimension of intelligence, wisdom may be associated with age. When people are asked to name someone in their lives whom they considered wise, they are more likely to point to a grandparent, an uncle or aunt, or a parent, rather than to a teenager or young adult. Why? Because it typically takes years and repeated experiences to appreciate the needs of the community, the advantages of solutions in which everyone wins, the drawbacks of self-serving decisions, and the delicate art of balancing multiple perspectives (Nair, 2003). That is, it takes time and experience to acquire a high degree of wisdom.

Creativity

Creativity is the ability to produce ideas that are both original and valuable (Paulus & Nijstad, 2003). Like wisdom, creativity reflects collective, as well as personal, values. Societies benefit from the creativity of their members; indeed, creativity plays a key role in technological, scientific, and artistic advances. Thus, it is not surprising that different cultures define and appreciate creativity in different ways (Johnson et al., 2003). Creativity often requires verbal and mathematical skills in Western culture, for example, while it depends more on the ability to appreciate and interact with nature in certain other cultures (Runco, 2004).

Psychologists who study creativity and intelligence typically believe that a high intellectual aptitude is necessary but not sufficient for creativity (Silvia, 2008; Sternberg & Lubart, 2003). People who score high on intelligence tests tend to score high on tests of creativity, but beyond a certain point (that is, beyond an intelligence test score of about 120), the correlation between intelligence and creativity diminishes. Research has shown, for example, that on average, exceptionally creative architects, musicians, scientists, and engineers do not score higher on intelligence tests than do their less creative colleagues (MacKinnon & Hall, 1972). Thus, it appears that there is more to creativity than that which intelligence tests measure.

Theorists and researchers have pointed to various personal qualities as being key to creativity (Runco, 2004; Sternberg, 2003). At the top of the list is *intrinsic motivation*, an internal drive to create. Also cited frequently are *imagination*—an ability and willingness to reexamine problems in new ways—and a *game personality*, one that tolerates ambiguity, risk, and initial failure. Other useful qualities include complex thinking, broad attention, expertise in relevant fields, broad interests, high energy, independence, and self-confidence.

creativity the ability to produce ideas that are both original and valuable.

Creativity around the world Different cultures encourage different kinds of creativity. A woman who can decorate a customer's hand with a beautiful henna design in India (*left*) is considered highly creative and intelligent in her country, while an American man who addresses his firm's production needs by developing a complex computer model (*right*) is called a "creative genius" by his colleagues.

Creative environment? Students of the Paris Opera Ballet School train in a town near Paris, France.

Investigators have also found that creative thinking is, in fact, nurtured, inspired, and refined by creative environments (Fogarty, 2008; Amabile & Gryskiewicz, 1989). Creative environments share several qualities: they encourage people to be innovative; are relatively free of criticism; and provide freedom, creative role models, sufficient resources, and time to think and explore. Artist communities and schools for the performing arts aspire to be environments of this kind. Some such communities and schools succeed in this regard, while others become more demanding and competitive than nurturing. In addition, a creative environment need not be large or formal; it can exist in a supportive home, a positive work setting, or a comfortable class.

Personality Characteristics

Even the earliest researchers of intelligence noted a relationship between intelligence and personality, our unique patterns of experiencing and acting in the world. Although intelligence tests often seek to separate intellectual functioning from personal style, many theorists argue that the division is artificial, that personality characteristics are inherent to intellectual functioning (Mayer, 2009, 2008). Indeed, David Wechsler, a pioneer in intelligence testing, considered intelligence to be a manifestation of personality (Wechsler, 1961). He thought that emotional, motivational, and other personal characteristics (such as interest and volition) must be key components of any meaningful notion of intelligence.

Following Wechsler's lead, a number of today's theorists think of intelligence as the cognitive part of personality (Furnham & Monsen, 2009). Others propose a complex reciprocal relationship between intelligence and personality, with intellectual, emotional, and motivational variables repeatedly affecting each other in day-to-day behavior (Mayer, 2008; Haslam, 2007). Consistent with such notions, studies have found that negative emotional and motivational states can impair intellectual performance to some degree, especially when the intellectual tasks demand attention or quick recall. Conversely, certain personality factors, such as self-efficacy (the belief that one can master a demanding task) and a high need to achieve, often enhance performance on intellectual tasks (Lounsbury et al., 2009, 2003; Bates & Rock, 2004).

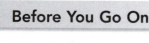

Before You Go On

What Do You Know?

4. What is emotional intelligence and how is it measured?
5. How does Robert Sternberg describe wisdom in relation to his triarchic theory of intelligence?
6. What are some factors that affect creativity?

What Do You Think? Suppose you were given the job of making up a test to assess social intelligence. What kinds of questions would you include on the test?

How Do We Measure Intelligence?

LEARNING OBJECTIVE 3 Identify important considerations in the construction of intelligence tests, discuss the history of intelligence testing, and describe some criticisms of intelligence tests.

For better or for worse, the history of intelligence theory is completely intertwined with the history of intelligence testing. That is, both the theories psychologists propose and the tests they devise affect how they understand intelligence. It was only about a century ago that researchers and statisticians first fashioned standardized tests and statistical methods with which to assess intelligence. In the West, one of the oldest and most enduring approaches to understanding and assessing intelligence is the psychometric approach. The **psychometric approach** attempts to measure intelligence with carefully constructed psychological tests, called *intelligence tests*.

Before talking in detail about some of the ways people have measured intelligence throughout history, it's worthwhile to think about what qualities make a good intelligence test. Knowing how psychologists build and use intelligence tests will help you make up your own mind about what these tests mean. Keep in mind, though, that much of the reason we are able to think about intelligence in such a sophisticated way today is that we have benefited from the insights and mistakes of the theorists and researchers we will be discussing later.

Intelligence Test Construction and Interpretation

Intelligence test constructors typically assume a comparative view of test scores. That is, intelligence is typically measured by comparing one person's test scores with another's. There is no absolute or independent measure of intelligence. Because of this comparative approach, a number of cautions arise. First, a test must function the same in different groups of people (so that individuals do not get different scores just because they are from different ethnic groups or different parts of the country). Second, the items on a test must relate both to one another and to the material of interest. To ensure that intelligence tests are grounded in sound scientific principles, psychologists design tests that adhere to three basic criteria: standardization, reliability, and validity (Lange & Iverson, 2008).

Standardization   If you were the only person taking a particular intelligence test, your score would mean very little. For your score to have meaning, it must be compared with the scores of people who have already taken the same test. This group of people is referred to as a *sample* population. If all subsequent test-takers follow the same procedures as those used by the sample population, then each individual's test score can be compared with the scores of the sample. The process of obtaining meaningful test scores from a sample population through the use of uniform procedures is called **standardization**.

Test results from large populations tend to follow particular patterns, called *distributions*. Scores on intelligence tests follow a **normal distribution** (or *normal curve*), a statistical pattern in which most people achieve fairly similar scores at or near the middle of the distribution while a small number earn low scores and an equally small number earn high scores. In graph form, these results form a bell-shaped pattern, often called a *bell curve* (see **Figure 10-4**).

In a normal distribution, the scores of most people fall in the vicinity of the **median** score (that is, the middle score). The scores that are higher or lower than the median keep declining in number as the scores extend farther and farther from the median. The very lowest and the very highest scores are found at the outer edges of the bell curve. The median score is but one indicator of a population's central tendencies. Others include the **mean**, or the average score, and the **mode**, the score that occurs most frequently in the population. If a sample is properly standardized into a normal distribution, the median, mean, and mode should be the same.

Reliability   The second criterion that is needed for a test to be of value is **reliability**. When a test is reliable, it consistently produces similar scores for the same test-takers over time. Psychologists have developed several ways to show that a test is reliable. One approach is to administer it once and then a second time, in either the same version or a version that is slightly different. If the scores on the two administrations agree for each individual, they are said to correlate highly. Another approach is to divide the items on

psychometric approach an approach to defining intelligence that attempts to measure intelligence with carefully constructed psychological tests.

standardization the use of uniform procedures in administering and scoring a test.

normal distribution a symmetrical, bell-shaped distribution in which most scores are in the middle with smaller groups of equal size at either end.

median the score exactly in the middle of a distribution.

mean the average score in a distribution.

mode the score that occurs most frequently in a distribution.

reliability the degree to which a test produces the same scores over time.

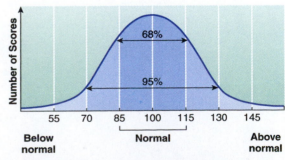

FIGURE 10-4 **The bell curve of intelligence scores** The distribution of scores on intelligence tests follows a statistical pattern called the bell curve. Most peoples' scores fall in the middle range, with a small number scoring at the extreme ends.

single test among two groups, and see whether each individual's scores on the two halves of the test correlate highly. Whatever the approach, the higher the statistical correlation between scores, the greater the reliability. Remember from Chapter 2 that a correlation can vary from a value of −1.00 to +1.00. A correlation of +1.00 indicates the highest degree of reliability.

Validity   A test with a high degree of reliability does not necessarily have high validity. **Validity** is the extent to which a test accurately measures or predicts what it is supposed to measure or predict. Suppose, for example, we use a broken scale to weigh the residents of a town and we weigh each resident multiple times. Assuming that, for each person, the scale repeatedly yields the same weight, the resulting weights would be said to have a high degree of reliability. The results, however, would have low validity because the weights offered by the broken scales are not accurate; that is, although everyone's weight would be uniformly reported, no one's reported weight would be correct. We would not know how much anyone actually weighs.

How can we determine the validity, or accuracy, of a test? Often we can simply look at the test's content. If you were to administer a test on Chinese grammar to assess students' mastery of French, the test would not demonstrate much **content validity**. By contrast, if you were taking flying lessons and your instructor tested you on your understanding of the instrument panel and other kinds of relevant information, the test would demonstrate high content validity.

We can also assess the validity of tests by correlating test scores with an external criterion that we have some confidence in—a correlation called a **validity coefficient**. If, for example, we believe that intelligent people will perform better at school (because of their higher intelligence), then we expect individuals' scores on a particular intelligence test to correlate with their school grades. The higher the validity coefficient, the more valid the test. A test need not just measure current performance. When high scores on an intelligence test continue to successfully predict high grades later in life, it is said to display high *predictive validity*.

"Unfortunately, all evidence of your son's intelligence is purely anecdotal."

History of Intelligence Testing

The first systematic attempts to measure intelligence were developed during the second half of the nineteenth century. The most influential approaches were those of Francis Galton in England and Alfred Binet in France. Later, in the United States, Lewis Terman and David Wechsler made important contributions.

Galton and *"Psychophysical Performance"*

Profoundly affected by the work of his half-cousin Charles Darwin, Francis Galton (1822–1911) sought to apply Darwin's ideas about evolution to the study of intelligence. He believed that by studying intellectual development, he could learn more about the evolution of the human species in general and the inheritance of intelligence in particular (Fancher, 2009, 2004). In particular, Galton sought to understand why some people appear to be more intelligent than others. If he could understand the evolutionary factors at work in such differences, he reasoned, then steps could be taken to improve the species.

Galton, who believed in a general intelligence factor, proposed that two qualities distinguish more gifted from less gifted people: a kind of psychic energy and a heightened sensitivity to external stimuli. His theory, termed the *theory of psychophysical performance*, held that people with more energy can perform more work and, in turn, develop greater intelligence. In addition, inasmuch as people gather information from their five senses, individuals who have more highly developed senses can take in more information (Kaufman, 2000). To more accurately gauge intelligence, Galton developed tests of an individual's sensory processing, motor skills, and reaction time.

Galton's work influenced many theorists. James McKean Cattell, in particular, later designed fifty psychophysical tests, expecting that the tests would support and extend Galton's ideas (Tulsky et al., 2003). Cattell tested skills, such as how fast people can move their arm over a specified distance and how many letters in a series they can remember. Ironically, Cattell's tests eventually helped to discredit Galton's notions rather than support them.

In his doctoral dissertation, one of Cattell's students, Clark Wissler, hypothesized that people would perform consistently well or consistently poorly across the various psychophysical tests and that those who did consistently well would display a higher level of general intelligence than those who performed poorly (Wissler, 1961). However, Wissler found that a given person's various test performances did not necessarily correlate either with each other or with academic performance. To determine whether each research participant's performances on various psychophysical tests were in fact correlated, Wissler has used *correlation coefficients*—a statistical method developed by Galton. Thus, the use of Galton's own statistical tool eventually helped to challenge his theory. Although, in general, his psychophysical theory of intelligence was not supported, certain of his specific physical measures have been found to relate to other measures of intelligence. Galton's use of motor skill measures and reaction time measures, for example, remain important aspects of modern intelligence testing.

Alfred Binet and the Binet-Simon Intelligence Test

At the same time that Galton and his followers were developing psychophysical theories and tests, Alfred Binet (1857–1911), along with his collaborator Theodosius Simon, were viewing intelligence and its measurement in a different way.

In 1904, the French government mandated compulsory education, and the Minister of Public Instruction in Paris formed a commission to devise a way to distinguish children with mental retardation from those who were unsuccessful in school for other reasons, such as behavioral problems. The idea was to assign intellectually capable children to regular classes and place those with mental retardation in special classes. To help determine the most appropriate type of class for each child, Binet and Simon devised the first widely applied intelligence tests.

Binet shared with Galton the notion of a general intelligence factor. However, regarding the psychophysical theory as "wasted time," he argued that the basis of intelligence is "judgment, otherwise called good sense, practical sense, initiative, the faculty of adapting one's self to circumstances. To judge well, to comprehend well, to reason well, these are the essential activities of intelligence." In short, Binet viewed intelligence as the "ability to demonstrate memory, judgment, reasoning, and social comprehension."

The tasks on Binet's intelligence test focused largely on language abilities, in contrast to the many nonverbal tasks devised by Galton. Binet also introduced the idea of **mental age**, the intellectual age at which a child is actually functioning. Mental age does not necessarily match chronological age. A child's mental age is indicated by the chronological age typically associated with his or her level of intellectual performance. Thus, the typical 11-year-old has a mental age of 11. A more intelligent 11-year-old, however, might have a mental age of 13, while a less intelligent 11-year-old might have a mental age of 9.

Binet did not believe his intelligence test necessarily measured a child's *inborn* level of intelligence. His goal was simply to predict a student's likelihood of success in school. And, in fact, he did find a strong correlation between performance on his test and performance in school. The test also correlated with scores on *achievement tests*—tests of knowledge about particular school subjects—although at a lower magnitude.

> " Intelligence is not to make no mistakes, but quickly to see how to make them good. "
>
> —*Bertholt Brecht, playwright*

validity the extent to which a test accurately measures or predicts what it is supposed to measure or predict.

content validity the degree to which the content of a test accurately represents what the test is intended to measure.

validity coefficient a correlation coefficient that measures validity by correlating a test score with some external criterion.

mental age the intellectual age at which a person is functioning, as opposed to chronological age.

intelligence quotient (IQ) Terman's measure of intelligence; the ratio of a child's mental age to his or her chronological age, multiplied by 100.

It is worth noting that Binet refused to use test scores to rank children. He felt that intelligence is too complex a phenomenon to draw meaningful conclusions about the *relative* intelligence among most children. It would be unfair to say, he argued, that one child of average intelligence, as measured by his test, was more intelligent than another child of average intelligence. However, Binet's concerns did not stop others from extending his test in ways that he neither anticipated nor advocated.

Lewis Terman and the Stanford-Binet Intelligence Test

Interest in Binet's work spread throughout the world, and Stanford University professor Lewis Terman (1877–1956) adapted the Binet-Simon intelligence test for use in the United States. He realized that some of the test items, originally developed to test French children, needed to be changed to better assess the intelligence of children in the United States. The age norms, for example, did not apply to the American school children in Terman's sample. This was an important early recognition of the influence of culture in intelligence testing. Terman called his new test the Stanford-Binet Intelligence Test (Hegarty, 2007; Feldhusen, 2003).

In developing his version of Binet's test, Terman decided to state the results not simply in terms of mental age, but as a measure that would relate mental to chronological age. Thus, the famous **intelligence quotient**, or **IQ**, was devised. To arrive at this measure of intelligence, Terman calculated the ratio of mental age to chronological age and multiplied that ratio by 100 (in order to remove the decimal point). Thus, returning to our earlier examples, the 11-year-old with average intelligence would earn an IQ of 100 (11/11 × 100), the more intelligent child would post an IQ of 118 (13/11 × 100), and the less intelligent child's IQ would be 82 (9/11 × 100).

In addition to adapting Binet's test for use in American schools, Terman had a larger goal—a goal that today we would consider reprehensible. He was an advocate of the nineteenth century *eugenics movement*, which sought to discourage people deemed as "unfit" from reproducing while encouraging "fit" individuals to have children. He believed that his IQ test could help determine the "fitness" of individuals to reproduce. He stated, "[T]he children of successful and cultured parents test higher than children from wretched and ignorant homes for the simple reason that their heredity is better." More generally, Terman believed that his test demonstrated that some groups of people are inherently less intelligent than others (Hegarty, 2007; Feldhusen, 2003).

As a result of eugenics research, the United States was one of the first countries to enact laws requiring individuals deemed "mentally retarded" or "mentally ill" to be sterilized. Nazi practices during World War II led to public distaste for eugenics, but some states kept these laws as late as 1980.

Working with agencies in the United States government, Terman also administered his test to newly arrived immigrants and to almost two million World War I army recruits. His student, Arthur Otis, developed nonverbal tasks for non-English speaking individuals. Some psychologists at the time believed that the results of these alternative versions of the intelligence test proved the inferiority of people whose origins were not Anglo-Saxon. In fact, the mass testing of immigrants helped lead to a 1924 law that greatly lowered the number of people allowed to enter the United States from Southern and Eastern Europe, while increasing the number from Northern and Western Europe. This is a vivid example of how nonscientific thinking (for example, prejudice and racism) can sometimes influence scientific thinking and political decision making. Despite such misuse of the early Stanford-Binet test, it remained for many years the leading intelligence testing instrument in the United States.

David Wechsler and the WAIS

As a young man inducted into the army during World War I, David Wechsler (1896–1981) was trained to administer and score the Stanford-Binet and other intelligence tests of the time. Over the course of his work, he came to recognize two key problems with the tests (Kaufman, 2000).

First, he realized that the distinction between mental and chronological age becomes less informative when testing adults. While it may be true that a considerable difference in intelligence is on display between an 8-year-old and a 13-year-old, a 5-year difference between adults tends to be meaningless. How much difference is there, for example, between the mental ability of a typical 30-year-old and a typical 35-year-old? Not much. Second, Wechsler, who was born in Romania and whose family emigrated to the United States when he was 6 years old, recognized the need for greater fairness when testing people who did not speak English or who spoke it poorly.

Over the course of his professional life, Wechsler devised a number of intelligence tests that took such problems into account. The first such test—the *Wechsler-Bellevue Intelligence Scale*—was published in 1939. Different versions of Wechsler's tests continue to be published by his associates to the present day (Lange & Iverson, 2008). The best known of these tests are the *Wechsler Adult Intelligence Scale (WAIS)* and the *Wechsler Intelligence Scale for Children (WISC)*. **Figure 10-5** shows sample items from the WAIS.

FIGURE 10-5 Items similar to those on the WAIS The widely used WAIS gives separate scores for verbal intelligence and performance as well as an overall intelligence score. (*Source:* Harcourt Assessment, Inc.)

Wechsler Adult Intelligence Scale (WAIS) Sample Items*

Test	Description	Example
Verbal Scale		
Information	Taps general range of information	On which continent is France?
Comprehension	Tests understanding of social conventions and ability to evaluate past experience	Why do people need birth certificates?
Arithmetic	Tests arithmetic reasoning through verbal problems	How many hours will it take to drive 150 miles at 50 miles per hour?
Similarities	Asks in what way certain objects or concepts are similar; measures abstract thinking	How are a calculator and a typewriter alike?
Digit span	Tests attention and rote memory by orally presenting series of digits to be repeated forward or backward	Repeat the following numbers backward: 2 4 3 5 1 8 6
Vocabulary	Tests ability to define increasingly difficult words	What does repudiate mean?
Performance scale		
Digit symbol	Tests speed of learning through timed coding tasks in which numbers must be associated with marks of various shapes	Shown: 1 2 3 4 Fill in: 4 2 1 3 
Picture completion	Tests visual alertness and visual memory through presentation of an incompletely drawn figure; the missing part must be discovered and named	Tell me what is missing: 
Block design	Tests ability to perceive and analyze patterns presenting designs that must be copied with blocks	Assemble blocks to match this design: 
Picture arrangement	Tests understanding of social situations through a series of comic-strip-type pictures that must be arranged in the right sequence to tell a story	Put this picture in the right order:  1 2 3
Object assembly	Tests ability to deal with part/whole relationships by presenting puzzle pieces that must be assembled to form a complete object	Assemble the pieces into a complete object: 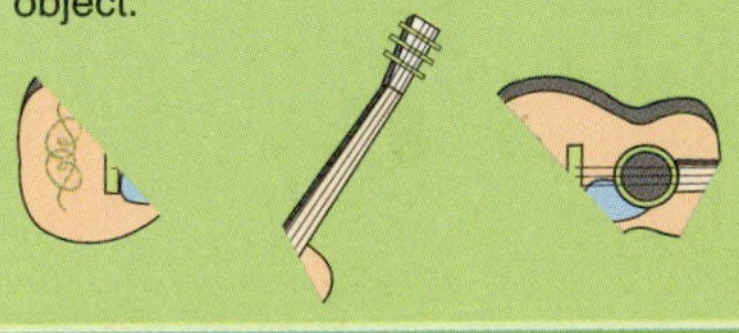

Wechsler borrowed much from the Stanford-Binet and other tests; however, his tests were less dominated by tasks requiring verbal ability. There are 11 subtests on the WAIS, some requiring verbal ability and others requiring nonverbal reasoning. Each individual who takes the test receives subtest scores, which are grouped into two main categories—a verbal score and a performance score. The individual also receives an overall score that Wechsler associated with the *g* factor. Wechsler also discarded the old formula for calculating an IQ score. Although he still called a person's overall score an *intelligence quotient,* or *IQ,* he derived the score from a normal distribution (discussed earlier in this chapter), rather than from a ratio—a change that has been adopted in most other intelligence tests.

Wechsler's tests resulted from his clinical experience, not from a clear theoretical position. However, he did come to develop a broad view of what intelligence means. In particular, he believed that it is more than success on test scores. To him, intelligence is at work as individuals try to manage the day-to-day aspects of life, interact with others, and perform at work. Wechsler's broad view of intelligence has gained momentum over the years. Indeed, as we suggested earlier, it lies at the center of most current theories of intelligence.

How Well Do Intelligence Tests Predict Performance?

The Stanford-Binet and the WAIS have very high degrees of reliability. The correlation coefficient for retakes of each test is about $+.90$. Furthermore, repeated measurements of IQ across the lifespan tend to correlate very highly (Larsen et al., 2008). Today's leading intelligence tests are also highly correlated with school performance—a validity coefficient of about $+.50$ (Sternberg et al., 2001). The correlations are even higher between IQ scores and the number of years of schooling that people complete (Ceci, 1991). These findings are especially relevant considering that IQ tests were originally designed to assess for school performance.

When we talk about IQ though, we often think about it in terms of defining general mental ability. After all, we still measure IQ for adults far past school age. This is so even though most of the tasks on any IQ test relate most strongly to school performance. Although these tasks are highly relevant to the types of challenges encountered in school—math, store of knowledge, reasoning—it is unclear to what degree they measure the many other types of intelligence that we have described in this chapter.

Research suggests you are just as likely to win a Nobel prize if you have an IQ of 130 as if you have an IQ of 180.

So what does IQ mean outside the classroom? Performance on intelligence tests correlates to some degree with other areas of functioning in life, such as occupational and social achievements, income, and health-related behaviors (Kuncel, Hezlett, & Ones, 2004; Lubinski, 2004). In a massive undertaking, researchers administered the same intelligence test to every 11-year-old child in Scotland in 1932 and 1947 and then followed the children's development and achievements as they moved through the lifespan (Deary et al., 2004). Performance on the IQ test at this young age was found to correlate to some degree with better health throughout life, greater independence during old age, and a longer lifespan. It would appear, then, that IQ testing does have some relevance beyond the school ages.

Cultural Bias and Stereotypes in Intelligence Testing

Though widely used and respected, intelligence tests are subject to many criticisms, both fair and unfair. One set of concerns involves *cultural bias* (Ford, 2008). As mentioned earlier, different cultures may have different ideas of intelligence. For example,

Sweating palms, rapid heartbeat, and mild nausea. That's what college-bound American high-school students have long experienced when sitting down before a bubble sheet—or computer screen— that could determine their futures. This rite of passage may become a relic of history as more colleges and universities make standardized achievement tests optional for admission.

As most college students know all too well, the *SAT* is a standardized test for college admissions, which purports to show whether a person will perform well in college. Since its introduction in 1901, its name has changed from the *Scholastic Aptitude Test* to the *Scholastic Assessment Test* to its present name, *The SAT Reasoning Test*. These changes reflect concerns about the test's ability to function as an intelligence test. The SAT's main rival is the ACT (American College Testing Program). But SAT's biggest problems lie not in its name nor its competitors, but rather in the test's possible biases, limited predictive values, and effects on student self-esteem (Lewin, 2009; St. Rose, 2009). Because of such problems, the time-honored college admission tool is under attack by educational groups and its future seems uncertain.

The SAT is meant to predict first-year grades in college. However, it explains only around 22 to 25 percent of the difference in freshman grades among students, leaving roughly three-quarters of the variance unexplained (Lewin, 2008; FairTest, 2007). A big part of that variance can be accounted for by high school grade point average (GPA), which is a better predictor of first-year grades than the SAT (Sternberg et al., 2006). SAT's producers therefore recommend that colleges use both high school GPA and SAT for admissions purposes (Kobrin et al., 2008). It has been found, however, that a combination of high school GPA and demographics, including race and social class, predicts college performance nearly as well as the GPA/SAT combination (Rothstein, 2004). This suggests that SAT scores may, in fact, largely be a fill-in for demographic variables, resulting in bias against low-income and minority students when SAT scores are used (Rothstein, 2004). In addition, the SAT tends to underestimate how well females will perform in college (FairTest, 2007).

Based on these and other concerns, the National Center for Fair and Open Testing, an advocacy group against the misuse of standardized tests, supports making standardized tests optional for admissions. They report that some colleges have already become test-optional, including highly selective schools, and that such schools have observed increased diversity in their applicant pools, with more first-generation, low-income, and minority students applying. In addition, most test-optional schools have found no decrease in the quality of their students as a result of the change (FairTest, 2007).

Others would prefer to keep the SAT and other such college admission tests in use, but to improve them. Highly regarded psychologist and educator Richard Atkinson (2001) has said, "We will never devise the perfect test: a test that accurately assesses students irrespective of parental education and income, the quality of local schools, and the kind of community students live in, but we can do better. We can do much better." With such sentiments in mind, SAT officials are trying to ensure that the SAT overcomes its limitations and continues to have relevance. They have, for example, funded a group of researchers, including noted psychologist Robert Sternberg, to produce and validate a standardized test based on Sternberg's triarchic theory of intelligence. So far, this augmented SAT test, which assesses *practical* and *creative* skills in addition to analytical skills, appears to be more predictive of first-year grades and less culturally biased than the current SAT (Sternberg et al., 2006). Whether these researchers further succeed at establishing the worth of the new test may determine whether future generations experience the nerve-wracking, stomach-churning battle with the bubble sheet that has long been synonymous with college applications.

Western intelligence tests emphasize abilities, such as logic, mathematical skill, and verbal fluency over abilities, such as getting along with others and fitting in with one's environment—abilities that are important in Chinese notions of intelligence. Such differences obviously make comparing intelligence across cultures challenging.

Furthermore, problems are not limited to comparing people from different countries but extend to comparing members of different subcultures within a single country. For example, although Wechsler made considerable efforts to standardize the WAIS and make it as unbiased as possible, critics noted several curious oversights in earlier versions of the test. Many

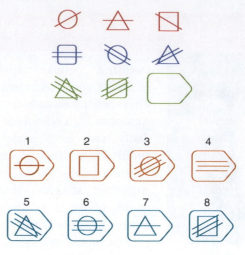

of its problem-solving questions reflected problems confronted in middle-class settings, for instance (Ford, 2008). In addition, until the most recent revisions of the WAIS, every time a picture of a person was used for a test item, the picture was of a white person.

In part to point out the culture-specific nature of intelligence testing, sociologist Adrian Dove created the Dove Counterbalance General Intelligence Test. Dove intended the test to be at least partly a satire of the notion that a culture-free intelligence test could ever be developed. It is likely that there will always be culture-based disagreements about intelligence tests and about what knowledge and skills are important.

Most people interested in the construction of intelligence tests have abandoned the idea of totally unbiased tests and instead try to design tests that do not put particular cultures at an absolute disadvantage. The Progressive Matrices Test attempts to achieve this goal in part by emphasizing abstract, nonverbal skills, for example. Some sample items from that test are shown in **Figure 10-6**.

A related testing issue involves **stereotype threat**, which occurs when people in a particular group perform poorly because they fear that their performance will conform to a negative stereotype associated with that group. Several studies have found that simply suggesting to students that they will not do well on a test because of their gender or race can lower their test scores (Steele & Aronson, 2004, 1995). In one particularly interesting study, researchers were able to use stereotype threat to manipulate the performance of Asian women on a math test (Ambady et al., 2004, 2001; Shih, Pittinsky, & Ambady, 1999). Some participants were encouraged to focus on their female identity, and they tended to perform less well on the test (in keeping with the stereotype that women are not good at math). Other participants had their attention focused on their Asian identity, and they tended to perform better (in keeping with the stereotype that Asians are good at math).

As psychologists' awareness and ability to detect bias grows, they are becoming increasingly able to construct tests that are more sensitive and more effective. We have, for example, already noted the efforts of developers of the WAIS to make their tests less culture-specific. Overall bias can be assessed both at the general level we have discussed here and also at a more detailed level. During test construction, today's tests are also assessed for *item bias*; if individuals from a particular gender or ethnic group miss an item with high frequency, that item is considered for elimination from the test. Similarly, certain questions may become less culturally relevant over time and must be exchanged for questions that better reflect current conditions. It appears that ongoing efforts to assess and challenge these sorts of bias have been somewhat successful in rendering generally nonbiased testing.

The power of stereotype threat In one study, Asian women who were encouraged to focus largely on their female identity performed poorly on a math test, while those who were led to focus on their Asian identity performed well on the math test.

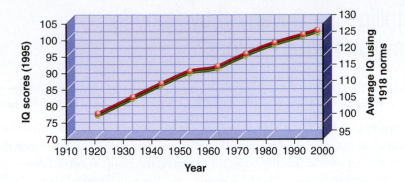

FIGURE 10-7 **The Flynn effect** Flynn demonstrated that intelligence scores have increased from 1918 to 1995. The right axis of the graph shows that if the 1918 scales were used today, the average IQ score in the United States would be 125. The left axis shows that if the 1995 scales were used, the average IQ score in 1918 would equate to a score of 76 today. *Source:* Adapted from Flynn, J. R. (1998). IQ gains over time: Toward finding the causes. In U. Neisser (Ed.), *The rising curve: Long-term gains in IQ and related measures* (p. 37). Washington, DC: American Psychological Association. Copyright © by the American Psychological Association. Reprinted by permission of the author.

Is Human Intelligence Increasing?

We have observed that the median score on intelligence tests, such as the Stanford-Binet and the WAIS is set at 100. To keep the median score at 100, the tests periodically must be *restandardized.* People taking the WAIS today, for example, are taking a version that has been reconstructed in recent years—not the version that David Wechsler designed originally.

Upon reviewing test scores over time, researchers have noticed something startling: intelligence test scores from around the world seem to be increasing, even though scores from other kinds of educational tasks and tests, such as college aptitude tests, are dropping (Nettelbeck & Wilson, 2004). Studies indicate that an average IQ score of 100 from 70 years ago would equate to a score of only 76 today. This puzzling phenomenon has been named the **Flynn effect,** after New Zealand researcher James Flynn (2007), who first discovered it (**Figure 10-7**).

Researchers do not fully understand why intelligence scores have increased over time (Cocodia et al., 2003). One possibility is that there is something wrong with the basic procedures, content, or nature of standardized intelligence tests. A more widely embraced explanation holds that intelligence is changeable and that, on average, people today exhibit higher intelligence than people in the past. Such improvements in intelligence might be related to improvements in education around the world, better nutrition, the development of more stimulating environments, reductions in childhood disease, or evolutionary shifts in genetic inheritance (Mingroni, 2007, 2004). It is also worth noting that some theorists believe that rising intelligence test performance is due to the greater test-taking sophistication of today's students. The problem with this explanation, however, is that the Flynn effect began before intelligence testing became as widespread as it is today.

stereotype threat a phenomenon in which people in a particular group perform poorly because they fear that their performance will conform to a negative stereotype associated with that group.

Flynn effect an observed rise in average IQ scores throughout the world over time.

Before You Go On

What Do You Know?
7. What three basic criteria are central to designing an intelligence test?
8. What was the original purpose of Binet's intelligence test?
9. How does mental age differ from chronological age?
10. What are some proposed causes of the Flynn effect?

What Do You Think?   How would you design a culture-free intelligence test?

Is Intelligence Governed by Genetic or Environmental Factors?

LEARNING OBJECTIVE 4 Review the contributions of heredity and environment to intelligence, and explain how emphasizing one factor or the other can affect social policy.

As you saw in Chapter 3, the nature/nurture debate centers on the question of whether particular qualities and behaviors result from genetic underpinnings or from the environment. Is a happy and healthy baby, for example, the result of robust genes, effective parental care and attention, or both? A similar question can be asked about intelligence. Do we inherit our intelligence from our parents? And if we do, does that mean that the environment has no influence, or can experiences, such as parenting, schooling, and familiarity with test taking have an effect? Later in this section, we will examine how various psychologists answer these questions. First, though, we'll consider important social questions that are raised by the search to identify the origin of intelligence.

What Are the Social Implications of the Nature/Nurture Debate?

If genes were clearly identified as the main determinant of intelligence, what might some of the social consequences be? In certain circles, such a finding might be taken to justify claims that some people are inherently superior to others. Perhaps some would even seek to create a social structure that assigned people to classes according to their parentage and restricted certain classes to certain social roles.

On the other hand, what if the environment were found to be more decisive in determining intelligence? Children from disadvantaged environments would be expected to lead disadvantaged lives and display, on average, lower intelligence, but then again, their environments and their intellectual level could be improved potentially. Would people who possess environmental advantages be willing to share them with those who are deprived, however?

Other difficult questions involving the nature/nurture debate and intelligence have been asked with respect to gender, ethnicity, and race. Perhaps the clearest example of the serious social consequences of such questions was the Nazi claim in the early twen-

Statistically, firstborn children appear to represent a majority of Nobel prize winners, classical music composers, and eminent psychologists. Children later in the birth order appear to be more prominent leaders and may, on average, be more creative (Plucker, 2003).

Environmental impact Research indicates that a stimulating environment can help facilitate the intellectual development of children whereas a deprived environment often has a negative impact.

cent of all differences observed in a population's intelligence test scores are due to genetic factors.

The statistical measure used to indicate the contribution of heredity to intelligence (or to any other characteristic) is the **heritability coefficient**, a number ranging from 0.00 to +1.00. A coefficient of 0.00 means that heredity has no impact on variations observed among people, whereas a coefficient of +1.00 means that heredity is the sole influence on the characteristic under investigation. The heritability coefficient for Huntington's Disease, in which genetic factors are totally responsible for the emergence of the disorder, is +1.00. In contrast, as we have just observed, the heritability coefficient for intelligence is +0.50—a figure that holds in studies conducted across the world, from the United States to Moscow, Japan, and India (Plomin & Spinath, 2004).

Findings from Molecular Biology   We know that genes contribute to intelligence, but do we know which genes are important? In recent years, new molecular biology techniques have enabled researchers to examine DNA sequences and genes. These techniques have already led to a detailed mapping (sequencing) of all genes in the human body, and they may lead eventually to the identification of the genes responsible for complex traits, such as intelligence. Although researchers do not yet know precisely which genes contribute to a person's intelligence, they have determined that more than one gene is involved (Plomin & Spinath, 2004). In fact, early indications are that numerous genes from various chromosomes may be at work—a polygenic effect—with each such gene accounting for only a small amount of intellectual potential.

Environmental Influences on Intelligence

If the heritability of intelligence is 50 percent, then environmental factors are responsible for the remaining 50 percent of differences in intelligence among people. The term *environment* can have a narrow or broad meaning. It can refer to our home setting, neighborhood, extended family, school, or socioeconomic group. It even can refer to biological events and experiences that a fetus confronts in its mother's uterus. Or, it can refer to the sum of all such contexts. Four environmental influences have received particular attention in the study of intelligence: family and home, culture, occupation, and schooling.

Family and Home Environment   The first environment to which we are exposed in life and the one that dominates our childhood is the family and home. Our parents' childrearing methods and other characteristics, our interactions with siblings, the objects in our houses, family trips—these are all parts of our family and home environment. Do such environmental factors affect children's intelligence?

Research has suggested a link between family and home environment and children's intelligence scores. A number of studies, for example, have examined the IQ scores of biological siblings and adoptive siblings. These investigations have found that when biological siblings are raised apart, the correlation between their IQ scores is +.22. In contrast, when children from different families are adopted and raised together, the correlation between their IQ scores is +.32 (Plomin & Spinath, 2004). If family and home environment did not affect intelligence levels, we would expect a near-zero correlation between the IQ scores of adoptive siblings. Instead, they display a higher correlation than that displayed by biological twins who are raised apart.

heritability the overall extent to which differences among people are attributable to genes.

heritability coefficient a correlation coefficient used to indicate the contribution of heredity to some characteristic, such as intelligence.

Animal studies suggest that organisms perform better on learning and intelligence tests when they are mildly hungry.

Early theories held that an individual's intellectual capacity was totally fixed at birth. The many examples presented throughout this chapter of how the environment can affect intelligence certainly challenge this early assumption. In par-

ticular, we now know that interventions of various kinds can improve intellectual functioning.

Two researchers, Robert Bradley and Bettye Caldwell, have examined the impact of the home environment on intelligence and identified several parenting approaches that may help raise the IQ scores of preschoolers (Bradley, Caldwell, & Corwyn, 2003; Bradley & Caldwell, 1984). In fact, these researchers claim that such approaches are better predictors of IQ scores than factors such as socioeconomic class or family structure. Current research seems to support their assertions. The parent to-do list includes:

- Be emotionally and verbally responsive and involved with the child.
- Avoid too much restriction and punishment.
- Organize the physical environment and the child's activity schedule.
- Provide appropriate play materials.
- Provide a variety of forms of daily stimulation.

Cultural Influences   Most definitions of intelligence include how well persons adapt to their environments. This criterion raises an important question: Does the definition of intelligence change across different cultural environments? Many researchers say yes, the definition of intelligence varies from culture to culture (Georgas, 2003).

Note that this is different from asking whether people from different parts of the world (or from different racial or ethnic groups) have different levels of intelligence. That question relates more to the idea of comparing general intelligence, whereas we here are more concerned with comparing the specific skill sets that constitute intelligence in different cultures. Researchers have found that the values of a society or cultural group often have powerful effects on the intellectual skills of its members. Rice farmers in Liberia, for example, are particularly skilled at estimating quantities of rice (Cole, Gay, & Glick, 1967); and children in Botswana, who are used to hearing stories, have good memories for the details of stories (Dube, 1982). These specific skills would improve individuals' ability to survive and thrive within their cultures and thus, would be valued components of intelligence within each culture. Such principles can apply within subcultures as well; as our case study at the beginning of the chapter demonstrates: a knowledge of fashion designers and the ability to walk a runway are prized skill sets in some subcultures within Western culture.

Most of the assumptions about intelligence that we have looked at thus far are Western-oriented. Western views of intelligence tend to be influenced by the Western value of individualism, while some other cultures place more emphasis on the community as a whole. Moreover, Westerners tend to equate high intelligence with rapid mental processing, whereas other cultures may value depth of thinking, however slowly it occurs (Sternberg et al., 1981). One study found that Taiwanese-Chinese theorists typically point to five factors at the root of intelligence: (1) a general cognitive factor; (2) interpersonal intelligence (knowing about others); (3) intrapersonal intelligence (knowing about oneself); (4) intellectual self-assertion; and (5) intellectual self-effacement (Yang & Sternberg, 1997). While the first three qualities are similar to factors in

Societal needs and intelligence An individual's particular expression of intelligence is often tied to the survival needs of his or her society. Rice farmers, such as these field workers during rice harvest, are often highly skilled at estimating quantities of rice and are admired for their high intelligence.

some Western definitions of intelligence, the final two are not. Also, Westerners often believe that intelligence further involves verbal skill and the ability to solve practical problems, features absent from the Chinese list.

Occupational Influences Researchers consistently have found a relationship between intelligence and job complexity. People of higher intelligence tend to work in more complex jobs (Ganzach, 2003; Ganzach & Pazy, 2001). An obvious explanation for this relationship is that individuals of higher intelligence can handle complex jobs more readily than less intelligent people and so are more likely to obtain and succeed in such positions.

Studies also suggest, however, that complex work may itself improve intelligence. In one study, for example, interviews with 3,000 men in various occupations seemed to indicate that more complex jobs lead to more "intellectual flexibility and independent judgment among employees" (Schooler, 2001; Kohn & Schooler, 1973). A job that requires workers to organize and interpret detailed financial data, for example, may help produce more intellectual know-how than one requiring workers to simply add up customer bills.

Why would more complex jobs enhance intellectual skills? Perhaps because holders of such jobs are forced to acquire a greater amount of complex information and knowledge (Kuncel et al., 2004)—the very kinds of information and knowledge that are measured on intelligence tests. The complexity factor may also help explain differences in IQ scores between urban and rural populations. A few generations ago, studies found that urban residents scored, on average, six IQ points higher than rural residents (Terman & Merrill, 1937; Seashore, Wesman, & Doppelt, 1950). One possible explanation for this difference is the greater complexity of the urban environment. More recently, the difference declined to about two points (Kaufman & Doppelt, 1976; Reynolds et al., 1987). It could be that changes in rural environments—less isolation, increased travel, mass communication, Internet access, improvements in schools, and increased use of technology on farms—have raised the level of complexity in these environments and, in turn, brought the IQ scores of rural citizens closer to those of city residents.

School Influences Researchers have determined that schooling is both a cause and consequence of intelligence (Fish, 2002; Sangwan, 2001). Children with higher intelligence test scores are more likely to be promoted from grade to grade, less likely to drop out of school, and more likely to attend college. In turn, schooling helps change mental abilities, including those measured on intelligence tests.

Researchers Stephen Ceci and Wendy Williams (2007, 1997) have demonstrated some interesting ties between intelligence scores and the amount of time spent in school. Students' IQ scores tend to rise during the school year and drop when schooling is discontinued or during summer vacation. Students who complete high school perform higher on intelligence tests than those who leave school early. And young children whose birthdays just make the cut-off for beginning school early earn higher intelligence scores than those of almost identical age who miss the cut-off and remain at home for an extra year.

Why might schooling help improve intelligence scores? In part because schools provide the opportunity both to acquire information (Who wrote *Moby Dick*? What is a square root, and how do you calculate it?) and to develop "systematic problem-solving, abstract thinking, categorization, sustained attention to material of little intrinsic interest, and repeated manipulation of basic symbols and operations"—skills measured on intelligence tests (Neisser, 1988, p.16).

Researchers have also shown that the *quality* of the school environment affects intellectual performance. In financially poor schools, children tend to learn less and in turn, tend to score significantly lower on IQ tests. One researcher reported that when

Which causes which? People in complex jobs, such as this engineer working in a telecommunications control room, are often highly intelligent. Does their high intelligence qualify them for more complex work or does the complex work increase their intelligence? Research has supported both explanations.

Times are changing An elderly farmer in Sweden sits in the doorway of his barn while working out his agricultural needs on a laptop. Some psychologists believe that the increased use of technology on farms helps account for the recent closing of the gap between the I.Q. scores of urban and rural populations.

Schooling and intellectual performance This teacher in the Philippines gives a lesson to her class of 59 second grade students. On average, children who attend financially poor schools perform less well on intelligence tests.

African-American students from a poor school in Georgia moved to Philadelphia, their IQ scores improved (Lee, 1961). Clearly, such findings argue for better schools so that each child can work in as enriching an environment as possible.

Group Differences in IQ Scores

Recall that at the beginning of this section we discussed *The Bell Curve,* in which the authors argued that group differences in IQ may be due largely to genetic factors. We went on to discuss findings that intelligence is, indeed, heritable, but that environment plays a significant role as well. Let us now look more closely at group differences in IQ scores.

There are two trends on which most researchers of group differences in intelligence agree (Lynn, 2008; Hunt & Carlson, 2007; Fish, 2002). First, racial groups do indeed differ in their average scores on intelligence tests. Second, high-scoring people (and groups) are more likely to attain high levels of education and income. In one review conducted decades ago, 52 researchers agreed that the IQ bell curve for Americans is centered around a score of 100 for white Americans and 85 for African Americans, with scores for different subgroups of Hispanic Americans falling in between (Avery et al., 1994). Similarly, researchers have noted that European New Zealanders tend to outscore native Maori New Zealanders, Israeli Jews outscore Israeli Arabs, and people with good hearing outscore the hearing impaired (Zeidner, 1990). What can we make of such trends?

Two important issues about group differences can be clarified by means of an analogy offered by geneticist Richard Lewontin (2001, 1982, 1976). Suppose you start with 100 plant seeds from the same source and divide them into two groups. You plant one group of seeds in a flowerpot filled with poor soil and the other group in a flowerpot filled with fertile soil. What differences would you expect between the groups of seeds as they grow into plants? As shown in **Figure 10-8**, you should see two kinds of variation: variation between the two groups and variation within each group. When evaluating these variations, we need to keep in mind two principles that also apply to evaluating group differences in intelligence scores:

1. *Environment contributes to variation between the groups.* The plants growing in poor soil vary from the ones growing in good soil, even though all of the plants came from the same mixture of seed. For example, the plants raised in poor soil are, on average, shorter than those raised in fertile soil. This difference is probably attributable to the environment. In short, optimal environments tend to produce optimal plants, and deficient environments tend to produce less successful plants. Similarly, on average, groups that now display lower average IQ scores have been raised in worse environments than the groups with higher scores.

FIGURE 10-8 **Lewontin's plant analogy of intelligence** If two groups of plants start out from the same source of seeds (genetics), but one group is given a better environment, the differences in height between the two groups would be mainly determined by environmental conditions. The analogy applies when evaluating group differences in IQ scores.

Group 1: poor soil | **Group 2:** fertile soil

2. *An average variation between groups cannot be applied to individuals within each group.* In our plant example, even though on average the plants growing in poor soil are shorter than those growing in good soil, some of the poor-soil plants will be taller than others. Some will probably even be taller the average plant in the good soil. These differences probably are attributable to normal genetic variation, since all the plants in a given pot share the same environment.

Again, this principle applies to people as well as plants. You cannot deduce anything about the intelligence of one person based on the mean scores of that individual's group. Even Herrnstein and Murray (1994), the authors of *The Bell Curve*, granted that "millions of Blacks have higher IQs than the average White." Failing to distinguish between individual performance and group norms can mislead people, produce incorrect expectations, and cause social injustices.

With this analogy in mind, let us return to the question of IQ scores and group differences. Researcher Joel Myerson and his colleagues (1998) examined the intelligence scores of African American and white American students from eighth grade through college and found that from the eighth grade through the early high school years, the average score of the white American students increased, whereas the average score of the African American students decreased. The gap between the two groups was at its widest at about the time both groups took their college admission tests. During college, however, the scores of the African American students increased more than four times as much as the scores of the white American students. The researchers concluded that "as black and white students complete more grades in high-school environments that differ in quality, the gap in cognitive test scores widens. At the college level, however, where black and white students are exposed to educational environments of comparable quality...many Blacks are able to make remarkable gains, closing the gap in test scores."

Such research suggests that public policy aimed at making more equitable resources available throughout society would lead to more similar intelligence test scores across different groups (Williams et al., 2004). Of course, this raises yet another important question: Do efforts to equalize educational experiences and other environmental resources actually improve intelligence? We will consider next the effects of *environmental enrichment*—providing disadvantaged children with more stimulating environments at home and at school.

> "When schools flourish, all flourishes."
> —*Martin Luther, German theologian and reformer*

Does Environmental Enrichment Make a Difference?

Studies have indicated that young children from poor families typically receive less intellectual stimulation than do children from wealthier homes (Arnold & Doctoroff, 2003). They have, on average, far fewer books and educational toys, for example, and their parents read to them less. Only half of preschoolers from families on public assistance have alphabet books, compared with 97 percent of children from wealthy homes (Mason et al., 1990; McCormick & Mason, 1986). It appears that their early environmental limitations may place poor children at a severe disadvantage when it comes to developing intellectual and academic skills.

We can see this problem particularly clearly in institutional settings such as orphanages and in foster homes. (Nelson et al., 2009, 2007; Nelson, 2007). During the early 1980s, psychologist J. McVicker Hunt (1982) conducted work in a poor Iranian orphanage. In an effort to improve the lives of children in the orphanage and, in turn, improve their development, he offered a program of "tutored human enrichment." He found that such early interventions did indeed help improve the cognitive functioning of the children. In other work, however, he clarified that early instruction of this kind helps to

Getting a head start Two toddlers enjoy the individualized attention provided by their teacher and their ultra-stimulating classroom environment in a Head Start program in Mississippi.

improve the intellectual capacities only of children who have been living in deprived environments, not of those who have already been living in enriched environments.

Based on findings such as Hunt's, *Project Head Start,* a federally funded preschool program, was launched in 1965. The program, which has served more than 22 million disadvantaged children since its inception and now serves around one million each year, aims to enhance children's performances in school and beyond by helping to develop their cognitive and social skills as early as possible (Olsen & DeBoise, 2007; Ripple et al., 1999). The program continues to enjoy significant community and political support.

Does Head Start work? Researchers have assessed its success by comparing children who have enrolled in the program with same-aged counterparts who have not. Studies indicate that programs, such as Head Start do indeed produce at least short-term cognitive gains among disadvantaged children (Arnold & Doctoroff, 2003). Two investigations found, for example, that children who participated in early childhood educational programs were by mid-adolescence more than a grade ahead of a matched control group of children who had not been in the programs (Zigler & Berman, 1983; Lazar & Darlington, 1982). The early education participants also scored higher on various tests of scholastic achievement.

Head Start and similar programs also appear to increase children's readiness for school, thus reducing the need for children to repeat grades or to be placed in special-education classes. Although some research suggests that the IQ changes and academic benefits resulting from these early education programs may diminish over time, other studies indicate that, at the very least, the programs enhance emotional intelligence,

Is There Really a Mozart Effect?

"Push me, Dad. Mozart was pushed."

For the past 15 years, a notion has been floating around that listening to the music of Mozart will significantly increase a person's intelligence and that the earlier in life one is exposed to such music, the greater the intellectual impact. The phenomenon is called the "Mozart effect," and it has spurred many parents to surround their young children with such music. In some families, the composer's music is even introduced during the prenatal months. The idea of a Mozart effect is exciting and even inspiring. But there is one small problem. It has no basis in fact.

So where did the notion come from? Back in 1993, a research team investigated whether performances by participants on a test of abstract spatial reasoning could be influenced by listening to classical music (Rauscher, Shaw, & Ky, 1993). The participants were administered three different spatial tests—one after listening to a sonata by Mozart, another after listening to repetitive relaxation music, and a third after sitting in silence. The researchers found that the spatial test scores of the participants rose 9 points after they had listened to Mozart. Almost immediately, exciting reports about the Mozart phenomenon spread throughout the world.

It is critical to note that the effect of this music on the participants' performances was temporary—15 minutes at most. Moreover, there was no effect on any other kind of intellectual task or on general intelligence. But such details were lost as the findings worked their way into the media. Hundreds of news stories and, later, books proclaimed the *permanent* impact of classical music—particularly Mozart's music—on *general learning* and on *general intelligence.* The governor of Georgia even proposed in his 1998 state budget that $105,000 be allocated to provide every child in the state with a CD of classical music.

Over the past decade, many studies have been conducted on the relationship between music and cognitive functioning. The findings have been mixed, although some suggest that music, perhaps by its effects on mood and on arousal, can sometimes have temporary and modest effects on certain kinds of cognitive performances (Thompson, Husaine, & Schellenberg, 2001). But none of these studies has even come close to suggesting that classical music—by Mozart or anyone else—actually makes you smarter. Nevertheless, in the world of pop culture, this particular beat goes on.

instill a more positive attitude toward learning, reduce school dropouts, and even decrease later criminality (Siegler, 2003).

Early intervention programs can extend beyond school settings. They can include going into the homes of young children; working with their parents; adding stimulating toys, books, and tools to the home; and otherwise enriching the home and community environments. It appears that such home-bound programs often help increase children's cognitive achievements. One extensive research project has clarified that enrichment-intervention programs of various kinds achieve greater success when they (1) begin earlier in life and continue; (2) are more intensive (more hours per day and more days per year); and (3) include programs for maintaining positive attitudes and behaviors (Ramey & Ramey, 2007).

Before You Go On

What Do You Know?

11. What are the main arguments of *The Bell Curve*?

12. About what percentage of intelligence is thought to be genetically determined, and what evidence supports this claim?

13. What types of environmental factors have been shown to affect intelligence?

What Do You Think?
Considering the material you have read about test construction, heritability, and cultural differences, what type of learning environment would maximize the intelligence of all individuals?

Intelligence *What Happens in the* B R A I N ?

LEARNING OBJECTIVE 5 Describe how brain size, number of neurons, processing speed, brain activity, and cortical thickness relate to intelligence.

So far in this chapter, we have explored several important questions concerning the nature, measurement, and sources of intelligence. We now add another question: What happens in the brain when we exhibit intelligence? Have researchers, for example, detected relationships between specific brain activities or specific brain structures and intelligence? To answer this question, let's look at four areas of investigation: brain size, brain speed, brain activity, and cortical thickness (Reynolds et al., 2008; Vernon et al., 2000).

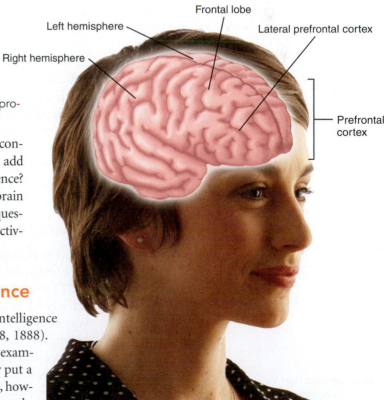

Brain Size, Number of Neurons, and Intelligence

Researchers have been exploring correlations between brain size and intelligence since the mid-nineteenth century (Ash & Gallup, 2008; Galton, 1948, 1888). Initially, limitations in technology hampered meaningful outcomes. For example, researchers could only study the brains of corpses, which certainly put a damper on testing their intelligence. Today's neuroimaging technologies, however, allow scientists to measure brain size and brain activity in living people.

Some neuroimaging findings over the past few decades have indeed suggested a possible correlation between brain size and mental functioning, but most studies of this issue fail to support this notion (Choi et al., 2008; Vernon et al., 2000, 1990). As we noted in Chapter 4, the overall size of the brain appears to be more closely related to the size of the body than to intelligence. The main exception to this is people with extremely small or extremely large brains, each of whom are more likely to exhibit mental deficiencies than are people whose brain sizes fall within the normal range.

Regardless of brain size, does the total number of neurons in a brain predict intellectual functioning? Apparently not. After all, there are, on average, 16 percent more neurons in male brains than female brains, but most research has found no difference in IQ scores between men and women. On the other hand, intelligence may be related to the number of neurons in particular brain regions. Studies have suggested, for example, that general intelligence may be tied to the number of neurons in the brain's frontal lobes (Tranel et al., 2008). All other things being equal, people with more such neurons seem to perform better on intelligence tests.

Brain Speed and Intelligence

Researchers often analyze the bioelectrical activity of the brain by using an *electroencephalogram (EEG)*, a device that places sensors on the outside of an individual's head and records his or her *brain waves*. EEG research has allowed investigators to see whether intelligence is correlated with brain speed—the speed with which the brain responds successfully to various stimuli, tasks, and events (Sternberg, 2003; Deary & Stough, 1997, 1996).

One procedure, for example, involves the speed at which people process stimuli that are flashed before their eyes. In a typical study, the experimenter briefly flashes an incomplete stimulus on one side of a screen, then quickly flashes a more complete stimulus on the other side. Viewers are asked to indicate which side the complete image appeared on. It typically takes only a fraction of a second for anybody to correctly answer this question. Still, some people are quicker than others, and those who perceive the correct image more quickly (as indicated by their EEG readings) tend to score higher on intelligence tests (especially on perceptual tasks) than those whose reactions are a bit slower. In short, more intelligent people may be physiologically wired to acquire and utilize information more quickly than others.

In a related line of research, several investigators have found significant correlations between IQ scores and **nerve conduction velocity (NCV)**, the speed with which electrical impulses are transmitted along nerve fibers and across synapses (Sternberg, 2003; Vernon et al., 2000; Reed & Jensen, 1992). Both the NCV and EEG findings fit well with studies showing that highly intelligent people are, on average, able to make decisions more quickly than less intelligent people (Tulsky & O'Brien, 2008).

Brain Activity and Intelligence

Another biological approach to the study of intelligence examines how active people's brains are when solving intellectual problems. A *positron emission tomography (PET)* scan is a type of neuroimaging technology that can reveal where and how actively the brain is metabolizing, or breaking down, glucose at any given moment. Very active areas of the brain show up as red and orange on a PET scan's color-coded pictures, while less active areas show up as green and blue. PET scans have generally revealed lower activity in the brains of people who are performing well on an intellectual task and higher activity in the brains of those who are performing poorly (Raichle, 2005; Haier, 2003; Posner et al., 2002). Thus, some researchers suggest that the brains of higher-performing people do not need to work as hard as the brains of

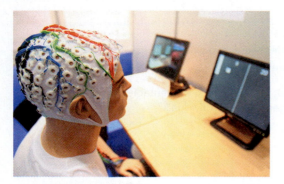

Speedier brains? People who score higher on intelligence tests tend to perceive correct images more quickly, as indicated by EEG readings.

nerve conduction velocity (NCV) the speed with which electrical impulses are transmitted along nerve fibers and across synapses.

lower-performing people—that is, their brains are more efficient (Grabner et al., 2003; Neubauer & Fink, 2003).

Although high intellectual performance seems to be related to an overall reduction in brain activity, PET scans have revealed that particular areas of brain activity are at work during certain types of intellectual tasks. Investigator John Duncan and his colleagues conducted a PET scan on thirteen men and women while they were taking an intelligence test (Duncan, 2001; Duncan et al., 2000). They found that for each individual, the brain activity during the test was concentrated in the left lateral prefrontal cortex and the right lateral prefrontal cortex—brain regions located toward the front and outer sides of the brain's two hemispheres. When a test-taker was performing verbal tasks on the test, the *left* lateral prefrontal cortex was activated (Remember from Chapters 4 and 9 that language is processed predominantly in the left hemisphere of the brain). During spatial tasks, both the left lateral prefrontal cortex and the right lateral prefrontal cortex were activated. It is worth noting that the prefrontal cortex, which sends and receives information to and from numerous other brain sites, may help people keep track of several thoughts at the same time, solve problems, produce new ideas, and filter out unimportant information.

While such studies are interesting, we must keep in mind that they do not clarify the causal relationships at work. Do people of higher intelligence display less brain activity overall, despite experiencing more activity in the prefrontal cortex, because they are smart, for example, or are people smart because their brain activity is more efficient? Or are both brain activity and intelligence related to yet a third causal factor that researchers have yet to discover?

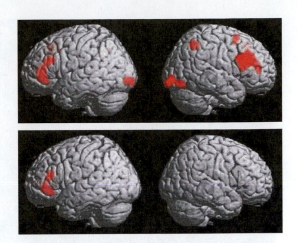

The prefrontal cortex and performance on intelligence tests The study by John Duncan and his colleagues (2000) found that the left lateral prefrontal cortex is active during the performance of a range of cognitive tasks. These PET scans from the study reveal that the left and right lateral prefrontal cortices are both active during spatial tasks (top row), while activity during verbal tasks tends to center in the left lateral prefrontal cortex (bottom row).

Cortical Thickness and Intelligence | How we *Develop*

We have seen that various brain features, such as the number of neurons, brain speed, and brain activity, may be tied to intelligence. A related issue is whether *brain development* is related to the development of intelligence. A highly publicized study by researcher Philip Shaw and his colleagues sought to answer this question (Shaw et al., 2008, 2006).

In a longitudinal study, the Shaw team performed brain scans on 309 children and teenagers between the ages of 6 and 19, with each participant scanned every two years. The scans revealed that throughout childhood and adolescence, individuals display changes in the thickness of the *cortex*—the folded outer layer of the brain—changes that have implications for the development of intelligence.

The study found that children begin with a thin cortex, which thickens over the years and then begins to thin down and continues thinning through adolescence. These changes in thickness are consistent with what is known about neural pruning during development. As we observed in Chapters 3 and 4, the brains of very young children produce a large number of neural synapses and neurons. Then, as the children grow older, their brains prune down the neural connections that are not being used and perhaps reduce the actual number of neurons as well, leaving the individuals with a much lower number of connections and, perhaps, neurons in their teenage and adult years. It is believed that a thick cortex may reflect a higher number of neural connections and neurons, whereas a thin cortex may reflect a lower number; so as adolescence approaches and pruning occurs, the cortex becomes thinner.

The study further found this pattern of changes in cortical thickness to be clearest in the prefrontal regions, the brain areas whose activity has been tied closely to intellectual activity. Thus, it appears that the development of intelligence may involve a process of synaptic and neural growth and then pruning, particularly in the prefrontal cortex—a process that is reflected by changes in cortical thickness throughout childhood and adolescence.

At one time, the Guinness Book of World Records *listed Kim Ung-yong as the person in the world with the highest IQ. Kim Ung-yong scored 210 on the Stanford-Binet and reportedly began to study differential calculus at the age of 3.*

Moving up the ladder As children develop, they move toward greater intellectual independence—for example, from a child who is read stories by her mother to a young woman who produces and reads her own reports. Over the same period of time, the individual's brain is undergoing synaptic pruning and other key changes.

Beyond this general picture, Shaw and his colleagues found that the participants who were most intelligent showed a pattern of cortical thickening and thinning that was different from the pattern shown by participants with lower intelligence. That is, the highly intelligent individuals began with a rather thin cortex during early childhood, and the cortex gradually thickened until the age of 11 or 12, at which time thinning began and continued into the late teenage years. In contrast, the participants with lower intelligence began with a somewhat thicker cortex, which then further thickened until the age of 8, at which time the thinning began. Assuming that all of this reflects growth and pruning of synapses and perhaps of neurons as well, particularly in the prefrontal cortex, it may be that the processes of growth and pruning unfold over a much longer developmental span in highly intelligent people than they do in less intelligent individuals, perhaps because more complex and sophisticated neural circuits are being constructed (Vedantam, 2006).

Are such brain changes over the course of childhood and adolescence genetically predetermined? Once again, the answer is "Not necessarily." We observed in Chapters 3 and 4 that the formation and pruning of neural networks are closely tied to interactions with the environment. Moreover, earlier in this chapter, we observed that enriching the environments of deprived young children often increases their intellectual performances. It could be that people with particularly high intelligence tend to be raised in rich social and learning environments and that this kind of environmental stimulation contributes heavily to the pattern of cortical thickness change that such individuals displayed in the study by Shaw and his colleagues.

Before You Go On

What Do You Know?

14. How are brain size and number of neurons related to intelligence?
15. How do researchers measure the speed of information processing in the brain?
16. Is efficient processing linked to relatively lower or relatively higher activity in the brain?
17. What is the role of cortical thickness in the development of intelligence?

What Do You Think? Can you think of any other ways to explain why the brains of people who are performing better on intelligence tests are often less active than those of people who are doing poorly?

Extremes in Intelligence HOW we Differ

Making music A young man with Down's syndrome is the percussionist in a community orchestra (left), while a child prodigy sings opera to an appreciative audience at a school for the arts (right).

LEARNING OBJECTIVE 6 Discuss mental retardation and giftedness.

Earlier in the chapter, we mentioned that intelligence, as measured by IQ tests, follows a normal distribution—that is, a distribution shaped like a bell curve. At either end of this curve are a small number of people who score either much lower or much higher than the people who make up the large middle. At the lower end are people who are diagnosed with mental retardation, and at the higher end are those who are intellectually gifted (**Figure 10-9**).

Mental Retardation

Most individuals demonstrate sufficient levels of intelligence to survive on their own and to succeed quite well. But the intellectual and adaptive functioning of some persons is well below that of most other people. These individuals are said to display **mental retardation**, a combination of general intellectual functioning that is well below average, and poor adaptive behavior (APA, 2000). That is, in addition to having an IQ score of 70 or below, the individuals experience great difficulty in areas such as communication, home living, self-direction, work, and safety (APA, 2000).

We have already observed that IQ tests and scores may be biased in various ways. Certainly then, diagnoses of mental retardation based on such tests can be subject to error (Kanaya et al., 2003). Thus, to properly diagnose mental retardation, mental-health professionals must observe the functioning of an individual in his or her everyday environment, taking both the person's background and the community's standards into account.

The most consistent sign of mental retardation is very slow learning (Hodapp & Dykens, 2003; Kail, 1992). Other areas of difficulty include attention, short-term memory, planning, and language. These difficulties vary, of course, according to the level of mental retardation.

The American Psychiatric Association (2000) describes four levels of mental retardation: mild (IQ 50–70), moderate (IQ 35–49), severe (IQ 20–34), and profound (IQ below 20). The American Association of Mental Retardation prefers to identify degrees of mental retardation according to the level of support the person needs—intermittent, limited, extensive, or pervasive.

mental retardation term describing individuals who display general intellectual functioning that is well below average and, at the same time, poor adaptive behavior.

Mild Retardation Around 80 to 85 percent of all people with mental retardation fall into the category of mild retardation (Leonard & Wen, 2002; APA, 2000). They are sometimes called "educably retarded" because they can profit from education and can support themselves as adults. Mild mental retardation is not usually recognized until children enter school and take intelligence tests. These individuals have reasonable language, social, and play skills, but they need assistance when under stress—a limitation that becomes increasingly apparent as academic and social demands increase. Often the intellectual performance of individuals with mild mental retardation improves with age; some even stop meeting the criteria for the label after they leave school (Sturmey, 2008). Their jobs tend to be unskilled or semiskilled.

Research has linked mild mental retardation mainly to the home environment, particularly poor and unstimulating environments, inadequate parent-child interactions, and insufficient learning experiences during a child's early

FIGURE 10-9 Extreme scores in intelligence A small but equal number of people score at the extreme low and extreme high end of the IQ range. (*Source:* Anastasi & Urbina, 1997)

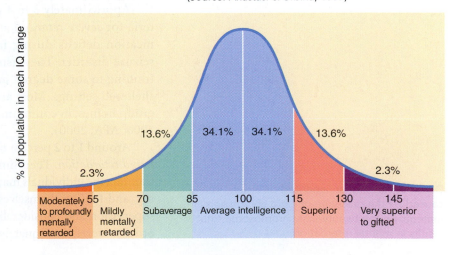

years (Sturmey, 2008; Stromme & Magnus, 2000). In addition, studies suggest that a mother's moderate drinking, drug use, or malnutrition during pregnancy may lower her child's intellectual potential (Ksir et al., 2008; Stein et al., 1972).

Severe retardation and special needs A seven-year-old lies by his teacher at a training center in China for children with disorders such as severe mental retardation, autism, and cerebral palsy.

Moderate, Severe, and Profound Retardation When Things Go Wrong

Although mild mental retardation is considered a variation in human functioning by many psychologists, the other levels of retardation—moderate, severe, and profound—are viewed by most as disorders. Moreover, whereas the primary factors in mild retardation seem to be related to the home environment, moderate, severe, and profound levels of retardation are caused largely by factors such as genetically based chromosomal and metabolic abnormalities, significant prenatal alcohol or drug use by mothers, prenatal maternal infections such as rubella and syphilis, complications during or after delivery, and injuries and severe infections during early childhood (Sturmey, 2008; Hodapp & Dykens, 2003).

In fact, severe and profound levels of mental retardation often appear as part of larger syndromes that include severe physical handicaps. The physical problems are often even more limiting than the individual's low intellectual functioning and in some cases can be fatal. Given such causes, moderate, severe, and profound levels of retardation are typically viewed as neurological disorders.

Around 10 percent of persons with mental retardation receive a label of *moderate retardation.* They receive their diagnosis early in life, typically demonstrating clear deficits in language development and play during their preschool years. By middle school, significant delays in the acquisition of reading and number skills and deficits in adaptive skills become apparent. By adulthood, however, many individuals with moderate mental retardation are able to communicate and care for themselves adequately, benefit from vocational training, and work in unskilled or semiskilled jobs. Most of these individuals also function well in the community if they have some degree of supervision (Bebko & Weiss, 2006; APA, 2000).

Many persons with moderate mental retardation have **Down syndrome**, the most common of the chromosomal disorders leading to mental retardation. Fewer than 1 of every 1,000 live births result in Down syndrome, but this rate increases greatly when the mother's age is over 35. The syndrome usually is caused by the presence of extra chromosomal material on the twenty-first chromosome. The additional material disturbs normal development, resulting in characteristic features such as a small head, flat face, slanted eyes, high cheekbones, and reduced intellectual functioning (Teicher et al., 2008). Most individuals with Down syndrome are very affectionate with family members. More generally they display the same range of personality characteristics as people in the general population.

Approximately 3 to 4 percent of people with mental retardation meet the criteria for *severe retardation.* They typically demonstrate basic motor and communication deficits during infancy. Many have an increased vulnerability to brain seizure disorder. They usually require careful supervision, profit from vocational training to some degree, and can perform only basic work tasks in structured and sheltered settings. Most are able to function well in the community if they live in group homes, in community nursing homes, or with their families (Bebko & Weiss, 2006; APA, 2000).

Around 1 to 2 percent of people with mental retardation receive a diagnosis of *profound retardation.* Their limitations are very noticeable at birth or early infancy. With training, the individuals may develop or improve basic skills such as walking, some talking, and feeding themselves. They require a very structured environment, with close supervision and considerable help, including a close relationship with a caregiver, in order to develop adequately (Sturmey, 2008; APA, 2000).

Down syndrome an inherited disorder, usually caused by the presence of extra chromosomal material on the twenty-first chromosome, that results in mental retardation.

Giftedness

Psychologists do not agree on how to define *giftedness*. Some use IQ tests as the sole criterion, defining the top 1 or 2 percent of the tested population as gifted. As you may remember from Chapter 3, for example, Lewis Terman defined gifted people as those with IQ scores above 140, and in a famous longitudinal study, he followed a group of gifted research participants over the course of their lifetime (Terman & Oden, 1959; Terman, 1925).

Other researchers and educators have added criteria such as school success or career achievement to IQ scores when defining giftedness. Indeed, many of the participants in Terman's study, who became known as the "Termites," achieved extraordinary success as scientists, scholars, businessmen, and professionals.

Other definitions of intelligence have led to still other definitions of giftedness. Howard Gardner, whom we discussed earlier in the chapter, suggests that people can be gifted with high intelligence in any one of the multiple intelligences he has identified. He would consider a highly talented athlete or musician to be as gifted as a math or verbal whiz.

Despite such varying definitions, researchers have tried to look for common characteristics among gifted people. Among their findings:

- *Environment can contribute to giftedness.* Many gifted people are raised in nurturing and stimulating environments. Terman's Termites, for example, were typically members of the upper socioeconomic families, and they received many years of education. It is worth noting that, contrary to stereotype, most gifted children are not pushed by demanding parents. Families do, however, tend to center much attention on such children. Typically, the parents first recognize the budding giftedness of their children and then support it by providing high-level intellectual or artistic stimulation. Parents of gifted children also tend to have higher expectations of themselves, model hard work for their children, and grant the children high degrees of independence.

- *Gifted people are often intrinsically motivated.* It appears that children who are gifted at piano playing, violin playing, chess, bridge, athletics, and the like typically experience a deep, intrinsic motivation to master such domains and subject themselves to many hours of deliberate practice. Perhaps the high motivation of these children drives them and sustains their practice efforts. However, research has failed to show that gifted abilities necessarily precede extensive practice. Does this mean that a person of average intelligence and above-average motivation can readily become a concert pianist or astrophysicist? No. Other research indicates that hard work, intensive training, perseverance, and practice alone rarely lead to giftedness. In short, motivation and hard work seem to be necessary but not sufficient requirements for the development of giftedness.

- *Some people gifted in academic or other forms of intelligence may not be equally gifted with social and emotional intelligence.* Some psychologists have observed that gifted children often display disproportionate social and emotional difficulties, especially during adolescence. Many are socially isolated and introverted. In fact, a number of academically gifted children try to hide their giftedness in an attempt to fit in with others. Girls seem more likely than boys to do this.

Educating the gifted A gifted nine-year-old girl sits in her college algebra class in Nashville, Tennessee. The algebra is apparently a snap for her, but getting in and out of the adult sized desk chair can be a problem.

Before You Go On

What Do You Know?

18. What are the four levels of mental retardation, and which is most common?
19. What are some causes of mental retardation?
20. Is high IQ the only criterion for giftedness?

What Do You Think? How might environment produce the effect of mental retardation? Do you think this effect could be reversed? If so, how? If not, why?

Summary

What Do We Mean by Intelligence?

LEARNING OBJECTIVE 1   Describe various ways in which intelligence has been defined, and summarize the current thinking on whether intelligence is general or specific.

- Scholars early in the twentieth century defined *intelligence* as the ability to learn and to meet the demands of the environment effectively. Later, other scholars added to this definition the ability to understand and control one's mental activities, called *metacognition*.

- A central issue in defining intelligence is whether it is a single, general factor or a cluster of different abilities. Charles Spearman hypothesized that a general factor, or *g factor*, underlies all mental abilities, while Lewis Thurstone argued that intelligence is made up of seven distinct *primary mental abilities*.

- Although most theorists today agree that intelligence does include a *g* factor, modern theorists such as Howard Gardner, Robert Sternberg, and Stephen Ceci have tended to deemphasize the *g* factor and focus on specific abilities, or *s factors*.

Additional Types of Intelligence

LEARNING OBJECTIVE 2   Discuss several proposed types of intelligence that go beyond intellectual functioning.

- Other theorists have broadened the definition of intelligence further to include emotional intelligence, social intelligence, wisdom, creativity, and personality.

How Do We Measure Intelligence?

LEARNING OBJECTIVE 3   Identify important considerations in the construction of intelligence tests, discuss the history of intelligence testing, and describe some criticisms of intelligence tests.

- The *psychometric approach* to studying intelligence attempts to measure intelligence with carefully constructed psychological tests.

- To ensure that intelligence tests are grounded in sound scientific principles, psychologists design tests that adhere to three basic criteria: *standardization*, *reliability*, and *validity*.

- Early pioneers of intelligence testing include Francis Galton, who proposed the theory of psychophysical performance, and Francis Binet, who developed a test to predict children's success in school.

- Adapting Binet's work for use in the United States, Lewis Terman constructed the Stanford-Binet Intelligence Test and devised the *intelligence quotient (IQ)*.

- David Wechsler broadened the usefulness of intelligence testing by developing the Wechsler Adult Intelligence Scale (WAIS), along with several other tests.

- Both the Stanford-Binet and the WAIS have high degrees of reliability. Performance on intelligence tests also correlates highly with school performance and to some degree with other areas of functioning in life, such as occupational achievements.

- Although widely used, intelligence tests are subject to several criticisms. One issue involves the culture-specific nature of the tests, which may produce bias. A related problem is *stereotype threat*.

- Intelligence test scores from around the world have increased over time, a phenomenon known as the *Flynn effect*. Possible explanations include potential problems with the procedures, content, or nature of the tests and improvements in education, nutrition, health, or environments.

Is Intelligence Governed by Genetic or Environmental Factors?

LEARNING OBJECTIVE 4   Review the contributions of heredity and environment to intelligence, and explain how emphasizing one factor or the other can affect social policy.

- The nature/nurture debate as applied to intelligence has important social implications, exemplified by the controversial book *The Bell Curve*, whose authors argued that group differences in IQ are likely due at least in part to genetic factors.

- Family studies and research in molecular biology have indicated that heredity does play a major role in intelligence. Researchers estimate that the *heritability* of intelligence is about 50 percent.

- Environmental factors that affect intelligence include family and home, overall culture, occupation, and schooling.

- Group differences in IQ scores enable us only to make distinctions between groups, not to reach any conclusions about an individual within a group.

- Studies have confirmed that environmental enrichment for members of disadvantaged groups is effective in producing at least short-term cognitive gains.

Intelligence *What Happens in The Brain*

LEARNING OBJECTIVE 5 Describe how brain size, processing speed, glucose metabolism, and cortical thickness relate to intelligence.

- Neuroimaging studies suggest that overall brain size is not correlated with intelligence. The number of neurons in certain brain regions, such as the frontal lobes, may be related to intellectual functioning.

- The speed with which the brain responds to stimuli, which can be measured by means of EEGs and *nerve conduction velocity (NCV)*, also correlates with intelligence.

- PET scans, which show what areas of the brain are active at a particular moment, have generally revealed lower activity in the brains of people performing well on an intellectual task and higher activity in the brains of people performing poorly, suggesting that the brains of the higher performers may be more efficient.

- It appears that the development of intelligence involves a process of neuron growth and then neuron pruning, particularly in the prefrontal cortex—a process that is reflected by a distinct pattern of change in cortical thickness throughout childhood and adolescence

Extremes In Intelligence

LEARNING OBJECTIVE 6 Discuss mental retardation and giftedness.

- The two extremes of intelligence, as measured by IQ tests, are represented by mental retardation and giftedness.
- Mental retardation is classified as mild (IQ 50–70), moderate (IQ 35–49), severe (IQ 20–34), and profound (IQ below 20).
- Home environmental causes of mental retardation include poor and unstimulating environments and inadequate parent-child interactions. These causes have been associated in particular with mild retardation, though they may also be at work in more severe cases.
- Other causes of retardation include genetically based chromosomal abnormalities, certain prenatal conditions in the mother, complications at delivery, and injuries and infections during early childhood. These causes have been associated in particular with moderate to profound levels of retardation.
- *Down Syndrome* is a genetic abnormality resulting in mental retardation.
- Psychologists do not agree on how to define giftedness but often identify gifted persons as having IQs at the top 1 or 2 percent of the tested population.
- Environment can contribute to giftedness, and gifted people are often highly motivated. However, academically gifted people may not be equally gifted with social and emotional intelligence.

Key Terms

intelligence 312

metacognition 312

factor analysis 312

g factor 312

s factor 312

primary mental abilities 312

theory of multiple
   intelligences 315

triarchic theory of intelligence 315

bioecological model of
   intelligence 316

emotional intelligence 316

creativity 319

psychometric approach 321

standardization 321

normal distribution 321

median 321

mean 321

mode 321

reliability 321

validity 323

content validity 323

validity coefficient 323

mental age 323

intelligence quotient (IQ) 324

stereotype threat 329

Flynn effect 329

heritability 333

heritability coefficient 333

nerve conduction velocity
   (NCV) 340

mental retardation 343

Down syndrome 344

CUT/ACROSS CONNECTION

What Happens in the
BRAIN?

- A larger number of neurons in particular brain areas, such as the frontal lobes, may be associated with higher intellectual functioning.
- How fast the brain responds to stimuli also correlates with intelligence. It may be that some people are wired to acquire information more quickly than others.
- PET scans have shown that the brains of people performing well on an intellectual task are less actve than those of people performing poorly—that is, the brains of the high-performing people may not need to work as hard.

When Things Go
Wrong

- Most psychologists view moderate, severe, and profound levels of mental retardation as mental disorders.
- Biological factors are primarily responsible for moderate, severe, and profound retardation. Severe and profound retardation often are part of larger syndromes that include severe physical handicaps.
- Although children with moderate retardation display significant delays in school, special-education programs can help them to succeed in many areas. By adulthood, they can generally function well at work and in the community with supervision.

HOW we Differ

- Intelligence, as measured by IQ tests, follows a distribution shaped like a bell curve. At one end of this curve are those diagnosed with mental retardation, and at the other are those considered intellectually gifted.
- Mental retardation involves a combination of lower general intellectual functioning and poorer adaptive behavior. The most consistent sign of mental retardation is very slow learning.
- Mild retardation, the most common kind, is linked primarily to home environmental causes, such as poor and unstimulating environments during early life.
- Often, intellectual giftedness is defined only in terms of IQ scores and doesn't take other forms of intelligence into account. Thus, an intellectually gifted person may be quite low in emotional or social intelligence.

How we Develop

- As noted in Chapter 3, children's brains actually lose neurons and synapses as the children grow into adolescence. This developmental process is reflected in a thinning of the cortex.
- The developmental pattern of cortical thickening and thinning is different in more intelligent children than in less intelligent children. In highly intelligent children, the process takes longer.
- These brain changes may be the result of environmental interactions, genetic factors, or both. Indeed, we know that enriching the environment of deprived children can improve their intellectual performance.

www.wileyplus.com

Video Lab Exercise

Psychology Around Us

General Intelligence versus Specific Intelligence

Who's More Intelligent?

After reading this chapter, you can appreciate that defining and measuring intelligence is one of psychology's most controversial, complex, and challenging tasks. Where do *you* stand on the issue of intelligence? On what basis do you conclude that someone is intelligent? And how do your notions of intelligence compare to those proposed by the various theorists and researchers in this chapter?

In this video lab exercise, you'll be looking at a bunch of people in action and deciding if they are intelligent, how they are intelligent, and why you believe they are intelligent. Over the course of your work, you'll come to appreciate even more the difficulties—some would say the misguidedness—at work in the field of intelligence and intelligence testing. In addition, along the way, this lab exercise will help you to appreciate the power, impact, and dangers of intelligence labels.

As you are working on this on-line exercise, consider the following questions:

- How do your assessments of intelligence compare to each of the leading theories on intelligence?
- Are cognitive, emotional, and creative intelligence related?
- Does intelligence increase over the course of a person's life? Can it increase once a person reaches adulthood?
- Is intelligence related to wisdom? conscientiousness? achievement? likeability? social perceptions and expectations?

CHAPTER 11

Motivation

chapter outline

- Theories of Motivation
- Biological Motivations: Hunger
- Biological Motivations: Sex
- Psychological Motivations: Affiliation and Achievement

Hot Dogging: A Different Kind of Competition

Takeru Kobayashi is world-renowned for eating hot dogs. The young Japanese man has repeatedly broken the world record, regularly scarfing down over 50 hot dogs in a single sitting, sometimes in as little as 12 minutes. Kobayashi reportedly suffers from arthritis of the jaw, related to incorrectly aligned wisdom teeth and years of competitive eating (he also holds the record for eating the most cow brains). He cannot open or close his mouth without pain. Nonetheless, he has been determined to continue his career in competitive hot dog eating.

In one recent year, Kobayashi's record was broken by an American competitor, Joey Chestnut. Kobayashi was determined to take back his crown. A month later the two met. Kobayashi, reportedly in great pain, managed to eat 63 hot dogs in that contest. Unfortunately for him, Chestnut's personal best was 66. Kobayashi was unable to regain his title (Gilger, 2007). Despite his pain, Kobayashi remains determined to compete again (Hackworth, 2007).

Stories such as this make us wonder what motivates an individual to engage in such odd behavior. Surely no one eats that many hot dogs in one sitting because they are hungry. In fact, eating so much at one time is more likely to cause revulsion and stomach pain than it is to produce a feeling of satisfaction. Psychologists define **motivation** as a condition that directs behavior usually toward a goal (Watts, 2003). For any

given circumstance, your behavior is probably the consequence of a combination of several **motives**—your needs or desires. If you consider the many behaviors you engage in throughout your day-to-day life, your motivations are sometimes related to the fulfillment of basic biological needs but more often are the result of complicated factors involving past experience and learning.

Motivation differs a lot from person to person. Your fellow students differ in their motivation to study. This

Hot dogging The driven former champion Takeru Kobayashi bites one of the many hot dogs that await him at the Nathan's Famous Fourth of July International Hot Dog Eating Contest.

motivation an internal state or condition that directs behavior.

motive a need or desire.

instincts inborn behavioral tendencies, activated by stimuli in our environments.

homeostasis a tendency of the body to maintain itself in a state of balance or equilibrium.

accounts for some of the variation in performance within classes. The reasons for these differences are very complex and often difficult to investigate scientifically. Variation in the degree to which people experience biological drives is also evident and has been the subject of much investigation. In particular, relatively large differences in food intake and sexual behavior are obvious among humans in the absence of any abnormality.

Kobayashi, and others like him, are more likely motivated by something other than the fulfillment of hunger pangs. Maybe they feel a need for the rewards of attention, social recognition, and fame, and have learned that competing in eating contests is one way to get those rewards. Or perhaps the competition itself is the reason they do it. Contestants may want to be pushed to do their best, even if it is in a field few people enter. Of course, money and prizes are at least part of the reason Kobayashi competes. Most likely, we would need a combination of reasons to explain his behavior.

We'll see in this chapter that psychologists have developed a number of theories that explain how our motivation drives and guides our behavior. Researchers have discovered a great deal about how the body and brain signals work to motivate us to fulfill some of our basic biological motives. We'll take a look at how even common biological motives, such as hunger, can interact with our experiences and thoughts to lead to specific behaviors. We'll discuss how these processes develop and what happens when things go wrong—when we become motivated to do things that aren't in our best interests.

Theories of Motivation

LEARNING OBJECTIVE 1 Compare and contrast major theories of motivation.

Like all of us, psychologists are interested in explaining people's behavior. There are several theories of motivation, each of which takes a different approach to explain what compels individuals to act as they do (**Table 11-1**). As we'll see, however, no single theory has yet been able to provide a complete explanation of what motivates us to engage in our many different behaviors.

Instinct Theory

Instinct theory maintains that behaviors originate from a set of behavioral blueprints, or **instincts** (Fancher, 1996). Instinctive behaviors are inborn and activated by particular environmental stimuli. A good example of instinctual motivation can be observed in the maternal behavior in female rats. Virgin female rats typically ignore or avoid unfamiliar rat pups. In some instances, virgin females will even commit infanticide. However, the same rat that reacted with indifference or violence when exposed to pups prior to giving birth will engage in a rich repertoire of maternal behavior once her own babies are born. She will build a nest, and lick, groom, retrieve, huddle over, and nurse her pups. These behaviors are not learned by the animal nor are there any external incentives for engaging in them. They occur automatically as a result of changes in hormone levels that coincide with delivering a litter of rat pups (Kinsley et al., 2008).

Many of our own basic motives are inborn. Some of the most critical for survival, such as eating, are present at birth (Colson, Meek, & Hawdon, 2008). Although the range of foods considered to be rewarding changes substantially from the time we're babies until our adult lives (infants will readily eat baby food and formula, both of which adults typically consider bland and unappealing), the basic motivation to eat when hungry persists throughout life.

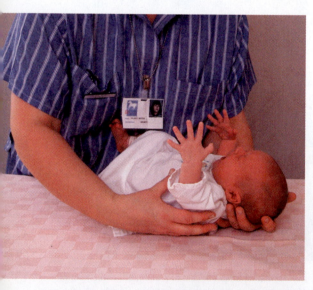

The moro reflex A nurse checks the moro reflex of a 1-day-old girl. In this reflex, babies react to loud noises or to a sense of being dropped by throwing their arms outward and bringing them together as if trying to grasp something.

TABLE 11-1 Major Theories of Motivation

Theory	Approach
Instinct	Behavior is motivated by instincts that are inborn and which are activated by environmental stimuli
Drive reduction	Motivation originates from biological needs to maintain the body in a state of balance or equilibrium
Arousal	Behavior is motivated by the need to achieve optimum levels of arousal
Incentive	Behavior is motivated by internal (intrinsic) or external (extrinsic) incentives or rewards
Hierarchy of needs	When different motives compete, basic survival needs must be satisfied first before we are motivated to satisfy higher level needs such as belonging and self-esteem

Another inborn human motivation is to form social contacts. As we saw in Chapter 5, babies are born with a well-developed sense of smell that lets them recognize the particular scent of their mothers (Porter & Winberg, 1999). We are also born with reflexes that allow us to engage in primitive social behavior. The rooting reflex, discussed in Chapter 3, for example, involves turning the head and using the mouth to search for a nipple. Rooting not only helps a baby to eat, but it allows the infant to seek contact with other people. Combined with the ability to recognize their mothers by smell, rooting enables babies to start establishing close relationships with their mothers (Swain et al., 2007). As the baby grows, new abilities emerge, such as smiling, laughing, reaching arms out to be carried, and talking. All of these further encourage the formation of social bonds, thus increasing the chance of survival (Messinger & Fogel, 2007; Broad, Curley, & Keverne, 2006). As with eating, the nuances of this basic motivation change as we grow. For example, instead of seeking mother love, we seek romantic love. The motivation to be socially connected remains strong throughout life, however.

Although instinct theory can explain some of our behavior and a substantial proportion of animal behavior, instincts don't account for all behavior, even in relatively simple creatures, such as rats (Clark, Broadbent, & Squire, 2008). In fact, studies on learning and memory would be impossible to carry out on laboratory animals if all of their behavior was innate. The animals would never need to learn or remember anything.

Instinct theory also has trouble explaining differences among individuals (Bevins, 2001). Among humans, for example, some of us seek out experiences that others avoid or even find painful. Consider adventurers who have climbed Mount Everest, a grueling and dangerous activity. Conversely, some individuals avoid experiences that others find rewarding and pleasurable. Catholic priests and nuns, for example, forego marriage and biological parenthood to fulfill their obligations to their church. Clearly, these behaviors are not driven by instincts. We need other explanations for these motivations.

Challenging a theory This bungee jumper takes off from a bridge and begins a wild—and seemingly dangerous—free fall, challenging the instinct theory along the way.

Drive-Reduction Theory

Drive-reduction theory is another attempt to account for motivation on the basis of internal biological factors. This theory is based on the concept of **homeostasis**, a tendency of the body to maintain itself in a state of balance or equilibrium (**Figure 11-1**). When

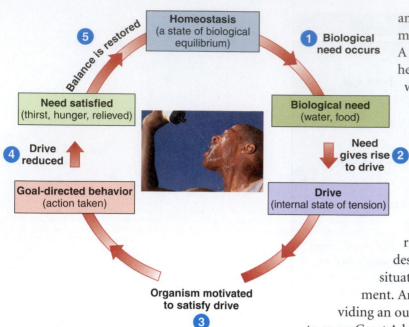

FIGURE 11-1 **Drive-reduction theory** When external factors alter our body's normal state of equilibrium, we are motivated to behave in ways that restore the balance.

Within the diagram:
- ⑤ Balance is restored
- **Homeostasis** (a state of biological equilibrium)
- ① **Biological need occurs**
- **Need satisfied** (thirst, hunger, relieved)
- **Biological need** (water, food)
- ④ **Drive reduced**
- ② Need gives rise to drive
- **Goal-directed behavior** (action taken)
- **Drive** (internal state of tension)
- **Organism motivated to satisfy drive** ③

an external factor alters the state of balance in the organism, a motivation arises to correct that balance (Stricker & Zigmond, 1986). A simple example of this can be seen in the response of the body to heat. When the temperature rises, your body perspires and you lose water. The perspiration evaporates and cools the surface of the skin, helping to maintain the temperature balance in the body. In addition, you may feel motivated to take actions that will hasten your return to an ideal body temperature, such as shedding some layers of clothing or getting a cool drink.

Drive-reduction theory works well to explain behaviors related to biological needs, such as cooling off when we're too hot. We engage in many behaviors, however, that do not appear to be motivated by a need to keep the body in a state of equilibrium (Schneider et al., 2007). In fact, some human behavior is designed to do just the opposite. Some people seek out adventurous situations that are designed to thrill and even terrorize for entertainment. Amusement park owners make millions of dollars every year providing an outlet for this sort of interest. It's difficult to explain the motivation to go on Great Adventure's Nitro roller coaster in terms of a need to restore the body to a state of equilibrium. Instead, the main purpose is to experience excitement by throwing riders suddenly *out* of a state of emotional equilibrium. That type of thrill-seeking behavior may be better described in terms of another theory.

Arousal Theory

Arousal theory maintains that motivation comes from a need to achieve an appropriate level of arousal (Jones, 2003). This theory is different from drive-reduction theory in that the motivation doesn't always arise from a need to reduce arousal back to a neutral state. While some situations, such as hunger or thirst, can elevate our arousal to uncomfortable levels that we try to reduce (by, for example, seeking food or drink), arousal theory states that we can also be motivated to elevate our arousal levels if they fall too low. Such under-arousal may stimulate us to seek out interesting and exciting situations (Maggini, 2000).

Arousal theory explains a number of behaviors that instinct and drive-reduction theories cannot. Consider the millions of dollars earned every year by paparazzi and the tabloids. Even though a rich knowledge in the latest celebrity gossip is unlikely to enhance

Challenging another theory These children scream with delight on an amusement park ride in the Coney Island section of Brooklyn, New York, demonstrating the limits of drive-reduction theory along the way.

your reputation, and could even cause embarrassment if your interest is discovered by people in the wrong circle, many of us seek out gossip information because we are generally curious. Curiosity often motivates us to seek out information, even if there is no other goal involved. Arousal theory would describe the behavior of people who follow celebrity gossip as an attempt to elevate our levels of arousal and interest.

You may have noticed arousal-increasing behaviors in your dog. Beau might explore new surroundings, watch a television show, or sniff another dog, for no apparent reason except to satisfy his curiosity. Scientists have long recognized that rodents also engage in behavior that does not appear to be goal-directed. As you read in Chapter 7, for example, if rats are exposed to a maze, they will navigate the apparatus and even learn its spatial characteristics without receiving rewards or punishments (Hughes, 2007). They appear to explore just because they find it interesting.

In addition to providing motivation, our arousal levels can systematically affect our performance on tasks we undertake. The **Yerkes-Dodson law** states that ideal performance

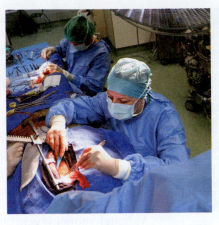

The Yerkes-Dodson law in action The worker on the left uses a knife to cut bread at a restaurant in Italy, while the surgeon on the right uses her sharp instrument to perform open-heart surgery. According to the Yerkes-Dodson law, a high level of physical arousal will help the restaurant worker's performance but probably not the surgeon's.

on a task occurs when our arousal level is right for the difficulty of the task. Task difficulty and arousal seem to be inversely related (**Figure 11-2**). That is, our performance on difficult tasks is optimal at relatively low arousal states, while our performance on easy tasks is optimal at high arousal states. This may be related to the fact that difficult tasks require more intense concentration that may be disrupted by highly arousing circumstances. Imagine, for example, that you are trying to finish writing a term paper. You may find it easier to focus on your writing if you are not highly aroused by a deadline looming only a few hours away. If, however, you are trying to read some really boring material (something other than this book, of course), you may need to periodically raise your arousal levels with snacks, stretch breaks, and the like, to help you focus on the task.

Incentive Theory

Some behaviors are **intrinsically motivating**, which means that engaging in the behavior is satisfying in and of itself (Schmitt & Lahroodi, 2008). For the rats described earlier, exploring mazes seems to be intrinsically motivating. For some people, eating hot dogs is intrinsically motivating. Although they may never enter a hot-dog-eating contest, they occasionally eat hot dogs simply for the pleasure they get out of doing so.

Other behaviors are driven by external motives, or **incentives**. Behavior that is motivated by external incentives is known as **extrinsically motivated**. Rats can be extrinsically motivated: They learn their way through a maze more quickly if provided with an incentive, such as food or a way to escape something unpleasant (such as water), than they do when no incentives are involved (Komaki, 2004).

Even when our motivation to behave in a certain way involves instinct, a drive to maintain homeostasis, or a motive to achieve an optimal level of arousal, it's clear that incentives play a major role in most human behavior. *Incentive theory* highlights the influence of external stimuli in behavior. Incentive theory would suggest that external rewards, such as public acclaim or financial prizes, contribute to the motivation of record-breaking hot dog eaters. A good deal of your own behavior as a student is probably also motivated by external factors, such as the desire to achieve high grades, graduate on time, and obtain a good job.

Incentives can be either primary or secondary and they can be rewarding or punitive.

- *Primary incentives* are rewards or punishments that are innate; we do not have to learn to either like or dislike them. Food is a primary reward, and pain is a primary punishment, for example. Most humans instinctually find food rewarding

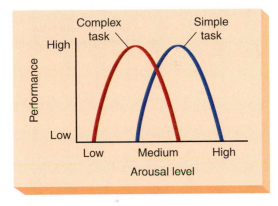

FIGURE 11-2 The Yerkes-Dodson law Our optimal performance on tasks is inversely related to our arousal level. We perform difficult tasks best when our arousal level is low and simple or boring ones best when our arousal level is high.

Yerkes-Dodson law ideal performance on a task occurs when the arousal level is optimized to the difficulty level.

intrinsic motivation engaging in a behavior simply for the satisfaction that is part of doing it.

incentives external motives that indirectly indicate reward.

extrinsic motivation engaging in a behavior due to the influence of factors outside ourselves.

The big payoff Although Joseph Hachem kisses a stack of money after winning $7.5 million at the World Series of Poker in Las Vegas, the money itself is not rewarding. Rather, it is what the money can buy, the prestige attached to winning so much, and the pride the big payoff instills in him.

and electric shock punishing. For that reason, these stimuli are likely to influence our behavior. There is an adaptive, or evolutionary, component to primary rewards and punishments. Typically, stimuli that increase our chances of survival and reproduction, such as food and sex, are rewarding, while those that are potentially harmful, such as anything painful, are punishing.

- *Secondary incentives* are cues that are viewed as rewarding or punishing as a result of learning about their association with other events. For example, most people are motivated to work to earn money. Money, in and of itself, is not rewarding. It becomes motivating to us when we learn its association with the rewarding goods, such as food, that money can buy.

Although money is generally considered to be a strong motivator, its effects differ greatly from person to person. Why is this? Scientists attribute the different motivational power of certain cues to *incentive salience,* how noticeable or important a particular incentive is to us (Berridge, 2007). Incentives can become more salient and more motivating after they become associated with specific emotions (Robinson & Berridge, 2001). Consider a person's motivation to work hard at a job. The first time we receive a paycheck, the things we purchase with the money may lead to happiness. This association of money with happiness may, in turn, motivate us to engage in behaviors designed to improve the chance of earning even more money, such as working harder. Alternatively, if your first work experience is a very negative one that becomes associated with boredom and unhappiness, your drive to pursue happiness through hard work is less likely to flourish. You may seek to avoid work altogether, or you may be motivated to look for a better and more gratifying job. Particularly for complex behaviors, such as working at a job, there can be many incentives that motivate different individuals. Some people work to avoid punishment, such as homelessness and shame, for example, while others work to receive rewards, such as money and pride.

Motivational theories that focus on incentives often take into consideration the distinction between "liking" and "wanting" (Berridge & Kringelbach, 2008). "Liking" refers to our experience of reward or pleasure that happens *at the moment* we are engaging in a particular behavior, while "wanting" refers to the anticipation of an experience that we expect will cause us pleasure. Having a pleasurable experience in the past often leads to wanting to repeat that experience again in the future. If you really like your first hot dog from a certain vendor, you might want more like it. You might even become motivated to walk an extra several blocks at lunchtime, just to visit that particular hot-dog vendor.

Neuroscientists have found that overlapping, but distinct, regions of our brains are involved in liking and wanting (Litman, 2005). Pleasure, or liking, is typically associated with systems of the brain that produce *opiates*. As we describe in Chapter 4, opiates, such as endorphins, are naturally-occurring neurochemicals that contribute to our feelings of pleasure. Eating, drinking, and sex—biological motivations that we discuss later in this chapter—are all associated with a release in opiates. Other experiences, such as intense physical exercise (for example, long distance running) can also stimulate the release of brain opiates, producing a phenomenon called "runner's high" (Boecker et al., 2008).

In addition to activating the brain-opiate system, rewarding stimuli typically stimulate the release of the neurotransmitter dopamine (Arias-Carrión & Pöppel, 2007; Berridge & Kringelbach, 2008; Arias-Carrión & Pöppel, 2007). As discussed in Chapter 4, dopamine is present in two major systems of the brain. One region is mostly important for movement and the other is important for reinforcement learning. The latter system consists of dopamine neurons in a region of the midbrain, called the ventral tegmental area, that send their axons to two key areas in the front of the brain: the *nucleus accumbens* and the *prefrontal cortex* (**Figure 11-3**). As we noted in Chapter 4, the nucleus accumbens is highly active in the experience of rewarding and pleasurable feelings (Carlezon & Thomas, 2009). The pathways of dopamine neurons from the ventral tegmental area to the nucleus accumbens and prefrontal cortex are not only activated during the reward experience, but they appear to be critical for future behavior directed toward that reward. In other words, the dopamine system plays a critical role in "wanting."

Although incentive theory explains how our behavior is shaped by external stimuli, not all of our behavior is motivated by wanting a reward or avoiding a punishment. Integrating incentive theory with other motivation theories is necessary to explain the complexity of motivation. For example, drive-reduction theory explains that eating to reduce the feeling of hunger maintains homeostasis and incentive theory explains the rewarding feelings associated with what you eat and the incentive to eat that food again in the future.

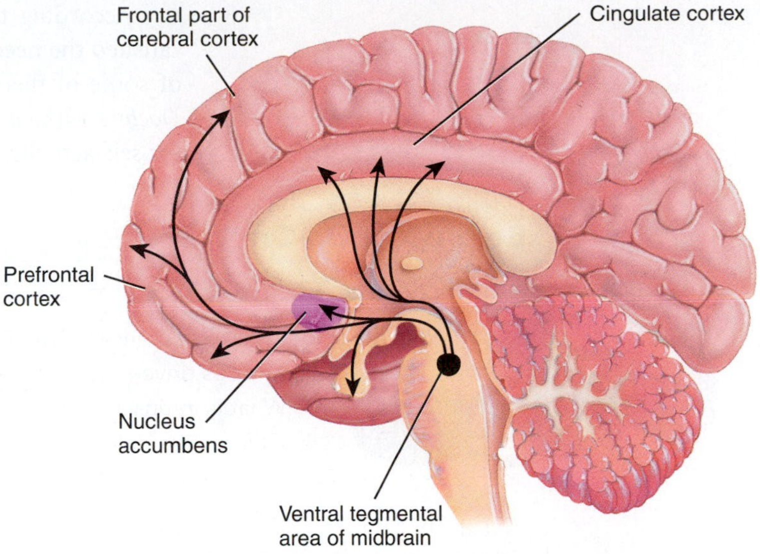

FIGURE 11-3 Reward pathways in the brain
Rewarding stimuli typically trigger dopamine neurons in the ventral tegmental area of the brain. The axons of these neurons project to the nucleus accumbens and the prefrontal cortex, activating rewarding and pleasurable feelings.

Multiple Motivations: Hierarchy of Needs

As we've seen, a combination of factors including innate and learned motives interact to drive behavior. Psychologists have also recognized that different motives can compete with one another (LaGraize et al., 2004). For instance, you might find it particularly difficult to concentrate on completing a homework assignment if you need to use the bathroom. The relative strength of certain motives and their ability to supersede one another led humanist psychologist Abraham Maslow to describe motives, or needs, in terms of a *hierarchy,* as we noted in the introductory chapter of this book (Maslow, 1978). Here, **Figure 11-4**, which you also observed in Chapter 1, shows Maslow's hierarchy of needs.

The most basic needs, such as the need to eat or drink, are at the bottom of the hierarchy pyramid. Unless these needs are satisfied, we find it difficult to generate motivation to engage in other behaviors. Above the basic needs are the safety needs: the need to feel secure and stable. It's important to realize that a balance exists between the first and second tier on the pyramid. It would not make sense for us to run out into traffic to stop the ice cream truck, acting primarily on our need to eat and bypassing the need for safety. That doesn't happen often, because food is usually not a matter of life or death in our culture. But humans, as well as other animals, will often take great risks to obtain food and water if they can't be obtained in a safer setting.

Above the safety needs is the need to feel love and to belong to a social group. This need motivates us to seek companionship in the form of friends and romantic partners. It motivates the creation of families and the formation of clubs and other social organizations. The social need varies considerably from species to species. The tree shrew, for example, lives a solitary life and only interacts with other tree shrews for purposes of mating. The mother tree shrew doesn't even sleep with her own babies! Humans vary from person to person, but as a species, we are highly social and our needs for human contact are often very strong motivators of our behavior.

Above the need to belong socially rests the need for a feeling of self-worth. This need motivates us to achieve at school, work, and in the home. Finally, at the top of the pyramid, rests the need for self-actualization. As our highest need, the need for self-actualization motivates us to live up to our potential and become the best we can be. For many people, this involves engaging in selfless, altruistic behavior, in the form of political activism or humanitarian behavior.

FIGURE 11-4 Maslow's hierarchy of needs A combination of needs, both innate and learned, drive our behavior and sometimes are in competition. Maslow identified the relative strengths of these needs and arranged them in a hierarchy. Basic survival needs at the base of the pyramid are the strongest and must be satisfied first before we are motivated to achieve our higher needs.

According to Maslow's theory, it is difficult to meet this need without having satisfied the needs below it on the pyramid. Even so, many people sacrifice fulfillment of some of their basic needs to meet higher needs. Physicians who are members of *Doctors without Borders*, for example, sacrifice their safety needs to fulfill their needs for self-actualization.

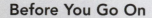

Before You Go On

What Do You Know?

1. What are some examples of instinctive motivations among humans?
2. How does drive-reduction theory differ from arousal theory?
3. What is intrinsic motivation and how does it differ from extrinsic motivation?
4. Give an example of a primary incentive and a secondary incentive.
5. What are the lowest level needs in the hierarchy of needs?

What Do You Think? Consider one of your favorite leisure-time activities, such as reading novels, playing videogames, or playing a sport. Whatever the activity, describe how each of the motivational theories discussed in this chapter would explain why you do it. Does any one theory describe your motivation best?

Biological Motivations: Hunger

LEARNING OBJECTIVE 2 Summarize physical and psychological factors that affect our levels of hunger and our eating behavior.

As we've noted, the drive to eat is biologically ingrained or instinctual. Even newborn babies show interest in feeding soon after they are born. The biological drive to eat remains in place throughout our lives since we need to eat to live. A person can generally last only about 40 days without food (Lieberson, 2004). Eating is not simply a matter of following an instinctive pattern of behavior to satisfy an inborn drive, however. As we'll see, a number of other factors play a role in motivating how much, what, when, and even where we are motivated to eat. First, let's explore what we know about the biology of eating.

Hunger: *What Happens in the* B R A I N ?

Hunger signals in our brains originate from several stimuli, including how full our stomachs are, the levels of nutrients circulating in our bloodstreams, and interacting with both of those signals, the activities of key parts of our brains.

Stomach Signals As you may have experienced, an empty stomach can trigger feelings of hunger. Physicians treating obese patients take advantage of the fact that physical signals produced by stretch receptors in the stomach are important for informing the brain to stop eating. These cues, called *satiety* signals, can be activated by surgically placing a balloon in the stomach. Since the stomach space is already partially occupied by the balloon, the stretch receptors will be activated even when the person eats a relatively small meal (Fernandes et al., 2007; Rigaud et al., 1995). Another technique that works on a similar principle is the surgical placement of a band around the stomach or physically stapling the stomach so that it is much smaller (Bowne et al., 2006). Many individuals who have undergone these procedures first lose weight, but then eventually gain it back, suggesting that, although signals from the stomach can

leptin a protein produced by fat cells that is important for regulating the amount of food eaten over long periods of time.

lateral hypothalamus a region of the hypothalamus important in signaling thirst and hunger.

ventromedial region of the hypothalamus a region of the hypothalamus important in signaling satiety.

influence the degree to which we are motivated to eat, these signals aren't the only mediators (Christou, Look, & Maclean, 2006).

Indeed, it turns out that satiety signals from the stomach are not even the most important hunger clues. People with no stomach at all, as a result of surgery for cancer, still experience hunger (Kamiji et al., 2009). Also, as you may have experienced, eating a small amount of food often stimulates additional hunger.

Chemical Signals   Eating occurs as a result of a complex interplay between hunger and satiety. Considerable evidence suggests that cues related to the metabolism of food can signal hunger or satiety (Erlanson-Albertsson, 2005; Wynne, Stanley, & Bloom, 2004). Some of these cues are related to levels of different chemicals produced in our blood when our bodies digest food. Two of the most well-researched of these are *glucose*, also known as blood sugar, and *lipids*, the products produced when our bodies break down fats from food. There are receptors for both glucose and lipids in the brain, which can influence hunger (Levin et al., 2004; Meister, 2000). Injections of glucose into the bloodstream, for instance, can reduce eating in experimental animals (Novin, Sanderson & Vanderweele 1974).

The protein **leptin** is another signal that appears to be important for regulating the amount of food eaten over long periods of time. Leptin is released from our fat cells as they grow larger. When receptors in the brain sense high levels of leptin, they in turn send signals that inhibit us from eating (Dhillon et al., 2006; Hommel et al., 2006). Obese animals and humans may be insensitive to leptin. Some evidence suggests that although they have higher blood levels of leptin than normal-weight individuals, they have fewer-leptin receptors in their brains, which may prevent the signal to stop eating from being generated soon enough (Bjornhelm et al., 2007; Farooqi et al., 2007).

Brain Signals   Within the brain, the hypothalamus is a key mediator of eating. As you can see in the brain illustration to the right, specific subregions in the hypothalamus have been linked to both hunger and satiety. The **lateral hypothalamus (LH)** is important for hunger. Rodents with damage to this area dramatically undereat; they need to be force-fed or they will starve to death (Petrovich et al., 2002). A nearby brain region, the **ventromedial region of the hypothalamus (VMH)**, has been shown to play an important role in satiety. Destruction of this region leads to overeating and obesity in rats (see **Figure 11-5**). Humans who develop brain tumors in the VMH also increase

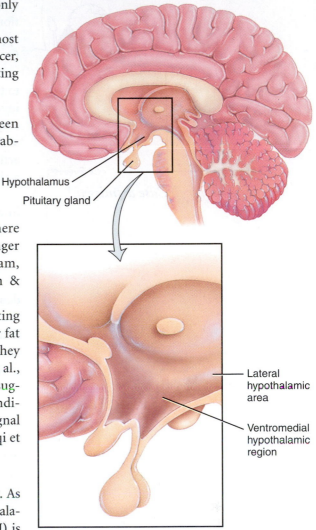

Hypothalamus
Pituitary gland

Lateral hypothalamic area

Ventromedial hypothalamic region

FIGURE 11-5 The VMH and obesity
The rat on the left had its ventromedial hypothalamus destroyed, which led to overeating and a dramatic increase in its body weight.

"You were hungry? Case dismissed."

their food intake and become markedly heavier (Yadav et al., 2009). A genetic condition in humans, known as Prader-Willi syndrome, is associated with an insatiable appetite leading to obesity. This condition is believed to arise, at least in part, from dysfunction of the hypothalamus (Hinton et al., 2006; Holland et al., 1993).

The identification of these two brain regions as important for feeding behavior led to the formation of the *dual-center theory of motivation*. This idea proposes that activity in one area serves to inhibit the area that serves the opposite function. For example, an empty stomach and low blood-glucose may stimulate the LH to motivate us to eat, while at the same time, inhibiting satiety signals from the VMH. Once the stretch receptors are activated and blood-glucose reaches a certain level, the VMH would once again become active and it would inhibit the LH.

Subsequent research, however, has shown that these brain regions influence eating in a more complicated way through the action of a hormone called *insulin* (Plum, Belgardt, & Brüning, 2006; Woods et al., 2006). The VMH appears to be important for modulating the levels of insulin in the blood. Insulin helps the body to metabolize and use glucose. Damage to the VMH can increase insulin levels. High insulin levels, in turn, cause our fat cells to store more glucose and grow. Studies of animals with lesions or damage in the VMH, show that they experience increases in fat deposits, regardless of the amount of food they eat (Yadav et al., 2009). So, it is not just a matter of the VMH failing to provide these animals with a satiety signal. They are actually short on blood sugar, or glucose. Because they store energy from glucose as fat more rapidly than undamaged animals, the signals of satiety, such as an increase in blood-glucose level, don't occur. As a result, the animals continue eating.

As we've stressed throughout this book, however, it's important to remember that no single area of the brain acts alone, especially in a complex behavior, such as eating. Along with the hypothalamus, several additional brain regions participate in eating. Our ability to taste food certainly plays a role in eating, for example. As described in Chapter 5, taste information is processed in the regions of the prefrontal cortex. Disgust cues related to the presentation of unpalatable food involve the insular cortex, a region situated close to the prefrontal cortex (Roman, Lin, & Reilly, 2009; Roman & Reilly, 2007).

Not only are many areas of the brain involved in eating, but the brain circuitry involved in our eating behavior is also active in a variety of motivational situations. Pathways important for general reward, punishment, and disgust under other circumstances interact with brain regions that specifically process visual, olfactory, and gustatory information to modulate eating (Rolls, 2007; De Araujo et al., 2003). For example, the same part of our brain that is active when we are enjoying the lovely scent of a flower might also be involved when we are enticed by the aroma wafting from our favorite hot dog stand.

Hunger: HOW we Differ

In addition to our basic biological need to eat, several psychological factors affect how hungry we feel and how much we eat. As we saw in the case of competitive hot-dog eaters, for example, people are often motivated to eat—sometimes to eat a great deal—even when they are not particularly hungry. Individual desires other than hunger obviously motivate competitive eaters and often affect the rest of us, too. Cultural and social influences also affect our eating behavior.

Culture plays a role not only in the types of foods that people enjoy and what times of the day we prefer to eat, but also in how much we

eat. For example, in Korea, where a meal often consists of many communal side dishes, it is considered proper etiquette to try a little food from each. People in India often skip breakfast, but in Ireland, breakfast is a large meal, often including porridge, eggs, and bacon. Food is also strongly associated with social interactions. Studies have shown that people eat considerably more when they are in a social setting, particularly when it is a relatively large gathering, compared to when eating alone (Lumeng & Hillman, 2007). People with schedules that involve business meetings and social engagements over meals are likely to eat more than those whose schedules do not include meetings at mealtimes, for example. This may be due to the fact that meals take longer with more participants, as well as the fact that people may pay less attention to restricting their diets when they are engaged in conversation (Pliner et al., 2006).

Some researchers have also suggested that we each have an individual **body weight set point**. Researchers have long recognized that as adults, our weights tend to stabilize near a certain general level. We may fluctuate in a small range around that weight, but we typically return to the original set point, even after major deviations from it (Pasquet & Apfelbaum, 1994). This is particularly evident when people diet. A reduction in body weight is often followed by a rebound back toward the original weight. The *Practically Speaking* feature discusses why so many dieters fail to achieve lasting weight loss. This isn't always the case, however. Some people do undergo dramatic weight changes in one direction or another and maintain their new weights for a considerable period of time. People who maintain a lower body weight typically make permanent changes in their eating habits and persistently monitor their weight (Dansinger et al., 2005; Warziski et al., 2008; Dansinger et al., 2005).

Other research suggests, however, that body weight set point is not the only factor at play in determining how much we eat. The availability of food we like also plays a role. Many individuals in societies such as much of the United States, where food is plentiful, find their weights steadily creeping up over the years (Philipson, 2001). This can be seen with laboratory rodents, too. Presenting them with a wide array of highly palatable foods will cause more eating and weight gain (**Figure 11-6**) (Hagan et al., 2002). This suggests that a firm body weight set point doesn't exist in experimental animals or humans. When presented with highly palatable food and a diminishing level of activity, most people have a tendency to put on weight as they age.

body weight set point a weight that individuals typically return to even after dieting or overeating.

"A man seldom thinks with more earnestness of anything than he does of his dinner.**"**

—*Samuel Johnson, writer*

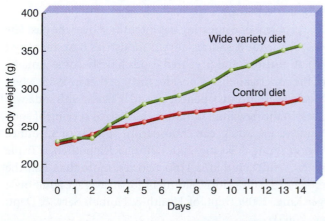

FIGURE 11-6 **Food variety and obesity** Research suggests that body weight set point is not the only factor determining the amount of food eaten by humans or animals. When rats are given a wide variety of highly palatable foods, they will eat more and become obese (Sclafani & Springer, 1976).

Hunger: When Things Go Wrong

We have seen that our motivation to eat is very complex, affected not only by intricate biological processes but also influenced by psychological, social, and cultural influences. As with any complex system, we face the potential for problems in our eating behavior. Two of the most common problems include obesity, often related to too much eating, and eating disorders, which often involve eating too little.

Obesity **Obesity**, a condition of extreme overweight, is determined on the basis of a weight-to-height ratio, called the **body mass index (BMI)**. Adults with a BMI of 30 or higher are considered obese, and those with BMIs between 25 and 30 are categorized as *overweight* (NIH, 1998, 2009). Obesity is a major health problem in the United States. Nearly two thirds of the American population now falls into the categories of overweight or obese. Being overweight or obese is associated with a variety of health problems, most notably diabetes and heart disease (Poirier et al., 2006; Huang, 2005). In addition to the physical risks they face, obese people are also more likely than those of normal weight to suffer from mood disorders, such as depression and anxiety. As the box describes, obese people are also often the victims of discrimination.

Some people become obese as a result of medical conditions. Researchers estimate, however, that medical conditions cause only about 1 to 5 percent of all cases of obesity and seem to be the result of a biological abnormality unrelated to overeating (Harvey et al., 2005). In the vast majority of people, obesity is caused by overeating.

Why is it so common to overeat? One answer to this question may be found by considering the evolutionary perspective. Early people evolved under conditions of unpredictable food availability. At times when food was plentiful, after a successful hunt or during a time when weather conditions led to an abundance of edible plants, it was surely advantageous to overeat in preparation for subsequent food deprivation. Overeating would lead to fat storage that increased the chances of survival throughout periods when food was scarce. In many of today's developed cultures, especially the United States, where inexpensive high-calorie food is readily available, this built-in adaptive mechanism is being activated in a chronic and maladaptive way. Intermittent overeating followed by periods of fasting has been replaced by chronic, continuous overeating.

The problem of overeating has intensified over the past few decades, as the food and restaurant industries have increased the size of portions and prepared foods have become a mainstay of the American diet. Consider the fact that in 1955, when McDonald's restaurants opened, a regular size adult's soda was 7 ounces. In the new millennium, a child-sized serving of soda is 12 ounces, and adults can choose from 16-, 21- or 32-ounce beverages (Young & Nestle, 2002). Burger King offers a Triple Whopper® sandwich that is 1160 calories, more than half the recommended daily calorie allotment for an average adult male (Burger King, 2009; Dept. of Health & Human Serv. & Dept. of Agr., 2005).

Bigger portions, bigger waists The size and calorie count of meals and drinks at fast food restaurants have increased dramatically over the past several decades.

Consumer behavior research strongly suggests that Americans appreciate large-size portions because they appear to be a good value (Ledikwe, Ello-martin, & Rolls 2005). It's very difficult to regulate the amount of food you ingest when the portions are so much larger than those recommended for maintaining a healthy weight. The massive oversizing of portions common today has, for many of us, led to an increase in energy intake, as measured in calories, without a corresponding change in energy expenditure. As a result, people gain weight.

Once people become accustomed to ingesting very large amounts of food, scaling back to sensible-sized portions can feel like deprivation. Many nutritionists often suggest that dieters eat their food from smaller plates to avoid feeling that the reduced portions are meager. This trick alone is typically not sufficient to support a substantial weight loss, however.

In fact, billions of dollars are spent every year on dieting programs and products that are designed to help overweight individuals lose weight and keep it off (Cleland et al., 1997). However, diet programs are often unsuccessful for long-term weight change. For this reason, many experts suggest that the best way to combat obesity is to prevent its occurrence (Bendelius, 2004; Mogan, 1984). Some approaches to obesity prevention may be suggested by identifying the risk factors for developing obesity. Although the majority of Americans are now overweight, only about one third are obese (CDC, 2009). Why are some people more prone to obesity than others? The answer seems to involve multiple factors.

One substantial contributor to obesity is genes. Adoption and twin studies have shown that a good deal of the variation in obesity can be attributed to genetics. Adopted individuals studied tend to have the body mass indexes that more closely resemble the BMIs of their biological parents than those of their adoptive parents (Sørensen et al., 1992; Moll, Burns, & Lauer, 1991). Moreover, identical twins separated at birth are as similar in body weight as those that were raised together (Price & Gottesman, 1991). This strongly suggests that genetics play a major role in determining obesity. Scientists do not completely understand exactly how our genes might predispose us to become obese. Some possibilities include inheriting a larger than normal number of fat cells, a lower metabolic rate (the speed at which we break down and burn the calories in food), or, as we saw earlier in the chapter, an abnormal leptin gene.

Genetics alone cannot explain the rise in obesity over the past few decades in this country, however. Genes may predispose people to become overweight, but the environment must be conducive to overeating in order for them to realize this potential. As we've seen, social and cultural factors contribute to our eating behavior. The social aspect of overeating is evident in recent findings that humans are much more likely to gain weight if they have an overweight friend, even if that person lives far away and the number of shared meals is minimal (Christakis & Fowler, 2007). This suggests that having overweight friends produces less resistance to gaining weight, perhaps because weight gain becomes associated with the positive stimulus of friendship. Obesity (especially among women) is also much more common among members of lower socioeconomic groups than in higher socioeconomic groups (McLaren, 2007). Researchers have suggested that this may be the result of less education about nutrition, fewer healthy food choices, and less social pressure to be thin (Monteiro et al., 2004).

Although obesity can significantly reduce the quality of life, people can be overweight for decades before the negative health effects become evident. Eating disorders on the other end of the spectrum, those that involve eating too little, can lead rather abruptly to emergency situations and even death.

Eating Disorders: Anorexia Nervosa and Bulimia Nervosa
Anorexia nervosa is a condition in which individuals are preoccupied with the notion that they are fat or will become fat. To combat these thoughts, people with anorexia engage in extreme dieting, often eating fewer than 500 calories per day (Sadock & Sadock, 2008). The restricted eating associated with anorexia generally leads to extreme weight loss, which can be very dangerous. People who lose too much weight are likely to suffer illnesses and imbalances in their blood chemistry. In as many as 10 percent of cases, anorexic weight loss leads to death (Steinhausen, 2002).

You can calculate your body mass index using the National Institute of Health's online calculator: http://www.nhlbisupport.com/bmi.

Genes or environment? Research clearly suggests that obesity is related to genes, but there is also evidence that the eating habits of parents and other family members can play a major role in the development of this problem.

obesity overweight; characterized as a body mass index of over 30.

body mass index (BMI) weight-to-height ratio.

anorexia nervosa eating disorder in which individuals undereat and have a distorted body image of being overweight.

Fighting a social stigma
Participants protest at a rally against size discrimination, seeking to speak out against the taunting and discrimination that plagues many obese people.

Obesity is acceptable and even considered to be desirable in some cultures. For example, in the African nation of Mauritania, parents have been known to force feed their daughters with high-calorie food to make them gain weight so that they will be more attractive to prospective suitors. While this practice may be on its way out, given that nation's recent recognition that obesity is unhealthy, Mauritanians certainly hold a different standard of beauty from the ideals prevalent in the United States.

In the United States, the media often dictate a certain standard of beauty, particularly for women. Young, slender women are considered desirable. The thin standard of beauty is becoming more and more extreme. Top female models and beauty pageant queens weigh 23 percent less than the average woman, compared to 8 percent less twenty-five years ago (Sheppird, 2009). Ironically, as the ideal weight is shrinking, the actually numbers on most people's scales are increasing (CDC, 2009).

Not only do people in the United States consider overweight people to be less attractive than thinner people, we also seem to ascribe a number of other unfavorable characteristics to people who are obese. Although overweight people are often considered to be "friendly" and "happy," they are also judged more often as "lazy," "stupid," and "incompetent" than are people of normal weight (Puhl et al., 2008; Friedman et al., 2005). Obese individuals are more often turned down for jobs (NAAFA, 2009). This discrimination can even affect normal-weight individuals associated with obese people. One study looked at the hiring rate of normal-weight job applicants who happened to be sitting next to an obese person just before their interview (Hebl & Mannix, 2003). They were less likely to be hired! Perhaps unsurprisingly, obese people are also more likely than normal-weight people to suffer from depression and anxiety (Friedlander et al., 2003).

In recent years, several organizations have attempted to combat this prejudice by supporting the obese and lobbying the government to pass laws against obesity discrimination. There are no national antiweight discrimination laws yet. At the state level, Michigan's Elliott-Larsen Civil Rights Act protects against weight discrimination (State of Michigan, 1976). Although it is the only state that currently prohibits weight discrimination, an antidiscrimination bill has been proposed in Massachusetts that would protect people from discrimination of weight and height. Several cities have incorporated categories such as "personal appearance" into their existing human rights legislation (NAAFA, 2009).

It's important to realize that there are major differences between people who diet, even those who do so continuously, and those with anorexia. People with anorexia have a distorted body image. Even when they are dangerously thin, they still think of themselves as fat and often cannot be convinced to increase their calorie intake.

Anorexia can begin as early as puberty (Hudson et al., 2007). Statistics suggest that about 1 in 100 young women in the United States has anorexia. It is much more common in females than males, although recent years have seen an increase in the number of males diagnosed with the condition (Hudson et al., 2007).

The causes of anorexia are complex, but it is most common in cultures where food is prevalent and social pressure exists for people to be thin (Makino, Tsuboi & Dennerstein, 2004). Similarly, many theorists have noted, with alarm, that today's media and fashion industry glamorize dangerously thin models. Anorexia often coexists with other anxiety disorders, such as obsessive-compulsive disorder, which we discussed in Chapter 9, suggesting that anorexia is just one of several possible outlets for a more general psychological disturbance.

Treatment of anorexia may involve hospitalization if extreme weight loss has occurred. Patients receive nutritional counseling to help restore a healthy weight. In addition, cognitive-behavioral therapy, which attempts to help patients develop a healthier body image, is used (Berkman et al., 2006). Adolescents with anorexia may also benefit from family therapy (Keel & Haedt, 2008).

bulima nervosa eating disorder in which individuals binge and then engage in purging type behavior.

Bulimia nervosa is a disorder in which individuals consume excessive calories and then go to extremes to prevent those calories from contributing to weight gain. People with bulimia typically rid themselves of excess food by inducing vomiting or diarrhea or by engaging in intensive exercise (Sigel, 2008). This cycle of bingeing followed by purging defines bulimia. Although people with anorexia often engage in bulimic behavior in order to prevent weight gain, most people with bulimia do not appear to be underweight. Some are even overweight (Probst et al., 2004). Like anorexia, bulimia is more common among females than males. Studies suggest that about 4 out of 100 young women in the United States have bulimia (APA, 2000).

The causes of bulimia are difficult to pinpoint. Like anorexia, bulimia is associated with other psychological disturbances, including OCD (Godart et al., 2007; Kaye et al., 2004). A significant number of people with bulimia have also engaged in other damaging behaviors, such as cutting themselves (Favaro et al., 2008).

Unlike anorexia, bulimia is typically not life-threatening. However, it can produce unwanted medical and dental problems, such as constipation from overuse of laxatives and tooth decay from excessive vomiting (Cremoni et al., 2009; Aranha, de Paula Eduardo, & Cordás, 2008). The psychological effects of bulimic behavior can be even more damaging than the physical ones. Because people with bulimia are generally ashamed of their binge-purge behaviors, they generally carry out these behaviors privately and make attempts to hide the evidence and keep their condition a secret. This secrecy, as well as the syndrome itself, often contribute to anxiety and depression (Pettersen, Rosevinge, & Ytterhus, 2008; Hayaki, Friedman, & Brownell, 2002).

Treatment of bulimia requires that patients admit that the problem exists and talk openly about it. Effective treatments for bulimia include behavioral modification, in which healthier eating behaviors are rewarded and cognitive therapy, which attempts to help people with bulimia develop healthier views of themselves and their eating patterns (Wilson & Shafran, 2005; Bailer et al., 2004). Antidepressant drug treatments have also been found to be effective, particularly when combined with behavioral or cognitive therapy (Romano et al., 2002).

Dangerous trend Here Brazilian model Ana Carolina Reston models an outfit in a 2005 fashion show. She died one year later at the age of 21, weighing 88 pounds, of complications from anorexia nervosa. Her death underscores a dangerous trend in the fashion industry toward using increasingly thin models.

Before You Go On

What Do You Know?
6. Describe three main categories of biological hunger signals.
7. What nonbiological factors affect our eating behavior?
8. What is obesity and what factors can contribute to it?
9. What are the characteristics of anorexia nervosa and bulimia nervosa?

What Do You Think?
As a public-health effort to combat obesity, several U.S. states and locations have begun to require restaurants to provide calorie and other nutritional information about food on their menus. What are some potential advantages and disadvantages of providing this information to diners?

Biological Motivations: Sex

LEARNING OBJECTIVE 3 Describe factors that affect our sexual motivation and behavior.

Another basic motivation is sex. From an evolutionary perspective, engaging in sexual behavior is highly adaptive. The continuation of the species depends on it (unless biotechnology takes over!). However, most sexual behavior does not occur with the goal of procreating in mind. Actually, the opposite seems to be true. Humans often engage in sexual behavior while taking steps to avoid conception. Humans, as well as other animals, seek out and engage in sexual behavior because it is a primary drive—it's pleasurable and rewarding.

Sex: Psychological and Social Factors

Although there is a basic biological instinct to engage in sexual activity, sexual motivation is strongly governed by social cues. In some species of animals, only select members of the social group reproduce. Among honeybees, for example, only the queen bee of each hive reproduces, while the other bees work to maintain the living environment (Wenseleers et al., 2004). In other groups, such as marmoset monkeys, dominant females in a social group procreate, and the other females help to raise the dominant's babies. Subordinate females must wait until a change occurs in the social order (perhaps the dominant will get old and sick and lose her rank) before they can reproduce (Barrett, Abbott & George, 1993).

Among humans, cultural factors play an important role in determining our choice and number of sexual partners, our range of sexual practices, and the age at which sexual activity typically begins. For instance, some societies, such as certain Nigerian tribes, practice polygamy, an arrangement in which men have multiple wives. Other societies, such as the Naxi of China, practice polyandry, an arrangement in which women have multiple male sexual partners (Yan, 1986).

Societies also vary in the sexual practices that are considered taboo or unacceptable. For example, in many states in the United States, it's a crime for an adult to have sex with a 16-year-old (even a consenting one), but in some Middle Eastern countries, the earliest age of marriage (and its consummation) is 9 years old (Admon, 2009; Norman-Eady, Reinhart, & Martino, 2003).

Some sexual taboos seem to be almost universal, however, suggesting that they may be rooted in human evolution. One example of this is the incest taboo. In most cultures, incest, or having sex with close relatives, is forbidden. It's illegal for siblings to marry in most countries throughout the world. In one case in Germany, for example, a biological brother and sister who were brought up separately, then met and fell in love as young adults were sentenced to prison after marrying (Connolly, 2007).

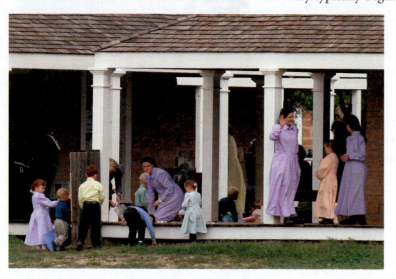

Of national concern Mothers and their children gather in San Angelo, Texas in April 2008, after they were uprooted from the nearby Yearning for Zion ranch, where they had been living in a polygamous community. For a few weeks, their plight received enormous national attention.

Why is sex between siblings so universally forbidden? From an evolutionary viewpoint, there are at least two possible reasons. First, procreation between closely related individuals increases the likelihood of passing on defective genes, particularly recessive ones. Early societies that forbade incest may have been genetically stronger than those that did not. Second, incest taboos put pressure on societies to interact with neighboring cultures. Historically, this meant that tribal elders would bargain about marrying their children to one another. In the process, the two tribes might increase general commerce and enhance the access to food and other forms of wealth for both groups (Leavitt, 1989; Johnson & Earle, 1987). According to these views, avoiding sex with close relatives enhances the chances for survival of a group of people. Cultural regulation of our biological drive toward sexual behavior may also have emerged because it serves the purpose of promoting our survival as a group.

Although norms vary from culture to culture, as we have seen, all cultures do approve certain sexual practices while condemning others. Within nations, many religious, ethnic, and other subcultural groups also influence the sexual behavior of their members. In many societies, sex is not acceptable unless the couple's relationship is considered legitimate, in many cases until marriage (ICASD, 2007). In the United States, the sexual revolution of the 1960s and 1970s loosened many social restrictions on premarital sex. Today, over 95 percent of people in the United States have sex before marriage (Finer, 2007) and about 10 percent of couples living together are unmarried (U.S. Census Bureau, 2008). The number of young adults with multiple sexual partners has also increased. By the time most individuals reach their early 20s, they have had three to four sexual partners (Mosher, Chandra, & Jones 2005). Some sexual behaviors, such as homosexual relationships, remain controversial in the United States.

Sex: What Happens in the Body and Brain

Changes in societal views of sex grew, in part, from psychology research on sexual behavior. One of the most influential sex researchers was biologist Alfred Kinsey. Realizing that many of his college students were uneducated about basic sexual practices, Kinsey switched his field of study from insect behavior to human sexual behavior in the 1940s (Bullough, 2004). He then undertook a massive project, interviewing thousands of people to collect data on the sexual practices of ordinary Americans. Kinsey's work was widely publicized and led to the realization that many "normal" Americans engaged in sexual behavior that was not considered to be conventional at the time, including oral sex, anal sex, and having multiple partners (Brown & Fee, 2003).

Sex: What Happens in the Body   During the 1950s and 1960s, researchers William Masters and Virginia Johnson brought the study of sexual behavior into the laboratory. Masters and Johnson recorded some of the first physiological data in humans during sex. They studied the sexual responses of both men and women and described four phases of the human sexual response, as shown in **Figure 11-7** (Masters & Johnson, 1966).

- *Excitement* This is the beginning of arousal and it can last up to several hours. Heart rate quickens.

- *Plateau* At this phase, breathing and pulse rates increase. Muscles tense and a flush may appear across the chest.

- *Orgasm* Muscle tension and blood pressure reach a peak. This is quickly followed by climax, which is a series of muscle contractions (the intensity varies, particularly among women).

- *Resolution* Muscles relax and heart rate returns to normal. While men have a refractory period after an orgasm, during which they cannot ejaculate, women may have additional orgasms.

In the 1970s, sex therapist Helen Kaplan incorporated an additional element to the beginning of the sexual response cycle. Kaplan believed that *desire*—basically, whether or not you're "in the mood"—was a necessary condition to motivate an individual to become

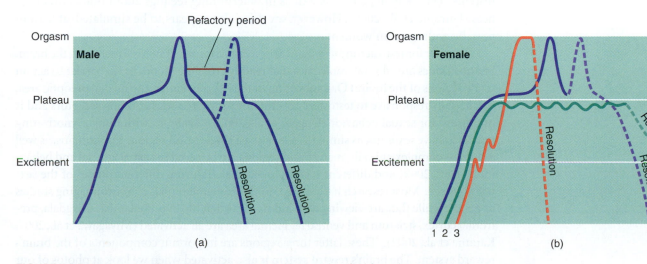

FIGURE 11-7 **Human sexual responses** Masters and Johnson identified four phases in sexual response. Part (a) illustrates the typical pattern in males. Women experience greater variability in their sexual response. Part (b) shows three female patterns.

"You're wasting your time. I'm asexual."

excited (Kaplan, 1977). The research of Masters and Johnson and those that followed, such as Kaplan, was particularly influential to U.S. society, because it encouraged women to enjoy sex, which was previously considered to be inappropriate (Weiss, 2000). Masters and Johnson's research also dispelled myths about aging and sexual behavior. Prior to their research, the conventional view was that sexual behavior was the realm of young to middle-aged adults and that after a certain age, sexual behavior was minimal, if not physically impossible. As a result of Masters and Johnson's research, as well as others that followed, the current view is that sexual behavior can continue throughout old age, providing a person remains physically healthy and can find a willing partner (Waite et al., 2009; DeLamater & Karraker, 2009).

Although the work of the early sex researchers was highly controversial at the time it was conducted and their methods have been questioned since then (Cochran, Mosteller, & Tukey, 1953), the publicity these researchers received had lasting effects of increasing awareness of sexual behavior and altering societal standards of what is considered "normal" (Gagnon, 1975). This body of psychology research emphasized that sexual behavior is a wholesome and healthy activity, another major change in thinking compared to earlier, more restrictive attitudes. It also encouraged later researchers to explore our physiological responses, including what happens in the brain during sex.

What Happens in the
Sex: B R A I N ?

Reproductive hormones are clearly important factors in modulating sexual behavior (Raskin et al., 2009; Kudwa et al., 2006; Berman, 2005). In males, the testes and adrenal glands produce male sex hormones collectively referred to as *androgens*. In females, the ovaries produce the female sex hormones (estrogen and progesterone). Even though androgens are referred to as male sex hormones, they are produced by the adrenal glands of females too. Like all other hormones, these molecules are released in the blood stream and travel throughout the body. In men, blood levels of androgens, particularly testosterone, are linked positively to sex drive (Bancroft, 2005; Simon et al., 2005). On average, sex drive in males declines with advancing age as testosterone levels drop, although as we have seen, aging does not preclude sexual interest and activity (Feldman et al., 2002). In women, the story appears to be a bit more complicated—estrogen levels are important for the physiological aspects of the sexual response (Frank et al., 2008) as well as in determining feelings about one's attractiveness (Durante et al., 2009). However, sex drive also appears to be simulated, at least in part, by androgens in women.

In order for testosterone to enhance motivation for sex, it needs to act upon the brain. Sex hormones are all small molecules that readily cross the blood–brain barrier to act on many regions of the brain. One subregion of the hypothalamus, the medial preoptic area, is especially responsive to testosterone – this area is rich in sex hormone receptors and is important for sexual behavior (Dugger et al., 2007). Again, as with hunger, motivating people to have sex is not as simple as activating a single brain region. For humans, as well as for less complex animals, many brain regions are involved in sexual arousal and behavior (Toates, 2009) and different regions are activated during different phases of the sexual response. Most research has focused on the excitement phase. Neuroimaging studies of people while they are viewing erotic films show that the hypothalamus, amygdala, prefrontal cortex, striatum and ventral tegmental area are all activated (Miyagawa et al., 2007; Karama et al., 2002). These latter three regions are important components of the brain's reward system. The brain's reward system is also activated when we look at photos of our romantic partner's faces, suggesting that this area is importantly involved in responding to rewarding stimuli that are not necessarily erotic (Fisher et al., 2005). During the orgasm phase, one study in males found that in addition to the ventral tegmental area, the cerebellum is activated (Holstege et al., 2003). While the involvement of the cerebellum in this phase of sexual activity remains a mystery, there may be links to the role of this brain region in emotional processing.

Neuroimaging studies show that we can get aroused just by watching sexual behavior. When people view videos of sex acts, or merely imagine them, parts of their brains associated with the *mirror neuron system*, such as the parietal and frontal lobes, are activated (Mouras et al., 2008; Shmuelof & Zohary, 2007; Gallese et al., 1996). As described in Chapter 9, the mirror neuron system is made up of areas of the brain that, when we watch another person engage in a specific activity, are activated in the same way as when we actually do the same activity ourselves (Rizzolatti & Craighero, 2004). Thus, watching other people engage in sexual behavior activates some of the same regions of the viewer's brain that would be active if the viewer were actually having sex. This activation makes viewers feel sexually aroused simply from watching.

Even if we do not consciously see an erotic picture or film, we can become aroused. In one study, researchers presented a series of photos to participants. Some of the photos were sexual, and these were rapidly shown and removed before the viewer was consciously aware. Even though viewers did not remember seeing anything, neuroimaging showed activation of regions of the brain associated with arousal and reward (Childress, 2008). Sexual behavior is essential for survival of the species, and the rapid activation of brain regions by subtle sexual cues ensures that we are motivated to have sex.

Sex: HOW we Differ

Gender Identity Before we consider individual differences in sexuality, we need to address the most basic of differences in this domain, whether or not we are male or female. Early in prenatal life, it's impossible to tell whether the fetus is a boy or girl (unless a chromosomal analysis is done). After a certain developmental stage, if the fetus is genetically male (its sex chromosomes are XY), it will develop testes. In the absence of testes, the fetus will develop ovaries. In other words, development of a female fetus is a default program that happens if the signals to masculinize aren't present.

The testes release *testosterone* which travels throughout the body. In certain organs, this hormone is converted to one of two other hormones, *dihydrotestosterone (DHT)* or, surprisingly, to estrogen. As shown in the accompanying box, DHT is important for masculinizing the external genitalia—this is the hormone that causes a male fetus to grow a penis. Testosterone can be converted to estrogen in the central nervous system, and some evidence suggests that estrogen along with testosterone then *masculinizes* the brain: they set up brain functioning that is, on average, characteristic of male brains. Since estrogen is considered to be a female reproductive hormone, its involvement in *masculinization* seems contradictory—leading scientists to recognize that the tradititional view of estrogen as the female sex hormone and testosterone as the male sex hormone was probably an oversimplification. Estrogen's role in masculinization also raises the question of why the female fetus, which produces estrogen directly from its ovaries, doesn't end up with a masculinized brain. The answer to this question is that female fetuses are protected against their own estrogen and the estrogen produced by the mother, because they make a protein that binds to estrogen and prevents it from masculinizing the brain.

Masculinization of the brain occurs in the hypothalamus, the brain region important for coordinating reproductive hormone release from the pituitary. Masculinization also occurs in brain regions important for nonreproductive behaviors, such as those

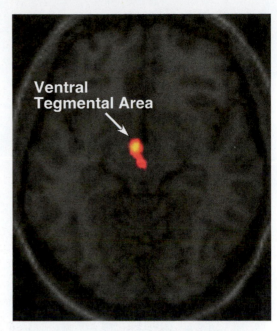

Ventral Tegmental Area

The brain, sexual arousal, and rewards Gazing at a photo of one's romantic partner activates the ventral tegmental area (VTA), (shown in yellow on this fMRI image). The VTA is activated during sexual activity as well as when looking at photos of loved ones for which there is no sexual interest, showing that this brain area is associated with learning about rewarding stimuli in general.

important for regulating aggression. Exposure to specific hormones during fetal life may also determine whether humans identify with being a male or female. Indeed, girls with a medical condition that exposes them during the fetal stage to masculine levels of hormones may later engage in play behavior that is more like boys than it is like girls (Hines and Kaufman, 1994).

In some cases, babies arrive with ambiguous genitalia, and the issue of gender identity isn't readily resolved. Sometimes an XX baby, because of the hormones it was exposed to in utero, will be born with an enlarged clitoris that resembles a penis. Other times, an XY baby will arrive with a smaller than normal penis. People with ambiguous genitalia are now referred to as intersex (this term has largely replaced the old name hermaphrodite). After determining the genetic sex of the baby, physicians and parents need to make decisions about how to proceed.

In the past, psychologists and healthcare providers believed that gender identity is determined mostly by the environment. In other words, if a child is treated like a boy (or girl), then he/she will grow up to identify with that gender. As a result, several individuals with ambiguous genitalia received treatment to make their external genitalia appear to be more "normal". For example, boys without fully developed penises underwent surgery and were raised as girls. In some cases, this treatment backfired and the surgically created "girls" grew up very unhappy with their gender assignment and eventually underwent treatment to live the remainder of their lives as males. Today, doctors and scientists generally believe that gender identity is largely determined by biology and that hormones present early in life contribute to masculinization (or by default, feminization) of the brain.

In still other kinds of cases, external gender characteristics appear to be the opposite of gender identity. That is, the individual appears to be one sex but identifies strongly with the other sex. Although it's not entirely clear how this disconnect occurs, it's possible that hormones responsible for masculinizing the body are not working synchronously with those that do so to the brain.

Gender Differences in Sexuality   Although each of us has our own preferences, beliefs, and behaviors, there do seem to be some differences between men and women when it comes to sex. Males and females differ in characteristics they perceive as attractive in a mate and in the stimuli that arouse them. Their fantasies and desired numbers of partners may also differ.

Evolutionary psychologists suggest that much of how heterosexual men and women interact with the opposite sex is the result of thousands of years of evolution designed to maximize our chances of survival and reproductive success. Men desire youthful, attractive mates because those attributes signal good odds for reproductive success; women are attracted to men who are dependable and strong because they will most likely be able to protect and care for children.

In addition to what makes someone attractive, men and women also differ in what arouses them. It may not be surprising, for example, that men, on average, are aroused more quickly than women by visual stimuli (Stoléru et al., 1999). After all, *Playboy* magazine has made millions of dollars on this very premise. Women, on the other hand, respond more strongly than men do to physical contact and verbal expression. This may be because arousal in women is more often influenced by their relationship with a partner, as well as their own self-image, than it is in men (Peplau, 2003).

Even women's sexual fantasies are more commitment-oriented (Ellis & Symons, 1990) and they tend to have fewer fantasies than men (Byers, Purdon, & Clark, 1998). In one study, surveyors asked college students, "Have you had sex with over a thousand different partners in your imagination?" Males in the study were four times more likely than females to say yes (Ellis & Symons, 1990). The frequency of men's arousal and the number of their fantasies have led many psychologists to conclude that men generally

Different needs and preferences A couple stares out the window after a sexual encounter. Given gender differences regarding sexual needs, attraction, arousal, and fantasies, their thoughts may be in different places at this particular moment.

have a higher sex drive. In fact, men tend to rate their own sex drives as higher than women rate theirs (Baumeister, Catanese, & Vohs, 2001).

It's important to realize that reported gender differences in sexual desire and sexual activity may reflect biases in reporting. On surveys and during interviews, women may downplay their sexual desires and behaviors because of perceived social constraints. Conversely, males may be more likely to exaggerate such feelings and behaviors to fulfill imagined expectations for men. There is no question that women and men are judged differently by society when it comes to sex. In movies, for example, women with high sex drives are often portrayed as dangerous or emotionally unstable while men with low sex drives are often the subject of ridicule. These perceptions may influence the way that people respond to questions about their sex lives. In reality though, women and men may be more alike than researchers once thought. A University of Southern California study of undergraduates did not find a significant difference between women and men in their desired number of partners (Miller et al., 2002).

Sexual Orientation   Most people are **heterosexual**; they are sexually attracted to members of the opposite sex. Approximately 10 percent of males and 2 percent of females identify themselves as **homosexual**, or attracted to members of their own sex. Why are some people attracted to members of the opposite sex while others are attracted to members of the same sex? Arguments about this topic have been heated and often reflect a nature-nurture debate.

Since homosexuality is considered by some religious and political groups to be immoral, a common position of such organizations has been that homosexuality is a choice or lifestyle selected by an individual on the basis of exposure to aberrant experiences while growing up (Lawson, 1987). Some theorists have suggested that homosexuals are more likely than heterosexuals to have experienced homosexual activity as youngsters or were not treated in a gender appropriate way while growing up. Other theories explain homosexuality in terms of abnormal relationships with the opposite sex parent (Bieber et al., 1962).

Alfred Kinsey believed that sexual orientation was on a continuum, with many people fitting between the two extremes of exclusively heterosexual and exclusively homosexual (Kinsey, Pomeroy, & Martin, 1949). Kinsey's theory is controversial, but it does

heterosexual sexual attraction to members of the opposite sex.

homosexual sexual attraction to members of one's own sex.

Turnim-Man: When "Girls" Become Men

Some individuals carry a genetic mutation that leads to a lack of the enzyme necessary for conversion of testosterone to DHT. Genetically male individuals with *5-alpha reductase deficiency* are born with feminized external genitalia. They are often raised as girls but once puberty sets in and secondary sex characteristics develop, it becomes evident that they are not becoming women. Voices deepen, facial hair develops and the external genitalia enlarge. This genetic condition is relatively rare in open societies but clusters of 5-alpha reductase deficiency exist in closed communities in which most individuals are related genetically. One such community is located in Papua New Guinea. Perhaps because this condition is more common (Imperato-McGinlay et al., 1991) and also because medical treatments are scarce in this region, the people have developed an acceptance of 5-alpha reductase deficiency individuals. Even if they were raised as girls, they often transition into manhood without significant psychological difficulties. In Papua New Guinea there is even a special name for these people—Turnim-man (one language of Papua New Guines is pidgin English and it's not difficult to discern what this name means). The relative ease with which the "Turnim-man" accept manhood probably occurs because the brain has already been masculinized by estrogen and the community is accepting of individuals moving from girlhood to manhood. It's not surprising, however, that such transitions are more difficult in western societies, where gender differences are often emphasized and medical intervention to correct whatever is considered to be "abnormal" has been prevalent.

suggest that sexual orientation is changeable. Based on this idea, numerous organizations have devised treatment programs to "convert" homosexuals to heterosexuality. Such programs make the assumption that if a person living as a homosexual is, in fact, at least part heterosexual, intervention can cause the person to increase the heterosexual-to-homosexual ratio—that is, to emphasize in his or her life heterosexual behaviors and thoughts (Murphy, 1992; Pattison & Pattison, 1980). In fact, in the late 1960s, the Masters and Johnson Institute sponsored such a program and reported conversions among the majority of participants (Masters & Johnson, 1979). These findings have not been supported, and current research strongly suggests that homosexuality is biologically based and cannot be "cured." If anything, such attempts can be damaging to the individual, since they typically produce feelings of shame and embarrassment (Cramer et al., 2008; Haldeman, 1994).

As part of a growing realization that homosexuality occurs naturally in some people, the American Psychiatric Association removed homosexuality from its designation as a psychological disorder in 1973. Additional evidence that homosexuality is a natural, biological phenomenon comes from repeated observations of homosexual behavior throughout the animal kingdom. Homosexuality has been reported in both male and female birds (including one celebrated case of a homosexual penguin at the Central Park Zoo in New York City), as well as among bonobos, a type of chimpanzee (Roughgarden, 2004; Smith, 2004).

Although the exact influences leading to sexual orientation remain unknown, considerable evidence suggests our orientation has a biological basis. Researchers have studied the intertwined influences of genes, hormones, and anatomical brain differences.

- *Genes* Studies suggest a strong genetic influence on sexual orientation. In other words, homosexuality tends to run in families (Bailey & Pillard, 1991; Buhrich, Bailey, & Martin, 1991). The correlation is greatest among monozygotic, or identical, twins. If one twin is homosexual, the other is also likely to have that orientation. Some evidence suggests this link exists even if the twins are raised apart (Eckert et al., 1986). As with many other traits, however, genetics do not completely determine sexual orientation; even among pairs of identical twins who share the same genes, some pairs differ in orientation. Furthermore, a genetic link isn't at all apparent for most people with homosexual orientations (Långström et al., 2008). Researchers have therefore considered other biological factors.

- *Hormones* Some studies suggest that some homosexual males may experience different hormone levels before birth compared to heterosexual males. Studies have shown that having an older brother increases the odds of male homosexuality. With each additional older brother, the likelihood of homosexuality increases (Blanchard, 2004; Blanchard, 2001). In the case of younger brothers with homosexual orientations, some researchers suggest that the mother's immune system may sometimes react to male sex hormones while she is carrying a male fetus, such that in subsequent pregnancies, maternal antibodies will lessen the "masculinizing" action of hormones on the brain of the younger brother. Although this hypothesis cannot account for the majority of homosexual individuals, studies examining brain differences support the possibility that prenatal hormone exposure may be an important factor for some individuals (Rahman, 2005; Williams et al., 2000).

- *Brain anatomy* A sex difference exists in the anterior, or front, part of the hypothalamus. This region is twice as large in heterosexual men as it is in women (Orikasa, Kondo, & Sakuma, 2007). A similar size difference exists in this brain region between heterosexual men and homosexual men. The anterior hypothalamuses of homosexual men are, on average, more similar in size to those of women than to those of heterosexual men, suggesting that individual differences

Gay marriage and the law Two women cross a Boston street with great joy on their faces after being married at a Unitarian church immediately after same-sex marriage was declared legal in Massachusetts in 2004.

in masculinizing factors (most likely hormones) may contribute to changes in brain anatomy that ultimately lead to homosexual or heterosexual behavior (LeVay, 1991).

Society is gradually becoming more tolerant of homosexuality. Up until 2004, same-sex marriage was illegal in all 50 states, but now a few states, including Massachusetts and Iowa, allow it. Still, same-sex marriage is a hotly debated topic among religious and political groups. Roughly half of the population still believes it is wrong for two men or two women to say, "I do" (Pew Forum, 2003).

Sex When Things Go Wrong

Although sexual activity brings great pleasure to most people, it can pose significant problems for some. Four kinds of sexual problems or disorders may occur: sexual dysfunctions, paraphilias, gender identity disorder, and medical problems.

Sexual Dysfunctions *Sexual dysfunctions* are disorders in which people cannot respond normally in key areas of sexual functioning, making it difficult or impossible to enjoy sexual intercourse. As you read earlier, the human sexual response consists of several phases. Sexual dysfunctions typically affect one or more of these phases.

Two of the sexual dysfunctions—hypoactive sexual desire disorder and sexual aversion disorder—center on how much sexual desire a person experiences. People with *hypoactive sexual desire disorder* lack interest in sex and, in turn, display very little sexual activity. As many as 16 percent of men and 33 percent of women may display this dysfunction (Maurice, 2007; Laumann et al., 2005, 1999). People with *sexual aversion disorder* find sex distinctly unpleasant or repulsive. Indeed, sexual overtures may sicken, disgust, or frighten them. Apparently aversion to sex is relatively uncommon, particularly among men (Wincze et al., 2008; Maurice, 2007).

There are two sexual dysfunctions that affect the excitement phase of the sexual response cycle: female sexual arousal disorder (once referred to as "frigidity") and male erectile disorder (once called "impotence"). Women with a *female sexual arousal disorder* are persistently unable to attain or maintain proper lubrication or genital swelling during sexual activity (Basson, 2007; Heiman, 2007). Estimates of its prevalence vary, but most studies agree that more than 10 percent of women experience it (Laumann et al., 2005, 1999, 1994; Bancroft et al., 2003). Men with *male erectile disorder* persistently fail to attain or maintain an adequate erection during sexual activity. This problem occurs in about 10 percent of the male population (Laumann et al., 2005, 1999). Most such men are over the age of 50, largely because so many cases are associated with ailments of older adults (Cameron et al., 2005). However, according to surveys, half of all adult men experience erectile difficulty during intercourse at least some of the time.

Dysfunctions of the orgasm phase of the sexual response cycle are rapid ejaculation, male orgasmic disorder, and female orgasmic disorder. A man suffering from *rapid, or premature, ejaculation* persistently reaches orgasm and ejaculates with very little sexual stimulation before, on, or shortly after penetration, and before he wishes to. As many as 30 percent of men in the United States experience rapid ejaculation at some time (Jannini & Lenai, 2005). Many young men experience this disfunction but it is not solely a young man's problem. Research suggests that men of any age may suffer from rapid ejaculation (Althof, 2007). A man with *male orgasmic disorder* is repeatedly unable to reach orgasm or is very delayed in reaching orgasm after normal sexual excitement. The disorder occurs in 8 percent of men (Hartmann & Waldinger, 2007; Laumann et al., 2005, 1999). Similarly, women with *female orgasmic disorder* rarely reach orgasm or

"To quote my broker, 'Past results are no guarantee of future performance.'"

generally experience a very delayed one. Studies indicate that 10 percent or more of women have never had an orgasm, either alone or during intercourse, and at least another 9 percent rarely have orgasms (LoPiccolo, 2004, 1995; Bancroft et al., 2003). In contrast, half of all women experience orgasm in intercourse at least fairly regularly (LoPiccolo & Stock, 1987).

Each of the sexual dysfunctions may be caused by a combination of biological and psychological factors. In the biological realm, for example, abnormal hormone activity can adversely affect sexual functioning and various medications can interfere with sex drive and behavior. Problematic psychological factors include feelings of depression, anxiety, or anger; inaccurate beliefs about sex; and stressors such as job pressure or relationship problems. Masters and Johnson (1970) found two psychological factors to be particularly common among men with sexual dysfunctions—*performance anxiety* and *spectator role*. They found that once some men experience erectile or orgasmic problems, they start to worry about the possibility of failing to have erections or orgasms during their sexual encounters (performance anxiety). As a result, instead of relaxing during such encounters, they keep observing themselves and their performances. They become judges and spectators rather than sexually aroused participants, and their ability to engage in sexual activity declines.

Today's treatments for sexual dysfunctions can be traced to the publication of Masters and Johnson's landmark book *Human Sexual Inadequacy* in 1970. Their *sex therapy* program has grown into a complex approach which now includes a combination of cognitive-behavioral, couple, and family techniques that you will read more about in Chapter 16 (Leiblum, 2007; Bach et al., 2001). In recent years, drug therapies have been added to the sex treatment approaches, triggered by the enormous success of drugs such as *sildenafil* (trade name Viagra) in the treatment of male erectile disorder.

Paraphilias *Paraphilias* are disorders in which people have repeated and intense sexual urges or fantasies or display sexual behaviors in response to objects or situations that society considers inappropriate. Some of the most common paraphilias are fetishism, exhibitionism, voyeurism, pedophilia, and sexual sadism. For most paraphilias, men with the disorders greatly outnumber women.

People with *fetishism* display recurrent intense sexual urges or behaviors that involve the use of a nonliving object. The object—women's underwear, shoes, and boots are particularly common—may be touched, smelled, worn, or used in some other way while the individual masturbates or has intercourse (Marshall et al., 2008).

A person with *exhibitionism* has recurrent urges to expose his genitals to another person, almost always a member of the opposite sex. He rarely attempts to initiate sexual activity with the person to whom he exposes himself; rather he wants to produce shock or surprise. Sometimes an exhibitionist will expose himself in a particular neighborhood at particular hours. In one survey of 2,800 men, 4.3 percent reported that they perform exhibitionistic behavior (Långström & Seto, 2006).

An individual with *voyeurism* has recurrent and intense urges to secretly observe unsuspecting people as they undress or to spy on couples having intercourse. The person may also masturbate during the act of observing or when thinking about it afterward but does not generally seek to have sex with the observed person.

People with *pedophilia* gain sexual gratification by watching, touching, or engaging in sexual acts with prepubescent children, usually 13 years old or younger. Some individuals with this disorder are satisfied by material such as children's underwear ads; others seek out child pornography; and some are driven to actually watch, fondle, or engage in sexual activities with children (Durkin & Hundersmarck, 2008). Both boys and girls can be pedophilia victims, but research suggests that two-thirds of them are girls (Doctor & Neff, 2001).

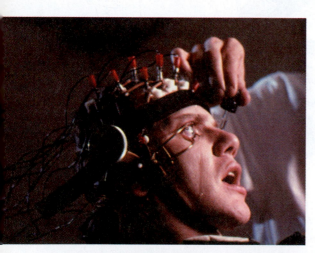

Sexual sadism and the cinema In a famous scene from the movie *A Clockwork Orange*, Alex, a sexual sadist, is forced to watch violent images while experiencing severe stomach cramps, in the hope that he will develop an aversion to sexually violent acts.

Some people with pedophilia also exhibit distorted thinking, such as "It's all right to have sex with children as long as they agree" (Roche & Quayle, 2007). Similarly, it is not uncommon for pedophiles to blame the children for adult–child sexual contacts or to assert that the children benefited from the experience (Durkin & Hundersmarck, 2008).

Most pedophilic offenders are imprisoned or forced into treatment if they are caught (Stone et al., 2000). Clearly, they are committing child sexual abuse when they have sexual contact with a child. Moreover, there are now many residential registration and community notification laws across the United States that help law enforcement agencies and the public account for and control where convicted child sex offenders live and work.

A person with *sexual sadism* is intensely sexually aroused by the thought or act of inflicting suffering on others by dominating, restraining, blindfolding, cutting, strangling, mutilating, or even killing the victim. Many carry out sadistic acts with a consenting partner; some, however, act out their urges on nonconsenting victims (Marshall et al., 2008). A number of rapists and sexual murderers, for example, exhibit sexual sadism. The key to their arousal is suffering by the victim.

A number of explanations have been proposed for the various paraphilias, but none has received much research support (Abramowitz, 2008). Moreover, none of the current treatments for these disorders has met with clear success (Roche & Quayle, 2007).

Gender Identity Disorder Most people feel like and identify themselves as males or females—an identity that is consistent with the gender to which they are born. But psychologists have come to appreciate that many people do not experience such gender clarity. They have *transgender experiences*—a sense that their actual gender identity is different from the gender category to which they were born physically, or that it lies outside the usual male versus female categories (Carroll, 2007). Many of today's psychologists believe that, in many cases, transgender feelings reflect alternative, rather than disordered, ways of experiencing one's gender identity. And, indeed, a number of people with transgender experiences come to terms with their gender inconsistencies, blend gender in some way, and become comfortable with their atypical gender identity. However, others experience extreme unhappiness with their given gender and may seek treatment for their problem. These individuals receive a diagnosis of *gender identity disorder*. People with gender identity disorder would like to get rid of their primary and secondary sex characteristics—many of them find their own genitals repugnant—and acquire the characteristics of the other sex (APA, 2000). Men with the disorder outnumber women by around 2 to 1.

Some children experience gender identity disorder (Carroll, 2007; Zucker, 2005). Like adults with this disorder, the children feel uncomfortable about their assigned sex and deeply desire to be members of the opposite sex. Surveys of mothers indicate that about 1 to 2 percent of young boys wish to be a girl, and 3 to 4 percent of young girls wish to be a boy (Carroll, 2007; Zucker & Bradley, 2005). This childhood pattern usually disappears by adolescence or adulthood, but in some cases it develops into adult gender identity disorder (Cohen-Kettenis, 2001).

The causes of gender identity disorder are not understood. In addition, treatment for the disorder has been very controversial. Many adults with this disorder receive *hormone treatments* to change their sexual characteristics (Andreasen & Black, 2006; Hepp et al., 2002; Bradley, 1995). Physicians prescribe *estrogen* for male patients, causing breast development, loss of body and facial hair, and change in body fat distribution. Similarly, women with gender identity disorder are treated with *testosterone*. For other individuals, however, this is not enough, and they pursue one of the most hotly debated practices in medicine: *sex-change*, or *sexual reassignment*, *surgery* (Andreasen & Black, 2006; Hepp et al., 2002). The operation itself includes, for men, amputation of the penis, creation of an artificial vagina, and face-changing plastic surgery. For women, surgery may include bilateral mastectomy and hysterectomy. Studies in Europe have suggested that 1 of every 30,000 men and 1 of

Breaking a barrier Actress and television personality Vladimir Luxuria, physically a male, offers a gesture of victory after her election to the Italian parliament in 2006, the highest legislative office ever attained by a transgender individual.

every 100,000 women may seek sex-change surgery (Carroll, 2007; Bakker et al., 1993). In the United States, more than 6,000 persons may have undergone this surgical procedure (Doctor & Neff, 2001). Some clinicians consider such surgery to be a humane solution, while others believe that sexual reassignment is an inappropriate approach for a complex disorder (Olsson & Moller, 2003).

Medical Problems   Sexual activity is not without risks. People who have sex without contraception face the risk of unintended or unwanted pregnancies. Unprotected sex also leaves participants at risk of contracting sexually transmitted infections (STIs), including HIV, the virus linked to AIDS. Other common STIs include chlamydia, which is the most frequently reported; gonorrhea; genital herpes; and human papillomavirus (HPV). Most individuals with an STI have no symptoms. Using condoms can greatly reduce the chances of contracting most STIs, and women younger than 26 years of age can receive a vaccine to protect against most of the HPV strains that cause cervical cancers, but abstaining from sex is the only way to entirely prevent infection (CDC, 2008; Markowitz et al., 2006).

Half of all new cases of HIV are contracted before the age of 25 (CDC, 2001). Because of the public health threats posed by HIV/AIDS, as well as other STIs and teen pregnancies, sex education for secondary school students has become an important priority in the United States (Luker, 2007; Dailard, 2001). Sex education programs generally take one of two major approaches. One, called comprehensive sex education, includes teaching about contraception and safer sex measures, such as condom use, to prevent sexually transmitted infections. The other approach provides less information on the specifics of contraception and disease prevention, focusing instead on promoting abstinence from intercourse, generally until marriage.

Many political and religious organizations support abstinence programs, suggesting that the detailed information provided in comprehensive programs actually encourages sexual activity among teens (Gaul, 2007). (Until 2009, the U.S. government provided funding only to school districts that offered abstinence-only education.) Proponents of comprehensive education respond that research evidence does not support the claim that sex education increases sexual activity (Trenholm et al., 2007). In fact, teenagers in either type of program are just as likely to engage in sex (Brückner & Bearman, 2005).

Promoters of comprehensive programs further point out that abstinence education takes a negative, disapproving view of premarital sex. They note that feelings of shame and embarrassment about sexual activity can actually increase the likelihood of *unprotected* sex (Kay & Jackson, 2008; Brückner & Bearman, 2005). Planning ahead for contraception and condom use is more often associated with open attitudes about sexual activity than with feelings of guilt. The first large analysis of the effectiveness of comprehensive sex education found that it reduces teen pregnancy by 50 percent, compared to either abstinence-only education or no sex education at all (Kohler, Manhart & Lafferty, 2008). The American Psychological Association says that well-rounded sex education also reduces the risk of HIV infection, whereas abstinence-only programs may actually increase the risk of getting HIV (APA, 2005).

A signature moment   An important turning point in changing the public's attitudes toward AIDS and its victims came in 1991 when the enormously popular and respected professional basketball player Magic Johnson announced at this press conference that he had been diagnosed HIV positive.

Before You Go On

What Do You Know?

10. What aspects of sexual behavior are affected by our cultural standards?
11. What are the phases of the sexual response cycle described by Masters and Johnson and what happens at each one?
12. What biological factors has research found to be related to sexual orientation?
13. Identify four kinds of sexual problems or disorders and give an example of each.
14. How do comprehensive sex education and abstinence education differ?

What Do You Think?   Describe the specific cultural standards for sexual behavior that affect your peer group.

Psychological Motivations: Affiliation and Achievement

LEARNING OBJECTIVE 4 Describe factors that influence our psychological motivations for affiliation and achievement.

In the previous sections, we talked about biological motivations. Recall Maslow's hierarchy of needs though and you will see that we are also motivated by nonbiological needs. The need to belong and the need for self-worth are psychological motivations that are just as important to our health and happiness.

Just as it may be difficult to focus on achieving in school if you are hungry, your focus may be affected if the more basic psychological need of *affiliation*, or belonging, is not met.

Affiliation

Going to college is, for many students, their first experience away from home for a prolonged period of time. Suddenly, you are on your own, without the support and comfort of your family. Those first few weeks can be quite stressful, until students become acquainted with their new surroundings and meet new people.

Being part of a social group, whether it is a family or a group of friends or an organization, helps us define who we are and allows us to feel secure about our place in the world. This need has evolved from the evolutionary advantage that groups had in being able to provide food and protection, compared to individuals living alone (Diener & Seligman, 2002).

From the moment we are born, we seek a connection with others. As we learned previously, instinct theory explains that infants automatically seek out their mother's breast and this "rooting" reflex reinforces the infant's chances of survival. As we develop, relationships with friends and, later, with significant others help to raise our self-esteem. Men and women in long-term, healthy relationships have less depression and live longer (Holt-Lunstad, Birmingham, & Jones, 2008). Even elderly spouses who provide more care to each other live longer than those who are less considerate of each other (Kaplan & Kronick, 2006).

Affiliation: When Things Go Wrong Our motivation to belong may also explain why some individuals remain in abusive relationships and join gangs. The fear of social exclusion is a powerful motivator. In fact, when people feel excluded, the anterior cingulate cortex in the frontal cortex is activated (Eisenberger, Lieberman, & Williams, 2003). Recall that this same area responds to physical pain.

The need to be affiliated with others is routinely exploited as a means of punishment or torture during war and even in prisons in the United States. So profound is our motivation to be around others that the effects of long-term isolation are not only disturbing, they often lead to permanent psychological damage. One study of inmates at a California prison (Haney, 2008) found that months of isolation can literally cause a person to become catatonic, or competely nonresponsive. Another study composed of over 200 interviews of prisoners who had been confined to solitary cells found that one-third became psychotic, losing contact with reality (Grassian, 1983).

Affiliation with others is an essential psychological need. When we are denied contact with other humans, we are not only unable to satisfy biological needs but we also lose our motivation to pursue our highest level needs: self-worth and self-actualization. We are no longer driven to achieve.

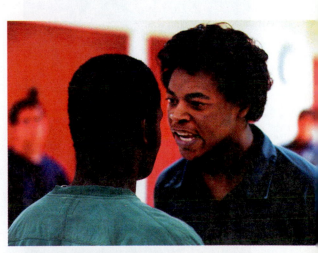

Trying to make gang membership less attractive
In an effort to reduce gang recruitments, many communities arrange for "at risk" teenagers to visit nearby prisons where inmates, such as this individual, make it very clear that gang life led to their present imprisonment. However, research has not consistently indicated that such prevention programs are successful.

Achievement

The fact that you are reading this book means that you are motivated to go to school, study, and obtain a degree. You may even pursue additional degrees or you may graduate and find a job. No matter what path you take, to satisfy the needs at the top of Maslow's pyramid, self-worth and self-actualization, you need to feel competent, engage with others, and possess control over your own life. **Self-determination** theory says that competence, relatedness, and autonomy are instinctive and that they give purpose and meaning to life (Ryan & Deci, 2002). Not all psychologists agree with this theory, though. As you'll see later in this section, other cultures, such as the Chinese, place less importance on autonomy, instead valuing collective effort.

As you might expect, incentives often play a role in motivating us to achieve. In school, you may be motivated intrinsically by curiosity to learn new information. In other words, the behavior may be engaging in and of itself. Or you may be motivated extrinsically by incentives. For instance, your reason for studying hard in this course may be because you are hoping to be rewarded with an *A* at the end of the semester. When achievement is motivated by incentives, it is often associated with competition. People who place too much value on rewards are more likely to suffer when they fail (Sheldon et al., 2004). If they succeed, they may think that the reward, and not their motivation, was the reason for their success. In contrast, psychologists associate intrinsic motivation with the qualities of self-determination theory: competence, relatedness, and autonomy. When you strive to do well for yourself, you enjoy yourself more (Blumenfeld, Kempler, & Krajcik, 2006). See "What Happens in the Brain When We're Motivated to Run a Marathon" on the following pages for a display of what happens in the brain when we strive to achieve in the realm of physical exercise.

Achievement: How we *Develop* Social, or nonbiological motivations, especially those that involve incentives, are not present at birth but are learned. In fact, often, incentive motivations involve inhibiting basic biological drives to obtain the reward. Consider a restaurant server trying to earn money in his or her job. If the server acted on biological instincts and ate the food off the customer's plate, then it would be difficult to keep the job and earn money.

Delaying gratification is especially important for some of the goals you set as a student. Earning a college degree takes a long period of time, during which you often set aside immediate pleasures, such as social activities, in favor of studying. This type of self-control isn't present in very small children, but instead develops over time. The ability to delay gratification requires not just an understanding of the relative worth of the rewards but also an ability to control impulses. Impulse control also develops over time. While playing, toddlers often get into physical fights over sharing toys, whereas preschool and kindergarten-age children react this way less and less.

Developmental psychologists have tested the ability to delay gratification in the laboratory by offering children of varying ages the choice of getting a reward right away or waiting some amount of time to get a better reward. For example, researchers might offer a child the choice of receiving a single M&M immediately or getting a whole bag of M&Ms if they wait 30 minutes. Studies have shown that children display a wide range in the ability to delay gratification; some are much more able to do so than others (Lemmon & Moore, 2007). Related research also suggests that the ability to delay gratification in a laboratory setting may be predictive of success in other realms, including in academic and social settings (Mischel, Shoda, & Rodriguez, 1989).

One likely explanation for the fact that very young children lack the skills necessary to work toward long-term goals and delay instant gratification along the way is that their brains are not yet developed in key areas related to these tasks. The prefrontal cortex is not yet myelinated in children, and the adult levels of synapses connecting them to other neurons are not reached until after puberty. The prefrontal cortex is not only important for mediating reward signals, but also for planning and carrying out complicated tasks that involve several steps toward the achievement of a long-term goal. This may provide some explanation for the common observation that, compared to adults, teenagers are more likely to engage in risky behavior, jeopardizing their futures for instant gratification.

You may find that as you get older, it is easier to set your sights on goals far in the future, including several years away. You realize that your actions in the here and now will contribute to your situation in the future. These are mature thought processes that cannot occur without an intact prefrontal cortex.

Achievement: HOW we Differ Just as psychological and social factors influence our motivation to achieve, so does culture. For instance, one of the elements of self-determination theory, autonomy, does not seem to be essential to individuals who are part of collectivist cultures (Triandis, 2002). As we noted in Chapter 1, people from collectivist cultures tend to view achieving as a cooperative group as preferable to achieving on one's own. Individuals may be motivated to succeed in order to make their organization, team, or country proud, for example, rather than to garner individual recognition for themselves.

Motivation, whether biological or psychological, is complex and inextricably linked with other cognitive processes, such as memory and emotion. In trying to understand why we do the things we do, it is important to remember that society and culture play important roles as well. Whether undertaking the challenge of a hot-dog eating contest or trying to ace a psychology course, our behaviors illustrate that our survival is dependent on the need for purpose.

Collectivist achievement Residents of an Amish community in Pennsylvania help build a new barn for one of their neighbors, a common activity in this collectivist culture which values cooperative achievements over individual ones.

Before You Go On

What Do You Think?
15. Why are we motivated to be socially connected?
16. What are the components of self-determination theory?
17. How do intrinsic and extrinsic motives influence achievement?
18. How does delay of gratification help us reach goals?

What Do You Know? Describe a long-term goal you have and how you might achieve that goal by dividing it into several smaller, short-term goals.

When We're Motivated to Run a Marathon

A marathon is a 26.2 mile race that generally requires months of preparation. Many people follow strict regimens to help them prepare. Runners eagerly sign up for marathons all across the world, in all kinds of weather. What might motivate people to run?

When we are motivated to run for personal achievement, the reward learning pathway—the brain regions involved in basic biological reward, such as the ventral tegmental area, the nucleus accumbens, and the prefrontal cortex – is engaged. In addition, areas that are important for storing the memories of your past running experiences, such as the hippocampus and neocortex, are likely to be involved. The prefrontal cortex is also important for enabling us to attend to our goals and respond flexibly to changes in the terrain as we run. Will you beat your personal best?

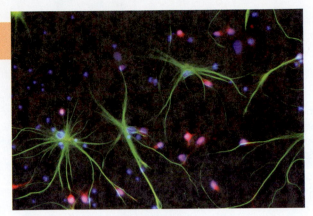

REAPING THE BENEFITS

Long-term exercise increases the number of glial cells (shown here stained with green fluorescent dyes) in the prefrontal cortex, a brain region important for reward learning and cognitive function. Glial cells assist with synaptic function and provide growth factors to sustain neurons, so an increase in their number may improve prefrontal function, potentially enhancing the rewards of running.

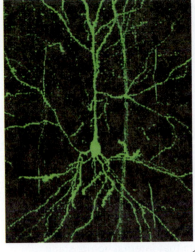

GROWING NEURONS WHILE YOU BUILD MUSCLE

One of the long-term benefits of getting in shape by running is that exercise stimulates the growth of new dendrites and new synaptic connections in the neocortex (shown here in this temporal lobe pyramidal neuron stained with a fluorescent dye). More connections likely translates into greater brain function, enhancing learning and memory.

GETTING THE BLOOD FLOWING

Aerobic exercise increases your heart rate, which sends more blood throughout your body as well as to the brain. Increased blood flow in runners is particularly evident in the hippocampus, shown here in colors on this brain scan. Since the hippocampus is important for anxiety regulation, increased blood flow may contribute to the calming and mood elevating effects often associated with exercise.

Ventral tegmental area

Prefrontal cortex

Nucleus accumbens

Temporal lobe

Hippocampus

Summary

Theories of Motivation

LEARNING OBJECTIVE 1 Compare and contrast major theories of motivation.

- Several theories offer explanations for our motivation but no single theory can explain all our behavior.
- Instinct theory, which suggests that environmental cues stimulate inborn behavioral instincts, best explains motivation that serves basic biological drives, such as eating, drinking, and sex.
- Drive-reduction theory suggests that internal homeostatic mechanisms produce balance within the body by reducing arousal stemming from unmet basic biological needs.
- Arousal theory explains why we sometimes seek to increase, arousal levels. The Yerkes-Dodson law proposes that task performance is best if our arousal level matches that needed for a task.
- Incentive learning produces extrinsic motivation to engage in experiences that do not fulfill basic biological drives. Primary and secondary incentives may both be involved. Different incentives motivate different people.
- Incentive motivation involves brain systems associated with pleasure, incentive learning, and the neurochemical opiate dopamine.
- Maslow proposed that we are motivated by a hierarchy of needs, in which basic survival needs must be satisfied before higher-level needs for belonging, achievement, and self-actualization.

Biological Motivations: Hunger

LEARNING OBJECTIVE 2 Summarize physical and psychological factors that affect our levels of hunger and our eating behavior.

- Hunger, our motivation to eat, is created by the interaction of signals from our stomachs, levels of food-related chemicals in our blood, and brain activity, particularly in the hypothalamus.
- Culture and individual differences interact with our basic biological need for food to determine what foods we will eat, when and with whom we like to eat, and how much we eat.
- Obesity is a major public health problem in the United States. It is usually caused by overeating, which can result from an interaction between genes and the environment.

- Anorexia nervosa is an eating disorder in which individuals believe they are fat and eat too little. Bulimia nervosa is an eating disorder in which people binge on food, then to purge themselves of the food before it can add weight to their bodies.

Biological Motivations: Sex

LEARNING OBJECTIVE 3 Describe factors that affect our sexual motivation and behavior.

- Sexual practices vary widely as a result of cultural influences. Research consistently shows much variety in normal sexual behavior throughout healthy adulthood.
- Sex researchers have described a four-stage sexual response cycle.
- Testosterone and other hormones affect our motivation toward sexual behavior. Many parts of our brains become active during sexual arousal and behavior.
- Four types of sexual problems may occur: sexual dysfunctions, paraphilias, gender identity disorder, and medical problems.
- Sex education programs for teens attempt to reduce their risks of sexually-transmitted infections and pregnancy. Two approaches are comprehensive sex education and abstinence programs.

Psychological Motivations: Affiliation and Achievement

LEARNING OBJECTIVE 4 Describe factors that influence our psychological motivations for affiliation and achievement.

- Affiliation represents our need to interact with others, not only for survival but also for self-worth.
- Isolation puts people at risk of psychological impairments.
- Self-determination theory suggests that we need competence, relatedness, and autonomy to realize our potential.
- Achievement through intrinsic motivation does not involve incentives.
- Individuals who are able to delay gratification can focus on goals and ignore distractions.

Key Terms

CUT/ACROSS CONNECTION

What Happens in the B R A I N ?

- Rewards can lead our brains to release natural painkilling neurochemicals called opiates, the same ones responsible for the so-called "runner's high."
- Damage to different parts of the hypothalamus can lead to either severe overeating or undereating.
- When we see erotic videos or pictures, mirror neurons in the brain activate just as though we were having sex ourselves.

When Things Go *Wrong*

- Two-thirds of people in the United States are overweight.
- Restricted eaters, people who use external cues, such as calorie counts to control their eating, are more likely than nonrestricted eaters to binge after they've eaten a small amount of a high-calorie food.
- Long-term isolation from other people can lead people to develop severe psychological problems.
  - At least 10 percent of men experience erectile disorder and at least 10 percent of women experience sexual arousal disorder.

HOW we Differ

- We eat more in social settings, with other people, than we do when we were alone.
- Men are more likely to fantasize about having lots of sexual partners, but the number of partners men and women say they would like to have in real life is close to the same.
- People in collectivist societies value achievement that contributes to one's groups more highly than individual achievements.

How we *Develop*

- Even as young children, people vary in their ability to delay immediate gratification in exchange for larger rewards later. Some can do it, some cannot.
- Delaying immediate gratification in order to achieve long-term goals may get easier with age for most children and teens, because parts of their brain associated with planning are still developing.

View this in Action

WILEY PLUS +

www.wileyplus.com

Video Lab Exercise

Psychology Around Us

Eating, Body Satisfaction, and Eating Disorders

You Are What You Eat?

In certain respects, eating is the simplest human motive to understand. We must eat or we will die. Yet, it also has become the most complex of human needs in Western society, because, for women, eating is intertwined with issues such as self-concept, self-control, mood, and social engagement. Indeed, some have argued that it is almost impossible to grow up female in Western society and not have a range of upsetting, self-destructive, and deflating attitudes toward food and eating.

In this video exercise, you'll observe several individuals involved in situations that relate to eating and weight. You'll compare the needs and attitudes of the individuals; consider the impact of their attitudes on eating behavior, self-image, mood, and the like; and search for the sources of such attitudes. You'll also come to appreciate that the food attitudes of "normal" females in Western society and females with eating disorders are remarkably similar.

As you are working on this on-line exercise, consider the following questions:

- Do the psychological and biological eating needs of women in Western society complement each other, or do they conflict?
- Given the attitudes of women in Western society toward food and eating, why is obesity a major problem?
- Why do most diets fail?
- Why is the prevalence of eating disorders on the rise in Western society?

CHAPTER 12

Emotion

chapter outline

Emotion in the Driver's Seat

"Road-Rage Accusations Fly over Death," trumpeted the headline to a story detailing how an outburst of violent emotion had sparked a fatal chain of events that resulted in the death of Gregory Moore, a 27-year-old man from San Jose, California.

The chain apparently began when 44-year-old Michael David Shannon persisted in tailgating a car driven by Leslie Holsten, a San Jose woman traveling with her 2-year-old son. After the two cars stopped at a traffic signal, Holsten refused to pull away when the light turned green, hoping to put an end to Shannon's tailgating. In response, Shannon tapped the rear bumper of Holsten's car with his truck. Outraged, Holsten put on the emergency brake, got out of her car, and—after a heated exchange—slapped Shannon's face. According to the deputy district attorney, Shannon then stepped hard on the gas and shoved Holsten's car into the intersection before speeding away.

Only seconds later, Shannon found himself behind another slow-moving vehicle, this time a utility truck. The driver of the truck had slowed down to copy Shannon's license plate number after witnessing Shannon's hit-and-run action against Holsten. Already agitated from the altercation with Holsten, Shannon accelerated around the utility truck. Unable to see what lay beyond the utility truck until it was too late, Shannon's vehicle slammed into a third car, this one driven by Christine Hawley. Gregory Moore, a passenger riding with Hawley, was killed instantly.

Road rage has been defined as an incident in which an angry or impatient motorist or passenger intentionally injures or kills another motorist, passenger, or pedestrian, or threatens to injure or kill another motorist, passenger, or pedestrian (Smart et al., 2007; Rathbone & Huckabee, 1999). Although anger is a common and often adaptive human experience, the explosive and dangerous anger on display in cases of road rage shows how extreme, powerful, and even uncontrollable human emotions can become in certain circumstances.

Of course, anger and rage are not the only emotions people experience, and more often than not, experiencing an emotion does not lead to tragic consequences. In fact, today alone, you have undoubtedly experienced several different emotions—perhaps including happiness, surprise, or fear—and you may even be experiencing clear, readily identified emotions as you read this chapter (hopefully boredom is not one of them). What exactly happens when we experience an emotion? Where do emotions come from? Are emotions meaningful, or are they just noise cluttering up our better judgment? Might even negative emotions be good for us? We will address all these issues in this chapter, but first let's examine a more basic question: What is emotion?

What Is Emotion?

LEARNING OBJECTIVE 1 Define emotion and discuss the components, measurement, and functions of emotion.

Despite all the attention psychologists give to emotion, they have had difficulty agreeing on exactly what an emotion is. Over 500 words in the English language refer to various aspects or forms of emotions, from *affect,* to *mood,* to *feeling,* so perhaps it is not surprising that a unified definition has eluded scientists (Averill, 1980). Nevertheless, psychologists continue to believe that human emotion is one of psychology's most important topics.

Components of Emotion

Most of today's theorists define an **emotion** as an individual state that occurs in response to either an external or an internal event and that typically involves three separate but intertwined components:

1. A *physiological component*—changes in bodily arousal, such as increased heart rate, body temperature, and respiration.
2. A *cognitive component*—the subjective appraisal and interpretation of one's feelings and one's surrounding environment.
3. A *behavioral component*—the expression of emotion through verbal or nonverbal channels, such as smiling, frowning, whining, laughing, reflecting, or slouching.

Let's look more closely at each of these components. Remember, though, that when we experience an emotion, all three are at work.

Physiological Component   The physiological component of emotion refers to the bodily arousal we feel when experiencing a particular emotion, whether it is positive or negative. When, for example, you are nervous about giving a class presentation or going out on a first date, you may notice that your heart beats faster, your hands sweat, and your mouth becomes dry. These physical manifestations of anxiety are produced by your *autonomic nervous system (ANS),* shown in **Figure 12-1**. As described in Chapter 4, the ANS is responsible for regulating various bodily functions and the activity of specific organs, glands, and muscles. Other physiological changes that might occur as we experience an emotion include increased blood pressure, increased blood sugar, pupil dilation, and the inhibition of intestinal action.

Because emotions vary in intensity, some emotions may be accompanied by several physiological changes, while others may involve only a few. If, for example, you are anxious about going out with someone for the first time, you will likely experience less intense and fewer physiological reactions than if you are trying to escape from a fire in a crowded concert hall. The reason for these differences has to do with the *sympathetic nervous system,* the subdivision of the ANS that mobilizes internal resources and primes the organism to take swift action for survival—the *fight-or-flight response.* When waiting for a new date to arrive, your heart may beat faster and your palms may sweat because that is your body's way of signifying the importance of the situation to you. When, however, you need to flee a burning building, more emotional arousal and energy are needed, and the body produces a more intense physiological response. Like fear and anxiety, emotions such as happiness, excitement, and surprise also involve activation of the sympathetic nervous system. Here, too, the intensity of the physiological arousal and the number of bodily changes depend on the nature of the situation.

Emotional ingredients Head football coach John Fox of the Carolina Panthers shows his anger over a referee's call in various ways, including his red face (physiological component), his stated appraisal that a bad call had placed his team in danger of losing (cognitive component), and his yelling at the referee and keeping his fists clenched (behavioral components).

emotion an intrapersonal state that occurs in response to either an external or an internal event and typically involves a physiological component, a cognitive component, and a behavioral component.

Sympathetic Nervous System *Prepares the body for action*		Parasympathetic Nervous System *Returns the body to normal state*
Pupils dilate	**Eyes**	Pupils constrict
Salivation decreases	**Mouth**	Salivation increases
Perspires; goose bumps	**Skin**	Dries up; no goose bumps
Breathing rate increases	**Lungs**	Breathing rate decreases
Accelerates	**Heart**	Slows
Release stress hormones	**Adrenal glands**	Decrease release of stress hormones
Decreased motility	**Digestion**	Increased motility
Blood vessels constrict; blood sugar increases	**Blood**	Blood vessels dilate; blood sugar drops
Perspires	**Palms**	Dries up

FIGURE 12-1 Emotion and the autonomic nervous system The physiological changes we experience in emotion are controlled by the autonomic nervous system. The sympathetic branch arouses the body in situations of anxiety or danger. The parasympathetic branch returns the body to its normal state.

Following an intense physiological reaction, the other component of the ANS, the *parasympathetic nervous system*, works to calm the body down and attempts to conserve energy by returning the organism to a normal state. Later, we will see how various areas of the brain and the endocrine system are involved in each of these processes.

Cognitive Component   The cognitive component of emotion refers to both the evaluative thoughts people have about their emotional experiences (such as "I feel bad") and the appraisal of the events that are producing the emotions. Our interpretation of an event not only helps bring about an emotional reaction but also influences how intensely we will experience that emotion. Consider the event of coming face to face with a grizzly bear. If the grizzly bear is just a cub and is safely behind a protective barrier at the National Zoo, you will probably appraise the situation as pleasant and experience an emotion such as happiness. If, however, a full-grown grizzly bear were to appear in front of you on a hiking trail in the Canadian Rockies, you would likely appraise the situation as life-threatening and experience, among other emotions, very intense fear.

In addition to appraising the situation that gives rise to a particular emotion, people also interpret and evaluate the emotion itself, further shaping how they experience that emotion. If you love to ride roller coasters or amusement park horror rides, you will most likely interpret the bodily arousal you feel while going into a big drop as excitement and thrill. If, in contrast, you dread roller coasters but are talked into riding one by friends, you will likely label that same bodily arousal as fear.

Behavioral Component   When you experience an emotion, you not only have particular thoughts and bodily sensations, but also express and reveal that emotion. You do so through body language, such as facial expressions, gestures, and body posture, as well as through verbal expression. For example, happiness is almost universally expressed with a smile (Leppänen & Hietanan, 2007). Conversely, someone who is frustrated may cross his arms and shrug his shoulders; someone who is angry may clench her teeth and furrow her eyebrows; and a person who is sad may frown, slump, and avoid eye contact.

Research suggests that there are several facial expressions that most people are able to identify accurately. Paul Ekman, a pioneer in the study of emotion and facial expressions, conducted a series of studies in which participants were asked to identify which emotion an individual was experiencing on the basis of the individual's facial cues (Cohn, Ambadar, & Ekman, 2007; Ekman, 2003; Ekman & Friesen, 1975). Ekman and

If you asked people whether they preferred to feel fear or love, the answer would be obvious—right? Then consider this: The adjusted box office revenues of the top 25 horror films surpass those of the top 25 romances by over a billion dollars—even with Titanic, the highest-grossing movie of all time, included among the romances (MPAA).

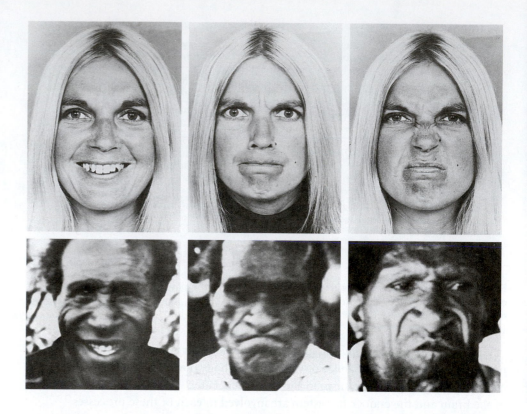

Universal recognition In one study, Paul Ekman traveled to parts of New Guinea where he found that members of the Fore tribe could readily identify the emotions of happiness, anger, and disgust expressed on a Westerner's face (*top row*). Similarly, he found that college students in the United States easily recognized the same emotions when they were expressed on a Fore tribe member's face (*lower row*).

his colleagues found six fundamental emotions that typically can be identified by research participants: anger, sadness, happiness, surprise, fear, and disgust. In fact, some research suggests that the ability to identify the facial expressions for these emotions is genetically programmed (Izard, 2009, 1997, 1977). This would explain why even persons from different countries and cultures readily recognize the same emotions depicted in photographs of facial expressions (Ekman et al., 1987; Ekman & Friesen, 1986).

Although less fundamental to emotional expression than nonverbal emotional behaviors, verbal expression of emotion is also important (Rimé, 2007). Studies asking respondents to recall a recently experienced emotion from memory found that more than 90 percent of them had already talked with someone about that emotion (Luminet et al., 2000). And, when it comes to emotions, once people get started, it's hard for them to stop talking; after someone discloses an emotional experience to another person, that person often discusses it with yet a third person. Researchers Veronique Christophe and Bernard Rimé (2001, 1997) reported that this so-called *secondary social sharing* occurs in more than two-thirds of cases. The likelihood of sharing experiences increases with the intensity of the reported emotion.

An interesting aspect of behavioral expressions of emotion is that just by pretending to express the emotion, people may begin to experience that emotion—a phenomenon you'll come across again later in this chapter. It is worth noting here because it suggests a strong interdependency among the three components of emotion. As we shall soon see, this complex relationship makes the development of a comprehensive theory of emotion a daunting endeavor.

Measurement of Emotions

Researchers typically use three kinds of information to measure an individual's emotions: (1) behavioral displays of emotion, (2) self-reports of emotion, and (3) physiological reactions.

Behavioral displays of emotion are most often observed by objective raters. These displays typically include obvious acts, such as fighting, fleeing, or making sexual advances. Behavioral displays may also include facial expressions. Researchers often observe behavioral displays in role-playing situations. The researchers evoke particular emotional responses from participants by showing them a film, giving them a small gift, or manipulating them in some other way (Isen, 2008, 2004, 1993), and then measure how well the participants perform on tasks of various kinds.

Self-ratings are the most widely used approach to measuring a person's emotional experience. The use of such measures is based on the premise that the best way to evaluate emotional states is to simply ask individuals how they are feeling. Many questionnaires and surveys have been published throughout the years that ask people to provide ratings for how happy, afraid, content, anxious, or depressed they are. The *Positive and Negative Affect Schedule* (*PANAS*), for example, is a measure of various emotional states (Watson & Tellegen, 1985). It contains a list of adjectives, such as *cheerful, angry, sad, happy,* and *timid,* and asks individuals to rate how much they are feeling each emotional state on a scale from 1 ("very slightly") to 5 ("extremely"). Self-report scales such as this offer a fast and convenient measure of emotional experiences. However, self-reports may be inaccurate at times, as they provide only a limited picture of a person's total emotional experience and rely on a person's ability to properly identify and describe an emotional experience.

In recent years, researchers have developed several techniques for measuring an individual's *psychophysiological reactions* to stimuli and have begun using such measures to assess emotional experiences (Santerre & Allen, 2007; Bradley, Cuthbert, & Lang, 1991). This approach is based on the premise that emotions vary biologically from one another (Bradley & Lang, 2007, 2000). These new tools allow the measurement of emotion to go beyond questionnaire-based assessments and may provide a more thorough and accurate report of many of the processes involved in the experience of emotion (Sloan, 2004). Psychophysiological approaches include facial electromyography and assessments of heart rate, skin conductance, and the startle reflex.

- *Facial electromyography (EMG)* A facial EMG measures muscle contractions in specific areas of the face that occur when a person is exposed to an emotionally charged stimulus, such as a pleasant or unpleasant picture. Studies have found that emotional reactions to unpleasant stimuli, such as pictures of mutilated bodies, are often associated with greater activity of the muscles used in frowning. That is, when we are exposed to distressing stimuli, we tend to lower and contract our eyebrows (Sloan et al., 2002; Lang et al., 1993). Conversely, when individuals are shown pleasant stimuli, such as scenic images or sexually provocative pictures, they display heightened activity of the facial muscles responsible for smiling.

- *Heart rate* Reductions in heart rate have been observed when individuals are presented with unpleasant stimuli, whereas pleasant stimuli are associated with accelerations in heart rate (Löw et al., 2008; Bradley & Lang, 2000: Bradley, Cuthbert, & Lang, 1990).

- *Skin conductance* We tend to perspire when we are emotionally aroused. One technique developed to detect and measure emotional arousal involves placing a large electrode on part of the palm of a person's hand and determining from readings of the electrode how well the skin of the hand conducts electrical activity. Such skin conductance—or electrical resistance of the skin—reflects increased perspiration, so a higher conductance reading means greater arousal of emotions. Readings of skin conductance are a very useful indicator of emotional arousal (either positive or negative) and of sympathetic nervous system activity.

- *Startle reflex* An additional physiological indicator of emotional reactivity is the *startle reflex*, an involuntary movement (an eye blink, for example) that is brought on by the onset of a sudden stimulus, such as a loud burst of noise. Researchers usually measure startle reflexes by placing tiny electrodes on the muscle just below a

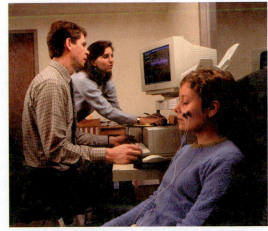

Detecting facial changes EMG measurements indicate that each emotion is accompanied by a distinct set of facial muscle contractions.

person's eye, and assessing the magnitude of involuntary eye blinks that occur when people are startled while viewing pleasant and unpleasant pictures. Studies have revealed that eye blinks that occur while people are viewing unpleasant pictures are larger than those that occur while they are viewing pleasant pictures (Bradley et al., 2007, 1990; Mallan & Lipp, 2007; Bradley, Cuthbert, & Lang, 1991). Odd as it may seem, startle response fluctuations appear to be a very reliable measure of whether people tend to react to life situations with levels of emotional arousal.

Although psychophysiological measures of emotion are in some respects more valid and reliable indicators of emotional states than behavioral displays and self-ratings, most investigators of emotion agree that the complexity of emotion is best measured by using multiple approaches. Thus, the integration of all three types of measures provides the richest picture of a person's overall emotional experience.

Functions of Emotions

Since ancient times, philosophers have often considered emotion inferior to reason, but modern researchers who study emotion have emphasized its positive effects. William James (1842–1910), perhaps the most influential emotion researcher of the last 150 years, declared that, without emotion, consciousness and cognition would be "void of human significance" (1890, p. 471). Just as Technicolor® breathed life into the black-and-white images of early films, emotions provide color to our every experience and lie at the heart of what makes life worth living. Can you imagine riding a roller coaster without expe-

Emotional Decision Making

Wary of strangers Children often rely unconsciously on their emotional states when making decisions about people, particularly strangers, in social situations.

Emotions were once thought to be unimportant to rational decisions, but it appears that in many situations they may, in fact, provide more guidance to us than do our conscious evaluations, even when we are unaware of them (LeDoux, 1996).

Consider the case of Boswell, a man with amnesia so severe that he could not retain any newly acquired knowledge for longer than 60 seconds (Tranel & Damasio, 1993). He could not remember the faces of the caregivers, professionals, or family members who visited him regularly over the 15 years of his amnesia. Nevertheless, he preferred some of his regular caregivers over others. By manipulating Boswell's experiences with his daily caregivers so that one acted as a "good guy," another as a "bad guy," and a third as a "neutral guy", researchers discovered that the emotional content of his daily encounters helped guide Boswell's behavior. He preferred the good and neutral guys to the bad guy. The researchers concluded that Boswell's emotions served an adaptive function; they unconsciously protected him from "'bad guys" who might do him harm.

In everyday life, most of us also experience and are influenced by similar "gut" feelings or intuitions of which we may not be consciously aware. Children often seem to be particularly well-tuned to such feelings, especially about strangers. And adults often unconsciously rely on their emotional states when they make "snap" decisions about people in social situations. In fact, if we're asked to remember an encounter with a stranger, most of us have less difficulty recalling how we felt about that individual than remembering the person's hair color or clothes ensemble (Zajonc, 1980).

Unconscious emotional processing is not always a good thing. Although it may offer protection against menacing social situations, it can also exacerbate social problems by leading to prejudice (DeSteno et al., 2004). One study, for example, demonstrated that angry emotions increased the likelihood of participants agreeing with prejudiced statements about unfamiliar social groups, or *outgroups* (Greenwald & Banaji, 1995). So, while it often makes sense to pay attention to our gut feelings about individuals, it is also important to apply rational thought as we move through life forming judgments and making decisions.

riencing exhilaration (or fear)? How about watching your favorite movie, playing your favorite sport, or spending time with your best friends without feeling some happiness or satisfaction? Without emotions, our most enjoyable activities and experiences might not seem very rewarding. Emotions can serve cognitive, behavioral, and social functions.

Cognitive Functions One function of emotions is to help us organize our memories. As we discussed in Chapter 8, for example, memories associated with emotional content are much easier to recall (Abercrombie et al., 2008). Emotions also help us to prioritize our concerns, needs, or goals in a given moment (Morris, 1992). The information we gain from noticing our emotions may help us form judgments and make decisions (Gohm & Clore, 2002). A strong feeling of fear if you encounter a grizzly bear while out gathering berries in the woods can make it easy to decide which is more important to you, fleeing the bear or filling up your berry basket. As the box on emotional decision making describes, our emotions also guide our judgments in far more everyday circumstances.

Behavioral Functions Emotions, whether positive or negative, can not only help us perform cognitive tasks, such as remembering relevant information, prioritizing our goals, and making decisions, they can also organize our behavior. Generally speaking, we act to minimize our experience of negative emotions and maximize our experience of positive emotions. Such actions can involve basic behaviors, including diverting our attention away from unpleasant or disgusting images in favor of more neutral or positive images, as well as more complex behaviors, such as procrastination. You've probably noticed a correlation between how terrible you believe the experience of working on a homework assignment will be and how long you delay before starting that assignment. In contrast, tasks that we find enjoyable or pleasurable, such as spending time with a boyfriend or girlfriend, are very easy to find time for and hard to delay. In this way, our emotions can help us organize our behaviors (although admittedly in ways that sometimes run counter to our self-interest).

Some theorists describe emotions as messengers that serve a valuable information function, telling us how to respond appropriately to events in our environments (Frijda, 2007, 1986; Parrott, 2004, 2001). Many theorists also believe that particular emotions are associated with predictable patterns of behavior, sometimes called *action tendencies*, that help us to adapt and survive in our social and physical environments (Frijda, 2007, 1986; Gross, 1998; Lang, Bradley, & Cuthbert, 1998). Specific action tendencies associated with key emotions include the following:

- *Happiness* When people who engage in rewarding behaviors or positive interactions feel happiness and joy, they will likely continue to engage in those behaviors or interactions; happiness and joy also signal to people that particular goals have been attained (Carver, 2004; Fredrickson, 2001).

- *Embarrassment* often evokes forgiveness and motivates reconciliation and adherence to social norms (Parrott, 2004, 2001; Keltner & Kring, 1998). Consider, for example, a scenario in which a young employee asks an overweight co-worker when she is due, only to discover that she is not pregnant. Embarrassment may not only lead the unfortunate inquirer to apologize profusely, but also help to ensure that he or she will not make such a careless remark again. Similarly, guilt directs people's awareness toward their transgressions and may trigger conciliatory efforts, personal change, and self-improvement.

- *Anger* signals the presence of injustice and prompts aggression (as we saw at the beginning of this chapter), as well as other self-protective behaviors (Mayer & Salovey, 2004, 1997).

“Human behavior flows from three main sources: desire, emotion, and knowledge.”

–Plato, Greek philosopher

"Let's do this again next week" Emotions can be viewed as messengers that predict particular *action tendencies*. Given that bathing their dog in an outside tub brings this family so much joy, they are likely to repeat the activity again and again.

Research suggests that the avoidance of negative emotion is typically a more powerful motivator than the achievement of positive emotion (Cacioppo & Berntsen, 1994).

- *Anxiety* directs a person's attention toward potential threats and motivates appropriate action to avoid or cope with them (Öhman, 2000).
- *Sadness* may signal the loss of positive relationships and help people to seek needed support and assistance from others (Oatley & Jenkins, 1996; Campos et al., 1989).

Social Functions   Another important function of emotions appears to be coordination of relationships. Emotions form the foundations of relationships by helping us develop a sense that we like and trust another person. In one study, for example, viewers assigned more positive ratings of friendliness and competence to people who showed a sincere smile in their yearbook photographs than to those whose pictures had fake smiles or no smiles (Harker & Keltner, 2001).

Emotions, even when they're negative, can also improve the quality of our relationships. Research suggests, for example, that the more a married couple talk about their feelings, the happier they are (Gottman & Levenson, 1988). In contrast, keeping our emotions inside may get in the way of our ability to form lasting relationships. One study found that participants who habitually kept their emotions to themselves were more likely to report problems with closeness and sharing in intimate relationships than people who talked about their emotions (Gross & John, 2003).

In an experimental study of this idea, researchers asked pairs of unacquainted women to watch a documentary clip designed to produce disgust, anger, and sadness (Butler et al., 2003). Following the clip, the researchers asked the women to interact with each other (see **Figure 12-2**). Half of the participants had been asked to suppress their emotional reactions to the documentary, and these participants later demonstrated heightened physiological arousal and reported less rapport with their partners. Similarly, the partners of these suppressors felt less rapport, liked their partners less than partners who did not suppress, and were less willing to form a friendship with the partners. In short, the opportunity to express negative emotions led to more positive social encounters, indicating that emotional expressiveness may have a direct impact on feelings of intimacy.

	During documentary	After documentary	
Pair 1	Asked to suppress emotional reactions	→	Less responsive interaction
Pair 2	Not asked to suppress emotional reactions	→	More responsive interaction

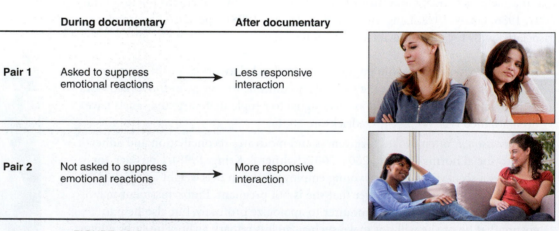

FIGURE 12-2 Emotional expressiveness improves the quality of relationships In one study of the social function of emotion, pairs of women watched a disturbing documentary clip. One group was asked to suppress their emotional reactions while watching the clip, the other half was not instructed to do so. After the documentary, when the pairs were asked to interact with each other, those who had suppressed their emotions were less responsive and felt less rapport with their partners. The study demonstrated that suppressed emotions can lead to poor social relations (Butler et al., 2003).

Before You Go On

What Do You Know?

1. What system produces the bodily arousal associated with emotions?
2. What three types of information are most commonly used by researchers to measure emotions?
3. Name four physiological indicators of emotional state.
4. What are the major functions of emotion?

What Do You Think? Think about the road-rage incident described in our opening example and describe what you think the physiological, cognitive, and behavioral components of the various drivers might have been.

Where Do Emotions Come From?

LEARNING OBJECTIVE 2 Discuss the major theories of emotion.

Since the birth of psychology, a number of theories have been proposed to explain how emotions occur and what causes them: the James-Lange theory, the Cannon-Bard theory, the Schacter and Singer two-factor theory, the cognitive-mediational theory, and the facial-feedback theory. Each theory proposes a different twist on the sequence of an emotional episode and each emphasizes a particular component of emotion (physiological, cognitive, or behavioral). In addition, evolutionary theory has important things to say about the origins of emotion.

James-Lange Theory

As we observed earlier, William James was the earliest and one of the most influential psychologists to study emotion. James took issue with the conventional common-sense explanation of emotion, which suggests that an event triggers an emotion, which leads to physiological changes, followed by a behavioral response to the situation. Looking at the road-rage example that began this chapter, the common sense explanation would suggest that Michael Shannon became angry in response to Leslie Holsten's driving. As a result, we can imagine that his heart started beating faster and his face became flushed and red. Once he experienced this high arousal, he began tailgating Holsten.

James (1884, 1890) argued that emotions proceed differently. He suggested that an emotion begins with (1) the perception of an environmental situation or event, followed by (2) the elicitation of physiological and behavioral changes, which are then (3) processed by the cortex and converted into felt emotion. In other words, Shannon did not become angry and then, as a result, experience high physiological arousal; instead, he experienced high physiological arousal and interpreted it as anger. James believed that our physiological response to a stimulus occurs prior to, and provides the basis for, the experience of a particular emotion.

In 1885, a Danish physiologist, Carl Lange (1834–1900), published a theory of emotion that was very similar to James's. Both theorists believed that there is no emotion to experience without a physiological component (Davidson, Jackson, & Kalin, 2000). Their views are collectively referred to as the **James-Lange theory of emotion**.

Although the two theories are very similar, they do have a few key differences. Whereas James believed there is a place for cognition in the context of an emotional episode, Lange viewed mental activity as having little to do with emotion. Lange (1885) postulated instead that the *vasomotor center*, a collection of nerves and muscles that cause the blood vessels

James-Lange theory of emotion a theory proposing that felt emotions result from physiological changes, rather than being their cause.

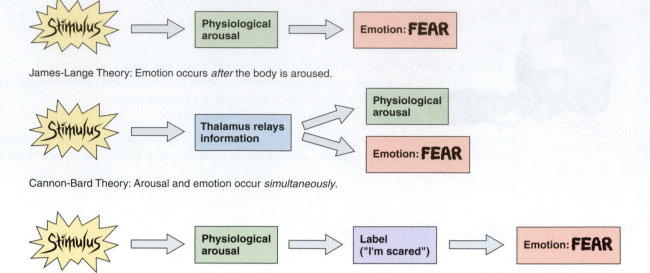

James-Lange Theory: Emotion occurs *after* the body is aroused.

Cannon-Bard Theory: Arousal and emotion occur *simultaneously*.

Schachter and Singer's Two-Factor Theory: Both physiological arousal *and* a cognitive label determine the emotion experienced.

FIGURE 12-3 **Three major theories of emotion**

to constrict or dilate, is the root cause of all emotion: "We owe all the emotional side of our mental life, our joys and sorrows, our happy and unhappy hours, to our vasomotor system." **Figure 12-3** compares the James-Lange theory with the two theories that we'll turn to next, the Cannon-Bard theory and the Schachter and Singer two-factor theory.

Cannon-Bard Theory

The James-Lange theory of emotion produced quite a stir in the fields of psychology and physiology, and much research was published disputing various pieces of it. The leading critic of the James-Lange theory was Harvard psychologist Walter Cannon (1871–1945). Central to Cannon's criticism was the James-Lange theory's notion that *visceral organs*—that is, our internal organs in which physiological arousal occurs, such as the heart—can produce complex emotional experiences. Pointing to a number of research findings, Cannon disputed the accuracy of the James-Lange theory on five different points:

1. *Total separation of the visceral organs from the central nervous system does not alter emotional behavior.* Cannon cited research on dogs and cats whose vasomotor centers had been disconnected from their central nervous systems. Even without the vasomotor center that Lange believed to be of utmost importance, cats and dogs continued to display aggression and rage in the usual way. Similarly, more recent studies indicate that most human patients with spinal cord injuries continue to experience emotional excitability that is similar to their functioning prior to injury; some actually report an increase in the intensity of particular emotions (Bermond et al., 1991; Chwalisz, Diener, & Gallager, 1988).

2. *The same visceral changes often occur in different emotional states and in nonemotional states.* Recall that the arousal associated with emotions arises from the sympathetic nervous system. Cannon argued that, because the activity of the sympathetic nervous system is typically general and nonspecific, several emotions probably share similar patterns of visceral activity. Cannon further noted that certain nonemotional events, such as fever, produce patterns of sympathetic nervous system activity that are similar to the patterns that accompany emotions, although they are not experienced as emotions.

3. *The viscera are rather insensitive structures.* According to Cannon, "We can feel the thumping of the heart because it presses against the chest wall, we can also feel the throbbing of the blood vessels because they pass through tissues well supplied with sensory nerves . . . [but], normally, the visceral processes are extraordinarily undemonstrative" (1927, p. 111).

4. *Visceral changes are too slow to be the source of emotional feeling.* Cannon argued that the amount of time it takes for the body's vasomotor system to communicate with the brain and send impulses back to the rest of the body is too slow "to be the occasion for the appearance of affective states" (1927, p. 112).

5. *Artificially inducing visceral changes does not produce strong emotions.* Citing research by the Spanish psychologist Gregorio Marañón (1924), Cannon pointed out that the injection of adrenaline, a stimulant, into the bloodstream of research participants, which activates the sympathetic nervous system and produces visceral changes characteristic of intense emotions, does not lead to discrete and identifiable emotional reactions.

"I'm sorry, I didn't hear what you said. I was listening to my body."

Following his critique of the James-Lange theory, Cannon (1927) offered his own explanation of emotion, which was later elaborated on by Philip Bard (1934), an American physiologist. This theory, often referred to as the **Cannon-Bard theory of emotion**, states that when we perceive an emotionally stirring event, the *thalamus*, a key brain structure, simultaneously relays information about the event to both the sympathetic nervous system and to the parts of the brain that are active in thought and decision making. As a result, the subjective experience of emotion and the activation of the sympathetic nervous system (that is, bodily arousal) occur simultaneously (see Figure 12-4 again). According to the Cannon-Bard theory, Michael Shannon would have simultaneously experienced both rage and physiological arousal when he perceived Leslie Holsten in front of his car, blocking his way.

Schachter and Singer's Two-Factor Theory

In 1962, Stanley Schachter and Jerome Singer, social psychologists at Columbia University, published a landmark study that helped change psychology's understanding of emotion. According to Schachter and Singer (1962), earlier theories had neglected to consider the influence of cognition, or thought processes, in our emotional experiences. Physiological differences alone are too subtle to define specific emotional states, said these researchers; it is our cognitive appraisal of the immediate situation that provides a label ("I am afraid") for our bodily feelings. According to **Schachter and Singer's two-factor theory of emotion**, "It is the cognition which determines whether the state of physiological arousal will be labeled as 'anger,' 'joy,' 'fear,' or 'whatever'" (Schachter & Singer, 1962, p. 380). Schachter and Signer suggested that, although physiological arousal is *necessary* for an emotion to occur, in fact determining the intensity of the emotional experience, it's up to our cognitive faculties to determine our specific emotional state (see Figure 12-4).

If we were to apply Schachter and Singer's two-factor theory to Michael Shannon's case, we would assume that the severity of his actions was determined by his level of physiological arousal. If his arousal had been mild or moderate, he might have appraised the situation differently ("Stuck in traffic again") and might have responded in a mildly angry or frustrated way (perhaps cursing in the privacy of his car or raising his middle finger at Holsten). Instead, however, we would presume that he experienced intense physiological arousal and appraised the situation in a way that led to anger ("That woman is purposely getting in my way"), making him respond in ways that ultimately had fatal consequences.

Cannon-Bard theory of emotion a theory proposing that the subjective experience of emotion and the activation of the sympathetic nervous system (that is, bodily arousal) occur simultaneously.

Schachter and Singer's two-factor theory of emotion a theory proposing that an emotional state is a function of both physiological arousal and cognition.

Schachter and Singer's two-factor theory also suggests that, when the cause of our physical arousal is not immediately clear to us, we use cues from our surroundings to help us identify a cause. This can lead to mislabeling physical arousal from a nonemotional source as an emotion. Schacter and Singer conducted one of psychology's most famous experiments at the University of Minnesota to test this idea (see **Figure 12-4**). They told undergraduate research participants that the study was examining the effects of a vitamin supplement (called *Suproxin*) on vision. When the students arrived at the lab, they were met by an experimenter and told that they would be receiving a small injection of Suproxin and then would complete several vision tests. The participants then received an injection of either epinephrine (adrenalin) or a placebo (saline solution). By producing physiological arousal, the epinephrine injections mimicked sympathetic nervous system activation. Among those who received epinephrine, one-third (the *informed group*) were told they might experience side effects, such as palpitations, trembling, and facial flushing; one-third (the *deceived group*) were told they would experience no side effects; and one-third (the *misinformed group*) were told they would experience side effects that were not in fact likely to occur, such as headaches. All the participants in the placebo group were told they would have no side effects from their injections. After the participants were given the drug, a confederate of the experimenters' entered the room and acted either euphoric or angry. These manipulations allowed Schachter and Singer to create a scenario in which participants experienced bodily arousal either with or without plausible explanations for it.

As Schachter and Singer's two-factor theory had predicted, students who received an epinephrine injection but were not given a proper explanation for their bodily arousal (the deceived and misinformed groups) later reported feelings of anger or euphoria. In contrast, students in the epinephrine condition who were told to anticipate various symptoms of sympathetic nervous system activity (informed group) did not experience anger or euphoria—they were immune to any effects of the arousal manipulation. Clearly, the label of an emotion is influenced by whether or not a person has an appropriate explanation for his or her arousal.

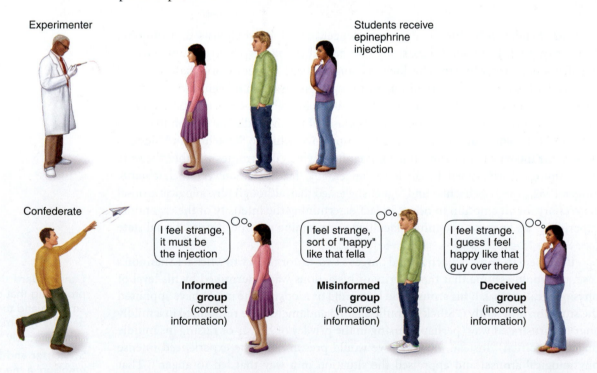

FIGURE 12-4 **Testing the two-factor theory** In the absence of correct information, participants in the deceived and misinformed groups who received the epinephrine injection concluded that they were feeling happy, like the confederate who had acted euphoric.

Schachter and Singer's two-factor theory served to redirect the focus of emotion research toward the role of cognitive factors. Indeed, a number of studies have since provided indirect evidence for their two-factor theory. In one study, for example, male participants were confronted by an attractive female (a confederate of the researchers) and asked to complete questionnaires. Males confronted by the woman while crossing the Capilano Suspension Bridge in British Columbia, Canada—a long, narrow footbridge constructed of wooden boards and wire cables suspended 100 feet above the river—reported being more attracted to the female confederate than males who met the same woman on a wider, sturdier bridge only 10 feet above the river (Dutton & Aron, 1974). The researchers concluded that the men on the Capilano Bridge had experienced anxious arousal because of the height of the bridge and had misinterpreted this arousal as sexual attraction—findings consistent with Schachter and Singer's two-factor theory.

Cognitive-Mediational Theory

One theory that built on Schachter and Singer's ideas was developed by Richard Lazarus, an influential psychologist at the University of California, Berkeley. As we shall see in Chapter 14, Lazarus spent much of his career investigating the role of appraisal in people's reactions to stress (Lazarus, 2007; Lazarus et al., 1965; Lazarus & Alfert, 1964). Eventually, Lazarus came to believe that appraisal must play a similar role in emotional experiences that it plays in stress reactions. Unlike Schachter and Singer's two-factor theory, Lazarus' theory holds that appraisal affects not only how people interpret physical arousal, but also the level of arousal itself. As such, the **cognitive-mediational theory of emotion** views cognitive interpretations of events as playing a still broader role in the experience of emotion.

In one of his early studies, for example, Lazarus and his colleagues had participants watch stressful films (featuring, for example, skin-piercing rituals among Australian tribesmen) while their autonomic nervous system activity was measured and their subjective reports of stress were recorded. Some of the viewers were told "the people in this film were not hurt or distressed by what is happening," while others were told, "many of the people you see in this film suffered severe pain and infection from these rituals." By influencing the way the participants construed what was happening in the films, Lazarus and his colleagues found they could greatly alter the participants' physiological activity and subjective stress reactions while viewing. That is, appraisal serves as a *cognitive mediator* between environmental stimuli and people's reaction to those stimuli (Lazarus, 2007, 1993).

Facial-Feedback Theory

We mentioned earlier, in discussing the behavioral component of emotion, that people may begin to experience an emotion just by pretending to express it. Related to this observation is the **facial-feedback theory of emotion**, which is derived from Charles Darwin's early (1872) notion that muscular activity can either strengthen or lessen the experience of emotion. According to the current facial-feedback perspective, our subjective experiences of emotion are influenced by sensory feedback we receive from the activity of our facial muscles, our **facial efference** (Izard, 2007, 1997, 1977; Tomkins, 1962). Thus, facial expressions not only express a given emotion but also intensify the physiological experience of that emotion.

In one study, for example, participants were directed to move their facial muscles into certain positions, without directly being told which emotions they were expressing. The facial changes produced significant changes in their autonomic nervous system arousal, as indicated by increases in their heart rates, skin conductance,

Echoes of the Capilano Bridge study This young man and woman run into each other for the first time while looking out from a wooden-boarded, not-so-sturdy footbridge that stands high above the water. If surveyed by a nosy researcher, each of them would probably report being more attracted to the other than they would if they had met on a sturdier and lower (i.e., less arousing) bridge.

cognitive-mediational theory of emotion a theory proposing that cognitive interpretations, particularly appraisals, of events are the keys to experiences of emotion.

facial-feedback theory of emotion a theory proposing that subjective experiences of emotion are influenced by sensory feedback from facial muscular activity, or *facial efference*.

facial efference sensory feedback from facial muscular activity.

and finger temperatures (Ekman, Levenson, & Friesen, 1983). In a related study, research participants held pens in their mouths while rating the funniness of cartoons (Strack, Martin, & Stepper, 1988). This approach enabled the experimenters to manipulate the participants' facial expressions without calling attention to their facial activity or to the emotions normally associated with that activity. People directed to hold the pen in their teeth made a face similar to a smile, while those directed to hold the pen with their lips were unable to smile (**Figure 12-5**). Sure enough, individuals who held the pen in their teeth found the cartoons funnier than those who held the pen in their lips.

The facial-feedback theory of emotion has also been supported by studies of the *Duchenne smile*, named after French neurologist Guillaume Duchenne. Duchenne observed that smiles reflecting genuine emotion involve the activity of certain muscles near the mouth and the eyes, whereas more artificial "social smiles" involve only muscles near the mouth (see **Figure 12-6**). One experiment found that participants who displayed genuine, Duchenne smiles while viewing a positive film clip displayed greater physiological arousal and experienced more positive emotion than other participants (Soussignan, 2002).

How might facial expressions produce physiological arousal and the subjective experience of emotion? Several explanations have been proposed. It may be that facial expressions serve as *relays* between an emotionally stirring event and a resulting subjective experience of emotion. Indeed, the psychologist Silvan Tomkins (1962) argued that emotionally stirring stimuli activate an inborn, almost reflexive "affect program" that sends signals throughout the body by motor and circulatory pathways, bypassing the parts of the brain involved in cognition. The body reacts to these signals in forms, such as facial expressions (smiles, frowns) and other activities, which then supply sensory feedback to the brain, producing the experience of an emotion. Tomkins (1992, 1980) further argued that receptors in the face change position when people contract their facial muscles and that this sensory information is also sent to the brain, ultimately leading to a felt emotion.

Another theory is that patterns of facial muscle activity change the temperature of blood entering the brain and by doing so affect neuron activity in the brain, eventually producing particular emotional states. In one study, researchers had research participants repeat a series of vowel sounds, *i, e, o, a, ü, ah,* and *u*, while measuring

FIGURE 12-5 Testing the facial-feedback theory When you hold a pen between your teeth, you activate facial muscles that are associated with a smile and you are more likely to report pleasant feelings than if you held the pen between your lips (Strack, Martin, & Stepper, 1988).

"A smile is the universal welcome."

—Max Eastman, American writer

FIGURE 12-6 **Genuine versus artificial smiles** Real or Duchenne smiles reflect genuine emotion and involve muscles near the mouth and the eyes (left). Social or artificial smiles involve only muscles near the mouth (right).

blood temperature in the participants' brains (Zajonc, Murphy, & Inglehart, 1989). The researchers hypothesized that the pronunciation of *e* and *ah* would produce muscular patterns similar to that of a smile and an expression of surprise, respectively. Similarly, the long *u* sound, *ü*, was expected to mimic aspects of facial expressions associated with negative emotions. The results showed that facial efference of this kind did indeed produce negative and positive feelings, as well as corresponding changes in brain blood temperature. Apparently, saying the long *u* sound restricts peoples' ability to breathe through their noses. Breathing through the nose generally cools our blood before it reaches our brains. Because participants in the Zajonc study were breathing less through their noses, they experienced a rise in brain blood temperature, and, along with that, a rise in negative emotions. In contrast, the pronunciation of *e* and *ah* increases nose breathing, allowing the cooling of blood traveling to the brain, and ultimately produces positive emotional experiences—a pattern also confirmed by participants in this study.

It is important to note that none of the theories just discussed seems to explain emotion completely. As psychologist Robert Zajonc has said, "It is unlikely that all emotions have the same etiology, are characterized by the same affective and cognitive processes, . . . or have the same underlying neuroanatomical structure and neurochemical actions" (Zajonc et al., 1989, p. 412). Thus, one emotional experience may result largely from of a singular source, such as physiological arousal, cognitive appraisal, or facial expression, while others may be the product of a combination of these factors.

Evolutionary Theory

Over the past 50 years, a number of theorists have suggested that emotions are innate, prewired responses that have evolved over millions of years, from lower species to humans (Izard, 2007; Cosmides & Tooby, 2000; Plutchik, 1980). This perspective is based on the evolutionary theory of Charles Darwin, described in Chapter 1.

In 1872, having noted the similarities in emotional expression across and within species throughout the world, Darwin published *The Expression of the Emotions in Man and Animals*. Here he argued that emotional expression in both people and animals serves a *communicative* function that is essential to survival. Emotional expressions may, for example, warn others of danger, dissuade enemies from attacking, or signal sexual receptiveness (Seyfarth & Cheney, 2003; LeDoux, 1996).

Evolutionary psychologists argue that certain emotions have been passed down through the generations because they have played an integral role in the survival of our

basic emotions a group of emotions prepro-grammed into all humans regardless of culture.

species (Nesse & Ellsworth, 2009; Nesse, 1990). It may even be that each emotion corresponds to a particular situation that has occurred repeatedly throughout the course of evolution and that each emotion increases an individual's ability to cope with the adaptive challenges that arise in such a situation (see **Table 12-1**). For example, organisms that experienced fear when confronted by predators most likely survived at a much higher rate than those that experienced calm during such interactions. Over time, as this situation was repeated, fear became a characteristic response to danger and, eventually, an innate, prewired, and automatic response. Such patterns of emotionality have been genetically passed on to us from generations of ancestors, making our lives much easier than if we were required to learn about every aspect of our environmental surroundings without their guidance.

Much of the research support for an evolutionary explanation of emotion centers on the universal and innate nature of facial expressions of emotion. As we observed earlier, Paul Ekman and his colleagues have conducted a series of studies on facial expressions of emotion (Cohn et al., 2007; Ekman, 2003; Ekman & Friesen, 1971). They have found that individuals from many different cultural and language backgrounds, when presented with photographs of different facial expressions, are fairly accurate at selecting the emotions being expressed. Individuals from places such as Estonia, Ethiopia, Turkey, and Japan, for example, similarly recognize facial expressions of happiness, anger, fear, disgust, surprise, and sadness (Ekman et al., 1987). One study even found that the inhabitants of isolated villages in Papua, New Guinea—who had never seen a photograph, magazine, film, or television—recognized facial expressions of emotion with the same degree of accuracy as individuals from countries exposed to Western media (Ekman & Friesen, 1971).

Based on research on the universality of certain facial expressions and the evolution of emotion, a number of theorists have suggested that some innate, **basic emotions** are preprogrammed into all people, regardless of culture or country of origin. Tomkins (1962) has proposed that there are eight basic emotions: surprise, interest, joy, rage, fear, disgust, shame, and anguish. Other notable theorists have proposed similar lists (Frijda, 1986; Plutchik, 1980; Izard, 1977). Indeed, it appears that infants typically display the facial expressions of such fundamental emotions very early in life (Izard, 1994). Even children who are born without sight display facial expressions similar to those of sighted children of the same age (Galati et al., 2003; Goodenough, 1932).

TABLE 12-1 Evolutionary Links Between Emotion and Behavior in Humans and Other Animals

Situation	Emotion	Survival function
Threat	Fear, terror, anxiety	Fight, flight
Obstacle	Anger, rage	Biting, hitting
Potential mate	Joy, ecstasy, excitement	Courtship, mating
Loss of valued person	Sadness, grief	Crying for help
Sudden novel object	Surprise	Stopping, attending

Source: Plutchik, 1980.

Before You Go On

What Do You Know?
5. What was the key idea in the James-Lange theory of emotion?
6. What were Cannon's arguments disputing this idea?
7. What element did Schachter and Singer's two-factor theory add to explanations of what determines emotional experience?
8. What is facial efference?
9. What does it mean to say that emotions have been shaped by natural selection?

What Do You Think? Recall a powerful emotional experience you have had. Which of theories of emotion detailed in this chapter seems to best explain your experience? Is one theory sufficient?

Emotion How we *Develop*

LEARNING OBJECTIVE 3 Contrast the cognitive theory of emotional development with the differential emotions theory.

We have discussed several ideas about how emotions evolved in the human species, but what about how emotions develop in each individual as that person grows from infant to adult? Next, we will discuss two contrasting theories of emotional development. One holds that emotions unfold as a consequence of neural and cognitive development, while the other argues that emotions themselves help spur neural growth and the development of cognitive processes.

As you will see, research on facial expressions, which we discussed in the preceding section, plays a role in both theories.

Lewis's Cognitive Theory of Emotional Development

Developmental psychologist Michael Lewis has proposed a cognitive theory of emotional development suggesting that most emotions can be experienced and expressed only *after* particular cognitive abilities have developed. According to Lewis (2008, 2007, 2005, 1992), children are born with a limited capacity for emotional experience—a capacity that expands enormously over the first three years of life, culminating eventually in the development of a full range of emotions.

As you may have observed, newborn infants often vacillate between only a few *mood states*, appearing either distressed (when hungry, tired, lonely, or in need of changing) or content (when satiated, rested, and secure). Although they display startle reactions in the presence of sudden, loud noises, and show signs of hunger at the sight of food, their emotional responses remain rather undifferentiated until certain milestones in their cognitive development have been achieved. According to Lewis, those key cognitive milestones include the abilities to perceive and discriminate stimuli, to recall memories of past events and compare them with current situations, and to be aware of themselves and compare themselves with others (Lewis, 2008, 2007, 2005, 1992).

By the time babies are 3 months of age, their emotional repertoire has expanded to include happiness and excitement at the sight of familiar objects and faces and sadness at the loss of positive stimuli, such as a parent's attention. In addition, infants begin to demonstrate disgust during this time, characterized by spitting out unpleasant-tasting objects (Lewis, 2000). Between 4 and 6 months, infants begin to express anger when they are frustrated and surprise when confronted with situations that are unexpected.

differential emotions theory a theory holding that particular emotions or sets of emotions become more prominent during specific life stages as they serve stage-related developmental processes.

By 7 to 8 months of age, most infants display fearfulness. According to Lewis (2000), fearfulness emerges only after infants develop the ability to compare a fear-eliciting event with an internal representation of a similar event that was previously encountered. When, for example, 8-month-old children see an adult, they compare the adult's face with their internal representations or memories of adult faces that they have previously encountered. Based on this comparison, they determine whether the adult is a stranger, and so someone to fear, or a familiar person who can be trusted. Thus, by 8 months of age, after they have developed the cognitive abilities to recall and compare stimuli, most infants exhibit the fundamental emotions—anger, sadness, happiness, surprise, fear, and disgust—identified in studies of facial expressions (Ekman & Friesen, 1986, 1975).

For the next year of life, an infant's emotional development remains stable. No new emotions emerge, although those in the current repertoire are enhanced. From 18 to 24 months, however, children reach the cognitive milestone of paying attention to themselves, and this eventually gives rise to *objective self-awareness*, an ability to look at themselves as objects, with a clear understanding that they are separate from other people (Lewis, 2000). Such cognitive development enables them to experience so-called *emotions of self-consciousness*, such as envy, empathy, and embarrassment.

A final cluster of emotions emerge between the second and third year of life, following the achievement of another cognitive milestone—the capacity to compare one's behavior against external or internal standards, which eventually include such points of comparison as parents, teachers, and personal ideals (Lewis, 2008, 2007, 1992). These emotions, which Lewis calls *self-conscious evaluative emotions*, include pride, shame, and guilt. Although emotional development continues well into adolescence and beyond, and is further shaped by external factors, such as cultural rules, the most significant growth and achievement of emotional milestones is complete by the age of 3.

Izard's Differential Emotions Theory

Emotion researcher Carroll Izard suggests that emotions, rather than emerging as a result of cognitive development, actually help trigger the achievement of social and cognitive milestones. In his **differential emotions theory**, Izard argues that emotions have evolved largely to help individuals develop and that emotions aid in the successful completion of various stages of development (Izard, 2007, 1991, 1977; Abe & Izard, 1999).

During the third or fourth month of life, for example, the emotional experiences of an infant and caregiver play off each other more and more, giving rise to two emotional milestones of infancy: the ability to regulate emotions and the formation of attachment bonds with caregivers. The infant's achievement of these emotional milestones, in turn, triggers the emergence of exploratory behaviors. Feeling secure that their parents are nearby and available, infants increasingly are able to examine their surroundings. Similarly, Izard argues that emotional interactions of one kind or another eventually help trigger the achievement of such later cognitive and social milestones as the acquisition of moral standards, the ability to make social comparisons, the emergence of a self-concept, and the ability to think abstractly (Izard, 2007; Abe & Izard, 1999).

Before You Go On

What Do You Know?

10. What cognitive milestones did Lewis identify as keys to emotional development in infants?
11. In Izard's view, what is the developmental relationship between cognition and emotion?

What Do You Think?   Imagine a toddler showing interest and happiness as she examines her reflection in a mirror with her mother nearby. How would you explain her emotions in terms of Lewis's cognitive-mediational theory? Izard's differential emotions theory?

Just as evolution has helped shape the nature of human emotions, thousands of years of natural selection have helped mold and re-mold the human brain, enabling it to adapt to an ever-changing environment. The brain has not evolved as a single unified entity; rather, different parts have evolved at different times, each at its own pace. Thus, the brain structures involved in emotion are located in several different regions of the brain, rather than in a unified "emotion center." The cluster of brain structures that are activated when we are confronted by a rattlesnake, for example, is different from the cluster of structures that springs into action when we feel lust or love toward someone.

Recent neuroscience research suggests that when committed Democrats and Republicans are asked to evaluate negative information about their chosen presidential candidate, brain activity increases in parts of their brains associated with emotion rather than in the cognitive decision-making areas of their brains.

Early Theories

As we observed earlier, Walter Cannon (1927, 1929) and Phillip Bard (1928, 1929, 1934) were among the first to propose that the brain plays a key role in the production of emotional states. Their view was supported by research in which they removed structures from the brains of cats, piece by piece, trying to pinpoint the area responsible for rage. They found that the removal of the *hypothalamus* affected this emotional response more than the removal of any other structure, and they concluded that this brain structure was the emotion center of the brain (see **Figure 12-7**). They proposed that emotional stimuli first pass through sensory channels, such as vision and hearing, to the *thalamus*, a brain structure located above the hypothalamus. As we saw in Chapter 5, the thalamus serves as a relay station for a great deal of incoming information in the brain. According to Cannon and Bard, the thalamus sends the emotional information simultaneously to the hypothalamus and to the *cerebral cortex*, the region of the brain responsible for complex functions. The hypothalamus processes this information and produces

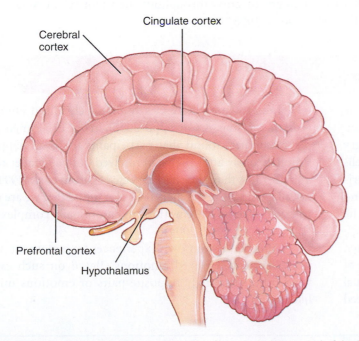

FIGURE 12-7 Brain structures linked to emotion This figure indicates several of the brain parts that have been tied to emotion by various theories.

a bodily response, while the cerebral cortex converts the information into a feeling—the conscious experience of emotion.

In 1937, an anatomy researcher named James Papez expanded Cannon and Bard's theory by suggesting that incoming sensory information is actually split by the thalamus into two *streams of information*. A *stream of thinking* is sent to the cerebral cortex for processing, while a *stream of feeling* is routed to the hypothalamus. The two streams eventually are reunited in the hypothalamus and a full emotional experience is produced (Dalgleish, 2004; LeDoux, 1996).

Conducting research during the same period as Papez, two other scientists, Heinrich Klüver and Paul Bucy, found evidence that the brain's *temporal lobes* also play a key role in emotion. In the course of research on vision, these two researchers found that monkeys whose temporal lobes had been removed became unusually tame and fearless (Klüver & Bucy, 1937). Although Klüver and Bucy had not been investigating emotions per se, their finding suggested that much of the processing of emotional stimuli may take place in the temporal lobes.

In 1949, Paul MacLean coined the term *limbic system* to describe a system of structures of the brain that work together in creating emotions. The limbic system includes the thalamus, hypothalamus, hippocampus, cingulate cortex, amygdala, and prefrontal cortex—some of the same structures of interest to the earlier emotion researchers. Because it includes many structures that are also present in less complex mammals, MacLean believed that the limbic system continues to be responsible for primitive brain functions, such as emotion, and that it, in fact, evolved in order to help humans control their emotional functioning. Eventually, MacLean (1970) further suggested that our most basic emotions, such as fear and aggression, actually are processed in areas of the brain that evolved even earlier: the brainstem and cerebellum.

Current Research

Although MacLean's notion that the limbic system plays an important role in emotions has been supported by numerous studies, recent research indicates that his ideas were not entirely correct. Research now indicates that the limbic system alone does not control emotion. Instead, as mentioned at the beginning of this section, emotional processes are controlled by a number of areas throughout the brain (Cain & LeDoux, 2008; Schiller et al., 2008; LeDoux, 1996).

Mixed Emotions

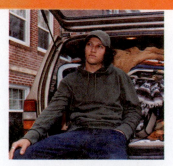

We often think of emotions as opposing pairs. For example, you might be either sad *or* happy, angry *or* calm. Common experience tells us, however, that often we experience *mixed emotions*, degrees and combinations of emotions that lie in between such pairs of opposites.

As you've seen in this chapter, positive and negative emotional experiences may reflect activation of different areas of the brain, particularly different areas of the prefrontal cortex (LeDoux, 1995). If so, it seems to imply that we could indeed feel both positive and negative emotions simultaneously.

Studies demonstrate clearly that such mixed emotions exist (Larsen, McGraw, & Cacioppo, 2001). In one experiment, for example, researchers found that participants felt both happy and sad simultaneously after they had received both a smaller reward and a smaller loss than they had expected (Larsen et al., 2004). Perhaps not surprisingly, researchers have also found that we are most likely to experience mixed emotions in emotionally complex situations (Larsen, et al., 2007, 2004).

Think about your own experiences for a moment. When have you experienced mixed emotions? Based on such experiences, what other seemingly opposite pairs of emotions might we be likely to mix?

Recently, considerable research has focused on the roles of the amygdala and the cerebral cortex in the experience of emotion, particularly the emotion of fear. In fact, according to the influential neuroscientist Joseph LeDoux (2008, 1996), the amygdala is "the hub" of fear in the brain. This almond-shaped structure located in front of the hippocampus is believed to have a direct connection with the thalamus, which allows for almost instantaneous processing of fear-related stimuli (see **Figure 12-8**). If you were to stumble upon a snake while on a hiking trail, your thalamus would send the visual information directly to your amygdala, which would immediately produce bodily arousal and begin to prepare your body for danger. At the same time, the thalamus would also send the visual image of the snake to the visual center of your cerebral cortex, which would process the information and then send that additional assessment to the amygdala as well. In a sense, the initial activation of the amygdala enables your brain to initiate a fear response before you even have a chance to think about the snake in front of you! As you may notice, this order of events is consistent with the early James-Lange theory that perceptions of environmental events produce physiological arousal and behavioral changes prior to the processing of that information by the cerebral cortex.

Current research has repeatedly highlighted the importance of the amygdala in the conditioning and recognition of fear. It appears, for example, that individuals with damage to their amygdalas do not easily learn fear responses to various stimuli in the laboratory, although people whose amygdalas are intact readily learn these responses (Angrilli et al., 2008, 1996; Bechara et al., 1995). Moreover, in other research, it has been found that the amygdala becomes active when individuals look at pictures of faces depicting fear, but not when they observe faces depicting happiness (Morris et al., 1996). Conversely, people whose amygdalas are damaged cannot recognize facial expressions of fear, even though their ability to recognize facial expressions of other emotions remains intact (Berntson et al., 2007; Adolphs et al., 1994).

Most people with phobias—severe, sometimes disabling fears—can't remember what happened to cause their fear. LeDoux's theory suggests they might not remember because they responded so quickly. They might have an emotional memory of the event but no cognitive memory they can access.

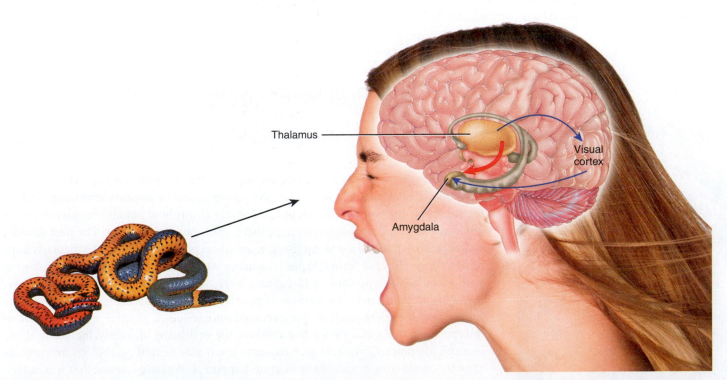

FIGURE 12-8 The brain's shortcut for fear When sensory input arrives at the thalamus, the thalamus sends it along a fast route to the amygdala and along a slower route to the visual cortex. The shortcut direct to the amygdala allows us to react instantly before thinking (LeDoux, 2008, 1996).

Whereas the amygdala seems to be devoted primarily to fear, it appears that the *prefrontal cortex*, an area of the cerebral cortex, plays a role in the production of a range of both positive and negative emotions. One neuroimaging study found, for example, that participants displayed heightened activity in the right prefrontal cortex when they experienced negative emotions and in their left prefrontal cortex when they experienced positive emotions (Sutton & Davidson, 2000; Sutton et al., 1997). Similarly, other studies indicated that participants with damage to the left brain had a greater incidence of depression than did individuals with damage to the right brain. Still other research found that when people who were very anxious about social situations anticipated giving a public speech, the right prefrontal cortex showed increased activation (Davidson et al., 2000). This pattern of findings has led some researchers to wonder whether positive and negative emotions might be governed by two independent brain systems. Further explorations in this area might help explain why some people appear to be characteristically positive and upbeat—and often, as a result, more extroverted and risk-taking—while other people have a more depressive or negative outlook on life.

Research is also beginning to suggest that the prefrontal cortex may further be involved in *coordinating* emotional responses. Whereas the amygdala is responsible for the rapid processing of emotional information, particularly fear-related stimuli, the prefrontal cortex may serve the role of an emotional guide, turning emotional impulses into carefully planned and deliberate actions (Cain & LeDoux, 2008; LeDoux, 1996).

Before You Go On

What Do You Know?

12. What did Cannon and Bard identify as the emotion center of the brain, and why?

13. How did MacLean combine the findings of earlier research?

14. According to recent research, what region of the brain is especially important in the experience of fear?

What Do You Think? Why do you think identifying the parts of the brain responsible for emotion was difficult for early researchers? Why is such research more doable today?

What About Positive Emotions?

LEARNING OBJECTIVE 5 Identify some factors that influence whether or not a person is happy.

After reading about the work of early emotion researchers, you have begun to think that psychologists have a great deal to say about unpleasant or negative emotions, such as fear, anxiety, anger, and sadness, but less to say about how people experience pleasant, positive emotions, including happiness, pride, and excitement. The past decade, however, has witnessed a striking rise in research on positive emotions, particularly happiness. As you'll recall from Chapter 1, a major new trend in the field of psychology is to focus on positive psychology (Seligman, 2007; Seligman & Steen, 2005). *Positive psychology* is the study and enhancement of positive feelings, including happiness and optimism; positive traits, such as perseverance and wisdom; positive abilities, such as interpersonal skills; and virtues that enhance the well-being of society, including altruism and tolerance. Consistent with this important new field of psychology, researchers are now conducting numerous studies on happiness. We have learned that it is indeed one of the most important and adaptive of human emotions.

In fact, regarding happiness, the news seems to be quite good. Research indicates that people's lives are, in general, more upbeat than psychologists used to think. In fact,

TABLE 12-2 Happiness Levels Around the World, 2000–2008

How much people enjoy their lives as a whole, on a scale of 0 to 10			
Iceland	8.5	France	6.5
Denmark	8.4	Vietnam	6.5
Colombia	8.1	Greece	6.4
Switzerland	8.1	Japan	6.4
Mexico	8.0	Peru	6.4
Finland	7.8	China	6.3
Australia	7.7	Philippines	6.3
Norway	7.7	Iran	6.0
Sweden	7.7	South Africa	6.0
Canada	7.6	Bolivia	5.9
Argentina	7.5	India	5.9
Ireland	7.5	Dominican Republic	5.7
Netherlands	7.5	Ecuador	5.7
Brazil	7.4	Ghana	5.7
Costa Rica	7.3	Lebanon	5.6
New Zealand	7.3	Hungary	5.5
Germany	7.2	Kosovo	5.5
Spain	7.2	Turkey	5.5
Venezuela	7.2	Russia	5.4
United Arab Emirates	7.1	Bosnia	5.3
Britain	7.1	Kenya	5.2
Guatemala	7.0	Egypt	5.1
Malta	7.0	Afghanistan	4.7
Saudi Arabia	7.0	Iraq	4.3
United States of America	**7.0**	Pakistan	4.3
Belize	6.9	Chad	4.2
Chile	6.8	Togo	4.1
Italy	6.8	Angola	4.0
Israel	6.7	Zimbabwe	3.3
Jamaica	6.6	Tanzania	3.2

Source: Adapted from Veenhoven, R., Average happiness in 144 nations 2000–2008, *World Database of Happiness*, RankReport 2009-1c, Internet: worlddatabaseofhappiness.eur.nl

most people around the world say they're happy—including most of those who are poor, unemployed, elderly, and disabled (Table 12-2) (Becchetti & Santoro, 2007; Pugno, 2007; Wallis, 2005). Consider the following results:

- Wealthy people appear only slightly happier than those of modest means (Easterbrook, 2005; Diener et al., 1993).

- Although early studies suggested only a minimal relationship between age and happiness (Myers & Diener, 1997; Inglehart, 1990), recent studies have found that, provided they remain healthy, people over 65 actually report more happiness and less negative emotion than do younger people (Mroczek & Spiro, 2007, 2005; Mroczek, 2004).

- Over 90 percent of people with quadriplegia say they're glad to be alive, and overall, people with spinal cord injuries report feeling only slightly less happy than other people (Diener & Diener, 1996).

"For me, music making is the most joyful activity possible, the most perfect expression of any emotion."

—Luciano Pavarotti, Italian opera tenor

Think about what you've been doing and experiencing during the past four weeks. Then report how much you experienced each of the following feelings, using the scale below. For each item, select a number from 1 to 5, and write that number on the line next to the feeling:

1 Very rarely or never
2 Rarely
3 Sometimes
4 Often
5 Very often or always

_2_ Positive (1)   _4_ Unpleasant (9)
_5_ Negative (2)   _1_ Happy (10)
_2_ Good (3)   _4_ Sad (11)
_5_ Bad (4)   _4_ Angry (12)
_1_ Pleasant (5)   _2_ Afraid (13)
_1_ Contented (6)   _2_ Loving (14)
_2_ Interested (7)   _5_ Depressed (15)
_5_ Stressed (8)   _1_ Joyful (16)

A Pleasant feelings: Add up your scores on items 1, 3, 5, 6, 7, 10, 14, and 16 (8 items), and place your score here: _12_

B Unpleasant feelings: Add up your scores on items 2, 4, 8, 9, 11, 12, 13, and 15 (8 items), and place your score here: _364_

Pleasant feelings

8–13	Extremely low pleasant feelings
14–18	Very low
19–23	Low
24–27	Moderate
28–30	High
31–35	Very high
36–40	Extremely high pleasant feelings

Unpleasant feelings

8–11	Extremely low unpleasant feelings
12–16	Very low
17–20	Low
21–25	Moderate
26–28	High
29–31	Very high
32–40	Extremely high unpleasant feelings

Your happiness balance

Besides your overall pleasant feelings and unpleasant feelings scores, you can also examine the relation between the two, in what is called "hedonic balance," or the amount of pleasant feelings you experience minus the amount of unpleasant feelings.

Subtract your Unpleasant Feelings Score from your Pleasant Feelings Score and put your answer here: _____

Balance scores

24 to 32	Very happy
16 to 23	Happy
5 to 15	Slightly happy
4 to –3	Neutral, mixed
–4 to –12	Somewhat unhappy
–13 to –23	Very unhappy
–24 to –32	Extremely unhappy

Individual emotion items

Besides the summed scores and their balance score, you can also examine individual items.

You ought to be feeling general positive feelings, such as "good" or "positive," the majority of the time, unless some bad event has just occurred in your life. If you are not feeling positive, good, or pleasant most of the time, and only experience these feelings rarely, you should examine why.

Similarly, you should be experiencing negative feelings a minority of the time. If you feel stressed sometimes, but not often, you may feel that this is acceptable. But for some feelings, such as "depressed" and "angry," it is usually most beneficial to feel these emotions only rarely or very rarely.

Do any of your individual emotions stand out? That is, which of the positive feelings do you have less often? If you are interested and positive most of the time, this is a very good sign. When you examine your negative feelings, are there any that you feel substantially more often? If you are frequently afraid, angry, sad, depressed, or stressed, are there steps you can take to reduce those emotions?

Source: Reprinted with permission from Ed Diener and Robert Biswas-Diener, _Happiness: Unlocking the Mysteries of Psychological Wealth_ (Malden, MA: Blackwell Publishing, 2008), pp. 237–239.

Men and women are equally likely to declare themselves satisfied or very happy. Overall, only one person in ten reports being "not too happy" (Myers, 2000; Myers & Diener, 1996). And only one in seven reports waking up unhappy (Wallis, 2005).

Of course, some people are indeed happier than others. Those who are generally happy seem to remain happy from decade to decade, regardless of job changes, moves, and family changes (Becchetti & Santoro, 2007; Myers & Diener, 1996). Such people adjust to negative events and return to their usual cheerful state within a few months (Diener et al., 2007, 1992). Conversely, unhappy people are not cheered much in the long term even by positive events. Some theorists believe that people have a "happiness set point" to which they consistently return, despite life's ups and downs. However, this notion is not always supported by research (Diener et al., 2007; Lucas, 2007).

Some studies suggest that one's sense of happiness may have a genetic component (Roysamb, 2006; Lykken & Tellegen, 1996). Indeed, one of the most dominant factors in determining happiness may be temperament. Twin studies have found that twins' ratings of happiness are generally similar, and other researchers have reported that the single best predictor of future happiness is past happiness (Diener & Lucas, 1999). These findings may suggest that a temperamental predisposition to look at life optimistically is more important than an individual's life situation.

Research also indicates that happiness is linked to our personality characteristics and our typical ways of cognitively interpreting events (Diener et al., 2007; Stewart et al., 2005; Diener, 2000). Happy people are, for example, generally optimistic, outgoing, curious, and tender-minded. They also tend to possess high self-esteem, be spiritual, be goal directed, and have a sense of perseverance and of control over their lives (Peterson et al., 2007; Sahoo et al., 2005; Diener & Seligman, 2002).

It appears that good relationships are related to happiness and satisfaction. Married people tend to be happier than single people (although this effect may be stronger for men than for women) (Myers, 2000; DeNeve, 1999). And in what may or may not be surprising news to you, college students who have close friends and significant others are happier than college students who do not (Diener & Seligman, 2002).

No age limit People who are happy when younger tend to remain happy as they age. On average, older people are as likely as younger people to be happy, perhaps more likely.

A longitudinal study published in the journal Science found that highly optimistic people had a 55 percent reduced risk of death from any cause and a 23 percent reduced risk of heart problems, compared with highly pessimistic people.

Before You Go On

What Do You Know?

15. Why do some researchers suggest that we may have a happiness "set point"?

16. What are some of the life circumstances positively related to happiness and satisfaction?

What Do You Think? How would you advise a friend who asked you for tips on how he or she could be happier?

Emotion HOW we Differ

LEARNING OBJECTIVE 6 Identify and discuss the emotional dimensions on which people may differ.

People experience their emotions in a variety of ways. Some researchers suggest that patterns in these variations may have important implications for how we adapt to circumstances in our environments. As we discussed in Chapter 10, for example, people high in *emotional intelligence*—the ability to recognize, produce, and understand

Same situation, different emotions As the faces and body language of these two partygoers reveal, people often react to the same situation very differently.

emotions—can use emotions to promote their intellectual and emotional growth, as well as for purposes of reasoning, problem solving, and emotion management (Grewal, Brackett, & Salovey, 2006; Mayer & Salovey, 2004, 1997).

Before we can make use of our emotions, however, we must feel them. Researchers have identified some common patterns in how different people experience emotions, as well as differences among individuals in our ability to regulate our emotions. We'll also see in this section that psychologists have investigated gender and cultural differences in emotion.

Patterns of Emotionality

A good deal of research has focused on three features of our emotional responding: the clarity of our emotions, the attention we pay to them, and the intensity with which we feel emotions. In different individuals, these three characteristics combine into identifiable clusters or patterns of emotional responding.

Emotional Clarity   *Clarity* in understanding one's emotions has been described as the ability to accurately identify and distinguish one's emotions (Barrett et al., 2001). Vague representations of emotional experiences as being either pleasant or unpleasant often leave individuals without clear strategies for reducing or enhancing particular emotions or for navigating particular social circumstances (Gohm, 2003). If, however, we are able to accurately identify and distinguish emotions (say, guilt and anger), we can better understand the causes of those emotions, the context in which they occur, and the most appropriate responses to make in particular situations (Barrett et al., 2007, 2001).

Attention to Emotions   A process closely related to emotional clarity is *attention to emotion*, which has been described as a person's tendency to take notice of, value, and focus on his or her emotions and moods (Gohm, 2003). People who are aware of and attend more to their emotions typically have greater access to them and greater ability to use them in positive and meaningful ways. Conversely, persons who tend to ignore emotions or deem them irrelevant are less able to identify or control them (Gohm, 2003). Through instruction and practice, individuals can become more skilled at attending to their emotions, but such improvements may be limited by the individuals' inborn sensitivity to visceral and other physiological changes that occur within their bodies (Larsen, 2000).

Emotional Intensity   **Emotional intensity** refers to the characteristic strength with which an individual typically experiences emotions. Of course, the magnitude of our emotions is related to the magnitude of the emotional stimuli that we encounter. Nevertheless, some individuals may react intensely to a mild experience (say, a bad grade on a minor homework assignment), while others may barely respond to situations that most individuals would find extremely upsetting (such as a failing grade in a required class). Research has confirmed that individuals who report heightened levels of emotional intensity display stronger emotional responses to the same emotional stimulus than do individuals who report low intensity (Larsen & Diener, 1987).

Many theorists believe that emotional intensity is a stable trait that generalizes across different kinds of emotions (Charles & Piazza, 2007; Bachorowski & Braaten, 1994; Larsen & Diener, 1987). In support of this notion, studies have found that people who react to positive daily life events with strong positive emotions (say, great joy) also tend to react to negative life events with strong negative emotions (such as intense anger), while those who react to positive events with mild positive emotions react to negative life events with mild negative emotions (Larsen, Diener, & Emmons, 1986; Diener et al., 1985).

emotional intensity the characteristic strength with which an individual typically experiences emotion.

Some people who experience emotions very intensely worry that their emotions are too influential and try to dampen their mood states, especially when they are experiencing negative emotions (Gohm, 2003). Such people may also find it uncomfortable to focus on their emotions too long. Conversely, individuals who experience low levels of emotional intensity often find it hard to identify their feelings and may therefore have less access to the useful information provided by emotions. Small wonder that some theorists believe *moderate* emotional intensity to be the ideal level in most circumstances.

Emotion Styles Using a statistical technique called *cluster analysis*, emotion researcher Carol Gohm (2003) identified four common patterns of emotional responding that combine different levels of emotional clarity, attention, and intenisty: hot, cool, overwhelmed, and cerebral.

- The *hot* cluster consists of individuals who experience their emotions intensely (high intensity), value and attend to their emotions regularly (high attention), and identify and describe their emotions readily (high clarity).
- In contrast, individuals in the *cool* cluster display low emotional intensity, attention, and clarity.
- The *overwhelmed* cluster is made up of individuals who display average emotional attention, high emotional intensity, and low emotional clarity.
- People in the *cerebral* cluster show high emotional clarity, average emotional attention, and low emotional intensity.

Touched by music The pure ecstasy on the face of this gentleman as he listens to a musical recording suggests that he may generally display high degrees of emotional intensity, attentiveness, and recognition—the so-called "hot" cluster of emotional responding .

Comparisons of these four patterns suggest that people in the hot cluster generally react more strongly to emotional situations than do those characterized as cool, cerebral, or overwhelmed. Even though overwhelmed individuals react less strongly than hot individuals to emotional situations, they worry intensely about the influence of mood in their lives and so are more likely than hot, cool, or cerebral people to try to reduce their emotions when in emotionally charged situations. In one study, for example, researchers subtly produced different moods in participants (Gohm, 2003). Following the mood-producing procedures, participants who fit into the overwhelmed emotional cluster reported strong beliefs about the influence of their moods on their judgments and also made more frequent attempts than other kinds of participants did to reduce their mood states.

According to Gohm, people who are confused about their emotions yet feel their emotions intensely are likely to experience particular discomfort. Frequently, they are flooded with intense emotions that they would like to regulate, but they lack the ability to identify the emotions accurately, making such emotion regulation difficult to achieve. In contrast, research suggests that individuals who experience intense negative emotions yet possess the ability to differentiate among their emotions tend to regulate their emotions in ways that are adaptive and ultimately more comfortable (Barrett et al., 2001).

Regulation of Emotions

Let's look more closely at the regulation of emotions. Because emotions have "the capacity to either enhance or undermine effective functioning," reducing or otherwise regulating them is often necessary (Thompson, 1994, p. 25). When, for example, emotions occur at inopportune times, are too intense, or run counter to one's goals, dampening them through some form of emotion regulation may be the most desirable response. In fact, we often exert considerable control over our emotions, using various strategies to help influence what emotions we have, when we have them, and how we experience them (Hien et al., 2009; Gross & John, 2003; Gross, 1998).

emotion dysregulation unhealthy attempts to regulate emotion.

display rules cultural expectations that prescribe how, when, and by whom emotions should be expressed.

Efforts to regulate emotions begin very early in life and continue throughout the lifespan (Cicchetti, Ganiban, & Barnett, 1991). Theorists have suggested that the presence or absence of stressors early in a person's life, the person's temperament, and the models available in the person's family and in social settings may influence how he or she comes to perceive and experience emotions. Depending on such factors, individuals may develop either adaptive or maladaptive styles of regulation (Linehan & Dexter-Mazza, 2008; Linehan, 1993).

Unhealthy attempts to regulate one's emotions are referred to as **emotion dysregulation** (Chapman, Leung, & Lynch, 2008; Linehan, 1993). Dysregulation occurs when efforts at regulation inadvertently prevent us from effectively adapting to our life circumstances or negatively influence our overall well-being. Someone who tries to control his or her emotions by *suppressing* them may find the strategy helpful in the short run, particularly when it decreases the intensity of a strongly negative emotion. Continuing to suppress emotions in situation after situation, however, may eventually backfire, reducing the person's ability to adjust to life circumstances or to attain goals (Cole & Hall, 2008; Carver & Scheier, 1998).

It is difficult to specify what constitutes adaptive or maladaptive emotional regulation, because emotions depend so much on context. Although suppression of emotions is often a bad thing, there are some occasions when emotions should be suppressed or, at least, modulated. For example, even though sharing private information about ourselves often helps us develop intimacy with someone, too much disclosure can on occasion lead to distress and ambivalence on the listener's part (Christophe & Rimé, 1997). Indeed, most of us can recall instances in which we felt very uncomfortable when people we hardly knew shared a little bit too much about themselves. Research indicates that relationships benefit from an emphasis on positive emotion in the early stages. Over time, though, the rules change, and our friendships depend on a balance of positive and negative information. In one study, strangers were found to focus on happiness-related topics when interacting, while friends focused on both happiness- and anger-related topics (Clark & Taraban, 1991).

Gender Differences in Emotion

One of the more enduring stereotypes in Western society is that women are inherently more "emotional" than men (Fischer & Manstead, 2000). Whereas men traditionally have been seen as "calm, cool, and rational" in emotional situations, women have been viewed as being more emotionally intense and more likely to express their feelings openly. Consistent with these stereotypical views, women typically report that they express emotions more than men do and that they experience emotions more intensively (John & Gross, 2007; Gross & John, 1998; Grossman & Wood, 1993). In one self-report study, for example, female participants reported experiencing more intense emotions than male participants did, as well as expressing more positive and negative emotions (Gross & John, 1998). Such differences between the genders also have been observed when researchers observe the social interactions, facial expressions, and verbalizations of males and females (Brody, 1999; Dimberg & Lundquist, 1990).

Although, at first glance, these findings seem to support the stereotypical view that women are biologically more emotional than men, alternative interpretations are certainly possible. It may be, for example, that when women report experiencing and expressing their emotions more intensely than men, they are being influenced by **display rules**—cultural expectations that prescribe how, when, and by whom emotions should be expressed. In families and society at large, for example, expressions of anger are more socially acceptable for males than they are for females. Similarly, as we shall see in Chapter 14, society deems it more acceptable for females to express nurturing emotions such as love and warmth (Safdar et al., 2009: Brody, 1999). One study found that women more often conform to *feminine* display rules, including the suppression of neg-

> «A real gentleman, even if he loses everything he owns, must show no emotion.»
>
> –*Fyodor Dostoevsky, Russian writer*

ative emotions and the expression of positive emotions, whereas men more often conform to *masculine* display rules, such as the suppression of positive emotions and the expression of negative emotions (Simpson & Stroh, 2004). Another study found a relationship between participants' acceptance of societal norms and their experiences of emotionality (Grossman & Wood, 1993). For example, female participants who believed that women should experience emotions more intensely than men do tended to actually experience their own emotions with greater intensity than male participants did.

It appears that when cultural display rules are removed from the equation, many of the male-female differences in emotionality disappear. For example, studies have found fewer differences between the emotional experiences of men and women in countries with a greater focus on female empowerment and male-female equality (Fischer et al., 2004). In short, it may be that men and women are actually wired for similar patterns of emotionality but have learned from society to experience and express their emotions differently.

Cultural and Ethnic Differences in Emotion

Emotionality does not vary from culture to culture as much as one might expect. Earlier, we observed that people from cultures across the world tend to display emotions with the same facial expressions and to interpret facial expressions of emotionality in a consistent way. It is true that some cultures do differ in the *language* of emotionality; for example, in Gidjingali, an Australian aboriginal language, only one word, *gurakadj*, is available to describe a range of fearful emotions, from terror, horror, and dread to apprehension and timidity; and in Ecuador, the Quichua people lack any word at all for remorse (Tousignant, 1984; Hiatt, 1978). However, there is, for the most part, considerable overlap from culture to culture with respect to the primary categories used to classify emotions.

When differences between cultural groups are observed, they commonly are due to differences in display rules. Early research, for example, found that Japanese and American participants differed in how the presence of another person affected their expression of negative emotion. When they were left alone, both Japanese and American participants displayed similar expressions of anger, disgust, fear, and sadness in reaction to a negative stimulus. However, when an experimenter remained seated in the room, the Americans continued to exhibit expressions of negative emotions, while the Japanese participants masked their negative emotions with smiles. These differences probably occurred because the Japanese participants were conforming to a culture-specific display rule that prohibits the expression of negative emotions in the presence of a higher-status individual. In Japan's collectivist society, group harmony, cohesion, and cooperation are valued first and foremost, with individual needs and individualistic traits, such as uniqueness and autonomy

In Japan, pharmaceutical companies had a hard time making headway with treatments for mild depression because the Japanese considered depression a bad word. In response, companies changed their marketing language to target depression as a medical illness called kokoro no kaze ("cold of the soul"). Physician referrals for depression skyrocketed 46 percent between 1999 and 2003 (New York Times, 2004).

considered secondary (Matsumoto et al., 1998). Thus, the Japanese participants in this study may have been smiling in the presence of the experimenter to display harmony and respect for the experimenter's status (Safdar et al., 2009; Ekman, 1972; Friesen, 1972).

Among the various ethnic groups within the United States, studies have found few differences in the experience and expression of emotion. In a study comparing the emotions of Chinese Americans and Mexican Americans, Chinese-American participants reported feeling less emotion than Mexican-American participants did in response to emotionally charged stimuli. However, no emotional differences were found between the two groups when the participants' physiological and behavioral responses to the stimuli were examined (Soto, Levenson, & Ebling, 2005). Similarly, in a study that compared Hmong Americans and European Americans, members of the two cultural groups displayed similar physiological patterns of arousal and facial expressions and reported similar emotional experiences in response to an emotion-inducing exercise (Tsai et al., 2002). Still other studies have found that Chinese-Americans and European-Americans report similar kinds of emotions and show similar levels of physiological arousal during performance of interpersonal tasks and discussions of relationship conflicts (Tsai et al., 2006, 2004, 2002).

Before You Go On

What Do You Know?
17. What is emotional clarity?
18. What factors may influence the techniques a person uses to control his or her emotions?
19. What are display rules and how do they affect emotional differences?

What Do You Think?
Build your own emotional profile by estimating your levels of emotional intelligence, clarity, attention, intensity, and regulation. How easy or difficult do you believe it would be to change your emotional profile?

Disorders of Emotion When Things Go Wrong

LEARNING OBJECTIVE 7 Describe how malfunctions in emotional processes are related to psychological disorders.

Earlier, we observed that people differ from one another in the clarity, attention, intensity, and regulation of their emotions. It turns out that extreme manifestations of these features of emotion may contribute to psychological disturbances of one kind or another.

- *Clarity of emotions* Researchers have found that people who are largely unable to identify and describe their emotions, commonly referred to as *alexithymia,* often confuse their emotions with symptoms of medical problems and develop numerous bodily fears and health complaints (Cox et al., 1994).

  - *Attention to emotions* People who attend to their emotions too much, a pattern called *hypervigilance,* tend to be more anxious than other people (Vujanovic et al., 2007; Swinkels & Giuliano, 1995). Because of their heightened self-focus, they keep noticing signs of arousal that other people are not even aware of, and they repeatedly appraise such arousal in ways that cause them constant worry.

- *Intensity of emotions* People who experience too little emotion may be incapable of caring deeply for and relating effectively with other people. An extreme form of this problem is found among individuals with *antisocial personality disorder*, a pattern that we'll be examining more in Chapter 13. People who display this pattern seem to experience little or no guilt or anxiety, and thus are more likely to violate the needs of other people and less likely to learn from the adverse consequences of their actions (Cleckley, 1941). Indeed, studies reveal that when such persons are exposed in the laboratory to unpleasant stimuli, they experience little emotion intensity at all (Patrick, 1994; Patrick, Bradley, & Lang, 1993).

- *Regulation of emotions* People who suffer from an extreme dysregulation of their emotions often develop self-defeating ways of trying to bring order to their emotional lives (Bradley, 2000). As you'll see in Chapter 13, for example, people with *borderline personality disorder* experience a severe inability to regulate their intense emotions. They may show impulsivity or even resort to self-mutilation in what many theorists view as dysfunctional attempts to regulate their intense emotional reactions (Nock & Prinstein, 2004; Gratz, 2003; APA, 2000). Similarly, research suggests that women with bulimia nervosa (discussed in Chapter 11) experience their emotions as particularly dysregulated, leading many theorists to conclude that binge-eating and purging behavior represent maladaptive attempts by those individuals to deal with their chaotic emotions (Safer, Telch, & Agras, 2001; Westen & Harnden-Fischer, 2001).

Given that emotional irregularities can disrupt functioning so severely, many observers believe that all psychological disorders involve some degree of disturbance in emotional functioning (Gard & Kring, 2009; Yuan & Kring, 2009; Kring & Bachorowski, 1999). For certain psychological disorders, however, emotional disturbances seem to be the central and defining features of the problem. These disorders, sometimes called *emotional disorders*, include the *anxiety disorders* and *mood disorders*.

Anxiety Disorders

As you have seen in this chapter, although everyday experiences of fear and anxiety are not pleasant, they often have an adaptive function: they prepare us for action—for "fight-or-flight"—when danger threatens. They may, for example, lead us to drive more cautiously in a storm or work harder at our jobs. Unfortunately, some people suffer such disabling fear and anxiety that they cannot lead normal lives. They are said to have an *anxiety disorder*.

Anxiety disorders are the most prevalent of all mental disorders. In the United States around 18 percent of adults currently suffer from one or more of the anxiety disorders, and 29 percent of all people develop an anxiety disorder during their lives (Koury & Rapaport, 2007; Kessler et al., 2005). Four prominent anxiety disorders are *phobias, generalized anxiety disorder, panic disorder,* and *obsessive-compulsive disorder*.

Phobias A **phobia** is a persistent and unreasonable fear of a particular object, activity, or situation. Everyone has areas of special fear, and it is normal for a person to be upset by some things more than other things. A phobia, however, is more intense, persistent, and disruptive than such common fears (APA, 2000).

The most widely accepted explanation for the onset of phobias is that they are acquired by conditioning—primarily *classical conditioning* (Field, 2006; Rowa et al., 2006), the learning process described in Chapter 7. As you'll recall, in classical conditioning, two events that occur close together in time become closely associated in a person's mind, so that the person eventually reacts similarly to both of them. Classical conditioning is also used to treat phobias, through a technique called *systematic desensitization* that helps people learn to react with less fear to the object or situation of their phobias.

Generalized Anxiety Disorder People with **generalized anxiety disorder** experience excessive anxiety under most circumstances and seem to worry all the time. They usually feel restless, keyed-up, or on edge; have difficulty concentrating; experience muscle tension; and have sleep problems (Calleo et al., 2009).

phobia a persistent and unreasonable fear of a particular object, activity, or situation.

generalized anxiety disorder an anxiety disorder in which people feel excessive anxiety and worry under most circumstances.

The most common phobic object in the world is the spider. An intense fear of these arthropods is called arachnophobia.

panic attacks periodic, short bouts of panic.

obsessive-compulsive disorder (OCD) an anxiety disorder in which obsessions or compulsions feel excessive or unreasonable, cause great distress, take up much time, or interfere with daily functions.

depression a persistent sad state in which life seems dark and its challenges overwhelming.

mania a persistent state of euphoria or frenzied energy.

unipolar depression a mood disorder that includes only depression.

bipolar disorder a mood disorder in which periods of mania alternate with periods of depression.

cognitive triad a pattern of thinking in which individuals repeatedly interpret their experiences, themselves, and their futures in negative ways that lead them to feel depressed.

Earlier in this chapter, we observed that emotions can be influenced by how people interpret their situations. People with generalized anxiety disorder apparently have a cognitive bias that leads them to interpret almost every situation as threatening. According to research, they approach each situation with anxiety-provoking assumptions that they are in imminent danger. For example, people with generalized anxiety disorder may operate by rules of thought such as, "a situation or a person is unsafe until proven to be safe," or, "it is always best to assume the worst" (Beck & Weishaar, 2008; Ellis, 2008).

Related research also suggests that individuals with generalized anxiety disorder are unable to tolerate uncertainty: they believe that any chance of a negative event occurring, no matter how unlikely, means that the event is going to occur. Given their intolerance of uncertainty, the individuals worry whenever an outcome is less than certain—which, in fact, most outcomes in life are (Dugas et al., 2009, 2004, 1998). Think of when you become attracted to someone and how you then feel prior to your first text message or first call with that person. The concern that you experience in such instances—the sense of almost unbearable uncertainty—is how people with generalized anxiety disorder feel most of the time.

Some neuroimaging studies suggest that people with generalized anxiety disorder may have impairments in areas of the limbic system of the brain, including the amygdala, prefrontal cortex, and cingulate cortex (McClure et al., 2007).

Panic Disorder   Although anyone is capable of reacting with panic when a real threat looms up suddenly, people with *panic disorder* repeatedly experience **panic attacks**—periodic, short bouts of panic that occur suddenly and often without provocation, reach a peak within 10 minutes, and gradually pass. The attacks may feature palpitations of the heart, tingling in the hands or feet, shortness of breath, sweating, hot and cold flashes, trembling, chest pains, faintness, and dizziness. Indeed, during a panic attack many people fear they will die, go crazy, or lose control.

It appears that panic-prone people are more attentive to their bodily sensations than other individuals, experience more intense bodily sensations, and are more inclined to misinterpret their sensations (Nardi et al., 2008, 2001). Research suggests that when these people experience certain sensations—for example, shifts in blood pressure, rises in heart rate, or carbon dioxide increases in the blood—they typically misinterpret them as signs of a medical catastrophe (Casey et al., 2004). Rather than understanding the probable cause of their sensations as "overexerting myself" or "my queasiness about an upcoming test," panic-prone people grow increasingly upset, fear the worst, lose all perspective, and rapidly plunge into panic. For example, many people with panic disorder seem to "overbreathe," or hyperventilate, in stressful situations. Such breathing makes them think that they are in danger of suffocation, and so they panic (Dratcu, 2000).

Neuroimaging studies have further linked panic reactions to a brain circuit that includes the amygdala, hypothalamus, and locus coeruleus (Ninan & Dunlop, 2005; Mezzasalma et al., 2004). Researchers believe that this brain circuit, which normally helps regulate the rise and fall of situationally-provoked fear reactions, functions improperly in people who experience panic disorder, allowing fear to escalate into full-blown panic attacks, even in the absence of real threats (Maron et al., 2005, 2004; Gray & McNaughton, 1996).

Obsessive-Compulsive Disorder   As we discussed in Chapter 9, *obsessions* are persistent thoughts, ideas, impulses, or images that seem to invade a person's consciousness. *Compulsions* are repetitive and rigid behaviors or mental acts that people feel they must perform in order to prevent or reduce anxiety. A diagnosis of **obsessive-compulsive disorder (OCD)** may be made when obsessions or compulsions feel excessive or unreasonable, cause great distress, take up much time, or interfere with daily functions.

Obsessive-compulsive disorder is considered an anxiety disorder because the obsessions cause people who have this disorder intense anxiety, while their compulsions are aimed at preventing or reducing anxiety. In addition, their anxiety rises if they try to resist their obsessions or compulsions. Recent research suggests that a brain circuit involved with converting information from our senses into thoughts and actions may malfunction in people with OCD (Stein & Fineberg, 2007; Szeszko et al, 2005). Not surprisingly, this circuit includes some of the anxiety-linked structures that we have come across throughout this chapter: the cingulate cortex, the thalamus, and the amygdala (Stein & Fineberg, 2007).

Mood Disorders

Most people's moods are transient. Their feelings of happiness or sadness rise and fall in response to daily events. In contrast, the moods of people with mood disorders last a long time, color all of their interactions with the world, and interfere with normal functioning.

Depression and *mania* are the key emotions in mood disorders. **Depression** is a markedly sad state in which life seems dark and its challenges overwhelming. **Mania**, the opposite of depression, in many ways, is a state of frenzied energy in which people may have an exaggerated belief that they can do and accomplish anything. Mania is a much more intense emotion than happiness, the positive emotion that we looked at earlier. Most people with a mood disorder suffer only from depression, a pattern called **unipolar depression**. Others experience periods of mania that alternate with periods of depression, a pattern called **bipolar disorder**. In this section, we'll focus only on unipolar depression.

Everyone is vulnerable At a 1999 White House conference, famous CBS newsman Mike Wallace and Tipper Gore, wife of then-Vice President Al Gore, discussed their past experiences with clinical depression. Wallace's depression was triggered by a lengthy civil trial, Gore's by her son's near fatal accident.

Clinical depression produces severe and long-lasting psychological pain that often intensifies over time. Those who suffer from it may lose their will to carry out life's activities; some even lose their will to live. Episodes of depression often, but certainly not always, seem to be triggered by stressful events (Paykel, 2003).

Seven percent of adults in the United States currently suffer from severe depression and 5 percent more have mild depression (Taube-Schiff & Lau, 2008; Vasiliadis et al., 2007; Kessler et al., 2005). Altogether, 17 percent of adults experience an episode of severe unipolar depression during their lives. Women are at least twice as likely as men to experience episodes of severe depression. As many as 26 percent of women may have an episode during their lives, compared with 12 percent of men.

Depression is one of clinical psychology's most studied problems, and as a result, a range of explanations for this disorder have been offered. Two of the best supported explanations focus on two factors that we have looked at repeatedly throughout our discussions of emotions: cognitive factors and biological factors.

Cognitive Factors   Depression has been linked strongly to two problematic cognitive tendencies. The first is a biased, negative way of viewing the world. Psychologist Aaron Beck argues that the thinking of depressed people takes three forms, which he calls the **cognitive triad**: the individuals repeatedly interpret their experiences, themselves, and their futures in negative ways that lead them to feel depressed (Beck & Weishaar, 2008; Beck, 2002, 1967). A depressed person might focus attention on the negative events in his or her life, feel that he or she is to blame for those events, and conclude that there is no hope of improvement in the future.

A second cognitive problem for depressed people, according to Beck, is illogical thinking. They commonly draw *arbitrary inferences*, for example—negative conclusions based on little evidence. A person with depression might be walking through a library, pass someone who is reading a book, and conclude, "That person is avoiding looking at me." Such illogical thinking, along with the cognitive triad, increases the likelihood that depressed people will keep interpreting their situations negatively, and in turn, continue to experience depressive emotions. Many studies have confirmed that the cognitive triad and illogical thinking processes are at work in depressed people (Ridout et al., 2009, 2003).

Biological Factors Since the 1950s, an enormous body of research has found that people with low brain activity of the neurotransmitters *serotonin* and *norepinephrine* are prone to develop depression (Carlson, 2008; Julien, 2008). Indeed, the most commonly prescribed medications for depression increase the activity of these brain chemicals.

In recent years, brain imaging studies have also pointed to several interconnected brain structures that may work together as members of a "depression circuit." These include structures that have been linked to general emotions, especially negative ones—the prefrontal cortex and the amygdala—as well as the hippocampus and an area located within the cingulate cortex (Carlson, 2008; Insel, 2007; Mayberg, 2006).

Anxiety disorders and mood disorders are among the most common psychological disorders for which people seek treatment. As a result, many treatment approaches exist for these problems, and we shall discuss these in Chapter 16. In the meantime, it is worth keeping in mind that whether emotions "go wrong" (as in the case of these disorders), "go right" (as with happiness and other positive emotions), or elude categorization as right or wrong, emotions certainly are a critical part of human functioning. Indeed, as we mentioned early in this chapter and have since observed again and again, emotions have an impact on nearly every aspect of our lives.

Before You Go On

What Do You Know?

20. Extreme variations of which individual differences in emotion have been linked to psychological disorders?
21. List and describe four major anxiety disorders.
22. What is the cognitive triad?

What Do You Think?
Analyze a character from a film you have seen or a book you have read who has one of the disorders described in this chapter. Is the information provided in the text consistent with what you know of the character?

Summary

What Is Emotion?

LEARNING OBJECTIVE 1 Define emotion and discuss the components, measurement, and functions of emotion.

- An *emotion* is an intrapersonal state that occurs in response to an external or internal event and includes three components: a *physiological component*, a *cognitive component*, and a *behavioral component*.
- To measure emotion, researchers typically use three kinds of information: people's *behavioral displays of emotion*, *self-reports of emotion*, and *physiological reactions*.
- Emotions serve many functions. They add color to our lives, give us information about important events in the environment, stir us to action when necessary, and help us to coordinate relationships with others.

Where Do Emotions Come From?

LEARNING OBJECTIVE 2 Discuss the major theories of emotion.

- The conventional *common sense explanation of emotion* holds that an event triggers an emotion, which leads to physiological changes, followed by a response to the situation.
- In contrast, the *James-Lange theory* proposes that the emotion we feel *results* from bodily and behavioral responses to environmental stimuli, rather than causing those responses.
- According to the *Cannon-Bard theory*, physiological arousal by itself cannot produce complex emotional experiences. Rather, the perception of an emotionally stirring event simultaneously sends messages to parts of the brain responsible for the subjective experience of emotion and physiological arousal.

- *Schachter and Singer's two-factor theory* holds that an emotional state is a function of both physiological arousal and cognition.
- Building on Schachter and Singer's two-factor theory, *cognitive-mediational theory* proposes that cognitive interpretations, and particularly appraisals, of events are in fact the keys to the experience of emotions.
- The *facial-feedback theory* of emotion, based on the ideas of Darwin, holds that facial expressions that occur in response to stimuli provide feedback to the brain that helps to shape emotional experience.
- *Evolutionary theorists* believe that emotions have been shaped by natural selection and that certain emotions have been passed down because of their role in the survival of our species.

Emotion *How We Develop*

LEARNING OBJECTIVE 3 Contrast the cognitive theory of emotional development with the differential emotions theory.

- According to Lewis's *cognitive theory of emotional development*, emotions unfold in infants as a consequence of neural and cognitive development, with the most significant development achieved by the age of three.
- In contrast, Izard's *differential emotions theory* holds that emotions, rather than emerging as a result of cognitive development, actually help to trigger cognitive development. In this view, emotions serve stage-related developmental processes.

Emotion What Happens in the Brain

LEARNING OBJECTIVE 4 Identify the main brain structures that have been associated with emotion.

- Early researchers Cannon and Bard believed that emotional stimuli are routed by the *thalamus* to the *cerebral cortex* and the *hypothalamus*, which they considered the emotion center of the brain.
- Papez noted that the process was more complex and proposed that the *cingulate cortex* and the *hippocampus* are also involved, providing integration functions.
- Klüver and Bucy found evidence that the *temporal lobes* play a role in the processing of emotional stimuli.
- MacLean proposed that a collection or brain areas, which he collectively called the *limbic system*, are responsible for primitive brain functions, such as emotion.
- Considerable current research has focused on the roles of the *amygdala* and the *cerebral cortex* in the experience of emotion.

What about Positive Emotions?

LEARNING OBJECTIVE 5 Identify some factors that influence whether or not a person is happy.

- Researchers have tended to focus on negative emotions, in part because of difficulties in measuring positive emotions.
- Identifying what makes people happy can also be difficult. Research has shown that good relationships, employment, goal-directed behavior, religious belief, and good health are among the things that can make people happy. In particular though, temperament and personality predict happiness.

Emotion *How We Differ*

LEARNING OBJECTIVE 6 Identify and discuss the emotional dimensions on which people may differ.

- Individuals show important differences in *emotional intelligence, emotional clarity, attention to emotions, emotional intensity,* and *regulation of emotions* and also display patterns of emotional responsiveness that remain relatively stable across situations.
- Women often report being more emotionally expressive than men and experiencing emotions more intensely, but these gender differences are highly influenced by cultural *display rules* and may not reflect inherent patterns of emotionality.
- Emotionality does not vary greatly from culture to culture, although there may be differences in display rules and the language of emotionality.

Disorders of Emotion

LEARNING OBJECTIVE 7 Describe how malfunctions in emotional processes are related to psychological disorders.

- Extremes in the intensity, clarity, attention to, regulation of, and expression of emotion may contribute to psychological disturbances.
- Anxiety disorders, characterized by excessive emotions of fear or worry, include *phobias, generalized anxiety disorder, panic disorder,* and *obsessive-compulsive disorder.*
- Mood disorders include *depression,* marked by an inescapable sad mood, and *mania,* a maladaptive extreme version of happiness. Depression is very common. Research shows that, as with normal emotions, both cognitive and biological factors contribute.

Key Terms

CUT/ACROSS CONNECTION

What Happens in the B R A I N ?

- The amygdala plays a key role in the onset of emotions, particularly fear. Its activation enables the brain to initiate a fear reaction before other brain areas even start to process the fear-arousing situation.
- People whose amygdalas are damaged cannot recognize other people's facial expressions of fear.
- The prefrontal cortex plays a key role in both positive and negative emotions. Negative emotions may be linked to high activity in the right prefrontal cortex, while positive emotions may be tied to greater activity in the left prefrontal cortex.
- Whereas the amygdala is responsible for the rapid processing of emotional information, the prefrontal cortex may serve as more of an emotional coordinator and guide, turning emotional impulses to deliberate actions.

When Things Go Wrong

- Around 18 percent of adults in the United States display one or more of the anxiety disorders each year— such as phobias, generalized anxiety disorder, panic disorder, and obsessive-compulsive disorder.
- Almost 7 percent of adults in the United States display severe depression each year and 5 percent experience mild depression.
- The various emotional disorders have each been tied to abnormalities in a particular brain circuit. The panic disorder circuit, for example, apparently includes the amygdala, hypothalamus, and locus coeruleus, and the depression circuit includes the amygdala, prefrontal cortex, hippocampus, and cingulate cortex.
  - The various emotional disorders have also each been linked to cognitive factors, such as misinterpretations of bodily sensations in panic disorder, and biased and illogical thinking in depression.

HOW we Differ

- People differ in how clearly they can identify their emotions, how attentive they are to their emotions, and how intense their emotions feel.
- People seem to display either a hot, cool, overwhelmed, or cerebral emotional style, based on their levels of emotional clarity, their attention to their emotions, and the intensity with which they feel emotions.
- Women may not really be all that much more emotional than men. Rather, individuals may following social *display rules* about the appropriateness of their particular gender expressing emotions.
- Our culture helps determine the display rules we follow. In one study, American and Japanese participants displayed similar expressions of anger, disgust, and fear when alone. However, when seated with an experimenter, the Japanese individuals masked their negative emotions, while the Americans continued to express their negative feelings.
- Women are at least twice as likely as men to experience severe depression.

How we Develop

- The range of emotions in newborns is largely undifferentiated. Infants vacillate largely between general distress and general contentment.
- Babies express happiness, excitement, and disgust by 3 months of age, anger by 4 to 6 months, and fearfulness by 7 to 8 months.
- Children experience emotions of self-consciousness, such as envy, empathy, and embarrassment, by 18 to 24 months of age, and self-conscious evaluative emotions such as pride, shame, and guilt by 24 to 30 months.
- Some research suggests that the achievement of various cognitive stages enables certain emotions to emerge, while other research finds that the emergence of various emotions helps trigger cognitive and social development, such as the development of moral standards and a self-concept.

Psychology Around Us

The Role of Arousal in Emotion

Identifying (and Misidentifying) Your Emotions

Stanley Schachter and Jerome Singer's classic study of emotions showed that cognitive interpretations of one's own arousal are a key part of the emotional experience. This video lab exercise will help you experience and appreciate their important findings first hand.

The exercise requires two different sessions. In one session, you'll sit down at your computer while in a caffeine-free, arousal-free state. While in this state, you'll be looking at upsetting or uplifting videos and photos and rate your emotions throughout these observations. For the other session, you'll be sitting down at your computer immediately after you have, in the normal course of your life, stimulated your brain and body with exercise, coffee, soda, or the like (whichever is your usual stimulator of choice). You'll then observe a set of comparable upsetting or uplifting videos and photos and again rate your emotions during your observations.

Over the course of the exercise, you'll feel and react the same way that the participants did in Schachter and Singer's study, and you'll come to appreciate first-hand the principles of the two-factor theory. Most importantly, you'll better recognize the separate roles played by physical arousal, cognitive interpretation, and behavior in the experience of emotions.

As you are working on this on-line exercise, consider the following questions:

* Why was Schachter and Singer's research so stunning to the field and to the public when it was first published?
* How does the two-factor theory of emotion compare to the other theories of emotion?
* Does the two-factor theory apply to some emotions or some levels of emotionality more than to others?
* Schachter and Singer's study had important methodological advantages over this lab exercise. What were they and why did this exercise have to take a somewhat different route?

CHAPTER 13

Personality

Chapter Outline

- Historic Perspectives on Personality • Understanding Personality Today: Traits versus Situations

- Biological Foundations of Personality • Personality *How We Differ*

- Personality Disorders • Personality Assessment

Not So Identical Twins

Tamara Rabi is a city girl, raised Jewish. Adriana Scott is Catholic and raised in the suburbs. Talking to them as they sit side-by-side in a room on campus, you can tell they grew up in different communities. Dark-haired Tamara is dressed in the somber shades of downtown Manhattan, while Adrianna sports sculpted hair, straightened teeth, and a white fur-lined jacket. Adriana has a car, while Tamara does not.

The two students are at neighboring universities on Long Island, New York. They share a birthday, they are exactly the same height, and they both love hip-hop.

The most important thing they share is the same Mexican mother. Separated shortly after birth and given up for adoption in the U.S., for most of their lives they had no idea that, somewhere out there, was an identical twin.

But they have many similarities in spite of growing up in different homes. They're both night people, they both love to dance, they both want to have a boy and a girl (in that order) and they both use Pantene® shampoo. They're both "B" students, even though Tamara attended a top private school and Adriana went to public school. And the subject that gives them both the most trouble? Math. They look remarkably alike, but they're not exactly alike. Tamara has a birthmark over her right eyebrow and Adriana had braces for five years. Plus, Tamara says she's a little more outgoing than Adriana, who admits she's a very shy person (Wells, 2004).

What makes us who we are? How do we explain the striking similarities between Tamara and Adriana? Are they an interesting coincidence, or do they reveal something fundamental about the nature of personality?

Personality refers to the unique characteristics that account for our enduring patterns of inner experience and outward behavior. You probably do a lot of thinking about personality. Have you ever taken an online quiz to figure out which movie celebrity or superhero you most resemble? Maybe you've filled out a quiz in *Cosmopolitan* to determine how much of a pushover you are (and, because of the gender contribution to personality, you probably won't admit that you take *Cosmo* quizzes if you're a guy). Maybe you've also spent time thinking and talking about the varying personalities of your friends. Thinking about people's unique characteristics allows us to give context to their behavior and to try to predict how they might react in a given situation.

Psychological research has historically focused on the divide between nature and nurture explanations of personality development. Increasingly, however, psychologists and biologists have come to acknowledge that environmental experience and biological mechanisms interact to shape personality. In this chapter, we will first explore key historic perspectives on personality. We'll then look at contemporary research and at the importance of both biological and environmental factors in the development of personality. Next, we'll examine whether personality differs depending on gender and culture, and describe several personality disorders. Finally, we will discuss how psychologists assess personality in individuals.

Historic Perspectives on Personality

LEARNING OBJECTIVE 1 Summarize the main ideas of the psychoanalytic and humanistic views of personality development.

For the greater part of the twentieth century, two schools of thought, *psychoanalytic theory* and *humanistic theory*, coexisted with little overlap, in part because they offered such contrasting views of what it meant to be human. Recall from Chapter 1 that psychoanalytic theory emphasized the notion of unconscious, instinctual, often dark desires that have to be held in check. Humanistic psychological approaches instead emphasized the essential goodness of humankind. Although research has demonstrated flaws in both theories, it is impossible to appreciate modern personality theories without first considering the contributions of psychoanalytic and humanistic thought.

Freud and Psychoanalytic Theory

Recall from earlier chapters that the psychoanalytic model was formulated by the Viennese neurologist Sigmund Freud (1856–1939) at the beginning of the twentieth century. In Freud's view, the personality forms as a result of struggles between primal needs and social or moral restraints.

The Structure of Personality   Essential to Freud's ideas about how a personality develops are his views of the conscious and unconscious mind. To Freud, the mind is a little like an iceberg, with only the top of the massive entity visible to the outside world (see **Figure 13-1**). Three levels of consciousness contain the information stored in our minds, and only a small portion of that information is available to normal awareness.

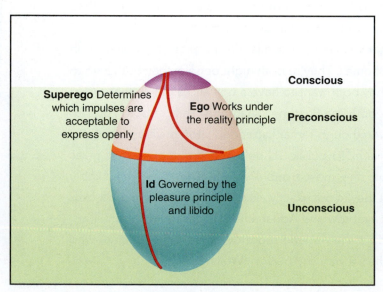

FIGURE 13-1 **Freud's view of the mind** According to Freud, the mind has three levels of consciousness, and the content stored in the unconscious level is especially important for personality development.

1. The topmost level is the *conscious* mind, composed of the thoughts and feelings of which we are aware at any given moment.

2. The second level, just below the surface, is the *preconscious*, which contains mental content that can be easily brought into the conscious mind if it is attended to. For example, your mother's birthday or your plans for this evening remain in your preconscious until you need to use the information, at which point the information is transferred into your conscious awareness.

3. The deepest level, the *unconscious*, contains most of the content of our minds. We are unaware of this content and cannot become aware of it except under special circumstances.

The unconscious is particularly important to the development of personality. Freud identified three central forces in personality development: basic instinctual drives (which he called the *id*), rational thoughts (the *ego*), and moral limits (the *superego*). Figure 13-1 shows the relationship of these three forces to the conscious, preconscious, and unconscious portions of the mind.

The **id** is present at birth and represents basic instinctual needs and desires, such as those related to eating, sleeping, sex, and comfort. These impulses are governed by the *pleasure principle*; that is, they constantly strive for gratification. Freud believed that most of these basic impulses have sexual overtones and that sexual energy, which he called *libido*, fuels the id. Due to the simple nature of the id's needs and its urgent demand for satisfaction, it is often described as immature and childlike. The id resides largely in the unconscious; it is not readily available to consciousness.

The **ego** develops as children grow older and begin to learn that their id impulses cannot always be satisfied. The ego works under the *reality principle*—the awareness that it is not always possible or acceptable to have all wants and desires met. Much like the id, the ego is responsible for satisfying impulses, but instead of demanding immediate and direct gratification, the ego first assesses what is realistically possible. Freud essentially saw the ego as the rational, problem-solving force that constantly strives to keep id-based impulses from bursting forth in a destructive manner. You might conclude that the ego is largely a product of the conscious mind, but Freud believed that it works both consciously and unconsciously, as shown in Figure 13-1.

The **superego**, which also forms during childhood, is in charge of determining which impulses are acceptable to express openly and which are unacceptable. The super-ego develops as children observe the behaviors of those in their families and their culture. As children, we *internalize*—or unconsciously adopt—the values and norms embodied in those behaviors and begin to evaluate ourselves with respect to them. The superego's standards of right and wrong comprise our moral code and remain stable over the course of our lives. Our superego might therefore be thought of as our *conscience*—an entity that leads us to feel guilt and sometimes even anxiety. Like the ego, the superego resides in both the conscious and the unconscious mind.

According to Freud, the ego acts as a mediator between the id and superego, balancing the powerful desires of the id with the moral standards of the superego. Freud believed that the three forces are always in conflict to some degree, usually at an unconscious level. Personality problems and even psychological disorders may result if a person is not able to find acceptable compromises.

Freud's Psychosexual Stages: How we *Develop* Freud believed that as the id, the ego, and the superego work with and against one another, children move through stages that result in the development of personality. The two drives that influence these stages most strongly are *sexuality* and *aggression*. To Freud, these drives are the most likely to cause internal conflict because they are the ones that most often fall

personality the unique characteristics that account for enduring patterns of inner experience and outward behavior.

id according to psychoanalytic theory, the personality element representing basic instinctual drives, such as those related to eating, sleeping, sex, and comfort.

ego according to psychoanalytic theory, a personality element that works to help satisfy the drives of the id while complying with the constraints placed on behavior by the environment.

superego according to psychoanalytic theory, a personality element in charge of determining which impulses are acceptable to express openly and which are unacceptable; develops as we observe and internalize the behaviors of others in our culture.

Oral personality in the making? Freud proposed that individuals whose nurturance needs are not adequately met during infancy may become fixated and develop an oral personality style. They may, for example, be inclined to suck their thumbs, even during later childhood, chew their nails, smoke cigarettes, and show signs of dependence.

TABLE 13-1 Freud's Psychosexual Stages

Stage	Erogenous zone	Key conflict or experience	Symptoms of fixation
Oral (0-18 months)	Mouth	Weaning	Dependency on pleasures of the mouth; also general dependence on mother
Anal (18 months-3 years)	Anus	Toilet training	Excessive neatness, orderliness, stubbornness, stingy, controlling
Phallic (3-6 years)	Genitals	Attraction to opposite sex parent	Sexual role rigidity or confusion
Latency (6 years to puberty)	None	Repression of sexual impulses; identification with same sex parent	No fixations for this stage
Genital (puberty-adult)	Genitals	Establishing mature sexual relations and emotional intimacy	Sexual dysfunction and unsatisfactory relationships

under social and moral constraints and the ones that are most likely to be left unsatisfied. Accordingly, the stages of development are termed **psychosexual stages** and several are named after specific *erogenous zones,* or pleasure-producing areas of the body. As shown in **Table 13-1**, Freud labeled the stages *oral, anal, phallic, latency,* and *genital.*

The psychosexual stages function as learning periods. Children must successfully complete, or *resolve*, the issues of each stage to form a healthy personality. As children move into a new stage, they must cope with new demands from the environment and conflicting internal feelings. If they do not successfully resolve the conflicts that arise, they may become *fixated*, or mentally stuck at that stage of development. Freud hypothesized that a fixation may affect all subsequent development.

Freud linked fixation at different psychosexual stages to the development of distinct, sometimes abnormal, personality characteristics. For instance, Freud believed that a boy in the phallic stage focuses on his penis and a girl on her lack of a penis (so-called *penis envy*). A boy entering the phallic stage also begins to feel sexual attraction toward his mother and jealous rage toward her love interest, his father. Freud called these feelings the *Oedipus complex*, after the character in Greek mythology who inadvertently killed his father and married his mother. At the same time, the boy fears that his father will punish him for his feelings, perhaps by cutting off his main zone of pleasure, his penis (so-called *castration anxiety*). These feelings, of course, are unconscious, and the child's attempts to resolve the conflicts they create also occur largely at the unconscious level. If children fail to resolve such conflicts, they may suffer from **neuroses**, Freud's term for abnormal behavior patterns characterized by anxiety, depression, and other such symptoms.

Anxiety and Defense Mechanisms   We've seen that internal conflict, often resulting in anxiety, is central to personality development in psychoanalytic theory. Because humans cannot constantly live in an unsettled state of anxiety, they must have some effective methods for handling it. This realization forms the basis for one of Freud's major contributions to how human beings think about themselves: **defense mechanisms**. Freud described defense mechanisms as unconscious tactics employed by our egos to protect us from anxiety. **Table 13-2** lists and describes some defense mechanisms.

Repression is the most basic defense mechanism. This strategy keeps unpleasant memories or thoughts buried deep within our unconscious minds, protecting us from the difficult and painful process of facing them. Another frequently used defense mechanism, and one that has entered into our common vocabulary, is **denial**. This occurs

"I ran across something today you don't see much anymore—a guilty conscience."

TABLE 13-2 Some Common Defense Mechanisms

Mechanism	Description	Example
Repression	Keeping unpleasant memories or thoughts buried in the unconscious	Forgetting the details of a tragic accident
Denial	Refusing to recognize an unpleasant reality	Refusing to admit an addiction
Rationalization	Creating a socially acceptable excuse to justify unacceptable behavior	Justifying cheating on taxes because "everyone does it"
Reaction formation	Not acknowledging unacceptable impulses and overemphasizing their opposite	Overpraising a sibling's accomplishment even though resentful
Projection	Transferring one's unacceptable qualities or impulses to others	Not trusting a coworker and believing the coworker does not trust you
Displacement	Diverting one's impulses to a more acceptable target	Yelling at family members after being yelled at by your boss
Sublimation	Channeling socially unacceptable impulses into acceptable activities	Redirecting aggressive behavior by becoming a professional fighter
Regression	Reverting to immature ways of responding	Throwing a tantrum when frustrated
Identification	Enhancing self esteem by imagining or forming alliances with others	Joining groups for their prestige value
Intellectualization	Ignoring troubling emotional aspects by focusing on abstract ideas or thoughts	Discussing various economic theories while ignoring the pain of losing your job

when a person simply refuses to recognize an existing situation. A person who gambles constantly, for example, may claim that she doesn't really gamble that much or that, even if she does, it isn't a problem. It's important to remember that, as stated above, defense mechanisms are unconscious tactics. Thus, the gambler in our example is not consciously making excuses for her behavior when she practices denial.

Evaluating Freud's Theories   Many of Freud's basic ideas have been incorporated into the intellectual foundations of psychology and continue to influence the development of the field (Solms, 2007, 2004; Westen, 1998). However, since the mid-twentieth century, when the popularity of psychoanalytic theory was at its highest, Freud's theories have come under significant criticism in the scientific community. The scholar Anthony Grayling recently wrote, for example, "Philosophies that capture the imagination never wholly fade . . . but as to Freud's claims upon truth, the judgment of time seems to be running against him" (Grayling, 2003). Such criticism is largely due to the fact that the key principles of psychoanalytic theory are based on observations that cannot be readily tested by scientific methods.

Freud based his theories on the cases of patients he treated in his private practice as a neurologist. When presented with puzzling symptoms, Freud pieced together clues from the patient's childhood to try to identify the cause. For example, one of his patients—a five-year-old boy called "Little Hans"—had developed an intense fear of horses (Freud, 1909). Freud came to believe that the boy's anxiety was a product of his psychosexual development related to his relationship with his father. In a lengthy summary of his treatment of Hans, Freud described his procedure for helping the father and son learn to address the repressed feelings that were leading to Hans's anxiety.

psychosexual stages according to psychoanalytic theory, stages in the development of personality; the stages—labeled oral, anal, phallic, latency, and genital—are primarily influenced by sexuality and aggression.

neurosis an abnormal behavior pattern caused by unresolved conflicts between the id, ego, and superego.

defense mechanisms unconscious tactics employed by the ego to protect the individual from anxiety.

repression the most basic defense mechanism; the process of keeping unpleasant memories or thoughts buried deep within the unconscious mind.

denial a defense mechanism; the process of refusing to recognize an existing situation.

Setting the stage Freud was among the first theorists to hold that parent-child relationships influence how people feel about themselves and how they handle intimacy as adults. It is obvious which of the interactions pictured here represents a healthier approach to correcting a child's mistakes, according to Freud.

Freud's case studies, such as that of "Little Hans," are effective at characterizing and classifying certain types of observed behaviors. Indeed, Freud's theories can provide an explanation for almost any type of observed behavior. For example, we might say that a man who keeps getting into fist fights is redirecting angry, unresolved feelings of aggression toward his parents onto his various acquaintances in life. At the same time, we might say that another man, who is unhappy but not hostile, is repressing those same feelings of aggression. In both cases, we have explained the man's behavior (or nonbehavior). But recall that psychologists seek to predict as well as to describe and explain. Based only on the knowledge that a particular man has unresolved feelings of aggression toward his parents, could we predict whether or not he will be prone to hostile and fighting relationships? Probably not. This lack of predictive power is a key weakness of psychoanalytic theory.

Additionally, many of Freud's observations were based on a very small and select population of upper-class individuals from nineteenth century Vienna. This raises questions about the theory's cross-cultural validity and highlights the fact that Freud's ideas were based on his particular—and at times narrow—views of sexuality, parenting norms, and gender roles.

At the same time, Freud's supporters argue that it is unfair to criticize psychoanalytic theory for not holding up to scientific testing when it was never intended to act as a predictive model. Rather, Freud's fundamental claim was that individuals can find meaning from looking into their past (Rieff, 1979).

On the positive side, many aspects of Freud's theory remain relevant today, such as the idea that our relationships with our parents can influence how we form intimate emotional relationships in adulthood (Black & Schutte, 2006). In addition, some studies on defense mechanisms suggest that they are observable and can have important functions in both development and psychological disorders (Bouchard & Thériault, 2003; Perry, Hoglend, & Shear, 1998).

Perhaps most importantly, Freud's ideas spurred the first inquiries into the functioning of the conscious and unconscious aspects of the mind and how they relate to behavior. The study of the unconscious mind has accelerated in the last two decades. As you learned in Chapters 6 and 8, numerous studies indicate that much of the information processed by the mind remains unconscious and that people rely on a variety of automatic processes to function in the world.

Other Psychodynamic Theories

Moving beyond inferiority Adler proposed that a child's inevitable experiences of helplessness produce early feelings of inferiority, which can lead to a lifelong sense of inferiority or to a lifelong quest for completeness and superiority.

Over time, some of Freud's followers became critical of his ideas and split away to form their own schools of thought, becoming what are called *neo-Freudians*. Three of Freud's most notable followers were Alfred Adler, Carl G. Jung, and Karen Horney. Although their new theories departed from Freud's in important ways, each held on to Freud's basic belief that human functioning is shaped by interacting, or *dynamic,* underlying psychological forces. All such theories, including Freud's, are thus referred to as *psychodynamic theories.*

Alfred Adler   Unlike Freud, Alfred Adler (1870–1937) believed that social needs and conscious thoughts are more important to human behavior than sexual needs and other unconscious motivations. Adler was particularly interested in how feelings of *inferiority* motivate behavior. In Adler's view, almost everyone has some feelings of inferiority stemming from childhood experiences of helplessness. People often make special efforts to compensate for or mask those painful feelings. Adler focused, in particular, on how feelings of inferiority are channeled into a quest for superiority. Although Adler's school of *individual psychology* has not had a major impact on personality theory, his ideas about how the need for power shapes human behavior have gained momentum in contemporary research.

Carl Jung   Carl G. Jung (1875–1961), unlike Adler, agreed with Freud's views on the importance of the unconscious. However, he added a new dimension: the collective unconscious. In Jung's system, the unconscious has two parts. The *personal unconscious,* formed from individual experiences, is similar to the unconscious as seen by Freud. The *collective unconscious,* though, is not a private entity like the personal unconscious. Instead, it is a cumulative storehouse of inherited memories shared by all humankind. Jung called these shared memories *archetypes.* According to Jung, archetypes are reflected in symbols and images that appear in the art, literature, and religions of all cultures. The archetype of the hero, for example, can be found in the stories of almost any cultural tradition.

Jung's *analytical psychology* also differed from psychoanalytic theory in the emphasis placed on sexuality and aggression. Jung acknowledged the importance of these forces but argued that the unconscious also includes drives toward joy, creativity, and internal harmony. Indeed, the search for harmony is a central theme of Jung's theory. He believed that each of us seeks to integrate the mind's various conscious and unconscious elements into a coherent whole, which he termed the *self.*

The positive drives of personality One-hundred-year-old artist Frances Dunham Catlett speaks about her work at a reception celebrating her "century of creativity." Carl Jung believed that unconscious drives toward joy and creativity are powerful forces in personality.

PRACTICALLY SPEAKING   Jung in the Business World

In the 1940s, a mother-daughter team, Katharine Cook Briggs and Isabel Briggs Myers, both psychologists, created the Myers-Briggs Type Indicator (MBTI). Today it is one of the most well-known personality tests. Employers in various job fields, employment agencies, and job counselors distribute the questionnaire to several million individuals each year (Furnham, 2008). The test is popular because it describes how we interact with our environment as well as with other people. This knowledge can be extremely useful for a manager in charge of a team of employees from diverse backgrounds, for example.

The MBTI is based on Carl Jung's theory of personality types and it describes personality in terms of individual preferences for perceiving and judging the world (Kennedy & Kennedy, 2004). Do you prefer a more social or solitary environment? How do you interpret the information you take in? When you make a decision, do you first think about it logically or emotionally? Are you open to several possibilities? Your answers describe your basic preferences and, theoretically, reveal a lot about the kinds of jobs you would most enjoy (Myers et al., 1998). Knowing your preferences may also provide clues about your strengths and weaknesses at work. One thing the MBTI cannot inform you or a prospective employer about is your abilities (McCrae & Costa, 1989). It cannot tell you how well you will perform a particular job.

Most psychologists warn against basing career decisions only on the MBTI (Gardner & Martinko, 1996; Abella & Dutton, 1994). Although the test may inform you that you meet the criteria of an introverted type, this does not mean that you should avoid that sales job you were coveting. Your categorization as an introvert does not mean that you are totally lacking in extraversion qualities. Moreover, success at the job depends on many variables beyond extraversion or other such personality traits. And finally, for most jobs, there are a variety of different approaches that can lead to success.

self-actualization the need of humans to fulfill their full and special potential; the highest-level of need in Maslow's hierarchy of needs.

positive psychology an area of psychology focusing on positive experiences and healthy mental functioning.

self-concept a pattern of self-perception that remains consistent over time and can be used to characterize an individual.

unconditional positive regard acceptance without terms or conditions.

Karen Horney   Karen Horney (1885–1952), another neo-Freudian, accepted many of the basic principles of psychoanalysis but went on to develop her own orientation and school of psychoanalytic training. Horney agreed with Freud that anxiety-provoking experiences in childhood can lead to lasting psychological problems, but she was particularly interested in what she called *basic anxiety,* which develops in children who experience extreme feelings of isolation and helplessness. Basic anxiety, in Horney's view, sets the stage for later neuroses.

Perhaps Horney's greatest disagreement with Freud related to the role of cultural influences on behavior. To Freud, the basic conflicts that shape development are universal, but Horney observed distinct differences in personality structure between patients from Europe and those from the United States. She came to believe that cultural differences play a more important role in development than traditional psychoanalytic theory acknowledged. Horney rejected Freud's theories about penis envy, suggesting that what Freud was really detecting was women's envy of men's power—power that came from cultural norms, not inherent differences.

Humanistic Theories

Psychodynamic theorists, particularly Freud, generally believed that personality development is driven by forces beyond our control. Humanistic psychologists offered a different view: one that emphasized the potential of individuals and highlighted each person's consciousness, free will, and other special human qualities. Let's consider the ideas of two key humanistic theorists: Abraham Maslow (1908–1970) and Carl Rogers (1902–1987).

Abraham Maslow   As we mentioned in Chapter 1, Abraham Maslow believed that humans are basically good and that there is in each individual an urge to grow and fulfill his or her potential. Maslow proposed that personality arises from people's striving to meet their needs (Leontiev, 2008). As you saw in Chapters 1 and 11, these needs are arranged hierarchically, beginning with the need for basic physiological necessities, such as food and shelter, and becoming increasingly complex. Only after our basic needs have been met can we address more subtle needs and strive to attain more complex things. Our highest-level need is **self-actualization**—the need to fulfill our full and special potential as human beings. Maslow described self-actualization as, "the full use and exploitation of talents, capacities, [and] potentialities" (1970, p. 150). He suggested that psychologists had become overly focused on biological drives and needs, overlooking the role of high-level processes and the need for more complex forms of fulfillment.

Unlike Freud, Maslow believed that more could be learned from individuals who were healthy and well adjusted than from those who were experiencing psychological problems. In fact, he based his notion of self-actualized individuals on notable historical figures who appeared to lead rich and healthy lives: Albert Einstein and Eleanor Roosevelt, for example. The characteristics that define self-actualized people are the ability to recognize the needs and desires of others, the willingness to respond to the uniqueness of people and situations rather than responding in mechanical or fixed ways, an emotionally deep connection with a few people, spontaneity and creativity, and the ability to resist the urge to conform while still responding to reality.

More recently, some of Maslow's ideas were taken up by psychologist Mihaly Csikszentmihalyi (2003, 1998). Csikszentmihalyi studied *peak experiences*—moments in which people experience intense clarity of perception, feelings of joy and excitement, and a suspended sense of time and reality. Maslow thought that such moments usually occur when a person becomes totally engrossed in an activity, such as when we hear a beautiful piece of music or experience the beauty of nature. Csikszentmihalyi's

Candidates for self-actualization Maslow proposed that self-actualized people also recognize the needs of others and seek to address them. He believed that full self-actualization is rare, but some of today's humanists consider Microsoft founder Bill Gates and rock star Bono to be candidates for this distinction, given their worldwide humanitarian and charitable undertakings.

writing on peak experiences reflect psychologists' growing interest in **positive psychology**, the study of positive experiences and healthy mental functioning that we discussed in Chapter 12 (Baumgardner & Crothers, 2009; Seligman & Csikszentmihalyi, 2000). Such ideas also have been influential in sports psychology. Basketball players, for example, talk about "hitting the zone"—reaching a point where they feel they can't miss or the hoop seems twice as big.

Carl Rogers   Carl Rogers, like Maslow, believed that human nature is fundamentally positive and that people strive for self-actualization (Rogers, 2008, 1963). However, Rogers based his theory of personality around the concept of the *self* rather around a hierarchy of needs. For Rogers, **self-concept** is a pattern of perception that remains consistent over time and can be used to characterize an individual. Our self-concept is related both to how we see ourselves and to how others see us. Because self-concept develops in part based on how we are perceived by others, as children we need **unconditional positive regard**—acceptance without terms or conditions—from parents or other adults to develop healthy self-concepts.

The idea of unconditional positive regard became a central part of Rogers's therapeutic practice. He believed that, over the course of development, many children form *conditions of worth*, a perception that they must meet certain standards in order to gain the love of their parents or other important figures. These conditions of worth, often rigid or harsh in nature, can hold over into adulthood and act as a negative force that prevents a person from reaching his or her full potential. Not surprisingly, in Roger's *client-centered therapy,* discussed in Chapter 1, he worked with clients to create an atmosphere of openness, honesty, and absence of judgment, regardless of the specific type of psychological problems the persons were experiencing. He believed that only in such an atmosphere can individuals begin to put aside the conditions of worth that lie at the root of their personal maladaptive functioning.

"Just remember, son, it doesn't matter whether you win or lose—unless you want Daddy's love."

Evaluating Humanistic Theories   Many critics fault the humanistic theories for their overly positive focus, saying that they are simplistic and that they ignore the role of psychological dysfunction in society. In addition, it has been difficult for researchers to conduct controlled studies on such abstract concepts as self-actualization and unconditional positive regard. However, humanistic theories have had a pervasive influence on the field of psychology. As mentioned above, and elsewhere in the textbook, researchers in positive psychology are giving new attention to questions about how human beings can achieve their full potential for happiness. It remains to be seen how humanistic psychology will contribute to this ongoing discussion.

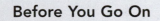

Before You Go On

What Do You Know?

1. In Freudian theory, how does a neurotic personality develop?
2. What is repression?
3. What are some common criticisms of psychoanalytic theory?
4. How did Jung's idea of the unconscious differ from Freud's?
5. What is a key difference between psychoanalytic and humanist thinking?

What Do You Think?   What would fit into your description of a fully self-actualized person? Can you think of anyone who matches this description?

personality traits tendencies to behave in certain ways that remain relatively constant across situations.

superfactor a fundamental dimension of personality made up of a related cluster of personality traits.

Understanding Personality Today: Traits versus Situations

LEARNING OBJECTIVE 2 Compare and contrast trait theories of personality with situational theories.

If you were asked to describe your best friend's personality, you might use words, such as *funny, caring,* and *outgoing.* Indeed, an investigation conducted in 1936 revealed that in the English language alone, there are 4,500 words to describe personality (Allport & Odbert, 1936). Many of today's personality theories are based on the premise that people's personalities are made up of collections of **personality traits**—tendencies to behave in certain ways that remain relatively constant across situations. More precisely, personality traits describe our general dispositions, and those dispositions lead to our behaviors. If people are generally enthusiastic, for example, they may display their trait of enthusiasm by approaching their homework with gusto or singing out as they walk down the street. Of course, as many theorists point out, it is often difficult to pinpoint aspects of an individual's personality that are entirely consistent across time and situations. Here, we'll examine some of the work that has been done on the influence of traits and situational factors on personality.

Trait Theories

Human beings are natural trait theorists. It appears, though, that we are likely to explain our own behavior in situational terms and others' behavior in terms of personality traits (this tendency, called the *fundamental attribution error,* is discussed further in Chapter 14). For example, you didn't finish your paper because you were busy studying for two tests in your other classes. That guy over there, however, didn't finish his paper because he was disinterested or disorganized. Thinking about others' behavior in terms of traits helps make their behavior predictable and gives us a sense of how our interactions with them might go.

It was trait theorists such as Gordon Allport (1897–1967) and Hans Eysenck (1916–1997) who first proposed that *central traits* affect a broad range of an individual's behavior. Among researchers, it is difficult to pinpoint a standard definition for central traits. Generally speaking, however, trait theorists assume that people have innate tendencies to respond to situations in certain ways (traits), that these tendencies can be linked together to form broad habits (central traits), and that such principles can be used to form the foundation of a scientifically testable theory. A man named Jason, for example, may have a lot of traits. He may be cheerful, friendly, lazy, disorganized, and talkative. According to the early trait theorists, however, only a few of his traits will dominate his behaviors, while others will be at work less often. Jason may be cheerful in most situations, from home to school and from changing a lightbulb to playing basketball (central trait), but lazy only when it comes to cleaning his house. Let's look at the ideas of Allport and Eysenck next and then move on to the influential *five-factor theory* of personality.

Gordon Allport   The influential personality theorist Gordon Allport believed that psychoanalysis "may plunge too deep, and that psychologists would do well to give full recognition to *manifest* motives before probing the unconscious" (1968, pp. 383–384). Unlike Freud, Allport did not believe that behavior is necessarily related to unconscious tensions; rather, it can be quite healthy and organized. Over the course of his long and distinguished career, Allport emphasized the unity and uniqueness of the individual, and he believed that the present is more important than the past in understanding personality. Allport conducted detailed case studies that sought to reveal the unique collection of traits at play for each individual. Because much of his work was based on case studies, his ideas have sometimes been criticized by other trait theorists who use empir-

> " I am what is mine. Personality is the original personal property. "
>
> —*Norman O. Brown,*
> *American writer and philosopher*

ical investigations to identify the traits that run through large populations. Nevertheless, his work on personality factors provided the starting point for many empirical studies.

Hans Eysenck and Factor Analysis The British psychologist Hans Eysenck was a strong proponent of using reliable statistical measures to test psychological principles. To Eysenck, it was vital to develop a theory that could be scientifically tested. As a result, he strove to develop adequate measures of personality traits and, specifically, measures of their biological foundations. He hoped that eventually theorists would be able to identify clear correlations between traits and behaviors and underlying biological systems.

Eysenck made particular use of *factor analysis*—which, as you may recall from Chapter 10, is a statistical method for analyzing correlations among variables. The use of factor analysis marked a significant turning point in the scientific study of personality theory. In the past, psychologists such as Freud and Allport had relied on case studies and on their own intuition to form ideas about personality structure. Although factor analysis can also be influenced by the decisions and interpretations of a given researcher, the method provides a much more objective way of identifying relationships between variables.

Eysenck used factor analysis to identify traits that cluster together to form fundamental dimensions of personality, which he called **superfactors** (**Figure 13-2**). Eysenck eventually identified three basic superfactors:

- *Extraversion*—the degree to which a person is outgoing and enjoys interacting with others. An *extravert* has personality traits such as impulsiveness, sociability, and assertiveness. At the other end of the spectrum, an *introvert* displays traits such as thoughtfulness, reliability, and passivity.
- *Neuroticism*—the degree to which a person tends to experience negative emotions, also known as *mental instability*.
- *Psychoticism*—the degree to which a person is vulnerable to developing the serious disorders known as *psychoses*, in which contact with reality is lost in key ways.

Eysenck saw each of these superfactors—and the individual character traits of which each is composed—as existing on a continuum, with each person displaying a certain degree of each superfactor.

Although Eysenck depended on factor analysis to determine how personality traits cluster together, he gathered information on the traits themselves through the use of questionnaires. He administered his *Eysenck Personality Questionnaire* to people in hundreds of countries. The results indicated that his superfactors correspond to basic personality types across many cultures (Eysenck, 2002, 1992, 1990).

The fictional detective Sherlock Holmes was asked by his friend Dr. Watson how he had deduced that a certain man was intellectual. "For answer Holmes clapped the [man's] hat upon his head. It came right over the forehead and settled upon the bridge of his nose. 'It is a question of cubic capacity,' said he; 'a man with so large a brain must have something in it.'"

—A. Conan Doyle, Adventure of the Blue Carbuncle

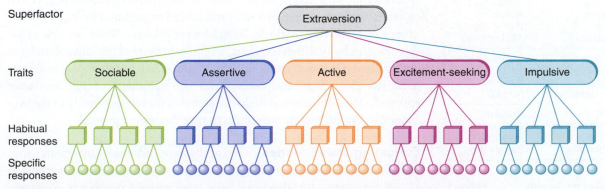

FIGURE 13-2 Eysenck's model of personality Eysenck used factor analysis to identify traits that cluster together. He described three basic trait clusters, which he called superfactors. Each superfactor, such as extraversion shown here, is made up of specific traits, and in turn each trait is made up of habitual and specific responses.

Spotting the superfactors The fundamental dimensions of personality cited in the Big Five Model and other theories of personality are each on display in this photo of people passing through an airport waiting area. Can you identify examples of these key trait categories?

Because Eysenck believed that personality traits were biologically based, he also studied the biological basis of personality traits. His belief in the biological roots of personality has been supported by a number of studies. Several investigations of twins, for example, suggest that genetics play a significant role in how individuals score on the extraversion superfactor (Heath, Cloninger, & Martin, 1994; Pergadia et al., 2006). A number of studies of hormones, blood pressure, and brain activity support the notion that biological factors are linked to the superfactors at least to some degree (Eysenck, 1990).

Eysenck's work has had an enormous influence on personality theory and research. His early emphasis on empirical research set the stage for much of the current research on personality. Moreover, Eysenck's personality tests have been translated into many languages, and his ideas and findings have influenced such diverse fields as education, aesthetics, politics, and psychopathology. Finally, he was one of the first psychologists to systematically investigate the possible biological basis of personality traits, an area of investigation that, as we shall see, has become a significant force in the field.

The Five-Factor Model   A number of factor analysis studies have derived more than three higher-order dimensions of personality, or superfactors (Poropat, 2009; Boyle, 2008; Saggino & Kline, 1996). The five-factor model identifies five major trait categories, popularly known as *the Big Five* (see **Figure 13-3**): *agreeableness* (versus disagreeableness); *extraversion* (versus introversion); *neuroticism* or *emotional instability* (versus stability); *conscientiousness* or *dependability* (versus irresponsibility); and *openness to experience* or *imaginativeness* (versus unimaginativeness). A helpful way to memorize these five factors is with the acronym OCEAN (openness, conscientiousness, extraversion, agreeableness, and neuroticism).

If you look closely, you'll notice that Eysenck's dimensions of extraversion and neuroticism are also found among the Big Five superfactors. His third dimension, *psychoticism*, however, does not appear in the five-factor model. That dimension was originally thought by Eysenck to serve as a marker of psychotic tendencies, and people with schizophrenia were indeed found to score high on this dimension. However, many people who score high on Eysenck's psychoticism dimension do not become psychotic and, in fact, they also display particular traits that are found within the Big Five superfactors of agreeableness and conscientiousness (Saggino, 2000).

Despite such differences, Eysenck would probably be happy to learn that trait theory has been reenergized in recent years, thanks largely to the popularity of the **five-factor theory**. Although some theorists argue that additional factors should be added to the list of five, a great many researchers believe that individual differences in personality can indeed be captured by the five broad categories of this theory (Boyle, 2008; McCrae & Costa, 2003). Because of the theory's popularity with researchers, a significant body of relevant research has accumulated (Cooper & Sheldon, 2002). This research has attempted to answer questions about both the validity and the usefulness of the five-factor approach. Most of the research discussed next thus relates directly to the five-factor theory, although some applies to trait theories in general.

Big Five Traits	Low Scorers	High Scorers
1 **O**penness	Practical Uncreative Incurious Conforming	Imaginative Creative Curious Independent
2 **C**onscientiousness	Disorganized Careless Lazy Late	Organized Careful Disciplined Punctual
3 **E**xtraversion	Retiring Passive Sober Reserved	Sociable Active Fun-loving Affectionate
4 **A**greeableness	Ruthless Suspicious Critical Uncooperative	Soft-hearted Trusting Lenient Helpful
5 **N**euroticism	Calm Unemotional Secure Self-satisfied	Anxious Emotional Insecure Self-pitying

FIGURE 13-3 The five-factor model of personality Studies using factor analysis have identified five broad categories of traits, known as *the Big Five*. Many researchers believe that individual differences in personality can be captured by these five categories.

Evaluating Trait Theories   One of the issues addressed by research into trait theories is whether they apply to a variety of cultures. As we mentioned, Eysenck found that his superfactors described basic types across a number of countries. In addition, there is growing evidence that people in many cultures display personality types that can be captured by at least three of the Big Five superfactors and sometimes by all five (Nye et al., 2008; Saucier, Hampson, & Goldberg, 2000; De Raad et al., 1998).

A second question involves how powerful personality traits are. Consider an interesting study conducted to determine whether people are "naturally" expressive or inexpressive (DePaulo et al., 1992). To evaluate a person's ability to control his or her expressiveness, the experimenters asked subjects to act either very expressively or very inexpressively while discussing a topic. Interestingly, even when asked to feign expressiveness, naturally inexpressive people showed less expression than did expressive people in their natural state. Similarly, when naturally expressive subjects were asked to act inexpressively, they were still more expressive than naturally inexpressive individuals. Clearly, traits are often quite powerful. Even when people want to behave in a manner that conflicts with a particular trait, they may have trouble doing so.

A third question is whether traits, and the behaviors they produce, remain stable across situations. The answer appears to be sometimes yes and sometimes no. In a classic investigation conducted in the early 1980s, investigators observed college students and rated their levels of *conscientiousness*, based on behaviors ranging from being punctual to completing assignments on time and tidying their rooms (Mischel & Peake, 1982). The researchers found that levels of conscientiousness were relatively stable across *similar* situations but not particularly consistent across very different situations. That is, persons who are punctual for class will likely be punctual for dates, because those situations and their demands are similar. However, individuals who are punctual may not necessarily keep their rooms clean. Although both of these situations require conscientiousness, the situations are quite different, leading to inconsistent displays of conscientiousness for some people.

Yet another question is whether traits, and the behaviors they dictate, are stable over time. Studies indicate that personality traits are more stable over a short period of time than over a span of years (Srivastava et al., 2003). People who conscientiously show up on time for an appointment today are likely to be punctual for appointments next week and next month. But today's punctuality is not as likely to predict punctuality a year or two from now.

Similarly, traits often show inconsistency across a person's lifespan, especially as individuals travel from childhood to adulthood (Fleeson, 2007, 2001). For example, people who score high during their teenage years on the *openness* superfactor (adventurous, imaginative, and untraditional), may display less openness in their fifties. Researchers disagree on why such lifespan changes occur. Some believe that they reflect intrinsic, biologically based maturation (McCrae, 2002), while others hold that they have more to do with changes in an individual's social environment (Srivastava et al., 2003). Either way, it is worth noting that once a person reaches adulthood, lifespan fluctuations seem to lessen, and traits become increasingly stable across the adult years (Roberts & Del Vecchio, 2000; Caspi & Roberts, 1999).

The predictive value of a model is another issue of concern to researchers. Although trait theories do not necessarily claim to serve as a device for predicting what will happen in a person's life, it is tempting to apply them in this way. In fact, the idea that personality factors may be able to predict broad outcomes dates back many years. One longitudinal investigation found that the Big Five superfactor *conscientiousness* can help predict the length of a person's life (Kern & Friedman, 2008). In this study, a large number of children were followed for 70 years by several researchers. When the children were 11 years old, their parents and teachers rated them on various personality dimensions, and subsequent records were kept about these individuals and the causes of their eventual deaths. It turned out that, on average, those who had been rated as conscientious lived significantly longer than those who had not been rated as conscientious. To explain this finding, the researchers speculated that conscientiousness is related to a broad pattern of health-related behaviors, such as not smoking and not drinking—behaviors that add up over a lifetime. Similarly, research has

five-factor theory an empirically derived trait theory that proposes five major trait categories: agreeableness/disagreeableness, extraversion/introversion, neuroticism/stability, conscientiousness/irresponsibility, and openness to experience/unimaginativeness.

Another benefit of conscientiousness An elderly teacher carefully demonstrates to a student how to operate woodwork equipment both safely and productively. Studies indicate that, on average, conscientious people live longer than less responsible individuals.

suggested that certain personality attributes may be predictive of marital satisfaction. One study found, for example, that high agreeableness greatly increases the chances of having a happy and satisfying marriage (Botwin et al., 1997) as do conscientiousness, emotional stability, and intellectual openness.

Finally, researchers have been interested in whether traits are inherited. As suggested earlier, case studies of monozygotic, or identical, twins who have been reared apart seem to suggest that genetic factors can have a strong influence on personality. In addition, a growing number of empirical studies indicate that heredity plays a role in many dimensions of personality (Krueger et al., 2008; Plomin & Caspi, 1999). Based on such studies, the heritability of personality traits has been estimated at around 40 percent (Pervin, Cervone, & John, 2005). In short, it appears that there is a strong genetic contribution to personality.

Situationism and Interactionism

Traits obviously play an important role in behavior. As we have just seen, traits can be predictive, powerful, and consistent forces in our lives. But are traits the single key to behavior? Apparently not. As we have also just observed, traits show more consistency and are more predictive in the short run than in the long run and across similar situations than across dissimilar situations. Clearly, there is more to behavior than traits alone. Personality theorists have wrestled with the relative importance of traits and situational factors, and as you will see, many have come to the conclusion that both are important (Fleeson, 2007).

The Situationist Approach   Over the years, as research identified the limits of trait theory and indicated the importance of situational factors, a number of personality theorists began to embrace a view called **situationism**—the notion that behavior is governed primarily by the variables in a given situation rather than by internal traits (Mischel, 2004). These theorists acknowledged that personality factors come into play when people are making choices, reacting to events, or displaying other behaviors. Nevertheless, the theorists argued, situational "pushes" and "pulls" rule in most instances.

The behaviorist B. F. Skinner, discussed in earlier chapters with regard to learning and operant conditioning, could be said to have viewed personality from a situationist perspective. Indeed, Skinner believed that human behavior was completely shaped by environmental factors. What we call *personality,* Skinner saw as simply a certain consistency in what he called *response tendencies.* By that, Skinner meant that we approach life in a certain way because certain responses have been rewarding to us in the past while certain other responses have not. That is, we tend to favor, or repeat, responses that have previously helped us gain a desired outcome or avoid an undesired one. Whereas a trait theorist might look at your presence in college as some combination of intelligence, conscientiousness, and perhaps a little neuroticism, Skinner would say that you studied because you found academic achievement to be rewarding or because studying served to keep your parents happy. Because these outcomes were sufficiently motivating, you developed a general response tendency to persist at studying, which led you to respond consistently in academic situations.

Situationism has a strong appeal. As we already mentioned, human beings appear predisposed to explain their own behavior in situational terms, although they tend to explain others' behavior in terms of traits. How often have you responded "it depends" when somebody has asked how you would handle a situation? Certainly, we do not like to think of ourselves as "trait machines"—robots who behave as if we were preprogrammed.

The famous behaviorist B. F. Skinner cited Freud more than he cited any other psychologist in his works. Skinner once applied to be psychoanalyzed at a Boston institute but was turned down because of a long waiting list.

At the same time, though, we must note that there really can be no such thing as *pure* situational factors in human behavior. Consider, for instance, Skinner's perspective on reward. As you saw in Chapter 7, Skinner defined a *reinforcer* as something that leads you to engage in a behavior more often. In other words, what is a reinforcer to you may not be a reinforcer to someone else. Theorists argue that even in the context of reinforcement principles, it is still *people* who choose, manipulate, interpret, and react to the situations—or reinforcements— they meet. It's hard to believe, for example, that a particular student puts off every single essay assignment until the very last minute because his or her reinforcers always line up in that direction. Ultimately, even as we acknowledge the power and influence of situations, we must acknowledge the power and influence of people and their personalities. Thus, it is not surprising that more and more of today's psychologists believe that the most appropriate models are those that try to integrate both personality variables and situational factors to explain behavior.

The Interactionist Perspective   One such model, **interactionism**, focuses on interactions between people and situations. At the center of the interactionist model is the idea that people influence the situations they encounter. According to this model, the choices you make, such as being at your present college or enrolled in your present classes, are functions of underlying personality traits. Let's say, for example, introversion leads you to choose a school with really small classes—a choice that you suspect would make it more comfortable for you to participate in class—or a school with really large classes—a choice that you believe would make it easier for you to go unnoticed in class. Such choices are likely to result in self-fulfilling prophecies. If you choose the school with big classes, for example, the large class sizes will indeed help ensure that you can remain quiet in class and continue your introverted style. This idea that individual and situational variables interact suggests a way of moving beyond the trait-versus-situation controversy.

One key example of interactionist theory is cognitive psychologist Albert Bandura's social-cognitive theory (Bandura, 2008, 2006), which you read about in Chapter 7. Bandura is famous for introducing the concepts of modeling and self-efficacy to the study of human behavior and personality. As you'll recall, *modeling*, also known as *observational learning*, is a process by which people, especially as young children, learn to respond to particular situations by observing and imitating the behavior of others. *Self-efficacy* refers to people's personal beliefs about their ability to achieve the goals they pursue. The higher your self-efficacy, the more likely you are to pursue a goal and, ultimately, to be reinforced by the outcome of your efforts.

How do these concepts influence personality? Through a process Bandura called *reciprocal determinism*. In Bandura's way of thinking, the external environment, internal mental events (such as one's beliefs and expectations), and behavior all interact with one another, as shown in **Figure 13-4**. How, for example, might your current presence in college be explained? Bandura might note that as a child you observed your parents or friends studying or working hard and as a result you engaged in similar behavior when you entered the school environment. Perhaps you were praised by teachers or your parents for good grades, which reinforced that behavior. You may in turn have developed a confident belief that you were a good student and curious about and open to new experiences, and your high level of self-efficacy may have led you to persist in behaviors (listening, completing your homework, studying) that further led to desired reinforcements (praise, good grades, positive self-image). Get that all rolling, and here you are.

The major advantage of this perspective over other theories of personality is that Bandura's theory, with its special emphasis on observable variables, such as models,

situationism the view that behavior is governed primarily by the variables in a given situation rather than by internal traits.

interactionism a view emphasizing the relationship between a person's underlying personality traits and the reinforcing aspects of the situations in which they choose to put themselves.

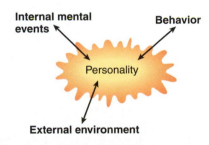

FIGURE 13-4 Bandura's theory of reciprocal determinism In Bandura's view, personality is determined by the interaction of the external environment, internal mental events, and behavior.

Film and television are powerful mediums in the entertainment industry. The stories conveyed in movies and TV shows can make us laugh, cry, or even get angry. But can they fundamentally affect our personality or influence how we act? This is a subject of much debate among parents, psychologists, and government organizations, such as the Federal Communications Commission (FCC).

In 2007, the FCC released a report regarding violent programming on TV (FCC, 2007). Although the report did not go so far as to describe what types of programming should be barred from TV, it did express concern over the relationship between aggression on TV and in real life. In one study, movie clips of violent acts were shown to university students to see whether the brain's response to aggression changes with repeated viewing. The researchers found that a region of the brain partly responsible for regulating aggression was less active after repeated exposure to violence (Kelly et al., 2007). Such findings have appropriately raised concern among scientists and the public. At the same time, it is important to recognize that although the average American views 200,000 dramatized acts of violence by the age of 18, most college-aged individuals are far from violent (Finley, 2007). In short, as we noted in Chapter 7, TV and movie viewing may indeed have a potential relationship to aggressive behavior, and perhaps to other undesirable behaviors as well, but other factors, such as parental and peer influences, may play an even more powerful role (Kim et al., 2006; Collins, 2005).

TV programs and films appear to have at least some influence on harmful and risky behavior, but can they also affect us in a positive way? A study of the effect of the movie *Super Size Me* – an exposé on overeating in the United States — showed that undergraduates who viewed the film were more conscientious about their food choices afterward (Cottone & Byrd-Bredhenner, 2007). However, the study did not examine whether long-term, permanent changes in eating behavior occurred.

Film and television are frequently blamed for negatively influencing the behavior of children and adolescents. Research suggests that such attributions may indeed have merit. At the same time, however, personality and behavior are complex, and a variety of genetic and environmental factors interact to influence who we are. In most cases, the content of movies and TV shows probably plays only a supporting role.

behaviors, goals, and outcomes, is readily testable. There is a vast amount of data linking both modeling and self-efficacy to personality development and change across the lifespan (Borgen & Betz, 2008; Walsh, 2007).

With an interactionist perspective in mind, personality researchers have recently uncovered a new kind of consistency in human affairs: not trait consistency, not situation consistency, but *disposition-situation* consistency. They have discovered that interactive effects between dispositions (traits) and situations are common and that disposition-situation relationships often show stability (Mischel, 2004; Shoda & Lee Tiernan, 2002). Such stability would be reflected by the statement, "Tamara is more outgoing than her sister when she decides to go for a run but less outgoing than her sister when visiting a museum in order to please her friends." This notion of stable patterns of disposition-situation relationships is just beginning to influence thinking relating to personality development.

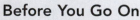

Before You Go On

What Do You Know?

6. What is factor analysis and with which school of personality theory is it most associated?
7. What are the Big Five personality factors?
8. How do situationism and interactionism differ?

What Do You Think?   How might Skinner and Bandura each view someone's failure to quit smoking?

Biological Foundations of Personality

LEARNING OBJECTIVE 3 Discuss the heritability of personality traits and some of the neural systems that may be involved in the expression of personality.

You've just seen that the trait-versus-situation debate has moved toward an interactionist view. As we mentioned earlier, the traditional nature-nurture debate has changed in much the same way. In recent years, many researchers have been trying to understand the *relative* contributions of genetic and environmental factors to the development of personality. Other researchers have been investigating what brain structures and other neurological factors affect personality patterns.

How Much Do Genetic Factors Contribute to Personality? | How we *Develop*

As we have seen throughout this book, situations in which twins are separated very early in life and raised in different families afford researchers a unique opportunity to separate the effects of genetics, shared family and social environments, and nonshared environments. Perhaps the most famous of these twin adoption studies is the *Minnesota Study of Twins Reared Apart* (MISTRA) (Johnson et al., 2007; Bouchard & Pedersen, 1998). This investigation focused on 59 pairs of identical twins who had been raised in different families and 47 pairs of fraternal twins raised in the same household. Recall that identical twins have exactly the same genetic structure, while fraternal twins are no more genetically similar than nontwin siblings.

The twins who participated in the study spent six days taking personality and intelligence tests. The identical twins proved to be substantially more similar on every psychological dimension than the fraternal twins. These results suggest that shared environments are less important than genetic factors to the development of temperament and many personality traits, although shared environments certainly do contribute (Zawadzki et al., 2001).

Some broad traits appeared to have particularly strong genetic links (see **Figure 13-5**). For example, in twin studies of personality the superfactor *agreeableness* from the Big Five scale had an estimated heritability coefficient of .40, and the heritability coefficient of the superfactor *openness* was estimated to be .55 (Bouchard, 2004). Among more specific traits, the heritability coefficient for *warmth* was estimated to be .23, while that for *excitement* was estimated to be .36 (Jang et al., 1998; Loehlin, 1992).

The Minnesota Twin Study has been embraced by the media for its straightforward findings. It is easy, however, to misinterpret the meaning of heritability statistics. Based on their findings, for example, the study's authors have estimated that the heritability coefficient of IQ is close to .70 (other studies suggest that it is closer to .50). This is commonly misinterpreted to mean that IQ is 70 percent genetic and 30 percent environmental. In fact, however—as noted in Chapter 10—the heritability statistic is related to the total variance in a population rather than to the development of IQ on an individual level. That is, a heritability coefficient of .70 means that 70 percent of all differences observed in the tested population are due to genetic factors.

Some researchers have suggested that certain behavioral tendencies, which are expressions of personality, may also have an inherited component. For instance, genetic factors may contribute to an individual's tendency to watch television (Prescott et al., 1991). Even more complex behaviors, such as the tendency to get a divorce (McGue & Lykken, 1992) and to develop alcoholism (Froehlich et al., 2000; Pickens et al., 1991), have been

Separated at birth Identical twins Gerald Levy and Mark Newman were separated at birth and did not meet or know of each other's existence until adulthood. In the interim, they had both become firemen and developed a range of very similar personality characteristics, mannerisms, interests, and hobbies.

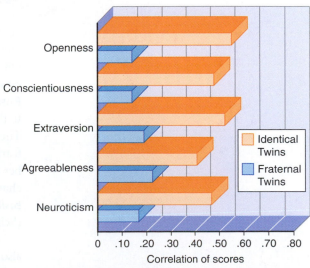

FIGURE 13-5 Heritability of the Big Five traits among twins Studies comparing identical twins (who share 100 percent of their genes) and fraternal twins reveal that the Big Five personality traits have a strong genetic component (Loehlin, 1992).

phrenology a method of assessing a person's mental and moral qualities by studying the shape of the person's skull.

found to be partially heritable. Of course, no single gene is at work in traits or in behaviors such as these. More likely, multiple genes interact and affect an individual's broad biological systems, and these systems contribute to the traits or behaviors in question.

Whatever the genetic pathway, even strong proponents of a genetic model now recognize that environmental experiences also play a critical role in how personality factors are expressed. Recall that Eysenck considered personality traits to be biologically based and proposed that the superfactor psychoticism served as a marker of psychotic tendencies, such as schizophrenia. Even Eysenck, however, discovered that persons who are predisposed to high levels of psychoticism will not necessarily develop schizophrenia. Their environmental experiences help determine whether they will become disabled by their genetic disposition or channel that disposition into more productive behaviors.

What Happens in the
Personality B R A I N ?

Although twin studies have suggested links between genes and personality, these studies do not provide precise information about what biological systems affect personality patterns. The search for such systems dates back to Franz Joseph Gall (1758–1828). Gall developed the theory of **phrenology**, a method of assessing a person's mental and moral qualities by studying the shape of the skull. He believed he could pinpoint specific parts of the brain that were responsible for distinct personality qualities (**see Figure 13-6**), and the practice became quite widespread between 1820 and 1850. Although Gall's techniques were later shown to be inaccurate, his ideas about the localization of brain functions and the role of the brain in personality continue to influence neurological science. Many researchers are currently attempting to uncover how brain structures, neurotransmitters, and other factors influence personality (Joseph, 2007). Much of this research focuses on specific personality traits, but a new line of study is also examining higher-order personality variables, such as moral inclinations and self-concept.

Left hemisphere

Right hemisphere

Prefrontal cortex

Amygdala

Research on Neural Systems and Personality Many studies suggest that certain *brain structures* help to regulate personality. As we have observed in previous chapters (Chapter 12, for example) the amygdala, a structure in the limbic system, plays a key role in emotionality, motivation, and the processing of negative stimuli, especially stimuli that activate fear and avoidance responses (Haas et al., 2007; Adolphs, Russell, & Tranel, 1999). Brain imaging studies have shown that people with damage to the amygdala have difficulty becoming conditioned to fear stimuli (Le Doux, 1999). The damage may prevent the amygdala from responding to stimuli that normally excite fearful responses in people without amygdala damage. Such studies have spurred a number of psychologists to theorize that children who display an inhibited personality—characterized by shyness and fear of the unfamiliar—may have amygdalas that are *too easily* activated, causing the children to be aroused by unfamiliar situations too readily (Schwartz, Snidman, & Kagan, 1999).

As you have already observed in earlier chapters, *cerebral hemisphere dominance* may also contribute in subtle ways to personality. Some studies have hinted that people whose right hemisphere is dominant experience more negative emotions and traits, such as withdrawal and inhibition, while those whose left hemisphere is dominant display more positive emotions and traits, such as extraversion (Davidson, 1998). One study found, for example, that participants who were generally sad and withdrawn displayed less activity in the left side of their prefrontal cortex—the part of the brain responsible for planned actions and thought and, in part, for emotional reactions to stress (Davidson & Fox, 1989). Moreover, the link between hemisphere dominance and personality may appear at a very early age. Psychologists have studied the brains of infants who show high levels of distress when separated from their mothers. Results indicate that such infants tend to display heightened activity in the right-side prefrontal cortex (Harman & Fox, 1997).

Neurotransmitter activity has also been linked to some personality variables. As mentioned earlier in this book, the neurotransmitter dopamine helps regulate the "pleasure pathway" (Dreher et al., 2009; Volkow & Fowler, 2000). It is central to the brain's reward systems. High dopamine activity in the reward centers, for example, has been associated with positive emotions, high energy, and lack of inhibition, while low activity of this neurotransmitter has been linked to anxiety, inhibition, and low energy levels (Zuckerman, 2007, 1995). Similarly, low serotonin activity has been associated with depression, violent behavior, and impulsivity (Knutson et al., 1998). In addition, the important hormone cortisol, secreted by the adrenal cortex to help regulate reactions to threatening experiences, has also been tied to personality. In Jerome Kagan's famous 1994 study of inhibited children (discussed in Chapter 3), he measured the blood cortisol levels of children as they were reacting to stress situations. He found that the children with inhibited personalities tended to have higher cortisol stress reactions to unfamiliar situations.

Organizing Research Findings Numerous studies have looked at the link between biological processes and personality, yielding findings that are complex and often confusing. One of the most compelling methods for organizing these findings has been suggested by the researchers Lee Anna Clark and David Watson, who grouped personality types into three broad categories of temperament (Watson et al., 2008; Clark & Watson, 1999), similar to the superfactors proposed by Eysenck and the Big Five theorists.

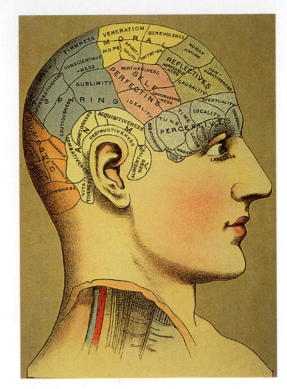

FIGURE 13-6 Bumps, lumps, and personality
Franz Gall proposed that personality could be determined by measuring the bumps on a person's skull, and he diagramed the areas associated with particular personality traits. While his assumptions were wrong, his idea that brain functions are localized is true.

- *Negative emotionality* Individuals who have high levels of negative emotionality are thought to experience more negative emotions and see the world as distressing, whereas those low on this dimension are relatively peaceful and have higher levels of satisfaction.

- *Positive emotionality* Measures of positive emotionality are thought to represent a person's engagement with their environment. High scorers are social individuals who lead active lives and exhibit enthusiasm, while low scorers are shyer and have less energy and self-confidence.

- *Disinhibition versus constraint* The disinhibition/constraint dimension reflects how we regulate our various emotions. People high in disinhibition have difficulty controlling their emotional responses and tend to be impulsive, living for the moment rather than in a careful and controlled manner.

Note that negative emotionality and positive emotionality are two separate dimensions. These two types of emotionality are not necessarily at opposite ends of a spectrum. A person may score high on both, low on both, or high on one and low on the other.

Scores on the three dimensions are broadly related to particular lifestyle patterns (see Figure 13-7). Individuals high in negative emotionality are more likely to experience feelings such as anger, contempt, and guilt, while those high in positive emotionality tend to experience positive emotions such as joy, excitement, and pride. Some problematic lifestyle patterns may be found among individuals who score high on the disinhibition dimension. These individuals, who are high in impulsivity and do not act with long-term consequences in mind, tend to get poorer grades in school, perform more poorly in their jobs, and engage in riskier activities, such as drinking and using illegal drugs. Interestingly, "morning people" are more likely to be high in positive emotionality, while many "night owls" are high on the disinhibition dimension (Clark & Watson, 1999).

FIGURE 13-7 The biology of personality Clark and Watson grouped the findings from personality studies into three dimensions of temperament. Research evidence suggests that biological processes are at the root of these temperament dimensions.

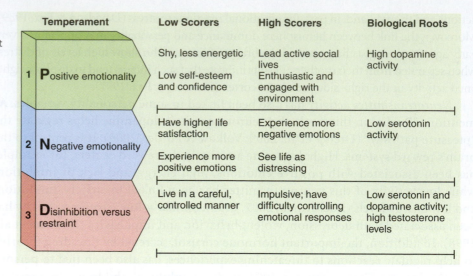

Temperament	Low Scorers	High Scorers	Biological Roots
1 **P**ositive emotionality	Shy, less energetic Low self-esteem and confidence	Lead active social lives Enthusiastic and engaged with environment	High dopamine activity
2 **N**egative emotionality	Have higher life satisfaction Experience more positive emotions	Experience more negative emotions See life as distressing	Low serotonin activity
3 **D**isinhibition versus restraint	Live in a careful, controlled manner	Impulsive; have difficulty controlling emotional responses	Low serotonin and dopamine activity; high testosterone levels

《Don't you just love being with someone who's recklessly impulsive?》

—*Homer Simpson,* The Simpsons

《Actually, it's aged me terribly.》

—*Marge Simpson, Homer's wife*

Evidence suggests that different biological processes may be at the root of these three dimensions. Levels of positive emotionality appear to be associated with higher dopamine activity (Clark & Watson, 1999; Depue & Collins, 1999). Although less is known about the biological system linked to the regulation of negative emotionality, this dimension is thought to be primarily tied to low serotonin activity (Clark & Watson, 1999). The biological roots of disinhibition appear to be more complicated. Low serotonin activity seems to contribute to aggressiveness and to increase a person's likelihood of abusing substances, while low dopamine activity contributes to thrill seeking and impulsivity, other features of the disinhibition dimension—almost as if individuals need to seek outside thrills to make up for deficiencies in their dopamine-activated pleasure pathways (Clark & Watson, 1999). Testosterone also comes into play in disinhibition. High levels of this hormone have been associated with aggressiveness and competitiveness, prominent characteristics of the disinhibition dimension (Carré et al., 2009).

Interpreting Research Findings Although research findings suggest links between brain functioning and personality, we must, as always, take care in interpreting these findings. The links just discussed are not usually straightforward, and personality traits are never the result of a single biological process. The activity of one neurotransmitter—say, serotonin—is, at most, *partially* responsible for the regulation of a trait or emotion. Clearly, the relationships between biology and personality that have been discovered represent only a glimpse of the complex neurological system.

In addition, it is important to remember that the patterns of brain activity that we have observed have not been shown to provide a causal explanation of traits. Particular biological processes associated with personality may themselves be the results of environment and experience. As you have seen, for example, studies indicate that life experiences, even very early ones, may affect both biological make-up and personality patterns, present and future. One study of rhesus monkeys found that baby monkeys who had endured high levels of abuse and rejection by their mothers displayed lower levels of serotonin activity in adulthood. Moreover, the lower their level of serotonin activity in adulthood, the more likely they were to abuse their own offspring (Maestripieri et. al, 2006). Clearly, environmental factors, even at an early age, greatly affect the neurobiological system, and that impact can be enduring.

In summary, we must be very careful about the conclusions we draw from genetic and neurological personality research. First, we must keep in mind that the brain operates as a system, and personality reflects activity in a number of regions, as well as the expression of multiple genes (Bouchard, 2004). Second, we must recall that one gene may interact with other genes and affect a variety of personality dimensions (Livesley, Jang, & Vernon, 2003). Third, we need to recognize that the environment affects the operation and impact of both genetic and biological processes, and those processes in turn affect how individuals interact with their environment. Given the complex, bidirectional relationships that occur between traits, biological factors, the environment, and behavior, the only certain conclusion that can be drawn is that much more research is needed before we can truly understand the nature and causes of personality.

Before You Go On

What Do You Know?

9. What do we mean when we say that the Big Five dimension of openness has a heritability coefficient of .55?

10. What is thought to be the role of the amygdala in the development of inhibited personalities?

11. What are the three categories of temperament proposed by Clark and Watson?

12. Why is it necessary to be careful in interpreting research findings associating particular personality traits with particular biological substances or structures?

What Do You Think? Many of the same brain structures are involved in both emotion and personality. Discuss what you think this suggests about the relationship between emotion and personality.

Personality HOW weDiffer

LEARNING OBJECTIVE 4 Explain how gender and cultural differences can affect personality.

We've focused so far on ideas about how personality unfolds. Let's turn now to the question of group differences in personality, examining gender differences and differences among different cultures and subcultures.

Gender Differences

The 1992 book *Men Are from Mars, Women Are from Venus* has sold more than six million copies in the United States and been translated into 40 languages. The book's premise that men and women are entirely different clearly struck a responsive chord. But how accurate is this notion?

Research into Gender Differences A number of studies suggest that the widespread belief in inherent personality differences between men and women may be no more than a myth. Recent broad reviews of studies on gender differences in personality, cognitive abilities, and leadership have found that the similarities between men and women far outnumber the differences (Hyde, 2008, 2007, 2005). Differences among individuals of each gender are much larger than differences between males and females (Costa, Terracciano, & McCrae, 2001). Beyond all this, gender researchers have begun to note the importance of *context* in investigations of psychological gender differences. The situational and social context of a study—for instance, the male-to-female ratio in the experimental room—can greatly influence the nature and size of observed gender differences (Bussey & Bandura, 1999; Eagly & Wood, 1999). Many psychologists rightly stress that incorrect conclusions about certain gender differences can perpetuate stereotypes and improperly affect men and women at work, at home, and in their professional lives (Barnett & Rivers, 2004).

Nevertheless, we must be clear that some consistent sex differences have been documented. For example, women, on average, tend to be more accurate than men at assessing emotion in other people (McClure, 2000). The psychologist Carol Gilligan—who,

A caring life Operating against the stereotype that females are consistently more nurturing than males, animal shelter worker Sam Wheeler has devoted much of his life to loving and caring for unfortunate dogs and cats.

along with Karen Horney, was one of the first theorists to focus on how women differ psychologically from men—argued that women and men, in fact, view the world differently, although she also emphasized that one perspective is not superior to the other (Gilligan, 2004). Gilligan, whom you first met in Chapter 3, believes that women are more attuned to interpersonal concerns when making moral decisions, while men are more likely to base such decisions on laws or abstract principles. Building on this idea, she has found that men, on average, score higher on traits that reflect individuality and autonomy, while women score higher on ones that emphasize social connectedness (Gilligan, 1982). Similarly, some investigations have indicated that women tend to display more nurturing behaviors (Feingold, 1994).

After statistically comparing the results of many studies relating to gender differences in personality, psychologist Janet Hyde (2008, 2005) found only a handful of variables on which females and males differed consistently. Those that she did find, however, seem to be important. Levels of aggression—particularly physical aggression—were somewhat higher among males. In addition, males were quite different from females on measures of motor performance and sexuality, and males and females had strikingly different attitudes about sex in casual, uncommitted relationships—men were more open to sex in such instances. As we noted in Chapter 11, the data on gender differences in sexual attitudes may be influenced by research participants' awareness that society expects men and women to behave in certain ways sexually. Still, it is clear that, overall, differences in aggression and attitudes may lead to significant differences in the expression of personality.

Why Do Gender Differences in Personality Exist? Knowing about gender differences is similar to looking at the results of a personality assessment—both provide descriptions but do little to explain *why* certain patterns exist and what those patterns may say about future behavior. A number of theories attempt to explain the personality differences observed in men and women.

One theory explains these differences in sociocultural terms. After all, a person's self-concept, life goals, and values all develop in a social context. According to **social role theory**, girls and boys develop different personal styles, behaviors, and skills based largely on the division of labor between the sexes and the resulting differences in gender role expectations (Eagly & Koenig, 2006; Eagly, 1987). In other words, males and females develop the personality attributes that are best suited for the roles that they typically occupy. Some theorists believe that play behavior in childhood helps teach gender roles and expectations. Young boys are expected to play competitive games, for example, and often are given aggressive-type action figures as toys. Girls, in contrast, are encouraged to play games that emphasize nurturing and interacting with peers.

Family and social relationships may also contribute to the development of personality differences between boys and girls. As children interact with their families and peers, they form ideas about gender role expectations based on how those other individuals react to their behaviors. Particularly important, the reactions of others teach children what behaviors and ideas are not appropriate to their gender role (Henley, 1977). A little boy may, for example, face disapproval if he plays with dolls rather than action figures.

Broad cultural practices, often a reflection of religious and philosophical beliefs, are also significant in the development of male-female differences. Traditionally, men held a position of higher power than women in most societies, and this power structure had a "trickle-down" effect on smaller units of behavior. Women, for example, often were limited to certain roles, such as child rearing, domestic work, and particular occupations (nurse, teacher, secretary). It may be that women were more likely to develop certain personality traits as a result of these constraints. Consider, for example, the superior abilities of women, on aver-

social role theory theory that gender differences occur because girls and boys develop different behaviors and skills based largely on differences in gender role expectations.

age, to read emotions and to perform in the social realm. Individuals who are in positions of less power or privilege may need to develop their skills at recognizing interpersonal cues and spotting the emotions of those in power in order to better address their own needs (Eagly & Koenig, 2006; Tavris, 1991; Eagly 1987).

A number of theorists further propose that cultural norms influence how men and women form their self-schemas. As we discussed in Chapter 3, *schemas* are ways we organize knowledge. A *self-schema* is an individual's cognitive framework for the knowledge he or she has about himself or herself. When we need to process new information about ourselves or our interactions, we refer to these schemas for guidance. A number of studies suggest that men are more likely to have self-schemas that emphasize autonomy and independence, while women are more likely to have collectivist or relationship-based schemas (Bekker & van Assen, 2008). One team of researchers further hypothesized that an individual's self-esteem would be directly related to how well he or she lived up to gender-dependent schemas—a hypothesis supported by a study they conducted (Josephs, Markus, & Tarafodi, 1992). Research participants who believed that they equaled or surpassed most of their peers in gender-specific skills and abilities had consistently higher levels of self-esteem.

In addition to such sociocultural factors, biological factors may play a role in gender differences in personality. In Chapter 4, for example, we discussed the nature and importance of *hemispheric lateralization* in the brain. It turns out that males and females may exhibit different degrees of hemispheric lateralization. Male brains tend to be more functionally lateralized than female brains: In male brains, one hemisphere is relatively dominant for various kinds of processing, while female brains appear to be more integrated (Everhart et al., 2001; Saucier & Elias, 2001). Still other studies have found that the sex hormones, testosterone and estrogen, which are available in different amounts and often act differently in males and females, have major influences on behavior and personal tendencies, leading many theorists to believe that they also contribute to gender differences in personality (Hines, 2004; Dabbs et al., 2001, 1997).

In male-female conversations, women laugh 126 percent more often than men.

In summary, it is true that, on the one hand, many of our society's beliefs about male-female personality differences are incorrect or overstated. A number of psychologists worry that the Mars-Venus myth of massive gender differences serves to perpetuate harmful misconceptions. Highlighting differences between men and women, for example, may support prejudicial beliefs and discriminatory practices against women (Hyde, 2005). On the other hand, it is also true that that there is potential danger in not acknowledging the real differences that do exist between the genders. Such denial, argue a number of theorists, may serve to downplay the unique strengths and gifts of each gender. Perhaps the most appropriate response to this debate was offered by the psychologist Diane Halpern, past president of the American Psychological Association. There may be limited differences between males and females, Halpern stated, but "differences are not deficiencies" (Halpern, 2000).

Differences Among Cultural Groups

Around the world, each culture is characterized by its own values, beliefs, and to some degree, patterns of behaviors. These features help guide members of the cultural group, teaching them what they should value in life, how they should treat others in their group, and how they should view themselves in relation to society. Cultures also form their own ideas about what is important in life, and these ideas can vary widely. For example, the term *self-esteem,* so important in American culture, is not even found in a number of languages. Clearly, people who live in a society that does not emphasize self-esteem are less likely than Americans to spend their lives striving for it. Similarly, in North America and Western Europe, a person's goals and life path are often influenced by the culture's emphasis on autonomy and accomplishment, whereas in Asian cultures there is greater emphasis on contributing to a community and honoring one's family.

Some of the most comprehensive cross-cultural research has focused on personality development in individualist and collectivist cultures. As we observed in Chapter 12, most collectivist cultures consider the needs of the group more important than the needs of the individual. With this orientation comes heightened emphasis on the role of the individual within his or her family and on social relationships in general. In turn, the individual is more likely to strive to help maintain the social order and to exhibit humility in social interactions (Triandis, 2001; Triandis et al., 1990). Collectivist values are particularly found in African, Latin American, Asian, and Middle Eastern cultures (Buda & Elsayed-Elkhouly, 1998).

In contrast, individualist cultures value individual achievement, freedom, and success. The self is seen as independent, and each individual is thought to possess a set of psychological qualities that are distinct from those of others. Unlike collectivist cultures, individualist cultures consider individual attainment more important than the needs and values of others. Indeed, competition between individuals is valued. Countries known for this type of structure are Great Britain, the United States, and Australia.

Cross-cultural psychologists have uncovered some interesting personality variations between collectivist and individualist cultures (Oyserman et al., 2002, 2000; Schmitt et al., 2007). One large, multination study found that people in collectivist cultures tend to score higher on measures of agreeableness, for example, while people from individualist cultures score higher on measures of extraversion and openness (Hofstede & McCrae, 2004).

Happiness and success may also be defined differently from culture to culture. In collectivist societies, contentment is related to harmony in interpersonal relationships, and this emphasis affects behavior (Kitayama & Markus, 2000). Interpersonal behaviors are tailored to the feelings and needs of others (Kashima et al., 1992). A strong sense of reciprocity and a responsibility to return favors shapes personal styles, behaviors, life goals, and measures of success. In such a culture, a sense of accomplishment comes not from individual achievements but from strong commitment to family, community, or company.

In contrast, people in more individualist cultures are less constrained by a tightly knit social network and enjoy greater personal freedom. They value their privacy and place a premium on individual human rights. Interestingly, some studies have found that people in individualist cultures report greater happiness than those in collectivist cultures (Kuppens, Realo, & Diener, 2008; Diener, Diener, & Diener, 1995). At the same time, however, individualist societies have higher rates of divorce, homicide, and stress-related disease than collectivist ones (Triandis 2001; Popenoe, 1993; Triandis et al., 1988).

People's sense of their own personalities also differs across cultures. Individuals in collectivist cultures, for example, do not use traits to describe themselves as often as those in individualist cultures. Studies have shown that when students are asked to complete the phrase "I am . . . ," those from the United States are more likely to answer using a personal trait (say, "I am friendly" or "I am honest"), while those from cultures with a collectivist orientation are more likely to describe themselves in a social manner (for example, "I am a member of the psychology department") (Cousins, 1989; Triandis, 2001, 1989). In light of such findings, some have argued that Western personality measures, such as the Big Five superfactors, are of limited usefulness in studying behavior in collectivist cultures (Church & Katigbak, 2000).

The interplay of culture and personality is also evident when people move from one environment to another. As a person becomes entrenched in a new cultural context, he or she typically absorbs the norms and values of the society. Indeed, research has revealed that when individuals move from a collectivist culture to an individualist one, their personal and behavioral patterns change. One study, for example, looked at

> "Nurture shapes nature."
> —Albert Bandura, psychologist

> "Different people bring out different aspects of one's personality."
> —Trevor Dunn, musician and composer

Different values, different personalities The different ways in which these business meetings are being conducted in the United States and Japan reflect the different values and personalities at work in individualist and collectivist cultures. Goals and personal styles in an individualist culture emphasize striving for autonomy, individual achievement, and high self-esteem. In contrast, those on display in a collectivist culture emphasize the community, cooperation, and honoring one's family.

the personality traits of Chinese students who were enrolled in universities in North America (McCrae et al., 1998). Those students who had been in North America the longest, and had presumably been more exposed to Western culture, showed higher levels of extraversion and had personality profiles more similar to those of other North Americans.

Interestingly, some people who come from bicultural backgrounds seem to develop the ability to "frame switch"—that is, to change back and forth between cultural frameworks as they interpret experiences. This suggests that they may have internalized the belief systems of both cultures (Hong et al., 2000). It is not yet clear what implications frame switching has for the ties between culture and personality. This is, however, an important question as the world moves each day toward greater cultural integration.

Differences Among Subcultures

Subcultures within larger cultural groups may also have their own sets of beliefs and practices. An interesting example is the variation we can see among the geographic regions of the United States, each of which has a distinct cultural identity. Although the U.S. culture as a whole is considered individualist, for example, regions vary in the strength of this orientation. The culture of the "Deep South" is relatively collectivist, a characteristic thought to stem from a history of conservative religious principles and nomadic farming, a type of farming in which groups of farmers keep moving to different pastures with their herds. Similarly, the Southwest is thought to have a culture that is relatively collectivist, perhaps because it has large Hispanic and Native American populations that tend toward collectivism. In contrast, the Great Plains and the Western mountain states are distinctly individualist, a cultural pattern that can be traced to the single family settlers who originally developed the land.

An example of the impact that culture may have on personal characteristics and individual behaviors can be found in the "culture of honor" in the southern United States (Vandello, Cohen, & Ransom, 2008; Nisbett & Cohen, 1996; Cohen & Nisbett, 1994). A belief common among Southern white men is that "honor"— which in this context means a reputation for strength and toughness—is key and that even violence is acceptable in order to protect one's honor. One study sought to determine how this broad code translates into the personal styles, perceptions, and reactions of individuals (Cohen et al., 1996). The researchers found that when southern white men were insulted, they were much more likely than uninsulted southern white men and insulted northern white men, to believe that the insult hurt their reputation and honor, to have elevated cortisol levels, to be primed for future aggression, and to behave in a domineering and physically aggressive way in subsequent situations (Cohen et al., 1996). Correspondingly, southern white men have a higher incidence of homicide than do northern men in cases where the homicides are triggered by seemingly trivial arguments (Cohen & Nisbett, 1994).

Culture, Socioeconomic Environment, and Personality

A key aspect of culture is the socioeconomic environment. Even in the most prosperous nations, there are distinct differences in living conditions between those in the lowest and highest income brackets. These differences have actually increased across the world in recent years (Autor, Katz, & Kearney, 2006). Although the relationship between socioeconomic conditions and personality traits has received relatively little attention, investigations conducted to date suggest that it is an important topic (Caspi, 2002; Caspi, Bem, & Elder, 1989). At the very least, it appears that living conditions have a direct impact on how and whether certain personality traits translate into behaviors.

One study assessed the impulsivity of a population of 13-year-old males in the city of Pittsburgh (Lynam et al., 2000). The teens in the study came from a mixture of backgrounds, from wealthy households to poverty-stricken neighborhoods, and their socioeconomic status was found to have a clear link to the outcomes of individual differences in impulsivity. Among boys who lived in poor neighborhoods, those who displayed high levels of impulsivity were much more likely to engage in delinquent behaviors than those who displayed low levels of impulsivity. In contrast, among boys from high-socioeconomic-status neighborhoods, behavioral differences between those with low and high impulsivity were negligible. To explain these findings, the investigators reasoned that poor neighborhoods produce many more triggers for delinquent acts, whereas community structures in affluent neighborhoods may offer limited opportunities for antisocial activities. In short, particular personality characteristics will result in particular behaviors only if certain situational triggers also are in place.

Socioeconomic class, impulsivity, and behavior
School children walk across the graffiti-covered yard of their financially troubled school. Research suggests that impulsive boys from poor neighborhoods may be more likely to engage in delinquent behaviors than impulsive boys from wealthier communities.

Before You Go On

What Do You Know?
13. What personality differences between men and women have researchers identified?

14. How does social role theory explain these differences?

15. What are some of the primary differences between the values of collectivist and individualist cultures and how do these differences affect personality?

16. How does the socioeconomic environment affect personality?

What Do You Think?
Think about the personality traits of a number people of you know. Include people of different gender and different cultural or subcultural groups. Do personalities seem to differ more on a group level or on an individual level among these acquaintances? How would you explain your observation?

Personality Disorders — When Things Go **Wrong**

personality disorder an inflexible pattern of inner experience and outward behavior that causes distress or difficulty with daily functioning.

LEARNING OBJECTIVE 5 Define personality disorder, and describe some features of narcissistic, antisocial, and borderline personality disorders.

Karen and I met two years earlier when I placed an ad in a newspaper for a new roommate. At first, things were a lot of fun, but then she would become really depressed off and on, and . . . well, weird. I thought we were having fun living together, discovering that we liked a lot of the same movies and music and things. Then one night, about two months after she moved in, I was getting ready to go out with a friend, and Karen demanded to know where I was going. She wanted to know who I was seeing, what I was doing, and then she tried to make me feel guilty for going out. "Fine, just leave," she pouted. She complained that we were no longer spending any time together, which was ridiculous because we had just spent a whole day at an art museum. When I pointed that out, she got hysterical, yelling at me, telling me that I only cared about myself.

When I came home that night, it was really scary. There was a little blood on the floor, and it made a trail that led to her bedroom door. When I banged on the door to see if she was all right, she said that she'd accidentally cut herself making a sandwich, and everything was fine.

Dealing with her was starting to take a lot out of me. Then she started dating this guy, Eric, and I thought things were getting better. Karen was spending almost no time at home, and when I did see her, she would gush about how incredibly happy she was—I mean, this was just weeks after she met him—how deep their relationship was and how perfect everything was. She was sure he was "the one."

I should have seen what was coming next, but, like an idiot, I didn't. Eric left her, and she was totally my problem again. She stayed home and cried for days at a time. She made me take care of her, telling me she was too depressed to do anything for herself. She even fantasized about the violent things she would do to Eric when she felt up to it, and cursed a blue streak while talking about him. After Eric, there was Ahmad, then James, then Stefan. Always the same story, always the same ending. And always with me in the middle—having to smile while she gushed endlessly about the latest relationship, or having to pick up the pieces when the relationship would end.

What does this description tell us about Karen? Was she the victim of emotionally distressing circumstances, or was her self-destructive behavior the result of dysfunctional personal characteristics? It appears that Karen's initial positive feelings and excitement about someone new in her life were invariably followed by a turbulent phase of emotional outbursts and an eventual falling out. This pattern suggests that Karen may have a **personality disorder**, an inflexible pattern of inner experience and outward behavior that causes distress or difficulty with daily functioning. Such patterns are enduring and differ markedly from the experiences and behaviors usually expected of people (APA, 2000).

As we suggested earlier in this chapter, each of us has a distinct personality and specific personality traits. Yet, for most of us, this distinct personality is also flexible. We are affected by situational factors, and we learn from our experiences. As we interact with our environment, we try out various responses to see which are more effective. This flexibility is missing in people who have a personality disorder.

Personality disorders usually become evident during adolescence or early adulthood, although some begin during childhood (APA, 2000). Between 9 and 13 percent of the general population of the United States are believed to display a personality disorder (O'Connor, 2008; Lenzenweger et al., 2007).

As in Karen's case, the effects of a personality disorder can sometimes be so subtle that they are initially unnoticeable. It may take multiple encounters over time for the

Disregarding others Financier Bernard Madoff was sentenced to 150 years in prison in 2009 after defrauding thousands of investors of billions of dollars. Many psychologists have proposed that Madoff meets the clinical criteria for a personality disorder, perhaps antisocial personality disorder.

maladaptive symptoms to become recognizable. Nevertheless, they have a significant impact on the individual's functioning in school, at work, and in social and romantic relationships. Many theorists have attempted to uncover the origins of personality disorders, and have highlighted factors such as the roles of biological predispositions, early experiences of abuse and neglect, and the pressures of poverty or otherwise harsh social environments (Bollini & Walker, 2007; Millon & Grossman, 2007; Patrick, 2007).

The American Psychiatric Association's diagnostic and classification system identifies ten personality disorders, and organizes them into three broad categories, or groups (APA, 2000) (see Table 13-3). The first group is marked by odd or eccentric behaviors and includes the *paranoid*, *schizoid*, and *schizotypal* personality disorders. The second group includes personality disorders that involve dramatic or emotional behavior: *antisocial*, *borderline*, *histrionic*, and *narcissistic* personality disorders. The third group features disorders characterized by high levels of anxiety and fear, including the *avoidant*, *dependent*, and *obsessive-compulsive* personality disorders. A look at the three most widely studied of these disorders—narcissistic personality disorder, antisocial person-

> "Personality disorders . . . are the only things left in psychiatry where people think you are bad."
>
> —*Gary Flaxenberg, psychiatrist*

TABLE 13-3 The Major Personality Disorders

Marked by odd or eccentric behavior
Paranoid: Exaggerated suspicion and distrust of others; assumption that others' motives are hostile; highly guarded and emotionally withdrawn
Schizoid: Detachment from social relationships; flat emotional expression; cold or indifferent to others
Schizotypal: Behavior that is odd or peculiar; unusual cognitive or perceptual experiences; acute discomfort with close relationships
Involve dramatic or emotional behavior
Antisocial: Extreme disregard for others; relationships are dishonest, deceitful, and exploitive; typically impulsive and reckless
Borderline: Severe instability in emotion and self-concept; impulsive and self-destructive behavior
Histrionic: Excessive need to be noticed and the center of attention; emotions shallow and changeable; engagement with others superficial
Narcissistic: Characterized by high degree of self interest and self-importance; callous attitude toward others
Characterized by high levels of fear and anxiety
Avoidant: Extreme feelings of inadequacy; avoidance of social activities; inhibited personal relationships; hypersensitive to criticism
Dependent: Excessive need to be cared for by others; clinging and submissive behavior; difficulty making decisions
Obsessive-compulsive: Preoccupied with perfectionism and control at the expense of flexibility or enjoyment; excessive devotion to work and productivity

Source: DSM-IV-TR, APA, 2000

ality disorder, and borderline personality disorder—reveals how disabling such disorders can be and how powerfully they can disrupt the lives of the people who have them, as well as their family members and friends.

Narcissistic Personality Disorder

People with **narcissistic personality disorder** might be described by others as being highly self-important and craving admiration. Narcissistic individuals often have an unrealistically inflated view of their abilities and accomplishments, and they are highly defensive and easily agitated when criticized or outdone by others. They tend to have a callous attitude and are only interested in others as a means of advancing their own interests or status (O'Connor, 2008). It is estimated that around 1 percent of adults displays narcissistic personality disorder, up to three-quarters of them male (Levy et al., 2007).

Psychologists are divided on the possible causes of narcissistic behavior. Some argue that individuals with this personality disorder are actually using a mask of self-importance to try to protect themselves from persistent and intense feelings of rejection, unworthiness, and wariness (Bornstein, 2005). Other theorists, however, believe that narcissistic behaviors are a genuine expression of inflated self-regard that may have developed when the individuals were treated too positively early in life and did not learn to acknowledge their personal limits (Sperry, 2003). Still others suggest that modern Western culture may help foster an atmosphere of narcissism by assigning too much importance to the trait of high self-esteem as a key to happiness and success (Levy et al., 2007).

Although individuals with narcissism are self-centered and insensitive, many manage to achieve professional success. Researchers Arijit Chatterjee and Donald Hambrick (2006) of Pennsylvania State University conducted a study of 111 CEOs (chief executive officers) in the computer and software industries and found unexpectedly high rates of narcissism in this group. They also found that the CEOs' narcissistic qualities often contributed to extreme and volatile organizational performances.

Lookin' at me People with narcissistic personality disorder have an unrealistically inflated view of themselves, are interested exclusively in their own needs and interests, and crave attention.

Antisocial Personality Disorder

Individuals with **antisocial personality disorder**, most of whom are male, show an extreme and callous disregard for the feelings and rights of others. They typically exhibit impulsivity, egocentrism, and recklessness, along with a superficial charm. Dishonesty and deceit are at the root of their relationships. Indeed, they often form relationships with the intent of exploiting others for material gain or personal gratification. Many are irritable, aggressive, and quick to start fights, and a large number commit criminal acts (APA, 2000). According to surveys, 2 to 3.5 percent of people in the United States qualify for a diagnosis of antisocial personality disorder (O'Connor, 2008). Moreover, cross-cultural research has shown that antisocial patterns of symptoms are found in both Eastern and Western cultures (Zoccolillo et al., 1999).

Adoption studies have uncovered interesting evidence on how heredity and environment may jointly influence the development of antisocial behavior. It appears that environmental factors, such as ineffective parenting and criminality in parents, play a role—but only if a child's biological parents have also manifested antisocial tendencies (Paris, 2001). Children whose biological parents are criminals but who are adopted into families with law-abiding parents show a slightly elevated rate of criminal behavior. However, children from that same biological background who are adopted into families of criminals are much more likely to

narcissistic personality disorder a personality disorder characterized by a high degree of self-interest and a high, often unrealistic, degree of self-importance.

antisocial personality disorder a personality disorder characterized by extreme and callous disregard for feelings and rights of others.

Unthinkable Friends of the victims of the 1999 Columbine High School shooting embrace at a memorial service.

On the morning of April 16, 2007, the deadliest shooting in U.S. history occurred at Virginia Tech when a senior killed 33 students and professors and injured 29 before shooting himself. Mass killings in schools have received considerable attention since the Columbine High School massacre in 1999, and investigators have found that most of them are premeditated and carefully planned (Robertz, 2007).

For its part, the media has regularly tied such school shootings to the playing of videogames—the two students who orchestrated the Columbine killings were, for example, avid players of Doom. But, it turns out that the behavior of student-killers is not so easily explained. Three years after Columbine, the Secret Service and the Department of Education published a joint report that looked at 37 school shootings over the past three decades (Vossekuil et al., 2002). Only 12 percent of the school shooters had any interest in videogames. Similarly, the Virginia Tech shooter had almost no exposure to videogames.

If videogames are not a major factor in most school shootings, what are the causes of these violent outbursts? Recent studies of the relationship between school shootings and videogames have found that family violence is more of a risk factor than fictional violence (Ferguson, 2008; Kutner & Olson, 2008). Low self-esteem, depression, and antisocial personality patterns are also factors. In addition, as we observed earlier in the book, adolescent shooters have often been the victims of bullying or rejection, and some have fantasized for quite a while about revenge for "perceived offenses" (Robertz, 2007).

In light of the Virginia Tech shootings and other such incidents, the federal government has searched for ways to help prevent future shootings (Leavitt et al., 2007). The Departments of Health, Education, and Justice issued a report that expressed concern about access to firearms, especially among individuals with a history of mental disorders, such as the Virginia Tech shooter. The report also recommended increased awareness of the warning signs of potential attacks, such as a student describing plans to hurt others on a website. The hope is that identifying and addressing problems early on may prevent students with mental health problems from reaching a point where there is no turning back.

---

engage in illegal behaviors (Nigg & Goldsmith, 1994). This research illustrates, once again, how genetic predispositions may be expressed differently in different social environments.

Psychologists also have looked deeper into the biological mechanisms that may underlie antisocial behavior. It appears that individuals with antisocial personality disorder have difficulty regulating their impulses and the expression of these impulses (Patrick, 2007; Zlotnick, 1999). Researchers have theorized that this difficulty may result from an underresponsive autonomic nervous system (Gaynor & Baird, 2007; Schachter & Latane, 1964). The idea stemmed partly from the observation that individuals with antisocial personality disorder are relatively unaffected by punishment, either physical or social.

To test this theory, a study was conducted in which participants were given electric shocks (Lykken, 1995). Those with antisocial personality disorder had difficulty learning to avoid the physical discomfort of the shocks. They seemed to experience little or no fear and so were unable to learn tasks that depended on arousal and fear. When, however, these individuals were administered injections of adrenaline—that is, when fear-like arousal was artificially induced—they did learn to avoid the unpleasant shocks. This suggests that an underresponsive autonomic nervous system may be inhibiting the individuals' ability to become appropriately engaged in the environment.

Borderline Personality Disorder

Let's return to the case study that opened this section. Based on her roommate's description, Karen appears to be emotionally volatile, particularly when it comes to her relationships. Particularly in the early stages of a relationship, she tends to see the men in her life as "perfect," but they inevitably fall from grace. Karen also appears to have a high sensitivity to feeling abandoned, which leads to emotional outbursts. She may even cut herself or cause some other harm as a way of dealing with that negative emotion. Her outbursts and moodiness are off-putting to the roommate and most others in her life. All these features suggest that Karen may be displaying **borderline personality disorder**.

Borderline personality disorder is characterized by severe instability in mood and self-concept, which in turn contributes to a high level of instability in relationships (APA, 2000). Borderline personality disorder is often thought of as an emotion dysregulation disturbance (discussed in Chapter 12), because the individuals who experience it report enormous difficulty managing the onset or intensity of their emotional reactions (Sherry & Whilde, 2008; Berenbaum et al., 2003). They may often engage in very impulsive or potentially dangerous activities, including self-mutilation, suicidal threats or behaviors, alcohol or drug abuse, and unsafe or risky sexual behavior. Some clinical theorists consider these features to be dysfunctional attempts by sufferers to regulate their intense emotional reactions (Linehan & Dexter-Mazza, 2008).

Between 1 and 2.5 percent of the population display borderline personality disorder, 75 percent of them women (Sherry & Whilde, 2008). Psychological explanations often focus on childhood experiences of abandonment or neglect. Research has found that many people with borderline personality disorder report histories of loss, neglect, death, and divorce. Some also report histories of physical or sexual abuse (Sansone et al., 2005; Yen et al., 2002).

In addition to these potential environmental influences, some evidence suggests a genetic predisposition to this disorder. It has been found, for example, that close relatives of persons with borderline personality disorder are five times more likely than other people to have the disorder (Bradley et al., 2007; Torgerson, 2000).

Biological factors have been associated with high levels of impulsiveness—a characteristic shown by many people with borderline personality disorder. Indeed, people with borderline personality disorder and lower-than-normal serotonin levels are more likely than other people to commit aggressive acts against themselves or someone else (Norra et al., 2003). Borderline personality disorder is also associated with disrupted sleep, similar to what is seen in depression (Siever & Davis, 1991).

borderline personality disorder a personality disorder characterized by severe instability in emotions and self-concept and high levels of volatility.

Before You Go On

What Do You Know?

17. What is a personality disorder?

18. What are the three groups of personality disorders recognized by DSM-IV-TR?

19. What is the most intensively studied personality disorder and what behaviors characterize it?

What Do You Think? Personality disorders are popular subjects of fiction. Think about films or television programs that you've seen recently, and try to find examples of each of the personality disorders discussed in this section.

Personality Assessment

LEARNING OBJECTIVE 6 Describe the two major types of personality tests and give examples of each.

Go to almost any pop-culture Internet site or flip open any newspaper or popular magazine and you will likely find evidence of people's desire to understand, describe, and use personality traits. Horoscopes, personality quizzes, and even clairvoyants offer personality-based analyses and advice to thousands of people worldwide. The fact that devices such as horoscopes have been shown to be unreliable has done little to diminish their popularity.

Of course, there are also more formal tools for assessing personality, and these tools are used in a variety of important contexts. Clinicians use personality assessment tools to learn more about their clients' problems. Researchers may use them to conduct personality research or to help select participants for their studies. Employers and job counselors often use such tools to help predict the suitability of potential employees for various positions. Scores on traits such as conscientiousness have, for example, been used to predict absenteeism, misconduct, and termination (Organ & Ryan, 1995). The personality tests used most frequently by these professionals are *personality inventories* and *projective tests*.

Personality Inventories

Personality inventories are questionnaires that require individuals to respond to a series of true-or-false or agree-disagree statements designed to measure various aspects of

---

PRACTICALLYSPEAKING   Evaluating Personality Quizzes

Are you dating a person with a narcissistic personality? What is your "pizza personality"? What kind of podcast are you? Personality quizzes fascinate and entertain millions of people. Magazines as varied as *Cosmopolitan* and *Time* publish personality quizzes all the time and the Internet has numerous websites dedicated to helping you to better understand yourself.

Below are some of pop-culture quiz types that you are most likely to stumble across:

- *Scenario quizzes* ask the question: When this happens, how do you react? Popular topics are love and rela-

tionships. The claim is that the answers you choose can reveal personal qualities that you may not normally attribute to yourself.

- *Preference quizzes* pose questions on a variety of topics, from your favorite color to how you write to what time of day you like best. The claim here is that your answers illustrate enduring and broad traits such as extraversion or creativity.

- *Relational quizzes* ask you open-ended questions about how you would react to specific, imaginary events. For example, "If you saw someone being robbed, what would you do?" The claim behind these quizzes is that your responses can tell you a lot about your values and your self-concept, or how you see yourself.

Almost all psychologists recommend treating such pop-culture personality quizzes as entertainment at most. They may be fun, but they typically emerge from the minds of enterprising individuals or organizations, rarely undergo testing or research of any kind, and often are misleading. Always keep in mind that you should not base important decisions on the results of such quizzes and that forming insights or views about yourself based on the results of the tests is likely to be a big mistake.

- Conflicts result in anxiety, and Freud believed that we use unconscious tactics called defense mechanisms to protect ourselves from this anxiety.
- Humanist theorists, including Abraham Maslow and Carl Rogers, emphasized people's basic goodness and their ability to fulfill their potential.
- Maslow proposed that personality arises from people's striving to meet their needs. Human needs are arranged hierarchically, with self-actualization at the top level.
- Rogers based his theory of personality on his ideas about the importance of self-concept. He believed that children need unconditional positive regard to develop healthy self-concepts.

Understanding Personality Today: Traits versus Situations

LEARNING OBJECTIVE 2   Compare and contrast trait theories of personality with situational theories.

- Personality traits are tendencies to behave in certain ways that remain relatively constant across situations.
- Hans Eysenck, using factor analysis, identified three personality superfactors: extraversion, neroticism, and psychoticism.
- Other trait theorists proposed the five-factor theory, which identified five major trait categories: agreeableness, extraversion, neuroticism, conscientiousness, and openness to experience.
- Although traits play an important role in behavior, they can be inconsistent over time and across different situations, causing some theorists to embrace situationism—the view that behavior is governed primarily by the variables in a given situation rather than by internal traits. The behaviorist B. F. Skinner took this view.
- Interactionism focuses on interactions between persons and situations. Albert Bandura's social-cognitive theory is an example of interactionist theory. In Bandura's view, the environment, internal mental events, and behavior all interact to affect behavior through the process of reciprocal determinism.

Biological Foundations of Personality

LEARNING OBJECTIVE 3   Discuss the heritability of personality traits and some of the neural systems that may be involved in the expression of personality.

- Twin studies, such as the Minnesota Study of Twins Reared Apart, suggest that many personality traits have strong genetic links.
- Certain brain structures, neurotransmitters, and hormones have been associated with personality variables.
- In interpreting links between genes, physiological factors, and personality, it is important to remember that the relationships are complex and multidirectional.

Personality *How We Differ*

LEARNING OBJECTIVE 4   Explain how gender and cultural differences can affect personality.

- Although research has found many more similarities than differences between men's and women's personalities, some consistent differences have been identified.

- Sociocultural factors are thought to play an important role in gender differences in personality. According to social role theory, for example, boys and girls develop different behaviors and skills based largely on the division of labor between the sexes and the resulting differences in gender role expectations.
- Cross-cultural research into personality has focused on personality development in individualist and collectivist cultures. Some traits observed in these cultures reflect differing cultural values.

Personality Disorders

LEARNING OBJECTIVE 5   Define personality disorder, and describe some features of narcissistic, antisocial, and borderline personality disorders.

- A personality disorder is an inflexible pattern of inner experience and outward behavior that causes distress or difficulty with daily functioning. The American Psychological Association has outlined ten personality disorders in its guide for therapists.
- People with narcissistic personality disorder are highly self-important and often have unrealistically inflated views of their abilities and accomplishments. They are callous toward others and easily upset when criticized.
- Antisocial personality disorder is marked by an extreme and callous disregard for the feelings and rights of others. People with this disorder typically exhibit impulsivity, egocentrism, and recklessness, along with a superficial charm.
- Borderline personality disorder is characterized by severe instability in mood and self-concept, which contribute to a high level of instability in relationships.

Personality Assessment

LEARNING OBJECTIVE 6   Describe the two major types of personality tests and give examples of each.

- Personality inventories are questionnaires that require individuals to respond to a series of true-or-false or agree-disagree statements designed to measure various aspects of personality.
- Two widely used personality inventories are the Minnesota Multiphasic Personality Inventory 2 (MMPI-2), which is typically used to assess abnormal personality characteristics and inclinations, and the NEO (Neuroticism, Extraversion, Openness) Personality Inventory Revised (NEO-PI-R), which evaluates traits associated with the five-factor theory of personality.
- Projective tests are intended to tap into a person's unconscious mind by having him or her interpret ambiguous stimuli. In the case of the Rorschach Inkblot Test, the stimuli are inkblots; in the case of the Thematic Apperception Test (TAT), they are black-and-white drawings.

Key Terms

CUT/ACROSS CONNECTION

What Happens in the BRAIN?

- Phrenologists in the nineteenth century incorrectly believed that the shape of an individual's skull could reveal his or her personal and moral characteristics.
- Some studies suggest that, on average, people whose right brain hemisphere is dominant tend to be less extraverted than people whose left hemisphere is dominant.
- On average, people with generally high dopamine activity in their brain's reward learning pathway tend to be less inhibited, less anxious, and more energetic than those with lower dopamine activity throughout that pathway.

When Things Go Wrong

- At least 9 percent of people in the United States may display a personality disorder.
- Research has found that people with antisocial personality disorder, who consistently show callous disregard for the feelings and rights of others, have difficulty regulating their impulses and are relatively unaffected by punishment.
- People with borderline personality disorder, characterized by severe instability in one's moods and relationships, are particularly likely to engage in self-cutting and other seemingly impulsive actions. Such behaviors may represent dysfunctional attempts to deal with their intense emotional reactions.

HOW we Differ

- Personality similarities between men and women far outnumber the differences between them.
- Two personality variables on which males and females tend to differ are aggression and interpersonal sensitivity, with males being higher on the former, on average, and females being higher on the latter.
- People from collectivist cultures tend to score higher on measures of agreeableness while those from individualistic cultures tend to score higher on extraversion and desire for individual success.

How we Develop

- Identical twins tend to be substantially more similar on many personality characteristics than are fraternal twins, even if the twins have been raised apart.
- Particularly strong ties have been found between genetic inheritance and the personality characteristics of openness, extraversion, neuroticism, and agreeableness.
- Freud believed that individuals whose needs are not adequately addressed in their early years may become fixated at an early stage of development and go on to display an oral, anal, or phallic personality style throughout life. Research has not provided much support for this theory.

Video Lab Exercise

Psychology Around Us

The Five-Factor Personality Model in Action

Spotting Personality Traits

One of the leading models of personality is the *five-factor model*, which holds that people's personalities can be represented by their scores on five superfactors, each of which consists of numerous specific trait categories. Alright then, let's start identifying different personalities.

In this video lab exercise, you'll observe friends interacting in multiple situations. One of your jobs will be to spot the specific traits of each individual and determine the individual's corresponding scores on each of the superfactors. While doing this, you'll also be examining whether the identified personality traits can be accounted for better by situational factors, distinguishing trait-caused behaviors from situation-caused behaviors, and considering the role of culture and gender in personality. By the end of the exercise, you'll appreciate that personality assessments are far from exact, regardless of whether you are applying a formal personality model or your own implicit personality theory.

As you are working on this on-line exercise, consider the following questions:

- Can the trait-versus-situation question ever be firmly resolved in evaluating personality?
- Which personality traits seem most likely to be tied to genetic inheritance?
- How might the brain regulate personality?
- How can we know when an individual's personality profile actually reflects a broad personality disorder?

CHAPTER 14

Social Psychology

chapter outline

Social Psychology in a Storm

The city of New Orleans, Louisiana, is built largely on a delta marsh and much of it sits below sea level. It is surrounded on its south by the Mississippi River, on its north by Lake Pontchartrain, and on its east by Lake Borgne. Although an extensive system of river levees was built to protect the city from flooding, it was feared for decades that a strong storm, such as a category five hurricane, could overwhelm the city's levee system and plunge the city underwater.

On August 23, 2005, a tropical depression formed over the Bahamas that quickly swelled to a category five storm. As the storm strengthened over the next several days and crossed Florida into the Gulf of Mexico, a mandatory evacuation of New Orleans was ordered. Unfortunately, the evacuation plans that had been designed by the Federal Emergency Management Agency (FEMA) and state and local agencies for just such a catastrophe proved inadequate. According to these plans, it would be up to individuals and private caretakers to find a way out of the city in the event of a catastrophe. However, as the hurricane named Katrina approached the city, most forms of mass transportation had to be shut down, and rental car and private bus facilities were overwhelmed by the demand for evacuation vehicles. As a result, thousands of people, particularly poor people who did not own cars, had no way to get out of the city and were forced to stay behind.

The situation became even more desperate in New Orleans by the end of the first day of the storm, as the city's levee system failed. Water began filling the city. Before long, 80 percent of the city was completely flooded. More and more of the people who had not evacuated worked their way to the huge Superdome, which had been designated a shelter, and to some smaller "last-resort shelters." Unfortunately, to their surprise, these shelters offered woefully inadequate provisions—little food, few beds, and limited medical aid.

Many heart-wrenching stories emerged from this chaos and devastation. Many people, desperate for food and other supplies began to break in to stores that had been abandoned by their owners and staff and take the goods that were on the shelves. Hearing about this looting, along with the other events of the disaster, people throughout the United States wondered what they would do in such a situation.

The British poet John Donne's famous words, "No man is an island," highlight the interconnectedness of humankind. We live in a world of approximately 6.5 billion people, and each and every day we influence and are influenced by others. Social psychologists devote themselves to the study of human interconnectedness. Unlike many areas of psychology, which focus on areas of individual difference, such as temperament and personality, social psychology is based on the belief that "it is not so much the kind of person a man is, as the kind of situation in which he finds himself that determines how he will act" (Milgram, 2004, p. 101).

We might think of social psychology in a general way as the scientific study of how people are affected by other

The social impact This resident of Biloxi, Mississippi watches over his friend's house in the wake of Hurricane Katrina. Among its many effects, the storm greatly influenced how victims behaved toward each other, both positively and negatively.

people. This informal definition covers considerable territory. Many aspects of an individual's functioning may be affected by others—thoughts, feelings, and behaviors may each reflect the influence of the social environment. Moreover, the influence of others may be direct or indirect.

Let's again consider Hurricane Katrina. As they responded to the storm, people either worsened or improved the plight of others in innumerable ways. You will read about some of these events later in the chapter. The events in New Orleans affected not only the city's residents but also people who watched the events unfold on television or over the Internet, triggering dramatic changes in how people perceive various institutions within our society.

Given the many ways in which people can affect one another, the pioneering psychologist Gordon Allport (1954), whom we also discussed in the previous chapter, offered a more detailed definition of social psychology that is embraced by most persons in the field. That is, **social psychology** seeks to understand, explain, and predict how our thoughts, feelings, and behavior are influenced by the actual, imagined, or implied presence of others (Allport, 1985).

Which pieces of this definition should social psychologists focus on? Over the years, certain topics have received particular attention. Many social psychologists have concerned themselves with **social cognition**—how people perceive and interpret themselves and others in their social world. They have examined, for example, the *attitudes* people hold and the *attributions* that people make. Other social psychologists have paid more attention to *social forces* and *social interactions*. We'll discuss each of these areas on the following pages, and then examine what happens in the brain during social functioning. We'll conclude the chapter with a description of disorders of social behavior.

Social Cognition: Attitudes

LEARNING OBJECTIVE 1 Explain how attitudes form and change and what role they play in behavior.

There are few things in our world that we do not evaluate in some form or another. On some evaluations, people tend to agree. For example, most people believe that poverty is bad, that horror movies are scary, and that Tiger Woods is an extraordinary golfer. On other topics, people are more divided—such as the proper role of government in people's lives, the best ice cream flavor, and the advisability of legalizing drugs. Psychologists refer to our relatively stable and enduring evaluations of things and people as **attitudes** (Albarracin et al., 2005).

According to the **ABC model of attitudes**, attitudes have three components, as shown in **Figure 14-1** (van den Berg et al., 2006; Eagly & Chaiken, 1998):

* The *affective* component—how we feel toward an object.
* The *behavioral* component—how we behave toward an object.
* The *cognitive* component—what we believe about an object.

Before September 11, 2001, many Americans held the attitude that their everyday world was safe from terrorism. They felt secure (affective component), went to work each day confident that terrorism would not touch their lives (behavioral component), and believed they were safe (cognitive component). Similarly, before Hurricane Katrina,

social psychology an area of psychology that seeks to understand, explain, and predict how people's thoughts, feelings, and behaviors are influenced by the actual, imagined, or implied presence of others.

social cognition the way in which people perceive and interpret themselves and others in their social world.

attitudes relatively stable and enduring evaluations of things and people.

ABC model of attitudes a model proposing that attitudes have three components: the affective component, the behavioral component, and the cognitive component.

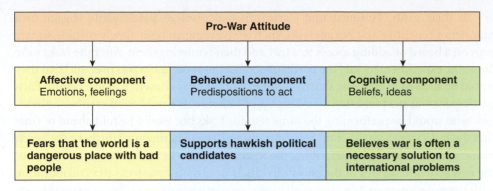

Pro-War Attitude		
Affective component Emotions, feelings	**Behavioral component** Predispositions to act	**Cognitive component** Beliefs, ideas
Fears that the world is a dangerous place with bad people	**Supports hawkish political candidates**	**Believes war is often a necessary solution to international problems**

FIGURE 14-1 **The ABC model of attitudes**

most residents of New Orleans felt safe and secure and went about their lives accordingly. Clearly, then, attitudes can change. We'll explain how that can happen later in this section; but first, let's discuss how attitudes form in the first place.

Attitudes | How we *Develop*

Early in life, parents play a major role in shaping children's beliefs and opinions about things and people (Day et al., 2006). As we observed in Chapter 3, socialization is the process by which children acquire beliefs and behaviors considered desirable or appropriate by the family to which they belong. You are reading this textbook right now because you have been socialized in a number of ways—perhaps to believe in the value of a college education or the need for hard work to achieve your goals. This socialization may have occurred by direct transmission (your parents lecturing you about these values) or in subtler ways. Perhaps your mother or father praised you for your grades or punished you for not doing your homework. Over time, you might generalize these individual experiences into an overall attitude about the value of what you are doing.

As children mature, their peers, their teachers, and the media influence their attitudes more prominently (Prislin & Wood, 2005). Children observe their classmates and take note of the rewards and punishments those students reap from their behavior. If a child sees a classmate rejected by the rest of the class for making disparaging remarks about a particular ethnic group, for example, the child may develop an attitude that such remarks are inappropriate and unacceptable. Similarly, seeing a favorite television character get whatever he wants by bullying people might foster an attitude that aggression is an acceptable way to achieve one's goals.

How Do Attitudes Change?

Once we've internalized a particular attitude—that is, once we've made it our own—how rigid and long lasting is that attitude? Can people experience a change of heart? In a classic social psychology experiment in the late 1950s, researchers Leon Festinger and J. Merrill Carlsmith (1959) demonstrated that when we are subtly manipulated into doing or saying something that is contrary to our private attitudes, we often change our attitudes to match the new action or statement. If, for example, a woman must make a presentation on the merits of managed-care health systems when she in fact favors health-care reform, she may later report—and believe—that she actually favors the existing managed-care systems.

Shaping attitudes Many school-age children today support recycling. What influences in the media and the general culture may have helped to shape this child's attitude?

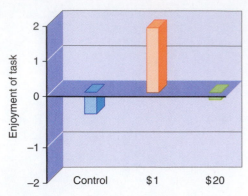

FIGURE 14-2 **Cognitive dissonance** After describing a boring task as fun, participants in Festinger and Carlsmith's study were asked to rate their own enjoyment of the task on a scale of −5 to +5. Those paid $1 for praising the task rated the task as more enjoyable than those paid $20 for praising it.

Serious dissonance The contradiction between this nurse's professional commitment to fight cancer and her smoking behavior may produce noxious feelings of dissonance. To reduce these feelings, she may adopt a belief such as "I have an addiction to smoking that overrides my better judgment."

In their study, Festinger and Carlsmith had research participants engage in a number of repetitive and boring tasks, such as spending an hour slowly turning square pegs on a board or adding spools to a tray and then removing them. After the tasks were done, the experimenters told the participants that the experiment was over and that they would be allowed to go home shortly—but in truth the experiment had just begun! Each participant was next told that a new group of individuals would soon arrive—individuals who would be performing the same tedious tasks but would be told ahead of time that the tasks were actually "fun" and "intriguing." The experimenter further asked each participant to help out by describing the upcoming tasks as fun and exciting to one of the new individuals. (All of the new individuals were in fact confederates collaborating with the experimenters.) In almost all cases, the participants agreed to prepare the new individuals for an enjoyable experience. In addition, some of the participants were told they would be paid one dollar for helping out in this way, while others were told they would receive twenty dollars.

After presenting the positive spiel about the tedious tasks to the new individuals, the participants were interviewed by the experimenters about how enjoyable they themselves actually believed the tasks to be. This was, in fact, Festinger and Carlsmith's central area of interest. Many of the participants reported that they actually had found the tasks to be quite enjoyable! Even more fascinating, it was those who had been paid one dollar for "talking up" the tasks who reported the tasks to be most enjoyable—not those who had been paid twenty dollars (see **Figure 14-2**).

How could participants come to find the mind-numbing tasks of this study enjoyable? Why did those paid less money to convince someone else that the tasks were enjoyable find the tasks *more* enjoyable than those paid more money to do so? Theorists have offered two possible answers to these questions.

Cognitive Dissonance Theory Festinger (1957) proposed that when we hold two contradictory beliefs, or when we hold a belief that contradicts our behavior, we experience a state of emotional discomfort, or **cognitive dissonance**. This state is so unpleasant that we are motivated to reduce or eliminate it. One way of removing dissonance is to modify our existing beliefs. In Festinger and Carlsmith's study, cognitive dissonance theory would hold that the conflict between the participants' initial attitudes about the tasks (that the tasks were boring and trivial) and their later behavior (telling someone that the tasks were enjoyable) resulted in cognitive dissonance, and this unpleasant state motivated them to change their attitudes about the tasks in positive directions.

But what about the differing results for the participants in the one-dollar condition and those in the twenty-dollar condition? According to dissonance theory, the participants in the twenty-dollar condition experienced less dissonance because they had sufficient justification for their behavior. Since they were well paid to say that the tasks were enjoyable, they could tell themselves, "I said the experiment was fun because I got money for saying it." (Twenty dollars was quite a bit more money in the late 1950s than it is today.) Thus, these participants experienced little or no discrepancy between their attitudes and their behavior. In contrast, those who received only a dollar for their positive statements had insufficient justification for their behavior and so experienced a marked discrepancy and uncomfortable feelings of dissonance. These participants managed to reduce the uncomfortable feelings by modifying their beliefs about the tasks— that is, by later reporting (and indeed, believing) "the tasks really were kind of interesting."

Festinger's theory of cognitive dissonance has received support from literally hundreds of studies (Cooper et al., 2005, 2004). Furthermore, it has significant implications for many events and strategies in real life. For example, a growing number of today's parents financially reward their children for working on their homework. The parents' hope is that such rewards will move doing homework ahead of attractive alternatives, such as texting, listening to iPods, or playing computer games, and that the children will come to willingly complete and even enjoy homework. However, cognitive dissonance theory warns that such strategies are likely to backfire. Children who are given explicit financial rewards—especially sizeable ones—will likely know exactly why they are doing their homework. That is, they will experience little or no dissonance between their attitude toward homework ("homework is the pits!") and their act of doing homework. In turn, they will not be inclined to change their unfavorable view about doing homework.

The Self-Perception Alternative   Cognitive dissonance theory fits some instances of attitude change, but not others. In many cases, we seem to form and change attitudes in the absence of internal discomfort. You might think, for example, that you are alert, but after yawning, you might decide, "I'm tired"—not because of a need to reduce emotional tension brought about by the discrepancy between the attitude ("I'm alert") and the behavior (a yawn) but simply because the yawn was informative. Thus, psychologist Daryl Bem developed the **self-perception theory** of attitude change (Bem, 1972). This theory minimizes the role of emotional discomfort and suggests that when we are uncertain of our attitudes, we simply infer what our attitudes are by observing our own behavior, much as outsiders might observe us. According to Bem, our behaviors are often clues from which we deduce our attitudes—we might decide we like roller coasters because we keep riding them, or we might decide we hate spinach because we keep spitting it out.

Which is correct—the cognitive dissonance or the self-perception explanation of attitude change? Historically, this has been a source of great debate in social psychology, but research has clarified that each may be more relevant in particular situations (Cooper et al., 2004; Petty et al., 2003; Fazio et al., 1977). Festinger's theory of cognitive dissonance seems more applicable to situations in which we behave in ways that are strikingly out of character for us, whereas Bem's self-perception theory may be at work in situations where we behave only slightly out of character or our attitudes are not all that clear to begin with.

Do Attitudes Influence Behavior?

If we know someone's attitudes, does that mean we can predict that person's behavior? It turns out that the attitudes people express are not necessarily related to how they actually behave (Fazio & Roskos-Ewoldsen, 2005; Cooper et al., 2004; Eagly & Chaiken, 1998). In the 1930s, a time when many Americans held very negative attitudes toward the Chinese, sociologist Richard LaPiere conducted a field study in which he had a Chinese couple travel across the United States and visit over 250 hotels and restaurants (LaPiere, 1934). Although managers at over 90 percent of the establishments indicated in a questionnaire that they would not serve Chinese guests, only one of the establishments visited by the Chinese couple actually refused them service. In fact, most of the hotels and restaurants provided above-average service.

Of course attitudes do sometimes predict behavior. Research has uncovered various factors that affect the extent to which attitudes will predict behaviors (Fabrigar et al., 2006; Fazio & Roskos-Ewoldsen, 2005; Cooper et al., 2004). One of the leading factors is *attitude specificity*. The more specific an attitude, the more likely it is to predict behavior. If a young woman specifically loves Justin Timberlake, for example, she is more likely to download his album the first day it is released than someone who loves pop music more broadly. Another factor is *attitude strength*. Stronger attitudes predict behavior more accurately than weak or vague attitudes.

cognitive dissonance a state of emotional discomfort people experience when they hold two contradictory beliefs or hold a belief that contradicts their behavior.

self-perception theory a theory suggesting that when people are uncertain of their attitudes, they infer what the attitudes are by observing their own behavior.

"Believe what I do, not what I say" Many people who endorse healthful eating and better fitness on surveys actually consume huge quantities of junk food in their daily meals.

Are People Honest About Their Attitudes?

One reason that attitudes fail to consistently predict behaviors is that people often *misrepresent* their attitudes. In fact, analyses of most self-report questionnaires—the tools usually used by researchers to measure attitudes—cannot distinguish genuine attitudes from false ones (Carels et al., 2006; Cobb, 2002; Rosenberg, 1969). Why would people misrepresent their attitudes? There appear to be several reasons.

The Social Desirability Factor Often, people state attitudes that are *socially desirable* rather than accurate. A person who privately does not trust people of a particular ethnic background, for example, may not acknowledge having this attitude for fear of being judged unfavorably by others. To eliminate the social desirability factor and measure people's attitudes, psychologists have sometimes employed the *bogus pipeline* technique (Jones & Sigall, 1971). Here, a research participant is connected to a nonfunctioning device that looks like a polygraph (lie-detector machine) and is told that the device can detect deception. When individuals are connected to such a device, they are more likely to report their attitudes truthfully (Nier, 2005; Roese & Jamieson, 1993).

In one bogus pipeline study, investigators asked students about socially sensitive issues, such as how frequently they drank, smoked, had sex, and used illicit drugs (Tourangeau et al., 1997). Participants in one group were hooked up to a device and told that it could detect inaccurate answers. This belief apparently made the participants more honest. The students hooked up to the machine reported performing socially sensitive behaviors relatively frequently. Control participants, who were not hooked up to the device, answered in more socially desirable ways, reporting lower frequencies of the behaviors in question.

Implicit Attitudes Another problem that researchers run into when trying to measure attitudes, is that people are not always *aware* of their true attitudes (Bassili & Brown, 2005). In their own minds, employers may believe that applicants of all ethnicities deserve a fair interview process. But when interviewing individuals from ethnic backgrounds other than their own, the same employers may, in fact, engage in less eye contact, maintain greater physical distance, and offer less interview time than when interviewing applicants whose backgrounds are similar to their own. In such cases, the employers may have difficulty trusting people of different backgrounds, but this attitude has not reached their conscious awareness (Baron & Banaji, 2006; Bassett et al., 2005; Greenwald et al., 2002, 1998). When attitudes, such as these lie below the level of conscious awareness, they are called **implicit attitudes**. The finding that people have implicit attitudes is reminiscent of the following observation by the famous Russian writer Fyodor Dostoyevsky:

> *Every man has reminiscences which he would not tell to everyone but only his friends. He has other matters in his mind which he would not reveal even to his friends, but only to himself, and that in secret. But there are other things which a man is afraid to tell even to himself, and every decent man has a number of such things stored away in his mind.*

As you might imagine, measuring attitudes that the holder is not aware of presents a challenge for researchers. To get at implicit attitudes, researchers have employed the *Implicit Association Test (IAT)*, which uses a person's reaction times to help gauge his or her implicit attitudes. The IAT consists of three stages.

1. *First, a person is exposed to two broad categories—say, "dog" and "cat." The person is asked to categorize certain words as belonging in the "dog" category or the "cat" category—for example, fire hydrant and litter box.*
2. *Next, the person is asked to categorize words as either pleasant or unpleasant. These words are again fairly obvious, such as "poison" and happiness.*

3. *Finally, the categories are combined, and the person is asked to identify a series of words as either more dog-related/pleasant or more cat-related/unpleasant; the categories are later reversed to be cat/pleasant and dog/unpleasant. The assumption is that if a person implicitly believes that dogs are more desirable than cats, the person should be quicker to identify pleasant words during the dog/pleasant combination, because the association between pleasant things and dogs is stronger. It will take this person slightly longer to make the dog/unpleasant association because it requires more effort. Similarly, cat people should respond quicker to the cat/pleasant combination.*

If you want to see how an Implicit Association Test works, go online to www.implicit.harvard.edu and take one for yourself. You can be part of a research study with tens of thousands of participants.

You might find this logic convoluted and hard to accept. However, researchers have found that many white Americans who characterize themselves as not prejudiced have quicker reaction times to white American/pleasant and African American/ unpleasant identifications than to white American/unpleasant and African American/pleasant ones. Such implicit attitudes appear to be stable over time, and they have been useful predictors of both subtle indicators of discomfort, such as turning one's eyes away during a conversation with someone of another race, and overt acts of racism, such as the use of slurs, physical violence, and snubbing (Rudman & Ashmore, 2007). The IAT has also been used by researchers to detect bias against elderly people, overweight people, women, and other groups.

Stereotypes and Prejudice

In the wake of Hurricane Katrina, millions of people began reaching out with contributions and charity to help the suffering people in Louisiana, Alabama, and Mississippi. It was during a special charity drive, which aired on all the major television networks, that controversial rap star Kanye West made a highly provocative statement about the disaster:

> *I hate the way they portray us in the media. You see a black family, it [the media] says, "they're looting." You see a white family, it says, "they're looking for food." And, you know, it's been five days [waiting for federal help] because most of the people are black. …*

Racial bias In the aftermath of Hurricane Katrina, newspapers carried many photos of desperate people taking food from local food stores. The news caption that accompanied the photo on the left (of an African American) stated that the man had just finished "looting a grocery store," whereas the one that accompanied the photo on the right (white Americans) said that the two individuals had just finished "finding bread and soda at a local grocery store."

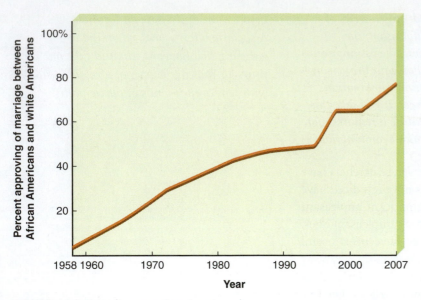

FIGURE 14-3 **Prejudice over time** Americans have expressed greater approval of interracial marriage over the last 50 years, yet studies show that subtle biases remain (Gallup Poll, 2007).

In part, West was talking about *stereotypes*. Most of us are familiar with the notion of **stereotypes**—generalized impressions about people or groups of people based on the social category they occupy. Stereotypes can be based on age, race, region of origin, political or religious beliefs, or any other group characteristic.

Although stereotypes may be positive or negative, there is little doubt that there is a strong relationship between stereotypes and **prejudice**—negative attitudes toward individuals from another group. Research suggests that prejudice in the form of overt racism and sexism has decreased over time in the United States (see **Figure 14-3**), but subtle biases remain (Sue et al., 2007; Dovidio, et al., 2002). For example, as noted earlier, many white Americans who characterize themselves as not prejudiced respond to the Implicit Association Test in a way that suggests they have some implicit negative attitudes toward African Americans.

Psychologists believe that the human tendency to identify with a group is one of the main contributors to stereotypes and prejudice. As humans, we generally categorize ourselves in terms of similarities to some people and differences from others. Understanding ourselves as members of a particular group (our *in-group*) offers us some insight into who we are. Similarly, perceiving people outside our group as members of other groups (*out-groups*) gives us information—not necessarily valid information—about who they are. As we'll discuss in more detail later, human beings appear to have a cognitive predisposition to see things associated with themselves as good and things not associated with themselves as less good.

Evolutionary psychologists have suggested that stereotypes and prejudice may have had some adaptive value, as our ancestors probably prized being able to quickly recognize members of their own tribe based on superficial information. Early humans needed to quickly identify other figures as friends or foes, and general appearance would have been an easy way to accomplish this goal. Evolutionary psychologists also have suggested that we may be prewired to think of people whom we perceive to be different from us as inferior, which may cause or justify our decisions to exclude or demean them.

A view called the *realistic conflict theory* relies on somewhat more recent history to explain how prejudice comes into play. According to this theory, the amount of actual conflict between particular in-groups and out-groups determines the degree of prejudice or discrimination between those groups. An example is the difficult history of conflict between white Americans and African Americans. Given that history, proponents of realistic conflict theory might have predicted that the media would indeed discriminate against impoverished African-American survivors of Hurricane Katrina, as Kanye West and others later claimed they did.

Rather than focusing on historical antecedents, another view, the **social identity theory**, emphasizes social cognitive factors that come into play in prejudice. Social identity theory proposes that prejudice emerges through three processes:

1. *Social categorization*, in which a person affiliates with a particular group as a way of figuring out how to act and react in the world.

2. *Social identity*, in which the person forms an identity within the group.

3. *Social comparison*, in which the group member compares the group favorably with other groups and in turn derives a sense of positive well-being from looking at himself or herself as superior in some way.

stereotypes generalized impressions about a person or a group of people based on the social category they occupy.

prejudice negative stereotypical attitudes toward individuals from another group.

social identity theory a theory that emphasizes social cognitive factors in the onset of prejudice.

Attitudes and the Power of Persuasion

Earlier, we discussed how attitudes form and change. Advertisers have taken a strong interest in these processes. In fact, billions of advertising dollars are devoted each year to helping people develop particular attitudes toward products or services. If you wouldn't dream of using any computer but a MacBook Pro®, or if you much prefer Coke® over Pepsi® (or vice versa), that attitude probably has been created in part through persuasion—the advertiser's best efforts to convince you that its product is far superior to anyone else's and that you must have it. Politicians running for office, interest groups looking to increase their influence, and any number of others also use persuasive techniques regularly. Indeed, most of us have had occasion to try to persuade someone else to come around to our way of thinking.

For persuasion to occur, a few elements must be present. There must be, of course, a *message*, somebody to transmit the message (the *source*), and somebody to receive it (the *receiver*). In attempting to make a message persuasive, the source can use methods that follow either a central route or a peripheral route (**Figure 14-4**).

Central Route versus Peripheral Route

The *central route* to persuasion emphasizes the content of the message, using factual information and logical arguments to persuade. This method requires a fair amount of effort on the receiver's part and is more commonly used for matters of some significance. If you were trying to decide whether to buy a Mac or a PC, you might be willing to spend considerable time in careful deliberation of all the facts. After all, a computer is an expensive item and an important purchase. You might not be as interested in thinking hard about whether to buy Coke or Pepsi, though, or about which brand of shampoo to purchase.

The *peripheral route* relies on more superficial information. When you respond to peripheral appeals, you're responding to such factors as how attractive the spokesperson is and how amusing or engaging the message is. As might be expected, decisions based on central routes to persuasion are more likely to last than decisions based on the peripheral route.

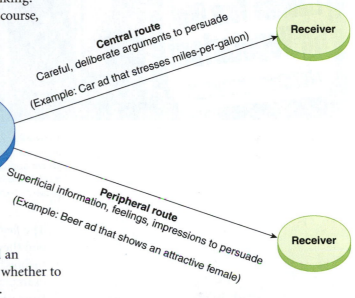

FIGURE 14-4 **Two routes to persuasion**

Aids to Persuasion Beyond the route chosen, a number of other factors can also make a message more or less persuasive. Characteristics of the *source* are important. We are more likely to be persuaded by a source who is rated as more knowledgeable or more likable, for example. In addition, if we think of the source as more similar to us, we're more likely to be persuaded by the message. (This is part of the reason why presidential candidates often try to emphasize their middle-class folksiness by speaking in shopping malls and grocery stores.) Finally, at least in some instances, people are more likely to find a source credible and persuasive when the source presents both sides of an issue.

Sometimes, the key to persuasion rests on an interaction between audience characteristics and source characteristics. If, for example, a source is trying to win the favor of an intelligent or highly motivated audience, an emphasis on logic and on supporting data is more likely to carry the day. If addressing a less intelligent or less interested audience, however, the source might have more success with a glossy, superficial presentation and a good haircut.

A number of *specific techniques* can further improve the chances of successfully persuading others. We'll mention only a few here. You have probably been exposed to some of these strategies (and you may even have used some of them).

Tools of persuasion The organization *People for the Ethical Treatment of Animals (PETA)* has run many campaigns to persuade consumers to stop eating meat and go vegetarian. Which of the above approaches is more likely to help change the minds of meat eaters—the scantily dressed model who holds a sign while posing inside a cage *(left)* or the spokesperson who systematically presents facts and figures on the merits of a vegetarian lifesyle *(right)*?

- The *foot-in-the-door technique* involves getting someone to agree to a small request and then following up with a much larger one. The idea is that the person will be inclined to grant the second request because of having granted the first one. For example, you might first ask to borrow your parents' car for an hour and then later ask to borrow it for the weekend.

- The *door-in-the-face technique* reverses this behavior. The technique involves making an absurd first request that will obviously be turned down and following it with a more moderate request. A teenager might ask his or her parents, "Will you buy me a motorcycle?", and then follow up with "Just kidding, but can I borrow $50?" as the parents sigh in relief.

- *Appeals to fear* can be powerful. We frequently see these appeals in antismoking campaigns and the like. In order to work, however, an appeal to fear must make receivers truly believe that something bad will happen to them if they don't comply with the source's request.

Barriers to Persuasion Other strategies can interfere with persuasion. Again, we'll mention only a few.

- Forewarning an audience that you will be trying to persuade them of something will immediately raise their defenses. Although listeners in this situation may make subtle shifts toward your way of thinking, they are unlikely to change their attitudes as much as individuals who are not told that they are about to hear a persuasive speech.

- Beginning with a weak argument instead of a strong one can make subsequent arguments seem weaker. Starting off a request to your professor for a paper extension by arguing that you simply need to catch up on your sleep might lead the professor to interpret your subsequent (stronger) argument—that you've been up for days working on midterms in three other classes—as more of an excuse than a valid argument.

Sigmund Freud's nephew, Edmund Bernays, is credited with helping to create modern advertising. Bernays applied psychoanalytic theory to link products with emotions. For example, told by psychoanalysts that women smoked less than men because cigarettes were phallic symbols of men's power, Bernays designed campaigns in the 1920s presenting smoking as a women's rights issue, calling cigarettes "torches of freedom." Smoking among women skyrocketed.

Social Cognition: Attributions

LEARNING OBJECTIVE 2 Discuss how people make attributions to explain their own behavior and the behavior of others.

There has been much debate about the exact nature of the looting that happened in the wake of Hurricane Katrina. It appears that some looters were simply taking advantage of the situation to steal whatever they could carry. It is clear, however, that many of the looters would never have considered breaking into a store if they had not found themselves in a desperate situation in need of food.

As the looting became more widespread, many storeowners stayed behind to defend their stores at gunpoint. It was hard to separate rumor from fact as communications in the city broke down and unsupported, sometimes wild, stories surfaced on news reports. Supposed eyewitnesses told, for example, of roving gangs in the streets, wild gun battles, snipers shooting at aid workers, and out-of-control violence.

Throughout the United States, individuals formed distinct opinions as they tried to understand the unrest that they were witnessing or hearing about. Horrified by the tales of violence in New Orleans, many initially took the stance that looting was wrong in all cases. However, as days passed and it became clear that people remaining in New Orleans were in a desperate state, with no help in sight, people around the country began to ask themselves what they would do in a similar situation. Many, for the first time in their lives, found themselves believing that a number of the people they saw looting on their television screens might simply be doing what they had to do.

In many ways, we are all lay psychologists, continually trying to explain what we see in our social worlds so that we can make sense of events and predict what will happen in the future. We attempt to figure out *why* people, including ourselves, do things. Social psychologists refer to these causal explanations as **attributions**, and they are interested in what influences our attributions and how such attributions affect our subsequent decisions, feelings, and behaviors (Silvera & Laufer, 2005; Stewart, 2005).

"Your Honor, we the jury blame the victim."

Dispositional and Situational Attributions

Attributions may fall into one of two categories. *Dispositional*, or *internal*, *attributions* focus on peoples' traits as the cause of their behavior. In contrast, *situational*, or *external*, *attributions* focus on environmental factors as the cause of behavior. If you fail

attributions causal explanations of behavior.

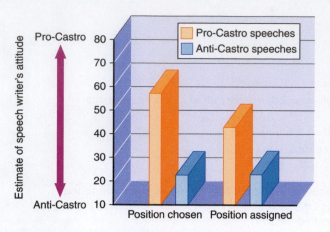

FIGURE 14-5 The fundamental attribution error
Even when told that pro-Castro or anti-Castro speechwriters had been randomly assigned their positions, research participants assumed that each speechwriter truly believed what he or she had written (Jones & Harris, 1967).

fundamental attribution error the tendency to use dispositional attributions to explain the behavior of other people.

actor-observer effect the discrepancy between how we explain other people's behavior (dispositionally) and how we explain our own behavior (situationally).

an examination, you might make a dispositional attribution that you failed because you were not smart enough. Instead, though, you might tell yourself that the test was unfair and that your neighbor's music was so loud the night before that you couldn't get a good night's sleep—situational attributions.

What determines whether we make dispositional or situational attributions? Research suggests that when explaining *other* people's behavior, we tend to rely more heavily on dispositional attributions. In a famous study in the 1960s, researchers had participants read a speech that expressed either support for or opposition to Cuban leader Fidel Castro. They then asked each participant to rate the extent to which the speechwriter was pro-Castro (Jones & Harris, 1967). Participants who read a speech supportive of Castro naturally rated the speechwriter as pro-Castro, and those who read a speech critical of Castro naturally rated the speechwriter as anti-Castro. These were dispositional attributions; the participants reasoned that the speeches reflected internal characteristics of the speechwriters. But then the participants were told that the speechwriters had been randomly assigned to write either a pro- or anti-Castro speech. In other words, the participants were given a reason to make a situational attribution rather than a dispositional one. Remarkably, even then, the participants rated speechwriters who had written supportive speeches as very pro-Castro and speechwriters who had written critical speeches as very anti-Castro (see **Figure 14-5**).

Social psychologist Lee Ross (2001, 1977) has referred to our reliance on dispositional attributions to explain the behavior of other people as the **fundamental attribution error**. When we are almost hit by a speeding driver, we are likely to conclude that the driver is reckless and irresponsible, even though, in fact, he or she might have been racing to the hospital to see a stricken child. When we meet a woman who is not very talkative, we may conclude that she is shy and introverted, when in fact she might be a normally friendly sort who has a terrible cold. When a waiter provides unsatisfactory service, we may assume that he is disorganized, even though the fault may lie in the restaurant's kitchen or in the policies of management (Cowley, 2005).

In contrast, as we have already suggested, we tend to rely more heavily on situational attributions when explaining our own behavior. Recall our example about failing an examination. Although you might make the dispositional attribution that you aren't smart enough, you're more likely to make a situational attribution and blame your failure on the unfairness of the exam and your noisy neighbor. Research has repeatedly shown this tendency.

The Actor-Observer Effect

Social psychologists refer to the discrepancy between how we explain other people's behavior and how we explain our own behavior as the **actor-observer effect** (Jones & Nisbett, 1971). The idea is that as *actors,* we tend to make situational attributions about our behaviors; and as *observers,* we tend to make dispositional attributions (**Figure 14-6**). Several explanations have been offered as to why this is so. For one thing, as actors, we have information about ourselves that observers don't have. We know from experience, for example, that we don't act the same way in every situation. For another thing, observers tend to focus on the actor, while actors need to focus more on situations. Think about a baseball game. As a fan (observer), you might watch the batter closely. But if you were the batter (actor), you'd need to pay attention to the ball, the other players, and many other aspects of your surroundings. Interestingly, if people are shown videotapes of their own behavior—that is, if they become observers—they tend to make more dispositional attributions about the causes of their behavior (Storms, 1973). That is, the video enables them to switch from actors to observers, and their explanations for their behaviors switch correspondingly.

The observer

Dispositional attribution

Focuses on the personality of the actor

"He's goes up to the bar a lot; he must have a drinking problem."

The Actor

Situational attribution

Focuses attention on external factors

"People keep picking up my drink whenever I put it down."

FIGURE 14-6 **The actor-observer effect** We tend to explain our own behavior in terms of external factors (situational attributions), and others' behavior in terms of their internal characteristics (dispositional attributions).

As an example of the actor-observer effect, consider a class exercise developed by social psychologist Susan Fiske (2010). She tells her students, "Rate on a scale from 1 (low) to 10 (high) to what extent each of the following are reasons you chose your college."

- I had a wish to please my parents.
- I desired to get away from home.
- I wanted to go where my friends went.
- I liked the location of my college.
- I decided to go to a prestigious college.
- I was looking to find a marriage partner.
- I wanted a good social life.

After the students have completed these ratings, Fiske instructs them, "Next rate all the reasons that the *typical* student at your college picked it."

Take a break from reading, and complete this exercise yourself. Then compare your ratings of your reasons for attending your college with your ratings of other students' reasons. Did your ratings follow a pattern? If you are like most of the students in Fiske's classes, you thought the reasons on the list described the typical student's decision better than they described yours. If that's the case, your ratings illustrate the actor-observer effect. Each of the reasons on the list is a dispositional attribution, relating to something internal to the person. As Fiske observes, "People see themselves as having rich, deep, and adaptive personalities, able to express almost any [behavior] or its opposite, depending on the circumstances. *Other* people, of course, are ruled by their personalities" (Fiske, 2010, p. 116).

Exceptions to the Rule

Despite the trend just described, we do not *always* attribute other people's behaviors to their personalities. When we know that just about everyone would react the same way in a given situation, we will likely conclude that a person's behavior in that situation is situationally caused. When most persons are robbed at gunpoint, for example, they (wisely) hand over their money. Thus, a particular robbery victim's surrender of money will usually be attributed to the powerful situational factors.

Similarly, if we are given detailed information about situational pressures, we may attribute the behavior of other people to situational factors. Think back, once again, to the events surrounding Hurricane Katrina. Initially, most television viewers assumed that all New Orleans residents who had stayed at home rather than evacuate to another

Researchers have found that depressed individuals sometimes have a more realistic perception of themselves and their abilities, a phenomenon known as depressive realism, or the sadder-but-wiser hypothesis.

city were stubborn, or foolish, or both. However, when information later revealed that thousands of the city's residents were too poor to own a car and that all public transportation systems had shut down, most viewers shifted to a situational explanation for the residents' behavior.

By the same token, we do not *always* attribute our own behavior to situational factors. Let's say, for example, that you do poorly on an examination and complain that the questions were "too hard" and the grading unfair. You are, as we would expect, making a situational attribution for your poor performance. But suppose you get a good mark on the next examination. Will you explain your success by pointing out how easy the exam questions were or how generous the grading was? Not likely.

Consistent with this point, social psychologists have noted that when we explain our own behavior, we are able, and often likely, to fluctuate between situational and dispositional attributions, depending on which puts us in a better light. In other words, we tend to attribute our successes to internal causes and our failures to external ones—a phenomenon referred to as the **self-serving bias** (Johnston & Lee, 2005; Miller & Ross, 1975). Research also has indicated that the direction of our attributions can be influenced by factors such as our moods and emotions, motives, prejudices and stereotypes, and cultural background (Forgas & Locke, 2005; Lieberman et al., 2005; Sadler et al., 2005; Sherman et al., 2005).

Before You Go On

What Do You Know?

6. How do dispositional and situational attributions differ?
7. What is the fundamental attribution error?
8. What are some exceptions to the actor-observer effect?

What Do You Think?   How do you think empathy might affect the actor-observer effect?

Social Forces

LEARNING OBJECTIVE 3 Describe the power of conformity and obedience in shaping people's behavior.

As bad as conditions were in the last-resort shelters after Hurricane Katrina, they were even worse in the New Orleans Convention Center. A small group of people had decided to make their way to this facility, even though it had not been designated a shelter. Others followed, until the convention center filled with thousands of displaced souls. Those people waited for days for food and support to come. However, because the convention center had never been formally designated a shelter, federal and state agencies did not even know anyone was there. Not until days later, when television and news reporters "found" those in the center, were they included in the city's relief efforts.

Given the chaos and uncertainty in the aftermath of Hurricane Katrina, it is understandable that people would look for any sign of what to do or how to get help. The fact that a small group of people decisively sought shelter at the Convention Center, even in the absence of any information about whether that was a good choice or not, was more than sufficient to influence many other people to seek shelter there. Even in more normal situations, *social forces* such as these exert a powerful influence on our behaviors and beliefs. Often, for example, people conform to the behaviors and opinions of others, especially when those behaviors and opinions reflect a majority position. We'll discuss the social forces of conformity and obedience in this section. First, though, let's examine the related topics of *norms* and *social roles*.

Norms and Social Roles

Recall that, in the aftermath of Hurricane Katrina, people around the country learned that seemingly desperate people were breaking into stores, while some storeowners were defending their property at gunpoint. Such reports made most people feel very unsettled. One reason for their discomfort was that such behaviors seemed to represent a breakdown of social values and compassion. Another reason was that the behaviors defied people's social expectations. Respectable citizens are not supposed to break into stores and carry off goods, and storeowners are supposed to sell merchandise, not take the law into their own hands. These expectations arise from the norms and roles of our society.

Norms Society is filled with rules about how everyone is supposed to act. These conventions, referred to as **norms**, provide order and predictability. Some norms are *explicit,* or stated openly. We all know, for example, that we are supposed to stop our car when we come to a red light. Other norms are *implicit.* These norms are not openly stated, but we are still aware of them. You probably weren't taught as a child to face the front of an elevator, for instance, but when's the last time you stepped into an elevator where all the passengers had their backs to the doors?

We can also classify norms as descriptive or injunctive (Larimer et al., 2005, 2004, 2003; Eagly & Karau, 2002). *Descriptive norms* are agreed-on expectations about what members of a group *do,* while *injunctive norms* are agreed-on expectations about what members of a group *ought to do.* Consider the behavior of museum patrons, for example. The pristine appearance of the typical museum, along with signs throughout the building, regularly reminds patrons not to litter in this setting. Virtually all museum goers abide by this rule, making it a descriptive norm (Kallgren, Reno, & Cialdini, 2000; Cialdini et al., 1991). Now consider the behavior of people walking outdoors. They, too, are expected to not litter; but in this arena, the no-litter norm is less explicit and more often ignored. Still, it is an expectation about what people *ought* to do, so it is an injunctive norm.

Friendly reminder This sign along a Nevada highway looks like a warning regarding a real law, but, on closer inspection, you'll see that it is just a clever reminder of the community's injunctive norm against littering. Such reminders often have a beneficial impact.

social role a set of norms ascribed to a person's social position; expectations and duties associated with the individual's position in the family, at work, in the community, and in other settings.

People are more likely to abide by injunctive norms if the norms are called to their attention. For example, people walking through a neighborhood with litter cans and antilittering signs are more likely to become aware of and follow the community's injunctive antilittering norm. In one study of this phenomenon, researchers passed out handbills to pedestrians. Each pedestrian received a handbill promoting either the importance of not littering, the wisdom of saving electricity by turning off lights, or the responsibility of each citizen to vote (Cialdini et al., 1991). Only 10 percent of the pedestrians who had been given the antilittering pamphlet crumpled and threw the handbill to the ground after they had finished reading it, compared with 20 percent of those who had been given the "lights out" or "voting" handbill.

Social Roles A **social role** is a set of norms ascribed to a person's social position—expectations and duties associated with the individual's position in the family, at work, in the community, and in other settings (Glass, 2005; Alexander & Wood, 2000; Sarbin & Allen, 1968). The role of police officers, for example, is to maintain law and order. The role of parents is to nurture, rear, and teach their children and prepare them for life outside the family.

Roles often have a positive impact on people and society. Indeed, they are critical for the smooth functioning of society. They can, however, also confine people. Just as many Hollywood actors complain of being "typecast" and prevented from demonstrating their versatility, people in various positions are often limited by their prescribed social roles. Many observers argue, for example, that traditional Western gender roles are oppressive for women.

When individuals in a particular group try to step out of the social roles assigned to members of that group, they may be met with negative reactions and evaluations (Morfei et al., 2004). For example, traditional Western gender roles ascribe more *communal* characteristics to women—that is, ones associated with the welfare of other people—and more *agentic* characteristics to men—that is, those associated with assertiveness, control, and confidence (Mosher & Danoff-Burg, 2008, 2005; Eagly & Koenig, 2006). In short, women in the West are expected to be caring and men to be assertive and self-assured.

Gossiping About People We Don't Even Know

As we noted in Chapter 11, some observers believe that, as a society, we like gossip. In earlier eras, people relied on word of mouth or newspapers to find out what their fellow humans were doing. Today we have the Internet, where gossip sites provide many followers with updated postings of the latest goings-on in Hollywood (KCET, 2007).

Just what makes our society so preoccupied with celebrity happenings? Some researchers suggest that this interest has evolutionary roots (McAndrew, 2008). A shared focus on the comings and goings of others may help bond us together into social groups and, over time, strong group affiliation probably helped to enhance safety, improve the chances of successfully bearing and raising children, and the like, thus ensuring continuation of the species (Dunbar, 2004). But why celebrities? According to some theorists, humans have come to view anyone they see frequently as an important member of their social group, even if they don't actually know the person—and we certainly see celebrities frequently. In addition, since modern society is quite mobile, celebrities may be the "friends" we have most in common with the people around us, thus providing a source of conversation and affiliation in our social groups (McAndrew, 2008).

In addition, gossip may serve to teach and enforce social norms (Baumeister, Zhang, & Vohs, 2004). Recall, for example, when entertainer Britney Spears was sharply sanctioned by society for shaving off her hair in 2007 (Marikar, 2007). A dominant American social norm is that females should not choose to be bald. If any young American children had been unaware of that norm, they learned a clear lesson by witnessing the ostracism Spears faced after her act.

Although few people want to admit that they're a gossip (McAndrew, 2008), it appears that many of us want—and may even need—to talk about other people, even ones we don't know.

Women are often judged harshly when they step outside their gender role. One study found, for example, that when a female manager was described to research participants as "successful," the individuals rated the woman as more hostile, selfish, quarrelsome, and subjective than successful male managers (Heilman, Block, & Martell, 1995). It is small wonder that women's advancement in the business world has often been limited (Abele, 2003). Women make up 46 percent of all workers in the United States, and possess 51 percent of bachelor's degrees and 45 percent of advanced degrees. Nevertheless, on average, they occupy lower-ranking positions and earn less income than men (U.S. Bureau of Labor Statistics, 2001; U.S. Bureau of the Census, 2000). In Fortune 500 companies, women constitute only 0.4 percent of the Chief Executive Officers (CEOs) and 4 percent of the five highest earning officers (Catalyst, 2000).

Social roles affect not only how others think about us but also how we think about ourselves and how we act toward others. In 1971, Philip Zimbardo and his colleagues at Stanford University studied the power of roles in a study famously known as *The Stanford Prison Experiment*, although it did not actually follow an experimental design (Zimbardo, 2006, 1972). The basement of the university's psychology department was converted into a mock prison, and 24 male students were randomly assigned to play the roles of either prisoners or guards for what was supposed to be two weeks. "Guards" were given batons, uniforms, and mirrored sunglasses and were told that it was their responsibility to run the prison. "Prisoners" wore smocks and small chains around their ankles and were referred to by assigned numbers instead of by name. To the researchers' horror, within hours the "guards" had settled comfortably into their new roles and had begun humiliating their "prisoner" peers. Some actually tormented the prisoners, imposed physical punishments on them, and denied bathroom privileges and food to prisoners who were "out of line." The study, clearly out of hand, raised many ethical questions and had to be shut down after just six days.

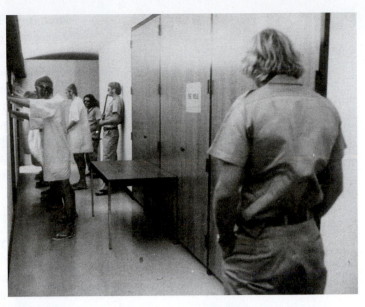

The power of social role playing In the famous Stanford University prison study, most of the students who were assigned to play prison guards engaged in at least some abuses of power, while those assigned to prisoner roles typically became passive, depressed, and disorganized.

Roles, Gender, and Social Skills HOW we Differ   There is a popular belief in Western society that, on average, women are more skilled socially than men, more sensitive emotionally, more expressive, and more focused on social relationships. In fact, research has supported this notion over the years (Eagly & Koenig, 2006). In a wide range of social psychology studies, it has been found, for example, that female participants tend to read nonverbal social cues more accurately than male participants, are more expressive with their faces and bodies during interactions, feel more empathy for the emotional experiences of others, and act friendlier in group discussions. For their part, male participants tend to focus more narrowly on the tasks at hand in group activities than do female participants, to emerge as leaders (as opposed to social facilitators) in group activities, and to adopt more authoritarian and less participative styles when they take on leadership roles.

Why is this gender difference in the social realm? Although researchers have not fully sorted out the issue, one of the most common explanations points to social roles (Eagly & Wood, 2006). As we observed above, traditional Western gender roles ascribe more communal characteristics to women—including expectations that they should be friendly, unselfish, concerned about others, and emotionally expressive—and more agentic characteristics to men—including expectations that they will be assertive, independent, and controlling. According to social role theory, people are inclined to behave in ways that are consistent with the expectations tied to their roles. Moreover, over the course of their lives, as people enact their social roles, their skills in the assigned realm become sharper and their corresponding attitudes more deeply

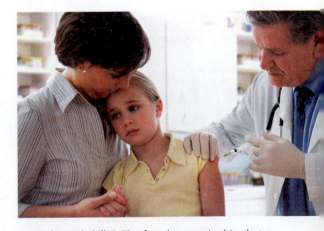

Special social skills? The female nurse in this photo demonstrates heightened sensitivity and other social skills while the male physician focuses on the task at hand without paying much attention to the child's social needs. Why are gender differences in social skills less pronounced today than in years past?

ingrained. Thus, the theory goes, women learn to be more interested and skilled in the social realm than men do.

Of course, as you are well aware, traditional gender roles have been undergoing considerable change in recent decades. Enormous numbers of women, for example, have competed in the work world and many men have taken on domestic and caretaking responsibilities and adopted more people-oriented attitudes and concerns. Not surprisingly, along with these changes in roles and expectations, social psychologists have been finding fewer and smaller gender differences in their studies of social skill, empathy, leadership, and the like. To be sure, such differences still exist in many research undertakings, as social role theory would predict, but there is clearly a shift occurring.

Conformity

Conformity is the tendency to yield to real or imagined group pressure. Investigators have been studying conformity for more than 60 years. Early work on this phenomenon was done by social psychologist Theodore Newcomb (1943). In a classic study, Newcomb examined the political views of students at Bennington College as they progressed through school. Although Bennington College is well known for the politically liberal leanings of many of its faculty members, it was attended during the Great Depression in the 1930s largely by children from conservative families. Newcomb found that as the students progressed through college, immersed in the Bennington culture, their political views grew more and more liberal. Moreover, these liberal views endured well into late adulthood, confirmed by interviews conducted 25 and 50 years later (Alwin, Cohen, & Newcomb, 1991; Newcomb et al., 1967).

Laboratory studies tell a similar story. Imagine that you agree to participate in a psychology experiment on "perceptual judgments." You and six other participants are seated around a table—you are seated second from the end—and the experimenter presents two cards to the group. The card on the left, Card A, displays a single vertical line, whereas the card on the right, Card B, displays three vertical lines of various lengths (see **Figure 14-7**). The experimenter asks each participant which of the three lines on Card B is equal in length to the line on Card A. When it is your turn, you immediately recognize that the second line on Card B matches the one on Card A. Thus, after the five participants seated ahead of you indicate that the second line on Card B is equal in length to the line on Card A, you do the same. Another set of cards is presented, and again everyone agrees. The straightforward task is moving along easily and comfortably.

Then something odd happens. On the third round, you again readily note which line on Card B matches the line on Card A—it's pretty clear that it's line 3 this time—but you are shocked to hear that the first person called upon by the experimenter answers, "line 1." You think to yourself "he needs an eye exam," but then the second person responds the same as the first. You rub your eyes, blink, and squint, but still you see that it's line 3 that matches the length of the line on Card A. After the five people ahead of you have all selected line 1, it is your turn to respond. What will you say?

In fact, this classic study, conducted by social psychologist Solomon Asch (1955), was not about perceptual judgments at all but rather was an investigation of conformity. In the study, the other "participants" were actually confederates, coached by the experimenter to give uniformly wrong answers on the third round and thereafter. Asch found that when the responses of the confederates were incorrect, almost 75 percent of the real participants conformed to the group norm and gave an incorrect response.

Asch also varied the procedures in his experiment to reveal what group features might affect this "tyranny of the majority" (Martin & Hewstone, 2001), and others have followed with similar work. One key factor is group *unanimity*. The presence of even one dissenting group member dramatically reduces the likelihood that participants will

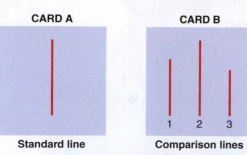

CARD A   **CARD B**

Standard line   Comparison lines

FIGURE 14-7 The perceptual judgment task in Asch's conformity study Asch's participants were asked which line (1, 2, or 3) was the same length as the standard line. Despite the obvious and correct choice (line 2), when the confederates gave the wrong answer, almost 75 percent of the participants conformed and gave the wrong answer, too.

conform to an incorrect group norm (Prislin & Wood, 2005). The *size* of the group also affects its influence. Groups with fewer than four members, for example, do not seem to bring about a powerful conformity effect (see **Figure 14-8**). Many laboratory studies on conformity have been conducted since Asch's pioneering undertaking (Abrams et al., 2005, 2000, 1990). The findings of most such studies are similar to Asch's—they demonstrate the strong effects of social pressure.

Obedience

In the studies of conformity just discussed, there were no leaders in the groups—just peers. In addition, there were no consequences for incorrect responses. No fines were imposed, nobody was hurt, and nobody had to account for or defend their decisions. But what about situations in which people are working under an authority figure or in which they must pay a price for making an incorrect decision? Classic work by researcher Stanley Milgram has offered important, and unsettling, insights into situations of this kind. Milgram was studying **obedience** which occurs when people follow direct commands, usually given by an authority figure.

Milgram's Experiment   Milgram's (1963) study is perhaps the most famous and controversial experiment in the history of psychology (Blass, 2007, 2004). Imagine that you've agreed to participate in this experiment. You arrive at the designated location and are met by a stern-looking man in a lab coat. The man introduces you to the mild-mannered "Mr. Wallace" and explains that the two of you are participating in a study of the effects of punishment on learning. One of you will be randomly assigned the role of "teacher"; and the other, the role of "learner." You are then given the "teacher" role. Although you are not aware of it, the assignment of roles has not been random at all. "Mr. Wallace" is a collaborator in league with the experimenter, who is really only interested in your behavior.

The experimenter takes the two of you to an adjacent room, where Mr. Wallace is prepped for his role as learner. He is told to roll up his right shirt sleeve, and the investigator attaches an electrode to his wrist. His arm is strapped down "to prevent excessive movement," and electrode paste is applied "to prevent blisters or burns." You are informed that the electrode is connected to a shock generator in the other room (**Figure 14-9**).

The two of you are told that you (as the teacher) will recite a list of word pairs. After going through the entire list, you will recite only the first word of each pair, followed by four options. Mr. Wallace will indicate which option is the correct match for the first word by pulling one of four levers. If the response is incorrect, you will administer an electric shock. Mr. Wallace mumbles something about having a heart condition, but that comment is more or less ignored by the experimenter.

You are taken to another room, unable to see Mr. Wallace, and are seated in front of a metallic, box-shaped instrument, covered with knobs and switches and labeled "Shock Generator." You notice that each switch on the shock generator's control panel is identified by a voltage—ranging from 15 volts to 450 volts—and a label—ranging from "slight shock"(15 volts) to "danger: extreme shock" (375 volts) to "XXX" (450 volts). The experimenter explains that whenever you push down a switch, Mr. Wallace will receive the corresponding shock, and this shock will stop as soon as you push the switch back up.

You are to communicate with Mr. Wallace through a microphone intercom, as the rooms are "partially soundproof." When he responds by pulling one of the four levers, one of four lights on top of the shock generator will light up. You are to administer a shock to Mr. Wallace whenever he responds incorrectly. With each successive incorrect

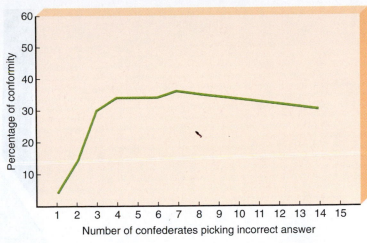

FIGURE 14-8 Group size and conformity A key factor in conformity is group size. Asch found that the conformity effect is not strong when the group's size is less than four members (Asch, 1955).

conformity the tendency to yield to social pressure.

obedience the act of following direct commands, usually given by an authority figure.

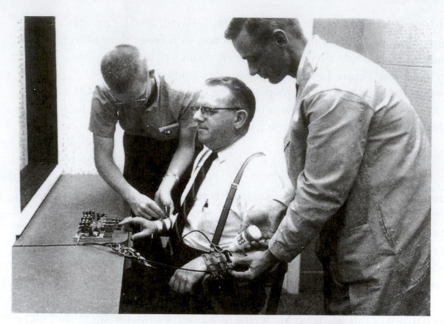

FIGURE 14-9 **Milgram's learner and the shock generator** Most people believe that they would not administer shocks to a person crying out in protest, but Milgram's experiment found otherwise.

“Obedience is due only to legitimate powers.”

*“*Obedience is due only to legitimate powers.*”*

–Jean-Jacques Rousseau,
French philosopher and writer

response, you are to move up one switch on the shock generator, administering what the labels suggest are increasingly powerful—and dangerous—shocks.

After Mr. Wallace offers his first incorrect response, you flick the switch identified as "15 volts." The machine springs to life, with bright red lights flashing and an ominous buzzing noise filling the air. As Mr. Wallace continues to offer incorrect responses, you are instructed to administer increasingly powerful shocks. Through the wall, you can hear Mr. Wallace moan and say things, such as "Get me out of here!" Any time you express reluctance to go on, the experimenter confidently states "Please continue" or even "You have no choice; you must go on." After a while, Mr. Wallace stops responding to your word prompts. The experimenter tells you to treat the failure to respond as an incorrect response and administer another shock (you're up to 450 volts, or "XXX," by now). Mr. Wallace lets out an agonized scream and yells, "Let me out of here! I have heart problems!" You hear and feel Mr. Wallace banging on the adjacent wall. Then he is completely silent. There are no further responses to your word prompts or to the shocks you administer.

As you are reading about this study, you are probably saying to yourself that you would have refused to go on with the experiment very early on. Most people who learn about this study have that reaction. Indeed, before the study became famous, its

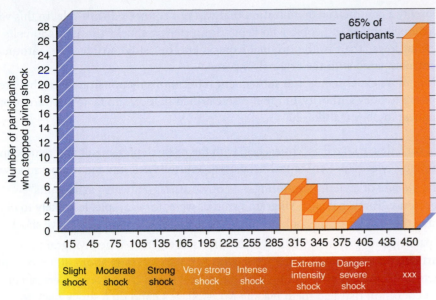

FIGURE 14-10 The results of Milgram's obedience experiment Milgram found that no participant stopped administering shocks before the 300-volt mark and that the vast majority (65 percent) continued administering shocks to the highest level (Milgram, 1963).

procedures were described to psychologists, and they predicted that only 1 percent of participants would continue with the experiment all the way through 450 volts. Astonishingly, Milgram found that 65 percent of the participants continued with the experiment all the way through the 450 volts label, and no participant stopped before the 300-volt mark (see **Figure 14-10**).

The Milgram Controversy It is no wonder that Milgram's study is one of psychology's most controversial. The study revealed something profoundly disturbing about human nature—namely, that we are inclined to obey authority, even if it means betraying our own personal morality. Milgram demonstrated that it is not just a cruel and sadistic fringe of the population that can inflict pain and suffering on innocent victims; two-thirds of the population might hurt others if ordered to do so by an authority figure. Milgram (1974) went on to explain the atrocities committed by Nazi Germany within the context of his remarkable findings, although a number of theorists have questioned the appropriateness of such a leap (Miller, 2004).

Initially, many refused to believe that Milgram's findings provided an accurate representation of people's readiness to inflict suffering. Critics attacked the experiment on various grounds. Most notably, the participants in the original study were all male. Some speculated that women might be less inclined to obey commands to inflict pain on others. Additionally, a number pointed out that the study had been conducted at Yale University. Had it been carried out at a less prestigious locale, they argued, the participants might have been less likely to obey the experimenter's commands. Finally, many questioned the ethical implications of the research.

Follow-Up Studies Milgram spent the years following the publication of his controversial findings conducting variations of the original experiment in order to further clarify the nature of obedience (Milgram, 1974). To the surprise of many people, he found that female participants were no more likely to defy an experimenter's commands than the male participants in the original experiment. Milgram also set up an alternative site for his experiment, the "Research Associates of Bridgeport"—

"I was just following orders."
—Adolf Eichmann, high-ranking official in Nazi Germany and self-proclaimed Jewish Specialist, at his 1961 war criminal trial

supposedly a commercial organization that was not connected with Yale. In this variation, the percentage of people who kept administering shocks through 450 volts was somewhat lower than in the original experiment, but still considerable—around 50 percent, compared with the original 65 percent.

Milgram's experiments and subsequent replications demonstrated just how ready people are to obey authority, but they also clarified that certain factors *reduce* people's willingness to obey (Lüttke, 2004).

- If a confederate served as "co-teacher" with the research participant and refused to continue, over 90 percent of the real participants followed suit and disobeyed as well.
- The *salience* of a victim's suffering—its obviousness—affects participants' obedience. Participants in Milgram's studies were, for example, less likely to obey when they could see the look on Mr. Wallace's face with each successive shock.
- A participant's *proximity* to the victim affects obedience. When Milgram's participants were seated in the room with Mr. Wallace, only about 40 percent of them continued to obey through 450 volts. Still fewer (30 percent) were obedient in a condition that had them placing Mr. Wallace's hand on a shock plate to administer the shock.

Of course, there are many occasions in life where it is quite useful and even advantageous to obey commands. During military maneuvers, surgical procedures, theater productions, and sporting competitions, for example, a lack of obedience may result in chaos or disaster. However, Milgram's study demonstrates the dark side of obedience. In a letter to another social psychologist, Milgram wrote, "Certainly, obedience serves numerous productive functions, and you may wonder why I focus on its destructive potential. Perhaps it is because this has been the most striking and disturbing expression of obedience in our time" (Blass, 2004).

Before You Go On

What Do You Know?
9. What are norms and what is their function in society?
10. What did Solomon Asch's experiments on conformity reveal?
11. What is the central difference between the concepts of conformity and obedience?

What Do You Think?   In both Asch's and Milgram's experiments, the presence of another person who would either go against the group or refuse to obey the authority figure made it more likely that the research participant would do so as well. How would you explain this phenomenon?

Social Relations

LEARNING OBJECTIVE 4 Review major concepts in the areas of group dynamics, helping behavior, aggression, and interpersonal attraction.

Many social psychologists have been interested in social relations. Some have studied *group dynamics*—how membership or participation in a group influences our thoughts and behaviors. Still others have attempted to determine when people choose to help others and when they ignore others' needs. Other social psychologists have examined aggression and interpersonal attraction, trying to understand why people behave aggressively and how people come to like or love others in their social world.

Group Dynamics

A **group** is an organized, stable collection of individuals in which the members are aware of and influence one another and share a common identity. Groups members are thus *interdependent*—that is, the behavior of one group member affects the behavior of the other members. Let's consider several topics related to groups and group dynamics: *group productivity, the social facilitation effect, social loafing, group polarization,* and *groupthink.*

Group Productivity One issue of interest to social psychologists is what makes groups productive. Not surprisingly, they have found that the optimal group size for productivity depends on the task at hand (Steiner, 1972).

- When a group confronts an *additive task,* its members must perform parallel actions. For example, to clear a property of snow after a storm, all members of a work crew must shovel snow. For such tasks, group productivity increases directly with group size.

- In contrast, a group faced with a *conjunctive task* is only as productive as its weakest member. If, for example, group members are hiking together up a mountain, they can travel only as fast as the slowest person in the group. In this situation, a greater number of group members does not necessarily yield better performance.

- A *disjunctive task* requires a single solution. In such undertakings, the most competent person in the group is likely to provide the solution. Larger groups are typically more productive for disjunctive tasks, because a larger group is more likely to have a superstar member who can solve the problem at hand.

- *Divisible tasks* involve the simultaneous performance of several different activities. When groups confront such tasks, no single person works on all phases of the undertaking; thus, the different strengths of group members complement one another. For divisible tasks, larger groups tend to be more productive.

Social Facilitation In many instances, our performance is enhanced when we are in the presence of others. This is one of the oldest observations in social psychology. In the late 1890s, psychologist Norman Triplett noted that cyclists tend to go faster when in the presence of other cyclists than when alone—even when they are not in competition with one another. To test his hypothesis that the presence of others can enhance individual performance, Triplett (1898) conducted an experiment in which he had children wind a fishing reel either all alone or side-by-side with other children. Triplett found that children winding side-by-side worked substantially quicker than children winding by themselves. This phenomenon was later labeled **social facilitation** and its study was expanded to include not just physical tasks but also mental tasks (such as solving puzzles and doing math problems).

As social facilitation has been studied over the years, researchers have learned that people's performance in the presence of others is more complicated than Triplett first believed. In fact, for some tasks, and for some people, performing in the presence of others can impair—rather than enhance—performance (Uziel, 2007; Strauss, 2002; Aiello & Douthitt, 2001). Trying to make sense of these contradictory findings, psychologist Robert Zajonc (1965) proposed that the presence of others elevates our arousal level, which in turn facilitates performance on simple, well-learned tasks but interferes with performance on complicated tasks. Zajonc's theory has received support from numerous studies and observations of both humans and animals (Bargh, 2001; Platania & Moran, 2001; Zentall & Levine, 1972).

group an organized, stable collection of individuals in which the members are aware of and influence one another and share a common identity.

social facilitation an effect in which the presence of others enhances performance.

Improving each other's performance Without realizing it, these two friends probably run faster when they jog together than when they each jog alone—the result of social facilitation.

In recent years, theorists have focused less on the mere presence of others and more on individuals' *interpretations* of and *reactions* to the presence of others (Aiello & Douthitt, 2001; Bond, 2000; Bond & Titus, 1983). If, for example, individuals do not like or trust other persons in their group, their own contributions to a group project may suffer. In addition, if people believe that other group members are disregarding their ideas or efforts, their own performance in the group may decline (Fiske, 2010; Paulus et al., 2002, 1993).

Social Loafing   Groups are often formed in hopes that an interconnected body of people can energize and motivate every individual member. However, these hopes are not always realized. How many times when working in a group have you noticed that one or two of the group members are not pulling their weight? **Social loafing**—also known as *free riding*—refers to the phenomenon in which people exert less effort on a collective task than they would on a comparable individual task (Liden et al., 2004; Latane et al., 1979).

Social loafing seems to rear its ugly head most in large groups (Liden et al., 2004). It is most likely to occur when certain group members lack motivation to contribute, feel isolated from the group, calculate the cost of contributing as too high, or view their own contributions as unnecessary (Chidambaram & Tung, 2005; Shepperd, 1995, 1993). Research suggests that people from Western cultures are more inclined to display social loafing than people from Eastern cultures, and men are more likely to do so than women (Fiske, 2004).

Fortunately, social loafing can be minimized. When, for example, groups are highly *cohesive*—when group members all desire and value membership in the group—the social loafing phenomenon all but disappears (Hoigaard et al., 2006; Liden et al., 2004). Additionally, social loafing is reduced when group members are each explicitly reminded of their uniqueness and importance (Asmus & James, 2005), when they are given specific and challenging goals (Ling et al., 2005), when the output of each member is publicly identified (Williams et al., 1981), and when the members are given clear norms and comparison standards for their work (Hoigaard et al., 2006; Paulus et al., 2002). Finally, alertness tends to decrease social loafing, whereas fatigue tends to increase it (Hoeksema-van Orden, Gaillard, & Buunk, 1998).

Group Polarization   Have you ever begun talking about one of your favorite bands with a bunch of friends with similar musical tastes and found yourself liking the band even more by the end of the conversation? When an initial tendency of individual group members is intensified following group discussion, **group polarization** occurs (Abrams et al., 2001; Isenberg, 1986). This phenomenon is not simply an example of conformity. With group polarization, the attitudes and inclinations of the individual group members are already in place, and they become more intense and more extreme as a result of the group interaction (Cooper et al., 2004).

Group polarization has been studied most often with regard to racial and ethnic bias and social and political attitudes (Prislin & Wood, 2005; Billings et al., 2000). When, for example, researchers have placed individuals with highly prejudiced attitudes in a group to discuss racial issues, the attitudes of the individuals tend to become still more prejudiced (Myers & Bishop, 1970). In similar work, it has been found that the attitudes of women with moderate leanings toward feminism become more strongly feminist following group discussions (Myers, 1975).

Groupthink   Groups often come together to solve specific problems and make decisions. We noted earlier that group cohesiveness can prevent social loafing—but sometimes, groups can become *too* cohesive and single-minded, and the group's decision making can lead to disaster. A classic example occurred in the early 1960s, when the United States government was determined to overthrow the communist government that Fidel Castro had instituted in Cuba. The U.S. government had trained a small group of Cuban exiles as part of a military operation to overthrow Castro. Proponents of the

social loafing a phenomenon in which people exert less effort on a collective task than they would on a comparable individual task; also known as *free riding*.

group polarization the intensification of an initial tendency of individual group members brought about by group discussion.

groupthink a form of faulty group decision making that occurs when group members strive for unanimity and this goal overrides their motivation to realistically appraise alternative courses of action.

plan predicted that once this small militia touched down in Cuba at the Bay of Pigs, the Cuban citizens would rise up and join them. Instead, the operation collapsed, with no support from the Cuban people and no further help from the U.S. government. As a result of the failed invasion, anti-American sentiment around the globe increased, as did Castro's influence in Latin America and Cuba's ties with the Soviet Union.

Psychologist Irving Janis (1972), after examining the flawed decision-making process that went into the Bay of Pigs invasion, attributed the fiasco to **groupthink**, which he defined as a form of faulty group decision making that occurs when group members strive too hard for unanimity. The goal of achieving a consensus among all group members overrides the need to realistically appraise alternative courses of action. Clearly, groupthink can have undesired consequences (Henningsen et al., 2006; Baron, 2005; Whyte, 2000).

Janis identified a number of conditions that set the stage for groupthink: (1) strong similarity in group members' backgrounds and ideologies, (2) high group cohesiveness, (3) high perceived threat, (4) elevated stress, (5) insulation from outside influence, and (6) a directive leader. Group members experience an illusion of invulnerability and have an unquestioned belief in the group's inherent morality. Typically, group members exert direct pressure against any member who expresses strong disagreement, and members protect the group from information that might shatter the shared conviction that their decisions are effective and moral (Janis, 1982).

Groupthink may have been operating among government officials in the months and even years leading up to the Hurricane Katrina disaster. Officials at the Federal Emergency Management Agency (FEMA) were well aware that New Orleans could suffer grave damage if hit by a major hurricane. In fact, they predicted that a storm powerful enough to top the New Orleans levees would displace more than a million people. Despite this grim projection and the apparent recognition that an effective evacuation plan was not in place in New Orleans, officials remained upbeat about their level of preparedness for such a hurricane. Although outside experts expressed serious concerns—concerns that turned out to be well founded—officials in charge maintained that FEMA, along with state and local agencies, was well equipped to handle a major storm and manage its aftermath. Dissenting voices were largely ignored.

Having identified the phenomenon of groupthink, Janis went on to propose measures that a group can take to safeguard against it. First, the leader of the group should encourage members to air objections and doubts and should accept criticisms of the group's judgments. Additionally, various group members should be assigned the role of "devil's advocate," arguing against the group's favored position. Finally, outside experts should be invited to group meetings and encouraged to challenge the group's core views and decisions.

Research conducted since Janis first proposed his theory suggests that groupthink is a complicated phenomenon—probably more complicated than Janis initially realized. The conditions that he believed set the stage for groupthink do not always result in unwarranted unanimity (Baron, 2005). Nor do his proposed safeguards always prevent groupthink. At the same time, research and observations clearly indicate that the phenomenon of groupthink is widespread. Not only does it often affect decision making in important policy-setting groups, as Janis recognized, but it also influences decision making in mundane and temporary groups and groups working on trivial matters (Baron, 2005; Eaton, 2001; Whyte, 2000).

Helping Behavior

When people are in need, we tend to offer our help, as an expression of **altruism** or of another social motive. After the 9/11 terrorist attacks, for example, people gave their time, money, and support to those affected by the attacks. The number of people

A consequence of groupthink? In 2003 the space shuttle Columbia disintegrated during re-entry over Texas, killing all seven crew members. Just two days before the disaster, a NASA engineer had warned his supervisors of possible catastrophes on re-entry, but his message was not forwarded up the chain of command. How might groupthink have been involved in this mishandling of the warning?

altruism self-sacrificing behavior carried out for the benefit of others.

Social Relations **485**

Responding to tragedy Almost immediately after a series of terrorist bombs ripped through passenger trains in Madrid, Spain in 2004, killing 191 people and injuring 1800 others, Spanish citizens such as these began lining up to donate blood to the victims. Altruism? Possibly. But social psychologists point out that egoistic motives may also be at work during the early reactions to tragedies of this kind.

donating blood to the Red Cross doubled in the month following the attacks, and by the end of September 2001, $115 million had been donated to the September 11 Fund (Piferi, Jobe, & Jones, 2006). Similarly, as we observed earlier, private contributions reached unprecedented levels after Hurricane Katrina. Social psychologists have studied various aspects of such helping behavior.

Why Do We Help? Altruism refers to self-sacrificing behavior carried out for the benefit of others. To be altruistic, behavior must be motivated by concern for persons in need, without concern for oneself (Post, 2005; Puka, 2004). Thus, engaging in self-sacrificing behavior to avoid a sense of guilt or donating to charity for tax purposes would not be considered altruistic behavior. Such acts, which are motivated by a desire to reduce one's own personal distress or to receive rewards, are sometimes called *egoistic helping behaviors* (Batson et al., 2004, 1997; Khalil, 2004).

When we engage in helping behavior, our motives can be entirely altruistic, entirely egoistic, or some combination of the two. Surveys have revealed that in the *immediate* aftermath of the 9/11 terrorist attacks, actions such as giving blood, money, and goods and offering prayers were associated with both altruistic and egoistic motives (Piferi et al., 2006). People's motivations for giving ranged from wanting to ease the suffering of others to hoping to reduce their own attack-induced distress and seeking to reassure themselves that other people would also help them if they were in need. In contrast, *sustained* giving after the attacks—that is, giving after one or more years—was associated only with altruistic motives.

Research further indicates that certain factors increase the likelihood of altruistic behavior. When people empathize and identify with the individuals in need, they are more likely to behave altruistically (Batson et al., 2004, 1997; Batson & Weeks, 1996). Similarly, people tend to display more altruism when they take the perspective of victims (Mikulincer et al., 2005; Underwood & Moore, 1982). Not surprisingly, then, people who are generally trusting and outward-looking and who form secure attachments in their relationships are most likely to perform altruistic behaviors (Mikulincer et al., 2005; Mikulincer & Shaver, 2005).

Bystander Apathy Imagine you are in a life-threatening situation and desperately need the help of others. If you could choose, would you prefer that one or two people were nearby or that a large number of people were present? If you are like most people, you probably would prefer the larger number. After all, that would mean more potential helpers. In fact, however, this may be the more dangerous choice. It turns out that, in many circumstances, the more people present in a situation where help is required, the less likely it is that any one person will give that help (Fischer et al., 2006; Garcia et al., 2002; Batson, 1991).

On March 13, 1961, a woman named Kitty Genovese was stabbed to death over the course of 30 minutes in the New York borough of Queens, while at least 38 neighbors and other onlookers failed to intervene. This famous murder was followed by a public outcry demanding an explanation for the lack of intervention by others, including a *New York Times* article with the headline: "Thirty-Eight Who Saw Murder Didn't Call the Police" (Gansberg, 1964). Initially, many observers concluded that these 38 bystanders must have had a host of personality flaws that prevented them from helping. But were they really callous and uncaring?

Social psychologists John Darley and Bibb Latané were less interested in the personality traits of these onlookers than with features of the situation that might have kept them from providing help. In a series of studies examining the impact of the presence of others on helping behavior, Darley and Latané repeatedly demonstrated that we are, in fact, more likely to intervene when we are *alone* than when others are also present. In one of their studies, for example, participants found themselves in a situation where

Diffusion of responsibility People are less likely to stop and help an apparently lost child if they are part of a large crowd than if they are walking alone on a street. Why? When many others are present, we are not as likely to feel the full burden of responsibility.

they smelled smoke (contrived by the experimenters) while either alone or in the presence of others. When other people were present in the room, fewer than 40 percent of the participants got up to report the smoke. In contrast, 75 percent of the participants reported smelling smoke when no one else was in the room (see **Figure 14-11**) (Latané & Darley, 1968). In another experiment by the two researchers, participants were placed in a situation in which they overheard a person (actually an actor) in another room having a seizure. The more people the participants believed could also hear the individual having the seizure, the less quickly they acted to help (Darley & Latané, 1968).

This phenomenon has been termed *bystander apathy*. Researchers in addition to Darley and Latané have observed group apathy of this kind under a wide variety of conditions, including situations in which a person's belongings were seemingly stolen in a library (Shaffer et al., 1975), graffiti was written on an elevator wall (Chekroun & Brauer, 2002), and drunk driving was about to take place (Rabow et al., 1990).

What must occur in order for bystanders to intervene on someone else's behalf? Apparently, several steps are involved (Fischer et al., 2006; Darley, 2000; Latané & Darley, 1970). Bystanders must: (1) notice the event, (2) interpret the event as an emergency, (3) feel personal responsibility for acting, (4) consider what form of assistance is needed, and (5) implement action.

Some theorists have focused on the third step, *feeling a sense of personal responsibility*, as the key to bystander apathy. They suggest that the presence of a large number of people in an emergency situation creates a *diffusion of responsibility*. When others are present, we feel that we do not bear the full burden of responsibility, and thus we feel less compelled to act. We may also assume that someone else must be taking action. This was exactly what many individuals concluded as they observed bodies of Hurricane Katrina victims floating past them or decaying in the streets of New Orleans—they concluded that other people would soon be collecting the bodies. Of course, when everyone in a crisis assumes that others will be taking responsibility for constructive action, no one intervenes. In extreme cases, such as that of Kitty Genovese, tragedy can result.

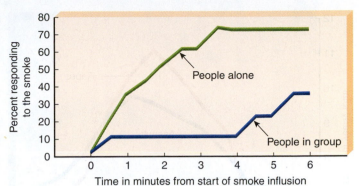

FIGURE 14-11 Bystander intervention People are more likely to intervene to help when they are alone than in a group. In the presence of others, people feel less compelled to act, a phenomenon called *bystander apathy* (Darley & Latané, 1968).

Aggression

In social psychological terms, *aggression* describes a broad category of behaviors, including physical and verbal attacks, intended to do harm to another. Aggression appears to have at least some biological underpinnings. Twin studies indicate that two identical twins are more likely to share the trait of violent temper than fraternal twins, suggesting a genetic component (Baker et al., 2007; Miles & Carey, 1997; Rowe et al., 1999). High levels of the hormone testosterone have been linked with higher levels of aggression, as have low levels of the neurotransmitter serotonin. Indeed, the persons most likely to be involved with violent crime are muscular young men with below-average intelligence, high levels of testosterone, and low levels of serotonin (Dabbs et al., 2001).

That said, under the right circumstances, we are apparently all capable of aggressive acts. One major hypothesis explaining aggression in humans—the *frustration-aggression hypothesis*—holds that we become aggressive in response to frustration (Dollard et al., 1939). As suggested in Chapter 12, any emotional stressor that impedes our progress or prevents achievement of some goal elicits frustration. Aggression, then, might be a cue to push harder in order to achieve that goal.

This theory was later expanded to include the notion that any unpleasant event, ranging from experiencing a bad odor or an annoying sound to hearing bad news, leads to activation of the sympathetic nervous system (Berkowitz, 1989). Recall from Chapter 12 that activation of the sympathetic nervous system is associated with both anger and

Relational aggression On average, women are more likely than men to express their anger with relational aggression (for example, ignoring the person who has angered them).

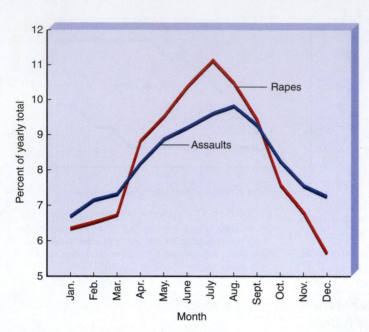

FIGURE 14-12 Aggression by time of year Studies of data in North America and Europe over the last hundred years show that aggression is highest in the hottest months of the year (Anderson, 1989).

fear and with the fight-or-flight response. This theory suggests that if you have translated this activation to aggressive (fight) behavior in the past, and the outcome has had a desired effect, you will continue to engage in that aggressive behavior.

Other factors influencing aggression probably result from both biology and environment (**Figure 14-12**). For example, as we have observed previously, men tend to be more aggressive than women—at least in some respects. Women are more likely to engage in acts of *relational aggression*, such as snubbing, gossiping, and otherwise excluding others as a means of venting frustration or anger (Archer, 2005). However, men are more likely to engage in *direct aggression*, which includes direct physical and verbal abuse. In fact, the vast majority of violent offenders are male (Halpern, 2000). Because this disparity shows up very early in childhood, it may be at least partially attributable to biological gender differences. However, it is probably also affected by social norms within our society, where men are permitted more than women to express anger and act aggressively.

Alcohol has also been found to increase aggressive behavior for both biological and psychological reasons. The effects of the drug may reduce inhibitions and so make people more likely to engage in violence or verbal abuse. However, people have been shown to become more aggressive even if they only think that they've had alcohol to drink, suggesting that they are responding to social expectations about how people act when they have been drinking.

Interpersonal Attraction

Why are we attracted to some people and not others? What's the difference between liking someone and loving someone? These are questions central to the study of interpersonal attraction. Interpersonal attraction operates at three levels: *cognitively*, we think certain things about the other person; *affectively*, we experience particular feelings toward him or her; and *behaviorally*, we act in certain ways toward the person (Orbuch & Sprecher, 2003; Berscheid & Walster, 1978).

Liking   *Liking* refers to fondness and affection for another person. Research has revealed five key factors that lead to liking someone.

1. *Similarity*—The more similar to us we perceive someone to be, the more likely we are to develop a fondness for that person (Lankau, Riordan, & Thomas, 2005; Bates, 2002). In addition, the more similar people are, the likelier it is that their fondness for one another will last a long time (Byrne, 1971).
2. *Proximity*—We tend to like people whom we encounter frequently more than those we do not encounter often, and we tend to like familiar people more than unfamiliar people (Smith & Weber, 2005; Swap, 1977). How many times have you eventually come to like a song you disliked when you first heard it? Our feelings toward people often operate in a similar fashion.
3. *Self-disclosure*—We tend to initially like people who disclose personal information to us (Dindia, 2000; Taylor et al., 1981), and we tend to disclose more to people whom we initially like (Certner, 1973; Worthy et al., 1969).
4. *Situational factors*—The situations in which we encounter other people greatly affect how much we like them. It has been suggested, for example, that we like people when we experience rewards while in their presence (Lott & Lott, 1974). Furthermore, a shared humorous experience seems to be a powerful way of forging closeness with a stranger (Fraley & Aron, 2004; Lyttle, 2001). The famous playwright Oscar Wilde once said, "Laughter is not at all a bad beginning for a friendship."

"I do not believe that friends are necessarily the people you like the best. They are merely the people who got there first."
—Peter Ustinov, actor

5. *Physical attractiveness*—People of all ages, even babies, prefer to look at and be near attractive people (Smith & Weber, 2005; Langlois & Stephan, 1981; Dion & Berscheid, 1974). Not surprisingly, then, physical attractiveness may affect likeability.

What kinds of studies have led researchers to these conclusions? Let's examine a few of the investigations into the last factor mentioned above, physical attractiveness. In a study by social psychologist Elaine Walster and her colleagues (1966), the experimenters randomly paired participants to be dates at a dance. During a break in the dance, the participants were asked to rate how much they liked their partners. Overall, the more attractive the partner, the more likeable he or she was reported to be.

In other studies, an attractive middle-aged person was judged to be more outgoing and more pleasant than a less attractive middle-aged individual (Adams & Huston, 1975); physically attractive college students were found to be more popular than less attractive ones among members of the same sex (Byrne et al., 1968); and attractive fifth-grade students were rated more popular by their classmates than less attractive students (Cavior & Dokecki, 1969).

Finally, one study examined the joint impact of two factors—physical attractiveness and similarity—on liking (Byrne et al., 1970). The experimenters prearranged lab dates for participants, varying both attractiveness and similarity of attitudes on certain issues. Upon their arrival, the dates were sent to a student lounge to talk for 20 minutes and then instructed to return to the lab. In the laboratory, the experimenters then measured how much the date pairs liked each other by having the participants fill out a questionnaire and by observing how close together the date pair stood when they reentered the lab. It turned out that the measures of liking were indeed related to both how attractive the dates were and how similar their attitudes were.

Loving Whereas liking someone involves a sense of fondness, loving is associated with a more extreme affection. When we *love* someone, we experience a strong, passionate attachment to that person. Some see loving as simply an extreme form of liking—with degree of attraction being the key distinction—whereas others see loving as a qualitatively different phenomenon (Watts & Stenner, 2005; Sternberg, 2004, 1987).

Let's first consider the question of what functions love serves. Freud viewed love as *sublimated sexual energy*—that is, a transformation of sexual desire into a more socially acceptable form (Fenchel, 2006). Evolutionary theorists emphasize love's role in propagating the species (Brumbaugh & Fraley, 2006; Wilson, 1981). According to these theorists, strong passionate attachments have ensured that over time, parents would stay together and raise their children together.

Still other theorists argue that love's most important value is to help provide companionship, emotional support, and even protection throughout the lifespan (Mikulincer et al., 2008; Mikulincer & Goodman, 2006). Loving relationships have in fact been associated with improved health (Levin, 2000). Such relationships provide us with people to confide in—and not being able to confide our troubles to someone has been associated with a host of health problems (Pennebaker, 2004, 2003, 1990; Pennebaker et al., 2004). This may be one reason why recently widowed individuals are more vulnerable to disease than individuals of similar age who have not lost a spouse (Troyer, 2006; Daggett, 2002).

What are the building blocks of love? Decades ago, social psychologist Zick Rubin (1970) emphasized three elements of love: attachment, caring, and intimacy. *Attachment* refers to the individual's need or desire for the physical

New approach, same criteria Two people meet in a speed dating program at Bondi Beach in Australia. Speed dating is a relatively new form of social engagement in which large numbers of men and women are rotated to meet many potential partners over a series of short 3 to 8 minute "dates." What kinds of partners do speed daters choose most often? Those who are attractive and hold attitudes similar to those of the selectors.

"Don't you understand? I love you! I need you! I want to spend the rest of my vacation with you!"

triangular theory of love a theory that love is composed of three elements: intimacy, passion, and commitment; proposed by Robert Sternberg.

presence and emotional support of the other person; *caring* is a feeling of concern and responsibility for him or her; and *intimacy* involves the desire for close, confidential communication with the other individual.

Using this definition of love, Rubin (1973) designed a self-report scale that he hoped would be able to measure love and distinguish it from liking. The scale included *love* items, such as "If I could never be with _____, I would feel miserable" and "I feel I can confide in _____ about virtually everything," along with *like* items, such as "I think that _____ is usually well-adjusted" and "_____ is the sort of person whom I myself would like to be." In one study, Rubin had dating couples fill out this scale, alone and confidentially, focusing on their date partner in their ratings. He found that friends and lovers both scored high on the like items, but friends did not score high on the love items.

In another study, Rubin had volunteer couples come to his laboratory and sit across from each other while awaiting the start of the experiment. His assistants secretly observed the couples from behind a one-way mirror to determine which ones gazed into each other's eyes, a sign of love according to conventional wisdom. As expected, the partners who had scored high on Rubin's love scale gazed lovingly at each other more than did partners who had scored low on the scale.

Another psychologist, Robert Sternberg, whom you met back in Chapter 10, has proposed the **triangular theory of love**, which holds that love is composed of *intimacy*, *passion*, and *commitment* (Sternberg & Weis, 2006; Sternberg, 2004, 1986). Here, *intimacy* refers once again to feelings that promote closeness and connection, *passion* involves intense desires for union with the other person, and *commitment* refers to the decision to maintain the relationship across time. According to Sternberg, the extent and quality of each of these three components determines the nature of a particular loving relationship.

In fact, Sternberg distinguishes eight kinds of love, each reflecting a particular combination of the three components (Table 14-1). For example, purely *romantic* love consists of much intimacy and passion with little commitment. In contrast, couples who experience *companionate* love are high on intimacy and commitment but low on passion. Couples who experience *consummate* love are high on all three components;

TABLE 14-1 Sternberg's Eight Kinds of Love

Kind of Love	Intimacy	Passion	Commitment
Non-Love	✗	✗	✗
Liking	✓	✗	✗
Infatuated love	✗	✓	✗
Empty love	✗	✗	✓
Romantic love	✓	✓	✗
Companionate love	✓	✗	✓
Fatuous love	✗	✓	✓
Consummate love	✓	✓	✓

Source: (Sternberg, 1987) Figure 17-2: From R. J. Sternberg (1987). The triangle of love: Intimacy, passion, commitment. New York: Basic Books. Copyright © 1987 by Basic Books. Reprinted with the permission of the publisher.

and those with *empty* love are high on commitment only. Sternberg also believes these relationships change over time, peaking at different points.

A number of social psychologists propose that relationships proceed through *stages* as the participants move from the fondness and affection of liking to the intimacy and commitment of loving. One theory, for example, cites four stages: exploration, bargaining, commitment, and institutionalization (Backman, 1990, 1981). In the *exploration* stage, the partners try out the possible rewards and costs of a relationship. During the *bargaining* stage, they implicitly negotiate the terms of the relationship. That is, they "feel out" its ground rules—which behaviors are rewarding, which cost too much, and how the joint benefits of the relationship can be maximized. During the third stage, *commitment*, the partners grow increasingly dependent on each other. Finally, in the *institutionalization* stage, shared expectations emerge, and the relationship is recognized by the partners (and by others) as exclusive. Other theorists have proposed different specific stages, but most agree that relationships do tend to proceed step-by-step as they deepen from liking to loving, with each stop marked by changing understandings, behaviors, and feelings (Yela, 2006; Berscheid, 1983).

What determines *how* we love? Many theorists suggest that the way we express and experience love is a direct outgrowth of our early experiences with caregivers (Hazan & Shaver, 2004, 1994, 1987). For example, as we observed in Chapter 3, young children seem to express one of several kinds of attachment in their relationships with their parents (Ainsworth, 1979). It appears that adults display similar types of attachment in their romantic relationships. Using the attachment model, researchers Cindy Hazan and Phillip Shaver have proposed three types of lovers.

- Those with *secure* attachment styles find it relatively easy to become close to others and are comfortable depending on lovers and being depended on. They do not fear becoming too close or being abandoned.

Falling in Limerence

Have you been in love? If yes, what did it feel like? Did you think about the object of your affection constantly? Did you intensely fear that the person would reject you? Did you even have an aching feeling in your chest? If so, the reality may have been that you weren't in love. You were in *limerence* (Tennov, 1999).

Based on interviews with over 500 individuals conducted in the 1960s and 1970s, psychologist Dorothy Tennov coined the term *limerence* to describe the ultimate, obsessive form of romantic love. According to Tennov, limerence lasts, on average, two years. A person may experience it many times, only once, or never in a lifetime. The most notable component of limerence is constant, intrusive thinking about the object of affection, whom Tennov referred to as the limerent object, or LO (Reynolds, 1993). Tennov claimed that when people first fall into limerence, they spend about 30 percent of their day thinking about the LO. A few months later, they are thinking about the LO 100 percent of the time (*Time*, 1980).

The reality is, limerence can be problematic. Not only do romantic relationships suffer if one partner is in limerence while the other is not, but friendships and familial relationships can also become strained by the limerent's preoccupation with the LO. Some observers have even compared limerence to substance dependence.

Some psychologists believe that limerence is so disruptive it should be categorized as a psychological disorder for which people shoud get clinical help. They argue that people in limerence who do seek treatment are often incorrectly diagnosed with generalized anxiety disorder, depression, or obsessive-compulsive disorder (OCD) (Wakin & Vo, 2008).

Some brain research supports the view that limerence is not a usual state. Neuroscientists have found that people who are newly "in love" have activity levels of the neurotransmitter serotonin similar to the levels found in individuals with OCD. In addition, people who have fallen in love within the past six months have elevated levels of the stress hormone cortisol (Anathasawamy, 2004).

What do you think? Is the heart-pounding state that fuels romance novels and movies, actually a psychological disorder?

- Those with *avoidant* attachment styles are somewhat uncomfortable being close to others and have difficulty trusting others and depending on them. In fact, they become nervous when others want to become closer to them.
- Those with *anxious-ambivalent* attachment styles worry that their lovers are less interested in closeness than they are. These insecure individuals are preoccupied with concerns that their partners do not really love them or will not stay with them. Sometimes their demands for security in relationships wind up pushing people away.

In their research, Hazan and Shaver found that approximately 53 percent of adults in relationships display a secure attachment style, 26 percent an avoidant attachment style, and 20 percent an anxious-ambivalent attachment style.

Before You Go On

What Do You Know?

12. What is groupthink and under what conditions is it most likely to occur?

13. How does altruistic helping behavior differ from egoistic helping behavior?

14. How does the presence of other people affect the likelihood that a bystander will intervene on behalf of someone who needs help?

15. What are some of the biological underpinnings of aggressive behavior?

16. What are the three components of Robert Sternberg's triangular theory of love and how do they interact in relationships?

What Do You Think? Think about a relationship you have had with a friend—someone you really like. Analyze the development of that relationship with reference to each of the key factors discussed in this section.

What Happens in the
Social Functioning B R A I N ?

LEARNING OBJECTIVE 5 Describe the major findings of social neuroscience about regions of the brain particularly important to our social functioning.

Throughout this book, you have seen that with the help of brain-scanning procedures, researchers have tied many areas of psychological functioning, such as memory or emotions, to particular neural circuits—collections of neurons that communicate with each other. The study of social functioning is no different. Indeed, there has been so much work to uncover what happens in the brain when people are thinking and behaving socially that the field of study has been given a special title, *social neuroscience,* and the combination of brain regions that operate together when people function socially has also been given a special name in some circles, the "social brain."

One of the early clues for helping researchers to identify regions of the brain that may be at work in social cognition and behavior came from evolutionary psychology (Adolphs, 2009, 2003). Beginning with the observation that a unique and critically important area of human functioning is social cognition—particularly the ability to infer what is going on (intentions, feelings, and thoughts) inside the minds of other people—scientists decided to pay special attention to those regions that are newer and/or bigger in human brains than in the brains of other animals. Their suspicion was that these regions may be the ones that play key roles in social functioning.

Not surprisingly, several of the brain regions that, according to brain scans, are very active during social cognition and behavior are indeed particularly large in the human brain. For example, the *prefrontal cortex,* the part of the frontal cortex that is closest to the front of the head, is much larger in humans than in other animals. As we observed in Chapter 4, the entire frontal cortex is somewhat larger in the human brain than in the brains of less complex animals. But the prefrontal cortex is particularly larger (Semendeferi et al., 2002).

Social cognitions and behaviors rely on many of the psychological functions that we have examined throughout this book. They require, for example, rapid identification of social stimuli and signals (for example, recognition of people), rapid retrieval of memories (to help us remember who is a friend and who is a foe), the ability to recognize the perspective of others, anticipation of others' behaviors, experiences of emotion and empathy, and moral and other evaluations of situations (to help us decide, for example, whether prosocial behavior is in order) (Adolphs, 2009). Thus, some of the brain regions that are highly active during social functioning turn out to be ones that we have come across in our chapters on language and thought, memory, emotion, and the like. To date, social neuroscientists have identified the following brain regions as among the key players in social functioning:

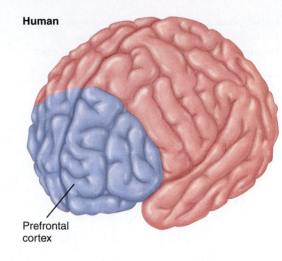

- *Orbitofrontal cortex*—a subregion of the prefrontal cortex, it is involved in social reasoning, reward evaluation, reading other people, and eliciting emotional states (Stuss et al., 2001).

- *Ventromedial prefrontal cortex*—another subregion of the prefrontal cortex, it plays a key role in the processing of rewards and punishments, interpreting nonverbal social information (such as facial expressions), making social and moral assessments and decisions, and feeling empathy (Koenigs et al., 2007; Shamay-Tsoory et al., 2005).

- *Insula*—a region of the cortex that is located beneath the frontal cortex, it plays a key role in empathy and in reading others. The insula is activated when we observe others in physical or emotional pain and immediately feel that pain ourselves (Keysers & Gazzola, 2007).

- *Amygdala*—a brain region that is located in the temporal lobe, it is, as we have seen, actively involved in the control of emotions. In social functioning, it helps us to identify the emotional facial expressions of other people and to pay particular attention to stimuli that may be unpredictable, potentially rewarding, or potentially punishing (Whalen et al., 2009; Whalen, 1998).

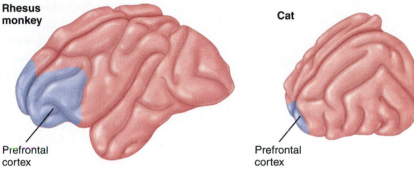

Across the species The prefrontal cortex of human beings is larger than that of other animals and is, at the same time, very active during social behavior, suggesting that it plays an important role in human social functioning.

We still have much to learn about how these and other regions operate together to help people function socially. Social neuroscientists are also still trying to identify the precise neural networks that enable us to so readily carry out the social cognitions and behaviors examined throughout this chapter. Considering how little researchers knew about the relationship between the brain and social functioning just a decade ago, however, the progress made and knowledge gained in recent years is quite remarkable.

Before You Go On

What Do You Know?
17. What is social neuroscience and what is the "social brain"?
18. Which brain regions have been identified as particularly important to our social functioning?

What Do You Think?
If you were a neuroscientist looking for parts of the brain that are important to social functioning, how would you decide where to look first?

social phobia a disorder involving severe, persistent, and irrational fears of social situations in which embarrassment may occur.

avoidant personality disorder a disorder involving extreme discomfort and inhibition in social relationships.

Disorders of Social Functioning

When Things Go **Wrong**

LEARNING OBJECTIVE 6 Describe the major features of social phobias, avoidant personality disorder, dependent personality disorder, and antisocial personality disorder.

Social psychology's various theories and studies all include the implicit notion that people are *socially motivated* (Forgas, Williams, & Laham 2005). That is, they are interested in, concerned about, and influenced by the behaviors, opinions, and feelings of other people; they want to understand others; and they need other people in their lives. Such social needs and behaviors are, however, impaired for some people, leading to significant problems in their relationships and interactions.

Psychologists have identified several types of disorders whose symptoms interfere with the ability to function normally in the social sphere. We have already looked at one such disorder, antisocial personality disorder, in the previous chapter. In two other disorders, social phobia and avoidant personality disorder, individuals are excessively afraid to interact with other people. In contrast, persons with dependent personality disorder have an abnormal need to please and be accepted by others. And finally, those with autism, a severe disorder, are extremely unresponsive to others and uncommunicative, among other symptoms.

Social Phobias and Avoidant Personality Disorder

People with a **social phobia** have severe, persistent, and irrational fears of social situations in which embarrassment may occur. A social phobia may be specific, such as a fear of talking in public or writing in front of others, or it may be general, such as a wide-ranging fear of functioning poorly in front of others. This disorder can severely impair how the person participates in groups, relationships, and bystander situations—some of the key social contexts that we have examined in this chapter. It appears that around 7 percent of people in countries throughout the western world—around three women for every two men—currently experience a social phobia (Ruscio et al., 2008; Kessler et al., 2005).

It is not clear why or how social phobias develop. Traditionally, the fear has been explained, like most other phobias, as a learned reaction—largely the result of modeling or classical conditioning (discussed in Chapter 7). For example, many young children whose parents display fearful reactions to other persons (and particularly to the judgments of others) may acquire similar fear reactions simply by observing the parents' anxious responses (Mineka & Zinbarg, 1998). In recent years, however, many theorists have come to believe that social phobias may also have biological, even genetic, roots. Several studies suggest, for example, that certain infants are born with a style of social inhibition or shyness that may increase their risk of developing this disorder (Kagan et al., 2007; Kagan & Snidman, 2004, 1999, 1991; Smoller et al., 2003).

People with **avoidant personality disorder** are very uncomfortable and inhibited in social relationships, overwhelmed by feelings of inadequacy, and extremely sensitive to negative evaluation (APA, 2000). They have an extreme fear of being criticized or rejected and so they actively avoid various forms of social contact. Many people with this disorder consider themselves unappealing or inferior. They may have few or no close friends, though they would certainly like to have intimate relationships. Often, they feel depressed and lonely. It is estimated that between 1 and 2 percent of adults have avoidant personality disorder (Mattia & Zimmerman, 2001; APA, 2000).

Words are not always the answer In 2004, Austrian author Elfriede Jelinek won the Nobel Prize in literature, but her social phobia prevented her from attending the Nobel festivities. Instead, she had to accept the award and present her Nobel lecture by video transmission.

Dependent Personality Disorder

Earlier in this chapter, when we examined the famous series of experiments by Stanley Milgram, we observed that people may become excessively obedient under certain circumstances. People with **dependent personality disorder**, however, are excessively obedient under *all* circumstances. They have a wide-ranging, excessive need to be taken care of (APA, 2000). Correspondingly, they are clinging and obedient, and fear separation from their parents, spouses or friends. At the center of this disorder is a difficulty with separation. The individuals feel devastated when close relationships end, and they quickly seek out new relationships to fill the void. They may even hold on desperately to relationships with partners who physically or psychologically abuse them.

People with dependent personality disorder rely on others so much that they cannot make the smallest decision for themselves. They seek help for even the simplest matters and experience extreme feelings of inadequacy and helplessness. They seldom dispute the opinions of other people, and they allow others to make important decisions for them, including where to live, what job to have, and which neighbors to befriend (APA, 2000). Because they are so fearful of rejection, they are extraordinarily sensitive to disapproval and they keep trying to measure up to other people's expectations and wishes, even volunteering for unpleasant or degrading tasks or agreeing to do things that they know are wrong. Over 2 percent of people may display dependent personality disorder (Mattia & Zimmerman, 2001).

Autism

Individuals with **autism** are extremely unresponsive to others, uncommunicative, repetitive, and rigid. Their symptoms appear early in life, typically before 3 years of age. At least one in 600 and as many as one in 160 children display the disorder, an estimate that includes cases of autism-like disorders (Teicher et al., 2008).

Around 80 percent of all cases occur in boys. The vast majority of children with the disorder remain severely disabled into adulthood. In most cases, even the highest-functioning adults with autism continue to have significant problems showing closeness, empathy, and support in their social relationships and communications and have limited interests and activities (Baron-Cohen & Wheelwright, 2003).

A lack of responsiveness—including extreme aloofness, little interest in other people, low empathy, and inability to share attention with others—is generally considered the central feature of autism (Gillis & Romanczyk, 2007). In addition, individuals with the disorder typically have severe language and communication problems (for example, failing to speak, displaying poor language skills, or using odd speech patterns). They may have problems naming objects, employing a proper tone when talking, or using language for conversational purposes. Children with the disorder also may be unable to play in a varied, spontaneous way. They typically fail to include others in their play or to make social experiences part of their play behavior. More generally, they often fail to see themselves as others see them and make no effort to imitate or be like others (Kasari et al., 2006; Siegel & Ficcaglia, 2006). Finally, the motor movements of people with autism are often unusual. Many, for example, flap their arms, twist their hands and fingers, rock, and make faces—acts called *self-stimulatory behaviors*. Some individuals also perform *self-injurious behaviors*, such as repeatedly banging their head against a wall, pulling their hair, or biting themselves.

Asperger's Disorder   A variation of autism, sometimes referred to as an *autism-spectrum disorder*, is **Asperger's disorder**. Here individuals experience many of the same kinds of social deficits, impairments in expressiveness, and restricted and repetitive behaviors that are on display in autism, but at the same time they often have relatively

dependent personality disorder a disorder involving a pervasive, excessive need to be taken care of and a fear of separation.

autism a severe disorder marked by extreme unresponsiveness, poor communication skills, and very repetitive and rigid behaviors.

Asperger's disorder a disorder in which persons have major social impairments yet maintain relatively normal intellectual, adaptive, and language skills.

Picture of autism This individual with autism engages in self-stimulatory behavior (rapidly moving his fingers in front of his eyes), a common behavior among people with the disorder. This symptom adds to the social impairments that mark autism, such as unresponsiveness to others, limited capacity for imaginative play, poor communication, and severe relationship deficits.

normal intellectual, adaptive, and language skills (Siegel & Ficcaglia, 2006). Individuals with Asperger's disorder often want to fit in and interact with others, but their social limitations make it difficult for them to do so. Instead they may seem awkward and unaware of conventional social rules (ASA, 2006). Although these individuals must contend with deficits throughout their lives, many are—in contrast to those with autism—able to complete a high level of education, such as college or trade school. Many also successfully hold jobs and have romantic—even marital—relationships (ASA, 2005).

Causes and Treatments of Autism A variety of explanations have been offered for autism. Some theorists propose that people with the disorder have a key perceptual or cognitive disturbance that makes normal communication and interactions impossible. One influential explanation holds, for example, that they fail to develop a *theory of mind*—an awareness that other people base their behaviors on their own beliefs, knowledge, and other mental states, not on information that they have no way of knowing (Hale & Tager-Flusberg, 2005; Frith, 2000). As you'll recall from Chapter 9, developing a theory of mind is critical to proper development.

A number of theorist believe that this and other cognitive limitations have their roots in early biological problems—problems that prevent proper cognitive development. Although a detailed biological understanding of autism has yet to emerge, some promising leads have been found. First, studies of the relatives of people with autism have suggested a *genetic factor* in this disorder. The prevalence of autism is as high as 6 to 8 per 100 among siblings of those with this disorder (Gillis & Romanczyk, 2007), a rate much higher than the general population's. Other studies have also linked autism to *prenatal difficulties* or *birth complications* (Teicher et al., 2008; Rodier, 2000). The chances of developing autism are higher when the mother contracted rubella (German measles) during pregnancy, came into contact with toxic chemicals before or during pregnancy, or had complications during labor or delivery. In addition, researchers have identified specific *biological abnormalities* that may contribute to autism. Certain studies have pointed to the cerebellum, for example (Teicher et al., 2008; DeLong, 2005). Apparently, abnormal development in this brain region occurs early in the life of people with autism. Similarly, brainscans indicate that many individuals with autism have increased brain volume and white matter (Wicker, 2008) and abnormalities in the brain's limbic system, brain stem nuclei, and amygdala (Gillis & Romanczyk, 2007). People with autism may also experience reduced activity in the brain's temporal and frontal lobes when they perform language and motor initiation tasks—tasks that, as you'll recall, normally involve activity by the brain's left hemisphere (Escalante, Minshew, & Sweeney, 2003).

Although treatment can help people with autism adapt better, no treatment yet known totally reverses this disorder. The treatments of most help are behavioral therapy, communication training, and parent training. Psychotropic drugs and certain vitamins have also sometimes helped when combined with other approaches (Teicher et al., 2008).

Before You Go On

What Do You Know?

19. What are the key features of social phobias, avoidant personality disorder, and dependent personality disorder?

20. Describe some of the ways in which individuals with autism show a lack of responsiveness.

What Do You Think? Disorders that interfere with social functioning are among the most disabling of problems. Why?

Summary

Social Cognition: Attitudes

LEARNING OBJECTIVE 1   Explain how attitudes form and change and what role they play in behavior.

- *Attitudes* are relatively stable and enduring evaluations of things and people. According to the *ABC model*, they have affective, behavioral, and cognitive components.
- Parents play a major role in shaping children's attitudes. In older children, peers, teachers, and the media also exert an influence.
- Leon Festinger proposed that people change their attitudes when they experience *cognitive dissonance*—a state of emotional discomfort that arises when a person holds two contradictory beliefs or holds a belief inconsistent with his or her behavior.
- The *self-perception theory* of attitude change minimizes the role of emotional discomfort and suggests that people simply infer what their attitudes are by observing their own behavior.
- The attitudes people express are not necessarily related to their behavior. In part, this is because people sometimes misrepresent their attitudes. They may wish to express socially desirable attitudes or they may not be aware of what their *implicit attitudes* really are.
- *Stereotypes* and *prejudice* arise in part from the human tendency to identify with a group. Various explanations of prejudice come from evolutionary theories, realistic conflict theory, and social identity theory.
- People use persuasion techniques to try to influence the attitudes of others. The central route to persuasion emphasizes the content of the message, while the peripheral route depends on more superficial appeals, such as the appearance of the spokesperson.

Social Cognition: Attributions

LEARNING OBJECTIVE 2   Discuss how people make attributions to explain their own behavior and the behavior of others.

- *Attributions*, or causal explanations of behavior, can be *dispositional* (internal) or *situational* (external).
- People tend to attribute their own behavior to situational factors and the behavior of others to dispositional factors. The reliance on dispositional factors to explain others' behavior is the *fundamental attribution error*.
- According to the *actor-observer effect*, this discrepancy exists because people make situational attributions as actors and dispositional attributions as observers.
- People sometimes attribute only their failures to situational factors and attribute their successes to dispositional factors, called the *self-serving bias*.

Social Forces

LEARNING OBJECTIVE 3   Describe the power of conformity and obedience in shaping people's behavior.

- Society establishes rules, or *norms*, about how people are supposed to act. *Social roles* are sets of norms ascribed to particular social positions. Norms and roles are critical to the smooth functioning of society but also place limits on individuals.
- *Conformity* is the tendency to yield to real or imagined group pressure. In a famous series of experiments, Solomon Asch found that 75 percent of research participants yielded to implicit group pressure to conform to an incorrect judgment.
- Unlike conformity, *obedience* involves following direct orders, usually from an authority figure. Experiments by Stanley Milgram found that 65 percent of subjects continued to follow orders to administer what they believed to be dangerous electric shocks.

Social Relations

LEARNING OBJECTIVE 4   Review major concepts in the areas of group dynamics, helping behavior, aggression, and interpersonal attraction.

- The *social facilitation* effect occurs when the presence of others enhances a person's performance. Research shows that this effect holds for simple, well-learned tasks; but the presence of others can impair performance on more complicated tasks.
- With *social loafing*, people in a group exert less effort on a task than they would if performing the task alone.
- *Group polarization* is a phenomenon in which group discussion intensifies the already-held opinions of group members and produces a shift toward a more extreme position.
- Groups with certain characteristics—a strong similarity among members, high group cohesiveness, high-perceived threat, elevated stress, insulation from outside influence, and a directive leader—may become victims of *groupthink*, a faulty decision-making process in which group members strive for unanimity at the expense of realistically appraising alternative courses of action.
- Helping behavior is of two types: *altruism*, which is motivated by concern for others, and egoistic helping behavior, which is motivated by a desire to reduce one's own distress or receive rewards.
- People are more likely to engage in helping behavior when alone than when in the presence of others. Theorists propose that the presence of others may create a diffusion of responsibility, in which no single individual feels personal responsibility for acting.
- *Aggression* describes a broad range of behaviors intended to do harm to another. Aggression has some biological underpinnings.

In addition, the frustration-aggression hypothesis proposes that aggression arises in response to frustration.

- Factors that lead to liking another person include similarity, proximity, self-disclosure, situational factors, and physical attractiveness.
- One description of love includes three elements: attachment, caring, and intimacy. Another, Sternberg's *triangular theory of love*, holds that love is composed of intimacy, passion, and commitment, which combine in varying degrees.
- Similar to young children, adults display three types of attachment in love relationships: secure attachment, avoidant attachment, and anxious-ambivalent attachment.

Social Functioning
What Happens in the Brain?

LEARNING OBJECTIVE 5   Describe the major findings of social neuroscience about regions of the brain particularly important to our social functioning.

- Social neuroscience is the specialty of neuroscience that studies how the brain works during social functioning. Social functioning is so important and uniquely human that social neuroscientists

have given the name "social brain" to the combination of brain areas that are particularly active in social functioning.

- The orbitofrontal cortex, ventromedial prefrontal cortex, insula, and amygdala all have been identified as especially important in social functioning and researchers continue to try to pinpoint neural connections related to social functioning.

Disorders of Social Functioning

LEARNING OBJECTIVE 6   Describe the major features of social phobias, avoidant personality disorder, dependent personality disorder, and autism.

- People with *social phobias* have severe, persistent, and irrational fears of social situations in which embarrassment may occur.
- *Avoidant personality disorder* involves extreme discomfort and inhibition in social relationships.
- People with *dependent personality disorder* display a pervasive, excessive need to be taken care of and a fear of separation.
- *Autism* is a severe disorder marked by extreme unresponsiveness, poor communication skills, and very repetitive and rigid behaviors.

Key Terms

CUT/ACROSS CONNECTION

What Happens in the BRAIN?

- There has been so much research on the brain's role in social functioning that there is now a branch of neuroscience called *social neuroscience*.
- The prefrontal cortex, much larger in humans than most animals, houses many of the structures important in social functioning.
- High levels of aggression have been linked with a combination of high testosterone activity and low serotonin activity.

When Things Go Wrong

- Around seven out of every hundred people in the U.S. experience phobias related to certain social circumstances.
  - Another 1 or 2 percent, who have avoidant personality disorders, fear social relationships in general.
    - In contrast, at least 2 percent of the population display dependent personality disorder.
    - As many as 1 in every 160 individuals may have autism or an autism-like disorder.

HOW we Differ

- Females and males who act outside their societies' gender roles may face harsh reactions.
- Studies show that, on average, women in the United States are more socially skilled than men.
- People who are trusting and outward–looking and who form secure attachments in their relationships are more likely to perform altruistic behaviors.
- Both men and women are aggressive, but males are, on average, more likely to engage in direct, physical and verbal aggression, while female aggression is more likely, on average, to be relational, such as snubbing someone.

How we Develop

- Childhood socialization can lead us to develop long-lasting attitudes, including stereotypes and prejudice.
- Part of our socialization as children involves learning our society's norms. Once learned, our norms can influence our behavior for life.
- Although autism is sometimes referred to as a childhood disorder, it is in fact a lifespan disorder for most individuals.

View this in Action

WILEY PLUS

www.wileyplus.com

Video Lab Exercise

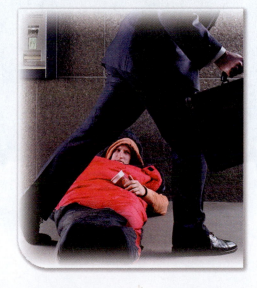

Psychology Around Us

Helping Behavior and Bystander Apathy

Good Intentions Are Not Enough

Most of us like to think of ourselves as caring people who always stand ready to help those in distress. But, under certain circumstances, many people—indeed, most people—fail to act as helpful bystanders in situations that seem to cry out for the involvement of others. Helping a lost child, coming to the aid of car crash victims, helping someone who is being beaten—these are but a few of the situations in which bystanders—such as you or I—may sometimes fail to act.

Let's see when you are a good Samaritan and when you are not. In this video lab exercise, you'll become a bystander in various situations, and you'll see how your prosocial behavior changes as bystander factors are changed one-by-one. In a world where we typically think "I would never act that way" upon reading or hearing about undesirable, apathetic behaviors, you'll probably be surprised at what you are (or are not) capable of.

As you are working on this on-line exercise, consider the following questions:

- What factors determine whether bystanders will be apathetic or choose to act?
- What role does *diffusion of responsibility* play in the bystander apathy phenomenon?
- What defense mechanisms or dissonance principles might apathetic bystanders need to employ later?
- Might there also be personality factors that cause some people to come to the aid of others particularly quickly?

CHAPTER 15

Stress, Coping, and Health

chapter outline

Just Work Harder

Nina sits at her desk, unable to concentrate. Her English paper is due on Wednesday, but her computer screen remains blank. She knows she needs to get started, but she is having a hard time. All sorts of thoughts are flying through her head, and each one makes her chest tighten and makes her want to curl up into a ball and shut her eyes.

She has to leave for her job in less than an hour. She desperately needs the bus to be on time. Chris, her boss, has told her that if she is late again, he'll "have to find someone more reliable." And then there is the letter she just got from her parents asking—once again—about her grades. She is the first child in her family to go to college, and her parents have been driving her crazy. She's glad that they're so excited, but don't they realize that asking for weekly updates only puts more pressure on her?

In fact, things aren't going so well in some of her classes. She's good at chemistry; but she finds English, especially writing, very difficult. "Just work harder," her parents have told her, as if she weren't trying as hard as she could. Her public speaking class is a disaster: She actually had to leave in the middle of her last speech, fighting back tears.

The more trouble she has, the more she feels like just going out with her friends at night. In fact, she's gone out every night this week, always telling herself, "I'll get started on my paper tomorrow." Even though she knows she can't put her paper off any longer, she's agreed to see a movie tonight after work with some people from school.

Then there is the recent break-up with her boyfriend, Henry. She feels bad about the way their relationship ended. One night when she was late for work and in a panic, he called her and teasingly refused to let her off the phone. After a few minutes, she called him a jerk and hung up on him. It wasn't the first time she'd lashed out at him, and even though she tried to apologize the next day, he said he didn't want to deal with her moods anymore.

"All right, let's try to get it together," she tells herself. "Come up with a game plan." She decides to jog to the restaurant, avoiding bus delays and getting some exercise to boot. Moreover, in the few minutes she has before she must

stress state brought on by any situation that threatens or appears to threaten a person's sense of well-being, thus challenging the individual's ability to cope.

stressor a situation or circumstance that triggers the stress response.

acute stressor a stressful situation or circumstance that happens in the short term and has a definite endpoint.

chronic stressor a stressful situation or circumstance that is more long term and often lacks a definite endpoint.

leave for work, she forces herself to start typing. Before too long, she has two paragraphs on the screen. At least it's a start. She is finally thinking and acting constructively.

You don't need a textbook to tell you that Nina is experiencing stress. After all, you've probably been in a similar place—too much to do, too little time, too many expectations, too little certainty about what to do next. Obviously, Nina feels stress because she has lots of work to do and is running out of time. But she also has feelings of stress connected to something otherwise pleasant—the opportunity to socialize with friends. Something as minor as an English paper, as pleasant as the prospect of an evening out, or as awful as a life-threatening medical condition can prompt feelings of stress.

Stress affects us both physically and psychologically. Recall how you felt the last time you were stuck in a traffic jam on your way to someplace important. Chances are you had physical and psychological reactions—you may have been frustrated and angry, your stomach may have been tied up in knots, and you may even have pounded on the steering wheel or yelled. Because stress affects us this way, it can damage our health.

The effects of stress on psychological and physical health have made it a subject of major interest. Thousands of researchers are studying it. Some are trying to clarify what makes situations stressful. Others are studying how stress affects the body. Still others are trying to figure out what responses help people to cope with stress and lessen its toll. This chapter examines what researchers have learned about the sources and effects of stress. It also looks at ways to deal with stress, noting that certain kinds of behavior—such as Nina's jog to work or her decision to simply start writing her paper—can help people reduce stress or cope with it more effectively.

What Is Stress?

LEARNING OBJECTIVE 1 Define stress and describe the ways in which people experience stress and the kinds of situations that typically cause stress.

You probably throw around the word *stress* all the time, but have you thought about what it actually means? The term has been defined in various ways, so we'll begin our examination of stress with a definition. We will then discuss the ways in which people experience stress and the kinds of situations that cause stress.

Stress and Stressors

Stress is a state brought on by any situation that threatens or appears to threaten a person's sense of well-being, thus challenging the person's ability to cope. A situation or circumstance that triggers the stress response is called a **stressor**. Stressors can be *acute* or *chronic*. An **acute stressor** is short term and has a definite endpoint—for example, a near miss in heavy traffic. A **chronic stressor** is long term and often lacks a definite endpoint—for example, dealing over time with a high-pressure job.

Obviously, our definition of stress is rather broad—literally anything can cause stress. The breadth of the definition takes into account the wide range of situations that people experience as stressful, from daily pressures at work and school to more catastrophic events, such as health crises, natural disasters, and terrorist attacks. At the same time, the definition calls attention to the emotional experience of stress and how individualized stress is. A number of psychological factors help to determine the degree to which something will stress us out. For example, our appraisal

His face says it all A trader on the floor of the New York Stock Exchange shows all the earmarks of stress as he follows the numbers on the board, waiting desperately for a favorable moment to make his move.

of our ability (or inability) to cope with that situation is an important factor in how stressed we get. A pop quiz in Spanish may not be stressful to a student who is up-to-date in the course, but a student who has been putting off assignments and is far behind will find a surprise quiz quite stressful. It is our *perception* of threat that triggers the emotional state we connect to stress. If we do not perceive a situation as threatening, we will not feel particularly stressed. We'll look soon at more psychological factors in stress, but before that, let's examine the different ways that people experience stress.

Ways of Experiencing Stress

By definition, people who experience stress feel threatened and challenged. But these threats and challenges come in different forms. Certainly, soldiers in combat, students whose grades are falling, and children whose parents are unhappy with them face different kinds of stress. Psychologists have in fact distinguished four kinds of stress experience: *frustration, pressure, conflict,* and *danger.* These kinds of stress are not mutually exclusive.

Feeling Frustrated   You finally find a parking spot, and someone pulls into it just ahead of you. You try to register for a course, and it is full. You work hard, but you get a C on the test. Whenever we find ourselves thwarted in the pursuit of a goal, we experience **frustration**. Life is full of frustration; it is one of our most familiar kinds of stress. Frustration can be caused by acute stressors, such as those in the situations just described and by chronic stressors. Persons who have chronic illnesses or disabilities, for example, are likely to feel frustrated that they cannot do more. All of these experiences are bound up with the notion of trying to achieve something and having a barrier to our progress. Barriers to progress generate stress.

Feeling Pressured   We all encounter a certain amount of **pressure**—the expectation that we should act in a certain way. The pride felt by Nina's parents over their daughter's admission to college is a source of pressure, and her boss's expectation that she should arrive at work on time is another.

Pressure often comes from within. Some individuals have such high expectations of themselves that they are constantly under self-imposed stress. Think of the sources of pressure in your own life. What standards do you set for yourself academically and socially? Are you driven to achieve in athletics? How much pressure do you experience as a result of such expectations? Stress that comes from within is often more difficult to cope with than stress imposed by others. It may not be easy to meet the deadline for turning in a term paper, but at least when you do so, the pressure will be off. By contrast, if you set yourself a rigid standard of perfection, you may never find release from this internal pressure.

Pressure also varies along with the task and situation. One set of studies, for example, used the presence of an audience to provide pressure for participants who were performing a task. When the task was fairly simple, the participants were not affected by the presence of the audience—their performance was about the same, audience or no audience. When the task was more complex, however, the individuals performed significantly better without the pressure of an audience (Wan & Huon, 2005; Butler & Baumeister, 1998; Baumeister, 1984). Still other research has found a strong correlation between feelings of pressure and symptoms of distress.

Feeling Conflicted   The stress our friend Nina felt was not simply the result of pressure from her parents. It also resulted in part from her desire to do two things at the same time: (1) study to earn good grades and (2) have time to go out with her friends. In situations such as this, we experience **conflict**—discomfort brought about by two or more

frustration an emotion people experience when thwarted in pursuit of a goal.

pressure an expectation or demand that someone act in a certain way.

conflict discomfort brought about by two or more goals or impulses perceived to be incompatible.

goals or impulses that we perceive to be incompatible. There are three basic types of conflict: *approach-approach*, *avoidance-avoidance*, and *approach-avoidance* (see **Figure 15-1**) (Miller, 1959; Lewin, 1935).

- As its name implies, **approach-approach conflict** occurs when we must choose between two equally desirable options. Should we have the chocolate cake or the blueberry pie? Should we buy the red backpack or the black one? In many cases, approach-approach conflicts are easy to resolve (you can't really lose with either choice) and so, not especially stressful.

- **Avoidance-avoidance conflicts** are somewhat more stressful because here the choice is between two equally undesirable outcomes. Should you clean the garage or do the laundry? You may be tempted to do neither. If you deal with this kind of conflict by deciding to procrastinate, postpone, or avoid the choice, however, you are particularly likely to experience stress (Shafir & Tversky, 2002).

Sports and Pressure

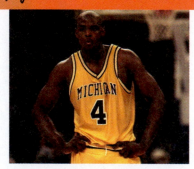

A costly error A dejected Chris Webber looks on as his team loses the NCAA Championship game.

Eleven seconds remained in the 1993 NCAA Division I Men's Basketball Championship game. For the second year in a row the University of Michigan was losing, but this time they were only down by two points. All-American Chris Webber grabbed a defensive rebound and suddenly Michigan had a chance to tie the game or even go ahead. After a stutter step, Webber brought the ball down the court. He paused for a moment, then desperately gestured for a time-out. However, Michigan had no time outs remaining, and calling for a time out when none remains is penalized by loss of possession of the ball and a technical foul. Whistles blew, and moments later Michigan had lost the championship once again.

What happened to Webber and to myriad other athletes who have made mental errors in high-pressure situations? When does pressure aid athletic performance and when does it impair it? These questions have been the subject of much study and a number of explanations have been offered, but a clear understanding of the effects of pressure on athletes remains elusive (Weinberg & Gould, 2003).

We do know that performance pressure results when athletes feel strongly about the outcome of an event and believe that their own performance will have an impact on that outcome (Wallace, Baumeister, & Vohs, 2005). We also know that this pressure can result in increased physiological and psychological arousal. But insights start to drop off when we try to predict the precise relationship between such arousal and performance.

For years, psychologists believed that the relationship probably follows the principle of the Yerkes-Dodson law. As we observed in Chapter 11, this psychological "law," developed in 1908 by psychologists Robert Yerkes and John Dodson, holds that performances on tasks of any kind increase along with physical or mental arousal—up to a point—but, once an optimal, moderate level of arousal is passed, performances decrease more and more. Applying this law to athletic performances, it is generally believed that if an athlete is not aroused, his or her performance will suffer, and that if he or she is too aroused, performance will also suffer. Optimal performance is thought to occur only in the presence of a moderate level of arousal (Yerkes & Dodson, 1908). Over the years, research has better supported an alternative version of the Yerkes-Dodson law, particularly in the realm of athletic performance. This alternative model holds that the level of arousal at which optimal performance occurs is a *zone* (not a single point) and varies from athlete to athlete. Some cross-country runners, for example, will perform best if they take naps right before a race while their teammates will do best if they listen to hard-core music, visualize their opponents, and stretch intensely before the race (Hanin, 1997).

A different line of research has clarified that coaches can play a large role in helping athletes cope with performance pressure. Since anxiety tends to be lowest in athletes who believe in their performance abilities and are self-assured, coaches apparently can help by facilitating feelings of confidence – by, for example, providing frequent, genuine encouragement and by fostering a positive environment regardless of whether things have gone well or mistakes have occurred (Weinberg & Gould, 2003). Here again, however, such rules may vary from athlete to athlete. Some athletes respond better to certain coaching syles and techniques, while others respond better to alternative syles and techniques.

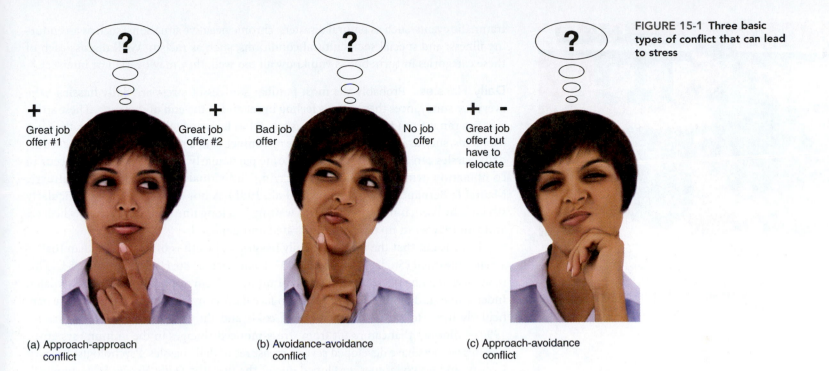

| + | | + | - | | - | + | - |
| Great job offer #1 | | Great job offer #2 | Bad job offer | | No job offer | Great job offer but have to relocate |

(a) Approach-approach conflict

(b) Avoidance-avoidance conflict

(c) Approach-avoidance conflict

FIGURE 15-1 Three basic types of conflict that can lead to stress

- In an **approach-avoidance conflict**, any available choice has both desirable and undesirable qualities, rendering us ambivalent and indecisive. In some situations, this sort of conflict may involve only one choice with both positive and negative features. Recall, for example, Nina's decision to go out with her friends. On the one hand, she knew that if she went, she'd enjoy herself; on the other hand, she also knew she wouldn't be able to work on her paper. In other situations, more than one option may be involved. Should you buy a car that is expensive but fuel-efficient, for example, or a less expensive gas guzzler? Approach-avoidance conflicts are on display in many of our most agonizing decisions. Often people worry for some time about how to resolve them and experience considerable stress along the way.

Feeling Endangered   Life-threatening situations understandably produce stress, making us feel endangered. The adrenaline rush we experience when a car in front of us suddenly stops, forcing us to swerve and slam on the brakes, is characteristic of this kind of stress. Similarly, such stress is experienced by people who face combat or are trapped in a fire. Natural disasters may also be life threatening and, in turn, stressful.

Terrorism poses a special danger to life and in turn produces stress. The deadly violence of a terrorist attack leaves survivors and those who grieve for lost loved ones with feelings of uncertainty, sadness, and fear, making them vulnerable to the onset of stress disorders (Delahanty, 2007; Bleich et al., 2003; Ursano et al., 2003). Indeed, terrorism may have long-term psychological effects. Because of past run-ins with terrorism, a New Yorker may experience a sense of life-threatening fear at the sight of a plane in the sky, for example, or a person from the Middle East may cringe at the sound of a bus backfiring.

Kinds of Stressors

Just as there are different ways of experiencing stress, there are different types of stressors. Indeed, stressors vary widely—from discrete life events to chronic stressors. Moreover, they can be mild, extreme, or anywhere in between. As you will see later in this chapter, what is stressful for one person may not be stressful for another. Still, there are several kinds of events that are likely to produce feelings of stress whenever they are experienced: daily hassles, such as traffic jams; life changes, such as the loss of a job;

approach-approach conflict conflict that occurs when a person must choose between two equally desirable options.

avoidance-avoidance conflict conflict that occurs when a person must choose between two equally undesirable options.

approach-avoidance conflict conflict that occurs when any available choice has both desirable and undesirable qualities.

"Put it back!" Although raising a family is certainly a blessing in many ways, the onslaught of daily hassles experienced by parents of young children often leaves them feeling overwhelmed and more than a little tense.

Even positive changes can be stressful Completing their airborne marriage ceremony, this man and woman kiss while freefalling toward the ground. Even more conventional marriages produce a high degree of stress according to research using the Social Readjustment Rating Scale.

traumatic events, such as natural disasters; chronic negative situations, such as an enduring illness; and special sociocultural conditions, such as racism. We'll discuss each of these categories in turn; but as you know all too well, they may overlap or intersect.

Daily Hassles Probably the most familiar sources of stress are **daily hassles**—the everyday annoyances that leave us feeling upset and at the end of our rope. These stressors can range from minor irritations, such as lost keys or a talkative coworker, to major problems, such as intense work pressure or conflict with a romantic partner. Over time, daily hassles can add up. They may become particularly stressful when they occur in combination with other stressors, leaving individuals overwhelmed (Boutreyre, Maurel & Bernaud, 2007; De Longis et al., 1982). A hot day may not be particularly stressful by itself, but combine it with waiting in a long line to renew a driver's license, and you may wind up feeling exasperated and depleted.

It turns out that the impact of daily hassles on health is often greater than that of a major life event (Stuart & Garrison, 2002; Ivancevich, 1986; Holahan et al., 1984). This is because ongoing stress may impair our immune system responses, as we shall see later. Indeed, one study found that people who face daily commutes in heavy traffic are particularly likely to miss work because of colds and flu (Novaco, Stokols & Milanesi, 1990)—illnesses that can result from stress-induced changes in the immune system.

Researchers have developed several measures of daily hassles. Psychologist Richard Lazarus and his colleagues developed one of the first, the *Daily Hassles Scale,* in which subjects are asked to consider a list of hassles, indicate which ones they have experienced over the past month, and report how stressful each event felt (Kanner et al., 1981). Measuring the impact of daily hassles is difficult, because people vary widely in how they experience and weigh such stressors (Kohn, 1996). Nevertheless, some daily hassles seem to be universally upsetting, including time pressures, cash-flow problems, feelings of being cheated after purchasing something, conflicts with romantic partners, mistreatment by friends, and poor evaluations at work.

Some daily hassle scales have targeted the experiences of college students (Cardilla, 2008; D'Angelo & Wierzbicki, 2003; Kohn et al., 1990). Such scales have paid special attention to the impact of exams (Edwards & Trimble, 1992; Abella & Heslin, 1989; Folkman & Lazarus, 1985). Feelings of stress tend to be strongest just before an exam and continue (though to a lesser extent) as students wait to receive their grades and as they later try to cope with the results.

Life Changes Another common source of stress is change. Those early weeks in a new school, for example, are usually quite stressful, even if they are also exciting. In the first weeks of college, students need to figure out what classes to take, where classrooms are located, what is expected of them, and where to buy books (as well as how to pay for them). At the same time, they are meeting many new people. Trying to find our way in new relationships can be even more complicated and challenging than finding our way to class.

Life changes—shifts in life circumstances that require adjustment of some kind—were among the first sources of stress studied. In 1967, investigators Thomas Holmes and Richard Rahe set out to develop a way to systematically measure how much stress people experience. They compiled a list of 43 events that were likely to change a person's life and therefore cause stress. These events ranged from the death of a spouse, to minor violations of the law, to taking a vacation. Based on ratings by participants, the researchers assigned a point value to each event, ranging from 1 to 100 points, or *life-change units (LCUs).* The point value for each event corresponded to the amount of upset and adjustment the event typically produced. The death of a spouse received a score of 100 LCUs on the scale, for example, whereas a change in responsibilities at work was 29 LCUs, and taking a vacation came in at 13 LCUs.

With this 43-item list, called the *Social Readjustment Rating Scale (SRRS),* Holmes and Rahe set about conducting studies on the impact of stress on people's lives. First they had individuals complete the scale to determine how much stress they were under. Participants were asked to check off all those events that had occurred in their lives over a certain time period, usually the past year. Then the total number of life-change units was added up, with the sum indicating the amount of stress the person had been under. A total score of 150 LCUs or less indicated relatively little stress; 150 to 199 indicated mild stress; 200 to 299 suggested moderate stress; and over 300 pointed to major life stress. The life events from the SRRS and their ratings are listed in Table 15-1. Notice that a life-changing event need not be an undesirable one. A number of the events on the SRRS are positive, and some can be either positive or negative. A change in living conditions, for example, may reflect a move upward or downward in life.

Think back to our chapter opener. There, we learned that Nina recently broke up with her boyfriend, an event that would receive a score of 65 LCUs on Holmes and Rahe's scale. In addition, she has been experiencing troubles with her boss (23 LCUs), school pressures (39 LCUs), and new social activities (18 LCUs). Since she is a relatively new student, we can assume that she changed schools (20 LCU's) and residences (19 LCUs) fairly recently. Add in her outstanding personal achievement of being the first in her family to go to college (28 LCUs), and her LCU score totals 212—a moderate level of stress over a short period of time.

We pointed out that the Social Readjustment Rating Scale includes positive as well as negative life events. Nevertheless, the scale has been criticized for looking at many more negative events than positive ones (McLean & Link, 1994). Because of this, the scale may not give a complete picture of the effects of life change on stress levels.

daily hassles everyday annoyances that contribute to higher stress levels.

life changes shifts in life circumstances that require adjustment of some kind.

TABLE 15-1 The Social Readjustment Rating Scale

To score your susceptibility to stress on this scale, add up the life change units for the events you experienced in the last year. Scores of 150 or less indicate little stress; 150–199 mild stress; 200–299 moderate stress; and over 300 major life stress.

Life events	Life change units	Life events	Life change units
Death of spouse	100	Son or daughter leaving home	29
Divorce	73	Trouble with in-laws	29
Marital separation	65	Outstanding personal achievement	28
Jail term	63	Spouse begins or stops work	26
Death of a close family member	63	Begin or end school	26
Personal injury or illness	53	Change in living conditions	25
Marriage	50	Revision of personal habits	24
Fired at work	47	Trouble with boss	23
Marital reconciliation	45	Change in work hours or conditions	20
Retirement	45	Change in residence	20
Change in health of family member	44	Change in schools	20
Pregnancy	40	Change in recreation	19
Sex difficulties	39	Change in church activities	19
Gain of a new family member	39	Change in social activities	18
Business readjustment	39	Mortgage or loan for lesser purchase (car, major appliance)	17
Change in financial state	38	Change in sleeping habits	16
Death of a close friend	37	Change in number of family get-togethers	15
Change to different line of work	36	Change in eating habits	15
Change in number of arguments with spouse	35	Vacation	13
Mortgage or loan for major purchase	31	Christmas	12
Foreclosure on mortgage or loan	30	Minor violations of the law	11
Change in responsibilities at work	29		

Source: Reprinted from *Journal of Psychosomatic Research,* Vol. III; Holmes and Rahe: "The Social Readjustment Rating Scale," 213–218, 1967, with permission from Elsevier.

Another shortcoming of the SRRS is that it does not apply equally to all populations. In developing the scale, Holmes and Rahe sampled mostly white Americans. Less than 5 percent of their participants were African Americans. Subsequent research has found that white Americans and African Americans often rank life events differently. For example, although both groups rank the death of a spouse as the most stressful life event, African Americans rank personal injury or illness and major changes in work responsibilities or living conditions much higher than do white Americans (Komaroff, Masuda & Holmes, 1989, 1986). Similarly, certain types of events, such as the death of a family member, loss of a job, credit problems, and change in residence, are generally more stressful for women than for men (Miller & Rahe, 1997).

Life Changes | How we *Develop* Although feelings of stress may be similar for both young and old, the life changes that evoke these feelings apparently differ widely from age group to age group. As you have just seen, the most powerful stressors (in decreasing order) on the SRRS, a largely adult scale, are death of a spouse, divorce, marital separation, jail term, death of a close family member, and personal injury or illness. But what about younger age groups?

Researchers have developed special scales to measure life events and stress among college students (Renner & Mackin, 2002; Crandall et al., 1992). They have found that the most stressful life event for this population is the death of a family member or friend, much like the top life stressor for adults. Beyond this event, however, the leading life stressors for college students are ones that are tied to college life. They are (again in decreasing order) having to take multiple tests, enduring finals week, applying to graduate school, being a victim of crime, having assignments in all classes due on the same day, and breaking up with a boyfriend or girlfriend.

Moving to still younger individuals, researchers have found that the leading life stressors for children overlap to some degree with those of adults and college students, but, here again, they largely reflect issues unique to childhood (Ryan-Wenger, Sharrer, & Campbell, 2005; Neff & Dale, 1996; Coddington, 1984, 1972; Yamamoto, 1979). Across various scales, the leading stressors for school-aged children are taking tests, having excessive homework, being made fun of or bullied, feeling left out, getting bad grades, getting in trouble, fighting with family members or friends, experiencing the death or illness of someone close, and doing something embarrassing.

It is worth noting that the kinds of life events that produce stress tend to shift as children develop (Vasey et al., 1994). As children move from 5 years old to 12 years old, physical-type events (for example, getting sick) become less stressful, behavioral events (getting into trouble) become more stressful, and psychosocial events (fighting with friends) also become more stressful.

Finally, life stressors seem to change from generation to generation (Ryan-Wenger et al., 2005). In the 1990s a number of new childhood stressors worked their way into children's life stress scales—for example, being bullied and experiencing violence in school. Similarly, during the 2000s, several other powerful childhood stressors have emerged, such as having too many things to do and performing poorly at sports and games.

Traumatic Events Life changes are stressful because they disrupt the routines of our lives. **Traumatic events** are more extreme disruptions—unexpected events that have the power to change the way we view the world. The terrorist attack on the World Trade Center on September 11, 2001, is an example of the stress-inducing power of a single, cataclysmic event. A natural disaster, such as Hurricane Katrina, or a rape or violent assault may also have such power.

Early separation This soldier consoles his young daughter prior to his departure for Iraq. Research suggests that family military separations of this kind often take an enormous emotional toll on the children who are left behind.

Traumatic events can have profound and long-lasting effects. Victims may experience a sense of helplessness, depression, anxiety, numbness, and disorientation (Overmier & Murison, 2005; Carr, 2000). The effects can last for years. In fact, some victims of extraordinarily traumatic events develop **posttraumatic stress disorder (PTSD)**, a condition characterized by persistent, frightening thoughts or memories of the traumatic events, along with anxiety, depression, and other symptoms. We'll discuss this disorder further later in the chapter.

Although traumatic events are usually of short duration, some can be ongoing. Suffering ongoing physical or sexual abuse or living with an alcoholic spouse or parent are examples of long-lasting traumatic events. These, too, can leave victims withdrawn and experiencing recurring mental images, anxiety, and depression.

Chronic Negative Situations   A negative situation may become particularly stressful if it continues over a long, perhaps indefinite, period of time (Schmidt et al., 2009). People living in a war zone, for example, confront the fearful possibility of an attack as they go about their daily lives, attending school, shopping, or taking the bus to work. Similarly, people who live in poverty face constant concerns about meeting their basic needs and paying their debts (Freeman, 1984). An ongoing negative home environment—marked by endless arguments with a spouse or child, for example—may produce considerable stress, and so may enduring workplace problems, such as continually feeling underpaid, unappreciated, bored, or in danger of being fired (Rossi et al., 2009; Krantz, Berntsson & Lundberg, 2005; Lundberg, 2000).

Chronic illnesses can also produce much stress over time. Such illnesses may not only cause pain but also impose limitations and produce feelings of mortality and uncertainty in people's lives. The patients themselves are not the only ones affected by chronic illnesses. Their caregivers also experience stress. Thus, parents of children with special needs—whether enduring illnesses, physical handicaps, mental retardation, or other conditions—often experience stress. So do the growing numbers of adults who must take care of aging parents or spouses. In fact, research indicates that such caregivers often suffer from depression, drink excessively, are sleep deprived, and engage in fewer healthful behaviors, such as exercise (O'Rourke et al., 2003; Yoon, 2003; Zarit & Gaugler, 2000).

The physical environment may also provide chronic stressors. Chronic noise, for example, often leads to tension and upset (Evans, 2001). Similarly, chronic overcrowding leads to higher bodily arousal and makes it difficult for people to calm down (Fleming et al., 1987). (We'll discuss bodily arousal and stress later in this chapter.) Chronic environmental stressors may interact with each other. A noisy roommate, for example, may be both a physical and a social stressor. The roommate's loud stereo may bombard you and leave you with frequent headaches; at the same time, the tense relationship that develops between the two of you may produce further stress.

Special Sociocultural Conditions   Special sociocultural conditions, such as those faced by members of ethnic minority groups who confront prejudice regularly, can be sources of stress (Liang et al., 2009). Minority-group members face special challenges and stressors as they try to navigate through the dominant culture. An immigrant worker, for example, has to adjust to new ways of doing things, learn a new language, and often contend with poverty and the stress of a crowded living situation. In addition, members of minority groups often have to try to balance the demands of two cultures—their own culture and that of the dominant culture in which they live. If they are not proficient in the language or nuances of the dominant culture, they may also experience the stress of isolation and of having limited access to the main channels of communication within the dominant culture (Mino, Profit, & Pierce, 2000).

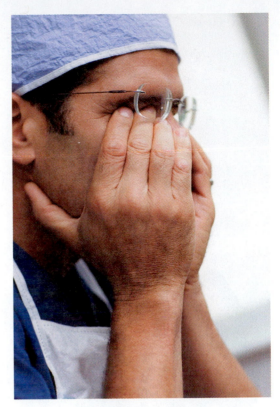

Chronic job stress Certain jobs produce chronic stress. Research reveals, for example, that physicians, particularly those whose specialties deal largely with lifethreatening medical problems, often experience enormous work pressure and strain.

traumatic events unexpected events severe enough to create extreme disruptions.

posttraumatic stress disorder (PTSD) an anxiety disorder experienced in response to a major traumatic event, characterized by lingering and persistent, frightening thoughts or memories of the traumatic events, along with anxiety, depression, and other symptoms.

Living in an atmosphere of racism—even if it occurs in subtle forms—is a particularly difficult sociocultural condition. Many members of minority groups receive the message that they are inferior. While this message is rarely stated outright, it may be on display in the lesser services, jobs, and consideration that are part of their minority status. As minority group members increasingly achieve success in the dominant culture, another source of stress can emerge: they may find themselves having to decode their interactions with the dominant culture. Consider Jonathan, an African-American man who is working in the advertising department of a large department store. It is Jonathan's job to produce ads for a special sale of fall clothing. His boss, who is white, doesn't think much of the two ideas Jonathan has proposed and tells him so. In addition to feeling disappointed and perhaps angry about the rejection of his ideas, Jonathan may experience the further stress of wondering whether his boss was reacting to his color. The suspicions, confusion, and vigilance experienced by minority group members as they maneuver their way through interactions with majority group members is often invisible to those in the majority group (Profit, Mino, & Pierce, 2000).

Before You Go On

What Do You Know?

1. What is the difference between an acute stressor and a chronic stressor?
2. What are the four types of stress experiences?
3. Define the three basic types of conflict.
4. What are daily hassles and what is their impact on health?
5. What is the Social Readjustment Rating Scale?

What Do You Think?
What kinds of situations do you find especially stressful? How do they compare with what your friends find stressful? What do variations in the experience of stress tell us about stress and stressors?

Responding to Stress

LEARNING OBJECTIVE 2 Describe the physiological, emotional, and cognitive responses to stress, and explain how individual responses to stress differ.

We've looked at the kinds of experiences that cause stress. Let's turn next to what happens to people when they experience stress. Responses to stress fall into three general types: physiological, emotional, and cognitive. As you might expect, people vary greatly in their responses.

Physiological Responses to Stress *What Happens in the* B R A I N ?

Think about how you come to know that you are under stress. Typically, your breathing and heart rate quicken, you begin to sweat, your mouth gets dry, and your stomach tightens. What's happening is that your brain has perceived a challenge and is sending signals to your body to prepare to meet it. Sweating, dry mouth, and stomach tightness are some of the immediate physical effects of stress, but these effects are actually indicators of more basic physiological responses. We examine these responses next and illustrate them in **Figure 15-2**.

The Fight-or-Flight Response   You may remember the physiologist Walter Cannon from our discussion of theories of emotion in Chapter 12. Cannon was the first theo-

Under fire This marine fighting in Afghanistan yells to other marines after an IED (Improvised Explosive Device) goes off while they are under enemy fire. Fewer individuals feel more endangered on a daily basis than combat soldiers.

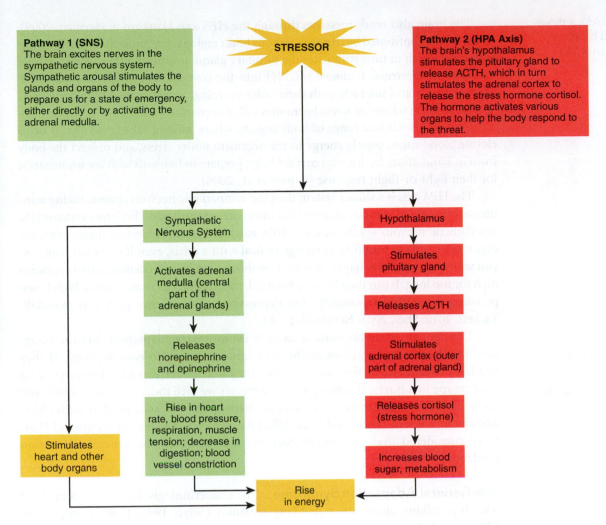

STRESSOR

Sympathetic Nervous System

Hypothalamus

Activates adrenal medulla (central part of the adrenal glands)

Stimulates pituitary gland

Releases norepinephrine and epinephrine

Releases ACTH

Stimulates heart and other body organs

Rise in heart rate, blood pressure, respiration, muscle tension; decrease in digestion; blood vessel constriction

Stimulates adrenal cortex (outer part of adrenal gland)

Releases cortisol (stress hormone)

Increases blood sugar, metabolism

Rise in energy

FIGURE 15-2 The physiological response to stress As shown in this flow chart, the brain sends messages to the endocrine glands and bodily organs through the sympathetic nervous system (SNS) pathway and the hypothalamic-pituitary-adrenal (HPA) axis.

rist to connect the bodily arousal associated with emotional responses to the need to fight or flee. According to Cannon (1932), the fight-or-flight response is a series of physiological reactions throughout the sympathetic nervous system and the endocrine system that mobilize an organism to either attack or escape an enemy. The process begins in the brain. The brain sends messages to the endocrine glands and bodily organs along two different routes. One is through the sympathetic nervous system, which as you recall is a division of the autonomic nervous system (ANS). The other is through the hypothalamic-pituitary-adrenal (HPA) axis.

When we confront a dangerous situation, within seconds the brain sends messages to the sympathetic nervous system, and these nerves directly stimulate organs of the body (the heart, for example). The nerves also influence organs indirectly by stimulating the adrenal glands (located at the tops of the kidneys), particularly the inner layer of those glands, an area called the *adrenal medulla*. The adrenal medulla, in turn, releases the chemicals epinephrine and norepinephrine (otherwise known as adrenaline and noradrenaline) into the bloodstream, where they are carried to various organs and muscles, further arousing the organism and enabling it to fight or flee. Normally, the biological changes associated with the fight-or-flight response subside around 15 minutes after the threatening situation eases.

The brain also sends messages through the HPA axis (Jankord & Herman, 2009). When we are confronted by stressors, various brain regions communicate with the hypothalamus, which in turn stimulates the pituitary gland, prompting the gland to release the *adrenocorticotropic hormone (ACTH)* into the bloodstream. ACTH travels to the adrenal glands and interacts with their outer covering, an area called the *adrenal cortex,* causing the release of stress hormones called *cortisol.*

Cortisol travels to a range of body organs, where, among other activities, it helps elevate blood sugar, supply energy to the organism under stress, and protect the body from inflammation. In this way, cortisol helps prepare individuals who are under stress for their fight-or-flight response (Lupien et al., 2006).

The HPA axis is a slower system than the sympathetic nervous system, taking minutes as opposed to seconds to have a big influence on the body. These two systems (the sympathetic nervous system and the HPA axis), activated in tandem, insure that the organism is able to mobilize its energy to deal with a crisis, even if it takes a while. As you will see later in the chapter, however, problems can arise if cortisol activity remains high for too long. It can then become harmful, contributing in some cases to high blood pressure, inflammation, anxiety, and depression, among other problems (Kendall-Tackett, 2010; Sher, 2003; Nemeroff, 1998).

Some theorists argue that the fight-or-flight response may be a largely male response, and suggest that evolution may have selected a "tend-and-befriend" response to cope with stress in females (Taylor et al., 2000).

The fight-or-flight response is an early evolutionary adaptation. You can imagine how this kind of reaction might have come in handy to early humans. If they suddenly came upon a saber-toothed tiger, they were better able to either overwhelm it or escape in a hurry. But many of the stressors we face today are more subtle and more chronic—homework stress, employment pressures, relationship difficulties, and any number of other conditions. What happens when a stressor is chronic? Hans Selye considered that question in forming his theory of the general adaptation syndrome.

The General Adaptation Syndrome The endocrinologist Hans Selye is credited with first talking about stress in living creatures (Selye, 1993, 1956, 1936). In his laboratory, Selye exposed animals to a variety of stressors. No matter what the stressor—mild shock, pain, restraint, heat, cold—he found that the animals displayed the same pattern of response—a consistent pattern that he labeled *stress* (a term he borrowed from engineers, who use it when they discuss forces that affect the structural integrity of the things they build). Selye believed we respond in much the same ways to stress, whatever its source. This insight was particularly important, because it means that, although our responses to different stressors might vary in degree, we are responding in the same basic way to all of them.

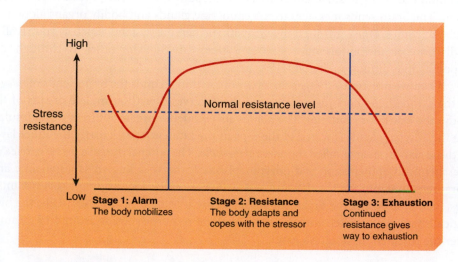

FIGURE 15-3 The general adaptation syndrome Seyle proposed that the body's physiological response to prolonged stress has three stages.

A different approach The real Patch Adams, physician and clown, talks here to the sister of a hospitalized child.

In a 1998 film, Robin Williams donned a white coat and a red clown nose and took a new brand of medicine to movie theatres around the world. He was playing real-life physician Patch Adams, who believes that the medical community has failed to embrace the use of laughter and humor to aid in health and healing (Marsh, 2008). While this may be a feel-good sentiment, is there actual support for the notion that laughter is the best medicine?

For a while, research in medicine and psychology seemed to support a laughter-health link. One study found, for example, that after watching a humorous film, participants who had laughed at and enjoyed the film showed decreases in stress and improvements in their immune system activity (Bennett, 1998). On the basis of such supportive findings, psychologists offered various explanations for how laughter might improve health (McCreaddie & Wiggins, 2008; Godfrey, 2004). Some such explanations suggested that there is a *direct* link between laughter and health. One proposal, for example, held that laughter may increase blood flow, thereby reducing blood pressure. Another proposal argued that 100 laughs can provide an aerobic workout equal to fifteen minutes on an exercise bike. Still other scientists suggested that the link between laughter and health is an *indirect* one. One popular proposal, for example, suggested that humor results in greater social support, thereby aiding health, and that humor may help heal by bringing down a person's stress level.

In recent years, however, a closer look at this body of research has revealed that support for the humor-health link is less clear and perhaps more questionable than first thought. It appears that many of the studies on this subject have been plagued with methodological problems and some well-done studies have failed to support the link (McCreaddie & Wiggins, 2008; Martin, 2001). A clearer verdict on the strength of this relationship and on the theories that seek to explain it await the results of some current and future research undertakings.

In the meantime, there is nothing in the literature to suggest laughter is bad for one's health, and many health and humor experts have offered tips on how to increase one's daily quota of good humor. They suggest, for example, browsing through the humor section of a local bookstore; keeping a humor journal filled with funny newspaper headlines, bumper stickers, and notes about humorous events; and reading cartoons daily, making sure to save and post the ones that tickle your funny bone the most (Godfrey, 2004). Sounds like a solid prescription for a laughter-filled life, even if it doesn't necessarily make you healthier!

Selye also noticed that if stressors continue, the organism's body progresses through three stages of response: alarm, resistance, and finally, exhaustion. He called this three-stage response to stress the **general adaptation syndrome (GAS)** (see **Figure 15-3**).

1. When an organism is first exposed to a threat, it reacts with *alarm* and becomes aroused physically as it prepares to face the challenge by fighting or fleeing. In short, the first stage of the general adaptation syndrome corresponds to the fight-or-flight response.

2. If the threat continues, the organism's body undergoes further changes in an attempt to stabilize itself—a second wave of adaptation that Selye called *resistance*. The organism's level of arousal remains elevated, though slightly lower than during the initial alarm phase, as it adjusts to the stressor. If new stressors are introduced during this stage, the body is less able to marshal the energy needed to address them. According to Selye, this makes the body vulnerable to *diseases of adaptation*—health problems, such as high blood pressure, asthma, and illnesses associated with impaired immune function.

3. If the organism is exposed to the stressor for still longer periods of time, its resistance gradually gives way to the third stage, *exhaustion*. In this stage, the body is depleted of energy and has little ability to resist. If the threat continues, the organism can suffer organ damage or death.

Alarm can save lives As the 2005 typhoon Matsa suddenly grew in strength in Shanghai, China, this couple immediately moved into an alarm mode, struggling to flee the onslaught of wind and rain as quickly as possible.

Students who have gone through final exams often have firsthand experience with Selye's general adaptation syndrome. As the exams approach, most students experience alarm. When they gear up and begin patterns of late-night studying, the students are entering the resistance phase. By the end of the exam period, many students feel as if they are heading toward exhaustion, and, in fact, a number catch colds or develop other illnesses at the end of the school year. If you haven't gone through a final exam period yet—well, now you have something to look forward to.

Although the principles of Selye's theory are widely accepted today, some theorists have questioned his claim that the stress response is the same no matter what the stressor (Lupien et al., 2007, 2006). They point out that although Selye used many kinds of stressors in his experiments with animals, all were physical—pain, heat, cold, and so forth. This has led some theorists to suggest that the precursors of stress are much more specific than Selye thought, and in fact measurable and predictable. As we shall soon see, psychological factors also play an important part in our stress experience.

Emotional Responses to Stress

Bodily arousal is only one dimension of our reaction to stressors. When people feel threatened by an event or situation, they typically experience a change in mood or emotions as well. Let's briefly revisit Nina, the stressed-out student from the chapter opener. As the stressors in her life mounted, Nina felt increasingly dejected (she wanted to curl up in a ball), annoyed (her inquisitive parents were "driving her crazy"), anxious (she had to leave her public speaking class in the middle of a speech), and angry (during an argument with Henry, she called him a jerk).

Note that most of Nina's emotional responses to stress were negative. This is typical of people under stress. Researchers have found that the more stress a person experiences, the more negative his or her emotions (Lazarus, 2007, 1999, 1993; D'Angelo & Wierzbicki, 2003). People who generally live under severe stress tend to be more anxious, depressed, or otherwise upset than those who have relatively stress-free lives. Even within the course of a day, people feel more negative when short-term stressors emerge. Conversely, as daily stressors subside, people's moods take an upward turn (van Eck, Nicholson, & Berkhof, 1998).

It was once thought that certain negative emotions—anxiety and depression—were more likely than others to emerge during stress. However, researchers have learned that, in fact, a range of different negative emotions may accompany stress, depending on individuals' personal styles and on the stress-inducing situations. The most common emotional reactions include anxiety, fear, and apprehension; dejection and grief; annoyance, anger, and rage; guilt; shame; disgust; and jealousy (Lazarus, 2007, 1993, 1991; Sher, 2003).

Cognitive Responses to Stress

As we noted at the beginning of the chapter, a key feature of stress is how we appraise both the challenging situation and our ability to handle that situation. If asked to speak publicly, for example, one person may be excited and pleased at the opportunity, while another may be fearful and anxious (see "What Happens in the Brain When Public Speaking Stresses Us Out" on the following pages). Sometimes, as in the fear of public speaking, this appraisal is stable—that is, people tend to react consistently to the prospect of speaking before a group. In other situations, however, the appraisal depends on the person's present psychological state. We may appraise a missing car key as much more stressful on the day of a final exam than on a less eventful day.

Remember Richard Lazarus and his cognitive-mediational theory of emotions, discussed in Chapter 12? Lazarus believed that emotion is aroused by a combination of

"No, I don't need an alarm clock— anxiety is my alarm clock."

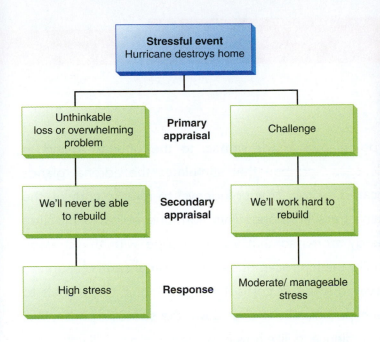

Stressful event
Hurricane destroys home

Unthinkable loss or overwhelming problem	**Primary appraisal**	Challenge
We'll never be able to rebuild	**Secondary appraisal**	We'll work hard to rebuild
High stress	**Response**	Moderate/ manageable stress

FIGURE 15-4 The cognitive-mediational theory of stress Our level of stress largely depends on how we appraise a threat and evaluate our abilities to cope with it.

two elements—an environmental event and a person's motives and beliefs. In fact, much of his early work was focused specifically on stress, and he identified two steps in how we experience stress (see **Figure 15-4**).

In the first step, **primary appraisal**, we examine the stressor and assess how severe it is. We may identify the stressor as a future danger (a threat), a current situation to be confronted and overcome (a challenge), or a loss or harm. The way we appraise the stressor in this first step can have important consequences for how we attempt to deal with it. Nina, for example, appraised her term paper as a threat to be avoided rather than a challenge to be overcome.

In the second step, we evaluate our own resources and ability to cope with the threat, challenge, or loss. This step is called **secondary appraisal**. Perceiving ourselves as lacking the resources to deal with a problem will elevate its threat level. Conversely, by reminding ourselves of what resources we have, we can decrease the threat level quickly. Consider Nina's more positive attitude when she mustered her resources and produced a few paragraphs of her paper.

One common factor in these appraisals is that the degree to which we feel in control of a situation affects how dangerous or stressful it feels. Perceptions of control (or lack of control) can greatly influence our appraisal of a stressor and, in turn, our experience of stress. Persons who believe that they can exert control over a particular stressor will experience less stress than individuals who feel no such control. A study of residents in a nursing home, for example, found that persons who were given more control over their lives (deciding when to attend a movie, for example, or where to receive visitors) experienced less overall stress than residents given little control. Perhaps not so coincidentally, the residents with control were twice as likely to still be alive 18 months after the study began (Langer & Rodin, 2004; Rodin & Langer, 1977).

It is important, of course, that our sense of control be realistic. People with life-threatening illnesses such as cancer or heart disease who think that they can control their disease with unproven remedies may feel less stress initially, but they are not likely to be healthier for their efforts. Patients with such illnesses can, however, experience a realistic sense of control (and a lower level of stress) by managing specific aspects of their diseases (seeking out useful medical information, for example), taking part in treatment decisions, controlling some of their emotions, and seeking closer relationships with their loved ones (Thompson et al., 1993).

primary appraisal appraisal of a stressor to determine how severe it is; the first stage in Richard Lazarus's description of how people experience stress.

secondary appraisal appraisal of one's personal resources and ability to cope with a stressor; the second stage in Richard Lazarus's description of how people experience stress.

When Public Speaking Stresses Us Out

If you're like most people, you feel stressed out when you have to give a speech in public. What's happening in the brain while you're feeling this pressure? Although you are not in physical danger, your brain is responding to the presence of an audience as if you were. Brain signals activate the sympathetic nervous system—resulting in increased heart rate, sweaty palms, and a dry mouth. In the brainstem, the locus coeruleus increases arousal by changing activity in its widespread projections throughout the brain. The amygdala and cortex process sensory stimuli that in turn activate stress systems. The hypothalamus sends signals to the pituitary gland to release a hormone that stimulates the adrenal glands (located on top of your kidneys) to release cortisol, the main stress hormone. This hormone helps to mobilize energy stores so that you can cope with the stressor. Finally, the hippocampus and prefrontal cortex recognize elevated levels of cortisol and send inhibitory signals to the hypothalamus to shut down the stress response. Will the audience realize how nervous you are or will you come across as cool, calm and collected?

COPING WITH STRESS OVER THE LONG TERM

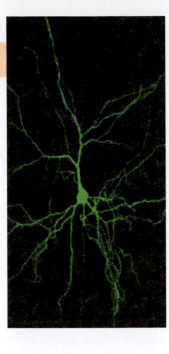

Activation of stress hormone systems is adaptive in the short-term because they can help focus attention and increase energy sources. If negative stress goes on for too long, however, it can become detrimental to the brain. Chronic stress results in a reduction in the size of prefrontal cortex pyramidal neurons (shown here stained with a fluorescent dye) as well as diminished performance on cognitive tasks associated with this brain region.

LEARNING TO ENJOY PUBLIC SPEAKING

With repeated experiences, most people find public speaking less frightening and some even begin to enjoy it. When stress has a reward-ing component to it, the brain's response switches from negative to positive. Even with elevated stress hormones, neurons are not dam-aged and they even start to grow. Studies have shown that rewarding stress can stimulate the production of new neurons in the hippocampus (shown here stained with red fluo-rescent dye).

Locus coeruleus

Hypothalamus

Prefrontal cortex

Pituitary

Amygdala

Hippocampus

SHUTTING DOWN THE STRESS RESPONSE

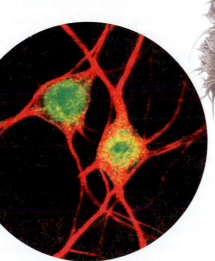

To reduce the risks associated with long-term exposure to elevated stress hormones and to enable stress systems to reset themselves for future use with new experiences, the brain has stress hormone receptors (shown here stained with a green fluorescent dye). These receptors, located in the hippocampus, prefrontal cortex and hypothalamus, work to turn the system off and restore the brain to its normal resting state.

Bewitched, bothered, and bewildered As these three young men struggle with the demands of a computer game they are playing, each displays a different reaction: one seems overwhelmed *(left)*, another frustrated and angry *(middle)*, and the other unfazed *(right)*.

Individual Responses to Stress HOW we Differ

It should be clear by now that when it comes down to it, how stressed someone gets in a particular situation often depends on whom we're talking about. You probably have friends who collapse at the slightest hint of trouble and other friends who are experts in crisis management. Perhaps you have other friends who just let trouble roll off their backs without even a suggestion of worry.

Individuals are unique in many ways. Each of us has a particular biological makeup, a preferred style of interpretation, and a favored cluster of personality traits. In addition, we each operate within a particular social context. These individual differences profoundly influence our physical, emotional, and cognitive responses to stress. Researchers have spent considerable energy examining four areas of individuality and their relationships to stress: *autonomic reactivity*, *explanatory style*, *personality*, and *social support*.

Autonomic Reactivity and Stress Earlier, we observed that the autonomic nervous system (ANS), particularly the sympathetic nervous system, plays a key role in stress reactions. When a person confronts a stressor, the ANS stimulates organs throughout the body, triggering feelings of physical arousal. As you might expect, people differ in how intensely the ANS responds to stressors. In some, the ANS tends to be highly reactive across various situations and springs into action even in response to mild stressors. In others, the ANS is less reactive and so less likely to respond even to fairly significant stressors. Such basic differences in *autonomic reactivity* may cause some people to experience stress reactions more often or more intensely than other people, even in the face of identical environmental threats (Cohen & Hamrick, 2003).

To illustrate, let's look at cardiovascular responses to stress, which include blood pressure and heart rate. In a number of studies, researchers have measured the cardiovascular reactions of individuals confronting stressors, such as difficult cognitive or social tasks (Sgoifo et al., 2003; Malkoff et al., 1993; Sherwood, 1993). Across a variety of situations, certain participants repeatedly display high-cardiovascular reactivity, while others consistently exhibit low-cardiovascular reactions.

Differences in autonomic reactivity may help explain why people seem to display characteristic stress reactions. One person may always respond to perceived threats by perspiring profusely and being gripped by a sense of dread, for example, while another typically breathes faster and has difficulty concentrating yet perspires very little. Similarly, differences in autonomic reactivity may help explain why some people always seem relaxed, while others typically experience tension even when confronting minimal threats (Spielberger, 1985, 1972, 1966).

Explanatory Style and Stress The characteristic manner in which we explain events, our *explanatory style*, can make a difference in how we appraise and respond to stressors. People with generally *optimistic* explanatory styles tend to believe that, despite setbacks, things will improve (Peterson & Steen, 2009, 2002). Those with generally *pessimistic* explanatory styles have a gloomier appraisal—they believe that if things can go wrong, they usually will go wrong.

Imagine two people, each failing to make the varsity soccer team. Both feel disappointed and sad. One says to herself, "I'll never make it. I'm such a dud. I should never have tried out. It was stupid of me to think I was any good at soccer." In contrast, the other individual says, "At least I tried. If I do track in the spring, I can improve my speed and make the team next year. Meanwhile, I'll talk to the coach and find out how I can improve." It is likely that the latter individual—the more optimistic one—will experience less stress than the former.

Research has supported the idea that optimistic and pessimistic explanatory styles influence stress reactions (Chang et al., 2008; Carver & Sheier, 1999). When optimistic research participants appraise stressful situations, they are more likely than pessimists to recognize the positive features and to perceive the situations as manageable (Aspinwald, Richter, & Hoffman, 2001). In turn, they typically experience lower levels of stress (Chang, 2002). Similarly, it turns out that optimists are more likely to seek out social support during stressful events and to employ constructive coping techniques (Iwanaga et al., 2004). (We'll discuss the importance of social support later in this section.)

Of course, few people are exclusively pessimistic or exclusively optimistic, although they may lean in one direction or other. In fact, some individuals develop an "optimistic brand of pessimism." These individuals believe that things will go wrong but, at the same time, hope that they won't: "I probably will fail to make the soccer team, but maybe I'll get lucky. If I play my best and the others have problems, I might have a chance." Still other persons are "defensive pessimists." They anticipate negative outcomes largely to help protect themselves from disappointment (Norem & Illingworth, 2004). Deep down, they hold out hope for the best and so manage to preserve a degree of optimism.

Personality and Stress Our personalities often help set the tone for how we appraise and react to stressors (Vollrath, 2001). People who are generally timid will likely greet a stressor with more alarm than people who are generally bold. Similarly, our ongoing levels of anger, depression, curiosity, and the like will influence our stress reactions. Nina's breakup, for example, appeared to be precipitated by her general tendency to react to stressors by becoming moody and critical.

One personality style that has received particular study is the *hardy personality*, sometimes called the *stress-resistant personality* (Maddi, 2007; Bartone, 2003; Oulette & Di Placido, 2001; Kobasa, 1990, 1987). Individuals with such personalities welcome challenges and are willing to commit themselves and take control in their daily lives. Generally, they greet stressors as opportunities for growth rather than as crises and perceive stressors as less severe than nonhardy individuals. Not surprisingly, hardy persons also seem to experience fewer and less intense feelings of stress (Beasley et al., 2003).

At the other end of the stress continuum are people with personality styles that appear to make them more prone to stress. In the late 1950s, two cardiologists, Meyer Friedman and Raymond Rosenman (1959) reported that many of their heart patients seemed to share similar personality traits: they were consistently angry, cynical, hard-driving, impatient, and time conscious. They were also competitive, ambitious, and in a hurry to do many things at once. Friedman and Rosenman claimed that individuals with this personality style, which they labeled **Type A**, interact with the world in a way that produces continual stress (Jamal & Baba, 2003; Smith & Gallo, 2001; Miller, 2000; Friedman & Rosenman, 1959). In contrast, people who display **Type B** personalities are more relaxed, less aggressive, and less worried about time. People with this personal style are thought to experience lower levels of stress. In fact, most people fall between these two extremes, leaning toward one or the other but showing features of both personality patterns.

Researchers later suggested there might be a third personality pattern, **Type C**. People with this personality type are pleasant and peace loving but have a hard time expressing or acknowledging negative feelings (Temoshok et al., 2008; Temoshok, 2003). Although their positive attitudes might be thought to protect them from stress, persons with Type C behavior patterns are actually particularly vulnerable. When angry, Type C personalities tend to turn the anger inward. They also tend to take losses and relationship problems particularly hard. We'll talk more about Type A and Type C personality types when we discuss the relationship between stress and health later in the chapter.

Some two thousand years ago, the Roman poet Horace wrote, "In times of stress, be bold and valiant."

Type A a personality type characterized by competitiveness, impatience, and anger and hostility.

Type B a personality type that is less aggressive, more relaxed, and less hostile than Type A.

Type C a personality type characterized by difficulty in expressing or acknowledging negative feelings.

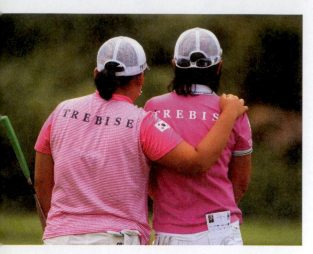

Social support can make the difference A Korean golfer comforts her playing partner as the latter is sizing up a difficult putt on the 18th green of the Women's World Cup of Golf in 2008. The partner went on to sink the putt.

Social Support and Stress As we think back to Nina's struggle at the beginning of the chapter, we may notice that she seemed to be going through her difficulties alone, without much social support. She did not feel free to turn to family members, and she did not appear to have close friends in whom she could confide. In fact, family and social relationships seemed to add to her experience of stress. Would Nina have felt better if she could have turned to family members or friends for support? The answer is yes, according to numerous studies and observations (Taylor, 2008, 2007, 2006).

Social relationships can be paradoxical. On the one hand, as in Nina's case, negative interactions with relatives and friends can be sources of significant stress (Lepore et al., 1991). On the other hand, studies have resoundingly indicated that social relationships and support help prevent or reduce stress reactions (Cohen & Janicki-Deverts, 2009; Cohen, 2004).

The positive impact of social support on stress was first revealed in animal studies. In a famous investigation, for example, twin goats were subjected to a stressful conditioning task. One goat worked in isolation and the other worked in the presence of its mother. The goat working in isolation reacted with greater anxiety and stress than did its twin goat (Liddell, 1950). In another study, a group of mice had to "share" a common feeding place, which created a persistent state of territorial conflict (Henry & Cassel, 1969). In one condition, the mice in the group were strangers, while in the other, the mice were from the same litter. The former group showed more signs of stress than did the latter.

Studies of humans have revealed a similar role for social support in stress reactions (Taylor, 2008, 2007, 2006). It has been found, for example, that when faced with various job stressors, from work overload to job conflict, workers who can rely on their supervisors, coworkers, and spouses for emotional and practical support often experience less distress than workers without such support (Beehr et al., 2003). Other studies suggest that having an intimate, confiding relationship with someone, whether that be a spouse, close friend, or other individual, provides the strongest kind of social support (Cohen & Wills, 1985).

Why do people who have strong social support seem to experience less stress? Researchers are not sure. Such support may increase people's self-confidence or self-esteem as they confront stressors. It may provide individuals under stress with a greater sense of control or greater optimism that everything will turn out well. Alternatively, social feedback may change people's perspectives as they face stressors, alter their perceptions of threat, or reduce their appraisal of a stressor's importance. Finally, it may be that the reassuring presence of close friends or relatives helps to reduce the kinds of bodily arousal and negative emotions that normally feed stress reactions (Taylor, 2008, 2007, 2006).

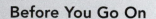

Before You Go On

What Do You Know?

6. How do the sympathetic nervous system and hypothalamic-pituitary-adrenal pathways influence our experience of stress?
7. What happens in each stage of the general adaptation syndrome?
8. What is the difference between primary appraisal and secondary appraisal?
9. How does autonomic reactivity affect how different people experience stress?
10. What are the characteristics of the hardy personality type?

What Do You Think?
Can you think of any advantages to having a Type A personality? A Type C personality? Can you think of any disadvantages to having a Type B personality?

Coping With Stress

coping efforts to manage, reduce, or tolerate stress.

LEARNING OBJECTIVE 3 Discuss and evaluate several ways in which people cope with stress.

We've seen that a number of individual differences contribute to how stressed we become. Once we feel stressed, we also differ in our efforts to manage the situation. What do you do when you feel stressed? If you feel overloaded or overburdened, do you lie in bed, worrying about all that you have to do, unable to get started? Or do you start making lists and timetables? If you are in a traffic jam, do you pound the steering wheel, or do you instead try to find an interesting radio station or play your favorite CD? Faced with the terrifying prospect of a chemistry midterm, do you call a friend to study or light a cigarette?

Our efforts to manage, reduce, or tolerate stress are called **coping**. Although most people use this term to convey constructive efforts ("I'm coping with the situation"), a coping response may be either adaptive or maladaptive in a given situation (Kleinke, 2007; Folkman & Moskowitz, 2004). For a person faced with failing grades, for example, going out and partying is a less adaptive coping response than spending extra time studying. Each of us has preferred styles of coping that we tend to apply across various situations (Aldwin, 2007; Folkman & Moskowitz, 2004; Carver & Scheier, 2003, 1994). A person may use different coping responses in different situations, however, and some *coping-flexible* individuals are more able than others to depart from their preferred coping styles to meet the demands at hand. Let's look at some of the more common coping styles.

Lashing Out

As stressors pile up, people often say that they feel "as if they're going to explode." Thus, it is not surprising that some individuals do in fact explode—psychologically or physically. They react to stress by lashing out at other people with angry words or behaviors. Around one-quarter of adults report such reactions (Kanner, 1998).

Lashing out often occurs after a series of stressors has taken place. The particular event that triggers an aggressive outburst may seem relatively mild in itself, but for the individual under siege, it is the last straw. Recall how Nina, the beleaguered student in our case opener, blew up at her boyfriend, Henry, during a phone conversation, calling him names and hanging up on him. Henry's crime? He had refused to let her off the phone. Ordinarily, this teasing might not have elicited such a strong reaction. But Nina was feeling pressure from her boss, her parents, and the demands of her schoolwork. Nina's explosive reaction isn't surprising when we consider the cumulative impact of these multiple stressors.

Everyone is capable of lashing out at others in the face of stress. For most people, it is an occasional and temporary reaction, performed before they have time to think about things and decide how to act more constructively. For some people, however, lashing out is a characteristic mode of coping. Recall that Nina had been in the habit of lashing out at Henry. These outbursts were, in fact, a key reason that Henry decided to break up with her.

Angry outbursts, although sometimes understandable, are not typically a constructive way of dealing with stress. Such outbursts may harm relationships, produce psychological or physical damage, and lead to additional stress. Theorists and clinicians once believed that expressions of anger were cathartic, or cleansing—that is, if people expressed their anger and "got their frustrations out of their system," they would feel better and be able to move forward constructively. It turns out, however, that excessive or continuous expressions of anger usually cause further outbursts (Tavris, 2003, 1989). In one study, experimenters induced anger in participants and then directed one group of angry participants to hit a punching bag and the other group of angry individuals to sit quietly (Bushman et al., 1999). Later in the experiment, the "punching bag" participants were found to behave much more aggressively than the "sit quiet" individuals.

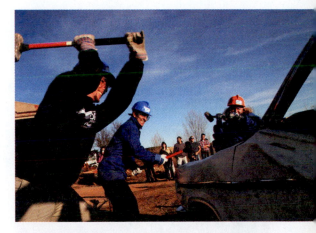

But does it work? In Spain, certain consulting organizations have advised clients such as these men to smash cars (or computers, TVs, or mobile phones) with sledge hammers as a way of fighting stress. The approach has caught on throughout the country, but research has not found that lashing out or venting anger are necessarily effective coping strategies.

In the long term, lashing out can harm or destroy a person's social support network, as in the example of Nina and Henry. As mentioned earlier, social support is a primary defense against stress. By driving away those who could help with stress-related problems, such as anxiety and depression, a person will likely make those problems worse.

Self-Defense

In some instances, people run away from—that is, physically leave—stressors through such actions as dropping a difficult class, changing jobs, or ending a troubled relationship. More commonly, people try to make a "psychological getaway." You may recall Aesop's story of the fox and the grapes. A fox was trying to get some grapes, but they were hanging too high on a vine, and he couldn't reach them. Eventually, after trying for most of the afternoon, the fox gave up, saying, "they're probably sour anyway." Leaving aside the question of why a fox wants grapes in the first place, the fox's behavior in this story is an example of *reaction formation*—saying or doing the opposite of what one actually believes—one of Freud's defense mechanisms.

Recall from Chapter 13 that defense mechanisms are unconscious strategies that people use to defend against anxiety. Freud explained such behavior in psychoanalytic terms. Today, though, the notion of defense mechanisms is widely embraced even by theorists outside the psychoanalytic model. Many psychologists believe that people often cope with stress—whether consciously or unconsciously—by engaging in defensive behaviors. These theorists also agree that the defensive behaviors often involve a high degree of self-deception.

Although everyone reacts to stressors with defensive behaviors on occasion, some people use such behaviors regularly. In fact, certain individuals display what theorists describe as a *repressive coping style* (Langens & Moerth, 2003; Brown et al., 1996). They consistently deny negative feelings and discomfort and try to push such emotions out of awareness.

Is the use of defense mechanisms—whether occasional or continual—a helpful way to cope with stress? Sometimes, it probably is. We can all think of instances when it would be best to simply put something out of our mind, particularly if we don't have any control over the outcome (for example, waiting for our grade on a recent exam). In other instances, however, defensive coping is not constructive. After all, while we spend our time defending and avoiding, the problem typically continues (Holahan & Moos, 1990, 1985). The conflict with a roommate, the course paper that needs writing, and the medical problem that needs attention continue as stressors and may even intensify.

It is also worth noting that defensive coping can be difficult to achieve. Research has found that people with a repressive coping style often fail to fully repress their feelings of stress (Pauls & Stemmler, 2003; Brown et al., 1996). While research participants were watching an upsetting film, for example, experimenters measured their autonomic nervous system responses. Although participants with a repressive coping style reported feeling less stress than other participants did, their autonomic responses were actually higher (for example, their heart rates and blood pressure were higher throughout the film). It may be that repressive coping behaviors mask stress rather than eliminate it. Or perhaps the higher autonomic activity associated with repressive coping indicates that such repression requires considerable physical effort. Either way, it is not surprising that people with this coping style have been found to experience more medical problems than people who use other coping styles do (Coy, 1998).

Self-Indulgence

Many individuals use self-indulgent coping strategies, such as overeating, smoking cigarettes, and consuming drugs and alcohol (Steptoe, 2000). Nina went partying with her friends, for example, to deal with the stress created by her paper-writing assignment.

"You can avoid reality, but you cannot avoid the consequences of avoiding reality."

—*Ayn Rand, Russian-American writer*

Such strategies may help people feel better in the short term, but in most instances they fail to change the challenge at hand and so have little long-term benefit. In fact, such responses are often associated with poor adjustment and depression and anxiety (Folkman & Moskowitz, 2004; Aspinwall & Taylor, 1992).

If the problem at hand is transient and simple—recovering from a drive home in a blinding snowstorm, for example—the self-indulgence of having a bowl of ice cream or a beer may indeed help a stressed person to calm down. If, however, the problem is more complex—a term paper due next week—self-indulgence is unlikely to be an effective

How Can You Manage Stress?

Mass relaxation A group of 150 students in Bejing, China receive stress relief training to help them relax during their upcoming college entrance examinations.

Stress is often unavoidable. The traffic jams, life changes, and occasional natural disasters that create stress are not going to miraculously disappear. The issue, then, is how to handle stress. Is there a way to lessen its impact so that cortisol levels, blood pressure, and the like do not soar? The answer, according to many psychologists and studies, is yes (Folkman & Moskowitz, 2004). As this chapter has already begun to suggest, there are quite a few things you can do the next time you anticipate or begin to feel the heart-pounding symptoms of stress.

Exercise, Meditation, and Relaxation

One of the best ways to manage physiological responses to stress is to exercise (Steptoe, 2000). In fact, it appears that people who exercise regularly reap not only physical benefits, such as lowering the activity of stress hormones (Rejeski & Thompson, 2007; Rejeski et al., 1992, 1991), but also psychological benefits, such as increases in self-confidence. Similarly, research indicates that some of those who learn to quiet their thoughts and relax their muscles through meditation and relaxation training experience reductions in stress hormone activity, blood pressure, and anxiety levels (Cardoso et al., 2009; Stetter & Kupper, 2002).

Social Support

Seeking the support of others, whether in the form of assistance or a sympathetic ear, is another way to ease the effects of stress. Simply knowing that friends or family will be available when needed is a form of social support (Taylor, 2008, 2007, 2006; Pierce, Sarason, & Sarason, 1996). It appears that social support helps ease the effects of stress in at least two ways—by helping to reduce the actual number and impact of threatening situations and by providing practical, problem-focused assistance when stress does occur.

Religion

For many people, religion is of major help in dealing with stress. As we have observed in this chapter, one reason for this may be the social support that the individuals derive from religion (Folkman & Moskowitz, 2004). Religion and religious communities can, for example, serve as antidotes to feelings of aloneness and may also provide a sense of order as people face the uncertainties of life. In addition, religious beliefs may offer explanations for stressful events that make those events seem less threatening or overwhelming to many people (Packer, 2000).

Self-Disclosure

Self-disclosure, the sharing of emotions and experiences with others, can also help people deal with stress. Up to a point, self-disclosure serves to release stress—consider the phrase "getting things off my chest"—but it is more than simply the venting of emotion. It helps people to channel emotions into a cohesive narrative, making stressors easier to process and deal with (Foa & Kozak, 1986). In addition, by putting fearful, angry, or uncomfortable feelings into language and "bouncing them off" of other people, individuals are forced to think about and perhaps better address those feelings (Smyth & Pennebaker, 2001). Of course, the effectiveness of self-disclosure is tied to the ability of others to understand the problems a person is going through. Rape victims or former prisoners of war, for example, may discover that certain relatives or friends simply cannot comprehend what they are going through. In such cases, the feedback they receive ("Gee, that's really rough, but I am sure you'll feel better soon") may feel empty, unhelpful, and in some cases even painful.

problem-focused coping coping strategies focused on dealing directly with the stressor, such as by changing the stressor in some way.

emotion-focused coping coping strategies focused on changing one's feelings about the stressor.

coping strategy. Eating, drinking, shopping, watching television, or surfing the Internet will not make the problem go away. In fact, it may produce still greater pressure and higher stress: while one indulges, the paper's due date keeps getting closer. Moreover, certain self-indulgent strategies, such as cigarette smoking, excessive alcohol consumption, drug use, and extreme overeating, have serious health effects. Nevertheless, surveys show that self-indulgence is on the rise as a coping response (Young, 2009, 2004, 1998, 1996).

Constructive Strategies

It is possible, of course, to cope with stress constructively rather than lashing out at others or engaging in self-defense or self-indulgence. Psychologists Richard Lazarus and Susan Folkman (1984) use the terms *problem-focused coping* and *emotion-focused coping* to distinguish two kinds of constructive strategies. Which of these strategies we are likely to use depends in part on the nature of the problem (Stanton et al., 2009, 2002; Folkman & Moskowitz, 2004). For example, we could try to hit the highway at 4:00 A.M. as a way of dealing with morning traffic, but it is probably more practical to learn how to react calmly and philosophically to rush-hour tie-ups. Conversely, when a tornado watch is posted, figuring out how to calm down may not be as fruitful as deciding whether to leave town or head for the cellar.

In **problem-focused coping**, the person's efforts are aimed at dealing directly with the stressor in some way. For example, the late-to-work Nina might ask her boss to assign her to a different work shift so that she has more time to get to work. Or she might look for a new job closer to campus. Or she might devise a plan to buy a car, so that she can save time traveling to work. In any case, by dealing directly with the stressor, she can begin to reduce its effects.

But what about the noisy two-year-old next door who keeps interrupting your efforts to relax in the backyard? Or the grief resulting from the loss of a loved one? These are not stressors that readily yield to a problem-focused approach. When we can exert little control over stressors, we may instead try to change how we feel toward the stressors, thus limiting their negative effects—an approach called **emotion-focused coping** by Lazarus and Folkman.

In some cases, emotion-focused coping may involve *cognitive reappraisal*—finding a way to reinterpret the negative aspects of a situation so that they are less upsetting (Harvey, 2008; Lechner et al., 2008; Gross, Richards, & John, 2006; Gross & John, 2003; Wortman et al., 1992). People who are trying to come to terms with the death of a loved one or with some other catastrophic loss often look for ways to find positive meaning or purpose in their loss (Folkman & Moskowitz, 2004). Similarly, people may reinterpret threatening situations as challenges or tests, rather than catastrophes. The loss of a job, for example, might be viewed as a new beginning or new opportunity (Folkman & Moskowitz, 2000). As we shall see later, strong religious beliefs help some individuals make such cognitive reappraisals.

Changing how we think or feel about a stressor can also be a useful tactic for less traumatic stressors, such as tests and traffic jams. Rather than becoming increasingly upset over a traffic jam, for example, you may be able to shrug it off—saying, in effect, "It won't be great if I'm late, but I'll survive."

> " The greatest weapon against stress is our ability to choose one thought over another. "
>
> *—William James, American psychologist and philosopher*

Before You Go On

What Do You Know?

11. How can lashing out negatively affect our management of stressors?
12. What is a repressive coping style?
13. Identify and describe two forms of constructive coping.

What Do You Think?   Do you tend to use constructive coping strategies, or do your responses tend to be more maladaptive? Do you adapt your coping style to the situation, or do you tend to use the same style across many different situations? How could you improve your coping style?

Stress and Health

Explain how stress can cause physical illness, and discuss situations in which stress may be beneficial.

We have seen that stress has a profound effect on bodily functioning. Thus, it should come as no surprise that researchers have found strong relationships between stress and health—or, more accurately, between stress and illness (Groer et al., 2010). Scientists' appreciation of this relationship unfolded slowly. Back in the 1930s and 1940s, researchers began to recognize that certain medical illnesses are caused by an interaction of psychological factors (particularly stress-related factors) and biological factors, rather than by biological factors alone. These special illnesses were given the label *psychosomatic* or *psychophysiological diseases.* By the 1960s, a number of medical illnesses were considered psychosomatic diseases. Among the most prominent were ulcers, asthma, tension and migraine headaches, and hypertension.

As the list of psychosomatic diseases grew, medical researchers began to suspect that stress might, in fact, be at work in a wide range of medical illnesses, not just in a special few. Their suspicions changed to near certainty when studies revealed that stress often contributes to coronary heart disease, the leading cause of death in the United States. Researchers continue to investigate how stress is connected to various illnesses, as well as how stress brings about its effects on body systems.

Coronary Heart Disease

Coronary heart disease involves a blocking of the coronary arteries—the blood vessels that surround the heart and are responsible for carrying oxygen to the heart muscle. The term actually refers to several problems, including blockage of the coronary arteries and *myocardial infarction* ("heart attack"). Together, such problems are the leading cause of death in men over the age of 35 and women over the age of 40 in the United States, accounting for close to one million deaths each year, around 40 percent of all deaths in the nation (CDC, 2009). Research has shown that most cases of coronary heart disease are related to an interaction of psychological factors, such as job stress, and physiological factors, such as high cholesterol, obesity, hypertension, smoking, and lack of exercise (CDC, 2009).

Earlier, we discussed the Type A personality, which was identified by two cardiologists, Friedman and Rosenman. These doctors argued that the stress-producing behavior of people with Type A personalities makes them more likely to develop coronary heart disease. In fact, the Type A personality is also known in many circles as the *coronary-prone personality*. People with the more relaxed Type B behavior pattern exhibit lower levels of stress and less coronary disease (See **Figure 15-5**.) In a pioneering study of more than three thousand men, Friedman and Rosenman (1974) separated healthy men in their forties and fifties into Type A and Type B groups and then followed their health over a period of eight years. The doctors found that more than twice as many of the Type A men developed coronary heart disease. Subsequent studies found similar correlations among women (Haynes et al., 1980).

As research continued into the link between Type A behavior and coronary heart disease, many investigators found that while a connection existed, it was weaker than that reported by Friedman and Rosenman (Gallacher et al., 2003). It now appears that only some of the Type A characteristics are related strongly to heart disease (Ben Zur, 2002; Krantz & McCeney, 2002). In particular, research has identified the importance of negative emotions. Hostility, which includes not just feelings of anger but also enduring cognitive patterns of mistrust and cynicism, seems to be espe-

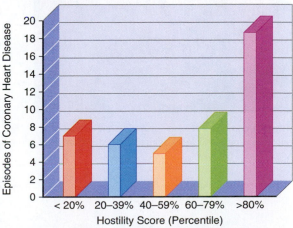

FIGURE 15-5 **Type A personality and hostility** A key characteristic of the Type A personality is chronic hostility. People with this personality style interact with others in a way that produces continual high levels of stress and increases their risk of coronary heart disease (Niaura et al., 2002).

JAMES PAUL SMYTHE
1914 – 1992

NEVER SICK
A DAY IN HIS
LIFE — AND
NOW THIS

Internal combat This scanning electron micrograph shows a cancer cell *(red)* being attacked by natural killer T-cells *(yellow).*

cially important (Smith & Gallo, 2001). People who score high on measures of hostility tend to experience greater stress and to have an increased risk of developing coronary heart disease, as well as other serious medical illnesses (Kendall-Tacket, 2010; Niaura et al., 2002; Miller et al., 1996).

Life Change and Illness

Earlier, we observed that in the 1960s researchers Thomas Holmes and Richard Rahe opened the door to investigations of life changes and stress when they designed the Social Readjustment Rating Scale (SRRS). The higher a person's score on the scale, as measured in life-change units (LCUs), the more change the person has been going through and, correspondingly, the more stress he or she has been experiencing.

With the SRRS, Holmes and Rahe decided to examine the relationship between life stress and the onset of illness. They found that the LCU scores of sick people during the year before they became ill were considerably higher than those of healthy people (Holmes & Rahe, 1989, 1967). In fact, if a person's life changes totaled more than 300 LCUs over the course of a year, that person was likely to develop a serious health problem.

The SRRS has been revised by researchers over the years (Hobson & Delunas, 2001; Hobson et al., 1998; Miller & Rabe, 1997). Using various scales, studies have tied a variety of life stressors to a wide range of physical problems, from upper respiratory infection to cancer (Cohen, 2005; Taylor, 2004). Generally, the greater the amount of life stress, the higher the likelihood of medical illness. Some researchers have even found a relationship between stress and death. Widows and widowers, for example, have an elevated risk of death during their period of bereavement (Rees & Lutkin, 1967; Young et al., 1963).

Stress and the Immune System

Research clearly shows that stress can result in various medical disorders. But exactly how does this effect come about? What is it about stress that makes it a threat to health? An area of study called **psychoneuroimmunology** has tried to answer this question by examining the links between stress, the immune system, and health (Kendall-Tackett, 2010; Kiecolt-Glaser et al., 2002).

The **immune system** is the body's system of organs, tissues, and cells that identify and destroy foreign invaders, such as bacteria and viruses, as well as cancer cells. An important group of cells in the immune system are **lymphocytes**, white blood cells that circulate through the lymphatic system and the bloodstream. When stimulated by bacterial or viral invaders, lymphocytes act to help the body fight the invaders. There are various kinds of lymphocytes. One kind, for example, is *natural killer T-cells,* lymphocytes that seek out and destroy body cells that have been infected by viruses.

Researchers believe that severe stress can negatively affect the activity of lymphocytes, slowing them down and thus reducing a person's ability to fight off viral and bacterial infections (see **Figure 15-6**) (Ader et al., 2001). In a pioneering study, Roger Bartrop and his colleagues (1977) in New South Wales, Australia, compared the immune systems of 26 people whose spouses had died eight weeks earlier to those of 26 similar participants whose spouses had not died. Blood samples showed that lymphocyte functioning was significantly slower in the bereaved people than in the nonbereaved individuals. Similarly, other studies have shown poor immune system functioning in persons who are exposed to long-term stressors, such as people who must provide care for relatives with Alzheimer's disease (Kiecolt-Glaser et al., 2002, 1996, 1991).

In short, during periods when healthy people confront unusual levels of stress, their immune systems slow down, so that they become susceptible to illness. If stress adversely affects our very capacity to fight off illness, it is not surprising that Holmes and Rahe and other researchers have found a relationship between life stress and a wide range of illnesses. Several factors seem to influence whether and when stress will lead to immune system problems. A number of biochemical changes must occur in order for stress to have such an impact. Certain behavioral changes, personality styles, and social circumstances may also play a role.

Biochemical Activity   Remember that when stressors first appear, the sympathetic nervous system springs into action. Its activity includes an increase in the release of norepinephrine throughout the brain and body. Apparently, beyond supporting the activity of the sympathetic nervous system, norepinephrine can eventually help slow the functioning of the immune system (Carlson, 2008; Lekander, 2002). During periods of low stress, norepinephrine travels to particular lymphocyte receptors, binds to them, and gives a message for the lymphocytes to increase activity. As stress rises and continues, however, the chemical travels to other receptors on the lymphocytes, binds to them, and gives an inhibitory message—a signal for the lymphocytes to stop their activity. Thus, the release of norepinephrine increases immune functioning at low levels of stress, but it slows down immune functioning in the face of higher and continuing stress.

Similarly, the stress hormone cortisol lowers immune system functioning during periods of extended stress. Recall that when people are under stress, their adrenal glands release cortisol. Initially, the release of this hormone stimulates body organs into action. After stress continues for 30 minutes or more, however, the stress hormone travels to particular receptor sites in the body, binds to these sites, and gives inhibitory messages meant to help calm down the stressed body (Manuck et al., 1991). Some of these receptor sites are located on the lymphocytes. When the cortisol binds to such receptors, its inhibitory messages slow down the activity of the immune system (Bellinger et al., 1994). Again, a chemical that initially helps people to deal with stress eventually acts to slow the immune system.

Another action of cortisol is to stimulate an increase in the production of *cytokines*—proteins that bind to receptors throughout the body and play a key role in the immune system. At early levels of stress, the cytokines help fight infection. But as stress continues, the continuing production and spread of cytokines leads to inflammation throughout the body (Kendall-Tackett, 2010; McEwen, 2002). *Inflammation* is an immune response characterized by swelling, heat, redness, and pain. Chronic inflammation of this kind may contribute to heart disease, stroke, and other illnesses.

Finally, investigators have learned that patterns of immune system responding vary from individual to individual (Marsland et al., 2002). Certain individuals experience more profound immune system slowdowns in the face of stress than other individuals do. Moreover, these individual differences in immune system functioning tend to be consistent across stressful situations. Thus, some stressed persons are more likely than others to develop infections and other diseases. Let's look next at some individual factors that may be responsible for differences in immune system functioning.

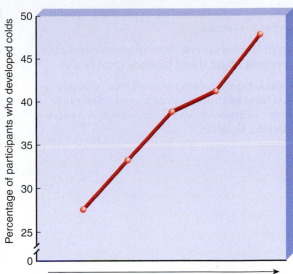

Percentage of participants who developed colds

General level of psychological stress in participants' lives

FIGURE 15-6 Stress and the common cold Researchers have examined the links between stress and illness. One study found that when healthy inoculation volunteers were exposed to a cold virus, those who reported generally the highest levels of stress in their lives were most likely to come down with a cold and to develop worse symptoms (Cohen et al., 1991).

psychoneuroimmunology an area of study focusing on links between stress, the immune system, and health.

immune system the body's system of organs, tissues, and cells that identify and destroy foreign invaders, such as bacteria and viruses, as well as cancer cells.

lymphocytes white blood cells that circulate through the body and destroy foreign invaders and cancer cells; important components of the immune system.

distress stress caused by unpleasant situations or circumstances.

eustress the optimal level of stress needed to promote physical and psychological health.

inoculation exposing oneself to a relatively low level of stress in a controlled situation in order to improve later performance in a more stressful situation.

Healthy communities This group of Native Americans perform a "blanket toss" ceremony in which they form a ring around a blanket and use it to hurl group members into the air. Communities that share activities and remain close knit often have lower illness rates than other communities.

Behavior, Personality, and Social Support Stress may trigger a series of behavioral changes that affect the immune system indirectly (Kalueff & La Porte, 2008). People under chronic stress may, for example, become anxious or depressed, perhaps even develop an anxiety or mood disorder. In turn, they may eat poorly, exercise less, have trouble sleeping, or smoke or drink. Such behaviors are all known to slow down the immune system (Irwin & Cole, 2005; Kiecolt-Glaser & Glaser, 2002, 1999, 1988).

An individual's personality may also help determine how much the immune system is affected by stress. Studies suggest that people who typically respond to life stress with optimism, effective coping, and resilience tend to experience better immune system functioning and to be better prepared to combat illness (Kendall-Tackett, 2010; Taylor, 2006, 2004).

Several studies have actually noted a relationship between certain personality characteristics and cancer (Hjerl et al., 2003). People exhibiting the Type C behavior pattern appear to be more at risk for cancer. Recall that people with the Type C personality have trouble acknowledging negative feelings and may be particularly vulnerable to stress. In addition, some studies have found that patients with certain forms of cancer who display a helpless or repressive coping style tend to have less successful recoveries than patients who express their emotions. It is important to note, however, that other studies have found no relationship between personality and cancer outcome (Urcuyo et al., 2005; Garssen & Goodkin, 1999).

Some researchers have identified a connection between religiousness and health. Specifically, studies have found that regular church attendance is correlated with a decreased risk of death over a particular period (Ellison et al., 2000). A few studies have also linked religiousness to better immune system functioning (Folkman & Moskowitz, 2004; Koenig & Cohen, 2002). Although the relationship between church attendance and health is not well understood, it appears to result at least in part from the social support people receive from others in their religious group.

More generally, research indicates that social support helps to protect us from the effects of stress. People who have little social support and feel lonely tend to experience poorer immune functioning when stressed than other people do (Curtis et al., 2004; Cohen, 2002). Conversely, it appears that social support helps protect people from stress, poor immune system functioning, and illness and helps improve recovery from illness or surgery (Matsumoto & Juang, 2008; Cohen, 2002; Kiecolt-Glaser et al., 2002). Some studies have even suggested that patients with certain kinds of cancer who receive social support or supportive therapy often display better immune system functioning and, in turn, have more successful recoveries than patients without such social help (Spiegel & Fawzy, 2002).

The stress-reducing benefits of social support can be seen in the health of people who grow up in close-knit communities. One early study explored the low rate of stress-related illnesses among residents of the town of Roseto, Pennsylvania (Wolf, 1969). The death rate from coronary heart disease in this town was considerably lower than that in the general population, despite the fact that the residents' eating, smoking, and exercise patterns were similar to those in communities with much higher coronary death rates. Clearly, something special was responsible for the residents' good health. That something turned out to be Roseto's positive social environment. An Italian enclave, Roseto was home to extremely close, supportive, and traditional families. Relatives, friends, and local priests were always available to help out with any kind of problem. During the 1970s, Roseto's younger generation began to marry people from other backgrounds and move away. Church attendance also dropped. These social changes resulted in less social support throughout the community. Perhaps not surprisingly, the rate of heart attacks in the community increased (Greenberg, 1978).

The Benefits of Stress

It might be hard to believe, given the litany of problems that we've identified here, but stress can be positive. In fact, when Selye first identified stress as a concept, back in 1936, he actually drew a distinction between unpleasant stressors and pleasant stressors. How can a stressor be pleasant? Think about waiting for a call from someone you met at a party last night; it can be stressful, but in an exciting way. Unpleasant stressors, according to Selye, cause **distress**—the kind of unpleasant stress on which we've generally been focusing up to now. Pleasant stressors, in contrast, cause *eustress*.

A key benefit of stress is that it helps promote positive development. Remember in Chapter 3 when we discussed some theorists' notion that parents can actually stunt a baby's development by meeting all the baby's needs and that there is some optimal level of frustration that facilitates development? Researchers have suggested that similar principles apply across the lifespan. That is, adverse events and the stress that they produce can force you to confront challenges, adapt to your environment, and build up strength and resilience (Tennen & Affleck, 2009, 2005, 2002; Harvey, 2008).

Today, **eustress** is defined not in terms of the stressor but in terms of the stress level—it is the optimal level of stress that promotes physical and psychological health (Nelson & Cooper, 2005). But what exactly is an optimal level of stress? We can think about this question in a couple of ways. First, exposing yourself to a smaller level of stress in a controlled situation can improve your performance in a more stressful situation, a process called **inoculation**. If you call one friend to talk through what you want to say to another friend with whom you've been fighting, you're inoculating yourself.

As we have seen previously, another way of considering what constitutes an optimal level of stress involves looking at the relationship between stress and performance. As shown in **Figure 15-7**, researchers have found that stress can actually facilitate performance on a task, depending on the complexity of the task.

- *Performance of very easy tasks can benefit from a high level of stress.* For example, the videogame Tetris® involves very little cognitive complexity and very low stakes, but as the computer starts dropping the pieces faster, it will get your attention and help you stay focused on the game.

- *A moderately difficult task benefits from a moderate level of stress.* Too low, and you won't get excited enough to perform your best. Too high, and you'll be more likely to lose your focus or perform poorly.

- *For a complex task, low stress leads to the optimal performance.* Consider that next time you decide to make dinner for a few friends and don't leave quite enough time to get your house cleaned and everything prepared before they arrive. You might do better ordering out.

Stress inoculation? Why is this Marine Corps drill instructor screaming at this poor recruit? The logic behind this time-honored training technique is that intense stressors experienced during basic training will build mental strength and resilience and make individuals more effective in actual combat.

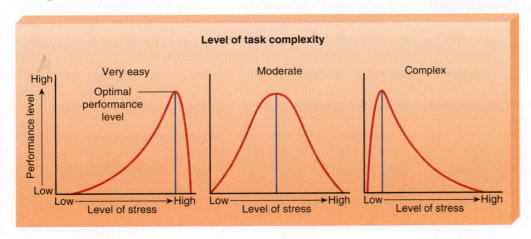

FIGURE 15-7 **Stress and performance** Stress can actually benefit performance, depending on the complexity of the task. On very complex tasks, a low level of stress is optimal for performing your best; on very easy tasks, a high stress level helps you stay focused.

Before You Go On

What Do You Know?

14. How has stress been linked with coronary heart disease?
15. What is the connection between life changes and illness?
16. How does stress affect the immune system?
17. What factors influence whether stress will have this effect?
18. What are some beneficial effects of stress?

What Do You Think?
Try to recall five events in your life or in the lives of your family members and friends that suggest a relationship between stress and illness. Having now read this chapter, how might you account for those events and relationships?

Posttraumatic Stress Disorder When Things Go

LEARNING OBJECTIVE 5 Describe the symptoms and causes of posttraumatic stress disorder, and discuss some risk factors for developing it.

As we have seen, stress, when moderate and handled constructively, can serve us well. But it can also work against us. In addition to leading to physical diseases, it can contribute to various psychological disorders, from depression to sexual dysfunctions. Moreover, it plays a central role in *posttraumatic stress disorder*, or *PTSD*, mentioned earlier in the chapter.

Symptoms of PTSD

In posttraumatic stress disorder, persons who have confronted an extraordinarily stressful event—combat, rape, earthquake, airplane crash, automobile accident—experience a number of severe psychological symptoms lasting for months or even years. (Keane, Marx, & Sloan, 2009). They have lingering reactions of intense fear and helplessness. They may be battered by memories, dreams, or nightmares connected to the traumatic event and may repeatedly try to avoid activities, thoughts, feelings, or conversations that remind them of the event. Many also feel detached from other people, some lose interest in activities that once brought enjoyment, and some feel dazed. A number of individuals with the disorder are easily startled, develop sleep problems, and have trouble concentrating. They may also feel extreme guilt because they survived the traumatic event while others did not. Here a Vietnam combat veteran describes some of these symptoms years after he returned home:

A new battle These combat veterans are trying to overcome their posttraumatic stress disorders by participating in group therapy sessions at a Veterans Administration treatment program in California.

I can't get the memories out of my mind! The images come flooding back in vivid detail, triggered by the most inconsequential things, like a door slamming or the smell of stir-fried pork. Last night I went to bed, was having a good sleep for a change. Then in the early morning a storm-front passed through and there was a bolt of crackling thunder. I awoke instantly, frozen in fear. I am right back in Vietnam, in the middle of the monsoon season at my guard post. I am sure I'll get hit in the next volley and convinced I will die. My hands are freezing, yet sweat pours from my entire body. I feel each hair on the back of my neck standing on end. I can't catch my breath and my heart is pounding. I smell a damp sulfur smell.

(Davis, 1992)

What Events Cause PTSD?

While any traumatic event can trigger PTSD, certain events are particularly likely to do so. Among the most common are combat, natural disasters, and abuse and victimization (Keane et al., 2009). People who are victims of terrorism, for example, or who live with a fear of terrorism, often experience posttraumatic stress symptoms (Tramontin & Halpern, 2007). Most of us will forever remember the events of September 11, 2001, when hijacked airplanes crashed into the World Trade Center in New York City and damaged the Pentagon in Washington, D.C. One effect of these terrorists attacks is a lingering psychological effect that they have had on the people who were directly affected and their family members, as well as on millions of others who watched images of the disasters on their television sets throughout that day. Numerous studies indicate that posttraumatic stress reactions were common in the days, months, and years following the attacks, and that these symptoms have, in many cases, continued to the present day (Marshall et al., 2007; Schlenger et al., 2002).

Who Develops PTSD?

Almost 4 percent of people in the United States experience posttraumatic stress disorder in any given year—8 percent experience it during their lifetimes (Burijon, 2007; Kessler et al., 2005). The disorder can occur at any age, even in childhood (Balaban, 2009). Women are at least twice as likely as men to develop PTSD (Koch & Haring, 2008).

Although anyone who experiences an unusual trauma will be affected by it, only some people develop posttraumatic stress disorder (McNally, 2001). To understand the development of this disorder more fully, researchers have looked at the same stress-related factors that we have come across throughout this chapter—and they have come up with promising leads.

Is anyone immune? Most people who experience extraordinary traumatic events are capable of developing PTSD. Even rescue workers at the site of disasters often develop the disorder. Nevertheless, all things being equal, some people seem particularly prone to PTSD in the aftermath of traumatic events.

Biological Factors   As we have observed, stressors trigger biochemical reactions throughout the brain and body. Apparently, in the face of extraordinarily threatening stressors, some people develop particularly strong biochemical reactions—reactions that continue well beyond a short-term fight-or-flight period. It appears that such individuals are more likely than others to experience a posttraumatic stress disorder (Yehuda, 2009; Kellner & Yehuda, 1999). Consistent with this notion, researchers have found abnormal activity of the stress hormone cortisol and the neurotransmitter norepinephrine in the urine and blood of combat soldiers, rape victims, concentration camp survivors, and survivors of other traumatic events (Burijon, 2007; Delahanty et al., 2005). Indeed, some studies suggest that people who develop PTSD have exaggerated sympathetic nervous system responses and blunted HPA axis responses to stress (Yehuda, 2001; Yehuda et al., 1998). There is also some evidence that once a posttraumatic stress disorder sets in, the individual's continuing biochemical arousal may eventually shrink the hippocampus, one of the brain

Detecting PTSD in children The Sesame Street Muppet Rosita tells children in New York about "You Can Ask," a program that seeks to identify and deal with stress in children. The program was first formed in the aftermath of the September 11, 2001 terrorist attacks.

areas that helps control the body's stress hormones, thus further locking in the disorder (Carlson, 2008; Mirzaei et al., 2005). At the same time, it is worth noting that, according to some research, people who are more susceptible to developing PTSD may have a smaller hippocampus to begin with (Gilbertson et al., 2002).

Personality, Childhood Experiences, and Social Support   Earlier, we observed that people with certain personality styles or coping styles are particularly likely to react to threats with stress and to develop medical problems. Similarly, such styles increase the likelihood of developing a posttraumatic stress disorder (Burijon, 2007; Chung et al., 2005). It turns out, for example, that rape victims who had psychological problems or difficult life situations before their sexual assault are more likely than other such victims to develop PTSD (Darvres-Bornoz et al., 1995). So too are war veterans who had psychological problems before they went into combat (Dikel et al., 2005). In addition, people who typically view life's negative events as beyond their control are more likely than others to develop posttraumatic stress symptoms after criminal assaults (Taylor, 2006; Regehr et al., 1999). People with less resilient, or less hardy, personality styles appear more likely to develop a posttraumatic stress disorder than those with more resilient styles (Maddi, 2007; Bartone, 2003).

Studies have also suggested that certain childhood experiences increase the risk of later posttraumatic stress disorders (Alter & Hen, 2009; Rapee & Bryant, 2009). People whose childhoods have been characterized by poverty appear more likely to develop this disorder when later confronting horrific events. So are people whose parents displayed psychological disorders and who experienced assault, abuse, or catastrophe at a young age (Koch & Haring, 2008; Ozer et al., 2003).

Finally, the social environment may influence whether victims of traumatic events develop posttraumatic stress disorders. Earlier, we saw that inadequate social support can intensify stress reactions and slow down immune system functioning. Thus, it is not surprising that people with weak social support systems are also more likely to develop a posttraumatic stress disorder after a traumatic event (Charuvastra & Cloitre, 2008; Ozer et al., 2003) For example, rape victims who feel loved, cared for, and accepted by their friends and relatives tend to recover more successfully. So do those treated with dignity by the criminal justice system (Murphy, 2001; Sales et al., 1984).

Before You Go On

What Do You Know?

19. What are some symptoms of posttraumatic stress disorder?

20. What factors put a person at heightened risk for developing posttraumatic stress disorder following a traumatic event?

What Do You Think?   One form of therapy for combat veterans suffering from posttraumatic stress disorder is getting together regularly in groups to discuss their experiences. What might be the benefits of this type of therapy?

Summary

What Is Stress?

LEARNING OBJECTIVE 1 Define stress and describe the ways in which people experience stress and the kinds of situations that typically cause stress.

- *Stress* is a state brought on by any situation that threatens or appears to threaten a person's sense of well-being, thus challenging the person's ability to cope. A situation that triggers the stress response is a *stressor*. A stressor may be *acute* (short term) or *chronic* (long term).
- People may experience stress as frustration, pressure, conflict, or danger.
- Kinds of stressors include daily hassles, life changes (which can be measured by use of the Social Readjustment Rating Scale), traumatic events, chronic negative situations, and special sociocultural conditions.

Responding to Stress

LEARNING OBJECTIVE 2 Describe the physiological, emotional, and cognitive responses to stress, and explain how individual responses to stress differ.

- There are two main physiological pathways of stress—the sympathetic nervous system and the hypothalamic-pituitary-adrenal axis. Both lead to activation of the fight-or-flight response, which is an immediate response to a stressor.
- Hans Selye first described the effects of chronic stress, which he called the general adaptation syndrome (GAS). The syndrome has three stages: alarm, resistance, and exhaustion.
- Emotional responses to stress generally involve negative emotions. The more stress a person experiences, the more negative the emotions.
- Cognitive appraisal is an important element in responses to stress. Richard Lazarus identified two steps in this process: *primary appraisal*, in which people assess the severity of the stressor, and *secondary appraisal*, in which they evaluate how well they can cope with it.
- Individuals vary greatly in their responses to stress. Areas of difference include autonomic activity, explanatory style, personality, and availability of social support.

Coping with Stress

LEARNING OBJECTIVE 3 Discuss and evaluate several ways in which people cope with stress.

- *Coping* describes efforts to manage, reduce, or tolerate stress.
- Dealing with stress by lashing out at others, using defense mechanisms such as repression, and engaging in self-indulgent behaviors such as smoking or drinking alcohol, can be destructive when used in excess.
- More constructive coping strategies include directly confronting a stressor in hopes of changing the situation (*problem-focused coping*) and changing how you feel or think about the stressor to reduce its impact (*emotion-focused coping*).

Stress and Health

LEARNING OBJECTIVE 4 Explain how stress can cause physical illness, and discuss situations in which stress may be beneficial.

- Stress can increase risk for a number of health problems. People with *Type A* personalities are prone to stress and appear to be at greater risk for coronary heart disease than the more relaxed *Type B* personalities. Using the Social Readjustment Rating Scale, researchers have found that stress-producing life changes also increase the risk of illness.
- *Psychoimmunology* is an area of study that examines the links between stress, the immune system, and health.
- Severe stress may interfere with the activity of *lymphocytes*, a component of the immune system that helps the body to overcome invaders, such as bacteria and viruses.
- Stress-related biochemical changes in the body, such as changes in the activity of norepinephrine and cortisol, can eventually slow the functioning of the immune system.
- Behavior, personality, and social support are additional factors affecting how much the immune system is slowed down by stress.
- Unlike *distress*, or negative stress, *eustress* offers benefits. Optimal levels of stress can promote the development of resilience and facilitate performance, especially for easy or moderately difficult tasks.

Posttraumatic Stress Disorder

LEARNING OBJECTIVE 5 Describe the symptoms and causes of posttraumatic stress disorder, and discuss some risk factors for developing it.

- Posttraumatic stress disorder is characterized by persistent, frightening thoughts or memories of a traumatic event, along with anxiety, depression, and other symptoms.
- Combat, natural disasters, and abuse and victimization are among the events most likely to cause posttraumatic stress disorder.
- Not everyone affected by unusual trauma develops posttraumatic stress disorder. Factors that affect the likelihood of developing the disorder include biological factors, personality factors, childhood experiences, and the availability of social support.

Key Terms

CUT/ACROSS CONNECTION

What Happens in the BRAIN?

- In the face of danger or stress, the brain and body respond with a fight-or-flight response, particularly among males.
- The brain reacts to danger or stress by both activating the sympathetic nervous system and setting in motion the HPA axis.
- The brains and bodies of stressed people may progress through three stages: alarm, resistance, and, if the danger continues too long, exhaustion.
- The release of norepinephrine and stress hormones can be helpful and protective when people experience short-term stress, but physically debilitating when people experience high, longer-term stress

When Things Go Wrong

- People with high levels of hostility and certain other Type A personality characteristics are at greater risk for coronary heart disease.
- Significant life changes occurring over a limited period of time may contribute to a slowdown in immune system functioning and the onset of various medical problems.
- In any given year almost 4 percent of people in the United States experience PTSD. Around 8 percent experience this disorder at some point in their lives.
- People with generally abnormal stress hormone and norepinephrine reactions, weak social supports, or a general sense of helplessness in life appear more likely than other people to develop PTSD in the face of an extraordinary and traumatic event.

HOW we Differ

- The brains and bodies of women may react to danger or stress with a "tend-and-befriend" response rather than a "fight-or-flight" response.
- People with highly reactive ANSs, pessimistic explanatory styles, Type A personality styles, or weak social supports display, on average, more intense stress reactions than other people.
- Optimists are more likely than pessimists to seek out social support during stressful events and to employ constructive coping techniques.
- Optimists, constructive copers, and resilient people tend to experience better immune system functioning and better health than other people.

How we Develop

- As children move from 5 years old to 12 years old, physical events (e.g., getting sick) feel less stressful to them while behavioral events (e.g., getting into trouble) and psychosocial events (e.g., fighting with friends) arouse more stress.
- The leading stressors for school-aged children include taking tests, having excessive homework, being bullied or made fun of, feeling left out, getting in trouble, and fighting with family members or friends.
- The leading stressors for college students include having to take multiple tests, enduring finals week, applying to graduate school, being a crime victim, having multiple assignments due the same day, and breaking up with a boyfriend or girlfriend.
- Children who live in poverty or who experience assault, abuse, or catastrophe have an increased vulnerability to developing PTSD as adults.

Video Lab Exercise

Psychology Around Us

Reacting to and Dealing With Stress

Stressing Out

It's hard to fully identify our reactions during a stressful event or to identify our coping mechanisms. We are, after all, too busy feeling stressed and dealing with stressors at hand. In this video lab exercise, however, your involvement with stress will be "virtual," allowing you just enough psychological space to observe your reactions and coping mechanisms at the same time that you are experiencing stress.

While observing various stressful situations and placing yourself firmly in those situations, you'll be required to identify the features of your stress reaction. You'll also be guided down a decision tree during which you will decide how you would deal and cope with the pressures and frustrations you are confronting. While doing all this, you'll compare your reactions and coping mechanisms to those of other people and categorize them using the terms laid out in the chapter. Along the way, you'll learn a lot about your personal ways of feeling and coping with stress, and the merits or drawbacks of your approach.

As you are working on this on-line exercise, consider the following questions:

- What kind of stressors do people confront and what are the components of stress?
- Why do certain situations feel more stressful than others, and why do some people feel more stressed than others by a given situation?
- What's going on in the brain and body as we confront stressors?
- What are the various ways in which people try to manage, reduce, or tolerate stress? Do those approaches work?

CHAPTER 16

Psychological Disorders and Their Treatments

Chapter Outline

- Defining, Classifying, and Diagnosing Psychological Abnormality
- Models of Psychological Abnormality • The Neuroscience Model
- The Psychodynamic Model • The Behavioral Model
- The Cognitive Model • The Humanistic-Existential Model
- Formats of Therapy • Does Therapy Work?
- Abnormal Psychology: Social and Cultural Forces • Some Final Thoughts on Psychology

Depressed and Lost

Diane Markos, a 38-year-old single female, was referred [to a new therapist] for depression. Within a period of three months, she had lost 15 pounds, and she felt tired all the time. She had withdrawn herself from nearly all her usual social activities, and she openly acknowledged thoughts of overdosing on pills. Previous psychotherapy and treatment with antidepressant medication had produced no improvement.

This change occurred shortly after the breakup of a relationship she had been having with a man for approximately two years. She now saw herself as fat . . . , unattractive, and doomed to be a spinster. Although she had never had a wide circle of friends, the past two years had seen her social contacts become even more limited. Other than the few evenings that she spent with her boyfriend, she had gradually managed to work herself into a life of all work and no play, and she was intensely lonely.

Diane lived alone and worked full-time as a pediatric nurse while pursuing a master's degree in nursing part time. Although she was a straight-A student, she had had numer-

ous interpersonal difficulties with fellow students and instructors. Her relations with coworkers were similarly troubled. Although she had a reputation as a good staff nurse, she had never been able to hold supervisory positions for any length of time without interpersonal conflicts.

Diane's early family history provided some clues to the sources of her current difficulties. She was the eldest of three children and was frequently expected to play the role of caretaker for her younger siblings. She felt that her parents' love was contingent on her playing the role of "mother's little helper." She felt that her sister and brother had been allowed to lead a much more carefree childhood.

In short, Diane saw her past and present as an unhappy life of servitude, rejection, and failure. And she could envision no other scenario for her future. She felt quite hopeless, and was therefore considered to be a serious suicidal risk by her new therapist (Spitzer et al., 1983).

Throughout this book we have examined the nature of behavior and mental functioning, from sensations to memory to personality. Most of our discussions have looked at "normal" functioning. Indeed, our mental life and behavior are fascinating and complex even when they proceed without going astray. However, as we have repeatedly observed throughout the book, functioning often does go astray. We are immediately reminded of this as we read about Diane Markos. Most of us would agree that her depressed mood, isolated behavior, and negative thinking are far from constructive or functional.

We have already come across the leading psychological disorders while reading the *When Things Go Wrong* sections throughout this book. In Chapter 3: Human Development, we saw how children and adolescents with *conduct disorder* display excessive aggression. In Chapter 4: Neuroscience, we learned how profoundly lives are affected by neurological disorders such as *Parkinson's disease, Huntington's disease,* and *multiple sclerosis.* In Chapter 5: Sensation and Perception, we observed how difficult it is to live with various kinds of *pain disorders.* We considered the discomforts of *sleep disorders* and the perils of *substance abuse and dependence* in Chapter 6: Consciousness and the impact of *ADHD* and *learning disorders* in Chapter 7: Learning. We examined the the heartbreak of *Alzheimer's disease* and the mysteries of *dissociative disorders* in Chapter 8: Memory and the disruptions caused by *schizophrenia* in Chapter 9: Language and Thought. We observed the difficulties posed by *moderate, severe,* and *profound mental retardation* in Chapter 10: Intelligence, by *eating disorders* and *sexual disorders* in Chapter 11: Motivation, and by *anxiety disorders* and *mood disorders* in Chapter 12: Emotion. And, finally, we learned about the significant life disruptions brought on by *personality disorders* in Chapter 13: Personality, by social fears and autism in Chapter 14: Social Psychology, and by *posttraumatic stress disorder* in Chapter 15: Stress, Coping, and Health.

In this chapter, we'll be looking further at the topic of abnormal psychological functioning. First, we'll see that although most people believe they know abnormal functioning when they see it, it is, in fact, a difficult concept to define. Next, we'll explore the various ways in which psychologists identify, distinguish, and explain the various kinds of abnormal functioning. Similarly, we'll examine how mental health practitioners try to help the individuals whose behaviors, thoughts, or emotions are dysfunctional—individuals known as *clients* or *patients* when seen in mental health settings. And, finally, we'll consider how social and cultural forces may contribute to the onset and nature of abnormal functioning.

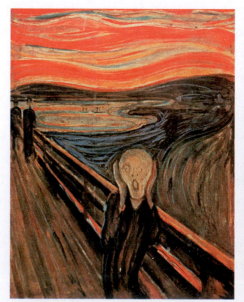

Art and psychological disorders Many of our greatest paintings focus on psychological dysfunction. Two of the most famous are *The Scream*, by Edvard Munch, which brings symptoms of anxiety and panic to life, and *Portrait of Dr. Gachet*, by Vincent van Gogh, about depression.

Edvard Munch, "The Scream"/Burstein Collection/©Corbis/©2009 The Munch Museum/The Munch-Elligsen Group /Artists Rights Society (ARS), NY

Defining, Classifying, and Diagnosing Psychological Abnormality

abnormal psychology the scientific study of psychological disorders.

LEARNING OBJECTIVE 1 List the common features of most definitions of abnormal functioning and describe how psychological disorders are classified and diagnosed.

Diane Markos's emotions, behaviors, and thoughts appear to be abnormal, the result of a state sometimes called *psychological dysfunction, psychopathology,* or *mental illness.* The field devoted to the scientific study of psychological disorders is usually called **abnormal psychology**. As in the other areas of psychology, researchers in this field, called *clinical researchers,* gather information systematically so that they may describe, explain, and predict the phenomena they study. The knowledge that they acquire is then used by *clinical practitioners,* or *clinicians,* whose role is to detect, assess, and treat abnormal patterns of functioning.

Abnormal psychological functioning is a pervasive problem in this country, as indicated in **Figure 16-1**. It has been estimated that in a given year as many as 30 percent of the adults and 20 percent of the children and adolescents in the United States experience serious psychological disturbances and are in need of clinical treatment (Kessler et al., 2007, 2005, 1994; Kazdin, 2003, 2000). The numbers and rates in other countries are similar. Furthermore, many people go through periods of great tension, upset, or other forms of psychological discomfort in their lives, and at such times experience at least some of the distress found in psychological disorders. Although the special pressures of modern life may contribute to psychological dysfunctioning, they are not its main cause. Records demonstrate that every society over the course of history has witnessed psychological abnormality.

Although many definitions of abnormality have been proposed over the years, none is universally accepted (Boysen, 2007). Nevertheless, most of the definitions have key features in common, often called "the four *D*s": deviance, distress, dysfunction, and danger:

- *Deviance* Behavior, thoughts, and emotions are considered abnormal when they differ from a society's ideas about proper functioning. Judgments of deviance and abnormality vary from society to society. A society that values competition and dominance may embrace aggressive behavior, whereas one that emphasizes cooperation may consider such behavior unacceptable and even abnormal. Moreover, a society's values may change over time, leading to a new societal view of what is psychologically abnormal. For example, a woman's participation in athletics, academia, or business was considered

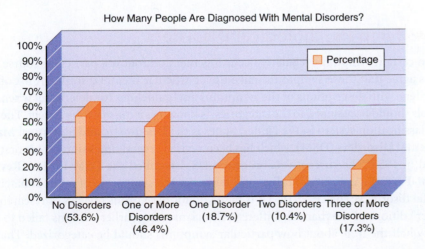

FIGURE 16-1 How many people are diagnosed with mental disorders? Nearly half the people in the United States each year experience symptoms that qualify for a diagnosis of at least one mental disorder.

Does dysfunction equal abnormality? A Tibetan man sets himself on fire to protest China's occupation of Tibet. In this context, such personal dysfunctioning does not, by itself, indicate that he is experiencing a psychological disorder.

highly unusual and inappropriate a hundred years ago. Today that behavior is valued.

- *Distress* According to many clinical theorists, behaviors, ideas, or emotions usually must also cause distress or unhappiness before they can be considered abnormal. Diane Markos feels upset and burdened most of the time by her deviant feelings and thoughts and the impact they are having on her life.

- *Dysfunction* Abnormal behavior also tends to interfere with daily functioning. It upsets people so that they cannot take proper care of themselves, interact well with others, or work effectively. As we saw in the opening case, Diane's behaviors have contributed to social isolation, problems at work, and conflicts at school. At the same time, dysfunction alone does not necessarily indicate psychological abnormality. Certain individuals, such as Gandhi or the Dalai Lama, may fast or deprive themselves in other ways of things they need as a protest against social injustice. Rather than receiving a clinical label, they are usually viewed as people to be admired.

- *Danger* Some people with psychological dysfunctioning become dangerous to themselves or others. If, for example, individuals are consistently hostile or confused, they may put themselves, family members, or friends at risk. Recall that Diane Markos's thoughts of overdosing on pills have led her therapist to consider her a serious suicide risk. It is important to note, however, that although danger is often cited as a feature of abnormal psychological functioning, research indicates that it is actually the exception rather than the rule (Freedman et al., 2007). Despite popular views, most people who are greatly troubled or even out of touch with reality pose no immediate danger to themselves or anyone else.

As our discussion suggests, the definition of abnormality depends heavily on social norms and values. In fact, each society chooses general criteria for defining abnormality and then uses those criteria to assess particular cases. At the same time, a society may have difficulty distinguishing between an abnormality that requires help and an eccentricity that should not be the concern of other people. We often see or hear about people who behave in ways we consider strange, such as an individual who lives alone with dozens of animals and avoids interacting with other people. The behavior of such individuals is clearly deviant, and it may lead to distress and dysfunction, yet many clinicians would judge it to be eccentric rather than abnormal.

Given the difficulties that we have just been discussing, how do psychologists determine which experiences constitute or do not constitute a psychological disorder, and how do they distinguish among various disorders? In large part, they rely upon *classification* and *diagnosis*.

Classifying Psychological Disorders

When certain symptoms regularly occur together and follow a particular course, clinicians agree that those symptoms make up a particular mental disorder. A list of such disorders, with descriptions of the symptoms and guidelines for determing when individuals should be assigned to the categories, is known as a *classification system*. The leading classification system in the United States is the **Diagnostic and Statistical Manual of Mental Disorders (DSM)**, which has been revised several times since it was first published in 1952. The current version of the DSM is called the **DSM-IV Text Revision (DSM-IV-TR)** (APA, 2000). It lists and describes the symptoms of approximately 400 mental disorders. The DSM-IV-TR is based on more rigorous reviews of research than earlier editions of the manual. Different clinicians using earlier editions failed to agree nearly half the time about how particular symptoms should be categorized. That rate

Made for each other A bride with real scorpions on her gown kisses her groom, who has a real centipede in his mouth. She holds the world record for staying in a cage with 3,400 scorpions for 32 days, he for staying with 1,000 centipedes for 28 days. Eccentric? Yes. Mentally disordered? Probably not.

has been greatly, although far from completely, reduced among users of the current version of the DSM (Keenan et al., 2007; Lyneham et al., 2007).

When clinicians decide that a person's symptoms fit the criteria for a particular disorder, they are making a **diagnosis**. Many clinicians use the the DSM-IV-TR to help them diagnose their clients' problems. Assigning a diagnosis suggests that the client's pattern of dysfunction is basically the same as patterns displayed by many other people, has been observed and researched in numerous studies, and has responded to certain kinds of treatment. Clinicians can then apply what is generally known about the disorder to the client with whom they are working (Compas & Gotlib, 2002). The current version of the DSM makes it easier for clinicians to make such assumptions than earlier versions did, although certainly not all diagnoses lead to predictable patterns among individuals (Dosen, 2005; Faravelli et al., 2005). We shall discuss some of the risks of diagnosis for clients in the box, "Can Assessment and Diagnosis Cause Harm?"

DSM-IV-TR actually consists of two lists of clinical disorders. One list, called *Axis I*, is a long list of *syndromes*, or clusters of symptoms, that typically cause marked impairment (see **Table 16-1**). Some of the most frequently diagnosed disorders listed on Axis I are the anxiety disorders and mood disorders. The other list in DSM-IV-TR, called *Axis II*, is a short list of long-standing problems that frequently limit or make life difficult for persons There are only two groups of Axis II disorders: *mental retardation* and *personality disorders*. Although people with psychological problems usually fit a category from either Axis I or Axis II, they may meet criteria for disorders from both axes and may receive a diagnosis from each axis.

Diagnostic and Statistical Manual of Mental Disorders (DSM) leading classification system for psychological disorders in the United States.

DSM-IV-TR the current version of the DSM.

diagnosis a clinician's determination that a person's cluster of symptoms represents a particular disorder.

PRACTICALLYSPEAKING   Can Assessment and Diagnosis Cause Harm?

Power of labeling In 2005 mental health groups protested and successfully halted the production of "Crazy for You" bears, a new line of Vermont Teddy Bears. Their concern was that such derogatory labels contribute to negative stereotypes and the stigmatization of people with psychological problems.

Although mental health terms such as anxiety, depression, and schizophrenia are as common as can be in the media, public discourse, and even daily conversations, it turns out that accurate diagnoses of these and other psychological disorders are often elusive in the clinical field. It appears that even with effective assessment techniques and carefully researched classification categories, clinicians sometimes arrive at a wrong conclusion or diagnosis (Rohrer, 2005).

Indeed, studies have sometimes revealed enormous errors in assessment and diagnosis, particularly in hospitals (Caetano & Babor, 2007; Chen et al., 1996). In one study, skilled clinicians were asked to reevaluate the diagnoses of 131 patients at a mental hospital in New York (Lipton & Simon, 1985). Whereas 89 of the patients had originally received a diagnosis of schizophrenia when they were hospitalized, only 16 received it upon reevaluation. And while 15 patients initially had been given a diagnosis of mood disorder, 50 received that label on reevaluation.

Beyond the possibility of misdiagnosis, the sheer act of classifying people can lead to unfortunate results. Diagnostic labels can, for example, become self-fulfilling prophecies. When people are diagnosed as having a mental disorder, others may view and react to them in ways that actually make them act more "sick" or disturbed. Furthermore, our society attaches a stigma, or negative prejudice, to abnormality (Spagnolo et al., 2008; Corrigan, 2007). People with such labels may find it hard to get a job, particularly one with a high level of responsibility, or to be accepted socially. In short, such labels may stick for a long time.

Given these problems, some clinicians have argued for doing away with assessment and diagnosis (Gurman & Messer, 2003). Others, however, believe that classification and diagnosis are essential to understanding and treating people with psychological difficulties. They suggest that we must simply work to increase what is known about psychological disorders and improve assessment and diagnostic techniques (Cunningham, 2000).

TABLE 16-1 Disorders in DSM-IV-TR

Category	Description	Disorders Included in This Category	For More Information in This Text, Refer to These Chapters
Disorders usually first diagnosed in infancy, childhood, and adolescence	Disorders in this group tend to emerge and sometimes dissipate before adult life.	• Pervasive developmental disorders, such as autism and Asperger's disorder • Learning disorders • Attention-deficit hyperactivity disorder • Conduct disorder • Separation anxiety disorder.	3, 4, 7, 14
Delirium, dementia, amnesic, and other cognitive disorders	These disorders are dominated by impairment in cognitive functioning.	• Alzheimer's disease • Huntington's disease	4, 8
Mental disorders due to a general medical condition	These mental disorders are caused primarily by a general medical disorder.	• Mood disorder due to a general medical condition	4, 5
Substance-related disorders	These disorders are brought about by the use of substances that affect the central nervous system.	• Alcohol use disorders • Opioid use disorders • Amphetamine use disorders • Cocaine use disorders • Hallucinogen use disorders	6
Schizophrenia and other psychotic disorders	In this group of disorders, functioning deteriorates until the individual reaches a state of psychosis, or loss of contact with reality.	• Schizophrenia	9
Mood disorders	Disorders in this group are marked by severe disturbances of mood that cause people to feel extremely and inappropriately sad or elated for extended periods of time.	• Major depressive disorder • Bipolar disorders	12
Anxiety disorders	Anxiety is the predominant disturbance in this group of disorders.	• Generalized anxiety disorder • Phobias • Panic disorder • Obsessive-compulsive disorder • Acute stress disorder • Posttraumatic stress disorder	7, 9, 12, 14, 15
Somatoform disorders	These disorders are marked by physical symptoms that apparently are caused primarily by psychological rather than physiological factors.	• Conversion disorder • Somatization disorder • Hypochondriasis	5, 15
Dissociative disorders	These disorders are characterized by significant changes in consciousness, memory, identity, or perception, without a clear physical cause.	• Dissociative amnesia • Dissociative fugue • Dissociative identity disorder (multiple personality disorder)	8

TABLE 16-1 Disorders in DSM-IV-TR (Continued)

Category	Description	Disorders Included in This Category	For More Information in This Text, Refer to These Chapters
Eating disorders	People with these disorders display abnormal patterns of eating that significantly impair their functioning.	• Anorexia nervosa • Bulimia nervosa	11
Sexual disorders and gender identity disorder	These are disorders in sexual function, behavior, or preferences.	• Sexual dysfunctions • Paraphilias • Gender identity disorder	11
Sleep disorders	People with these disorders display chronic sleep problems.	• Primary insomnia • Primary hypersomnia • Sleep-terror disorder • Sleepwalking disorder	6
Impulse-control disorders	People with these disorders are chronically unable to resist impulses, drives, or temptations to perform certain acts that are harmful to themselves or to others.	• Pathological gambling • Kleptomania • Pyromania • Intermittent explosive disorder	9, 12
Psychological factors affecting medical condition	These disorders, also called psychophysiological disorders, result from an interaction of psychological and biological factors.	• Ulcer • Asthma • Hypertension • Coronary heart disease	5, 15
Personality disorders	People with these disorders display pervasive, inflexible, enduring, and deviant personality traits and behaviors.	• Paranoid, schizoid, schizotypal, antisocial, borderline, histrionic, narcissistic, avoidant, dependent, and obsessive-compulsive personality disorders	13, 14
Mental retardation	This disorder is marked by general intellectual functioning that is significantly below average and significant limitations in adaptive functioning, or day-to-day living.		10

Based on her pattern of symptoms, Diane Markos would probably receive a diagnosis of a mood disorder from Axis I: *major depressive disorder*. A clinician might also make note of the fact that Diane avoided social activities and relationships. If the clinician judged that Diane had in fact spent a lifetime avoiding other people, largely because she feared they might judge her or criticize her, the clinician might further assign her an Axis II diagnosis of *avoidant personality disorder*. When people qualify for two or more diagnoses, they are said to display **comorbidity**. Such multiple diagnoses may come from the two different axes, as in Diane's case, or they may come from the same axis. A person may, for example, receive Axis I diagnoses of major depression *and* panic disorder (one of the anxiety disorders).

comorbidity condition in which a person's symptoms qualify him or her for two or more diagnoses.

clinical interview assessment technique involving a face-to-face encounter between the clinician and the person being assessed.

analog observation observation in an artificial setting, such as a clinical office or a laboratory.

naturalistic observation observation of individuals in everyday settings.

self-monitoring when individuals monitor their own symptoms.

Diagnosing Psychological Disorders

In order to determine that a client displays certain symptoms and qualifies for a particular DSM-IV-TR diagnosis, clinicians must *assess* the individual. Clinical assessment is used to determine precisely how and why a person is behaving abnormally and how that person may be helped. The hundreds of clinical assessment techniques and tools that have been developed fall into three categories: *clinical interviews, observations,* and *tests*.

Clinical Interviews   Most of us believe that an ideal way to get to know people is to meet with them face-to-face. Similarly, a **clinical interview** is a face-to-face encounter (Sommers-Flanagan & Sommers-Flanagan, 2007, 2003). Unsurprisingly, just about every practitioner begins with an interview as the key part of the assessment process.

Interviews can be either unstructured or structured or a combination of the two (O'Brien & Tabaczynski, 2007; Rabinowitz et al., 2007). In an *unstructured* clinical interview, the clinician asks open-ended questions such as as "What brings you here today?" or "Would you tell me about yourself?" The lack of structure allows the interviewer to follow leads and pursue key topics that could not be anticipated beforehand. In a *structured* clinical interview, clinicians ask carefully prepared questions. Sometimes they use a published *interview schedule*, a standard set of questions targetted for all interviews. A structured format helps guarantee that clinicians will gather the same kinds of useful information in all their interviews (Grant et al., 2004).

Although interviews often yield valuable information, this assessment technique has key limitations (Hersen & Thomas, 2007). Clients may intentionally mislead interviewers in order to present themselves in a positive light or to avoid discussing unflattering events, especially considering that the interview is often the first time the individual has laid eyes on the clinican. Often, people may be unable to give an accurate report in their interview simply because of their problems. Individuals who suffer from depression, for example, view themselves very negatively and may describe themselves as poor students or inadequate parents when that is far from accurate. During her interview with her new therapist, for example, Diane inaccurately described herself as overweight, unattractive, unintelligent, and ineffective.

Interviewers also make mistakes in judgment that can influence the information they gather. Their biases, including race, gender, and age biases, may also affect their interpretations of what a client is saying (Ungar et al., 2006; McFarland et al., 2004). An interviewer might also fail to ask relevant questions as part of the interview or might be prone to make certain diagnoses due to bias.

Clinical interviewing In this part of his initial meeting with a child, a clinician conducts an unstructured interview.

The interaction between client and clinician can also affect information gathered in interviews (Wood et al., 2002). People respond to various interviewers in different ways, giving less information to a cold interviewer, for example, than to a warm and supportive interviewer (Quas et al, 2007). Similarly, a clinician's race, sex, age, and appearance may alter a client's responses (Springman et al., 2006).

Clinical Observations   Another strategy in the assessment of abnormal functioning is the systematic observation of behavior. In one technique, **analog observation**, clinicians observe clients in an artificial setting, such as a therapy office or laboratory. In another, called **naturalistic observation**, practitioners observe the clients in their everyday environments. Finally, in **self-monitoring**, clients observe themselves.

Just about every assessment involves at least some simple version of analog observations. After all, during the initial interview, the clinician attends to the person's various behaviors to see how they confirm or affect the data the client is reporting.

However, analog observations can also be much more involved, and they are often aided by special equipment, such as a video recorder or one-way mirror (Haynes, 2001). Analog observations may center on children and parents interacting, married couples trying to settle a disagreement, or fearful people trying to approach an object they find frightening.

Naturalistic clinical observations usually take place in homes, schools, institutions such as hospitals and prisons, or community settings. In most cases they center on parent-child, sibling-child, or teacher-child interactions and on fearful, aggressive, or disruptive behavior (Murdock et al., 2005). These observations may be made by *participant observers,* people in the client's environment who report what they observe to the clinician. Although these observations can be helpful, they are used less often than analog observations because they can be difficult or impractical to manage.

Although important information can be learned from actually seeing behavior, clinical observations have key limitations (Connor-Greene, 2007). Clinicians may, for example, make errors in their observations. Alternatively, a client's behavior may be affected by the very presence of the observer (Kamphaus & Frick, 2002). If students in a classroom become aware that someone special is watching them, they may alter their usual behavior, trying, for example, to create a good impression.

In self-monitoring, people observe themselves and record the frequency of certain behaviors, feelings, or thoughts as they are occuring (Wright & Truax, 2008). How often, for instance, does a man have an urge to drink alcoholic beverages or an anxious person have worrisome thoughts? What circumstances bring those feelings about? Although useful in many ways, self-monitoring also has certain limitations. When people monitor themselves, they often change their behaviors unintentionally (Otten, 2004). Smokers, for example, often cut down on the number of cigarettes they smoke when they are monitoring themselves.

Clinical Tests   **Clinical tests** are tools for gathering information about certain aspects of a person's mental functioning, from which broader conclusions about the person can be drawn (Gregory, 2004). More than 500 clinical tests are currently in use throughout the United States.

Although all of today's clinicians use interviews and at least informal kinds of observation to help assess and diagnose clients, most do not typically conduct formal testing. On a number of occassions, however, a client's pathology is severe, the case proves complicated, or the person's symptoms do not readily fit into one of the available diagnostic categories. In such cases, the clinician may indeed administer clinical tests or refer the client to a testing expert. The tests that are most commonly used in the clinical arena are ones that we have already examined throughout this textbook, including projective tests and personality inventories (Chapter 13: Personality), intelligence tests (Chapter 10: Intelligence), and neuroimaging tests, or brain scans (Chapter 4: Neuroscience).

In addition, clinical testing may include a *response inventory*, a test or questionnaire that measures just *one* specific area of functioning, such as emotions or social skills (Osman et al., 2008). Given her difficulties, Diane's therapist might decide to administer to her the *Beck Depression Inventory,* a widely used affective (emotion-focused) response inventory. In this test, clients rate their level of sadness and its effect on various aspects of their functioning. One question asks respondents to rate their level of suicidal ideas from 0 to 3, for example, with 0 being "I don't have any thoughts of killing myself," and 3 being, "I would kill myself if I had the chance." Unfortunately, with the notable exceptions of this test and a few others, most response inventories are improvised as a need arises, without being tested carefully for accuracy and consistency (Weis & Smenner, 2007). Correspondingly, their use by clinicians to help assess psychopathology is limited.

Looking on In this observation, a clinician observes a child interacting with his teacher and classmates.

clinical tests devices for gathering information about a person's psychological functioning.

Models of Abnormality

LEARNING OBJECTIVE 2 Identify the major models used by psychologists to explain abnormal functioning.

Over the course of our lives, each of us has developed a perspective that helps us make sense of the things other people say and do. The perspectives that scientists use to explain phenomena are known as *models*, or *paradigms* (Kuhn, 1962). To understand how a clinical theorist explains disorders, we must know which model shapes his or her view of abnormal functioning. Thus in the following sections we'll be examining today's most influential clinical models—the neuroscience, psychodynamic, behavioral, cognitive, and humanistic-existential models.

As we discuss each model, we will also be observing how clinicians who subscribe to that model address therapy, or treatment. **Therapy** is a procedure designed to change abnormal behavior into more normal behavior. According to theorist Jerome Frank (1973), all forms of therapy have three key features: (1) a *sufferer* who seeks relief from the *healer*; (2) a trained, socially accepted healer; and (3) a *series of contacts* between the healer and the sufferer, through which the healer, sometimes with the aid of a group, tries to produce certain changes in the sufferer's emotions, attitudes, and behaviors. We will discuss how effective the therapies are, and the various factors that affect them. See **Table 16-2** for a summary of the major models of abnormality and their related therapeutic approaches.

The Neuroscience Model *What Happens in the* B R A I N ?

LEARNING OBJECTIVE 3 Describe neuroscience views of abnormal functioning and major brain therapies.

therapy (treatment) procedures designed to change abnormal functioning to more normal functioning.

Neuroscientists view abnormal behavior as an illness brought about by a malfunctioning brain (Lambert & Kinsley, 2005). They also conclude that medical treatment techniques, such as drugs, can relieve many people's psychological problems.

TABLE 16-2 Summary of Views of Abnormal Functioning and Treatment

	Causes of Abnormal Functioning	Goals of Therapy	Therapy Techniques	Strengths	Weaknesses
Neuroscience Approaches	Structural or biochemical malfunctions in the brain	Improve structural or biochemical functioning, relieve symptoms	Psychotropic drugs, electroconvulsive therapy (ECT), neurosurgery	Often effective for people whose problems don't respond to other treatments.	• Side effects • Not always effective • May neglect nonbiological problems of clients
Psychodynamic Approaches	Unconscious conflicts, often rooted in childhood	Discover source of conflicts and resolve them	Free association; therapist analysis of resistance, transference, dreams; catharsis; and working through problems	• Offered first major alternative to biological views • Sees abnormal functioning as rooted in same processes as normal • Model for many other treatments	Research does not support effectiveness of therapies
Behavioral Approaches	Abnormal behaviors acquired through conditioning or modeling	Learn more functional behaviors	Systematic desensitization; aversion therapy; operant conditioning, including token economies; therapist modeling, including social-skills training	• Research often supports behavioral explanations of causes and effectiveness of treatments	• Effects of treatment may not last long after treatment stops • May neglect unobservable cognitive processes
Cognitive Approaches	Maladaptive ways of thinking	Change harmful thinking patterns to more useful ones	Rational-emotive therapy; cognitive therapy; cognitive-behavioral techniques	Research supports cognitive theories about problems in thinking and effectiveness of treatments	Thinking problems may result from, not cause, abnormal functioning
Humanistic and Existential Approaches	Distorted views of self prevent personal growth or decision making	Provide support for honest self-appraisal, acceptance, and self-actualization	Client-centered therapy; Gestalt therapy, including skillful frustration, role-playing, rules, and games; existential therapy	• Recognize positive human goals • Recognize distinctly human values and needs	• Little research to test effectiveness

Neuroscience Views of Abnormal Behavior

As we have seen throughout the textbook, researchers have discovered connections between certain psychological or neurological disorders and problems in specific structures of the brain. One such disorder is Huntington's disease, a disorder marked by violent emotional outbursts, memory loss, suicidal thinking, involuntary body movements, and absurd beliefs (Paulsen, 2009). Huntington's disease has been linked to the loss of cells in the brain region called the *striatum*. Another such disorder is Parkinson's disease, a degenerative disease which, as we described in Chapter 4, is marked by decreasing control over voluntary movements of the body (Jankovic & Aguilar, 2008). This disease has been tied to the death of certain neurons in the region called the *substantia nigra*.

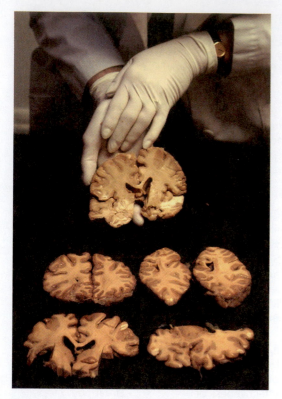

Extreme antisocial disorders and the brain Forensic psychiatrist Helen Morrison displays slices of the brain of John Wayne Gacy, who murdered at least 33 boys and young men between 1972 and 1978. Post mortem examinations have not revealed clear links between abnormal brain structure and the extreme antisocial patterns exhibited by Gacy and other serial killers.

Neuroscientists have also linked some mental disorders to deficient or excessive activity of different neurotransmitters. Certain anxiety disorders, for example, seem to be related to insufficient activity of the neurotransmitter *gamma aminobutyric acid*, or *GABA* (Garrett, 2009). Schizophrenia appears related to excessive activity of the neurotransmitter *dopamine*. And neuroscientists have also investigated the role of low activity of the neurotransmitters *norepinephrine* and *serotonin* in depression.

In addition to focusing on neurotransmitters, neuroscience researchers have learned that mental disorders are sometimes related to abnormal hormonal activity in the body's endocrine system (see Chapter 4). Abnormal secretions of the hormone cortisol, for example, have been tied to anxiety and mood disorders.

What causes these problems with brain anatomy and chemical functioning? Two factors have received particular attention from clinical theorists in recent years: *genetics* and *viral infections*.

Studies suggest that genetic inheritance plays a key role in mood disorders, schizophrenia, mental retardation, Alzheimer's disease, and other mental disorders. Yet, in most cases, researchers have not been able to identify the specific genes responsible for these problems. It appears that in most cases no single gene is responsible for a particular behavioral or mental disorder (Joseph, 2006). Instead, many genes combine to help produce our actions and reactions, both functional and dysfunctional.

Another possible source of abnormal brain structure or biochemical dyfunctioning appears to be viral infections. Some research suggests, for example, that schizophrenia, the disorder marked by hallucinations and other departures from reality, may be related to exposure to certain viruses before birth or during childhood (Meyer et al., 2008). The studies suggest that a damaging virus may enter the brain of a fetus or young child and then remain quiet there until the individual reaches puberty or young adulthood. At that time, activated by hormonal changes, by another infection, or by stressful life events, the virus may set in motion the symptoms of schizophrenia. In addition to schizophrenia, research has sometimes linked viruses to anxiety and mood disorders (Dale et al., 2004; Kim et al., 2004).

Brain Therapies

Brain therapies use chemical and physical methods to help people overcome their psychological problems. The clinical practitioners who apply such approaches are usually *psychiatrists*, therapists whose training includes medical school. The three principal kinds of brain interventions are *drug therapy, electroconvulsive therapy*, and *psychosurgery*. Drug therapy is by far the most common of these approaches.

Drug Therapy Since the 1950s, researchers have discovered several kinds of effective **psychotropic drugs**, drugs that act primarily on the brain and in many cases help to relieve the symptoms of mental disorders (Julien, 2008). We have touched on many of these medications throughout this book. The drugs have radically changed the outlook for people with various mental disorders and are now used widely, as the first-line treatment for a disorder or in conjunction with psychotherapy or other interventions. Table 16-3 lists and describes some of the key psychotropic drugs. In addition, see "What Happens in the Brain When a Depressed Person Takes an Antidepressant" on the next pages.

Although medication has proven to be very effective in the treatment of many disorders, it does not work for everyone. Recall, for example, that Diane did not show any improvement when administered drug therapy. Furthermore, some of the drugs have serious undesirable side effects that must be weighed against the good the drugs can do. For example, certain antipsychotic drugs, given mainly to people with schizophrenia, may produce severe movement abnormalities, such as severe shaking, bizarre-looking contractions of the face and body, and extreme restlessness (Combs et al., 2008). Fortunately, in recent decades, researchers have developed a new group of antipsychotic drugs, called *atypical antipsychotic drugs,* that are not nearly as likely to produce these

psychotropic drugs medications that act primarily on the brain.

electroconvulsive therapy (ECT) use of electric shock to trigger a brain seizure in hopes of relieving abnormal functioning.

psychosurgery brain surgery, often used in hopes of relieving abnormal functioning.

trephining prehistoric practice of chipping a hole in the skull of a person who was behaving strangely, with the idea of letting the demons out.

lobotomy surgical practice of cutting the connections between the frontal lobe and the lower centers of the brain.

TABLE 16-3 Commonly Prescribed Psychotropic Drugs

Symptom	Type of Medication	Examples
Psychosis (loss of touch with reality)	Antipsychotics	chlorpromazine (Thorazine), clozapine (Clozaril)
Depression	Antidepressants	trazodone (Desyrel), amitriptyline (Elavil), phenelzine (Nardil), fluoxetine (Prozac), paroxetine (Paxil), sertraline (Zoloft), venlafaxine (Effexor)
Mania	Mood stabilizers	lithium (Lithonate)
Anxiety	Anxiolitics	benzodiazepines (Valium, Xanax)
	Antidepressants	fluoxetine (Prozac)

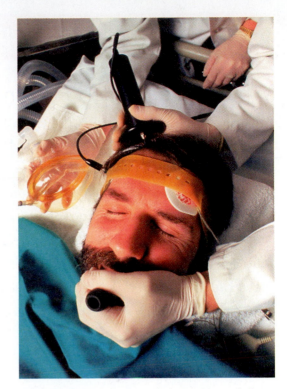

ECT today As we can see with this patient, today's ECT treatments are conducted with considerable medical care and many safety precautions, and include procedures that help patients sleep through the procedure.

unpleasant and dangerous effects and are often more effective than the conventional antipsychotic drugs (Julien, 2008).

As their ability to map the brain and connect its functioning with human behavior progresses further, neuroscientists believe that they will eventually be able to pinpoint the actions of medications so that the drugs focus only on the malfunctioning areas or connections in the brain, increasing the effectiveness and reducing harmful or annoying side effects of psychotropic drugs.

Electroconvulsive Therapy Another form of biological treatment used today, primarily for people who have severe depression, is **electroconvulsive therapy (ECT)**, a technique first developed in the 1930s. Here, two electrodes are attached to a patient's forehead and 65 to 140 volts of electricity are briefly passed through the brain. The procedure produces a brain seizure that lasts up to a few minutes. After an average of seven to nine ECT sessions, spaced two or three days apart, many patients feel considerably less depressed. ECT helps approximately 70 percent of depressed patients to improve (Garrett, 2009; Richard & Lyness, 2006).

ECT is currently administered less often than it was in the past. The procedure can negatively affect short-term memory. Most such memories return, but some people who have gone through ECT report memory difficulties for the rest of their lives (Wang, 2007). With the growing success of antidepressant medications and of certain forms of psychotherapy, fewer depressed patients now need this form of treatment. Nevertheless, ECT is still applied when people have a severe depressive episode that is unresponsive to other forms of treatment (Eschweiler et al., 2007), which makes its high success rate all the more impressive.

Psychosurgery Throughout the book, we have mentioned **psychosurgery**—brain-surgery procedures that can help some people with psychological disorders. Actually, the first use of brain surgery as a treatment for mental disorders was **trephining**, the prehistoric practice of chipping a hole in the skull of a person who behaved strangely. Many modern forms of psychosurgery are derived from a technique known as a **lobotomy**, in which the surgeon cuts the connections between the brain's frontal lobes and the lower centers of the brain. Lobotomies were widely used for a few decades after the procedure was developed in the 1930s. It became clear by the late 1950s, however, that lobotomies were not as effective as many psychosurgeons had been claiming. Moreover, many patients who had undergone the surgery later suffered irreversible effects, including seizures, extreme listlessness, stupor, and in some cases death (Barahal, 1958). Thus, use of this procedure declined during the 1960s.

Early roots of psychosurgery? The hole in this 5,100-year-old skull indicates that the individual underwent trephining, cutting away a circular section of the skull. Some historians believe that trephination was done to release the evil spirits that were thought to be responsible for mental dysfunctioning.

When a Depressed Person Takes an Antidepressant

When people have symptoms of depression so severe that they interfere with normal functioning, physicians will sometimes prescribe the use of antidepressant medication. Some of the most commonly prescribed antidepressants are called selective serotonin reuptake inhibitors (SSRIs). The primary action of these drugs is to increase the availability of the neurotransmitter serotonin in the brain. Neurons that make serotonin are present in the brainstem raphe nuclei. These neurons send axon projections to the cortex, hippocampus, and amygdala, among other regions. SSRIs have a multitude of effects on these brain regions, although the precise mechanism(s) by which the drugs alleviate symptoms of depression is not known. How might antidepressant drugs work?

RESTORING BRAIN ACTIVITY TO NORMAL LEVELS

The prefrontal cortex of depressed individuals shows reduced activity and a lower than normal level of blood flow. Some studies suggest that antidepressants ultimately raise activity in this brain region (shown on this brain scan in yellow) and restore blood flow to levels observed in nondepressed individuals. Similar findings have been reported for the amygdala.

BLOCKING SEROTONIN REUPTAKE

By blocking key receptors, SSRIs prevent the reuptake, or retention, of serotonin by presynaptic neurons (shown in this illustration), thus freeing the neurotransmitter to better activate brain regions that are targets of serotonin axons, including the hippocampus and cerebral cortex. Depression relief, however, usually does not occur until someone has taken the drug for a few weeks, suggesting that some other mechanism may also be responsible for improving mood.

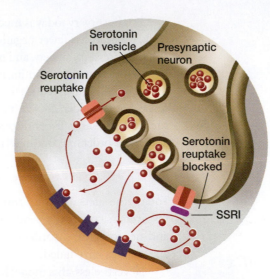

Serotonin in vesicle
Presynaptic neuron
Serotonin reuptake
Serotonin reuptake blocked
SSRI

Amygdala
Hippocampus
Prefrontal cortex
Raphe nuclei

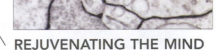

REJUVENATING THE MIND

Antidepressant use stimulates the production of synapses in the hippocampus (shown here in this electron micrograph, with the asterisk indicating a postsynaptic site). The hippocampus plays a role in cognitive function and in regulating anxiety (a feature in many cases of depression). The growth of new synapses may refresh this important brain region, enabling the formation of new connections to support a more positive outlook.

Psychosurgery today is much more precise than the lobotomies of the past (Aouizerate et al., 2006). It has fewer negative effects and is apparently beneficial for some people with severe depression, anxiety, and obsessive-compulsive disorders. Researchers have also begun to experiment with implanting electrodes deep within the brain, to stimulate particular brain regions and, in turn, reduce the symptoms of such disorders as depression and Parkinson's disease (Burkholder, 2008, Mayberg et al., 2005). Although promising, at the present time, such implants are still considered experimental and are used infrequently, usually only after a severe disorder has continued for years without responding to any other form of treatment.

The Neuroscience Model in Perspective

Today the neuroscience model of mental dysfunctioning is highly regarded. Its researchers constantly produce valuable new information about various psychological and neurological disorders, and brain treatments often bring great relief when other approaches have failed.

Nevertheless, this model has limitations. As we have observed, the brain treatments are capable of producing significant side effects. Another concern about the neuroscience model is that some proponents seem to expect that biological factors and brain interventions alone can explain and treat all abnormal behaviors. This view neglects the complex interplay of biological and nonbiological factors such as a person's environmental experiences (Kosslyn & Rosenberg, 2004). Indeed, as we have seen throughout the textbook, the connections in our brains unfold partly in response to the experiences that we keep having throughout our lives, beginning back in the womb.

Just as negative experiences can interact with brain activity to produce abnormal functioning, evidence is mounting that positive experiences, including psychotherapy, also affect the brain. One study found that people with depression who responded to psychotherapy came to show brain responses similar to those of healthy, nondepressed individuals, while depressed individuals who did not respond to psychotherapy continued to show the brain patterns that typically accompany depression (Okamoto et al., 2006). Just as behavior can respond to changes in our brain chemistry, so too can our brain chemistry responds to changes in behavior.

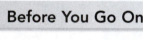

Before You Go On

What Do You Know?

6. What are the major types of brain problems that are linked to abnormal functioning?
7. What are the three main categories of brain treatments?

What Do You Think?   Are today's clinicians and their clients too reliant on drugs as a treatment? Why or why not?

The Psychodynamic Model

LEARNING OBJECTIVE 4 Describe Freud's view and other psychodynamic views of the causes and treatments of abnormal functioning and summarize the influence of the psychodynamic approach.

The psychodynamic model has its roots in Sigmund Freud's theories. Psychodynamic theorists look at people's unconscious internal processes and conflicts as the source of abnormal functioning. Therapy includes helping clients become aware of their internal conflicts and the effects they have on the client.

Psychodynamic Views of Abnormal Behavior

As we observed in Chapter 13: Personality, psychodynamic theorists believe that a person's behavior is determined largely by underlying psychological forces of which the person is not consciously aware. Abnormal behaviors or symptoms are viewed as the consequences of conflicts between these forces or as unconscious attempts to solve such conflicts and lessen some painful inner turmoil.

Freud, Psychosexual Stages, and Abnormality *How we Develop*

Recall from our discussion in Chapter 13 that Freud proposed that if a child's environment prevents his or her id, ego, and superego from maturing properly or interacting effectively, the child can become *fixated*, or entrapped, at an early stage of development. Such fixations affect all subsequent development and may set in motion abnormal functioning. Freud would have suggested that the family pressures Diane Markos experienced during her early years caused an imbalance among her id, ego, and superego, as she was forced to put aside many of her own id needs and to act in a mature, ego-dominated manner beyond her years. Freud would certainly have looked upon such childhood pressures and deprivations as possible roots for her adult depression.

As we observed in Chapter 13, Freud believed that severe clashes between the id, ego, and superego are particularly likely to emerge during the stages of early life that he called the oral, anal, and phallic stages, and that such clashes may set the stage for later abnormal functioning.

Anal personality? According to Freud, when an individual's neat and orderly personality is as extreme as this woman's (prior to storing her knickknacks, she organizes them carefully before her and enters each item on a computer file), fixation at the anal stage of development may be operating.

- *Oral Stage (birth to 18 months)* Freud suggested that if mothers consistently fail to gratify the nurturance needs of their children during this period, the children may become fixated at the oral stage, unable to grow beyond their oral needs. They may be particularly prone to develop depression and anxiety, and their personalities and behaviors may display an "oral character" throughout their lives: extreme dependence, extreme mistrust, or perhaps overindulgence in eating, smoking, drinking, and other forms of substance abuse.

- *Anal Stage (18 months to 3 years)* Freud believed that parents who use disapproval and withdrawal of love as tools to help toilet train their children may inadvertently cause them to feel great shame and to lose self-esteem, and an anal fixation may result. Children with an anal fixation may develop into adults with an "anal character," prone to be stubborn, contrary, stingy, overcontrolling, orderly, meticulous, punctual, and hateful of waste. They may be particularly prone to develop obsessive-compulsive patterns of dysfunction.

- *Phallic Stage (3 to 6 years)* According to Freud, if children are punished too harshly for sexual behavior during this stage, or if they are subtly encouraged to pursue their desire for the parent of the opposite sex that occurs during this period, their sexual development may suffer. As Freud saw it, they might later develop a sexual orientation different from the norm, fear sexual intimacy, be overly seductive, or have other difficulties in romantic relationships. Moreover, because the superego emerges during the phallic stage, children who become fixated at this stage may suffer pervasive feelings of guilt throughout their lives.

Other Psychodynamic Approaches to Abnormal Functioning

As we also saw in Chapter 13, several of Freud's colleagues disagreed with key aspects of his theories. As a result, there are now a number of different psychodynamic explanations and treatments for abnormal functioning.

Ego psychologists believe that the ego is a more independent and powerful force than Freud recognized. For example, Erik Erikson (1902–1994), whom you met in Chapter 3: Human Development, believed that a person develops an integrated sense of self, called the *ego identity*, and that each stage of life presents a crisis that challenges the ego.

Setting the stage Object relations theorists believe that early relationships in life, particularly with parents, are a key to adult functioning.

"It's that same dream,
where I'm drowning in a bowl of noodles."

Object relations theorists, on the other hand, believe people are motivated primarily by a need to establish relationships with others, known as *objects*. They propose that severe problems in early relationships with primary caregivers may result in abnormal development and psychological problems (Luborsky et al., 2008; Kernberg, 2005, 1997).

Psychodynamic Therapies

A variety of psychodynamic therapies are now practiced, ranging from classical Freudian psychoanalysis to modern therapies based on object relations theory. All share the goals of helping clients to uncover past traumatic events and the inner conflicts that have resulted from them, to settle those conflicts, and to resume interrupted personal development. Although they might focus on and try to settle different conflicts, the psychodynamic therapists of different theoretical persuasions use similar techniques.

Techniques of Psychodynamic Therapies   All psychodynamic therapists try to subtly guide the therapeutic discussions so that the clients discover their underlying problems for themselves. To help them do so, the therapists rely on such techniques as *free association, therapist interpretation, catharsis,* and *working through*.

- *Free Association* In psychodynamic therapies the client is responsible for initiating and leading each discussion. The therapist tells the individual to describe any thought or feeling that comes to mind, even if it seems unimportant. This is the process known as **free association**. The therapist probes the client's associations, expecting that they will eventually reveal unconscious events and unearth the dynamics underlying the individual's problem.

- *Therapist Interpretation* Psychodynamic therapists share their interpretations of a client's associations with the client when they think the individual is ready to hear them. The interpretations of three phenomena—*resistance, transference,* and *dreams*—are thought to be of special value.

  - *Resistance* Individuals demonstrate **resistance** when they encounter a block in their free associations or change the subject so as to avoid a potentially painful discussion. The therapist remains on the lookout for resistance, which is usually unconscious, and may point it out to the client and interpret it.

  - *Transference* Psychodynamic therapists also believe that clients act and feel toward the therapist as they do toward important figures in their lives, past and present. By interpreting this **transference** behavior, therapists may help individuals better understand how they unconsciously feel toward a parent or some other key person in their lives.

  - *Dream interpretation* Freud (1924) called dreams the "royal road to the unconscious." He believed that repression and other defense mechanisms operate ineffectively during sleep. Thus a client's dreams, correctly interpreted, can help reveal the person's unconscious instincts, needs, and wishes.

- *Catharsis* Psychodynamic therapists believe that individuals must experience **catharsis**, a reliving of past, repressed feelings, if they are to resolve internal conflicts and overcome their problems. Emotional catharsis must accompany intellectual insight for genuine progress to be achieved.

- *Working Through* A single session of interpretation and catharsis will not change a person. For deep and lasting insight to be gained, the client and therapist must *work through*, or examine the same issues over and over across many sessions, each time with new and sharper clarity.

Short-Term Psychodynamic Therapy   An increased demand by the public and by insurance companies for time-limited psychotherapies has resulted in several efforts to

free association psychodynamic therapy technique of allowing clients to freely talk about whatever they want.

resistance when clients encounter a block in their free associations or change the subject so as to avoid a potentially painful discussion.

transference process through which clients act and feel toward the therapist as they did toward important figures in their childhood.

catharsis reliving of past repressed feelings as means of settling internal conflicts and overcoming problems.

make psychodynamic therapy shorter, more efficient, and more cost-effective. In short versions of this therapy, clients focus on a single problem—a *dynamic focus*—such as excessive dependence on other people (Charman, 2004). The therapist and client center discussions on this problem throughout the treatment and work only on the psychodynamic issues that relate to it. A relatively small number of studies have tested the effectiveness of these short-term psychodynamic therapies, but their findings do suggest that the approaches are sometimes quite helpful (Present et al., 2008).

The Psychodynamic Model in Perspective

Freud and his followers helped change the way abnormal functioning is viewed (Corey, 2008). Primarily because of their work, many different kinds of theorists today look for explanations outside biological processes. Psychodynamic theorists have also helped us to understand that abnormal functioning may emerge from the same processes as normal functioning. Psychological conflict is a universal experience; it leads to abnormal functioning only if the conflict becomes excessive.

Freud and his followers were also the first practitioners to demonstrate the value of systematically applying theory and techniques to treatment. Their systems of therapy were the first to clarify the potential of psychological, as opposed to biological, treatment and have served as a starting point for many other psychological treatments.

Systematic research, however, has generally failed to support the effectiveness of most psychodynamic therapies. For the first half of the twentieth century, the value of these approaches was supported principally by the case studies of enthusiastic psychodynamic clinicians and by uncontrolled research studies. Controlled investigations have been conducted only since the 1950s, and only a minority of these have found psychodynamic therapies to be more effective than no treatment or placebo treatments (Prochaska & Norcross, 2007).

Before You Go On

What Do You Know?

8. According to Freud, what causes people to become fixated at early stages of psychological development?
9. Describe the key views of ego psychologists and object relations theorists.
10. List and describe psychodynamic therapy techniques.

What Do You Think?   At what stage of development do you think Freud might say Diane Markos is fixated?

The Behavioral Model

LEARNING OBJECTIVE 5 Describe behavioral views of the causes and treatments of abnormal functioning and summarize the influence of the behavioral approach.

As we observed in Chapter 7: Learning, behavioral theorists use learning principles to explain human functioning—principles that focus on how the environment changes a person's behaviors. Many learned behaviors are constructive and adaptive, helping people to cope with daily challenges and to lead satisfying lives. However, abnormal and undesirable behaviors also can be learned. According to the behavioral model, these behaviors are acquired by the same principles of learning as adaptive behaviors. As described in Chapter 7, for example, phobias may occur as a result of classical conditioning that pairs a previously neutral object with an unconditioned stimulus that creates fear.

Behaviorists also suggest that many of the behaviors we learn through operant conditioning processes of reward and punishment are abnormal ones. For example, some people may learn to abuse alcohol and drugs because initially such behaviors brought feelings of calm,

"Virtual" desensitization Virtual reality software enables phobic clients to more vividly experience their feared objects and situations, such as flying in an airplane, during desensitization.

Looking at a building with outside elevators

Approaching a bank of elevator doors

Pressing the elevator call button

Doors open to empty elevator

Stepping onto elevator with a few other people

Most   In a crowded elevator as doors close

Amount of anxiety

comfort, or pleasure (Ksir et al., 2008). Others may develop or continue to display disordered eating patterns partly because of praise they receive for a thinner appearance (Wilson, 2008).

Modeling, in which we learn by observing others, can also lead to abnormality. Recall from Chapter 7 the famous study in which children learned from a model to behave aggressively toward a Bobo doll, an inflatable clown (Bandura, Ross, & Ross, 1963). Similarly, children of psychologically dysfunctional people may themselves develop maladaptive reactions because of their exposure to such parental models.

Behavioral Therapies

The goal of behavioral therapy is to identify the client's specific problem-causing behaviors and to replace them with more appropriate or adaptive behaviors. Behavioral techniques fall into three categories: *classical conditioning*, *operant conditioning*, and *modeling*.

Classical Conditioning Techniques   Classical conditioning treatments are intended to change clients' dysfunctional reactions to stimuli. One treatment, described in Chapter 7, is *systematic desensitization*, a step-by-step process of teaching people with phobias to react with calm instead of fear to the objects or situations they dread (Wolpe, 1997, 1995, 1990). Clients first learn deep-muscle relaxation. Then, they construct a *fear hierarchy*, a list of objects or situations, starting with those that are minimally feared and ending with the ones that are most fearsome (see **Figure 16-2**). For a client with a phobia of elevators, for example, looking at an elevator on the outside of a building a block away might be low on the fear hierarchy, and watching the elevator doors close while inside the elevator might be near the top. Clients then, either in imagination or physically, confront each item on the hierarchy while they are in a state of deep relaxation, starting with the least fearful before moving on to scarier items higher on the list.

Research has repeatedly found that systematic desensitization and other classical conditioning techniques reduce phobic reactions more effectively than placebo treatments or no treatment at all (Buchanan & Houlihan, 2008). These approaches have also been helpful in treating several other kinds of problems, including sexual dysfunctions, posttraumatic stress disorder, agoraphobia, and asthma attacks (Koch & Haring, 2008).

In an opposite use of classical conditioning known as **aversion therapy**, clients acquire anxiety responses to stimuli that the individuals have been finding too attractive. This approach has been used with people who want to stop excessive drinking, for example, as shown in **Figure 16-3** (Owen-Howard, 2001). In repeated sessions the clients may be given an electric shock, a nausea-producing drug, or some other noxious stimulus whenever they reach for a drink. Aversion therapy has also been applied to help eliminate such undesirable behaviors as self-mutilation in autistic children, paraphilias, and smoking (George & Weinberger, 2008; Krueger & Kaplan, 2002). The effects of this approach have, however, typically been short-lived.

Operant Conditioning Techniques   In operant conditioning treatments, therapists consistently provide rewards for appropriate behavior and withhold rewards for inappropriate behavior. This technique has been employed frequently, and often successfully, with hospitalized patients experiencing psychosis (Spiegler & Guevremont, 2003; Paul & Lentz, 1977; Ayllon & Azrin, 1965). When such patients talk coherently and behave normally, they are rewarded with food, privileges, attention, or something else they value. Conversely, they receive no rewards when they speak bizarrely or display other psychotic behaviors.

Parents, teachers, and therapists have successfully used operant conditioning techniques to change problem behaviors in children (such as repeated tantrums) and to teach skills

FIGURE 16-2 Fear hierarchy Systematic desensitization uses classical conditioning principles to reduce a person's fears. Starting with the least stressful situation on his fear hierarchy, a man with a fear of riding in an elevator is exposed to each item on the hierarchy while applying relaxation techniques.

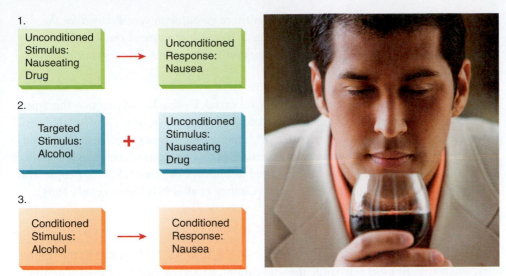

FIGURE 16-3 Aversion therapy Aversion therapy uses classical conditioning principles to create a negative response to a stimulus a person would like to avoid, such as alcohol. Here a man savors a drink just before the effects of a nauseating drug begin.

to individuals with autism or mental retardation (Spiegler & Guevremont, 2003). Rewards in such cases have included food, recreation time, social rewards, and television watching.

Operant conditioning techniques typically work best in institutions or schools, where a person's behavior can be reinforced systematically throughout the day. Often a whole ward or classroom is converted into an operant conditioning arena. Such programs are referred to as **token economy** programs because in many of them desirable behavior is reinforced with tokens that can later be exchanged for food, privileges, or other rewards (Ayllon & Azrin, 1968).

Behavioral techniques based on operant conditioning have also been useful for depression (Farmer & Chapman, 2009; Lewinsohn et al., 1990). Because depression is often associated with a decline in pleasant activities and withdrawal, therapists will often work with depressed individuals to identify activities the clients enjoy and then guide the individuals to systematically add the activities back into their lives. For example, a behavioral therapist seeing Diane Markos might help her set goals to engage regularly in leisure activities that she enjoys, such as reading, going to a movie, or spending time with friends.

Modeling Techniques   Modeling therapy was first developed by the pioneering social learning theorist Albert Bandura (1977, 1969). Therapists demonstrate appropriate behaviors for clients, who, through a process of imitation and rehearsal, acquire the ability to perform the behaviors in their own lives. It has been found, for example, that when therapists repeatedly display calm emotions while confronting objects that are feared by phobic clients, many clients are able to overcome their phobias (Rosenthal & Bandura, 1978; Bandura, Adams, & Beyer, 1977).

Behavioral therapists have also used modeling in combination with other techniques to help people acquire or improve their social skills and assertiveness. In an approach called **social skills training**, for example, therapists point out the social deficits of clients and then role-play social situations with the clients. Ultimately, the clients practice the behaviors in real-life situations. In the following role-playing session, the client is a male college student who has difficulty making dates with women:

> **Client:** *By the way, [Pause] I don't suppose you want to go out Saturday night?*
>
> **Therapist:** *Up to actually asking for the date you were very good. However, if I were the girl, I think I might have been a bit offended when you said, "By the way." It's like your asking her out is pretty casual. Also, the way you phrased the question, you were*

aversion therapy therapy designed to help clients to acquire anxiety responses to stimuli that the clients have been finding too attractive.

token economy operant conditioning therapy program in which participants receive tokens (that can be traded for rewards) when they display desired behaviors.

social skills training behavioral therapy technique in which therapists serve as models and teachers to help clients acquire desired social behaviors.

kind of suggesting to her that she doesn't want to go out with you. Pretend for the moment I'm you. Now, how does this sound: "There is a movie at the Varsity Theater this Saturday that I want to see. If you don't have other plans, I'd very much like to take you." (Rimm & Masters, 1979, p. 74)

Using a combined strategy of modeling, rehearsal, feedback, and practice, therapists have successfully taught social and assertion skills to shy, passive, or socially isolated people, as well as to people who have a pattern of bursting out in rage or violence after building up resentment (rather than asserting themselves) over perceived social slights (Fisher et al., 2004). The approach has also been used to improve the social skills of people who are depressed, alcoholic, obese, or anxious (Cooney et al., 1991; Hersen et al., 1984).

The Behavioral Model in Perspective

One of the appeals of the behavioral model is that its theories can be tested in the laboratory, whereas most psychodynamic theories cannot. Experimenters have used the principles of conditioning to produce clinical symptoms in research participants, suggesting that psychological disorders may in fact develop through learning. Moreover, research has indicated that behavioral treatments can be helpful to people with specific fears, compulsive behaviors, social deficits, mental retardation, and other problems (Wilson, 2008).

Nevertheless, the model has certain weaknesses. Although behavioral researchers have produced specific symptoms in the laboratory, there is still no clear evidence that people acquire psychological disorders because of improper conditioning in the world outside the lab. Behavioral therapies also display limitations. The improvements that occur in the therapist's office do not always extend to real life. Nor do they always last without continued therapy.

Finally, critics argue that the behavioral view is too simplistic, that its concepts do not fully account for the complexity of behavior. In the 1960s and 1970s, a number of behaviorists began to point out that our behavior is not all observable; we also engage in *cognitive* behaviors, such as anticipating or interpreting stimuli or responses in our environments. These behaviorists proposed *cognitive-behavioral theories* and *therapies* that also took unseen cognitive behaviors into account. Today, many theorists and researchers combine principles from both the behavioral model and the cognitive model, the model to which we will turn next.

We're all familiar with token economies The token economies applied in various mental health settings operate just like the star system that most of us were exposed to in elementary school. At school, however, good work was rewarded with stars instead of tokens, and numerous stars added up to a certificate instead of privileges, treats, or other rewards.

Before You Go On

What Do You Know?

11. What are systematic desensitization and aversion therapy?
12. What principles and procedures are involved in a token economy program?
13. How does social skills training work?

What Do You Think?
Does changing behavior fully treat people's disorders?

The Cognitive Model

LEARNING OBJECTIVE 6 Describe cognitive theorists' views of the causes and treatments of abnormal functioning and summarize the influence of the cognitive approach.

According to the cognitive model, to understand human behavior, we must understand the content and process of human thought. Cognitive therapists also believe that if dysfunctioning people can start to think differently, they can overcome their difficulties.

Cognitive Views of Abnormal Behavior

When people display abnormal patterns of functioning, clinical cognitive theorists assume that cognitive problems are to blame. Abnormal functioning can result from several kinds of cognitive problems: maladaptive attitudes, specific upsetting thoughts, and illogical thinking processes.

Maladaptive Attitudes The pioneering clinical theorist Albert Ellis (1913-2007) proposed that each of us holds a unique set of attitudes about ourselves and our world that serve to guide us through life and determine our reactions to the various situations we encounter. However, some people's attitudes are largely *irrational*, guiding them to act and react in ways that are inappropriate and that reduce their chances of happiness. Ellis called these **basic irrational assumptions**.

Some people, for example, irrationally assume that they are failures if they are not loved or approved of by every person they know. An otherwise successful presentation in the classroom can, for example, make them sad or anxious because one listener seems bored. The basic irrational assumption sets the stage for a life hampered by tension and disappointment.

According to Ellis (2008, 1962), other irrational assumptions include the idea that one should be a high achiever in all possible respects to consider oneself worthwhile or the idea that it is catastrophic when things are not the way we would like them to be. People may also believe that they have little ability to control their sorrows and disturbances, or that they need to depend upon someone stronger than themselves.

Diane Markos held some basic irrational assumptions that may have made her particularly vulnerable to depression. Her case study further stated:

> Many of her [problems] seemed to stem from underlying attitudes that recurred with such regularity that she and the therapist were able to group them under general themes, such as: "If I care for others, they should/must care for me," or "If something good happens to me, I'll have to pay for it later with pain," or "People either love me or hate me." Once these themes became clear to the patient, she was able to see the basis of much of her depressed thinking. (Spitzer et al., 1983, p. 129).

Specific Upsetting Thoughts Clinical cognitive theorists believe that *specific upsetting thoughts* may also contribute to abnormal functioning. As we confront the many situations that arise in life, a range of thoughts come into our minds, some comforting, others upsetting. As we noted in Chapter 12, Aaron Beck, another pioneer of the model, has called these unbidden cognitions **automatic thoughts** (Beck & Weishaar, 2008). In cases of depression, according to Beck, a person's stream of automatic thoughts is consistently negative, and collectively takes the form of a **cognitive triad** that includes negative thoughts about 1) oneself, 2) one's experiences, and 3) the future, as shown in **Figure 16-4**.

Illogical Thinking Processes As we also saw in Chapter 12, Beck has further found that some people continuously think in illogical ways and keep drawing self-defeating and even pathological conclusions (Beck & Weishaar, 2008). He has identified the illogical thinking processes most characteristic of depression, including the following ones:

- *Selective perception*, seeing only the negative features of an event
- *Magnification*, exaggerating the importance of undesirable events
- *Overgeneralization*, drawing broad negative conclusions on the basis of a single insignificant event.

Diane's Markos's therapist noted repeated examples of illogical thinking that helped predispose Diane to depressive reactions:

basic irrational assumptions maladaptive assumptions about oneself and one's world that increase the likelihood of psychological dysfunctioning.

automatic thoughts specific upsetting thoughts that occur unbidden.

cognitive triad a combination of negative thoughts about 1) one's self, 2) the world, and 3) the future, that has been linked to depression.

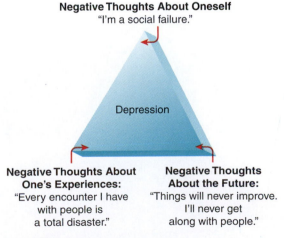

Negative Thoughts About Oneself
"I'm a social failure."

Depression

Negative Thoughts About One's Experiences:
"Every encounter I have with people is a total disaster."

Negative Thoughts About the Future:
"Things will never improve. I'll never get along with people."

FIGURE 16-4 Cognitive triad of depression According to Aaron Beck, a regular pattern of these three types of negative thoughts increases vulnerability to depression.

FIGURE 16-5 **Cognitive restructuring** This cognitive strategy can help clients change self-defeating thinking and, in turn, open the door to new, more positive life experiences.

When she finally did get a B from her professor, she concluded that she had failed miserably. There was no recognition of any middle ground between total academic success and total academic failure. Moreover, she tended to magnify the importance of events like this as if they were an indictment of her as a total human being (Spitzer et al., 1983, p. 129).

Cognitive Therapies

Cognitive therapists try to help clients recognize and change their faulty thinking processes. Because different forms of abnormality involve different kinds of cognitive dysfunctioning, a number of cognitive strategies have been developed.

Ellis's Rational-Emotive Therapy   In line with his belief that irrational assumptions give rise to abnormal functioning, Albert Ellis developed an approach called **rational-emotive therapy** (Ellis, 2008, 2005, 1962). Therapists help clients to identify the irrational assumptions that govern their emotional responses and to change those assumptions into constructive ways of viewing themselves and the world. This technique, in which clients learn to replace negative interpretations with more positive notions, is known as *cognitive restructuring* (see **Figure 16-5**).

In his own practice, Ellis would point out to clients their irrational assumptions in a blunt, confrontational, and often humorous way, and then he would model the use of alternative assumptions. After criticizing a young man's perfectionistic standards, for example, he might say, "So what if you did a lousy job on that paper? It's important to realize that one lousy paper simply means one lousy paper, and no more than that!" Ellis gave clients homework assignments requiring them to observe their assumptions at work in their everyday lives and to think of ways to test the rationality of the assumptions. He also had clients rehearse new assumptions during therapy and apply them at home and work.

Similarly, Diane's therapist asked her to make and test real-life predictions based on her irrational assumptions. She went to singles bars to test her assumption that all men found her unattractive, for example. Her assumption that she was undesirable was disproved when, contrary to her prediction that she would be ignored, several men asked her to dance (Spitzer et al., 1983, p. 129).

Rational-emotive therapists have cited numerous studies in support of this approach (Ellis, 2008, 2005). In particular, clients with social anxiety who are treated with this therapy improve more than socially anxious clients who receive no treatment or placebo treatments (McEvoy, 2007).

Beck's Cognitive Therapy   Aaron Beck independently developed a system of therapy that is similar to Ellis's rational-emotive therapy. Called simply **cognitive therapy**, this approach has been most widely used with people who are depressed (Beck & Weishaar, 2008). Cognitive therapists help clients to identify the negative thoughts and errors in logic that pervade their thinking and, according to Beck, give rise to feelings of depression. The therapists also teach clients to challenge their dysfunctional thoughts, try new interpretations, and apply alternative ways of thinking in their daily lives. Once again, we can see these strategies at work in the therapy conducted with Diane:

The therapy actively challenged the logical basis for many of these ideas, and gradually the patient was able to incorporate this reality testing into her own thinking. The therapist asked her to write down her most depressing thoughts and then examine their validity herself. Initially he coached her to ask certain key questions about the thoughts, such as:

"What is the evidence for this?"

"Am I seeing things only in a black-or-white fashion?"

"Am I taking things out of context?"

"What kind of distortion in my thinking could this be?"

(Spitzer et al., 1983, pp. 129-130)

Around two-thirds of depressed people who are treated with Beck's cognitive approach improve, significantly more than those who receive no treatment and about the same as those who receive biological treatments (Taube-Schiff & Lau, 2008; Hollon et al., 2006, 2005, 2002). Beck's cognitive therapy has also been successfully applied to a number of other disorders.

rational-emotive therapy Ellis's cognitive therapy technique designed to help clients discover and change the irrational assumptions that govern their emotions, behaviors, and thinking.

cognitive therapy Beck's cognitive therapy technique designed to help clients recognize and change their dysfunctional thoughts and ways of thinking.

The Cognitive Model in Perspective

The cognitive model has appealed to a wide range of therapists. In addition to the behaviorists who now include cognitive concepts in their theories about learning, many theorists from varied backgrounds embrace a model that sees thought as the main cause of normal and abnormal behavior. Research supports this appeal. Investigators have found that people with psychological disorders do, indeed, often display the kinds of assumptions and errors in thinking described in the cognitive theories (Ingram et al., 2007).

Another reason for the popularity of the cognitive model is the strong performance of cognitive and cognitive-behavioral therapies. Such approaches have proved very effective for treating depression, panic disorder, sexual dysfunctions, and a number of other psychological disorders (Beck & Weishaar, 2008; Landon & Barlow, 2004).

At the same time, the cognitive model, too, has its limitations. First, although disturbed cognitive functioning is found in many psychological disorders, its precise role has yet to be determined. The cognitions at work in psychologically-troubled people could often be a result rather than a cause of their difficulties. Second, although cognitive therapies are certainly effective for many problems, they do not help everyone (Sharf, 2008). Also, because cognitive therapies are often packaged with behavioral techniques, it is unclear what is the active ingredient of treatment; does the client improve because of cognitive skill development, behavioral exposures and activation, or a combination of these approaches?

"I could sit here all day thinking about my problems."

Before You Go On

What Do You Know?

14. What is the cognitive triad that has been linked to depression?

15. What do therapists help clients to do in rational-emotive therapy?

16. What is cognitive therapy?

What Do You Think? We all sometimes have irrational assumptions or upsetting thoughts, though they don't usually cause psychological disorders. What irrational assumptions and thoughts do you occasionally have?

The Humanistic-Existential Model

LEARNING OBJECTIVE 7 Describe humanistic and existential views of abnormal functioning and therapy and evaluate the influence of these approaches.

Humanistic and existential theorists are usually grouped together because of their common focus on the broader dimensions of human existence. However, there are important differences between them. As we observed in Chapter 13: Personality, *humanists*, the more optimistic of the two groups, believe that we are all born with a natural inclination to fulfill our potential for goodness and growth (Maslow, 1970). We will be able to do so, however, only if we can honestly appraise and accept our strengths and weaknesses and find positive personal values to live by. According to humanists, people who habitually deceive themselves and create a distorted view of the things that happen to them are likely to suffer some degree of psychological dysfunction.

Rogers's Humanistic Theory and Therapy

According to humanist Carl Rogers (2007, 1987, 1951), the road to dysfunction starts early in life. Recall from Chapter 13, Rogers's claim that we all have a basic need to receive **unconditional positive regard** from the significant other people in our lives, particularly our parents. Rogers believed that children who do not receive unconditional positive regard acquire **conditions of worth**, a sense that they must meet certain standards in order to gain the love of their parents or other important figures. Recall in this regard Diane Markos feeling that her parents' love was conditional upon her helping out in the care and upkeep of the family.

Harsh or rigid conditions of worth can prevent a person from reaching his or her full potential. People may deny or distort thoughts and actions that do not measure up to their conditions of worth, creating a warped view of themselves and their experiences. Eventually, they may not know what they are genuinely feeling or needing, or what values and goals would bring satisfaction to their lives. Moreover, they spend so much energy trying to protect their self-image that little is left to devote to self-actualizing. Psychological dysfunction in one form or another is inevitable.

Clinicians who practice Rogers's **client-centered therapy** try to create a positive climate in which clients can look at themselves honestly and acceptingly (Raskin, Rogers, & Witty, 2008; Rogers, 2000, 1992, 1957). The therapist must display three important qualities throughout the therapy:

* *unconditional positive regard*—full and warm acceptance for the client.
* *accurate empathy*—skillful listening, including restatements of the client's own comments.
* *genuineness*—sincere communication.

According to Rogers, clients will feel accepted by their therapists in this kind of atmosphere. They will eventually come to value their own emotions, thoughts, and behaviors once again, and so they will be freed from the insecurities that have been preventing self-actualization. The following interaction shows a therapist using the qualities Roger advocates:

Client: *When I meet somebody, I wonder what he's actually thinking of me. Then later on I wonder how I match up to what he's come to think of me.*

Therapist: *You feel that you're pretty responsive to the opinions of other people . . .*

An alternative source of unconditional positive regard Based on the Rogerian principle that unconditional positive regard is highly therapeutic, pet therapy has become a widely applied intervention to help reduce the depression of elderly nursing home residents, medically ill people, and developmentally disabled individuals. In this approach, individuals interact with various kinds of nonjudgmental animals.

Client: *In a way, but some things just seem illogical. I'm afraid I'm not very clear here but that's the way it comes.*

Therapist: *That's all right. You say just what you think (Snyder, 1947, pp. 2–24).*

Carl Rogers was committed to clinical research, and his commitment helped promote the systematic study of treatment. Client-centered therapy has not performed well in research, however (Sharf, 2008). Although some studies report improvements among people who receive this therapy, most controlled studies find it to be of limited effectiveness. Overall, however, Rogers's therapy has had a positive influence on the clinical field (Raskin et al., 2008; Kirschenbaum, 2004). As one of the first major alternatives to psychodynamic therapy, it helped open up the field to new approaches.

Gestalt Theory and Therapy

Gestalt therapy, another humanistic approach, was developed in the 1950s by clinical theorist Frederick (Fritz) Perls (1893–1970). Gestalt therapists, like client-centered therapists, move clients toward self-recognition and self-acceptance (Yontef & Jacobs, 2008). But unlike client-centered therapists, they often try to do this by challenging and frustrating the clients. Perls's favorite techniques included skillful frustration, role playing, and numerous rules, exercises, and games.

- *Skillful frustration* Gestalt therapists consistently refuse to meet their clients' expectations or demands, helping the clients to see how often they try to manipulate others into meeting their needs.

- *Role playing* Gestalt therapists often have clients act out various roles. A person may be instructed to be another person, an object, an alternate self, or even a part of the body. Role playing can become very intense, as individuals are encouraged to fully express their feelings. They may cry out, scream, kick, or pound. Eventually they are expected to "own," or accept, feelings that previously made them uncomfortable.

Gestalt techniques Gestalt therapists often guide clients, such as this man, to express their needs and feelings to an extreme through role playing and other exercises. In this session, the client moves from "strangling" a pillow (*left*) to banging the pillow, to hugging it (*right*). The pillow may represent a person about whom the client has mixed feelings.

unconditional positive regard a therapist's (or another person's) full and warm acceptance for a client.

conditions of worth a perception that persons must meet certain standards in order to gain the love of their parents or other important figures.

client-centered therapy humanistic therapy designed to help clients experience unconditional positive regard and look at themselves honestly and acceptingly.

- *Rules* are intended to ensure that clients look at themselves closely. In certain versions of Gestalt therapy, for example, clients may be required to use "I" language instead of "it" language. They must say, "I am sad" rather than "The situation is depressing."
- *Exercises and games* are intended to help clients recognize the depth of their feelings, the meaning of particular behaviors, and the effect of their behaviors on others. In the exaggeration game, for example, clients must repeatedly exaggerate some gesture or verbal behavior—perhaps a phrase that they use regularly.

Because Gestalt therapists believe that subjective experiences and self-awareness defy objective measurement, controlled research has rarely been conducted on their approach (Yontef & Jacobs, 2008; Strumpfel, 2006, 2004). Recently, Gestalt techniques have become important parts of other treatments that refer to themselves as *emotion-focused* and emphasize attention to one's current emotional experiences as a way to reduce anxiety, depression, and other psychological difficulties (Greenberg & Goldman, 2008).

Existential Theories and Therapy

Existentialists agree with humanists that human beings must have an accurate awareness of themselves and live subjectively meaningful—"authentic"—lives in order to be well adjusted. These theorists do not agree, however, that people are naturally inclined to live constructively. In fact, they believe that from birth we have the freedom either to confront our existence and give meaning to our lives or to run away from that responsibility.

According to existentialists, many people become intimidated by the pressures of society and look to others for guidance and authority. They surrender their personal freedom of choice and "hide" from responsibility for their lives and decisions (Mendelowitz & Schneider, 2008). These people are left with empty, inauthentic lives. Their primary emotions are anxiety, frustration, and depression.

Existential therapists encourage clients to accept responsibility for their lives and their problems. They help clients to recognize their freedom so that they may choose a different path and live more meaningful lives (Mendelowitz & Schneider, 2008). Existential therapists place great emphasis on the relationship between therapist and client and try to create an atmosphere of honesty and shared learning and growth.

Patient:	*I don't know why I keep coming here. All I do is tell you the same thing over and over. I'm not getting anywhere.*
Doctor:	*I'm getting tired of hearing the same thing over and over, too.*
Patient:	*Maybe I'll stop coming.*
Doctor:	*It's certainly your choice.*
Patient:	*What do you think I should do?*
Doctor:	*What do you want to do? (Keen, 1970, p. 200)*

Thus an existential therapist might help Diane Markos become more aware of the ways in which she repeatedly holds others, such as her parents, teachers, and coworkers, responsible for her problems. The therapist would probably seek to increase her focus on her own goals and her own control over her life.

Like gestalt therapists, existential therapists do not typically believe that experimental methods can properly test the effectiveness of their treatments (Mendelowitz & Schneider, 2008). In fact, they hold that research dehumanizes individuals by reducing them to test measures. Thus, little controlled research has been done to clarify the effectiveness of this approach.

The Humanistic-Existential Model in Perspective

The humanistic-existential model appeals to many in the clinical field. By recognizing the special challenges of human existence, both humanistic and existential theories highlight an aspect of psychological life that is typically missing from the other models (Wampold, 2007). In addition, the factors that they say are critical to positive functioning—self-acceptance, personal values, personal meaning, and personal choice—certainly seem to be lacking in many people with psychological disorders.

Such virtues aside, the broad issues of human fulfillment at the core of this model are hard to research. Only recently have properly controlled studies been conducted by humanistic researchers. These studies in fact suggest that the therapies can be beneficial in some cases (Schneider, 2008; Cain, 2007). This emerging interest in research by some proponents of the humanistic-existential model may soon lead to clearer insights about these perspectives and treatment approaches.

Before You Go On

What Do You Know?
17. What are the key characteristics therapists should display in client-centered therapy?
18. What technniques are part of Gestalt therapy?
19. What are the main goals of existential therapy?

What Do You Think? What kind of clients and what kind of problems do you think would benefit most from humanistic and existentialist therapies?

Formats of Therapy

LEARNING OBJECTIVE 8 Describe commonly used formats of therapy.

Thus far our discussions of therapy have centered on treatment conducted by an individual therapist with an individual client. In fact, **individual therapy** is the oldest of the modern therapy formats. Other formats, often used as alternatives to individual therapy, include *group therapy*, *family* and *couple therapy*; and *community treatment*. Therapists may apply their favored techniques and principles in each of these formats, whether they be psychodynamic, behavioral, or other techniques. In addition, special strategies have been developed for use in the nonindividual formats.

Group Therapy

In **group therapy** a therapist sees several clients who have similar problems at the same time. Group therapy became a popular format for treating people with psychological problems after World War II when growing demand for psychological services forced therapists throughout the United States and Europe to look for time-saving alternatives to individual therapy. Many therapists now specialize in group therapy, and countless others conduct therapy groups as one aspect of their practice. A survey of clinical psychologists, for example, revealed that almost one-third of them practice group therapy to some degree (Norcross & Goldfried, 2005).

Typically, group members meet together with a therapist and discuss the problems or concerns of one or more of the members. Groups are often created with particular client populations in mind; for example, there are groups for people with alcoholism,

individual therapy oldest of the modern psychotherapy formats in which the therapist sees the client alone.

group therapy psychotherapy format in which a therapist sees several clients who have similar problems at the same time.

self-help groups groups consisting of people who have similar problems and come together to help and support one another without the direct leadership of a professional clinician.

family therapy a format in which therapists meet with all members of a family in order to help the whole family to change.

family systems theory theory that each family has its own implicit rules, relationship structure, and communication patterns that shape the behavior of the individual members.

couple therapy (sometimes called *marital therapy*) a therapy format in which a therapist works with two people who are in a long-term relationship.

community mental health treatment treatment programs that emphasize community care, including an emphasis on prevention.

for those who are physically handicapped, and for people who are divorced, abused, or bereaved.

On the basis of his own work and on a number of group investigations, a leading group-therapy theorist Irvin Yalom suggests that successful forms of group therapy share certain "curative" features (Vinogradov, Cox, & Yalom, 2003):

1. Guidance: they usually provide information and advice for members.
2. Identification: they provide models of appropriate behavior.
3. Group cohesiveness: they offer an atmosphere of solidarity in which members can learn to take risks and accept criticism.
4. Universality: members discover that other people have similar problems.
5. Altruism: members develop feelings of self-worth by helping others.
6. Catharsis: members develop more understanding of themselves and of others and learn to express their feelings.
7. Skill building: members acquire or improve social skills.

One form of group treatment that is in wide use today is **self-help groups**, groups made up of people who have similar problems and come together to help and support one another without the direct leadership of a professional clinician (Mueller et al., 2007; Weiss et al., 2005). These groups have become increasingly popular over the last few decades. Today there are between 500,000 and 3 million such groups in the United States alone, attended by 4 percent of the population. Self-help groups address a wide assortment of issues, including alcoholism and other forms of drug abuse, compulsive gambling, bereavement, overeating, phobias, child abuse, medical illnesses, rape victimization, unemployment, and divorce. It is estimated that 25 million Americans will participate in self-help groups during their lives (Davison et al., 2000).

Self-help groups are popular for several reasons. Many participants have lost confidence in the ability of clinicians and social institutions to help with their particular problems (Silverman, 1992). For example, Alcoholics Anonymous, the well-known network of self-help groups for people dependent on alcohol, was developed in 1934 in response to the general ineffectiveness of clinical treatments for alcoholism. Still other people are drawn to self-help groups because they find them less threatening and less stigmatizing than therapy groups.

Because groups—from conventional group therapies to self-help groups—vary so widely, it has been difficult to assess their effectiveness. Research does indicate, how-

Range of formats Individual therapy (left) used to be the only format used in treatment for psychological problems. Today, the approach has been joined by other formats such as group therapy (middle) and couple therapy (right).

ever, that group therapy is of help to many clients, often as helpful as individual therapy (Shaughnessy et al., 2007; Dies, 2003). It appears that candid feedback is usually useful for group members as long as a balance is struck between positive and negative feedback.

Family Therapy

In the 1950s several clinicians developed **family therapy**, a format in which therapists meet with all members of a family, point out problematic behavior and interactions between the members, and help the whole family to change (Goldenberg & Goldenberg, 2008). Most family therapists meet with family members as a group, but some choose to see them separately. Either way, the family is viewed as the unit under treatment. Like group therapists, family therapists may follow the principles of any of the major theoretical models. Whatever their orientation, however, most also adhere to some of the principles of **family systems theory**. Family systems theory holds that each family has its own implicit rules, relationship structure, and communication patterns that shape the behavior of the individual members, including dysfunctional behavior. For one family member to change, the family system must be changed.

Family therapies are often helpful to individuals, although research has not yet clarified how helpful, nor has any one type of family therapy emerged as consistently more helpful than the others (Goldenberg & Goldenberg, 2008; Alexander et al., 2002). Some studies have found that as many as 65 percent of individuals treated with family approaches improve, but other studies have found much lower success rates.

Couple Therapy

In **couple therapy**, also known as **marital therapy**, the therapist works with two people who are in a long-term relationship, focusing on the structure and communication patterns in their relationship (Harway, 2005). Often this format of therapy involves a husband and wife, but the couple need not be married or even living together. Similarly, they need not be heterosexual; some therapists specialize in working with same-sex couples.

Although some degree of discord occurs in any long-term relationship, there is growing evidence that many adults in our society experience serious marital problems. The divorce rate across North America and Europe is now close to 50 percent of the marriage rate and has been climbing steadily in recent decades (Lewin, 2004). Only one-third of Americans who married a few decades ago are now still married and proclaiming their marriages to be "very happy." Many of those who live together without marrying seem to have similar levels of relationship disharmony (Harway, 2005).

Like group and family therapy, couple therapy may be conducted with any therapy orientation (Shadish & Baldwin, 2005). People treated in couple therapy seem to show greater improvement in their relationships than people who fail to receive such treatment, but no one form of couple therapy stands out as better than the others (Harway 2005; Gollan & Jacobson, 2001). Two-thirds of treated couples display improved marital functioning, but fewer than half of those who are treated achieve "distress-free" relationships.

Community Treatment

Community mental health treatment programs offer people with psychological problems, including those with severe disorders, services from nearby agencies rather than distant facilities or institutions, as was the case historically. A key feature of community treatment is *prevention*. Clinicians reach out to clients rather than wait for them,

"What do you mean we don't communicate? I sent you e-mail on Monday."

Community mental health in action This man with both schizophrenia and bipolar disorder is moving into his own apartment, a key step in his recovery.

an approach that is often very successful (Hage et al., 2007). Community workers identify three types of prevention—*primary, secondary,* and *tertiary.*

- *Primary prevention* consists of efforts to improve community functioning and policies. The goal here is to prevent psychological disorders altogether. Community workers may lobby for better child-care facilities in the community, consult with a district school board to help develop a curriculum, or offer mental health fairs or workshops on stress reduction (Bloom, 2008; LeCroy, 2005).
- *Secondary prevention* consists of detecting and treating psychological disorders in the early stages, before they reach serious levels. Community workers may work with teachers, clergy, or police to help them identify early signs of psychological dysfunction and teach them how to refer people for treatment (Ervin et al., 2007).
- *Tertiary prevention* aims to provide effective treatment immediately so that moderate or severe disorders do not become chronic problems. Unfortunately, although community agencies are able to offer tertiary care for millions of people with moderate problems, low funding often prevents them from providing care for hundreds of thousands with severe disorders (Weisman, 2004; Humphreys & Rappaport, 1993).

Before You Go On

What Do You Know?
20. What are self-help groups?
21. What is the main assumption of family systems theory?
22. Describe primary, secondary, and tertiary prevention.

What Do You Think? Which therapy format appeals to you most? Least? Why? Are certain formats better suited for particular problems or client personalities?

Does Therapy Work?

LEARNING OBJECTIVE 9 Summarize research on the effectiveness of therapy.

Altogether, as many as 400 forms of therapy are currently practiced (Corsini, 2008). The most important question to ask about each of them is whether it really helps people overcome their psychological problems. **Therapy outcome studies**, which measure the effects of various treatments, typically ask one of three questions:

1. *Is therapy in general effective?* Studies reveal that therapy is often more helpful than no treatment or placebo treatments. One early review statistically summarized the results of 375 separate, controlled studies, covering a total of almost 25,000 people seen in a wide assortment of therapies (Smith, Glass, & Miller, 1980; Smith & Glass, 1977). According to this statistical analysis, shown in **Figure 16-6**, the average person who received treatment was better off than 75 percent of the untreated control clients. Other analyses have found similar relationships between treatment and improvement (Bickman, 2005).

2. *Are particular therapies generally effective?* A number of studies have found that each of the major forms of therapy is of some help to clients, certainly more help than a placebo treatment (Prochaska & Norcross, 2006). Other research has compared these therapies to one another and found that no one form of therapy generally stands out over all others (Luborsky et al., 2003, 1975). If different kinds of therapy are similarly successful overall, it may be that they in fact share common features (Bickman, 2005). Surveys of highly successful therapists suggest that, regardless of their particular orientations, successful therapists tend to do similar

therapy outcome studies research that looks at the effects of various treatments.

things: 1) provide feedback to clients, 2) help clients focus on their own thoughts and behavior, 3) pay careful attention to the way they and their clients interact, and 4) try to build a sense of self-mastery in their clients (Portnoy, 2008; Korchin & Sands, 1983).

3. *Are particular therapies effective for certain problems?* In recent years researchers have found that particular therapies are especially effective at treating certain disorders. Behavioral therapies, for example, seem to be the most effective of all treatments for phobias, cognitive-behavioral therapies are particularly helpful in cases of depression, and drug therapy is the most helpful treatment for schizophrenia (Wilson, 2008; Tryon, 2005; Weiden & Kane, 2005). Moreover, some studies show that certain clinical problems, such as panic disorder and obsessive-compulsive disorder, often respond best to *combined* approaches (deMaat et al., 2007; TADS, 2007). As a result, there is a movement afoot in the clinical field that calls for the clarification and increased use of *evidence-based*, or *empirically supported, therapies* (Pope & Wedding, 2008). The evergrowing number of proponents of this movement call for properly controlled investigations into which treatments are most effective for which problems, and many argue that clients should receive only those therapies that have been well supported by such research.

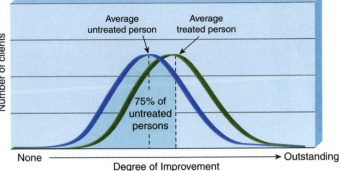

FIGURE 16-6 Is therapy generally effective? An analysis of 375 studies of treatment effectiveness shows that the average person who gets treatment of any kind is better off after treatment than a similar person who does not get treatment.

PRACTICALLYSPEAKING How to Choose a Therapist

Selecting the right therapist is obviously a very important decision. Even if your insurance plan provides only a limited list of potential therapists to choose from or your financial situation dictates that you receive treatment at a nearby mental health center, you still have some choice regarding which of the available therapists you'd like to work with.

Here's a list of key questions to consider when selecting a therapist. You should direct some of questions to the potential therapists themselves.

- *Where can you get names of skilled potential therapists?* Ask a professional whom you trust—a psychologist you know, a family physician, or the like—for recommendations. Many states or cities also provide relevant information and lists.
- *What is the professional status of the potential therapists?* Are they clinical psychologists, psychiatrists, social workers, or counselors? Are they licensed/certified?

- *What is the experience level of the potential therapists?* Their overall experience in the field? Their specific experience and success rate with your kind of problem?
- *What is the treatment orientation of the potential therapists?* Are they psychodynamic, behavioral, cognitive, humanistic, existential, or eclectic? How do they approach problems such as yours?
- *What is the success rate of their treatment orientation for problems such as yours?* Reading this chapter or an abnormal psychology textbook should help you with this question.
- *Do the potential therapists believe in psychotropic medication as part of therapy in certain cases?* Can they arrange for medication consults if needed?
- *How do the potential therapists match up on personal variables that are important to you?* What is their gender, age, personality, and the like? Although such factors do not necessarily affect a therapist's ability to help, you may personally feel that the variables could affect your comfort level or confidence in the therapy process.
- *Once you are in therapy, are you comfortable with the way things are going?* Does the therapist seem attentive, interested, and engaged? Does the therapist's approach continue to make sense to you? Do you feel you are making progress? Don't be afraid to change therapists if, after a reasonable period of time, you are not making progress. In most such instances, you are not failing at therapy. The therapy is failing you.

Before You Go On

What Do You Know?

23. What does research show about whether or not therapy is generally effective?
24. What do effective therapists have in common?
25. What does research show about the effectiveness of particular therapies for certain problems?

What Do You Think? If a person feels that his or her treatment is not helping, is it likely to be worthwhile for that person to try to change therapists or treatment methods? Why or why not?

Abnormal Psychology: Social and Cultural Forces

LEARNING OBJECTIVE 9 Describe the influences of social and cultural forces in the prevalence and treatment of psychological disorders.

According to many theorists, abnormal behavior and its treatments are best understood in light of the social and cultural forces brought to bear on an individual. The unique characteristics of a given society may create special stresses that heighten the likelihood of abnormal functioning in its members. Researchers have, for example, found relationships between abnormal functioning and factors such as widespread social change, socioeconomic class membership, and cultural background.

Social Change

When a society undergoes major change, the mental health of its members can be greatly affected. Societies undergoing rapid urbanization, for example, usually show a rise in mental disorders, although it is not known which features of urbanization—overcrowding, technological change, social isolation, migration, and so forth—are most to blame (Ghubash, Hamdi, & Bebbington, 1992). Similarly, societies in the throes of economic depression often display rises in rates of clinical depression and suicide (SAMHSA, 2009; Hammer, 1993), which may be explained in part by an increase in unemployment and the resulting loss of self-esteem and personal security.

Socioeconomic Class HOW we Differ

Studies have found that rates of psychological abnormality, especially severe abnormality, are three times higher among members of the lower socioeconomic classes than among members of the higher ones (Byrne et al., 2004; Dohrenwend et al., 1992). Perhaps the special pressures of lower-class life help explain this relationship. Poverty is linked to many stresses, including high rates of crime, unemployment, overcrowding, and even homelessness, as well as inferior medical care and limited educational opportunities. Of course, a relationship between low socioeconomic class and psychological disorders does necessarily mean that poverty causes disorders. It could be that people who display significant mental disturbances become less effective at work, earn less money, and as a result *drift downward* to the lower socioeconomic classes.

The economy and mental health Thousands of Filipino job seekers line up at a 2009 job fair in Manila. Unemployment and poverty seem to be strongly linked to psychological dysfunction.

Cultural Factors HOW weDiffer

Many theorists believe that human behavior, including abnormal behavior, is understood most fully by examining an individual's unique cultural context, including the values of that culture and the external pressures faced by members of the culture (Sue & Sue, 2003; Johnson, 1990). As we have seen throughout this book, the cultural groups in the United States that have been studied most often are ethnic and racial minority groups (African American, Hispanic American, Native American, and Asian American groups) along with economically disadvantaged persons, women, and homosexual individuals. Each of these groups faces special pressures in society that may help produce feelings of stress and, in some cases, abnormal functioning. Moreover, membership in these groups often overlaps.

Researchers have found, for example, that the prejudice and discrimination confronted by many minority group members may contribute to various forms of abnormal functioning (Jackson et al., 2004; Simons et al., 2002). Women are at least twice as likely as men to experience anxiety and depressive disorders (McSweeney, 2004). African Americans experience especially high rates of anxiety disorders (Blazer et al., 1991). Hispanic Americans have elevated rates of PTSD (Pole et al., 2005, 2001). And Native Americans manifest extremely high alcoholism and suicide rates (Beals et al., 2005; Kinzie et al., 1992). Racial and sexual prejudice and related problems certainly may help explain these differences (McSweeney, 2004; Vega et al., 2004; Winston, 2004).

It is also the case that members of ethnic and racial minority groups tend to improve less in clinical treatment than members of majority groups (Ward 2007; Smedley & Smedley, 2005). Moreover, worldwide studies have found that minority clients use mental health services less often than members of majority groups (Wang et al., 2006; Kung, 2004). Sometimes, a language barrier, cultural beliefs, or lack of information about available services may prevent the individuals from finding help; often, however, such persons are not able to afford quality treatment. In a number of cases, minority individuals do not trust the establishment, and so may rely instead on other remedies that are available in their cultural environment (Smedley & Smedley, 2005).

Because of such trends, a number of clinicians now practice **culture-sensitive therapies**, approaches that focus largely on the unique issues faced by members of minority groups (Prochaska & Norcross, 2007; Wyatt & Parham, 2007). These approaches often include features such as (1) educating or raising the consciousness of minority-group clients about the impact of the dominant culture and of their own culture on their behaviors and views of themselves, (2) helping clients to express suppressed anger and pain, and (3) helping clients to make choices and achieve a bicultural balance that feel right for them. Therapies centered on the special pressures of being a woman in Western society, called **gender-sensitive**, or **feminist**, **therapies**, include similar features.

Another cultural factor that has received much attention from clinical researchers and therapists in recent years is religion. For years, clinical scientists tended to view religion as a negative factor in mental health, but today many theorists are looking carefully at the possible roles religion may play in psychological functioning and mental health (Blanch, 2007; Richards & Bergin, 2004, 2000). Researchers have studied possible links between religious faith and mental health and have learned that spirituality may be psychologically helpful to many people. Studies have found, for example, that genuinely spiritual people tend, on average, to be less lonely, pessimistic, depressed, or anxious than other people (Loewenthal, 2007; Bergin & Richards, 2001). Moreover, as we observed in Chapter 15: Stress, Coping, and Health, such individuals often seem to cope better with major life stressors and appear less likely to abuse drugs or to attempt suicide. As we noted in Chapter 15, these findings may reflect the close communities that religious people often live in, the feelings of hope or acceptance with which they confront major stressors, or yet other factors.

culture-sensitive therapies psychotherapy approaches that focus largely on the unique issues faced by members of minority groups.

gender-sensitive therapies (also *feminist therapies*) psychological treatment that centers on the special pressures of being a woman in Western society.

Pressures of discrimination In 2009 these dancers performed at an all-day antiracism concert in Britain entitled "Love Music, Hate Racism." Multicultural research suggests that prejudice and discrimination can contribute to abnormal functioning.

In line with such findings, many therapists now make a point of including spiritual issues when treating religious clients (Raab, 2007; Shafranske & Sperry, 2005) and some also encourage clients to use their spiritual resources to help them cope with current stresses and dysfunctioning.

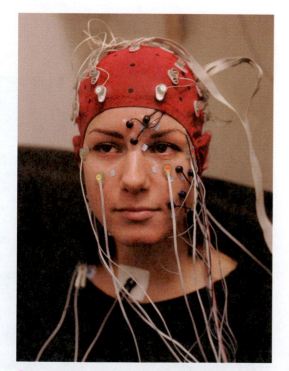

Before You Go On

What Do You Know?

26. What aspects of social change have been linked to increases in abnormal functioning?

27. What are two possible explanations for the strong link between low socioeconomic status and high levels of abnormal functioning?

28. How do culture-sensitive approaches differ from other models of psychotherapy?

What Do You Think?
Until recent years, clinical psychologists failed to consider what roles cultural pressures and issues might play in the development and treatment of psychological problems. Why do you think this was so? What problems might this oversight have caused in the clinical field?

Some Final Thoughts About the Field of Psychology

It is ironic that we end this book with a chapter on abnormal psychology because early on we noted that many people automatically think of abnormal psychology when they hear the term psychology. But, as you have seen throughout the book, psychology is, in fact, a broad field that studies all kinds of mental processes and behavior. And, as you have also observed, all of those processes and behaviors—both normal and abnormal—are rather awe-inspiring. For example, while disorders of memory, such as Alzheimer's disease or dissociative identity disorder, are certainly fascinating, normal acts of memory—our very ability to encode, store, and retrieve so many experiences and pieces of information in the first place—are no less fascinating and remarkable.

Psychology is a wide-ranging and complex field consisting of many subareas—from sensation and perception to social psychology—each of which seeks to explain particular aspects of mental functioning from a particular angle. Collectively, these many subareas and their bodies of research have provided us with an impressive understanding of mental processes and behavior. But it is important to recognize that this understanding is at a very early stage of development. There are many miles to go in our quest to more fully understand the phenomena at hand.

Perhaps the most important feature of psychological study today—and one that offers enormous promise for the future—is that the subareas are increasingly being viewed as closely connected areas of study, each of which helps to inform the others and all of which can, collectively, provide a more integrated, complete, and accurate understanding of mental processes and behavior. It is, for example, no longer a matter of choosing between neuroscience, cognitive psychology, and social psychology to understand how and why people behave (or don't behave) when passing by an accident scene, but rather of determining how these interacting subfields jointly account for that behavior. In short, psychology is becoming a truly integrated field. Given this critical course correction, one can only imagine how many insights and breakthroughs regarding mental processes and behavior lie ahead.

Covering all the angles To fully understand a mental process such as "intruding thoughts," today's psychologists study the phenomenon at many levels, from measuring the brain waves of individuals while their minds wander (seen here) to determining the possible childhood roots of such thoughts.

Summary

Defining, Classifying, and Diagnosing Psychological Abnormality

LEARNING OBJECTIVE 1   List the common features of most definitions of abnormal functioning and describe how psychological disorders are classified and diagnosed.

- The study of psychological disorders is usually called *abnormal psychology*. *Clinical researchers* conduct studies in abnormal functioning, and *clinical practitioners*, or *clinicians*, diagnose and treat people with psychological problems.

- Definitions of psychological disorders often include the "four Ds:" deviance, distress, dysfunction, and danger.

- The *Diagnostic and Statistical Manual of Mental Disorders (DSM)* (current version *DSM-IV-TR*) is the leading classification system in the United States.

- Clinicians use structured and unstructured *clinical interviews*; *analog*, *naturalistic*, and *self-report* observations; and a variety of *clinical tests* to diagnose people's disorders. Clinicians often combine information gathered from each of these sources.

Models of Psychological Abnormality

LEARNING OBJECTIVE 2   Identify the major models used by psychologists to describe abnormal functioning.

- Clinicians use five major models to explain abnormal functioning, including the biological, psychodynamic, behavioral, cognitive, and humanistic-existential models.

- All therapies have three features in common: (1) a sufferer who seeks relief from the healer; (2) a trained, socially accepted healer; and (3) a series of contacts between the healer and the sufferer, through which the healer, sometimes with the aid of a group, tries to produce certain changes in the sufferer's emotions, attitudes, and behaviors.

The Neuroscience Model

LEARNING OBJECTIVE 3   Describe neuroscience views of abnormal functioning and major brain therapies.

- The neuroscience model views abnormal functioning as a result of malfunctions in brain structure or chemical activity. Malfunctions can be caused by injuries or other factors, including genetics or viruses.

- *Drug therapy*, *electroconvulsive therapy (ECT)*, and *psychosurgery* are the three major brain treatments. All can bring relief, but each carries a risk of sometimes severe side effects. The neuroscience model has had a positive impact on the clinical field. At the same time, it has some key limitations.

The Psychodynamic Model

LEARNING OBJECTIVE 4   Describe Freud's view and other psychodynamic views of the causes and treatments of abnormal functioning and summarize the influence of the psychodynamic approach.

- Psychodynamic theorists view abnormal functioning as the result of unconscious conflicts that may have originated in our early development. Freud focused on fixations during the oral, anal, and phallic stages of development, while other theorists have focused on difficulties in ego development or our relationships with others.

- Psychodynamic therapy techniques include *free association*; therapist interpretation of *resistance*, *transference*, and *dreams*; *catharsis*; and repeatedly *working through* issues. Recent developments in psychodynamic therapy include short-term therapy.

- The psychodynamic approach has had a lasting influence on the conduct of treatment and was the first to offer an alternative to biological explanations of abnormal functioning. But the effectiveness of psychodynamic therapy is not well supported by research.

The Behavioral Model

LEARNING OBJECTIVE 5   Describe behavioral views of the causes and treatments of abnormal functioning and summarize the influence of the behavioral approach.

- Behavioral theorists suggest that abnormal behaviors develop via the same processes as more adaptive behaviors: classical conditioning, operant conditioning, and modeling.

- Behavioral treatments, aimed at replacing abnormal behaviors with more functional ones, are also based on learning processes. Systematic desensitization and *aversion therapy* rely on classical conditioning. *Token economies* follow the principles of operant conditioning, and *social skills training* uses modeling.

- Research suggests that behavioral therapies are often effective, although they do not always bring lasting change outside therapy. Moreover, some behaviorists do not focus on unobservable behaviors, such as thoughts.

The Cognitive Model

LEARNING OBJECTIVE 6   Describe cognitive theorists' views of the causes and treatments of abnormal functioning and summarize the influence of the cognitive approach.

- Cognitive theorists believe that abnormal functioning can result from disordered thoughts, including *basic irrational assumptions*, specific upsetting thoughts, and illogical thinking processes.

- *Rational-emotive therapy* focuses on helping clients to identify their maladaptive assumptions, test them, and change them. Similarly, cognitive therapy guides clients to challenge their maladaptive attitudes, automatic thoughts, and illogical thinking. Research supports the effectiveness of cognitive therapy for depression and certain other disorders.

- The cognitive view is quite popular today, and research suggests that cognitive treatment is often effective. It is still not clear, however, whether psychological disorders create or result from maladaptive thoughts.

The Humanistic-Existential Model

LEARNING OBJECTIVE 7 Describe humanistic and existential views of abnormal functioning and therapy and evaluate the influence of these approaches.

- Humanists suggest that people are vulnerable to psychological disorders when they develop inaccurate views of their worth or goals in life.
- Therapists practicing Carl Rogers' *client-centered therapy* try to provide *unconditional positive regard*, *accurate empathy*, and *genuineness*, so that clients come to value their own emotions thoughts and behaviors. Gestalt therapists use skillful frustration, role playing, rules, and games to help clients recognize and accept their needs and goals.
- Existentialist therapies focus on helping clients discover their personal freedom of choice and take responsibility for making choices.
- Only recently have humanistic and existential therapies begun to undergo systematic research. Early research suggests they can be beneficial for some clients.

Formats of Therapy

LEARNING OBJECTIVE 8 Describe commonly used formats of therapy.

- *Individual therapy*, in which practicioners meet with one client at a time, is the oldest of the modern therapy formats.
- In *group therapy* several clients with similar problems meet with a single therapist at the same time. *Self-help groups* are similar, but conducted without the leadership of a therapist. Both types of groups can be helpful for certain clients.
- *Family therapy* treats all members of a family, together or individually, and therapists usually consider the family as a system. Two

people in a long-term relationship can seek *couple therapy* to help address issues in their relationship.

- *Community mental health treatment* focuses on preventing abnormal functioning through 1) primary prevention—policies that reduce psychological risk in a community; 2) secondary prevention—treating minor problems before they become serious; and 3) tertiary prevention—providing prompt treatment for moderate and severe disorders so they do not become long-term problems.

Does Therapy Work?

LEARNING OBJECTIVE 9 Summarize research on the effectiveness of therapy.

- In general, receiving therapy is more likely to help people with psychological disorders than going without treatment. Research has found that each of the major forms of therapy is of some help to clients, although research also indicates that particular therapies are often best suited for certain disorders.
- Successful therapists often share similar effective elements in their approaches, regardless of their particular orientations.

Abnormal Psychology: Social and Cultural Forces

LEARNING OBJECTIVE 10 Describe the influences of social and cultural forces in the prevalence and treatment of psychological disorders.

- Rapid urbanization or economic upheaval can lead to increases in abnormal functioning in a society.
- Abnormal functioning is more common among people in lower socioeconomic groups. The stresses of poverty may increase the risk of disorders or perhaps disorders contribute to an inability to function at higher socioeconomic levels.
- Many psychologists focus on the influences and pressures faced by members of different cultures, particularly minority ethnic and racial groups. Women, members of ethnic minority groups, people in low socioeconomic classes, and homosexual individuals face pressures that sometimes contribute to psychological dysfunctioning. *Culture-sensitive* and *gender-sensitive therapy* approaches help clients become aware of and react adaptively to the cultural pressures and issues they face.

Key Terms

CUT/ACROSS CONNECTION

What Happens in the
B R A I N ?

- Biochemical and structural abnormalities in the brain have been linked to certain psychological disorders.
- Psychoactive drugs are one of the most common treatments for psychological disorders today.
- ECT is one of the clinical field's most effective treatments for depression.
- Today's psychosurgery traces its roots back to the prehistoric practice of chipping a hole in a person's skull to let demons out.

HOW we Differ

- It appears that culture, gender, sexual orientation, and socioeconomic status can all affect a person's risk of developing psychological problems.
- Women are twice as likely as men to experience severe depression, African Americans have elevated rates of anxiety disorders, Hispanic Americans have elevated rates of alcoholism, and Native Americans have unusually high rates of alcoholism and suicide.
- Genuinely spiritual people are, on average, less likely to display psychological disorders, a trend that may be linked to social and cultural factors, as well as to the positive expectations and interpretations of spiritual people.

When Things Go
Wrong

- Every year, nearly a third of U.S. adults, and about one in five children, have a psychological problem severe enough to need treatment.
  - There are over 400 different types of therapies practiced in the U.S. today.
  - Various kinds of treatments are more likely to be helpful than going without treatment, although certain treatments appear to be particularly helpful for certain disorders.

How we *Develop*

- Many psychodynamic and other theorists suggest that our earliest relationships with our primary caregivers serve as models for relationships that we use for the rest of our lives.
- Contracting certain viruses early in life, even before birth, may contribute to psychological disorders that don't appear until early adulthood.
- Freud believed that improper toilet training of children could lead them to have obsessive-compulsive habits as adults.
- Psychodynamic therapists believe it's common for clients to feel and behave toward their therapist as they did toward important figures in their childhood (or in their current lives), a process called *transference*.

Video Lab Exercise

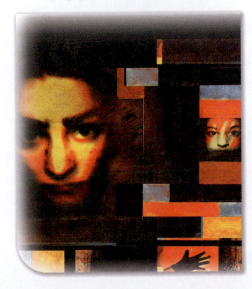

Psychology Around Us

Assessing and Treating Psychological Dysfunctioning

Therapist for a Day

How good are you at identifying psychological dysfunctioning? What treatments do you have confidence in? And what effects might your preferred treatments have on clients in need? This video lab exercise will answer those questions, as you play "therapist for a day."

In this exercise, you'll consider the interview responses of individuals with psychological problems, and, using decision-trees, you'll arrive at tentative diagnoses. You will then devise treatment programs for these individuals and their problems and try to justify your suggestions. Along the way, you'll see how your treatment plans compare to ones devised by clinical practitioners and learn about their likelihood of success. You will also come to appreciate the roles and limitations of using psychotropic drugs as part of treatment.

As you are working on this on-line exercise, consider the following questions:

- How useful is the process of diagnosis in general and that of DSM-IV-TR in particular?
- Which treatments are particularly effective for particular problems?
- What are the limitations and undesired effects of psychological labeling?
- Why are there a range of graduate training programs that can lead to becoming a mental health practitioner?

Glossary

A

ABC model of attitudes a model proposing that attitudes have three components: the affective component, the behavioral component, and the cognitive component.

abnormal psychology the scientific study of psychological disorders.

absolute pitch the ability to recognize or produce any note on a musical scale.

absolute refractory period a short time after an action potential, during which a neuron is completely unable to fire again.

absolute threshold the minimal stimulus necessary for detection by an individual.

academic psychology branch of psychology focusing on research and instruction in the various areas or fields of study in psychology.

accommodation one of two ways of acquiring knowledge, defined by Piaget as the alteration of pre-existing mental frameworks to take in new information.

action potential a sudden positive change in the electrical charge of a neuron's axon. Also known as a spike, or firing, action potentials rapidly transmit an excitatory charge down the axon.

activation-synthesis model theory that dreams result from brain's attempts to synthesize or organize random internally generated signals and give them meaning.

actor-observer effect the discrepancy between how we explain other people's behavior (dispositionally) and how we explain our own behavior (situationally).

acute stressor a stressful situation or circumstance that happens in the short term and has a definite endpoint.

adaptive theory of sleep theory that organisms sleep for the purposes of self-preservation, to keep away from predators that are more active at night.

addiction psychological or physical compulsion to take a drug, resulting from regular ingestion and leading to maladaptive patterns of behavior and changes in physical response.

ageusia inability to taste.

agrammatism a neurological condition arising from damage to a brain region just anterior to Broca's area where the patient is incapable of using words in grammatical sequence.

alcoholism long-term pattern of alcohol addiction.

algorithm problem-solving strategy that always leads to a solution.

allele variation of a gene.

altruism self-sacrificing behavior carried out for the benefit of others.

Alzheimer's disease most common form of dementia, usually beginning with mild memory problems, lapses of attention, and problems in language and progressing to difficulty with even simple tasks and recall of long-held memories.

amnestic disorders organic disorders in which memory loss is the primary symptom.

amygdala brain area involved in processing information about emotions, particularly fear.

amyotrophic lateral sclerosis (ALS or Lou Gehrig's disease) neurological disease that causes degeneration of motor neurons in the spinal cord, leading to loss of movement and eventual death.

analog observations observations of individuals in an artificial setting, such as a clinical office or a laboratory.

anorexia nervosa eating disorder in which individuals undereat and have a distorted body image of being overweight.

anosmia inability to smell.

anterograde amnesia ongoing inability to form new memories after an amnesia-inducing event.

antisocial personality disorder a personality disorder characterized by extreme and callous disregard for feelings and rights of others.

applied psychology branch of psychology applying psychological principles to practical problems in other fields, such as education, marketing, or industry.

approach-approach conflict conflict that occurs when a person must choose between two equally desirable options.

approach-avoidance conflict conflict that occurs when any available choice has both desirable and undesirable qualities.

Asperger's disorder a disorder in which persons have major social impairments yet maintain relatively normal intellectual, adaptive, and language skills.

assimilation   one of two ways of acquiring knowledge, defined by Piaget as the inclusion of new information or experiences into pre-existing schemata.

association cortex   areas of the neocortex responsible for complex functions, including higher-order sensory processing, thinking, and planning.

associative learning   learning that involves forming associations between stimuli.

attachment   a close emotional bond to another person, such as a baby to a caregiver.

attention deficit disorder (ADD)   a disorder characterized by an inability to pay attention.

attention deficit hyperactivity disorder (ADHD)   a disorder characterized by an inability to pay attention, accompanied by excessive activity.

attitudes   relatively stable and enduring evaluations of things and people.

attributions   causal explanations of behavior.

autism   a severe disorder marked by extreme unresponsiveness, poor communication, and very repetitive and rigid behaviors.

automatic processing   encoding of information with little conscious awareness or effort.

automatic thoughts   specific upsetting thoughts that occur unbidden.

autonomic nervous system   portion of the peripheral nervous system that includes the sympathetic and parasympathetic nervous systems.

availability heuristic   judging easily-recalled events as more common.

aversion therapy   therapy designed to help clients to acquire anxiety responses to stimuli that the clients have been finding too attractive.

avoidance-avoidance conflict   conflict that occurs when a person must choose between two equally undesirable options.

avoidant personality disorder   a disorder involving extreme discomfort and inhibition in social relationships.

axon   the part of the neuron that carries information away from the cell body toward other neurons.

axon terminal   the end of a neuron's axon, from which neurotransmitters are released.

B

babbling   babies' production of meaningless sounds.

basic emotions   a group of emotions preprogrammed into all humans regardless of culture.

basic irrational assumptions   maladaptive assumptions about oneself and one's world that increase the likelihood of psychological dysfunctioning.

basilar membrane   structure in the cochlea where the hair cells are located.

behavior   activities of an organism, often in response to environmental cues.

behavior modification   a planned effort to change behavior.

behavioral genetics   subfield of psychology looking at the influence of genes on human behavior.

behaviorism   the systematic study and manipulation of observable behavior; also, a branch of psychological thought.

biases   distorted beliefs based on a person's subjective sense of reality.

bioecological model of intelligence   Ceci's theory that intelligence is a function of the interactions among innate potential abilities, environmental context, and internal motivation.

bipolar disorder   a mood disorder in which periods of mania alternate with periods of depression.

body mass index (BMI)   weight-to-height ratio.

body weight set point   a weight that individuals typically return to even after dieting or overeating.

borderline personality disorder   a personality disorder characterized by severe instability in emotions and self-concept and high levels of volatility.

bottom-up processing   perception that proceeds by transducing environmental stimuli into neural impulses that move onto successively more complex brain regions.

brainstem (or **medulla**)   the part of the brain closest to the spinal cord that serves basic functions.

Broca's aphasia   a neurological condition arising from damage to Broca's area where the patient is unable to produce coherent speech.

Broca's area   brain region located in the frontal lobe that's important for speech production.

bulima nervosa   eating disorder in which individuals binge and then engage in purging-type behavior.

C

Cannon-Bard theory of emotion   a theory proposing that the subjective experience of emotion and the activation of the sympathetic nervous system (that is, bodily arousal) occur simultaneously.

case study   study focusing on a single person.

catharsis   reliving of past repressed feelings as means of settling internal conflicts and overcoming problems.

cellular clock theory   theory suggesting that we age because our cells have built-in limits on their ability to reproduce.

central nervous system   the brain and spinal cord.

cerebellum   part of the brain, near the back of the head, important for motor coordination.

child-directed speech speech characterized by exaggerated emotional responses and a slower pace that is common among caregivers communicating with babies and young children.

chromosomes strands of DNA; each human being has 46 chromosomes, distributed in pairs.

chronic stressor a stressful situation or circumstance that is relatively long term and often lacks a definite endpoint.

chunking grouping bits of information together to enhance ability to hold that information in working memory.

circadian rhythm pattern of sleep-wake cycles that in human beings roughly corresponds to periods of daylight and night.

client-centered therapy humanistic therapy designed by Carl Rogers to help clients experience unconditional positive regard and look at themselves honestly and acceptingly.

clinical and counseling psychology the study of abnormal psychological behavior and interventions designed to change that behavior.

clinical interview assessment technique involving a face-to-face encounter between the clinician and the person being assessed.

clinical tests devices for gathering information about a person's psychological functioning.

cochlea fluid-filled structure in the inner ear, contains the hair cells.

codominance in a heterozygous combination of alleles, both traits are expressed in the offspring.

cognition mental processes of thinking and knowing.

cognitive control the ability to direct thought in accord with one's intentions.

cognitive development changes in thinking that occur over the course of time.

cognitive dissonance a state of emotional discomfort people experience when they hold two contradictory beliefs or hold a belief that contradicts their behavior.

cognitive neuroscience study of mental processes and how they relate to the biological functions of the brain.

cognitive psychology field of psychology studying mental processes as forms of information processing, or the ways in which information is stored and operated in our minds.

cognitive therapy therapy approach designed to help clients recognize and change their dysfunctional thoughts and ways of thinking.

cognitive triad a pattern of thinking in which individuals repeatedly interpret their experiences, themselves, and their futures in negative ways that lead them to feel depressed.

cognitive-mediational theory of emotion a theory proposing that cognitive interpretations, particularly appraisals, of events are the keys to experiences of emotion.

cohort-sequential design blended cross-sectional and longitudinal research, designed to look at both how individuals from different age groups compare to one another and also follow them over time.

collectivist culture whose members focus more on the needs of the group and less on individual desires.

community mental health treatment treatment programs that emphasize community care, including an emphasis on prevention.

comorbidity condition in which a person's symptoms qualify him or her for two or more diagnoses.

compulsions repetitive and rigid behaviors or mental acts that people feel they must perform in order to prevent or reduce anxiety.

concrete operations Piagetian stage during which children are able to talk about complex relationships, such as categorization and cause and effect, but are still limited to understanding ideas in terms of real-world relationships.

conditioned response (CR) a response elicited by a conditioned stimulus; it is usually the same as the unconditioned response.

conditioned stimulus (CS) a neutral stimulus that eventually elicits the same response as an unconditioned stimulus with which it has been paired.

conditioned taste aversion a form of classical conditioning whereby a previously neutral stimulus (often an odor or taste) elicits an aversive reaction after it's paired with illness (nausea).

conditions of worth a perception that a person must meet certain standards in order to gain the love of his or her parent or other important figures.

conduct disorder clinical disorder in children and adolescents associated with emotional and behavioral problems, such as rule-breaking, trouble with limit-setting from authority figures, bullying and fighting with other people, and cruelty.

cones photoreceptors responsive to colors.

confirmation bias tendency to look for information that meets our expectations.

conflict discomfort brought about by two or more goals or impulses perceived to be incompatible.

conformity the tendency to yield to social pressure.

consciousness immediate personal awareness of ongoing mental processes, behaviors, and environmental events.

conservation the understanding that certain properties of an object (such as volume and number) remain the same despite changes in the object's outward appearance.

content validity the degree to which the content of a test accurately represents what the test is intended to measure.

continuous reinforcement when behavior is reinforced every time it occurs.

control group group in an experiment that has not been or will not be exposed to the independent variable.

convergence inward movement of the eyes to view objects close to oneself.

coping efforts to manage, reduce, or tolerate stress.

corpus callosum bundle of axons that allows communication from one side of the neocortex to the other.

correlation predictable relationship between two or more variables.

correlation coefficient statistic expressing the strength and nature of a relationship between two variables.

couple therapy (sometimes called **marital therapy**) a therapy format in which a therapist works with two people who are in a long-term relationship.

creativity the ability to produce ideas that are both original and valuable.

critical periods points in development when an organism is extremely sensitive to environmental input, making it easier for the organism to acquire certain brain functions and behaviors.

cross-sectional design research comparisons of groups of different-aged people to one another.

cultural psychology the study of how cognitive processing varies across different populations.

cultural universality behaviors and practices that occur across all cultures.

culture a set of shared beliefs and practices that are transmitted across generations.

culture-sensitive therapies psychotherapy approaches that seek to address the unique issues faced by members of minority groups.

D

daily hassles everyday annoyances that contribute to higher stress levels.

deafness loss or lack of hearing.

debriefing supplying full information to participants at the end of their participation in a research study.

decay theory theory of forgetting, suggesting memories fade over time due to neglect or failure to access over long period of time.

decision making evaluating and choosing from among options.

deductive reasoning reasoning proceeding from broad basic principles applied to specific situations.

defense mechanisms unconscious tactics employed by the ego to protect the individual from anxiety.

dementia severe memory problems combined with losses in at least one other cognitive function, such as abstract thinking or language.

dendrites the parts of neurons that collect input from other neurons.

denial a defense mechanism; the process of refusing to recognize an existing situation.

deoxyribonucleic acid (DNA) molecules in which genetic information is enclosed.

dependent personality disorder a disorder involving a pervasive, excessive need to be taken care of and a fear of separation.

dependent variable condition or event in an experiment that you expect to change as a result of variations in the independent variable.

depressants class of drugs that slow the activity of the central nervous system.

depression a persistent sad state in which life seems dark and its challenges overwhelming.

descriptive research methods studies that allow researchers to demonstrate a relationship between the variables of interest, without specifying a causal relationship.

developmental psychology the study of changes in behavior and mental processes over time and the factors that influence the course of those changes.

developmental psychopathology the study of how problematic behaviors evolve as a function of a person's genetics and early experiences and how those early problematic issues affect the person at later life stages.

diagnosis a clinician's determination that a person's cluster of symptoms represents a particular disorder.

Diagnostic and Statistical Manual of Mental Disorders (DSM) leading classification system for psychological disorders in the United States.

difference threshold or **just noticeable difference** the minimal difference between two stimuli necessary for detection of a difference between the two.

differential emotions theory a theory holding that particular emotions or sets of emotions become more prominent during specific life stages as they serve stage-related developmental processes.

discrete trait trait that results as the product of a single gene pairing.

display rules cultural expectations that prescribe how, when, and by whom emotions should be expressed.

dissociation a splitting of consciousness into two dimensions.

dissociative amnesia psychological disorder characterized by inability to recall important information, usually of an upsetting nature, about one's life.

dissociative disorders psychological disorder characterized by major loss of memory without a clear physical cause.

dissociative fugue psychological disorder characterized by loss of memory of personal identity and details of one's past life and flight to an entirely different location.

dissociative identity disorder psychological disorder characterized by the development of two or more distinct personalities.

distress stress caused by unpleasant situations or circumstances.

dominant trait trait that is expressed in a phenotype, no matter whether the genotype is homozygous or heterozygous for the trait.

dopamine neurotransmitter plentiful in brain areas involving movement and rewards.

double-blind procedure study in which neither the participant nor the researcher knows what treatment or procedure the participant is receiving.

Down syndrome an inherited disorder, usually caused by the presence of extra chromosomal material on the twenty-first chromosome, that results in mental retardation.

DSM-IV-TR the current version of the Diagnostic and Statistical Manual (DSM).

dyscalculia an inability to readily acquire information about mathematics.

dyslexia a learning disability that involves deficits in learning to read and write.

E

effortful processing encoding of information through careful attention and conscious effort.

ego according to psychoanalytic theory, a personality element that works to help satisfy the drives of the id while complying with the constraints placed on behavior by the environment.

egocentrism flaws in a child's reasoning based on his or her inability to take other perspectives.

electroconvulsive therapy (ECT) use of electric shock to trigger a brain seizure in hopes of relieving abnormal functioning.

emotion an intrapersonal state that occurs in response to either an external or an internal event and typically involves a physiological component, a cognitive component, and a behavioral component.

emotion dysregulation unhealthy attempts to regulate emotion.

emotion-focused coping coping strategies focused on changing one's feelings about the stressor.

emotional intelligence an individual's ability to perceive, express, assimilate, and regulate emotion.

emotional intensity the characteristic strength with which an individual typically experiences emotion.

empirical able to be tested in objective ways.

encoding a basic activity of memory, involving the recording of information in our brain.

endocrine system the system that controls levels of hormones throughout the body.

endorphins naturally-occurring pain-killing chemicals (neurotransmitters) in the brain.

enkephalins naturally-occurring pain-killing chemicals (neurotransmitters) in the brain.

episodic memory a person's memory of personal events or episodes from his or her life.

equifinality the idea that different individuals can start out from different places and wind up at the same outcome.

equilibrium balance in a mental framework.

eustress the optimal level of stress needed to promote physical and psychological health.

evolutionary psychology field of study believing that the body and brain are products of evolution and that genetic inheritance plays an important role in shaping the complete range of thoughts and behaviors.

experiment controlled observation, in which researchers manipulate the presence or amount of the independent variable to see what effect it has on the dependent variable.

experimental group group in an experiment that is exposed to the independent variable.

explicit memory memory that a person can consciously bring to mind, such as one's date of birth.

extinction reduction of a conditioned response after repeated presentations of the conditioned stimulus alone.

extrinsic motivation engaging in a behavior due to the influence of factors outside ourselves.

F

facial efference sensory feedback from facial muscular activity.

facial-feedback theory of emotion a theory proposing that subjective experiences of emotion are influenced by sensory feedback from facial muscular activity, or facial efference.

factor analysis a statistical method for determining whether certain items on a test correlate highly, thus forming a unified set, or cluster, of items.

family systems theory theory that each family has its own implicit rules, relationship structure, and communication patterns that shape the behavior of the individual members.

family therapy a treatment format in which therapists meet with all members of a family in order to help the whole family to change.

five-factor theory an empirically derived trait theory that proposes five major trait categories: agreeableness/disagreeableness, extraversion/introversion, neuroticism/stability, conscientiousness/irresponsibility, and openness to experience/unimaginativeness.

fixed interval schedule reinforcement occurs every time a specific time period has elapsed.

fixed ratio schedule reinforcement occurs after a specific number of responses.

flashbacks recurrence of the sensory and emotional changes after the LSD has left the body.

flashbulb memory detailed and near-permanent memories of an emotionally significant event, or of the circumstances surrounding the moment we learned about the event.

Flynn effect an observed rise in average IQ scores throughout the world over time.

forgetting the inability to recall information that was previously encoded into memory.

formal operations Piaget's final stage of cognitive development; the child achieves formal adult reasoning and the ability to think about things that don't have a concrete reality.

fovea center of the retina, containing only cones, where vision is most clear.

free association psychodynamic therapy technique of allowing clients to freely talk about whatever they want.

free nerve endings sensory receptors that convert physical stimuli into touch, pressure, or pain impulses.

free-radical theory theory suggesting we age because special negatively charged oxygen molecules become more prevalent in our body as we get older, destabilizing cellular structures and causing the effects of aging.

frontal cortex lobe of the neocortex involved in many functions including movement and speech production.

frustration an emotion people experience when thwarted in pursuit of a goal.

functional fixedness tendency to view objects as having only one function.

functionalism belief that mental processes have purpose and focus of study should be on how the mind adapts those purposes to changing environments.

fundamental attribution error the tendency to use dispositional attributions to explain the behavior of other people.

G

g factor a theoretical general factor of intelligence underlying all distinct clusters of mental ability; part of Spearman's two-factor theory of intelligence.

gate control theory of pain suggests that certain patterns of neural activity can close a "gate" to keep pain information from traveling to parts of the brain where it is perceived.

gender-sensitive therapies (or **feminist therapies**) psychological treatment geared to the special pressures of being a woman in Western society.

general adaptation syndrome (GAS) a three-stage response to stress identified by Hans Selye; the stages are alarm, resistance, and exhaustion.

generalized anxiety disorder an anxiety disorder in which people feel excessive anxiety and worry under most circumstances.

genes basic building blocks of our biological inheritance.

genotype a person's genetic inheritance.

Gestalt psychology field of psychology arguing that we have inborn tendencies to structure what we see in particular ways and to structure our perceptions into broad perceptual units.

glia the cells that, in addition to neurons, make up the nervous system.

group an organized, stable collection of individuals in which the members are aware of and influence one another and share a common identity.

group polarization the intensification of an initial tendency of individual group members brought about by group discussion.

group therapy psychotherapy format in which a therapist sees several clients who have similar problems at the same time.

groupthink a form of faulty group decision making that occurs when group members strive for unanimity and this goal overrides their motivation to realistically appraise alternative courses of action.

gustatory sense our sense of taste.

H

habituation process in which individuals respond less strongly to a stimulus after it is presented to them over and over again.

hair cells sensory receptors that convert sound waves into neural impulses.

hallucinogens substances that dramatically change one's state of awareness, causing powerful changes in sensory perception.

hemispheres halves of the brain.

heritability the overall extent to which differences among people are attributable to genes.

heritability coefficient a correlation coefficient used to indicate the contribution of heredity to some characteristic, such as intelligence.

heterosexual sexual attraction to members of the opposite sex.

heterozygous parents contribute two different alleles to offspring.

heuristic shortcut thinking strategy.

hippocampus brain region important for certain types of learning and memory.

homeostasis   a tendency of the body to maintain itself in a state of balance or equilibrium.

homosexual   sexual attraction to members of one's own sex.

homozygous   both parents contribute the same genetic material for a particular trait.

humanistic psychology   theory of psychology that seeks to give greater prominence to the special and unique features of human functioning.

Huntington's disease   inherited neurological disorder that results in the death of neurons in the striatum.

hypnagogic state   state a presleep period often characterized by vivid sensory phenomena.

hypnosis   a seemingly altered state of consciousness during which individuals can be directed to act or experience the world in unusual ways.

hypothalamus   brain structure important for motivation and control of the endocrine system.

hypothesis   a general statement about the way variables relate that is objectively falsifiable.

hypothetico-deductive reasoning   process of modern science where scientists begin with an educated guess about how the world works, and then set about designing small controlled observations to support or invalidate that hypothesis.

I

id   according to psychoanalytic theory, the personality element representing basic instinctual drives, such as those related to eating, sleeping, sex, and comfort.

immune system   the body's system of organs, tissues, and cells that identify and destroy foreign invaders, such as bacteria and viruses, as well as cancer cells.

implicit attitude   an attitude of which the person is unaware.

implicit memory   knowledge that we have stored in memory that we are not typically aware of or able to recall at will.

incentives   external motives that indirectly indicate reward.

independent variable   condition or event in an experiment that is thought to be a factor in changing another condition or event.

individual therapy   oldest of the modern psychotherapy formats in which the therapist sees the client alone.

individualistic   culture that places the wants or desires of the person over the needs of the group.

inductive reasoning   reasoning process proceeding from small specific situations to more general truths.

information processing   means by which information is stored and operated internally.

information-processing model   view of memory suggesting that information moves among three memory stores during encoding, storage, and retrieval.

information-processing theory   developmental theory focusing on how individuals take in and use information from their environment; also a theory that dreams are a form of information processing in which the mind attempts to sort out and organize the day's experiences and to fix them in memory.

informed consent   requirement that researchers give as much information as possible about the purpose, procedures, risks, and benefits of the study so that a participant can make an informed decision about whether or not to participate.

inoculation   exposing oneself to a relatively low level of stress in a controlled situation in order to improve later performance in a more stressful situation.

insight learning   a sudden realization of a solution to a problem or leap in understanding new concepts.

insomnia   sleep disorder characterized by a regular inability to fall asleep or stay asleep.

instincts   inborn behavioral tendencies, activated by stimuli in our environments.

institutional review board (IRB)   research oversight group that evaluates research to protect the rights of participants in the study.

intelligence   the ability to learn, to meet the demands of the environment effectively, and to understand and control one's mental activities.

intelligence quotient (IQ)   measure of intelligence, originally computed as the ratio of a child's mental age to his or her chronological age, multiplied by 100.

interactionism   a view emphasizing the relationship between a person's underlying personality traits and the reinforcing aspects of the situations in which they choose to put themselves.

interference theory   theory that forgetting is influenced by what happens to people before or after they take information in.

intermittent or **partial reinforcement**   a schedule of reinforcement where the behavior is only followed by reinforcement some of the time.

interneuron   neuron that typically has a short axon and serves as a relay between different classes of neurons. In the spinal cord, interneurons communicate with both sensory and motor neurons.

intrinsic motivation   engaging in a behavior simply for the satisfaction that is part of doing it.

introspection   method of psychological study endorsed by Wundt and his followers, involving careful evaluation of mental processes and how they expand simple thoughts into complex ideas.

ion channels pores in the cell membrane that open and close to allow certain ions into and out of the cell.

J

James-Lange theory of emotion a theory proposing that felt emotions result from physiological changes, rather than being their cause.

L

language a set of symbols used to communicate.

language comprehension the process of understanding spoken, written, or signed language.

language production the process of using movement to produce speech. Language production can also encompass signing by using hand signals.

lateral hypothalamus a region of the hypothalamus important in signaling thirst and hunger.

law of effect behaviors leading to rewards are more likely to occur again, while behaviors producing unpleasantness are less likely to occur again.

learned helplessness a situation in which repeated exposure to inescapable punishment eventually produces a failure to make escape attempts.

learning a lasting change caused by experience.

learning curve a graph that shows change in performance on a learning task over time.

learning disability a specific deficiency in one aspect of cognitive function while other aspects function normally.

leptin a protein produced by fat cells that is important for regulating the amount of food eaten over long periods of time.

lexical meaning dictionary meaning of a word.

life changes shifts in life circumstances that require adjustment of some kind.

linguistic relativity hypothesis suggests that the vocabulary available for objects or concepts in a language influences how speakers of that language think about them.

lobotomy surgical practice of cutting the connections between the frontal lobe and the lower centers of the brain.

long-term memory the memory system in which we hold all of the information we have previously gathered, available for retrieval and use in a new situation or task.

long-term potentiation (LTP) a form of synaptic change in which the repeated stimulation of certain nerve cells in the brain greatly increases the likelihood that the cells will respond strongly to future stimulation.

longitudinal design research following the same people over a period of time by administering the same tasks or questionnaires and seeing how their responses change.

lucid dreams dreams in which the sleeper fully recognizes that he or she is dreaming, and occasionally actively guides the outcome of the dream.

lymphocytes white blood cells that circulate through the body and destroy foreign invaders and cancer cells; important components of the immune system.

M

mania a persistent state of euphoria or frenzied energy.

maturation the unfolding of development in a particular sequence and time frame.

mean arithmetic average of a set of scores in a distribution.

median the score exactly in the middle of a distribution.

meditation technique designed to turn one's consciousness away from the outer world toward one's inner cues and awareness.

Meissner's corpuscles sensory receptors that convert physical stimuli about sensory touch on the fingertips, lips, and palms.

memory the faculty for recalling past events and past learning.

memory span maximum number of items that can be recalled in correct order.

menopause series of changes in hormonal function occurring in women during their 50s, which lead to the end of the menstrual cycle and reproductive capabilities.

mental age the intellectual age at which a person is functioning, as opposed to chronological age.

mental imagery picturing things in your mind.

mental processes activities of our brain when engaged in thinking, observing the environment, and using language.

mental retardation term describing individuals who display general intellectual functioning that is well below average and, at the same time, poor adaptive behavior.

mental set tendency to use problem-solving strategies that have worked in the past.

Merkel's discs sensory receptors that convert information about light to moderate pressure on the skin.

metacognition the ability to think about, understand, and control one's own thoughts.

mirror neurons neurons located in the frontal and parietal cortex, which respond similarly when the individual engages in an activity and when the individual watches someone else engage in the activity.

miscarriage discharge of the fetus from the uterus before it is able to function on its own

mnemonic devices techniques used to enhance the meaningfulness of information, as a way of making them more memorable.

mode the score that occurs most frequently in a distribution.

modeling   mimicking others' behavior.

monocular cues   visual clues about depth and distance that can be perceived using information from only one eye.

morpheme   the smallest unit of meaning in language.

motivation   an internal state or condition that directs behavior.

motive   a need or desire.

motor skills   ability to control our bodily movements.

multifinality   the idea that children can start from the same point and wind up in any numbers of other outcomes.

multiple sclerosis   neurological disease that causes a loss of myelin on the axons of neurons.

myelin   a fatty, white substance, formed from glial cells, that insulates the axons of many neurons.

myelination   development of fatty deposits on neurons that allow electric impulses to pass through neurons more efficiently.

N

narcissistic personality disorder   a personality disorder characterized by a high degree of self-interest and a high, often unrealistic, degree of self-importance.

narcolepsy   sleep disorder marked by uncontrollable urge to fall asleep.

naturalistic observation   observation of individuals in everyday settings.

negative correlation   relationship in which scores on one variable increase as scores on another variable decrease.

negative punishment   removal of a pleasant stimulus as a consequence of a behavior.

negative reinforcement   removal of a negative consequence as a result of behavior.

neocortex   the largest portion of the brain, responsible for complex behaviors including language and thought.

nerve conduction velocity (NCV)   the speed with which electrical impulses are transmitted along nerve fibers and across synapses.

neural circuits (or **neural networks**)   collections of neurons that communicate with one another.

neural tube   area of an embryo from which the CNS arises.

neurofibrillary tangles   twisted protein fibers found *within* the cells of the hippocampus and certain other brain areas.

neurogenesis   the production of new neurons.

neuroimaging   techniques that allow for studying brain activity by obtaining visual images in awake humans.

neuron   a nerve cell.

neuroscience   study of psychological functions by looking at the nervous system and related biological foundations of those functions. Previously known as *psychobiology*.

neurosis   an abnormal behavior pattern caused by unresolved conflicts between the id, ego, and superego.

neurotransmitter receptors   proteins in the membranes of neurons that bind to neurotransmitters.

neurotransmitters   specialized chemicals that travel across synapses to allow communication between neurons.

nonassociative learning   learning that does not involve forming associations between stimuli.

nonREM sleep (NREM)   Stages 1 through 4 of normal sleep pattern.

nonverbal communication   body language.

norepinephrine   neurotransmitter important for arousal and attention.

normal distribution   a symmetrical, bell-shaped distribution in which most scores are in the middle with smaller groups of equal size at either end.

norms   social rules about how members of a society are expected to act.

nucleus accumbens   a brain area important for motivation and reward.

O

obedience   the act of following direct commands, usually given by an authority figure.

obesity   overweight; characterized as a body mass index of over 30.

object permanence   an infant's realization that objects continue to exist even when they are outside one's immediate sensory awareness.

observational learning learning that occurs without overt training in response to watching behavior.

obsessive-compulsive disorder (OCD)   a mental disorder associated with repeated abnormal anxiety-provoking thoughts and/or repeated ritualistic-like behaviors.

occipital cortex   lobe of the neocortex at the back of the skull, important for processing very visual information.

odorants   airborne chemicals that are detected as odors.

olfactory bulb   the first region where olfactory information reaches the brain on its way from the nose.

olfactory receptor neurons   sensory receptor cells that convert chemical signals from odorants into neural impulses that travel to the brain.

olfactory sense   our sense of smell.

operant (or **instrumental conditioning**)   a form of associative learning whereby behavior is modified depending on its consequences.

operationalize   to develop a working definition of a variable that allows you to test it.

operations   Piagetian description of a child's ability to hold an idea in his or her mind and mentally manipulate it.

opioids class of drugs derived from the sap of the opium poppy.

optic nerve the bundle of axons of ganglion cells that carries visual information from the eye to the brain.

ossicles tiny bones in the ear called the *hammer*, *anvil*, and *stirrup*.

oval window a membrane separating the ossicles and the inner ear, deflection of which causes a wave to form in the cochlea.

overregularization the process by which elementary school children apply learned grammatical rules to improperly "correct" an irregular verb.

P

Pacinian corpuscles sensory receptors that respond to vibrations and heavy pressure.

panic attacks periodic, short bouts of panic.

papillae bumps on the tongue that contain clumps of taste buds.

parallel distributed-processing (PDP) (or connectionist) model theory of memory suggesting information is represented in the brain as a pattern of activation across entire neural networks.

parasympathetic nervous system the division of the autonomic nervous system active during restful times.

parietal cortex lobe of the neocortex involved in processing information related to touch and complex visual information, particularly about locations.

Parkinson's disease neurological disease that involves the death of dopaminergic neurons in the substantia nigra, leading to tremors, muscle rigidity, and other motor problems.

Pavlovian or **classical conditioning** a form of associative learning whereby a neutral stimulus is paired with a salient stimulus so that eventually the neutral stimulus predicts the salient stimulus.

perception recognition and identification of a sensory stimulus.

perceptual constancies our top-down tendency to view objects as unchanging, despite shifts in the environmental stimuli we receive.

perfect correlation a relationship in which two variables are exactly related; that is, low, medium, and high scores on both variables are always exactly related.

peripheral nervous system the nerves that extend throughout our bodies outside the central nervous system.

personality the unique characteristics that account for enduring patterns of inner experience and outward behavior.

personality disorder an inflexible pattern of inner experience and outward behavior that causes distress or difficulty with daily functioning.

personality inventory a paper-and-pencil questionnaire designed to assess various aspects of personality.

personality traits tendencies to behave in certain ways that remain relatively constant across situations.

phenotype the observable manifestation of a person's genetic inheritance.

phobia a persistent and unreasonable fear of a particular object, activity, or situation.

phoneme the smallest unit of language, an individual sound.

phonology the study of how individual sounds or phonemes are used to produce language.

photoreceptors the sensory receptor cells for vision, located in the retina.

phrenology an unsubstantiated method of assessing a person's mental and moral qualities by studying the shape of the person's skull.

pituitary gland brain structure that plays a central role in controlling the endocrine system.

placenta nutrient-rich structure that serves to feed the developing fetus.

plasticity change in the nervous system.

polygenic trait trait that manifests as the result of the contributions of multiple genes.

pons part of the brain anterior to the brainstem that includes the locus coeruleus.

positive correlation relationship in which scores on two variables increase together (or decrease together).

positive psychology an area of psychology focusing on positive experiences and healthy mental functioning.

positive punishment presentation of an unpleasant consequence following a behavior.

positive reinforcement presentation of a pleasant consequence following a behavior.

postsynaptic potentials electrical events in postsynaptic neurons, that occur when a neurotransmitter binds to one of its receptors.

posttraumatic stress disorder (PTSD) an anxiety disorder experienced in response to a major traumatic event, characterized by lingering and persistent, frightening thoughts or memories of the traumatic events, along with anxiety, depression, and other symptoms.

pragmatics the practical aspects of language usage, including speech pace, gesturing, and body language.

preconsciousness level of awareness in which information can become readily available to consciousness if necessary.

prefrontal cortex portion of the frontal cortex involved in higher-order thinking, such as memory, moral reasoning, and planning.

prejudice negative stereotypical attitudes toward individuals from another group.

prenatal period period of development stretching from conception to birth.

preoperational stage according to Piaget, a developmental stage during which the child begins to develop ideas of objects in the external world and the ability to work with it in his or her mind.

pressure an expectation or demand that someone act in a certain way.

primary appraisal appraisal of a stressor to determine how severe it is; the first stage in Richard Lazarus's description of how people experience stress.

primary mental abilities seven distinct mental abilities identified by Thurstone as the basic components of intelligence.

primary reinforcer reinforcer that is intrinsically pleasurable.

primary sex characteristics changes in body structure that occur during puberty that have to do specifically with the reproductive system, including the growth of the testes and the ovaries.

priming activation of one piece of information, which in turns leads to activation of another piece, and ultimately to the retrieval of a specific memory.

private speech a child's self-talk, which Vygotsky believed the child uses to regulate behavior and internal experiences.

proactive interference competing information that is learned before the forgotten material, preventing its subsequent recall.

problem solving determining how to reach a goal.

problem-focused coping coping strategies focused on dealing directly with the stressor, such as by changing the stressor in some way.

projective test a personality assessment device intended to tap a person's unconscious by presenting the person with an ambiguous stimulus and asking the person to interpret what the stimulus means.

proximodistal growth from more central areas of the body to parts at the outer edges.

psychoactive drugs chemicals that affect awareness, behavior, sensation, perception, or mood.

psychoanalytic theory psychological theory that human mental processes are influenced by the competition among unconscious forces.

psychology the study of mental processes and behaviors.

psychometric approach an approach to defining intelligence that attempts to measure intelligence with carefully constructed psychological tests.

psychoneuroimmunology an area of study focusing on links between stress, the immune system, and health.

psychosexual stages according to psychoanalytic theory, stages in the development of personality; the stages—labeled oral, anal, phallic, latency, and genital—are primarily influenced by sexuality and aggression.

psychosurgery brain surgery, often used in hopes of relieving abnormal functioning.

psychotropic drugs medications that act primarily on the brain.

puberty development of full sexual maturity during adolescence.

psychosurgery brain surgery, often used in hopes of relieving abnormal functioning.

punishment an unpleasurable experience that produces a decrease in a certain behavior.

R

random selection choosing a sample in such a way that everyone in the population of interest has an equal chance of being involved in the study.

rapid eye movement sleep (REM) stage of sleep associated with rapid and jagged brain-wave patterns, increased heart rate, rapid and irregular breathing, rapid eye movements, and dreaming.

rational-emotive therapy Ellis's cognitive therapy technique designed to help clients discover and change the irrational assumptions that govern their emotions, behaviors, and thinking.

recall tasks memory tasks in which people are asked to produce information using little or no retrieval cues.

recessive trait trait that is only expressed if a person carries the same two genetic alleles (e.g., is homozygous for the trait).

reciprocal socialization the transactional relationship between parent and child.

recognition tasks memory tasks in which people are asked to identify whether or not they have seen a particular item before.

reflexes programmed physical reactions to certain cues that do not require any conscious thought to perform.

rehearsal conscious repetition of information in an attempt to make sure the information is encoded.

reinforcement learning process in which the consequence resulting from a behavior will increase or decrease the likelihood that the behavior will occur again.

reinforcer an experience that produces an increase in a certain behavior.

relative refractory period just after the absolute refractory period during which a neuron can only fire if it receives a stimulus stronger than its usual threshold level.

reliability the degree to which a test produces the same scores over time.

replication repeated testing of a hypothesis to insure that the results achieved in one experiment are not due to chance.

representativeness heuristic assumes that individuals share characteristics of category of which they are a member.

repression the most basic defense mechanism; the process of keeping unpleasant memories or thoughts buried within the unconscious mind.

resilience the ability to recover from or avoid the serious effects of negative circumstances.

resistance when clients encounter a block in their free associations or change the subject so as to avoid a potentially painful discussion.

responses ways we react to stimuli.

resting potential the electrical charge of a neuron when it is at rest.

restorative theory of sleep theory that we sleep in order to allow the brain and body to restore certain depleted chemical resources and eliminate chemical wastes that have accumulated during the waking day.

reticular formation a brain structure important for sleep and wakefulness.

retina a specialized sheet of nerve cells in the back of the eye containing the sensory receptors for vision.

retinal disparity the slight difference in images processed by the retinas of each eye.

retrieval a basic activity of memory, involving recovery of information when we need it later.

retrieval cues words, sights, or other stimuli that remind us of the information we need to retrieve from our memory.

retroactive interference learning of new information that disrupts access to previously recalled information.

retrograde amnesia inability to remember things that occurred before an organic event.

reward-deficiency syndrome theory that people might abuse drugs because their reward learning pathway is not readily activated by usual life events.

reward learning pathway brain circuitry that is important for learning about rewarding stimuli.

risk factors biological and environmental factors that contribute to problematic outcomes.

rods photoreceptors most responsive to levels of light and dark.

Ruffini's end-organs sensory receptors that respond to heavy pressure and joint movement.

S

s factor a theoretical specific factor uniquely tied to a distinct mental ability or area of functioning; part of Spearman's two-factor theory of intelligence.

sample the group of people studied in an experiment, used to stand in for an entire group of people.

scaffolding developmental adjustments that adults make to give children the help that they need, but not so much that the children fail to move forward.

Schachter and Singer's two-factor theory of emotion a theory proposing that an emotional state is a function of both physiological arousal and cognition.

schemas knowledge bases that we develop based on prior exposure to similar experiences or other knowledge bases.

schemata Piaget's proposed mental structures or frameworks for understanding or thinking about the world.

schizophrenia a mental disorder characterized by disorganized thoughts, lack of contact with reality, and sometimes hallucinations.

secondary appraisal appraisal of one's personal resources and ability to cope with a stressor; the second stage in Richard Lazarus's description of how people experience stress.

secondary reinforcer reinforcer that is associated with primary reinforcers.

secondary sex characteristics changes that occur during puberty and that differ according to gender, but are not specifically related to the reproductive system.

sedative-hypnotic drugs class of drugs, the members of which produce feelings of relaxation and drowsiness.

self-actualization the need of humans to fulfill their full and special potential; the highest-level of need in Maslow's hierarchy of needs.

self-concept a pattern of self-perception that remains consistent over time and can be used to characterize an individual.

self-determination competence, relatedness and autonomy.

self-help groups groups consisting of people who have similar problems and come together to help and support one another without the direct leadership of a professional clinician.

self-monitoring when individuals monitor their own symptoms.

self-perception theory a theory suggesting that when people are uncertain of their attitudes, they infer what the attitudes are by observing their own behavior.

self-serving bias the tendency people have to attribute their successes to internal causes and their failures to external ones.

semantic code cognitive representation of information or an event based on the meaning of the information.

semantic memory a person's memory of general knowledge of the world.

semantics the study of how meaning in language is constructed of individual words and sentences.

senile plaques sphere-shaped deposits of a protein known as *beta-amyloid* that form in the spaces *between* cells in the hippocampus, cerebral cortex, and certain other brain regions, as well as in some nearby blood vessels.

sensation   the act of using our sensory systems to detect environmental stimuli.

sensitive period   a time during development after which it becomes more difficult to develop certain capabilities.

sensitization   a form of nonassociative learning whereby a strong stimulus results in an exaggerated response to the subsequent presentation of weaker stimuli.

sensory adaptation   the process whereby repeated stimulation of a sensory cell leads to a reduced response.

sensory memory   memory involving detailed, brief sensory image or sound retained for a brief period of time.

sensory receptor cells   specialized cells that convert a specific form of environmental stimuli into neural impulses.

sensory transduction   the process of converting a specific form of environmental stimuli into neural impulses.

serotonin   neurotransmitter involved in activity levels and mood regulation.

shaping   introducing new behavior by reinforcing small approximations of the desired behavior.

situationism   the view that behavior is governed primarily by the variables in a given situation rather than by internal traits.

sleep apnea   sleep disorder characterized by repeatedly ceasing to sleep during the night, depriving the brain of oxygen and leading to frequent awakenings.

sleep spindles   bursts of brain activity lasting a second or two; occur during Stage 2 sleep.

social cognition   the way in which people perceive and interpret themselves and others in their social world.

social facilitation   an effect in which the presence of others enhances performance.

social identity theory   a theory that emphasizes social cognitive factors in the onset of prejudice.

social loafing   a phenomenon in which people exert less effort on a collective task than they would on a comparable individual task; also known as free riding.

social neuroscience   study of social functioning and how it is tied to brain activity.

social phobia   a disorder involving severe, persistent, and irrational fears of social situations in which embarrassment may occur.

social psychology   an area of psychology that seeks to understand, explain, and predict how people's thoughts, feelings, and behaviors are influenced by the actual, imagined, or implied presence of others.

social role   a set of norms ascribed to a person's social position; expectations and duties associated with the individual's position in the family, at work, in the community, and in other settings.

social role theory   theory that gender differences occur because girls and boys develop different behaviors and skills based largely on the differences in gender role expectations.

social skills training   behavioral therapy technique in which therapists serve as models and teachers to help clients acquire desired social behaviors.

socially desirable responding   tailoring answers on personality inventories to try to create a good impression.

sociobiologists   theorists who believe humans have a genetically innate concept of how social behavior should be organized.

somatic nervous system   all the peripheral nerves that transmit information about the senses and movement to and from the central nervous system.

somatosensory strip   an area of the parietal cortex that processes tactile information coming from our body parts.

sound waves   vibrations of the air in the frequency of hearing.

source misattribution   remembering information, but not the source it came from; can lead to remembering as true information from unreliable sources.

spacing effect   facilitated encoding of material through rehearsal situations spread out over time.

spatial navigation learning   learning that involves forming associations among stimuli relevant to navigating in space.

spinal cord   portion of the central nervous system that extends from the base of the brain and mediates sensory and motor information.

spontaneous recovery   re-emergence of a conditioned response some time after extinction has occurred.

stage   developmental point at which organisms achieve certain levels of functioning.

standard deviation   statistical index of how much scores vary within a group.

standardization   the use of uniform procedures in administering and scoring a test.

state-dependent memory   memory retrieval facilitated by being in the same state of mind in which you encoded the memory in the first place.

stem cell   undifferentiated cell that can divide to replace itself and create new cells that have the potential to become all other cells of the body, including neurons.

stereotype threat   a phenomenon in which people in a particular group perform poorly because they fear that their performance will conform to a negative stereotype associated with that group.

stereotype threat   awareness of a negative stereotype that affects oneself and often leads to impairment in performance.

stereotypes   generalized impressions about a person or a group of people based on the social category they occupy.

stimulants substances that increase the activity of the central nervous system.

stimuli elements of the environment that trigger changes in our internal or external states.

stimulus generalization when similar stimuli elicit the same response as a conditioned stimulus after classical conditioning has occured.

storage a basic activity of memory, involving retention (whether brief or long) of information for later use.

stress state brought on by any situation that threatens or appears to threaten a person's sense of well-being, thus challenging the individual's ability to cope.

stressor a situation or circumstance that triggers the stress response.

striatum a brain area that works with the substantia nigra to enable fluid movements.

structuralism belief that mind is a collection of sensory experiences and that study should be focused on mental processes rather than explanation of mechanisms underlying those processes.

subpersonalities alternate personalities developed in dissociative identity disorder, each with a unique set of memories, behaviors, thoughts, and emotions.

substantia nigra brain region important in fluidity of movement and inhibiting movements.

superego according to psychoanalytic theory, a personality element in charge of determining which impulses are acceptable to express openly and which are unacceptable; develops as we observe and internalize the behaviors of others in our culture.

superfactor a fundamental dimension of personality made up of a related cluster of personality traits.

suprachiasmatic nucleus (SCN) small group of neurons in the hypothalamus responsible for coordinating the many rhythms of the body.

survey study in which researchers give participants a questionnaire or interview them.

sympathetic nervous system the division of the autonomic nervous system activated under conditions of stress.

synapses tiny spaces between the axon terminal of one neuron and the next neuron through which communication occurs.

synaptic pruning developmental reduction of neuronal connections, allowing stronger connections to flourish.

synaptic vesicles membrane-bound spheres in the axon terminals of neurons where neurotransmitters are stored before their release.

synaptogenesis the process of forming new synapses.

syntax the grammatical positioning of words in a sentence.

systematic desensitization a process used to extinguish phobias through gradual and relaxed exposure to the feared object or situation.

T

taste buds clusters of sensory receptor cells that convert chemical signals from food into neural impulses that travel to the brain.

telegraphic speech speech that consists of minimalistic sentences. This form of speech characterizes early toddlerhood and is the first evidence of sentence formation.

temperament biologically-based tendencies to respond to certain situations in similar ways throughout our lifetimes.

temporal cortex part of the neocortex important in processing sounds, in speech comprehension, and in recognizing complex visual stimuli, such as faces.

teratogens environmental risks to a fetus's development during gestation.

thalamus an area of the brain that serves as a relay station for incoming sensory information.

theories ideas about laws that govern phenomena.

theory of mind a recognition that other people base their opinions on their own perspectives, not on information that is unavailable to them.

theory of multiple intelligences theory that there is no single, unified intelligence, but instead several independent intelligences arising from different portions of the brain.

therapy (treatment) procedures designed to change abnormal functioning to more normal functioning.

therapy outcome studies research that looks at the effects of various treatments.

token economy operant conditioning therapy program in which participants receive tokens (that can be traded for rewards) when they display desired behaviors.

tolerance mark of physical dependence on drug, in which a person needs to take incrementally larger doses of the drug to achieve the same effect.

tonotopic map representation in the auditory cortex of different sound frequencies.

top-down processing perception processes led by cognitive processes, such as memory or expectations.

transference process through which clients act and feel toward the therapist as they did (or do) toward important figures from their past or present.

traumatic events unexpected events severe enough to create extreme disruptions.

trephining prehistoric practice of chipping a hole in the skull of a person who was behaving strangely, with the idea of letting the demons out.

triangular theory of love   a theory that love is composed of three elements: intimacy, passion, and commitment; proposed by Robert Sternberg.

triarchic theory of intelligence   Sternberg's theory that intelligence is made up of three interacting components: internal, external, and experiential components.

tympanic membrane   the ear drum.

Type A   a personality type characterized by competitiveness, impatience, and anger and hostility.

Type B   a personality type that is less aggressive, more relaxed, and less hostile than Type A.

Type C   a personality type characterized by difficulty in expressing or acknowledging negative feelings.

U

unconditional positive regard   a parent's, therapist's, or other person's full and warm acceptance of an individual, without terms or conditions.

unconditioned response (UR)   a response naturally elicited by an unconditioned stimulus; it is not learned.

unconditioned stimulus (US)   a stimulus that on its own elicits a response.

unconscious   hypothesized repository of thoughts, feelings and sensations outside human awareness, thought in some theories to have a strong bearing on human behavior.

unconscious state   state in which information is not easily accessible to conscious awareness.

unipolar depression   a mood disorder that includes only depression.

V

validity   the extent to which a test accurately measures or predicts what it is supposed to measure or predict.

validity coefficient   a correlation coefficient that measures validity by correlating a test score with some external criterion.

variable   condition, event, or situation that is studied in an experiment.

variable interval schedule   reinforcement occurs after varying amounts of time.

variable ratio schedule   the number of responses required for reinforcement varies.

ventromedial region of the hypothalamus   a region of the hypothalamus important in signaling satiety.

voluntarism   belief that much of behavior is motivated and that attention is focused for an explicit purpose.

W

wear-and-tear theory   theory suggesting we age because use of our body wears it out

Wernicke's aphasia   a neurological condition associated with damage to Wernicke's area where a person cannot understand language.

Wernicke's area   an area of the temporal cortex important for helping us understand language.

withdrawal symptoms   unpleasant and sometimes dangerous symptoms produced by reducing intake of a drug after a person has become addicted to it.

working memory   a short-term memory store that can hold about seven items at once.

Y

Yerkes-Dodson law   ideal performance on a task occurs when the arousal level is optimized to the difficulty level.

Z

zone of proximal development   the gap between what a child could accomplish alone and what the child can accomplish with help from others.

zygote   single cell resulting from successful fertilization of the egg by sperm.

References

A

Abe, J. A. & Izard, C. E. (1999). The developmental functions of emotions: An analysis in terms of differential emotions theory. *Cognition and Emotion, 13*, 523-549.

Abele, A. E. (2003). The dynamics of masculine-agentic and feminine-communal traits: Findings from a prospective study. *Journal of Personality and Social Psychology, 85*(4): 768-776.

Abella, K., & Dutton, S. (1994). Questions and answers. *Typeworks.*

Abella, R. & Heslin, R. (1989). Appraisal processes, coping and the regulation of stress-related emotions in a college examination. *Basic and Applied Social Psychology, 10:* 311-327.

Abercrombie, H. C., Chambers, A. S., Greischar, L., & Monticelli, R. M. (2008). Orienting, emotion, and memory: Phasic and tonic variation in heart rate predicts memory for emotional pictures in men. *Neurobiology of Learning and Memory, 90*(4), 644-650.

Abosch, A. & Cosgrove, G. R. (2008). Biological basis for the surgical treatment of depression. *Neurosurgical Focus. 25*(1): E2.

Abramowitz, J. S. (2008). Is nonparaphilic compulsive sexual behavior a variant of OCD? In J. S. Abramowitz, D. McKay, & S. Taylor (Eds.), *Obsessive-compulsive disorder: Subtypes and spectrum conditions.* Oxford, England: Elsevier.

Abramowitz, J. S., McKay, D., & Taylor, S. (Eds.). (2008). *Obsessive-compulsive disorder: Subtypes and spectrum conditions.* Oxford, England: Elsevier.

Abrams, D., Hogg, M. A., & Marques, J. M. (2005). A social psychological framework for understanding social inclusion and exclusion. *The social pshychology of inclusion and exclusion.* (pp. 1-23) New York, NY: Psychology Press.

Abrams, D., Marques, J. M., Bown, N., & Henson, M. (2000). Pro-norm and anti-norm deviance within and between groups. *Journal of Personality and Social Psychology, 78*(5), 906-912.

Abrams, D., Wetherell, M., Cochrane, S., Hogg, M. A. et al., (1990). Knowing what to think by knowing who you are: Self-categorization and the nature of norm formation, conformity and group polarization. *British Journal of Social Psychology, 29*(2), 97-119.

Abrams, D., Wetherell, M., Cochrane, S., Hogg, M. A., & Turner, J. C. (2001). Knowing what to think by knowing who you are: Self-categorization and the nature of norm formation, conformity and group polarization. In M. A. Hogg & D. Abrams (eds.), *Intergroup relations: Essential readings.* (pp. 270-288). New York, NY: Psychology Press.

Accolla, R., Bathellier, B., Petersen, C.C., & Carleton, A. (2007). Differential spatial representation of taste modalities in the rat gustatory cortex. *The Journal of Neuroscience, 27*, 1396-404.

Acebo, C., Sadeh, A., Seifer, R., Tzischinsky, O., Hafer, A., & Carskadon, M. A. (2005). Sleep/wake patterns derived from activity monitoring and maternal report for healthy 1 to 5-year-old children. *Sleep, 28*, 1568-77.

Acosta, M. C., Haller, D. L., & Schnoll, S. H. (2005). Cocaine and stimulants. In R. J. Frances, A. H. Mack, & S. I. Miller (Eds.), *Clinical textbook of addictive disorders (3rd ed.).* New York, NY: Guilford Press.

Acredolo, L. & Goodwyn, S. (1988). Symbolic gesturing in normal infants. *Child Development, 59:* 450-66.

Adams, G. R. & Huston, T. L. (1975). Social perception of middle-aged persons varying in physical attractiveness. *Developmental Psychology, 11:* 657-658.

Ader, R., Felten, D. L., & Cohen, N. (Eds.). (2001). *Psychoneuroimmunology* (3rd ed., Vols. 1 & 2). San Diego, CA: Academic Press.

Admon, Y. (2009). Rising Criticism of Child Bride Marriages in Saudi Arabia. The Middle East Media Research Institute. Downloaded on June 26, 2009 from: http://memri.org/bin/articles.cgi?Page=archives&Area=ia&ID=IA50209.

Adolphs, R. (2003). Cognitive neuroscience of human social behaviour. *Nature Reviews Neuroscience, 4*(3): 165-178.

Adolphs, R. (2009). The social brain: Neural basis of social knowledge. *Annual Review of Psychology, 60:* 693-716.

Adolphs, R., Russell, J., & Tranel, D. (1999). A role for the human amygdala in recognizing emotional arousal from unpleasant stimuli. *Psychological Science, 10:* 167-171.

Adolphs, R., Tranel, D., Damasio, H., & Damasio, A. (1994). Impaired recognition of emotion in facial expressions following bilateral damage to the human amygdala. *Nature, 372*, 669-672.

Aftanas, L. I. & Golosheikin, S. A. (2003). Changes in cortical activity in altered states of consciousness: The study of meditation by high-resolution EEG. *Human Physiology, 29*(2), 143-151.

Aggleton, J. P. & Shaw, C. (1996). Amnesia and recognition memory: A reanalysis of psychometric data. *Neuropsychologia, 34* (1), 51-62.

Aiello, J. R. & Douthitt, E. A. (2001). Social facilitation from Triplett to electronic performance monitoring. *Group Dynamics: Theory, Research, and Practice, 5:* 163-180.

Ainsworth, M. D. (1985). Patterns of attachment. *Clinical Psychologist, 38*(2), 27-29.

Ainsworth, M. D. S. (1967), *Infancy in Uganda: Infant care and the growth of love,* Baltimore, MD: Johns Hopkins University Press.

Ainsworth, M. D. S. (1979). Attachment as related to mother-infant interaction. In J. S. Rosenblatt, R. A. Hinde, C. Beer, & M. Busnel (eds.), *Advances in the study of behavior (Vol. 9).* Orlando, FL: Academic Press.

Ainsworth, M. S. (1993). Attachment as related to mother-infant interaction. *Advances in Infancy Research, 8*, 1-50.

al Absi, M. & Rokke, P.D. (1991). Can anxiety help us tolerate pain? *The Journal of Pain, 46*, 43-51.

Albarracin, D., Zanna, M. P., Johnson, B. T., & Kumkale, G. T. (2005). Attitudes: Introduction and scope. *The handbook of attitudes.* (pp. 3-19) Mahwah, NJ: Lawrence Erlbaum Associates Publishers.

Alcaro, A., Huber, R., & Panksepp, J. (2008). Behavioral Functions of the Mesolimbic Dopaminergic System: an Affective Neuroethological Perspective. *Brain Research Reviews, 56(2)*: 283-321.

Aldwin, C. M. (2007). *Stress, coping, and development: An integrative perspective (2nd ed.)* New York, NY: Guilford Press.

Alessio, A., Bonilha, L., Rorden, C., Kobayashi, E., Min, L. L., Damasceno, B. P., et al. (2006). Memory and language impairments and their relationships to hippocampal and perirhinal cortex damage in patients with medial temporal lobe epilepsy. *Epilepsy & Behavior, 8(3)*, 593-600.

Alessio, A., Kobayashi, E., Damasceno, B. P., Lopes-Cendes, I., & Cendes, F. (2004). Evidence of memory impairment in asymptomatic individuals with hippocampal atrophy. *Epilepsy & Behavior, 5(6)*, 981-987.

Alexander, J. F., Sexton, T. L., & Robbins, M. S. (2002). The developmental status of family therapy in family psychology intervention science. In H. A. Liddle, D. A. Santiseban, R. F. Levant, & J. H. Bray (Eds.), *Family psychology: Science-based interventions* (pp. 17-40) Washington, DC: American Psychological Association.

Alexander, M. G. & Wood, W. (2000). Women, men, and positive emotions: A social role interpretation. In A. H. Fischer (ed.), *Gender and emotion: Social psychological perspectives.* (pp. 189-210) New York, NY: Cambridge University Press.

Alloway, T. P., & Alloway, R. G. (2008). Working memory: Is it the new IQ? Nature Proceedings. Retrieved on May 6, 2009, from http://precedings. nature.com/documents/2343/version/1.

Allport, F. H. (1920). The influence of the group upon association and thought. *Journal of Experimental Psychology, 3:* 159-182.

Allport, G. 1968. *The Person in Psychology.* Boston, MA: Beacon Press.

Allport, G. W. (1935). Attitudes. In C. Murchison (ed.), *A Handbook of Social Psychology* (pp. 798-844). Worcester, MA: Clark University Press.

Allport, G. W. (1954). *The nature of prejudice Oxford,* England: Addison-Wesley.

Allport, G. W. (1985). The historical background of social psychology. In G. Lindzey & E. Aronson (eds.), *Handbook of Social Psychology* (Vol. 1, 3rd ed., pp. 1-46). New York, NY: Random House.

Allport, G. W. & Odbert, H. S. (1936). Traitnames. A psycho-lexical study. *Psychological Monographs, 47:* 171.

Alter, M. D., & Hen, R. (2009). Serotonin, sensitive periods, and anxiety. *Stress-induced and fear circuitry disorders: Advancing the research agenda for DSM-V.* (pp. 159-173). Arlington, VA: American Psychiatric Publishing, Inc.

Althof, S. E. (2007). Treatment of rapid ejaculation: Psychotherapy, pharmacotherapy, and combined therapy. *Principles and practice of sex therapy (4th ed.).* (pp. 212-240) New York, NY: Guilford Press.

Alvarez-Buylla, A., Seri, B., & Doetsch, F. (2002). Identification of neural stem cells in the adult vertebrate brain. *Brain Research Bulletin.* 57: 751-8.

Alwin, D. F., Cohen, R. L., & Newcomb, T. M. (1991). *Political Attitudes over the Life-Span: The Bennington Women After Fifty Years.* Madison, WI: The University of Wisconsin Press.

Alzheimer's Association. (2009). Alzheimer's Disease: Facts and Figures. Retrieved May 6, 2009, from http://www.alz.org/national/documents/report_alzfactsfigures2009.pdf.

Amabile, T. M. & Gryskiewicz, N. D. (1989). The creative environment scales: Work environment inventory. *Creativity Research Journal, 2(4),* 231-253.

Ambady, N., Paik, S. K., Steele, J., Owen-Smith, A., & Mitchell, J. P. (2004). Deflecting negative self-relevant stereotype activation: The effects of individuation. *Journal of Experimental Social Psychology, 40(3),* 401-408.

Ambady, N., Shih, M., Kim, A., & Pittinsky, T. L. (2001). Stereotype susceptibility in children: Effects of identity activation on quantitative performance. *Psychological Science, 12(5),* 385-390.

American Psychiatric Association. (2000). *Diagnostic and statistical manual of mental disorders DSM-IV-R (4th ed.).* Washington, DC: American Psychiatric Association.

American Psychological Association (2002). Ethical principles of psychologists and code of conduct. *American Psychologist, 57,* 1060-1073.

American Psychological Association. (2008). *Graduate study in psychology.* Washington, DC.

American Psychological Association. (2009). *Center for workforce studies.* Washington, DC.

American Psychological Association. (2005). Resolution In Favor of Empirically Supported Sex Education and HIV Prevention Programs for Adolescents. Downloaded on May 22, 2009 from: http://www.apa.org/ releases/sexed_resolution.pdf.

American Psychological Association. (2009). Report: APA Board of Scientific Affairs, Committee on Animal Research and Ethics. APA Online. Retrieved from http://www.apa.org/science/animal2.html

American Society of Plastic Surgeons. (2008). 2008 Quick Facts. Downloaded on May 22, 2009 from: http://www.plasticsurgery.org/Media/stats/2008-quick-facts-cosmetic-surgery-minimally-invasive-statistics.pdf.

Anastasi, A., & Urbina, S. (1954). *Psychological testing (7th ed.)* Englewood Cliffs, NJ: Prentice Hall, Inc.

Anathaswamy, A. (2004). Hormones converge for couples in love. New Scientist. Retrieved December 19, 2008 from http://www. newscientist.com/article/dn4957-hormones-converge-for-couples-in-love.html.

Anderson, C. A. (1989). Temperature and aggression: Ubiquitous effects of heat on occurrence of human violence. *Psychological Bulletin,* 106(1), 74-96.

Anderson, D. (1994). *Breaking the tradition on college campuses: Reducing drug and alcohol misuse.* Fairfax, VA: George Mason University Press.

Anderson, S. W., Bechara, A., Damasio, H., Tranel, D., & Damasio, A. R. (1999). Impairment of social and moral behavior related to early damage in human prefrontal cortex. *Nature Neuroscience, 2(11):* 103-7.

Andreasen, N. C. & Black, D. W. (2006). *Introductory textbook of psychiatry (4th ed.).* Washington, DC: American Psychiatric Publishing.

Angell, J. R. (1903a). A preliminary study of the localization of sound. *Psychological Review, 10,* 1-18.

Angell, J. R. (1911). Usages of the terms mind, consciousness, and soul. *Psychological Bulletin, 8,* 46-47.

Angier, N. (2001, May 20). Bully for you. Why push comes to shove. *New York Times,* Sect. 4. p. 1.

Angrilli, A., Bianchin, M., Radaelli, S., Bertagnoni, G., & Pertile, M. (2008). Reduced startle reflex and aversive noise perception in patients with orbitofrontal cortex lesions. Neuropsychologia 46(4), 1179-1184.

Angrilli, A., Mauri, A., Palomba, D., Flor, H., Birbaumer, N., Sartori, G., & di Paola, F. (1996). Startle reflex and emotion modulation impairment after a right amygdala lesion. *Brain: A Journal of Neurology, 119,* 1991-2000.

Angulo, M. C., Le Meur, K., Kozlov, A. S., Charpak, S., & Audinat, E. (2008). GABA, a forgotten gliotransmitter. *Progress in Neurobiology, 86:* 297-303.

Anthony, J. C., Arria, A. M., & Johnson, E. O. (1995). Epidemiological and public health issues for tobacco, alcohol, and other drugs. In J. M. Oldham & M. B. Riba (Eds.), *American Psychiatric Press review of psychiatry (Vol. 14).* Washington, DC: American Psychiatric Press.

Aouizerate, B., Rotge, J. Y., Martin-Guehl, C., Cuny, E., Rougier, A., Guehl, D., et al. (2006). A systematic review of psychosurgical treatments for obsessive-compulsive disorder: Does deep brain stimulation represent the future trend in psychosurgery? *Clinical Neuropsychiatry: Journal of Treatment and Evaluation,* 3(6), 391-403.

Apostolova, L. G. & Cummings, J. L. (2008). Neuropsychiatric aspects of Alzheimer's disease and other dementing illnesses. In S. C. Yudofsky & R. E. Hales (Eds.), *The American psychiatric publishing textbook of neuropsychiatry and behavioral neurosciences (5ᵗʰ ed.).* Washington, DC: American Psychiatric Publishing.

Archer, J. (2005). Are women or men the more aggressive sex? In S. Fein, G. R. Goethals, & M. J. Sandstrom (eds.), *Gender and aggression: Interdisciplinary perspectives.* Mahwah, NJ: Erlbaum.

Arias-Carrión, Ó., & Pöppel, E. (2007). Dopamine, learning, and reward-seeking behavior. *Acta Neurobiologiae Experimentalis (Warsaw), 67(4):* 481-488.

Aristotle (1941). *The basic works of Aristotle* (R. McKeon, Ed.). New York, NY: Random House.

Armstrong, V., Brunet, P. M., Chao, H., Nishimura, M., Poole, H. L., & Spector, F. J. (2006). What is so critical?: A commentary on the reexamination of critical periods. *Development and Psychobiology, 45,* 326-331.

Arnold, D. H. & Doctoroff, G. L. (2003). The early education of socioeconomically disadvantaged children. *Annual Review of Psychology, 54,* 517-545.

Artero, S., Ancelin, M., Portet, F., Dupuy, A., Berr, C., Dartigues, J., Tzourio, C., Rouaud, O., Poncet, M., Pasquier, F., Auriacombe, S., Touchon, J., & Ritchie, K. (2008). Risk profiles for mild cognitive impairment and progression to dementia are gender specific. *Journal of Neurology, Neurosurgery & Psychiatry, 79*(9), 979-984.

Asch, S. E. (1955). Opinions and social pressure. *Scientific American:* 31-35.

Aschersleben, G., Hofer, T., Jovanovic, B. (2008). The link between infant attention to goal-directed action and later theory of mind abilities. *Developmental Science; 11*(6): 862-8.

Aserinsky, E. (1996). Memories of famous neuropsychologists: The discovery of REM sleep. *Journal of the History of the Neurosciences, 5*(3), 213-227.

Ash, J. & Gallup Jr., G. G. (2008). Brain size, intelligence, and paleoclimatic variation. In G. Geher & G. Miller (Eds.), *Mating intelligence: Sex, relationships, and the mind's reproductive system.* (pp. 313-335), Mahwah, NJ: Lawrence Erlbaum Associates Publishers.

Aslin, R. N., Jusczyk, P. W., & Pisoni, D. B. (2000). Speech and auditory processing during infancy: Constraints on and precursors to language. In D. Kuhn & R. S. Siegler (Eds.), *Handbook of Child Psychology, Volume 2, Cognition, Perception, and Language* (5ᵗʰ ed., p. 147-198). New York, NY: John Wiley & Sons, Inc.

Asmus, C. L. & James, K. (2005). Nominal group technique, social loafing, and group creative project quality. *Creativity Research Journal, 17*(4): 349-354.

Aspinwall, L. G., Richter, L., & Hoffman III, R. R. (2001). Understanding how optimism works: An examination of optimists' adaptive moderation of belief and behavior. *Optimism & pessimism: Implications for theory, research, and practice.* (pp. 217-238) Washington, DC: American Psychological Association.

Associated Press. (2006). Brazil Model Who Battled Anorexia Dies. *The Washington Post.* Washington, D.C.

Atkinson, R. C. (1975). Mnemotechnics in second-language learning. *American Psychologist, 30*(8), 821-828.

Atkinson, R. C. (Feb. 18, 2001). "Standardized tests and access to American universities." Presentation at 2001 Robert Atwell Distinguished Lecture, 83ʳᵈ Annual Meeting of the American Council on Education. Washington, DC.

Atkinson, R. C. (Dec. 2001). "Achievement versus aptitude tests in college admissions." Presentation at University of California at Los Angeles.

Augustine, K. (2007). Near-death experiences with hallucinatory features. *Journal of Near-Death Studies, 26*(1), Fall, 3-31.

Auld, J. M. (2007). Review of hypnosis and communication in dental practice. *Australian Journal of Clinical & Experimental Hypnosis, 35*(2), 248-250.

Austin, E. J., Parker, J. D. A., Petrides, K. V., & Saklofske, D. H. (2008). Emotional intelligence. In G. J. Boyle, G. Matthews, & D. H. Saklofske (Eds.), *The SAGE handbook of personality theory and assessment, vol 1: Personality theories and models.* (pp. 576-596). Thousand Oaks, CA: Sage Publications.

Autism Society of America (ASA). (2005). Asperger's syndrome. Retrieved from www.autism-society.org.

Autism Society of America (ASA). (2006). Asperger's syndrome. Retrieved from www.autism-society.org.

Autor, D., Katz, L., & Kearney, M. (2006). The polarization of the U.S. labor market. *American Economic Review, 96:* 189-194.

Averill, J. R. (1980). A constructivist view of emotion. In R. Plutchik & H. Kellerman (Eds.), *Theories of emotion* (Vol. 1, pp. 305-340). New York, NY: Academic Press.

Avery, R. D. et al. (1994, December 13). Mainstream science on intelligence. *Wall Street Journal,* editorial page (356).

Axelrod, F.B. (2004). Familial dysautonomia. *Muscle & Nerve, 29,* 352-63.

Ayllon, T., & Azrin, N. H. (1965). The measurement and reinforcement of behavior of psychotics. *Journal of the Experimental Analysis of Behavior, 8*(6), 357-383.

B

Baars, B. J. (1986). *The cognitive revolution in psychology.* New York, NY: Guilford Press.

Baars, B. J. (2003). How brain reveals mind: Neuroimaging supports the central role of conscious experience. *Journal of Consciousness Studies, 10,* 100-114.

Baars, B. J., Banks W. P., & Newman J. B. (Eds.). (2003). *Essential sources in the scientific study of consciousness.* Cambridge, MA: MIT Press.

Bach, A. K., Wincze, J. P., & Barlow, D. H. (2001). Sexual dysfunction. *Clinical handbook of psychological disorders: A step-by-step treatment manual (3rd ed.).* (pp. 562-608) New York, NY: Guilford Press.

Bachorowski, J. & Braaten, E. B. (1994). Emotional intensity: Measurement and theoretical implications. *Personality and Individual Differences, 17,* 191-199.

Backhaus, J., Hoeckesfeld, R., Born, J., Hohagen, F., & Junghanns, K. (2008) Immediate as well as delayed post learning sleep but not wakefulness enhances declarative memory consolidation in children. *Neurobiology of Learning & Memory, 89,* 76-80.

Backman, C. W. (1981). Attraction in interpersonal relationships. In M. Rosenberg & R. Turner (eds.), *Social Psychology: Sociological Perspectives.* New York, NY: Basic Books.

Backman, C. W. (1990). Attraction in interpersonal relationships. In M. Rosenberg & R. H. Turner (eds.), *Social Psychology: Sociological Perspectives.* (pp. 235-268). New Brunswick, NJ: Transaction Publishers.

Baddeley, A. D. (1990). *Human memory: Theory and practice* Needham Heights, MA: Allyn & Bacon.

Baer, L., Rauch, S. L., Ballantine, H. T., Jr., Martuza, R., Cosgrove, R., Cassen, E., Giriunas, I, Manzo, P. A., Dimino, C., Jenike, M. A. Cingulotomy for intractable obsessive-compulsive disorder. Prospective long-term follow-up of 18 patients. *Arch General Psychiatry, 52*(5): 384-92.

Bailer, U., de Zwaan, M., Leisch, F., Strnad, A., Lennkh-Wolfsberg, C., El-Giamal, N., et al. (2004). Guided self-help versus cognitive-behavioral group therapy in the treatment of bulimia nervosa. *The International Journal of Eating Disorders, 35*(4): 522-37.

Bailey, J. M. & Pillard, R. C. (1991). A genetic study of male sexual orientation. *Archives of General Psychiatry, 48*(12): 1089-1096.

Baillargeon, R. (1987). Object permanence in 3- and 4-month-old infants. *Developmental Psychology, 23,* 655-664.

Baker, L. A., Jacobson, K. C., Raine, A., Lozano, D. I., & Bezdjian, S. (2007) Genetic and environmental bases of childhood antisocial behavior: A multi-informant twin study. *Journal of Abnormal Psychology, 116:* 219-235.

Bakin, J. S., South, D. A., & Weinberger, N. M. (1996). Induction of receptive field plasticity in the auditory cortex of the guinea pig during instrumental avoidance conditioning. *Behavioral Neuroscience, 110,* 905-13.

Bakker, A., van Kestren, P. J., Gooren, L. J. G., & Bezemer, P. D. (1993). The prevalence of transsexualism in the Netherlands. *Acta Psychiatrica Scandinavica, 87,* 237-238.

Balaban, V. (2009). Assessment of children. *Effective treatments for PTSD: Practice guidelines from the international society for traumatic stress studies (2nd ed.).* (pp. 62-80). New York, NY: Guilford Press.

Balaraman, S. (1962). Color vision research and the trichromatic theory: a historical review. *Psychological Bulletin, 59,* 434-48.

Bancroft, J. (2005). The endocrinology of sexual arousal. *The Journal of Endocrinology, 186*(3): 411-27.

Bancroft, J., Loftus, J., & Long, J. S. (2003). Distress about sex: A national survey of women in heterosexual relationships. *Archives of Sexual Behavior, 32*(3), 193-208.

Bandura, A. (1977). Self-efficacy: Toward a unifying theory of behavioral change. *Psychological Review, 84*(2), 191-215.

Bandura, A. (1978). Social learning theory of aggression. *The Journal of Communication, 28*(3):12-29.

Bandura, A. (2006). Toward a psychology of human agency. *Perspectives on Psychological Science, 1:* 164-180.

Bandura, A. (2008). Reconstrual of "free will" from the agentic perspective of social cognitive theory. In J. Baer, J. C. Kaufman, & R. F. Baumeister (eds.), *Are We Free? Psychology and Free Will.* (86-127). New York, NY: Oxford University Press.

Bandura, A., Adams, N. E., & Beyer, J. (1977). Cognitive processes mediating behavioral change. *Journal of Personality and Social Psychology, 35*(3), 125-139.

Bandura, A., & Rosenthal, T. (1966). Vicarious classical conditioning as a function of arousal level. *Journal of Personal and Social Psychology, 3,* 54-62.

Bandura, A., Ross, D., & Ross, S. A. (1961). Transmission of aggression through imitation of aggressive models. *Journal of Abnormal and Social Psychology, 63,* 575-82.

Bandura, A., Roth, D., & Ross, S. (1963). Imitation of film-mediated aggressive models. *Journal of Abnormality and Social Psychology, 66,* 3-11.

Bandura, A. (1969). *Principles of behavior modification.* Oxford, England: Holt, Rinehart, & Winston.

Bandura, A. (1969). Social learning of moral judgments. *Journal of Personality and Social Psychology, 11*(3), 275-279.

Banks, M. S. & Salapatek, P. (1983). Infant Visual Perception. In M. M. Haith & J. J. Campos (Eds.), *Handbook of Psychology* (pp. 435-571). New York, NY: Wiley.

Barahal, H. S. (1958). 1000 prefrontal lobotomies: A five to ten year follow-up study. *Psychiatric Quarterly, 32,* 653-690.

Barash, D. P. (1979). *The whispering within: Evolution and the origin of human nature.* New York, NY: Viking Press/Penguin Books.

Bard, P. (1928). A diencephalic mechanism for the expression of rage with special reference to the central nervous system. *American Journal of Physiology, 84,* 490-513.

Bard, P. (1929). The central representation of the sympathetic nervous system: As indicated by certain physiological observations. *Archives of Neurology and Psychiatry, 22,* 230-246.

Bard, P. (1934). The neuro-humoral basis of emotional reactions. In C. Murchinson (Ed.), *Handbook of general experimental psychology* (pp. 264-311). Worcester, MA: Clark University Press.

Bargh, J. A. (1997). The automaticity of everyday life. In R. S. Wyer, Jr. (ed.), *The Automaticity of Everyday Life: Advances in Social Cognition* (Vol. 10, 1-61). Mahwah, NJ: Erlbaum.

Bargh, J. A. (2001). The psychology of the mere. In J. A. Bargh & D. K. Apsley (eds.), *Unraveling the Complexities of Social Life: A Festschrift in Honor of Robert B. Zajonc.* (pp. 25-37). Washington, D.C.: American Psychological Association.

Barlow, D. H. (2002). *Anxiety and its disorders: The nature and treatment of anxiety and panic (second edition).* New York, NY: Guilford Press.

Barnabé-Heider, F. & Frisén, J. (2008). Stem cells for spinal cord repair. *Cell Stem Cell, 3:* 16-24.

Barnes, L. L., Wilson, R. S., Bienias, J. L., Schneider, J. A., Evans, D. A., & Bennett, D. A. (2005). Sex differences in the clinical manifestations of alzheimer disease pathology. *Archives of General Psychiatry, 62*(6), 685-691.

Barnett, R. & Rivers, C. (2004). *Same Difference: How Gender Myths Are Hurting Our Relationships, Our Children, and Our Jobs.* New York, NY: Basic Books.

Barnett, S. M., & Ceci, S. J. (2005). The role of transferable knowledge in intelligence. *Cognition and intelligence: Identifying the mechanisms of the mind.* (pp. 208-224) New York, NY: Cambridge University Press.

Barnier, A. J., McConkey, K. M., & Wright, J. (2004). Posthypnotic amnesia for autobiographical episodes: Influencing memory accessibility and quality. *International Journal of Clinical and Experimental Hypnosis, 52,* 260-279.

Baron, R. S. (2005). So right it's wrong: Groupthink and the ubiquitous nature of polarized group decision making. In M. P. Zanna (ed.), *Advances in Experimental Social Psychology, Vol. 37.* (pp. 219-253) San Diego, CA: Elsevier Academic Press.

Baron-Cohen, S. & Wheelwright, S. (2003). The Friendship Questionnaire: An investigation of adults with Asperger syndrome or high-functioning autism, and normal sex differences. *Journal of Autism and Developmental Disorders, 33,* 509-517.

Barrett, J., Abbott, D. H., & George, L. M. (1993). Sensory cues and the suppression of reproduction of subordinate female marmoset monkeys. *Journal of Reproduction and Fertility. 97(1):* 301-310.

Barrett, L. F., Gross, J. J., Christensen, T. C., & Benvenuto, M. (2001) Knowing what you're feeling and knowing what to do about it: Mapping the relation between emotion differentiation and emotion regulation. *Cognition and Emotion, 15,* 713-724.

Barrett, L. F., Mesquita, B., Ochsner, K. N., & Gross, J. J. (2007). The experience of emotion. *Annual Review of Psychology, 58,* 373-403.

Bartone, P. T. (2003). Hardiness as a resilience resource under high stress conditions. *Promoting capabilities to manage posttraumatic stress: Perspectives on resilience.* (pp. 59-73) Springfield, IL: Charles C. Thomas Publisher.

Bartrop, R. W., Lockhurst, E., Lazarus, L., Kiloh, L. G., & Penny, R. (1977). Depressed lymphocyte function after bereavement. *Lancet, 1,* 834-836.

Bartoshuk, L.M., Duffy, V.B., & Miller, I.J. (1994). PTC/PROP tasting: anatomy, psychophysics, and sex effects. *Physiology Behavior, 56,* 1165-71.

Bartoshuk, L.M., Duffy, V.B., Reed, D., & Williams A. (1996). Supertasting, earaches and head injury: genetics and pathology alter our taste worlds. *Neuroscience and Biobehavioral Reviews, 20,* 79-87.

Baruss, I. (2003). *Alterations of consciousness: An empirical analysis for social scientists.* Washington, DC: American Psychological Association.

Basak, C., Boot, W. R., Voss, M. W., & Kramer, A. F. (2008). Can training in a real-time strategy video game attenuate cognitive decline in older adults? *Psychology and Aging, 23(4),* 765-777.

Bass, B. M. (2002). Cognitive, social, and emotional intelligence of transformational leaders. In R. E. Riggio, S. E. Murphy & F. J. Pirozzolo (Eds.), *Multiple intelligences and leadership.* (pp. 105-118) Mahwah, NJ: Lawrence Erlbaum Associates Publishers.

Bassett, R. L., Van Nikkelen-Kuyper, M., Johnson, D., Miller, A., Carter, A., & Grimm, J. P. (2005). Being a good neighbor: Can students come to value homosexual persons? *Journal of Psychology and Theology, 33(1),* 17-26.

Bassili, J. N. & Brown, R. D. (2005). Implicit and explicit attitudes: Research, challenges, and theory. In D. Albarracín, B. T. Johnson & M. P. Zanna (Eds.), *The handbook of attitudes.* (pp. 543:574). Mahwah, NJ: Lawrence Erlbaum Associates Publishers.

Basson, R. (2007). Sexual desire/arousal disorders in women. *Principles and practice of sex therapy (4th ed.).* (pp. 25-53) New York, NY: Guilford Press.

Bates, J. E. (1989). Concepts and measures of temperament. In G. A. Kohnstamm, J. E. Bates, & M. K. Rothbart (Eds.), *Temperament in childhood* (pp. 3-26). Oxford, England: John Wiley & Sons, Inc.

Bates, R. (2002). Liking and similarity as predictors of multi-source ratings. *Personnel Review, 31(5),* 540-552.

Bates, T. C., & Rock, A. (2004). Personality and information processing speed: Independent influences on intelligent performance. *Intelligence, 32(1),* 33-46.

Batson, C. D. (1991). *The altruism question: Towards a social psychological answer.* Hillsdale, NJ: Lawrence Erlbaum Associates.

Batson, C. D., Ahmad, N., & Stocks, E. L. (2004). Benefits and liabilities of empathy-induced altruism. In A. G. Miller (ed.), *The social psychology of good and evil.* (pp. 359-385). New York, NY: Guilford Press.

Batson, C. D., Sanger, K., Garst, E., Kang, M., Rubchinsky, K., & Dawson, K. (1997). Is empathy-induced helping due to self-other merging? *Journal of Personality and Social Psychology, 73:* 495-509.

Batson, C. D. & Weeks, J. L. (1996). Mood effects of unsuccessful helping: Another test of the empathy-altruism hypothesis. *Personality and Social Psychology Bulletin, 22:* 148-157.

Battmer, R.D., Linz, B., & Lenarz, T. (2009). A review of device failure in more than 23 years of clinical experience of a cochlear implant program with more than 3,400 implantees. *Otology & Neurotology, 30,* 455-63.

Bauer, R. A. (1952). *The new man in Soviet psychology.* Cambridge, MA: Harvard University Press.

Baumeister, R. F. (1984). Choking under pressure: Self-consciousness and paradoxical effects of incentives on skillful performance. *Journal of Personality and Social Psychology, 46(3),* 610-620.

Baumeister, R. F. (2004). Sexual economics: Sex as female resource for social exchange in heterosexual interactions. *Personality and Social Psychology Review, 8(4):* 339-363.

Baumeister, R. F., Bratslavsky, E., Finkenauer, C., & Vohs, K. D. (2001). Bad is stronger than good. *Review of General Psychology 5(4),* 323-370.

Baumeister, R. F., Catanese, K. R., & Vohs, K. D. (2001). Is there a gender difference in strength of sex drive? Theoretical views, conceptual distinctions, and a review of relevant evidence. *Personality and Social Psychology Review, 5:* 242-273.

Baumeister, R. F., Zhang, L., & Vohs, K. D. (2004). Gossip as cultural learning. *Review of General Psychology, 8(2):* 111-121.

Baumgardner, S. R. & Crothers, M. K. (2009). *Positive psychology.* Upper Saddle River, NJ: Prentice Hall/Pearson Education.

Baumrind, D. (1991). The influence of parenting style on adolescent competence and substance use. *The Journal of Early Adolescence, 11,* 56-95.

BBC. (2006). Italy pact to stop skinny models. Downloaded on June 26, 2009 from: http://news.bbc.co.uk/2/hi/europe/6204865.stm.

BBC. (2006). Madrid bans waifs from catwalks. Downloaded on June 26, 2009 from: http://news.bbc.co.uk/2/hi/europe/5341202.stm.

Beals, J., Manson, S. M., Whitesell, N. R., Spicer, P., Novins, D. K., & Mitchell, C. M. (2005). Prevalence of DSM-IV disorders and attendant help-seeking in 2 American Indian reservation populations. *Archives of General Psychiatry, 62*(1), 99-108.

Beasley, M., Thompson, T., & Davidson, J. (2003). Resilience in responses to life stress: The effects of coping style and cognitive hardiness. *Personality and Individual Differences, 34*(1), 77-95.

Bebko, J. M. & Weiss, J. A. (2006). Mental retardation. In M. Hersen & J. C. Thomas (Series Eds.) & R. T. Ammerman (Vol. Ed.), *Comprehensive handbook of personality and psychopathology, Vol. 3: Child psychopathology.* Hoboken, NJ: John Wiley & Sons, Inc.

Becchetti, L. & Santoro, M. (2007). The income-unhappiness paradox: A relational goods/Baumol disease explanation. In P. L. Porta & L. Bruni (Eds.), *Handbook on the economies of happiness.* Northampton, MA: Edward Elgar Publishing.

Bechara, A., Tranel, D., Damasio, H., Adolphs, R., Rockland, C., & Damasio, A. R. (1995). Double dissociation of conditioning and declarative knowledge relative to the amygdala and hippocampus in humans. *Science, 269,* 1115-1118.

Beck, A. T. (1967). *Depression: Clinical, experimental and theoretical aspects.* New York, NY: Harper & Row.

Beck, A. T. (2002). Cognitive models of depression. In R. L. Leahy & E. T. Dowd (Eds.), *Clinical advances in cognitive psychotherapy: Theory and applications.* New York, NY: Springer.

Beck, A. T. & Weishaar, M. E. (2008). Cognitive therapy. In R. J. Corsini & D. Wedding (Eds.), *Current psychotherapies (8th edition).* Belmont, CA: Brooks Cole.

Bédard, P., and Sanes, J. N. (2009). Gaze and hand position effects on finger movement related human brain activation. *Journal of Neurophysiology. Vol. 101*(2), 834-842.

Beehr, T. A., Farmer, S. J., Glazer, S., Gudanowski, D. M., & Nair, V. N. (2003). The enigma of social support and occupational stress: Source congruence and gender role effects. *Journal of Occupational Health Psychology, 8*(3), 220-231.

Beilin, H. (1992). Piaget's enduring contribution to developmental psychology. *Developmental Psychology, 28,* 191-204.

Bekker, M. H. J. & van Assen, Marcel A. L. M. (2008). Autonomy-connectedness and gender. *Sex Roles, 59*(7-8): 532-544.

Bellinger, D. L., Madden, K. S., Felten, S. Y., & Felten, D. L. (1994). Neural and endocrine links between the brain and the immune system. In C. S. Lewis, C. O'Sullivan, & J. Barraclough (Eds.), *The psychoimmunology of cancer: Mind and body in the fight for survival.* Oxford, England: Oxford University Press.

Bem, D. J. (1972). Self-perception theory. In L. Berkowitz (Ed.), *Advances in Experimental Social Psychology. Vol. 6.* New York: Academic Press.

Bem, D. J. & McConnell, H. K. (1970). Testing the self-perception explanation of dissonance phenomena: On the salience of premanipulation attitudes. *Journal of Personality and Social Psychology, 14:* 23-31.

Bendelius, J. (2004). Prevention: the best way to help our kids avoid the obesity epidemic. *School Nurse News, 21*(3): 32-3.

Benedict, C., Dimitrov, S., Marshall, L., & Born, J. (2007). Sleep enhances serum interleukin-7 concentrations in humans. *Brain Behavior and Immunity, 21*(8), 1058-1062.

Benjamin Jr. L. T. (Ed.) (1997) *A history of psychology: Original sources and contemporary research (2nd ed.).* New York, NY: Mcgraw-Hill Book Company.

Benjamin Jr., L. T. (2007). *A brief history of modern psychology.* Malden, MA: Blackwell Publishing.

Bennett, C. M., & Baird, A. A. (2006). Anatomical changes in the emerging adult brain: A voxel-based morphometry study. *Human Brain Mapping, 27,* 766-777.

Bennett, M. P. (1998). The effect of mirthful laughter on stress and natural killer cell cytotoxicity. US: ProQuest Information & Learning). *Dissertation Abstracts International: Section B: The Sciences and Engineering, 58* (7), 3553.

Bensafi, M., Sobel, N., & Khan, R. M. (2007). Hedonic-specific activity in piriform cortex during odor imagery mimics that during odor perception. *Journal of Neurophysiology, 98,* 3254-62.

Ben-Zur, H. (2002). Associations of type A behavior with the emotional traits of anger and curiosity. *Anxiety, Stress & Coping: An International Journal, 15*(1), 95-104.

Berenbaum, H. & Barch, D. (1995). The categorization of thought disorder. *Journal of Psycholinguist Research, 24,* 349-76.

Berenbaum, H., Raghavan, C., Huynh-Nhu, L., Vernon, L.L., & Gomez, J.J. (2003). A taxonomy of emotional disturbances. *Clinical Psychology: Science and Practice, 10,* 206-226.

Bergin, A. E., & Richards, P. S. (2001). Religious values and mental health. In A. E. Kazdin (Ed.), *Encyclopedia of psychology.* New York, NY: American Psychological Association & Oxford University Press.

Berkman, N. D., Bulik, C. M., Brownley, K. A., Lohr, K. N., Sedway, J. A., Rooks, A., et al. (2006). Management of eating disorders. Evidence report/technology assessment No. 135. *AHRQ Publication No. 06-E010.*

Berkowitz, L. (1989). Frustration-aggression hypothesis: Examination and reformulation. *Psychological Bulletin, 106:* 59-73.

Berman, J. R. (2005). Physiology of female sexual function and dysfunction. *International Journal of Impotence Research, 17 Suppl 1:* S44-51.

Bermond, B., Nieuwenhuyse, B., Fasotti, L., & Schuerman, J. (1991). Spinal cord lesions, peripheral feedback, and intensities of emotional feelings. *Cognition & Emotion, 5,* 201-220.

Bermudez, P., Lerch, J.P., Evans, A.C., & Zatorre, R.J. (2009). Neuroanatomical correlates of musicianship as revealed by cortical thickness and voxel-based morphometry. *Cerebral Cortex, 19,* 1583-96.

Berntson, G. G., Bechara, A., Damasio, H., Tranel, D., & Cacioppo, J. T. (2007). Amygdala contribution to selective dimensions of emotion. *Social Cognitive Affective Neuroscience, 2*(2), 123-129.

Berr, C., Wancata, J., & Ritchie, K. (2005). Prevalence of dementia in the elderly in Europe. *Eur. Neuropsyhopharmacology, 15*(4), 463-471.

Berridge, K. C. (2007). The debate over dopamine's role in reward: The case for incentive salience. *Psychopharmacology, 191*(3): 391-431.

Berridge, K. & Kringelbach, M. (2008). Affective neuroscience of pleasure: Reward in humans and animals. *Psychopharmacology, 199*(3): 457-480.

Berry, J. W. (1992). *Cross-cultural psychology, research and applications.* New York, NY: Cambridge University Press.

Berscheid, E. (1983). Interpersonal attraction. In. G. Lindzey & E. Aronson (eds.), *Handbook of Social Psychology (3rd ed.).* Reading, MA: Addison-Wesley.

Berscheid, E. & Walster, E.H. (1978). Interpersonal attraction. In G. Lindzey & E. Aronson (eds.), *Handbook of Social Psychology* (Vol. 2, pp. 413-484). New York, NY: Random House.

Bertini, M., Ferrara, M., De Gennaro, L., Moroni, F., De Gasperis, M., Babiloni, C., Rossini, P. M., Vecchio, F., & Curcio, G. (2007).

Directional information flows between brain hemispheres during presleep wake and early sleep stages. *Cerebral Cortex, 17*(8), 1970-1978.

Bickman, L. (2005). A common factors approach to improving mental health services. *Mental Health Services Research, 7*(1), 1-4.

Billings, L. S., Vescio, T. K., & Biernat, M. (2000). Race-based social judgment by minority perceivers. *Journal of Applied Social Psychology, 30*(2): 221-240.

Bisaga, A. (2008). Benzodiazepines and other sedatives and hypnotics. In H.D. Kleber & M. Galanter (Eds.), *The American Psychiatric Publishing textbook of substance abuse treatment (4th ed.).* Arlington, VA: American Psychiatric Publishing.

Bissette, G., Seidler, F. J., Nemeroff, C. B., & Slotkin, T. A. (1996). High affinity choline transporter status in Alzheimer's disease tissue from rapid autopsy. In R. J. Wurtman, S. Corkin, J. H. Growdon, & R. M. Nitsch (Eds.), *The neurobiology of Alzheimer's disease.* New York, NY: New York Academy of Sciences.

Bitterman, M. E. (2006). Classical conditioning since pavlov. *Review of General Psychology, 10*(4), 365-376.

Björkman, B., Arnér, S., & Hydén, L.C. (2008). Phantom breast and other syndromes after mastectomy: eight breast cancer patients describe their experiences over time: a 2-year follow-up study. *The Journal of Pain, 9,* 1018-25.

Black, K. A. & Schutte, E. D. (2006) Recollections of being loved: Implications of childhood experiences with parents for young adults' romantic relationships. *Journal of Family Issues, 27:* 1459-1480.

Blanch, A. (2007). Integrating religion and spirituality in mental health: The promise and the challenge. *Psychiatric Rehabilitation Journal, 30*(4), 251-260.

Blanchard, R. (2001). Fraternal birth order and the maternal immune hypothesis of male homosexuality. *Hormonal Behavior 40(2):* 105-114.

Blanchard, R. (2004). Quantitative and theoretical analyses of the relation between older brothers and homosexuality in men. *Journal of Theoretical Biology, 230(2);* 173-187.

Blass, T. (2004). *The Man Who Shocked the World: The Life and Legacy of Stanley Milgram.* New York, NY: Basic Books.

Blass, T. (2007). Unsupported allegations about a link between Milgram and the CIA: Tortured reasoning in a question of torture. *Journal of the History of the Behavioral Sciences, 43:* 199-203.

Blazer, D. G., Hughes, D., George, L. K., Swartz, M., & Boyer, R. (1991). Generalized anxiety disorder. In L. N. Robins & D. A. Regier (Eds.), *Psychiatric disorders in America: The Epidemiologic Catchment Area Study.* New York, NY: Maxwell Macmillan International.

Bleich, A., Gelkopf, M., & Solomon, Z. (2003). Exposure to terrorism, stress-related mental health symptoms, and coping behaviors among a nationally representative sample in israel. *JAMA: Journal of the American Medical Association, 290*(5), 612-620.

Bliss, T. V. & Lomo, T. (1973). Long-lasting potentiation of synaptic transmission in the dentate area of the anaesthetized rabbit following stimulation of the perforant path. *The Journal of Physiology, 232,* 331-56.

Bloom, L. (1970). *Language development: Form and function in emerging grammars.* Cambridge, MA: MIT Press.

Bloom, M. (2008). Principles and approaches to primary prevention. In T. P. Gullotta & G. M. Blau (Eds.), *Handbook of childhood behavioral issues: Evidence-based approaches to prevention and treatment* (pp. 107-122). New York: Routledge/Taylor & Francis Group.

Blum, K., Braverman, E. R., Holder, J. M., Lubar, J. F., Monastra, V. J., Miller, D., et. al. (2000). Reward deficiency syndrome: A biogenetic model for the diagnosis and treatment of impulsive, addictive, and compulsive behaviors. *Journal of Psychoactive Drugs, 32* (Suppl.), 1-68.

Blumenfeld, P., Kempler, T., & Krajcik, J. (2006). Motivation and cognitive engagement in learning environments. In R. K. Sawyer (Ed.), *The Cambridge handbook of the learning sciences* (pp. 475-488). Cambridge, MA: Cambridge University Press.

Bock, P. (2005). Infant science: How do babies learn to talk. *Pacific Northwest: The Seattle Times Magazine,* March 6, 2005.

Boecker, H., Sprenger T., Spilker, M. E., Henriksen, G., Koppenhoefer, M., Wagner, K. J., Valet, M., Berthele, A., & Tolle, T. R. (2008). The runner's high: Opioidergic mechanisms in the human brain. *Cerebral Cortex, 18*(11): 2523-31.

Boldyrev, A. A. & Johnson, P. (2007). Free radicals and cell signaling in Alzheimer's disease. *Journal of Alzheimer's Disease, 11*(2), 141.

Bollini, A. M. & Walker, E. F. (2007). Schizotypal personality disorder. In W. O'Donohue, K. A. Fowler, & S. O. Lilienfeld (eds.), *Personality Disorders: Toward the DSM-V.* (81-108). Thousand Oaks, CA: Sage Publications.

Bonanno, G. A. (2004). Loss, trauma, and human resilience: Have we underestimated the human capacity to thrive after extremely aversive events? *American Psychologist, 59,* 20-28.

Bonanno, G. A. (2005). Clarifying and extending the construct of adult resilience. *American Psychologist, 60,* 265-267.

Bonanno, G. A. (2008). Loss, trauma, and human resilience: Have we underestimated the human capacity to thrive after extremely aversive events? *Psychological Trauma: Theory, Research, Practice, and Policy, S*(1), 101-113.

Bond Jr., C. F. (2000). Social facilitation. In A. E. Kazdin (ed.), *Encyclopedia of Psychology, vol. 7.* (pp. 338-440). Washington, D.C.: American Psychological Association.

Bond, C. F. & Titus, L. J. (1983). Social facilitation: A meta analysis of 241 studies. *Psychological Bulletin, 94:* 265-292.

Boon, B., Stroebe, W., Schut, H., & Ijntema, R. (2002). Ironic processes in the eating behaviour of restrained eaters. *British Journal of Health Psychology, 7(1):* 1-10.

Bord-Hoffman, M. A. & Donius, M. (2005). Loss in height: When is it a problem? *AAACN Viewpoint.*

Borgen, F. H. & Betz, N. E. (2008). Career self-efficacy and personality: Linking career confidence and the healthy personality. *Journal of Career Assessment, 16(1):* 22-43.

Borkovec, T. D., Alcaine, O. M., & Behar, E. (2004). Avoidance theory of worry and generalized anxiety disorder. In R. G. Heimberg, C. L. Turk, & D. S. Mennin (Eds.) *Generalized anxiety disorder: Advances in research and practice* (pp. 77-108). New York, NY: Guilford.

Bornstein, M. H., Tal, J., Rahn, C., Galperin, C. Z., Pecheux, M., Lamour, M., Azuma, H., Toda, S., Ogino, M., & Tamis-LeMonda, C. S. (1992). Functional analysis of the contents of maternal speech to infants of 5 and 13 months in four cultures: Argentina, France, Japan, and the United States. *Developmental Psychology, 28,* 593-603.

Bornstein, R. F. (2005). Psychodynamic theory and personality disorders. In S. Strack (ed.), *Handbook of personology and psychopathology*. (164-180) Hoboken, NJ: John Wiley & Sons Inc.

Bornstein, R. F. (2007). Might the Rorschach be a projective test after all? Social projection of an undesired trait alters Rorschach oral dependency scores. *Journal of Personality Assessment, 88(3):* 354-367.

Botton, A. (2006). *The Architecture of Happiness*. Pantheon: London, England.

Botwin, M. D., Buss, D. M., & Shackelford, T. K. (1997). Personality and mate preferences: Five factors in mate selection and marital satisfaction. *Journal of Personality, 65:* 107-136.

Bouchard, G., & Thériault, V. J. (2003). Defense mechanisms and coping strategies in conjugal relationships: An integration. *International Journal of Psychology, 38(2):* 79-90.

Bouchard, T. & Pedersen N. (1999). Twins reared apart: Nature's double experiment. In (Ed.) M. LaBuda and E. Grigorenko *On the Way to Individuality: Current Methodological Issues in Behavior Genetics*, ed. MC LaBuda, EL Grigorenko (pp. 71-93). Commack, NY: Nova Science Press.

Bouchard, T. J., Jr. (1984). Twins reared together and apart: What they tell us about human diversity. In S. W. Fox (Ed.), *Individuality and determinism: Chemical and biological bases* (pp.147-178). New York, NY: Plenum.

Bouchard, T., Jr. (2004). Genes, environment, and personality. *Science, 264:* 1700-1701.

Bourne, L. E., Dominowski, R. L., & Loftus, W. F. (1979). *Cognitive processes*. Englewood Cliffs, NJ: Prentice Hall.

Bourque, C. W. (2008). Central mechanisms of osmosensation and systemic osmoregulation. *Nature Reviews Neuroscience, 9(7),* 519-31.

Bouteyre, E., Maurel, M., & Bernaud, J-L. (2007). Daily hassles and depressive symptoms among first year psychology students in France: The role of coping and social support. *Stress and Health: Journal of the International Society for the Investigation of Stress, 23:* 93-99.

Bower, G. H. (1981). Mood and memory. *American Psychologist, 36(2),* 129-148.

Bower, G. H. (2008). The evolution of a cognitive psychologist: A journey from simple behaviors to complex mental acts. *Annual Review of Psychology, 59,* 1-27.

Bower, G. H. & Forgas, J. P. (2001). Mood and social memory. In J. P. Forgas (Ed.), *Handbook of affect and social cognition*. (pp. 95-120) Mahwah, NJ: Lawrence Erlbaum Associates Publishers.

Bowlby, J. (1958), The nature of the child's tie to his mother. *International Journal of PsychoAnalysis,* XXXIX, 1-23.

Bowlby, J. (1959). Separation anxiety. *International Journal of Psycho-Analysis,* XLI, 1-25. Bowlby, J. (1969), *Attachment and loss, Vol. 1: Attachment*. New York, NY: Basic Books.

Bowlby, J. & Robertson, J. (1952). A two-year-old goes to hospital. Proceedings of the Royal Society of Medicine, 46, 425-427.

Bowne, W. B., Julliard, K., Castro, A. E., Shah, P., Morgenthal, C. B., Ferzli, G. S., et al. (2006). Laparoscopic gastric bypass is superior to adjustable gastric band in super morbidly obese patients. *Archives of Surgery, 141:* 683-689.

Boyle, G. J. (2008). Critique of the five-factor model of personality. In G. J. Boyle, G. Matthews, & D. H. Saklofske (eds.), *The SAGE Handbook of Personality Theory and Assessment, Vol 1: Personality Theories and Models*. (295-312) Sage Publications.

Boysen, G. A. (2007). An evaluation of the DSM concept of mental disorder. *Journal of Mind and Behavior, 28(2),* 157-173.

Brach, J. S., FitzGerald, S., Newman, A. B., Kelsey, S., Kuller, L., VanSwearingen, J. M., & Kriska, A. M. (2003). Physical activity and functional status in community-dwelling older women. *Archives of Internal Medicine, 163,* 2565-2571.

Braden, W. R. (1994). Homies: A study of peer-mentoring among African-American males in chicago in relation to adult education. ProQuest Information & Learning: US. *Dissertation Abstracts International Section A: Humanities and Social Sciences, 54* (8), 2843.

Bradley, M. M., Cuthbert, B. N., & Lang, P. J. (1990). Startle reflex modification: Emotion or attention? *Psychophysiology, 27,* 513-522.

Bradley, M. M., Cuthbert, B. N., & Lang, P. J. (1991). Startle and emotion: Lateral acoustic probes and the bilateral blink. *Psychophysiology, 28,* 285-295.

Bradley, M. M. & Lang, P. J. (2000). Measuring emotion: Behavior, feeling, and physiology. In R. D. Lane & L. Nadel (Eds.), *Cognitive neuroscience of emotion* (pp.242-276). New York, NY: Oxford University Press.

Bradley, M. M. & Lang, P. J. (2007). Emotion and motivation. In J. T. Cacioppo, L. G. Tassinary, & G. G. Berntson (Eds.), *Handbook of psychophysiology (3rd ed.)*. (pp. 581-607) New York, NY: Cambridge University Press.

Bradley, R. H. & Caldwell, B. M. (1984). The HOME inventory and family demographics. *Developmental Psychology, 20(2),* 315-320.

Bradley, R. H., Caldwell, B. M., & Corwyn, R. F. (2003). The child care HOME inventories: Assessing the quality of family child care homes. *Early Childhood Research Quarterly, 18(3),* 294-309.

Bradley, R., Conklin, C. Z., & Westen, D. (2007). Borderline personality disorder. In W. O'Donohue, K. A. Fowler, & S. O. Lilienfeld (eds.), *Personality Disorders: Toward the DSM-V*. (167-201) Sage Publications.

Bradley, S. D., Angelini, J. R., & Lee, S. (2007). Psychophysiological and memory effects of negative political ads: Aversive, arousing, and well remembered. *Journal of Advertising, 36(4),* 115-127.

Bradley, S. J. (1995). Psychosexual disorders in adolescence. In J. M. Oldham & M. B. Riba (Eds.), *American Psychiatric Press review of psychiatry (Vol. 14)*. Washington, DC: American Psychiatric Press.

Brainerd, C. J., Reyna, V. F., & Ceci, S. J. (2008). Developmental reversals in false memory: a review of data and theory. *Psychological Bulletin. 134(5):* 764-7.

Breland, K. & Breland, M. (1961). The misbehavior of organisms. *American Psychologist, 16,* 681-684.

Bretherton, I. (1992). The origins of attachment theory: John Bowlby and Mary Ainsworth. *Developmental Psychology, 28,* 759-775.

Brickman, P. & Campbell, D. T. (1971). Hedonic relativism and planning the good society. In M. H. Apley (Ed.), *Adaptation-level theory: A symposium* (pp. 287-302). New York, NY: Academic Press.

Brislin, R. W. & Keating, C. F. (1976). Cultural Differences in the Perception of a Three-Dimensional Ponzo Illusion. *Journal of Cross-Cultural Psychology, 7,* 397-412.

Broad, K. D., Curley, J. P., & Keverne, E. B. (2006). Mother-infant bonding and the evolution of mammalian social relationships. *Philosophical Transactions of the Royal Society of London. Series B, Biological sciences, 361(1476):* 2199-214.

Brody, L. R. (1999). *Gender, emotion and the family*. Cambridge, MA: Harvard University Press.

Brooks, J., & Lewis, M. (1976). Infants' responses to strangers: Midget, adult, and child. *Child Development, 47*, 323-332.

Brosnan, S. F. & De Waal, F. B. (2003). Monkeys reject unequal pay. *Nature, 425*, 297-9.

Brown, D. E. (1991). *Human Universals.* New York, NY: McGraw-Hill.

Brown, L. L., Tomarken, A. J., Orth, D. N., Loosen, P. T., Kalin, N. H., & Davidson, R. J. (1996). Individual differences in repressive-defensiveness predict basal salivary cortisol levels. *Journal of Personality and Social Psychology, 70*(2), 362-371.

Brown, T. M. & Fee, E. (2003). Sexual behavior in the human male. *American Journal of Public Health, 93*(6).

Brownell, K. D. & Rodin, J. (1994). Medical, metabolic, and psychological effects of weight cycling. *Archives of Internal Medicine, 154:* 1325-30.

Bruckner, H. & Bearman, P. S. (2005). After the Promise: The STD consequences of adolescent virginity pledges. *Journal of Adolescent Health, 36:* 272-8

Brumbaugh, C. C. & Fraley, R. C. (2006). The evolution of attachment in romantic relationships. In M. Mikulincer, & G. S. Goodman (eds.), *Dynamics of romantic love: Attachment, caregiving, and sex.* (pp. 71-101). New York, NY: Guilford Press.

Bryan, W. L. & Harter, N. (1897). Studies in the psychology of the telegraphic language. *Psychological Review, 4*, 27-53.

Buchanan, J. A., & Houlihan, D. (2008). The use of in vivo desensitization for the treatment of a specific phobia of earthworms. *Clinical Case Studies, 7*(1), 12-24.

Buchner, A. & Brandt, M. (2003). The principle of multiple memory systems. In R. H. Kluwe, G. Lüer, & F. Rösler (Eds.), *Principles of learning and memory.* (pp. 93-111) Cambridge, MA: Birkhäuser.

Buchsbaum, G. & Gottschalk, A. (1983). Trichromacy, opponent colours coding and optimum colour information transmission in the retina. *Proceedings of The Royal Society of London. Series B, Containing Papers of a Biological Character, 220*, 89-113.

Buck, L.B. (1996). Information coding in the vertebrate olfactory system. *Annual Reviews in the Neurosciences, 19*, 517-44.

Buda, R. & Elsayed-Elkhouly, S. M. (1998). Cultural differences between Arabs and Americans: Individualism-collectivism revisited. *Journal of Cross-Cultural Psychology, 29:* 487-492.

Buhrich, N., Bailey, M. J., & Martin, N. G. (1991). Sexual orientation, sexual identity, and sex-dimorphic behaviors in male twins. *Behavior Genetics, 21(1):* 75-96.

Bullough, V. L. (2004). Sex will never be the same: The contributions of Alfred C. Kinsey. *Archives of Sexual Behavior, 33(3):* 277-86.

Burger King. (2009). Burger King USA Nutritionals. Downloaded on June 25, 2009 from: http://www.bk.com/Nutrition/PDFs/Nutritional Brochure.pdf.

Burgess, J. L. (2001). Phosphine exposure from a methamphetamine laboratory investigation. *Journal of Toxicology and Clinical Toxicology, 39*, 165.

Burijon, B. N. (2007). *Biological bases of clinical anxiety.* New York, NY: W. W. Norton & Company.

Burkholder, A. (2008). Jolting the brain fights deep depression. *CNN.com/health*, May 2, 2008.

Bush, G., Valera, E. M., & Seidman, L. J. (2005). Functional neuroimaging of attention-deficit/hyperactivity disorder: a review and suggested future directions. *Biological Psychiatry, 57*, 1273-84.

Bushman, B. J., Baumeister, R. F., & Stack, A. D. (1999). Catharsis, aggression, and persuasive influence: Self-fulfilling or self-defeating prophecies? *Journal of Personality and Social Psychology, 76*(3), 367-376.

Buss, D. M. (1999). *Evolutionary psychology: The new science of the mind.* Boston, MA: Allyn & Bacon.

Buss, D. M. (Ed.) (2005). *The handbook of evolutionary psychology.* Hoboken, NJ: John Wiley & Sons.

Buss, D. M. (2009). The great struggles of life: Darwin and the emergence of evolutionary psychology. *American Psychologist, 64*(2), 140-148.

Bussey, K. & Bandura, A. (1999) Social cognitive theory of gender development and differentiation, *Psychological Review, 106:* 676-713.

Button, L. A. (2008). Effect of social support and coping strategies on the relationship between health care-related occupational stress and health. *Journal of Research in Nursing, 13*(6), 498-524.

Butler, E. A., Egloff, B., Wilhelm, F. H., Smith, N. C., Erickson, E. A., & Gross, J. J. (2003). The social consequences of expressive suppression. *Emotion, 3*(1), 48-67.

Butler, J. L., & Baumeister, R. F. (1998). The trouble with friendly faces: Skilled performance with a supportive audience. *Journal of Personality and Social Psychology, 75*(5), 1213-1230.

Byers, E. S., Purdon, C., & Clark, D. A. (1998). Sexual intrusive thoughts of college students. *Journal of Sex Research, 35:* 359-369.

Byrd-Bredbenner, C., Murray, J., & Schlussel, Y. R. (2005). Temporal changes in anthropometric measurements of idealized females and young women in general. *Women & Health, 41(2):* 13-30.

Byrne, B. M., Oakland, T., Leong, F. T. L., van, D. V., Hambleton, R. K., Cheung, F. M., & Bartram, D. (2009). A critical analysis of cross-cultural research and testing practices: Implications for improved education and training in psychology. *Training and Education in Professional Psychology, 3*(2), 94-105.

Byrne, D. (1971). *The attraction paradigm.* New York, NY: Academic Press.

Byrne, D., Ervin, C., & Lamberth, J. (1970). Continuity between the experimental study of attraction and real-life computer dating. *Journal of Personality and Social Psychology, 16:* 157-165.

Byrne, D., London, O., & Reeves, K. (1968). The effects of physical attractiveness, sex, and attitude similarity on interpersonal attraction. *Journal of Personality, 36:* 259-271.

Byrne, M., Agerbo, E., Eaton, W. W., & Mortensen, P. B. (2004). Parental socio-economic status and risk of first admission with schizophrenia: A Danish national register based study. *Social Psychiatry and Psychiatric Epidemiology, 39*(2), 87-96.

C

Cacioppo, J. T., & Berntson, G. G. (1994). Relationship between attitudes and evaluative space: A critical review, with emphasis on the separability of positive and negative substrates. *Psychological Bulletin, 115*(3), 401-423.

Caetano, R., & Babor, T. F. (2007). Diagnosis of alcohol dependence in epidemiological surveys: An epidemic of youthful alcohol dependence or a case of measurement error? In P. J. Sirovatka, D. A. Regier, J. B. Saunders, & M. A. Schuckit (Eds.), *Diagnostic issues in substance use disorders: Refining the research agenda for DSM-V* (pp. 195-201). Washington, DC: American Psychiatric Association.

Cahill, L., Prins, B., Weber, M., & McGaugh, J. L. (1994). Beta-adrenergic activation and memory for emotional events. *Nature, 371*(6499), 702-704.

Cain, C. K. & LeDoux, J. E. (2008). Emotional processing and motivation: In search of brain mechanisms. In A. J. Elliot (Ed.), *Handbook of approach and avoidance motivation.* (pp. 17-34) New York, NY: Psychology Press.

Cain, D. J. (2007). What every therapist should know, be and do: Contributions from humanistic psychotherapies. *Journal of Contemporary Psychotherapy, 37*(1), 3-10.

Calder, A.J., Beaver, J.D., Davis, M.H., van Ditzhuijzen, J., Keane, J., & Lawrence, A.D. (2007). Disgust sensitivity predicts the insula and pallidal response to pictures of disgusting foods. *The European Journal of Neuroscience, 25,* 3422-8.

Calleo, J., Stanley, M. A., Greisinger, A., Wehmanen, O., Johnson, M., Novy, D., Wilson, N., & Kunik, M. (2009). Generalized anxiety disorder in older medical patients: Diagnostic recognition, mental health management and service utilization. *Journal of Clinical Psychology in Medical Settings, 16*(2), 178-185.

Cameron, A., Rosen, R. C., & Swindle, R. W. (2005). Sexual and relationship characteristics among an internet-based sample of U.S. men with and without erectile dysfunction. *Journal of Sex & Marital Therapy, 31*(3), 229-242.

Cameron, H. A. & McKay, R. D. (2001). Adult neurogenesis produces a large pool of new granule cells in the dentate gyrus. *Journal of Comparative Neurology.* 435: 406-17.

Campos, J. J., Campos, R. G., & Barrett, K. C. (1989). Emergent themes in the study of emotional development and emotion regulation. *Developmental Psychology, 25*(3), 394-402.

Cannon, W. B. (1929). *Bodily changes in pain, hunger, fear, and rage,* Vol. 2. New York, NY: Appleton.

Cannon, W. B. (1932). *Effects of strong emotions.* Oxford: Univ. Chicago Press.

Cannon, W. B. (1932). *The wisdom of the body* New York, NY: W. W. Norton & Co.

Cannon, W. B. (1987). The James-Lange theory of emotions: A critical examination and an alternative theory. *The American Journal of Psychology, 100,* 567-586. *(Paper originally published in 1927.)*

Cardeña, E. & Gleaves, D. H. (2007). Dissociative disorders. In M. Hersen, S. M. Turner, & D. C. Beidel (Eds.). *Adult psychopathology and diagnosis (5ᵗʰ ed.).* Hoboken, NJ: John Wiley & Sons Inc.

Cardilla, K. (2008). Personality vulnerabilities, coping, and depression: A multi-method daily diary study of college students' coping with daily hassles. US: ProQuest Information & Learning). *Dissertation Abstracts International: Section B: The Sciences and Engineering, 69* (5-), 3294.

Cardoso, R., Souza, E. d., & Camano, L. (2009). Meditation in health: Definition, operationalization, and technique. *Stress and quality of working life: The positive and the negative.* (pp. 143-166). Charlotte, NC: Information Age Publishing.

Carels, R. A., Cacciapaglia, H. M., Rydin, S., Douglass, O. M., & Harper, J. (2006). Can social desirability interfere with success in a behavioral weight loss program? *Psychology & Health, 21*(1): 65-78.

Carey, B. (2008). Lotus therapy. *New York Times Online.* Retrieved from http://www.nytimes.com/2008/05/27/health/research/27budd.html

Carey, B. (2009). The afterlife of near-death. *The New York Times, 158*(54, 559).

Carlson, N. R. (2008). *Foundations of physiological psychology (7ᵗʰ edition).* Boston MA: Pearson.

Carlsson, A. & Lindqvist, M. (1963). Effect of chlorpromazine o haloperidol on formation of 3-methoxytyramine and normetanephrine in mouse brain. *Acta Pharmcol Toxicol (Copenh), 20,* 140-4.

Carpendale, J. I. M. (2000). Kohlberg and Piaget on stages and moral reasoning. *Developmental Review, 20,* 181-205.

Carr, V. S. (2000). Stress effects of earthquakes. In G. Fink (ed.), *Encyclopedia of stress, Vol. 2* (1-4). New York, NY: Academic Press.

Carré, J. M., Putnam, S. K., & McCormick, C. M. (2009). Testosterone responses to competition predict future aggressive behaviour at a cost to reward in men. *Psychoneuroendocrinology, 34(4)*: 561-570.

Carroll, R. A. (2007). Gender dysphoria and transgender experiences. In S.R. Leiblum (Ed.), *Principles and practice of sex therapy (4ᵗʰ ed.).* (pp. 477-508) New York, NY: Guilford Press.

Carskadon, M. A. (Ed.). (2002). *Adolescent sleep patterns: Biological, social and psychological influences.* New York, NY: Cambridge University Press.

Carter, C. S., Botvinick, M. M., & Cohen, J.D. (1999). The contribution of the anterior cingulate cortex to executive processes in cognition. *Rev Neurosci. 10,* 49-57.

Carver, C.S. (2004). Self-regulation of action and affect. In R. F. Baumeister & K. D. Vohs (Eds.), *Handbook of self-regulation: Research, theory, and applications* (pp. 13-39). New York, NY: Guilford Press.

Carver, C. S. & Scheier, M. (1999). Optimism. In C. R. Snyder (ed.), *Coping: The Psychology of What Works,* New York, NY: Oxford University Press.

Carver, C. S. & Scheier, M. F. (1998). *On the self-regulation of behavior.* New York, NY: Cambridge University Press.

Carver, C. S., & Scheier, M. (2003). Optimism. *Positive psychological assessment: A handbook of models and measures.* (pp. 75-89). Washington, DC: American Psychological Association. doi:10.1037/10612-005.

Carver, C. S., & Scheier, M. F. (1994). Situational coping and coping dispositions in a stressful transaction. *Journal of Personality and Social Psychology, 66*(1), 184-195.

Casey, L. M., Oei, T. P. S., & Newcombe, P. A. (2004). An integrated cognitive model of panic disorder: The role of positive and negative cognitions. *Clinical Psychology Review, 24*(5), 529-555.

Caspi, A. (1998). Personality development across the life course. In W. Damon & N. Eisenberg (Eds.), *Handbook of child psychology: Vol. 3, Social emotional, and personality development* (5ᵗʰ ed., pp. 311-388). New York, NY: John Wiley & Sons, Inc.

Caspi, A. (2002). Social selection, social causation, and developmental pathways: Empirical strategies for better understanding how individuals and environments are linked across the life course. In L. Pulkkinen & A. Caspi (eds.), *Paths to Successful Development; Personality in the Life Course* (281-301). Cambridge, UK: Cambridge University Press.

Caspi, A., Bem, D. J., & Elder, G. H., Jr. (1989). Continuities and consequence of interactional styles across the life course. *Journal of Personality, 57*: 375-406.

Caspi, A. & Roberts, B. W. (1999). Personality change and continuity across the life course. In L. A. Pervin & O. P. John, *Handbook of Personality Theory and Research* (Vol. 2, 300-326). New York, NY: Guilford Press.

Catalyst. (2000). *Census of women corporate officers and top earners*. New York, NY: Catalyst.

Catania, K. C., & Remple, F. E. (2004). Tactile foveation in the star-nosed mole. *Brain, Behavior and Evolution, 63*(1), 1-12.

Catrambone, R. (1998). The subgoal learning model: creating better examples so that students can solve novel problems. *Journal of Experimental Psychology: General*, 127, 355-76.

Cavallini, E., Pagnin, A., & Vecchi, T. (2003). Aging and everyday memory: The beneficial effect of memory training. *Archives of Gerontology and Geriatrics, 37*(3), 241-257.

Cavior, N., & Dokecki, P. R. (1971). Physical attractiveness of self concept: A test of mead's hypothesis. *Proceedings of the Annual Convention of the American Psychological Association*, 6, 319-320.

Ceci, S. J. (1991). How much does schooling influence general intelligence and its cognitive components? A reassessment of the evidence. *Developmental Psychology, 27*(5), 703-722.

Ceci, S. J. (2003). Cast in six ponds and you'll reel in something: Looking back on 25 years of research. *American Psychologist, 58*(11), 855-864.

Ceci, S. J., & Williams, W. M. (1997). Schooling, intelligence, and income. *American Psychologist, 52*(10), 1051-1058.

Ceci, S. J., & Williams, W. M. (2007). Little g: Prospects and constraints. *European Journal of Personality, 21*(5), 716-718.

Ceci, S. J., Fitneva, S. A., & Gilstrap, L. L. (2003). Memory development and eyewitness testimony. In A. Slater & G. Bremner (Eds.), *An introduction to developmental psychology.* (pp. 283-310) Malden, MA: Blackwell Publishing.

Ceci, S. J., Rosenblum, T., de Bruyn, E., & Lee, D. Y. (1997). A bio-ecological model of intellectual development: Moving beyond h². *Intelligence, heredity, and environment.* (pp. 303-322) New York, NY: Cambridge University Press.

Cenci, M. A. (2007). Dopamine dysregulation of movement control in L-DOPA-induced dyskinesia. *Trends in Neurosciences, 30*: 236-43.

Centers for Disease Control and Prevention (CDC). (2001). Young People at Risk: HIV/AIDS Among America's Youth. Downloaded on May 23, 2009 from: www.cdc.gov/hiv/pubs/facts/youth.pdf.

Centers for Disease Control and Prevention (CDC). (2008) *Sexually Transmitted Disease Surveillance, 2007.* Atlanta, GA: U.S. Department of Health and Human Services.

Centers for Disease Control and Prevention (CDC). (2008). *Chronic liver disease/cirrhosis.* Hyattsville, MD: NCHS.

Centers for Disease Control and Prevention (CDC). (2009). Health, United States, 2008, Table 75. Downloaded on May 20, 2009 from: http://www.cdc.gov/nchs/data/hus/hus08.pdf#075.

Certner, B. C. (1973). Exchange of self-disclosures in same-sexed groups of strangers. *Journal of Consulting and Clinical Psychology, 40*: 292-297.

Cetas, J.S., Saedi, T., & Burchiel, K.J. (2008). Destructive procedures for the treatment of nonmalignant pain: a structured literature review. *Journal of Neurosurgery*, 109, 389-404.

Chandler, M. J. & Carpendale, J. I. (1998). Inching toward a mature theory of mind. In M. D. Ferrari & R. J. Sternberg (Eds.), *Self-awareness: Its nature and development* (pp. 148-190). New York, NY: Guilford Press.

Chang, E. C. (2002). Optimism-pessimism and stress appraisal: Testing a cognitive interactive model of psychological adjustment in adults. *Cognitive Therapy and Research, 26*(5), 675-690.

Chang, R., Chang, E. C., Sanna, L. J., & Hatcher, R. L. (2008). Optimism and pessimism as personality variables linked to adjustment. *The SAGE handbook of personality theory and assessment, vol 1: Personality theories and models.* (pp. 470-485). Thousand Oaks, CA: Sage Publications, Inc.

Chao, R. (2001). Extending research on the consequences of parenting style for Chinese Americans and European Americans. *Child Development*, 2, 1832-1843.

Chapman, A. L., Leung, D. W., & Lynch, T. R. (2008). Impulsivity and emotion dysregulation in borderline personality disorder. *22*(2), 148-164.

Charman, D. P. (Ed.). (2004). *Core processes in brief psychodynamic psychotherapy: Advancing effective practice.* Mahwah, NJ: Lawrence Erlbaum.

Charles, S. T. & Piazza, J. R. (2007). Memories of social interactions: Age differences in emotional intensity. *Psychology and Aging, 22*(2), 300-309.

Charuvastra, A., & Cloitre, M. (2008). Social bonds and posttraumatic stress disorder. In S. Fiske, D. L. Schacter, & R. Sternberg (Eds.), *Annual review of psychology (Vol. 59).* Palo Alto, CA: Annual reviews.

Chatterjee, A. & Hambrick D. (2006). It's All About Me: Narcissistic CEOs and Their Effects on Company Strategy and Performance. Manuscript submitted for publication.

Chekroun, P. & Brauer, M. (2002). The bystander effect and social control behavior: The effect of the presence of others on people's reactions to norm violations. *European Journal of Social Psychology, 32*(6): 853-866.

Chen, Y. R., Swann, A. C., & Burt, D. B. (1996). Stability of diagnosis in schizophrenia. *American Journal of Psychiatry, 153*(5), 682-686.

Chess, S. & Thomas, A. (1996). *Temperament: Theory and Practice.* New York: Brunner-Mazel. Cicchetti, D. & Rogosch, F.A. (1996). Equifinality and multifinality in developmental psychopathology. *Development and Psychopathology, 8*(4), 597-600.

Chidambaram, L. & Tung, L. L. (2005). Is out of sight, out of mind? An empirical study of social loafing in technology-supported groups. *Information Systems Research, 16*(2): 149-168.

Childress, A. R., Ehrman, R. N., Wang, Z., Li, Y., Sciortino, N., Hakun, J., et al. (2008). Prelude to passion: Limbic activation by "unseen" drug and sexual cues. *PLoS ONE, 3*(1): e1506.

Chin, J. H., Ma, L., MacTavish, D., & Jhamandas, J. H. (2007). Amyloid beta protein modulates glutamate-mediated neurotransmission in the rat basal forebrain: Involvement of presynaptic neuronal nicotinic acetylcholine and metabotropic glutamate receptors. *Journal of Neuroscience, 27*(35), 9262-9269.

Choi, Y. Y., Shamosh, N. A., Cho, S. H., DeYoung, C. G., Lee, M. J., Lee, J., et al. (2008). Multiple bases of human intelligence revealed by cortical thickness and neural activation. *Journal of Neuroscience, 28*(41), 10323-10329.

Chomsky, N. (1959). A review of B. F. Skinner's verbal behavior. *Language*, 35, 26-58.

Chomsky, N. (1964). The development of grammar in child language: Formal discussion. *Monographs of the Society for Research in Child Development*, 29, 35-9.

Chomsky, N. (2005). Editorial: Universals of human nature. *Psychotherapy and Psychosomatics, 74*(5), 263-268.

Christakis, N. A. & Fowler, J. H. (2007). The spread of obesity in a large social network over 32 years. *New England Journal of Medicine, 357*: 370-9.

Christian, K. M. & Thompson, R. F. (2003). Neural substrates of eye-blink conditioning: acquisition and retention. *Learning & Memory, 10*, 427-55.

Christophe, V. & Rimé, B. (1997). Exposure to the social sharing of emotion: Emotional impact, listener responses and secondary social sharing. *European Journal of Social Psychology, 27*(1), 37-54.

Christophe, V. & Rimé, B. (2001). Exposure to the social sharing of emotion: Emotional impact, listener responses and secondary social sharing. In W. G. Parrott (Ed.), *Emotions in social psychology: Essential readings.* (pp. 239-250) New York, NY: Psychology Press.

Christou, N. V., Look, D., & Maclean, L. D. (2006). Weight gain after short- and long-limb gastric bypass in patients followed for longer than 10 years. *Annals of Surgery, 244*(5): 734-40.

Chung, M. C., Dennis, I., Easthope, Y., Werrett, J., & Farmer, S. (2005). A multiple-indicator multiple-case model for posttraumatic stress reactions: Personality, coping, and maladjustment. *Psychosomatic Medicine, 67*(2), 251-259.

Church, A. T. & Katigbak, M. S. (2000). Trait psychology in the Philippines. *American Behavioral Scientist, 44*: 73-94.

Chwalisz, K., Diener, E., & Gallagher, D. (1988). Autonomic arousal feedback and emotional experience: Evidence from the spinal cord injured. *Journal of Personality and Social Psychology, 54*, 820-828.

Cialdini, R. B., Kallgren, C. A., & Reno, R. R. (1991). A focus theory of normative conduct: A theoretical refinement and reevaluation of the role of norms in human behavior. In M. P. Zanna (ed.), *Advances in Experimental Social Psychology (Vol. 24)* (pp. 201-234). New York: Academic Press.

Cicchetti, D., Ganiban, J., & Barnett, D. (1991). Contributions from the study of high-risk populations to understanding the development of emotion regulation. In J. Garber & K. A. Dodge (Eds.), *The development of emotion regulation and dysregulation.* (pp. 15-48) New York, NY: Cambridge University Press.

Cicchetti, D., & Rogosch, F. A. (1996). Equifinality and multifinality in developmental psychopathology. *Development and Psychopathology, 8*(4), 597-600.

Clark, L. & Watson, D. (1999). Temperament: A new paradigm for trait psychology. In L. A. Pervin & O. P. John (eds.), *Handbook of Personality* (2nd. ed., 399-423). New York, NY: Guilford Press.

Clark, M. S. & Taraban, C. (1991). Reactions to and willingness to express emotion in communal and exchange relationships. *Experimental Social Psychology, 27*(4), 324-336.

Clark, R. E., Broadbent, N. J., & Squire, L. R. (2008). The hippocampus and spatial memory: Findings with a novel modification of the water maze. *Journal of Neuroscience, 27*(25): 6647-6654.

Cleary, Anne M. (2008). Recognition Memory, Familiarity, and Déjà vu Experiences. *Current Directions in Psychologial Science. 17*(5): 353-57.

Cleckley, H. (1941). *The mask of sanity; an attempt to reinterpret the so-called psychopathic personality.* St. Louis, MO: Mosby.

Cleland, R., Graybill, D., Hubbard, V., Khan, L., Stern, J., Wadden, T., Weinsier, R., & Yanovski, S. (1997). Commercial weight loss products and programs: What consumers stand to gain and lose. *Public Conference on the Information Consumers Need to Evaluate Weight Loss Products and Programs.* Downloaded on June 26, 2009 from: http:// www.ftc.gov/os/1998/03/weightlo.rpt.htm#1.%20Consumers%20Are %20Not.

Clements, A. M., Rimrodt, S.L., Abel, J.R., Blankner, J.G., Mostofsky, S.H., Pekar, J.J., Denckla, M.B., & Cutting, L. E. (2006). Sex differences in cerebral laterality of language and visuospatial processing. *Brain Language, 98*, 150-8.

Clements, C. M. & Sawhney, D. K. (2000). Coping with domestic violence: control attributions, dysphoria, and hopelessness. *Journal of Traumatic Stress, 13*, 219-40.

Cobb, M. D. (2002). Unobtrusively measuring racial attitudes: The consequences of social desirability effects. ProQuest Information & Learning: US). *Dissertation Abstracts International Section A: Humanities and Social Sciences, 62* (8): 2869.

Cochran, W. G., Mosteller, F., & Tukey, J. W. (1953). Some statistical problems of the Kinsey Report. *Journal of the American Statistical Association, 48*: 673-716.

Cocodia, E. A., Kim, J., Shin, H., Kim, J., Ee, J., Wee, M. S. W., & Howard, R. W. (2003). Evidence that rising population intelligence is impacting in formal education. *Personality and Individual Differences, 35*(4), 797-810.

Coddington, R. D. (1972). The significance of life events as etiologic factors in the disease of children, II: A study of a normal population. *Journal of Psychosomatic Research, 16*: 205-213.

Coddington, R. D. (1984). Measuring the stressfulness of a child's environment. In J. H. Humphrey, *Stress in Childhood.* New York, NY: AMS Press.

Coetzer, B.R. (2004). Obsessive-compulsive disorder following brain injury: A review. *International Journal of Psychiatric Medicine., 34*(4), 363-377.

Cohen, D. & Nisbett, R. E. (1994). Self-protection and the culture of honor: Explaining southern homicide. *Personality and Social Psychology Bulletin, 20*: 551-567.

Cohen, S. (2002). Psychosocial stress, social networks, and susceptibility to infection. In H. G. Koenig & H. J. Cohen (Eds.), *The link between religion and health: Psychoneuroimmunology and the faith factor* (pp. 101-123). New York, NY: Oxford University Press.

Cohen, S. (2004). Social relationships and health. *American Psychologist, 59*(8), 676-684.

Cohen, S., & Hamrick, N. (2003). Stable individual differences in physiological response to stressors: Implications for stress-elicited changes in immune related health. *Brain, Behavior, and Immunity, 17*(6), 407-414.

Cohen, S., Hamrick, N., Rodriguez, M. S., Feldman, P. J., Rabin, B. S., & Manuck, S. B. (2002). Reactivity and vulnerability to stress-associated risk for upper respiratory illness. *Psychosomatic Medicine, 64*(2), 302-310.

Cohen, S. (2005). Psychological stress, immunity and upper respiratory infections. In G. Miller & E. Chen (Eds.), *Current directions in health psychology.* Upper Saddle River, NJ: Pearson.

Cohen, S., Alper, C. M., Doyle, W. J., Adler, N., Treanor, J. J., & Turner, R. B. (2008). Objective and subjective socioeconomic status and susceptibility to the common cold. *Health Psychology, 27*(2), 268-274.

Cohen, S., Doyle, W. J., Turner, R. B., Alper, C. M., & Skoner, D. P. (2003). Emotional style and susceptibility to the common cold. *Psychosomatic Medicine, 65*, 652-657.

Cohen, S. & Herbert, T.B. (1996). Health psychology: Psychological factors and physical disease from the perspective of human psychoneuroimmunology. *Annual Review of Psychology, 47,* 113-142.

Cohen, S. & Herbert, T., Henley, N. M. (1977). *Body politics: Power, sex, and nonverbal communication.* Englewood Cliffs, NJ: Prentice Hall.

Cohen, S., & Janicki-Deverts, D. (2009). Can we improve our physical health by altering our social networks? *Perspectives on Psychological Science, 4*(4), 375-378.

Cohen, S., Janicki-Deverts, D., & Miller, G. E. (2007). Psychological stress and disease. *JAMA: Journal of the American Medical Association, 298*(14), 1685-1687.

Cohen, S. & Herbert, T. (1996). Health psychology: Psychological factors and physical disease from the perspective of human psychoneuroimmunology. *Annual Review of Psychology, 47,* 113-142.

Cohen, S., Tyrell, D. A. J., & Smith, A. P. (1991). Psychological stress and susceptibility to the common cold. *The New England Journal of Medicine, 325:* 606-612.

Cohen, S., & Wills, T. A. (1985). Stress, social support, and the buffering hypothesis. *Psychological Bulletin, 98*(2), 310-357.

Cohen-Kettenis, P. (2001). Gender identity disorder in DSM? *Journal of the American Academy of Child & Adolescent Psychiatry, 40*(4), 391.

Cohn, J. F., Ambadar, Z., & Ekman, P. (2007). Observer-based measurement of facial expression with the facial action coding system. In J. A. Coan & J. J. B. Allen (Eds.), *Handbook of emotion elicitation and assessment.* (pp. 203-221) New York, NY: Oxford University Press.

Cole, D.A. & Turner, J.E., Jr. (1993). Models of cognitive mediation and moderation in child depression. *Journal of Abnormal Psychology, 102*(2), 271-281.

Cole, M. (1996). *Cultural Psychology: A once and future discipline.* Cambridge, MA: Harvard University Press.

Cole, M., Gay, J., & Glick, J. (1967). A cross-cultural study of clustering in free recall. *Psychonomic Bulletin, 1*(2), 18.

Cole, P. M. & Hall, S. E. (2008). Emotion dysregulation as a risk factor for psychopathology. In T. P. Beauchaine & S. P. Hinshaw (Eds.), *Child and adolescent psychopathology.* (pp. 265-298) Hoboken, NJ: John Wiley & Sons, Inc.

Coleman, S. R. (2007). Pavlov and the equivalence of associability in classical conditioning. *Journal of Mind and Behavior, 28*(2), 115-133.

Collins, R. L. (2005). Sex on television and its impact on American youth: Background and results from the RAND television and adolescent sexuality study. *Child and Adolescent Psychiatric Clinics of North America, 14*(3), 371-385.

Colson, S. D., Meek, J. H., & Hawdon, J. M. (2008). Optimal positions for the release of primitive neonatal reflexes stimulating breastfeeding. *Early Human Development, 84*(7): 441-9.

Colvin, M. K. & Gazzaniga, M. S. (2007). Split-brain cases. In S. Schneider & M. Velman (Eds.) *The Blackwell companion to consciousness.* (pp. 181-193). Malden, MA: Blackwell Publishing.

Combs, D. R., Basso, M. R., Wanner, J. L., & Ledet, S. N. (2008). Schizophrenia. In M. Hersen & J. Rosqvist (Eds.), *Handbook of psychological assessment, case conceptualization and treatment, Vol. 1: Adults* (pp. 352-402). Hoboken, NJ: John Wiley & Sons.

Community Epidemiology Work Group (CEWG). (2004). *Trends in drug abuse, Vol. 1: Proceedings of the community epidemiology work group. NIH Pub. No 04-5364.* Washington, DC: U.S. Government Printing Office.

Compas, B. E. (2004). Processes of risk and resilience during adolescence: Linking contexts and individuals. In R. M. Lerner, & L. Steinberg (Eds.), *Handbook of adolescent psychology (2nd ed.).* (pp. 263-296). Hoboken, NJ: John Wiley & Sons Inc.

Compas, B. E., & Gotlib, I. H. (2002). *Introduction to clinical psychology: Science and practice.* Boston, MA: McGraw-Hill.

Connolly, K. (2007). Brother and sister fight German's incest laws. *The Guardian,* Tuesday, February 27, 2007.

Connolly, T. & Zeelenberg, M. (2002). Regret in decision making. *Current Directions in Psychol Science, 11,* 212-6.

Connor-Greene, P. A. (2007). Observation or interpretation: Demonstrating unintentional subjectivity and interpretive variance. *Teaching of Psychology, 34*(3), 167-171.

Cook, M. (2001). Memory and complex skills. In J. Noyes, & M. Bransby (Eds.), *People in control: Human factors in control room design.* (pp. 17-33) Edison, NJ: Institution of Electrical Engineers.

Cooke, B. M. & Woolley, C. S. (2005). Gonadal hormone modulation of dendrites in the mammalian CNS. *Journal of Neurobiology.* 64: 34-46.

Cooney, J. W., & Gazzaniga, M. S. (2003) Neurological disorders and the structure of human consciousness. *Trends in Cognitive Sciences, 7,* 161-165.

Cooney, N. L., Kadden, R. M., Litt, M. D., & Getter, H. (1991). Matching alcoholics to coping skills or interactional therapies: Two-year follow-up results. *Journal of Consulting and Clinical Psychology, 59*(4), 598-601.

Cooper, J., Kelly, K. A., & Weaver, K. (2004). Attitudes, norms, and social groups. In M. B. Brewer & M. Hewstone (eds.), *Social Cognition.* (pp. 244-267). Malden, MA: Blackwell Publishing.

Cooper, J., Mirabile, R., & Scher, S. J. (2005). Actions and attitudes: The theory of cognitive dissonance. In T. C. Brock & M. C. Green (eds.), *Persuasion: Psychological Insights and Perspectives, 2nd ed.* (pp. 63-79). Thousand Oaks, CA: Sage Publications.

Cooper, M. L. & Sheldon, M. S. (2002). Seventy years of research on personality and close relationships: Substantive and methodological trends over time. *Journal of Personality, 70:* 783-812.

Cooper, R. (1994). Normal sleep. In R. Cooper (Ed.), *Sleep.* New York, NY: Chapman & Hall.

Cooper, R. P. & Aslin, R. N. (1994). Developmental differences in infant attention to the spectral properties of infant-directed speech. *Child Development, 65,* 1663-77.

Cooper, S. J. (2005). Donald O. Hebb's synapse and learning rule: a history and commentary. *Neuroscience and Biobehavioral Reviews, 28,* 851-74.

Corey, G. (2008). *Theory and practice of counseling and psychotherapy* (8th ed.). Belmont, CA: Brooks/Cole.

Corkin, S. (1984). Lasting consequences of bilateral medial temporal lobectomy: Clinical course and experimental findings in H.M. *Seminars in Neuroscience, 4,* 249-259.

Corrigan, P. W., Larson, J. E., & Kuwabara, S. A. (2007). Mental illness stigma and the fundamental components of supported employment. *Rehabilitation Psychology, 52*(4), 451-457.

Corrigan, P. W., Watson, A. C., Otey, E., Westbrook, A. L., Gardner, A. L., Lamb, T. A., & Fenton, W. S. (2007). How do children stigmatize people with mental illness? *Journal of Applied Social Psychology, 37*(7), 1405-1417.

Corsini, R. J. (2008). Introduction. In R. J. Corsini & D. Wedding (Eds.), *Current psychotherapies* (8th ed.). Belmont, CA: Thomson Brooks/Cole.

Cosmides, L. & Tooby, J. (2000). Evolutionary psychology and the emotions. In M. Lewis & J. M. Haviland-Jones (Eds.), *Handbook of Emotions, Second Edition* (pp. 91-115). New York, NY: The Guilford Press.

Costa, P. T., Jr., Terracciano, A., & McCrae, R. R. (2001). Gender differences in personality traits across cultures: Robust and surprising findings. *Journal of Personality and Social Psychology, 81:* 322-331.

Costa-Mattioli, M., Sossin, W. S., Klann, E., & Sonenberg, N. (2009). Translational control of long-lasting synaptic plasticity and memory. *Neuron, 61:* 10-26.

Cottone, E. & Byrd-Bredbenner, C. (2007). *Knowledge and Psychosocial Effects of the Film Super Size Me on Young Adults. JADA; 107(7).*

Cousins, S. D. (1989). Culture and selfhood in Japan and the U.S. *Journal of Personality and Social Psychology, 56:* 124-131.

Covington, M. A., He, C., Brown, C., Naçi, L., McClain, J. T., Fjordbak, B. S., Semple, J., & Brown, J. (2005). Schizophrenia and the Structure of language: the linguist's view. *Schizophrenia Research, 77,* 85-98.

Cowan, N. & Chen, Z. (2009). How chunks form in long-term memory and affect short-term memory limits. In A. S. C. Thorn & M. P. A. Page (Eds.), *Interactions between short-term and long-term memory in the verbal domain.* (pp. 86-107) New York, NY: Psychology Press.

Cowley, E. (2005). Views from consumers next in line: The fundamental attribution error in a service setting. *Journal of the Academy of Marketing Science, 33*(2): 139-152.

Cox, B. J., Kuch, K., Parker, J. D. A., Shulman, I. D., & et al. (1994). Alexithymia in somatoform disorder patients with chronic pain. *Journal of Psychosomatic Research, 38*(6), 523-527.

Coy, T. V. (1998). The effect of repressive coping style on cardiovascular reactivity and speech disturbances during stress. US: ProQuest Information & Learning). *Dissertation Abstracts International: Section B: The Sciences and Engineering, 58* (8-), 4512.

Cramer, R. J., Golom, F. D., LoPresto, C. T., & Kirkley, S. M. (2008). Weighing the evidence: empirical assessment and ethical implications of conversion therapy. *Ethics & Behavior, 18(1):* 93-114.

Crandall, C. S., Preisler, J. J., & Aussprung, J. (1992). Measuring life events stress in the lives of college students: The Undergraduate Stress Questionnaire (USQ). *Journal of Behavioral Medicine, 15*(6), 627-662.

Crisp, M. (2001, April 8). Sticks & stones: "New Kid" puts comic spin on a serious situation. *Sunday News* (Lancaster, PA), p. H-1.

Critchley, H. D., Elliott, R., Mathias, C. J., & Dolan, R. J. (2000). Neural activity relating to generation and representation of galvanic skin conductance responses: A functional magnetic resonance imaging study. *Journal of Neuroscience, 20,* 3033-40.

Crowley, S. J., Acebo, C., & Carskadon, M. A. (2007). Sleep, circadian rhythms, and delayed phase in adolescence. *Sleep Medicine, 8,* 602-612.

Csikszentmihalyi, M. (1998). *Finding flow: The psychology of engagement with everyday life.* Basic Books.

Csikszentmihalyi, M. (2003). *Good business: Leadership, flow, and the making of meaning.* New York, NY: Penguin Books.

Cuffe, S. P., McKeown, R.E., Addy, C. L., & Garrison, C. Z. (2005, February). Family psychosocial risk factors in a longitudinal epidemiological study of adolescents. *Journal of American Academic Child Adolescent Psychiatry, 44,* 121-129.

Cukan, A. (2001, March 8). Confronting a culture of cruelty. General feature release. United Press International.

Cumming, P. (2009). *Imaging dopamine.* New York, NY: Cambridge University Press.

Cummings, M. J. (2003). Shakespeare and medicine. Retrieved March 13, 2009: http://www.cummingsstudyguides.net/xMedicine.html

Cuninkova, L., & Brown, S. A. (2008). Peripheral circadian oscillators: Interesting mechanisms and powerful tools. *Molecular and biophysical mechanisms of arousal, alertness, and attention.* (pp. 358-370) Malden, MA: Blackwell Publishing.

Cunningham-Owens, D. G. (2000). The challenges of diagnosis and continuing patient assessment. *Inter. J. Psychiat. Clin. Pract., 4*(Suppl. 1), S13-S18.

Curtis, R., Groarke, A. M., Coughlan, R., & Gsel, A. (2004). The influence of disease severity, perceived stress, social support and coping in patients with chronic illness: A 1-year follow-up. *Psychology, Health, and Medicine, 9*(4), 456-475.

Curzi-Dascalova, L. & Challamel, M. J. (2000) Neurophysiological basis of sleep development. In G. M. Loughlin, J. L. Carroll, & C. L. Marcus (Eds.) Sleep and Breathing in Children. *A Developmental Approach* (pp. 3-37). New York, NY: Marcel Dekker.

Cynkar, A. (2007, June). The changing gender composition of psychology. *Monitor on Psychology, 38*(6), 46.

D

Dabbs, J. & Hargrove, M. (1997). Age, testosterone, and behavior among female prison inmates. *Psychosomatic Medicine, 59:* 477-80.

Dabbs Jr., J. M., Bernieri, F. J., Strong, R. K., Campo, R., & Milun, R. (2001). Going on stage: Testosterone in greetings and meetings. *Journal of Research of Personality, 35*(1), 27-40.

Dabbs Jr., J. M., Riad, J. K., Chance, S. E. (2001). Testosterone and ruthless homicide. *Personality and Individual Differences, 31*(4), 599-603.

Daggett, L. M. (2002). Living with loss: Middle-aged men face spousal bereavement. *Qualitative Health Research, 12*(5): 625-639.

Dale, R. C., Heyman, I., Surtees, R. A., Church, A. J., Giovannoni, G., Goodman, R., et al. (2004). Dyskinesias and associated psychiatric disorders following streptococcal infections. *Archives of Disease in Childhood, 89*(7), 604-610.

Dalgleish, T. (2004). The emotional brain. *Nature Reviews: Neuroscience, 5,* 582-589.

Dalton, P. (2000). Psychophysical and behavioral characteristics of olfactory adaptation. *Chemical Senses, 25,* 487-92.

Damasio, A. (1994). *Descartes' error.* New York, NY: Grosset/Putnam.

Damasio, A. (1999). *The feeling of what happens: Body and emotion in the making of consciousness.* New York, NY: Harcourt.

Damasio, A. (2003). *Looking for Spinoza: Joy, sorrow and the feeling brain.* New York, NY: Harcourt.

Damasio, A. R. & Geschwind, N. (1984). The neural basis of language. *Annual Review of Neuroscience, 7,* 127-47.

Damasio, H., Tranel, D., Grabowski, T., Adolphs, R., & Damasio, A. (2004). Neural systems behind word and concept retrieval. *Cognition. 92:* 179-229.

Damsa, C., Kosel, M., & Moussally, J. (2009). Current status of brain imaging in anxiety disorders. *Current Opinion in Psychiatry, 22*(1), 96-110.

D'Angelo, B., & Wierzbicki, M. (2003). Relations of daily hassles with both anxious and depressed mood in students. *Psychological Reports, 92*(2), 416-418.

Dansinger, M. L., Gleason, J. A., Griffith, J. L., Selker, H. P., & Schaefer, E. J. (2005). Comparison of the Atkins, Ornish, Weight Watchers, and Zone diets for weight loss and heart disease risk reduction: A randomized trial. *JAMA, 293*(1): 43-53.

Darley, J. M. (2000). Bystander phenomenon. In A. E. Kazdin (ed.), *Encyclopedia of Psychology, vol. 1.* (pp. 493-495). Washington, D.C.: American Psychological Association.

Darley, J. M. & Latane, B. (1968). Bystander intervention in emergencies: Diffusion of responsibility. *Journal of Personality and Social Psychology, 8:* 377-383.

Darvres-Bornoz, J., Lemperiere, T., Degio-vanni, A., & Gaillard, P. (1995). Sexual victimization in women with schizophrenia and bipolar disorder. *Social Psychiatry and Psychiatric Epidemiology, 30*(2), 78-84.

Darwin, C. R. (1872). *The expression of emotions in man and animals.* London: John Murray.

Davidson, R. J. (1998). Affective style and affective disorders: Perspectives from affective neuroscience. *Cognition and Emotion, 12:* 307-330.

Davidson, R. J. & Fox, N. A. (1989). Frontal brain asymmetry predicts infants' response to maternal separation. *Journal of Abnormal Psychology, 98:* 127-131.

Davidson, R. J., Jackson, D. C., & Kalin, N. H. (2000). Emotion, plasticity, context, and regulation: Perspectives from affective neuroscience. *Psychological Bulletin, 126,* 890-909.

Davies, I. R. & Corbett, G. G. (1997). A cross-cultural study of colour grouping: evidence for weak linguistic relativity. *British Journal of Psychology, 88,* 493-517.

Davis, M. (1992). Analysis of aversive memories using the fear potentiated startle paradigm. In N. Butters & L. R. Squire (Eds.), *The neuropsychology of memory* (2nd ed.). New York, NY: Guilford Press.

Davison, K.P., Pennebaker, J.W., & Dickerson, S.S. (2000). Who talks? The social psychology of illness support groups. *American Psychologist, 55*(2), 205-217.

Dawson, T. L. (2002). New tools, new insights: Kohlberg's moral judgement stages revisited. *International Journal of Behavioral Development, 26*(2), 154-166.

Day, D. M., Peterson-Badali, M., & Ruck, M. D. (2006). The relationship between maternal attitudes and young people's attitudes toward children's rights. *Journal of Adolescence, 29*(2): 193-207.

De Araujo, Ivan E. T., Rolls, Edmund T., Kringelbach, Morten L., McGlone, Francis, & Phillips, Nicola. (2005). Taste-olfactory convergence, and the representation of pleasantness of flavour, in the human brain. *European Journal of Neuroscience, 18:* 2059-2068.

De Coteau, T. J., Hope, D. A., & Anderson, J. (2003). Anxiety, stress, and health in northern plains native americans. *Behavior Therapy, 34*(3), 365-380.

De Longis, A., Coyne, J. C., Dakof, G., Folkman, S., & Lazarus, R. S. (1982). Relationships of daily hassles, uplifts, and major life events to health status. *Health Psychology, 1:* 119-136.

De Raad, B., Perugini, M., Hrebickova, M., & Szarota, P. (1998). Lingua franca of personality: Taxonomies and structures based on the psycholexical approach. *Journal of Cross-Cultural Psychology, 29:* 212-232.

de Villers-Sidani, E., Chang, E. F., Bao, S., & Merzenich, M. M. (2007). Critical Period Window for Spectral Tuning Defined in the Primary Auditory Cortex (A1) in the Rat. *The Journal of Neuroscience, 27,* 180-9.

De Vries, R. (1969). Constancy of genetic identity in the years three to six. *Monograph of the Society for Research in Child Development, 34* (Serial No. 127).

Deary, I. J. & Stough, C. (1996). Intelligence and inspection time: Achievements, prospects, and problems. *American Psychologist, 51*(6), 599-608.

Deary, I. J. & Stough, C. (1997). Looking down on human intelligence. *American Psychologist, 52*(10), 1148-1150.

Deary, I. J., Whiteman, M. C., Starr, J. M., Fox, H. C., & Whalley, L. J. (2004). The impact of childhood intelligence on later life: Following up the scottish mental surveys of 1932 and 1947. *Journal of Personality and Social Psychology, 86*(1), 130-147.

Deeley, Q., Daly, E., Surguladze, S., Tunstall, N., Mezey, G., Beer, D., Ambikapathy, A., Robertson, D., Giampietro, V., Brammer, M., Clarke, A., Dowsett, J., Fahy, T., Phillips, M. & Murphy, D. (2006) Facial emotion processing in criminal psychopathy: Preliminary functional magnetic resonance imaging study. *British Journal of Psychiatry, 189,* 533-9.

DeFelipe, J. (2002). Sesquicentenary of the birthday of Santiago Ramón y Cajal, the father of modern neuroscience. *Trends in Neurosciences, 25,* 481-4.

Deffenbacher, K. A., Bornstein, B. H., McGorty, E. K., & Penrod, S. D. (2008). Forgetting the once-seen face: Estimating the strength of an eyewitness's memory representation. *Journal of Experimental Psychology: Applied, 14*(2), 139-150.

Delahanty, D. L. (2007). Are we prepared to handle the mental health consequences of terrorism? *American Journal of Psychiatry, 164:* 189-191.

Delahanty, D. L., Nugent, N. R., Christopher, N. C., & Walsh, M. (2005). Initial urinary epinephrine and cortisol levels predict acute PTSD symptoms in child trauma victims. *Psychoneuroendocrinology, 30*(2), 121-128.

DeLamater, J., & Karraker, A. (2009). Sexual functioning in older adults. *Current Psychiatry Reports, 11*(1): 6-11.

DeLong, G. R. (2005). The cerebellum in autism. In M. Coleman (Ed.). *The neurology of autism.* New York, NY: Oxford University Press.

De Maat, S. M., Dekker, J., Schoevers, R. A., & de Jonghe, F. (2007). Relative efficacy of psychotherapy and combined therapy in the treatment of depression: A meta-analysis. *European Psychiatry, 22*(1), 1-8.

Dement, W. C., & Vaughan, C. (1999). *The promise of sleep: A pioneer in sleep medicine explores the vital connection between health, happiness, and a good night's sleep.* New York, NY: Dell.

Demo, D. H., Allen, K. R., & Fine, M. A. (Eds.). (2000). *Handbook of family diversity.* New York, NY: Oxford University Press.

DeNeve, K. M. (1999). Happy as an extraverted clam? The role of personality for subjective well-being. *Current Directions in Psychological Science, 8*(5), 141-144.

DePaulo, B. M., Blank, A. L., Swaim, G. W., & Hairfield, J. G. (1992). Expressiveness and expressive control. *Personality and Social Psychology Bulletin, 18:* 276-285.

Depue, R. & Collins (1999). Neurobiology of the Structure of Personality: Dopamine, facilitation of incentive motivation, and extraversion. *Behavioral and Brain Sciences, 22:* 491-569.

Depue, R. A. & Morrone-Strupinsky, J. V. (2005). A neurobehavioral model of affiliative bonding: implications for conceptualizing a human trait of affiliation. *The Behavioral and Brain Sciences, 28(3):* 313-50; discussion 350-95.

DeSteno, D., Dasgupta, N., Bartlett, M. Y., & Cajdric, A. (2004). Prejudice from thin air: The effect of emotion on automatic intergroup attitudes. *Psychological Science, 15(5),* 319-324.

Dhillon, H., Zigman, J. M., Ye, C., Lee, C. E., McGovern, R. A., Tang, V., et al. (2006). Leptin directly activates SF1 neurons in the VMH, and this action by leptin is required for normal body-weight homeostasis. *Neuron, 49(2): 191-203.*

Diener, E. (2000). Subjective well-being: The science of happiness and a proposal for a national index. *American Psychologist, 55* (1), 34-43.

Diener, E. & Diener, C. (1996). Most people are happy. *Psychological Science, 7*(3), 181-185.

Diener, E., Diener, M., & Diener, C. (1995). Factors predicting the subjective well-being of nations. *Journal of Personality and Social Psychology, 69:* 851-864.

Diener, E., Larsen, R. J., Levine, S., & Emmons, R. A. (1985). Frequency and intensity: The underlying dimensions of affect. *Journal of Personality and Social Psychology, 48,* 1253-1265.

Diener, E., Sandvik, E., & Larsen, R. (1985). Age and sex effects for emotional intensity. *Developmental Psychology, 21,* 542-546.

Diener, E., Sanvik, E., Pavot, W., & Fujita, E. (1992). Extraversion and subjective well-being in a U.S. national probability sample. *Journal of Research in Personality, 26*(3), 205-215.

Diener, E., Sanvik, E., Seidlitz, L., & Diener, M. (1993). The relationship between income and subjective well-being: Relative or absolute? *Social Indicators Research, 28*(3), 195-223.

Diener, E. & Lucas, R. E. (1999). Personality and subjective well-being. In D. Kahneman, E. Diener, & N. Schwarz (Eds.), *Well-being: The foundations of hedonic psychology.* (pp. 213-229) New York, NY: Russell Sage Foundation.

Diener, E. & Seligman, M. E. (2002). Research Report. *Psychology, 13(1):* 81-84.

Diener, E. & Seligman, M. E. P. (2002). Very happy people. *Psychological Science, 13*(1), 81-84.

Dies, R. R. (2003). Group psychotherapies. In A. S. Gurman & S. B. Messer (Eds.), *Essential psychotherapies: Theory and practice* (2nd ed.). New York, NY: Guilford Press

Dietary Reference Intakes (DRIs): Recommended Intakes for Individuals. (2004). Food and Nutrition Board, Institute of Medicine, National Academy of Sciences-New York.

Dietrich, C., Swingley, D., & Werker, J. F. (2007). Native language governs interpretation of salient speech sound differences at 18 months. *Proceedings of the National Acadamy Sciences, USA, 104,* 27-31.

Dikel, T. N., Engdahl, B., & Eberly, R. (2005). PTSD in former prisoners of war: Prewar, wartime, and postwar factors. *Journal of Traumatic Stress, 18*(1), 69-77.

Dimberg, U. & Lundquist, L. (1990). Gendeer differences in facial reactions to facial expressions. *Biological Psychology, 30,* 151-159.

Dindia, K. (2000). Sex differences in self-disclosure, reciprocity of self-disclosure, and self-disclosure and liking: Three meta-analyses reviewed. In S. Petronio (ed.), *Balancing the Secrets of Private Disclosures.* (pp. 21-35). Mahwah, NJ: Lawrence Erlbaum Associates Publishers.

Dion, K. K. & Berscheid, E. (1974). Physical attractiveness and peer perception among children. *Sociometry, 37:* 1-12.

Disorders in the National Comorbidity Survey Replication. *Archives in General Psychiatry, 62,* 617-627.

Dittmar, H. & Howard, S. (2004). Thin-ideal internalization and social comparison tendency as moderators of media models' impact on women's body-focused anxiety. *Journal of Social and Clinical Psychology. 23(6):* 786-91.

Djordjevic, J., Jones-Gotman, M., De Sousa, K., & Chertkow, H. (2008). Olfaction in patients with mild cognitive impairment and Alzheimer's disease. *Neurobiology of Aging, 29,* 693-706.

Doctor, R. M. & Neff, B. (2001). Sexual disorders. In H. S. Friedman (Ed.), *Specialty articles from the encyclopedia of mental health.* San Diego, CA: Academic Press.

Dodgen, C. E. (2005). *Nicotine dependence: Understanding and applying the most effective treatment interventions* Washington, DC: American Psychological Association.

Doetsch, F. (2003). The glial identity of neural stem cells. *Nature Neuroscience.* 6: 1127-34.

Dohrenwend, B. P., Levav, I., Shrout, P. E., Schwartz, S., & al, e. (1992). Socioeconomic status and psychiatric disorders: The causation-selection issue. *Science, 255*(5047), 946-952.

Dohrenwend, B., Pearlin, L., Clayton, P., Hamburg, B., Dohrenwend, B. P., Riley, M., & Rose, R. (1982). Report on stress and life events. In G. R. Elliott & C. Eisdorfer (eds.), *Stress and Human Health: Analysis and Implications of Research.* New York, NY: Springer.

Dollard, J., Miller, N. E., Doob, L. W., Mowrer, O. H., & Sears, R. R. (1939). *Frustration and aggression.* New Haven, CT: Yale University.

Donahue, E. M., Robins, R. W., Roberts, B. W., & John, O. P. (1993). The divided self: Concurrent and longitudinal effects of psychological adjustment and social roles on self-concept differentiation. *Journal of Personality and Social Psychology, 64:* 834-846.

Donaldson, Z. R. & Young, L. J. (2008). Oxytocin, vasopressin, and the neurogenetics of sociality. *Science, 322:* 900-4.

Dorahy, M. J. & Huntjens, R. J. C. (2007). Memory and attentional processes in dissociative identity disorder: A review of the empirical literature. In D. Spiegel, E. Vermetten, & M. Dorahy (Eds.), *Traumatic dissociation: Neurobiology and treatment.* Washington, DC: American Psychiatric Publishing.

Dorman, C. & Gaudiano, P. (1995). Motivation. M. Arbib, *Handbook of brain theory and neural networks* (591-594). Cambridge, MA: MIT Press.

Dosen, A. (2005). Applying the development perspective in the psychiatric assessment and diagnosis of persons with intellectual disability: Part II—Diagnosis. *Journal of Intellectual Disability Resesarch, 49*(1), 9-15.

Doty, R. I. (1986). Odor-guided behavior in mammals. *Experentia, 42,* 257-71.

Dovidio, J. F., Gaertner, S. L., Kawakami, K., & Hodson, G. (2002). Why can't we all just get along? Interpersonal biases and interracial distrust. *Cultural Diversity and Ethnic Minority Psychology: 8,* 88-102.

Dovidio, J. F. & Penner, L. A. (2004). Helping and altruism. In M. B. Brewer & M. Hewstone (eds.), *Emotion and Motivation.* (pp. 247-280). Malden, MA: Blackwell Publishing.

Doweiko, H. E. (2006). *Concepts of chemical dependency (6th ed.).* Belmont, CA: Thomson Brooks/Cole.

Drachman, D. A. (2006). Aging of the brain, entropy, and Alzheimer disease. *Neurology, 67,* 1340-1352.

Dratcu, L. (2000). Panic, hyperventilation and perpetuation of anxiety. *Progress in Neuro-Psychopharmacology & Biological Psychiatry, 24*(7), 1069-1089.

Dreher, J., Kohn, P., Kolachana, B., Weinberger, D. R., & Berman, K. F. (2009). Variation in dopamine genes influences responsivity of the human reward system. *PNAS Proceedings of the National Academy of Sciences of the United States of America, 106*(2): 617-622.

Drug Abuse Warning Network (DAWN). (2008). Publications and tables from DAWN Emergency Department Data. Retrieved November 24, 2008, from www.dawninfo.net.

Dubé, A.A., Duquette, M., Roy, M., Lepore, F., Duncan, G., & Rainville, P. (2009). Brain activity associated with the electrodermal reactivity to acute heat pain. *NeuroImage, 45,* 169-80.

Dube, E. F. (1982). Literacy, cultural familiarity, and "intelligence"as determinants of story recall. In U. Neisser (Ed.), *Memory observed: Remembering in natural contexts* (pp. 274-292) New York, NY: Freeman.

Duckworth, A. L. & Seligman, M. E. (2005). Self-discipline outdoes IQ in predicting academic performance of adolescents. *Psychological science: A journal of the American Psychological Society / APS, 16*(12): 939-44.

Dugas, M. J., Buhr, K., & Ladouceur, R. (2004). The role of intolerance of uncertainty in etiology and maintenance. In R. G. Heimberg, C. L. Turk, & D. S. Mennin (Eds.), *Generalized anxiety disorder: Advances in research and practice.* New York, NY: Guilford Press.

Dugas, M. J., Francis, K., & Bouchard, S. (2009). Cognitive behavioural therapy and applied relaxation for generalized anxiety disorder: A time series analysis of change in worry and somatic anxiety. *Cognitive Behaviour Therapy, 38*(1), 29-41.

Dugas, M. J., Gagnon, F., Ladouceur, R., & Freeston, M. H. (1998). Generalized anxiety disorder: A preliminary test of a conceptual model. *Behavior Research and Therapy, 36*(2), 215-226.

Dugger, B. N., Morris, J. A., Jordan, C. L., & Breedlove, S. M. (2007). Androgen receptors are required for full masculinization of the ventromedial hypothalamus (VMH) in rats. *Hormones and Behavior, 51*(2): 195-201.

Dunbar, R. I. M. (2004). Gossip in evolutionary perspective. *Review of General Psychology, 8*(2): 100-110.

Duncan, J. (2001). Frontal lobe function and the control of visual attention. In J. Braun, C. Koch & J. L. Davis (Eds.), *Visual attention and cortical circuits.* (pp. 69-88) Cambridge, MA: The MIT Press.

Duncan, J., Seitz, R.J., Kolodny, J., Bor, D., Herzog, H., Ahmed, A., Newell, F.N., & Emslie, H. (2000). A neural basis for general intelligence. *Science. Vol 289*(5478), Jul 2000, 457-460.

Dupont, R. L. & Dupont, C. M. (2005). Sedatives/hypnotics and benzodiazepines. In R.J. Frances, A.H. Mack, & S.I. Miller (Eds.), *Clinical textbook of addictive disorders (3rd ed.).* New York, NY: Guilford Press.

Durante, Kristina M., & Li, Norman P. (2009). Oestradiol level and opportunistic mating in women. *Proceedings of the Royal Society of London: Biology Letters. 5*(2): 19-182.

Durkin, K. F., & Hundersmarck, S. (2008). Pedophiles and child molesters. *Extreme deviance.* (pp. 144-150) Thousand Oaks, CA: Pine Forge Press/Sage Publications Co.

Dutton, D. G. & Aron, A. P. (1974). Some evidence for heightened sexual attraction under conditions of high anxiety. *Journal of Personality and Social Psychology, 23,* 510-517.

E

Eagly, A. H. & Chaiken, S. (1993). *The psychology of attitudes.* Fort Worth, TX: Harcourt Brace Jovanovich.

Eagly, A. H. & Chaiken, S. (1998). Attitude structure and function. In D. T. Gilbert, St. T. Fiske, & G. Lindzey (eds.), *The handbook of social psychology* (4th Ed., pp. 269-322). New York, NY: McGraw-Hill.

Eagly, A. H., & Karau, S. J. (2002). Role congruity theory of prejudice toward female leaders. *Psychological Review, 109:* 573-598.

Eagly, A. H. & Koenig, A. M. (2006). Social role theory of sex differences and similarities: Implication for prosocial behavior. In K. Dindia, & D. J. Canary (eds.), *Sex differences and similarities in communication, 2nd ed.* (161-177) Mahwah, NJ: Lawrence Erlbaum Associates Publishers.

Eagly, A. H. & Wood, W. (1999). The origins of sex differences in human behavior: Evolved dispositions versus social roles. *American Psychologist, 54:* 408-423.

Eagly, A.H., & Wood, W. (2006). Three ways that data can misinform: Inappropriate partialling, small samples, any anyway, they're not playing our song. *Psychological Inquiry, 17*(2), 131-137.

Earleywine, M. (2007). *Pet politics: Marijuana and the costs of prohibition.* New York, NY: Oxford University Press.

Easterbrook, G. (2005). The real truth about money. *Time, 165*(3), January 17, 2005, A32-A34.

Eating Disorders Coalition. (2007). Eating Disorders Fact Sheet. Downloaded on June 26, 2009 from: http://www.eatingdisorders coalition.org/documents/TalkingpointsEatingDisordersFactSheet.pdf.

Eaton, J. (2001). Management communication: The threat of groupthink. *Corporate Communications, 6*(4): 183-192.

Eckert, E. D., Bouchard, T. J., Bohlen, J., & Heston, L. L. (1986). Homosexuality in monozygotic twins reared apart. *The British Journal of Psychiatry, 148:* 421-425.

Edelstein, B. A., Stoner, S. A., & Woodhead, E. (2008). Older adults. In M. Hersen & J. Rosqvist (Eds.), *Handbook of Psychological Assessment, Case Conceptualization and Treatment, Volume 1, Adults.* Hoboken, NJ: John Wiley & Sons, Inc.

Edery-Halpern, G. & Nachson, I. (2004). Distinctiveness in flashbulb memory: Comparative analysis of five terrorist attacks. *Memory, 12*(2), 147-157.

Edin, F., Macoveanu, J., Olesen, P., Tegnér, J., & Klingberg, T. (2007). Stronger synaptic connectivity as a mechanism behind development of working memory-related brain activity during childhood. *Journal of Cognitive Neuroscience, 19*(5), 750-760.

Edwards, J. M. & Trimble, K. (1992). Anxiety, coping, and academic performance. *Anxiety, Stress, and Coping, 5:* 337-350.

Edwards, W. (1977). How to Use Multiattribute Utility Measurement for Social Decision Making. *IEEE Transactions on Systems, Man and Cybernetics, 17,* 326-40.

Edwards, W. & Newman, J. R. (1986). Multiattribute Evaluation. In H. R. Arkes & K. R. Hammond (Eds.), *Judgment and Decision Making: An Interdisciplinary Reader* (pp, 17-34). New York, NY: Cambridge University Press.

Eimas, P. D. (1975). Developmental studies in speech perception. In L. B. Cohen & P. Salapatek (Eds.), *Infant Perception: From Sensation to Cognition.* (pp. 193-231). New York, NY: Academic Press.

Eimas, P., Siqueland, E.R., Jusczyk, P., & Vigorito, J. (1971). Speech perception in infants. *Science 171,* 303-6.

Eisenberger, N. I., Lieberman, M. D., & Williams, K. D. (2003). Does rejection hurt? An FMRI study of social exclusion. *Science, 302:* 290-292.

Ekman, P. (1972). Universal and cultural differences in facial expressions of emotions. In J. Cole (Ed.), *Nebraska Symposium on Motivation, 1971: Vol. 19.* Lincoln, NE: University of Nebraska Press.

Ekman, P. (2003). *Emotions revealed: Recognizing faces and feelings to improve communication and emotional life.* New York: Times Books.

Ekman, P. & Friesen, W. V. (1975). *Unmasking the face: A guide to recognizing emotions from facial clues.* Oxford, England: Prentice Hall.

Ekman, P. & Friesen, W. V. (1986). A new pan-cultural facial expression of emotion. *Motivation and Emotion, 10,* 159-168.

Ekman, P., Friesen, W. V., O'Sullivan, M., Chan, A., et al. (1987). Universals and cultural differences in the judgments of facial expressions of emotion. *Journal of Personality and Social Psychology, 53,* 712-717.

Ekman, P., Levenson, R. W., & Friesen, W. V. (1983). Autonomic nervous system activity distinguishes among emotions. *Science, 221,* 1208-1210.

Elliott, J. (2007, February 26). Professor researches cell phone usage among college students. Retrieved from http://www.physorg.com/news 91732046.html.

Elliott-Larsen Civil Rights Act. (1976). State of Michigan. Downloaded on May 25, 2009 from: http://www.michigan.gov/documents/act_453_ elliott_larsen_8772_7.pdf.

Ellis, A. (1962). *Reason and emotion in psychotherapy.* Secaucus, NJ: Lyle Stuart.

Ellis, A. (2005). Rational-emotive therapy. In R. Corsini & D. Wedding (Eds.), *Current psychotherapies* (7th ed., pp. 166-201). Boston, MA: Thomson/Brooks-Cole.

Ellis, A. (2008). Rational emotive behavior therapy. In R. J. Corsini & D. Wedding (Eds.), *Current psychotherapies (8th edition).* Belmont, CA: Thomson Brooks/Cole.

Ellis, B. J. & Symons, D. (1990). Sex differences in sexual fantasy: An evolutionary psychological approach. *Journal of Sex Research, 27:* 527-555.

Ellison, C. G., Hummer, R. A., Cormier, S., & Rogers, R. G. (2000). Religious involvement and mortality risk among african american adults. *Research on Aging, 22*(6), 630-667.

Ely, R. (1997). Language and literacy in the school years. In J. Berko Gleason (Ed.), *The development of language* (4th ed, pp. 398-439). Boston, MA: Allyn and Bacon.

Emery, N. J., Dally, J. M. & Clayton, N. S. (2004). Western scrub-jays (Aphelocoma californica) use cognitive strategies to protect their caches from thieving nonspecifics, *Animal Cognition, 7,* 37-43.

Empson, J. (1993). *Sleep and dreaming (2nd rev. ed.).* Hertfordshire, England: Harvester Wheatsheaf.

Empson, J. (2002). *Sleep and dreaming (3rd edition).* Palgrave MacMillian.

Erickson, K. I., Prakash, R. S., Voss, M. W., Chaddock, L., Hu, L., Morris, K. S., White, S. M., Wojcicki, T. R., McAuley, E., & Kramer, A. F. (2009). Aerobic fitness is associated with hippocampal volume in elderly humans. *Hippocampus.* Epub ahead of print.

Erikson, E. (1968). *Identity, youth and crisis.* New York, NY: W. W. Norton & Company.

Erikson, E. H. (1950). *Childhood and society.* New York: W. W. Norton & Co.

Erikson, E. H. (1984). Reflections on the last stage—and the first. *Psychoanalytic Study of Children, 39,* 155-165.

Erikson, E. H. (1985). *The life cycle completed: A review* New York, NY: W.W. Norton & Co.

Erlanson-Albertsson, C. (2005). Appetite regulation and energy balance. *Acta Paediatrica (Norway), Supplement, 94*(448): 40-1.

Erten-Lyons, D., Woltjer, R. L., Dodge, H., Nixon, R., Vorobik, R., Calvert, J. F., Leahy, M., Montine, T., & Kaye, J. (2009). Factors associated with resistance to dementia despite high alzheimer disease pathology. *Neurology, 72*(4), 354-360.

Ervin, R. A., Schaughency, E., Matthews, A., Goodman, S. D., & McGlinchey, M. T. (2007). Primary and secondary prevention of behavior difficulties: Developing a data-informed problem-solving model to guide decision making at a school-wide level. *Psychology in the Schools, 44*(1), 7-18.

Escalante, P. R., Minshew, N. J., & Sweney, J.A. (2003). Abnormal brain lateralization in high-functioning autism. *Journal of Autism and Developmental Disorders, 33,* 539-543.

Eschweiler, G. W., Vonthein, R., Bode, R., Huell, M., Conca, A., Peters, O., et al. (2007). Clinical efficacy and cognitive side effects of bifrontal versus right unilateral electroconvulsive therapy (ECT): A short-term randomised controlled trial in pharmaco-resistant major depression. *Journal of Affective Disorders, 101*(1-3), 149-157.

Espie, C. A. (2002). Insomnia: Conceptual issues in the development, persistence, and treatment of sleep disorders in adults. *Annual Review of Psychology, 53,* 215-243.

Evans, G. W. (2001). Environmental stress and health. In A. Baum, T. A. Revenson & J. E. Singer (eds.), *Handbook of Health Psychology* (365-385). Mahwah, New Jersey: Lawrence Erlbaum Associates.

Everhart, D. E., Shucard, J. L., Quatrin, T., & Shucard, D. W. (2001). Sex-related differences in event-related potentials, face recognition, and facial affect processing in prepubertal children. *Neuropsychology, 15:* 329-341.

Ewing, J. A. (1984). Detecting alcoholism: the CAGE questionnaire. *Journal of the American Medical Association (JAMA),* 252, 1905-1907.

Eysenck, H. J. (1990). Biological dimensions of personality. In L. A. Pervin (ed.), *Handbook of Personality: Theory and Research* (244-276). New York, NY: Guilford.

Eysenck, H. J. (1992). Four ways five-factors are not basic. *Personality and Individual Differences, 13:* 667-673.

Eysenck, H. J. (2002). *The Dynamics of Anxiety & Hysteria: An Experimental Application of Modern Learning Theory to Psychiatry.* New Brunswick, NJ: Transaction Publishers.

F

Fabrigar, L. R., Petty, R. E., Smith, S. M., & Crites Jr., S. L. (2006). Understanding knowledge effects on attitude-behavior consistency: The role of relevance, complexity, and amount of knowledge. *Journal of Personality and Social Psychology, 90*(4): 556-577.

FairTest: The National Center for Fair & Open Testing. (2007). *SAT I: A faulty instrument for predicting college success.* Retrieved September

15, 2009, from http://www.fairtest.org/sat-i-faulty-instrument-predicting-college-success.

Fancher, R. E. (1996). *Mind in conflict. pioneers in psychology.* (393-394). New York, NY: W. W. Norton & Company, Inc.

Fancher, R. E. (2004). The concept of race in the life and thought of Francis Galton. In A. S. Winston (Ed.), *Defining difference: Race and racism in the history of psychology.* (pp. 49-75) Washington, DC: American Psychological Association.

Fancher, R. E. (2009). Scientific cousins: The relationship between Charles Darwin and Francis Galton. *American Psychologist, 64(2),* 84-92.

Farah, M. J., Levinson, K.L., & Klein, K.L. (1995). Face perception and within-category discrimination in prosopagnosia. *Neuropsychologia, 33,* 661-74.

Faravelli, C., Ravaldi, C., & Truglia, E. (2005). Unipolar depression. In C. Faravelli, D.J. Nutt, J. Zohar, & E. J. L. Griez (Eds.), *Mood disorders: Clinical management and research issues* (pp. 79-101). New York, NY: Wiley.

Farbman, A. I. (1997). Injury-stimulated neurogenesis in sensory systems. *Advances in Neurology, 72:* 157-161.

Farmer, R. F., & Chapman, A. L. (2008). *Behavioral interventions in cognitive behavior therapy: Practical guidance for putting theory into action.* Washington, DC: American Psychological Association.

Farooqi, I. S., Wangensteen, T., Collins, S., Kimber, W., Matarese, G., Keogh, J. M., et al. (2007). Clinical and molecular genetic spectrum of congenital deficiency of the leptin receptor. *The New England Journal of Medicine, 356(3):* 237-47.

Farvolden, P. & Woody, E. Z. (2004). Hypnosis, memory, and frontal executive functioning. *International Journal of Clinical and Experimental Hypnosis, 52(1),* 3-26.

Favaro, A., Santonastaso, P., Monteleone, P., Bellodi, L., Mauri, M., Rotondo, A., et al. (2008). Self-injurious behavior and attempted suicide in purging bulimia nervosa: associations with psychiatric comorbidity. *Journal of Affective Disorders, 105(1-3):* 285-9.

Fazio, R. H. & Roskos-Ewoldsen, D. (2005). Acting as we feel: When and how attitudes guide behavior. In T. C. Brock & M. C. Green (eds.), *Persuasion: Psychological Insights and Perspectives, 2nd ed.* (pp. 41-62). Thousand Oaks, CA: Sage Publications.

Fazio, R. H., Zanna, M. P., & Cooper, J. (1977). Dissonance and self perception: An integrative view of each theory's proper domain of application. *Journal of Experimental Social Psychology, 13:* 464-479.

Federal Communications Commission (FCC). (2007). *Report on Violent Television Programming and Its Impact On Children.* (1-39). Washington, D.C.

Feingold, A. (1994) Gender differences in personality: A meta-analysis. *Psychological Bulletin, 116:* 429-456.

Feldhusen, J. F. (2003). Lewis M. Terman: A pioneer in the development of ability tests. In Zimmerman B.J. & Schunk, D.H. (Eds.), *Educational psychology: A century of contributions.* (pp. 155-169) Mahwah, NJ: Erlbaum.

Feldman, D. E., & Brecht, M. (2005). Map plasticity in somatosensory cortex. *Science, 310(5749),* 810-815.

Feldman, D. H. (2003). Cognitive development in childhood. In R. M. Lerner, M. A. Easterbrooks & J. Mistry (Eds.), *Handbook of psychology: Developmental psychology, vol. 6.* (pp. 195-210). Hoboken, NJ: John Wiley & Sons Inc.

Feldman, H. A., Longcope, C., Derby, C. A., Johannes, C. B., Araujo, A. B., Coviello, A. D., et al. (2002). Age trends in the level of serum testosterone and other hormones in middle-aged men: Longitudinal results from the Massachusetts male aging study. *Journal of Clinical Endocrinology & Metabolism, 87(2):* 589 -598.

Feldman, M. D. & Christensen, J. F. (2007). *Behavioral Medicine* (Third ed., p. 475). NY, NY: McGraw-Hill Professional.

Fenchel, G. H. (2006). *Psychoanalytic reflections on love and sexuality.* Lanham, MD: University Press of America.

Fenn, K. M., Nusbaum, H. C., & Margoliash, D. (2003). Consolidation during sleep of perceptual learning of spoken language. *Nature, 425(6958),* 614-616.

Fenske, J. N. & Schwenk, T. L. (2009). Obsessive Compulsive Disorder: diagnosis and management. *American Family Physician, 80,* 239-45.

Fenson, L., Dale, P. S., Reznick, J. S., Bates, E., Thal, D. J., & Pethick, S. J. (1994). Variability in early communicative development. *Monographs of the Society for Research in Child Development, 59,* 1-185.

Ferguson, C. J. (2008). The school shooting/violent video game link: Causal Relationship or moral panic? *Journal of Investigative Psychology and Offender Profiling, 5:* 25-37.

Fernald, A., Taeschner, T., Dunn, J., Papousek, M., Boysson-Bardies, B., & Fukui, I. (1989). A cross-language study of prosodic modifications in mothers' and fathers' speech to preverbal infants. *Journal of Child Language, 16,* 477-502.

Fernandes, M., Atallah, A. N., Soares, B. G., Humberto, S., Guimarães, S., Matos, D., et al. (2007). Intragastric balloon for obesity. *Cochrane Database of Systematic Reviews (Online), (1):* CD004931.

Festinger, L. (1957). *A Theory of Cognitive Dissonance.* Stanford, CA: Stanford University Press.

Festinger, L. & Carlsmith, J. M. (1959). Cognitive consequences of forced compliance. *Journal of Abnormal and Social Psychology, 58:* 203-210.

Field, A. E., Manson, J. E., Laird, N., Williamson, D. F., Willett, W. C., E, A., et al. (2004). Weight Cycling and the Risk of Developing Type 2 Diabetes among Adult Women in the United States. Obesity Research.

Field, A. P. (2006). Is conditioning a useful framework for understanding the development and treatment of phobias? *Clinical Psychology Review, 26(7),* 857-875.

Field, A. P. & Nightingale, Z. C. (2009). Test of time: what if little Albert had escaped? *Clinical Child Psychology and Psychiatry, 14,* 311-9.

Finckh, U. (2001). The dopamine D2 receptor gene and alcoholism: Association studies. In D. P. Agarwal & H. K. Seitz (Eds.), *Alcohol in health and disease.* New York, NY: Marcel Dekker.

Finer, L. B. (2007). Trends in premarital sex in the United States, 1954-2003. *Public Health Reports, 122:* 73-78.

Finley, L. L. (2007). *The Encyclopedia of Juvenile Violence.* (291) Westport, CT: Greenwood Publishing Group.

Finnegan, L. P. & Kandall, S. R. (2008). Perinatal substance abuse. In H. D. Kleber & M. Galanter (Eds.), *The American Psychiatric Publishing textbook of substance abuse treatment (4th ed.).* Washington, DC: American Psychiatric Publishing.

Fischer, A. H. & Manstead, A. S. R. (2000). The relation between gender and emotions in different cultures. In A. H. Fischer (Ed.), *Gender and emotion: Social psychology perspectives* (pp. 71-94). New York, NY: Cambridge University Press.

Fischer, A. H., Rodriguez Mosquera, P. M., van Vianen, A. E. M., & Manstead, A. S. R. (2004). Gender and culture differences in emotion. *Emotion, 4*(1), 87-94.

Fischer, P., Greitemeyer, T., Pollozek, F., & Frey, D. (2006). The unresponsive bystander: Are bystanders more responsive in dangerous emergencies? *European Journal of Social Psychology, 36*(2): 267-278.

Fish, J. M. (Ed.) (2002). *Race and intelligence: Separating science from myth.* Mahwah, NJ: Lawrence Erlbaum Associates Publishers.

Fisher, H., Aron, A., & Brown, L. L. (2005, Dec. 5). Romantic love: an *f*MRI study of a neural mechanism for mate choice. *Journal of Comparative Neurology 493*(1), 58-62.

Fisher, P. H., Masia-Warner, C., & Klein, R. G. (2004). Skills for social and academic success: A school-based intervention for social anxiety disorder in adolescents. *Clinical Child and Family Psychological Review., 7*(4), 241-249.

Fiske, S. T. (2004). *Social beings: A core motives approach to social psychology.* Hoboken, NJ: John Wiley & Sons, Inc.

Fiske, S. T. (2010). *Social beings: Core motives in social psychology, Second Edition.* Hoboken, NJ: John Wiley & Sons.

Fitch, M. T. & Silver, J. (2008). CNS injury, glial scars, and inflammation: Inhibitory extracellular matrices and regeneration failure. *Experimental Neurology.* 209: 294-301.

Fleeson, W. (2001). Towards a structure- and process-integrated view of personality: Traits as density distributions of states. *Journal of Personality and Social Psychology, 80:* 1011-1027.

Fleeson, W. (2007). Situation-based contingencies underlying trait-content manifestation in behavior. *Journal of Personality, 75(4):* 825-862.

Fleming, I., Baum, A., Davidson, L., Rectanus, E., & McArdle, S. (1987). Chronic stress as a reactivity factor in physiologic reactivity to challenge. *Health Psychology, 11:* 221-237.

Flynn, J. R. (2000). *How to defend humane ideals: Substitutes for objectivity* Lincoln, NE: University of Nebraska Press.

Flynn, J. R. (2007). *What is intelligence? Beyond the Flynn effect.* New York, NY: Cambridge University Press.

Flynn, J. R. (2008). *Where have all the liberals gone? race, class, and ideals in America.* New York, NY: Cambridge University Press.

Foa, E. & Kozak, M. (1986). Emotional processing of fear: Exposure to corrective information. *Psychological Bulletin, 99:* 20-35.

Focus Adolescent Services (FAS). (2008). Teen Violence. ONLINE: Focusas.com

Fodor, E. M. & Carver, R. A. (2000). Achievement and power motives, performance feedback, and creativity. *Journal of Research in Personality, 34:* 380-396.

Fodor, J. (2007). The revenge of the given. In B. P. McLaughlin, & J. Cohen (Eds.), *Contemporary debates in philosophy of mind.* (pp. 105-116) Malden, MA: Blackwell Publishing.

Fodor, J. A. (1968). *Psychological explanation: An introduction to the philosophy of psychology.* New York, NY: Random House.

Fodor, J. A. (2006). "Précis of the modularity of mind". In J. L. Bermúdez (Ed.), *Philosophy of psychology: Contemporary readings.* (pp. 513-523) New York, NY: Routledge/Taylor & Francis Group.

Fogarty, R. (2008). The intelligence-friendly classroom: It just makes sense. In B. Z. Presseisen (Ed.), *Teaching for intelligence (2nd ed.).* (pp. 142-148) Thousand Oaks, CA: Corwin Press.

Folkman, S. & Lazarus, R. S. (1985). If it changes it must be a process: Study of emotion and coping during three stages of a college examination. *Journal of Personality and Social Psychology, 48:,* 150-170.

Folkman, S. & Moskowitz, J. T. (2000). Positive affect and the other side of coping. *American Psychologist, 55:* 647-654.

Folkman, S., & Moskowitz, J. T. (2000). Stress, positive emotion, and coping. *Current Directions in Psychological Science, 9*(4), 115-118.

Folkman, S., & Moskowitz, J. T. (2004). Coping: Pitfalls and promise. *Annual Review of Psychology, 55,* 745-774.

Fontana, D. (2007). Meditation. In M. Velmans & S. Schneider (Ed.), *The Blackwell companion to consciousness.* Malden, MA: Blackwell Publishing.

Ford, D. Y. (2008). Intelligence testing and cultural diversity: The need for alternative instruments, policies, and procedures. In J. L. VanTassel-Baska (Ed.), *Alternative assessments with gifted and talented students.* (pp. 107-128) Waco, TX: Press.

Forgas, J. P. (2008). Affect, cognition, and social behavior: The effects of mood on memory, social judgments, and social interaction. In M. A. Gluck, J. R. Anderson, & S. M. Kosslyn (Eds.), *Memory and mind: A festschrift for Gordon H. Bower.* (pp. 261-279) Mahwah, NJ: Lawrence Erlbaum Associates Publishers.

Forgas, J. P. & Locke, J. (2005). Affective influences on causal inferences: The effects of mood on attributions for positive and negative interpersonal episodes. *Cognition & Emotion, 19*(7): 1071-1081.

Forgas, J. P., Williams K. D. and Laham S. M. (Eds.). (2005). *Social motivation: Conscious and unconscious processes.* New York, NY: Cambridge University Press.

Foster, J. D. (2009, March, 16). Mass Murder is Nothing to Fear. Message posted to Psychology Today. Downloaded on July 11, 2009 from: *http://www.psychology-today.com/blog/the-narcissus-in-all-us/200903/mass-murder-is-nothing-fear.* (1975). Requests and responses in children's speech. *J Child Lang, 2,* 41-60.

Fowers, B. J. (2003). Reason and human finitude: In praise of practical wisdom. *American Behavioral Scientist, 47*(4), 415-426.

Fowers, B. J. (2005). Practical wisdom as the heart of professional ethics. *Virtue and psychology: Pursuing excellence in ordinary practices.* (pp. 177-201) Washington, DC: American Psychological Association.

Fowers, B. J. (2005). Practical wisdom: The heart of virtue and psychology. *Virtue and psychology: Pursuing excellence in ordinary practices.* (pp. 107-128) Washington, DC: American Psychological Association.

Fozard, J., Wolf, E., Bell, B., Farland, R., & Podolsky, S. (1977). Visual perception and communication. In J. Birren & K. Schaie (Eds.), *Handbook of the psychology of aging.* New York, NY: Van Nostrand Reinhold.

Fraley, B. & Aron, A. (2004). The effect of a shared humorous experience on closeness in initial encounters. *Personal Relationships, 11:* 61-78.

Frank, J. D. (1973). *Persuasion and healing* (Rev. ed.). Baltimore, MD: Johns Hopkins University Press.

Frank, J., Mistretta, P., & Will, J. (2008). Diagnosis and treatment of female sexual dysfunction. *American Family Physician, 77*(5): 635-642.

Franklin, R. J & Ffrench-Constant, C. (2008). Remyelination in the CNS: from biology to therapy. *Nature Reviews Neuroscience.* 9: 839-55.

Fredericks, L. E. (2001). *The use of hypnosis in surgery and anesthesiology: Psychological preparation of the surgical patient.* Springfield, IL: Charles C. Thomas Publisher.

Fredriksen, K., Rhodes, J., Reddy, R., & Way, N. (2004). Sleepless in Chicago: Tracking the Effects of Adolescent Sleep Loss During the Middle School Years. *Child Development, 75*, 84-95.

Fredrickson, B. L. (2001). The role of positive emotions in positive psychology: The broaden-and-build theory of positive emotions. *56*(3), 218-226.

Freedman, R., Ross, R., Michels, R., Appelbaum, P., Siever, L., Binder, R., et al. (2007). Psychiatrists, mental illness, and violence. *American Journal of Psychiatry, 165*(9), 1315-1317.

Freedman, V. A., Aykan, H., & Martin, L. G. (2001). Aggregate changes in severe cognitive impairment among older Americans: 1993 and 1998. *Journal of Gerontology, 56B*, S100-S111.

Freeman, H. L. (1984). Housing. In. H. L. Freeman (ed.), *Mental Health and the Environment* (197-225). London: Churchill Livingston.

Freud, S. (1900). *The Interpretation of Dreams.*

Freud, S. (1909). Analysis of a phobia in a five-year-old boy. S. E., 10: 5-149.

Freud, S. (1924). The loss of reality in neurosis and psychosis. In *Sigmund Freud's collected papers* (Vol. 2, pp. 272-282). London: Hogarth Press.

Frey, K. S., Hirschstein, M. K., Snell, J. L., Edstrom, L. V., MacKenzie, E. P., & Broderick, C. J. (2005). Reducing playground bullying and supporting beliefs: An experimental trial of the Steps to Respect program. *Developmental Psychology, 41*, 479-491.

Friedlander, S. L., Larkin, E. K., Rosen, C. L., Palermo, T. M., & Redline, S. (2003). Decreased quality of life associated with obesity in school-aged children. *Archives of Pediatrics & Adolescent Medicine, 157*(12): 1206-11.

Friedman, H.S., Tucker, J.S., Schwartz, J.E., Tomlinson-Keasey, C., Martin, L.R., Wingard, D.L., Criqui, M.H. (1995). Psychosocial and behavioral predictors of longevity: The aging and death of the "Termites". *American Psychologist, 50*, 69-78.

Friedman, K. E., Reichmann, S. K., Costanzo, P. R., Zelli, A., Ashmore, J. A., Musante, G. J., et al. (2005). Weight stigmatization and ideological beliefs: relation to psychological functioning in obese adults. *Obesity research, 13*(5): 907-16.

Friedman, M. & Rosenman, R. H. (1959). Association of a specific overt behavior pattern with increases in blood cholesterol, blood clotting time, incidence of arcus senilis and clinical coronary artery disease. *Journal of the American Medical Association, 169*: 1286-1296.

Friedman, M., & Rosenman, R. (1974). *Type A behavior and your heart.* New York, NY: Knopf.

Friesen, W. V. (1972). *Cultural differences in facial expressions in a social situation: An experimental test of the concept of display rules.* Unpublished doctoral dissertation. San Francisco, CA: University of California.

Frieze, I. H. & Bookwala, J. (1996). Coping with unusual stressors: Criminal victimization. In M. Zeidner & N. S. Endler (eds.), *Handbook of coping: Theory, research, applications* (303-321). New York, NY: John Wiley & Sons, Inc.

Frijda, N. H. (1986). *The emotions.* Cambridge, MA: Cambridge University Press.

Frijda, N. H. (2007). *The laws of emotion.* Mahwah, NJ: Lawrence Erlbaum Associates.

Frith, C. (2003). The scientific study of consciousness. In M.A. Ron & T.W. Robbins (Eds.), *Disorders of brain and mind 2*, New York, NY: Cambridge University Press.

Frith, U. (2000). Cognitive explanations of autism. In K. Lee (Ed.), *Childhood cognitive development: The essential readings. Essential readings in developmental psychology.* Malden, MA: Blackwell.

Froehlich, J. C., Zink, R. W., Li, T., & Christian, J. C. (2000). Analysis of heritability of hormonal responses to alcohol in twins: Beta-endorphin as a potential biomarker of genetic risk for alcoholism. *Alcoholism: Clinical and Experimental Research, 24*(3): 265-277.

Fry, C. J. (1988). Left-handedness and tongue-rolling ability. *Perceptual and Motor Skills, 67*(1), 168-170.

Furnham, A. (2008). *Personality and intelligence at work: Exploring and explaining individual differences at work.* Hove: Psychology Press/Taylor & Francis (UK).

Furnham, A. & Monsen, J. (2009). Personality traits and intelligence predict academic school grades. *Learning and Individual Differences, 19*(1), 28-33.

G

Gadsden, V., & Ray, A. (2003). Father's role in children's academic achievement and early literacy. *ERIC Clearinghouse on Early Education and Parenting.* Retrieved December 22, 2008 from http://www.ericdigests.org/2004-3/role.html

Gaffan, D. (2003). Against memory systems. In A. Parker, A. Derrington, & C. Blakemore (Eds.), *The physiology of cognitive processes.* (pp. 234-251) New York, NY: Oxford University Press.

Gagnon, J. H. (1975). Sex research and social change. *Archives of Sexual Behavior, 4*(2).

Gais, S., Hüllemann, P., Hallschmid, M., & Born, J. (2006). Sleep-dependent surges in growth hormone do not contribute to sleep-dependent memory consolidation. *Psychoneuroendocrinology, 31*(6), 786-791.

Galanter, E. (1962). Contemporary Psychophysics. *The Journal of Applied Psychology, 92*, 1524-41.

Galati, D., Sini, B., Schmidt, S., & Tinti, C. (2003). Spontaneous facial expressions in congenitally-blind and sighted children aged 8-11. *Journal of Visual Impairment and Blindness, 97*, 418-428.

Gallacher, J. E. J., Sweetnam, P. M., Yarnell, J. W. G., Elwood, P. C., & Stansfeld, S. A. (2003). Is type A behavior really a trigger for coronary heart disease events? *Psychosomatic Medicine, 65*(3), 339-346.

Gallese, V., Fadiga, L., Fogassi, L., & Rizzolatti, G. (1996). Action recognition in the premotor cortex. *Brain. 119*(2): 593-609.

Gallup, G. G. (1970). Chimpanzees: Self-recognition. *Science, 167*, 86-87.

Galton, F. (1948). Co-relations and their measurement, chiefly from anthropometric data, 1888. In W. Dennis (Ed.), *Readings in the history of psychology.* (pp. 336-346) East Norwalk, CT: Appleton-Century-Crofts.

Gansberg, M. (1964, March 27). Thirty-eight who saw murder didn't call the police. *New York Times.*

Gantt, W. H. (1980). Review of the shaping of a behaviorism (B.F. Skinner). *The Pavlovian Journal of Biological Science, 15*, 42-4.

Ganzach, Y. & Pazy, A. (2001). Within occupation sources of variance in incumbent perception of job complexity. *Journal of Occupational and Organizational Psychology, 74*(1), 95-108.

Ganzach, Y. (2003). Intelligence, education, and facets of job satisfaction. *Work and Occupations, 30*(1), 97-122.

Garcia, E., Godoy-Izquierdo, D., Godoy, J.F., Perez, M., & Lopez-Chicheri, I. (2007). Gender differences in pressure pain threshold in a repeated measures assessment. *Psychology: Health, & Medicine, 12,* 567-79.

Garcia, J., Lasiter, P. S., Bermudez-Rattoni, F., & Deems, D. A. (1985). A general theory of aversion learning. *Annals of the New York Academy of Sciences, 443,* 8-21.

Garcia, S. M., Weaver, K., Moskowitz, G. B., & Darley, J. M. (2002). Crowded minds: The implicit bystander effect. *Journal of Personality and Social Psychology, 83*(4): 843-853.

Garcia-Rill, E., Charlesworth, A., Heister, D., Ye, M., & Hayer, A. (2008). The developmental decrease in REM sleep: The role of transmitters and electrical coupling. *Sleep: Journal of Sleep and Sleep Disorders Research, 31*(5), 673-690.

Gard, D. E. & Kring, A. M. (2009). Emotion in the daily lives of schizophrenia patients: Context matters. *Schizophrenia Research.*

Gardner, H. (1993). *Multiple intelligences: The theory in practice.* New York, NY: Basic Books.

Gardner, H. (1993). Intelligence and intelligences: Universal principles and individual differences. *Archives De Psychologie, 61*(238), 169-172.

Gardner, H. (2004). *Frames of mind: The theory of multiple intelligences.* New York, NY: Basic Books.

Gardner, H. (2008). Who owns intelligence? In M. H. Immordino-Yang (Ed.), *The Jossey-Bass reader on the brain and learning.* (pp. 120-132) San Francisco, CA: Jossey-Bass.

Gardner, J., & Oswald, A. (2004). How is mortality affected by money, marriage, and stress? *Journal of Health Economics, 23*: 1181-1207.

Gardner, W. L. & Martinko, M. J. (1996). Using the Myers-Briggs Type Indicator to study managers: A literature review and research agenda. *Journal of Management, 22(1)*: 45-83.

Gariepy, J-L. & Blair, C. (2008). A biological window on psychological development. *Developmental Psychobiology, 50,* 1-3.

Garlow, S. J. (2002). Age, gender, and ethnicity differences in patterns of cocaine and ethanol use preceding suicide. *American Journal of Psychiatry, 159*(4), 615-619.

Garoff-Eaton R. J., Slotnick S. D., Schacter D. L. (2006). Not all false memories are created equal: The neural basis of false recognition. *Cerebral Cortex, 16,* 1645-52.

Garrett, B. (2008). *Brain and behavior: An introduction to biological psychology* (2nd ed.). Los Angeles, CA: Sage.

Garssen, B., & Goodkin, K. (1999). On the role of immunological factors as mediators between psychosocial factors and cancer progression. *Psychiatric Research, 85*(1), 51-61.

Garvey, C. (1974). Requests and responses in children's speech. *Journal of Child Language, 2,* 41-60.

Gaston, K. E. (1978). Interocular transfer of a visually mediated conditioned food aversion in chicks. *Behavioral Biology, 24,* 272-8.

Gaul, Moira. (2007). Testimony on D.C. Public Schools Sex Education. Family Research Council. Downloaded on May 25, 2009 from: http://www.frc.org/get.cfm?i=TS07L01

Gava, L., Valenza, E., Turati, C., & de Schonen, S. (2008). Effect of partial occlusion on newborns' face preference and recognition. *Developmental Science, 11*(4), 563-574.

Gaynor, S. T. & Baird, S. C. (2007). Personality disorders. In D.W. Woods & J.W. Kanter (eds.), *Understanding Behavior Disorders: A Contemporary Behavioral Perspective.* Reno, NV: Context Press.

Gazzaniga, M. S. (1983). Right hemisphere language following brain bisection: A twenty-year perspective. *American Psychologist, 38,* 525-537.

Gazzaniga, M. S. (1988). Brain modularity: Towards a philosophy of conscious experience. In A. J. Marcel & E. Bisiach (Eds.), *Consciousness in contemporary science.* New York, NY: Clarendon Press/Oxford University Press.

Gazzaniga, M. S. (1995). On neural circuits and cognition. *Neural Computation, 7*(1), 1-12.

Gazzaniga, M. S. (1995). Principles of human brain organization derived from split-brain studies. *Neuron 14,* 217-228.

Gazzaniga, M.S. (1995). The visual analysis of shape and form. *The cognitive neurosciences.* (pp. 339-350). Cambridge, MA: MIT Press.

Gazzaniga, M. S. (2000). Cerebral specialization and interhemispheric communication: Does the corpus callosum enable the human condition? *Brain, 123,* 1293-1326.

Gazzaniga, M. S. (2005). Forty-five years of split-brain research and still going strong. *Nature Reviews Neuroscience.* 6: 653-9.

Georgas, J. (2003). Cross-cultural psychology, intelligence, and cognitive processes. In J. Georgas, L. G. Weiss, F. J. R. van de Vijver, & D. H. Saklofske (Eds.), *Culture and children's intelligence: Cross-cultural analysis of the WISC-III.* (pp. 23-37) San Diego, CA: Academic Press.

George, T. P. & Weinberger, A. H. (2008). Nicotine and tobacco. In H. D. Kleber & M. Galanter (Eds.), *The American Psychiatric Publishing textbook of substance abuse treatment (4th ed.).* Washington, DC: American Psychiatric Publishing.

Gernsbacher, M. A. & Kaschak, M.P. (2003). Neuroimaging studies of language production and comprehension. *Annual Review of Psychology, 54,* 91-114.

Ghubash, R., Hamdi, E., & Bebbington, P. (1992). The Dubai community psychiatric survey: I. prevalence and socio-demographic correlates. *Social Psychiatry and Psychiatric Epidemiology, 27*(2), 53-61.

Gibbs, J. C., Basinger, K. S., Grime, R. L. & Snarey, J. R. (2007). Moral judgment development across cultures: Revisiting Kohlberg's universality claims. *Developmental Review, 27,* 443-500.

Gigerenzer, G. (2004). Fast and Frugal Heuristics: The tools of Founded Rationality. In D. J. Koehler & N. Harvey (Eds.), *Blackwell handbook of judgment and decision making* (pp. 62-88). Malden, MA: Blackwell Publishing.

Gigerenzer, G. & Goldstein, D. G. (1996). Reasoning the fast and frugal way: Models of bounded rationality. *Psychological Review, 103,* 650-69.

Gilbertson, M. W., Shenton, M. E., Ciszewski, A., Kasai, K., Lasko, N. B., Orr, S. P., & Pitman, R. K. (2002). Smaller hippocampal volume predicts pathologic vulnerability to psychological trauma. *Nature Neuroscience, 5*(11), 1242-1247.

Gilger, L. (2007). WOW! A WORLD WIENER WINNER: Californian stuffs way to new record in Tempe hot dog eating contest. *The Tribune.* Mesa, AZ.

Gilligan, C. (1982). *In a different voice: Psychological theory and women's development.* Cambridge, MA: Harvard University Press.

Gilligan, C. (2004). Recovering psyche: Reflections on life-history and history. *The Annual of Psychoanalysis, 32:* 131-147.

Gillis, J. M. & Romanczyk, R. G. (2007). Autism spectrum disorders and related developmental disabilities. In M. Hersen & A.M. Gross (Eds.), *Handbook of clinical psychology* (Vol.2). Hoboken, NJ: John Wiley & Sons.

Ginandes, C. (2006). The strategic integration of hypnosis and CBT for the treatment of Mind/Body conditions. In R. A. Chapman (Ed.),

The Clinical Use of Hypnosis in Cognitive Behavior Therapy: A Practitioner's Casebook. New York, NY: Springer Publishing Co.

Gingrich, K. J. & Byrne, J. H. (1985). Simulation of synaptic depression, posttetanic potentiation, and presynaptic facilitation of synaptic potentials from sensory neurons mediating gill-withdrawal reflex in Aplysia. *Journal of Neurophysiology, 53,* 652-69.

Gioia, G. (2007) Expert: Millions get concussions. Phill.com. Retrieved April 23, 2007.

Glaser, J., & Kihlstrom, J. F. (2005). Compensatory automaticity: Unconscious volition is not an oxymoron. In R. R. Hassin, J. S. Uleman, & J. A. Bargh (Eds.), *The new unconscious. Oxford series in social cognition and social neuroscience.* New York, NY: Oxford University Press.

Glass, J. (2005). Sociological perspectives on work and family. In S. M. Bianchi, L. M. Casper, & B. R. King (eds.), *Work, Family, Health, and Well-Being.* (pp. 215-229). Mahwah, NJ: Lawrence Erlbaum Associates Publishers.

Godart, N. T., Perdereau, F., Rein, Z., Berthoz, S., Wallier, J., Jeammet, P., et al. (2007). Comorbidity studies of eating disorders and mood disorders. Critical review of the literature. *Journal of Affective Disorders, 97(1-3):* 37-49.

Godfrey, J. R. (2004). Toward optimal health: The experts discuss therapeutic humor. *Journal of Women's Health, 13*(5): 474-479.

Goff, D. C. & Coyle, J. T. (2001). The Emerging Role of Glutamate in the Pathophysiology and Treatment of Scizophrenia. *American Journal of Psychiatry, 158,* 1367-77.

Gohm, C. L. (2003). Mood regulation and emotional intelligence: Individual differences. *Journal of Personality and Social Psychology, 84,* 594-607.

Gohm, C. L. & Clore, G. L. (2002). Four latent traits of emotional experience and their involvement in well-being, coping, and attributional style. *Cognition and Emotion, 16,* 495-518.

Goldenberg, I., & Goldenberg, H. (2008). Family therapy. In R. J. Corsini & D. Wedding (Eds.), *Current psychotherapies* (8th ed.). Belmont, CA: Thomson Brooks/Cole.

Goldberg, A E. (2008). Universal grammar? Or prerequisites for natural language? *Behavioral and Brain Sciences, 31,* 522-3.

Goldberg, R. F., Perfetti, C. A., & Schneider, W. (2006). Perceptual knowledge retrieval activates sensory brain regions. *Journal of Neuroscience, 26,* 4917-21.

Goldin-Meadow, S. (1999). The role of gesture in communication and thinking. *Trends in Cognitive Sciences, 3,* 419-29.

Goleman, D. (1995). *Emotional intelligence.* New York, NY: Bantam Books.

Goleman, D. (2006). *Social intelligence: The new science of human relationships.* New York, NY: Bantam Books.

Gollan J. K., & Jacobson N. S. (2002). Developments in couple therapy research. In H. A. Liddle, D. A. Santiseban, R. F. Levant, & J. H. Bray (Eds.), *Family psychology: Science-based interventions.* Washington, DC: American Psychological Association.

Gomes, G. (2003). A teoria Freudiana da consciencia/Freudian theory of consciousness. *Psicologia: Teoria e Pesquisa, 19*(2), 117-125.

González, A. R. A., Escobar-Córdoba, F., & Castañeda, G. C. (2007). Factores de riesgo para violencia y homicidio juvenil./Risk factors for juvenile violence and homicide. *Revista Colombiana de Psiquiatria, 36*(1), 78-97.

González J., Barros-Loscertales A., Pulvermüller F., Meseguer V., Sanjuán A., Belloch V., Avila C. (2006). Reading cinnamon activates olfactory brain regions. *Neuroimage, 32,* 906-12.

Goodenough, F. L. (1932). Expression of the emotions in a blind-deaf child. *Journal of Abnormal and Social Psychology, 27,* 328-333.

Goodman, R. S., Walton, K. G., Orme-Johnson, D. W., & Boyer, R. (2003). The transcendental meditation program: A consciousness-based developmental technology for rehabilitation and crime prevention. *Journal of Offender Rehabilitation, 36*(1-4), 1-33.

Goto Y., Grace A. A. (2008) Limbic and cortical information processing in the nucleus accumbens. *Trends in Neurosciences.* 31:552-8.

Gottfredson, L. S. (1997). Why *g* matters: The complexity of everyday life. *Intelligence, 24*(1), 79-132.

Gottman, J. M. & Levenson, R. W. (1988). The social psychophysiology of marriage. In P. Noller & M. A. Fitzpatrick (Eds.), *Perspectives on marital interaction.* (pp. 182-200) Multilingual Matters: Clevedon.

Goubet, N., Strasbaugh, K., & Chesney, J. (2007). Familiarity breeds content? Soothing effect of a familiar odor on full-term newborns. *Journal of Developmental and Behavioral Pediatrics, 28,* 189-94.

Gould, E. (2007). How widespread is adult neurogenesis in mammals? *Nature Reviews Neuroscience.* 8: 481-8.

Gould, E. (2007). Structural plasticity. In P. Andersen, R. Morris, D. Amaral, T. Bliss, J. O'Keefe (Eds.), *The hippocampus book.* New York, NY: Oxford University Press.

Gould, S. J. & Lewontin, R. C. (1979). The sandrels of San Marco and the Panglossian paradigm: A critique of the adaptation programme. *Proceedings of the Royal Society of London, Series B, 205,* 581-598.

Gourzis, P., Katrivanou, A., & Beratis, S. (2002). Symptomatology of the initial prodromal phase in schizophrenia. *Schizophrenia Bulletin, 28,* 415-29.

Grabner, R. H., Stern, E., & Neubauer, A. C. (2003). When intelligence loses its impact: Neural efficiency during reasoning in a familiar area. *International Journal of Psychophysiology, 49*(2), 89-98.

Grahn, J. A., Parkinson, J. A., & Owen, A. M. (2008). The cognitive functions of the caudate nucleus. *Progress in Neurobiology.* 86: 141-55.

Grant, B. F., Stinson, F. S., Dawson, D. A., Chou, P., Dufour, M. C., Compton, W., et al. (2004). Prevalence and co-occurrence of substance use disorders and independent mood and anxiety disorders: Results from the National Epidemiologic Survey on Alcohol and Related Conditions. *Archives of General Psychiatry, 61*(8), 807-816.

Grassian, S. (1983). Psychopathological Effects of Solitary Confinement. *American Journal of Psychiatry, 140:* 1450-1454

Gratz, K. L. (2003). Risk factors for and functions of deliberate self-harm: An empirical and conceptual review. *Clinical Psychology: Science and Practice, 10*(2), 192-205.

Gray, J. A. & McNaughton, N. (1996). The neuropsychology of anxiety: Reprise. In D. A. Hope (Ed.), *The Nebraska symposium on motivation (Vol. 43).* Lincoln, NE: University of Nebraska Press.

Grayling, A. (June, 2002). *Scientist or Storyteller?* The Guardian.

Graziano, M. S. (2006). The organization of behavioral repertoire in motor cortex. *Annual Review of Neuroscience, 29,* 105-134.

Greely, H., Sahakian, B., Harris, J., Kessler, R.C., Gazzaniga, M., Campbell, P., & Farah, M. J. (2008). Towards responsible use of cognitive-enhancing drugs by the healthy. *Nature, 456,* 702-5.

Greenberg, J. (1978). The Americanization of Roseto. *Science News, 113:* 378-382.

Greenberg, L. & Goldman, R. N. (2008). *Emotion-focused couples therapy*. Washington, D.C.: American Psychological Association.

Greene, R. R. (2008). Risk and resilience theory: A social work perspective. In R.R. Greene (Ed.), *Human behavior theory and social work practice (3rd edition)*. New Brunswick, NJ: Transaction Publishers.

Greenspan, R. J. (2003). RNA and memory: From feeding to localization. *Current Biology, 13*(4), R126-R127.

Greenwald, A. G. & Banaji, M. R. (1995). Implicit social cognition: Attitudes, self-esteem, and stereotypes. *Psychological Review, 102*: 4-27.

Greenwald, A. G., & Banaji, M. R. (1995). Implicit social cognition: Attitudes, self-esteem and stereotypes. *Psychological Review, 102*, 4-27.

Greenwald, A. G., Banaji, M. R., Rudman, L. A., Farnham, S. D., Nosek, B. A., & Mellott, D. S. (2002). A unified theory of implicit attitudes, stereotypes, self-esteem, and self-concept. *Psychological Review, 109*(1): 3-25.

Greenwald, A. G., McGhee, D. E., & Schwartz, J. L. K. (1998). Measuring individual differences in implicit cognition: The implicit association test. *Journal of Personality and Social Psychology: 74*, 1464-1480.

Gregory, R. J. (2004). *Psychological testing: History, principles, and applications*. Needham Heights, MA: Allyn and Bacon.

Grewal, D., Brackett, M., & Salovey, P. (2006). Emotional intelligence and the self-regulation of affect. In D. K. Snyder, J. Simpson, & J. N. Hughes (Eds.) *Emotion regulation in couples and families: Pathways to dysfunction and health*, pp. 37-55. Washington, DC: American Psychological Association.

Grilly, D. M. (2006). *Drugs and human behavior (5th ed.)*. Boston, MA: Pearson.

Groer, M., Meagher, M. W., & Kendall-Tackett, K. (2010). An overview of stress and immunity. *The psychoneuroimmunology of chronic disease: Exploring the links between inflammation, stress, and illness*. (pp. 9-22). Washington, DC: American Psychological Association.

Gross, C. G. (2005). Processing the facial image: a brief history. *American Psychologist*. 60: 755-63.

Gross, J. J., Richards, J. M., & John, O. P. 2006. Emotion regulation in everyday life. In: Snyder, D. K., Simpson, J. A., & Hughes, J. N. (eds.), *Emotion Regulation in Families: Pathways to Dysfunction and Health*. American Psychological Association, Washington, DC: pp. 13-35.

Grossman, M. & Wood, W. (1993). Sex differences in intensity of emotional experience: A social role interpretation. *Journal of Personality and Social Psychology, 65*, 1010-1022.

Group creativity: Innovation through collaboration. (2003). In P.B. Paulus, B. A. Nijstad (Eds.). New York, NY: Oxford University Press.

Gruneberg, M. M., & Sykes, R. N. (1993). The generalisability of confidence—accuracy studies in eyewitnessing. *Memory, 1*(3), 185-189.

Gruzelier, J. (2003). Contemporary hypnosis: Editorial commentary. *Contemporary Hypnosis, 20*(2), 57.

Guevara, R. E. (2008). A 13-year retrospective study on listeriosis in Los Angeles County, 1992-2004. *Dissertation Abstracts International: Section B: The Sciences and Engineering, 69*(1-B), 203.

Gurman, A.S., & & Messer, S. B. (Eds.) (2003). *Essential psychotherapies: Theory and practice (2nd ed.)*. New York, NY: Guilford Press.

Guyton, A. (2006). The body fluids and kidneys. In Textbook of medical physiology (pp. 291-414). Philadelphia, PA: WB Saunders Company.

Haas, B. W., Omura, K., Constable, R. T., & Canli, T. (2007). Emotional conflict and neuroticism: Personality-dependent activation in the amygdala and subgenual anterior cingulate. *Behavioral Neuroscience, 121(2)*: 249-256.

Habra, M. E., Linden, W., Anderson, J. C., & Weinberg, J. (2003). Type D personality is related to cardiovascular and neuroendocrine reactivity to acute stress. *Journal of Psychosomatic Research, 55*(3), 235-245.

Hackworth, M. (2007). Kobayashi loses: Hot dog title captured by Californian. Oakhurst, CA: *Sierra Star*.

Hagan, M. M., Chandler, P. C., Wauford, P. K., Rybak, R. J., & Oswald, K. D. (2003). The role of palatable food and hunger as trigger factors in an animal model of stress induced binge eating. *The International Journal of Eating Disorders, 34(2)*: 183-97.

Hage, S. M., Romano, J. L., Conyne, R. K., Kenny, M., Matthews, C., Schwartz, J. P., et al. (2007). Best practice guidelines on prevention practice, research, training, and social advocacy for psychologists. *The Counseling Psychologist, 35*(4), 493-566.

Haidt, J. (2004). The emotional dog gets mistaken for a possum. *Review of General Psychology*, 8, 283-290.

Haier, R. J. (2003). Brain imaging studies of intelligence: Individual differences and neurobiology. In R. J. Sternberg, J. Lautrey & T. I. Lubart (Eds.), *Models of intelligence: International perspectives*. (pp. 185-193) Washington, DC: American Psychological Association.

Haldeman, D. C. (1994). The practice and ethics of sexual orientation conversion. *Journal of Consulting and Clinical Psychology, 62(2)*: 221-227.

Hale, C. M. & Tager-Flusberg, H. (2005). Social communication in children with autism: The relationship between theory of mind and discourse development. *Autism, 9*(2), 157-178.

Hall, C. W., & Webster, R. E. (2002). Traumatic symptomatology characteristics of adult children of alcoholics. *Journal of Drug Education, 32*(3), 195-211.

Halle, M. (1990). Phonology. In D. N. Osherson and H. Lasnick (Eds.), *An Invitation to Cognitive Science, Vol. 1: Language*. Cambridge MA: MIT Press.

Halliday, G. (2004). Dreamwork and nightmares with incarcerated juvenile felons. *Dreaming, 14*(1), 30-42.

Hambrick, D. Z. & Engle, R. W. (2003). The role of working memory in problem solving. In J. E. Davidson & R. J. Sternberg (Eds.), *The psychology of problem solving*. (pp. 176-206) New York, NY: Cambridge University Press.

Hammer, T. (1993). Unemployment and mental health among young people: A longitudinal study. *Journal of Adolescence, 16*(4), 407-420 doi.

Hammond, D. C. (2008). Hypnosis as sole anesthesia for major surgeries: Historical & contemporary perspectives. *American Journal of Clinical Hypnosis, 51*(2), 101-121.

Haney, C. (1993). Infamous Punishment: The Psychological Effects of Isolation. *National Prison Journal, 8*, 367-368

Haney, M. (2008). Neurobiology of stimulants. In H. D. Kleber & M. Galanter (Eds.), *The American Psychiatric Publishing textbook of substance abuse treatment (4th ed.)*. Washington, DC: American Psychiatric Publishing.

Hanin, Y. L. (1997). Emotions and athletic performance: Individual zones of optimal functioning. *European Yearbook of Sport Psychology, 1*: 29-72.

Hankin, J. R. (2002). Fetal alcohol syndrome prevention research. *Alcohol Research and Health, 26*(1), 58-65.

Harker, L. & Keltner, D. (2001). Expressions of positive emotion in women's college yearbook pictures and their relationship to personality and life outcomes across adulthood. *Journal of Personality and Social Psychology 80*(1), 112-124.

Harman, C. & Fox, N. A. (1997). Frontal and attentional mechanisms regulating distress experience and expression during infancy. In N. A. Krasnegor, G. R. Lyon, & P. S. Goldman-Rakic (eds.), *Development of the Prefrontal Cortex: Evolution, Neurobiology, and Behavior.* (191-208) Baltimore, MD: Paul H Brookes Publishing.

Harper, C. C. & McLanahan, S. S. (2004, September). Father absence and youth incarceration. *Journal of Research on Adolescence, 14,* 369-397.

Harrison, Y. & Horne, J. A. (2000). The impact of sleep deprivation on decision making: A review. *Journal of Experimental Psychology: Applied, 6,* 236-249.

Hart, B. & Risley, T. R. (1995). *Meaningful differences in everyday parenting and intellectual development in young American children.* Baltimore, MD: Paul H. Brookes.

Hart, B. & Risley, T. R. (1995). *Meaningful differences in everyday experiences of young American children.* Baltimore, MD: Paul Brookes.

Hartmann, U., & Waldinger, M. D. (2007). Treatment of delayed ejaculation. *Principles and practice of sex therapy (4th ed.).* (pp. 241-276) New York, NY: Guilford Press.

Harvey, J. H. (2008). Growth through loss and adversity in close relationships. *Trauma, recovery, and growth: Positive psychological perspectives on posttraumatic stress.* (pp. 125-143). Hoboken, NJ: John Wiley & Sons Inc.

Harvey, N. L., Srinivasan, R. S., Dillard, M. E., Johnson, N. C., Witte, M. H., Boyd, K., et al. (2005). Lymphatic vascular defects promoted by Prox1 haploinsufficiency cause adult-onset obesity. *Nature genetics, 37(10)*: 1072-81.

Harway, M. (Ed.). (2005). *Handbook of couples therapy.* New York, NY: Wiley.

Haslam, N. (2007). *Introduction to personality and intelligence.* Thousand Oaks, CA: Sage Publications.

Hassin, R. R. (2005). Nonconscious control and implicit working memory. In R. R. Hassin, J. S. Uleman, & J. A. Bargh (Eds.), *The new unconscious.* (pp. 196-222) New York, NY: Oxford University Press.

Hauser, M. D., Chomsky, N., Fitch, W. T. (2002) The faculty of language: what is it, who has it, and how did it evolve? *Science, 298, 1569-79.*

Hawkins, R. D., Cohen, T. E., & Kandel, E. R. (2006). Dishabituation in Aplysia can involve either reversal of habituation or superimposed sensitization. *Learning & Memory, 13,* 397-403.

Hawkley, L. C., Berntson, G. G., Engeland, C. G., Marucha, P.T., Masi, C. M., & Cacioppo, J. T. (2005). *Canadian Psychology/Psychologie Canadienne, 46*(3), 115-125.

Haxel, B. R., Grant, L., & Mackay-Sim, A. (2008). Olfactory dysfunction after head injury. *The Journal of Head Trauma Rehabilitation, 23,* 407-13.

Hayaki, J., Friedman, M. A., & Brownell, K. D. (2002). Shame and severity of bulimic symptoms. *Eating Behaviors, 3(1):* 73-83.

Hayatbakhsh, M. R., Najman, J. M., McGee, T. R., Bor, W., & O'Callaghan, M. J. (2009). Early pubertal maturation in the prediction of early adult substance use: A prospective study. *Addiction, 104*(1), 59-66.

Haydon, P. G., Blendy, J., Moss, S. J, & Jackson, R. F. (2009). Astrocytic control of synaptic transmission and plasticity: a target for drugs of abuse? *Neuropharmacology.* 56 Suppl 1: 83-90.

Haynes, S. N. (2001). Clinical applications of analog behavioral observations: Dimensions of psychometric evaluations. *Psychological Assessment, 13*(1), 73-85.

Haynes, S. N. (2001). Introduction to the special section on clinical applications of analogue behavioral observation. *Psychological Assessment, 13*(1), 3-4.

Haynes, S. G., Feinleib, M., & Kannel, W. B. (1980). The relationship of psychosocial factors to coronary heart disease in the framingham study: III. eight-year incidence of coronary heart disease. *American Journal of Epidemiology, 111*(1), 37-58.

Hazan, C. & Shaver, P. (1987). Romantic love conceptualized as an attachment process. *Journal of Personality and Social Psychology, 52*(3): 511-524.

Hazan, C. & Shaver, P. R. (1994). Attachment as an organizational framework for research on close relationships. *Psychological Inquiry: 5*(1), 1-22.

Hazan, C. & Shaver, P. R. (1994). Deeper into attachment theory. *Psychological Inquiry, 5*(1): 68-79.

Hazan, C. & Shaver, P. R. (2004). Attachment as an organizational framework for research on close relationships. In H. T. Reis, & C. E. Rusbult (eds.), *Close relationships: Key readings.* (pp. 153-174) Philadelphia, PA: Taylor & Francis.

Headey, B. (2008). Life goals matter to happiness: A revision of set-point theory. *Social Indicators Research, 86*(2), 213-231.

Heath, A. C., Madden, P. A., Cloninger, C. R., & Martin, N. G. (1994). Genetic and environmental structure of personality. In C. R. Cloninger (ed.), *Personality and Psychopathology.* Washington, D.C.: American Psychiatric Press.

Hebb, D. O. (1960). The American revolution. *American Psychologist, 15,* 735-745.

Hebl, M. R. & Mannix, L. M. (2003). The weight of obesity in evaluating others: A mere proximity effect. *Personality and Social Psychology Bulletin, 29*(1): 28-38.

Hegarty, P. (2007). From genius inverts to gendered intelligence: Lewis Terman and the power of the norm. *History of Psychology, 10*(2), 132-155.

Heilman, M. E., Block, C. J., & Martell, R. F. (1995). Sex stereotypes: Do they influence perceptions of managers? *Journal of Social Behavior and Personality, 10*: 237-252.

Heiman, J. R. (2007). Orgasmic disorders in women. *Principles and practice of sex therapy (4th ed.).* (pp. 84-123) New York, NY: Guilford Press.

Heller, A. C., Amar, A. P., Liu, C. Y., & Apuzzo, M. L. (2006). Surgery of the mind and mood: a mosaic of issues in time and evolution. *Neurosurgery.* 59: 720-33

Helzer, J. E., Burnam, A., & McEvoy, L. T. (1991). Alcohol abuse and dependence. In L. N. Robins & D. S. Regier (Eds.), *Psychiatric disorders in America: The Epidemiological Catchment Area Study.* New York, NY: Free Press.

Henderson, H. A. & Wachs, T. D. (2007). Temperament theory and the study of cognitive-emotion interactions across development. *Developmental Review, 27,* 396-427.

Henley, N. M. (1977). *Body politics: Power, sex, and nonverbal communication.* Englewood Cliffs, NJ: Prentice Hall.

Henningsen, D. D., Henningsen, M. L. M., Eden, J., & Cruz, M. G. (2006). Examining the symptoms of groupthink and retrospective sensemaking. *Small Group Research, 37*(1): 36-64.

Henry, J. P., and Cassel, J. C. (1969). Psychosocial factors in essential hypertension: Recent epidemiologic and animal experimental evidence. *American Journal of Epidemiology, Sep; 90*(3): 171-200.

Hepp, U., Klaghofer, R., Burkhard, K., & Buddeberg, C. (2002). Treatment history of transsexual patients: A retrospective follow-up study. *Nervenarzt, 73*(3), 283-288.

Herberg, L. J., & Stephens, D. N. (1977). Interaction of hunger and thirst in the motivational arousal underlying hoarding behavior in the rat. *Journal of Comparative and Physiological Psychology, 91*(2), 359-64.

Herd, S. A., Banich, M. T., O'Reilly, R. C. (2006) Neural mechanisms of cognitive control: an integrative model of stroop task performance and FMRI data. *Journal of Cognitive Neuroscience. 18:* 22-32.

Hergenhahn, B. R. (2005). *An introduction to the history of psychology.* (5th ed.). Belmont, CA: Thomson Wadsworth.

Herlitz, A. & Rehnman, J. (2008). Sex Differences in Episodic Memory. *Current Directions in Psychological Science. 17*(1): 52-6.

Herrnstein, R. & Boring, E. (1966). *A source book in the history of psychology.* Cambridge, MA: Harvard University Press.

Herrnstein, R. J. & Murray, C. A. (1994). *The bell curve: Intelligence and class structure in american life.* New York, NY: Free Press.

Hersen, M., Bellack, A. S., Himmelhoch, J. M., & Thase, M. E. (1984). Effects of social skill training, amitriptyline, and psychotherapy in unipolar depressed women. *Behavioral Therapy, 15,* 21-40.

Hersen, M., & Thomas, J. C. (Eds.). (2007). *Handbook of clinical interviewing with adults.* Thousand Oaks, CA: Sage Publishing.

Hertzog, C. & Robinson, A. E. (2005). Metacognition and intelligence. In O. Wilhelm & R. W. Engle (Eds.), *Handbook of understanding and measuring intelligence.* (pp. 101-123). Thousand Oaks, CA: Sage Publications.

Hiatt, L. R. (1978). Classification of the emotions. In L. R. Hiatt (Ed.), *Australian aboriginal concepts* (pp. 182-187). Princeton, NJ: Humanities Press.

Hien, D., Litt, L. C., Cohen, L. R., Miele, G. M., & Campbell, A. (2009). Emotion regulation. *Trauma services for women in substance abuse treatment: An integrated approach.* (pp. 55-74) Washington, DC: American Psychological Association.

Higgins, E. S. & George, M.S. (2007). *The neuroscience of clinical psychiatry: The pathophysiology of behavior and mental illness.* Philadelphia, PA: Wolters Kluwer/Lippincott Williams & Wilkins.

Higgins, S. T., Heil, S. H., & Lussier, J. P. (2004). Clinical implications of reinforcement as a determinant of substance use disorders. *Annu. Rev. Psychol., 55,* 431-461.

Hilgard, E. R. (1982). Hypnotic susceptibility and implications for measurement. *International Journal of Clinical and Experimental Hypnosis, 30*(4), 394-403.

Hilgard, E. R. (1991). Suggestibility and suggestions as related to hypnosis. In J. F. Schumaker (Ed.), *Human suggestibility: Advances in theory, research, and application.* Florence, KY: Taylor & Frances/ Routledge.

Hilgard, E. R. (1992). Dissociation and theories of hypnosis. In E. Fromm & M.R. Nash (Eds.), *Contemporary hypnosis research.* New York, NY: Guilford Press.

Hilgard, E. R. (1992). Divided consciousness and dissociation. *Consciousness and Cognition: An International Journal, 1*(1), 16-31.

Hill, D. E., Yeo, R. A., Campbell, R. A., Hart, B., Vigil, J., & Brooks, W. (2003). Magnetic resonance imaging correlates of attention-deficit/hyperactivity disorder in children. *Neuropsychology, 17,* 496-506.

Hines, M. (2004). In A. Eagly, A. Beall, & R.Sternberg (Eds.) *The Psychology of Gender (2nd ed.).* New York, NY: Guilford Press

Hines, M., Kaufman, F. R. (1994) Androgen and the development of human sex-typical behavior: rough-and-tumble play and sex of preferred playmates in children with congenital adrenal hyperplasia (CAH). *Child Development, 65*(4):1042-53.

Hinshaw, S. P. (2002). Process, mechanism, and explanation related to externalizing behavior in developmental psychopathology. *Journal of Abnormal Child Psychology, 30,* 431-446.

Hinshaw, S. P. (2008). Developmental psychopathology as a scientific discipline: Relevance to behavioral and emotional disorders of childhood and adolescence. In T.P. Beauchaine & S.P. Hinshaw (Ed.), *Child and adolescent psychopathology.* Hoboken, NJ: John Wiley & Sons, Inc.

Hinton, E. C., Holland, A. J., Gellatly, M. S., Soni, S., & Owen, A. M. (2006). An investigation into food preferences and the neural basis of food-related incentive motivation in Prader-Willi syndrome. *Journal of Intellectual Disability Research, 50(9):* 633-42.

Hirata, S. (2009). Chimpanzee social intelligence: selfishness, altruism, and the mother-infant bond. *Primates, 50,* 2-11.

Hirschorn, M. (2007). The case for reality TV./The Atlantic Online/May, 2007.

Hitti, M. (2004). Brain chemicals suggest marijuana's effects. *WebMD.* Retrieved September 24, 2004, from my.webmd.com/content/ Article/94/102660.htm.

Hjerl, K., Andersen, E. W., Keiding, N., Mouridsen, H. T., Mortensen, P. B., & Jorgensen, T. (2003). Depression as a prognostic for breast cancer mortality. Journal of Consultation and Liaison Psychiatry, 44(1), 24-30.

Hobson, C. J., & Delunas, L. (2001). National norms and life-event frequencies for the revised social readjustment rating scale. *International Journal of Stress Management, 8*(4), 299-314.

Hobson, C. J., Kamen, J., Szostek, J., Nethercut, C. M., Tiedmann, J. W., & Wojnarowicz, S. (1998). Stressful life events: A revision and update of the Social Readjustment Rating Scale. *Interational Journal of Stress Management,* 5(1), 1-23.

Hobson, J. A. (2002) *Dreaming: An introduction to the science of sleep.* New York, NY: Oxford University Press.

Hobson, J. A. (2005). Sleep is of the brain, by the brain and for the brain. *Nature, 437,* 1254-1256.

Hobson, J. A. & McCarley, R. W. (1977). The brain as dream state generator: An activation-synthesis hypothesis of the dream process. *American Journal of Psychiatry, 134,* 1335-1348.

Hobson, J. A., Stickgold, R., & Pace-Schott, E. F. (1998). The neuropsychology of REM sleep dreaming. *Neuroreport: An International Journal for the Rapid Communication of Research in Neuroscience, 9*(3), R1-R14.

Hochman, J. (2001). A basic online search on the eidetic with PsycINFO, MEDLINE and ERIC. *Journal of Mental Imagery, 25*(1-2), 99-215.

Hodapp, R. M. & Dykens, E. M. (2003). Mental retardation (intellectual disabilities). In E. J. Mash & R.A. Barkley (Eds.), *Child psychopathology (2nd ed.).* New York, NY: Guilford Press.

Hoeft, F., Hernandez, A., McMillon, G., Taylor-Hill, H., Martindale, J. L., Meyler, A., Keller, T. A., Siok, W. T., Deutsch, G. K., Just, M. A., Whitfield-Gabrieli, S., & Gabrieli, J. D. (2006). Neural basis of dyslexia: a comparison between dyslexic and nondyslexic children equated for reading ability. *Journal of Neuroscience, 26,* 10700-8.

Hoeksema-van Orden, C. Y. D., Gaillard, A. W. K., & Buunk, B. P. (1998). Social loafing under fatigue. *Journal of Personality and Social Psychology, 75:* 1179-1190.

Hoffmann, J. P. (2002, May). The community context of family structure and adolescent drug use. *Journal of Marriage and Family, 64,* 314-330.

Hofstede, G. & McCrae, R. R. (2004). Culture and personality revisited: Linking traits and dimensions of culture. *Cross-Cultural Research, 38:* 52-88.

Hogan, J. & Hogan, R. (1993). *The ambiguity of conscientiousness.* Paper presented at the 8th annual conference of the Society for Industrial and Organizational Psychology, San Francisco.

Hoigaard, R., Säfvenbom, R., & Tonnessen, F. E. (2006). The relationship between group cohesion, group norms, and perceived social loafing in soccer teams. *Small Group Research, 37*(3): 217-232.

Holahan, C. J., & Moos, R. H. (1985). Life stress and health: Personality, coping, and family support in stress resistance. *Journal of Personality and Social Psychology, 49*(3), 739-747.

Holahan, C. J., & Moos, R. H. (1990). Life stressors, resistance factors, and improved psychological functioning: An extension of the stress resistance paradigm. *Journal of Personality and Social Psychology, 58*(5), 909-917.

Holahan, C. K., Holahan, C. J., & Belk, S. S. (1984). Adjustment in aging: The roles of life stress, hassles, and self-efficacy. *Health Psychology, 3:* 315-328.

Holland, A. J., Treasure, J., Coskeran, P., Dallow, J., Milton, N., & Hillhouse, E. (1993) Measurement of excessive appetite and metabolic changes in Prader-Willi syndrome. *International Journal of Obesity and Related Metabolic Disorders, 17:* 527-532.

Hollon, S. D., DeRubeis, R. J., Shelton, R. C., Amsterdam, J. D., Salomon, R. M., O'Reardon, J. P., et al. (2005). Prevention of relapse following cognitive therapy v. medications in moderate to severe depression. *Archives of General Psychiatry, 62,* 417-422.

Hollon, S. D., Haman, K. L., & Brown, L. L. (2002). Cognitive behavioral treatment of depression. In I. H. Gotlib & C. L. Hammen (Eds.), *Handbook of depression* (pp. 383-403). New York, NY: Guilford Press.

Hollon, S. D., Stewart, M. O., & Strunk D. (2006). Enduring effects for cognitive behavior therapy in the treatment of depression and anxiety. *Annual Review of Psychology, 57,* 285-315.

Holmes, T. H., & Rahe, R. H. (1967). The Social Readjustment Rating Scale. *Journal of Psychosomatic Research., 11,* 213-218.

Holmes, T. H., & Rahe, R. H. (1989). The Social Readjustment Rating Scale. In T. H. Holmes & E. M. David (Eds.), *Life change, life events, and illness: Selected papers.* New York, NY: Praeger.

Holstege, G., Georgiadis, J. R., Paans, A. M., Meiners, L. C., & Graaf, F. H. (2003). Brain activation during human male ejaculation. *Experimental Brain Research, 23*(27): 9185-9193.

Holyoak, K. J. & Morrison (2005). Analogy. In K. J. Holyoak & R. G. Morrison (Eds.), *The Cambridge Handbook of Thinking and Reasoning* (pp. 409-414). New York, NY: Cambridge University Press.

Hommel, J. D., Trinko, R., Sears, R. M., Georgescu, D., Liu, Z. W., Gao, X. B., Thurmon, J. J., Marinelli, M., & DiLeone, R. J. (2006) Leptin receptor signaling in midbrain dopamine neurons regulates feeding. *Neuron* 51:801-810.

Homosexuality and Sexual Orientation Disturbance: Proposed Change in DSM-II, 6th Printing, (44). Change. Arlington. (1973).

Hong, Y., Morris, M. W., Chiu, Y., & Benet-Martinez, V. (2000). Multicultural minds: A dynamic constructivist approach to culture and cognition. *American Psychologist, 55:* 709-717.

Honma, K. I., Hashimoto, S., Nakao, M., & Honma, S. (2003). Period and phase adjustments of human circadian rhythms in the real world. *Journal of Biological Rhythms, 18*(3), 261-270.

Hovakimyan, M., Haas, S. J., Schmitt, O., Gerber, B., Wree, A., & Andressen, C. (2008). Mesencephalic human neural progenitor cells transplanted into the adult hemiparkinsonian rat striatum lack dopaminergic differentiation but improve motor behavior. *Cells Tissues Organs.* 188: 373-83.

Howard, B. M., Zhicheng, M., Filipovic, R., Moore, A. R., Antic, S. D., & Zecevic, N. (2008). Radial glia cells in the developing human brain. *Neuroscientist.* 14: 459-73.

Howes, C. (1999). Attachment relationships in the context of multiple caregivers. In J. Cassidy, & P. R. Shaver (Eds.), *Handbook of attachment: Theory, research, and clinical applications.* (pp. 671-687). New York, NY: Guilford Press.

Huang, M. (2001). Cognitive abilities and the growth of high-IQ occupations. *Social Science Research, 30*(4), 529-551.

Huang, P. L. (2005). Unraveling the links between diabetes, obesity, and cardiovascular disease. *Circulation Research* 96: 1129-1131.

Hubel, D.H. & Wiesel, T.N. (1959). Receptive fields of single neurones in the cat's striate cortex. *The Journal of Physiology, 148,* 574-91.

Hublin, C., Kaprio, J., Partinen, M., & Koskenvuo, M. (1999). Limits of self-report in assessing sleep terrors in a population survey. *Sleep: Journal of Sleep Research & Sleep Medicine, 22*(1), 89-93.

Hublin, C., Kaprio, J., Partinen, M., & Koskenvuo, M. (2001). Parasomnias: Co-occurrence and genetics. *Psychiatric Genetics, 11*(2), 65-70.

Hudson, J. I., Hiripi, E., Pope, H. G., & Kessler, R. C. (2008). The prevalence and correlates of eating disorders in the national comorbidity survey replication. *Biol Psychiatry, 61*(3): 348-358.

Hudziak, J. & Bartels, M. (2008). Genetic and environmental influences on wellness, resilience, and psychopathology: A family-based approach for promotion, prevention, and intervention. In J.J. Hudziak (Ed.), *Developmental psychopathology and wellness: Genetic and environmental influences.* Washington, DC: American Psychiatric Publishing, Inc.

Hughes, L.F., McAsey, M.E., Donathan, C.L., Smith, T., Coney, P., & Struble, R.G. (2002). Effects of hormone replacement therapy on olfactory sensitivity: cross-sectional and longitudinal studies. *Climacteric, 5,* 140-50.

Hughes, R. N. (2007). Neotic preferences in laboratory rodents: issues, assessment, and substrates. *Neuroscience and Biobehavioral reviews, 31(3):* 441-64.

Humphreys, K., & Rappaport, J. (1993). From the community mental health movement to the war on drugs: A study in the definition of social problems. *American Psychologist, 48*(8), 892-901.

Hunt, E. & Carlson, J. (2007). Considerations relating to the study of group differences in intelligence. *Perspectives on Psychological Science, 2*(2), 194-213.

Hunt, J. M. (1982). Towawrd equalizing the developmental opportunities of infants and preschool children. *Journal of Social Issues, 38*(4), 163-191.

Hyde, J. S. (2005). The gender similarities hypothesis. *American Psychologist, 60*, 581-592

Hyde, J. S. (2007). New directions in the study of gender similarities and differences. *Current Directions in Psychological Science, 16*(5), 259-263.

Hyde, J. S. (2008, Spring). Men are from earth, women are from earth: The gender similarities hypothesis. *General Psychologist, 43*(1).

Hyde, M. & Power, D. (2006). Some ethical dimensions of cochlear implantation for deaf children and their families. *Journal of Deaf Studies and Deaf Education, 11*, 102-11.

Hyman Jr., I. E. & Kleinknecht, E. E. (1999). False childhood memories: Research, theory, and applications. In L. M. Williams & V. L. Banyard (Eds.), *Trauma & memory.* (pp. 175-188). Thousand Oaks, CA: Sage Publications.

Hymowitz, N. (2005). Tobacco. In R. J. Frances, A. H. Mack, & S. I. Miller (Eds.), *Clinical textbook of addictive disorders (3rd ed.).* New York, NY: Guilford Press.

I

Iacoboni, M., Molnar-Szakacs, I., Gallese, V., Buccino, G., Mazziotta, J. C., Rizzolatti, G. (2005). Grasping the intentions of others with one's own mirror neuron system. *PLoS Biol, 3*, 1-7.

Iadecola, C. & Nedergaard, M. (2007). Glial regulation of the cerebral microvasculature. *Nature Neuroscience.* 10: 1369-76.

Imperato-McGinley, J., Miller, M., Wilson, J. D., Peterson, R. E., Shackleton, C., Gajdusek, D. C. (1991). A cluster of male pseudohermaphrodites with 5 alpha-reductase deficiency in Papua New Guinea. *Clinical Endocrinology (Oxf). 34*(4):293-8.

Inglehart, R. (1990). *Culture shift in advanced industrial society.* Princeton, NJ: Princeton University Press.

Ingram, D. (1986). Phonological development: Production. In P. Fletcher & M. Garman (Eds.), *Language acquisition* (2nd ed., pp. 223-239). New York, NY: Cambridge University Press.

Ingram, R. E., Nelson, T., Steidtmann, D. K., & Bistricky, S. L. (2007). Comparative data on child and adolescent cognitive measures associated with depression. *Journal of Consulting Clinical Psychology, 75*(3), 390-403.

Inhelder, B. & Piaget, J. (1979) Procedures et structures [Procedures and structures] *Archives de Psychologie, 47*, 165-176.

Insel, T. R. (2007). Shining light on depression. *Science, 317*(5839), 757-758.

Institute for Laboratory Animal Research (ILAR). (2009). Home Page. Retrieved from http://dels.nas.edu/ilar_n/ilarhome/

Intelligence: New research. (2006). In Wesley L. V. (Ed.). Hauppauge, NY: Nova Science Publishers.

Irwin, M. (2001). Neuroimmunology of disordered sleep in depression and alcoholism. *Neuropsychopharmacology, 25*(suppl5), S45-S49.

Irwin, M. R., & Cole, J. C. (2005). Depression and psychonueroimmunology. In K. Vedhara & M. Irwin (Eds.), *Human psychoneuroimmunology.* Oxford, England: Oxford University Press.

Isacson, O. & Kordower, J. H. (2008). Future of cell and gene therapies for Parkinson's disease. *Annals of Neurology, 2*: S122-38.

Isen, A. M. (1993). Positive affect and decision making. In M. Lewis & J. M. Haviland (Eds.), *Handbook of emotions.* (pp. 261-277) New York, NY: Guilford Press.

Isen, A. M. (2004) Some perspectives on positive feelings and emotions: positive affect facilitates thinking and problem solving. In A. Manstead, N. Frijda, & A. Fischer (Eds.) *Feelings and emotions: The Amsterdam symposium,* pp. 263-281. New York, NY: Cambridge University Press.

Isen, A. M. (2008). Positive affect and decision processes: Some recent theoretical developments with practical implications. In C. P. Haugtvedt, P. M. Herr, & F. R. Kardes (Eds.), *Handbook of consumer psychology.* (pp. 273-296) New York, NY: Taylor & Francis Group/Lawrence Erlbaum Associates.

Isenberg, D. J. (1986). Group polarization: A critical review and meta-analysis. *Journal of Personality and Social Psychology, 50*: 1141-1151.

Ivancevich, J. M. (1986). Life events and hassles as predictors of health symptoms, job performance, and absenteeism. *Journal of Organizational Behavior, 7*: 39-51.

Iwanaga, M., Yokoyama, H., & Seiwa, H. (2004). Coping availability and stress reduction for optimistic and pessimistic individuals. *Personality and Individual Differences, 36*(1), 11-22.

Izard, C. E. (1977). *Human emotions.* New York, NY: Plenum Press.

Izard, C. E. (1991). *The psychology of emotions.* New York, NY: Plenum.

Izard, C. E. (1994). Innate and universal facial expressions: Evidence from developmental and cross-cultural research. *Psychological Bulletin, 115,* 288-299.

Izard, C. E. (1997). Emotions and facial expressions: A perspective from differential emotions theory. In J. A. Russell & J. M. Fernandez-Dols (Eds.), *The psychology of facial expression* (pp. 57-77). New York, NY: Cambridge University Press.

Izard, C. E. (2007). Basic emotions, natural kinds, emotion schemas, and a new paradigm. *Perspectives on Psychological Science, 2,* 260-280.

Izard, C. E. (2009). Emotion theory and research: Highlights, unanswered questions, and emerging issues. *Emotion Theory and Research, 60,* 1-25.

J

Jackson, J. S., Torres, M., Caldwell, C. H., Neighbors, H. W., Nesse, R. M., Taylor, R. J., et al. (2004). The National Survey of American Life: A study of racial, ethnic and cultural influences on mental disorders and mental health. *International Journal of Methods in Psychiatric Research, 13*(4), 196-207.

Jacobs, A. K. (2008). Components of evidence-based interventions for bullying and peer victimization. In R.G. Steele, T.D. Elkin, & M.C. Roberts (Eds.), *Handbook of evidence-based therapies for children and adolescents: Bridging science and practice.* New York, NY: Spriger.

Jacoby, L. L., Bishara, A. J., Hessels, S., & Toth, J. P. (2005). Aging, subjective experience, and cognitive control: Dramatic false remembering by older adults. *Journal of Experimental Psychology: General, 134*(2), 131-148.

Jamal, M., & Baba, V. V. (2003). Type A behavior, components, and outcomes: A study of canadian employees. *International Journal of Stress Management, 10*(1), 39-50.

James, W. (1884). What is emotion? *Mind, 19*, 188-205.

James, W. (1890). *The principles of psychology* (Vols. 1 & 2). New York, NY: Holt.

Jang, K., McCrae, R., Angleitner, A., Riemann, R., & Livesley, W. (1998). Heritability of facet-level traits in a cross-cultural twin sample: Support for a hierarchical model of personality. *Journal of Personality and Social Psychology, 74:* 1556-1565.

Janis, I. (1972). *Victims of Groupthink: A Psychological Study of Foreign-Policy Decisions and Fiascoes.* Boston, MA: Houghton Mifflin.

Janis, I. L. (1982). *Groupthink.* Boston, MA: Houghton Mifflin.

Jankord, R., & Herman, J. P. (2009). Limbic regulation of hypothalamo-pituitary-adrenocortical function during acute and chronic stress. *Stress, neurotransmitters, and hormones: Neuroendocrine and genetic mechanisms.* (pp. 63-74). New York, NY: New York Academy of Sciences; Wiley-Blackwell.

Jankovic, J. & Aguilar, L. G. (2008). Current approaches to the treatment of Parkinson's disease. *Neuropsychiatric Disease and Treatment.* 4: 743-57.

Jannini, E. & Lenai, A. (2005). Ejaculatory disorders; Epidemiology and current approaches to definition, classification and subtyping. *World Journal of Urology, 23*, 68-75.

Jarvis E. D. (2004) Learned birdsong and the neurobiology of human language. Ann N Y *Academy of Sciences, 1016*, 749-77.

Jastrow, J. (1929). Review of J. B. Watson, Ways of behaviorism, psychological care of infant and child, battle of behaviorism. *Science, 69*, 455-457.

Jefferson, D. J. (2005). America's most dangerous drug. *Newsweek, 146*(6), 40-48.

Jefferson, T., Herbst, J. H., & McCrae, R. R. (1998). Associations between birth order and personality traits: Evidence from self-report and observer ratings. *Journal of Research in Personality, 32*, 498-502.

Jensen, A. R. & Reed, T. E. (1992). The correlation between reaction time and the ponderal index. *Perceptual and Motor Skills, 75*(3), 843-846.

Ji, D. & Wilson, M. A. (2007). Coordinated memory replay in the visual cortex and hippocampus during sleep. *Nature Neuroscience, 10*, 100-7.

John, O. P. & Gross, J. J. (2007). Individual differences in emotion regulation. In J. J. Gross (Ed.), *Handbook of emotion regulation.* (pp. 351-372) New York, NY: The Guilford Press.

Johns, A. (2001). Psychiatric effects of cannabis. *British Journal of Psychiatry, 178*, 116-122.

Johnson, C. H., Elliott, J., Foster, R., Honma, K. I., & Kronauer, R. (2004). Fundamental properties of circadian rhythms. In J. C. Dunlap, J. J. Loros, et al. (Eds.), *Chronobiology: Biological timekeeping.* Sunderland, MA: Sinauer Associates, Inc.

Johnson, J. G., Cohen, P., Smailes, E. M., Kasen, S., & Brook, J. S. (2002). Television viewing and aggressive behavior during adolescence and adulthood. *Science, 295*, 2468-71.

Johnson, J. S. & Newport, E. L. (1989). Critical period effects in second language learning: The influence of maturational state on the acquisition of English as a second language. *Cognitive Psychology, 21*, 60-99.

Johnson, M. H. (2005). Sensitive periods in functional brain development: Problems and prospects. *Development and Psychobiology, 44*, 287-292.

Johnson, S. C., Farnworth, T., Pinkston, J. B., Bigler, E. D., & Blatter, D. D. (1994). Corpus callosum surface area across the human adult lifespan: effect of age and gender. *Brain Research Bulletin, 35(4).*

Johnson, S. D. (1990). Toward clarifying culture, race, and ethnicity in the context of multicultural counseling. *Journal of Multicultural Counseling and Development, 18*(1), 41-50.

Johnson, W., Bouchard Jr., T. J., Krueger, R. F., McGue, M., & Gottesman, I. I. (2004). Just one *g*: Consistent results from three test batteries. *Intelligence, 32*(1), 95-107.

Johnson, W., Bouchard Jr., T. J., McGue, M., Segal, N. L., Tellegen, A., Keyes, M., et al. (2007). Genetic and environmental influences on the verbal-perceptual-image rotation (VPR) model of the structure of mental abilities in the Minnesota study of twins reared apart. *Intelligence, 35(6):* 542-562.

Johnston, C. & Lee, C. M. (2005). Children's attributions for their own versus others' behavior: Influence of actor versus observer differences. *Journal of Applied Developmental Psychology, 26*(3): 314-328.

Johnston, L.D., O'Malley, P.M., Bachman, J.G., & Schulenberg, J.E. (2007). *Monitoring the future national results on adolescent drug use: Overview of key findings, 2006* (NIH Publication No. 07-6202). Bethesda, MD: National Institute on Drug Abuse.

Jones, B. E. (2003). Arousal systems. *Frontiers in Bioscience, 8*: 438-451.

Jones, E. E. & Harris, V.A. (1967). The attribution of attitudes. *Journal of Experimental Social Psychology, 3:* 1-24.

Jones, E. E. & Nisbett, R. E. (1971). *The Actor and the Observer: Divergent Perceptions of the Causes of Behavior.* Morristown, NJ: General Learning Press.

Jones, E. E. & Sigall, H. (1971). The bogus pipeline: A new paradigm for measuring affect and attitude. *Psychological Bulletin, 76:* 349-364.

Jones, E. G. (2007). Neuroanatomy: Cajal and after Cajal. *Brain Research Reviews.* 55: 248-55.

Jones, J. (1981). *Bad blood: The Tuskegee syphilis experiment: A tragedy of race and medicine.* New York, NY: The Free Press.

Jonides, J., Lewis, R. L., Nee, D. E., Lustig, C. A., Berman, M. G., & Moore, K. S. (2008). The mind and brain of short-term memory. *Annual Review of Psychology, 59*, 193-224.

Jonides, J., Sylvester, C. C., Lacey, S. C., Wager, T. D., Nichols, T. E., & Awh, E. (2003). Modules of working memory. In R. H. Kluwe, G. Lüer, & F. Rösler (Eds.), *Principles of learning and memory.* (pp. 113-134) Cambridge, MA: Birkhäuser.

Joseph, J. (2006). *The missing gene: Psychiatry, heredity, and the fruitless search for genes.* New York, NY: Algora Publishing.

Joseph, S. V. (2007). A study of the amplitudes and latencies of the brain stem and cortical auditory evoked potentials (AEP) in relation to the personality dimension of extraversion*. ProQuest Information & Learning: US. *Dissertation Abstracts International: Section B: The Sciences and Engineering, 68*(6) 4133.

Josephs, L. (1987). Dream reports of nightmares and stages of sleep. In H. Kellerman (Ed.), *The nightmare: Psychological and biological foundations.* New York, NY: Columbia University Press.

Josephs, R. A., Markus, H., & Tarafodi, R. W. (1992). Gender and self-esteem., *Journal of Personality and Social, 63:* 391-402.

Julien, C., Tremblay, C., Phivilay, A., Berthiaume, L., Emond, V., Julien, P., & Calon, F. (2008). High-fat diet aggravates amyloid-beta and tau pathologies in the 3xTg-AD mouse model. Neurobiol Aging. Epub ahead of print.

Julien, R. M., Advokat, C. D., & Comaty, J. E. (2008). *A primer of drug action: A comprehensive guide to the actions, uses, and side effects of psychoactive drugs (11th ed)*. New York, NY: Worth Publishers.

Just, M. A. & Carpenter, P. A. (2002). A capacity theory of comprehension: Individual differences in working memory. In T. A. Polk & C. M. Seifert (Eds.), *Cognitive modeling.* (pp. 131-177) Cambridge, MA: MIT Press.

K

Kabat-Zinn, J. (2005). *Wherever you go, there you are: Mindfulness meditation in everyday life.* New York, NY: Hyperion.

Kagan, J. (1999). Born to be shy? In R. Conlan (Ed.) *States of mind* (pp.29-51). New York, NY: John Wiley & Sons.

Kagan, J. (2001). Biological constraint, cultural variety, and psychological structures. In A. Harrington (Ed.) *Unity of knowledge: The convergence of natural and human science* (pp. 177-190). New York, NY: New York Academy of Sciences.

Kagan, J. (2008). Behavioral inhibition as a risk factor for psychopathology. In T. P. Beauchaine, & S. P. Hinshaw (Eds.), *Child and adolescent psychopathology.* (pp. 157-179). Hoboken, NJ: John Wiley & Sons Inc.

Kagan, J. & Snidman, N. (1991). Infant predictors of inhibited and uninhibited profiles. *Psychological Science, 2*(1), 40-44.

Kagan, J. & Snidman, N. (1999). Early childhood predictors of adult anxiety disorders. *Biological Psychiatry, 46*(11), 1536-1541.

Kagan, J., Snidman, N. (2004). *The long shadow of temperament.* Cambridge, MA: Belknap Press/Harvard University Press.

Kagan, J., Snidman, N., Kahn, V., & Towsley, S. (2007). The preservation of two infant temperaments into adolescence. *Monographs of the Society for Research in Child Development, 72*(2), 1-75.

Kahneman, D. & Tversky, A. (1979). Prospect theory: An Analysis of Decision Making Under Risk. *Econometrica, 47,* 263-92.

Kail, R. (1992). General slowing of information-processing by persons with mental retardation. *American Journal on Mental Retardation, 97*(3), 333-341.

Kail, R. V. (2003). Information processing and memory. In M. H. Bornstein, L. Davidson, C. L. M. Keyes & K. A. Moore (Eds.), *Well-being: Positive development across the life course.* (pp. 269-279). Mahwah, NJ: Lawrence Erlbaum Associates Publishers.

Kakigi, R., Hoshiyama, M., Shimojo, M., Naka, D., Yamasaki, H., Watanabe, S., Xiang, J., Maeda, K., Lam, K., Itomi, K., & Nakamura, A. (2000). The somatosensory evoked magnetic fields. *Progress in Neurobiology, 61,* 495-523.

Kalivas, P. W. & Nakamura, M. (1999). Neural systems for behavioral activation and reward. *Current Opinion in Neurobiology, 9,* 223-7.

Kallgren, C. A., Reno, R. R., & Cialdini, R. B. (2000). A focus theory of normative conduct: When norms do and do not affect behavior. *Personality and Social Psychology Bulletin, 26:* 1002-1012.

Kallio, S. & Revonsuo, A. (2003). Hypnotic phenomena and altered states of consciousness: A multilevel framework of description and explanation. *Contemporary Hypnosis, 20*(3), 111-164.

Kalueff A. V., and La Porte J. L. (Eds.) (2008), *Behavioral models in stress research*. Hauppauge, NY: Nova Biomedical Books.

Kamiji, M. M., Troncon, L. E., Suen, V. M., & de Oliveira, R. B. (2009). Gastrointestinal transit, appetite, and energy balance in gastrectomized patients. *The American Journal of Clinical Nutrition, 89(1):* 231-9.

Kamphaus, R. W., & Frick, P. J. (2002). *Clinical assessment of child and adolescent personality and behavior* (2nd ed.). Boston, MA: Allyn and Bacon.

Kanaya, T., Ceci, S. J., & Scullin, M. H. (2003). The rise and fall of IQ in special ed: Historical trends and their implications. *Journal of School Psychology, 41*(6), 453-465.

Kanaya, T., Scullin, M. H., & Ceci, S. J. (2003). The Flynn effect and U.S. policies: The impact of rising IQ scores on American society via mental retardation diagnoses. *American Psychologist, 58*(10), 778-790.

Kandel, E. R. (2001). The molecular biology of memory storage: a dialogue between genes and synapses. *Science, 294,* 1030-8.

Kandel, E. R. (2007). The new science of mind. In F. E. Bloom (Ed.), *Best of the brain from scientific american.* (pp. 68-75). Washington, DC: Dana Press.

Kanner, A. D., Coyne, J. C., Schaefer, C., & Lazarus, R. S. (1981). Comparison of two modes of stress measurement: Daily hassles and uplifts versus major life events. *Journal of Behavioral Medicine, 4:* 1-39.

Kanner, B. (1995) *Are You Normal?: Do You Behave Like Everyone Else?* New York, NY: St. Martin's Press.

Kant, I. (2003). Anthropology from a pragmatic point of view. *The history of psychology: Fundamental questions.* (pp. 127-140). New York, NY: Oxford University Press.

Kaplan, H., & Dove, H. (1987). Infant development among the ache of eastern paraguay. *Developmental Psychology, 23*(2), 190-198.

Kaplan, R. M., & Kronick, R. G. (2006). Marital status and longevity in the United States population. *Journal of Epidemiology & Community Health, 60*(9), 760-765.

Karama, S., Lecours, A. R., Leroux, J., Bourgouin, P., Beaudoin, G., Joubert, S., et al. (2002). Areas of brain activation in males and females during viewing of erotic film excerpts. *Human Brain Mapping, 16(1):* 1-13.

Karni, A., Tanne, D., Rubenstien, B. S., Askenasy, J. J. M. et al., (1994). Dependence on REM sleep of overnight improvement of a perceptual skill. *Science, 265*(5172), 679-682.

Kasari, C., Freeman, S., & Paprella, T. (2006). Joint attention and symbolic play in young children with autism: A randomized controlled intervention study. *Journal of Child Psychology and Psychiatry, 47,* 611-620.

Kashima, Y., Siegal, M., Tanaka, K., & Kashima, E. S. (1992). Do people believe behaviours are consistent with attitudes? Towards a cultural psychology of attribution processes. *British Journal of Social Psychology, 31:* 111-124.

Katz, R. V., Kegeles, S. S., Kressin, N. R., Green, L., James, S. A., Wang, M. Q., Russell, S. L., & Claudio, C. (2008). Awareness of the tuskegee syphilis study and the US presidential apology and their influence on minority participation in biomedical research. *American Journal of Public Health, 98*(6), 1137-1142.

Kauert, G. & Iwersen-Bergmann, S. (2004). Illicit drugs as cause of traffic crashes, focus on cannabis. *Sucht (German Journal of Addiction Research and Practice), 50*(5), 327-333.

Kaufman, A. S. (2000). Intelligence tests and school psychology: Predicting the future by studying the past. *Psychology in the Schools, 37*(1), 7-16.

Kaufman, A. S. (2000). Wechsler, David. In A. E. Kazdin (Ed.), *Encyclopedia of psychology, vol. 8.* (pp. 238-239) Washington, DC: American Psychological Association.

Kaufman, A. S. & Doppelt, J. E. (1976). Analysis of WISC-R standardization data in terms of the stratification variables. *Child Development, 47*(1), 165-171.

Kaufman, L. & Rock, I. (1989). The moon illusion thirty years later. In M. Hershenson (Ed.), *The moon illusion* (pp. 193-234). Hillsdale, NJ: Lawrence Erlbaum Assoc.

Kay, J. F. (2008). Sex, Lies & Stereotypes: How Abstinence-Only Programs Harm Women and Girls. Based on recommendations arising from the roundtable: Teaching Only Abstinence: Consequences for Girls and Society. New York, NY: Legal Momentum.

Kaye, W. (2008). Neurobiology of anorexia and bulimia nervosa. Purdue ingestive behavior research center symposium influences on eating and body weight over the lifespan: Children and adolescents. *Physiology & Behavior, 94(1):* 121-135.

Kaye, W. H. & Masters, K. (2004). Comorbidity of anxiety disorders with anorexia and bulimia nervosa. *Psychiatry: Interpersonal and Biological Processes, (8):* 2215-2221.

Kazdin, A. E. (2000). *Psychotherapy for children and adolescents: Directions for research and practice.* New York, NY: Oxford University Press.

Kazdin, A. E. (Ed.). (2003). *Methodological issues & strategies in clinical research* (3rd ed.). Washington, DC: American Psychological Association.

Kazdin, A. E. (2003). Problem-solving skills training and parent management training for conduct disorder. I A. E. Kazdin & J. R. Weisz (Eds.), *Evidence-based psychotherapies for children and adolescents.* New York, NY: Guilford Press.

KCET. (2007, May 24). *Life & times transcript.* Retrieved December 21, 2008 from http://www.kcet.org/lifeandtimes/archives/200705/20070524.php.

Keane, M. (2008, September 29). Texting overtakes voice in mobile phone usage. Retrieved from http://www.wired.com/epicenter/2008/09/texting-overtak/.

Keane, T. M., Marx, B. P., & Sloan, D. M. (2009). Post-traumatic stress disorder: Definition, prevalence, and risk factors. *Post-traumatic stress disorder: Basic science and clinical practice.* (pp. 1-19) Totowa, NJ: Humana Press.

Keel, P. K. & Haedt, A. (2008). Evidence-based psychosocial treatments for eating problems and eating disorders. *Journal of Clinical Child and Adolescent Psychology : The Official Journal for the Society of Clinical Child and Adolescent Psychology, American Psychological Association Division 53, 37(1):* 39-61.

Keen, E. (1970). *Three faces of being: Toward an existential clinical psychology.* By the Meredith Corp. Reprinted by permission of Irvington Publishers.

Keenan, J. P., Gallup, G. C., & Falk, D. (2003). *The face in the mirror: The search for the origins of consciousness.* New York, NY: HarperCollins Publishers.

Keenan, K., Wakschlag, L., Danis, B., Hill, C., Humphries, J., Duax, J., et al. (2007). Further evidence of the reliability and validity of DSM-IV ODD and CD in preschool children. *Journal of the American Academy of Child and Adolescent Psychiatry, 46,* 457-468.

Keith, S. J., Regier, D. A., & Rae, D. S. (1991). Schizophrenic Disorders. In L. N. Robins & D. A. Regier (Eds.), *Psychiatric Disorders in America:* *The Epidemiologic Catchment Area Study,* (pp. 33-52). New York, NY: Free Press.

Keller, C., Siegrist, M., & Gutscher, H. (2006). The role of the affect and availability of heuristics in risk communication. *Risk Analysis, 26,* 631-9.

Keller, F. S. (1973). *The Definition of Psychology* (2nd Ed.). Englewood Cliffs, NJ: Prentice Hall.

Kellman, P. J. & Arterberry, M. E. (1998). *The cradle of knowledge: Development of perception in infancy.* Cambridge, MA: MIT Press.

Kellner, M., & Yehuda, R. (1999). Do panic disorder and posttraumatic stress disorder share a common psychoneuroendocrinology? *Psychoneuroendocrinology, 24*(5), 485-504.

Kelly, C. R., Grinband, J., & Hirsch, J. (2007). Repeated exposure to media violence is associated with diminished response in an inhibitory frontolimbic network. *PLoS ONE, 2*(12), e1268.

Kelman, L. (2007). The triggers or precipitants of the acute migraine attack. *Cephalalgia, 27,* 394-402.

Keltner, D. & Kring, A. M. (1998). Emotion, social function, and psychopathology. *Review of General Psychology, 2,* 320-342.

Kendall-Tackett K. (Ed.) (2010), *The psychoneuroimmunology of chronic disease: Exploring the links between inflammation, stress, and illness.* Washington, DC: American Psychological Association.

Kendall-Tackett, K. (2010). Depression, hostility, posttraumatic stress disorder, and inflammation: The corrosive health effects of negative mental states. *The psychoneuroimmunology of chronic disease: Exploring the links between inflammation, stress, and illness.* (pp. 113-131). Washington, DC: American Psychological Association.

Kennedy, Q., Mather, M., & Carstensen, L. L. (2004). The role of motivation in the age-related positivity effect in autobiographical memory. *Psychological Science, 15*(3), 208-214.

Kennedy, R. B., & Kennedy, D. A. (2004). Using the Myers-Briggs Type Indicator in Career Counseling. *Journal of Employment Counseling,* 41: 38-44.

Kensinger, E. A. & Corkin, S. (2003). Memory enhancement for emotional words: Are emotional words more vividly remembered than neutral words? *Memory & Cognition, 31*(8), 1169-1180.

Kensinger, E. A., Ullmann, M. T., & Corkin, S. (2001). Bilateral medial temporal lobe damage does not affect lexical or grammatical processing. Evidence from amnesic patient H.M. *Hippocampus, 11*(4), 347-360.

Kern, M. L. & Friedman, H. S. (2008). Do conscientious individuals live longer? A quantitative review. *Health Psychology, 27*(5): 505-512.

Kernberg, O. F. (1997). Convergences and divergences in contemporary psychoanalytic technique and psychoanalytic psychotherapy. In J. K. Zeig (Ed.), *The evolution of psychotherapy: The third conference.* New York, NY: Brunner/Mazel.

Kernberg, O. F. (2005). Object relations theories and technique. In E. S. Person, A. M. Cooper, & G. O. Gabbard (Eds.), *The American Psychiatric Publishing textbook of psychoanalysis* (pp. 57-75). Washington, DC: American Psychiatric Publishing.

Kessler, R. C., Adler, L. A., Barkley, R., Biederman, J., Conners, C. K., Faraone, S. V. et al. (2005). Patterns and predictors of attention-deficit/hyperactivity disorder persistence into adulthood: Results from the National Comorbidity Survey Replication. *Biological Psychiatry, 57*(11), 1442-1451.

Kessler, R. C., Amminger, G. P., Aguilar-Gaxiola, S., Alongo, J., & Lee, S. (2007). Age of onset of mental disorders: A review of recent literature. *Current Opinions in Psychiatry, 20*(4), 359-364.

Kessler, R. C., Berglund, P., Demler, O., Jin, R., & Walters, E. E. (2005). Lifetime prevalence and age-of-onset distributions of DSM-IV disorders in the National Comorbidity Survey Replication. *Archives of General Psychiatry*, 62, 593-602.

Kessler, R. C., Chiu, W. T., Demler, O., Merikangas, K. R., & Walters, E. E. (2005). Prevalence, severity, and comorbidity of 12-month DSM-IV disorders in the National Comorbidity Survey Replication. *Archives of General Psychiatry, 62*, 617-627.

Kessels, R. P. C. & Postma, A. (2002). Verbal interference during encoding and maintenance of spatial information in working memory. *Current Psychology Letters: Behaviour, Brain & Cognition, 9*, 39-46.

Keysers, C. & Gazzola, V. (2007). Integrating simulation and theory of mind: From self to social cognition. *Trends in Cognitive Sciences, 11*(5): 194-196.

Khalil, E. L. (2004). What is altruism? *Journal of Economic Psychology, 25*(1): 97-123.

Kiecolt-Glaser, J. K., Dura, J. R., Speicher, C. E., Trask, O. J., & Glaser, R. (1991). Spousal caregivers of dementia victims: Longitudinal changes in immunity and health. *Psychosomatic Medicine, 53*, 345-362.

Kiecolt-Glaser, J. K., Glaser, R., Gravenstein, S., Malarkey, W. B., & Sheridan, J. (1996). Chronic stress alters the immune response to influenza virus vaccine in older adults. *Proceedings of the National Academy of Sciences, USA*, 93, 3043-3047.

Kiecolt-Glaser, J., McGuire, L., Robles, T. F., & Glaser, R. (2002). Psychoneuroimmunology and psychosomatic medicine: Back to the future. *Psychosomatic Medicine, 64*(1), 15-28.

Kiecolt-Glaser, J., McGuire, L., Robles, T. F., & Glaser, R. (2002). Psychoneuroimmunology: Psychological influences on immune function and health. *Journal of Consulting and Clinical Psychology*, 70(3), 537-547.

Kiecolt-Glaser, J. K., Glaser, R., Williger, D., et al. (1985). Psychosocial enhancement of immunocompetence in a geriatric population. *Health Psychology, 4*: 25-41.

Kihlstrom, J. F. (1999). The psychological unconscious. In L. A. Pervin & O. P. Oliver (Eds.), *Handbook of personality: Theory and research (2nd ed.)*. New York, NY: Guildford Press.

Kihlström, J. F. (2001). *Dissociative disorders*. New York, NY: Kluwer Academic/ Plenum.

Kihlstrom, J. F. (2002). The unconscious. In V. S. Ramachandran (Ed.), *Encyclopedia of the Human Brain, Vol. 4* (pp. 635-646). San Diego, CA: Academic.

Kihlstrom, J. F. (2006). Repression: A unified theory of a will-o'-the-wisp. *Behavioral and Brain Sciences, 29*(5), 523.

Kihlstrom, J. F. (2007). Consciousness in hypnosis. In P. D. Zelazo, M. Moscovitch, & E. Thompson (Eds.), *The Cambridge handbook of consciousness*. New York, NY: Cambridge University Press.

Kihlstrom, J. F., Beer, J. S., & Klein, S. B. (2003). Self and identity as memory. In M. R. Leary & J. P. Tangney (Eds.), *Handbook of self and identity*. (pp. 68-90) New York, NY: Guilford Press.

Kihlstrom, J. F. & Canter Kihlstrom, L. (1999). Self, sickness, somatization, and systems of care. In R. J. Contrada & R. D. Ashmore (Eds.), *Self, social identity, and physical health: Interdisciplinary explorations* (pp. 23-42). New York, NY: Oxford University Press. Read preprint.

Kihlstrom, J. F, Dorfman, J., & Park, L. (2007). Implicit and explicit memory and learning. In M. Velmans & S. Schneider (Eds.), *The Blackwell companion to consciousness*. Malden, MA: Blackwell Publishing.

Kihlstrom, J. F., Mulvaney, S., Tobias, B. A., & Tobis, I. P. (2000). The emotional unconscious. In E. Eich, J. F. Kihlstrom, et al. (Eds.), *Cognition and Emotion*, London, England: Oxford University Press.

Kim, J. L., Collins, R. L., Kanouse, D. E., Elliott, M. N., Berry, S. H., Hunter, S. B., Miu, A., & Kunkel, D. (2006). Sexual readiness, household policies, and other predictors of adolescents' exposure to sexual content in mainstream entertainment television. *Media Psychology, 8*(4), 449-471.

Kim, S. W., Grant, J. E., Kim, S. I., Swanson, T. A., Bernstein, G. A., Jaszcz, W. B., et al. (2004). A possible association of recurrent streptococcal infections and acute onset of obsessive-compulsive disorder. *Journal of Neuropsychiatry and Clinical Neuroscience, 16*(3), 252-260.

Kinsey, A. C., Pomeroy, W. B., & Martin, C. E. (1948). *Sexual Behavior in the Human Male*. Philadelphia, PA: Saunders.

Kinsey, A. C., Pomeroy, W. B., Martin, C. E., & Gebhard, P. H. (1953). *Sexual Behavior in the Human Female*. Philadelphia, PA: Saunders.

Kinsley, C. H., Bardi, M., Karelina, K., Rima, B., Christon, L., Friedenberg, J., et al. (2008). Motherhood induces and maintains behavioral and neural plasticity across the lifespan in the rat. *Archives of Sexual Behavior, 37(1)*: 43-56.

Kinzie, J., Leung, P., Boehnlein, J., & Matsunaga, D. (1992). Psychiatric epidemiology of an Indian village: A 19-year replication study. *Journal of Nervous and Mental Diseases, 180*(1), 33-39.

Kirschenbaum, H. (2004). Carl Rogers's life and work: An assessment on the 100th anniversary of his birth. Journal of Counseling and Development, 82(1), 116-124.

Kitayama, S., Markus, H. R., & Kurokawa, M. (2000). Culture, emotion, and well-being: Good feelings in Japan and the United States. *Cognition and Emotion, 14*: 93-124.

Kleber, H. D. & Galanter, M. (Eds.). (2008). *The American Psychiatric Publishing textbook of substance abuse treatment (4th ed.)*. Washington, DC: American Psychiatric Publishing.

Kleiner, S., Condor, B. (2007). *The Good Mood Diet: Feel Great While You Lose Weight*. New York, NY: Springboard Press.

Kleinke, C. L. (2007). What does it mean to cope? *The praeger handbook on stress and coping (vol.2)*. (pp. 289-308). Westport, CT: Praeger Publishers/Greenwood Publishing Group.

Kluger, J. (2007, October 29). *The power of birth order*. Time.

Klüver, H. & Bucy, P. C. (1937). "Psychic blindness" and other symptoms following bilateral temporal lobectomy in rhesus monkeys. *American Journal of Physiology 119*, 352-353.

Knight, B. G., Kaskie, B., Shurgot, G. R., & Dave, J. (2006). Improving the mental health of older adults. In J. E. Birren & K. W. Schaie (Eds.), *Handbook of the psychology of aging (6th ed.)*. San Diego, CA: Elsevier.

Knott, G. W., Holtmaat, A., Wilbrecht, L., Welker, E., & Svoboda, K. (2006). Spine growth precedes synapse formation in the adult neocortex in vivo. *Nature Neuroscience*. 9: 1117-24.

Knudson, E. I. (2004). Sensitive Periods in the Development of the Brain and Behavior. *Journal of Cognitive Neuroscience, 16*, 1412-25.

Knutson, B., Wolkowitz, O., Cole, S., Chan, T., Moore, E., Johnson, R., et al. (1998). Selective alteration of personality and social behavior by serotonergic intervention. *American Journal of Psychiatry, 155*: 373-379.

Kobasa, S. C. O. (1987). Stress responses and personality. *Gender and stress*. (pp. 308-329). New York, NY: Free Press.

Kobasa, S. C. O. (1990). Stress-resistant personality. *The healing brain: A scientific reader*. (pp. 219-230). New York, NY: Guilford Press.

Kobrin, J. L., Patterson, B. F., Shaw, E. J., Mattern, K. D., & Barbuti, S. M. (2008). *Validity of the SAT for predicting first-year college grade point average*. New York, NY: The College Board.

Koch, W. J., & Haring, M. (2008). Posttraumatic stress disorder. In M. Hersen & J. Rosqvist (Eds.), *Handbook of psychological assessment, case conceptualization, and treatment, Vol. 1: Adults* (pp. 263-290). Hoboken, NJ: John Wiley & Sons.

Koenig, H. G., & Cohen, H. J. (2002). Psychosocial factors, immunology, and wound healing. *The link between religion and health: Psychoneuroimmunology and the faith factor*. (pp. 124-138). New York, NY: Oxford University Press.

Koenigs, M., Young, L., Adolphs, R., Tranel, D., Cushman, F., Hauser, M., et al. (2007). Damage to the prefontal cortex increases utilitarian moral judgements. *Nature, 446*(7138): 908-911.

Kohlberg, L. (1963). The development of children's orientations toward a moral order: I. sequence in the development of moral thought. *Vita Humana, 6*(1-2), 11-33.

Kohlberg, L. (1994). The claim to moral adequacy of a highest stage of moral judgment. In B. Puka (Ed.), *The great justice debate: Kohlberg criticism*. (pp. 2-18). New York, NY: Garland Publishing.

Kohlberg, L. (2008). The development of children's orientations toward a moral order: I. sequence in the development of moral thought. *Human Development, 51*(1), 8-20.

Kohler, P. K., Manhart, L. E., & Lafferty, W. E. (2008). Abstinence-only and comprehensive sex education and the initiation of sexual activity and teen pregnancy. *Journal of Adolescent Health, 42*(4): 324-326.

Kohn, M. L. & Schooler, C. (1973). Occupational experience and psychological functioning: An assessment of reciprocal effects. *American Sociological Review, 38*(1), 97-118.

Kohn, P. M. (1996). On coping adaptively with daily hassles. In M. Zeidner and N. S. Endler (eds.), *Handbook of Coping: Theory, Research, Aapplications*. New York, NY: John Wiley & Sons, Inc.

Kohn, P. M., Lafreniere, K., & Gurevitch, M. (1990). The inventory of college students' recent life experiences: A decontaminated hassle scale for a special population. *Journal of Behavioral Medicine, 13:* 619-630.

Koivisto Hursti, U.K. (1999). Factors influencing children's food choice. *Annals of Medicine, Suppl, 1*, 26-32.

Kolb, B. & Whishaw, I. Q. (2009). *Fundamentals of human neuropsychology (6th ed.)*. New York, NY: Worth Publishers.

Komaroff, A. L., Masuda, M., & Holmes, T. H. (1986). The Social Readjustment Rating Scale: A comparative study of Negro, white, and Mexican Americans. *Journal of Psychosomatic Research., 12*, 121-128.

Komaroff, A. L., Masuda, M., & Holmes, T. H. (1989). The Social Readjustment Rating Scale: A comparative study of Black, white, and Mexican Americans. In T. H. Holmes and E. M. David (Eds.), *Life change, life events, and illness*. New York, NY: Praeger.

Komiyama, O., Wang, K., Svensson, P., Arendt-Nielsen, L., Kawara, M., & De Laat, A. (2009). Ethnic differences regarding sensory, pain, and reflex responses in the trigeminal region. *Clinical Neurophysiology, 120*, 384-9.

Koob, G. F., & LeMoal, M. (2008). Addiction and the brain antireward system. In S. Fiske, D. L. Schacter, & R. Sternberg (Eds.), *Annual review of psychology—Volume 59*. Palo Alto, CA: Annual reviews.

Korchin, S. J., & Sands, S. H. (1983). Principles common to all psychotherapies. In C. E. Walker (Ed.), *The handbook of clinical psychology*. Homewood, IL: Dow Jones-Irwin.

Kornhaber M. L. & Gardner, H. (2006). Multiple Intelligences: Developments in Implementation and Theory. In R. J. Sternberg & M. A. Constas (Eds.) *Translating theory and research into educational practice: Developments in content domains, large-scale reform, and intellectual capacity*. (pp. 255-276). Mahwah, NJ: Lawrence Erlbaum Associates Publishers.

Kosslyn, S. M. & Keonig, O. (1995). *Wet mind: The new cognitive neuroscience*. New York, NY: Free Press.

Kosslyn, S. M., & Rosenberg, R. S. (2004). *Psychology: The brain, the person, the world* (2nd ed.). Essex, England: Pearson Education Limited.

Kosten, T.R., George, T.P., & Kleber, H.D. (2005). The neurobiology of substance dependence: Implications for treatment. In R.J. Frances A.H. Mack, & S.I. Miller (Eds.), *Clinical textbook of addictive disorder* (3rd edition). New York, NY: Guilford Press.

Kosten, T.R., Sofuoglu, M., & Gardner, T.J. (2008). Clinical management: Cocaine. In H.D. Kleber & M Galanter (Eds.), *The American Psychiatric Publishing textbook of substance abuse treatment* (4th edition). Washington, DC: American Psychiatric Publishing.

Koury, M. A. & Rapaport, M. H. (2007). Quality of life impairment in anxiety disorders. In M. S. Ritsner & A. G. Awad (Eds.), *Quality of life impairment in schizophrenia, mood and anxiety disorders: New perspectives on research and treatment*. The Netherlands: Springer.

Krantz, D. S., & McCeney, M. K. (2002). Effects of psychological and social factors on organic disease: A critical assessment of research on coronary heart disease. *Annual Review of Psychology, 53*(1), 341-369.

Krantz, G., Berntsson, L., Lundberg, U. (2005). Total workload, work stress, and perceived symptoms in Swedish male and female white-collar employees. *European Journal of Public Health, 15:* 209-214.

Krebs, D. L., & Denton, K. (2006). Explanatory Limitations of Cognitive-Developmental Approaches to Morality. *Psychological Review, 113*, 672-675.

Kring, A. M. & Bachorowski, J. (1999). *Emotions and psychopathology, 13*(5), 575-599.

Krueger, R. F., South, S., Johnson, W., & Iacono, W. (2008). The heritability of personality is not always 50%: Gene-environment interactions and correlations between personality and parenting. *Journal of Personality, 76*(6): 1485-1522.

Krueger, R. G., & Kaplan, M. S. (2002). Behavioral and psychopharmacological treatment of the paraphilic and hypersexual disorders. *Journal of Psychiatric Practices, 8*(1), 21-32.

Krüetzen, M., Mann, J., Heithaus, M. R., Connor, R. C., Bejder, L. & Sherwin, W. B. (2005). Cultural transmission of tool use in bottlenose dolphins. *Proceedings of the National Academy of Sciences USA, 102*, 8939-43.

Ksir, C., Hart, C. L., & Oakley, R. (2008). *Drugs, society, and human behavior (12th ed.)*. Boston, MA: McGraw-Hill.

Kuboshima-Amemori, S. & Sawaguchi, T. (2007). Plasticity of the primate prefrontal cortex. *Neuroscientist, 13*, 229-40.

Kudwa, A. E., Michopoulos, V., Gatewood, J. D., & Rissman, E. F. (2006). Roles of estrogen receptors alpha and beta in differentiation of mouse sexual behavior. *Neuroscience, 138*(3): 921-8.

Kuhn, T. S. (1962). *The structure of scientific revolutions*. Chicago, IL: University of Chicago Press.

Kuncel, N. R., Hezlett, S. A., & Ones, D. S. (2004). Academic performance, career potential, creativity, and job performance: Can one construct predict them all? *Journal of Personality and Social Psychology, 86*(1), 148-161.

Kung, W. V. (2004). Cultural and practical barriers to seeking mental health treatment for Chinese Americans. *American Journal of Community Psychology, 32*(1), 27-43.

Kuppens, P., Realo, A., & Diener, E. (2008). The role of positive and negative emotions in life satisfaction judgment across nations. *Journal of Personality and Social Psychology, 95*(1): 66-75.

Kutner, L. & Olson, C. (2008). *Grand Theft Childhood: The Surprising Truth About Violent Video Games and What Parents Can Do*. New York, NY: Simon & Schuster.

Kyle, J. G. (1980). Auditory deprivation from birth—Clarification of some issues. *British Journal of Audiology 14*, 34-6.

L

LaBerge, S. (2007). Lucid dreaming. In D. Barrett & P. McNamara (Eds.), *The new science of dreaming: Volume 2. Content, recall, and personality correlates*. Westport, CT: Praeger Publishers/Greenwood Publishing Group.

Lachman, R., Lachman, J.L., & Butterfield, E.C. (1979). *Cognitive Psychology and Information Processing*. Hillsdale, NJ: Erlbaum.

Lack, L. C. & Bootzin, R. R. (2003). Circadian rhythm factors in insomnia and their treatment. In M. L. Perlis & K. L. Lichstein (Eds.), *Treating sleep disorders: Principles and practice of behavioral sleep medicine*. New York, NY: John Wiley & Sons, Inc.

Lagercrantz, H. & Changeux. J.P. (2009). The emergence of human consciousness: from fetal to neonatal life. *Pediatric Research, 65*, 255-60.

LaGraize, S. C., Borzan, J., Rinker, M. M., Kopp, J. L., & Fuchs, P. N. (2004). Behavioral evidence for competing motivational drives of nociception and hunger. *Neuroscience Letters, 372*(1/2): 30-34.

Lahey, B. B., Kupfer, D. L., Beggs, V. E., & Landon, D. (1982). Do learning-disabled children exhibit peripheral deficits in selective attention? An analysis of eye movements during reading. *Journal of Abnormal Child Psychology, 10*, 1-10.

Lahey, B. B. & Waldman, I. D. (2007). Personality dispositions and the development of violence and conduct problems. In D.J. Flannery, A.T. Vazsonyi, & I.D. Irwin (Eds.), *The Cambridge handbook of violent behavior and aggression*. New York, NY: Cambridge University Press.

Lakhan, S. E. (2007). Neuropsychological Generation of Source Amnesia: An Episodic Memory Disorder of the Frontal Brain. J. Med, 1. Retrieved from http://www.scientificjournals.org/journals2007/articles/1038.html.

Lamb, M. E., & Day, R. D. (Eds.). (2004). *Conceptualizing and measuring father involvement*. Mahwah, NJ: Erlbaum.

Lambert, K., & Kinsley, C. H. (2005). *Clinical neuroscience: The neurobiological foundations of mental health*. New York, NY: Worth Publishers.

Landon, T. M., & Barlow, D. H. (2004). Cognitive-behavioral treatment for panic disorder: Current status. *Journal of Psychiatric. Practices, 10*(4), 211-226.

Lang, P. J. (1993). The three systems approach to emotion. In N. Birbaumer & A. Öhman (Eds.), *The organization of motion* (pp. 18-30). Toronto, Canada: Hogrefe-Huber.

Lang, P. J., Bradley, M. M., & Cuthbert, B. N. (1998). Emotion, motivation, and anxiety: Brain mechanisms and psychophysiology. *Biological Psychiatry, 44*, 1248-1263.

Lang, P. J., Greenwald, M. K., & Bradley, M. M. (1993). Looking at pictures: Affective, facial, visceral, and behavioral reactions. *Psychophysiology, 30*, 261-273.

Lange, C. G. (1885). The mechanism of the emotions. Paper originally published in 1885 and reprinted in B. Rand (Ed.), *The classical psychologists* (pp. 672-684). Boston, MA: Houghton Mifflin (1921).

Lange, R. T. & Iverson, G. L. (2008). Concurrent validity of Wechsler adult intelligence scales—third edition index score short forms in the Canadian standardization sample. *Educational and Psychological Measurement, 68*(1), 139-153.

Langens, T. A., & Morth, S. (2003). Repressive coping and the use of passive and active coping strategies. *Personality and Individual Differences, 35*(2), 461-473.

Langer, E. J., & Rodin, J. (2004). The effects of choice and enhanced personal responsibility for the aged: A field experiment in an institutional setting. *The interface of social and clinical psychology: Key readings*. (pp. 339-348). New York, NY: Psychology Press.

Langlois, J. H. & Stephan, C. W. (1981). Beauty and the beast: The role of physical attractiveness in the development of peer relations and social behavior. In S. S. Brehm, S. M. Kassin, & F. X. Gibbons (eds.), *Developmental social psychology*. New York, NY: Oxford University Press.

Långström, N. & Seto, M.C. (2006). Exhibitionist and voyeuristic behavior in a Swedish national population survey. *Archives of Sexual Behavior, 35*, 27-435.

Lankau, M. J., Riordan, C. M., & Thomas, C. H. (2005). The effects of similarity and liking in formal relationships between mentors and protégés. *Journal of Vocational Behavior, 67*(2): 252-265.

Lanting, C.P., de Kleine, E., & van Dijk, P. (2009). Neural activity underlying tinnitus generation: results from PET and fMRI. *Hearing Research, 255*, 1-13.

LaPiere, R. (1934). Attitudes versus actions. *Social Forces, 13*: 230-237.

Larach, V. W., Zambroni, R. T., Mancini, H. R., Mancini, R. R., & Gallado, R. T. (1997). New strategies for old problems: Tardive dyskinesia (TD). Review and report on severe TD cases treated with clorapine, with 12, 8 and 5 years of video follow-up. *Schizophrenic Research, 28*: 231-46.

Larimer, M. E., Kilmer, J. R., & Lee, C. M. (2005). College student drug prevention: A review of individually-oriented prevention strategies. *Journal of Drug Issues, 35*(2): 431-456.

Larimer, M. E. & Neighbors, C. (2003). Normative misperception and the impact of descriptive and injunctive norms on college student gambling. *Psychology of Addictive Behaviors, 17*(3): 235-243.

Larimer, M. E., Turner, A. P., Mallett, K. A., & Geisner, I. M. (2004). Predicting drinking behavior and alcohol-related problems among fraternity and sorority members: Examining the role of descriptive and injunctive norms. *Psychology of Addictive Behaviors, 18*(3): 203-212.

Larsen, J. T., McGraw, A. P., & Cacioppo, J. T. (2001). Can people feel happy and sad at the same time? *Journal of Personality and Social Psychology, 81*(4), 684-696.

Larsen, J. T., McGraw, A. P., Mellers, B. A., & Cacioppo, J. T. (2004). The agony of victory and thrill of defeat: Mixed emotional reactions to disappointing wins and relieving losses. *Psychological Science, 15(5)*, 325-330.

Larsen, J. T., To, Y. M., & Fireman, G., (2007). Children's understanding and experience of mixed emotions. *Psychological Science, 18(2)*, 186-191.

Larsen, L., Hartmann, P., & Nyborg, H. (2008). The stability of general intelligence from early adulthood to middle-age. *Intelligence, 36(1)*, 29-34.

Larsen, R. J. (2000). Toward a science of mood regulation. *Psychological Inquiry, 11*, 129-141.

Larsen, R. J. & Diener, E. (1987). Affect intensity as an individual difference characteristic: A review. *Journal of Research in Personality, 21*, 1-39.

Larsen, R. J., Diener, E., & Emmons, R. A. (1986). Affect intensity and reactions to daily life events. *Journal of Personality and Social Psychology, 51*, 803-814.

Larson, E. B., Wang, L., Bowen, J. D., McCormick, W. C., Teri, L., Crane, P., & Kukull, W. (2006). Exercise is associated with reduced risk of incident dementia among persons 65 ears of age and older. *Annals of Internal Medicine, 144*, 73-81.

Lashley, K. S. (1929). *Brain mechanisms and intelligence: A quantitative study of injuries to the brain.* Chicago, IL: University of Chicago Press.

Lashley, K. S. (1948). Brain mechanisms and intelligence, 1929. In W. Dennis (Ed.), *Readings in the history of psychology.* (pp. 557-570). East Norwalk, CT: Appleton-Century-Crofts.

Lashley, K. S. (1988). In search of the engram. In J. A. Anderson, & E. Rosenfeld (Eds.), *Neurocomputing: Foundations of research.* (pp. 59-63) Cambridge, MA: MIT Press.

Laslo, P., Lipski, J., Nicholson, L. F., Miles, G. B., & Funk, G. D. (2001). GluR2 AMPA receptor subunit expression in motoneurons at low and high risk for degeneration in amyotrophic lateral sclerosis. *Experimental Neurology.* 169: 461-71.

Latane, B. & Darley, J. M. (1968). Group inhibition of bystander intervention in emergencies. *Journal of Personality and Social Psychology, 10*: 215-221.

Latane, B. & Darley, J. M. (1970). *The unresponsive bystander: Why doesn't he help?* Englewood Cliffs, NJ: Prentice Hall.

Latane, B., Williams, K., & Harkins, S. G. (1979). Many hands make light the work: The cause and consequences of social loafing. *Journal of Personality and Social Psychology, 37*: 822-832.

Laumann, E. O., Gagnon, J. H., Michael, R. T., & Michaels, S. (1994). *The social organization of sexuality.* Chicago, IL: University of Chicago Press.

Laumann, E. O., Paik, A., & Rosen, R. C. (1999). Sexual dysfunction in the United States: Prevalence and predictors. *JAMA: Journal of the American Medical Association, 281(6)*, 537-544.

Laumann, E.O., Nicolosi, A., Glasser, D.B., Paik, A., Gingell, C., Moreira, E., et al. (2005). Sexual problems among women and men aged 40-80 years: Prevalence and correlates identified in the Global Study of Sexual Attitudes and Behaviors. *International Journal of Impotence Research, 17*, 39-57.

Lavie, P. (2001). Sleep-wake as a biological rhythm. *Annual Review of Psychology, 52*, 277-303.

Lavoie, J. L. (2003). Minireview: Overview of the Renin-Angiotensin System—An Endocrine and Paracrine System. *Endocrinology, 144(6)*, 2179-2183.

Law, J., Masters, R., Bray, S. R., Eves, F., & Bardswell, I. (2003). Motor performance as a function of audience affability and metaknowledge. *Journal of Sport & Exercise Psychology, 25(4)*, 484-500.

Lawford, B. R., Young, R. McD., Rowell, J. A., Gibson, J. N., et al. (1997). Association of the D2 dopamine receptor A1 allele with alcoholism: Medical severity alcoholism and type of controls. *Biological Psychiatry, 41*, 386-393.

Lawson, R. (1987). Scandal in the Adventist-funded program to 'heal' homosexuals: Failure, sexual exploitation, official silence, and attempts to rehabilitate the exploiter and his methods. Paper presented at the annual convention of the American Sociological Association. Chicago, Illinois.

Lazar, I. & Darlington, R. B. (1982). Lasting effects of early education: A report from the consortium for longitudinal studies. *Monographs of the Society for Research in Child Development, 47(2-3)*, 1-151.

Lazarus, R. S. (1993). Why we should think of stress as a subset of emotion. *Handbook of stress: Theoretical and clinical aspects (2nd ed.).* (pp. 21-39). New York, NY: Free Press.

Lazarus, R. S. (1993). From psychological stress to the emotions: A history of changing outlooks. *Annual Review of Psychology, 44*, 1-21.

Lazarus, R. S. (1999). *Stress and emotion: A new synthesis.* New York, NY: Springer Publishing Co.

Lazarus, R. S. (2007). Stress and emotion: A new synthesis. In A. Monat, R. S. Lazarus, & G. Reevy (Eds.) *The Praeger handbook on stress and coping (vol.1)* pp. 33-51. Westport, CT: Praeger Publishers/ Greenwood Publishing Group.

Lazarus, R. S. & Alfert, E. (1964). The short-circuiting of threat by experimentally altering cognitive appraisal. *Journal of Abnormal and Social Psychology, 69*, 195-205.

Lazarus, R. S., Opton, E. M., Jr., Nomikos, M. S., & Rankin, N. O. (1965). The principle of short-circuiting of threat: Further evidence. *Journal of Personality, 33*, 622-635.

Leahey, T. H. (2000). *A History of Psychology.* (5th ed.) Upper Saddle River, NJ: Prentice Hall.

Leahey, T. H. (2005). Mind as a scientific object: A historical-philosophical exploration. In C. E. Erneling, & D. M. Johnson (Eds.), *The mind as a scientific object: Between brain and culture.* (pp. 35-78). New York, NY: Oxford University Press.

Leavitt, M. O., Spellings, M., & Gonzales, A. R. (2007). *Report to the President on Issues Raised by the Virginia Tech Tragedy.* Washington, D.C.

Lechner, S. C., Stoelb, B. L., & Antoni, M. H. (2008). Group-based therapies for benefit finding in cancer. *Trauma, recovery, and growth: Positive psychological perspectives on posttraumatic stress.* (pp. 207-231). Hoboken, NJ: John Wiley & Sons Inc.

Lechner, S. C., Tennen, H., & Affleck, G. (2009). Benefit-finding and growth. *Oxford handbook of positive psychology (2nd ed.).* (pp. 633-640). New York, NY: Oxford University Press.

Lecic-Tosevski, D., Gavrilovic, J., Knezevic, G., & Priebe, S. (2003). Personality factors and posttraumatic stress: Associations in civilians one year after air attacks. *Journal of Personality Disorders, 17(6)*, 537-549.

LeCroy, C. W. (2005). Building an effective primary prevention program for adolescent girls: Empirically based design and evaluation. *Brief Treatment and Crisis Interventtion, 5*(1), 75-84.

Ledikwe, J. H., Ello-martin, J. A., & Rolls, B. J. (2005). Portion sizes and the obesity epidemic. *Journal of Nutrition,* 135: 905-909.

LeDoux, J. (1996). *The emotional brain.* New York: Touchstone.

LeDoux, J. (2003). The emotional brain, fear, and the amygdala. *Cellular and Molecular Neurobiology, 23,* 727-38.

LeDoux, J. (2007). The amygdala. *Current Biology, 17*: R868-74.

LeDoux, J. E. (1995). Emotions: Clues from the brain. *Annual Review of Psychology, 46,* 209-235.

Ledoux, J. E. (1996). *The emotional brain: The mysterious underpinnings of emotional life.* New York, NY: Simon and Schuster.

LeDoux, J. E. (1998). Where the Wild Things Are. *The Emotional Brain (pp. 225-266).* New York, NY: Simon & Schuster.

LeDoux, J. E. (1999). The power of emotions. In R. Conlan (ed.), *States of Mind: New Discoveries about How Our Brains Make Us Who We Are.* New York: John Wiley & Sons, Inc.

LeDoux, J. E. (2000). Emotion circuits in the brain. *Annual Review of Neuroscience, 23,* 155-84.

LeDoux, J. E. (2008). Remembrance of emotions past. In M. H. Immordino-Yang (Ed.), *The Jossey-Bass reader on the brain and learning.* (pp. 151-179) San Francisco, CA: Jossey-Bass.

Lee, E. S. (1961). Negro intelligence and selective migration. In J. J. Jenkins & D. G. Paterson (Eds.), *Studies in individual differences: The search for intelligence.* (pp. 669-676) East Norwalk, CT: Appleton-Century-Crofts.

Lehrer, J. (2007). *Proust was a Neuroscientist.* Houghton Mifflin Harcourt.

Leiblum, S. R. (2007). Sex therapy today: Current issues and future perspectives. *Principles and practice of sex therapy (4th ed.).* (pp. 3-22) New York, NY: Guilford Press.

Lekander, M. (2002). Ecological immunology: The role of the immune system in psychology and neuroscience. *European Psychiatry, 7*(2), 98-115.

Lemmon, K. & Moore, C. (2007). The development of prudence in the face of varying future rewards. *Developmental Science, 10(4)*: 502-11.

Lenzenweger, M. F., Lane, M. C., Loranger, A. W., & Kessler, R. C. (2007). DSM-IV personality disorders in the national comorbidity survey replication. *Biological Psychiatry, 62(6)*: 553-564.

Leonard, H. & Wen, X. (2002). The epidemiology of mental retardation: Challenges and opportunities in the new millennium. *Mental Retardation and Developmental Disabilities Research Reviews, 7,* 117-134.

Leontiev, D. A. (2008). Maslow yesterday, today, and tomorrow. *Journal of Humanistic Psychology, 48(4)*: 451-453.

Lepore, S. J., Evans, G. W., & Palsane, M. N. (1991). Social hassles and psychological health in the context of chronic crowding. *Journal of Health and Social Behavior, 32*(4), 357-367.

Leppänen, J. M. & Hietanen, J. K. (2007). Is there more in a happy face than just a big smile? *Visual Cognition, 15*(4), 468-490.

Leuner, B., Falduto, J., & Shors, T. J. (2003). Associative memory formation increases the observation of dendritic spines in the hippocampus. *The Journal of Neuroscience, 23,* 659-65.

Leuner, B., Gould, E., & Shors, T. J. (2006) Is there a link between adult neurogenesis and learning? *Hippocampus, 16*(3): 216-24.

Levay, S. (1991). A difference in hypothalamic structure between heterosexual and homosexual men. *Science, 253*: 1034-1037.

Leventhal, E.A., Leventhal, H., Shacham, S., & Easterling, D.V. (1989). Active coping reduces reports of pain from childbirth. *Journal of Consulting and Clinical Psychology, 57,* 365-371.

Levi-Montalcini, R. (1988). *In Praise of Imperfection: My Life and Work.* New York, NY: Basic Books.

Levin, J. (2000). A prolegomenon to an epidemiology of love: Theory, measurement, and health outcomes. *Journal of Social & Clinical Psychology, 19*(1): 117-136.

Levy, K. N., Reynoso, J. S., Wasserman, R. H., & Clarkin, J. F. (2007). Narcissistic personality disorder. In W. O'Donohue, K. A. Fowler, & S. O. Lilienfeld (eds.), *Personality Disorders: Toward the DSM-V.* (233-277) Sage Publications.

Lewin, E. (2004). Does marriage have a future? *Journal of Marriage and Family, 66*(4), 1000-1006.

Lewin, K. (1935). *A dynamic theory of personality.* New York, NY: McGraw-Hill.

Lewin, T. (2008). Study finds little benefit in new SAT. *The New York Times.* 157(54, 345).

Lewinsohn, P. M., Clarke, G. N., Hops, H., & Andrews, J. (1990). Cognitive-behavioral treatment for depressed adolescents. *Behavior Therapy, 21,* 385-401.

Lewinsohn, P. M., Rohde, P., Teri, L., & Tilson, M. (1990, April). Presentation. Western Psychological Association.

Lewis, C., & Lamb. M. E. (2003). Fathers' influences on child development: The evidence from two-parent families. *European Journal of Psychology of Education, 18*(2), 211-228.

Lewis, M. & Brooks-Gunn, J. (1979). *Social cognition and the acquisition of self.* New York, NY: Plenum.

Lewis, M. (1991). Ways of knowing: Objective self-awareness or consciousness. *Developmental Review, 11,* 231-243.

Lewis, M. (1992). *Shame: The exposed self.* New York, NY: Free Press.

Lewis, M. (1995). Embarrassment: The emotion of self-exposure. In J. P. Tangney & K. W. Fischer (Eds.), *The self-conscious emotions: The psychology of shame, guilt, embarrassment, and pride* (pp. 198-218). New York, NY: The Guilford Press.

Lewis, M. (2000). The emergence of human emotions. In M. Lewis & J. M. Haviland-Jones (Eds.) *Handbook of Emotions, Second Edition* (pp. 265-280). New York, NY: The Guilford Press.

Lewis, M. (2005). Origins of the self-conscious child. In W. R. Crozier, & L. E. Alden (Eds.), *The essential handbook of social anxiety for clinicians.* (pp. 81-98) Hoboken, NJ: John Wiley & Sons, Inc.

Lewis, M. (2007). Self-conscious emotional development. In J. L. Tracy, R. W. Robins, & J. P. Tangney (Eds.), *The self-conscious emotions: Theory and research.* (pp. 134-149) New York, NY: The Guilford Press.

Lewis, M. (2008). The emergence of human emotions. *Handbook of emotions (3rd ed.).* (pp. 304-319) New York, NY: Guilford Press.

Lewis, R. J., Derlega, V. J., Griffin, J. L., & Krowinski, A. C. (2003). Stressors for gay men and lesbians: Life stress, gay-related stress, stigma consciousness, and depressive symptoms. *Journal of Social and Clinical Psychology, 22*(6): 716-729.

Lewis-Harter, S. (2000). Psychosocial adjustment of adult children of alcoholics. A review of the recent empirical literature. *Clinical Psychology Review, 20*(3), 311-337.

Lewontin, R. (1976). Race and intelligence. In N.J. Block & G. Dworkin (Eds.), *The IQ controversy: Critical readings.* New York, NY: Pantheon.

Lewontin, R. (1982). *Human diversity*. New York, NY: Scientific American Library.

Lewontin, R. C. (1976). Science and politics: An explosive mix. *PsycCRITIQUES, 21*(2), 97-98.

Lewontin, R. C. (2001). Gene, organism and environment. *Cycles of contingency: Developmental systems and evolution.* (pp. 59-66) Cambridge, MA: The MIT Press.

Li, W., Howard, J.D., Parrish, T.B., & Gottfried, J.A. (2008). Aversive learning enhances perceptual and cortical discrimination of indiscriminable odor cues. *Science, 319*, 1842-5.

Lian, J., Goldstein, A., Donchin, E., & He, B. (2002). Cortical potential imaging of episodic memory encoding. *Brain Topography, 15*(1), 29-36.

Liddell, H. S. (1950). Animal origins of anxiety. *Feelings and emotions; the mooseheart symposium.* (pp. 181-188) New York, NY: McGraw-Hill.

Liang, C. T. H., Alvarez, A. N., Juang, L. P., & Liang, M. X. (2009). The role of coping in the relationship between perceived racism and racism-related stress for asian americans: Gender differences. *Asian American Journal of Psychology*, S(1), 56-69.

Liden, R. C., Wayne, S. J., Jaworski, R. A., & Bennett, N. (2004). Social loafing: A field investigation. *Journal of Management, 30*(2): 285-304.

Lieberman, M. D., Jarcho, J. M., & Obayashi, J. (2005). Attributional inference across cultures: Similar automatic attributions and different controlled corrections. *Personality and Social Psychology Bulletin, 31*(7): 889-901.

Lieberson, A. D. (2004). How long can a person survive without food? *Scientific American.* Downloaded on June 25 from: http://www.scientificamerican.com/article.cfm?id=how-long-can-a-person-sur.

Liem, D.G. & Mennella, J.A. (2003). Heightened sour preferences during childhood. *Chemical Senses, 28*, 173-80.

Lilienfeld, S. O., Wood, J. M., & Garb, H. N. (2000). The scientific status of projective techniques. *Psychological Science in the Public Interest, 1*: 27-66.

Lindsay, D. S., Hagen, L., Read, J. D., Wade, K. A., & Garry, M. (2004). True photographs and false memories. *Psychological Science, 15*(3), 149-154.

Linehan, M. M. (1993). *Cognitive-behavioral treatment of borderline personality disorder* New York, NY: The Guilford Press.

Linehan, M. M. & Dexter-Mazza, E. (2008). Dialectical behavior therapy for borderline personality disorder. In D. H. Barlow (Ed.), *Clinical handbook of psychological disorders: A step-by-step treatment manual (4th ed.).* (pp. 365-420) New York, NY: The Guilford Press.

Ling, K., Beenen, G., Ludford, P., Wang, X., Chang, K., Li, Z., Cosley, D., Frankowski, D., Terveen, L., Rashid, A.M., Resnick, P., & Kraut, R. (2005). Using social psychology to motivate contributions to online communities. *Journal of Computer-mediated Communication, 10*: article 10.

Linville, P. W., Fischer, G. W., & Fischhoff, B. (1993). AIDS risk perceptions and decision biases. In J. B. Pryor & G. D. Reeder (Eds.), *The Social psychology of HIV infection.* Hillsdale, NJ: Lawrence Erlbaum Associates.

Lipsitt, L. P., Pederson, L. J., & Delucia, C. A. (1966). Conjugate reinforcement of operant responding in infants. *Psychonomic Science, 4*(2), 67-68.

Lipton, A. A., & Simon, F. S. (1985). Psychiatric diagnosis in a state hospital: Manhattan State revisited. *Hospital and Community Psychiatry, 36*(4), 368-373.

Litman, J. (2005). Curiosity and the pleasures of learning: Wanting and liking new information. *Cognition & Emotion, 19*(6): 793-814.

Livesley, W., Jang, K., & Vernon, P. (2003). Genetic Basis of Personality Structure. In I. B. Weiner (Series Ed.), T. Millon, & M. J. Lerner (Vol. Eds.), *Handbook of Psychology: Vol. 5. Personality and Social Psychology,* (59-84).

Llinás, R. R. (2001). *I of the vortex: From neurons to self.* Cambridge, MA: MIT Press.

Llinás, R. R., & Ribary, U. (2001). Consciousness and the brain: The thalamocortical dialogue in health and disease. *Annals of the New York Academy of Sciences, 929*, 166-175.

Locke, E. A. (2007). The case for inductive theory building. *Journal of Management, 33*(6), 867-890.

Loehlin, J.C. (1992). *Genes and environment in personality development.* Newbury Park, CA: Sage.

Loessl, B., Valerius, G., Kopasz, M., Hornyak, M., Riemann, D., & Voderholzer, U. (2008). Are adolescents chronically sleep-deprived? An investigation of sleep habits of adolescents in the southwest of Germany. *Child: Care, Health and Development, 34*, 549-556.

Loewenstein, R. J. (2007). Dissociative identity disorder: Issues in the iatrogenesis controversy. In D. Spiegel, E. Vermetten, & M. Dorahy (Eds.), *Traumatic dissociation: Neurobiology and treatment.* Washington, DC: American Psychiatric Publishing.

Loewenthal, K. (2007). *Religion, culture and mental health.* New York, NY: Cambridge University Press.

Loewi, O. (1957). On the background of the discovery of neurochemical transmission. *Journal of Mount Sinai Hospital, N Y, 24*, 1014-6.

Loftus, E. F. (2005). Planting misinformation in the human mind: A 30-year investigation of the malleability of memory. *Learning & Memory, 12*(4), 361-366.

Loftus, E. F. & Loftus, G. R. (1980). On the permanence of stored information in the human brain. *American Psychologist, 35*(5), 409-420.

Loftus, E. F., Miller, D. G., & Burns, H. J. (1978). Semantic integration of verbal information into a visual memory. *Journal of Experimental Psychology: Human Learning and Memory, 4*(1), 19-31.

Lopez, J. F., Chalmers, D., Little, K. Y., & Watson, S. J. (1998). Regulation of 5HT1a receptor, glucocorticoid and mineralocorticoid receptor in rat and human hippocampus: Implications for the neurobiology of depression. *Biological Psychiatry, 43*: 547-573.

LoPiccolo, J. (1995). Sexual disorders and gender identity disorders. In R. J. Comer, *Abnormal Psychology* (2nd edition). New York: W.H. Freeman.

LoPiccolo, J. (2004). Sexual disorders affecting men. *Handbook of primary care psychology.* (pp. 485-494) New York, NY: Oxford University Press.

LoPiccolo, J. & Stock, W. E. (1987). Sexual function, dysfunction, and counseling in gynecological practice. In Rosenwaks, F. Benjamin, & M. L. Stone (Eds.). *Gynecology.* New York: Macmillan.

Lorenz, K. (1937/1957). The conception of instinctive behavior. In C. H. Skiller (Ed. & Trans.), *Instinctive behavior* (pp. 129-175). New York, NY: International Universities Press.

Lott, A. J. & Lott, B. E. (1974). The role of reward in the formation of positive interpersonal attitudes. In T. L. Huston (ed.), *Foundation of Interpersonal attraction* (pp. 171-189). New York, NY: Academic Press.

Lounsbury, J. W., Fisher, L. A., Levy, J. J., & Welsh, D. P. (2009). An investigation of character strengths in relation to the academic success of college students. *Individual Differences Research, 7*(1), 52-69.

Lounsbury, J. W., Sundstrom, E., Loveland, J. M., & Gibson, L. W. (2003). Intelligence, "big five" personality traits, and work drive as predictors of course grade. *Personality and Individual Differences, 35*(6), 1231-1239.

Lourenç, O. & Machado, A. (1996). In defense of Piaget's theory: A reply to 10 common criticisms. *Psychological Review, 103*, 143-164.

Lövheim, H., Sandman, P., Karlsson, S., & Gustafson, Y. (2009). Sex differences in the prevalence of behavioral and psychological symptoms of dementia. *International Psychogeriatrics, 21*(3), 469-475.

Löw, A., Lang, P. J., Smith, J. C., & Bradley, M. M. (2008). Both predator and prey: Emotional arousal in threat and reward. *Psychological Science, 19*(9), 865-873.

Lowry, C. A., Hale, M. W., Evans, A. K., Heerkens, J., Staub, D. R., Gasser, P. J., & Shekhar, A. (2008). Serotonergic systems, anxiety, and affective disorder: focus on the dorsomedial part of the dorsal raphe nucleus. *Annals of the New York Academy of Sciences.* 1148: 86-94.

Lu, L., and Shih, J. (1997) Personality and happiness: Is mental health a mediator? *Personality and Individual Differences, 22*, 249-56.

Lubinski, D. (2004). Introduction to the special section on cognitive abilities: 100 years after Spearman's (1904) "'General intelligence,' objectively determined and measured.". *Journal of Personality and Social Psychology, 86*(1), 96-111.

Luborsky, E. B., O'Reilly-Landry, M., & Arlow, J. A. (2008). Psychoanalysis. In R. J. Corsini & D. Wedding (Eds.), *Current psychotherapies* (8th ed.). Belmont, CA: Thomson Brooks/Cole.

Luborsky, L., Rosenthal, R., Diguer, L., Andrusyna. T. P., Levitt, J. T., Seligman, D. A., Berman, J. S., & Krause, E. D. (2003). Are some psychotherapies much more effective than others? *Journal of Applied and Psychoanalytic Studies, 5*(4), 455-460.

Luborsky, L., Singer, B., & Luborsky, L. (1975). Comparative studies of psychotherapies. *Archives of General Psychiatry, 32*, 995-1008.

Lucas, R. E. (2007). Adaptation and the set point model of subjective well-being: Does happiness change after major life events? *Current Directions in Psychological Science, 16*(2), 75-79.

Luh, C. W. (1922). The conditions of retention. *Psychological Monographs, 31.*

Luker, K. (2007). *When Sex Goes to School: Warring Views on Sex—and Sex Education—Since the Sixties.* New York, NY: Norton and Company.

Lumeng, J. C. & Hillman, K. H. (2007). Eating in larger groups increases food consumption. *Archives of Disease in Childhood, 92*(5): 384-7.

Luminet, O., Bouts, P., Delie, F., Manstead, A. S. R., & Rimé, B. (2000). Social sharing of emotion following exposure to a negatively valenced situation. *Cognition and Emotion 14*(5), 661-688.

Lundberg, U. (2000). Workplace stress. In G. Fink (ed.), *Encyclopedia of Stress, Vol. 3* (684-692). New York, NY: Academic Press.

Lundqvist, T. (2005). Cognitive consequences of cannabis use: Comparison with abuse of stimulants and heroin with regard to attention, memory and executive functions. *Pharmacol Biochem Behav., 81*, 330-391.

Luo, L. & O'Leary, D. D. (2005). Axon retraction and degeneration in development and disease. *Annual Review of Neuroscience.* 28: 127-56.

Lupien, S. J., Maheu, F., Tu, M., Fiocco, A., & Schramek, T. E. (2007). The effects of stress and stress hormones on human cognition: Implications for the field of brain and cognition. *Brain and Cognition, 65*(3), 209-237.

Lupien, S. J., Ouelle-Morin, I., Hupback, A., Walker, D., Tu, M. T., & Buss, C. (2006). Beyond the stress concept: Allostatic load—a developmental biological and cognitive perspective. In: D. Cicchetti (ed.), *Handbook Series on Developmental Psychopathology* (784-809). New York, NY: John Wiley & Sons.

Lüttke, H. B. (2004). Experimente unter dem milgram-paradigma. [experiments within the milgram paradigm.]. *Gruppendynamik Und Organisationsberatung, 35*(4): 431-464.

Lykken, D. & Tellegen, A. (1996). Happiness is a stochastic phenomenon. *7*(3), 186-189.

Lykken, D. T. (1995). *The antisocial personalities.* Mahwah, NJ: Lawrence Erlbaum Associates.

Lynam, D., Caspi, A., Moffitt, T., Wikstrom, P., Loeber, R., & Novak, S. (2000) The interaction between impulsivity and neighborhood context on offending: The effects of impulsivity are stronger in poorer neighborhoods. *Journal of Abnormal Psychology, 109:* 563 -574.

Lynch, G., Larson, J., Staubli, U., Ambros-Ingerson, J., & Granger, R. (1991). Long-term potentiation and memory operations in cortical networks. In R. G. Lister & H. J. Weingartner (Eds.), *Perspectives on cognitive neuroscience.* (pp. 110-131) New York, NY: Oxford University Press.

Lyneham, H. J., Abbott, M. J., & Rapee, R. M. (2007). Interrater reliability of the anxiety disorders interview schedule for DSM-IV: Child and parent version. *Journal of the American Academy of Child and Adolescent Psychiatry, 46*, 731-736.

Lynn, A. B. (2008). *The EQ interview: Finding employees with high emotional intelligence* New York: AMACOM.

Lynn, S. J. & Kirsch, I. (2006). Smoking cessation. In S. J. Lynn & I. Kirsch, *Essentials of clinical hypnosis: An evidence-based approach. Dissociation, trauma, memory, and hypnosis book series.* Washington, DC: American Psychological Association.

Lyttle, J. (2001). The effectiveness of humor in persuasion: The case of business ethics training. *Journal of General Psychology, 128*(2): 206-216.

Lytton, W. W., Omurtag, A., Neymotin, S. A., & Hines, M. L. (2008). Just-in-time connectivity for large spiking networks. *Neural Computation, 20*(11), 2745-2756.

M

MacDonald, M., Jamshidi, P., & Campbell, K. (2008). Infrequent increases in stimulus intensity may interrupt central executive functioning during rapid eye movement sleep. *Neuroreport: For Rapid Communication of Neuroscience Research, 19*(3), 309-313.

MacKinnon, D.W. & Hall, W.B. (1972). Intelligence and creativity. *Proceedings, XVIIth International Congress of Applied Psychology* (Volume 2, 1883-1888). Brussels: Editest.

MacLean, P. D. (1970). The triune brain, emotion and scientific bias. In F.O. Schmidt (Ed.), *The neurosciences: Second study program* (pp. 336-349). New York, NY: Rockefeller University Press.

Maddi, S. R. (2007). The story of hardiness: Twenty years of theorizing, research, and practice. *The praeger handbook on stress and cop-*

ing (vol.2). (pp. 327-340). Westport, CT: Praeger Publishers/ Greenwood Publishing Group.

Maestripieri, D., Higley, J., Lindell, S., Newman, T., McCormack, K., & Sanchez, M. (2006). Early maternal rejection affects the development of monoaminergic systems and adult abusive parenting in rhesus macaques (Macaca mulatta). *Behavioral Neuroscience, 120:* 1017-24.

Magee, J. C. & Teachman, B. A. (2007). Why did the white bear return? Obsessive-compulsive symptoms and attributions for unsuccessful thought suppression. *Behavior Research and Therapy 45,* 2884-98.

Maggini, C. (2000). Psychobiology of boredom. *CNS Spectrums, 5*(8): 24-7.

Maguire, E. A., Gadian, D. G., Johnsrude, I. S., Good, C. D., Ashburner, J., Frackowiak, R. S., & Frith, C. D. (2000). Navigation-related structural change in the hippocampi of taxi drivers. *Proceedings of the National Academy of Sciences USA, 97,* 4398-403.

Main, M., & Solomon, J. (1990). Discovery of a new, insecure-disorganized/disoriented attachment pattern. In T. B. Brazelton & M. Yogman (Eds.), *Affective development in infancy* (pp. 121-160). Norwood, NJ: Ablex.

Makino, M., Tsuboi, K., & Dennerstein, L. (2004). Prevalence of eating disorders: A comparison of western and non-western countries. *Medscape General Medicine 6(3):* 49.

Maldonado, J. R. & Spiegel, D. (2007). Dissociative disorders. In S. C. Yudofsky, J. A. Bourgeois, & R.E. Hales (Eds.), *The American Psychiatric Publishing Board prep and review guide for psychiatry.* Washington, DC: American Psychiatric Publishing.

Malkoff, S. B., Muldoon, M. F., Zeigler, Z. R., & Manuck, S. B. (1993). Blood platelet responsivity to acute mental stress. *Psychosomatic Medicine, 55*(6), 477-482.

Mallan, K. M. & Lipp, O. V. (2007). Does emotion modulate the blink reflex in human conditioning? Startle potentiation during pleasant and unpleasant cues in the picture-picture paradigm. *Psychophysiology, 44,* 737-748.

Mandler, J. M. (2004). *Foundations of the mind.* New York: Oxford.

Mann, K., Pankok, J., Connemann, B., & Röschke, J. (2003). Temporal relationship between nocturnal erections and rapid eye movement episodes in healthy men. *Neuropsychology, 47*(2), 109-114.

Mannen, T., Iwata, M., Toyokura, Y., & Nagashima, K. (1982). The Onuf's nucleus and the external anal sphincter muscles in amyotrophic lateral sclerosis and Shy-Drager syndrome. *Acta Neuropathologica.* 58: 255-60.

Manuck, S. B., Cohen, S., Rabin, B. S., Muldoon, M. F., & Bachen, E. A. (1991). Individual differences in cellular immune responses to stress. *Psychological Science, 2,* 1-5.

Marañon, G. (1924). Contribution a l'etude de l'action emotive de l'adrenaline. *Rev. Francmse Endocrinol, 2,* 301-325.

Maratsos, M. (2000). More overregularizations after all: New data and discussion on Marcus, Pinker, Ullman, Hollander, Rosen & Xu. *Journal of Child Language, 27,* 183-212.

Marcia, J. E. (1994). The empirical study of ego identity. In H. A. Bosma, T. L. G. Graafsma, H. D. Grotevant & D. J. de Levita (Eds.), *Identity and development: An interdisciplinary approach.* (pp. 67-80) Thousand Oaks, CA: Sage Publications.

Marcia, J. E. (2007). Theory and measure: The identity status interview. In M. Watzlawik, & A. Born (Eds.), *Capturing identity: Quantitative and qualitative methods.* (pp. 1-14). Lanham: University Press of America.

Maren, S. (2005) Synaptic mechanisms of associative memory in the amygdala. *Neuron, 47,* 783-6.

Marijuana Policy Project. (2008). *State-by-state medical marijuana laws: How to remove the threat of arrest.* Washington, DC: Marijuana Policy Project.

Marikar, S. (2007, February 19). Bald and broken: Inside Britney's shaved head. *ABC News.* Retrieved December 21, 2008 from http://abcnews.go.com/Entertainment/Health/story?id=2885048.

Marín, O. & Rubenstein, J. L. (2003). Cell migration in the forebrain. *Annual Review of Neuroscience.* 26: 44183.

Market Opinion Research International (MORI). (1999, May). Poll on animal experimentation. *New Scientist.*

Market Opinion Research International (MORI). (2005, January). *Use of animals in medical research for coalition for medical progress.* London.

Markus, H. R., Plaut, V. C., & Lachman, M. E. (2004). Well-being in america: Core features and regional patterns. In O. G. Brim, C. D. Ryff & R. C. Kessler (Eds.), *How healthy are we?: A national study of well-being at midlife.* (pp. 614-650). Chicago, IL:University of Chicago Press.

Maron, E., Kuikka, J. T., Shlik, J., Vasar, V., Vanninen, E., & Tiihonen, J. (2004). Reduced brain serotonin transporter binding in patients with panic disorder. *Psychiatric Research and Neuroimaging, 132*(2), 173-181.

Maron, E., Nikopensius, T., Koks, S., Altmae, S., Heinaste, E., Vabrit, K., et al. (2005). Association study of 909 candidate gene polymorphisms in panic disorder. *Psychiatric Genetics, 15*(1), 17-24.

Marsh, E. J. (2007). Retelling is not the same as recalling: Implications for memory. *Current Directions in Psychological Science, 16,* 16-20.

Marsh, J. (2008). Playing doctor: An interview with Patch Adams. *Greater Good Magazine, 4*(4). Retrieved December 21, 2008 from http://greatergood.berkeley.edu/greatergood/2008spring/Q_A054.html

Marshall, R. D., Bryant, R. A., Amsel, L., Suh, E. J., Cook, J. M., & Neria, Y. (2007). The psychology of ongoing threat: Relative risk appraisal, the september 11 attacks, and terrorism-related fears. *American Psychologist, 62*(4), 304-316.

Marshall, W. L., Serran, G. A., Marshall, L. E., & O'Brien, M. D. (2008). Sexual deviation. *Handbook of psychological assessment, case conceptualization, and treatment, (Vol. 1): Adults.* (pp. 590-615) Hoboken, NJ: John Wiley & Sons Inc.

Marsland, A. L., Bachen, E. A., Cohen, S., Rabin, B., & Manuck, S. B. (2002). Stress, immune reactivity and susceptibility to infectious disease. *Physiology & Behavior, 77*(4-5), 711-716.

Martin, C. M. (2008). A meta-analytic investigation of the relationship between emotional intelligence and leadership effectiveness. ProQuest Information & Learning: US). *Dissertation Abstracts International Section A: Humanities and Social Sciences, 69* (2), 530.

Martin, N. (2009). The roles of semantic and phonological processing in short-term memory and learning: Evidence from aphasia. In A. S. C. Thorn & M. P. A. Page (Eds.), *Interactions between short-term and long-term memory in the verbal domain.* (pp. 220-243) New York, NY: Psychology Press.

Martin, R. & Hewstone, M. (2001). Conformity and independence in groups: Majorities and minorities. In M. A. Hogg & R. S. Tindale (Eds.), *Blackwell Handbook of Social Psychology: Group Processes* (pp. 209-234). Malden, MA: Blackwell.

Martin, R. & Hull, R. (2007). The case study perspective on psychological research. In D.E. Halpern, R.J. Sternberg, & H.L. Roediger, III (Eds.), *Critical thinking in psychology.* New York, NY: Cambridge University Press.

Martin, R. A. (2001). Humor, laughter, and physical health: Methodological issues and research findings. *Psychological Bulletin, 127*(4): 504-519.

Martinez, Jr., J. L. & Derrick, B. E. (1996). Long-term potentiation and learning. *Annual Review of Psychology, 47,* 173-203.

Masataka, N. (1998). motherese in Japanese sign language by 6-month-old hearing infants. *Developmental Psychology, 34,* 241-6.

Masling, J. (2004). A storied test. *PsycCRITIQUES* [np].

Maslow, A. (1970). *Motivation and personality.* (Vol. 2, Second Ed.). New York, NY: Harper and Row.

Maslow, A. (1970). *Motivation and personality* (rev. ed.). New York, NY: Harper & Row.

Mason, J. M., Kerr, B. M., Sinha, S., & McCormick, C. (1990). Shared book reading in an early start program for at-risk children. *National Reading Conference Yearbook, 39,* 189-198.

Masters, W. H. & Johnson, V.E. (1970). *Human sexual inadequacy.* Boston, MA: Little, Brown.

Masters, W. H. & Johnson, V. (1979). *Homosexuality in perspective.* Boston, MA: Little, Brown.

Masters, W. H. & Johnson, V. E. (1981). *Human sexual response.* New York, NY: Bantam Books.

Matsumoto, D., Takeuchi, S., Andayani, S., Kouznetsova, N., & Krupp, D. (1998). The contribution of individualism vs. collectivism to cross-national differences in display rules. *Asian Journal of Social Psychology, 1,* 147-165.

Matsumoto, M. & Hikosaka, O. (2009). Two types of dopamine neuron distinctly convey positive and negative motivational signals. *Nature, 459,* 837-41.

Matsumoto, D., & Juang, L. (2008). *Culture and psychology* (4th ed.). Australia: Thomson Wadsworth.

Mattia, J. I. & Zimmerman, M. (2001). Epidemiology. In W. J. Livesley (Ed.), *Handbook of personality disorders: Theory, research, and treatment.* New York, NY: Guilford Press.

Maurer, D. & Salapatek, P. (1976). Developmental changes in the scanning of faces by young infants. *Child Development, 47,* 523-527.

Maurice, W. L. (2007). Sexual desire disorders in men. *Principles and practice of sex therapy (4th ed.).* (pp. 181-211) New York, NY: Guilford Press.

Mayberg, H. S. (2006). Defining neurocircuits in depression. *Psychiatric Annals, 36,* 259-266.

Mayberg, H. S., Lozano, A. M., Voon, V., McNeely, H. E., Seminowicz, D., Hamani, C., et al. (2005). Deep brain stimulation for treatment-resistant depression. *Neuron, 45,* 651-660.

Maybery, M. T. & Do, N. (2003). Relationships between facets of working memory and performance on a curriculum-based mathematics test in children. *Educational and Child Psychology, 20*(3), 77-92.

Mayer, J. D. (2008). Personal intelligence. *Imagination, Cognition and Personality, 27*(3), 209-232.

Mayer, J. D. (2009). Personal intelligence expressed: A theoretical analysis. *Review of General Psychology, 13*(1), 46-58.

Mayer, J. D., Roberts, R. D., & Barsade, S. G. (2008). Human abilities: Emotional intelligence. *Annual Review of Psychology, 59,* 507-536.

Mayer, J. D. & Salovey, P. (1997). What is emotional intelligence? In P. Salovey & D. Sluyter (Eds.), *Emotional development and emotional intelligence: Educational implications* (pp. 3-31). New York, NY: Basic Books.

Mayer, J. D. & Salovey, P. (2004). What is emotional intelligence? In P. Salovey, M. A. Brackett, & J. D. Mayer (Eds.), *Emotional intelligence: Key readings on the Mayer and Salovey model.* (pp. 29-59) Port Chester, NY: Dude Publishing.

Mayer, J. D., Salovey, P., Caruso, D. R., & Sitarenios, G. (2003). Measuring emotional intelligence with the MSCEIT V2.0. *Emotion, 3*(1), 97-105.

Mayer, J. D., Salovey, P., & Caruso, D. R. (2008). Emotional intelligence: New ability or eclectic traits? *American Psychologist, 63*(6), 503-517.

Mayer, S. J. (2005). The early evolution of Jean Piaget's clinical method. *History of Psychology, 8,* 262-382.

McAndrew, F. T. (2008, October). The science of gossip: Why we can't stop ourselves. *Scientific American.* Retrieved December 21, 2008 from http://www.sciam.com/article.cfm?id=the-science-of-gossip.

McCabe, P., (1987). Desired and experienced levels of premarital affection and sexual intercourse during dating. *Journal of Sex Research, 23:* 23-33.

McClure, E. B. (2000). A meta-analytic review of sex differences in facial expression processing and their development in infants, children, and adolescents. *Psychological Bulletin, 126:* 424-453.

McClure, E. B., Monk, C. S., Nelson, E. E., Parrish, J. M., Adler, A., Blair, R. J., Fromm, S., Charney, D. S., Leibenluft, E., Ernst, M., & Pine, D. S. (2007). Abnormal attention modulation of fear circuit function in pediatric generalized anxiety disorder. *Archives of General Psychiatry, 64*(1), 97-106.

McCormick, C.E. and Mason, J.M., 1986. Intervention procedures for increasing preschool children's interest in and knowledge about reading. In: Teale, W.H. and Sulzby, E., Editors, 1986. *Emergent literacy: Writing and reading,* pp. 90-115. NJ: Ablex, Norwood.

McCrae, R. R. (2002). The maturation of personality psychology: Adult personality development and psychological well-being. *Journal of Research in Personality, 36(4):* 307-317.

McCrae, R. R., & Costa, P. T. (1989). Reinterpreting the Myers-Briggs Type Indicator from the perspective of the five-factor model of personality. *Journal of Personality, 57*(1): 17-40.

McCrae, R. R. & Costa, P.T. (2003). *Personality in adulthood: A five-factor theory perspective* (2nd Edition). New York, NY: Guilford.

McCrae, R. R., Yik, M. S. M., Trapnell, P. D., Bond, M. H., & Paulhus, D. L. (1998). Interpreting personality profiles across cultures: Bilingual, acculturation and peer rating studies of Chinese undergraduates. *Journal of Personality and Social Psychology, 74:* 1041-1055.

McCreaddie, M., & Wiggins, S. (2008). The purpose and function of humour in health, health care, and nursing: A narrative review. *Journal of Advanced Nursing, 61*(6): 584-595.

McCrink, K., & Wynn, K. (2004). Large-number addition and subtraction by 9-month-old infants. *Psychological Science, 15*(11), 776-781.

McEvoy, P. M. (2007). Effectiveness of cognitive behavioural group therapy for social phobia in a community clinic: A benchmarking study. *Behavior Research Therapy, 45*(12), 3030-3040.

McEwen, B. S. (2001). Plasticity of the hippocampus: adaptation to chronic stress and allostatic load. *Annals of the New York Academy of Sciences.* 933: 265-77.

McEwen, B. S. & Lasley, E. N. (2002). *The End of Stress as We Know It.* New York, NY: Joseph Henry Press.

McEwen, B. S. (2002). Protective and damaging effects of stress mediators: The good and bad sides of the response to stress. *Metabolism, 51* (Suppl 1), 2-4.

McEwen, D. P., Jenkins, P. M., & Martens, J. R. (2008). Olfactory cilia: our direct neuronal connection to the external world. *Current Topics in Developmental Biology, 85,* 333-70.

McFarland, L. A., Ryan, A. M., Sacco, J. M., & Kriska, D. (2004). Examination of structured interview ratings across time: The effects of applicant race, rater race, and panel composition. *Journal of Management, 30*(4), 435-452.

McFarlane, T., Carter, J., & Olmsted, M. (2005). Eating disorders. In M. M. Antony, D. R. Ledley, & R. G. Heimberg (Eds.), *Improving outcomes and preventing relapse in cognitive-behavioral therapy* (pp. 268-305). New York, NY: Guilford Press.

McGaha, A. C. & Korn, J. H. (1995). The emergence of interest in the ethics of psychological research with humans. *Ethics & Behavior, 5,* 147-159.

McGaugh, J. L. (1999). The perseveration-consolidation hypothesis: Mueller and pilzecker, 1900. *Brain Research Bulletin, 50*(5-6), 445-446.

McGaugh, J. L. (2003). *Memory and emotion: The making of lasting memories* New York, NY: Columbia University Press.

McGue, M. & Lykken, D. T. (1992). Genetic influence on risk of divorce. *Psychological Science, 3(6):* 368-373.

McKelvie, S. J. & Drumheller, A. (2001). The availability heuristic with famous names: A replication. *Perceptual and Motor Skills, 92,* 507-16.

McKinley, M. J., Denton, D. A., Oldfield, B. J., De Oliveira, L. B., & Mathai, M. L. (2006). Water intake and the neural correlates of the consciousness of thirst. *Seminars in nephrology, 26*(3), 249-57.

McLean, D. E., & Link, B. G. (1994). Unraveling complexity: Strategies to refine concepts, measures, and research designs in the study of life events and mental health. *Stress and mental health: Contemporary issues and prospects for the future.* (pp. 15-42) New York, NY: Plenum Press.

McSweeney, S. (2004). Depression in women. In L. Cosgrove & P. J. Caplan (Eds.), *Bias in psychiatric diagnosis* (pp. 183-188). Northvale, NJ: Jason Aronson.

McNally, R. J. (2001). Vulnerability to anxiety disorders in adulthood. In R. E. Ingram & J. M. Price (Eds.), *Vulnerability to psychopathology: Risk across the lifespan* (pp. 304-321). New York, NY: Guilford Press.

Mech, L. D. & Boitani, L. (2003). *Wolves: behavior, ecology, and conservation.* Chicago, IL: University of Chicago Press.

Meece, J. L., Anderman, E. M., & Anderman, L. H. (2006). Classroom goal structure, student motivation, and academic achievement. *Annual Review of Psychology, 57,* 487-503.

Mellers, B. A., Schwartz, A., & Cooke, A. D. (1998). Judgment and decision making. *Annual Review of Psychology, 49,* 447-77.

Mellers, B. A., Schwartz, A., Ho, K., & Ritov, L. (1997). Decision affect theory: Emotional reactions to the outcomes of risky options. *Psychological Science, 8,* 423-9.

Meltzer, M. (2007). Leisure and innocence: The eternal appeal of the stoner movie. *Slate.*

Melzack, R.(1999). From the gate to the neuromatrix. *The Journal of Pain, Suppl 6,* S121-6.

Mendelowitz, E., & Schneider, K. (2008). Existential psychotherapy. In R. J. Corsini & D. Wedding (Eds.), *Current psychotherapies* (8th ed.). Belmont, CA: Thomson Brooks/Cole.

Mendelson, J. (1967). Lateral hypothalamic stimulation in satiated rats: the rewarding effects of self-induced drinking. *Science, 157*(792), 1077-9.

Merlo, A., & Schotter, A. (2003). Learning by not doing: An experimental investigation of observational learning. *Games and Economic Behavior, 42,* 116-36.

Messinger, D. & Fogel, A. (2007). The interactive development of social smiling. *Advances in Child Development and Behavior, 35:* 327-66.

Mesulam, M.M. (1981). A cortical network for directed attention and unilateral neglect. *Annals of Neurology, 10,* 309-25.

Meyer, U., Nyffeler, M., Schwendener, S., Knuesel, I., Yee, B. K., & Feldon, J. (2008). Relative prenatal and postnatal maternal contributions to schizophrenia-related neurochemical dysfunction after in utero immune challenge. *Neuropsychopharmacology, 33*(202), 441-456.

Meyer-Luehmann, M., Spires-Jones, T., Prada, C., Garcia-Alloza, M., de Calignon, A., Rozkalne, A., Koenigsknecht-Talboo, J., Holtzman, D. M., Bacskai, B. J., & Hyman, B. T. (2008). Rapid appearance and local toxicity of amyloid-β plaques in a mouse model of alzheimer's disease. *Nature, 451*(7179), 720-724.

Mezzasalma, M. A., Valenca, A. M., Lopes, F. L., Nascimento, I., Zin, W. A., & Nardi, A. E. (2004). Neuroanatomy of panic disorder. *Revista Brasileira de Psiquiatria, 26*(3), 202-206.

Michel, G. F. & Tyler, A. N. (2005). Critical period: A history of the transition from questions of when, to what, to how. *Development and Psychobiology, 46,* 156-162.

Mikulincer M., & Goodman G. S. (Eds.). (2006). *Dynamics of romantic love: Attachment, caregiving, and sex.* New York, NY: Guilford Press.

Mikulincer, M. & Shaver, P. R. (2005). Attachment security, compassion, and altruism. *Current Directions in Psychological Science, 14*(1): 34-38.

Mikulincer, M., Shaver, P. R., & Gillath, O. (2008). A behavioral systems perspective on compassionate love. *The science of compassionate love: Theory, research, and applications,* (pp. 225-256). Wiley-Blackwell.

Mikulincer, M., Shaver, P. R., Gillath, O., & Nitzberg, R. A. (2005). Attachment, caregiving, and altruism: Boosting attachment security increases compassion and helping. *Journal of Personality and Social Psychology, 89*(5): 817-839.

Miles, D. R., & Carey, G. (1997). Genetic and environmental architecture on human aggression. *Journal of Personality and Social Psychology, 72*(1), 207-217.

Milgram, S. (1963). Behavioral study of obedience. *Journal of Abnormal and Social Psychology, 67:* 371-378.

Milgram, S. (1974). *Obedience to Authority: An Experimental View.* New York, NY: Harper and Row.

Miller, A. G. (2004). What can the Milgram obedience experiments tell us about the holocaust? Generalizing from the social psychology laboratory. In A. G. Miller (ed.), *The Social Psychology of Good and Evil.* (pp. 193-239). New York, NY: Guilford Press.

Miller, D. B. & O'Callaghan, J.P. (2005) Aging, stress and the hippocampus. *Ageing Research Review, 4:* 123-140.

Miller, D. T. & Ross, M. (1975). Self-serving biases in the attribution of causality: Fact or fiction? *Psychological Bulletin, 82:* 213-225.

Miller, G. A. (1956). The magical number seven, plus or minus two: Some limits on our capacity for processing information. *Psychological Review, 63*(2), 81-97.

Miller, G. A. (1978). The acquisition of word meaning. *Child Development, 49*, 999-1004.

Miller, J. G. (1984). Culture and the development of everyday social explanation. *Journal of Personality and Social Psychology, 46*: 961-978.

Miller, L. C., Putcha, A., & Pederson, W. C. (2002). Men's and women's mating preferences: Distinct evolutionary mechanisms? *Current Directions in Psychological Science, 11*: 88-93.

Miller, M. A., & Rahe, R. H. (1997). Life changes scaling for the 1990s. *Journal of Psychosomatic Research, 43*(3), 279-292.

Miller, N. E. (1959). Liberalization of basic S-R concepts: Extensions to conflict behavior, motivation, and social learning. In S. Koch (ed.), *Psychology: A study of a Science, Vol. 2.* New York, NY: McGraw-Hill.

Miller, T. Q. (2000). Type A behavior. In G. Fink (ed.), *Encyclopedia of Stress, Vol. 3* (623-24). New York, NY: Academic Press.

Miller, T. Q., Smith, T. W., Turner, C. W., Guijarro, M. L., & Hallet, A. J. (1996). A meta-analytic review of research on hostility and physical health. *Psychological Bulletin, 119*: 322-348.

Millon, T. & Grossman, S. (2007). *Moderating severe personality disorders: A personalized psychotherapy approach.* Hoboken, NJ: John Wiley & Sons Inc.

Mills, J. S. & Palandra, A. (2008). Perceived caloric content of a preload and disinhibition among restrained eaters. *Appetite, 50*(2-3): 240-5.

Mineka, S. & Zinbarg, R. (1998). Experimental approaches to the anxiety and mood disorders. In J. G. Adair, D. Bélanger, & K. L. Dion (eds.), *Advances in Psychological Science, Vol. 1: Social, Personal, and Cultural Aspects.* (pp. 429-454) Psychology Press/Erlbaum (UK) Taylor & Francis: Hove.

Mineka, S. & Zinbarg, R. (2006). A contemporary learning theory perspective on the etiology of anxiety disorders: It's not what you thought it was. *American Psychologist, 61*, 10-26.

Mingroni, M. A. (2004). The secular rise in IQ: Giving heterosis a closer look. *Intelligence, 32*(1), 65-83.

Mingroni, M. A. (2007). Resolving the IQ paradox: Heterosis as a cause of the flynn effect and other trends. *Psychological Review, 114*(3), 806-829.

Mino, I., Profit, W. E., & Pierce, C. M., (2000). Minorities and stress. In G. Fink (ed.), *Encyclopedia of stress, Vol. 3* (771-776). New York, NY: Academic Press.

Mirescu, C. & Gould, E. (2006). Stress and adult neurogenesis. *Hippocampus, 16*, 233-8.

Mirzaei, S., Gelpi, E., Roddrigues, M., Knoll, P., & Gutierrez-Lobos, K. (2005). Progress in post-traumatic stress disorder research. In T. A. Corales (Ed.), *Focus on posttraumatic stress disorder research* (pp. 157-177). Hauppauge, NY: Nova Science Publishers.

Mischel, W. & Peake, P. K. (1982). Beyond deja vu in the search for cross-situational consistency. *Psychological Review, 89*: 730-755.

Mischel, W. (2004). Toward an integrative science of the person. *Annual Review of Psychology, 55*: 1-22.

Mischel, W., Shoda, Y., & Rodriguez, M. L. (1989). Delay of Gratification in Children. *Science, 244*: 933-8.

Mitchell, C. M., Kaufman, C.E., Beals, J., et. al. (2004). Equifinality and multifinality as guides for prevention interventions: HIV risk/protection among American Indian young adults. *Journal of Primary Prevention, 25*(4), 491-510.

Miyagawa, Y., Tsujimura, A., Fujita, K., Matsuoka, Y., Takahashi, T., Takao, T., et al. (2007). Differential brain processing of audiovisual sexual stimuli in men: comparative positron emission tomography study of the initiation and maintenance of penile erection during sexual arousal. *NeuroImage, 36*(3): 830-42.

Mogan, J. (1984). Obesity: prevention is the treatment. *Patient Education and Counseling, 6*(2): 73-6.

Moll, P. P., Burns, T. L., & Lauer, R. M. (1991). The genetic and environmental sources of body mass index variability: The Muscatine ponderosity family study. *The American Journal of Human Genetics, 49*: 1243-1255.

Monat A., Lazarus R. S. (Eds.) (1991). *Stress and coping: An anthology (3rd ed.).* New York, NY: Columbia University Press.

Monteiro, C. A., Moura, E. C., Conde, W. L., & Popkin, B. M. (2004). Public Health Reviews: Socioeconomic status and obesity in adult populations of developing countries: a review. *Bulletin of the World Health Organization, 84*(12): 940-6.

Moody, R.A. (1975). *Life after life.* VA: Mockingbird Books.

Moorcroft, W. H. (2003). *Understanding sleep and dreaming.* New York: Springer.

Morfei, M. Z., Hooker, K., Carpenter, J., Mix, C., & Blakeley, E. (2004). Agentic and communal generative behavior in four areas of adult life: Implications for psychological well-being. *Journal of Adult Development, 11*(1): 55-58.

Morgan, M. A., Romanski, L. M., & LeDoux, J. E. (1993). Extinction of emotional learning: contribution of medial prefrontal cortex. *Neuroscience Letters, 163*, 109-13.

Moriceau, S. & Sullivan, R. M. (2006). Maternal presence serves as a switch between learning and attraction in infancy. *Nature Neuroscience, 9*, 1004-6.

Morin, C. M. & Espie, C. A. (2003). *Insomnia: A clinical guide to assessment and treatment.* New York: Kluwer Academic/Plenum Publishers.

Morris, R. G. (1990). Toward a representational hypothesis of the role of hippocampal synaptic plasticity in spatial and other forms of learning. *The Cold Spring Harbor Symposia on Quantitative Biology, 55*, 161-73.

Morris, W. N. (1992). A functional analysis of the role of mood in affective systems. In M. S. Clark (Ed.), *Emotion* (pp. 256-293). Thousand Oaks, CA: Sage Publications, Inc.

Morton, J., & Johnson, M. H. (1991). Conspec and Conlern—A Two-Process Theory of Infant Face Recognition. *Psychological Review, 98*, 164-181.

Moser, E. I., Kropff, E., & Moser, M. B. (2008). Place cells, grid cells, and the brain's spatial representation system. *Annual Review of Neuroscience.* 31: 69-89.

Moser, M. B., Trommald, M., & Andersen, P. (1994). An increase in dendritic spine density on hippocampal CA1 pyramidal cells following spatial learning in adult rats suggests the formation of new synapses. *Proceedings of the National Academy of Sciences USA, 91*, 12673-5.

Moser, M. B., Trommald, M., Egeland, T., & Andersen, P. (1997). Spatial training in a complex environment and isolation alter the spine distribution differently in rat CA1 pyramidal cells. *The Journal of Comparative Neurology, 380*, 373-81.

Mosher, C. E. & Danoff-Burg, S. (2005). Agentic and communal personality traits: Relations to attitudes toward sex and sexual experiences. *Sex Roles, 52*(1-2): 121-129.

Mosher, C. E. & Danoff-Burg, S. (2008). Agentic and communal personality traits: Relations to disordered eating behavior, body shape concern, and depressive symptoms. *Eating Behaviors, 9*(4): 497-500.

Mosher, W. D., Chandra, A., & Jones, J. (2005). Sexual Behavior and Selected Health Measures: Men and Women 15-44 Years of Age, United States, 2002. Advance Data From Vital Health Statistics (362).

Motivala, S. J., & Irwin, M. R. (2007). Sleep and Immunity: Cytokine Pathways Linking Sleep and Health Outcomes. *Current Directions in Psychological Science,16,* 21-25.

Mouras H., Stolérus, Moulier, V., Pélégrini-Issac, M., Rouxel, R., Grandjean, B., Glutron, D., Bittoun, J. (2008). Activation of mirror-neuron system by erotic video clips predicts degree of induced erection: an fMRI study. *Neuroimage, 42,* 1142-1150.

Mroczek, D. K. (2004). Positive and negative affect at midlife. In O. G. Brim, C. D. Ryff, & R. C. Kessler (Eds.), *How healthy are we? A national study of well-being at midlife.* (pp. 205-226) Chicago, IL: University of Chicago Press.

Mroczek, D. K. & Spiro III, A. (2005). Change in life satisfaction during adulthood: Findings from the Veterans affairs normative aging study. *Journal of Personality and Social Psychology, 88*(1), 189-202.

Mroczek, D. K., & Spiro III, A. (2007). Personality change influences mortality in older men. *Psychological Science, 18*(5), 371-376.

Mueller, S. E., Petitjean, S., Boening, J., & Wiesbeck, G. A. (2007). The impact of self-help group attendance on relapse rates after alcohol detoxification in a controlled study. *Alcohol Alcoholism, 42*(2), 108-112.

Mueser, K. T., Crocker, A.G., Frisman, L.B., Drake, R.E., Covell, N.H., & Essock, S.M. (2006). Conduct disorder and antisocial personality disorder in persons with severe psychiatric and substance use disorders. *Schizophrenia Bulletin, 32*(4), 626-636.

Munger, B.L. & Ide, C. (1988). The structure and function of cutaneous-sensory receptors. *Archives of Histology and Cytology, 51,* 1-34.

Murdock, S. G., O'Neill, R. E., & Cunningham, E. (2005). A comparison of results and acceptability of functional behavioral assessment procedures with a group of middle school students with emotional/behavioral disorders (E/BD). *Journal of Behavior Education, 14*(1), 5-18.

Murphy, J. G., McDevitt-Murphy, M. E., & Barnett, N. P. (2005). Drink and be merry? Gender, life satisfaction, and alcohol consumption among college students. *Psychology of Addictive Behaviors, 19,* 184-191.

Murphy, T. (1992). Redirecting sexual orientation: Techniques and justifications. *Journal of Sex Research, 29:* 501-523.

Murphy, W. J. (2001). The Victim Advocacy and Research Group: Serving a growing need to provide rape victims with personal legal representation to protect privacy rights and to fight gender bias in the criminal justice system. *Journal of Social Distress and the Homeless, 10*(1), 123-138.

Myers, D. G. (1975). Discussion-induced attitude polarization. *Human Relations, 28*(8), 699-714.

Myers, D. G. (2000). The funds, friends, and faith of happy people. *American Psychologist, 55*(1), 56-67.

Myers, D. G. & Bishop, G.D. (1970). Discussion effects on racial attitudes. *Science, 169:* 778-779.

Myers, D. G. & Diener, E. (1996). The pursuit of happiness. *Scientific American,* pp. 70-72.

Myers, I., McCaulley, M., Quenk, N. L., & Hammer, A. L. (1998). *Manual: A guide to the development and use of the Myers-Briggs type indicator. (3rd ed).* Palo Alto, CA: Consulting Psychologists Press.

Myerson, J., Rank, M. R., Raines, F. Q., & Schnitzler, M. A. (1998). Race and general cognitive ability: The myth of diminishing returns to education. *Psychological Science, 9*(2), 139-142.

Myrick, H. & Wright, T. (2008). Clinical management of alcohol abuse and dependence. In H. D. Kleber & M. Galanter (Eds.), *The American psychiatric publishing textbook of substance abuse treatment (4th ed.).* Washington, DC: American Psychiatric Publishing.

N

Nair, E. (2003). Hindsight lessons aka experiential wisdom: A review of the XXV ICAP. *Applied Psychology: An International Review, 52*(2), 165-174.

Nairne, J. S. (2003). Sensory and working memory. In A. F. Healy & R. W. Proctor (Eds.), *Handbook of psychology: Experimental psychology, vol. 4.* (pp. 423-444) Hoboken, NJ: John Wiley & Sons, Inc.

Nakamichi, N., Kato, E., Kojima, Y., & Itoigawa, N. (1998). Carrying and washing of grass roots by free-ranging Japanese macaques at Katsuyama. *Folia Primatologica, Basel, 69,* 35-40.

Nardi, A. E., Valença, A. M., Nascimento, I., Freire, R. C., Veras, A. B., de-Melo-Neto, V. L., Lopes, F. L., King, A. L., Soares-Filho, G., Mezzasalma, M. A., Rassi, A., & Zin, W. A. (2008). A caffeine challenge test in panic disorder patients, their healthy first-degree relatives and healthy controls. *Depression and Anxiety, 25*(10), 847-853.

Nash, J. M. (1997). Addicted. *Time,* 68-76.

National Association to Advance Fat Acceptance. (2009). Weight Discrimination Laws. Downloaded on May 25, 2009 from: http://www.naafaonline.com/dev2/education/laws.html.

National Center on Addiction and Substance Abuse at Columbia University (NCASA). (2007, March). *Wasting the best and the brightest: Substance abuse at America's colleges and universities.* Washington, DC.

National Fatherhood Initiative (NFI) (2009). The father factor: Facts of fatherhood. Retrieved from http://www.fatherhood.org/father_factor.asp

National Institute of Neurological Disorders and Stroke (NINDS). (2006). Narcolepsy fact sheet. Bethesda, MD.

Neckelmann, D., Mykletun, A., & Dahl, A. A. (2007). Chronic insomnia as a risk factor for developing anxiety and depression. *Sleep, 30*(7), 873-880.

Nee, D. E., Berman, M. G., Moore, K. S., & Jonides, J. (2008). Neuroscientific evidence about the distinction between short- and long-term memory. *Current Directions in Psychological Science, 17*(2), 102-106.

Neff, E. J. A. & Dale, J. C. (1996). Worries of school-age children. *Journal of the Society of Pediatric Nurses, 1:* 27-32.

Neisser, U. (1967). *Cognitive psychology.* New York, NY: Appleton-Century-Crofts.

Neisser, U. (Ed.) (1998). *The rising curve: Long-term gains in IQ and related measures.* Washington, DC: American Psychological Association.

Nelson, C. A. (2007). A neurobiological perspective on early human deprivation. *Child Development Perspectives 1,* 13-18.

Nelson, C. A., Zeanah, C. H., Fox, N. A., Marshall, P. J., Smyke, A. T., & Guthrie, D. (2007). Cognitive recovery in socially deprived young children: The Bucharest Early Intervention Project. *Science, 318*, 1937-1940.

Nelson, D. & Cooper, G. (2005). Stress and health: A positive direction. *Stress and Health: Journal of the International Society for the Investigation of Stress, 21*: 73-75.

Nelson, H. (2008). Menopause. *Lancet, 371*(9614), 760-770.

Nelson, III, C. A., Furtado, E. A., Fox, N. A., & Zeanah, Jr. C. H. (2009). The deprived brain. *American Scientist, 97*(3), 222-229.

Nelson, J. K. & Bennett, C. S. (2008). Introduction: Special issue on attachment. *Clinical Social Work Journal, 36*, 3-7.

Nelson, K. R., Mattingly, M., Lee, S. A., & Schmitt, F. A. (2006). Does the arousal system contribute to near death experience? *Neurology, 66*(7), 1003-1009.

Nemeroff, C. B. (1998). The neurobiology of depression. *Scientific American, 278*: 42-49.

Nesse, R. M. (1990). Evolutionary explanations of emotions. *Human Nature, 1*, 261-289.

Nesse, R. M. & Ellsworth, P. C. (2009). Evolution, emotions, and emotional disorders. *American Psychologist, 64*(2), 129-139.

Nestler, E. J. (2004). Molecular mechanisms of drug addiction. *Neuropharmacology.* 1: 24-32.

Nettelbeck, T., & Wilson, C. (2004). The flynn effect: Smarter not faster. *Intelligence, 32*(1), 85-93.

Neubauer, A. C. & Fink, A. (2003). Fluid intelligence and neural efficiency: Effects of task complexity and sex. *Personality and Individual Differences, 35*(4), 811-827.

Neuschatz, J. S., Preston, E. L., & Toglia, M. P. (2005) Comparison of the efficacy of two name-learning techniques: Expanding rehearsal and name-face imagery. *American Journal of Psychology, 118,* 79-101.

Newcomb, T. M. (1943). *Personality and social change.* New York, NY: Dryden.

Newcomb, T. M., Koening, K. E., Flacks, R., & Warwick, D. P. (1967). *Persistence and change: Bennington College and its students after 25 years.* New York, NY: John Wiley & Sons, Inc.

Niaura, R., Todaro, J. F., Stroud, L., Spiro III, A., Ward, K. D., & Weiss, S. (2002). Hostility, the metabolic syndrome, and incident coronary heart disease. *Health Psychology, 21*(6), 588-593.

Nier, J. A. (2005). How dissociated are implicit and explicit racial attitudes? A bogus pipeline approach. *Group Processes & Intergroup Relations, 8*(1): 39-52.

Nigg, J. T. & Goldsmith, H. H. (1994). Genetics of personality disorders: Perspectives from personality and psychopathology research. *Psychology Bulletin, 115,* 346-380.

Nilsson, B. (1979). The occurrence of taste buds in the palate of human adults as evidenced by light microscopy. *Acta Odontologica Scandinavica, 37,* 253-8.

Ninan, P. T. & Dunlop, B. W. (2005). Neurobiology and ethiology of panic disorder. *Journal of Clinical Psychiatry, 66*(Suppl. 4), 3-7.

Nisbett, R. E., and Cohen, D. (1996). *Culture of honor.* Boulder, CO: Westview Press.

Nishina, A., Juvonen, J., & Witkow, M.R. (2005). Sticks and stones may break my bones, but names will make me feel sick. The psychosocial, somatic, and scholastic consequences of peer harassment. *Journal of Clinical Child and Adolescent Psychology, 34*(1), 37-48.

Nishitani, S., Miyamura, T., Tagawa, M., Sumi, M., Takase, R., Doi, H., Moriuchi, H., & Shinohara, K. (2009). The calming effect of a maternal breast milk odor on the human newborn infant. *Neuroscience Research, 63,* 66-71.

Nock, M. K. & Prinstein, M. J. (2004). A functional approach to the assessment of self-mutilative behavior. *Journal of Consulting and Clinical Psychology, 72,* 885-890.

Norcross, J. C., & Goldfried, M. R. (Eds.). (2005). *Handbook of psychotherapy integration* (2nd ed.). New York, NY: Oxford University Press.

Norem, J. K. (2001). *The positive power of negative thinking.* New York, NY: Basic Books.

Norem, J. K., & Illingworth, K. S. S. (2004). Mood and performance among defensive pessimists and strategic optimists. *Journal of Research in Personality, 38*(4), 351-366.

Norgren, R., Hajnal, A., & Mungarndee, S.S. (2006). Gustatory reward and the nucleus accumbens. *Physiology & Behavior, 89,* 531-5.

Norman, D. A. (1988). *The psychology of everyday things.* New York, NY: Basic Books.

Norman-Eady, S., Reinhart, C., & Martino, P. (2003). Statutory Rape Laws by State. OLR Research Report. Downloaded on June 26, 2009 from: http://www.cga.ct.gov/2003/olrdata/jud/rpt/2003-R-0376.htm.

Norra, C., Mrazek, M., Tuchtenhagen, F., Gobbele, R., Buchner, H., Sass, H., & Herpertz, S. C. (2003). Enhanced intensity dependence as a marker of low serotonergic neurotransmission in borderline personality disorder. *Journal of Psychiatric Research, 37*(1): 23-33.

Novaco, R. W., Stokols, D., & Milanesi, L. (1990). Objective and subjective dimensions of travel impedance as determinants of commuting stress. *American Journal of Community Psychology, 18*: 231-257.

Novick, L.R. & Bassok, M. (2005). Problem solving. In K. J. Holyoak & R. G. Morrison (Eds.), *The Cambridge handbook of thinking and reasoning* (pp. 321-350). New York, NY: Cambridge University Press.

Novin, D., Sanderson, J. D., & Vanderweele, D. A. (1974). The effect of isotonic glucose on eating as a function of feeding condition and infusion site. *Physiology & Behavior, 13*(1): 4.

NSDUH. (2007). *National survey on drug use.* Washington, DC: Department of Health and Human Services, Substance Abuse and Mental Health Services Administration, Office of Applied Studies.

NSDUH. (2008). *National survey on drug use.* Washington, DC: Department of Health and Human Services, Substance Abuse and Mental Health Services Administration, Office of Applied Studies.

Numazaki, M. & Tominaga, M. (2004). Nociception and TRP Channels. *Current Drug Targets: CNS and Neurological Disorders, 3,* 479-85.

Nunn, J. A., Gregory, L. J., Brammer, M., Williams, S. C. R., Parslow, D. M., Morgan, M. J., Morris, R. G., Bullmore, E. T., Baron-Cohen, S., & Gray, J. A. (2002). Functional magnetic resonance imaging of synesthesia: Activation of V4/V8 by spoken words. *Nature Neuroscience, 5*(4), 371-375.

Nye, C. D., Roberts, B. W., Saucier, G., & Zhou, X. (2008). Testing the measurement equivalence of personality adjective items across cultures. *Journal of Research in Personality, 42*(6): 1524-1536.

O

Oatley, K., & Jenkins, J. M. (1996). *Understanding emotions.* Malden, MA: Blackwell Publishing.

O'Brien, C. P. (2008). The CAGE questionnaire for detection of alcoholism: A remarkably useful but simple tool. *JAMA: Journal of the American Medical Association, 300*(17), 2054-2056.

O'Brien, W. H., & Tabaczynski, T. (2007). Unstructured interviewing. In J. C. Thomas & M. Hersen (Eds.), *Handbook of clinical interviewing with children*. Thousand Oaks, CA: Sage Publications.

O'Connor, B. P. (2008). Other personality disorders. In M. Hersen & J. Rosqvist (eds.), *Handbook of psychological assessment, case conceptualization, and treatment, Vol 1: Adults.* (pp. 438-462) Hoboken, NJ: John Wiley & Sons, Inc.

O'Craven, K. M. & Kanwisher, N. (2000). Mental imagery of faces and places activates corresponding stimulus-specific brain regions. *Journal of Cognitive Neuroscience 12*, 1013-23.

O'Keefe, J. (1990). A computational theory of the hippocampal cognitive map. *Progress in Brain Research, 83*, 301-12.

O'Malley, A., O'Connell, C., & Regan, C. M. (1998). Ultrastructural analysis reveals avoidance conditioning to induce a transient increase in hippocampal dentate spine density in the 6 hour post-training period of consolidation. *Neuroscience, 87*, 607-13.

Oatley, K. & Jenkins, J. M. (1992). Human emotions: Function and dysfunction. *Annual Review of Psychology, 43*, 55-85.

Oesterle, S., Hill, K. G., Hawkins, J. D., Guo, J., Catalano, R. F., & Abbott, R. D. (2004). Adolescent heavy episodic drinking trajectories and health in young adulthood. *Journal of Studies on Alcohol, 65*, 204-212.

Ogden, C. L., D, P., Carroll, M. D., & Mcdowell, M. A. (2007). Obesity Among Adults in the United States— No Statistically Significant Change Since 2003-2004. *NCHS Data Brief*.

Öhman, A. (2000). Fear and anxiety: Evolutionary, cognitive, and clinical perspectives. In M. Lewis & J. M. Haviland-Jones (Eds.), *Handbook of emotions, 2nd ed.* (pp. 573-593). New York, NY: Guilford Press.

Okamoto, Y., Kinoshita, A., Onoda, K., Yoshimura, S., Matsunaga, M., Takami, H., Yamshita, H., Ueda, K., Suzuki, S., & Yamawaki, S. (2006). Functional brain basis of cognition in major depression. *Japanese Journal of Psychonomic Science. 25:* 237-243.

Okie, S. (2005). Medical marijuana and the Supreme Court. *New England Journal of Medicine, 353*(7), 648-651.

Olsen, L. & DeBoise, T. (2007). Enhancing school readiness: The Early Head Start model. *Children and Schools, 29*, 47-50.

Olsson, S. E. & Moller, A. R. (2003). On the incidence and sex ratio of transsexualism in Sweden. *Archives of Sexual Behavior, 32*(4), 381-386.

Ophira, E., Nassb, C., and Wagner, A. D. (2009) Cognitive control in media multitaskers *PNAS 2009 106*:15583-15587

Oppenheimer, D. M. (2004). Spontaneous discounting of availability in frequency judgment tasks. *Psychological Science, 15*, 100-5.

Orbuch, T. L. & Sprecher, S. (2003). Attraction and interpersonal relationships. In J. Delamater (Ed.), *Handbook of social psychology.* (pp. 339-362) New York, NY: Kluwer Academic/Plenum Publishers.

Organ, D. & Ryan, K. (1995). A meta-analytic review of attitudinal and dispositional predictors of organizational citizenship behavior. *Personnel Psychology, 48:* 775-802.

Orikasa, C., Kondo, Y., & Sakuma, Y. (2007). Transient transcription of the somatostatin gene at the time of estrogen-dependent organization of the sexually dimorphic nucleus of the rat preoptic area. *Endocrinology, 148:* 1144-1149.

O'Rourke, N., Cappeliez, P., & Guindon, S. (2003). Depressive symptoms and physical health of caregivers of persons with cognitive impairment: Analysis of reciprocal effects over time. *Journal of Aging and Health, 15*(4), 688-712.

Osaka, N. (2003). Working memory-based consciousness: An individual difference approach. In N. Osaka (Ed.) *Neural Basis of Consciousness,* pp. 27-44.

Osaka, N. (Ed.). (2003). *Neural basis of consciousness.* Amsterdam, Netherlands: John Benjamins Publishing Company.

Osman, A., Barrios, F. X., Gutierrez, P. M., Williams, J. E., & Bailey, J. (2008). Psychometric properties of the Beck Depression Inventory-II in nonclinical adolescent samples. *Journal of Clinical Psychology, 64*(10), 83-102.

Otten, K. L. (2004). An analysis of a classwide self-monitoring approach to improve the behavior of elementary students with severe emotional and behavioral disorders. *Dissertation. Abstracts International: Section. A: Humananities and Social Sciences, 65*(3-A), 893.

Otis, L. S. (1974). The facts on transcendental meditation: III. If well-integrated but anxious, try TM. *Psychology Today, 7*(11), 45-46.

Ouellette, S. C. (1993). Inquiries into hardiness. In L. Goldberger & S. Beznitz (Eds.), *Handbook of stress: Theoretical and clinical aspects* (2nd ed.). New York, NY: Free Press.

Ouellette, S. C., & DiPlacido, J. (2001). Personality's role in the protection and enhancement of health: Where the research has been, where it is stuck, how it might move. In A. Baum, T. A. Revenson, & J. E. Singer (Eds.), *Handbook of health psychology*. Mahwah, NJ: Lawrence Erlbaum.

Overmier, B. J. & Murison, R. (2005). Trauma and resulting sensitization effects are modulated by psychological factors. *Psychoneuroendocrinology, 30:* 965-973.

Owen-Howard, M. (2001). Pharmacological aversion treatment of alcohol dependence. I. Production and prediction of conditioned alcohol aversion. *American Journal of Drug and Alcohol Abuse, 27*(3), 561-585.

Oyserman, D., Coon, H. M., & Kemmelmeier, M. (2002a) Rethinking individualism and collectivism: Evaluation of theoretical assumptions and meta-analyses. *Psychological Bulletin, 128:* 3-72.

Oyserman, D., Kemmelmeier, M., & Coon, H. M. (2002b) Cultural Psychology, a new look: Reply to Bond (2002), Fiske (2002), Kityama (2002), and Miller (2002). *Psychological Bulletin, 128:* 110-117.

Ozer, E. J., Best, S. R., Lipsey, T. L., & Weiss, D. S. (2003). Predictors of posttraumatic stress disorder and symptoms in adults: A meta-analysis. *Psychology Buletin., 129*(1), 52-73.

Öztekin, I., McElree, B., Staresina, B. P., & Davachi, L. (2009). Working memory retrieval: Contributions of the left prefrontal cortex, the left posterior parietal cortex, and the hippocampus. *Journal of Cognitive Neuroscience, 21*(3), 581-593.

P

Packer, S. (2000). Religion and stress. In G. Fink (ed.), *Encyclopedia of Stress, Vol. 3* (348-355). New York, NY: *Academic Press*.

Page, R. M., & Brewster, A. (2009). Depiction of food as having drug-like properties in televised food advertisements directed at children: Portrayals as pleasure enhancing and addictive. *Journal of Pediatric Health Care, 23*(3), 150-158.

Paine, S., Gander, P. H., & Travier, N. (2006). The epidemiology of Morningness/Eveningness: Influence of age, gender, ethnicity, and socioeconomic factors in adults (30-49 years). *Journal of Biological Rhythms, 21*(1), 68-76.

Palkovitz, R., Copes, M.A., & Woolfolk, T.N. (2001). It's like . . . you discover a new sense of being: Involved fathering as an evoker of adult development. *Men & Masculinities, 4*(1), 49-69.

Palumbo, S.R. (1978). *Dreaming and memory: A new information processing model.* New York, NY: *Basic Books.*

Panko, T. L. (2005). Pathways from childhood conduct problems to adult criminality. Student paper at Rochester Institute of Technology.

Paris, J. (2001). Cultural risk factors in personality disorders. In J.F. Schumaker & T. Ward (es.), *Cultural cognition and psychopathology.* Westport, CT: Praeger.

Park, D. & Gutchess. A. (2006). The cognitive neuroscience of aging and culture. *Current Directions in Psychological Science, 15,* 105-108.

Park, D. C., Lautenschlager, G., Hedden, T., Davidson, N.S., Smith, A.D., & Smith, P. (2002). Models of visuospatial and verbal memory across the adult life span. *Psychology & Aging, 17*(2), 299-320.

Park, D. C., & Reuter-Lorenz, P. (2009). The adaptive brain: Aging and neurocognitive scaffolding. *Annual Review of Psychology, 60,* 173-196.

Parke, R. D. (1995). Fathers and families. In M. H. Bornstein (Ed.), *Handbook of parenting, vol. 3: Status and social conditions of parenting.* (pp. 27-63). Mahwah, NJ: Lawrence Erlbaum Associates.

Parrott, W. G. (2001). Implications of dysfunctional emotions for understanding how emotions function. *Review of General Psychology, 5,* 180-186.

Parrott, W. G. (2004). The nature of emotion. In M. B. Brewer & M. Hewstone (Eds.), *Emotion and motivation.* (pp. 5-20) Malden, MA: Blackwell Publishing.

Pasquet, P. & Apfelbaum, M. (1994). Recovery long-term. *American Journal of Physiology*, 861-863.

Patil, S. T., Zhang, L., Martenyi, F., Lowe, S. L., Jackson, K. A., Andreev, B. V., Avedisova, A. S., Bardenstein, L. M., Gurovich, I. Y., Morozova, M. A., Mosolov, S. N., Neznanov, N. G., Reznik, A. M., Smulevich, A. B., Tochilov, V. A., Johnson, B. G., Monn, J. A., & Schoepp, D. D. (2007). Activation of mGlu2/3 receptors as a new approach to treat schizophrenia: a randomized Phase 2 clinical trial. *Nature Medicine, 13,* 1102-7.

Paton, C. & Beer, D. (2001). Caffeine: The forgotten variable. *International Journal of Psychiatry in Clinical Practice, 5*(4), 231-236.

Patrick, C. J. (1994). Emotion and psychopathy: Startling new insights, Psychophysiology, *31*(4), 319-330.

Patrick, C. J. (2007). Antisocial personality disorder and psychopathy. In W. O'Donohue, K. A. Fowler, & S. O. Lilienfeld (eds.), *Personality Disorders: Toward the DSM-V.* (109-166). Thousand Oaks, CA: Sage Publications.

Patrick, C. J., Bradley, M. M., & Lang, P. J. (1993). Emotion in the criminal psychopath: Startle reflex modulation. *Journal of Abnormal Psychology, 102*(1), 82-92.

Pattison, E. & Pattison, M. (1980). "Ex-gays": Religiously mediated change in homosexuals. *American Journal of Psychiatry, 137:* 1553-1562.

Paul, G. L., & Lentz, R. (1977). *Psychosocial treatment of the chronic mental patient.* Cambridge, MA: Harvard University Press.

Pauls, C. A., & Stemmler, G. (2003). Repressive and defensive coping during fear and anger. *Emotion, 3*(3), 284-302.

Paulsen, J. S. (2009). Functional imaging in Huntington's disease. *Experimental Neurology.* Jan 3. [Epub ahead of print]

Paulus, P. B., Dugosh, K. L., Dzindolet, M. T., Coskun, H., & Putnam, V.L. (2002). Social and cognitive influences in group brainstorming: Predicting production gains and losses. In W. Stroebe & M. Hewston (eds.), *European Review of Social Psychology (Vol. 12,* pp. 299-325). Chichester: John Wiley & Sons, Inc.

Paulus, P. B., Dzindolet, M. T., Poletes, G., & Camacho, L.M. (1993). Perception of performance in group brainstorming: The illusion of group productivity. *Personality and Social Psychology Bulletin, 19:* 78-79.

Paulus, P. B. & Nijstad, B. A. (Eds.) (2003). *Group creativity: Innovation through collaboration.* New York, NY: *Oxford University Press.*

Paus, T., Zijdenbos, A., Worsley, K., Collins, D. L., Blumenthal, J., Giedd, J. N., et al. (1999). Structural maturation of neural pathways in children and adolescents: In vivo study. *Science, 283*(5409), 1908-1911.

Pause, B.M., Sojka, B., Krauel, K., Fehm-Wolfsdorf, G., & Ferstl, R. (1996). Olfactory information processing during the course of the menstrual cycle. *Biological Psychology, 44,* 31-54.

Paykel, E. S. (2003). Life events and affective disorders. *Acta Psychiatrica Scandinavica, 108,* 61-66.

Paykel, E. S. (2003). Life events: Effects and genesis. *Psychological Medicine, 33*(7), 1145-1148.

Payne, J. W. & Bettman, J. R. (2004). Walking with the scarecrow: The Information-processing Approach to Decision Research. In D. J. Koehler & N. Harvey (Eds.), *Blackwell handbook of judgment and decision making* (pp. 110-132). Malden, MA: Blackwell Publishing.

Pennebaker, J. (1990). *Opening up: The healing power of confiding in others.* New York, NY: *William Morrow.*

Pennebaker, J. W. (2003). The social, linguistic and health consequences of emotional disclosure. In J. Suls & K. A. Wallston (eds.), *Social Psychological foundations of health and illness.* (pp. 288-313) Malden, MA: Blackwell Publishing.

Pennebaker, J. W. (2004). Theories, therapies, and taxpayers: On the complexities of the expressive writing paradigm. *Clinical Psychology: Science and Practice, 11*(2): 138-142.

Pennebaker, J. W., Kiecolt-Glaser, J., & Glaser, R. (2004). Disclosure of traumas and immune function: Health implications for psychotherapy. In R. M. Kowalski & M. R. Leary (eds.), *The interface of social and clinical psychology: Key readings.* (pp. 301-312) New York, NY: Psychology Press.

Peplau, L. A. (2003). Human Sexuality: How Do Men and Women Differ? *Current Directions in Psychological Science, 12,* 37-41.

Pereira, A. C., Huddleston, D. E., Brickman, A. M., Sosunov, A. A., Hen, R., McKhann, G. M., Sloan, R., Gage, F. H., Brown, T. R., & Small, S. A. (2007). An in vivo correlate of exercise-induced neurogenesis in the adult dentate gyrus. *Proceedings of the National Academy of Sciences of the United States of America.* 104: 5638-43.

Peretz, I., Cummings, S., & Dubé, M.P. (2007). The genetics of congenital amusia (tone deafness): a family-aggregation study. *American Journal of Human Genetics, 81,* 582-8.

Pergadia, M., Madden, P., Lessov, C., Todorov, A., Bucholz, K., Martin, N., & Heath, A. (2006). Genetic and environmental influences on extreme personality dispositions in adolescent female twins. *Journal of Child Psychology and Psychiatry, 47:* 902-915.

Perneczky, R., Drzezga, A., Boecker, H., Ceballos-Baumann, A. O., Granert, O., Förstl, H., Kurz, A., & Häussermann, P. (2008).

Activities of daily living, cerebral glucose metabolism, and cognitive reserve in Lewy body and Parkinson's disease. *Dementia and Geriatric Cognitive Disorders, 26*: 475-81.

Perry, J. C., Hoglend, P., Shear, K., Valliant, G. E., Horowitz, M., Kardos, M. E., Bille, H., & Kagan, D. (1998). Field trial of a diagnostic axis for defense mechanisms for DSM-IV. *Journal of Personality Disorders, 12*: 56-68.

Perry, W. G., Jr. (1970). *Forms of intellectual and ethical development in the college years: A scheme.* New York, NY: Holt, Rinehart & Winston.

Pervin, L. A., Cervone, D., & John, O. P. (2005). *Personality: Theory and research* (9th ed.). New York, NY: John Wiley & Sons, Inc.

Peterson, C., Ruch, W., Beermann, U., Park, N., & Seligman, M. E. P. (2007). Strengths of character, orientations to happiness, and life satisfaction. *Journal of Positive Psychology, 2*(3), 149-156.

Peterson, C., & Steen, T. A. (2002). Optimistic explanatory style. *Handbook of positive psychology.* (pp. 244-256) New York, NY: Oxford University Press.

Peterson, C., & Steen, T. A. (2009). Optimistic explanatory style. *Oxford handbook of positive psychology (2nd ed.).* (pp. 313-321) New York, NY: Oxford University Press.

Petrescu, N. (2008). Loud music listening. *McGill Journal of Medicine, 11*, 169-76.

Petrovich, G. D., Setlow, B., Holland, P. C., & Gallagher, M. (2002). Amygdalo-hypothalamic circuit allows learned cues to override satiety and promote eating. *Journal of Comparative Physiology, 22(19):* 8748-8753.

Pettersen, G., Rosenvinge, J. H., & Ytterhus, B. (n.d.). The "double life" of bulimia: patients' experiences in daily life interactions. *Eating Disorders, 16(3):* 204-11.

Petty, R. E., Wheeler, S. C., & Tormala, Z. L. (2003). Persuasion and attitude change. In T. Millon & M. J. Lerner (eds.), *Handbook of psychology: Personality and social psychology, Vol. 5.* (pp. 353-382) Hoboken, NJ: John Wiley & Sons Inc.

Pezdek, K. (2003). Event memory and autobiographical memory for the events of September 11, 2001. *Applied Cognitive Psychology, 17*(9), 1033-1045.

Pfaus, J. G., Kippin, T. E., & Coria-Avila, G. (2003). What can animal models tell us about human sexual response? *Annual Review of Sex Research, 14:* 1-63.

Pham, T. M., Winblad, B., Granholm, A. C., & Mohammed, A. H. (2002). Environmental influences on brain neutrophins in rats. *Pharmacology, Biochemistry, and Behavior, 73*, 167-75.

Philipson, T. (2001). The world-wide growth in obesity: an economic research agenda. *Health Economics, 10:* 1-7.

Phillips, J. L. (1975). *The origins of intellect: Piaget's theory.* London: W. H. Freeman and Company.

Piaget, J. (1965). *The moral judgment of the child.* New York, NY: Free Press.

Piaget, J. (1972). *[Essay on operative logic. (2nd ed.).]* Dunod: 75661 Paris Cedex 14.

Piaget, J. (1973). *Main trends in psychology.* London: Allen & Unwin.

Piaget, J. (1985). *The equilibration of cognitive structures: The central problem of intellectual development* (T. Brown & K. Thampy, Trans). Chicago, IL: *University of Chicago Press.*

Piaget, J. (2000). *Studies in reflecting abstraction.* (R. L. Campbell, Trans). Hove: Psychology Press.

Piaget, J. (2003). PART I: Cognitive development in children: Piaget: Development and learning. *Journal of Research in Science Teaching, 40*, S8-S18.

Pickens, R., Svikis, D., McGue, M., Lykken, D., Heston, L., & Clayton, P. (1991) Heterogeneity in the inheritance of alcoholism. *Archives of General Psychiatry, 48:* 19-28.

Pierce, G. R., Sarason, I. G., & Sarason, B. R. (1996). Coping and social support. In M. Zeidner & N. S. Endler (eds.), *Handbook of coping, theory, research, applications* (434-451). New York, NY: *John Wiley & Sons, Inc.*

Pierpaoli, W. (Ed.). (2005). *Reversal of aging: Resetting the pineal clock.* New York, NY: New York Academy of Sciences.

Piferi, R. L., Jobe, R. L., & Jones, W. H. (2006). Giving to others during national tragedy: The effects of altruistic and egoistic motivations on long-term giving. *Journal of Social and Personal Relationships, 23:* 171-184.

Pinker, S. (1994) *The language instinct.* New York, NY: HarperCollins.

Pinker, S. (1997) *How the mind works.* New York, NY: W. W. Norton & Co.

Pinker, S. (1999) *Words and rules: The ingredients of language.* New York, NY: HarperCollins.

Pinker, S. (2002) *The blank slate: The modern denial of human nature.* New York, NY: *Viking.*

Pinker, S. (2007) *The Stuff of Thought: Language as a Window into Human Nature.* New York, NY: *Viking.*

Pinker, S. & Jackendoff, R. (2005). The faculty of language: What's special about it? *Cognition, 95,* 201-36.

Pinkerman, J. E., Haynes, J. P., & Keiser, T. (1993). Characteristics of psychological practice in juvenile court clinics. *American Journal of Forensic Psychology, 11:* 3-12.

Piper, A. & Merskey, H. (2004). The persistence of folly: A critical examination of dissociative identity disorder. Part I. The excesses of an improbable concept *Canadian Journal of Psychiatry, 49*(9), 592-600.

Piper, A. & Merskey, H. (2004). The persistence of folly: Critical examination of dissociative identity disorder. Part II. The defence and decline of multiple personality or dissociative identity disorder. *Canadian Journal of Psychiatry, 49*(10), 678-683.

Piskulic, D., Olver, J. S., Norman, T. R., & Maruff, P. (2007). Behavioural studies of spatial working memory dysfunction in schizophrenia: a quantitative literature review. *Psychiatry Research, 150,* 111-21.

Platania, J. & Moran, G. P. (2001). Social facilitation as a function of mere presence of others. *Journal of Social Psychology, 141*(2): 190-197.

Pliner, P., Bell, R., Hirsch, E. S., & Kinchla, M. (2006). Meal duration mediates the effect of "social facilitation" on eating in humans. *Appetite, 46(2):* 189-98.

Plomin, R. & Caspi, A. (1999). Behavioral genetics and personality. In L. A. Pervin & O. P. John (eds.), *Handbook of personality: Theory and research.* New York, NY: *Guilford Press.*

Plomin, R. & Spinath, F. M. (2004). Intelligence: Genetics, genes, and genomics. *Journal of Personality and Social Psychology, 86*(1), 112-129.

Plucker, J. A. (Ed.). (2003). Human intelligence: Historical influences, current controversies, teaching resources. Retrieved, from http://www.indiana.edu/~intell

Plum, L., Belgardt, B. F., & Brüning, J. C. (2006). Central insulin action in energy and glucose homeostasis. *Insulin, 116(7).*

Plutchik, R. (1980). *Emotion: A psychoevolutionary synthesis.* New York, NY: Harper & Row.

Pobric, G., Mashal, N., Faust, M., & Lavidor, M. (2008). The role of the right cerebral hemisphere in processing novel metaphoric expressions: A transcranial magnetic stimulation study. *Journal of Cognitive Neuroscience, 20, 170-81.*

Poirier, P., Giles, T. D., Bray, G. A., Hong, Y., & Stern, J. S. (2006). Obesity and cardiovascular disease: Pathophysiology, evaluation, and effect of weight loss: An update of the 1997 American Heart Association Scientific Statement on Obesity and heart Disease from the Obesity Committee of the Council on Nutrition, Physical Activity, and Metabolism. *Circulation, 113:* 898-918.

Polivy, J., Coleman, J., & Herman, C. P. (2005). The effect of deprivation on food cravings and eating behavior in restrained and unrestrained eaters. *The International Journal of Eating Disorders, 38(4):* 301-9.

Pope, K. S., & Wedding, D. (2008). Contemporary challenges and controversies. In R. J. Corsini & D. Wedding (Eds.), *Current psychotherapies* (8th ed.). Belmont, CA: Thomson Brooks/Cole.

Popenoe, D. (1993). American family decline 1960-1990: A review and appraisal. *Journal of Marriage and the Family, 55:* 527-544.

Popper, K. (1963). *Conjectures and Refutations: The growth of scientific knowledge.* London: Routledge & Kegan Paul.

Popper, K. R. (1959). *The logic of scientific discovery.* Oxford: Basic Books.

Poropat, A. E. (2009). A meta-analysis of the five-factor model of personality and academic performance. *Psychological Bulletin, 135(2):* 322-338.

Porsolt, R. D. (2000). Animal models of depression: utility for transgenic research. *Reviews in the Neurosciences, 11, 53-8.*

Porter, R. & Winberg, J. (1999). Unique salience of maternal breast odors for newborn infants. *Neuroscience & Biobehavioral Reviews, 23(3):* 439-449.

Portnoy, D. (2008). Relatedness: Where existential and psychoanalytic approaches converge. In K. J. Schneider (Ed.), *Existential-integrative psychotherapy: Guideposts to the core of practice* (pp. 268-281). New York, NY: Routledge/Taylor & Francis Group.

Posner, M. I., Petersen, S. E., Fox, P. T., & Raichle, M. E. (2002). Localization of cognitive operations in the human brain. In D. J. Levitin (Ed.), *Foundations of cognitive psychology: Core readings.* (pp. 819-830) Cambridge, MA: MIT Press.

Post, S. G. (2005). Altruism, happiness, and health: It's good to be good. *International Journal of Behavioral Medicine, 12(2):* 66-77.

Postle, B. R. (2003). Context in verbal short-term memory. *Memory & Cognition, 31(8),* 1198-1207.

Prescott, C., Johnson, R.C., & McArdle, J. (1991). Genetic contributions to television viewing. *Psychological Science, 2:* 430-431.

Present, J., Crits-Christoph, P., Gibbons, M. B. C., Hearon, B., Ring-Kurtz, S., Worley, M., et al. (2008). Sudden gains in the treatment of generalized anxiety disorder. *Journal of Clinical Psychology, 64(1),* 119-126.

Pressley, M., Levin, J. R., & Delaney, H. D. (1982). The mnemonic keyword method. *Review of Educational Research, 52(1),* 61-91.

Price, G. R., Holloway, I., Räsänen, P., Vesterinen, M., & Ansari, D. (2007). Impaired parietal magnitude processing in developmental dyscalculia. *Current Biology, 17,* R1042-3.

Price, R. A. & Gottesman, I. I. (1991). Body fat in identical twins reared apart: Roles for genes and environment. *Behavior Genetics, 21(1):* 22903-22903.

Prinstein M. J., Dodge K. A. (Eds.) (2008) *Understanding peer influence in children and adolescents.* New York, NY: Guilford Press.

Prislin, R. & Wood, W. (2005). Social influence in attitudes and attitude change. In D. Albarracín, B. T. Johnson, & M. P. Zanna (Eds.), *The Handbook of Attitudes.* (pp. 671-705) Mahwah, NJ: Lawrence Erlbaum Associates Publishers.

Probst, M., Goris, M., Vandereycken, W., Pieters, G., Vanderlinden, J., Van Coppenolle, H., et al. (2004). Body composition in bulimia nervosa patients compared to healthy females. *European Journal of Nutrition, 43(5):* 288-96.

Prochaska, J. O., & Norcross, J. C. (2006). *Systems of psychotherapy: A transtheoretical analysis.* Pacific Grove, CA: Brooks/Cole.

Prochaska, J. O., & Norcross, J. C. (2007). *Systems of psychotherapy: A transtheoretical analysis* (6th ed.). Pacific Grove, CA: Brooks/Cole.

Profit, W. E., Mino, I., & Pierce, C. M. (2000). Stress in blacks. In G. Fink (ed.), *Encyclopedia of stress, Vol. 1* (324-330). New York, NY: Academic Press.

Pugno, M. (2007). The subjective well-being paradox: A suggested solution based on relational goods. In P. L. Porta & L. Bruni (Eds.), *Handbook on the economics of happiness.* Northampton: MA: Edward Elgar Publishing.

Puhl, R. M., Moss-Racusin, C. A, Schwartz, M. B., & Brownell, K. D. (2008). Weight stigmatization and bias reduction: perspectives of overweight and obese adults. *Health education research, 23(2):* 347-58.

Puka, B. (2004). Altruism and character. In D. K. Lapsley & D. Narvaez (Eds.), *Moral development, self, and identity.* (pp. 161-187) Mahwah, NJ: Lawrence Erlbaum Associates Publishers.

Q

Qiu, A., Crocetti, D., Adler, M., Mahone, E. M., Denckla, M. B., Miller, M. I., & Mostofsky, S. H. (2009). Basal ganglia volume and shape in children with attention deficit hyperactivity disorder. *The American Journal of Psychiatry, 166,* 74-82.

Quas, J. A., Malloy, L. C., Melinder, A., Goodman, G. S., D-Mello, M., & Schaaf, J. (2007). Developmental differences in the effects of repeated interviews and interviewer bias on young children's event memory and false reports. *Developmental Psychology, 43(4),* 823-837.

Quinnell, T. G., Farooqi, I. S., Smith, I. E., & Schneerson, J. M. (2007). Screening the human prepro-orexin gene in a single-centre narcolepsy cohort. *Sleep Medicine, 8(5),* 498-502.

Quirk, G. J. (2006). Extinction: new excitement for an old phenomenon. *Biological Psychiatry, 60,* 317-8.

Quirk, G. J., Garcia, R., & González-Lima, F. (2006). Prefrontal mechanisms in extinction of conditioned fear. *Biological Psychiatry, 60,* 337-43.

R

Raab, K. A. (2007). Manic depression and religious experience: The use of religion in therapy. *Mental Health, Religion and Culture, 10(5),* 473-487.

Raaijmakers, J. G. & Shiffrin, R. M. (1992). Models for recall and recognition. *Annual Review of Psychology, 43,* 205-234.

Raaijmakers, J. G. W. & Shiffrin, R. M. (2002). Models of memory. In H. Pashler & D. Medin (Eds.), *Steven's handbook of experimental psy-*

chology (3rd ed.), vol. 2: Memory and cognitive processes. (pp. 43-76) Hoboken, NJ: John Wiley & Sons, Inc.

Rabinowitz, J., Levine, S. Z., Brill, N., & Bromet, E. J. (2007). The premorbid adjustment scale structured interview (PAS-SI): Preliminary findings. *Schizophrenia Research, 90*(1-3), 255-257.

Rabow, J., Newcomb, M. D., Monto, M. A., & Hernandez, A. C. (1990). Altruism in drunk driving situations: Personal and situational factors in intervention. *Social Psychology Quarterly, 53*(3), 199-213.

Rafii, M. S. & Aisen, P. S. (2009). Recent developments in Alzheimer's disease therapeutics. *BMC Medicine. 7:* 7.

Rahman, Q. (2005). The neurodevelopment of human sexual orientation. *Neuroscience and Biobehavioral Rreviews, 29*(7): 1057-66.

Raichle, M. E. (2005). Imaging the human brain: Reflections on some emerging issues. In U. Mayr, E. Awh & S. W. Keele (Eds.), *Developing individuality in the human brain: A tribute to Michael I. Posner.* (pp. 109-123) Washington, DC: American Psychological Association.

Rainville, P., Duncan, G. H., Price, D. D., Carrier, B., & Bushnell, M. C. (1997). Pain affect encoded in human anterior cingulate but not somatosensory cortex. *Science, 277*(5328), 968-971.

Rainville, P., Hofbauer, R. K., Bushnell, M. C., Duncan, G. H., & Price, D. D. (2002). Hypnosis modulates activity in brain structures involved in the regulation of consciousness. *Journal of Cognitive Neuroscience, 14*(6), 887-901.

Rainville, P., Hofbauer, R. K., Paus, T., Duncan, G. H., Bushnell, M. C., & Price, D. D. (1999). Cerebral mechanisms of hypnotic induction and suggestion. *Journal of Cognitive Neuroscience, 11*(1), 110-125.

Raksion, D. H. (2007) Is consciousness in its infancy in infancy? *Journal of Consciousness Studies, 14*, 66-89.

Ramachandran, V.S. (2005). Plasticity and functional recovery in neurology. *Clinical Medicine, 5*, 368-73.

Ramey, C. T. & Ramey, S. L. (2007). Early learning and school readiness: Can early intervention make a difference? In G. W. Ladd (Ed.), *Appraising the human developmental sciences: Essays in honor of Merrill-Palmer quarterly.* (pp. 329-350) Detroit: Wayne State University Press.

Ramponi, C., Richardson-Klavehn, A., & Gardiner, J. M. (2007). Component processes of conceptual priming and associative cued recall: The roles of preexisting representation and depth of processing. *Journal of Experimental Psychology: Learning, Memory & Cognition, 33*, 843-862.

Rapee, R. M., & Bryant, R. A. (2009). Stress and psychosocial factors in onset of fear circuitry disorders. *Stress-induced and fear circuitry disorders: Advancing the research agenda for DSM-V.* (pp. 195-214) Arlington, VA: American Psychiatric Publishing, Inc.

Raskin, K., de Gendt, K., Duittoz, A., Liere, P., Verhoeven, G., Tronche, F., et al. (2009). Conditional inactivation of androgen receptor gene in the nervous system: Effects on male behavioral and neuroendocrine responses. *The Journal of Neuroscience: The Official Journal of the Society for Neuroscience, 29*(14): 4461-70.

Raskin, N. J., Rogers, C. R., & Witty, M. C. (2008). Client-centered therapy. In R. J. Corsini & D. Wedding (Eds.), *Current psychotherapies* (8th ed.). Belmont, CA: Thomson Brooks/Cole.

Ratey, J. J. (2001). *A user's guide to the brain: Perception, attention, and the four theaters of the brain.* New York, NY: Random House.

Rathbone, D. B. & Huckabee, J. C. (1999). *Controlling Road Rage.* AAA Foundation for Traffic Safety.

Raugh, M. R., & Atkinson, R. C. (1975). A mnemonic method for learning a second-language vocabulary. *Journal of Educational Psychology, 67*(1), 1-16.

Rauscher, F., Shaw, G., Ky, K. (1993). Music and spatial task performance. *Nature. 365*, 611.

Rawson, R.A. & Ling, W. (2008). Clinical management: Methamphetamine. In H. D. Kleber & M. Galanter (Eds.), *The American psychiatric publishing textbook of substance abuse treatment(4th ed.).* Washington, DC: American Psychiatric Publishing.

Read, J.P., Beattie, M., Chamberlain, R., & Merrill, J.E. (2008). Beyond the "binge" threshold: Heavy drinking patterns and their association with alcohol involvement indices in college students. *Addictive Behaviors, 33*(2), 225-234.

Reddy, L. & Kanwisher, N. (2006). Coding of visual objects in the ventral stream. *Current Opinion in Neurobiology, 16*, 408-14.

Redelmeier, D. A., Katz, J., & Kahneman, D. (2003). Memories of colonoscopy: a randomized trial. *Pain, 104*, 187-94.

Reed, T. E. & Jensen, A. R. (1992). Conduction velocity in a brain nerve pathway of normal adults correlates with intelligence level. *Intelligence, 16*(3-4), 259-272.

Rees, W. D., & Lutkin, S. G. (1967). Mortality of bereavement. *British Medical Journal*, 4, 13-16.

Regehr, C., Cadell, S., & Jansen, K. (1999). Perceptions of control and long-term recovery from rape. *Ameican. Journal of Orthopsychiatry*, 69(1), 110-115.

Regier, D. A., Narrow, W. E., Rae, D. S., Manderscheid, R. W., Locke, B. Z., & Goodwin, F. K. (1993). The de facto US mental and addictive disorders service system. Epidemiologic catchment area prospective 1-year prevalence rates of disorders and services. *Archives of General Psychiatry, 50*, 85-94.

Reid, P. J. (2009). Adapting to the human world: Dogs' responsiveness to our social cues. *Behavioral Processes, 80*, 325-33.

Reiff, P. (1979) *Freud: The Mind of a Moralist.* University of Chicago Press.

Rejeski, W. J., Gregg, E., Thompson, A., & Berry, M. (1991). The effects of varying doses of acute aerobic exercise on psychophysiological stress responses in highly trained cyclists. *Journal of Sport & Exercise Psychology, 13*(2), 188-199.

Rejeski, W. J., & Thompson, A. (2007). Historical and conceptual roots of exercise psychology. *Essential readings in sport and exercise psychology.* (pp. 332-347) Champaign, IL: Human Kinetics.

Rejeski, W. J., Thompson, A., Brubaker, P. H., & Miller, H. S. (1992). Acute exercise: Buffering psychosocial stress responses in women. *Health Psychology, 11*(6), 355-362.

Rekers, G. A. (1992). Development of problems of puberty and sex roles in adolescence. In Walker, C.E. & Roberts, M.C. (Eds.), H*andbook of clinical child psychology, Second Edition.* Oxford, England: John Wiley & Sons, Inc.

Renner, M. J., & Mackin, R. S. (2002). A life stress instrument for classroom use. *Handbook for teaching introductory psychology: Vol. 3: With an emphasis on assessment.* (pp. 236-238) Mahwah, NJ: Lawrence Erlbaum Associates Publishers.

Reynolds, C. R., Castillo, C. L., & Horton Jr., A. M. (2008). Neuropsychology and intelligence: An overview. In A. M. Horton Jr., & D. Wedding (Eds.), *The neuropsychology handbook (3rd ed.).* (pp. 70-86) New York, NY: Springer Publishing Co.

Reynolds, C. R., Chastain, R. L., Kaufman, A. S., & McLean, J. E. (1987). Demographic characteristics and IQ among adults: Analysis of the WAIS-R standardization sample as a function of the stratification variables. *Journal of School Psychology, 25*(4), 323-342.

Reynolds, S. E. (1993). "Limerence:" A new word and concept. *Psychotherapy: Theory, Research and Practice, 20*(1), 107-111.

Reznick, J. S. & Goldfield, B. A. (1992). Rapid change in lexical development in comprehension and production. *Developmental Psychology, 28,* 406-13.

Rheaume, C., & *Mitty, E. (2008). Sexuality and intimacy in older adults. Geriatric Nursing, 29*(5), 342-9.

Richard, I. H., & Lyness, J. M. (2006). An overview of depression. In D. V. Jeste & J. H. Friedman (Eds.), *Psychiatry for neurologists* (pp. 33-42). Totowa, NJ: Humana Press.

Richards, G. (2004). "It's an American thing": The "race" and intelligence controversy from a british perspective. *Defining difference: Race and racism in the history of psychology.* (pp. 137-169) Washington, DC: American Psychological Association.

Richards, P. S., & Bergin, A. E. (Eds.). (2000). Toward religious and spiritual competency for mental health professionals. In P. S. Richards & A. E. Bergin, *Handbook of psychotherapy and religious diversity.* Washington, DC: American Psychological Association.

Richards, P. S., & Bergin, A. E. (Eds.). (2004). *Casebook for a spiritual strategy in counseling and psychotherapy.* Washington, DC: American Psychological Association.

Richardson, R. D. (2006). *William James: In the maelstrom of American modernism.* Boston, MA: Houghton Mifflin Company.

Ridout, N., Astell, A. J., Reid, I. C., Glen, T., & O'Carroll, R. E. (2003). Memory bias for emotional facial expressions in major depression. *Cognition and Emotion, 17*(1), 101-122.

Ridout, N., Dritschel, B., Matthews, K., McVicar, M., Reid, I. C., & Carroll, R. E. (2009). Memory for emotional faces in major depression following judgement of physical facial characteristics at encoding. *Cognition and Emotion, 23*(4), 739-752.

Rigaud, D., Trostler, N., Rozen, R., Vallot, T., & Apfelbaum, M. (1995). Gastric distension, hunger, and energy intake after balloon implantation in severe obesity. *International Journal of Obesity and Related Metabolic Disorders: Journal of the International Association for the Study of Obesity, 19*(7): 489-95.

Rimé, B. (2007) The social sharing of emotion as an interface between individual and collective processes in the construction of emotional climates. *Journal of Social Issues, 63,* 307-322.

Rimm, D. C., & Masters, J. C. (1979). *Behavior therapy: Techniques and empirical findings* (2nd ed.). New York, NY: Academic Press.

Rissman, E. F. (2009). Roles of estrogen receptors alpha and beta in behavioral neuroendocrinology: Beyond Yin/Yang. *Journal of Neuroendocrinology, 20*(6): 873-879.

Rivers, I. N. (1997). Lesbian, gay and bisexual development: Theory, research and social issues. *Journal of Community & Applied Social Psychology, 7:* 329-344.

Rizzolatti, G. & Craighero, L. (2004). The mirror-neuron system. *Annual Review of Neuroscience. 27:* 169-192.

Rizzolatti, G. & Fabbri-Destro, M. (2008). The mirror system and its role in social cognition. *Current Opinions in Neurobiology, 18,* 179-84.

Roberts, B. W. & DelVecchio, W. F. (2000). The rank-order consistency of personality from childhood to old age: A quantitative review of longitudinal studies. *Psychological Bulletin, 126:* 3-25.

Roberts, B. W., Helson, R., & Klohnen, E. C. (2002). Personality developmental and growth in women across 30 years: Three perspectives. *Journal of Personality, 70,* 79-102.

Roberts, B. W., Walton, K. E., & Viechtbauer, W. (2006). Patterns of mean-level change in personality traits across the life course: A meta-analysis of longitudinal studies. *Psychology Bulletin, 132,* 1-25.

Robertz, F. J. (2007). Deadly dreams. *Scientific American Mind, 18(4):* 52-59.

Robins, R. W., Gosling, S. D. & Craik, K. H. (1999). An empirical analysis of trends in psychology. *American Psychologist, 54,* 117-128.

Robinson, T. E. & Berridge, K. C. (2001). Incentive-sensitization and addiction. *Addiction (England), 96(1):* 103-14.

Roche, B. & Quayle, E. (2007). Sexual disorders. In D.W. Woods & J.W. Kanter (Eds.), *Understanding behavior disorders; A contemporary behavioral perspective.* Reno, NV: Context Press.

Roche, S. M. & McConkey, K. M. (1990). Absorption: Nature, assessment, and correlates. *Journal of Personality and Social Psychology, 59*(1), 91-101.

Rodier, P. M. (2000, February). The early origins of autism. *Scientific American,* 56-63.

Rodin, J., & Langer, E. J. (1977). Long-term effects of a control-relevant intervention with the institutionalized aged. *Journal of Personality and Social Psychology, 35*(12), 897-902.

Roese, N. J. & Jamieson, D. W. (1993). Twenty years of bogus pipeline research: A critical review and meta-analysis. *Psychological Bulletin, 114:* 363-375.

Rogers, C. R. (1951). *Client-centered therapy.* Boston, MA: Houghton Mifflin.

Rogers, C. R. (1957). The necessary and sufficient conditions of therapeutic personality change. *Journal of Consulting and Clinical Psychology, 121,* 95-203.

Rogers, C. R. (1963). Actualizing tendency in relation to "motives" and to consciousness. In M. R. Jones (ed.), *Nebraska symposium on motivation.* (1-24) Oxford: University of Nebraska Press.

Rogers, C. R. (1987). Rogers, Kohut, and Erickson: A personal perspective on some similarities and differences. In J. K. Zeig (Ed.), *The evolution of psychotherapy.* New York, NY: Brunner/Mazel.

Rogers, C.R. (1992). The necessary and sufficient conditions of therapeutic personality change. *Journal of Consulting and Clinical Psychology, 60*(6), 827-832.

Rogers, C. R. (2000). Interview with Carl Rogers on the use of the self in therapy. In M. Baldwin (Ed.), *The use of self in therapy* (2nd ed., pp. 29-38). Binghamton, NY: Haworth.

Rogers, C. R. (2007). The basic conditions of the facilitative therapeutic relationship. *The handbook of person-centred psychotherapy and counselling.* (pp. 1-5) New York, NY: Palgrave Macmillan.

Rogers, C. R. (2007). The necessary and sufficient conditions of therapeutic personality change. *Psychotherapy: Theory, Research, Practice, Training, 44*(3), 240-248.

Rogers, C. R. (2008). The actualizing tendency in relation to 'motives' and to consciousness. In B. E. Levitt (ed.), *Reflections on human potential: Bridging the person-centered approach and positive psychology.* (17-32) Ross-on-Wye: PCCS Books.

Rogers, P. (2005). Caffeine and health. *Psychologist, 18*(1), 9.

Rogers, T. T. & McClelland, J. L. (2008). Précis of semantic cognition: A parallel distributed-processing approach. *Behavioral and Brain Sciences, 31*(6), 689-714.

Rohrer, G. E. (2005). The problem of assessment and diagnosis. In G. Rohrer, *Mental health and literature: Literary lunacy and lucidity* (pp. 1-23). Chicago, IL: Lyceum Books.

Rolls, E. T. (2007). Sensory processing in the brain related to the control of food intake. *The Proceedings of the Nutrition Society, 66(1):* 96-112.

Roman, C., Lin, J., & Reilly, S. (2009). Conditioned taste aversion and latent inhibition following extensive taste preexposure in rats with insular cortex lesions. *Brain Research, 1259:* 68-73.

Roman, C. & Reilly, S. (2007). Effects of insular cortex lesions on conditioned taste aversion and latent inhibition in the rat. *The European Journal of Neuroscience, 26(9):* 2627-32.

Romano, S. J. & Lee, J. S. (2002). A placebo-controlled study of fluoxetine in continued treatment of bulimia nervosa after successful acute fluoxetine treatment. *Psychiatry: Interpersonal and Biological Processes, (January):* 96-102.

Romeu, P. F. (2006). Memories of the terrorist attacks of September 11, 2001: A study of the consistency and phenomenal characteristics of flashbulb memories. *The Spanish Journal of Psychology, 9(1),* 52-60.

Rosario, E. R., & Pike, C. J. (2008). Androgen regulation of ß-amyloid protein and the risk of alzheimer's disease. *Brain Research Reviews, 57(2),* 444-453.

Rosenberg, M. J. (1969). The conditions and consequences of evaluation apprehension. In R. Rosenthal & R.S. Rosnow (Eds.), *Artifact in behavioral research.* New York, NY: Academic Press.

Rosenstein, D. & Oster, H. (1988). Differential facial responses to four basic tastes in newborns. *Child Development, 59,* 1555-68.

Rosenthal, T. L., & Bandura, A. (1978). Psychological modeling: Theory and practice. In S. L. Garfield & A. E. Bergin (Eds.), *Handbook of psychotherapy and behavior change: An empirical analysis* (2nd ed., pp. 621-658). New York, NY: Wiley.

Rosenthal, R., Rosnow, R. L. & Rubin, D. B. (2000). *Contrasts and effect sizes in behavioral research.* Cambridge, England: Cambridge University Press.

Rosenzweig, M. R. (1996). Aspects of the search for neural mechanisms of memory. *Annual Review of Psychology, 47,* 1-32.

Rosenzweig, M. R. & Bennett, E. L. (1996). Psychobiology of plasticity: effects of training and experience on brain and behavior. *Behavioral Brain Research, 78,* 57-65.

Ross, J. M. (2003). Preconscious defence analysis, memory, and structural change. *International Journal of Psychoanalysis, 84(1),* 59-76.

Ross, L. (1977). The intuitive psychologist and his shortcomings: Distortions in the attribution process. In L. Berkowitz (Ed.), *Advances in experimental social psychology* (Vol. 10). New York: Academic Press.

Ross, L. D. (2001). Getting down to fundamentals: Lay dispositionism and the attributions of psychologists. *Psychological Inquiry, 12:* 37-40.

Rossi A. M., Quick J. C. and Perrewe P. L. (Eds.) (2009). *Stress and quality of working life: The positive and the negative.* Charlotte, NC: Information Age Publishing.

Rothbart, M. K., & Bates, J. E. (2006). Temperament (6th ed.. In N. Eisenberg, W. Damon, & R. Lerner (Eds.). *Handbook of child psychology: Social, emotional, and personality development* (Vol. 3, pp. 99-166). Hoboken, NJ: John Wiley & Sons, Inc.

Rothstein, J. M. (2004). College performance predictions and the SAT. *Journal of Econometrics,* 121, 297-317.

Roughgarden, J. (2004). *Evolution's rainbow: diversity, gender, and sexuality in nature and people.* Berkeley, CA: *University of California Press.*

Rowa, K., McCabe, R. E., & Antony, M. M. (2006). Specific phobias. *Comprehensive handbook of personality and psychopathology: Vol. 2: Adult psychopathology.* (pp. 154-168) Hoboken, NJ: John Wiley & Sons Inc.

Rowe, D. C., Almeida, D. M., & Jacobson, K. C. (1999). School context and genetic influences on aggression in adolescence. *Psychological Science, 10(3),* 277-280.

Roysamb, E. (2006). Personality and well-being. *Handbook of personality and health.* (pp. 115-134) New York, NY: John Wiley & Sons Ltd.

Rubin, Z. (1970). Measurement of romantic love. *Journal of Personality and Social Psychology, 16:* 265-273.

Rubin, Z. (1973). *Liking and Loving.* New York: Holt, Rinehart & Winston.

Rudman, L. A. & Ashmore, R. D. (2007) Discrimination and the Implicit Association Test. *Group Processes and Intergroup Relations, 10:* 359-372.

Rugg, M. D., Henson, R. N. A., & Robb, W. G. K. (2003). Neural correlates of retrieval processing in the prefrontal cortex during recognition and exclusion tasks. *Neuropsychologia, 41(1),* 40-52.

Rugg, M. D. & Yonelinas, A. P. (2003). Human recognition memory: A cognitive neuroscience perspective. *Trends in Cognitive Sciences, 7(7),* 313-319.

Runco, M. A. (2004). Creativity. *Annual Review of Psychology, 55,* 657-687.

Rupke, S. J., Blecke, D., & Renfrow, M. (2006). Cognitive therapy for depression. *American Family Physician, 73,* 83-6.

Ruscio, A. M., Brown, T. A., Chiu, W. T., Sareen, J., Stein, M. B., & Kessler, R. C. (2008). Social fears and social phobia in the USA: Results from the National Comorbidity Survey Replication. *Psychological Medicine, 38(1),* 15-28.

Ryan, R. M., & Deci, E. L. (2000). Self-determination theory and the facilitation of intrinsic motivation, social development, and well-being. *The American Psychologist, 55(1),* 68-78.

Ryan-Wenger, N. A., Sharrer, V. W., & Campbell, K. K. (2005, July-August). Changes in children's stressors over the past 30 years. *Pediatric Nursing.*

Rymer, R. (1994). *Genie: A scientific tragedy.* New York, NY: Harper Paperbacks.

S

Sabbagh, M. A., Bowman, L. C., Evraire, L. E., Ito, J. M. Neurodevelopmental correlates of theory of mind in preschool children. *Child Development* 80(4): 1147-62.

Sacchi, D. L., Agnoli, F., & Loftus, E. F. (2007). Changing history: doctored photographs affect memory for past public events. *Applied Cognitive Psychology.*

Sachs, J. (2009). Communication Development in Infancy. In J. B. Gleason (Ed.), *The Development of Language* (7th ed., pp. 40-60). Columbus, OH: Allyn & Bacon.

Sack, R. L., Auckley, D., Auger, R. R., Carskadon, M. A., Wright Jr., K. P., Vitiello, M. V., & Zhdanova, I. V. (2007). Circadian rhythm sleep disorders: Part I, basic principles, shift work and jet lag disorders: An american academy of sleep medicine review. *Sleep: Journal of Sleep and Sleep Disorders Research, 30*(11), 1460-1483.

Sack, R. L., Auckley, D., Auger, R. R., Carskadon, M. A., Wright Jr., K. P., Vitiello, M. V., & Zhdanova, I. V. (2007). Circadian rhythm sleep disorders: Part II, advanced sleep phase disorder, delayed sleep phase disorder, free-running disorder, and irregular sleep-wake rhythm: An american academy of sleep medicine review. *Sleep: Journal of Sleep and Sleep Disorders Research, 30*(11), 1484-1501.

Sacks, O. (1985). *The Man Who Mistook His Wife For A Hat: And Other Clinical Tales.* New York, NY: Touchstone.

Sacks, O. (September 2007). The Abyss. The New Yorker. Retrieved May 7, 2009 from http://www.newyorker.com/reporting/2007/09/24/070924fa_fact_ sacks.

Sadeh, A., Mindell, J. A., Luedtke, K., & Wiegand, B. (2009). Sleep and sleep ecology in the first 3 years: A web-based study. *Journal of Sleep Research, 18*(1), 60-73.

Sadler, M. S., Lineberger, M., Correll, J., & Park, B. (2005). Emotions, attributions, and policy endorsement in response to the September 11th terrorist attacks. *Basic and Applied Social Psychology, 27*(3): 249-258.

Sadock, B. J. & Sadock, V. A. (2007). *Synopsis of psychiatry: Behavioral sciences/clinical psychiatry (10th ed.).* Philadelphia, PA: Wolters Kluwer/Lippincott Williams & Wilkins.

Sadock, V. A. & Kaplan, H. I. (2008). *Kaplan & Sadock's concise textbook of clinical psychiatry.* (Third Ed). Philadelphia, PA: Wolters Kluwer Health.

Saewyc, E. M., Skay, C. L., Pettingell, S. L., Reis, E. A., Bearinger, L., Resnick, M., et al. (2006). Hazards of stigma: The sexual and physical abuse of gay, lesbian, and bisexual adolescents in the United States and Canada. *Child Welfare*, 195-214.

Safdar, S., Friedlmeier, W., Matsumoto, D., Yoo, S. H., Kwantes, C. T., Kakai, H., et al. (2009). Variations of emotional display rules within and across cultures: A comparison between Canada, USA, and Japan. *Canadian Journal of Behavioural Science, 41*(1), 1-10.

Safer, D. L., Telch, C. F., & Agras, W. S. (2001). Dialectical behavior therapy for bulimia nervosa. *American Journal of Psychiatry, 158(4),* 632-634.

Saggino, A. (2000). The big three or the big five? A replication study. *Personality and Individual Differences, 28:* 879-886.

Saggino, A. & Kline, P. (1996). The location of the Myers-Briggs Type Indicator in personality factor space. *Personality & Individual Differences, 21:* 591-597.

Sahoo, F. M., Sahoo, K., & Harichandan, S. (2005). Five big factors of personality and human happiness. *Social Sciences. International, 21*(1), 20-28.

St. Jacques, P. L., Dolcos, F., & Cabeza, R. (2009). Effects of Aging on Functional Connectivity of the Amygdala for Subsequent Memory of Negative Pictures. *Psychological Science. 20*(1): 74-84.

St. Rose, A. (2009). An examination of the relationship between gender, race/ethnicity, socioeconomic status, and SAT performance. US: ProQuest Information & Learning). *Dissertation Abstracts International Section A: Humanities and Social Sciences, 69* (8), 3126.

Sales, E., Baum, M., & Shore, B. (1984). Victim readjustment following assault. *Journal of Social Issues, 40*(1), 117-136.

Salovey, P. & Grewal, D. (2005) The science of emotional intelligence. *Current Directions in Psychological Science, 14,* 281-285.

Salovey, P., Mayer, J. D., Caruso, D., & Lopes, P. N. (2003). Measuring emotional intelligence as a set of abilities with the Mayer-Slovey-Caruso emotional intelligence test. In S. J. Lopez & C. R. Snyder (Eds.), *Positive psychological assessment: A handbook of models and measures.* (pp. 251-265) Washington, DC: American Psychological Association.

SAMHSA. (2008, June 16). *National survey on drug use and health.* Washington, DC: Department of Health and Human Services.

SAMHSA. (2008, June 16). *Racial and ethnic groups: Reports and data.* Washington, DC: Department of Health and Human Services.

Sanberg, C. D., Jones, F. L., Do, V. H., Dieguez Jr., D., & Derrick, B. E. (2006). 5-HTla receptor antagonists block perforant path-dentate LTP induced in novel, but not familiar, environments. *Learning & Memory, 13*(1), 52-62.

Sande, G. N., Goethals, G. R., & Radloff, C. E. (1988). Perceiving one's own traits and others': The multifaceted self. *Journal of Personality and Social Psychology, 54:* 13-20.

Sanford, A.J., Fay, N., Stewart, A., & Moxey, L. (2002). Perspective in statements of quantity, with implications for consumer psychology. *Psychological Science, 13,* 130-4.

Sangwan, S. (2001). Ecological factors as related to IQ of children. *Psycho-Lingua, 31*(2), 89-92.

Sansone, R. A., Songer, D. A., & Miller, K. A. (2005). Childhood abuse, mental healthcare utilization, self-harm behavior, and multiple psychiatric diagnoses among inpatients with and without a borderline diagnosis. *Comprehensive Psychiatry, 46(2):* 117-120.

Santerre, C. & Allen, J. J. B. (2007) Methods for Studying the Psychophysiology of Emotion. In J. Rottenberg & S. L. Johnson (Eds.) *Emotion and psychopathology: Bridging affective and clinical science.* Washington, DC: American Psychological Association.

Sar, V., Akyuz, G. & Dogan, O. (2007). Prevalence of dissociative disorders among women in the general population. *Psychiatry Research, 149,* 169-176.

Sarbin, T. R. & Allen, V. L. (1968). Role theory. In G. Lindzey & E. Aronson (eds.), *Handbook of social psychology* (2nd ed., Vol. 1. pp.488-567). Reading, MA: Addison-Wesley.

Sareen, J., Enns, M. W., & Cox, B. J. (2004). Potential for misuse of sedatives. *American Journal of Psychiatry, 161,* 1722-1723.

Sathian, K. (2002). The buzz of consciousness. *Neurology, 59,* 800-801.

Saucier, D. M. & Elias, L. J. (2001). Lateral and sex differences in manual gesture during conversation. *Laterality, 6:* 239-245.

Saucier, G., Hampson, S. E., & Goldberg, L. R. (2000). Cross-language studies of lexical personality factors. In S. E. Hampson (ed.), *Advances in personality psychology, Vol. 1* (1-36). Hove, England: Psychology Press.

Sawka, M. N., Cheuvront, S. N., & Carter, R. (2005). Human water needs. *Nutrition Reviews, 63*(6 Pt 2), S30-9.

Scelfo, B., Sacchetti, B., & Strata, P. (2008). Learning-related long-term potentiation of inhibitory synapses in the cerebellar cortex. *Proceedings of the National Academy of Sciences USA, 105,* 769-74.

Schacter, D. L. (2001). *The seven sins of memory: How the mind forgets and remembers.* NY: Houghton.

Schachter, S. & Latane, B. (1964). Crime, cognition, and the autonomic nervous system. *Nebraska Symposium on Motivation, 12:* 221-275.

Schachter, S. & Singer, J. (1962). Cognitive, social, and physiological determinants of emotional state. *Psychological Review, 69,* 379-399.

Schienle, A., Schäfer, A., & Vaitl, D. (2008). Individual differences in disgust imagery: a functional magnetic resonance imaging study. *Neuroreport, 19,* 527-30.

Schiffman, H. R. (1996). *Sensation and perception* (4th ed.) New York, NY: John Wiley & Sons, Inc.

Schiller, D., Levy, I., Niv, Y., LeDoux, J. E., & Phelps, E. A. (2008). From fear to safety and back: Reversal of fear in the human brain. *The Journal of Neuroscience 28*(45), 11517-11525.

Schlenger, W. E., Caddell, J. M., Ebert, L., Jordan, B. K., Rourke, K. M., Wilson, D., et al. (2002). Psychological reactions to terrorist attacks. *JAMA, 288*(5), 581-588.

Schlinger, H. D. (2003). The myth of intelligence. *Psychological Record,* 53, 15-32.

Schmidt, M. V., Sterlemann, V., & Müller, M. B. (2009). Chronic stress and individual vulnerability. *Stress, neurotransmitters, and hormones: Neuroendocrine and genetic mechanisms.* (pp. 174-183). New York, NY: New York Academy of Sciences; Wiley-Blackwell.

Schmitt, D. P., Allik, J., Mccrae, R. R., & Benet-Martínez, V. (2007). The geographic distribution of big five personality traits: Patterns and profiles of human self-description across 56 nations. *Journal of Cross-Cultural Psychology, 38*(2): 173-212.

Schmitt, F. F. & Lahroodi, R. (2008). The epistemic value of curiosity. *Educational Theory, 58*(2): 125-149.

Schneider, K. J. (Ed.). (2008). *Existential integratative psychotherapy: Guideposts to the core of practice.* New York, NY: Routledge/Taylor & Francis Group.

Schneider, T. A., Butryn, T. M., Furst, D. M., & Masucd, M. A. (2007). A qualitative examination of risk among elite adventure racers, *Journal of Sport Behavior,* 408, 330-337.

Schon, J. (2003). Dreams and dreaming: Perspectives over the century. *Psychoanalytic Psychotherapy in South Africa, 11*(2), 1-23.

Schooler, C. (2001). The intellectual effects of the demands of the work environment. In R. J. Sternberg & E. L. Grigorenko (Eds.), *Environmental effects on cognitive abilities.* (pp. 363-380) Mahwah, NJ: Lawrence Erlbaum Associates Publishers.

Schuel, H., Burkman, L. J., Lippes, J., Crickard, K., Mahony, M. C., Guiffrida, A., et al. (2002). Evidence that anandamide-signalling regulates human sperm functions required for fertilization. *Molecular Reproduction and Development, 63,* 376-387.

Schultz, T. F. & Kay, S. A. (2003). Circadian clocks in daily and seasonal control of development. *Science, 301*(5631), 326-327.

Schunk, D. H. (1990). Goal setting and self-efficacy during self-regulated learning. *Educational Psychologist. 25*(1): 71-86.

Schwanenflugel, P. J., Akin, C., & Luh, W. (1992). Context availability and the recall of abstract and concrete words. *Memory & Cognition, 20*(1), 96-104.

Schwarting, R. K. W. (2003). The principle of memory consolidation and its pharmacological modulation. In R. H. Kluwe, G. Lüer, & F. Rösler (Eds.), *Principles of learning and memory.* (pp. 137-153) Cambridge, MA: Birkhäuser.

Schwartz, B., Ward, A., Monterosso, J., Lyubomirsky, S., White, K., & Lehman, D. R. (2002). Maximizing versus sacrificing: Happiness is a matter of choice. *Journal of Personality and Social Psychology, 83,* 1178-97.

Schwartz, C. E., Snidman, N., Kagan, J. (1999), Adolescent social anxiety as an outcome of inhibited temperament in childhood. *Journal of the American Academy of Child and Adolescent Psychiatry, 38*: 1008-1015.

Sclafani, A. & Springer, D. (1976). Dietary obesity in adult rats: Similarities to hypothalamic and human obesity syndromes. *Physiology and Behavior, 17*: 461-471.

Seashore, H., Wesman, A., & Doppelt, J. (1950). The standardization of the Wechsler intelligence scale for children. *Journal of Consulting Psychology, 14*(2), 99-110.

Seeck, M., Mainwaring, N., Ives, J., Blume, H., Dubuisson, D., Cosgrove, R., Mesulam, M. M., & Schomer, D. L. (1993). Differential neural activity in the human temporal lobe evoked by faces of family members and friends. *Annals of Neurology.* 34: 369-72.

Segal, R. A. (Ed.) (2000). *Hero myths.* Oxford, UK: Blackwell Publishers Ltd.

Seligman, M., Rashid, T. & Parks, A. (2006). Positive psychotherapy. *American Psychology, 61,* 774-788.

Seligman, M. E. P. & Steen, T. A. (2005). Positive psychology progress: Empirical validation of interventions. *Amer. Psychologist, 60*(5), 410-421.

Seligman, M. E. P. (2007). Coaching and positive psychology. *Australian Psychologist, 42*(4), 266-267.

Seligman, M. E., Weiss, J., Weinraub, M., & Schulman, A. (1980). Coping behavior: learned helplessness, physiological change and learned inactivity. *Behavioral Research Therapy, 18,* 459-512.

Seligman, M. P. & Csikszentmihalyi, M. (2000). Positive psychology. *American Psychologist, 55*: 5-14.

Selkoe, D. J. (1991). Amyloid protein and Alzheimer's disease. *Scientific American, 265,* 68-78.

Selkoe, D. J. (2000). The origins of Alzheimer's disease: A is for amyloid. *JAMA, 283*(12), 1615-1617.

Selkoe, D.J. (2002). Alzheimer's disease is a synaptic failure. *Science, 298*(5594), 789-791.

Selye, H. (1956). Stress and psychobiology. *Journal of Clinical & Experimental Psychopathology,* 17, 370-375.

Selye, H. (1956). *The stress of life.* New York, NY: McGraw-Hill.

Selye, H. (1993). History of the stress concept. *Handbook of stress: Theoretical and clinical aspects (2nd ed.).* (pp. 7-17) New York, NY: Free Press.

Semendeferi, K., Lu, A., Schenker, N., & Damasio, H. (2002). Humans and great apes share a large frontal cortex. *Nature Neuroscience, 5*(3): 272-276.

Sénéchal, M. & LeFevre, J. (2001). Storybook reading and parent teaching: Links to Language and Literacy Development. In P. R. Britto & J. Brooks-Gunn (Eds.), *The role of family literacy environments in promoting young children's emerging literacy skills: New directions for child and adolescent development* (pp. 39-52). San Francisco, CA: Jossey-Bass.

Seyfarth, R. M. & Cheney, D. L. (2003). Meaning and Emotion in Animal Vocalizations. In P. Ekman, J. J. Campos, J. J. Davidson, R. J. de Waal, & B. M. Frans (Eds) *Emotions inside out: 130 years after Darwin's: The expression of the emotions in man and animals,* pp. 32-55. New York, NY: New York University Press.

Sgoifo, A., Braglia, F., Costoli, T., Musso, E., Meerlo, P., Ceresini, G., & Troisi, A. (2003). Cardiac autonomic reactivity and salivary cortisol in men and women exposed to social stressors: Relationship with individual ethological profile. *Neuroscience and Biobehavioral Reviews, 27*(1-2), 179-188.

Shadish, W. R., & Baldwin, S. A. (2005). Effects of behavioral marital therapy: A meta-analysis of randomized controlled trials. *Journal of Consulting and Clinical Psychology, 73*(1), 6-14.

Shaffer, D. R., Rogel, M., & Hendrick, C. (1975). Intervention in the library: The effect of increased responsibility on bystanders' willingness to prevent a theft. *Journal of Applied Social Psychology, 5*(4), 303-319.

Shafir, E., & Tversky, A. (2002). Decision making. *Foundations of cognitive psychology: Core readings.* (pp. 601-620) Cambridge, MA: MIT Press.

Shafranske, E. P., & Sperry, L. (2005). Addressing the spiritual dimension in psychotherapy: Introduction and overview. In L. Sperry & E. P. Shafranske (Eds.). *Spiritually oriented psychotherapy.* Washington, DC: American Psychological Association.

Shamay-Tsoory, S., Tomer, R., Berger, B. D., Goldsher, D., & Aharon-Peretz, J. (2005). Impaired "affective theory of mind" is associated with right ventromedial prefrontal damage. *Cognitive and Behavioral Neurology, 18*(1): 55-67.

Sharf, R. S. (2008). *Theories of psychotherapy and counseling: Concepts and cases* (4th ed.). Belmont, NY: Thomson Brooks Cole.

Sharma, A., Nash, A.A., & Dorman, M. (2009). Cortical development, plasticity and re-organization in children with cochlear implants. *Journal of Communication Disorders, 42*, 272-9.

Shaughnessy, M. F., Main, D., & Madewell, J. (2007). An interview with Irvin Yalom. *North American Journal of Psychology, 9*(3), 511-518.

Shaver, P., & Hazan, C. (1994). Attachment. In A. L. Weber & J. H. Harvey (eds.), *Perspectives on close relationships.* Boston, MA: Allyn & Bacon.

Shaw, P., Eckstrand, K., Sharp, W., Blumenthal, J., Lerch, J. P., Greenstein, D., Clasen, L., Evans, A., Giedd, J., & Rapoport, J. L. (2007). Attention-deficit/hyperactivity disorder is characterized by a delay in cortical maturation. *Proceedings of the National Academy of Sciences USA, 104*, 19649-54.

Shaw, P., Greenstein, D., Lerch, J., Clasen, L., Lenroot, R., Gogtay, N., Evans, A., Rapoport, J., Giedd, J. (2006, March 30). Intellectual ability and cortical development in children and adolescents. *Nature, 440*(7084), 619-620.

Shaw, P., Kabani, N. J., Lerch. J. P., Eckstrand, K., Lenroot, R., Gogtay, N., Greenstein D., Clasen, L., Evans, A., Rapoport, J. L., Giedd, J. N., & Wise, S. P. (2008). Neurodevelopmental trajectories of the human cerebral cortex. *Journal of Neuroscience, 28*(14), 3586-3594.

Shaywitz S. E., Shaywitz B. A. (2005) Dyslexia (specific reading disability). *Biological Psychiatry, 57*, 1301-9.

Sheikh, A.A., Ramaswami, S., & Sheikh, K.S. (Eds.). (2007). *Healing with death imagery. Imagery and Human Development Series.* Amityville, NY: Baywood Publishing Co.

Sheldon, K. M., Ryan, R. M., Deci, E. L., & Kasser, T. (2004). The independent effects of goal contents and motives on well-being: it's both what you pursue and why you pursue it. *Personality and Social Psychology Bulletin, 30*(4): 475-86.

Sheline, Y. I., Gado, M. H., & Kraemer, H. C. (2003). Untreated depression and hippocampal volume loss. *American Journal of Psychiatry.* 160: 1516-8.

Shenefelt, P. D. (2003). Hypnosis-facilitated relaxation using self-guided imagery during dermatologic procedures. *American Journal of Clinical Hypnosis, 45*, 225-231.

Shepperd, J. A. (1993). Productivity loss in performance groups: A motivation analysis. *Psychological Bulletin, 113*: 67-81.

Shepperd, J. A. (1995). Remedying motivation and productivity loss in collective settings. *Current Directions in Psychological Science, 4*: 131-134.

Sher, L. (2003). Daily hassles, cortisol, and depression. *Australian and New Zealand Journal of Psychiatry, 37*(3), 383-384.

Sherman, J. W., Stroessner, S. J., Conrey, F. R., & Azam, O. A. (2005). Prejudice and stereotype maintenance processes: Attention, attribution, and individuation. *Journal of Personality and Social Psychology, 89*(4): 607-622.

Sherry, A. & Whilde, M. R. (2008). Borderline personality disorder. In M. Hersen & J. Rosqvist (eds.), *Handbook of Psychological Assessment, Case Conceptualization, and Treatment, Vol 1: Adults.* (403-437) Hoboken, NJ: John Wiley & Sons Inc.

Sherwood, A. (1993). Use of impedance cardiography in cardiovascular reactivity research. *Cardiovascular reactivity to psychological stress & disease.* (pp. 157-199) Washington, DC: American Psychological Association.

Sherwood, J. (2002). Supermodels and drugs: The truth. *The Independent.* Downloaded on June 26, 2009 from: http://www.independent.co.uk/ news/uk/crime/supermodels-and-drugs-the-truth-660474.html.

Sherwood, S. J. (2002). Relationship between the hypnagogic/hypnopompic states and reports of anomalous experiences. *Journal of Parapsychology, 66*(2), 127-150.

Shih, M., Pittinsky, T. L., & Ambady, N. (1999). Stereotype susceptibility: Identity salience and shifts in quantitative performance. *Psychological Science, 10*(1), 80-83.

Shin, L. M., Orr, S. P., Carson, M. A., Rauch, S. L., Macklin, M. L., Lasko, N. B., Peters, P. M., Metzger, L. J., Dougherty, D. D., Cannistraro, P. A., Alpert, N. M., Fishman, A. J., Pitman, R. K. (2004). Regional cerebral blood flow in the amygdala and medial prefrontal cortex during traumatic imagery in male and female Vietnam veterans with PTSD. *Archives of General Psychiatry, 61*, 168-76.

Shmuelof, L. & Zohary, E. (2007). Watching others' actions: Mirror representations in the parietal cortex. *The Neuroscientist, 13*: 667-672.

Shoda, Y. & LeeTiernan, S. (2002). What remains invariant?: Finding order within a person's thoughts, feelings, and behaviors across situations. In D. Cervone & W. Mischel, *Advances in Personality Science, 1*: 241-270.

Shors, T. J. (2009). Saving new brain cells. *Scientific American, 300*(3): 46-52, 54.

Siegel, B. & Ficcaglia, M. (2006). Pervasive developmental disorders. In M. Hersen & J.C. Thomas (Series Eds.) & R.T. Ammerman (Vol. Ed.), *Comprehensive handbook of personality and psychopathology, Vol. 3: Child psychopathology.* Hoboken, NJ: Wiley.

Siegel, J. M. (2005). Clues to the functions of mammalian sleep. *Nature, 437*, 1264-1271.

Siegler, R. S. (2003). Thinking and intelligence. In M. H. Bornstein, L. Davidson, C. L. M. Keyes & K. A. Moore (Eds.), *Well-being: Positive development across the life course.* (pp. 311-320) Mahwah, NJ: Lawrence Erlbaum Associates Publishers.

Siever, L. J., & Davis, K. L. (1991). A psychobiological perspective on the personality disorders. *American Journal of Psychiatry, 148*(12), 1647-1658.

Sigel, E. (2008). Eating disorders. *Adolescent Medicine: State of the Art Reviews, 19*(3): 547-72, xi.

Silvera, D. H. & Laufer, D. (2005). Recent developments in attribution research and their implications for consumer judgments and behavior. In F. R. Kardes, P. M. Herr, & J. Nantel (eds.), *Applying social cognition to consumer-focused strategy.* (pp. 53-77) Mahwah, NJ: Lawrence Erlbaum Associates Publishers.

Silverman, K., Evans, S. M., Strain, E. C., & Griffiths, R. R. (1992). Withdrawal syndrome after the double-blind cessation of caffeine consumption. *New England Journal of Medicine, 327*(16), 1109-1114.

Silverman, P. (1992). An introduction to self-help groups. In B.J. White & E.J. Madara (Eds.), *The self-help sourcebook: Finding & forming mutual aid self-help groups.* Denville, NJ: St. Clares-Riverside Medical Center.

Silvia, P. J. (2008). Another look at creativity and intelligence: Exploring higher-order models and probable confounds. *Personality and Individual Differences, 44*(4), 1012-1021.

Simon, H. A. (1957). *Models of man.* New York: John Wiley & Sons, Inc.

Simon, H. A. (1990). Invariants of human behavior. *Annual Review of Psychology, 41,* 1-20.

Simon, J., Braunstein, G., Nachtigall, L., Utian, W., Katz, M., Miller, S., et al. (2005). Testosterone patch increases sexual activity and desire in surgically menopausal women with hypoactive sexual desire disorder. *The Journal of Clinical Endocrinology and Metabolism, 90*(9): 5226-33.

Simons, R. L., Murry, V., McLoyd, V., Lin, K., Cutrona, C., & Conger, R. D. (2002). Discrimination, crime, ethnic identity, and parenting as correlates of depressive symptoms among african american children: A multilevel analysis. *Development and Psychopathology, 14*(2), 371-393.

Simpson, P. A. & Stroh, L. K. (2004). Gender differences: Emotional expression and feelings of personal inauthenticity. *Journal of Applied Psychology, 89,* 715-721.

Singer, J. L. (2003). Daydreaming, consciousness, and self-representations: Empirical approaches to theories of William James and Sigmund Freud. *Journal of Applied Psychoanalytic Studies, 5,* 461-483.

Sinton C. M., & McCarley, R. W. (2004). Neurophysiological mechanisms of sleep and wakefulness: a question of balance. *Seminars in Neurology, 24,* 211-223.

Sizemore, C. C. (1991). *A mind of my own: The woman who was known as "Eve" tells the story of her triumph over multiple personality disorder.* New York, NY: William Morrow.

Skinner, B. F. (1957). *Verbal behavior.* New York, NY: Appleton-Century-Crofts.

Skinner, B. F. (1958). Diagramming schedules of reinforcement. *Journal of the Experimental Analysis of Behavior, 1,* 67-8.

Skinner, B. F. & Morse, W. H. (1958). Fixed-interval reinforcement of running in a wheel. *Journal of the Experimental Analysis of Behavior, 1,* 371-9.

Sloan, D. M. (2004). Emotion regulation in action: Emotional reactivity in experiential avoidance. *Behaviour Research and Therapy, 42,* 1257-1270.

Sloan, D. M., Bradley, M. M., Dimoulas, E., & Lang, P. J. (2002). Looking at facial expressions: Dysphoria and facial EMG. *Biological Psychology, 60*(2-3), 79-90.

Slovic, P. (1990). Choice. In D. N. Osherson & E. E. Smith (Eds.), *An invitation to cognitive science: Vol. 3: Thinking.* Cambridge, MA: MIT Press.

Smart, R. G., Stoduto, G., Adlaf, E. M., Mann, R. E., & Sharpley, J. M. (2007). Road rage victimization among adolescents. *Journal of Adolescent Health, 41*(3), 277-282.

Smedley, A., & Smedley, B. D. (2005). Race as biology is fiction, racism as a social problem is real. *Ameican. Psychologist, 60*(1), 16-26.

Smith, A. B., Taylor, E., Brammer, M., Halari, R., & Rubia, K. (2008). Reduced activation in right lateral prefrontal cortex and anterior cingulate gyrus in medication-naïve adolescents with attention deficit hyperactivity disorder during time discrimination. *Journal of Child Psychology and Psychiatry, and Allied Disciplines, 49,* 977-85.

Smith, A. W. & Baum, A. (2003). The influence of psychological factors on restorative function in health and illness. In J. Suls & K. A. Wallston (Eds.), *Social psychological foundations of health and illness.* Malden, MA: Blackwell Publishing.

Smith, C. (1996). Sleep states, memory processes and synaptic plasticity. *Behavioural Brain Research, 78*(1), 49-56.

Smith, C. (2006). Symposium V—Sleep and learning: New Developments. *Brain and Cognition. 60*(3), 331-332.

Smith, D. (2004). Love That Dare Not Squeak Its Name. *The New York Times.* Downloaded on June 25, 2009 from: http://www.nytimes.com/2004/02/07/arts/07GAY.html.

Smith, M. L., & Glass, G. V. (1977). Meta-analysis of psychotherapy outcome studies. *American Psychologist, 32*(9), 752-760.

Smith, M. L., Glass, G. V., & Miller, T. I. (1980). *The benefits of psychotherapy.* Baltimore, MD: Johns Hopkins University Press.

Smith, R. A. & Weber, A. L. (2005). Applying social psychology in everyday life. In F. W. Schneider, J. A. Gruman, & L. M. Coutts (Eds.), *Applied Social Psychology: Understanding and Addressing Social and Practical Problems.* (pp. 75-99) Sage Publications.

Smith, T. W. & Gallo, L. C., (2001). Personality traits as risk factors for physical illness. In A. Baum, T. A. Revenson, & J. E. Singer (eds.), *Handbook of health psychology* (139-173). Mahwah, NJ: Erlbaum.

Smoller, J. W., Rosenbaum, J. F., Biederman, J., Kennedy, J., Dai, D., Racette, S. R. et al. (2003). Association of a genetic marker at the corticotropin-releasing hormone locus with behavioral inhibition. *Biological Psychiatry, 54*(12), 1376-1381.

Smyth, J. M. & Pennebaker, J. W. (2001). What are the health effects of disclosure? In A. Baum, T. A. Revenson, & J. E. Singer (eds.), *Handbook of health psychology* (339-348). Mahwah, NJ: Erlbaum.

Snarey, J. R. (1985). Cross-cultural universality of social-moral development: A critical review of Kohlbergian research. *Psychological Bulletin, 97,* 202-232.

Snyder, W. V. (1947). *Casebook of non-directive counseling.* Boston, MA: Houghton Mifflin.

Solantaus, T., & Salo, S. (2005). Paternal postnatal depression: Fathers emerge from the wings. *The Lancet, 365,* 2158-2159.

Solms, M. (2004). Is the brain more real than the mind? In A. Casement (ed.), *Who owns psychoanalysis?* (323-342) London: Karnac Books.

Solms, M. (2007). Freud returns. In F. E. Bloom (ed.), *Best of the Brain* from *Scientific American.* (pp. 35-46) Washington, D.C.: Dana Press.

Solms, M. (2007). The interpretation of dreams and the neurosciences. In L. Mayes, P. Fonagy, & M. Target (Eds.), *Developmental science and psychoanalysis: Integration and innovation. Developments in psychoanalysis.* London, England: Karnac Books.

Solomon, R.C. (2000). The philosophy of emotions. In M. Lewis & J.M. Haviland-Jones (Eds.) *Handbook of emotions, Second Edition* (pp. 3-15). New York, NY: The Guilford Press.

Somers, J. M., Goldner, E. M., Waraich, P., & Hsu, L. (2004). Prevalence studies of substance-related disorders: A systematic review of the literature. *Canadian Journal of Psychiatry, 49*(6).

Sommers, C. H. (2000). The war against boys. *The Atlantic.*

Sommers-Flanagan, J., & Sommers-Flanagan, R. (2003). *Clinical interviewing* (3rd ed.). New York, NY: Wiley.

Sommers-Flanagan, J., & Sommers-Flanagan, R. (2007). Our favorite tips for interviewing couples and families. *Psychiatric Clinics of North America, 30*(2), 275-281.

Soomro, G. M., Altman, D., Rajagopal, S., & Oakley-Browne, M. (2008). Selective serotonin re-uptake inhibitors (SSRIs) versus placebo for obsessive compulsive disorder (OCD). *Cochrane Database Syst Rev,* 1, CD001765.

Sørensen, T. I., Holst, C., Stunkard, A. J., & Skovgaard, L. T. (1992). Correlations of body mass index of adult adoptees and their biological and adoptive relatives. *International Journal of Obesity and Related Metabolic Disorders: Journal of the International Association for the Study of Obesity, 16*(3): 227-36.

Sorkhabi, N. (2005). Applicability of Baumrind's parent typology to collective cultures: Analysis of cultural explanations of parent socialization effects. *International Journal of Behavioral Development, 29,* 552-563.

Soto, D., Hodsoll, J., Rotshtein, P., & Humphreys, G. W. (2008). Automatic guidance of attention from working memory. *Trends in Cognitive, Sciences, 12*: 342-8.

Soto, J. A., Levenson, R. W., & Ebling, R. (2005). Cultures of moderation and expression: Emotional experience, behavior, and physiology in Chinese Americans and Mexican Americans. *Emotion, 5,* 154-165.

Soukup, J. E. (2006). Alzheimer's disease: New concepts in diagnosis, treatment, and management. In T.G. Plante (Ed.), *Mental disorders of the new millennium, Vol. 3: Biology and function.* Westport, CT: Praeger Publishers.

Soussignan, R. (2002). Duchenne smile, emotional experience, and autonomic reactivity: A test of the facial-feedback hypothesis. *Emotion, 2,* 52-74.

Spagnolo, A. B., Murphy, A. A., & Librera, L. A. (2008). Reducing stigma by meeting and learning from people with mental illness. *Psychiatric Rehabilitation Journal, 31*(3), 186-193.

Spain, J., Eaton, L., & Funder, D. (2000). Perspectives on personality: The relative accuracy of self versus others in the prediction of emotion and *behavior. Journal of Personality, 68:* 837-867.

Spanos, N. P., Mondoux, T. J., & Burgess, C. A. (1995). Comparison of multi-component hypnotic and non-hypnotic treatments for smoking. *Contemporary Hypnosis, 12*(1), 12-19.

Spearman, C. (1904). "General intelligence," objectively determined and measured. *American Journal of Psychology, 15*(2), 201-293.

Spearman, C. (1923). *The nature of "intelligence" and the principles of cognition.* Oxford: Macmillan.

Spearman, C. (1927). *The nature of intelligence and the principles of cognition. (2nd ed.)* Oxford: Macmillan.

Spearman, C. (1937). *Psychology down the ages.* Oxford: Macmillan.

Spearman, C. (1939). Thurstone's work reworked. *Journal of Educational Psychology, 30*(1), 1-16.

Sperling, G. (1960). The information available in brief visual presentation. *Psychological Monographs, 74*(11), 29.

Sperry, L. (2003). *Handbook of diagnosis and treatment of DSM-IV-TR personality disorders (2nd ed.)* New York, NY: Brunner-Routledge.

Sperry, R. W. (1982). Some effects of disconnecting the cerebral hemispheres. *Science, 217*(4566), 1223-1226.

Sperry, R. W. (1985). Consciousness, personal identity, and the divided brain. In D. F. Benson & E. Zaidel (Eds.), *The dual brain: Hemispheric specialization in humans.* New York, NY: Guilford Press.

Sperry, R. W. (1995). The future of psychology. *American Psychologist, 50*(7), 505-506.

Sperry, R. W. (1998). A powerful paradigm made stronger. *Neuropsychologia, 36*(10), 1063-1068.

Spiegel, D., & Fawzy, F. I. (2002). Psychosocial interventions and prognosis in cancer. In H. G. Koenig & H. J. Cohen (Eds.), *The link between religion and health: Psychoneuroimmunology and the faith factor* (pp. 84-100). New York, NY: Oxford University Press.

Spielberger, C. D. (1966). Theory and research on anxiety. In C. D. Spielberger (Ed.), *Anxiety and behavior.* New York, NY: Academic Press.

Spielberger, C. D. (1972). Anxiety as an emotional state. In C. D. Spielberger (Ed.), *Anxiety: Current trends in theory and research* (Vol. 1). New York, NY: Academic Press.

Spielberger, C. D. (1985). Anxiety, cognition, and affect: A state-trait perspective. In A. H. Tuma & J. Maser (Eds.), *Anxiety and the anxiety disorders.* Hillsdale, NJ: Lawrence Erlbaum.

Spiegler, M. D., & Guevremont, D. C. (2003). *Contemporary behavior therapy.* Belmont, CA: Thomson/Wadsworth.

Spitzer, R. L., Skodol, A., Gibbon, M., & Williams, J. B. W. (1983). *Psychopathology: A case book.* New York, NY: McGraw-Hill.

Springman, R. E., Wherry, J. N., & Notaro, P. C. (2006). The effects of interviewer race and child race on sexual abuse disclosures in forensic interviews. *Journal of Child Sexual Abuse, 15*(3), 99-116.

Squire, L. R. & Schacter, D. L. (Eds.) *Neuropsychology of memory (3rd ed.)*(2002). New York, NY: Guilford Press.

Squire, L. R., Stark, C. E., & Clark, R. E. (2004). The medial temporal lobe. *Annual Review of Neuroscience.* -27: 279-306.

Srivastava, A. S., Malhotra, R., Sharp, J., & Berggren, T. (2008). Potentials of ES cell therapy in neurodegenerative diseases. *Current Pharmaceutical Design.* 14: 3873-9.

Srivastava, S., John, O. P., Gosling, S. D., & Potter, J. (2003). Development of personality in early and middle adulthood: Set like plaster or persistent change? *Journal of Personality and Social Psychology, 84:* 1041-1053.

Sroufe, L. A. & Rutter, M. (1984). The domain of developmental psychopathology. *Child Development, 55,* 17-29.

Stanovich, K. E. (2008). *How to Think Straight about Psychology* (8th ed.). Boston, MA: Allyn & Bacon.

Stanton, A. L., Parsa, A., & Austenfeld, J. L. (2002). The adaptive potential of coping through emotional approach. *Handbook of positive psychology.* (pp. 148-158) New York, NY: Oxford University Press.

Stanton, A. L., Sullivan, S. J., & Austenfeld, J. L. (2009). Coping through emotional approach: Emerging evidence for the utility of processing and expressing emotions in responding to stressors. *Oxford handbook of positive psychology (2nd ed.).* (pp. 225-235) New York, NY: Oxford University Press.

Steele, C. M. & Aronson, J. (1995). Stereotype threat and the intellectual test performance of African Americans. *Journal of Personality and Social Psychology, 69*(5), 797-811.

Steele, C. M. & Aronson, J. A. (2004). Stereotype threat does not live by Steele and Aronson (1995) alone. *American Psychologist, 59*(1), 47-48.

Steg L., Buunk A. P. and Rothengatter T. (Eds.) (2008) *Applied social psychology: Understanding and managing social problems*(2008). New York, NY: Cambridge University Press.

Stehlin, I. B. (1996). Inside FDA: Office of Women's Health. *FDA Consumer Magazine, 30*(8).

Stein, D. J. (2008). Classifying hypersexual disorders: Compulsive, impulsive, and addictive models. *Psychiatric Clinics of North America, 31*(4), 587-591.

Stein, D. J. & Fineberg, N. A. (2007). *Obsessive-compulsive disorder.* Oxford, England: Oxford University Press.

Stein, Z., Susser, M., Saenger, G., & Marolla, F. (1972). Nutrition and mental performance. *Science, 178,* 708-713.

Steinberg, L. (2001). We know some things: Parent-adolescent relationships in retrospect and prospect. *Journal of Research on Adolescence, 11,* 1-19.

Steiner, I. D. (1972). *Group process and productivity.* New York: Academic Press.

Steinhausen, H. (2002). The outcome of anorexia nervosa in the 20th century. *American Journal of Psychiatry, 159:* 1284-1293.

Steller, H. (1995). Mechanisms and genes of cellular suicide. *Science.* 267: 1445-9.

Steptoe, A. (2000) Health behavior and stress. In G. Fink (ed.), *Encyclopedia of Stress, Vol. 2,* (322-326). New York: Academic Press.

Sternberg, R. J. (1986). A triangular theory of love. *Psychological Review, 93: 119-135.*

Sternberg, R. J. (1987). Liking versus loving: A comparative evaluation of theories. *Psychological Bulletin, 102:* 331-345.

Sternberg, R. J. (2003). A broad view of intelligence: The theory of successful intelligence. *Consulting Psychology Journal: Practice and Research, 55*(3), 139-154.

Sternberg, R. J. (2003). Biological intelligence. In R. J. Sternberg & E. L. Grigorenko (Eds.), *The psychology of abilities, competencies, and expertise.* (pp. 240-262) New York, NY: *Cambridge University Press.*

Sternberg, R. J. (2003). *Wisdom, intelligence, and creativity synthesized.* New York, NY: Cambridge University Press.

Sternberg, R. J. (2003). WICS: A model of leadership in organizations. *Academy of Management Learning & Education, 2*(4), 386-401.

Sternberg, R. J. (2004). A triangular theory of love. In H. T. Reis & C. E. Rusbult (Eds.), *Close relationships: Key readings.* (pp. 213-227) Philadelphia, PA: Taylor & Francis.

Sternberg, R. J. (2008). The balance theory of wisdom. In M. H. Immordino-Yang (Ed.), *The Jossey-Bass reader on the brain and learning.* (pp. 133-150) San Francisco, CA: Jossey-Bass.

Sternberg, R. J. & Grigorenko, E. L. (2001). Unified psychology. *American Psychologist, 56,* 1069-1079.

Sternberg, R. J., Grigorenko, E. L., & Bundy, D. A. (2001). The predictive value of IQ. *Merrill-Palmer Quarterly, 47*(1), 1-41.

Sternberg, R. J., Kaufman, J. C., & Grigorenko, E. L. (2008). *Applied intelligence.* New York, NY: Cambridge University Press.

Sternberg, R. J. & Lubart, T. E. (2003). The role of intelligence in creativity. In M. A. Runco (Ed.), *Critical creative processes.* (pp. 153-187) Cresskill: Hampton Press.

Sternberg, R. J. & The Rainbow Project Collaborators. (2006). The Rainbow Project: Enhancing the SAT through assessments of analytical, practical and creative skills. *Intelligence,* 34, 321-350.

Sternberg, R. J., Wagner, R. K., Williams, W. M., Horvath, J. A., & al, e. (1995). Testing common sense. *American Psychologist, 50*(11), 912-927.

Sternberg, R. J. & Weis, K. (2006) *The New Psychology of Love.* New Haven, CT: Yale University.

Stetter, F., & Kupper, S. (2002). Autogenic training: A meta-analysis of clinical outcome studies. *Applied Psychophysiology and Biofeedback, 27*(1), 45-98.

Stewart, A. E. (2005). Attributions of responsibility for motor vehicle crashes. *Accident Analysis & Prevention, 37*(4): 681-688.

Stickgold, R. & Walker, M. P. (2005). Memory consolidation and reconsolidation: What is the role of sleep? *Trends in Neurosciences, 28,* 408-15.

Stickgold, R. & Walker, M. P. (2007). Sleep-dependent memory consolidation and reconsolidation. *Sleep Medicine, 8,* 331-343.

Stoleru, S., Gregoire, M. C., Gerard, D., Decety, J., Lafarge, E., Cinotti, L., et al. (1999). Neuroanatomical correlates of visually evoked sexual arousal in human males. *Archives of Sexual Behavior, 28:* 1-21.

Stone, T. H., Winslade, W. J., & Klugman, C. M. (2000). Sex offenders, sentencing laws and pharmaceutical treatment: A prescription for failure. *Behavioral Sciences & the Law, 18*(1), 83-110.

Storms, M. S. (1973). Videotape of the attribution process: Reversing actors' and observers' points of view. *Journal of Personality and Social Psychology, 27:* 165-175.

Strack, F., Martin, L. L., & Stepper, S. (1988). Inhibiting and facilitating conditions of the human smile: A non-obtrusive test of the facial-feedback hypothesis. *Journal of Personality and Social Psychology, 54,* 768-777.

Stranahan, A. M, Khalil, D., & Gould, E. (2006). Social isolation delays the positive effects of running on adult neurogenesis, *Nature Neuroscience, 9:* 526-33.

Stranahan, A. M., Khalil, D., & Gould, E. (2007). Running induces widespread structural alterations in the hippocampus and entorhinal cortex. *Hippocampus, 17:* 1017-22.

Strauss, B. (2002). Social facilitation in motor tasks: A review of research and theory. *Psychology of Sport and Exercise, 3*(3): 237-256.

Stricker, E. M. & Zigmond, M. J. (1986). Brain monoamines, homeostasis, and adaptive behavior handbook of physiology: Intrinsic regulatory systems of the brain. Bethesda, MD: American Physiological Society, 677-696.

Stromme, P. & Magnus, P. (2000). Correlations between socioeconomic status, IQ and aetiology in mental retardation: A population-based study of Norwegian children. *Soc. Psychiat. Psychiatr. Epidemiol., 35*(1), 12-18.

Strümpfel, U. (2004). Research on gestalt therapy. *International Gestalt Journal, 27*(1), 9-54.

Strümpfel, U. (2006). *Therapie der gefüble: For-schungsbefunde zur gestalttherapie.* Cologne, Germany: Edition Huanistiche Psychologie.

Stuart, T. D., & Garrison, M. E. B. (2002). The influence of daily hassles and role balance on health status: A study of mothers of grade school children. *Women & Health, 36*(3), 1-11.

Sturmey, P. (2008). Adults with intellectual disabilities. In M. Hersen & J. Rosqvist (Eds.), *Handbook of psychological assessment, case conceptualization, and treatment, Vol. 1: Adults.* Hoboken, NJ: John Wiley & Sons, Inc.

Stuss, D. T., Gallup Jr., G. G., & Alexander, M. P. (2001). The frontal lobes are necessary for "theory of mind." *Brain: A Journal of Neurology, 124*(2): 279-286.

Substance Abuse & Mental Health Services Administration (SAMHSA) (2009). *A SAMHSA Guide: Getting through tough economic times*. Department of Health and Human Services.

Sue, D. W., Capodilupo, C. M., Torino, G. C. (2007). Racial microaggressions in everyday life: Implications for clinical practice. *American Psychologist, 62*: 271-286.

Sue, D. W., & Sue, D. (2003) *Counseling the culturally diverse: Theory and practice* (4th ed.). New York, NY: Wiley.

Sugita, M. (2006). Taste perception and coding in the periphery. *Cellular and Molecular Life Sciences, 63*, 2000-15.

Sullivan, P. F., Kendler, K. S., & Neale, M. C. (2003). Schizophrenia as a complex trait: evidence from a meta-analysis of twin studies. *Archives of General Psychiatry, 60*, 1187-92.

Sulloway, F. J. (1996). *Born to rebel: Birth order, family dynamics and creative lives*. New York, NY: Pantheon.

Sun, M. (Ed.)(2007). *New research in cognitive sciences*. Hauppauge, NY: Nova Science Publishers.

Sunil, A., Carter, G. T., & Steinborn, J. J. (2005). Clearing the air: What the latest Supreme Court decision regarding medical marijuana really means. *American Journal of Hospice & Palliative Medicine, 22(5)*, 327-329.

Super, C. M. (1976). Environmental effects on motor development: The case of african infant precocity. *Developmental Medicine & Child Neurology, 18*(5), 561-567.

Super, C. M. & Harkness, S. (1972). The infant's niche in rural Kenya and metropolitan America. In L. Adler (Ed.), *Issues in cross-cultural research*. New York, NY: Academic Press.

Super, C. M. & Harkness, S. (2002). Culture structures the environment for development. *Human Development, 45*, 270-274.

Sutton, S. K. & Davidson, R. J. (2000). Prefrontal brain electrical asymmetry predicts the evaluation of affective stimuli. *Neuropsychologia 38*(13), 1723-1733.

Sutton, S. K., Ward, R. T., Larson, C. L., Holden, J. E., Perlman, S. B., & Davidson, R. J. (1997). Asymmetry in prefrontal glucose metabolism during appetitive and aversive emotional states: An FDG-PET study. *Psychophysiology, 34*, S89.

Swain, J. E., Lorberbaum, J. P., Kose, S., & Strathearn, L. (2007). Brain basis of early parent-infant interactions: Psychology, physiology, and in vivo functional neuroimaging studies. *Journal of Child Psychology and Psychiatry, and Allied Disciplines, 48(3-4)*: 262-87.

Swap, W. C. (1977). Interpersonal attraction and repeated exposure to rewarders and punishers. *Personality and Social Psychology Bulletin, 3*: 248-251.

Swinkels, A., & Giuliano, T. A. (1995). The measurement and conceptualization of mood awareness: Monitoring and labeling one's mood states. *Personality and Social Psychology Bulletin, 21*(9), 934-949.

Szeszko, P. R., Ardekani, B. A., Ashtari, M., Malhotra, A. K., Robinson, D. G., Bilder, R. M., et al. (2005). White matter abnormalities in obsessive-compulsive disorder: A diffusion tensor imaging study. *Archives of General Psychiatry, 62*, 782-790.

Szpunar, K. K., Watson, J. M., & McDermott, K. B. (2007). Neural substrates of envisioning the future. *PNAS. 104*(2): 642-47.

Szymanski, D. M., Chung, Y. B., & Balsam, K. F. (2001). Psychosocial correlates of internalized homophobia in lesbians. *Measurement and Evaluation in Counseling and Development, 34*: 27-38.

T

Tager-Flusberg, H. (2001). Putting Words Together: Morphology and Syntax in the Preschool Years. In J. Berko Gleason (Ed.), *The development of language* (5th ed., pp. 116-212). Boston, MA: Allyn and Bacon.

Takahashi, J., Takagi, Y., & Saiki, H. (2009). Transplantation of embryonic stem cell-derived dopaminergic neurons in MPTP-treated monkeys. *Methods in Molecular Biology*. 482: 199-212.

Takano, K. & Tanno, Y. (2009). Self-rumination, self-reflection, and depression: self-rumination counteracts the adaptive effect of self-reflection. *Behaviour Research and Therapy, 47*, 260-4.

Talarico, J. M. & Rubin, D. C. (2003). Confidence, not consistency, characterizes flashbulb memories. *Psychological Science, 14*(5), 455-461.

Talarico, J. M. & Rubin, D. C. (2007). Flashbulb memories are special after all; in phenomenology, not accuracy. *Applied Cognitive Psychology, 21*(5), 557-578.

Talwar, V., Gordon, H. M., Lee, K. Lying in the elementary school years: verbal deception and its relation to second-order belief understanding. *Developmental Psychology* 2007 May; 43(3): 804-10

Talwar, V., Lee, K. Social and cognitive correlates of children's lying behavior. *Child Development* 2008 Jul-Aug; 79(4): 866-81.

Tamis-LeMonda, C., & Cabrera, N. (Eds.). (2002). *Handbook of father involvement*. Mahwah, NJ: Erlbaum.

Tanaka, J., & Nomura, M. (1993). Involvement of neurons sensitive to angiotensin II in the median preoptic nucleus in the drinking response induced by angiotensin II activation of the subfornical organ in rats. *Experimental Neurology, 119*(2), 235-9.

Tandon, R., Belmaker, R. H., Gattaz, W. F., Lopez-Ibor, J. J., Okasha, A., Singh, B., Stein, D. J., Olie, J. P., Fleischhacker, W. W., & Moeller, H. J. (2008). World Psychiatric Association Pharmacopsychiatry Section statement on comparative effectiveness of antipsychotics in the treatment of schizophrenia. *Schizophrenia Research, 100*, 20-38.

Taube-Schiff, M. & Lau, M. A. (2008). Major depressive disorder. In M. Hersen & J. Rosqvist (Eds.), *Handbook of psychological assessment, case conceptualization and treatment, Vol. 1: Adults*. Hoboken, NJ: John Wiley & Sons, Inc.

Taube-Schiff, M., & Lau, M. A. (2008). Major depressive disorder. In M. Hersen & J. Rosqvist (Eds.), *Handbook of psychological assessment, case conceptualization, and treatment, Vol. 1: Adults* (pp. 319-351). Hoboken, NJ: John Wiley & Sons.

Tavris, C. (1989). *Anger: The misunderstood emotion (rev. ed.)*. New York, NY: Touchstone Books/Simon & Schuster.

Tavris, C. (1991). The mismeasure of woman: Paradoxes and perspectives in the study of gender. In J. D. Goodchilds (Ed.), *Psychological Perspectives on Human Diversity in America*. (87-136) Washington, D.C.: American Psychological Association.

Tavris, C. (2003). Uncivil rights--the cultural rules of anger. *Violence and society: A reader*. (pp. 3-14). Upper Saddle River, NJ: Prentice Hall/Pearson Education.

Taylor, D. A., Gould, R. J., & Brounstein, P. J. (1981). Effects of personalistic self-disclosure. *Personality and Social Psychology Bulletin, 7*: 487-492.

Taylor, D. J., McCrae, C. M., Gehrman, P., Dautovich, N., & Lichtein, K. L. (2008). Insomnia. In M. Hersen & J. Rosqvist (Eds.), *Handbook of psychological assessment, case conceptualization and treatment, Volume 1, Adults.* Hoboken, NJ: John Wiley & Sons, Inc.

Taylor, J., Iacono, W. G., & McGue, M. (2000). Evidence for a genetic etiology of early-onset delinquency. *Journal of Abnormal Psychology, 109,* 634-643.

Taylor, S. E. (2004). The accidental neuroscientist: Positive resources, stress responses, and course of illness. In G. G. Berntson & J. T. Cacioppo (Eds.), *Essays in social neuroscience* (pp. 133-141). Cambridge, MA: The MIT Press.

Taylor, S. E. (2006). *Health psychology (6th ed.).* New York, NY: McGraw Hill.

Taylor, S. E. (2006). Tend and befriend: Biobehavioral bases of affiliation under stress. *Current Directions in Psychological Science, 15*(6), 273-277.

Taylor, S. E. (2007). Social support. *Foundations of health psychology.* (pp. 145-171). New York, NY: Oxford University Press.

Taylor, S. E. (2008). From social psychology to neuroscience and back. *Journeys in social psychology: Looking back to inspire the future.* (pp. 39-54). New York, NY: Psychology Press.

Taylor, S. E., Klein, L. C., Gruenewald, T. L., Gurung, R. A. R., & Fernandes-Taylor, S. (2003). Affiliation, social support and biobehavioral responses to stress. *Social psychological foundations of health and illness.* (pp. 314-331). Malden: Blackwell Publishing.

Tedeschi, R. G., Park, C. L., & Calhoun, L. G. (1998). Posttraumatic growth: Conceptual issues. *Posttraumatic growth: Positive changes in the aftermath of crisis.* (pp. 1-22).Mahwah, NJ: Lawrence Erlbaum Associates Publishers.

Teicher, M. H., Andersen, S. L., Navalta, C. P., Tomoda, A., Polcari, A., & Kim, D. (2008). Neuropsychiatric disorders of childhood and adolescence. *The american psychiatric publishing textbook of neuropsychiatry and behavioral neurosciences (5th ed.).* (pp. 1045-1113) Washington, DC, US: American Psychiatric Publishing, Inc.

Temoshok, L. R. (2003). Congruence Matters: A Consideration of Adaptation and Appropriateness. *Advances in Mind-Body Medicine, 19:* 10-11.

Temoshok, L. R., Wald, R. L., Synowski, S., & Garzino-Demo, A. (2008). Coping as a multisystem construct associated with pathways mediating HIV-relevant immune function and disease progression. *Psychosomatic Medicine, 70*(5), 555-561.

Temoshok, L. R., Waldstein, S. R., Wald, R. L., Garzino-Demo, A., Synowski, S. J., Sun, L., & Wiley, J. A. (2008). Type C coping, alexithymia, and heart rate reactivity are associated independently and differentially with specific immune mechanisms linked to HIV progression. *Brain, Behavior, and Immunity, 22*(5), 781-792.

Tennen, H., & Affleck, G. (2002). Benefit-finding and benefit-reminding. *Handbook of positive psychology.* (pp. 584-597) New York, NY: Oxford University Press.

Tennen, H., & Affleck, G. (2009). Assessing positive life change: In search of meticulous methods. *Medical illness and positive life change: Can crisis lead to personal transformation?* (pp. 31-49) Washington, DC, US: American Psychological Association.

Tennen, H., Affleck, G., & Armeli, S. (2005). Personality and daily experience revisited. *Journal of Personality, 73*(6), 1465-1484.

Tennov, D. (1999). *Love and limerence: The experience of being in love.* (2nd edition). Chelsea, MI: Scarborough House.

Terman, L. M. (1925). *Genetic studies of genius. mental and physical traits of a thousand gifted children.* Oxford: Stanford Univ. Press.

Terman, L. M. & Merrill, M. A. (1937). *Measuring intelligence: A guide to the administration of the new revised Stanford-Binet tests of intelligence.* Oxford: Houghton Mifflin.

Terman, L. M. & Oden, M. H. (1959). *Genetic studies of genius. vol. V. the gifted group at mid-life.* Oxford: Stanford Univer. Press.

Thagard, P. & Kroon, F. W. (2006). Emotional consensus in group decision making. *Mind & Society, 5,* 85-104.

The National Weight Control Registry. (2009). http://www.nwcr.ws/ Research/default.htm

The Pew Forum on Religion and Public Life. (2003) Religious Beliefs Underpin Opposition to Homosexuality. Downloaded on May 24, 2009 from: http://pewforum.org/docs/?DocID=37.

The Report of the Model Health Inquiry. (2007). Fashioning a Healthy Future. Downloaded on June 26, 2009 from: http://www.model-healthinquiry.com/docs/The%20Report%20of%20the%20Model%20Health%20Inquiry,%20September%202007.pdf.

Thelen, E. (2001) Dynamic mechanisms of change in early perceptual-motor development. In J. L. McClelland & R. S. Siegler (Eds), *Mechanisms of cognitive development: Behavioral and neural perspectives.* (pp. 161-184). Mahwah, NJ: Lawrence Erlbaum Associates Publishers.

Theodorou, S. & Haber, P. S. (2005). The medical complications of heroin use. *Current Opinions in Psychiatry, 18*(3), 257-263.

Thigpen, C. H. & Cleckley, H. M. (1957). *The three faces of Eve.* New York: McGraw-Hill.

Thomas, A. K., Hannula, D. E., & Loftus, E. F. (2007). How self-relevant imagination affects memory for behaviour. *Applied Cognitive Psychology, 21*(1), 69-86.

Thomas, A. K. & Loftus, E. F. (2002). Creating bizarre false memories through imagination. *Memory & Cognition, 30*(3), 423-431.

Thomas, D. C., Elron, E., Stahl, G., Ekelund, B. Z., Ravlin, E. C., Cerdin, J., et al. (2008). Cultural intelligence: Domain and assessment. *International Journal of Cross Cultural Management, 8*(2), 123-143.

Thompson, R. A. (1994). Emotion regulation: A theme in search of a definition. *Monographs of the Society for Research in Child Development, 59,* 25-52.

Thompson, R. F. (2000). *The brain: A neuroscience primer (3rd ed.).* New York, NY: Worth Publishers.

Thompson, R. F. & Steinmetz, J. E. (2009). The role of the cerebellum in classical conditioning of discrete behavioral responses. *Neuroscience, 162, 732-55.*

Thompson, S. C., Sobolew-Shubin, A., Galbraith, M. E., Schwankovsky, L., & Cruzen, D. (1993). Maintaining perceptions of control: Finding perceived control in low-control circumstances. *Journal of Personality and Social Psychology, 64*(2), 293-304.

Thompson, W.F., Husain, G., & Schellenberg, E.G. (2001). Arousal, mood, and the Mozart effect. *Psychological Science, 12*(3), 248-251.

Thorndike, E. L. (1906). *The principles of teaching based on psychology.* New York, NY: A G Seiler.

Thorndike, E. L. (1920). The reliability and significance of tests of intelligence. *Journal of Educational Psychology, 11*(5), 284-287.

Thorndike, E. L. (1933). A proof of the law of effect. *Science, 77,* 173-5.

Thurstone, L. L. (1938). *Primary mental abilities* Chicago, IL: University of Chicago Press.

Time. (1980). Let's fall in limerence. *Time Magazine*. Retrieved December 19, 2008 from http://www.time.com/time/magazine/article/ 0,9171,952554-1,00.html

Tirri, K. & Nokelainen, P. (2008). Identification of multiple intelligences with the multiple intelligence profiling questionnaire III. *Psychology Science, 50*(2), 206-221.

Tither, J. M., & Ellis, B. J. (2008). Impact of fathers on daughterís age at menarche: A genetically and environmentally controlled sibling study. *Developmental Psychology, 44*(5), 1409-1420.

Toates, F. (2009). An integrative theoretical framework for understanding sexual motivation, arousal, and behavior. *Journal of Sex Research, 46(2):* 168-93.

Tolman, E. C. & Gleitman, H. (1949). Studies in spatial learning; place and response learning under different degrees of motivation. *Journal Experimental Psychol, 39,* 653-9.

Tomkins, S. S. (1962). *Affect, imagery, and consciousness.* New York, NY: Springer Publishing.

Tomkins, S. S. (1980). Affect as amplification: Some modifications in theory. In R. Plutchik & H. Kellerman (Eds.), *Emotion: Theory, Research and Experience* (pp.141-164). New York: Academic.

Tomkins, S. S. (1992). *Affect, imagery, consciousness, vol. 4: Cognition: Duplication and transformation of information.* New York, NY: Springer Publishing Co.

Torgersen, S. (2000). Genetics of patients with borderline personality disorder. *Psychiatric Clinics of North America, 23(1):* 1-9.

Tourangeau, R., Smith, T. W., & Rasinski, K. A. (1997). Motivation to report sensitive behaviors on surveys: Evidence from a bogus pipeline experiment. *Journal of Applied Social Psychology, 27:* 209-222.

Tousignant, M. (1984). *Pena in the Ecuadorian Sierra: A psychoanthropological analysis of sadness. Culture, Medicine, and Psychiatry, 8,* 381-398.

Townsend, F. (2000). Birth order and rebelliousness: Reconstructing the research in *Born to Rebel. Politics and the Life Sciences, 19*(2), 135-156.

Tramontin, M., & Halpern, J. (2007). The psychological aftermath of terrorism: The 2001 World Trade Center attack. In E. K. Carll (Ed.), *Trauma psychology: Issues in violence, disaster, health, and illness* (Vol. 1). Westport, CT: Praeger Publishers.

Tranel, D. & Damasio, A. R. (1993). The covert learning of affective valence does not require structures in hippocampal system or amygdala. *Journal of Cognitive Neuroscience, 5(1),* 79-88.

Tranel, D., Manzel, K., & Anderson, S. W. (2008). Is the prefrontal cortex important for fluid intelligence? A neuropsychological study using matrix reasoning. *Clinical Neuropsychologist, 22*(2), 242-261.

Travis, C. B., & Meltzer, A. L. (2008). Women's health: Biological and social systems. In F. L. Denmark & M. A. Paludi (Eds.), *Psychology of women: A handbook of issues and theories* (2nd ed., pp. 353-399). Westport, CT: Praeger Publishers.

Treatment for Adolescents with Depression Study Team, U.S.(TADS) (2007). The Treatment for Adolescents with Depression Study (TADS): Long-term effectiveness and safety outcomes. *Archives of General Psychiatry, 64*(10), 1132-1144.

Treisman, A. M., Kanwisher, N. G. (1998) Perceiving visually presented objects: recognition, awareness, and modularity. *Current Opinions in Neurobiology* 8:218-26.

Trenholm, C., Devaney, B., Fortson, K., Quay, L., Wheeler, J., Clark, M., et al. (2007). Impacts of Four Title V, Section 510 Abstinence Education Programs.

Triandis, H.C. (1989). Cross-cultural studies of individualism and collectivism. In J. Berman (ed.) *Nebraska Symposium.* Lincoln, NE: University of Nebraska Press (41- 130).

Triandis, H. C. (2001). Individualism-collectivism and personality. *Journal of Personality, 69*(6): 907-924.

Triandis, H. C. (2002). Individualism-Collectivism and Personality. *Journal of Personality. 69* (6): 907-924.

Triandis, H., Botempo, R., Villareal, M, Asai, M., & Lucca, N. (1988). Individualism and collectivism: Cross-cultural perspectives on self in group relationships. *Journal of Personality and Social Psychology, 54:* 332-336.

Triandis, H.C., McCusker, C., & Hui, C.H. (1990). Multimethod probes of individualism and collectivism. *Journal of Personality and Social Psychology, 59:* 1006-1020.

Triplett, N. (1898). The dynamogenic factors in pace-making and competition. *American Journal of Psychology, 9:* 507-533.

Troutt-Ervin, E. (1990). Application of keyword mnemonics to learning terminology in the college classroom. *Journal of Experimental Education, 59*(1), 31-41.

Troyer, J. M. (2006). Post-bereavement experiences of older widowers: A qualitative investigation. ProQuest Information & Learning: US. *Dissertation Abstracts International Section A: Humanities and Social Sciences, 66*(8): 3051.

Truett, K. R., Eaves, L. J., Walters, E. E., et al. (1994) A model system for analysis of family resemblance in extended kinships of twins. *Behavior Genetics,* 24(1), 35-49.

Tsai, J. L., Chentsova-Dutton, Y., Freire-Bebeau, L., & Przymus, D.E. (2002). Emotional expression and physiology in European Americans and Hmong Americans. *Emotion, 2,* 380-397.

Tsai, J. L., Levenson, R. W., & McCoy, K. (2006). Cultural and temperamental variation in emotional response. *Emotion, 6,* 484-497.

Tsai, J. L., Simeonova, D. I., & Watanabe, J. T. (2004). Somatic and social: Chinese Americans talk about emotion. *Personality and Social Psychology Bulletin, 30,* 1226-1238.

Tulsky, D. S. & O'Brien, A. R. (2008). The history of processing speed and its relationship to intelligence. In J. DeLuca & J. H. Kalmar (Eds.), *Information processing speed in clinical populations.* (pp. 1-28) Philadelphia, PA: Taylor & Francis.

Tulsky, D. S., Saklofske, D. H., & Ricker, J. H. (2003). Historical overview of intelligence and memory: Factors influencing the Wechsler scales. In D. S. Tulsky, D. H. Saklofske, G. J. Chelune, R. K. Heaton, & R. J. Ivnik (Eds.), *Clinical interpretation of the WAIS-III and WMS-III.* (pp. 7-41) San Diego, CA: Academic Press.

Tulving, E. (1974). Recall and recognition of semantically encoded words. *Journal of Experimental Psychology, 102*(5), 778-787.

Turkington, C. & Harris, J. R. (2001). *The Encyclopedia of memory and memory disorders (2nd edition).* New York, NY: Facts on File/Infobase Publishing.

Turkington, C. & Harris, J. R. (2009). *The Encyclopedia of the brain and brain disorders (3rd edition).* New York, NY: Facts on File/Infobase Publishing.

Tversky, A. (1972). Elimination by aspects: A theory of choice. *Psychological Review, 79,* 281-99.

Tversky, A. & Kahneman, D. (1974). Judgment under uncertainty: Heuristics and biases. *Science. 185,* 1124-31.

Tversky, A. & Kahneman, D. (1993). Probabilistic reasoning. In A. I. Goldman (Ed.), *Readings in Philosophy and Cognitive Science* (pp. 43-68). Cambridge, MA: MIT Press.

Twemlow, S.W., Fonagy, P., & Sacco, F.C. (2003). Modifying social aggression in schools. *Journal of Applied Psychoanalytical Studies, 5*(2), 211-222.

Tryon, W. W. (2005). Possible mechanisms for why desensitization and exposure therapy work. *Clinical Psychological Review, 25*(1), 67-95.

U

Ulrich, R.S. (1984). View through a window may influence recovery from surgery. *Science, 224,* 420-21.

Underwood, B. & Moore, B. (1982). Perspective-taking and altruism. *Psychological Bulletin, 91:* 143-173.

Ungar, W. J., Mirabelli, C., Cousins, M., & Boydell, K. M. (2006). A qualitative analysis of a dyad approach to health-related quality of life measurement in children with asthma. *Social Science and Medicine,* 63(9), 2354-2366.

Ungerleider, L.G. & Haxby, J.V. (1994) What and where in the human brain. *Current Opinion in Neurobiology, 4,* 157-65.

U.S. Bureau of Labor Statistics. (2001). *News: The employment situation: July 2001* (Table A-1: Employment status of the civilian population by sex and age). Retrieved May 16, 2006, from http://www.bls.gov/news.release/ pdf/empsit.pdf.

U.S. Bureau of the Census. (2000). *Current population reports: Educational attainment in the United States: March 2000* (Table 1: Educational attainment of the population 15 years and over, by age, sex, race, and Hispanic origin). Retrieved May 16, 2006, from http://www.census.gov/population/socdemo/education/p20-536/tab01.txt.

U.S. Census Bureau. (2008). Families and Living Arrangements Current Population Survey Report. Downloaded on May 23, 2009 from: http://www.census.gov/population/www/socdemo/hh-fam.html.

Urcuyo, K. R., Boyers, A. E., Carver, C. S., & Antoni, M. H. (2005). Finding benefit in breast cancer: Relations with personality, coping, and concurrent well-being. *Psychology of Health.,* 20(2), 175-192.

Ursano, R. J., McCarroll, J. E., & Fullerton, C. S. (2003). Traumatic death in terrorism and disasters: The effects on posttraumatic stress and behavior. *Terrorism and disaster: Individual and community mental health interventions.* (pp. 308-332) New York, NY: Cambridge University Press.

Urry, H. L, Nitschke, J. B., Dolski, I., Jackson, D. C., Dalton, K. M., Mueller, C. J., Rosenkranz, M. A., Ryff, C. D., Singer, B. H., & Davidson, R. J. (2004). Making a life worth living: neural correlates of well-being. *Psychological Science.* 15(6): 367-72.

Uziel, L. (2007). Individual differences in the social facilitation effect: A review and meta-analysis. *Journal of Research in Personality, 41:* 579-601.

V

van den Berg, Manstead, A. S. R., van, d. P., & Wigboldus, D. H. J. (2006). The impact of affective and cognitive focus on attitude formation. *Journal of Experimental Social Psychology, 42*(3): 373-379.

Van der Werf, Y. D., Witter, M. P., & Groenewegen, H. J. (2002). The intralaminar and midline nuclei of the thalamus. Anatomical and functional evidence for participation in processes of arousal and awareness. *Brain Research Reviews, 39,* 107-140.

Van Dongen, H. P. A., Maislin, G., Mullington, J. M., & Dinges, D. F. (2003). The cumulative cost of additional wakefulness: Dose-response effects on neurobehavioral functions and sleep physiology from chronic sleep restriction and total sleep deprivation. *Sleep: Journal of Sleep and Sleep Disorders Research, 26*(2), 117-126.

Van Dongen, H. P., Mott, C. G., Huang, J-K., Mollicone, D. J., McKenzie, F. D., & Dinges, D. F. (2007). Optimization of biomathematical model predictions for cognitive performance impairment in individuals: Accounting for unknown traits and uncertain states in homeostatic and circadian processes. *Sleep: Journal of Sleep and Sleep Disorders Research, 30,* 1129-1143.

Vandello, J. A., Cohen, D., & Ransom, S. (2008). U.S. southern and northern differences in perceptions of norms about aggression: Mechanisms for the perpetuation of a culture of honor. *Journal of Cross-Cultural Psychology, 39*(2): 162-177.

Vandrey, R. G., Budney, A. J., Hughes, J. R., & Liquori, A. (2008). A within-subject comparison of withdrawal symptoms during abstinence from cannabis, tobacco, and both substances. *Drug and Alcohol Dependence.* 92(1-3), 48-54.

van Eck, M., Nicolson, N. A., & Berkhof, J. (1998). Effects of stressful daily events on mood states: Relationship to global perceived stress. *Journal of Personality and Social Psychology, 75*(6), 1572-1585.

Vasey, M.W., Crnic, K.A., & Carter, W.G. (1994). Worry in childhood: A developmental perspective. *Cognitive Therapy Research, 18*(6): 529-549.

Vasiliadis, H. J., Lesage, A., Adair, C., Wang, P. S., & Kessler, R. C. (2007). Do Canada and the United States differ in prevalence of depression and utilization of services? *Psychiatric Services, 58*(1), 63-71.

Vedantam, S. (2006, March 30). Brain development and intelligence linked, study says. *The Washington Post,* A13.

Vega, W. A., Sribney, W. M., Aguilar-Gaxiola, S., & Kolody, B. (2004). 12-month prevalence of DSM-III-R psychiatric disorders among mexican americans: Nativity, social assimilation, and age determinants. *Journal of Nervous and Mental Disease,* 192(8), 532-541. doi.

Vernon, P. A., Wickett, J. C., Bazana, P. G., & Stelmack, R. M. (2000). The neuropsychology and psychophysiology of human intelligence. In *Handbook of intelligence.* (pp. 245-264) New York, NY: Cambridge University Press.

Vernon-Feagans, L., Hammer, C. S., Miccio, A. & Manlove, E. (2003). Early Language and Literacy Skills in Low-Income African American and Hispanic children. In S. B. Neuman & D. K. Dickinson (Eds.), *Handbook of early literacy research,* Volume 1 (pp. 192-206). New York, NY: Guilford Press Publications.

Vertes, R. P. & Eastman, K. E. (2003). The case against memory consolidation in REM sleep. In E. F. Pace-Schott, M. Solms, M. Blagrove, & S. Harnad (Eds.), *Sleep and dreaming: Scientific advances and reconsiderations.* New York, NY: Cambridge University Press.

Viggiano, D., Ruocco, L. A., Arcieri, S., & Sadile, A. G. (2004). Involvement of norepinephrine in the control of activity and attentive processes in animal models of attention deficit hyperactivity disorder. *Neural Plasticity.* 11: 133-49.

Vinogradov, S., Cox, P. D., & Yalom, I. D. (2003). Group therapy. In S. C. Yudofsky & R. E. Hales (Eds.), *The American Psychiatric Publishing textbook of clinical psychiatry.* New York, NY: Wiley.

Viswesvaran, C. & Ones, D. (1999). Meta-analysis of fakability estimates: Implications for personality measurement. *Educational and Psychological Measurement, 54:* 197-210.

Volkow, N. & Fowler, J. (2000). Addiction, a disease of compulsion and drive: involvement of the orbitofrontal cortex. *Cerebral Cortex, 10:* 318-325.

Vollrath, M. (2001). Personality and stress. *Scandinavian Journal of Psychology*, 42(4), 335-347.

Volz, J. (2000). Successful aging. The second 50. *APA Monitor, 31,* 24-28.

Voss, J. L. & Paller, K. A. (2009). An electrophysiological signature of unconscious recognition memory. *Nature Neuroscience.* 12(3): 349-55.

Vossekuil, B., Fein, R. A., Reddy, M. Borum, R., & Modzeleski, W. (2002). *The final report and findings of the safe school initiative: Implications for the prevention of school attacks in the United States.* Washington, D.C.

Vujanovic, A. A., Zvolensky, M. J., Bernstein, A., Feldner, M. T., & McLeish, A. C. (2007). A test of the interactive effects of anxiety sensitivity and mindfulness in the prediction of anxious arousal, agoraphobic cognitions, and body vigilance. *Behaviour Research and Therapy*, 45(6), 1393-1400.

Vygotsky, L. (1978). *Mind in society: Development of higher psychological processes.* Cambridge, MA: Harvard University Press.

Vygotsky, L. S. (1991). Genesis of the higher mental functions. In P. Light, S. Sheldon & M. Woodhead (Eds.), *Learning to think.* (pp. 32-41). Florence: Taylor & Frances/Routledge.

Vygotsky, L. S. (2004). Imagination and creativity in childhood. *Journal of Russian & East European Psychology*, 42(1), 7-97.

W

Wadden, T., D., F. G., Letizia, K. A., & Mullen, J. L. (1990). Long-term effects of dieting on resting metabolic rate in obese outpatients. *The Journal of the American Medical Association, 264(6):* 707-711.

Waite, L. J., Laumann, E. O., Das, A., & Schumm, L. P. (2009). Sexuality: measures of partnerships, practices, attitudes, and problems in the national social life, health, and aging study. *The Journals of Gerontology. Series B, Psychological Sciences and Social Sciences.* Downloaded on June 26, 2009 from: http://www.ncbi.nlm.nih.gov/pubmed/19497930.

Wakin, A. & Vo, D. B. (2008). *Love-variant: The Wakin-Vo I.D.R. model of limerence.* Retrieved December 19, 2008 from http://www.inter-disciplinary.net/ptb/persons/pil/pil2/wakinvo%20paper.pdf

Walenski, M., Mostofsky, S. H. & Ullman, M. T. Speeded processing of grammar and tool knowledge in Tourette's syndrome. *Neuropsychologia, 45,* 2447-60.

Walker, L. J. (2006). Gender and morality. In. M. Killen & J. G. Smetana, (Eds). *Handbook of moral development.* Mahwah, NJ: Lawrence Erlbaum Associates, pp. 93-115.

Wall, B. (2008). *Working relationships: Using emotional intelligence to enhance your effectiveness with others (rev. ed.).* Palo Alto, CA: Davies-Black Publishing.

Wall, T. L., Shea, S. H., Chan, K. K., & Carr, L. G. (2001). A genetic association with the development of alcohol and other substance use behavior in Asian Americans. *Journal of Abnormal Psychology*, 110(1), 173-178.

Wallace, B., & Persanyi, M. W. (1989). Hypnotic susceptibility and familial handedness. *Journal of General Psychology, 116*(4), 345-350.

Wallace, H. M., Baumeister, R. F., & Vohs, K. D. (2005). Audience support and choking under pressure: A home disadvantage? *Journal of Sports Sciences, 23*(4): 429-438.

Wallace, V., Menn, L., & Yoshinaga-Itano, C. (1999). Is babble the gateway to speech for all children? A longitudinal study of children who are deaf or hard of hearing. *Volta Review, 100,* 121-48.

Wallerstein, R. S. (2006). The relevance of freud's psychoanalysis in the 21st century: Its science and its research. *Psychoanalytic Psychology, 23*(2), 302-326.

Wallis, C. (2005). The new science of happiness. *Time, 165*(3), A2-A9.

Walsh, W. B. (2007). Introduction: Special section on self-efficacy, interests, and personality. *Journal of Career Assessment, 15(2):* 143-144.

Walster, E., Aronson, E., & Abrahams, D. (1966). On increasing the persuasiveness of a low prestige communicator. *Journal of Experimental Social Psychology, 2:* 73-79.

Wampold, B. E. (2007). Psychotherapy: The humanistic (and effective) treatment. *American Psychologist*, 62(8), 857-873.

Wan, C. Y. & Huon G. F. (2005). Performance degradation under pressure in music: An examination of attentional processes. *Psychology of Music, 33:* 155-172.

Wang, Qi, & Conway, Martin A. (2004). The stories we keep: Autobiographical memory in American and Chinese middle-aged adults. *Journal of Personality.* 72(5): 911-38.

Wang, P. S., Demler, O., Olfson, M., Pincus, H. A., Wells, K. B., & Kessler, R. C. (2006). Changing profiles of service sectors used for mental health care in the United States. *American Journal of Psychiatry*, 163(7), 1187-1198.

Wang, X. (2005). Discovering spatial working memory fields in prefrontal cortex. *Journal of Neurophysiology*, 93(6), 3027-3028.

Ward, E. C. (2007). Examining differential treatment effects for depression in racial and ethnic minority women: A qualitative systematic review. *JAMA*, 99(3), 265-274.

Ward, J. (2007, October 29). We are all Larry David. *New Yorker.* http://www.newyorker.com/talk/2007/10/29/071029ta_talk_ward.

Warziski, M. T., Sereika, S. M., Styn, M. A., Music, E., & Burke, L. E. (2008). Changes in self-efficacy and dietary adherence: The impact on weight loss in the PREFER study. *Journal of Behavioral Medicine, 31(1):* 81-92.

Wason, P. C. (1960). On the failure to eliminate hypotheses in a conceptual task. *Quarterly Journal of Experimental Psychology, 12,* 129-40.

Waterfield, R. (2000). *The first philosophers: The Presocratics and the Sophists.* New York, NY: Oxford University Press.

Waterhouse, J. M. & DeCoursey, P. J. (2004). The relevance of circadian rhythms for human welfare. In J. C. Dunlap, J. J. Loros, et al. (Eds.), *Chronobiology: Biological timekeeping.* Sunderland, MA: Sinauer Associates, Inc.

Watson, D. & Tellegen, A. (1985). Towards a consensual structure of mood. *Psychological Bulletin, 98,* 219-235.

Watson, D., Clark, L. A., & Chmielewski, M. (2008). Structures of personality and their relevance to psychopathology: II. Further articulation of a comprehensive unified trait structure. *Journal of Personality, 76(6);* 1545-1586.

Watt, T. T. (2002). Marital and cohabiting relationships of adult children of alcoholics: Evidence from the National Survey of Family and Households. *Journal of Family Issues, 23*(2), 246-265.

Watts, S. & Stenner, P. (2005). The subjective experience of partnership love: A Q methodological study. *British Journal of Social Psychology, 44*(1): 85-107.

Weale, R. (1982). *Focus on vision.* Cambridge, MA: Harvard University Press.

Weaver, C. M., Borkowski, J.G., & Whitman, T.L. (2008). Violence breeds violence: Childhood exposure and adolescent conduct problems. *Journal of Community Psychology, 36*(1), 96-112.

Wechsler, D. (1961). Cognitive, conative, and non-intellective intelligence. In J. J. Jenkins & D. G. Paterson (Eds.), *Studies in individual differences: The search for intelligence.* (pp. 651-660) East Norwalk, CT: Appleton-Century-Crofts.

Wechsler, H., Davenport, A., Dowdall, G., Moeykens, B., & Castillo, S. (1994). Health and behavioral consequences of binge drinking in college. *JAMA, 272*(21), 1672-1677.

Wechsler, H., Dowdall, G. W., Davenport, A., & Castillo, S. (1995). Correlates of college student binge drinking. *American Journal of Public Health, 85*(7), 921-926.

Wechsler, H., Lee, J. E., Kuo, M., & Lee, H. (2000). College binge drinking in the 1990s: A continuing problem: Results of the Harvard School of Public Health 1999 College Alcohol Study. *Journal of American College Health, 48*(5), 199-210.

Wechsler, H., Lee, J. E., Kuo, M., Seibring, M., Nelson, T. F., & Lee, H. (2002). Trends in alcohol use, related problems and experience of prevention efforts among US college students 1993 to 2001: Results from the 2001 Harvard School of Public Health college alcohol study. *Journal of American College Health, 50,* 203-217.

Wechsler, H. & Nelson, T. F. (2008). What we have learned from the Harvard School of Public Health College Alcohol Study: Focusing attention on college student alcohol consumption and the environmental conditions that promote it. *Journal of Studies on Alcohol and Drugs, 69,* 481-490.

Wechsler, H., Seibring, M., Liu, I. C., & Ahl, M. (2004). Colleges respond to student binge drinking: Reducing student demand or limiting access. *Journal of American College Health, 52*(4), 159-168, 159-168.

Weiden, P. J., & Kane, J. M. (Eds.). (2005). Optimizing pharmacotherapy to maximize outcome in schizophrenia: What is effectiveness with antipsychotic medications? *Journal of Clinical Psychiatry, 66*(1), 122-128.

Weight-control Information Network. (2008). Weight Cycling. Bethesda.

Weinberg, R. S. & Gould, D. (2003). *Foundations of sport and exercise psychology.* Champaign, IL: Human Kinetics.

Weiner, I. B. & Greene, R. L. (2008). *Handbook of personality assessment.* Hoboken, NJ: John Wiley & Sons, Inc.

Weinraub, M., Horvath, D. L., Gringlas, M.B. (2002). Single parenthood. In M.H. Bornstein (Ed.), *Handbook of parenting: Vol. 3. Being and becoming a parent (2nd edition).* Mahwah, NJ: Erlbaum.

Weis, R., & Smenner, L. (2007). Construct validity of the Behavior Assessment system for Children (BASC) Self-Report of Personality: Evidence from adolescents referred to residential treatment. *Journal of Psychoeducational Assessment, 25*(2), 111-126.

Weisberg, R. W. (1999). Creativity and Knowledge: A challenge to theories. In R. J. Sternberg (Ed.), *Handbook of creativity* (pp. 227-250). New York, NY: Cambridge University Press.

Weiskrantz, L. (1997). *Consciousness lost and found: A neuropsychological exploration.* London, England: Oxford University Press.

Weiskrantz, L. (2000). Blindsight: Implications for the conscious experience of emotion. In R. D. Lane & L. Nadel (Eds.), *Cognitive neuroscience of emotion.* London, England: Oxford University Press.

Weiskrantz, L. (2002). Prime-sight and blindsight. *Consciousness and Cognition: An International Journal, 11*(4), 568-581.

Weisman, R. L. (Ed.). (2004). Introduction to the special section on integrating community mental health and the criminal justice systems for adults with severe mental illness: Bridges and barriers. *Psychiatric Quarterly, 75*(2), 105-106.

Weiss, J. (2000). To have and to hold: marriage, the baby boom, and social change. Chigago, IL: University of Chicago Press.

Weiss, J. M. & Glazer, H. I. (1975). Effects of acute exposure to stressors on sub-sequent avoidance-escape behavior. *Psychosomatic Medicine, 37,* 499-521.

Weiss, R.D., Griffin, M.L., Gallop, R.J., Najavits, L.M., Frank, A., Crits-Christoph, P., et al. (2005) The effect of 12-step self-help group attandance and participation on drug use outcomes among cocaine-dependent patients, *Drug and Alcohol Dependency. 77*(2), 177-184

Wellman, H. M. & Hickling, A. K. (1994). The mind's "I": Children's conception of the mind as an active agent. *Child Development, 65,* 1564-80.

Wells, G. L. & Loftus, E. F. (2003). Eyewitness memory for people and events. In A. M. Goldstein (Ed.), *Handbook of psychology: Forensic psychology, vol. 11.* (pp. 149-160) Hoboken, NJ: John Wiley & Sons, Inc.

Wells, G. L., Small, M., Penrod, S., Malpass, R. S., Fulero, S. M., & Brimacombe, C. A. E. (1998). Eyewitness identification procedures: Recommendations for lineups and photospreads. *Law and Human Behavior, 22*(6), 603-647.

Wells, M. (2004). Reunited twins embrace entwined future. *Electronic BBC News.* Retrieved November 29, 2006, from http://news.bbc.co.uk/2/ hi/americas/3343763.stm.

Wenseleers, T., Helanterä, H., Hart, A., & Ratnieks, F. L. (2004). Worker reproduction and policing in insect societies: an ESS analysis. *Journal of Evolutionary Biology, 17*(5): 1035-47.

Werker, J. F. (1989). Becoming a native listener: A developmental perspective on human speech perception. *American Scientist, 77,* 54-59.

Wertenbaker, L. (1981). *The human body-eye: Window to the world.* Washington, D.C.: U.S. News books.

Wesley, L.V. (Ed.). *Intelligence: New research.* Hauppauge, NY: Nova Science Publishers.

West, R. L., Bagwell, D. K., & Dark-Freudeman, A. (2008). Self-efficacy and memory aging: The impact of a memory intervention based on self-efficacy. *Aging, Neuropsychology, and Cognition, 15*(3), 302-329.

Westen, D. (1998). The scientific legacy of Sigmund Freud: Toward a psychodynamically informed psychological science. *Psychological Bulletin, 124:* 333-371.

Westen, D. & Harnden-Fischer, J. (2001). Personality profiles in eating disorders: Rethinking the distinction between axis I and axis II. *American Journal of Psychiatry, 158*(4), 547-562.

Whalen, P. J. (1998). Fear, vigilance, and ambiguity: Initial neuroimaging studies of the human amygdala. *Current Directions in Psychological Science, 7*(6): 177-188.

Whalen, P. J., Davis, F. C., Oler, J. A., Kim, H., Kim, M. J., & Neta, M. (2009). Human amygdala responses to facial expressions of emotion. In P. J. Whalen & E. A. Phelps (Eds.), *The human amygdala*. (pp. 265-288) New York, NY: Guilford Press.

Whitaker, R. (2002). *Mad in America: Bad science, bad medicine, and the enduring mistreatment of the mentally ill*. Cambridge, MA: Perseus.

Whitlock, J. R., Heynen, A. J., Shuler, M. G., & Bear, M. F. (2006). Learning induces long-term potentiation in the hippocampus. *Science, 313*, 1093-7.

Whyte, G. (2000). Groupthink. In A. E. Kazdin (Ed.), *Encyclopedia of Psychology, Vol. 4*. (pp. 35-38) Washington, D.C.: American Psychological Association.

Wicker, B. (2008). New insights from neuroimaging into the emotional brain in autism. In E. McGregor, M. Núñez, K. Cebula, & J.C. Gómez (Eds.), *Autism: An integrated view from neurocognitive, clinical, and intervention research*. Malden, MA: Blackwell Publishing.

Wickwire, E. M., Jr., Roland, M. M. S., Elkin, T. D., & Schumacher, J. A. (2008). Sleep disorders. In D. Reitman (Ed.), *Handbook of psychological assessment, case conceptualization, and treatment: Volume 2—Children and adolescents*. Hoboken, NJ: John Wiley & Sons, Inc.

Wieser, H.G. (2003). Music and the brain. Lessons from brain diseases and some reflections on the "emotional" brain. *Annals of the New York Academy of Sciences, 999*, 76-94.

Willerman, L., Schultz, R., Rutledge, J. N., & Bigler, E. D. (1991). In vivo brain size and intelligence. *Intelligence, 15*(2), 223-228.

Williams, K. D., Harkins, S. G., & Latane, B. (1981). Identifiability as a deterrent to social loafing: Two cheering experiements. *Journal of Personality and Social Psychology, 40*: 303-311.

Williams, T. J., Pepitone, M. E., Christensen, S. E., Cooke, B. M., Huberman, A. D., Breedlove, N. J., et al. (2000). Finger-length ratios and sexual orientation. *Nature, 404*: 455-456.

Williams, W. M., Papierno, P. B., Makel, M. C., & Ceci, S. J. (2004). Thinking like A scientist about real-world problems: The Cornell institute for research on children science education program. *Journal of Applied Developmental Psychology, 25*(1), 107-126.

Wilsey, B., Marcotte, T., Tsodikov, A., Millman, J., Bentley, H., Gouaux, B., & Fishman, S. (2008). A randomized, placebo-controlled, crossover trial of cannabis cigarettes in neuropathic pain. *The Journal of Pain, 9*(6), 506-521.

Wilson, D.A. (2001). Receptive fields in the rat piriform cortex. *Chemical Senses, 26*, 577-84.

Wilson, E. O. (1975). *Sociobiology: The New Synthesis*. Cambridge, MA: Harvard University Press.

Wilson, G. (1981). *The Coolidge effect: An evolutionary account of human sexuality*. New York: William Morrow.

Wilson, G. T. & Shafran, R. (2005) Eating disorders guidelines from NICE. *Lancet, 365*: 79-81.

Wilson, G. T. (2008). Behavior therapy. In R. J. Corsini & D. Wedding (Eds.), *Current psychotherapies* (8th ed.). Belmont, CA: Thomson Brooks/Cole.

Wilson, N. (2003). Commercializing mental health issues: Entertainment, advertising, and psychological advice. In S. O. Lilienfeld, S. J. Lynn & J. M. Lohr (Eds), *Science and pseudoscience in clinical psychology*. New York NY: Guilford Press.

Wimmer, H., & Perner, J. (1983). Beliefs about beliefs: Representation and constraining function of wrong beliefs in young children's understanding of deception. *Cognition, 13*(1), 103-128.

Wincze, J. P., Bach, A. K., & Barlow, D. H. (2008). Sexual dysfunction. *Clinical handbook of psychological disorders: A step-by-step treatment manual (4th ed.)*. (pp. 615-661) New York, NY: Guilford Press.

Windholz, G. (1987). Pavlov as a psychologist. A reappraisal. Pavlov Journal of Biological Sciences, 22, 103-12.

Winegar L. & Valsiner, J. (Eds.) (1992). *Children's development within the social context* (2 vols). Hillsdale, NJ: Erlbaum.

Winston, A. S. (Ed.). (2004). *Defining difference: Race and racism in the history of psychology*. Washington, DC: American Psychological Association.

Wissler, C. (1961). The correlation of mental and physical tests. In J. J. Jenkins & D. G. Paterson (Eds.), *Studies in individual differences: The search for intelligence*. (pp. 32-44) East Norwalk, CT: Appleton-Century-Crofts.

Wixted, J. T. (2004). The psychology and neuroscience of forgetting. *Annual Review of Psychology, 55*, 235-269.

Wolf, S. (1969). Psychosocial factors in myocardial infarction and sudden death. *Circulation, 39*: 74-83.

Wolosin, S. M., Richardson, M. E., Hennessey, J. G., Denckla, M. B., & Mostofsky, S. H. (2009). Abnormal cerebral cortex structure in children with ADHD. *Human Brain Mapping, 30*, 175-84.

Wolpe, J. (1990). *The practice of behavior therapy* (4th ed.). Elmsford, NY: Pergamon Press.

Wolpe, J. (1995). Reciprocal inhibition: Major agent of behavior change. In W. T. O'Donohue & L. Krasner (Eds.), *Theories of behavior therapy: Exploring behavior change*. Washington, DC: American Psychological Association.

Wolpe, J. (1997). From psychoanalytic to behavioral methods in anxiety disorders: A continuing evolution. In J. K. Zeig (Ed.), *The evolution of psychotherapy: The third conference*. New York, NY: Brunner/Mazel.

Wolpe, J. (1997). Thirty years of behavior therapy. *Behavior Therapy, 28*(4), 633-635.

Wood, J. M., Garb, H. N., Lilienfeld, S. O., & Nezworski, M. T. (2002). Clinical assessment. *Annual Review of Psychology, 53*(1): 519-543.

Woods, S. C., Lutz, T. A., Geary, N., & Langhans, W. (2006). Pancreatic signals controlling food intake; insulin, glucagon, and amylin. *Philosophical transactions of the Royal Society of London. Series B, Biological sciences, 361*(1471): 1219-35.

Wootton, J. (2008). Meditation and chronic pain. In J. F. Audette & A. Bailey (Eds.), *Integrative pain medicine: The science and practice of complementary and alternative medicine in pain management. Contemporary pain medicine*. Totowa, NJ: Humana Press.

Worthy, M., Gary, A. L., & Kahn, G. M. (1969). Self-disclosure as an exchange process. *Journal of Personality and Social Psychology, 13*: 59-63.

Wortman, C. B., & Silver, R. C. (1992). Reconsidering assumptions about coping with loss: An overview of current research. *Life crises and experiences of loss in adulthood*. (pp. 341-365) Hillsdale, NJ: Lawrence Erlbaum Associates, Inc.

Wright, S., & Truax, P. (2008). Behavioral conceptualization. In M. Hersen & J. Rosqvist (Eds.), *Handbook of psychological assessment, case conceptualization, and treatment, Vol. 1: Adults* (pp. 53-75). Hoboken, NJ: John Wiley & Sons.

Wu, W., Brickman, A. M., Luchsinger, J., Ferrazzano, P., Pichiule, P., Yoshita, M., Brown, T., DeCarli, C., Barnes, C. A., Mayeux, R., Vannucci, S. J., & Small, S. A. (2008). The brain in the age of old:

The hippocampal formation is targeted differentially by diseases of late life. *Annals of Neurology, 64*(6): 698-706.

Wyatt, G. W., & Parham, W. D. (2007). The inclusion of culturally sensitive course materials in graduate school and training programs. Psychotherapy: *Theory, Research, Practice and Training,* 22(2, Suppl.) Sum 1985, 461-468.

Wynn, K. (1992). Addition and subtraction by human infants. *Nature, 358*(6389), 749-750.

Wynn, K. (2002). Do infants have numerical expectations or just perceptual preferences?: Comment. *Developmental Science, 5*(2), 207-209.

Wynne, K., Stanley, S., & Bloom, S. (2004). The gut and regulation of body weight. *The Journal of Clinical Endocrinology and Metabolism, 89(6):* 2576-82.

Y

Yadav, R., Suri, M., Mathur, R., & Jain, S. (2009). Effect of ventromedial nucleus of hypothalamus on the feeding behavior of rats. *Journal of Clinical Biochemical Nutrition, 44(May):* 247-252.

Yahr, P. (1977). Social subordination and scent marking in male Mongolian gerbils (Meriones unguiculatus). *Animal Behavior, 25,* 292-7.

Yamamoto, K. (1979). Children's ratings of the stressfulness of experiences. *Developmental Psychology, 15:* 581-682.

Yan, R. (n.d.). *Marriage, family and social progress of China's minority nationalities* (79-87). Boston, MA: Beacon Press.

Yang, S. & Sternberg, R. J. (1997). Conceptions of intelligence in ancient Chinese philosophy. *Journal of Theoretical and Philosophical Psychology, 17*(2), 101-119.

Yang, S. & Sternberg, R. J. (1997). Taiwanese Chinese people's conceptions of intelligence. *Intelligence, 25*(1), 21-36.

Yehuda, R. (2001). Biology of posttraumatic stress disorder. *Journal of Clinical Psychiatry, 62,* 41-46.

Yehuda, R. (2009). Stress hormones and PTSD. *Post-traumatic stress disorder: Basic science and clinical practice.* (pp. 257-275). Totowa, NJ: Humana Press.

Yehuda, R., McFarlane, A. C., & Shalev, A. Y. (1998). Predicting the development of posttraumatic stress disorder from the acute response to a traumatic event. *Biological Psychiatry, 44*(12), 1305-1313.

Yela, C. (2006). The evaluation of love: Simplified version of the scales for yela's tetrangular model based on sternberg's model. *European Journal of Psychological Assessment, 22*(1): 21-27.

Yen, S., Sr., Shea, M. T., Battle, C. L., Johnson, D. M., Zlotnick, C., Dolan-Sewell, R., Skodol, A. E., Grilo, C. M., Gunderson, J. G., Sanislow, C. A., Zanarini, M. C., Bender, D. S., Rettew, J. B., & McGlashan, T. H. (2002). Traumatic exposure and posttraumatic stress disorder in borderline, schizotypal, avoidant and obsessive-compulsive personality disorders: Findings from the collaborative longitudinal personality disorders study. *Journal of Nervous and Mental Disease, 190*(8), 510-518.

Yerkes, R. M. & Dodson, J. D. (1908). The relation of strength of stimulus to rapidity of habit-formation. *Journal of Comparative Neurology and Psychology, 18:* 459-482.

Yontef, G., & Jacobs, L. (2008). Gestalt therapy. In R . J. Corsini & D. Wedding (Eds.), *Current psychotherapies* (8th ed.). Belmont, CA: Thomson Brooks/Cole.

Yoo, S. S., Hu, P. T., Gujar, N., Jolesz, F. A., & Walker, M. P. (2007). A deficit in the ability to form new human memories without sleep. *Nature Neuroscience, 10,* 385-92.

Yoon, H. (2003). Factors associated with family caregiver's burden and depression in korea. *International Journal of Aging & Human Development, 57*(4), 291-311.

Yoon, I. Y., Kripke, D. F., Elliott, J. A., Youngstedt, S. D., Rex, K. M., & Hauger, R. L. (2003). Age-related changes of circadian rhythms and sleep-wake cycles. *Journal of the American Geriatrics Society, 51*(8), 1085-1091.

Young, K. S. (1996). Psychology of computer use: XL. addictive use of the internet: A case that breaks the stereotype. *Psychological Reports, 79*(3), 899-902.

Young, K. S. (1998). Internet addiction: The emergence of a new clinical disorder. *CyberPsychology & Behavior, 1*(3), 237-244.

Young, K. S. (2004). Internet addiction: A new clinical phenomenon and its consequences. *American Behavioral Scientist, 48*(4), 402-415.

Young, K. S. (2009). Assessment and treatment of internet addiction. *The praeger international collection on addictions, vol 4: Behavioral addictions from concept to compulsion.* (pp. 217-234) Santa Barbara, CA: Praeger/ABC-CLIO.

Young, L. R. (2007) By any other name, it's still a supersize. MSNBC. Downloaded on June 25, 2009 from: http://www.msnbc.msn.com/id/20825325.

Young, M., Benjamin, B., & Wallis, C. (1963). Mortality of widowers. *Lancet, 2,* 454-456.

Yuan, J. W., & Kring, A. M. (2009). Dysphoria and the prediction and experience of emotion. *Cognition and Emotion, 23*(6), 1221-1232.

Z

Zajonc, R.B. (1965). Social facilitation. *Science, 149,* 269-274.

Zajonc, R. B. (1980). Feeling and thinking: preferences need no inferences. *American Psychologist, 35,* 151-175.

Zajonc, R. B., Heingartner, A., & Herman, E. M. (1969). Social enhancement and impairment of performance in the cockroach. *Journal of Personality and Social Psychology, 13:* 83-92.

Zajonc, R. B., Murphy, S. T., & Inglehart, M. (1989). Feeling and facial efference: Implications of the vascular theory of emotion. *Psychological Review, 96,* 395-416.

Zarit, S. H. & Gaugler, J. E. (2000). Stress and caregivers. In G. Fink (ed.), *Encyclopedia of stress, Vol. 1* (404-407). New York, NY: Academic Press.

Zatorre, R.J. (2003). Absolute pitch: a model for understanding the influence of genes and development on neural and cognitive function. *Nature Neuroscience, 6,* 692-5.

Zawadzki, B., Strelau W., Oniszczenko, W., Roemann, R., & Angleitner, A. (2001). Genetic and environmental influences on temperament. *European Psychologist, 6:* 272-286.

Zeidner, M. (1990). Perceptions of ethnic group modal intelligence: Reflections of cultural stereotypes or intelligence test scores? *Journal of Cross-Cultural Psychology, 21*(2), 214-231.

Zeidner, M. (1990). Some demographic and health correlates of trait anger in Israeli adults. *Journal of Research in Personality, 24*(1), 1-15.

Zelazo, P. D. (2004). The development of conscious control in childhood. *Trends in Cognitive Sciences, 8,* 12-17.

Zentall, T. R. & Levine, J. M. (1972). Observational learning and social facilitation in the rat. *Science, 178:* 1220-1221.

Zigler, E. & Berman, W. (1983). Discerning the future of early childhood intervention. *American Psychologist, 38*(8), 894-906.

Zimbardo, P. (2006). A situationist perspective on the psychology of evil: Understanding how good people are transformed into pe+rpetrators. In R. Falk, I. Gendzier, & R. J. Lifton (eds.), *Crimes of War: Iraq.* (pp. 366-369) New York, NY: Nation Books.

Zimbardo, P. G. (2006). On rethinking the psychology of tyranny: The BBC prison study. *British Journal of Social Psychology, 45*(1): 47-53.

Zimbardo, P.G. (1972). Psychology of imprisonment. *Transition/Society:* 4-8.

Zlotnick, C. (1999). Antisocial personality, affect dysregulation, and childhood abuse among incarcerated women. *Journal of Personality Disorders, 13:* 90-95.

Zoccolillo, M., Price, R., Ji, T., Hyun, C., & Hwu, H.-G. (1999). Antisocial personality disorder: Comparisons of prevalence, symptoms, and correlates in four countries. In P. Cohen, C. Slomkowski, & L.N. Robins (eds.), *Historical and geographical influences on psychopathology.* (249-277) Mahwah, NJ: Lawrence Erlbaum Associates Publishers.

Zucker, K. J. (2005). Gender identity disorder in children and adolescents. *Annual Review of Clinical Psychology, 1*(1), 467-492.

Zucker, K. J. & Bradley, S. J. (1995). *Gender identity disorder and psychosexual problems in children and adolescents.* New York, NY: Guilford Press.

Zuckerman M. (1995). Good and bad humors: biochemical bases of personality and its disorders. *Psychological Science, 6:* 325-332.

Zuckerman, M. (2007). Sensation seeking and risk. *Sensation seeking and risky behavior.* (51-72). Washington, D.C.: American Psychological Association.

Text and Illustration Credits

Chapter 1

Figure 1-4: Ciccarelli, Saundra K.; White, J. Noland, *Psychology*, 2nd Edition, © 2009, p. 18. Reprinted by permission of Pearson Education, Inc., Upper Saddle River, NJ. Figure 1-5: Ciccarelli, Saundra K.; White, J. Noland, *Psychology*, 2nd Edition, © 2009, p. 18. Reprinted by permission of Pearson Education, Inc., Upper Saddle River, NJ. Figure 1-6: Data from Summary Report: Doctorate Recipients from United States Universities (Selected years). National Research Council, National Opinion Research Center. This bar chart is based on information compiled by Center for Workforce Studies, APA (2009). Reproduced with permission.

Chapter 2

Figure 2-3: Adapted with permission of John Wiley & Sons, Inc., from Carpenter, S., & Huffman, K. (2008). *Visualizing psychology.* Hoboken, NJ: Wiley, p. 15.

Chapter 3

Figure 3-2: Adapted with permission of John Wiley & Sons, Inc., from Carpenter, S., & Huffman, K. (2008). *Visualizing psychology.* Hoboken, NJ: Wiley, p. 230. Table 3-4: Based on Berk, L. E. (2008). *Infants, children, and adolescents* (6th ed.) Boston, MA: Allyn & Bacon, Table 5.2, p. 188. Figure 3-5: Based on Weiten, W. (2007). *Psychology: Themes and variations* (7th ed.). Belmont, CA: Thomson Higher Education. Adapted by permission from Macmillan Publishers Ltd: *Nature*, K. Wynn, Addition and subtraction by human infants, vol. 358, pp. 749–750, © 1992. Figure 3-9: Paragraph excerpted from Lilienfeld, S., Lynn, S., Namy, L., & Wolf, N. (2009). *Psychology: From inquiry to understanding.* Boston, MA: Pearson/Allyn & Bacon. Figure 3-11: Adapted by permission from BMJ Publishing Group Limited. *Archives of Disease in Childhood*, J. M. Tanner, R. N. Whitehouse, and M. Takaislu, vol. 41, pp. 451–471, 1966.

Chapter 4

Figure 4-5: Adapted with permission of John Wiley & Sons, Inc., from Huffman, K. (2010). *Psychology in action* (9th ed.). Hoboken, NJ: Wiley, p. 64.

Chapter 5

Figure 5-6: Based on Carpenter, S., & Huffman, K. (2008). *Visualizing psychology.* Hoboken, NJ: Wiley, p. 91. Figure 5-8: Reprinted with permission of John Wiley & Sons, Inc., from Carpenter, S., & Huffman, K. (2008). *Visualizing psychology.* Hoboken, NJ: Wiley, p. 106. Figure 5-9: Reprinted with permission of John Wiley & Sons, Inc., from Carpenter, S., & Huffman, K. (2008). *Visualizing psychology.* Hoboken, NJ: Wiley, p. 107. Figure 5-13: Reprinted with permission of John Wiley & Sons, Inc., from Kowalski, R., & Westen, D. (2009). *Psychology* (5th ed.). Hoboken, NJ: Wiley, p. 138. Figure 5-15: Reprinted with permission of John Wiley & Sons, Inc., from Kowalski, R., & Westen, D. (2009). *Psychology* (5th ed.). Hoboken, NJ: Wiley, pp. 143, 144.

Chapter 6

Table 6-2: Adapted with permission of John Wiley & Sons, Inc., from Carpenter. S., & Huffman, K. (2008). *Visualizing psychology.* Hoboken, NJ: Wiley, p. 129.

Chapter 7

Figure 7-12: Adapted with permission of John Wiley & Sons, Inc., from Carpenter, S., & Huffman, K. (2008). *Visualizing psychology.* Hoboken, NJ: Wiley, p. 152. Figure 7-13: Based on Gazzaniga, M. S., & Heatherton, T. F. (2006). *Psychological science* (2nd ed.). New York, NY: WW Norton, p. 230.

Chapter 8

Figure 8-5: Based on Turkington & Harris, 2009, 2001. Figure 8-7: Data from Luh, 1922. Figure 8-9: Reprinted from Bahrick, Bahrick, and Wittlinger. (1978). Those unforgettable high school days. *Psychology Today.*

Chapter 9

Figure 9-2: Adapted with permission from Fenson, Dale, Reznick, et al. (1994). Variability in early communicative development. *Monographs of the Society for Research in Child Development, 59*(5, Serial No. 173), Blackwell Publishers; based on Lilienfeld, S., Lynn, S., Namy, L., & Wolf, N. (2009). *Psychology: From inquiry to understanding.* Boston, MA: Pearson/Allyn & Bacon, Figure 8-3, p. 325. Figure 9-3: Adapted from Reznick, J. S., and Goldfield, B. A. Rapid change in lexical development in comprehension and production. *Developmental Psychology, 28,* 406–413. Figure 9-4: Reprinted from *Cognitive Psychology*, 21, J.S. Johnson & E.L. Newport, Critical period effects in second language learning: The influence of maturational state on the acquisition of English as a second language, pp. 60-99, Copyright 1989, with permission from Elsevier.

Chapter 10

Table 10-1: Based on Gardner, H. (1993). *Multiple intelligences: The theory in practice.* New York, NY: Basic Books. Figure 10-5: Sample items similar to those found in the *Wechsler Adult Intelligence Scale,* Third Edition (WAIS-III). Copyright © 1997 NCS Pearson, Inc. Reproduced with permission. All rights reserved. "Wechsler Adult Intelligence Scale" and

"WAIS" are trademarks, in the US and/or other countries, of Pearson Education, Inc. or its affiliates. Figure 10-6: Sample items similar to those found in *Raven's Progressive Matrices (Advanced)*. Copyright © 1976, 1947, 1943 NCS Pearson, Inc. Reproduced with permission. All rights reserved. "Raven's Progressive Matrices and vocabulary scales" are trademarks, in the US and/or other countries, of Pearson Education, Inc. or its affiliates. Figure 10-7: Adapted from Weiten, W. (2007). *Psychology: Themes and variations* (7th ed.). Belmont, CA: Thomson Learning; Horgan, J. (1995). Get smart, take a test. *Scientific American, 273*(5), 1995, p. 14. Adapted with permission of Dmitry Schidlowsky Illustration. Figure 10-9: Based on Anastasi & Urbina, 1977.

Chapter 11

Figure 11-1: Adapted with permission of John Wiley & Sons, Inc., from Carpenter, S., & Huffman, K. (2008). *Visualizing psychology*. Hoboken, NJ: Wiley, p. 285. Figure 11-2: Based on Lilienfeld, S., Lynn, S., Namy, L., & Wolf, N. (2009). *Psychology: From inquiry to understanding*. Boston, MA: Pearson/Allyn & Bacon, p. 470. Figure 11-6: Based on Sclafani A & Springer D. (1976). Dietary obesity in adult rats; Similarities to hypothalamic and human obesity syndromes. *Physiology and Behavior, 17*, 461-471. From *Psychological Science*, 2nd Edition, by Michael S. Gazzaniga and Todd F. Heatherton. Copyright © 2006, 2003 by W. W. Norton & Company, Inc. Used by permission of W. W. Norton & Company, Inc. Available at Amazon.com. This selection may not be reproduced, stored in a retrieval system, or transmitted in any form or by any means without the prior written permission of the publisher. Figure 11-7: Reprinted with permission from Masters, W. H., & Johnson V. E. (1966). *Human sexual response*. Boston, MA: Little, Brown, p. 5. Copyright © 1966 by the Masters and Johnson Institute.

Chapter 12

Table 12-1: Adapted with permission of John Wiley & Sons, Inc., from Kowalski, R., & Westen, D. (2009). *Psychology* (5th ed.). Hoboken, NJ: Wiley, p. 361; data from Plutchik, R. (1980). *Emotions: A psychoevolutionary synthesis*. New York, NY: Harper & Row. Practically Speaking: Measuring Your Emotional Well-Being: Adapted with permission from Diener, E., & Biswas-Diener, R. (2008). *Happiness: Unlocking the mysteries of psychological wealth*. Malden, MA: Blackwell Publishing, pp. 237–239. Figure 12-8: Based on King, L. A. (2008). *The science of psychology: An appreciative view*. New York, NY: McGraw-Hill, p. 391. Table 12-2: Based on Veenhoven, R. *World database of happiness, average happiness in 144 nations 2000-2008, RankReport 2009-1c*, Erasmus University Rotterdam. Available at: http://worlddatabaseofhappiness.eur.nl. Assessed May 4, 2009.

Chapter 13

Figure 13-2: Adapted with permission from Eysenck, H. J. (1976). *The biological basis of personality*, p. 36. Courtesy of Charles C Thomas Publisher, Ltd., Springfield, Illinois; based on Weiten, W. (2007). *Psychology: Themes and variations* (7th ed.). Belmont, CA: Thomson Wadsworth. Figure 13-3: Adapted from Cattell (1974). Personality pinned down. *Psychology Today*, 44. Figure 13-5: Adapted with permission from Weiten. *ACP psychology—Themes and variations–FIU Edition*, 6E. © 2004 Wadsworth, a part of Cengage Learning, Inc. Reproduced by permission. www.cengage.com/permissions; based on data from Loehlin, J. C. (1992). *Genes and environment*

in personality development. Newbury Park, CA: Sage. Table 13-3: Based on American Psychiatric Association. (2000). *Diagnostic and statistical manual of mental disorders-IV-TR*. Washington, DC: APA.

Chapter 14

Figure 14-2: Adapted with permission of John Wiley & Sons, Inc., from Kowalski, R., & Westen, D. (2009). *Psychology* (5th ed.). Hoboken, NJ: Wiley, p. 614; based on Festinger, L., & Carlsmith, J. M. (1959). Cognitive consequences of forced compliance. *Journal of Abnormal and Social Psychology, 58*, 203–210. Figure 14-5: Adapted from Myers, D. G. (2002). *Social psychology* (7th ed.). New York, NY: Worth, Figure 3-2; data from Jones, E. E., & Harris, V.A. (1967). The attribution of attitudes. *Journal of Experimental Social Psychology, 3*, 1–24. Figure 14-8: Adapted from Asch, S. E. (1955). Opinions and social pressure. *Scientific American, 193*(5), 31–35. © 1955 by Scientific American, Inc. All rights reserved. Figure 14-10: Based on Milgram, S. (1963). Behavioral study of obedience. *Journal of Abnormal and Social Psychology, 67*, 371–378; and Weiten, W. (2007). *Psychology: Themes and variations* (7th ed.). Belmont, CA: Wadsworth, Figure 16-17, p. 658. Figure 14-11: Adapted from Myers, D. G. (2002). *Social psychology* (7th ed.). New York, NY: Worth, Figures 3-2 and 12-4; based on Darley, J. M., & Latane, B. (1968). Bystander intervention in emergencies: Diffusion of responsibility. *Journal of Personality and Social Psychology, 8*, 377–383. Figure 14-12: Adapted from Anderson, C. (1989). Temperature and aggression: Ubiquitous effects of heat on occurrence of human violence. *Psychological Bulletin, 106*, 74–96. Table 14-1: From R.J. Sternberg (1987). The triangle of love: Intimacy, passion, commitment. New York, NY: Basic Books. Copyright © 1987 by Basic Books. Reprinted with the permission of the author.

Chapter 15

Table 15-1: Reprinted from *Journal of Psychosomatic Research, 3*, T.H. Holmes & R.H. Rahe, The social readjustment rating scale, pp. 213-218, Copyright 1967, with permission from Elsevier. Figure 15-5: Adapted from Niaura, R., et al. (2002). Hostility, the metabolic syndrome, and incident coronary heart disease. *Health Psychology, 21*, 588–593. Figure 15-6: Based on Cohen, S., Tyrrell, D. A. J., & Smith, A. P. (1991). Psychological stress and susceptibility to the common cold. *The New England Journal of Medicine, 325*, 609. Figure 15-7: Based on Weiten, W. (2004). *Psychology: Themes and variations* (6th ed.). Belmont, CA: Wadsworth, Figure 13.5, p. 528.

Chapter 16

Figure 16-1: Based on Kessler, R. C., Chiu, W. T., Demler, O., & Walters, E. E. (2005). Prevalence, severity, and comorbidity of 12-month DSM-IV disorders in the National Comorbidity Survey Replication. *Archives of General Psychiatry, 62*, 617–627. Table 16-3: Reprinted with permission of John Wiley & Sons, Inc., from Kowalski, R., & Westen, D. (2009). *Psychology* (5th ed.). Hoboken, NJ: Wiley, p. 574. Figure 16-6: Based on Prochaska, J. O., & Norcross, J. C. (2003). *Systems of psychotherapy: A transtheoretical analysis* (5th ed.). Pacific Grove, CA: Brooks/Cole; Lambert, M. J., Weber, F. D., & Sykes, J. D. (1993, April). Psychotherapy versus placebo. Poster presented at the annual meeting of the Western psychological Association, Phoenix, AZ; and Smith, M. L., & Glass, G. V. (1977). Metaanalysis of psychotherapy outcome studies. *American Psychologist, 32*(9), 752–760.

Photo Credits

Chapter 1

Page 2: Jae Rew/Getty Images, Inc.; page 4 (top): Fredrik Skold/Getty Images, Inc.; page 4 (bottom): Stuart Freedman/©Corbis; page 7 (center): Mark Andersen/Rubberball/Getty Images, Inc.; page 7 (bottom): Lonely Planet Images/Zuma Press; page 8 (top): ©The New Yorker Collection 1993 Dana Fradon from cartoonbank.com. All Rights Reserved; page 8 (center): The Granger Collection; page 9 (bottom): The Art Archive/Down House Kent/Eileen Tweedy/The Kobal Collection, Ltd.; page 10 (bottom): Archives of the History of American Psychology-University of Akron; page 11: The Granger Collection; page 12: ©Rune Hellestad/Corbis; page 14: ©AP/Wide World Photos; page 15: Nina Leen/Time & Life Pictures/Getty Images, Inc.; page 16: Markus Botzek/zefa/©Corbis; page 17: Roger Ressmeyer/©Corbis; page 19 (top): Karen Kasmauski/©Corbis; page 19 (bottom): ©The New Yorker Collection 1986 J.B. Handelsman from cartoonbank.com. All Rights Reserved; page 20 (far left): Mitchell Kanashkevich/Getty Images, Inc.; page 20 (left): Vitoria Blackie/Getty Images, Inc.; page 20 (center): Theo Allofs/Masterfile; page 20 (right): Daniel Milnor/Masterfile; page 22: ©AP/Wide World Photos; page 23: Clemens Bilan/AFP/Getty Images, Inc.; page 27: Ian Berry/Magnum Photos, Inc.

Chapter 2

Page 30: Pando Hall/Getty Images, Inc.; page 32: Derek Blair/Getty Images, Inc.; page 33: Joe Raedle/Getty Images, Inc.; page 35: Colin Hawkins/Getty Images, Inc.; page 36 (top left): ER Productions/Brand X/©Corbis; page 36 (top right): Josef Lindau/©Corbis; page 36 (bottom): China Foto Press/Getty Images, Inc.; page 37 (bottom): Jonathan Alcorn/Getty Images, Inc.; page 38 (bottom): ©The New Yorker Collection 1994 Sam Gross from cartoonbank.com. All Rights Reserved; page 39: John Henley/©Corbis; page 40: John Rowley/Getty Images, Inc.; page 41: Jeff Greenberg/PhotoEdit; page 43 (top): Picture Partners/Alamy; page 46 (left): iStockphoto; page 46 (right): Mike/zefa/©Corbis; page 47: ©The New Yorker Collection 2006 P.C. Vey from cartoonbank.com. All Rights Reserved; page 48 (center): Image Source/Getty Images, Inc.; page 49: Greg Gibson/©AP/Wide World Photos; page 50: Milena Boniek/PhotoAlto/©Corbis; page 51 (top): I Dream Stock/Masterfile.

Chapter 3

Page 54: John Lund/Annabelle Breakey/Getty Images, Inc.; page 58 (top): ©The New Yorker Collection 2002 David Sipress from cartoonbank.com. All Rights Reserved; page 58 (bottom): Nina Leen/Time & Life Pictures/Getty Images, Inc.; page 59 (top): Robert van der Hilst/©Corbis; page 61: CNRI/Photo Researchers, Inc.; page 62: Bert Krages/Visuals Unlimited; page 64: Rubberball/Getty Images, Inc.; page 65 (top): Bonnier Alba; page 65 (center): Petit Format/Nestle/Photo Researchers; page 66: Spencer Grant/PhotoEdit; page 69: ©The New

Yorker Collection 1989 Lee Lorenz from cartoonbank.com. All Rights Reserved; page 71 (left): Doug Goodman/Photo Researchers, Inc.; page 71 (center): Doug Goodman/Photo Researchers, Inc.; page 71 (right): Laura Dwight/PhotoEdit; page 74: Masterfile; page 75: Pat LaCroix/Getty Images, Inc.; page 76: iStockphoto; page 77: Ellen B. Senisi/The Image Works; page 83: John Giustina/Getty Images, Inc.; page 86 (top): James Woodson/Getty Images, Inc.; page 87: Betsie van der Meer/zefa/©Corbis; page 88: LookatSciences/Phototake; page 91: Jessica Webb Sibley/©AP/Wide World Photos; page 90: Zach Gold/©Corbis; page 95: Ariel Skeley/Getty Images, Inc.

Chapter 4

Page 96: G. Tompkinson/Photo Researchers, Inc.; page 98: Courtesy Leigh Nystrom and Jonathan Cohen; page 99: Primary rat hippocampal neurons, courtesy of Dr LLewelyn Roderick, Dr Martin Bootman and Dr Paul Cuddon, The Babraham Institute, Cambridge, UK; page 100 (center): From Wikipedia, http://commons.wikimedia.org/wiki/File: Zwei_Verschiedene_Neurone.png; page 101: Riccardo Cassiani-Ingoni/Photo Researchers, Inc.; page 104: Dennis Kunkel/Phototake; page 106: Bob Pardue/Alamy; page 108 (bottom): iStockphoto; page 109: Courtesy Thomas Deerinck, NCMIR, University of California, San Diego; page 110: Hola Images/Getty Images, Inc.; page 111: Thomas Northcut/Getty Images, Inc.; page 112: Chad Slattery/Getty Images, Inc.; page 114: Asia Images Group/Getty Images, Inc.; page 115 (top left): From the collection of Jack and Beverly Wilgus. Image from Wikipedia.org; page 115 (top right): Harvard Medical School/©AP/Wide World Photos; page 116 (top): Masterfile; page 116 (bottom): Mark Nielsen; page 119 (top): Courtesy Elizabeth Gould; page 119 (bottom): Courtesy Becker Medical Library, Washington University School of Medicine; page 120 (bottom left): Danielle Wooten/Getty Images, Inc.; page 120 (bottom right): Michael Rosenfeld/Getty Images, Inc.; page 121: Dana Hursey Photography/Getty Images, Inc.; page 123: Courtesy ReNeuron; page 127: Owen Franken/©Corbis.

Chapter 5

Page 128: Masterfile; page 131 (center): ER Productions/©Corbis; page 134: Freudenrich, Visualizing A & P; page 135 (top left): Photo courtesy of Drs. Hang Hu and Ariel Agmon, Sensory Neuroscience Research Center, West Virginia University School of Medicine; page 135 (top right): Neuroscience Research Center, West Virginia University School of Medicine; page 135 (center): Masterfile; page 135 (bottom right): From Marco Tizzano et al. BMC Neuroscience 2008 9:110, Figure 5; ©2008 Tizzano et al.; licensee BioMed Central Ltd.; page 136 (top): Steve Prezant/©Corbis; page 136 (bottom): Paul Taylor/©Corbis; page 137: iStockphoto; page 138: Louie Psihoyos/©Corbis; page 139 (top): Patrick Sheandell O'Carroll/PhotoAlto/©Corbis; page 140: Owne Franken/©Corbis; page 142 (top): Ken Catania/Visuals Unlimited; page 142 (bottom): Keith Brofsky/Age Fotostock America, Inc.; page 143:

Robbie Jack/©Corbis; page 144: Stockbyte/Getty Images, Inc.; page 145 (top right): Jim Mone/©AP/Wide World Photos; page 147: Jose Luis Pelaez/©Corbis; page 148: George Steinmetz/©Corbis; page 149 (top): Getty Images, Inc.; page 149 (bottom): Gareth Brown/©Corbis; page 150 (top): Rene Macura/©AP/Wide World Photos; page 150 (bottom): ©Landov; page 152: Omikron/Photo Researchers, Inc.; page 154: Steven Senne/©AP/Wide World Photos; page 156: Kate Mitchell/©Corbis; page 157: M.C. Escher s Convex and Concave ©2009 The M.C. Escher Company-Holland. All rights reserved. www.mcescher.com; page 158: Margo Silver/Getty Images, Inc.; page 159 (top): Laura Dwight/©Corbis; page 159 (bottom): Ron Watts/©Corbis; page 160 (top): Billy Hustace/Getty Images, Inc.; page 163 (bottom): Londie Padelsky/Monsoon/Photolibrary/©Corbis.

Chapter 6

Page 164: Ron Krisel/Getty Images, Inc.; page 165: Jose Luis Pelaez, Inc./©Corbis; page 166: Damir Frkovic/Masterfile; page 167: John Burcham/Getty Images, Inc.; page 170 (center): Charles Gullung/Getty Images, Inc.; page 171: The New Yorker Collection 1983 Edward Frascino from cartoonbank.com. All Rights Reserved.; page 173 (center): Francoise Sauze/Photo Researchers, Inc.; page 176 (center): Masterfile; page 177: Science Photo Library/Photo Researchers, Inc.; page 178 (right): Jupiter Images/Getty Images, Inc.; page 178 (left): Life Boat/Getty Images, Inc.; page 180: Stockbyte/Getty Images, Inc.; page 181: Hank Morgan/Photo Researchers, Inc.; page 182: Harald Sund/Getty Images, Inc.; page 183: PM Images/Getty Images, Inc.; page 185 (top): Alistair Baker/©Corbis; page 185 (center): Julia Klee/©Corbis; page 186 (center): Louie Psihoyos/Science Faction/©Corbis; page 187: ©The New Yorker Collection 2000 Tom Cheney from cartoonbank.com. All Rights Reserved; page 188: Brad Barket/Getty Images, Inc.; page 190: Murat Taner/©Corbis; page 191: Catherine Karnow/©Corbis; page 193 (top): Bob Thomas/©Corbis; page 193 (bottom): The Granger Collection; page 195: Carol and Mike Werner/Phototake; page 189: Andrew Lichenstein/©Corbis; page 196: CP, Kevin Frayer/©AP/Wide World Photos; page 201: Newmann/©Corbis.

Chapter 7

Page 202: Masterfile; page 204: Tetra Images/©Corbis; page 205 (left): Mango Productions/©Corbis; page 205 (right): Simon Jarratt/©Corbis; page 206: Courtesy Columbia University, New York. Image from Wikipedia,http: //en.wikipedia.org/wiki/Aplysia_californica; page 207 (center): ©The New Yorker Collection 1998 Leo Collum from cartoonbank.com. All Rights Reserved; page 209: The Granger Collection, New York; page 210: Jose Luis Pelaez/Blend Images/Getty Images, Inc.; page 211: Courtesy Benjamin Harris; page 212: Alan and Sandy Carey/Photo Researchers, Inc.; page 213 (top left): Serge Kozak/©Corbis; page 213 (top right): Reprinted by permission of Elsevier from L. Goossen, et al., Amygdala Hyperfunction in Phobic Fear Normalizes After Exposure Biological Psychiatry, Volume 62, Issue 10, Pages 1119-1125, Figure 1.; page 213 (bottom right): ©James Balog Photography; page 217: Cynthia Dopkin/Photo Researchers; page 218: ©The New Yorker Collection 1993 Tom Cheney from cartoonbank.com. All Rights Reserved; page 219 (top): A. Witte/C. Mahaney/Getty Images, Inc.; page 219 (bottom): Dan McCoy/Rainbow/©Corbis; page 220: Jupiter Images/Thinkstock/Getty Images, Inc.; page 221 (center): Courtesy American Philosophical Society; page 222: Photograph by Frans de Waal from The Ape and the Sushi Master.; page 223 (top right):

Courtesy Albert Bandura; page 224 (top): David H. Wells/©Corbis; page 225 (top right): Dan Hallman/Getty Images, Inc.; page 226 (top left): PhotoDisc Green/Getty Images; page 226 (top right): ©Alexis Cheziere/CNRS/Phototeque; page 228: Masterfile; page 229 (top left): From Michael Petrides, J. Neurosci, 2003 Jul 2; 23 (13): 5945-52; page 229 (top right): Courtesy Elizabeth Gould; page 229 (center left): Courtesy Elizabeth Gould; page 229 (center right): Masterfile; page 230 (top): LookatSciences/Phototake; page 231: Digital Vision/Getty Images, Inc.; page 232 (bottom): Olivier Voisin/Photo Researchers, Inc.; page 233: Chuck Burton/©AP/Wide World Photos; page 237: Photodisc/Getty Images, Inc.

Chapter 8

Page 238: Chris Ryan/Age Fotostock America, Inc.; page 242 (top): Digital Vision/Getty Images, Inc.; page 243: ©The New Yorker Collection1996 Arnie Levin from cartoonbank.com. All Rights Reserved; page 244: Masterfile; page 245: Tom Stewart/©Corbis; page 246: Dong Yiming/BJCB/ChinaFotoPress/Getty Images, Inc.; page 247: Neo Vision/Getty Images, Inc.; page 248: Tetra Images/Getty Images, Inc.; page 249 (top left): Tomas Hajek/isifa/Getty Images, Inc.; page 252 (left): Ethan Miller/Getty Images, Inc.; page 252 (right): AAGAMIA/Getty Images, Inc.; page 253 (bottom): ©The New Yorker Collection 1990 Jack Ziegler from cartoonbank.com. All Rights Reserved; page 255: NBAE/Getty Images, Inc.; page 256: Spencer Platt/Getty Images, Inc.; page 259 (left): Chip Somodevilla/Getty Images, Inc.; page 259 (right): Jeff Hutchens/Getty Images, Inc.; page 260: Masterfile; page 261: Chuck Burton/©AP/Wide World Photos; page 262: Oscar Sosa/©AP/Wide World Photos; page 263 (top): Christina Koci Hernandez/©Corbis; page 264 (bottom left): William Fritsch/Alamy; page 264 (top right): PNC/Getty Images, Inc.; page 264 (center right): Stockbyte/Getty Images, Inc.; page 265 (top left): Courtesy Elizabeth Gould; page 265 (top right): Image provided courtesy of Roberto Cabeza, Duke University. From Cabeza, Cerebral Cortex, 2007, Figure 4. Reproduced with permission of Oxford University Press.; page 265 (bottom left): Masterfile; page 265 (bottom right): Courtesy Jeff Lichtman and Jean Livet; page 266: From Edward T. Bullmore, Neuroimage 22 (issue 4), 1704-1714, Figure 5; page 267: ©The New Yorker Collection 1983 Ed Fisher from cartoonbank.com. All Rights Reserved; page 269: Jason Szenes/epa/©Corbis; page 270: Science Source/Photo Researchers, Inc.; page 271: Andrew Holbrooke/©Corbis; page 272: St. Petersburg Times, Bill Serne/©AP/Wide World Photos; page 275: STOCK4B/Getty Images, Inc.

Chapter 9

Page 276: Masterfile; page 278: Hans Reinhard/©Corbis; page 280 (top): Pete Souza/White House/©Corbis; page 280 (bottom): Laura Dwight/©Corbis; page 282: Joe Bator/©Corbis; page 283: David Young-Wolff/PhotoEdit; page 284 (top): ©1993 by Russ Rymer. A portion of this book appeared in somewhat different form in th The New Yorker magazine. Reprinted by permission of HarperCollins Publishers; page 284 (bottom): Joe Castro/©AP/Wide World Photos; page 285: Asia Images Group/Getty Images, Inc.; page 286 (top): WDCN/Univ. College London/Photo Researchers, Inc.; page 286 (bottom): Rogelio Solis/©AP/Wide World Photos; page 287 (top): Digital Vision/Getty Images, Inc.; page 287 (bottom): Charlie Riedel/©AP/Wide World Photos; page 288 (top): ©The New Yorker Collection 1994 Frank Cotham from cartoonbank.com. All Rights Reserved; page 290 (top and center): David Lyons/Alamy; page 290 (top and right): Peter Holmes/Age Fotostock America, Inc.; page 291 (top left): From Yapeng Wang, Neuroimage 35(2): 862-70, Figure 1, 2007; page 291 (top right): From K.L. Sakai, Science 310 (5749): 815-9, Nov 4, 2005, figure 3; page 291 (bottom right): From D. Perani, Brain Mapp. 19(3): 170-82, Figure 2, 2003; page 293: ©Interfoto/Alamy; page 294 (left): Tom Grill/©Corbis; page 294 (right): Image Source/©Corbis; page 295: Image Source/©Corbis; page 296: Richard Hutchings/©Corbis; page 299 (top): Bryn Colton/Assignments Photographers/©Corbis; page 299 (bottom): Car Culture/©Corbis; page 301: Michael Nichols/NGS Image Sales; page 302 (top): Laura Doss/©Corbis; page 302 (bottom): ©The New Yorker Collection 1989 Robert Weber from cartoonbank.com. All Rights Reserved; page 303: George Lepp/©Corbis; page 304 (bottom): Dave Bowman/©AP/Wide World Photos; page 309: Gabe Palmer/©Corbis.

Chapter 10

Page 310: Influx Productions/Getty Images, Inc.; page 313: AFP/Getty Images, Inc.; page 314 (top): Taylor Hill/FilmMagic/Getty Images, Inc.; page 314 (center): Lynn Goldsmith/©Corbis; page 314 (bottom): Justin Sullivan/Getty Images, Inc.; page 318 (top): Getty Images, Inc.; page 318 (bottom): Michael Caulfield/Getty Images, Inc.; page 319 (left): Bruno Morandi/Getty Images, Inc.; page 319 (right): Paul Barton/©Corbis; page 320 (top): Francois Guillot/AFP/Getty Images, Inc.; page 322: ©The New Yorker Collection 2001 William Haefeli from cartoonbank.com. All Rights Reserved; page 327: ©AP/Wide World Photos; page 328: Bob Daemmrich/PhotoEdit; page 330 (right): Richard Schultz/©Corbis; page 330 (left): eyetrigger Pty Ltd/©Corbis; page 331: ©The New Yorker Collection 1994 Charles Barsotti from cartoonbank.com. All Rights Reserved; page 332: Rick Gershon/Getty Images, Inc.; page 334 (top): Marcus Mok/Getty Images, Inc.; page 334 (bottom): Matt Moyer/Getty Images, Inc.; page 335 (top): Lester Lefkowitz/Getty Images, Inc.; page 335 (center): Stefan Berg/Getty Images, Inc.; page 336: Romeo Gacad/AFP/Getty Images, Inc.; page 337: Jim West/PhotoEdit; page 338: ©The New Yorker Collection1989 Robert Weber from cartoonbank.com. All Rights Reserved; page 339: Masterfile; page 340: John MacDougall/AFP/Getty Images, Inc.; page 341: From J. Duncan, Science, 289 (5478): 457-460, July 21, 2000, Figures a and b; page 342 (top left): Peet Simard/©Corbis; page 342 (top right): Kristy-Anne Glubish/Design Pics/©Corbis; page 343 (top left): Markus Moellenberg/©Corbis; page 343 (top right): Hayley Madden/Redferns/Getty Images, Inc.; page 344: AFP/Getty Images, Inc.; page 345 (top right): The Tennessean, Rex Perry/©AP/Wide World Photos; page 349: Hill Street Studios/Getty Images, Inc.

Chapter 11

Page 350: Thomas Barwick/Digital Vision/Getty Images, Inc.; page 351: Mario Tama/Getty Images, Inc.; page 352: Jennie Woodcock/Reflections Photolibrary/©Corbis; page 353: Denny Allen/Getty Images, Inc.; page 354 (top): Shalom Ormsby/Blend Images/©Corbis; page 354 (bottom): Justin Lane/epa/©Corbis; page 355 (left): Massimo Borchi/©Corbis; page 355 (right): Thierry Dosogne/Getty Images, Inc.; page 356: R. Marsh Starks/Las Vegas Sun/Handout/Reuters/©Corbis; page 359: Courtesy Philip Teitelbaum; page 360 (top): ©The New Yorker Collection 2000 Charles Barsotti from cartoonbank.com. All Rights Reserved; page 360 (bottom): Greg Ceo/Getty Images, Inc.; page 361: UpperCut Images/Getty Images, Inc.; page 362 (top): Gary Salter/©Corbis; page 362 (bottom): Mark Peterson/©Corbis; page 363: Tim Boyle/Getty Images, Inc.; page 364: Stephen Ferry/Liaison/Getty Images, Inc.; page 365 (top): Eugenio Savio/©AP/Wide World Photos; page 365 (bottom): Don Hammond/Design Pics/©Corbis; page 366: Tony Gutierrez/©AP/Wide World Photos; page 368 (top): ©Robert Mankoff from cartoonbank.com. All Rights Reserved; page 368 (bottom): Courtesy Lucy L. Brown, Albert Einstein College of Medicine; page 370: Somos/Veer/Getty Images, Inc.; page 372: Winslow Townson/©AP/Wide World Photos; page 374 (top): ©J.C. Duffy from cartoonbank.com. All Rights Reserved; page 374 (bottom): Sunset Boulevard/©Corbis; page 375: Getty Images, Inc.; page 376 (top): Bill Nation/©Corbis; page 377 (top): Bob Krist/©Corbis; page 377 (bottom): Wisconsin State Journal, Craig Schreiner/©AP/Wide World Photos; page 378: Mascarucci/©Corbis; page 379 (top): William Albert Allard/Getty Images, Inc.; page 380: ©AIC/Age Fotostock America, Inc.; page 381 (top left): Nancy Kedersha/UCLA/Science Photo Library/Photo Researchers, Inc.; page 381 (top right): Courtesy Elizabeth Gould; page 381 (bottom left): Masterfile; page 381 (bottom right): From S. Small, et al., Proc Natl Acad Sci USA: 104(13): 5638-43, 2007; page 383 (bottom): Odilon Dimier/Photo Alto/©Corbis.

Chapter 12

Page 384: Glow Images/Age Fotostock America, Inc.; page 386: Streeter Lecka/Getty Images, Inc.; page 387: Mike Kemp/Getty Images, Inc.; page 388: Courtesy P. Ekman, Human Interaction Lab, University of California, San Francisco; page 389: Tom Stewart/©Corbis; page 390: Dann Tardif/©Corbis; page 391: George Shelley/©Corbis; page 392 (top): Alessandra Schellnegger/©Corbis; page 392 (bottom): Jose Luis Pelaez/Blend Images/©Corbis; page 395 (top): ©Peter Steiner from cartoonbank.com. All Rights Reserved; page 397: Dave & Les Jacobs/Blend Images/©Corbis; page 398: David Young-Wolff/Photoedit; page 399 (top): Courtesy Karen Huffman; page 399 (bottom): ©The New Yorker Collection 1999 Charles Barsotti from cartoonbank.com. All Rights Reserved; page 401 (center): Stretch Photography/Blend Images/Getty Images, Inc.; page 404: Erica Shires/©Corbis; page 405 (bottom left): Jack Goldfarb/Design Pics/©Corbis; page 405 (bottom right): Masterfile; page 406 (bottom): David Woods/©Corbis; page 409 (top): ©Corbis; page 410: Inspirestock/©Corbis; page 411: Edward Bock/©Corbis; page 413 (left): Kin Cheung/Reuters/©Corbis; page 413 (right): Jens Buettner/epa/©Corbis; page 414 (bottom): Ashley Cooper/©Corbis; page 417: Ron Edmonds/©AP/Wide World Photos; page 421: John Lund/Drew Kelly/Blend Images/©Corbis.

Chapter 13

Page 422: Digital Vision/Getty Images, Inc.; page 423: James Woodson/Digital Vision/Getty Images, Inc.; page 426: ©The New Yorker Collection 1991 Lee Lorenz from cartoonbank.com. All Rights Reserved; page 425: Masterfile; page 428 (top left): Image Source/©Corbis; page 428 (top right): Jose Luis Pelaez, Inc./Blend Images/©Corbis; page 428 (bottom): Anna Peisl/©Corbis; page 429 (top): Michael Macor/San Francisco Chronicle/©Corbis; page 429 (bottom): Cancan Chu/Getty Images, Inc.; page 430: PIERRE VERDY/AFP/Getty Images, Inc.; page 431 (top right): ©The New Yorker Collection 2001 Pat Byrnes from cartoonbank.com. All Rights Reserved; page 434: Baerbel Schmidt/Getty Images, Inc.; page 435: Ableimages/Getty Images, Inc.; page 438 (top): Peter Byrne/PA Wire /©AP/Wide World Photos; page 439: T.K. Wanstal/The Image Works; page 441: Bettmann/

©Corbis; page 443 (center): Lawrence Manning/©Corbis; page 443 (bottom): Latin Stock Collection/©Corbis; page 444: Roger Ressmeyer/©Corbis; page 445: Tim Pannell/©Corbis; page 447 (left): Creasource/©Corbis; page 447 (right): Tokyo Space Club/©Corbis; page 448: Ted Thai//Time Life Pictures/Getty Images, Inc.; page 449: Justin Lane/epa/©Corbis; page 451: Goodshoot/©Corbis; page 455 (top): Index Stock/Photolibrary; page 455 (bottom): Vincent McIndoe/Stock Illustration Source/Getty Images, Inc. No electronic rights; page 452: Mark Leffingwell/AFP/Getty Images, Inc.; page 454: Image Source/©Corbis; page 459: Image Source/©Corbis.

Chapter 14

Page 460: Steve Bloom/Taxi/Getty Images, Inc.; page 462: Frank Polich/Reuters/©Corbis; page 463: Jose Luis Peleaz/Blend Images/©Corbis; page 464: Spencer Grant/PhotoEdit; page 465: Michele Constantini/Photo Alto/©Corbis; page 467 (left): Dave Martin/©AP/Wide World Photos; page 467 (right): Chris Graythen/Getty Images, Inc.; page 470 (right): Tetra Images/Getty Images, Inc.; page 470 (left): Jay Directo/AFP/Getty Images, Inc.; page 471 (center): ©The New Yorker Collection 1992 Dana Fradon from cartoonbank.com. All Rights Reserved; page 473: Christine Schneider/©Corbis; page 475: Joseph Sohm/Visions of America/©Corbis; page 476: Image Source/Getty Images, Inc.; page 477 (top): Philip G. Zimbardo, Inc.; page 477 (bottom): Jose Luis Pelaez/Getty Images, Inc.; page 478: Rachel Watson/Photodisc/Getty Images, Inc.; page 480: ©1968 by Stanley Milgram. ©renewed 1993 by Alexandra Milgram. From the film OBEDIENCE, distributed by Penn State Media Sales; page 483: Rolf Bruderer/Blend Images/Getty Images, Inc.; page 484: Heide Benser/©Corbis; page 485: NASA/©AP/Wide World Photos; page 486 (top): ALBERT GEA/Reuters/©Corbis; page 486 (bottom): Ann Cutting/Getty Images, Inc.; page 489 (top): Sergio Dionisio/Getty Images, Inc.; page 489 (bottom): ©The New Yorker Collection 1997 Mike Twohy from cartoonbank.com. All Rights Reserved; page 491: ©Corbis; page 494: Jonas Ekstromer/©AP/Wide World Photos; page 495: Silvia Morara/©Corbis; page 499 (bottom): Jasper White/Getty Images, Inc.

Chapter 15

Page 500: BLOOMImage/Getty Images, Inc.; page 501: Mango Productions/©Corbis; page 502: Richard Drew/©AP/Wide World Photos; page 503: TIMOTHY A. CLARY/AFP/Getty Images, Inc.; page 504: Manny Millan/Sports Illustrated/Getty Images, Inc.; page 506 (top): Laura Dwight/©Corbis; page 506 (bottom): AFP/Getty Images, Inc.; page 508: Mark J. Rebilas/US Navy/ZUMA/©Corbis; page 509: Kevin Dodge/©Corbis; page 510 (bottom): Joe Raedle/Getty Images, Inc.; page 513 (top): Jessica Tefft/Zuma Press; page 513 (bottom): Viviane Moos/©Corbis; page 514: ©The New Yorker Collection 2008 Robert Mankoff from cartoonbank.com. All Rights Reserved; page 515: Mark Wilson/Getty Images, Inc.; page 516: Masterfile; page 517 (top left): Courtesy Jason J. Radley, Salk Institute for Biological Studies; page 517 (top right): Courtesy Elizabeth Gould; page 517 (bottom left): Image provided by Casper Hoogenraad (Erasmus Medical Center Rotterdam, The Netherlands; c.hoogenraad@erasmusmc.nl) and Harm Krugers (SILS-CNS, University of Amsterdam), The Netherlands, h.krugers@uva.nl; page 517 (bottom right): Masterfile; page 518:

ColorBlind Images/Getty Images, Inc.; page 520 (top): Richard Heathcote/Getty Images, Inc.; page 521: Susana Vera/Reuters/©Corbis; page 522: JLP/Jose Luis Pelaez/©Corbis; page 523: Xinhua Press/©Corbis; page 525: Stuart Pearce/Age Fotostock America, Inc.; page 526 (top): ©The New Yorker Collection 1992 Mike Twohy from cartoonbank.com. All Rights Reserved; page 526 (bottom): Jean Claude Revy/ISM/Phototake; page 528: Chris Arend/Getty Images, Inc.; page 529: Shannon Stapleton/Reuters/©Corbis; page 530: John Gibbins/San Diego Union-Tribune/Zuma Press; page 531: Tom Hood/©AP/Wide World Photos; page 532: Chris Hondros/Getty Images, Inc.; page 535: Stockbyte/Getty Images, Inc.

Chapter 16

Page 536: Justin Horrocks/iStockphoto; page 538 (left): Burstein Collection/©Corbis/©2009 The Munch Museum/The Munch-Ellingsen Group/Artists Rights Society (ARS), NY; page 538 (right): Bettmann/©Corbis; page 540 (top): Rajesh Nirgude/©AP/Wide World Photos; page 540 (bottom): Sukree Sukplang/Reuters/©Corbis; page 541: Toby Talbot/©AP/Wide World Photos; page 544: Spencer Grant/PhotoEdit; page 545: Spencer Grant/Photo Researchers, Inc.; page 548: M. Spencer Green/©AP/Wide World Photos; page 549 (top): Will & Deni McIntyre/Photo Researchers, Inc.; page 549 (bottom): Winfried Rothermel/©AP/Wide World Photos; page 550: Michael A. Keller/©Corbis; page 551 (top left): From Paul Keedwell, Journal of Psychopharmacology 23(7): 775-88, Figure 3, 2009, Sage Publications. ©2009 British Association for Psychopharmacology; page 551 (bottom left): MedioImages/Photodisc/Getty Images, Inc.; page 551 (bottom right): Courtesy Charles Nicholson, New York University School of Medicine; page 553 (top): Monalyn Gracia/©Corbis; page 553 (bottom): Radius Images/©Corbis; page 554: ©The New Yorker Collection 2005 Leo Cullum from cartoonbank.com. All Rights Reserved; page 555 (bottom): The Charlotte Observer, Christopher A. Record/©AP/Wide World Photos; page 557: Jon Feingersh/Blend Images/©Corbis; page 558 (top): David Young-Wolff/PhotoEdit; page 561 (center): ©The New Yorker Collection 2005 David Sipress from cartoonbank.com. All Rights Reserved; page 562: David Woods/©Corbis; page 563: Pascal Preti/Getty Images, Inc.; page 566 (center): Richard T. Nowitz/©Corbis; page 566 (left): Robin Nelson/PhotoEdit; page 566 (right): Comstock/Getty Images, Inc.; page 567: ©The New Yorker Collection Aaron Bacall from cartoonbank.com. All Rights Reserved; page 568 (top): M. Spencer Green/©AP/Wide World Photos; page 569: Jedd Cadge/The Image Bank/Getty Images, Inc.; page 570 (bottom): Romeo Ranoco/Reuters/Landov LLC; page 571: Steve Woods/epa/©Corbis; page 572: Chuck Stoody/©AP/Wide World Photos; page 575 (bottom): Images.com/©Corbis.

Before You Go On

Page 7 (center): Mark Andersen/Rubberball/Getty Images, Inc.; page 9 (center): iStockphoto; page 13 (bottom): iStockphoto; page 21: iStockphoto.

Cut Across Connection

Page 94: Photodisc/Getty Images, Inc.; page 126: Hill Street Studios/Getty Images, Inc.; page 163: Hola Images/Getty Images, Inc.

Name Index

Bauer, R. A., 15
Baum, A., 177
Baumeister, R. F., 371, 476, 503, 504
Baumgardner, S. R., 27, 431
Baumrind, D., 73, 74
Baylery, N., 26
Beals, J., 571
Bearman, P. S., 378
Beasley, M., 519
Bebbington, P., 570
Bebko, J. M., 344
Becchetti, L., 407, 409
Bechara, A., 405
Beck, A., 559, 561
Beck, A. T., 416, 417
Bédard, P., 116
Beehr, T. A., 520
Beer, D., 192
Beer, J. S., 239
Beilin, H., 72
Bekker, M. H. J., 445
Belgardt, B. F., 360
Bellinger, D. L., 527
Bem, D. J., 448, 465
Bendelius, J., 363
Benedict, C., 185
Benjamin, L. T., Jr., 10
Bennett, C. M., 86
Bennett, E. L., 226
Bennett, M., 72
Bennett, C. S., 513
Bensafi, M., 292
Ben-Zur, H., 525
Beratis, S., 305
Berenbaum, H., 305, 453
Bergin, A. E., 571
Berk, L. E., 68f
Berkhof, J., 514
Berkman, N. D., 364
Berkowitz, L., 487
Berman, J. R., 368
Berman, W., 338
Bermond, B., 394
Bermudez, P., 150
Bernaud, J.-L., 506
Bernays, E., 470
Berntson, G. G., 392, 405
Berntsson, L., 509
Berr, C., 269
Berridge, K., 356
Berridge, K. C., 355
Berry, J. W., 158
Berscheid, E., 488, 489, 491
Bertini, M., 180
Betz, N. E., 438
Bevins, R. A., 353
Beyer, J., 557
Bickman, L., 568
Bieber, I., 371
Billings, L. S., 484
Binet, A., 322, 323–324
Bisaga, A., 191

Bishop, G. D., 484
Bissette, G., 270
Biswas-Diener, R., 408
Bitterman, M. E., 15
Björkman, B., 145
Björnhelm, M., 359
Black, D. W., 375
Black, K. A., 428
Blair, C., 18
Blanch, A., 571
Blanchard, R., 372
Blass, T., 478, 482
Blazer, D. G., 571
Blecke, D., 304
Bleich, A., 505
Bliss, T. V., 226
Block, C. J., 477
Bloom, L., 281
Bloom, M., 568
Bloom, S., 359
Blum, K., 197
Blumenfeld, P., 378
Bock, P., 67
Boecker, H., 356
Boitani, L., 132
Boldyrev, A. A., 88
Bollini, A. M., 450
Bonanno, G. A., 27
Bond, C. F., 484
Bond, C. F., Jr., 484
Bono, 430
Bootzin, R. R., 178
Bord-Hoffman, M. A., 87
Borgen, F. H., 438
Bornstein, M. H., 283
Bornstein, R. F., 451, 456
Botton, A., 27
Botvinick, M. M., 294
Botwin, M. C., 436
Bouchard, T., 428, 439
Bouchard, T. J., Jr., 20, 442
Bourne, L. E., 295
Boutreyre, E., 506
Bower, G. H., 256
Bowlby, J., 72
Bowne, W. B., 358
Boyle, G. J., 434
Boyle, S., 32f
Boysen, G. A., 539
Braaten, E. B., 410
Brach, J. S., 87
Brackett, M., 410
Bradley, M. M., 389, 390, 391, 415
Bradley, R., 334, 453
Bradley, S. D., 390
Bradley, S. J., 375, 376
Braille, L., 160
Brandt, M., 230
Brauer, M., 487
Bretherton, I., 72
Brewster, A., 188
Briggs, K. C., 428

Brislin, R. W., 158
Broad, K. D., 353
Broadbent, N. J., 353
Brody, L. R., 412
Brooks-Gunn, J., 170
Brosnan, S. F., 222
Brown, D. E., 20
Brown, L. L., 522
Brown, R. D., 466
Brown, S. A., 178
Brown, T. M., 367
Brownell, K. D., 362, 365
Brückner, H., 376
Brumbaugh, C. C., 489
Brüning, J. C., 360
Bryan, W. L., 12
Bryant, R. A., 532
Buchanan, J. A., 556
Buchner, A., 230
Buchsbaum, G., 154
Buck, L. B., 132
Bucy, P., 404
Buda, R., 446
Buhrich, N., 372
Bullough, V. L., 367
Burgess, J. L., 194
Burijon, B. N., 531
Burkholder, A., 552
Burnman, A., 571
Burns, T. L., 363
Bush, G., 233
Bushman, B. J., 521
Buss, D. M., 19
Bussey, K., 443
Butler, E. A., 392
Butler, J. L., 503
Buunk, B. P., 484
Byers, E. S., 370
Byrd-Bredbenner, C., 438
Byrne, B. M., 18
Byrne, D., 488, 489
Byrne, J. H., 206
Byrne, M., 570

C

Cabrera, N., 74
Cacioppo, J. T., 392, 404
Cadwell, B., 334
Caetano, R., 541
Cahill, L., 257
Cain, C. K., 404, 406
Cain, D. J., 565
Cajal, R., 226
Cajal, S. R., 111
Calder, A. J., 137
Calkins, M. W., 25, 26
Calleo, J., 415
Cameron, A., 374
Cameron, H. A., 111, 119
Campbell, K. K., 508
Campos, J. J., 392

Subject Index

Homeostasis, 353–354
Homosexuality, 371–373
Homozygous traits, 63–64
Hormones, sexual orientation and, 372
Horney, Karen, 26, 430
Hostility, Type A personality and, 525–526
Hue, color vision and, 153–154
Human development
    adolescence and, 85–88
    adulthood and, 89–91
    aging and, 263
    attitudes and, 463
    birth order effects and, 66
    childhood and, 77–84
    cohort-sequential design and, 63
    consciousness and, 170
    critical periods and, 60–61
    cross-sectional design and, 61–62
    developmental milestones, 230
    developmental stages, 58–60
    emotions and, 401–402
    genetics and, 63–65
    hearing and, 149
    infancy and, 68–77
    intelligence, 341–342
    language and, 280–281
    learning and, 230
    longitudinal design and, 62
    maturation process and, 59
    metacognition and, 302–303
    nature vs. nurture, 59
    personality, 439–440
    prenatal development, 66–67
    psychosexual stages, 425–428, 553–554
    qualitative vs. quantitative shifts in,
        59–60
    sensitive periods and, 61
    sleep and, 183–184
    stages and, 58–60
    stress and, 508
    tactile senses and, 141–142
    taste and smell and, 137
    vision and, 159
Humanistic-existential model, 562–565
    client-centered therapy and, 562
    conditions of worth and, 562
    existential theories and therapy, 564
    Gestalt therapy, 563–564
    unconditional positive regard and, 562
Humanistic psychology, 17–18
Humanistic theories
    Abraham Maslow and, 430–431
    Carl Rogers and, 431
    evaluation of, 431
Humor-health link, 513
Hunger, 358–366
    anorexia nervosa and, 363–364
    body weight set point and, 361
    brain signals and, 359–360
    bulimia nervosa and, 365
    chemical signals and, 359
    cultural differences and, 360–361

obesity and, 362–364
    stomach signals and, 358
Huntington's disease, 123
Hyperalert hypnotic trance, 173
Hypnagogic hallucinations, 179
Hypnagogic state, 179
Hypnosis, 173–175
    brain's role in, 175
    common social and cognitive processes and,
        174–175
    dissociation and, 175
    divided consciousness and, 174
    explaining, 174–175
    hypnotic hallucinations, 174
    memory and, 262
    motor control and, 174
    openness and, 173
    posthypnotic amnesia, 174
    power of suggestion and, 173
    procedures and effects, 173–174
Hypnotic hallucinations, 174
Hypoactive sexual desire disorder, 373
Hypothalamic-pituitary-adrenal (HPA) axis, 110,
        512, 531
Hypothalamus
    emotions and, 403–404
    hunger and, 359–360
    role of, 110
    sleep and, 179
Hypotheses
    psychological research and, 38–39
    scientific method and, 33–34
    variables and, 39
Hypothetico-deductive approach, 33–34

I

Id, 425
Identity and role confusion, 87
Identity disorder, dissociative, 271
Ill-defined problems, 295
Illness and stress, 509
Illogical thinking processes, 559–560
Imaginary audience, 86
Imagination, 262–263, 319
Immune system, stress and, 526–529
Implicit Association Test (IAT), 466–467
Implicit attitudes, 466–467
Implicit memories, 172, 251–252
Imprinting, 60
Inborn temperament, 65
Incentive salience, 356
Incentive theory of motivation, 355–357
Incest taboo, 366
Independent variables, 39
Individual differences
    achievement, 379
    brain side and brain size, 120–122
    emotions and, 409–414
    gender and dementia, 270–271
    hearing and, 150
    hunger, 360–361

intelligence, 343–345
    language and, 287–289
    "owls and larks", 178
    parenting styles, 73–75
    personality and, 443–448
    sex, 369–373
    social skills and, 477–478
    stress, 518–520
    tactile senses and, 142–143
    taste and smell and, 137–138
Individual psychology (Adler), 429
Individual therapy, 565
Individualistic cultures. See also Cultural factors
    parenting style and, 76
    personality development and, 446–447
Inductive reasoning, 33
Infantile amnesia, 230
Infants
    brain growth and, 69–70
    cognitive development and, 71–74
    common newborn reflexes, 69
    emotional development and, 401–402
    motor development and, 70–71
    parenting styles and, 75–76
    physical development and, 68–71
    reflexes and, 69
    sleep and, 183
    social and emotional development and, 74–75
    taste and smell and, 137
Inferential statistics, 46
Inferiority, behavior and, 429
Inflammation, 527
Information encoding, 242–249
    automatic processing and, 243–244
    effortful processing and, 243–244
    eidetic (photographic) memory, 246
    forms of, 245–249
    into long-term memory, 245
    meaning and, 246–247
    mnemonic devices and, 247
    nonverbal information and, 246
    organization and, 248–249
    rehearsal and, 245
    schemas and, 248–249
    semantic codes and, 246
    into working memory, 244–245
Information hierarchy, memory and, 248
Information-processing theory, 72–74, 182
Information streams, 404
Informed consent, 49
Injunctive norms, 475
Inoculation, 529
Insight, 297
Insight learning, 221
Insomnia, 185
Instinct theory, motivation and, 352–353
Instincts, 352–353
Institutional Animal Care and Use Committee
        (IACUC), 51
Institutional review boards (IRBs), 49
Institutionalization, 491

O

Obedience, 479–482
Obesity, 362–364
    food variety and, 361
    genetics and, 362–363
    hypothalamus and, 359–360
    overeating and, 362
    stigma against, 364
Object permanence, cognitive development and, 72
Object-relation theorists, 182, 553–554
Objective self-awareness, 402
Observational learning, 222–223, 437
Obsessive-compulsive disorder (OCD), 304–305, 416–417
Occipital cortex, 112–113
Occupational influences, intelligence and, 335
Odorants, 132
Odors, 137–138
Oedipus complex, 426
Olfactory bulb, 133–134
Olfactory learning, 230
Olfactory receptor neurons, 132, 133
Olfactory sense, 132. *See also* Smell
Oligodendroglia, 101
Opening-up approach, meditation and, 176
Operant conditioning, 214–221
    law of effect and, 214
    learned helplessness and, 219–220
    negative punishment and, 217
    positive reinforcement and, 217
    primary reinforcers and, 216
    reinforcement and punishment, 215–216
    reinforcement schedules, 216–218
    reinforcer types and, 216
    secondary reinforcers, 216
    shaping and, 219
    teaching new behaviors and, 218–219
    techniques, 556–557
Operationalizing, 75
Opiates, 143–144
Opioids, 192
Opium, 192
Opponent process theory, 154
Oppositional defiant disorder, 91
Optic nerve, 152
Oral psychosexual stage, 553
Orbitofrontal cortex, 493
Organic memory disorders, 269–271
Ossicles, auditory sense and, 147
Outgroups, 390
Oval window, auditory sense and, 147
Ovaries, adolescent physical development and, 85
Overeating, 362
Overgeneralization, 559
Overregularization, 284

P

Pacinian corpuscles, 140
Pain. *See also* Tactile senses
    chronic, 143–144

cingulotomy and, 144
endorphins and, 143
enkephalins and, 143
familial dysautonomia and, 145
gate control theory of, 143
high pain threshold, 143
no pain, 144–145
opiates and, 143–144
reducing acute pain, 144
using brain to counteract, 140–141
Panic attacks, 416
Panic disorder, 416
Papillae, tongue, 133
Paradoxical sleep, 180
Parallel distributed-processing model of memory, 241–242
Parallel processing, 112, 168
Paraphilias, 374–375
Parasympathetic nervous system, 106, 387
Parenting styles, 75–77
Parietal cortex, 114
Parkinson's disease, 109, 123
Participant choice, research and, 39–40
Pavlov, Ivan, 15, 208
Pavlovian conditioning. *See* Classical conditioning
Peak experiences, 430
Pedophilia, 374
Penis envy, 426
Peptides, 110
Perception illusions, vision and, 158
Perceptual constancies, vision and, 158–159
Perfect correlation, 45
Performance anxiety, sexual, 374
Permissive parenting style, 77
Personal fable, 86
Personal unconscious, 429
Personality. *See also* Specific theories
    biological foundations of, 439–443
    brain function and, 440–443
    cancer and, 528
    cultural group differences and, 445–448
    disinhibition/constraint dimension and, 441–442
    five-factor model of personality, 434
    gender differences and, 443–445
    genetic factors and, 439–440
    hemispheric lateralization and, 445
    humanistic theories and, 430–431
    individual differences and, 443–448
    intelligence and, 320
    interactionist perspective and, 437–438
    inventories, 454–455
    negative emotionality and, 441–442
    neural systems and, 440–441
    phrenology and, 440
    positive emotionality and, 441–442
    projective tests and, 455–456
    psychoanalytic theory and, 424–428
    psychodynamic theories and, 428–430
    quizzes, 454
    self-schemas and, 445

    situationist approach and, 436–437
    social role theory and, 444
    socioeconomic environment and, 448
    stress and, 529
    subcultures and, 447–448
    television and movies influence on, 438
    trait theories and, 432–436
    Type A personality, 529
    Type B personality, 529
    Type C personality, 529
Personality disorders, 449–453
    antisocial personality disorder, 451–452
    borderline personality disorder, 452–453
    DSM-IV-TR classifications and, 450–451
    narcissistic personality disorder, 451
Persuasion, 469–470
Pessimistic explanatory styles, 518–519
Phallic stage, 553
Phantom limb sensations, 145
Philosophical roots, psychology and, 7–8
Phobias, 211–212, 415
Phonemes, 279
Phonology, 279
Photographic memories, 246
Photoreceptors, 152
Phrenology, 440
Physical and cognitive development, adulthood and, 89–90
Physical attractiveness, 489
Physical development
    adolescence and, 85–86
    childhood and, 75–76, 78
    infancy and, 68–71
    primary sex characteristics, 85
    puberty, 85
    secondary sex characteristics, 85
Physiologic component, emotions and, 386–387
Physiological responses to stress
    fight-or-flight response, 511–512
    general adaptation syndrome, 512–513
Piaget, Jean, 71–74
Piaget's concrete operational stage, 80
Piaget's formal operations stage, 86
Piaget's four stages of cognitive development, 72
Piaget's preoperational stage, 78–80
Piaget's theory, 71–74, 80–81
Pineal gland, sleep and, 179
Pitch, 146
Pituitary gland
    puberty and, 85
    role of, 110–111
    sleep and, 177
Place cells, 111
Place theory, auditory sense and, 147
Placenta, 66
Plant analogy of intelligence, 336–337
Plasticity, 104
Plato, 8
Pleasure principle, 425
Polygenic traits, human development and, 64
Pons, 109, 177
Ponzo illusion, 158